ALGEBRA

Exponents and Radicals

$$x^a x^b = x^{a+b} \qquad \frac{x^a}{x^b} = x^{a-b} \qquad x^{-a} = \frac{1}{x^a} \qquad (x^a)^b = x^{ab} \qquad \left(\frac{x}{y}\right)^a = \frac{x^a}{y^a}$$

$$x^{1/n} = \sqrt[n]{x} \qquad x^{m/n} = \sqrt[n]{x^m} = (\sqrt[n]{x})^m \qquad \sqrt[n]{xy} = \sqrt[n]{x}\sqrt[n]{y} \qquad \sqrt[n]{x/y} = \sqrt[n]{x}/\sqrt[n]{y}$$

Factoring Formulas

$$a^2 - b^2 = (a - b)(a + b) \qquad\qquad a^2 + b^2 \text{ does not factor over real numbers.}$$
$$a^3 - b^3 = (a - b)(a^2 + ab + b^2) \qquad a^3 + b^3 = (a + b)(a^2 - ab + b^2)$$
$$a^n - b^n = (a - b)(a^{n-1} + a^{n-2}b + a^{n-3}b^2 + \cdots + ab^{n-2} + b^{n-1})$$

Binomials

$$(a \pm b)^2 = a^2 \pm 2ab + b^2$$
$$(a \pm b)^3 = a^3 \pm 3a^2b + 3ab^2 \pm b^3$$

Binomial Theorem

$$(a + b)^n = a^n + \binom{n}{1}a^{n-1}b + \binom{n}{2}a^{n-2}b^2 + \cdots + \binom{n}{n-1}ab^{n-1} + b^n,$$

$$\text{where } \binom{n}{k} = \frac{n(n-1)(n-2)\cdots(n-k+1)}{k(k-1)(k-2)\cdots 3 \cdot 2 \cdot 1} = \frac{n!}{k!(n-k)!}$$

Quadratic Formula

The solutions of $ax^2 + bx + c = 0$ are

$$x = \frac{-b \pm \sqrt{b^2 - 4ac}}{2a}.$$

GEOMETRY

Parallelogram

$$A = bh$$

Triangle

$$A = \frac{1}{2}bh$$

Trapezoid
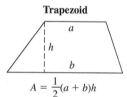

$$A = \frac{1}{2}(a + b)h$$

Circle

$$A = \pi r^2$$
$$C = 2\pi r$$

Sector
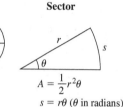

$$A = \frac{1}{2}r^2\theta$$
$$s = r\theta \ (\theta \text{ in radians})$$

Cylinder

$$V = \pi r^2 h$$
$$S = 2\pi rh$$
(lateral surface area)

Cone

$$V = \frac{1}{3}\pi r^2 h$$
$$S = \pi r\ell$$
(lateral surface area)

Sphere

$$V = \frac{4}{3}\pi r^3$$
$$S = 4\pi r^2$$

Equations of Lines and Circles

$$m = \frac{y_2 - y_1}{x_2 - x_1} \qquad \text{slope of line through } (x_1, y_1) \text{ and } (x_2, y_2)$$

$$y - y_1 = m(x - x_1) \qquad \text{point–slope form of line through } (x_1, y_1) \text{ with slope } m$$

$$y = mx + b \qquad \text{slope–intercept form of line with slope } m \text{ and } y\text{-intercept } (0, b)$$

$$(x - h)^2 + (y - k)^2 = r^2 \qquad \text{circle of radius } r \text{ with center } (h, k)$$

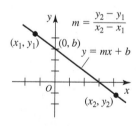

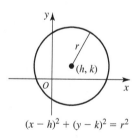

$$(x - h)^2 + (y - k)^2 = r^2$$

TRIGONOMETRY

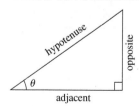

$$\cos \theta = \frac{\text{adj}}{\text{hyp}} \qquad \sin \theta = \frac{\text{opp}}{\text{hyp}} \qquad \tan \theta = \frac{\text{opp}}{\text{adj}}$$

$$\sec \theta = \frac{\text{hyp}}{\text{adj}} \qquad \csc \theta = \frac{\text{hyp}}{\text{opp}} \qquad \cot \theta = \frac{\text{adj}}{\text{opp}}$$

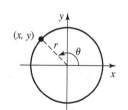

$$\cos \theta = \frac{x}{r} \qquad \sec \theta = \frac{r}{x}$$
$$\sin \theta = \frac{y}{r} \qquad \csc \theta = \frac{r}{y}$$
$$\tan \theta = \frac{y}{x} \qquad \cot \theta = \frac{x}{y}$$

(Continued)

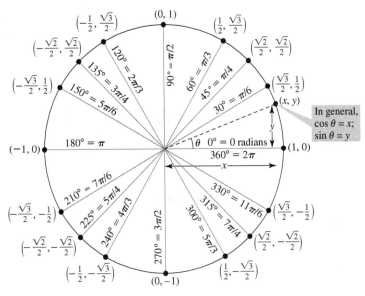

$(0, 1)$

$\left(-\frac{1}{2}, \frac{\sqrt{3}}{2}\right)$ $\left(\frac{1}{2}, \frac{\sqrt{3}}{2}\right)$

$\left(-\frac{\sqrt{2}}{2}, \frac{\sqrt{2}}{2}\right)$ $\left(\frac{\sqrt{2}}{2}, \frac{\sqrt{2}}{2}\right)$

$120° = 2\pi/3$ $90° = \pi/2$ $60° = \pi/3$

$135° = 3\pi/4$ $45° = \pi/4$

$\left(-\frac{\sqrt{3}}{2}, \frac{1}{2}\right)$ $150° = 5\pi/6$ $30° = \pi/6$ $\left(\frac{\sqrt{3}}{2}, \frac{1}{2}\right)$

(x, y)

$180° = \pi$ θ $0° = 0$ radians

$(-1, 0)$ $360° = 2\pi$ $(1, 0)$

$-x-$

In general,
$\cos \theta = x$;
$\sin \theta = y$

$210° = 7\pi/6$ $330° = 11\pi/6$

$\left(-\frac{\sqrt{3}}{2}, -\frac{1}{2}\right)$ $225° = 5\pi/4$ $315° = 7\pi/4$ $\left(\frac{\sqrt{3}}{2}, -\frac{1}{2}\right)$

$\left(-\frac{\sqrt{2}}{2}, -\frac{\sqrt{2}}{2}\right)$ $240° = 4\pi/3$ $270° = 3\pi/2$ $300° = 5\pi/3$ $\left(\frac{\sqrt{2}}{2}, -\frac{\sqrt{2}}{2}\right)$

$\left(-\frac{1}{2}, -\frac{\sqrt{3}}{2}\right)$ $\left(\frac{1}{2}, -\frac{\sqrt{3}}{2}\right)$

$(0, -1)$

Reciprocal Identities

$$\tan \theta = \frac{\sin \theta}{\cos \theta} \quad \cot \theta = \frac{\cos \theta}{\sin \theta} \quad \sec \theta = \frac{1}{\cos \theta} \quad \csc \theta = \frac{1}{\sin \theta}$$

Pythagorean Identities

$$\sin^2 \theta + \cos^2 \theta = 1 \quad \tan^2 \theta + 1 = \sec^2 \theta \quad 1 + \cot^2 \theta = \csc^2 \theta$$

Sign Identities

$$\sin(-\theta) = -\sin \theta \quad \cos(-\theta) = \cos \theta \quad \tan(-\theta) = -\tan \theta$$
$$\csc(-\theta) = -\csc \theta \quad \sec(-\theta) = \sec \theta \quad \cot(-\theta) = -\cot \theta$$

Double-Angle Identities

$$\sin 2\theta = 2 \sin \theta \cos \theta \qquad \cos 2\theta = \cos^2 \theta - \sin^2 \theta$$
$$= 2 \cos^2 \theta - 1$$
$$\tan 2\theta = \frac{2 \tan \theta}{1 - \tan^2 \theta} \qquad \qquad \qquad = 1 - 2 \sin^2 \theta$$

Half-Angle Formulas

$$\cos^2 \theta = \frac{1 + \cos 2\theta}{2} \qquad \sin^2 \theta = \frac{1 - \cos 2\theta}{2}$$

Addition Formulas

$$\sin(\alpha + \beta) = \sin \alpha \cos \beta + \cos \alpha \sin \beta \qquad \sin(\alpha - \beta) = \sin \alpha \cos \beta - \cos \alpha \sin \beta$$
$$\cos(\alpha + \beta) = \cos \alpha \cos \beta - \sin \alpha \sin \beta \qquad \cos(\alpha - \beta) = \cos \alpha \cos \beta + \sin \alpha \sin \beta$$
$$\tan(\alpha + \beta) = \frac{\tan \alpha + \tan \beta}{1 - \tan \alpha \tan \beta} \qquad \qquad \tan(\alpha - \beta) = \frac{\tan \alpha - \tan \beta}{1 + \tan \alpha \tan \beta}$$

Law of Sines

$$\frac{\sin \alpha}{a} = \frac{\sin \beta}{b} = \frac{\sin \gamma}{c}$$

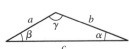

Law of Cosines

$$a^2 = b^2 + c^2 - 2bc \cos \alpha$$

Graphs of Trigonometric Functions and Their Inverses

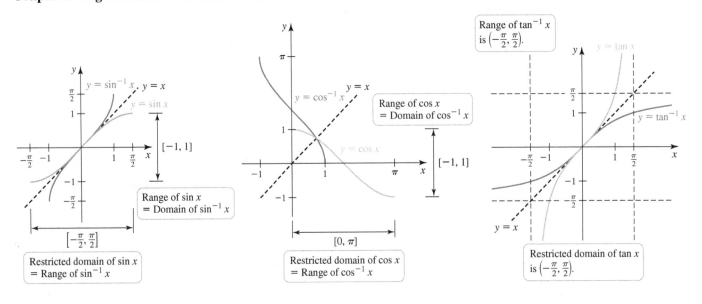

Calculus
Early Transcendentals
Volume1
with Student Solutions Manual

Fourth Custom Edition for the University of British Columbia

William Briggs, Lyle Cochran, and Bernard Gillett with
the assistance of Eric Schulz
Solutions Manual by Mark Woodward

Taken from:
Calculus: Early Transcendentals, Second Edition
by William Briggs, Lyle Cochran, and Bernard Gillett
with the assistance of Eric Schulz

Student's Solutions Manual, Single Variable
by Mark Woodward
for *Calculus: Early Transcendentals*, Second Edition
by William Briggs, Lyle Cochran, and Bernard Gillett

Cover Art: Courtesy Mark MacLean.

Taken from:

Calculus: Early Transcendentals, Second Edition
by William Briggs, Lyle Cochran, and Bernard Gillett with the assistance of Eric Schulz
Copyright © 2015, 2011 by Pearson Education, Inc.
501 Boylston Street, Suite 900, Boston, MA 02116

Student's Solutions Manual, *Single Variable*
by Mark Woodward
for *Calculus: Early Transcendentals,* Second Edition
by William Briggs, Lyle Cochran, and Bernard Gillett with the assistance of Eric Schulz
Copyright © 2015, 2011 by Pearson Education, Inc.

This special edition published in cooperation with Pearson Learning Solutions.

All trademarks, service marks, registered trademarks, and registered service marks are the property of their respective owners and are used herein for identification purposes only.

Pearson Learning Solutions, 501 Boylston Street, Suite 900, Boston, MA 02116
A Pearson Education Company
www.pearsoned.com

Printed in Canada

1 2 3 4 5 6 7 8 9 10 XXXX 17 16 15 14

000200010271903740

JHA

ISBN 10: 1-269-91047-7
ISBN 13: 978-1-269-91047-7

Contents

The following is taken from *Calculus: Early Transcendentals*, Second Edition
by William Briggs, Lyle Cochran, and Bernard Gillett with the assistance of Eric Schulz

4   Applications of the Derivative   236

9   Power Series   661

The following is taken from *Student's Solutions Manual, Single Variable* by Mark Woodward
for *Calculus: Early Transcendentals*, Second Edition by William Briggs, Lyle Cochran, and Bernard Gillett

Credits

Chapter opener art: Petr Vaclavek/Shutterstock

Chapter 1

Page 25, The Journal of Experimental Biology 203: 3745–3754, Dec. 2000. **Page 25,** The College Mathematics Journal 38, No. 1, Jan. 2007. **Page 25,** U.S. Fish and Wildlife Service. **Page 49,** The College Mathematics Journal 27, No. 4, Jan. 1996.

Chapter 2

Page 111, Arthur Koestler, The Act of Creation.

Chapter 3

Page 134, U.S. Bureau of Census. **Page 180,** J. Perloff MICROECONOMICS, Prentice Hall, 2012. **Page 206,** E.G. Hook and A. Lindsjo, Down Syndrome in Live Births by Single Year Maternal Age. **Page 213,** H. Ska la, The College Mathematics Journal, 28 Mar. 1997. **Page 223,** The College Mathematics Journal, 32, 4 Sept. 2001. **Page 228,** Calculus, Tom M. Apostol, Vol. 1, John Wiley & Sons, New York, 1967.

Chapter 4

Pages 237, 238, 239, 251, and 256, Thomas, George B.; Weir, Maurice D.; Hass, Joel; Giordano, Frank R., THOMAS' CALCULUS, EARLY TRANSCENDENTALS, MEDIA UPGRADE, 11th edition, © 2008 Printed and Electronically reproduced by permission of Pearson Education, Inc., Upper Saddle River, New Jersey. **Page 276,** Mathematics Teacher, Nov. 2002. **Page 278,** PROBLEMS FOR MATHEMATICIANS, YOUNG AND OLD by Paul R. Halmos. Copyright © 1991 Mathematical Association of America. Reprinted by permission. All rights reserved. **Page 279,** "Do Dogs Know Calculus?" by Tim Pennings from The College Mathematics Journal, Vol. 34, No. 3. Copyright © 2003 Mathematical Association of America. Reprinted by permission. All rights reserved. **Page 280,** "Energetic Savings and The Body Size Distributions of Gliding Mammals" Roman Dial, Evolutionary Ecology Research 5 2003: 1151–1162. **Page 280,** Calculus, Vol. 1, Tom M Apostol, John Wiley & Sons, 1967.

1

Functions

Chapter Preview   Mathematics is a language with an alphabet, a vocabulary, and many rules. Before beginning your calculus journey, you should be familiar with the elements of this language. Among these elements are algebra skills; the notation and terminology for various sets of real numbers; and the descriptions of lines, circles, and other basic sets in the coordinate plane. A review of this material is found in Appendix A. This chapter begins with the fundamental concept of a function and then presents the entire cast of functions needed for calculus: polynomials, rational functions, algebraic functions, exponential and logarithmic functions, and the trigonometric functions, along with their inverses. Before you begin studying calculus, it is important that you master the ideas in this chapter.

1.1 Review of Functions

Everywhere around us we see relationships among quantities, or **variables**. For example, the consumer price index changes in time and the temperature of the ocean varies with latitude. These relationships can often be expressed by mathematical objects called *functions*. Calculus is the study of functions, and because we use functions to describe the world around us, calculus is a universal language for human inquiry.

DEFINITION **Function**

A **function** f is a rule that assigns to each value x in a set D a *unique* value denoted $f(x)$. The set D is the **domain** of the function. The **range** is the set of all values of $f(x)$ produced as x varies over the entire domain (Figure 1.1).

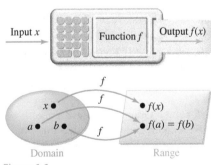

Figure 1.1

The **independent variable** is the variable associated with the domain; the **dependent variable** belongs to the range. The **graph** of a function f is the set of all points (x, y) in the xy-plane that satisfy the equation $y = f(x)$. The **argument** of a function is the expression on which the function works. For example, x is the argument when we write $f(x)$. Similarly, 2 is the argument in $f(2)$ and $x^2 + 4$ is the argument in $f(x^2 + 4)$.

QUICK CHECK 1 If $f(x) = x^2 - 2x$, find $f(-1)$, $f(x^2)$, $f(t)$, and $f(p - 1)$. ◄

The requirement that a function assigns a *unique* value of the dependent variable to each value in the domain is expressed in the vertical line test (Figure 1.2a). For example, the outside temperature as it varies over the course of a day is a function of time (Figure 1.2b).

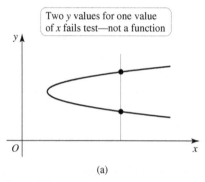
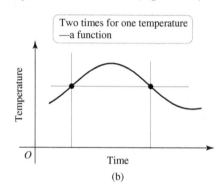

> Two y values for one value of x fails test—not a function

> Two times for one temperature —a function

(a)   (b)

Figure 1.2

> If the domain is not specified, we take it to be the set of all values of x for which f is defined. We will see shortly that the domain and range of a function may be restricted by the context of the problem.

> A set of points or a graph that does *not* correspond to a function represents a **relation** between the variables. All functions are relations, but not all relations are functions.

Vertical Line Test

A graph represents a function if and only if it passes the **vertical line test**: Every vertical line intersects the graph at most once. A graph that fails this test does not represent a function.

EXAMPLE 1 Identifying functions State whether each graph in Figure 1.3 represents a function.

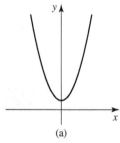
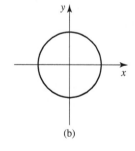
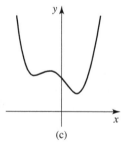
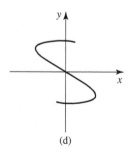

(a)   (b)   (c)   (d)

Figure 1.3

SOLUTION The vertical line test indicates that only graphs (a) and (c) represent functions. In graphs (b) and (d), there are vertical lines that intersect the graph more than once. Equivalently, there are values of x that correspond to more than one value of y. Therefore, graphs (b) and (d) do not pass the vertical line test and do not represent functions.   *Related Exercises 11–12* ◄

EXAMPLE 2 Domain and range Graph each function with a graphing utility using the given window. Then state the domain and range of the function.

> A window of $[a, b] \times [c, d]$ means $a \le x \le b$ and $c \le y \le d$.

a. $y = f(x) = x^2 + 1$; $[-3, 3] \times [-1, 5]$

b. $z = g(t) = \sqrt{4 - t^2}$; $[-3, 3] \times [-1, 3]$

c. $w = h(u) = \dfrac{1}{u - 1}$; $[-3, 5] \times [-4, 4]$

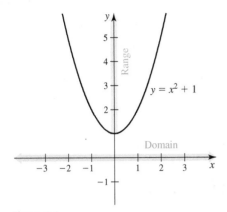

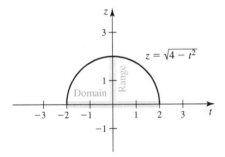

Figure 1.4

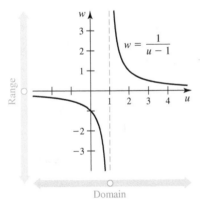

Figure 1.5

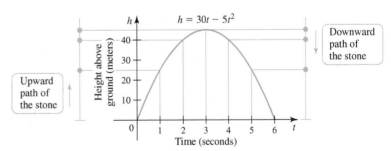

Figure 1.6

SOLUTION

a. Figure 1.4 shows the graph of $f(x) = x^2 + 1$. Because f is defined for all values of x, its domain is the set of all real numbers, written $(-\infty, \infty)$ or $\mathbb{R}$. Because $x^2 \geq 0$ for all x, it follows that $x^2 + 1 \geq 1$ and the range of f is $[1, \infty)$.

b. When n is even, functions involving nth roots are defined provided the quantity under the root is nonnegative (additional restrictions may also apply). In this case, the function g is defined provided $4 - t^2 \geq 0$, which means $t^2 \leq 4$, or $-2 \leq t \leq 2$. Therefore, the domain of g is $[-2, 2]$. By the definition of the square root, the range consists only of nonnegative numbers. When $t = 0$, z reaches its maximum value of $g(0) = \sqrt{4} = 2$, and when $t = \pm 2$, z attains its minimum value of $g(\pm 2) = 0$. Therefore, the range of g is $[0, 2]$ (Figure 1.5).

c. The function h is undefined at $u = 1$, so its domain is $\{u: u \neq 1\}$, and the graph does not have a point corresponding to $u = 1$. We see that w takes on all values except 0; therefore, the range is $\{w: w \neq 0\}$. A graphing utility does *not* represent this function accurately if it shows the vertical line $u = 1$ as part of the graph (Figure 1.6).

Related Exercises 13–20 ◄

EXAMPLE 3 **Domain and range in context** At time $t = 0$, a stone is thrown vertically upward from the ground at a speed of 30 m/s. Its height above the ground in meters (neglecting air resistance) is approximated by the function $h = f(t) = 30t - 5t^2$, where t is measured in seconds. Find the domain and range of f in the context of this particular problem.

SOLUTION Although f is defined for all values of t, the only relevant times are between the time the stone is thrown $(t = 0)$ and the time it strikes the ground, when $h = f(t) = 0$. Solving the equation $h = 30t - 5t^2 = 0$, we find that

$$30t - 5t^2 = 0$$
$$5t(6 - t) = 0 \qquad \text{Factor.}$$
$$5t = 0 \quad \text{or} \quad 6 - t = 0 \qquad \text{Set each factor equal to 0.}$$
$$t = 0 \quad \text{or} \quad t = 6. \qquad \text{Solve.}$$

Therefore, the stone leaves the ground at $t = 0$ and returns to the ground at $t = 6$. An appropriate domain that fits the context of this problem is $\{t: 0 \leq t \leq 6\}$. The range consists of all values of $h = 30t - 5t^2$ as t varies over $[0, 6]$. The largest value of h occurs when the stone reaches its highest point at $t = 3$ (halfway through its flight), which is $h = f(3) = 45$. Therefore, the range is $[0, 45]$. These observations are confirmed by the graph of the height function (Figure 1.7). Note that this graph is *not* the trajectory of the stone; the stone moves vertically.

> The dashed vertical line $u = 1$ in Figure 1.6 indicates that the graph of $w = h(u)$ approaches a *vertical asymptote* as u approaches 1 and that w becomes large in magnitude for u near 1.

Figure 1.7

Related Exercises 21–24 ◄

QUICK CHECK 2 State the domain and range of $f(x) = (x^2 + 1)^{-1}$. ◄

Composite Functions

Functions may be combined using sums $(f + g)$, differences $(f - g)$, products (fg), or quotients (f/g). The process called *composition* also produces new functions.

▶ In the composition $y = f(g(x))$, f is the *outer function* and g is the *inner function*.

> **DEFINITION Composite Functions**
>
> Given two functions f and g, the composite function $f \circ g$ is defined by $(f \circ g)(x) = f(g(x))$. It is evaluated in two steps: $y = f(u)$, where $u = g(x)$. The domain of $f \circ g$ consists of all x in the domain of g such that $u = g(x)$ is in the domain of f (Figure 1.8).

▶ You have now seen three different notations for intervals on the real number line, all of which will be used throughout the book:
  • $[-2, 3)$ is an example of interval notation,
  • $-2 \le x < 3$ is inequality notation, and
  • $\{x: -2 \le x < 3\}$ is set notation.

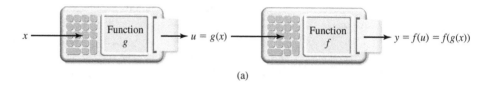

(a)

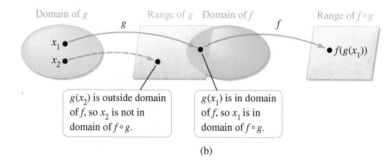

(b)

Figure 1.8

EXAMPLE 4 Composite functions and notation Let $f(x) = 3x^2 - x$ and $g(x) = 1/x$. Simplify the following expressions.

a. $f(5p + 1)$ **b.** $g(1/x)$ **c.** $f(g(x))$ **d.** $g(f(x))$

SOLUTION In each case, the functions work on their arguments.

a. The argument of f is $5p + 1$, so

$$f(5p + 1) = 3(5p + 1)^2 - (5p + 1) = 75p^2 + 25p + 2.$$

b. Because g requires taking the reciprocal of the argument, we take the reciprocal of $1/x$ and find that $g(1/x) = 1/(1/x) = x$.

c. The argument of f is $g(x)$, so

$$f(g(x)) = f\left(\frac{1}{x}\right) = 3\left(\frac{1}{x}\right)^2 - \left(\frac{1}{x}\right) = \frac{3}{x^2} - \frac{1}{x} = \frac{3 - x}{x^2}.$$

▶ Examples 4c and 4d demonstrate that, in general,
$$f(g(x)) \ne g(f(x)).$$

d. The argument of g is $f(x)$, so

$$g(f(x)) = g(3x^2 - x) = \frac{1}{3x^2 - x}.$$

Related Exercises 25–36 ◀

EXAMPLE 5 Working with composite functions Identify possible choices for the inner and outer functions in the following composite functions. Give the domain of the composite function.

a. $h(x) = \sqrt{9x - x^2}$ **b.** $h(x) = \dfrac{2}{(x^2 - 1)^3}$

SOLUTION

▶ Techniques for solving inequalities are discussed in Appendix A.

a. An obvious outer function is $f(x) = \sqrt{x}$, which works on the inner function $g(x) = 9x - x^2$. Therefore, h can be expressed as $h = f \circ g$ or $h(x) = f(g(x))$. The domain of $f \circ g$ consists of all values of x such that $9x - x^2 \ge 0$. Solving this inequality gives $\{x: 0 \le x \le 9\}$ as the domain of $f \circ g$.

b. A good choice for an outer function is $f(x) = 2/x^3 = 2x^{-3}$, which works on the inner function $g(x) = x^2 - 1$. Therefore, h can be expressed as $h = f \circ g$ or $h(x) = f(g(x))$. The domain of $f \circ g$ consists of all values of $g(x)$ such that $g(x) \neq 0$, which is $\{x: x \neq \pm 1\}$.

Related Exercises 37–40 ◄

EXAMPLE 6   More composite functions Given $f(x) = \sqrt[3]{x}$ and $g(x) = x^2 - x - 6$, find (a) $g \circ f$ and (b) $g \circ g$, and their domains.

SOLUTION

a. We have

$$(g \circ f)(x) = g(f(x)) = g(\underbrace{\sqrt[3]{x}}_{f(x)}) = (\underbrace{\sqrt[3]{x}}_{f(x)})^2 - \sqrt[3]{x} - 6 = x^{2/3} - x^{1/3} - 6.$$

Because the domains of f and g are $(-\infty, \infty)$, the domain of $f \circ g$ is also $(-\infty, \infty)$.

b. In this case, we have the composition of two polynomials:

$$(g \circ g)(x) = g(g(x))$$
$$= g(x^2 - x - 6)$$
$$= (\underbrace{x^2 - x - 6}_{g(x)})^2 - (\underbrace{x^2 - x - 6}_{g(x)}) - 6$$
$$= x^4 - 2x^3 - 12x^2 + 13x + 36.$$

The domain of the composition of two polynomials is $(-\infty, \infty)$.

Related Exercises 41–54 ◄

QUICK CHECK 3 If $f(x) = x^2 + 1$ and $g(x) = x^2$, find $f \circ g$ and $g \circ f$. ◄

EXAMPLE 7   Using graphs to evaluate composite functions Use the graphs of f and g in Figure 1.9 to find the following values.

a. $f(g(3))$ **b.** $g(f(3))$ **c.** $f(f(4))$ **d.** $f(g(f(8)))$

SOLUTION

a. The graphs indicate that $g(3) = 4$ and $f(4) = 8$, so $f(g(3)) = f(4) = 8$.

b. We see that $g(f(3)) = g(5) = 1$. Observe that $f(g(3)) \neq g(f(3))$.

c. In this case, $f(\underbrace{f(4)}_{8}) = f(8) = 6$.

d. Starting on the inside,

$$f(g(\underbrace{f(8)}_{6})) = f(\underbrace{g(6)}_{1}) = f(1) = 6.$$

Related Exercises 55–56 ◄

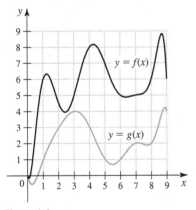

Figure 1.9

EXAMPLE 8   Using a table to evaluate composite functions Use the function values in the table to evaluate the following composite functions.

a. $(f \circ g)(0)$ **b.** $g(f(-1))$ **c.** $f(g(g(-1)))$

x	-2	-1	0	1	2
$f(x)$	0	1	3	4	2
$g(x)$	-1	0	-2	-3	-4

SOLUTION

a. Using the table, we see that $g(0) = -2$ and $f(-2) = 0$. Therefore, $(f \circ g)(0) = 0$.

b. Because $f(-1) = 1$ and $g(1) = -3$, it follows that $g(f(-1)) = -3$.

c. Starting with the inner function,

$$f(g(\underbrace{g(-1)}_{0}))) = f(\underbrace{g(0)}_{-2}) = f(-2) = 0.$$

Related Exercises 55–56 ◄

Secant Lines and the Difference Quotient

As you will see shortly, slopes of lines and curves play a fundamental role in calculus. Figure 1.10 shows two points $P(x, f(x))$ and $Q(x + h, f(x + h))$ on the graph of $y = f(x)$ in the case that $h > 0$. A line through any two points on a curve is called a **secant line**; its importance in the study of calculus is explained in Chapters 2 and 3. For now, we focus on the slope of the secant line through P and Q, which is denoted m_{sec} and is given by

$$m_{\text{sec}} = \frac{\text{change in } y}{\text{change in } x} = \frac{f(x + h) - f(x)}{(x + h) - x} = \frac{f(x + h) - f(x)}{h}.$$

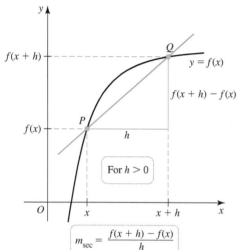

Figure 1.10

The slope formula $\dfrac{f(x + h) - f(x)}{h}$ is also known as a **difference quotient**, and it can be expressed in several ways depending on how the coordinates of P and Q are labeled. For example, given the coordinates $P(a, f(a))$ and $Q(x, f(x))$ (Figure 1.11), the difference quotient is

$$m_{\text{sec}} = \frac{f(x) - f(a)}{x - a}.$$

We interpret the slope of the secant line in this form as the **average rate of change** of f over the interval $[a, x]$.

EXAMPLE 9 Working with difference quotients

a. Simplify the difference quotient $\dfrac{f(x + h) - f(x)}{h}$, for $f(x) = 3x^2 - x$.

b. Simplify the difference quotient $\dfrac{f(x) - f(a)}{x - a}$, for $f(x) = x^3$.

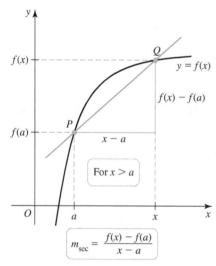

Figure 1.11

SOLUTION

a. First note that $f(x + h) = 3(x + h)^2 - (x + h)$. We substitute this expression into the difference quotient and simplify:

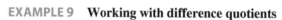

$$\frac{f(x + h) - f(x)}{h} = \frac{3(x + h)^2 - (x + h) - (3x^2 - x)}{h}$$

$$= \frac{3(x^2 + 2xh + h^2) - (x + h) - (3x^2 - x)}{h} \qquad \text{Expand } (x + h)^2.$$

$$= \frac{3x^2 + 6xh + 3h^2 - x - h - 3x^2 + x}{h} \qquad \text{Distribute.}$$

$$= \frac{6xh + 3h^2 - h}{h} \qquad \text{Simplify.}$$

$$= \frac{h(6x + 3h - 1)}{h} = 6x + 3h - 1. \qquad \text{Factor and simplify.}$$

▶ Treat $f(x + h)$ like the composition $f(g(x))$, where $x + h$ plays the role of $g(x)$. It may help to establish a pattern in your mind before evaluating $f(x + h)$. For instance, using the function in Example 9a, we have

$$f(x) = 3x^2 - x;$$
$$f(12) = 3 \cdot 12^2 - 12;$$
$$f(b) = 3b^2 - b;$$
$$f(\text{math}) = 3 \cdot \text{math}^2 - \text{math};$$

therefore,

$$f(x + h) = 3(x + h)^2 - (x + h).$$

▶ Some useful factoring formulas:

1. Difference of perfect squares:
    $$x^2 - y^2 = (x - y)(x + y).$$

2. Sum of perfect squares: $x^2 + y^2$ does not factor over the real numbers.

3. Difference of perfect cubes:
    $$x^3 - y^3 = (x - y)(x^2 + xy + y^2).$$

4. Sum of perfect cubes:
    $$x^3 + y^3 = (x + y)(x^2 - xy + y^2).$$

b. The factoring formula for the difference of perfect cubes is needed:

$$\frac{f(x) - f(a)}{x - a} = \frac{x^3 - a^3}{x - a}$$

$$= \frac{(x - a)(x^2 + ax + a^2)}{x - a} \qquad \text{Factoring formula}$$

$$= x^2 + ax + a^2. \qquad \text{Simplify.}$$

Related Exercises 57–66 ◄

EXAMPLE 10 Interpreting the slope of the secant line Sound intensity I, measured in watts per square meter (W/m^2), at a point r meters from a sound source with acoustic power P is given by $I(r) = \dfrac{P}{4\pi r^2}$.

a. Find the sound intensity at two points $r_1 = 10\,\text{m}$ and $r_2 = 15\,\text{m}$ from a sound source with power $P = 100\,\text{W}$. Then find the slope of the secant line through the points $(10, I(10))$ and $(15, I(15))$ on the graph of the intensity function and interpret the result.

b. Find the slope of the secant line through any two points $(r_1, I(r_1))$ and $(r_2, I(r_2))$ on the graph of the intensity function with acoustic power P.

SOLUTION

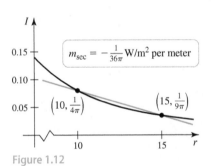

Figure 1.12

a. The sound intensity 10 m from the source is $I(10) = \dfrac{100\,\text{W}}{4\pi(10\,\text{m})^2} = \dfrac{1}{4\pi}\,\text{W/m}^2$. At 15 m, the intensity is $I(15) = \dfrac{100\,\text{W}}{4\pi(15\,\text{m})^2} = \dfrac{1}{9\pi}\,\text{W/m}^2$. To find the slope of the secant line (Figure 1.12), we compute the change in intensity divided by the change in distance:

$$m_{\text{sec}} = \frac{I(15) - I(10)}{15 - 10} = \frac{\dfrac{1}{9\pi} - \dfrac{1}{4\pi}}{5} = -\frac{1}{36\pi} \approx -0.0088\,\text{W/m}^2 \text{ per meter.}$$

The units provide a clue to the physical meaning of the slope: It measures the average rate at which the intensity changes as one moves from 10 m to 15 m away from the sound source. In this case, because the slope of the secant line is negative, the intensity *decreases* (slowly) at an average rate of $1/(36\pi)\,\text{W/m}^2$ per meter.

b.

$$m_{\text{sec}} = \frac{I(r_2) - I(r_1)}{r_2 - r_1} = \frac{\dfrac{P}{4\pi r_2^2} - \dfrac{P}{4\pi r_1^2}}{r_2 - r_1} \qquad \text{Evaluate } I(r_2) \text{ and } I(r_1).$$

$$= \frac{\dfrac{P}{4\pi}\left(\dfrac{1}{r_2^2} - \dfrac{1}{r_1^2}\right)}{r_2 - r_1} \qquad \text{Factor.}$$

$$= \frac{P}{4\pi}\left(\frac{r_1^2 - r_2^2}{r_1^2 r_2^2}\right)\frac{1}{r_2 - r_1} \qquad \text{Simplify.}$$

$$= \frac{P}{4\pi} \cdot \frac{(r_1 - r_2)(r_1 + r_2)}{r_1^2 r_2^2} \cdot \frac{1}{-(r_1 - r_2)} \qquad \text{Factor.}$$

$$= -\frac{P(r_1 + r_2)}{4\pi r_1^2 r_2^2} \qquad \text{Cancel and simplify.}$$

This result is the average rate at which the sound intensity changes over an interval $[r_1, r_2]$. Because $r_1 > 0$ and $r_2 > 0$, we see that m_{sec} is always negative. Therefore, the sound intensity $I(r)$ decreases as r increases, for $r > 0$.

Related Exercises 67–70 ◄

Symmetry

The word *symmetry* has many meanings in mathematics. Here we consider symmetries of graphs and the relations they represent. Taking advantage of symmetry often saves time and leads to insights.

DEFINITION Symmetry in Graphs

A graph is **symmetric with respect to the y-axis** if whenever the point (x, y) is on the graph, the point $(-x, y)$ is also on the graph. This property means that the graph is unchanged when reflected across the y-axis (Figure 1.13a).

A graph is **symmetric with respect to the x-axis** if whenever the point (x, y) is on the graph, the point $(x, -y)$ is also on the graph. This property means that the graph is unchanged when reflected across the x-axis (Figure 1.13b).

A graph is **symmetric with respect to the origin** if whenever the point (x, y) is on the graph, the point $(-x, -y)$ is also on the graph (Figure 1.13c). Symmetry about both the x- and y-axes implies symmetry about the origin, but not vice versa.

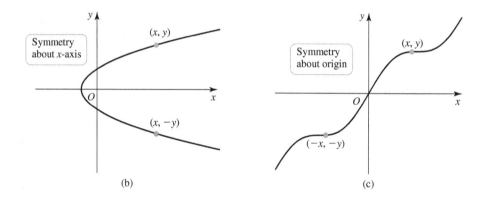

Figure 1.13

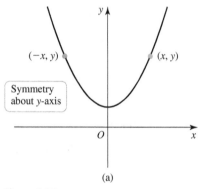

(a)

DEFINITION Symmetry in Functions

An **even function** f has the property that $f(-x) = f(x)$, for all x in the domain. The graph of an even function is symmetric about the y-axis.

An **odd function** f has the property that $f(-x) = -f(x)$, for all x in the domain. The graph of an odd function is symmetric about the origin.

Polynomials consisting of only even powers of the variable (of the form x^{2n}, where n is a nonnegative integer) are even functions. Polynomials consisting of only odd powers of the variable (of the form x^{2n+1}, where n is a nonnegative integer) are odd functions.

QUICK CHECK 4 Explain why the graph of a nonzero function is never symmetric with respect to the x-axis. ◄

EXAMPLE 11   Identifying symmetry in functions Identify the symmetry, if any, in the following functions.

a. $f(x) = x^4 - 2x^2 - 20$ **b.** $g(x) = x^3 - 3x + 1$ **c.** $h(x) = \dfrac{1}{x^3 - x}$

SOLUTION

a. The function f consists of only even powers of x (where $20 = 20 \cdot 1 = 20x^0$ and x^0 is considered an even power). Therefore, f is an even function (Figure 1.14). This fact is verified by showing that $f(-x) = f(x)$:

$$f(-x) = (-x)^4 - 2(-x)^2 - 20 = x^4 - 2x^2 - 20 = f(x).$$

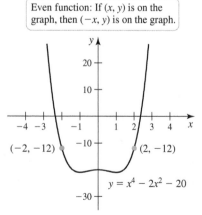

Even function: If (x, y) is on the graph, then $(-x, y)$ is on the graph.

$(-2, -12)$ $(2, -12)$

$y = x^4 - 2x^2 - 20$

Figure 1.14

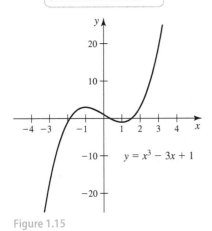

No symmetry: neither an even nor odd function.

$y = x^3 - 3x + 1$

Figure 1.15

▶ The symmetry of compositions of even and odd functions is considered in Exercises 95–101.

b. The function g consists of two odd powers and one even power (again, $1 = x^0$ is an even power). Therefore, we expect that g has no symmetry about the y-axis or the origin (Figure 1.15). Note that

$$g(-x) = (-x)^3 - 3(-x) + 1 = -x^3 + 3x + 1,$$

so $g(-x)$ equals neither $g(x)$ nor $-g(x)$; therefore, g has no symmetry.

c. In this case, h is a composition of an odd function $f(x) = 1/x$ with an odd function $g(x) = x^3 - x$. Note that

$$h(-x) = \frac{1}{(-x)^3 - (-x)} = -\frac{1}{x^3 - x} = -h(x).$$

Because $h(-x) = -h(x)$, h is an odd function (Figure 1.16).

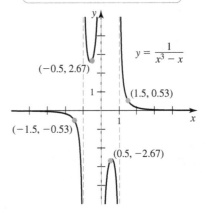

Odd function: If (x, y) is on the graph, then $(-x, -y)$ is on the graph.

$(-0.5, 2.67)$

$y = \dfrac{1}{x^3 - x}$

$(1.5, 0.53)$

$(-1.5, -0.53)$

$(0.5, -2.67)$

Figure 1.16

Related Exercises 71–80 ◄

SECTION 1.1 EXERCISES

Review Questions

1. Use the terms *domain, range, independent variable*, and *dependent variable* to explain how a function relates one variable to another variable.

2. Is the independent variable of a function associated with the domain or range? Is the dependent variable associated with the domain or range?

3. Explain how the vertical line test is used to detect functions.

4. If $f(x) = 1/(x^3 + 1)$, what is $f(2)$? What is $f(y^2)$?

5. Which statement about a function is true? (i) For each value of x in the domain, there corresponds one unique value of y in the range; (ii) for each value of y in the range, there corresponds one unique value of x in the domain. Explain.

6. If $f(x) = \sqrt{x}$ and $g(x) = x^3 - 2$, find the compositions $f \circ g, g \circ f, f \circ f$, and $g \circ g$.

7. Suppose f and g are even functions with $f(2) = 2$ and $g(2) = -2$. Evaluate $f(g(2))$ and $g(f(-2))$.

8. Explain how to find the domain of $f \circ g$ if you know the domain and range of f and g.

9. Sketch a graph of an even function f and state how $f(x)$ and $f(-x)$ are related.

10. Sketch a graph of an odd function f and state how $f(x)$ and $f(-x)$ are related.

Basic Skills

11–12. Vertical line test *Decide whether graphs A, B, or both represent functions.*

11.

12.

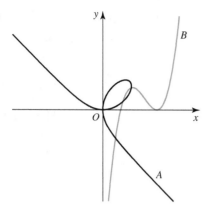

▣ 13–20. Domain and range *Graph each function with a graphing utility using the given window. Then state the domain and range of the function.*

13. $f(x) = 3x^4 - 10;$ $[-2, 2] \times [-10, 15]$

14. $g(y) = \dfrac{y + 1}{(y + 2)(y - 3)};$ $[-4, 6] \times [-3, 3]$

15. $f(x) = \sqrt{4 - x^2};$ $[-4, 4] \times [-4, 4]$

16. $F(w) = \sqrt[4]{2 - w};$ $[-3, 2] \times [0, 2]$

17. $h(u) = \sqrt[3]{u - 1};$ $[-7, 9] \times [-2, 2]$

18. $g(x) = (x^2 - 4)\sqrt{x + 5};$ $[-5, 5] \times [-10, 50]$

19. $f(x) = (9 - x^2)^{3/2};$ $[-4, 4] \times [0, 30]$

20. $g(t) = \dfrac{1}{1 + t^2};$ $[-7, 7] \times [0, 1.5]$

21–24. Domain in context *Determine an appropriate domain of each function. Identify the independent and dependent variables.*

21. A stone is thrown vertically upward from the ground at a speed of 40 m/s at time $t = 0$. Its distance d (in meters) above the ground (neglecting air resistance) is approximated by the function $f(t) = 40t - 5t^2$.

22. A stone is dropped off a bridge from a height of 20 m above a river. If t represents the elapsed time (in seconds) after the stone is released, then its distance d (in meters) above the river is approximated by the function $f(t) = 20 - 5t^2$.

23. A cylindrical water tower with a radius of 10 m and a height of 50 m is filled to a height of h. The volume V of water (in cubic meters) is given by the function $g(h) = 100\pi h$.

24. The volume V of a balloon of radius r (in meters) filled with helium is given by the function $f(r) = \frac{4}{3}\pi r^3$. Assume the balloon can hold up to 1 m³ of helium.

25–36. Composite functions and notation *Let $f(x) = x^2 - 4$, $g(x) = x^3$, and $F(x) = 1/(x - 3)$. Simplify or evaluate the following expressions.*

25. $f(10)$

26. $f(p^2)$

27. $g(1/z)$

28. $F(y^4)$

29. $F(g(y))$

30. $f(g(w))$

31. $g(f(u))$

32. $\dfrac{f(2 + h) - f(2)}{h}$

33. $F(F(x))$

34. $g(F(f(x)))$

35. $f(\sqrt{x + 4})$

36. $F\left(\dfrac{3x + 1}{x}\right)$

37–40. Working with composite functions *Find possible choices for the outer and inner functions f and g such that the given function h equals $f \circ g$. Give the domain of h.*

37. $h(x) = (x^3 - 5)^{10}$

38. $h(x) = \dfrac{2}{(x^6 + x^2 + 1)^2}$

39. $h(x) = \sqrt{x^4 + 2}$

40. $h(x) = \dfrac{1}{\sqrt{x^3 - 1}}$

41–48. More composite functions *Let $f(x) = |x|$, $g(x) = x^2 - 4$, $F(x) = \sqrt{x}$, and $G(x) = 1/(x - 2)$. Determine the following composite functions and give their domains.*

41. $f \circ g$

42. $g \circ f$

43. $f \circ G$

44. $f \circ g \circ G$

45. $G \circ g \circ f$

46. $F \circ g \circ g$

47. $g \circ g$

48. $G \circ G$

49–54. Missing piece *Let $g(x) = x^2 + 3$. Find a function f that produces the given composition.*

49. $(f \circ g)(x) = x^2$

50. $(f \circ g)(x) = \dfrac{1}{x^2 + 3}$

51. $(f \circ g)(x) = x^4 + 6x^2 + 9$

52. $(f \circ g)(x) = x^4 + 6x^2 + 20$

53. $(g \circ f)(x) = x^4 + 3$

54. $(g \circ f)(x) = x^{2/3} + 3$

55. Composite functions from graphs Use the graphs of f and g in the figure to determine the following function values.

a. $(f \circ g)(2)$ **b.** $g(f(2))$ **c.** $f(g(4))$
d. $g(f(5))$ **e.** $f(f(8))$ **f.** $g(f(g(5)))$

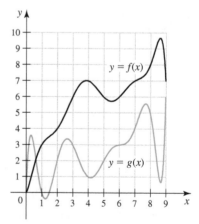

56. Composite functions from tables Use the table to evaluate the given compositions.

x	-1	0	1	2	3	4
$f(x)$	3	1	0	-1	-3	-1
$g(x)$	-1	0	2	3	4	5
$h(x)$	0	-1	0	3	0	4

a. $h(g(0))$ **b.** $g(f(4))$ **c.** $h(h(0))$
d. $g(h(f(4)))$ **e.** $f(f(f(1)))$ **f.** $h(h(h(0)))$
g. $f(h(g(2)))$ **h.** $g(f(h(4)))$ **i.** $g(g(g(1)))$
j. $f(f(h(3)))$

57–61. Working with difference quotients *Simplify the difference quotient* $\dfrac{f(x+h)-f(x)}{h}$ *for the following functions.*

57. $f(x) = x^2$

58. $f(x) = 4x - 3$

59. $f(x) = 2/x$

60. $f(x) = 2x^2 - 3x + 1$

61. $f(x) = \dfrac{x}{x+1}$

62–66. Working with difference quotients *Simplify the difference quotient* $\dfrac{f(x)-f(a)}{x-a}$ *for the following functions.*

62. $f(x) = x^4$

63. $f(x) = x^3 - 2x$

64. $f(x) = 4 - 4x - x^2$

65. $f(x) = -\dfrac{4}{x^2}$

66. $f(x) = \dfrac{1}{x} - x^2$

67–70. Interpreting the slope of secant lines *In each exercise, a function and an interval of its independent variable are given. The endpoints of the interval are associated with the points P and Q on the graph of the function.*

a. *Sketch a graph of the function and the secant line through P and Q.*

b. *Find the slope of the secant line in part (a), and interpret your answer in terms of an average rate of change over the interval. Include units in your answer.*

67. After t seconds, an object dropped from rest falls a distance $d = 16t^2$, where d is measured in feet and $2 \le t \le 5$.

68. After t seconds, the second hand on a clock moves through an angle $D = 6t$, where D is measured in degrees and $5 \le t \le 20$.

69. The volume V of an ideal gas in cubic centimeters is given by $V = 2/p$, where p is the pressure in atmospheres and $0.5 \le p \le 2$.

70. The speed of a car prior to hard braking can be estimated by the length of the skid mark. One model claims that the speed S in mi/hr is $S = \sqrt{30\ell}$, where ℓ is the length of the skid mark in feet and $50 \le \ell \le 150$.

71–78. Symmetry *Determine whether the graphs of the following equations and functions are symmetric about the x-axis, the y-axis, or the origin. Check your work by graphing.*

71. $f(x) = x^4 + 5x^2 - 12$

72. $f(x) = 3x^5 + 2x^3 - x$

73. $f(x) = x^5 - x^3 - 2$

74. $f(x) = 2|x|$

75. $x^{2/3} + y^{2/3} = 1$

76. $x^3 - y^5 = 0$

77. $f(x) = x|x|$

78. $|x| + |y| = 1$

79. **Symmetry in graphs** State whether the functions represented by graphs A, B, and C in the figure are even, odd, or neither.

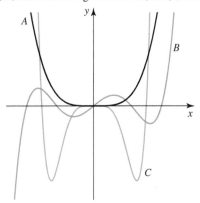

80. **Symmetry in graphs** State whether the functions represented by graphs A, B, and C in the figure are even, odd, or neither.

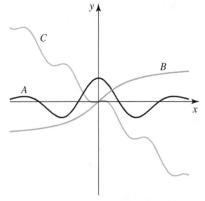

Further Explorations

81. **Explain why or why not** Determine whether the following statements are true and give an explanation or counterexample.

  a. The range of $f(x) = 2x - 38$ is all real numbers.

  b. The relation $y = x^6 + 1$ is *not* a function because $y = 2$ for both $x = -1$ and $x = 1$.

  c. If $f(x) = x^{-1}$, then $f(1/x) = 1/f(x)$.

  d. In general, $f(f(x)) = (f(x))^2$.

  e. In general, $f(g(x)) = g(f(x))$.

  f. By definition, $f(g(x)) = (f \circ g)(x)$.

  g. If $f(x)$ is an even function, then $c\,f(ax)$ is an even function, where a and c are nonzero real numbers.

  h. If $f(x)$ is an odd function, then $f(x) + d$ is an odd function, where d is a nonzero real number.

  i. If f is both even *and* odd, then $f(x) = 0$ for all x.

82. **Range of power functions** Using words and figures, explain why the range of $f(x) = x^n$, where n is a positive odd integer, is all real numbers. Explain why the range of $g(x) = x^n$, where n is a positive even integer, is all nonnegative real numbers.

83. **Absolute value graph** Use the definition of absolute value to graph the equation $|x| - |y| = 1$. Use a graphing utility to check your work.

84. **Even and odd at the origin**

  a. If $f(0)$ is defined and f is an even function, is it necessarily true that $f(0) = 0$? Explain.

  b. If $f(0)$ is defined and f is an odd function, is it necessarily true that $f(0) = 0$? Explain.

85–88. Polynomial calculations *Find a polynomial f that satisfies the following properties. (Hint: Determine the degree of f; then substitute a polynomial of that degree and solve for its coefficients.)*

85. $f(f(x)) = 9x - 8$

86. $(f(x))^2 = 9x^2 - 12x + 4$

87. $f(f(x)) = x^4 - 12x^2 + 30$

88. $(f(x))^2 = x^4 - 12x^2 + 36$

89–92. Difference quotients *Simplify the difference quotients* $\dfrac{f(x+h) - f(x)}{h}$ *and* $\dfrac{f(x) - f(a)}{x - a}$ *by rationalizing the numerator.*

89. $f(x) = \sqrt{x}$

90. $f(x) = \sqrt{1 - 2x}$

91. $f(x) = -\dfrac{3}{\sqrt{x}}$

92. $f(x) = \sqrt{x^2 + 1}$

Applications

93. Launching a rocket A small rocket is launched vertically upward from the edge of a cliff 80 ft off the ground at a speed of 96 ft/s. Its height (in feet) above the ground is given by $h(t) = -16t^2 + 96t + 80$, where t represents time measured in seconds.

  a. Assuming the rocket is launched at $t = 0$, what is an appropriate domain for h?

  b. Graph h and determine the time at which the rocket reaches its highest point. What is the height at that time?

94. Draining a tank (Torricelli's law) A cylindrical tank with a cross-sectional area of 100 cm² is filled to a depth of 100 cm with water. At $t = 0$, a drain in the bottom of the tank with an area of 10 cm² is opened, allowing water to flow out of the tank. The depth of water in the tank at time $t \geq 0$ is $d(t) = (10 - 2.2t)^2$.

  a. Check that $d(0) = 100$, as specified.

  b. At what time is the tank empty?

  c. What is an appropriate domain for d?

Additional Exercises

95–101. Combining even and odd functions *Let E be an even function and O be an odd function. Determine the symmetry, if any, of the following functions.*

95. $E + O$ **96.** $E \cdot O$ **97.** E/O **98.** $E \circ O$

99. $E \circ E$ **100.** $O \circ O$ **101.** $O \circ E$

102. Composition of even and odd functions from tables Assume f is an even function and g is an odd function. Use the (incomplete) table to evaluate the given compositions.

x	1	2	3	4
$f(x)$	2	−1	3	−4
$g(x)$	−3	−1	−4	−2

  a. $f(g(-1))$ **b.** $g(f(-4))$ **c.** $f(g(-3))$
  d. $f(g(-2))$ **e.** $g(g(-1))$ **f.** $f(g(0) - 1)$
  g. $f(g(g(-2)))$ **h.** $g(f(f(-4)))$ **i.** $g(g(g(-1)))$

103. Composition of even and odd functions from graphs Assume f is an even function and g is an odd function. Use the (incomplete) graphs of f and g in the figure to determine the following function values.

  a. $f(g(-2))$ **b.** $g(f(-2))$ **c.** $f(g(-4))$
  d. $g(f(5) - 8)$ **e.** $g(g(-7))$ **f.** $f(1 - f(8))$

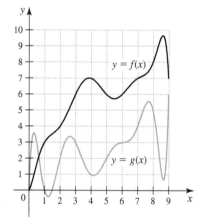

QUICK CHECK ANSWERS

1. $3, x^4 - 2x^2, t^2 - 2t, p^2 - 4p + 3$ **2.** Domain is all real numbers; range is $\{y : 0 < y \leq 1\}$.
3. $(f \circ g)(x) = x^4 + 1$ and $(g \circ f)(x) = (x^2 + 1)^2$
4. If the graph were symmetric with respect to the x-axis, it would not pass the vertical line test. ◄

1.2 Representing Functions

We consider four approaches to defining and representing functions: formulas, graphs, tables, and words.

Using Formulas

The following list is a brief catalog of the families of functions that are introduced in this chapter and studied systematically throughout this book; they are all defined by *formulas*.

> ➤ One version of the Fundamental Theorem of Algebra states that a nonzero polynomial of degree n has exactly n (possibly complex) roots, counting each root up to its multiplicity.

1. Polynomials are functions of the form

$$p(x) = a_n x^n + a_{n-1} x^{n-1} + \cdots + a_1 x + a_0,$$

where the **coefficients** $a_0, a_1, \ldots, a_n$ are real numbers with $a_n \neq 0$ and the nonnegative integer n is the **degree** of the polynomial. The domain of any polynomial is the set of all real numbers. An nth-degree polynomial can have as many as n real **zeros** or **roots**—values of x at which $p(x) = 0$; the zeros are points at which the graph of p intersects the x-axis.

2. **Rational functions** are ratios of the form $f(x) = p(x)/q(x)$, where p and q are polynomials. Because division by zero is prohibited, the domain of a rational function is the set of all real numbers except those for which the denominator is zero.

3. **Algebraic functions** are constructed using the operations of algebra: addition, subtraction, multiplication, division, and roots. Examples of algebraic functions are $f(x) = \sqrt{2x^3 + 4}$ and $g(x) = x^{1/4}(x^3 + 2)$. In general, if an even root (square root, fourth root, and so forth) appears, then the domain does not contain points at which the quantity under the root is negative (and perhaps other points).

> Exponential and logarithmic functions are introduced in Section 1.3.

4. **Exponential functions** have the form $f(x) = b^x$, where the base $b \neq 1$ is a positive real number. Closely associated with exponential functions are **logarithmic functions** of the form $f(x) = \log_b x$, where $b > 0$ and $b \neq 1$. Exponential functions have a domain consisting of all real numbers. Logarithmic functions are defined for positive real numbers.

   The **natural exponential function** is $f(x) = e^x$, with base $b = e$, where $e \approx 2.71828\ldots$ is one of the fundamental constants of mathematics. Associated with the natural exponential function is the **natural logarithm function** $f(x) = \ln x$, which also has the base $b = e$.

> Trigonometric functions and their inverses are introduced in Section 1.4.

5. The **trigonometric functions** are $\sin x$, $\cos x$, $\tan x$, $\cot x$, $\sec x$, and $\csc x$; they are fundamental to mathematics and many areas of application. Also important are their relatives, the **inverse trigonometric functions**.

6. Trigonometric, exponential, and logarithmic functions are a few examples of a large family called **transcendental functions**. Figure 1.17 shows the organization of these functions, which are explored in detail in upcoming chapters.

QUICK CHECK 1 Are all polynomials rational functions? Are all algebraic functions polynomials? ◄

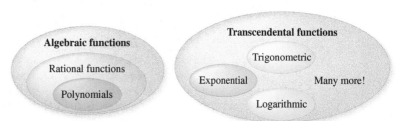

Figure 1.17

Using Graphs

Although formulas are the most compact way to represent many functions, graphs often provide the most illuminating representations. Two of countless examples of functions and their graphs are shown in Figure 1.18. Much of this book is devoted to creating and analyzing graphs of functions.

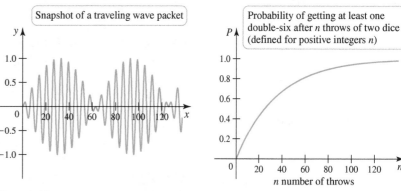

Figure 1.18

There are two approaches to graphing functions.

• Graphing calculators, tablets, and software are easy to use and powerful. Such **technology** easily produces graphs of most functions encountered in this book. We assume you know how to use a graphing utility.

• Graphing utilities, however, are not infallible. Therefore, you should also strive to master **analytical methods** (pencil-and-paper methods) in order to analyze functions and make accurate graphs by hand. Analytical methods rely heavily on calculus and are presented throughout this book.

The important message is this: Both technology and analytical methods are essential and must be used together in an integrated way to produce accurate graphs.

Linear Functions   One form of the equation of a line (see Appendix A) is $y = mx + b$, where m and b are constants. Therefore, the function $f(x) = mx + b$ has a straight-line graph and is called a **linear function**.

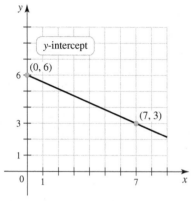

Figure 1.19

EXAMPLE 1   Linear functions and their graphs Determine the function represented by the line in Figure 1.19.

SOLUTION From the graph, we see that the y-intercept is $(0, 6)$. Using the points $(0, 6)$ and $(7, 3)$, the slope of the line is

$$m = \frac{3 - 6}{7 - 0} = -\frac{3}{7}.$$

Therefore, the line is described by the function $f(x) = -3x/7 + 6$.

Related Exercises 11–14 ◄

EXAMPLE 2   Demand function for pizzas After studying sales for several months, the owner of a pizza chain knows that the number of two-topping pizzas sold in a week (called the *demand*) decreases as the price increases. Specifically, her data indicate that at a price of $14 per pizza, an average of 400 pizzas are sold per week, while at a price of $17 per pizza, an average of 250 pizzas are sold per week. Assume that the demand d is a *linear* function of the price p.

a. Find the constants m and b in the demand function $d = f(p) = mp + b$. Then graph f.

b. According to this model, how many pizzas (on average) are sold per week at a price of $20?

SOLUTION

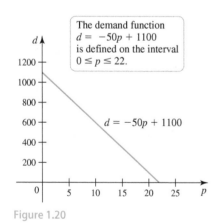

Figure 1.20

a. Two points on the graph of the demand function are given: $(p, d) = (14, 400)$ and $(17, 250)$. Therefore, the slope of the demand line is

$$m = \frac{400 - 250}{14 - 17} = -50 \text{ pizzas per dollar.}$$

It follows that the equation of the linear demand function is

$$d - 250 = -50(p - 17).$$

Expressing d as a function of p, we have $d = f(p) = -50p + 1100$ (Figure 1.20).

b. Using the demand function with a price of $20, the average number of pizzas that could be sold per week is $f(20) = 100$.

Related Exercises 15–18 ◄

➤ The units of the slope have meaning: For every dollar the price is reduced, an average of 50 more pizzas can be sold.

Piecewise Functions   A function may have different definitions on different parts of its domain. For example, income tax is levied in tax brackets that have different tax rates. Functions that have different definitions on different parts of their domain are called **piecewise functions**. If all the pieces are linear, the function is **piecewise linear**. Here are some examples.

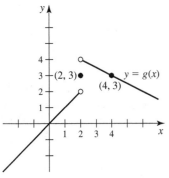

Figure 1.21

EXAMPLE 3 **Defining a piecewise function** The graph of a piecewise linear function g is shown in Figure 1.21. Find a formula for the function.

SOLUTION For $x < 2$, the graph is linear with a slope of 1 and a y-intercept of $(0, 0)$; its equation is $y = x$. For $x > 2$, the slope of the line is $-\frac{1}{2}$ and it passes through $(4, 3)$; so an equation of this piece of the function is

$$y - 3 = -\frac{1}{2}(x - 4) \quad \text{or} \quad y = -\frac{1}{2}x + 5.$$

For $x = 2$, we have $g(2) = 3$. Therefore,

$$g(x) = \begin{cases} x & \text{if } x < 2 \\ 3 & \text{if } x = 2 \\ -\frac{1}{2}x + 5 & \text{if } x > 2. \end{cases}$$

Related Exercises 19–22 ◄

EXAMPLE 4 **Graphing piecewise functions** Graph the following functions.

a. $f(x) = \begin{cases} \dfrac{x^2 - 5x + 6}{x - 2} & \text{if } x \neq 2 \\ 1 & \text{if } x = 2 \end{cases}$

b. $f(x) = |x|$, the **absolute value** function

SOLUTION

a. The function f is simplified by factoring and then canceling $x - 2$, assuming $x \neq 2$:

$$\frac{x^2 - 5x + 6}{x - 2} = \frac{(x - 2)(x - 3)}{x - 2} = x - 3.$$

Therefore, the graph of f is identical to the graph of the line $y = x - 3$ when $x \neq 2$. We are given that $f(2) = 1$ (Figure 1.22).

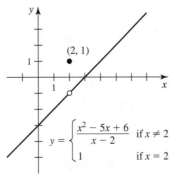

Figure 1.22

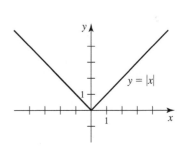

Figure 1.23

b. The absolute value of a real number is defined as

$$f(x) = |x| = \begin{cases} x & \text{if } x \geq 0 \\ -x & \text{if } x < 0. \end{cases}$$

Graphing $y = -x$, for $x < 0$, and $y = x$, for $x \geq 0$, produces the graph in Figure 1.23.

Related Exercises 23–28 ◄

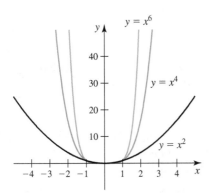

Figure 1.24

Power Functions Power functions are a special case of polynomials; they have the form $f(x) = x^n$, where n is a positive integer. When n is an even integer, the function values are nonnegative and the graph passes through the origin, opening upward (Figure 1.24). For

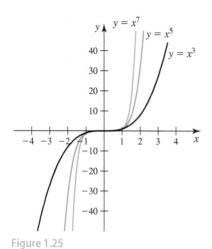

Figure 1.25

> Recall that if n is a positive integer,
> then $x^{1/n}$ is the nth root of x; that is,
> $f(x) = x^{1/n} = \sqrt[n]{x}$.

QUICK CHECK 3 What are the domain and range of $f(x) = x^{1/7}$? What are the domain and range of $f(x) = x^{1/10}$? ◄

odd integers, the power function $f(x) = x^n$ has values that are positive when x is positive and negative when x is negative (Figure 1.25).

QUICK CHECK 2 What is the range of $f(x) = x^7$? What is the range of $f(x) = x^8$? ◄

Root Functions   Root functions are a special case of algebraic functions; they have the form $f(x) = x^{1/n}$, where $n > 1$ is a positive integer. Notice that when n is even (square roots, fourth roots, and so forth), the domain and range consist of nonnegative numbers. Their graphs begin steeply at the origin and flatten out as x increases (Figure 1.26).

By contrast, the odd root functions (cube roots, fifth roots, and so forth) are defined for all real values of x and their range is all real numbers. Their graphs pass through the origin, open upward for $x < 0$ and downward for $x > 0$, and flatten out as x increases in magnitude (Figure 1.27).

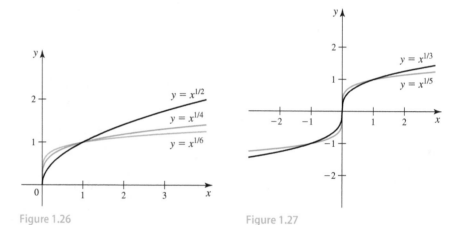

Figure 1.26

Figure 1.27

Rational Functions   Rational functions appear frequently in this book, and much is said later about graphing rational functions. The following example illustrates how analysis and technology work together.

EXAMPLE 5   Technology and analysis   Consider the rational function

$$f(x) = \frac{3x^3 - x - 1}{x^3 + 2x^2 - 6}.$$

a. What is the domain of f?

b. Find the roots (zeros) of f.

c. Graph the function using a graphing utility.

d. At what points does the function have peaks and valleys?

e. How does f behave as x grows large in magnitude?

SOLUTION

a. The domain consists of all real numbers except those at which the denominator is zero. A graphing utility shows that the denominator has one real zero at $x \approx 1.34$ and therefore, the domain of f is $\{x : x \neq 1.34\}$.

b. The roots of a rational function are the roots of the numerator, provided they are not also roots of the denominator. Using a graphing utility, the only real root of the numerator is $x \approx 0.85$.

c. After experimenting with the graphing window, a reasonable graph of f is obtained (Figure 1.28). At the point $x \approx 1.34$, where the denominator is zero, the function becomes large in magnitude and f has a *vertical asymptote*.

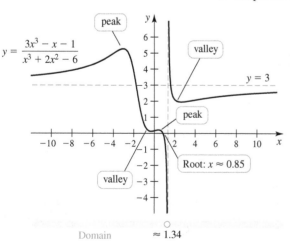

Figure 1.28

> ▶ In Chapter 3, we show how calculus is used to locate the local maximum and local minimum values of a function.

d. The function has two peaks (soon to be called *local maxima*), one near $x = -3.0$ and one near $x = 0.4$. The function also has two valleys (soon to be called *local minima*), one near $x = -0.3$ and one near $x = 2.6$.

e. By zooming out, it appears that as x increases in the positive direction, the graph approaches the *horizontal asymptote* $y = 3$ from below, and as x becomes large and negative, the graph approaches $y = 3$ from above.

Related Exercises 29–34 ◀

Using Tables

Sometimes functions do not originate as formulas or graphs; they may start as numbers or data. For example, suppose you do an experiment in which a marble is dropped into a cylinder filled with heavy oil and is allowed to fall freely. You measure the total distance d, in centimeters, that the marble falls at times $t = 0, 1, 2, 3, 4, 5, 6,$ and 7 seconds after it is dropped (Table 1.1). The first step might be to plot the data points (Figure 1.29).

Table 1.1

t (s)	d (cm)
0	0
1	2
2	6
3	14
4	24
5	34
6	44
7	54

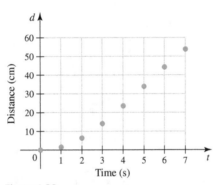

Figure 1.29

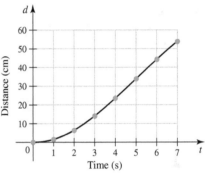

Figure 1.30

The data points suggest that there is a function $d = f(t)$ that gives the distance that the marble falls at *all* times of interest. Because the marble falls through the oil without abrupt changes, a smooth graph passing through the data points (Figure 1.30) is reasonable. Finding the best function that fits the data is a more difficult problem, which we discuss later in the text.

Using Words

Using words may be the least mathematical way to define functions, but it is often the way in which functions originate. Once a function is defined in words, it can often be tabulated, graphed, or expressed as a formula.

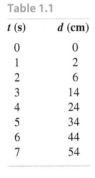

Figure 1.31

EXAMPLE 6 A slope function Let g be the **slope function** for a given function f. In words, this means that $g(x)$ is the slope of the curve $y = f(x)$ at the point $(x, f(x))$. Find and graph the slope function for the function f in Figure 1.31.

SOLUTION For $x < 1$, the slope of $y = f(x)$ is 2. The slope is 0 for $1 < x < 2$, and the slope is -1 for $x > 2$. At $x = 1$ and $x = 2$, the graph of f has a corner, so the slope is undefined at these points. Therefore, the domain of g is the set of all real numbers except $x = 1$ and $x = 2$, and the slope function (Figure 1.32) is defined by the piecewise function

$$g(x) = \begin{cases} 2 & \text{if } x < 1 \\ 0 & \text{if } 1 < x < 2 \\ -1 & \text{if } x > 2. \end{cases}$$

Related Exercises 35–38 ◀

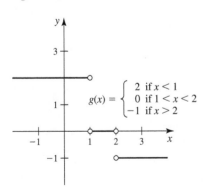

Figure 1.32

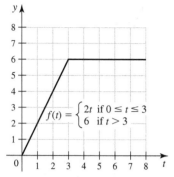

Figure 1.33

▶ Slope functions and area functions reappear in upcoming chapters and play an essential part in calculus.

EXAMPLE 7   **An area function** Let A be an **area function** for a positive function f. In words, this means that $A(x)$ is the area of the region bounded by the graph of f and the t-axis from $t = 0$ to $t = x$. Consider the function (Figure 1.33)

$$f(t) = \begin{cases} 2t & \text{if } 0 \le t \le 3 \\ 6 & \text{if } t > 3. \end{cases}$$

a. Find $A(2)$ and $A(5)$.

b. Find a piecewise formula for the area function for f.

SOLUTION

a. The value of $A(2)$ is the area of the shaded region between the graph of f and the t-axis from $t = 0$ to $t = 2$ (Figure 1.34a). Using the formula for the area of a triangle,

$$A(2) = \frac{1}{2}(2)(4) = 4.$$

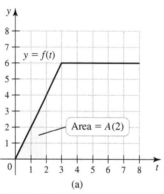

(a)

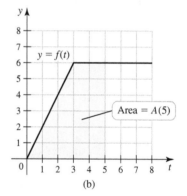

(b)

Figure 1.34

The value of $A(5)$ is the area of the shaded region between the graph of f and the t-axis on the interval $[0, 5]$ (Figure 1.34b). This area equals the area of the triangle whose base is the interval $[0, 3]$ plus the area of the rectangle whose base is the interval $[3, 5]$:

$$A(5) = \overbrace{\frac{1}{2}(3)(6)}^{\substack{\text{area of the} \\ \text{triangle}}} + \overbrace{(2)(6)}^{\substack{\text{area of the} \\ \text{rectangle}}} = 21.$$

b. For $0 \le x \le 3$ (Figure 1.35a), $A(x)$ is the area of the triangle whose base is the interval $[0, x]$. Because the height of the triangle at $t = x$ is $f(x)$,

$$A(x) = \frac{1}{2}xf(x) = \frac{1}{2}x\underbrace{(2x)}_{f(x)} = x^2.$$

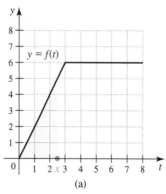

(a)

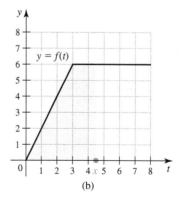

(b)

Figure 1.35

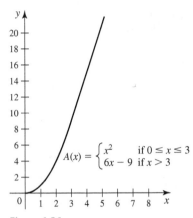

Figure 1.36

For $x > 3$ (Figure 1.35b), $A(x)$ is the area of the triangle on the interval $[0, 3]$ plus the area of the rectangle on the interval $[3, x]$:

$$A(x) = \underbrace{\frac{1}{2}(3)(6)}_{\substack{\text{area of the} \\ \text{triangle}}} + \underbrace{(x - 3)(6)}_{\substack{\text{area of the} \\ \text{rectangle}}} = 6x - 9.$$

Therefore, the area function A (Figure 1.36) has the piecewise definition

$$y = A(x) = \begin{cases} x^2 & \text{if } 0 \le x \le 3 \\ 6x - 9 & \text{if } x > 3. \end{cases}$$

Related Exercises 39–42 ◄

Transformations of Functions and Graphs

There are several ways to transform the graph of a function to produce graphs of new functions. Four transformations are common: *shifts* in the x- and y-directions and *scalings* in the x- and y-directions. These transformations, summarized in Figures 1.37–1.42, can save time in graphing and visualizing functions.

> The graph of $y = f(x) + d$ is the graph of $y = f(x)$ shifted vertically by d units (up if $d > 0$ and down if $d < 0$).

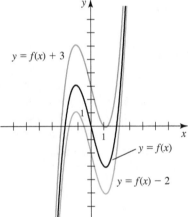

Figure 1.37

> The graph of $y = f(x - b)$ is the graph of $y = f(x)$ shifted horizontally by b units (right if $b > 0$ and left if $b < 0$).

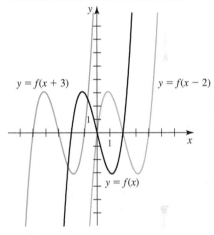

Figure 1.38

> For $c > 0$, the graph of $y = cf(x)$ is the graph of $y = f(x)$ scaled vertically by a factor of c (wider if $0 < c < 1$ and narrower if $c > 1$).

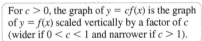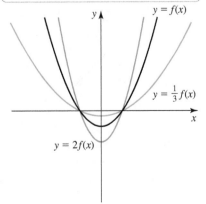

Figure 1.39

> For $c < 0$, the graph of $y = cf(x)$ is the graph of $y = f(x)$ scaled vertically by a factor of $|c|$ and reflected across the x-axis (wider if $-1 < c < 0$ and narrower if $c < -1$).

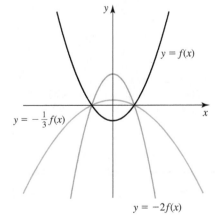

Figure 1.40

For $a > 0$, the graph of $y = f(ax)$ is the graph of $y = f(x)$ scaled horizontally by a factor of a (wider if $0 < a < 1$ and narrower if $a > 1$).

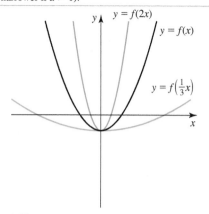

Figure 1.41

For $a < 0$, the graph of $y = f(ax)$ is the graph of $y = f(x)$ scaled horizontally by a factor of $|a|$ and reflected across the y-axis (wider if $-1 < a < 0$ and narrower if $a < -1$).

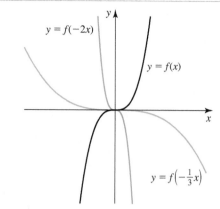

Figure 1.42

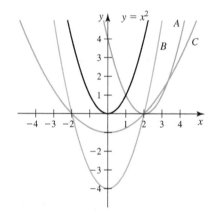

Figure 1.43

▶ You should verify that graph C also corresponds to a horizontal scaling and a vertical shift. It has the equation $y = f(ax) - 1$, where $a = \frac{1}{2}$.

QUICK CHECK 4 How do you modify the graph of $f(x) = 1/x$ to produce the graph of $g(x) = 1/(x + 4)$? ◄

EXAMPLE 8   Shifting parabolas The graphs A, B, and C in Figure 1.43 are obtained from the graph of $f(x) = x^2$ using shifts and scalings. Find the function that describes each graph.

SOLUTION

a. Graph A is the graph of f shifted to the right by 2 units. It represents the function
$$f(x - 2) = (x - 2)^2 = x^2 - 4x + 4.$$

b. Graph B is the graph of f shifted down by 4 units. It represents the function
$$f(x) - 4 = x^2 - 4.$$

c. Graph C is a wider version of the graph of f shifted down by 1 unit. Therefore, it represents $cf(x) - 1 = cx^2 - 1$, for some value of c, with $0 < c < 1$ (because the graph is widened). Using the fact that graph C passes through the points $(\pm 2, 0)$, we find that $c = \frac{1}{4}$. Therefore, the graph represents
$$y = \frac{1}{4} f(x) - 1 = \frac{1}{4} x^2 - 1.$$

Related Exercises 43–54 ◄

EXAMPLE 9   Scaling and shifting Graph $g(x) = |2x + 1|$.

SOLUTION We write the function as $g(x) = \left| 2\left(x + \frac{1}{2}\right) \right|$. Letting $f(x) = |x|$, we have $g(x) = f\left(2\left(x + \frac{1}{2}\right)\right)$. Therefore, the graph of g is obtained by scaling (steepening) the graph of f horizontally and shifting it $\frac{1}{2}$ unit to the left (Figure 1.44).

▶ Note that we can also write $g(x) = 2\left|x + \frac{1}{2}\right|$, which means the graph of g may also be obtained by a vertical scaling and a horizontal shift.

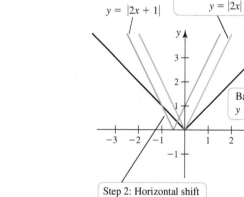

Figure 1.44

Related Exercises 43–54 ◄

SUMMARY   **Transformations**

Given the real numbers a, b, c, and d and the function f, the graph of $y = cf(a(x - b)) + d$ can be obtained from the graph of $y = f(x)$ in the following steps.

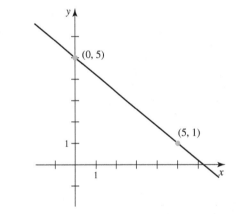

SECTION 1.2 EXERCISES

Review Questions

1. Give four ways that functions may be defined and represented.

2. What is the domain of a polynomial?

3. What is the domain of a rational function?

4. Describe what is meant by a piecewise linear function.

5. Sketch a graph of $y = x^5$.

6. Sketch a graph of $y = x^{1/5}$.

7. How do you obtain the graph of $y = f(x + 2)$ from the graph of $y = f(x)$?

8. How do you obtain the graph of $y = -3f(x)$ from the graph of $y = f(x)$?

9. How do you obtain the graph of $y = f(3x)$ from the graph of $y = f(x)$?

10. How do you obtain the graph of $y = 4(x + 3)^2 + 6$ from the graph of $y = x^2$?

Basic Skills

11–12. Graphs of functions *Find the linear functions that correspond to the following graphs.*

11.

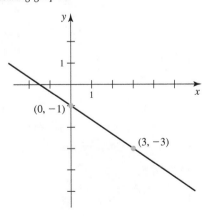

12.

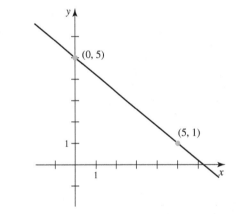

13. **Graph of a linear function** Find and graph the linear function that passes through the points $(1, 3)$ and $(2, 5)$.

14. **Graph of a linear function** Find and graph the linear function that passes through the points $(2, -3)$ and $(5, 0)$.

15. **Demand function** Sales records indicate that if Blu-ray players are priced at $250, then a large store sells an average of 12 units per day. If they are priced at $200, then the store sells an average of 15 units per day. Find and graph the linear demand function for Blu-ray sales. For what prices is the demand function defined?

16. **Fundraiser** The Biology Club plans to have a fundraiser for which $8 tickets will be sold. The cost of room rental and refreshments is $175. Find and graph the function $p = f(n)$ that gives the profit from the fundraiser when n tickets are sold. Notice that $f(0) = -\$175$; that is, the cost of room rental and refreshments must be paid regardless of how many tickets are sold. How many tickets must be sold to break even (zero profit)?

17. **Population function** The population of a small town was 500 in 2015 and is growing at a rate of 24 people per year. Find and graph the linear population function $p(t)$ that gives the population of the town t years after 2015. Then use this model to predict the population in 2030.

18. Taxicab fees A taxicab ride costs \$3.50 plus \$2.50 per mile. Let m be the distance (in miles) from the airport to a hotel. Find and graph the function $c(m)$ that represents the cost of taking a taxi from the airport to the hotel. Also determine how much it costs if the hotel is 9 miles from the airport.

19–20. Graphs of piecewise functions *Write a definition of the functions whose graphs are given.*

19.

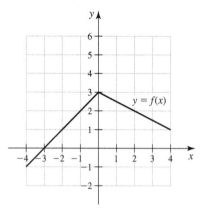

20.

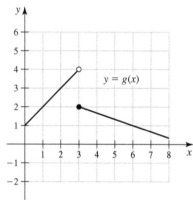

21. Parking fees Suppose that it costs 5¢ per minute to park at the airport with the rate dropping to 3¢ per minute after 9 P.M. Find and graph the cost function $c(t)$ for values of t satisfying $0 \le t \le 120$. Assume that t is the number of minutes after 8 P.M.

22. Taxicab fees A taxicab ride costs \$3.50 plus \$2.50 per mile for the first 5 miles, with the rate dropping to \$1.50 per mile after the fifth mile. Let m be the distance (in miles) from the airport to a hotel. Find and graph the piecewise linear function $c(m)$ that represents the cost of taking a taxi from the airport to a hotel m miles away.

23–28. Piecewise linear functions *Graph the following functions.*

23. $f(x) = \begin{cases} \dfrac{x^2 - x}{x - 1} & \text{if } x \ne 1 \\ 2 & \text{if } x = 1 \end{cases}$

24. $f(x) = \begin{cases} \dfrac{x^2 - x - 2}{x - 2} & \text{if } x \ne 2 \\ 4 & \text{if } x = 2 \end{cases}$

25. $f(x) = \begin{cases} 3x - 1 & \text{if } x \le 0 \\ -2x + 1 & \text{if } x > 0 \end{cases}$

26. $f(x) = \begin{cases} 3x - 1 & \text{if } x < 1 \\ x + 1 & \text{if } x \ge 1 \end{cases}$

27. $f(x) = \begin{cases} -2x - 1 & \text{if } x < -1 \\ 1 & \text{if } -1 \le x \le 1 \\ 2x - 1 & \text{if } x > 1 \end{cases}$

28. $f(x) = \begin{cases} 2x + 2 & \text{if } x < 0 \\ x + 2 & \text{if } 0 \le x \le 2 \\ 3 - x/2 & \text{if } x > 2 \end{cases}$

⊤ 29–34. Graphs of functions

  a. Use a graphing utility to produce a graph of the given function. Experiment with different windows to see how the graph changes on different scales. Sketch an accurate graph by hand after using the graphing utility.
  b. Give the domain of the function.
  c. Discuss interesting features of the function, such as peaks, valleys, and intercepts (as in Example 5).

29. $f(x) = x^3 - 2x^2 + 6$

30. $f(x) = \sqrt[3]{2x^2 - 8}$

31. $g(x) = \left| \dfrac{x^2 - 4}{x + 3} \right|$

32. $f(x) = \dfrac{\sqrt{3x^2 - 12}}{x + 1}$

33. $f(x) = 3 - |2x - 1|$

34. $f(x) = \begin{cases} \dfrac{|x - 1|}{x - 1} & \text{if } x \ne 1 \\ 0 & \text{if } x = 1 \end{cases}$

35–38. Slope functions *Determine the slope function for the following functions.*

35. $f(x) = 2x + 1$

36. $f(x) = |x|$

37. Use the figure for Exercise 19.

38. Use the figure for Exercise 20.

39–42. Area functions *Let $A(x)$ be the area of the region bounded by the t-axis and the graph of $y = f(t)$ from $t = 0$ to $t = x$. Consider the following functions and graphs.*

  a. Find $A(2)$.
  b. Find $A(6)$.
  c. Find a formula for $A(x)$.

39. $f(t) = 6$

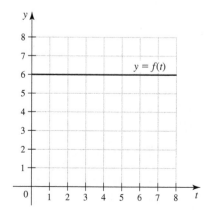

40. $f(t) = \dfrac{t}{2}$

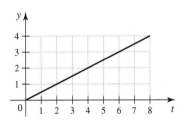

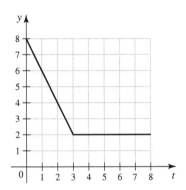

41. $f(t) = \begin{cases} -2t + 8 & \text{if } t \le 3 \\ 2 & \text{if } t > 3 \end{cases}$

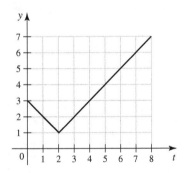

42. $f(t) = |t - 2| + 1$

43. Transformations of $y = |x|$ The functions f and g in the figure are obtained by vertical and horizontal shifts and scalings of $y = |x|$. Find formulas for f and g. Verify your answers with a graphing utility.

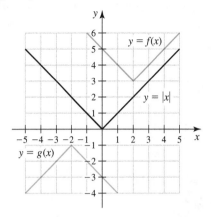

44. Transformations Use the graph of f in the figure to plot the following functions.

a. $y = -f(x)$ **b.** $y = f(x + 2)$
c. $y = f(x - 2)$ **d.** $y = f(2x)$
e. $y = f(x - 1) + 2$ **f.** $y = 2f(x)$

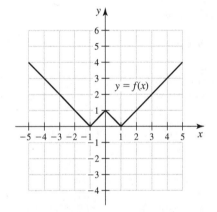

45. Transformations of $f(x) = x^2$ Use shifts and scalings to transform the graph of $f(x) = x^2$ into the graph of g. Use a graphing utility to check your work.

a. $g(x) = f(x - 3)$ **b.** $g(x) = f(2x - 4)$
c. $g(x) = -3f(x - 2) + 4$ **d.** $g(x) = 6f\left(\dfrac{x - 2}{3}\right) + 1$

46. Transformations of $f(x) = \sqrt{x}$ Use shifts and scalings to transform the graph of $f(x) = \sqrt{x}$ into the graph of g. Use a graphing utility to check your work.

a. $g(x) = f(x + 4)$ **b.** $g(x) = 2f(2x - 1)$
c. $g(x) = \sqrt{x - 1}$ **d.** $g(x) = 3\sqrt{x - 1} - 5$

47–54. Shifting and scaling *Use shifts and scalings to graph the given functions. Then check your work with a graphing utility. Be sure to identify an original function on which the shifts and scalings are performed.*

47. $f(x) = (x - 2)^2 + 1$

48. $f(x) = x^2 - 2x + 3$ (*Hint:* Complete the square first.)

49. $g(x) = -3x^2$

50. $g(x) = 2x^3 - 1$

51. $g(x) = 2(x + 3)^2$

52. $p(x) = x^2 + 3x - 5$

53. $h(x) = -4x^2 - 4x + 12$

54. $h(x) = |3x - 6| + 1$

Further Explorations

55. **Explain why or why not** Determine whether the following statements are true and give an explanation or counterexample.

   a. All polynomials are rational functions, but not all rational functions are polynomials.

   b. If f is a linear polynomial, then $f \circ f$ is a quadratic polynomial.

   c. If f and g are polynomials, then the degrees of $f \circ g$ and $g \circ f$ are equal.

   d. To graph $g(x) = f(x + 2)$, shift the graph of f 2 units to the right.

56–57. Intersection problems *Use analytical methods to find the following points of intersection. Use a graphing utility to check your work.*

56. Find the point(s) of intersection of the parabola $y = x^2 + 2$ and the line $y = x + 4$.

57. Find the point(s) of intersection of the parabolas $y = x^2$ and $y = -x^2 + 8x$.

58–59. Functions from tables *Find a simple function that fits the data in the tables.*

58.

x	y
−1	0
0	1
1	2
2	3
3	4

59.

x	y
0	−1
1	0
4	1
9	2
16	3

60–63. Functions from words *Find a formula for a function describing the given situation. Graph the function and give a domain that makes sense for the problem. Recall that with constant speed, distance = speed · time elapsed.*

60. A function $y = f(x)$ such that y is 1 less than the cube of x

61. Two cars leave a junction at the same time, one traveling north at 30 mi/hr, the other one traveling east at 60 mi/hr. The function $s(t)$ is the distance between the cars t hours after they leave the junction.

62. A function $y = f(x)$ such that if you ride a bike for 50 mi at x miles per hour, you arrive at your destination in y hours

63. A function $y = f(x)$ such that if your car gets 32 mi/gal and gasoline costs $\$x$/gallon, then $\$100$ is the cost of taking a y-mile trip

64. **Floor function** The floor function, or greatest integer function, $f(x) = \lfloor x \rfloor$, gives the greatest integer less than or equal to x. Graph the floor function, for $-3 \le x \le 3$.

65. **Ceiling function** The ceiling function, or smallest integer function, $f(x) = \lceil x \rceil$, gives the smallest integer greater than or equal to x. Graph the ceiling function, for $-3 \le x \le 3$.

66. **Sawtooth wave** Graph the sawtooth wave defined by

$$f(x) = \begin{cases} \vdots & \\ x + 1 & \text{if } -1 \le x < 0 \\ x & \text{if } 0 \le x < 1 \\ x - 1 & \text{if } 1 \le x < 2 \\ x - 2 & \text{if } 2 \le x < 3 \\ \vdots & \end{cases}$$

67. **Square wave** Graph the square wave defined by

$$f(x) = \begin{cases} 0 & \text{if } x < 0 \\ 1 & \text{if } 0 \le x < 1 \\ 0 & \text{if } 1 \le x < 2 \\ 1 & \text{if } 2 \le x < 3 \\ \vdots & \end{cases}$$

68–70. Roots and powers *Make a sketch of the given pairs of functions. Be sure to draw the graphs accurately relative to each other.*

68. $y = x^4$ and $y = x^6$

69. $y = x^3$ and $y = x^7$

70. $y = x^{1/3}$ and $y = x^{1/5}$

71. **Features of a graph** Consider the graph of the function f shown in the figure. Answer the following questions by referring to the points A–I.

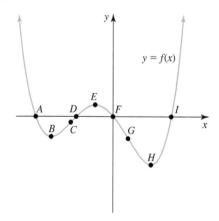

   a. Which points correspond to the roots (zeros) of f?

   b. Which points on the graph correspond to high points or peaks (soon to be called *local maximum* values of f)?

   c. Which points on the graph correspond to low points or valleys (soon to be called *local minimum* values of f)?

   d. As you move along the curve in the positive x-direction, at which point is the graph rising most rapidly?

   e. As you move along the curve in the positive x-direction, at which point is the graph falling most rapidly?

72. Features of a graph Consider the graph of the function g shown in the figure.

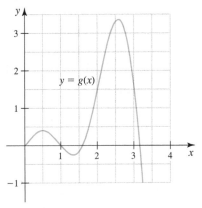

a. Give the approximate roots (zeros) of g.
b. Give the approximate coordinates of the high points or peaks (soon to be called *local maximum* values of f).
c. Give the approximate coordinates of the low points or valleys (soon to be called *local minimum* values of f).
d. Imagine moving along the curve in the positive x-direction on the interval $[0, 3]$. Give the approximate coordinates of the point at which the graph is rising most rapidly.
e. Imagine moving along the curve in the positive x-direction on the interval $[0, 3]$. Give the approximate coordinates of the point at which the graph is falling most rapidly.

Applications

73. Relative acuity of the human eye The **fovea centralis** (or **fovea**) is responsible for the sharp central vision that humans use for reading and other detail-oriented eyesight. The relative acuity of a human eye, which measures the sharpness of vision, is modeled by the function

$$R(\theta) = \frac{0.568}{0.331|\theta| + 0.568},$$

where θ (in degrees) is the angular deviation of the line of sight from the center of the fovea (see figure).

a. Graph R, for $-15 \leq \theta \leq 15$.
b. For what value of θ is R maximized? What does this fact indicate about our eyesight?
c. For what values of θ do we maintain at least 90% of our maximum relative acuity? (*Source: The Journal of Experimental Biology*, 203, Dec 2000)

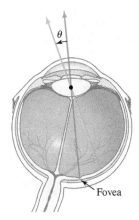

Fovea

74. Tennis probabilities Suppose the probability of a server winning any given point in a tennis match is a constant p, with $0 \leq p \leq 1$.

Then the probability of the server winning a game when serving from deuce is

$$f(p) = \frac{p^2}{1 - 2p(1 - p)}.$$

a. Evaluate $f(0.75)$ and interpret the result.
b. Evaluate $f(0.25)$ and interpret the result.
(*Source: The College Mathematics Journal* 38, 1, Jan 2007).

75. Bald eagle population Since DDT was banned and the Endangered Species Act was passed in 1973, the number of bald eagles in the United States has increased dramatically (see figure). In the lower 48 states, the number of breeding pairs of bald eagles increased at a nearly linear rate from 1875 pairs in 1986 to 6471 pairs in 2000.

a. Use the data points for 1986 and 2000 to find a linear function p that models the number of breeding pairs from 1986 to 2000 ($0 \leq t \leq 14$).
b. Using the function in part (a), approximately how many breeding pairs were in the lower 48 states in 1995?

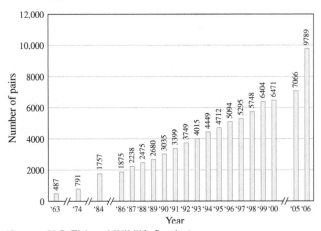

(*Source:* U.S. Fish and Wildlife Service)

76. Temperature scales

a. Find the linear function $C = f(F)$ that gives the reading on the Celsius temperature scale corresponding to a reading on the Fahrenheit scale. Use the facts that $C = 0$ when $F = 32$ (freezing point) and $C = 100$ when $F = 212$ (boiling point).
b. At what temperature are the Celsius and Fahrenheit readings equal?

77. Automobile lease vs. purchase A car dealer offers a purchase option and a lease option on all new cars. Suppose you are interested in a car that can be bought outright for $25,000 or leased for a start-up fee of $1200 plus monthly payments of $350.

a. Find the linear function $y = f(m)$ that gives the total amount you have paid on the lease option after m months.
b. With the lease option, after a 48-month (4-year) term, the car has a residual value of $10,000, which is the amount that you could pay to purchase the car. Assuming no other costs, should you lease or buy?

78. Surface area of a sphere The surface area of a sphere of radius r is $S = 4\pi r^2$. Solve for r in terms of S and graph the radius function for $S \geq 0$.

79. Volume of a spherical cap A single slice through a sphere of radius r produces a *cap* of the sphere. If the thickness of the cap is h, then its volume is $V = \frac{1}{3}\pi h^2 (3r - h)$. Graph the volume as a function of h for a sphere of radius 1. For what values of h does this function make sense?

80. Walking and rowing Kelly has finished a picnic on an island that is 200 m off shore (see figure). She wants to return to a beach house that is 600 m from the point P on the shore closest to the island. She plans to row a boat to a point on shore x meters from P and then jog along the (straight) shore to the house.

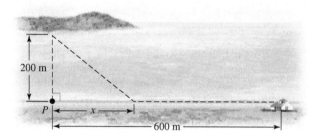

a. Let $d(x)$ be the total length of her trip as a function of x. Find and graph this function.

b. Suppose that Kelly can row at 2 m/s and jog at 4 m/s. Let $T(x)$ be the total time for her trip as a function of x. Find and graph $y = T(x)$.

c. Based on your graph in part (b), estimate the point on the shore at which Kelly should land to minimize the total time of her trip. What is that minimum time?

81. Optimal boxes Imagine a lidless box with height h and a square base whose sides have length x. The box must have a volume of 125 ft^3.

a. Find and graph the function $S(x)$ that gives the surface area of the box, for all values of $x > 0$.

b. Based on your graph in part (a), estimate the value of x that produces the box with a minimum surface area.

Additional Exercises

82. Composition of polynomials Let f be an nth-degree polynomial and let g be an mth-degree polynomial. What is the degree of the following polynomials?

a. $f \cdot f$ **b.** $f \circ f$ **c.** $f \cdot g$ **d.** $f \circ g$

83. Parabola vertex property Prove that if a parabola crosses the x-axis twice, the x-coordinate of the vertex of the parabola is halfway between the x-intercepts.

84. Parabola properties Consider the general quadratic function $f(x) = ax^2 + bx + c$, with $a \neq 0$.

a. Find the coordinates of the vertex in terms of a, b, and c.

b. Find the conditions on a, b, and c that guarantee that the graph of f crosses the x-axis twice.

85. Factorial function The factorial function is defined for positive integers as $n! = n(n - 1)(n - 2) \cdots 3 \cdot 2 \cdot 1$.

a. Make a table of the factorial function, for $n = 1, 2, 3, 4, 5$.

b. Graph these data points and then connect them with a smooth curve.

c. What is the least value of n for which $n! > 10^6$?

86. Sum of integers Let $S(n) = 1 + 2 + \cdots + n$, where n is a positive integer. It can be shown that $S(n) = n(n + 1)/2$.

a. Make a table of $S(n)$, for $n = 1, 2, \ldots, 10$.

b. How would you describe the domain of this function?

c. What is the least value of n for which $S(n) > 1000$?

87. Sum of squared integers Let $T(n) = 1^2 + 2^2 + \cdots + n^2$, where n is a positive integer. It can be shown that $T(n) = n(n + 1)(2n + 1)/6$.

a. Make a table of $T(n)$, for $n = 1, 2, \ldots, 10$.

b. How would you describe the domain of this function?

c. What is the least value of n for which $T(n) > 1000$?

QUICK CHECK ANSWERS

1. Yes; no   **2.** $(-\infty, \infty)$; $[0, \infty)$ **3.** Domain and range are $(-\infty, \infty)$. Domain and range are $[0, \infty)$.   **4.** Shift the graph of f horizontally 4 units to the left. ◄

1.3 Inverse, Exponential, and Logarithmic Functions

Exponential functions are fundamental to all of mathematics. Many processes in the world around us are modeled by *exponential functions*—they appear in finance, medicine, ecology, biology, economics, anthropology, and physics (among other disciplines). Every exponential function has an inverse function, which is a member of the family of *logarithmic functions*, also discussed in this section.

Exponential Functions

Exponential functions have the form $f(x) = b^x$, where the base $b \neq 1$ is a positive real number. An important question arises immediately: For what values of x can b^x be evaluated? We certainly know how to compute b^x when x is an integer. For example, $2^3 = 8$ and $2^{-4} = 1/2^4 = 1/16$. When x is rational, the numerator and denominator are interpreted as a power and root, respectively:

➤ $16^{3/4}$ can also be computed as $\sqrt[4]{16^3} = \sqrt[4]{4096} = 8$.

$$16^{3/4} = 16^{3/4} = (\sqrt[4]{16})^3 = 8.$$

▶ **Exponent Rules**

For any base $b > 0$ and real numbers x and y, the following relations hold:

E1. $b^x b^y = b^{x+y}$

E2. $\dfrac{b^x}{b^y} = b^{x-y}$

$\left(\text{which includes } \dfrac{1}{b^y} = b^{-y}\right)$

E3. $(b^x)^y = b^{xy}$

E4. $b^x > 0$, for all x

QUICK CHECK 1 Is it possible to raise a positive number b to a power and obtain a negative number? Is it possible to obtain zero? ◀

QUICK CHECK 2 Explain why $f(x) = \left(\dfrac{1}{3}\right)^x$ is a decreasing function. ◀

But what happens when x is irrational? For example, how should 2^π be understood? Your calculator provides an approximation to 2^π, but where does the approximation come from? These questions will be answered eventually. For now, we assume that b^x can be defined for all real numbers x and that it can be approximated as closely as desired by using rational numbers as close to x as needed. In Section 6.8, we prove that the domain of an exponential function is all real numbers.

Properties of Exponential Functions $f(x) = b^x$

1. Because b^x is defined for all real numbers, the domain of f is $\{x: -\infty < x < \infty\}$. Because $b^x > 0$ for all values of x, the range of f is $\{y: 0 < y < \infty\}$.

2. For all $b > 0$, $b^0 = 1$, and therefore $f(0) = 1$.

3. If $b > 1$, then f is an increasing function of x (Figure 1.45). For example, if $b = 2$, then $2^x > 2^y$ whenever $x > y$.

4. If $0 < b < 1$, then f is a decreasing function of x. For example, if $b = \frac{1}{2}$,

$$f(x) = \left(\frac{1}{2}\right)^x = \frac{1}{2^x} = 2^{-x},$$

and because 2^x increases with x, 2^{-x} decreases with x (Figure 1.46).

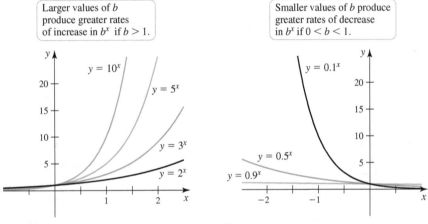

Figure 1.45

Figure 1.46

▶ The notation e was proposed by the Swiss mathematician Leonhard Euler (pronounced *oiler*) (1707–1783).

The Natural Exponential Function One of the bases used for exponential functions is special. For reasons that will become evident in upcoming chapters, the special base is e, one of the fundamental constants of mathematics. It is an irrational number with a value of $e = 2.718281828459\ldots$.

> **DEFINITION The Natural Exponential Function**
>
> The **natural exponential function** is $f(x) = e^x$, which has the base $e = 2.718281828459\ldots$.

The base e gives an exponential function that has a valuable property. As shown in Figure 1.47a, the graph of $y = e^x$ lies between the graphs of $y = 2^x$ and $y = 3^x$ (because $2 < e < 3$). At every point on the graph of $y = e^x$, it is possible to draw a *tangent line* (discussed in Chapters 2 and 3) that touches the graph only at that point. The natural exponential function is the only exponential function with the property that the slope of the tangent line at $x = 0$ is 1 (Figure 1.47b); therefore, e^x has both value and slope equal to 1 at $x = 0$. This property—minor as it may seem—leads to many simplifications when we do calculus with exponential functions.

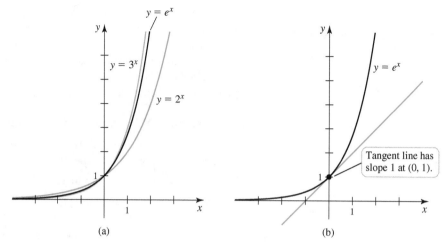

Figure 1.47

Inverse Functions

Consider the linear function $f(x) = 2x$, which takes any value of x and doubles it. The function that reverses this process by taking any value of $f(x) = 2x$ and mapping it back to x is called the *inverse function* of f, denoted f^{-1}. In this case, the inverse function is $f^{-1}(x) = x/2$. The effect of applying these two functions in succession looks like this:

$$x \xrightarrow{\ f\ } 2x \xrightarrow{\ f^{-1}\ } x$$

We now generalize this idea.

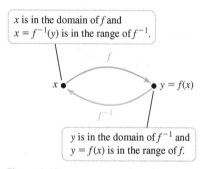

x is in the domain of f and $x = f^{-1}(y)$ is in the range of f^{-1}.

y is in the domain of f^{-1} and $y = f(x)$ is in the range of f.

Figure 1.48

▶ The notation f^{-1} for the inverse can be confusing. The inverse is not the reciprocal; that is, $f^{-1}(x)$ is not $1/f(x) = (f(x))^{-1}$. We adopt the common convention of using simply *inverse* to mean *inverse function*.

> **DEFINITION Inverse Function**
>
> Given a function f, its inverse (if it exists) is a function f^{-1} such that whenever $y = f(x)$, then $f^{-1}(y) = x$ (Figure 1.48).

QUICK CHECK 3 What is the inverse of $f(x) = \frac{1}{3}x$? What is the inverse of $f(x) = x - 7$? ◄

Because the inverse "undoes" the original function, if we start with a value of x, apply f to it, and then apply f^{-1} to the result, we recover the original value of x; that is,

$$f^{-1}(f(x)) = x.$$

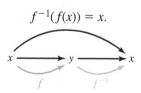

Similarly, if we apply f^{-1} to a value of y and then apply f to the result, we recover the original value of y; that is,

$$f(f^{-1}(y)) = y.$$

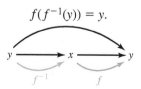

One-to-One Functions   We have defined the inverse of a function, but said nothing about when it exists. To ensure that f has an inverse on a domain, f must be *one-to-one* on that domain. This property means that every output of the function f must correspond to exactly one input. The one-to-one property is checked graphically by using the *horizontal line test*.

> **DEFINITION** **One-to-One Functions and the Horizontal Line Test**
>
> A function f is **one-to-one** on a domain D if each value of $f(x)$ corresponds to exactly one value of x in D. More precisely, f is one-to-one on D if $f(x_1) \neq f(x_2)$ whenever $x_1 \neq x_2$, for x_1 and x_2 in D. The **horizontal line test** says that every horizontal line intersects the graph of a one-to-one function at most once (Figure 1.49).

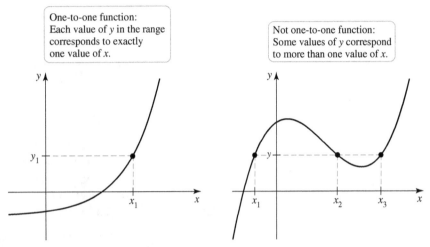

One-to-one function:
Each value of y in the range corresponds to exactly one value of x.

Not one-to-one function:
Some values of y correspond to more than one value of x.

Figure 1.49

For example, in Figure 1.50, some horizontal lines intersect the graph of $f(x) = x^2$ twice. Therefore, f does not have an inverse function on the interval $(-\infty, \infty)$. However, if the domain of f is restricted to one of the intervals $(-\infty, 0]$ or $[0, \infty)$, then the graph of f passes the horizontal line test and f is one-to-one on these intervals.

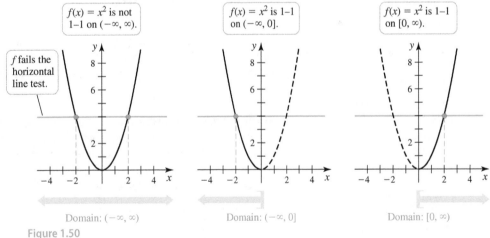

$f(x) = x^2$ is not 1–1 on $(-\infty, \infty)$.

f fails the horizontal line test.

$f(x) = x^2$ is 1–1 on $(-\infty, 0]$.

$f(x) = x^2$ is 1–1 on $[0, \infty)$.

Domain: $(-\infty, \infty)$ Domain: $(-\infty, 0]$ Domain: $[0, \infty)$

Figure 1.50

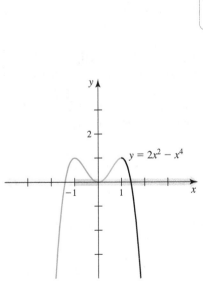

$y = 2x^2 - x^4$

Figure 1.51

EXAMPLE 1 **One-to-one functions** Determine the (largest possible) intervals on which the function $f(x) = 2x^2 - x^4$ (Figure 1.51) is one-to-one.

SOLUTION The function is not one-to-one on the entire real line because it fails the horizontal line test. However, on the intervals $(-\infty, -1]$, $[-1, 0]$, $[0, 1]$, and $[1, \infty)$, f is one-to-one. The function is also one-to-one on any subinterval of these four intervals.

Related Exercises 11–14 ◄

Existence of Inverse Functions   Figure 1.52a illustrates the actions of a one-to-one function f and its inverse f^{-1}. We see that f maps a value of x to a unique value of y. In turn, f^{-1} maps that value of y back to the original value of x. This procedure cannot be carried out if f is *not* one-to-one (Figure 1.52b).

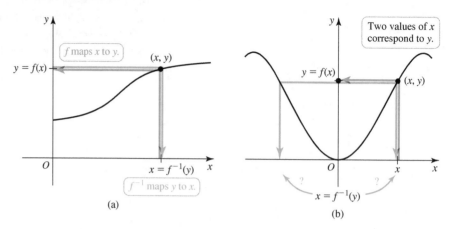

Figure 1.52

▶ The statement that a one-to-one function has an inverse is plausible based on its graph. However, the proof of this theorem is fairly technical and is omitted.

THEOREM 1.1   Existence of Inverse Functions

Let f be a one-to-one function on a domain D with a range R. Then f has a unique inverse f^{-1} with domain R and range D such that

$$f^{-1}(f(x)) = x \quad \text{and} \quad f(f^{-1}(y)) = y,$$

where x is in D and y is in R.

QUICK CHECK 4 The function that gives degrees Fahrenheit in terms of degrees Celsius is $F = 9C/5 + 32$. Why does this function have an inverse? ◄

EXAMPLE 2   Does an inverse exist? Determine the largest intervals on which $f(x) = x^2 - 1$ has an inverse function.

SOLUTION On the interval $(-\infty, \infty)$ the function does not pass the horizontal line test and is not one-to-one (Figure 1.53). However, if the domain of f is restricted to the interval $(-\infty, 0]$ or $[0, \infty)$, then f is one-to-one and an inverse exists.

Related Exercises 15–20 ◄

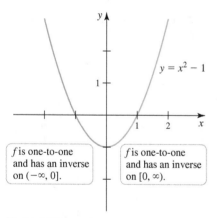

f is one-to-one and has an inverse on $(-\infty, 0]$.

f is one-to-one and has an inverse on $[0, \infty)$.

Figure 1.53

Finding Inverse Functions   The crux of finding an inverse for a function f is solving the equation $y = f(x)$ for x in terms of y. If it is possible to do so, then we have found a relationship of the form $x = f^{-1}(y)$. Interchanging x and y in $x = f^{-1}(y)$ so that x is the independent variable (which is the customary role for x), the inverse has the form $y = f^{-1}(x)$. Notice that if f is not one-to-one, this process leads to more than one inverse function.

PROCEDURE   **Finding an Inverse Function**

Suppose f is one-to-one on an interval I. To find f^{-1}:

1. Solve $y = f(x)$ for x. If necessary, choose the function that corresponds to I.
2. Interchange x and y and write $y = f^{-1}(x)$.

▶ Once you find a formula for f^{-1}, you can check your work by verifying that $f^{-1}(f(x)) = x$ and $f(f^{-1}(x)) = x$.

EXAMPLE 3 Finding inverse functions Find the inverse(s) of the following functions. Restrict the domain of f if necessary.

a. $f(x) = 2x + 6$

b. $f(x) = x^2 - 1$

SOLUTION

> ➤ A constant function (whose graph is a horizontal line) fails the horizontal line test and does not have an inverse.

a. Linear functions (except constant linear functions) are one-to-one on the entire real line. Therefore, an inverse function for f exists for all values of x.

Step 1: Solve $y = f(x)$ for x: We see that $y = 2x + 6$ implies that $2x = y - 6$, or

$$x = \frac{1}{2}y - 3.$$

Step 2: Interchange x and y and write $y = f^{-1}(x)$:

$$y = f^{-1}(x) = \frac{1}{2}x - 3.$$

It is instructive to verify that the inverse relations $f(f^{-1}(x)) = x$ and $f^{-1}(f(x)) = x$ are satisfied:

$$f(f^{-1}(x)) = f\left(\frac{1}{2}x - 3\right) = 2\underbrace{\left(\frac{1}{2}x - 3\right) + 6}_{f(x)\,=\,2x\,+\,6} = x - 6 + 6 = x,$$

$$f^{-1}(f(x)) = f^{-1}(2x + 6) = \underbrace{\frac{1}{2}(2x + 6) - 3}_{f^{-1}(x)\,=\,\frac{1}{2}x\,-\,3} = x + 3 - 3 = x.$$

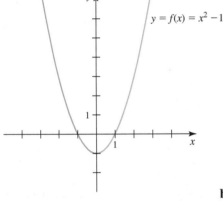

(a)

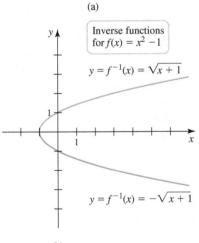

(b)

Figure 1.54

b. As shown in Example 2, the function $f(x) = x^2 - 1$ is not one-to-one on the entire real line; however, it is one-to-one on $(-\infty, 0]$ and on $[0, \infty)$ (Figure 1.54a). If we restrict our attention to either of these intervals, then an inverse function can be found.

Step 1: Solve $y = f(x)$ for x:

$$y = x^2 - 1$$
$$x^2 = y + 1$$
$$x = \begin{cases} \sqrt{y + 1} \\ -\sqrt{y + 1}. \end{cases}$$

Each branch of the square root corresponds to an inverse function.

Step 2: Interchange x and y and write $y = f^{-1}(x)$:

$$y = f^{-1}(x) = \sqrt{x + 1} \quad \text{or} \quad y = f^{-1}(x) = -\sqrt{x + 1}.$$

The interpretation of this result is important. Taking the positive branch of the square root, the inverse function $y = f^{-1}(x) = \sqrt{x + 1}$ gives positive values of y; it corresponds to the branch of $f(x) = x^2 - 1$ on the interval $[0, \infty)$ (Figure 1.54b). The negative branch of the square root, $y = f^{-1}(x) = -\sqrt{x + 1}$, is another inverse function that gives negative values of y; it corresponds to the branch of $f(x) = x^2 - 1$ on the interval $(-\infty, 0]$.   *Related Exercises 21–30* ◄

QUICK CHECK 5 On what interval(s) does the function $f(x) = x^3$ have an inverse? ◄

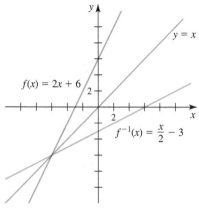

The function $f(x) = 2x + 6$ and its inverse $f^{-1}(x) = \frac{x}{2} - 3$ are symmetric about the line $y = x$.

Figure 1.55

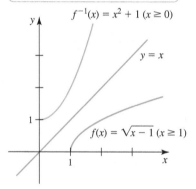

The function $f(x) = \sqrt{x - 1}$ $(x \geq 1)$ and its inverse $f^{-1}(x) = x^2 + 1$ $(x \geq 0)$ are symmetric about $y = x$.

Figure 1.56

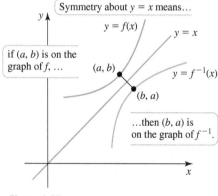

Symmetry about $y = x$ means...

if (a, b) is on the graph of f, ...

...then (b, a) is on the graph of f^{-1}.

Figure 1.57

Graphing Inverse Functions

The graphs of a function and its inverse have a special relationship, which is illustrated in the following example.

EXAMPLE 4 Graphing inverse functions Plot f and f^{-1} on the same coordinate axes.

a. $f(x) = 2x + 6$

b. $f(x) = \sqrt{x - 1}$

SOLUTION

a. The inverse of $f(x) = 2x + 6$, found in Example 3, is

$$y = f^{-1}(x) = \frac{1}{2}x - 3.$$

The graphs of f and f^{-1} are shown in Figure 1.55. Notice that both f and f^{-1} are increasing linear functions that intersect at $(-6, -6)$.

b. The domain of $f(x) = \sqrt{x - 1}$ is $[1, \infty)$ and its range is $[0, \infty)$. On this domain, f is one-to-one and has an inverse. It can be found in two steps:

Step 1: Solve $y = \sqrt{x - 1}$ for x:

$$y^2 = x - 1 \quad \text{or} \quad x = y^2 + 1.$$

Step 2: Interchange x and y and write $y = f^{-1}(x)$:

$$y = f^{-1}(x) = x^2 + 1.$$

The graphs of f and f^{-1} are shown in Figure 1.56. Notice that the domain of f^{-1} (which is $x \geq 0$) corresponds to the range of f (which is $y \geq 0$).

Related Exercises 31–40 ◄

Looking closely at the graphs in Figure 1.55 and Figure 1.56, you see a symmetry that always occurs when a function and its inverse are plotted on the same set of axes. In each figure, one curve is the reflection of the other curve across the line $y = x$. These curves have *symmetry about the line* $y = x$, which means that the point (a, b) is on one curve whenever the point (b, a) is on the other curve (Figure 1.57).

The explanation for the symmetry comes directly from the definition of the inverse. Suppose that the point (a, b) is on the graph of $y = f(x)$, which means that $b = f(a)$. By the definition of the inverse function, we know that $a = f^{-1}(b)$, which means that the point (b, a) is on the graph of $y = f^{-1}(x)$. This argument applies to all relevant points (a, b), so whenever (a, b) is on the graph of f, (b, a) is on the graph of f^{-1}. As a consequence, the graphs are symmetric about the line $y = x$.

Logarithmic Functions

Everything we learned about inverse functions is now applied to the exponential function $f(x) = b^x$. For any $b > 0$, with $b \neq 1$, this function is one-to-one on the interval $(-\infty, \infty)$. Therefore, it has an inverse.

DEFINITION Logarithmic Function Base b

For any base $b > 0$, with $b \neq 1$, the **logarithmic function base b**, denoted $y = \log_b x$, is the inverse of the exponential function $y = b^x$. The inverse of the natural exponential function with base $b = e$ is the **natural logarithm function**, denoted $y = \ln x$.

The inverse relationship between logarithmic and exponential functions may be stated concisely in several ways. First, we have

$$y = \log_b x \quad \text{if and only if} \quad b^y = x.$$

> Logarithms were invented around 1600 for calculating purposes by the Scotsman John Napier and the Englishman Henry Briggs. Unfortunately, the word *logarithm*, derived from the Greek for reasoning (*logos*) with numbers (*arithmos*), doesn't help with the meaning of the word. **When you see *logarithm*, you should think *exponent*.**

Combining these two conditions results in two important relations.

Inverse Relations for Exponential and Logarithmic Functions

For any base $b > 0$, with $b \neq 1$, the following inverse relations hold.

I1. $b^{\log_b x} = x$, for $x > 0$

I2. $\log_b b^x = x$, for real values of x

> **Logarithm Rules**
>
> For any base $b > 0$ ($b \neq 1$), positive real numbers x and y, and real numbers z, the following relations hold:
>
> **L1.** $\log_b xy = \log_b x + \log_b y$
>
> **L2.** $\log_b \dfrac{x}{y} = \log_b x - \log_b y$
>
> $\left(\text{includes } \log_b \dfrac{1}{y} = -\log_b y \right)$
>
> **L3.** $\log_b x^z = z \log_b x$
>
> **L4.** $\log_b b = 1$
>
> Specifically, these properties hold with $b = e$, in which case $\log_b x = \log_e x = \ln x$.

Properties of Logarithmic Functions   The graph of the logarithmic function is generated using the symmetry of the graphs of a function and its inverse. Figure 1.58 shows how the graph of $y = b^x$, for $b > 1$, is reflected across the line $y = x$ to obtain the graph of $y = \log_b x$.

The graphs of $y = \log_b x$ are shown (Figure 1.59) for several bases $b > 1$. Logarithms with bases $0 < b < 1$, although well defined, are generally not used (and they can be expressed in terms of bases with $b > 1$).

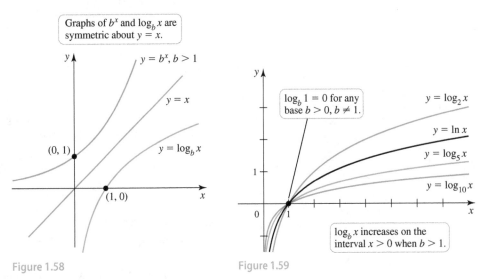

Figure 1.58   Figure 1.59

Logarithmic functions with base $b > 0$ satisfy properties that parallel the properties of the exponential functions on p. 27.

1. Because the range of b^x is $(0, \infty)$ the domain of $\log_b x$ is $(0, \infty)$.
2. The domain of b^x is $(-\infty, \infty)$, which implies that the range of $\log_b x$ is $(-\infty, \infty)$.
3. Because $b^0 = 1$, it follows that $\log_b 1 = 0$.
4. If $b > 1$, then $\log_b x$ is an increasing function of x. For example, if $b = e$, then $\ln x > \ln y$ whenever $x > y$ (Figure 1.59).

QUICK CHECK 6 What is the domain of $f(x) = \log_b(x^2)$? What is the range of $f(x) = \log_b(x^2)$? ◄

EXAMPLE 5   **Using inverse relations**   One thousand grams of a particular radioactive substance decays according to the function $m(t) = 1000e^{-t/850}$, where $t \geq 0$ measures time in years. When does the mass of the substance reach the safe level deemed to be 1 g?

SOLUTION Setting $m(t) = 1$, we solve $1000e^{-t/850} = 1$ by dividing both sides by 1000 and taking the natural logarithm of both sides:

$$\ln\left(e^{-t/850}\right) = \ln\left(\frac{1}{1000}\right).$$

> Provided the arguments are positive, we can take the $\log_b$ of both sides of an equation and produce an equivalent equation.

This equation is simplified by calculating $\ln(1/1000) \approx -6.908$ and observing that $\ln(e^{-t/850}) = -\dfrac{t}{850}$ (inverse property I2). Therefore,

$$-\frac{t}{850} \approx -6.908.$$

Solving for t, we find that $t \approx (-850)(-6.908) \approx 5872$ years.

Related Exercises 41–58 ◄

Change of Base

When working with logarithms and exponentials, it doesn't matter *in principle* which base is used. However, there are practical reasons for switching between bases. For example, most calculators have built-in logarithmic functions in just one or two bases. If you need to use a different base, then the change-of-base rules are essential.

Consider changing bases with exponential functions. Specifically, suppose you want to express b^x (base b) in the form e^y (base e), where y must be determined. Taking the natural logarithm of both sides of $e^y = b^x$, we have

$$\underbrace{\ln e^y}_{y} = \underbrace{\ln b^x}_{x \ln b} \quad \text{which implies that } y = x \ln b.$$

It follows that $b^x = e^y = e^{x \ln b}$. For example, $4^x = e^{x \ln 4}$. This result is derived rigorously in Section 6.8.

> A similar argument is used to derive more general formulas for changing from base b to any other positive base c.

The formula for changing from $\log_b x$ to $\ln x$ is derived in a similar way. We let $y = \log_b x$, which implies that $x = b^y$. Taking the natural logarithm of both sides of $x = b^y$ gives $\ln x = \ln b^y = y \ln b$. Solving for y gives

$$y = \log_b x = \frac{\ln x}{\ln b}.$$

Change-of-Base Rules

Let b be a positive real number with $b \neq 1$. Then

$$b^x = e^{x \ln b}, \text{ for all } x \quad \text{and} \quad \log_b x = \frac{\ln x}{\ln b}, \text{ for } x > 0.$$

More generally, if c is a positive real number with $c \neq 1$, then

$$b^x = c^{x \log_c b}, \text{ for all } x \quad \text{and} \quad \log_b x = \frac{\log_c x}{\log_c b}, \text{ for } x > 0.$$

EXAMPLE 6   Changing bases

a. Express 2^{x+4} as an exponential function with base e.

b. Express $\log_2 x$ using base e and base 32.

SOLUTION

a. Using the change-of-base rule for exponential functions, we have

$$2^{x+4} = e^{(x+4)\ln 2}.$$

b. Using the change-of-base rule for logarithmic functions, we have

$$\log_2 x = \frac{\ln x}{\ln 2}.$$

To change from base 2 to base 32, we use the general change-of-base formula:

$$\log_2 x = \frac{\log_{32} x}{\log_{32} 2} = \frac{\log_{32} x}{1/5} = 5 \log_{32} x.$$

The second step follows from the fact that $2 = 32^{1/5}$, so $\log_{32} 2 = \frac{1}{5}$.

Related Exercises 59–68 ◄

SECTION 1.3 EXERCISES

Review Questions

1. For $b > 0$, what are the domain and range of $f(x) = b^x$?

2. Give an example of a function that is one-to-one on the entire real number line.

3. Explain why a function that is not one-to-one on an interval I cannot have an inverse function on I.

4. Explain with pictures why (a, b) is on the graph of f whenever (b, a) is on the graph of f^{-1}.

5. Sketch a function that is one-to-one and positive for $x \geq 0$. Make a rough sketch of its inverse.

6. Express the inverse of $f(x) = 3x - 4$ in the form $y = f^{-1}(x)$.

7. Explain the meaning of $\log_b x$.

8. How is the property $b^{x+y} = b^x b^y$ related to the property $\log_b (xy) = \log_b x + \log_b y$?

9. For $b > 0$ with $b \neq 1$, what are the domain and range of $f(x) = \log_b x$ and why?

10. Express 2^5 using base e.

Basic Skills

11–14. One-to-one functions

11. Find three intervals on which f is one-to-one, making each interval as large as possible.

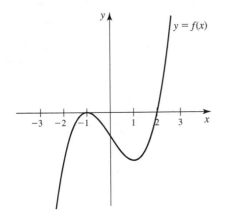

12. Find four intervals on which f is one-to-one, making each interval as large as possible.

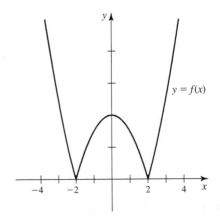

13. Sketch a graph of a function that is one-to-one on the interval $(-\infty, 0]$ but is not one-to-one on $(-\infty, \infty)$.

14. Sketch a graph of a function that is one-to-one on the intervals $(-\infty, -2]$, and $[-2, \infty)$ but is not one-to-one on $(-\infty, \infty)$.

15–20. Where do inverses exist? *Use analytical and/or graphical methods to determine the largest possible sets of points on which the following functions have an inverse.*

15. $f(x) = 3x + 4$

16. $f(x) = |2x + 1|$

17. $f(x) = 1/(x - 5)$

18. $f(x) = -(6 - x)^2$

19. $f(x) = 1/x^2$

20. $f(x) = x^2 - 2x + 8$ (*Hint:* Complete the square.)

21–28. Finding inverse functions

a. *Find the inverse of each function (on the given interval, if specified) and write it in the form $y = f^{-1}(x)$.*

b. *Verify the relationships $f(f^{-1}(x)) = x$ and $f^{-1}(f(x)) = x$.*

21. $f(x) = 2x$

22. $f(x) = \frac{1}{4}x + 1$

23. $f(x) = 6 - 4x$

24. $f(x) = 3x^3$

25. $f(x) = 3x + 5$

26. $f(x) = x^2 + 4$, for $x \geq 0$

27. $f(x) = \sqrt{x + 2}$, for $x \geq -2$

28. $f(x) = 2/(x^2 + 1)$, for $x \geq 0$

29. Splitting up curves The unit circle $x^2 + y^2 = 1$ consists of four one-to-one functions, $f_1(x)$, $f_2(x)$, $f_3(x)$, and $f_4(x)$ (see figure).

   a. Find the domain and a formula for each function.

   b. Find the inverse of each function and write it as $y = f^{-1}(x)$.

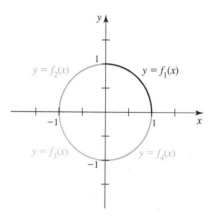

30. Splitting up curves The equation $y^4 = 4x^2$ is associated with four one-to-one functions $f_1(x)$, $f_2(x)$, $f_3(x)$, and $f_4(x)$ (see figure).

   a. Find the domain and a formula for each function.

   b. Find the inverse of each function and write it as $y = f^{-1}(x)$.

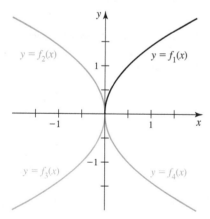

31–38. Graphing inverse functions *Find the inverse function (on the given interval, if specified) and graph both f and f^{-1} on the same set of axes. Check your work by looking for the required symmetry in the graphs.*

31. $f(x) = 8 - 4x$

32. $f(x) = 4x - 12$

33. $f(x) = \sqrt{x}$, for $x \geq 0$

34. $f(x) = \sqrt{3 - x}$, for $x \leq 3$

35. $f(x) = x^4 + 4$, for $x \geq 0$

36. $f(x) = 6/(x^2 - 9)$, for $x > 3$

37. $f(x) = x^2 - 2x + 6$, for $x \geq 1$ (*Hint:* Complete the square first.)

38. $f(x) = -x^2 - 4x - 3$, for $x \leq -2$ (*Hint:* Complete the square first.)

39–40. Graphs of inverses *Sketch the graph of the inverse function.*

39.

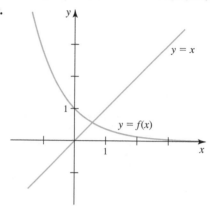

40.

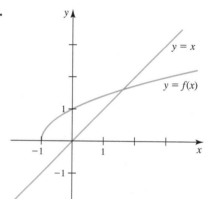

41–46. Solving logarithmic equations *Solve the following equations.*

41. $\log_{10} x = 3$

42. $\log_5 x = -1$

43. $\log_8 x = \frac{1}{3}$

44. $\log_b 125 = 3$

45. $\ln x = -1$

46. $\ln y = 3$

47–52. Properties of logarithms *Assume $\log_b x = 0.36$, $\log_b y = 0.56$, and $\log_b z = 0.83$. Evaluate the following expressions.*

47. $\log_b \dfrac{x}{y}$

48. $\log_b x^2$

49. $\log_b xz$

50. $\log_b \dfrac{\sqrt{xy}}{z}$

51. $\log_b \dfrac{\sqrt{x}}{\sqrt[3]{z}}$

52. $\log_b \dfrac{b^2 x^{5/2}}{\sqrt{y}}$

53–56. Solving equations *Solve the following equations.*

53. $7^x = 21$

54. $2^x = 55$

55. $3^{3x-4} = 15$

56. $5^{3x} = 29$

57. Using inverse relations One hundred grams of a particular radioactive substance decays according to the function $m(t) = 100\,e^{-t/650}$, where $t > 0$ measures time in years. When does the mass reach 50 grams?

58. Using inverse relations The population P of a small town grows according to the function $P(t) = 100\,e^{t/50}$, where t measures the number of years after 2010. How long does it take the population to double?

59–62. Calculator base change *Write the following logarithms in terms of the natural logarithm. Then use a calculator to find the value of the logarithm, rounding your result to four decimal places.*

59. $\log_2 15$ **60.** $\log_3 30$ **61.** $\log_4 40$ **62.** $\log_6 60$

63–68. Changing bases *Convert the following expressions to the indicated base.*

63. 2^x using base e

64. $3^{\sin x}$ using base e

65. $\ln |x|$ using base 5

66. $\log_2 (x^2 + 1)$ using base e

67. $a^{1/\ln a}$ using base e, for $a > 0$ and $a \neq 1$

68. $a^{1/\log_{10} a}$ using base 10, for $a > 0$ and $a \neq 1$

Further Explorations

69. Explain why or why not Determine whether the following statements are true and give an explanation or counterexample.

  a. If $y = 3^x$, then $x = \sqrt[3]{y}$.

  b. $\dfrac{\log_b x}{\log_b y} = \log_b x - \log_b y$.

  c. $\log_5 4^6 = 4 \log_5 6$.

  d. $2 = 10^{\log_{10} 2}$.

  e. $2 = \ln 2^e$.

  f. If $f(x) = x^2 + 1$, then $f^{-1}(x) = 1/(x^2 + 1)$.

  g. If $f(x) = 1/x$, then $f^{-1}(x) = 1/x$.

70. Graphs of exponential functions The following figure shows the graphs of $y = 2^x, y = 3^x, y = 2^{-x}$, and $y = 3^{-x}$. Match each curve with the correct function.

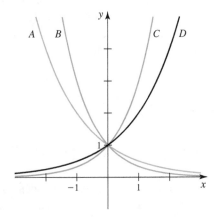

71. Graphs of logarithmic functions The following figure shows the graphs of $y = \log_2 x, y = \log_4 x$, and $y = \log_{10} x$. Match each curve with the correct function.

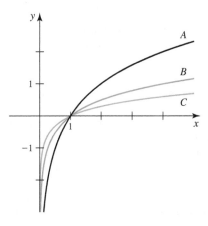

72. Graphs of modified exponential functions Without using a graphing utility, sketch the graph of $y = 2^x$. Then on the same set of axes, sketch the graphs of $y = 2^{-x}, y = 2^{x-1}, y = 2^x + 1$, and $y = 2^{2x}$.

73. Graphs of modified logarithmic functions Without using a graphing utility, sketch the graph of $y = \log_2 x$. Then on the same set of axes, sketch the graphs of $y = \log_2 (x - 1), y = \log_2 x^2$, $y = (\log_2 x)^2$, and $y = \log_2 x + 1$.

74. Large intersection point Use any means to approximate the intersection point(s) of the graphs of $f(x) = e^x$ and $g(x) = x^{123}$. (*Hint:* Consider using logarithms.)

75–78. Finding all inverses *Find all the inverses associated with the following functions and state their domains.*

75. $f(x) = (x + 1)^3$ **76.** $f(x) = (x - 4)^2$

77. $f(x) = 2/(x^2 + 2)$ **78.** $f(x) = 2x/(x + 2)$

Applications

79. Population model A culture of bacteria has a population of 150 cells when it is first observed. The population doubles every 12 hr, which means its population is governed by the function $p(t) = 150 \cdot 2^{t/12}$, where t is the number of hours after the first observation.

  a. Verify that $p(0) = 150$, as claimed.

  b. Show that the population doubles every 12 hr, as claimed.

  c. What is the population 4 days after the first observation?

  d. How long does it take the population to triple in size?

  e. How long does it take the population to reach 10,000?

80. Charging a capacitor A capacitor is a device that stores electrical charge. The charge on a capacitor accumulates according to the function $Q(t) = a(1 - e^{-t/c})$, where t is measured in seconds, and a and $c > 0$ are physical constants. The *steady-state charge* is the value that $Q(t)$ approaches as t becomes large.

  a. Graph the charge function for $t \geq 0$ using $a = 1$ and $c = 10$. Find a graphing window that shows the full range of the function.

  b. Vary the value of a while holding c fixed. Describe the effect on the curve. How does the steady-state charge vary with a?

c. Vary the value of c while holding a fixed. Describe the effect on the curve. How does the steady-state charge vary with c?

d. Find a formula that gives the steady-state charge in terms of a and c.

81. Height and time The height in feet of a baseball hit straight up from the ground with an initial velocity of 64 ft/s is given by $h = f(t) = 64t - 16t^2$, where t is measured in seconds after the hit.

a. Is this function one-to-one on the interval $0 \le t \le 4$?

b. Find the inverse function that gives the time t at which the ball is at height h as the ball travels *upward*. Express your answer in the form $t = f^{-1}(h)$.

c. Find the inverse function that gives the time t at which the ball is at height h as the ball travels *downward*. Express your answer in the form $t = f^{-1}(h)$.

d. At what time is the ball at a height of 30 ft on the way up?

e. At what time is the ball at a height of 10 ft on the way down?

82. Velocity of a skydiver The velocity of a skydiver (in m/s) t seconds after jumping from a plane is $v(t) = 600(1 - e^{-kt/60})/k$, where $k > 0$ is a constant. The *terminal velocity* of the skydiver is the value that $v(t)$ approaches as t becomes large. Graph v with $k = 11$ and estimate the terminal velocity.

Additional Exercises

83. Reciprocal bases Assume that $b > 0$ and $b \ne 1$. Show that $\log_{1/b} x = -\log_b x$.

84. Proof of rule L1 Use the following steps to prove that $\log_b xy = \log_b x + \log_b y$.

a. Let $x = b^p$ and $y = b^q$. Solve these expressions for p and q, respectively.

b. Use property E1 for exponents to express xy in terms of b, p, and q.

c. Compute $\log_b xy$ and simplify.

85. Proof of rule L2 Modify the proof outlined in Exercise 84 and use property E2 for exponents to prove that $\log_b (x/y) = \log_b x - \log_b y$.

86. Proof of rule L3 Use the following steps to prove that $\log_b x^z = z \log_b x$.

a. Let $x = b^p$. Solve this expression for p.

b. Use property E3 for exponents to express x^z in terms of b and p.

c. Compute $\log_b x^z$ and simplify.

87. Inverses of a quartic Consider the quartic polynomial $y = f(x) = x^4 - x^2$.

a. Graph f and estimate the largest intervals on which it is one-to-one. The goal is to find the inverse function on each of these intervals.

b. Make the substitution $u = x^2$ to solve the equation $y = f(x)$ for x in terms of y. Be sure you have included all possible solutions.

c. Write each inverse function in the form $y = f^{-1}(x)$ for each of the intervals found in part (a).

88. Inverse of composite functions

a. Let $g(x) = 2x + 3$ and $h(x) = x^3$. Consider the composite function $f(x) = g(h(x))$. Find f^{-1} directly and then express it in terms of g^{-1} and h^{-1}.

b. Let $g(x) = x^2 + 1$ and $h(x) = \sqrt{x}$. Consider the composite function $f(x) = g(h(x))$. Find f^{-1} directly and then express it in terms of g^{-1} and h^{-1}.

c. Explain why if g and h are one-to-one, the inverse of $f(x) = g(h(x))$ exists.

89–90. Inverses of (some) cubics *Finding the inverse of a cubic polynomial is equivalent to solving a cubic equation. A special case that is simpler than the general case is the cubic $y = f(x) = x^3 + ax$. Find the inverse of the following cubics using the substitution (known as Vieta's substitution) $x = z - a/(3z)$. Be sure to determine where the function is one-to-one.*

89. $f(x) = x^3 + 2x$

90. $f(x) = x^3 + 4x - 1$

91. Nice property Prove that $(\log_b c)(\log_c b) = 1$, for $b > 0$, $c > 0$, $b \ne 1$, and $c \ne 1$.

QUICK CHECK ANSWERS

1. b^x is always positive (and never zero) for all x and for positive bases b.   **2.** Because $(1/3)^x = 1/3^x$ and 3^x increases as x increases, it follows that $(1/3)^x$ decreases as x increases.   **3.** $f^{-1}(x) = 3x; f^{-1}(x) = x + 7$.   **4.** For every Fahrenheit temperature, there is exactly one Celsius temperature, and vice versa. The given relation is also a linear function. It is one-to-one, so it has an inverse function.   **5.** The function $f(x) = x^3$ is one-to-one on $(-\infty, \infty)$, so it has an inverse for all values of x.   **6.** The domain of $\log_b x^2$ is all real numbers except zero (because x^2 is positive for $x \ne 0$). The range of $\log_b x^2$ is all real numbers. ◄

1.4 Trigonometric Functions and Their Inverses

This section is a review of what you need to know in order to study the calculus of trigonometric functions. Once the trigonometric functions are on stage, it makes sense to present the inverse trigonometric functions and their basic properties.

Degrees	Radians
0	0
30	$\pi/6$
45	$\pi/4$
60	$\pi/3$
90	$\pi/2$
120	$2\pi/3$
135	$3\pi/4$
150	$5\pi/6$
180	π

Radian Measure

Calculus typically requires that angles be measured in **radians** (rad). Working with a circle of radius r, the radian measure of an angle θ is the length of the arc associated with θ, denoted s, divided by the radius of the circle r (Figure 1.60a). Working on a unit circle $(r = 1)$, the radian measure of an angle is simply the length of the arc associated with θ (Figure 1.60b). For example, the length of a full unit circle is 2π; therefore, an angle with a radian measure of π corresponds to a half circle $(\theta = 180°)$ and an angle with a radian measure of $\pi/2$ corresponds to a quarter circle $(\theta = 90°)$.

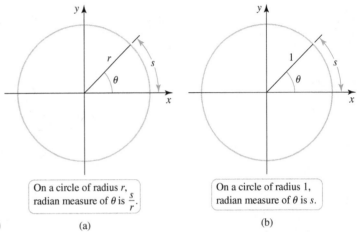

On a circle of radius r, radian measure of θ is $\dfrac{s}{r}$.

On a circle of radius 1, radian measure of θ is s.

Figure 1.60   (a)   (b)

QUICK CHECK 1 What is the radian measure of a 270° angle? What is the degree measure of a $5\pi/4$-rad angle? ◄

Trigonometric Functions

For acute angles, the trigonometric functions are defined as ratios of the lengths of the sides of a right triangle (Figure 1.61). To extend these definitions to include all angles, we work in an xy-coordinate system with a circle of radius r centered at the origin. Suppose that $P(x, y)$ is a point on the circle. An angle θ is in **standard position** if its initial side is on the positive x-axis and its terminal side is the line segment OP between the origin and P. An angle is positive if it is obtained by a counterclockwise rotation from the positive x-axis (Figure 1.62). When the right-triangle definitions of Figure 1.61 are used with the right triangle in Figure 1.62, the trigonometric functions may be expressed in terms of x, y, and the radius of the circle, $r = \sqrt{x^2 + y^2}$.

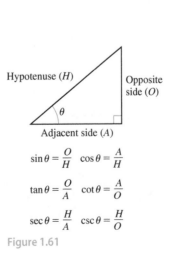

Hypotenuse (H)   Opposite side (O)

Adjacent side (A)

$$\sin\theta = \frac{O}{H} \quad \cos\theta = \frac{A}{H}$$

$$\tan\theta = \frac{O}{A} \quad \cot\theta = \frac{A}{O}$$

$$\sec\theta = \frac{H}{A} \quad \csc\theta = \frac{H}{O}$$

Figure 1.61

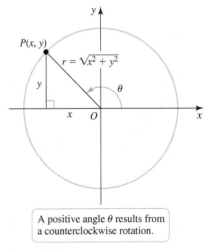

$P(x, y)$

$r = \sqrt{x^2 + y^2}$

A positive angle θ results from a counterclockwise rotation.

Figure 1.62

➤ When working on a unit circle ($r = 1$), these definitions become

$$\sin \theta = y \qquad \cos \theta = x$$

$$\tan \theta = \frac{y}{x} \qquad \cot \theta = \frac{x}{y}$$

$$\sec \theta = \frac{1}{x} \qquad \csc \theta = \frac{1}{y}$$

DEFINITION Trigonometric Functions

Let $P(x, y)$ be a point on a circle of radius r associated with the angle θ. Then

$$\sin \theta = \frac{y}{r}, \qquad \cos \theta = \frac{x}{r}, \qquad \tan \theta = \frac{y}{x},$$

$$\cot \theta = \frac{x}{y}, \qquad \sec \theta = \frac{r}{x}, \qquad \csc \theta = \frac{r}{y}.$$

To find the trigonometric functions of the standard angles (multiples of 30° and 45°), it is helpful to know the radian measure of those angles and the coordinates of the associated points on the unit circle (Figure 1.63).

➤ **Standard triangles**

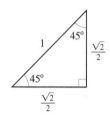

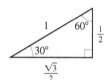

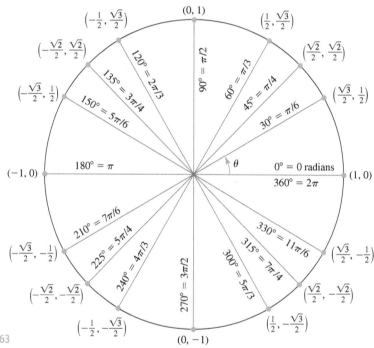

Figure 1.63

Combining the definitions of the trigonometric functions with the coordinates shown in Figure 1.63, we may evaluate these functions at any standard angle. For example,

$$\sin \frac{2\pi}{3} = \frac{\sqrt{3}}{2}, \qquad \cos \frac{5\pi}{6} = -\frac{\sqrt{3}}{2}, \qquad \tan \frac{7\pi}{6} = \frac{1}{\sqrt{3}}, \qquad \tan \frac{3\pi}{2} \text{ is undefined,}$$

$$\cot \frac{5\pi}{3} = -\frac{1}{\sqrt{3}}, \qquad \sec \frac{7\pi}{4} = \sqrt{2}, \qquad \csc \frac{3\pi}{2} = -1, \qquad \sec \frac{\pi}{2} \text{ is undefined.}$$

EXAMPLE 1 Evaluating trigonometric functions Evaluate the following expressions.

a. $\sin (8\pi/3)$ **b.** $\csc (-11\pi/3)$

SOLUTION

a. The angle $8\pi/3 = 2\pi + 2\pi/3$ corresponds to a *counterclockwise* revolution of one full circle (2π radians) plus an additional $2\pi/3$ radians (Figure 1.64). Therefore, this angle has the same terminal side as the angle $2\pi/3$, and the corresponding point on the unit circle is $(-1/2, \sqrt{3}/2)$. It follows that $\sin (8\pi/3) = y = \sqrt{3}/2$.

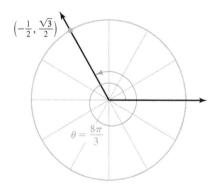

Figure 1.64

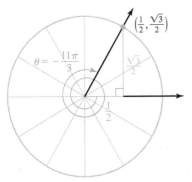

Figure 1.65

▶ In addition, to these identities, you should be familiar with the Law of Sines and the Law of Cosines. See Exercises 108 and 109.

b. The angle $\theta = -11\pi/3 = -2\pi - 5\pi/3$ corresponds to a *clockwise* revolution of one full circle (2π radians) plus an additional $5\pi/3$ radians (Figure 1.65). Therefore, this angle has the same terminal side as the angle $\pi/3$. The coordinates of the corresponding point on the unit circle are $(1/2, \sqrt{3}/2)$, so $\csc(-11\pi/3) = 1/y = 2/\sqrt{3}$.

Related Exercises 15–28 ◄

QUICK CHECK 2 Evaluate $\cos(11\pi/6)$ and $\sin(5\pi/4)$. ◄

Trigonometric Identities

Trigonometric functions have a variety of properties, called identities, that are true for all angles in their domain. Here is a list of some commonly used identities.

Trigonometric Identities

Reciprocal Identities

$$\tan\theta = \frac{\sin\theta}{\cos\theta} \qquad \cot\theta = \frac{1}{\tan\theta} = \frac{\cos\theta}{\sin\theta}$$

$$\csc\theta = \frac{1}{\sin\theta} \qquad \sec\theta = \frac{1}{\cos\theta}$$

Pythagorean Identities

$$\sin^2\theta + \cos^2\theta = 1 \qquad 1 + \cot^2\theta = \csc^2\theta \qquad \tan^2\theta + 1 = \sec^2\theta$$

Double- and Half-Angle Formulas

$$\sin 2\theta = 2\sin\theta\cos\theta \qquad \cos 2\theta = \cos^2\theta - \sin^2\theta$$

$$\cos^2\theta = \frac{1 + \cos 2\theta}{2} \qquad \sin^2\theta = \frac{1 - \cos 2\theta}{2}$$

QUICK CHECK 3 Use $\sin^2\theta + \cos^2\theta = 1$ to prove that $1 + \cot^2\theta = \csc^2\theta$. ◄

EXAMPLE 2 **Solving trigonometric equations** Solve the following equations.

a. $\sqrt{2}\sin x + 1 = 0$ **b.** $\cos 2x = \sin 2x$, where $0 \le x < 2\pi$

SOLUTION

▶ By rationalizing the denominator, observe that $\dfrac{1}{\sqrt{2}} = \dfrac{1}{\sqrt{2}} \cdot \dfrac{\sqrt{2}}{\sqrt{2}} = \dfrac{\sqrt{2}}{2}$.

a. First, we solve for $\sin x$ to obtain $\sin x = -1/\sqrt{2} = -\sqrt{2}/2$. From the unit circle (Figure 1.63), we find that $\sin x = -\sqrt{2}/2$ if $x = 5\pi/4$ or $x = 7\pi/4$. Adding integer multiples of 2π produces additional solutions. Therefore, the set of all solutions is

$$x = \frac{5\pi}{4} + 2n\pi \quad \text{and} \quad x = \frac{7\pi}{4} + 2n\pi, \qquad \text{for } n = 0, \pm 1, \pm 2, \pm 3, \dots.$$

b. Dividing both sides of the equation by $\cos 2x$ (assuming $\cos 2x \neq 0$), we obtain $\tan 2x = 1$. Letting $\theta = 2x$ gives us the equivalent equation $\tan\theta = 1$. This equation is satisfied by

$$\theta = \frac{\pi}{4}, \frac{5\pi}{4}, \frac{9\pi}{4}, \frac{13\pi}{4}, \frac{17\pi}{4}, \dots.$$

▶ Notice that the assumption $\cos 2x \neq 0$ is valid for these values of x.

Dividing by two and using the restriction $0 \le x < 2\pi$ gives the solutions

$$x = \frac{\theta}{2} = \frac{\pi}{8}, \frac{5\pi}{8}, \frac{9\pi}{8}, \text{and } \frac{13\pi}{8}.$$

Related Exercises 29–46 ◄

Graphs of the Trigonometric Functions

Trigonometric functions are examples of **periodic functions**: Their values repeat over every interval of some fixed length. A function f is said to be periodic if $f(x + P) = f(x)$, for all x in the domain, where the **period** P is the smallest positive real number that has this property.

Period of Trigonometric Functions

The functions $\sin \theta$, $\cos \theta$, $\sec \theta$, and $\csc \theta$ have a period of 2π:

$$\sin (\theta + 2\pi) = \sin \theta \qquad \cos (\theta + 2\pi) = \cos \theta$$
$$\sec (\theta + 2\pi) = \sec \theta \qquad \csc (\theta + 2\pi) = \csc \theta,$$

for all θ in the domain.

The functions $\tan \theta$ and $\cot \theta$ have a period of π:

$$\tan (\theta + \pi) = \tan \theta \qquad \cot (\theta + \pi) = \cot \theta,$$

for all θ in the domain.

The graph of $y = \sin \theta$ is shown in Figure 1.66a. Because $\csc \theta = 1/\sin \theta$, these two functions have the same sign, but $y = \csc \theta$ is undefined with vertical asymptotes at $\theta = 0, \pm\pi, \pm2\pi, \ldots$. The functions $\cos \theta$ and $\sec \theta$ have a similar relationship (Figure 1.66b).

The graphs of $y = \sin \theta$ and its reciprocal, $y = \csc \theta$

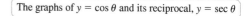

The graphs of $y = \cos \theta$ and its reciprocal, $y = \sec \theta$

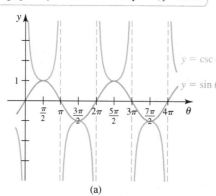

(a)

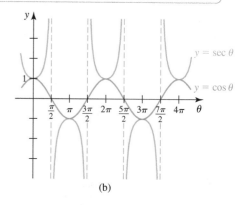

(b)

Figure 1.66

The graphs of $\tan \theta$ and $\cot \theta$ are shown in Figure 1.67. Each function has points, separated by π units, at which it is undefined.

The graph of $y = \tan \theta$ has period π.

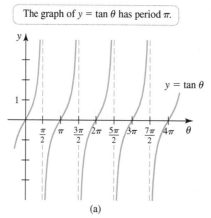

(a)

The graph of $y = \cot \theta$ has period π.

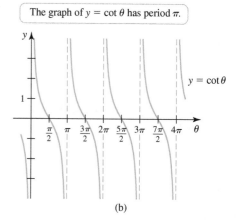

(b)

Figure 1.67

$$y = A \sin(B(\theta - C)) + D$$

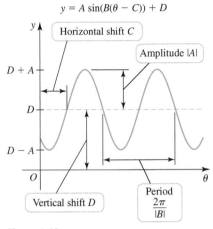

Figure 1.68

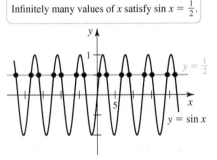

Figure 1.69

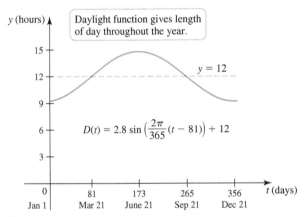

Figure 1.70

▶ The notation for the inverse trigonometric functions invites confusion: $\sin^{-1} x$ and $\cos^{-1} x$ do not mean the reciprocals of $\sin x$ and $\cos x$. The expression $\sin^{-1} x$ should be read "*angle whose sine is x*," and $\cos^{-1} x$ should be read "*angle whose cosine is x*." The values of $\sin^{-1} x$ and $\cos^{-1} x$ are angles.

Transforming Graphs

Many physical phenomena, such as the motion of waves or the rising and setting of the sun, can be modeled using trigonometric functions; the sine and cosine functions are especially useful. Using the transformation methods introduced in Section 1.2, we can show that the functions

$$y = A \sin (B(\theta - C)) + D \quad \text{and} \quad y = A \cos (B(\theta - C)) + D,$$

when compared to the graphs of $y = \sin \theta$ and $y = \cos \theta$, have a vertical stretch (or **amplitude**) of $|A|$, a period of $2\pi/|B|$, a horizontal shift (or **phase shift**) of C, and a **vertical shift** of D (Figure 1.68).

For example, at latitude 40° north (Beijing, Madrid, Philadelphia), there are 12 hours of daylight on the equinoxes (approximately March 21 and September 21), with a maximum of 14.8 hours of daylight on the summer solstice (approximately June 21) and a minimum of 9.2 hours of daylight on the winter solstice (approximately December 21). Using this information, it can be shown that the function

$$D(t) = 2.8 \sin \left(\frac{2\pi}{365} (t - 81) \right) + 12$$

models the number of daylight hours t days after January 1 (Figure 1.69; Exercise 100). The graph of this function is obtained from the graph of $y = \sin t$ by (1) a horizontal scaling by a factor of $2\pi/365$, (2) a horizontal shift of 81, (3) a vertical scaling by a factor of 2.8, and (4) a vertical shift of 12.

Inverse Trigonometric Functions

The notion of inverse functions led from exponential functions to logarithmic functions (Section 1.3). We now carry out a similar procedure—this time with trigonometric functions.

Inverse Sine and Cosine Our goal is to develop the inverses of the sine and cosine in detail. The inverses of the other four trigonometric functions then follow in an analogous way. So far, we have asked this question: Given an angle x, what is $\sin x$ or $\cos x$? Now we ask the opposite question: Given a number y, what is the angle x such that $\sin x = y$? Or what is the angle x such that $\cos x = y$? These are inverse questions.

There are a few things to notice right away. First, these questions don't make sense if $|y| > 1$, because $-1 \le \sin x \le 1$ and $-1 \le \cos x \le 1$. Next, let's select an acceptable value of y, say, $y = \frac{1}{2}$, and find the angle x that satisfies $\sin x = y = \frac{1}{2}$. It is apparent that infinitely many angles satisfy $\sin x = \frac{1}{2}$; all angles of the form $\pi/6 \pm 2n\pi$ and $5\pi/6 \pm 2n\pi$, where n is an integer, answer the inverse question (Figure 1.70). A similar situation occurs with the cosine function.

These inverse questions do not have unique answers because $\sin x$ and $\cos x$ are not one-to-one on their domains. To define their inverses, these functions are restricted to intervals on which they are one-to-one. For the sine function, the standard choice is $[-\pi/2, \pi/2]$; for cosine, it is $[0, \pi]$ (Figure 1.71). Now when we ask for the angle x on the interval $[-\pi/2, \pi/2]$ such that $\sin x = \frac{1}{2}$, there is one answer: $x = \pi/6$. When we ask for the angle x on the interval $[0, \pi]$ such that $\cos x = -\frac{1}{2}$, there is one answer: $x = 2\pi/3$.

We define the **inverse sine**, or **arcsine**, denoted $y = \sin^{-1} x$ or $y = \arcsin x$, such that y is the angle whose sine is x, with the provision that y lies in the interval $[-\pi/2, \pi/2]$. Similarly, we define the **inverse cosine**, or **arccosine**, denoted $y = \cos^{-1} x$ or $y = \arccos x$, such that y is the angle whose cosine is x, with the provision that y lies in the interval $[0, \pi]$.

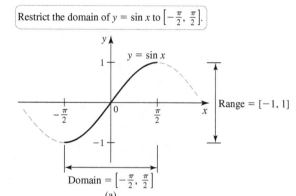

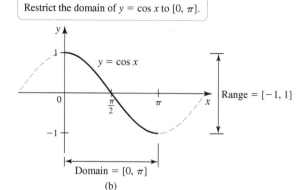

Figure 1.71

DEFINITION Inverse Sine and Cosine

$y = \sin^{-1} x$ is the value of y such that $x = \sin y$, where $-\pi/2 \leq y \leq \pi/2$.
$y = \cos^{-1} x$ is the value of y such that $x = \cos y$, where $0 \leq y \leq \pi$.
The domain of both $\sin^{-1} x$ and $\cos^{-1} x$ is $\{x: -1 \leq x \leq 1\}$.

Recall that any invertible function and its inverse satisfy the properties

$$f(f^{-1}(y)) = y \quad \text{and} \quad f^{-1}(f(x)) = x.$$

These properties apply to the inverse sine and cosine, as long as we observe the restrictions on the domains. Here is what we can say:

- $\sin(\sin^{-1} x) = x$ and $\cos(\cos^{-1} x) = x$, for $-1 \leq x \leq 1$.
- $\sin^{-1}(\sin y) = y$, for $-\pi/2 \leq y \leq \pi/2$.
- $\cos^{-1}(\cos y) = y$, for $0 \leq y \leq \pi$.

QUICK CHECK 4 Explain why $\sin^{-1}(\sin 0) = 0$, but $\sin^{-1}(\sin 2\pi) \neq 2\pi$. ◄

EXAMPLE 3   Working with inverse sine and cosine Evaluate the following expressions.

a. $\sin^{-1}(\sqrt{3}/2)$ **b.** $\cos^{-1}(-\sqrt{3}/2)$ **c.** $\cos^{-1}(\cos 3\pi)$ **d.** $\sin^{-1}\left(\sin \frac{3\pi}{4}\right)$

SOLUTION

a. $\sin^{-1}(\sqrt{3}/2) = \pi/3$ because $\sin(\pi/3) = \sqrt{3}/2$ and $\pi/3$ is in the interval $[-\pi/2, \pi/2]$.

b. $\cos^{-1}(-\sqrt{3}/2) = 5\pi/6$ because $\cos(5\pi/6) = -\sqrt{3}/2$ and $5\pi/6$ is in the interval $[0, \pi]$.

c. It's tempting to conclude that $\cos^{-1}(\cos 3\pi) = 3\pi$, but the result of an inverse cosine operation must lie in the interval $[0, \pi]$. Because $\cos(3\pi) = -1$ and $\cos^{-1}(-1) = \pi$, we have

$$\cos^{-1}(\underbrace{\cos 3\pi}_{-1}) = \cos^{-1}(-1) = \pi.$$

d. $\sin^{-1}\left(\underbrace{\sin \frac{3\pi}{4}}_{\sqrt{2}/2}\right) = \sin^{-1}\frac{\sqrt{2}}{2} = \frac{\pi}{4}$

Related Exercises 47–56 ◄

Graphs and Properties Recall from Section 1.3 that the graph of f^{-1} is obtained by reflecting the graph of f about the line $y = x$. This operation produces the graphs of the inverse sine (Figure 1.72) and inverse cosine (Figure 1.73). The graphs make it easy to compare the domain and range of each function and its inverse.

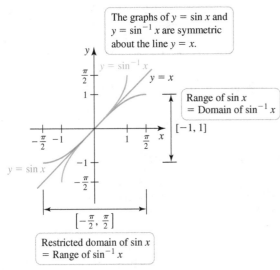

The graphs of $y = \sin x$ and $y = \sin^{-1} x$ are symmetric about the line $y = x$.

Range of $\sin x$ = Domain of $\sin^{-1} x$
$[-1, 1]$

$\left[-\frac{\pi}{2}, \frac{\pi}{2}\right]$
Restricted domain of $\sin x$ = Range of $\sin^{-1} x$

Figure 1.72

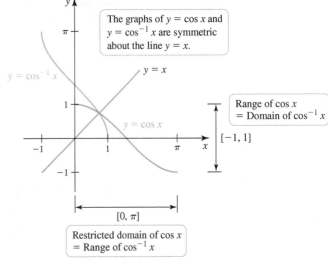

The graphs of $y = \cos x$ and $y = \cos^{-1} x$ are symmetric about the line $y = x$.

Range of $\cos x$ = Domain of $\cos^{-1} x$
$[-1, 1]$

$[0, \pi]$
Restricted domain of $\cos x$ = Range of $\cos^{-1} x$

Figure 1.73

EXAMPLE 4   Right-triangle relationships

a. Suppose $\theta = \sin^{-1}(2/5)$. Find $\cos \theta$ and $\tan \theta$.

b. Find an alternative form for $\cot\left(\cos^{-1}(x/4)\right)$ in terms of x.

SOLUTION

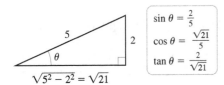

$\sin \theta = \frac{2}{5}$

$\cos \theta = \frac{\sqrt{21}}{5}$

$\tan \theta = \frac{2}{\sqrt{21}}$

$\sqrt{5^2 - 2^2} = \sqrt{21}$

Figure 1.74

a. Relationships between the trigonometric functions and their inverses can often be simplified using a right-triangle sketch. Notice that $0 < \theta < \pi/2$. The right triangle in Figure 1.74 satisfies the relationship $\sin \theta = \frac{2}{5}$, or, equivalently, $\theta = \sin^{-1}\frac{2}{5}$. We label the angle θ and the lengths of two sides; then the length of the third side is $\sqrt{21}$ (by the Pythagorean theorem). Now it is easy to read directly from the triangle:

$$\cos \theta = \frac{\sqrt{21}}{5} \quad \text{and} \quad \tan \theta = \frac{2}{\sqrt{21}}.$$

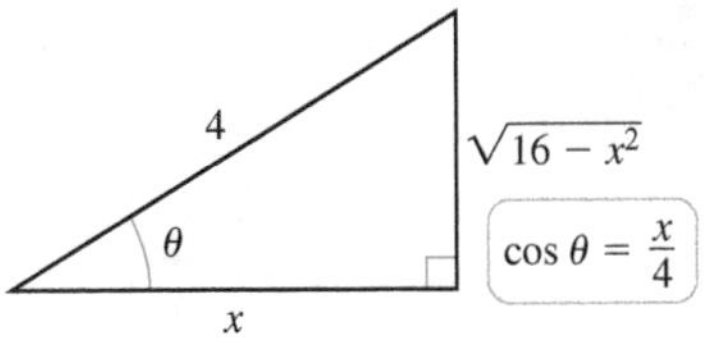

$\sqrt{16 - x^2}$

$\cos \theta = \frac{x}{4}$

Figure 1.75

b. We draw a right triangle with an angle θ satisfying $\cos \theta = x/4$, or, equivalently, $\theta = \cos^{-1}(x/4)$, where $x > 0$ (Figure 1.75). The length of the third side of the triangle is $\sqrt{16 - x^2}$. It now follows that

$$\cot\left(\underbrace{\cos^{-1}\frac{x}{4}}_{\theta}\right) = \frac{x}{\sqrt{16 - x^2}};$$

this relationship is valid for $|x| < 4$.   *Related Exercises 57–62* ◄

EXAMPLE 5   A useful identity Use right triangles to explain why $\cos^{-1} x + \sin^{-1} x = \pi/2$.

SOLUTION We draw a right triangle in a unit circle and label the acute angles θ and φ (Figure 1.76). These angles satisfy $\cos \theta = x$, or $\theta = \cos^{-1} x$, and $\sin \varphi = x$, or $\varphi = \sin^{-1} x$. Because θ and φ are complementary angles, we have

$$\frac{\pi}{2} = \theta + \varphi = \cos^{-1} x + \sin^{-1} x.$$

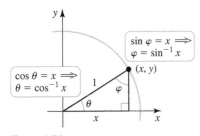

$\sin \varphi = x \implies \varphi = \sin^{-1} x$

$\cos \theta = x \implies \theta = \cos^{-1} x$

Figure 1.76

This result holds for $0 \le x \le 1$. An analogous argument extends the property to $-1 \le x \le 1$.

Related Exercises 63–66 ◄

Other Inverse Trigonometric Functions

The procedures that led to the inverse sine and inverse cosine functions can be used to obtain the other four inverse trigonometric functions. Each of these functions carries a restriction that must be imposed to ensure that an inverse exists.

• The tangent function is one-to-one on $(-\pi/2, \pi/2)$, which becomes the range of $y = \tan^{-1} x$.

• The cotangent function is one-to-one on $(0, \pi)$, which becomes the range of $y = \cot^{-1} x$.

• The secant function is one-to-one on $[0, \pi]$, excluding $x = \pi/2$; this set becomes the range of $y = \sec^{-1} x$.

• The cosecant function is one-to-one on $[-\pi/2, \pi/2]$, excluding $x = 0$; this set becomes the range of $y = \csc^{-1} x$.

The inverse tangent, cotangent, secant, and cosecant are defined as follows.

> ► Tables, books, and computer algebra systems differ on the definition of the inverse secant and cosecant. In some books, $\sec^{-1} x$ is defined to lie in the interval $[-\pi, -\pi/2)$ when $x < 0$.

DEFINITION   Other Inverse Trigonometric Functions

$y = \tan^{-1} x$ is the value of y such that $x = \tan y$, where $-\pi/2 < y < \pi/2$.
$y = \cot^{-1} x$ is the value of y such that $x = \cot y$, where $0 < y < \pi$.
The domain of both $\tan^{-1} x$ and $\cot^{-1} x$ is $\{x: -\infty < x < \infty\}$.

$y = \sec^{-1} x$ is the value of y such that $x = \sec y$, where $0 \le y \le \pi$, with $y \ne \pi/2$.
$y = \csc^{-1} x$ is the value of y such that $x = \csc y$, where $-\pi/2 \le y \le \pi/2$, with $y \ne 0$.
The domain of both $\sec^{-1} x$ and $\csc^{-1} x$ is $\{x: |x| \ge 1\}$.

The graphs of these inverse functions are obtained by reflecting the graphs of the original trigonometric functions about the line $y = x$ (Figures 1.77–1.80). The inverse secant and cosecant are somewhat irregular. The domain of the secant function (Figure 1.79) is restricted to the set $[0, \pi]$, excluding $x = \pi/2$, where the secant has a vertical asymptote. This asymptote splits the range of the secant into two disjoint intervals $(-\infty, -1]$ and $[1, \infty)$, which, in turn, splits the domain of the inverse secant into the same two intervals. A similar situation occurs with the cosecant function.

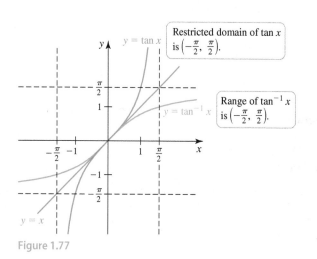

Figure 1.77

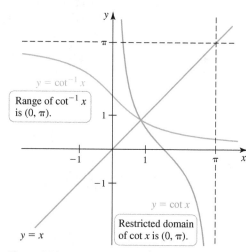

Figure 1.78

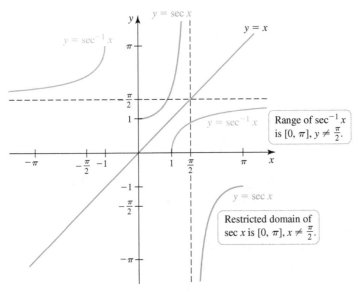

Figure 1.79

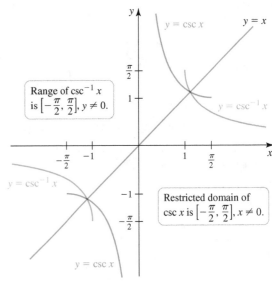

Figure 1.80

EXAMPLE 6 Working with inverse trigonometric functions Evaluate or simplify the following expressions.

a. $\tan^{-1}\left(-1/\sqrt{3}\right)$ **b.** $\sec^{-1}(-2)$ **c.** $\sin\left(\tan^{-1} x\right)$

SOLUTION

a. The result of an inverse tangent operation must lie in the interval $(-\pi/2, \pi/2)$. Therefore,

$$\tan^{-1}\left(-\frac{1}{\sqrt{3}}\right) = -\frac{\pi}{6} \quad \text{because} \quad \tan\left(-\frac{\pi}{6}\right) = -\frac{1}{\sqrt{3}}.$$

b. The result of an inverse secant operation when $x \leq -1$ must lie in the interval $(\pi/2, \pi]$. Therefore,

$$\sec^{-1}(-2) = \frac{2\pi}{3} \quad \text{because} \quad \sec\frac{2\pi}{3} = -2.$$

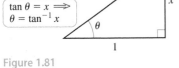

Figure 1.81

c. Figure 1.81 shows a right triangle with the relationship $x = \tan\theta$ or $\theta = \tan^{-1} x$, in the case that $0 \leq \theta < \pi/2$. We see that

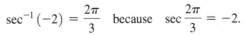
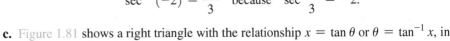

$$\sin\left(\underbrace{\tan^{-1} x}_{\theta}\right) = \frac{x}{\sqrt{1 + x^2}}.$$

The same result follows if $-\pi/2 < \theta < 0$, in which case $x < 0$ and $\sin\theta < 0$.

Related Exercises 67–82 ◄

QUICK CHECK 5 Evaluate $\sec^{-1} 1$ and $\tan^{-1} 1$. ◄

SECTION 1.4 EXERCISES

Review Questions

1. Define the six trigonometric functions in terms of the sides of a right triangle.

2. Explain how a point $P(x, y)$ on a circle of radius r determines an angle θ and the values of the six trigonometric functions at θ.

3. How is the radian measure of an angle determined?

4. Explain what is meant by the period of a trigonometric function. What are the periods of the six trigonometric functions?

5. What are the three Pythagorean identities for the trigonometric functions?

6. How are the sine and cosine functions related to the other four trigonometric functions?

7. Where is the tangent function undefined?

8. What is the domain of the secant function?

9. Explain why the domain of the sine function must be restricted in order to define its inverse function.

10. Why do the values of $\cos^{-1} x$ lie in the interval $[0, \pi]$?

11. Is it true that $\tan(\tan^{-1} x) = x$ for all x? Is it true that $\tan^{-1}(\tan x) = x$ for all x?

12. Sketch the graphs of $y = \cos x$ and $y = \cos^{-1} x$ on the same set of axes.

13. The function $\tan x$ is undefined at $x = \pm\pi/2$. How does this fact appear in the graph of $y = \tan^{-1} x$?

14. State the domain and range of $\sec^{-1} x$.

Basic Skills

15–22. Evaluating trigonometric functions *Evaluate the following expressions using a unit circle. Use a calculator to check your work. All angles are in radians.*

15. $\cos(2\pi/3)$
16. $\sin(2\pi/3)$
17. $\tan(-3\pi/4)$
18. $\tan(15\pi/4)$
19. $\cot(-13\pi/3)$
20. $\sec(7\pi/6)$
21. $\cot(-17\pi/3)$
22. $\sin(16\pi/3)$

23–28. Evaluating trigonometric functions *Evaluate the following expressions or state that the quantity is undefined. Use a calculator to check your work.*

23. $\cos 0$
24. $\sin(-\pi/2)$
25. $\cos(-\pi)$
26. $\tan 3\pi$
27. $\sec(5\pi/2)$
28. $\cot \pi$

29–36. Trigonometric identities

29. Prove that $\sec \theta = \dfrac{1}{\cos \theta}$.

30. Prove that $\tan \theta = \dfrac{\sin \theta}{\cos \theta}$.

31. Prove that $\tan^2 \theta + 1 = \sec^2 \theta$.

32. Prove that $\dfrac{\sin \theta}{\csc \theta} + \dfrac{\cos \theta}{\sec \theta} = 1$.

33. Prove that $\sec(\pi/2 - \theta) = \csc \theta$.

34. Prove that $\sec(x + \pi) = -\sec x$.

35. Find the exact value of $\cos(\pi/12)$.

36. Find the exact value of $\tan(3\pi/8)$.

37–46. Solving trigonometric equations *Solve the following equations.*

37. $\tan x = 1$
38. $2\theta \cos \theta + \theta = 0$
39. $\sin^2 \theta = \frac{1}{4}, 0 \le \theta < 2\pi$
40. $\cos^2 \theta = \frac{1}{2}, 0 \le \theta < 2\pi$
41. $\sqrt{2} \sin x - 1 = 0$
42. $\sin 3x = \frac{\sqrt{2}}{2}, 0 \le x < 2\pi$
43. $\cos 3x = \sin 3x, 0 \le x < 2\pi$
44. $\sin^2 \theta - 1 = 0$

45. $\sin \theta \cos \theta = 0, 0 \le \theta < 2\pi$
46. $\tan^2 2\theta = 1, 0 \le \theta < \pi$

47–56. Inverse sines and cosines *Without using a calculator, evaluate the following expressions or state that the quantity is undefined.*

47. $\sin^{-1} 1$
48. $\cos^{-1}(-1)$
49. $\tan^{-1} 1$
50. $\cos^{-1}\left(-\frac{\sqrt{2}}{2}\right)$
51. $\sin^{-1} \frac{\sqrt{3}}{2}$
52. $\cos^{-1} 2$
53. $\cos^{-1}\left(-\frac{1}{2}\right)$
54. $\sin^{-1}(-1)$
55. $\cos(\cos^{-1}(-1))$
56. $\cos^{-1}(\cos(7\pi/6))$

57–62. Right-triangle relationships *Draw a right triangle to simplify the given expressions. Assume $x > 0$.*

57. $\cos(\sin^{-1} x)$
58. $\cos(\sin^{-1}(x/3))$
59. $\sin(\cos^{-1}(x/2))$
60. $\sin^{-1}(\cos \theta)$, for $0 \le \theta \le \pi/2$
61. $\sin(2\cos^{-1} x)$ (*Hint:* Use $\sin 2\theta = 2 \sin \theta \cos \theta$.)
62. $\cos(2\sin^{-1} x)$ (*Hint:* Use $\cos 2\theta = \cos^2 \theta - \sin^2 \theta$.)

63–64. Identities *Prove the following identities.*

63. $\cos^{-1} x + \cos^{-1}(-x) = \pi$
64. $\sin^{-1} y + \sin^{-1}(-y) = 0$

65–66. Verifying identities *Sketch a graph of the given pair of functions to conjecture a relationship between the two functions. Then verify the conjecture.*

65. $\sin^{-1} x; \dfrac{\pi}{2} - \cos^{-1} x$
66. $\tan^{-1} x; \dfrac{\pi}{2} - \cot^{-1} x$

67–74. Evaluating inverse trigonometric functions *Without using a calculator, evaluate or simplify the following expressions.*

67. $\tan^{-1} \sqrt{3}$
68. $\cot^{-1}(-1/\sqrt{3})$
69. $\sec^{-1} 2$
70. $\csc^{-1}(-1)$
71. $\tan^{-1}(\tan(\pi/4))$
72. $\tan^{-1}(\tan(3\pi/4))$
73. $\csc^{-1}(\sec 2)$
74. $\tan(\tan^{-1} 1)$

75–80. Right-triangle relationships *Use a right triangle to simplify the given expressions. Assume $x > 0$.*

75. $\cos(\tan^{-1} x)$
76. $\tan(\cos^{-1} x)$
77. $\cos(\sec^{-1} x)$
78. $\cot(\tan^{-1} 2x)$
79. $\sin\left(\sec^{-1}\left(\dfrac{\sqrt{x^2 + 16}}{4}\right)\right)$
80. $\cos\left(\tan^{-1}\left(\dfrac{x}{\sqrt{9 - x^2}}\right)\right)$

81–82. Right-triangle pictures *Express θ in terms of x using the inverse sine, inverse tangent, and inverse secant functions.*

81.
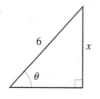

82.
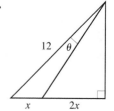

Further Explorations

83. Explain why or why not Determine whether the following statements are true and give an explanation or counterexample.

    a. $\sin(a + b) = \sin a + \sin b$.

    b. The equation $\cos \theta = 2$ has multiple real solutions.

    c. The equation $\sin \theta = \frac{1}{2}$ has exactly one solution.

    d. The function $\sin(\pi x/12)$ has a period of 12.

    e. Of the six basic trigonometric functions, only tangent and cotangent have a range of $(-\infty, \infty)$.

    f. $\dfrac{\sin^{-1} x}{\cos^{-1} x} = \tan^{-1} x$.

    g. $\cos^{-1}(\cos(15\pi/16)) = 15\pi/16$.

    h. $\sin^{-1} x = 1/\sin x$.

84–87. One function gives all six *Given the following information about one trigonometric function, evaluate the other five functions.*

84. $\sin \theta = -\dfrac{4}{5}$ and $\pi < \theta < 3\pi/2$

85. $\cos \theta = \dfrac{5}{13}$ and $0 < \theta < \pi/2$

86. $\sec \theta = \dfrac{5}{3}$ and $3\pi/2 < \theta < 2\pi$

87. $\csc \theta = \dfrac{13}{12}$ and $0 < \theta < \pi/2$

88–91. Amplitude and period *Identify the amplitude and period of the following functions.*

88. $f(\theta) = 2 \sin 2\theta$

89. $g(\theta) = 3 \cos(\theta/3)$

90. $p(t) = 2.5 \sin\left(\frac{1}{2}(t - 3)\right)$

91. $q(x) = 3.6 \cos(\pi x/24)$

92–95. Graphing sine and cosine functions *Beginning with the graphs of $y = \sin x$ or $y = \cos x$, use shifting and scaling transformations to sketch the graph of the following functions. Use a graphing utility to check your work.*

92. $f(x) = 3 \sin 2x$

93. $g(x) = -2 \cos(x/3)$

94. $p(x) = 3 \sin(2x - \pi/3) + 1$

95. $q(x) = 3.6 \cos(\pi x/24) + 2$

96–97. Designer functions *Design a sine function with the given properties.*

96. It has a period of 12 hr with a minimum value of -4 at $t = 0$ hr and a maximum value of 4 at $t = 6$ hr.

97. It has a period of 24 hr with a minimum value of 10 at $t = 3$ hr and a maximum value of 16 at $t = 15$ hr.

T 98. Field goal attempt Near the end of the 1950 Rose Bowl football game between the University of California and Ohio State University, Ohio State was preparing to attempt a field goal from a distance of 23 yd from the endline at point A on the edge of the kicking region (see figure). But before the kick, Ohio State committed a penalty and the ball was backed up 5 yd to point B on the edge of the kicking region. After the game, the Ohio State coach claimed that his team deliberately committed a penalty to improve the kicking angle. Given that a successful kick must go between the uprights of the goal posts G_1 and G_2, is $\angle G_1BG_2$ greater than $\angle G_1AG_2$? (In 1950, the uprights were 23 ft 4 in apart, equidistant from the origin on the end line. The boundaries of the kicking region are 53 ft 4 in apart and are equidistant from the y-axis. (*Source: The College Mathematics Journal 27, 4, Sep 1996*)

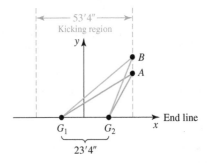

T 99. A surprising result The Earth is approximately circular in cross section, with a circumference at the equator of 24,882 miles. Suppose we use two ropes to create two concentric circles: one by wrapping a rope around the equator and another using a rope 38 ft longer (see figure). How much space is between the ropes?

Applications

100. Daylight function for 40° N Verify that the function

$$D(t) = 2.8 \sin\left(\frac{2\pi}{365}(t - 81)\right) + 12$$

has the following properties, where t is measured in days and D is the number of hours between sunrise and sunset.

    a. It has a period of 365 days.

    b. Its maximum and minimum values are 14.8 and 9.2, respectively, which occur approximately at $t = 172$ and $t = 355$, respectively (corresponding to the solstices).

    c. $D(81) = 12$ and $D(264) \approx 12$ (corresponding to the equinoxes).

101. Block on a spring A light block hangs at rest from the end of a spring when it is pulled down 10 cm and released. Assume the block oscillates with an amplitude of 10 cm on either side of its rest position with a period of 1.5 s. Find a trigonometric function

$d(t)$ that gives the displacement of the block t seconds after it is released, where $d(t) > 0$ represents downward displacement.

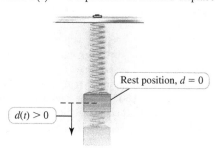

Rest position, $d = 0$

$d(t) > 0$

102. Approaching a lighthouse A boat approaches a 50-ft-high lighthouse whose base is at sea level. Let d be the distance between the boat and the base of the lighthouse. Let L be the distance between the boat and the top of the lighthouse. Let θ be the angle of elevation between the boat and the top of the lighthouse.

  a. Express d as a function of θ.
  b. Express L as a function of θ.

103. Ladders Two ladders of length a lean against opposite walls of an alley with their feet touching (see figure). One ladder extends h feet up the wall and makes a $75°$ angle with the ground. The other ladder extends k feet up the opposite wall and makes a $45°$ angle with the ground. Find the width of the alley in terms of h. Assume the ground is horizontal and perpendicular to both walls.

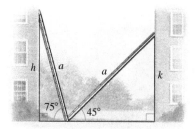

104. Pole in a corner A pole of length L is carried horizontally around a corner where a 3-ft-wide hallway meets a 4-ft-wide hallway. For $0 < \theta < \pi/2$, find the relationship between L and θ at the moment when the pole simultaneously touches both walls and the corner P. Estimate θ when $L = 10$ ft.

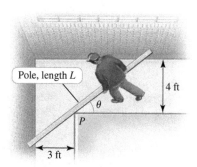

Pole, length L

4 ft

θ

P

3 ft

105. Little-known fact The shortest day of the year occurs on the winter solstice (near December 21) and the longest day of the year occurs on the summer solstice (near June 21). However, the latest sunrise and the earliest sunset do not occur on the winter solstice, and the earliest sunrise and the latest sunset do not occur on the summer solstice. At latitude $40°$ north, the latest sunrise occurs on January 4 at 7:25 A.M. (14 days after the solstice), and the earliest sunset occurs on December 7 at 4:37 P.M. (14 days before the solstice). Similarly, the earliest sunrise occurs on July 2 at 4:30 A.M. (14 days after the solstice) and the latest sunset occurs on June 7 at 7:32 P.M. (14 days before the solstice). Using sine functions, devise a function $s(t)$ that gives the time of sunrise t days after January 1 and a function $S(t)$ that gives the time of sunset t days after January 1. Assume that s and S are measured in minutes and $s = 0$ and $S = 0$ correspond to 4:00 A.M. Graph the functions. Then graph the length of the day function $D(t) = S(t) - s(t)$ and show that the longest and shortest days occur on the solstices.

106. Viewing angles An auditorium with a flat floor has a large flat-panel television on one wall. The lower edge of the television is 3 ft above the floor, and the upper edge is 10 ft above the floor (see figure). Express θ in terms of x.

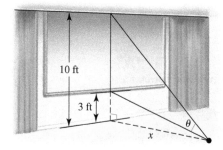

10 ft

3 ft

θ

x

Additional Exercises

107. Area of a circular sector Prove that the area of a sector of a circle of radius r associated with a central angle θ (measured in radians) is $A = \frac{1}{2} r^2 \theta$.

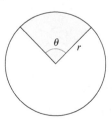

θ r

108. Law of cosines Use the figure to prove the law of cosines (which is a generalization of the Pythagorean theorem): $c^2 = a^2 + b^2 - 2ab \cos \theta$.

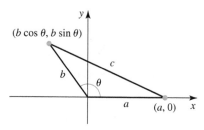

y

$(b \cos \theta, b \sin \theta)$

b c θ

a $(a, 0)$ x

109. Law of sines Use the figure to prove the law of sines:
$$\frac{\sin A}{a} = \frac{\sin B}{b} = \frac{\sin C}{c}.$$

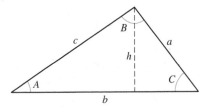

CHAPTER 1   REVIEW EXERCISES

1. **Explain why or why not** Determine whether the following statements are true and give an explanation or counterexample.

    a. A function could have the property that $f(-x) = f(x)$, for all x.
    b. $\cos(a + b) = \cos a + \cos b$, for all a and b in $[0, 2\pi]$.
    c. If f is a linear function of the form $f(x) = mx + b$, then $f(u + v) = f(u) + f(v)$, for all u and v.
    d. The function $f(x) = 1 - x$ has the property that $f(f(x)) = x$.
    e. The set $\{x : |x + 3| > 4\}$ can be drawn on the number line without lifting your pencil.
    f. $\log_{10}(xy) = (\log_{10} x)(\log_{10} y)$
    g. $\sin^{-1}(\sin(2\pi)) = 0$

2. **Domain and range** Find the domain and range of the following functions.

    a. $f(x) = x^5 + \sqrt{x}$ b. $g(y) = \dfrac{1}{y - 2}$
    c. $h(z) = \sqrt{z^2 - 2z - 3}$

3. **Equations of lines** In each part below, find an equation of the line with the given properties. Graph the line.

    a. The line passing through the points $(2, -3)$ and $(4, 2)$
    b. The line with slope $\frac{3}{4}$ and x-intercept $(-4, 0)$
    c. The line with intercepts $(4, 0)$ and $(0, -2)$

4. **Piecewise linear functions** The parking costs in a city garage are $2 for the first half hour and $1 for each additional half hour. Graph the function $C = f(t)$ that gives the cost of parking for t hours, where $0 \le t \le 3$.

Ⅱ 5. **Graphing absolute value** Consider the function $f(x) = 2(x - |x|)$. Express the function in two pieces without using the absolute value. Then graph the function by hand. Use a graphing utility to check your work.

6. **Function from words** Suppose you plan to take a 500-mile trip in a car that gets 35 mi/gal. Find the function $C = f(p)$ that gives the cost of gasoline for the trip when gasoline costs $p per gallon.

Ⅱ 7. **Graphing equations** Graph the following equations. Use a graphing utility to check your work.

    a. $2x - 3y + 10 = 0$
    b. $y = x^2 + 2x - 3$
    c. $x^2 + 2x + y^2 + 4y + 1 = 0$
    d. $x^2 - 2x + y^2 - 8y + 5 = 0$

8. **Root functions** Graph the functions $f(x) = x^{1/3}$ and $g(x) = x^{1/4}$. Find all points where the two graphs intersect. For $x > 1$, is $f(x) > g(x)$ or is $g(x) > f(x)$?

9. **Root functions** Find the domain and range of the functions $f(x) = x^{1/7}$ and $g(x) = x^{1/4}$.

10. **Intersection points** Graph the equations $y = x^2$ and $x^2 + y^2 - 7y + 8 = 0$. At what point(s) do the curves intersect?

11. **Boiling-point function** Water boils at $212°$ F at sea level and at $200°$ F at an elevation of 6000 ft. Assume that the boiling point B varies linearly with altitude a. Find the function $B = f(a)$ that describes the dependence. Comment on whether a linear function is a realistic model.

12. **Publishing costs** A small publisher plans to spend $1000 for advertising a paperback book and estimates the printing cost is $2.50 per book. The publisher will receive $7 for each book sold.

    a. Find the function $C = f(x)$ that gives the cost of producing x books.
    b. Find the function $R = g(x)$ that gives the revenue from selling x books.
    c. Graph the cost and revenue functions; then find the number of books that must be sold for the publisher to break even.

Ⅱ 13. **Shifting and scaling** Starting with the graph of $f(x) = x^2$, plot the following functions. Use a graphing calculator to check your work.

    a. $f(x + 3)$ b. $2f(x - 4)$ c. $-f(3x)$ d. $f(2(x - 3))$

14. **Shifting and scaling** The graph of f is shown in the figure. Graph the following functions.

    a. $f(x + 1)$ b. $2f(x - 1)$ c. $-f(x/2)$ d. $f(2(x - 1))$

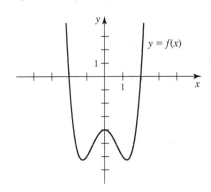

15. Composite functions Let $f(x) = x^3$, $g(x) = \sin x$, and $h(x) = \sqrt{x}$.

    a. Evaluate $h(g(\pi/2))$.   **b.** Find $h(f(x))$.
    c. Find $f(g(h(x)))$.   **d.** Find the domain of $g \circ f$.
    e. Find the range of $f \circ g$.

16. Composite functions Find functions f and g such that $h = f \circ g$.

    a. $h(x) = \sin(x^2 + 1)$ **b.** $h(x) = (x^2 - 4)^{-3}$
    c. $h(x) = e^{\cos 2x}$

17–20. Simplifying difference quotients *Evaluate and simplify the difference quotients* $\dfrac{f(x + h) - f(x)}{h}$ *and* $\dfrac{f(x) - f(a)}{x - a}$ *for each function.*

17. $f(x) = x^2 - 2x$ **18.** $f(x) = 4 - 5x$

19. $f(x) = x^3 + 2$ **20.** $f(x) = \dfrac{7}{x + 3}$

21. Symmetry Identify the symmetry (if any) in the graphs of the following equations.

    a. $y = \cos 3x$ **b.** $y = 3x^4 - 3x^2 + 1$
    c. $y^2 - 4x^2 = 4$

22–23. Properties of logarithms and exponentials *Use properties of logarithms and exponentials, not a calculator, for the following exercises.*

22. Solve the equation $48 = 6e^{4k}$ for k.

23. Solve the equation $\log_{10} x^2 + 3 \log_{10} x = \log_{10} 32$ for x. Does the answer depend on the base of the log in the equation?

24. Graphs of logarithmic and exponential functions The figure shows the graphs of $y = 2^x$, $y = 3^{-x}$, and $y = -\ln x$. Match each curve with the correct function.

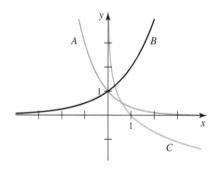

25–26. Existence of inverses *Determine the intervals on which the following functions have an inverse.*

25. $f(x) = x^3 - 3x^2$ **26.** $g(t) = 2 \sin(t/3)$

27–28. Finding inverses *Find the inverse on the specified interval and express it in the form $y = f^{-1}(x)$. Then graph f and f^{-1}.*

27. $f(x) = x^2 - 4x + 5$, for $x > 2$

28. $f(x) = 1/x^2$, for $x > 0$

29. Degrees and radians

    a. Convert $135°$ to radian measure.
    b. Convert $4\pi/5$ to degree measure.
    c. What is the length of the arc on a circle of radius 10 associated with an angle of $4\pi/3$ (radians)?

30. Graphing sine and cosine functions Use shifts and scalings to graph the following functions, and identify the amplitude and period.

    a. $f(x) = 4 \cos(x/2)$ **b.** $g(\theta) = 2 \sin(2\pi\theta/3)$
    c. $h(\theta) = -\cos(2(\theta - \pi/4))$

31. Designing functions Find a trigonometric function f that satisfies each set of properties. Answers are not unique.

    a. It has a period of 6 with a minimum value of -2 at $t = 0$ and a maximum value of 2 at $t = 3$.
    b. It has a period of 24 with a maximum value of 20 at $t = 6$ and a minimum value of 10 at $t = 18$.

32. Graph to function Find a trigonometric function f represented by the graph in the figure.

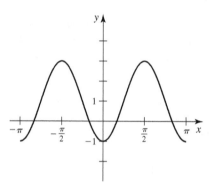

33. Matching Match each function a–f with the corresponding graphs A–F.

    a. $f(x) = -\sin x$ **b.** $f(x) = \cos 2x$
    c. $f(x) = \tan(x/2)$ **d.** $f(x) = -\sec x$
    e. $f(x) = \cot 2x$ **f.** $f(x) = \sin^2 x$

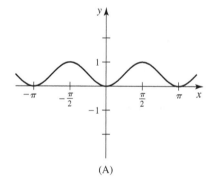

(A)

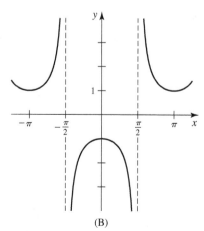

(B)

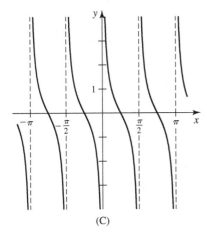

(C)

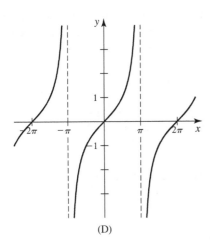

(D)

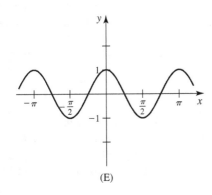

(E)

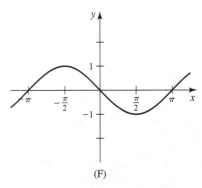

(F)

34–35. Intersection points *Find the points at which the curves intersect on the given interval.*

34. $y = \sec x$ and $y = 2$ on $(-\pi/2, \pi/2)$

35. $y = \sin x$ and $y = -\frac{1}{2}$ on $(0, 2\pi)$

36–42. Inverse sines and cosines *Evaluate or simplify the following expressions without using a calculator.*

36. $\sin^{-1}\frac{\sqrt{3}}{2}$ **37.** $\cos^{-1}\frac{\sqrt{3}}{2}$ **38.** $\cos^{-1}\left(-\frac{1}{2}\right)$

39. $\sin^{-1}(-1)$ **40.** $\cos\left(\cos^{-1}(-1)\right)$ **41.** $\sin\left(\sin^{-1}x\right)$

42. $\cos^{-1}(\sin 3\pi)$

43. Right triangles Given that $\theta = \sin^{-1}\frac{12}{13}$, evaluate $\cos\theta$, $\tan\theta$, $\cot\theta$, $\sec\theta$, and $\csc\theta$.

44–51. Right-triangle relationships *Draw a right triangle to simplify the given expression. Assume $x > 0$ and $0 \le \theta \le \pi/2$.*

44. $\cos\left(\tan^{-1}x\right)$ **45.** $\sin\left(\cos^{-1}(x/2)\right)$

46. $\tan\left(\sec^{-1}(x/2)\right)$ **47.** $\cot^{-1}(\tan\theta)$

48. $\csc^{-1}(\sec\theta)$ **49.** $\sin^{-1}x + \sin^{-1}(-x)$

50. $\sin\left(2\cos^{-1}x\right)$ (*Hint:* Use $\sin 2\theta = 2\sin\theta\cos\theta$.)

51. $\cos\left(2\sin^{-1}x\right)$ (*Hint:* Use $\cos 2\theta = \cos^2\theta - \sin^2\theta$.)

52. Stereographic projections A common way of displaying a sphere (such as Earth) on a plane (such as a map) is to use a *stereographic projection.* Here is the two-dimensional version of the method, which maps a circle to a line. Let P be a point on the right half of a circle of radius R identified by the angle φ. Find the function $x = F(\varphi)$ that gives the x-coordinate $(x \ge 0)$ corresponding to φ for $0 < \varphi \le \pi$.

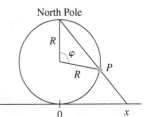

Chapter 1 Guided Projects

Applications of the material in this chapter and related topics can be found in the following Guided Projects. For additional information, see the Preface.

- Problem-solving skills
- Constant rate problems
- Functions in action I
- Functions in action II

- Supply and demand
- Phase and amplitude
- Atmospheric CO_2
- Acid, noise, and earthquakes

2

Limits

Chapter Preview All of calculus is based on the idea of a *limit*. Not only are limits important in their own right but they also underlie the two fundamental operations of calculus: differentiation (calculating derivatives) and integration (evaluating integrals). Derivatives enable us to talk about the instantaneous rate of change of a function, which, in turn, leads to concepts such as velocity and acceleration, population growth rates, marginal cost, and flow rates. Integrals enable us to compute areas under curves, surface areas, and volumes. Because of the incredible reach of this single idea, it is essential to develop a solid understanding of limits. We first present limits intuitively by showing how they arise in computing instantaneous velocities and finding slopes of tangent lines. As the chapter progresses, we build more rigor into the definition of the limit and examine the different ways in which limits arise. The chapter concludes by introducing the important property of *continuity* and by giving the formal definition of a limit.

2.1 The Idea of Limits

This brief opening section illustrates how limits arise in two seemingly unrelated problems: finding the instantaneous velocity of a moving object and finding the slope of a line tangent to a curve. These two problems provide important insights into limits on an intuitive level. In the remainder of the chapter, we develop limits carefully and fill in the mathematical details.

Average Velocity

Suppose you want to calculate your average velocity as you travel along a straight highway. If you pass milepost 100 at noon and milepost 130 at 12:30 P.M., you travel 30 miles in a half hour, so your **average velocity** over this time interval is $(30 \text{ mi})/(0.5 \text{ hr}) = 60 \text{ mi/hr}$. By contrast, even though your average velocity may be 60 mi/hr, it's almost certain that your **instantaneous velocity**, the speed indicated by the speedometer, varies from one moment to the next.

EXAMPLE 1 **Average velocity** A rock is launched vertically upward from the ground with a speed of 96 ft/s. Neglecting air resistance, a well-known formula from physics states that the position of the rock after t seconds is given by the function

$$s(t) = -16t^2 + 96t.$$

The position s is measured in feet with $s = 0$ corresponding to the ground. Find the average velocity of the rock between each pair of times.

a. $t = 1 \text{ s}$ and $t = 3 \text{ s}$ \qquad **b.** $t = 1 \text{ s}$ and $t = 2 \text{ s}$

SOLUTION Figure 2.1 shows the position function of the rock on the time interval $0 \le t \le 3$. The graph is *not* the path of the rock. The rock travels up and down on a vertical line.

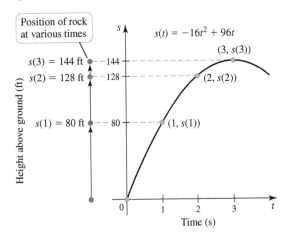

Figure 2.1

a. The average velocity of the rock over any time interval $[t_0, t_1]$ is the change in position divided by the elapsed time:

$$v_{av} = \frac{s(t_1) - s(t_0)}{t_1 - t_0}.$$

Therefore, the average velocity over the interval $[1, 3]$ is

$$v_{av} = \frac{s(3) - s(1)}{3 - 1} = \frac{144 \text{ ft} - 80 \text{ ft}}{3 \text{ s} - 1 \text{ s}} = \frac{64 \text{ ft}}{2 \text{ s}} = 32 \text{ ft/s}.$$

Here is an important observation: As shown in Figure 2.2a, the average velocity is simply the slope of the line joining the points $(1, s(1))$ and $(3, s(3))$ on the graph of the position function.

b. The average velocity of the rock over the interval $[1, 2]$ is

$$v_{av} = \frac{s(2) - s(1)}{2 - 1} = \frac{128 \text{ ft} - 80 \text{ ft}}{2 \text{ s} - 1 \text{ s}} = \frac{48 \text{ ft}}{1 \text{ s}} = 48 \text{ ft/s}.$$

Again, the average velocity is the slope of the line joining the points $(1, s(1))$ and $(2, s(2))$ on the graph of the position function (Figure 2.2b).

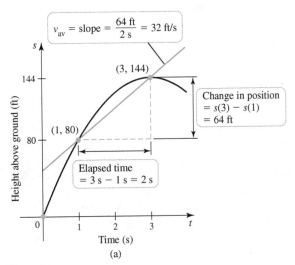
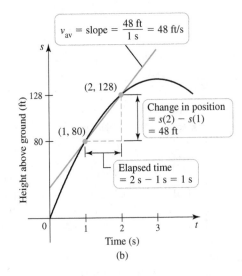

Figure 2.2

Related Exercises 7–14 ◀

➤ See Section 1.1 for a discussion of secant lines.

QUICK CHECK 1 In Example 1, what is the average velocity between $t = 2$ and $t = 3$? ◀

In Example 1, we computed slopes of lines passing through two points on a curve. Any such line joining two points on a curve is called a **secant line**. The slope of the secant line, denoted m_{sec}, for the position function in Example 1 on the interval $[t_0, t_1]$ is

$$m_{sec} = \frac{s(t_1) - s(t_0)}{t_1 - t_0}.$$

Example 1 demonstrates that the average velocity is the slope of a secant line on the graph of the position function; that is, $v_{av} = m_{sec}$ (Figure 2.3).

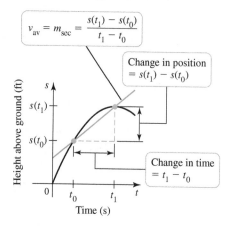

Figure 2.3

Instantaneous Velocity

To compute the average velocity, we use the position of the object at *two* distinct points in time. How do we compute the instantaneous velocity at a *single* point in time? As illustrated in Example 2, the instantaneous velocity at a point $t = t_0$ is determined by computing average velocities over intervals $[t_0, t_1]$ that decrease in length. As t_1 approaches t_0, the average velocities typically approach a unique number, which is the instantaneous velocity. This single number is called a **limit**.

QUICK CHECK 2 Explain the difference between average velocity and instantaneous velocity. ◀

EXAMPLE 2 **Instantaneous velocity** Estimate the instantaneous velocity of the rock in Example 1 at the *single* point $t = 1$.

SOLUTION We are interested in the instantaneous velocity at $t = 1$, so we compute the average velocity over smaller and smaller time intervals $[1, t]$ using the formula

$$v_{av} = \frac{s(t) - s(1)}{t - 1}.$$

Table 2.1

Time interval	Average velocity
$[1, 2]$	48 ft/s
$[1, 1.5]$	56 ft/s
$[1, 1.1]$	62.4 ft/s
$[1, 1.01]$	63.84 ft/s
$[1, 1.001]$	63.984 ft/s
$[1, 1.0001]$	63.9984 ft/s

Notice that these average velocities are also slopes of secant lines, several of which are shown in Table 2.1. For example, the average velocity on the interval $[1, 1.0001]$ is 63.9984 ft/s. Because this time interval is so short, the average velocity gives a good approximation to the instantaneous velocity at $t = 1$. We see that as t approaches 1, the average velocities appear to approach 64 ft/s. In fact, we could make the average velocity as close to 64 ft/s as we like by taking t sufficiently close to 1. Therefore, 64 ft/s is a reasonable estimate of the instantaneous velocity at $t = 1$.

Related Exercises 15–20 ◀

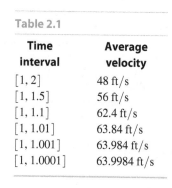

➤ The same instantaneous velocity is obtained as t approaches 1 from the left (with $t < 1$) and as t approaches 1 from the right (with $t > 1$).

In language to be introduced in Section 2.2, we say that the limit of v_{av} as t approaches 1 equals the instantaneous velocity v_{inst}, which is 64 ft/s. This statement is illustrated in Figure 2.4 and written compactly as

$$v_{inst} = \lim_{t \to 1} v_{av} = \lim_{t \to 1} \frac{s(t) - s(1)}{t - 1} = 64 \text{ ft/s}.$$

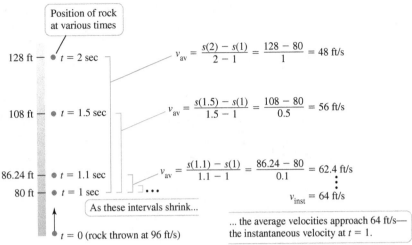

$$v_{av} = \frac{s(2) - s(1)}{2 - 1} = \frac{128 - 80}{1} = 48 \text{ ft/s}$$

$$v_{av} = \frac{s(1.5) - s(1)}{1.5 - 1} = \frac{108 - 80}{0.5} = 56 \text{ ft/s}$$

$$v_{av} = \frac{s(1.1) - s(1)}{1.1 - 1} = \frac{86.24 - 80}{0.1} = 62.4 \text{ ft/s}$$

$$v_{inst} = 64 \text{ ft/s}$$

Figure 2.4

> We define tangent lines carefully in Section 3.1. For the moment, imagine zooming in on a point P on a smooth curve. As you zoom in, the curve appears more and more like a line passing through P. This line is the *tangent line* at P. Because a smooth curve approaches a line as we zoom in on a point, a smooth curve is said to be *locally linear* at any given point.

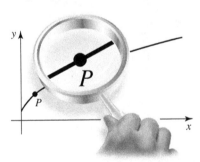

Slope of the Tangent Line

Several important conclusions follow from Examples 1 and 2. Each average velocity in Table 2.1 corresponds to the slope of a secant line on the graph of the position function (Figure 2.5). Just as the average velocities approach a limit as t approaches 1, the slopes of the secant lines approach the same limit as t approaches 1. Specifically, as t approaches 1, two things happen:

1. The secant lines approach a unique line called the **tangent line**.

2. The slopes of the secant lines m_{sec} approach the slope of the tangent line m_{tan} at the point $(1, s(1))$. Therefore, the slope of the tangent line is also expressed as a limit:

$$m_{tan} = \lim_{t \to 1} m_{sec} = \lim_{t \to 1} \frac{s(t) - s(1)}{t - 1} = 64.$$

This limit is the same limit that defines the instantaneous velocity. Therefore, the instantaneous velocity at $t = 1$ is the slope of the line tangent to the position curve at $t = 1$.

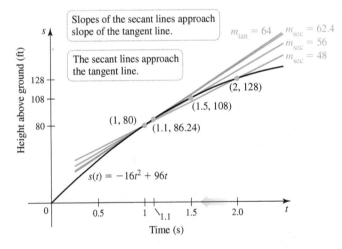

Figure 2.5

QUICK CHECK 3 In Figure 2.5, is m_{tan} at $t = 2$ greater than or less than m_{tan} at $t = 1$? ◄

The parallels between average and instantaneous velocities, on one hand, and between slopes of secant lines and tangent lines, on the other, illuminate the power behind the idea of a limit. As $t \to 1$, slopes of secant lines approach the slope of a tangent line. And as $t \to 1$, average velocities approach an instantaneous velocity. Figure 2.6 summarizes these two parallel limit processes. These ideas lie at the foundation of what follows in the coming chapters.

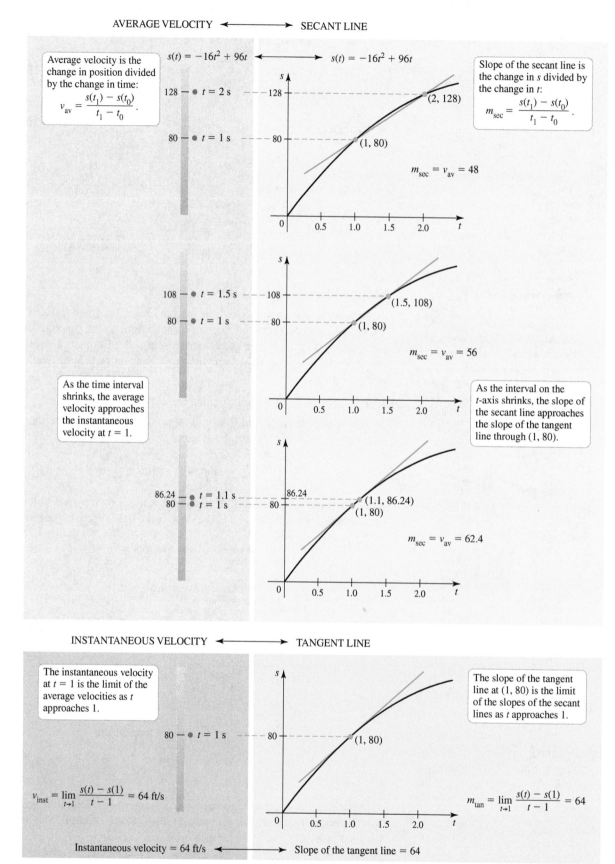

AVERAGE VELOCITY ←——————→ SECANT LINE

Average velocity is the change in position divided by the change in time:
$$v_{av} = \frac{s(t_1) - s(t_0)}{t_1 - t_0}.$$

$s(t) = -16t^2 + 96t$ ←——————→ $s(t) = -16t^2 + 96t$

Slope of the secant line is the change in s divided by the change in t:
$$m_{sec} = \frac{s(t_1) - s(t_0)}{t_1 - t_0}.$$

$128 — • \ t = 2$ s

$80 — • \ t = 1$ s

$(2, 128)$

$(1, 80)$

$m_{sec} = v_{av} = 48$

$108 — • \ t = 1.5$ s

$80 — • \ t = 1$ s

$(1.5, 108)$

$(1, 80)$

$m_{sec} = v_{av} = 56$

As the time interval shrinks, the average velocity approaches the instantaneous velocity at $t = 1$.

As the interval on the t-axis shrinks, the slope of the secant line approaches the slope of the tangent line through $(1, 80)$.

$86.24 — • \ t = 1.1$ s
$80 — • \ t = 1$ s

$(1.1, 86.24)$
$(1, 80)$

$m_{sec} = v_{av} = 62.4$

INSTANTANEOUS VELOCITY ←——————→ TANGENT LINE

The instantaneous velocity at $t = 1$ is the limit of the average velocities as t approaches 1.

The slope of the tangent line at $(1, 80)$ is the limit of the slopes of the secant lines as t approaches 1.

$80 — • \ t = 1$ s

$(1, 80)$

$$v_{inst} = \lim_{t \to 1} \frac{s(t) - s(1)}{t - 1} = 64 \text{ ft/s}$$

$$m_{tan} = \lim_{t \to 1} \frac{s(t) - s(1)}{t - 1} = 64$$

Instantaneous velocity = 64 ft/s ←——————→ Slope of the tangent line = 64

Figure 2.6

SECTION 2.1 EXERCISES

Review Questions

1. Suppose $s(t)$ is the position of an object moving along a line at time $t \geq 0$. What is the average velocity between the times $t = a$ and $t = b$?

2. Suppose $s(t)$ is the position of an object moving along a line at time $t \geq 0$. Describe a process for finding the instantaneous velocity at $t = a$.

3. What is the slope of the secant line that passes through the points $(a, f(a))$ and $(b, f(b))$ on the graph of f?

4. Describe a process for finding the slope of the line tangent to the graph of f at $(a, f(a))$.

5. Describe the parallels between finding the instantaneous velocity of an object at a point in time and finding the slope of the line tangent to the graph of a function at a point on the graph.

6. Graph the parabola $f(x) = x^2$. Explain why the secant lines between the points $(-a, f(-a))$ and $(a, f(a))$ have zero slope. What is the slope of the tangent line at $x = 0$?

Basic Skills

7. **Average velocity** The function $s(t)$ represents the position of an object at time t moving along a line. Suppose $s(2) = 136$ and $s(3) = 156$. Find the average velocity of the object over the interval of time $[2, 3]$.

8. **Average velocity** The function $s(t)$ represents the position of an object at time t moving along a line. Suppose $s(1) = 84$ and $s(4) = 144$. Find the average velocity of the object over the interval of time $[1, 4]$.

9. **Average velocity** The position of an object moving vertically along a line is given by the function $s(t) = -16t^2 + 128t$. Find the average velocity of the object over the following intervals.

    a. $[1, 4]$ b. $[1, 3]$
    c. $[1, 2]$ d. $[1, 1 + h]$, where $h > 0$ is a real number

10. **Average velocity** The position of an object moving vertically along a line is given by the function $s(t) = -4.9t^2 + 30t + 20$. Find the average velocity of the object over the following intervals.

    a. $[0, 3]$ b. $[0, 2]$
    c. $[0, 1]$ d. $[0, h]$, where $h > 0$ is a real number

11. **Average velocity** The table gives the position $s(t)$ of an object moving along a line at time t, over a two-second interval. Find the average velocity of the object over the following intervals.

    a. $[0, 2]$ b. $[0, 1.5]$
    c. $[0, 1]$ d. $[0, 0.5]$

t	0	0.5	1	1.5	2
$s(t)$	0	30	52	66	72

12. **Average velocity** The graph gives the position $s(t)$ of an object moving along a line at time t, over a 2.5-second interval. Find the average velocity of the object over the following intervals.

    a. $[0.5, 2.5]$ b. $[0.5, 2]$
    c. $[0.5, 1.5]$ d. $[0.5, 1]$

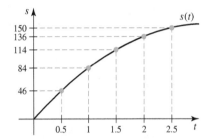

13. **Average velocity** Consider the position function $s(t) = -16t^2 + 100t$ representing the position of an object moving vertically along a line. Sketch a graph of s with the secant line passing through $(0.5, s(0.5))$ and $(2, s(2))$. Determine the slope of the secant line and explain its relationship to the moving object.

14. **Average velocity** Consider the position function $s(t) = \sin \pi t$ representing the position of an object moving along a line on the end of a spring. Sketch a graph of s together with a secant line passing through $(0, s(0))$ and $(0.5, s(0.5))$. Determine the slope of the secant line and explain its relationship to the moving object.

15. **Instantaneous velocity** Consider the position function $s(t) = -16t^2 + 128t$ (Exercise 9). Complete the following table with the appropriate average velocities. Then make a conjecture about the value of the instantaneous velocity at $t = 1$.

Time interval	$[1, 2]$	$[1, 1.5]$	$[1, 1.1]$	$[1, 1.01]$	$[1, 1.001]$
Average velocity					

16. **Instantaneous velocity** Consider the position function $s(t) = -4.9t^2 + 30t + 20$ (Exercise 10). Complete the following table with the appropriate average velocities. Then make a conjecture about the value of the instantaneous velocity at $t = 2$.

Time interval	$[2, 3]$	$[2, 2.5]$	$[2, 2.1]$	$[2, 2.01]$	$[2, 2.001]$
Average velocity					

17. **Instantaneous velocity** The following table gives the position $s(t)$ of an object moving along a line at time t. Determine the average velocities over the time intervals $[1, 1.01], [1, 1.001]$,

and $[1, 1.0001]$. Then make a conjecture about the value of the instantaneous velocity at $t = 1$.

t	1	1.0001	1.001	1.01
$s(t)$	64	64.00479984	64.047984	64.4784

18. Instantaneous velocity The following table gives the position $s(t)$ of an object moving along a line at time t. Determine the average velocities over the time intervals $[2, 2.01]$, $[2, 2.001]$, and $[2, 2.0001]$. Then make a conjecture about the value of the instantaneous velocity at $t = 2$.

t	2	2.0001	2.001	2.01
$s(t)$	56	55.99959984	55.995984	55.9584

19. Instantaneous velocity Consider the position function $s(t) = -16t^2 + 100t$. Complete the following table with the appropriate average velocities. Then make a conjecture about the value of the instantaneous velocity at $t = 3$.

Time interval	Average velocity
$[2, 3]$	
$[2.9, 3]$	
$[2.99, 3]$	
$[2.999, 3]$	
$[2.9999, 3]$	

20. Instantaneous velocity Consider the position function $s(t) = 3 \sin t$ that describes a block bouncing vertically on a spring. Complete the following table with the appropriate average velocities. Then make a conjecture about the value of the instantaneous velocity at $t = \pi/2$.

Time interval	Average velocity
$[\pi/2, \pi]$	
$[\pi/2, \pi/2 + 0.1]$	
$[\pi/2, \pi/2 + 0.01]$	
$[\pi/2, \pi/2 + 0.001]$	
$[\pi/2, \pi/2 + 0.0001]$	

Further Explorations

21–24. Instantaneous velocity *For the following position functions, make a table of average velocities similar to those in Exercises 19–20 and make a conjecture about the instantaneous velocity at the indicated time.*

21. $s(t) = -16t^2 + 80t + 60$ at $t = 3$

22. $s(t) = 20 \cos t$ at $t = \pi/2$

23. $s(t) = 40 \sin 2t$ at $t = 0$

24. $s(t) = 20/(t + 1)$ at $t = 0$

25–28. Slopes of tangent lines *For the following functions, make a table of slopes of secant lines and make a conjecture about the slope of the tangent line at the indicated point.*

25. $f(x) = 2x^2$ at $x = 2$

26. $f(x) = 3 \cos x$ at $x = \pi/2$

27. $f(x) = e^x$ at $x = 0$

28. $f(x) = x^3 - x$ at $x = 1$

29. Tangent lines with zero slope

    a. Graph the function $f(x) = x^2 - 4x + 3$.

    b. Identify the point $(a, f(a))$ at which the function has a tangent line with zero slope.

    c. Confirm your answer to part (b) by making a table of slopes of secant lines to approximate the slope of the tangent line at this point.

30. Tangent lines with zero slope

    a. Graph the function $f(x) = 4 - x^2$.

    b. Identify the point $(a, f(a))$ at which the function has a tangent line with zero slope.

    c. Consider the point $(a, f(a))$ found in part (b). Is it true that the secant line between $(a - h, f(a - h))$ and $(a + h, f(a + h))$ has slope zero for any value of $h \neq 0$?

31. Zero velocity A projectile is fired vertically upward and has a position given by $s(t) = -16t^2 + 128t + 192$, for $0 \le t \le 9$.

    a. Graph the position function, for $0 \le t \le 9$.

    b. From the graph of the position function, identify the time at which the projectile has an instantaneous velocity of zero; call this time $t = a$.

    c. Confirm your answer to part (b) by making a table of average velocities to approximate the instantaneous velocity at $t = a$.

    d. For what values of t on the interval $[0, 9]$ is the instantaneous velocity positive (the projectile moves upward)?

    e. For what values of t on the interval $[0, 9]$ is the instantaneous velocity negative (the projectile moves downward)?

32. Impact speed A rock is dropped off the edge of a cliff, and its distance s (in feet) from the top of the cliff after t seconds is $s(t) = 16t^2$. Assume the distance from the top of the cliff to the ground is 96 ft.

    a. When will the rock strike the ground?

    b. Make a table of average velocities and approximate the velocity at which the rock strikes the ground.

33. Slope of tangent line Given the function $f(x) = 1 - \cos x$ and the points $A(\pi/2, f(\pi/2))$, $B(\pi/2 + 0.05, f(\pi/2 + 0.05))$, $C(\pi/2 + 0.5, f(\pi/2 + 0.5))$, and $D(\pi, f(\pi))$ (see figure), find the slopes of the secant lines through A and D, A and C, and A and B. Then use your calculations to make a conjecture about the slope of the line tangent to the graph of f at $x = \pi/2$.

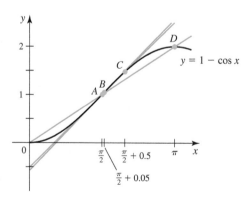

QUICK CHECK ANSWERS

1. 16 ft/s   **2.** Average velocity is the velocity over an interval of time. Instantaneous velocity is the velocity at one point of time.   **3.** Less than ◄

2.2 Definitions of Limits

Computing slopes of tangent lines and instantaneous velocities (Section 2.1) are just two of many important calculus problems that rely on limits. We now put these two problems aside until Chapter 3 and begin with a preliminary definition of the limit of a function.

> ▶ The terms *arbitrarily close* and *sufficiently close* will be made precise when rigorous definitions of limits are given in Section 2.7.

DEFINITION Limit of a Function (Preliminary)

Suppose the function f is defined for all x near a except possibly at a. If $f(x)$ is arbitrarily close to L (as close to L as we like) for all x sufficiently close (but not equal) to a, we write

$$\lim_{x \to a} f(x) = L$$

and say the limit of $f(x)$ as x approaches a equals L.

Informally, we say that $\lim_{x \to a} f(x) = L$ if $f(x)$ gets closer and closer to L as x gets closer and closer to a from both sides of a. The value of $\lim_{x \to a} f(x)$ (if it exists) depends on the values of f near a, but it does not depend on the value of $f(a)$. In some cases, the limit $\lim_{x \to a} f(x)$ equals $f(a)$. In other instances, $\lim_{x \to a} f(x)$ and $f(a)$ differ, or $f(a)$ may not even be defined.

EXAMPLE 1 Finding limits from a graph Use the graph of f (Figure 2.7) to determine the following values, if possible.

a. $f(1)$ and $\lim\limits_{x \to 1} f(x)$ **b.** $f(2)$ and $\lim\limits_{x \to 2} f(x)$ **c.** $f(3)$ and $\lim\limits_{x \to 3} f(x)$

SOLUTION

a. We see that $f(1) = 2$. As x approaches 1 from either side, the values of $f(x)$ approach 2 (Figure 2.8). Therefore, $\lim\limits_{x \to 1} f(x) = 2$.

b. We see that $f(2) = 5$. However, as x approaches 2 from either side, $f(x)$ approaches 3 because the points on the graph of f approach the open circle at $(2, 3)$ (Figure 2.9). Therefore, $\lim\limits_{x \to 2} f(x) = 3$ even though $f(2) = 5$.

c. In this case, $f(3)$ is undefined. We see that $f(x)$ approaches 4 as x approaches 3 from either side (Figure 2.10). Therefore, $\lim\limits_{x \to 3} f(x) = 4$ even though $f(3)$ does not exist.

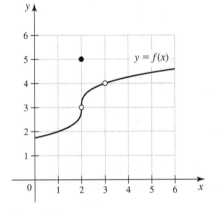

Figure 2.7

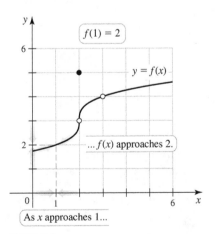

Figure 2.8

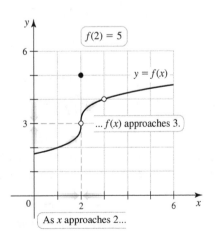

Figure 2.9

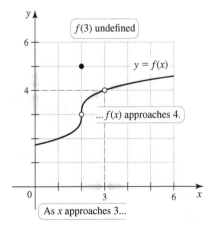

Figure 2.10

Related Exercises 7–10 ◀

QUICK CHECK 1 In Example 1, suppose we redefine the function at one point so that $f(1) = 1$. Does this change the value of $\lim_{x \to 1} f(x)$? ◄

In Example 1, we worked with the graph of a function to estimate limits. Let's now estimate limits using tabulated values of a function.

> ▶ In Example 2, we have not stated with certainty that $\lim_{x \to 1} f(x) = 0.5$. But this is a reasonable conjecture based on the numerical evidence. Methods for calculating limits precisely are introduced in Section 2.3.

EXAMPLE 2 **Finding limits from a table** Create a table of values of $f(x) = \dfrac{\sqrt{x} - 1}{x - 1}$ corresponding to values of x near 1. Then make a conjecture about the value of $\lim_{x \to 1} f(x)$.

SOLUTION Table 2.2 lists values of f corresponding to values of x approaching 1 from both sides. The numerical evidence suggests that $f(x)$ approaches 0.5 as x approaches 1. Therefore, we make the conjecture that $\lim_{x \to 1} f(x) = 0.5$.

Table 2.2   ⟶ 1 ⟵

x	0.9	0.99	0.999	0.9999	1.0001	1.001	1.01	1.1
$f(x) = \dfrac{\sqrt{x} - 1}{x - 1}$	0.5131670	0.5012563	0.5001251	0.5000125	0.4999875	0.4998751	0.4987562	0.4880885

Related Exercises 11–14 ◄

One-Sided Limits

The limit $\lim_{x \to a} f(x) = L$ is referred to as a *two-sided* limit because $f(x)$ approaches L as x approaches a for values of x less than a *and* for values of x greater than a. For some functions, it makes sense to examine *one-sided* limits called *right-sided* and *left-sided* limits.

> ▶ As with two-sided limits, the value of a one-sided limit (if it exists) depends on the values of $f(x)$ near a but not on the value of $f(a)$.

DEFINITION **One-Sided Limits**

1. **Right-sided limit** Suppose f is defined for all x near a with $x > a$. If $f(x)$ is arbitrarily close to L for all x sufficiently close to a with $x > a$, we write

$$\lim_{x \to a^+} f(x) = L$$

    and say the limit of $f(x)$ as x approaches a from the right equals L.

2. **Left-sided limit** Suppose f is defined for all x near a with $x < a$. If $f(x)$ is arbitrarily close to L for all x sufficiently close to a with $x < a$, we write

$$\lim_{x \to a^-} f(x) = L$$

    and say the limit of $f(x)$ as x approaches a from the left equals L.

EXAMPLE 3 **Examining limits graphically and numerically** Let $f(x) = \dfrac{x^3 - 8}{4(x - 2)}$. Use tables and graphs to make a conjecture about the values of $\lim_{x \to 2^+} f(x)$, $\lim_{x \to 2^-} f(x)$, and $\lim_{x \to 2} f(x)$, if they exist.

> ▶ Computer-generated graphs and tables help us understand the idea of a limit. Keep in mind, however, that computers are not infallible and they may produce incorrect results, even for simple functions (see Example 5).

SOLUTION Figure 2.11a shows the graph of f obtained with a graphing utility. The graph is misleading because $f(2)$ is undefined, which means there should be a hole in the graph at $(2, 3)$ (Figure 2.11b).

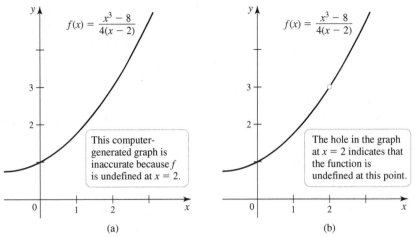

Figure 2.11

The graph in Figure 2.12a and the function values in Table 2.3 suggest that $f(x)$ approaches 3 as x approaches 2 from the right. Therefore, we write the right-sided limit

$$\lim_{x \to 2^+} f(x) = 3,$$

which says the limit of $f(x)$ as x approaches 2 from the right equals 3.

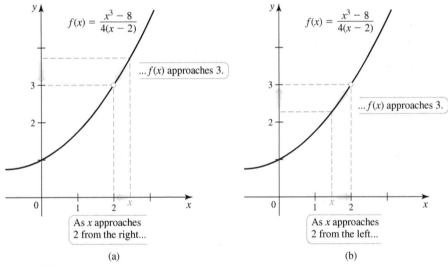

Figure 2.12

Table 2.3

x	1.9	1.99	1.999	1.9999	2.0001	2.001	2.01	2.1
$f(x) = \dfrac{x^3 - 8}{4(x - 2)}$	2.8525	2.985025	2.99850025	2.99985000	3.00015000	3.00150025	3.015025	3.1525

▶ Remember that the value of the limit does not depend on the value of $f(2)$. In Example 3, $\lim_{x \to 2} f(x) = 3$ despite the fact that $f(2)$ is undefined.

Similarly, Figure 2.12b and Table 2.3 suggest that as x approaches 2 from the left, $f(x)$ approaches 3. So we write the left-sided limit

$$\lim_{x \to 2^-} f(x) = 3,$$

which says the limit of $f(x)$ as x approaches 2 from the left equals 3. Because $f(x)$ approaches 3 as x approaches 2 from either side, we write the two-sided limit $\lim_{x \to 2} f(x) = 3$.

Related Exercises 15–18 ◄

Based on the previous example, you might wonder whether the limits $\lim_{x \to a^-} f(x)$, $\lim_{x \to a^+} f(x)$, and $\lim_{x \to a} f(x)$ always exist and are equal. The remaining examples demonstrate that these limits may have different values, and in some cases, one or more of these limits may not exist. The following theorem is useful when comparing one-sided and two-sided limits.

▶ Suppose P and Q are statements. We write P if and only if Q when P implies Q and Q implies P.

> **THEOREM 2.1   Relationship Between One-Sided and Two-Sided Limits**
> Assume f is defined for all x near a except possibly at a. Then $\lim_{x \to a} f(x) = L$ if and only if $\lim_{x \to a^+} f(x) = L$ and $\lim_{x \to a^-} f(x) = L$.

A proof of Theorem 2.1 is outlined in Exercise 44 of Section 2.7. Using this theorem, it follows that $\lim_{x \to a} f(x) \neq L$ if either $\lim_{x \to a^+} f(x) \neq L$ or $\lim_{x \to a^-} f(x) \neq L$ (or both). Furthermore, if either $\lim_{x \to a^+} f(x)$ or $\lim_{x \to a^-} f(x)$ does not exist, then $\lim_{x \to a} f(x)$ does not exist. We put these ideas to work in the next two examples.

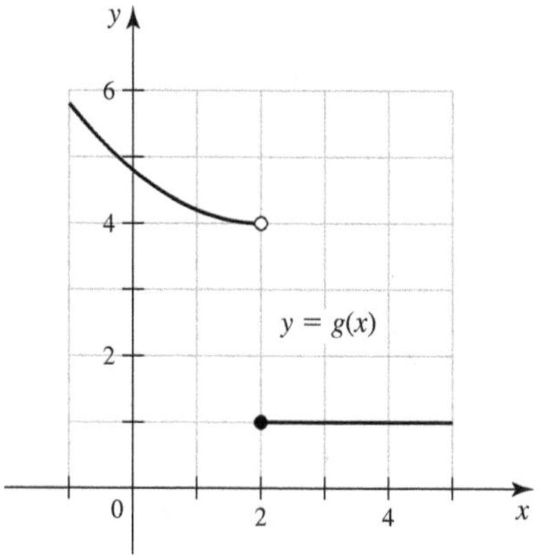

EXAMPLE 4   A function with a jump Given the graph of g in Figure 2.13, find the following limits, if they exist.

a. $\lim_{x \to 2^-} g(x)$ **b.** $\lim_{x \to 2^+} g(x)$ **c.** $\lim_{x \to 2} g(x)$

SOLUTION

a. As x approaches 2 from the left, $g(x)$ approaches 4. Therefore, $\lim_{x \to 2^-} g(x) = 4$.
b. Because $g(x) = 1$ for all $x \geq 2$, $\lim_{x \to 2^+} g(x) = 1$.
c. By Theorem 2.1, $\lim_{x \to 2} g(x)$ does not exist because $\lim_{x \to 2^-} g(x) \neq \lim_{x \to 2^+} g(x)$.

Related Exercises 19–24 ◄

Figure 2.13

EXAMPLE 5   Some strange behavior Examine $\lim_{x \to 0} \cos (1/x)$.

SOLUTION From the first three values of $\cos (1/x)$ in Table 2.4, it is tempting to conclude that $\lim_{x \to 0^+} \cos (1/x) = -1$. But this conclusion is not confirmed when we evaluate $\cos (1/x)$ for values of x closer to 0.

Table 2.4	
x	$\cos (1/x)$
0.001	0.56238
0.0001	−0.95216
0.00001	−0.99936
0.000001	0.93675
0.0000001	−0.90727
0.00000001	−0.36338

We might *incorrectly* conclude that $\cos (1/x)$ approaches -1 as x approaches 0 from the right.

The behavior of $\cos (1/x)$ near 0 is better understood by letting $x = 1/(n\pi)$, where n is a positive integer. By making this substitution, we can sample the function at discrete points that approach zero. In this case,

$$\cos \frac{1}{x} = \cos n\pi = \begin{cases} 1 & \text{if } n \text{ is even} \\ -1 & \text{if } n \text{ is odd.} \end{cases}$$

QUICK CHECK 2 Why is the graph of $y = \cos(1/x)$ difficult to plot near $x = 0$, as suggested by Figure 2.14? ◄

As n increases, the values of $x = 1/(n\pi)$ approach zero, while the values of $\cos(1/x)$ oscillate between -1 and 1 (Figure 2.14). Therefore, $\cos(1/x)$ does not approach a single number as x approaches 0 from the right. We conclude that $\lim\limits_{x \to 0^+} \cos(1/x)$ does *not* exist, which implies that $\lim\limits_{x \to 0} \cos(1/x)$ does not exist.

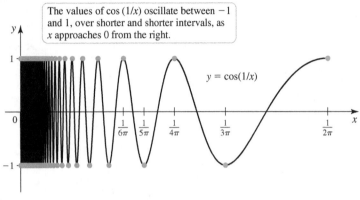

The values of $\cos(1/x)$ oscillate between -1 and 1, over shorter and shorter intervals, as x approaches 0 from the right.

$y = \cos(1/x)$

Figure 2.14

Related Exercises 25–26 ◄

Using tables and graphs to make conjectures for the values of limits worked well until Example 5. The limitation of technology in this example is not an isolated incident. For this reason, analytical techniques (paper-and-pencil methods) for finding limits are developed in the next section.

SECTION 2.2 EXERCISES

Review Questions

1. Explain the meaning of $\lim\limits_{x \to a} f(x) = L$.

2. True or false: When $\lim\limits_{x \to a} f(x)$ exists, it always equals $f(a)$. Explain.

3. Explain the meaning of $\lim\limits_{x \to a^+} f(x) = L$.

4. Explain the meaning of $\lim\limits_{x \to a^-} f(x) = L$.

5. If $\lim\limits_{x \to a^-} f(x) = L$ and $\lim\limits_{x \to a^+} f(x) = M$, where L and M are finite real numbers, then how are L and M related if $\lim\limits_{x \to a} f(x)$ exists?

6. What are the potential problems of using a graphing utility to estimate $\lim\limits_{x \to a} f(x)$?

Basic Skills

7. **Finding limits from a graph** Use the graph of h in the figure to find the following values or state that they do not exist.

    a. $h(2)$ **b.** $\lim\limits_{x \to 2} h(x)$ **c.** $h(4)$ **d.** $\lim\limits_{x \to 4} h(x)$ **e.** $\lim\limits_{x \to 5} h(x)$

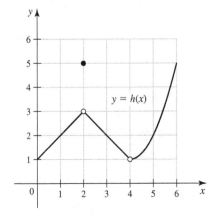

8. **Finding limits from a graph** Use the graph of g in the figure to find the following values or state that they do not exist.

    a. $g(0)$ **b.** $\lim\limits_{x \to 0} g(x)$ **c.** $g(1)$ **d.** $\lim\limits_{x \to 1} g(x)$

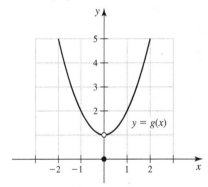

$y = g(x)$

9. **Finding limits from a graph** Use the graph of f in the figure to find the following values or state that they do not exist.

    a. $f(1)$ **b.** $\lim\limits_{x \to 1} f(x)$ **c.** $f(0)$ **d.** $\lim\limits_{x \to 0} f(x)$

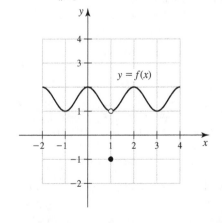

$y = f(x)$

10. Finding limits from a graph Use the graph of f in the figure to find the following values or state that they do not exist.

a. $f(2)$ b. $\lim\limits_{x \to 2} f(x)$ c. $\lim\limits_{x \to 4} f(x)$ d. $\lim\limits_{x \to 5} f(x)$

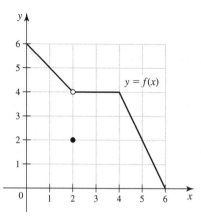

T 11. Estimating a limit from tables Let $f(x) = \dfrac{x^2 - 4}{x - 2}$.

a. Calculate $f(x)$ for each value of x in the following table.

b. Make a conjecture about the value of $\lim\limits_{x \to 2} \dfrac{x^2 - 4}{x - 2}$.

x	1.9	1.99	1.999	1.9999
$f(x) = \dfrac{x^2 - 4}{x - 2}$				
x	2.1	2.01	2.001	2.0001
$f(x) = \dfrac{x^2 - 4}{x - 2}$				

T 12. Estimating a limit from tables Let $f(x) = \dfrac{x^3 - 1}{x - 1}$.

a. Calculate $f(x)$ for each value of x in the following table.

b. Make a conjecture about the value of $\lim\limits_{x \to 1} \dfrac{x^3 - 1}{x - 1}$.

x	0.9	0.99	0.999	0.9999
$f(x) = \dfrac{x^3 - 1}{x - 1}$				
x	1.1	1.01	1.001	1.0001
$f(x) = \dfrac{x^3 - 1}{x - 1}$				

T 13. Estimating a limit numerically Let $g(t) = \dfrac{t - 9}{\sqrt{t} - 3}$.

a. Make two tables, one showing values of g for $t = 8.9, 8.99,$ and 8.999 and one showing values of g for $t = 9.1, 9.01,$ and 9.001.

b. Make a conjecture about the value of $\lim\limits_{t \to 9} \dfrac{t - 9}{\sqrt{t} - 3}$.

T 14. Estimating a limit numerically Let $f(x) = (1 + x)^{1/x}$.

a. Make two tables, one showing values of f for $x = 0.01, 0.001, 0.0001,$ and 0.00001 and one showing values of f for $x = -0.01, -0.001, -0.0001,$ and -0.00001. Round your answers to five digits.

b. Estimate the value of $\lim\limits_{x \to 0} (1 + x)^{1/x}$.

c. What mathematical constant does $\lim\limits_{x \to 0} (1 + x)^{1/x}$ appear to equal?

T 15. Estimating a limit graphically and numerically

Let $f(x) = \dfrac{x - 2}{\ln |x - 2|}$.

a. Graph f to estimate $\lim\limits_{x \to 2} f(x)$.

b. Evaluate $f(x)$ for values of x near 2 to support your conjecture in part (a).

T 16. Estimating a limit graphically and numerically

Let $g(x) = \dfrac{e^{2x} - 2x - 1}{x^2}$.

a. Graph g to estimate $\lim\limits_{x \to 0} g(x)$.

b. Evaluate $g(x)$ for values of x near 0 to support your conjecture in part (a).

T 17. Estimating a limit graphically and numerically

Let $f(x) = \dfrac{1 - \cos(2x - 2)}{(x - 1)^2}$.

a. Graph f to estimate $\lim\limits_{x \to 1} f(x)$.

b. Evaluate $f(x)$ for values of x near 1 to support your conjecture in part (a).

T 18. Estimating a limit graphically and numerically

Let $g(x) = \dfrac{3 \sin x - 2 \cos x + 2}{x}$.

a. Graph of g to estimate $\lim\limits_{x \to 0} g(x)$.

b. Evaluate $g(x)$ for values of x near 0 to support your conjecture in part (a).

T 19. One-sided and two-sided limits Let $f(x) = \dfrac{x^2 - 25}{x - 5}$. Use tables and graphs to make a conjecture about the values of $\lim\limits_{x \to 5^+} f(x)$, $\lim\limits_{x \to 5^-} f(x)$, and $\lim\limits_{x \to 5} f(x)$ or state that they do not exist.

T 20. One-sided and two-sided limits Let $g(x) = \dfrac{x - 100}{\sqrt{x} - 10}$. Use tables and graphs to make a conjecture about the values of $\lim\limits_{x \to 100^+} g(x)$, $\lim\limits_{x \to 100^-} g(x)$, and $\lim\limits_{x \to 100} g(x)$ or state that they do not exist.

T 21. One-sided and two-sided limits Use the graph of f in the figure to find the following values or state that they do not exist. If a limit does not exist, explain why.

a. $f(1)$ b. $\lim\limits_{x \to 1} f(x)$

c. $\lim\limits_{x \to 1^+} f(x)$ d. $\lim\limits_{x \to 1^-} f(x)$

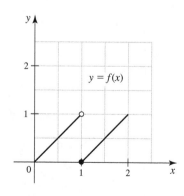

22. One-sided and two-sided limits Use the graph of g in the figure to find the following values or state that they do not exist. If a limit does not exist, explain why.

a. $g(2)$

b. $\lim_{x \to 2^-} g(x)$

c. $\lim_{x \to 2^+} g(x)$

d. $\lim_{x \to 2} g(x)$

e. $g(3)$

f. $\lim_{x \to 3^+} g(x)$

g. $\lim_{x \to 3^+} g(x)$

h. $g(4)$

i. $\lim_{x \to 4} g(x)$

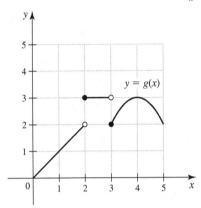

23. Finding limits from a graph Use the graph of f in the figure to find the following values or state that they do not exist. If a limit does not exist, explain why.

a. $f(1)$

b. $\lim_{x \to 1^-} f(x)$

c. $\lim_{x \to 1^+} f(x)$

d. $\lim_{x \to 1} f(x)$

e. $f(3)$

f. $\lim_{x \to 3^-} f(x)$

g. $\lim_{x \to 3^+} f(x)$

h. $\lim_{x \to 3} f(x)$

i. $f(2)$

j. $\lim_{x \to 2^-} f(x)$

k. $\lim_{x \to 2^+} f(x)$

l. $\lim_{x \to 2} f(x)$

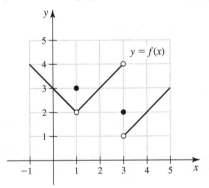

24. Finding limits from a graph Use the graph of g in the figure to find the following values or state that they do not exist. If a limit does not exist, explain why.

a. $g(-1)$

b. $\lim_{x \to -1^-} g(x)$

c. $\lim_{x \to -1^+} g(x)$

d. $\lim_{x \to -1} g(x)$

e. $g(1)$

f. $\lim_{x \to 1} g(x)$

g. $\lim_{x \to 3} g(x)$

h. $g(5)$

i. $\lim_{x \to 5^-} g(x)$

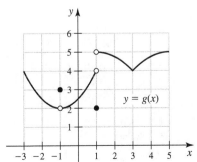

T 25. Strange behavior near $x = 0$

a. Create a table of values of $\sin(1/x)$, for $x = \dfrac{2}{\pi}, \dfrac{2}{3\pi}, \dfrac{2}{5\pi}, \dfrac{2}{7\pi}, \dfrac{2}{9\pi}$, and $\dfrac{2}{11\pi}$. Describe the pattern of values you observe.

b. Why does a graphing utility have difficulty plotting the graph of $y = \sin(1/x)$ near $x = 0$ (see figure)?

c. What do you conclude about $\lim_{x \to 0} \sin(1/x)$?

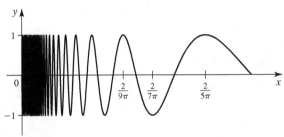

T 26. Strange behavior near $x = 0$

a. Create a table of values of $\tan(3/x)$ for $x = 12/\pi, 12/(3\pi), 12/(5\pi), \ldots, 12/(11\pi)$. Describe the general pattern in the values you observe.

b. Use a graphing utility to graph $y = \tan(3/x)$. Why do graphing utilities have difficulty plotting the graph near $x = 0$?

c. What do you conclude about $\lim_{x \to 0} \tan(3/x)$?

Further Explorations

27. Explain why or why not Determine whether the following statements are true and give an explanation or counterexample.

a. The value of $\lim_{x \to 3} \dfrac{x^2 - 9}{x - 3}$ does not exist.

b. The value of $\lim_{x \to a} f(x)$ is always found by computing $f(a)$.

c. The value of $\lim_{x \to a} f(x)$ does not exist if $f(a)$ is undefined.

d. $\lim_{x \to 0} \sqrt{x} = 0$.

e. $\lim_{x \to \pi/2} \cot x = 0$.

28–31. Sketching graphs of functions *Sketch the graph of a function with the given properties. You do not need to find a formula for the function.*

28. $f(1) = 0, f(2) = 4, f(3) = 6, \lim_{x \to 2^-} f(x) = -3, \lim_{x \to 2^+} f(x) = 5$

29. $g(1) = 0, g(2) = 1, g(3) = -2, \lim_{x \to 2} g(x) = 0,$
$\lim_{x \to 3^-} g(x) = -1, \lim_{x \to 3^+} g(x) = -2$

30. $h(-1) = 2, \lim_{x \to -1^-} h(x) = 0, \lim_{x \to -1^+} h(x) = 3,$
$h(1) = \lim_{x \to 1^-} h(x) = 1, \lim_{x \to 1^+} h(x) = 4$

31. $p(0) = 2, \lim_{x \to 0} p(x) = 0, \lim_{x \to 2} p(x)$ does not exist,
$p(2) = \lim_{x \to 2^+} p(x) = 1$

T 32–35. Calculator limits *Estimate the value of the following limits by creating a table of function values for $h = 0.01, 0.001,$ and $0.0001,$ and $h = -0.01, -0.001,$ and -0.0001.*

32. $\lim_{h \to 0} (1 + 2h)^{1/h}$

33. $\lim_{h \to 0} (1 + 3h)^{2/h}$

34. $\lim\limits_{h\to 0} \dfrac{2^h - 1}{h}$

35. $\lim\limits_{h\to 0} \dfrac{\ln(1+h)}{h}$

36. A step function Let $f(x) = \dfrac{|x|}{x}$, for $x \neq 0$.

  a. Sketch a graph of f on the interval $[-2, 2]$.

  b. Does $\lim\limits_{x\to 0} f(x)$ exist? Explain your reasoning after first examining $\lim\limits_{x\to 0^-} f(x)$ and $\lim\limits_{x\to 0^+} f(x)$.

37. The floor function For any real number x, the *floor function* (or *greatest integer function*) $\lfloor x \rfloor$ is the greatest integer less than or equal to x (see figure).

  a. Compute $\lim\limits_{x\to -1^-} \lfloor x \rfloor$, $\lim\limits_{x\to -1^+} \lfloor x \rfloor$, $\lim\limits_{x\to 2^-} \lfloor x \rfloor$, and $\lim\limits_{x\to 2^+} \lfloor x \rfloor$.

  b. Compute $\lim\limits_{x\to 2.3^-} \lfloor x \rfloor$, $\lim\limits_{x\to 2.3^+} \lfloor x \rfloor$, and $\lim\limits_{x\to 2.3} \lfloor x \rfloor$.

  c. For a given integer a, state the values of $\lim\limits_{x\to a^-} \lfloor x \rfloor$ and $\lim\limits_{x\to a^+} \lfloor x \rfloor$.

  d. In general, if a is not an integer, state the values of $\lim\limits_{x\to a^-} \lfloor x \rfloor$ and $\lim\limits_{x\to a^+} \lfloor x \rfloor$.

  e. For what values of a does $\lim\limits_{x\to a} \lfloor x \rfloor$ exist? Explain.

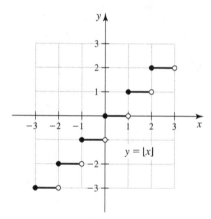

$y = \lfloor x \rfloor$

38. The ceiling function For any real number x, the *ceiling function* $\lceil x \rceil$ is the smallest integer greater than or equal to x.

  a. Graph the ceiling function $y = \lceil x \rceil$, for $-2 \leq x \leq 3$.

  b. Evaluate $\lim\limits_{x\to 2^-} \lceil x \rceil$, $\lim\limits_{x\to 1^+} \lceil x \rceil$, and $\lim\limits_{x\to 1.5} \lceil x \rceil$.

  c. For what values of a does $\lim\limits_{x\to a} \lceil x \rceil$ exist? Explain.

39–42. Limits by graphing *Use the zoom and trace features of a graphing utility to approximate the following limits.*

39. $\lim\limits_{x\to 0} x \sin\dfrac{1}{x}$

40. $\lim\limits_{x\to 1} \dfrac{18(\sqrt[3]{x} - 1)}{x^3 - 1}$

41. $\lim\limits_{x\to 1} \dfrac{9(\sqrt{2x - x^4} - \sqrt[3]{x})}{1 - x^{3/4}}$

42. $\lim\limits_{x\to 0} \dfrac{6^x - 3^x}{x \ln 2}$

Applications

43. Postage rates Assume that postage for sending a first-class letter in the United States is $0.44 for the first ounce (up to and including 1 oz) plus $0.17 for each additional ounce (up to and including each additional ounce).

  a. Graph the function $p = f(w)$ that gives the postage p for sending a letter that weighs w ounces, for $0 < w \leq 5$.

  b. Evaluate $\lim\limits_{w\to 3.3} f(w)$.

  c. Interpret the limits $\lim\limits_{w\to 1^+} f(w)$ and $\lim\limits_{w\to 1^-} f(w)$.

  d. Does $\lim\limits_{w\to 4} f(w)$ exist? Explain.

44. The Heaviside function The Heaviside function is used in engineering applications to model flipping a switch. It is defined as

$$H(x) = \begin{cases} 0 & \text{if } x < 0 \\ 1 & \text{if } x \geq 0. \end{cases}$$

  a. Sketch a graph of H on the interval $[-1, 1]$.

  b. Does $\lim\limits_{x\to 0} H(x)$ exist? Explain your reasoning after first examining $\lim\limits_{x\to 0^-} H(x)$ and $\lim\limits_{x\to 0^+} H(x)$.

Additional Exercises

45. Limits of even functions A function f is even if $f(-x) = f(x)$, for all x in the domain of f. Suppose f is even, with $\lim\limits_{x\to 2^+} f(x) = 5$ and $\lim\limits_{x\to 2^-} f(x) = 8$. Evaluate the following limits.

  a. $\lim\limits_{x\to -2^+} f(x)$

  b. $\lim\limits_{x\to -2^-} f(x)$

46. Limits of odd functions A function g is odd if $g(-x) = -g(x)$, for all x in the domain of g. Suppose g is odd, with $\lim\limits_{x\to 2^+} g(x) = 5$ and $\lim\limits_{x\to 2^-} g(x) = 8$. Evaluate the following limits.

  a. $\lim\limits_{x\to -2^+} g(x)$

  b. $\lim\limits_{x\to -2^-} g(x)$

47. Limits by graphs

  a. Use a graphing utility to estimate $\lim\limits_{x\to 0} \dfrac{\tan 2x}{\sin x}$, $\lim\limits_{x\to 0} \dfrac{\tan 3x}{\sin x}$, and $\lim\limits_{x\to 0} \dfrac{\tan 4x}{\sin x}$.

  b. Make a conjecture about the value of $\lim\limits_{x\to 0} \dfrac{\tan px}{\sin x}$, for any real constant p.

48. Limits by graphs Graph $f(x) = \dfrac{\sin nx}{x}$, for $n = 1, 2, 3$, and 4 (four graphs). Use the window $[-1, 1] \times [0, 5]$.

  a. Estimate $\lim\limits_{x\to 0} \dfrac{\sin x}{x}$, $\lim\limits_{x\to 0} \dfrac{\sin 2x}{x}$, $\lim\limits_{x\to 0} \dfrac{\sin 3x}{x}$, and $\lim\limits_{x\to 0} \dfrac{\sin 4x}{x}$.

  b. Make a conjecture about the value of $\lim\limits_{x\to 0} \dfrac{\sin px}{x}$, for any real constant p.

49. Limits by graphs Use a graphing utility to plot $y = \dfrac{\sin px}{\sin qx}$ for at least three different pairs of nonzero constants p and q of your choice. Estimate $\lim\limits_{x\to 0} \dfrac{\sin px}{\sin qx}$ in each case. Then use your work to make a conjecture about the value of $\lim\limits_{x\to 0} \dfrac{\sin px}{\sin qx}$ for any nonzero values of p and q.

QUICK CHECK ANSWERS

1. The value of $\lim\limits_{x\to 1} f(x)$ depends on the value of f only *near* 1, not at 1. Therefore, changing the value of $f(1)$ will not change the value of $\lim\limits_{x\to 1} f(x)$. **2.** A graphing device has difficulty plotting $y = \cos(1/x)$ near 0 because values of the function vary between -1 and 1 over shorter and shorter intervals as x approaches 0. ◄

2.3 Techniques for Computing Limits

Graphical and numerical techniques for estimating limits, like those presented in the previous section, provide intuition about limits. These techniques, however, occasionally lead to incorrect results. Therefore, we turn our attention to analytical methods for evaluating limits precisely.

Limits of Linear Functions

The graph of $f(x) = mx + b$ is a line with slope m and y-intercept b. From Figure 2.15, we see that $f(x)$ approaches $f(a)$ as x approaches a. Therefore, if f is a linear function, we have $\lim_{x \to a} f(x) = f(a)$. It follows that for linear functions, $\lim_{x \to a} f(x)$ is found by direct substitution of $x = a$ into $f(x)$. This observation leads to the following theorem, which is proved in Exercise 28 of Section 2.7.

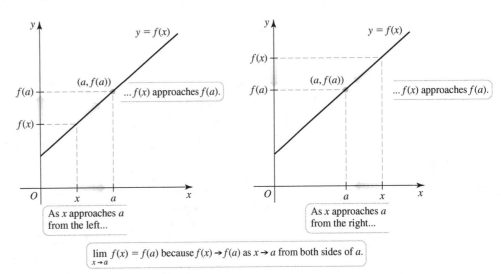

$\lim_{x \to a} f(x) = f(a)$ because $f(x) \to f(a)$ as $x \to a$ from both sides of a.

As x approaches a from the left...

As x approaches a from the right...

Figure 2.15

THEOREM 2.2   Limits of Linear Functions

Let a, b, and m be real numbers. For linear functions $f(x) = mx + b$,

$$\lim_{x \to a} f(x) = f(a) = ma + b.$$

EXAMPLE 1   Limits of linear functions Evaluate the following limits.

a. $\lim_{x \to 3} f(x)$, where $f(x) = \frac{1}{2}x - 7$

b. $\lim_{x \to 2} g(x)$, where $g(x) = 6$

SOLUTION

a. $\lim_{x \to 3} f(x) = \lim_{x \to 3} \left(\frac{1}{2}x - 7 \right) = f(3) = -\frac{11}{2}$

b. $\lim_{x \to 2} g(x) = \lim_{x \to 2} 6 = g(2) = 6$

Related Exercises 11–16 ◄

Limit Laws

The following limit laws greatly simplify the evaluation of many limits.

THEOREM 2.3   Limit Laws

Assume $\lim\limits_{x \to a} f(x)$ and $\lim\limits_{x \to a} g(x)$ exist. The following properties hold, where c is a real number, and $m > 0$ and $n > 0$ are integers.

1. Sum $\lim\limits_{x \to a} (f(x) + g(x)) = \lim\limits_{x \to a} f(x) + \lim\limits_{x \to a} g(x)$

2. Difference $\lim\limits_{x \to a} (f(x) - g(x)) = \lim\limits_{x \to a} f(x) - \lim\limits_{x \to a} g(x)$

3. Constant multiple $\lim\limits_{x \to a} (cf(x)) = c \lim\limits_{x \to a} f(x)$

4. Product $\lim\limits_{x \to a} (f(x)g(x)) = \left(\lim\limits_{x \to a} f(x) \right) \left(\lim\limits_{x \to a} g(x) \right)$

5. Quotient $\lim\limits_{x \to a} \left(\dfrac{f(x)}{g(x)} \right) = \dfrac{\lim\limits_{x \to a} f(x)}{\lim\limits_{x \to a} g(x)}$, provided $\lim\limits_{x \to a} g(x) \neq 0$

6. Power $\lim\limits_{x \to a} (f(x))^n = \left(\lim\limits_{x \to a} f(x) \right)^n$

7. Fractional power $\lim\limits_{x \to a} (f(x))^{n/m} = \left(\lim\limits_{x \to a} f(x) \right)^{n/m}$, provided $f(x) \geq 0$, for x near a, if m is even and n/m is reduced to lowest terms

---

> ➤ Law 6 is a special case of Law 7. Letting $m = 1$ in Law 7 gives Law 6.

A proof of Law 1 is outlined in Section 2.7. Laws 2–5 are proved in Appendix B. Law 6 is proved from Law 4 as follows.

For a positive integer n, if $\lim\limits_{x \to a} f(x)$ exists, we have

$$\lim_{x \to a} (f(x))^n = \lim_{x \to a} (\underbrace{f(x)\, f(x) \cdots f(x)}_{n \text{ factors of } f(x)})$$

$$= \underbrace{\left(\lim_{x \to a} f(x) \right) \left(\lim_{x \to a} f(x) \right) \cdots \left(\lim_{x \to a} f(x) \right)}_{n \text{ factors of } \lim\limits_{x \to a} f(x)} \qquad \text{Repeated use of Law 4}$$

$$= \left(\lim_{x \to a} f(x) \right)^n.$$

> ➤ Recall that to take even roots of a number (for example, square roots or fourth roots), the number must be nonnegative if the result is to be real.

In Law 7, the limit of $(f(x))^{n/m}$ involves the mth root of $f(x)$ when x is near a. If the fraction n/m is in lowest terms and m is even, this root is undefined unless $f(x)$ is nonnegative for all x near a, which explains the restrictions shown.

EXAMPLE 2   Evaluating limits Suppose $\lim\limits_{x \to 2} f(x) = 4$, $\lim\limits_{x \to 2} g(x) = 5$, and $\lim\limits_{x \to 2} h(x) = 8$. Use the limit laws in Theorem 2.3 to compute each limit.

a. $\lim\limits_{x \to 2} \dfrac{f(x) - g(x)}{h(x)}$ **b.** $\lim\limits_{x \to 2} (6f(x)g(x) + h(x))$ **c.** $\lim\limits_{x \to 2} (g(x))^3$

SOLUTION

a. $\lim\limits_{x \to 2} \dfrac{f(x) - g(x)}{h(x)} = \dfrac{\lim\limits_{x \to 2} (f(x) - g(x))}{\lim\limits_{x \to 2} h(x)}$ Law 5

$$= \dfrac{\lim\limits_{x \to 2} f(x) - \lim\limits_{x \to 2} g(x)}{\lim\limits_{x \to 2} h(x)} \qquad \text{Law 2}$$

$$= \dfrac{4 - 5}{8} = -\dfrac{1}{8}$$

b. $\lim\limits_{x \to 2} (6f(x)g(x) + h(x)) = \lim\limits_{x \to 2} (6f(x)g(x)) + \lim\limits_{x \to 2} h(x)$ Law 1

$= 6 \cdot \lim\limits_{x \to 2} (f(x)g(x)) + \lim\limits_{x \to 2} h(x)$ Law 3

$= 6\left(\lim\limits_{x \to 2} f(x)\right)\left(\lim\limits_{x \to 2} g(x)\right) + \lim\limits_{x \to 2} h(x)$ Law 4

$= 6 \cdot 4 \cdot 5 + 8 = 128$

c. $\lim\limits_{x \to 2} (g(x))^3 = \left(\lim\limits_{x \to 2} g(x)\right)^3 = 5^3 = 125$ Law 6

Related Exercises 17–24 ◄

Limits of Polynomial and Rational Functions

The limit laws are now used to find the limits of polynomial and rational functions. For example, to evaluate the limit of the polynomial $p(x) = 7x^3 + 3x^2 + 4x + 2$ at an arbitrary point a, we proceed as follows:

$$\lim_{x \to a} p(x) = \lim_{x \to a} (7x^3 + 3x^2 + 4x + 2)$$

$$= \lim_{x \to a} (7x^3) + \lim_{x \to a} (3x^2) + \lim_{x \to a} (4x + 2) \quad \text{Law 1}$$

$$= 7 \lim_{x \to a} (x^3) + 3 \lim_{x \to a} (x^2) + \lim_{x \to a} (4x + 2) \quad \text{Law 3}$$

$$= 7\underbrace{\left(\lim_{x \to a} x\right)^3}_{a} + 3\underbrace{\left(\lim_{x \to a} x\right)^2}_{a} + \underbrace{\lim_{x \to a} (4x + 2)}_{4a + 2} \quad \text{Law 6}$$

$$= 7a^3 + 3a^2 + 4a + 2 = p(a). \quad \text{Theorem 2.2}$$

As in the case of linear functions, the limit of a polynomial is found by direct substitution; that is, $\lim\limits_{x \to a} p(x) = p(a)$ (Exercise 91).

It is now a short step to evaluating limits of rational functions of the form $f(x) = p(x)/q(x)$, where p and q are polynomials. Applying Law 5, we have

$$\lim_{x \to a} \frac{p(x)}{q(x)} = \frac{\lim\limits_{x \to a} p(x)}{\lim\limits_{x \to a} q(x)} = \frac{p(a)}{q(a)}, \quad \text{provided } q(a) \neq 0,$$

which shows that limits of rational functions are also evaluated by direct substitution.

> ► The conditions under which direct substitution $\left(\lim\limits_{x \to a} f(x) = f(a)\right)$ can be used to evaluate a limit become clear in Section 2.6, when we discuss the important property of *continuity*.

THEOREM 2.4   Limits of Polynomial and Rational Functions
Assume p and q are polynomials and a is a constant.

a. Polynomial functions: $\lim\limits_{x \to a} p(x) = p(a)$

b. Rational functions: $\lim\limits_{x \to a} \dfrac{p(x)}{q(x)} = \dfrac{p(a)}{q(a)}$, provided $q(a) \neq 0$

QUICK CHECK 1 Evaluate $\lim\limits_{x \to 2} (2x^4 - 8x - 16)$ and $\lim\limits_{x \to -1} \dfrac{x - 1}{x}$. ◄

EXAMPLE 3   Limit of a rational function Evaluate $\lim\limits_{x \to 2} \dfrac{3x^2 - 4x}{5x^3 - 36}$.

SOLUTION Notice that the denominator of this function is nonzero at $x = 2$. Using Theorem 2.4b,

$$\lim_{x \to 2} \frac{3x^2 - 4x}{5x^3 - 36} = \frac{3(2^2) - 4(2)}{5(2^3) - 36} = 1.$$

Related Exercises 25–27 ◄

QUICK CHECK 2 Use Theorem 2.4b to compute $\lim\limits_{x \to 1} \dfrac{5x^4 - 3x^2 + 8x - 6}{x + 1}$. ◄

EXAMPLE 4   **An algebraic function** Evaluate $\lim\limits_{x \to 2} \dfrac{\sqrt{2x^3 + 9} + 3x - 1}{4x + 1}$.

SOLUTION Using Theorems 2.3 and 2.4, we have

$$
\begin{aligned}
\lim_{x \to 2} \frac{\sqrt{2x^3 + 9} + 3x - 1}{4x + 1}
&= \frac{\lim\limits_{x \to 2} \left(\sqrt{2x^3 + 9} + 3x - 1 \right)}{\lim\limits_{x \to 2} (4x + 1)} && \text{Law 5}\\[2ex]
&= \frac{\sqrt{\lim\limits_{x \to 2} (2x^3 + 9)} + \lim\limits_{x \to 2} (3x - 1)}{\lim\limits_{x \to 2} (4x + 1)} && \text{Laws 1 and 7}\\[2ex]
&= \frac{\sqrt{(2(2)^3 + 9)} + (3(2) - 1)}{(4(2) + 1)} && \text{Theorem 2.4}\\[2ex]
&= \frac{\sqrt{25} + 5}{9} = \frac{10}{9}.
\end{aligned}
$$

Notice that the limit at $x = 2$ equals the value of the function at $x = 2$.

Related Exercises 28–32 ◄

One-Sided Limits

Theorem 2.2, Limit Laws 1–6, and Theorem 2.4 also hold for left-sided and right-sided limits. In other words, these laws remain valid if we replace $\lim\limits_{x \to a}$ with $\lim\limits_{x \to a^+}$ or $\lim\limits_{x \to a^-}$. Law 7 must be modified slightly for one-sided limits, as shown in the next theorem.

THEOREM 2.3 (CONTINUED)   **Limit Laws for One-Sided Limits**
Laws 1–6 hold with $\lim\limits_{x \to a}$ replaced with $\lim\limits_{x \to a^+}$ or $\lim\limits_{x \to a^-}$. Law 7 is modified as follows. Assume $m > 0$ and $n > 0$ are integers.

7. Fractional power

a. $\lim\limits_{x \to a^+} (f(x))^{n/m} = \left(\lim\limits_{x \to a^+} f(x) \right)^{n/m}$, provided $f(x) \geq 0$, for x near a with $x > a$, if m is even and n/m is reduced to lowest terms

b. $\lim\limits_{x \to a^-} (f(x))^{n/m} = \left(\lim\limits_{x \to a^-} f(x) \right)^{n/m}$, provided $f(x) \geq 0$, for x near a with $x < a$, if m is even and n/m is reduced to lowest terms

---

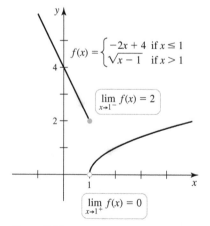

$$f(x) = \begin{cases} -2x + 4 & \text{if } x \leq 1 \\ \sqrt{x - 1} & \text{if } x > 1 \end{cases}$$

$\lim\limits_{x \to 1^-} f(x) = 2$

$\lim\limits_{x \to 1^+} f(x) = 0$

Figure 2.16

EXAMPLE 5   **Calculating left- and right-sided limits** Let

$$f(x) = \begin{cases} -2x + 4 & \text{if } x \leq 1 \\ \sqrt{x - 1} & \text{if } x > 1. \end{cases}$$

Find the values of $\lim\limits_{x \to 1^-} f(x)$, $\lim\limits_{x \to 1^+} f(x)$, and $\lim\limits_{x \to 1} f(x)$, or state that they do not exist.

SOLUTION The graph of f (Figure 2.16) suggests that $\lim\limits_{x \to 1^-} f(x) = 2$ and $\lim\limits_{x \to 1^+} f(x) = 0$. We verify this observation analytically by applying the limit laws. For $x \leq 1$, $f(x) = -2x + 4$; therefore,

$$\lim_{x \to 1^-} f(x) = \lim_{x \to 1^-} (-2x + 4) = 2. \quad \text{Theorem 2.2}$$

For $x > 1$, note that $x - 1 > 0$; it follows that

$$\lim_{x \to 1^+} f(x) = \lim_{x \to 1^+} \sqrt{x - 1} = 0. \quad \text{Law 7}$$

Because $\lim\limits_{x \to 1^-} f(x) = 2$ and $\lim\limits_{x \to 1^+} f(x) = 0$, $\lim\limits_{x \to 1} f(x)$ does not exist by Theorem 2.1.

Related Exercises 33–38 ◄

Other Techniques

So far, we have evaluated limits by direct substitution. A more challenging problem is finding $\lim_{x \to a} f(x)$ when the limit exists, but $\lim_{x \to a} f(x) \neq f(a)$. Two typical cases are shown in Figure 2.17. In the first case, $f(a)$ is defined, but it is not equal to $\lim_{x \to a} f(x)$; in the second case, $f(a)$ is not defined at all. In both cases, direct substitution does not work—we need a new strategy. One way to evaluate a challenging limit is to replace it with an equivalent limit that *can* be evaluated by direct substitution. Example 6 illustrates two common scenarios.

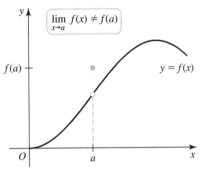
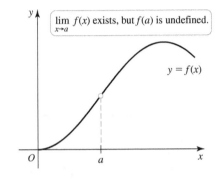

Figure 2.17

EXAMPLE 6 Other techniques Evaluate the following limits.

a. $\lim_{x \to 2} \dfrac{x^2 - 6x + 8}{x^2 - 4}$ **b.** $\lim_{x \to 1} \dfrac{\sqrt{x} - 1}{x - 1}$

SOLUTION

a. Factor and cancel This limit cannot be found by direct substitution because the denominator is zero when $x = 2$. Instead, the numerator and denominator are factored; then, assuming $x \neq 2$, we cancel like factors:

> The argument used in Example 6 relies on the fact that in the limit process, x approaches 2, but $x \neq 2$. Therefore, we may cancel like factors.

$$\frac{x^2 - 6x + 8}{x^2 - 4} = \frac{(x - 2)(x - 4)}{(x - 2)(x + 2)} = \frac{x - 4}{x + 2}.$$

Because $\dfrac{x^2 - 6x + 8}{x^2 - 4} = \dfrac{x - 4}{x + 2}$ whenever $x \neq 2$, the two functions have the same limit as x approaches 2 (Figure 2.18). Therefore,

$$\lim_{x \to 2} \frac{x^2 - 6x + 8}{x^2 - 4} = \lim_{x \to 2} \frac{x - 4}{x + 2} = \frac{2 - 4}{2 + 2} = -\frac{1}{2}.$$

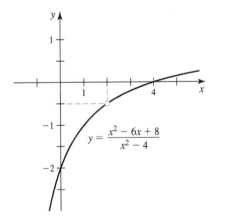
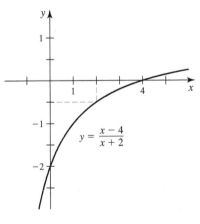

$$\lim_{x \to 2} \frac{x^2 - 6x + 8}{x^2 - 4} = \lim_{x \to 2} \frac{x - 4}{x + 2} = -\frac{1}{2}$$

Figure 2.18

> ▶ We multiply the given function by
>
> $$1 = \frac{\sqrt{x} + 1}{\sqrt{x} + 1}.$$

b. Use conjugates This limit was approximated numerically in Example 2 of Section 2.2; we conjectured that the value of the limit is $\frac{1}{2}$. Direct substitution fails in this case because the denominator is zero at $x = 1$. Instead, we first simplify the function by multiplying the numerator and denominator by the *algebraic conjugate* of the numerator. The conjugate of $\sqrt{x} - 1$ is $\sqrt{x} + 1$; therefore,

$$\frac{\sqrt{x} - 1}{x - 1} = \frac{(\sqrt{x} - 1)(\sqrt{x} + 1)}{(x - 1)(\sqrt{x} + 1)} \qquad \text{Rationalize the numerator; multiply by 1.}$$

$$= \frac{x + \sqrt{x} - \sqrt{x} - 1}{(x - 1)(\sqrt{x} + 1)} \qquad \text{Expand the numerator.}$$

$$= \frac{x - 1}{(x - 1)(\sqrt{x} + 1)} \qquad \text{Simplify.}$$

$$= \frac{1}{\sqrt{x} + 1}. \qquad \text{Cancel like factors assuming } x \neq 1.$$

QUICK CHECK 3 Evaluate

$$\lim_{x \to 5} \frac{x^2 - 7x + 10}{x - 5}. \blacktriangleleft$$

The limit can now be evaluated:

$$\lim_{x \to 1} \frac{\sqrt{x} - 1}{x - 1} = \lim_{x \to 1} \frac{1}{\sqrt{x} + 1} = \frac{1}{1 + 1} = \frac{1}{2}.$$

Related Exercises 39–52 ◄

An Important Limit

Despite our success in evaluating limits using direct substitution, algebraic manipulation, and the limit laws, there are important limits for which these techniques do not work. One such limit arises when investigating the slope of a line tangent to the graph of an exponential function.

EXAMPLE 7 Slope of a line tangent to $f(x) = 2^x$ Estimate the slope of the line tangent to the graph of $f(x) = 2^x$ at the point $P(0, 1)$.

SOLUTION In Section 2.1, the slope of a tangent line was obtained by finding the limit of slopes of secant lines; the same strategy is employed here. We begin by selecting a point Q near P on the graph of f with coordinates $(x, 2^x)$. The secant line joining the points $P(0, 1)$ and $Q(x, 2^x)$ is an approximation to the tangent line. To estimate the slope of the tangent line (denoted $m_{\tan}$) at $x = 0$, we compute the slope of the secant line $m_{\text{sec}} = (2^x - 1)/x$ and then let x approach 0.

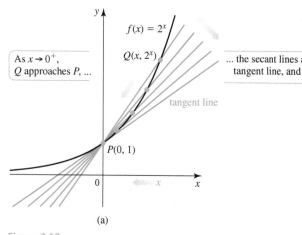

(a)

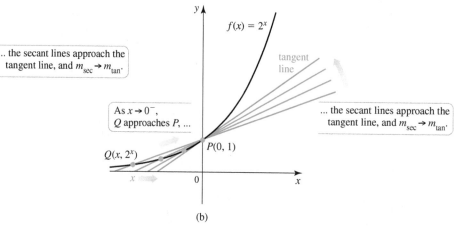

(b)

Figure 2.19

The limit $\lim_{x \to 0} \dfrac{2^x - 1}{x}$ exists only if it has the same value as $x \to 0^+$ (Figure 2.19a) and as $x \to 0^-$ (Figure 2.19b). Because it is not an elementary limit, it cannot be evaluated using the limit laws introduced in this section. Instead, we investigate the limit using numerical evidence. Choosing positive values of x near 0 results in Table 2.5.

Table 2.5

x		1.0	0.1	0.01	0.001	0.0001	0.00001
$m_{sec} = \dfrac{2^x - 1}{x}$		1.000000	0.7177	0.6956	0.6934	0.6932	0.6931

> Example 7 shows that
> $$\lim_{x \to 0} \frac{2^x - 1}{x} \approx 0.693.$$ The exact value
> of the limit is $\ln 2$. The connection
> between the natural logarithm and slopes
> of lines tangent to exponential curves is
> made clear in Chapters 3 and 6.

We see that as x approaches 0 from the right, the slopes of the secant lines approach the slope of the tangent line, which is approximately 0.693. A similar calculation (Exercise 53) gives the same approximation for the limit as x approaches 0 from the left.

Because the left-sided and right-sided limits are the same, we conclude that $\lim_{x \to 0} (2^x - 1)/x \approx 0.693$ (Theorem 2.1). Therefore, the slope of the line tangent to $f(x) = 2^x$ at $x = 0$ is approximately 0.693.

Related Exercises 53–54 ◀

The Squeeze Theorem

> The Squeeze Theorem is also called
> the Pinching Theorem or the Sandwich
> Theorem.

The *Squeeze Theorem* provides another useful method for calculating limits. Suppose the functions f and h have the same limit L at a and assume the function g is trapped between f and h (Figure 2.20). The Squeeze Theorem says that g must also have the limit L at a. A proof of this theorem is outlined in Exercise 54 of Section 2.7.

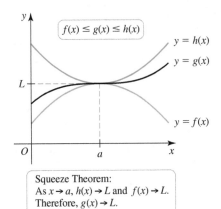

$f(x) \le g(x) \le h(x)$

$y = h(x)$

$y = g(x)$

$y = f(x)$

Squeeze Theorem:
As $x \to a$, $h(x) \to L$ and $f(x) \to L$.
Therefore, $g(x) \to L$.

Figure 2.20

THEOREM 2.5   The Squeeze Theorem
Assume the functions f, g, and h satisfy $f(x) \le g(x) \le h(x)$ for all values of x near a, except possibly at a. If $\lim_{x \to a} f(x) = \lim_{x \to a} h(x) = L$, then $\lim_{x \to a} g(x) = L$.

EXAMPLE 8   Sine and cosine limits A geometric argument (Exercise 90) may be used to show that for $-\pi/2 < x < \pi/2$,

$$-|x| \le \sin x \le |x| \quad \text{and} \quad 0 \le 1 - \cos x \le |x|.$$

Use the Squeeze Theorem to confirm the following limits.

a. $\lim_{x \to 0} \sin x = 0$ **b.** $\lim_{x \to 0} \cos x = 1$

> The two limits in Example 8 play a
> crucial role in establishing fundamental
> properties of the trigonometric functions.
> The limits reappear in Section 2.6.

SOLUTION

a. Letting $f(x) = -|x|$, $g(x) = \sin x$, and $h(x) = |x|$, we see that g is trapped between f and h on $-\pi/2 < x < \pi/2$ (Figure 2.21a). Because $\lim_{x \to 0} f(x) = \lim_{x \to 0} h(x) = 0$ (Exercise 37), the Squeeze Theorem implies that $\lim_{x \to 0} g(x) = \lim_{x \to 0} \sin x = 0$.

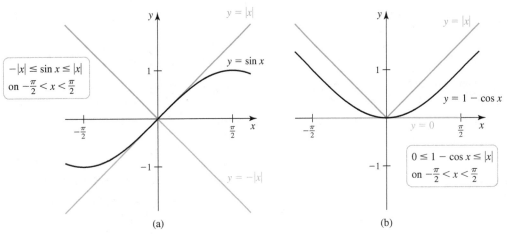

(a)   (b)

Figure 2.21

b. In this case, we let $f(x) = 0$, $g(x) = 1 - \cos x$, and $h(x) = |x|$ (Figure 2.21b). Because $\lim\limits_{x \to 0} f(x) = \lim\limits_{x \to 0} h(x) = 0$, the Squeeze Theorem implies that $\lim\limits_{x \to 0} g(x) = \lim\limits_{x \to 0} (1 - \cos x) = 0$. By the limit laws of Theorem 2.3, it follows that $\lim\limits_{x \to 0} 1 - \lim\limits_{x \to 0} \cos x = 0$, or $\lim\limits_{x \to 0} \cos x = 1$.

Related Exercises 55–58 ◄

EXAMPLE 9 Applying the Squeeze Theorem Use the Squeeze Theorem to verify that $\lim\limits_{x \to 0} x^2 \sin (1/x) = 0$.

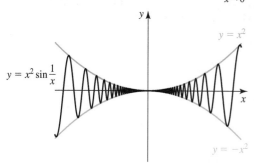

Figure 2.22

SOLUTION For any real number θ, $-1 \le \sin \theta \le 1$. Letting $\theta = 1/x$ for $x \ne 0$, it follows that

$$-1 \le \sin \frac{1}{x} \le 1.$$

Noting that $x^2 > 0$ for $x \ne 0$, each term in this inequality is multiplied by x^2:

$$-x^2 \le x^2 \sin \frac{1}{x} \le x^2.$$

These inequalities are illustrated in Figure 2.22. Because $\lim\limits_{x \to 0} x^2 = \lim\limits_{x \to 0} (-x^2) = 0$, the Squeeze Theorem implies that $\lim\limits_{x \to 0} x^2 \sin (1/x) = 0$.

Related Exercises 55–58 ◄

QUICK CHECK 4 Suppose f satisfies $1 \le f(x) \le 1 + \dfrac{x^2}{6}$ for all values of x near zero. Find $\lim\limits_{x \to 0} f(x)$, if possible. ◄

SECTION 2.3 EXERCISES

Review Questions

1. How is $\lim\limits_{x \to a} f(x)$ calculated if f is a polynomial function?

2. How are $\lim\limits_{x \to a^-} f(x)$ and $\lim\limits_{x \to a^+} f(x)$ calculated if f is a polynomial function?

3. For what values of a does $\lim\limits_{x \to a} r(x) = r(a)$ if r is a rational function?

4. Assume $\lim\limits_{x \to 3} g(x) = 4$ and $f(x) = g(x)$ whenever $x \ne 3$. Evaluate $\lim\limits_{x \to 3} f(x)$, if possible.

5. Explain why $\lim\limits_{x \to 3} \dfrac{x^2 - 7x + 12}{x - 3} = \lim\limits_{x \to 3} (x - 4)$.

6. If $\lim\limits_{x \to 2} f(x) = -8$, find $\lim\limits_{x \to 2} (f(x))^{2/3}$.

7. Suppose p and q are polynomials. If $\lim\limits_{x \to 0} \dfrac{p(x)}{q(x)} = 10$ and $q(0) = 2$, find $p(0)$.

8. Suppose $\lim\limits_{x \to 2} f(x) = \lim\limits_{x \to 2} h(x) = 5$. Find $\lim\limits_{x \to 2} g(x)$, where $f(x) \le g(x) \le h(x)$, for all x.

9. Evaluate $\lim\limits_{x \to 5} \sqrt{x^2 - 9}$.

10. Suppose

$$f(x) = \begin{cases} 4 & \text{if } x \le 3 \\ x + 2 & \text{if } x > 3. \end{cases}$$

Compute $\lim\limits_{x \to 3^-} f(x)$ and $\lim\limits_{x \to 3^+} f(x)$.

Basic Skills

11–16. Limits of linear functions *Evaluate the following limits.*

11. $\lim\limits_{x \to 4} (3x - 7)$ 12. $\lim\limits_{x \to 1} (-2x + 5)$ 13. $\lim\limits_{x \to -9} 5x$

14. $\lim\limits_{x \to 2} (-3x)$ 15. $\lim\limits_{x \to 6} 4$ 16. $\lim\limits_{x \to -5} \pi$

17–24. Applying limit laws *Assume $\lim\limits_{x \to 1} f(x) = 8$, $\lim\limits_{x \to 1} g(x) = 3$, and $\lim\limits_{x \to 1} h(x) = 2$. Compute the following limits and state the limit laws used to justify your computations.*

17. $\lim\limits_{x \to 1} (4f(x))$ 18. $\lim\limits_{x \to 1} \dfrac{f(x)}{h(x)}$

19. $\lim\limits_{x \to 1} (f(x) - g(x))$ 20. $\lim\limits_{x \to 1} (f(x)h(x))$

21. $\lim\limits_{x \to 1} \dfrac{f(x)g(x)}{h(x)}$ 22. $\lim\limits_{x \to 1} \dfrac{f(x)}{g(x) - h(x)}$

23. $\lim\limits_{x \to 1} (h(x))^5$ 24. $\lim\limits_{x \to 1} \sqrt[3]{f(x)g(x) + 3}$

25–32. Evaluating limits *Evaluate the following limits.*

25. $\lim\limits_{x \to 1} (2x^3 - 3x^2 + 4x + 5)$ 26. $\lim\limits_{t \to -2} (t^2 + 5t + 7)$

27. $\lim\limits_{x \to 1} \dfrac{5x^2 + 6x + 1}{8x - 4}$ 28. $\lim\limits_{t \to 3} \sqrt[3]{t^2 - 10}$

29. $\lim\limits_{b \to 2} \dfrac{3b}{\sqrt{4b + 1} - 1}$ 30. $\lim\limits_{x \to 2} (x^2 - x)^5$

31. $\displaystyle\lim_{x\to3}\frac{-5x}{\sqrt{4x-3}}$

32. $\displaystyle\lim_{h\to0}\frac{3}{\sqrt{16+3h}+4}$

33. One-sided limits Let

$$f(x) = \begin{cases} x^2 + 1 & \text{if } x < -1 \\ \sqrt{x+1} & \text{if } x \geq -1. \end{cases}$$

Compute the following limits or state that they do not exist.

a. $\displaystyle\lim_{x\to-1^-}f(x)$ **b.** $\displaystyle\lim_{x\to-1^+}f(x)$ **c.** $\displaystyle\lim_{x\to-1}f(x)$

34. One-sided limits Let

$$f(x) = \begin{cases} 0 & \text{if } x \leq -5 \\ \sqrt{25-x^2} & \text{if } -5 < x < 5 \\ 3x & \text{if } x \geq 5. \end{cases}$$

Compute the following limits or state that they do not exist.

a. $\displaystyle\lim_{x\to-5^-}f(x)$ **b.** $\displaystyle\lim_{x\to-5^+}f(x)$ **c.** $\displaystyle\lim_{x\to-5}f(x)$
d. $\displaystyle\lim_{x\to5^-}f(x)$ **e.** $\displaystyle\lim_{x\to5^+}f(x)$ **f.** $\displaystyle\lim_{x\to5}f(x)$

35. One-sided limits

a. Evaluate $\displaystyle\lim_{x\to2^+}\sqrt{x-2}$.
b. Explain why $\displaystyle\lim_{x\to2^-}\sqrt{x-2}$ does not exist.

36. One-sided limits

a. Evaluate $\displaystyle\lim_{x\to3^-}\sqrt{\frac{x-3}{2-x}}$.

b. Explain why $\displaystyle\lim_{x\to3^+}\sqrt{\frac{x-3}{2-x}}$ does not exist.

37. Absolute value limit Show that $\displaystyle\lim_{x\to0}|x|=0$ by first evaluating $\displaystyle\lim_{x\to0^-}|x|$ and $\displaystyle\lim_{x\to0^+}|x|$. Recall that

$$|x| = \begin{cases} x & \text{if } x \geq 0 \\ -x & \text{if } x < 0. \end{cases}$$

38. Absolute value limit Show that $\displaystyle\lim_{x\to a}|x|=|a|$, for any real number. (*Hint:* Consider the cases $a < 0$ and $a \geq 0$.)

39–52. Other techniques *Evaluate the following limits, where a and b are fixed real numbers.*

39. $\displaystyle\lim_{x\to1}\frac{x^2-1}{x-1}$

40. $\displaystyle\lim_{x\to3}\frac{x^2-2x-3}{x-3}$

41. $\displaystyle\lim_{x\to4}\frac{x^2-16}{4-x}$

42. $\displaystyle\lim_{t\to2}\frac{3t^2-7t+2}{2-t}$

43. $\displaystyle\lim_{x\to b}\frac{(x-b)^{50}-x+b}{x-b}$

44. $\displaystyle\lim_{x\to-b}\frac{(x+b)^7+(x+b)^{10}}{4(x+b)}$

45. $\displaystyle\lim_{x\to-1}\frac{(2x-1)^2-9}{x+1}$

46. $\displaystyle\lim_{h\to0}\frac{\frac{1}{5+h}-\frac{1}{5}}{h}$

47. $\displaystyle\lim_{x\to9}\frac{\sqrt{x}-3}{x-9}$

48. $\displaystyle\lim_{t\to3}\left(\left(4t-\frac{2}{t-3}\right)(6+t-t^2)\right)$

49. $\displaystyle\lim_{x\to a}\frac{x-a}{\sqrt{x}-\sqrt{a}}, a > 0$ **50.** $\displaystyle\lim_{x\to a}\frac{x^2-a^2}{\sqrt{x}-\sqrt{a}}, a > 0$

51. $\displaystyle\lim_{h\to0}\frac{\sqrt{16+h}-4}{h}$

52. $\displaystyle\lim_{x\to a}\frac{x^3-a^3}{x-a}$

T 53. Slope of a tangent line

a. Sketch a graph of $y = 2^x$ and carefully draw three secant lines connecting the points $P(0, 1)$ and $Q(x, 2^x)$, for $x = -3, -2$, and -1.
b. Find the slope of the line that passes through $P(0, 1)$ and $Q(x, 2^x)$, for $x \neq 0$.
c. Complete the table and make a conjecture about the value of $\displaystyle\lim_{x\to0^-}\frac{2^x-1}{x}$.

x	-1	-0.1	-0.01	-0.001	-0.0001	-0.00001
$\dfrac{2^x-1}{x}$						

T 54. Slope of a tangent line

a. Sketch a graph of $y = 3^x$ and carefully draw four secant lines connecting the points $P(0, 1)$ and $Q(x, 3^x)$, for $x = -2, -1, 1$, and 2.
b. Find the slope of the line that passes through $P(0, 1)$ and $Q(x, 3^x)$, for $x \neq 0$.
c. Complete the table and make a conjecture about the value of $\displaystyle\lim_{x\to0}\frac{3^x-1}{x}$.

x	-0.1	-0.01	-0.001	-0.0001	0.0001	0.001	0.01	0.1
$\dfrac{3^x-1}{x}$								

T 55. Applying the Squeeze Theorem

a. Show that $-|x| \leq x\sin\dfrac{1}{x} \leq |x|$, for $x \neq 0$.
b. Illustrate the inequalities in part (a) with a graph.
c. Use the Squeeze Theorem to show that $\displaystyle\lim_{x\to0}x\sin\frac{1}{x}=0$.

T 56. A cosine limit by the Squeeze Theorem It can be shown that

$$1 - \frac{x^2}{2} \leq \cos x \leq 1, \text{ for } x \text{ near } 0.$$

a. Illustrate these inequalities with a graph.
b. Use these inequalities to evaluate $\displaystyle\lim_{x\to0}\cos x$.

T 57. A sine limit by the Squeeze Theorem It can be shown that

$$1 - \frac{x^2}{6} \leq \frac{\sin x}{x} \leq 1, \text{ for } x \text{ near } 0.$$

a. Illustrate these inequalities with a graph.
b. Use these inequalities to evaluate $\displaystyle\lim_{x\to0}\frac{\sin x}{x}$.

T 58. A logarithm limit by the Squeeze Theorem

a. Draw a graph to verify that $-|x| \leq x^2 \ln x^2 \leq |x|$, for $-1 \leq x \leq 1$, where $x \neq 0$.
b. Use the Squeeze Theorem to evaluate $\displaystyle\lim_{x\to0}x^2 \ln x^2$.

Further Explorations

59. Explain why or why not Determine whether the following statements are true and give an explanation or counterexample. Assume a and L are finite numbers.

  a. If $\lim\limits_{x \to a} f(x) = L$, then $f(a) = L$.

  b. If $\lim\limits_{x \to a^-} f(x) = L$, then $\lim\limits_{x \to a^+} f(x) = L$.

  c. If $\lim\limits_{x \to a} f(x) = L$ and $\lim\limits_{x \to a} g(x) = L$, then $f(a) = g(a)$.

  d. The limit $\lim\limits_{x \to a} \dfrac{f(x)}{g(x)}$ does not exist if $g(a) = 0$.

  e. If $\lim\limits_{x \to 1^+} \sqrt{f(x)} = \sqrt{\lim\limits_{x \to 1^+} f(x)}$, it follows that

$$\lim_{x \to 1} \sqrt{f(x)} = \sqrt{\lim_{x \to 1} f(x)}.$$

60–67. Evaluating limits *Evaluate the following limits, where c and k are constants.*

60. $\lim\limits_{h \to 0} \dfrac{100}{(10h - 1)^{11} + 2}$

61. $\lim\limits_{x \to 2} (5x - 6)^{3/2}$

62. $\lim\limits_{x \to 3} \dfrac{\frac{1}{x^2 + 2x} - \frac{1}{15}}{x - 3}$

63. $\lim\limits_{x \to 1} \dfrac{\sqrt{10x - 9} - 1}{x - 1}$

64. $\lim\limits_{x \to 2} \left(\dfrac{1}{x - 2} - \dfrac{2}{x^2 - 2x} \right)$

65. $\lim\limits_{h \to 0} \dfrac{(5 + h)^2 - 25}{h}$

66. $\lim\limits_{x \to c} \dfrac{x^2 - 2cx + c^2}{x - c}$

67. $\lim\limits_{w \to -k} \dfrac{w^2 + 5kw + 4k^2}{w^2 + kw}$, for $k \neq 0$

68. Finding a constant Suppose

$$f(x) = \begin{cases} 3x + b & \text{if } x \leq 2 \\ x - 2 & \text{if } x > 2. \end{cases}$$

Determine a value of the constant b for which $\lim\limits_{x \to 2} f(x)$ exists and state the value of the limit, if possible.

69. Finding a constant Suppose

$$g(x) = \begin{cases} x^2 - 5x & \text{if } x \leq -1 \\ ax^3 - 7 & \text{if } x > -1. \end{cases}$$

Determine a value of the constant a for which $\lim\limits_{x \to -1} g(x)$ exists and state the value of the limit, if possible.

70–76. Useful factorization formula *Calculate the following limits using the factorization formula*

$$x^n - a^n = (x - a)(x^{n-1} + x^{n-2}a + x^{n-3}a^2 + \cdots + xa^{n-2} + a^{n-1}),$$

where n is a positive integer and a is a real number.

70. $\lim\limits_{x \to 2} \dfrac{x^5 - 32}{x - 2}$

71. $\lim\limits_{x \to 1} \dfrac{x^6 - 1}{x - 1}$

72. $\lim\limits_{x \to -1} \dfrac{x^7 + 1}{x + 1}$ (*Hint:* Use the formula for $x^7 - a^7$ with $a = -1$.)

73. $\lim\limits_{x \to a} \dfrac{x^5 - a^5}{x - a}$

74. $\lim\limits_{x \to a} \dfrac{x^n - a^n}{x - a}$, for any positive integer n

75. $\lim\limits_{x \to 1} \dfrac{\sqrt[3]{x} - 1}{x - 1}$ (*Hint:* $x - 1 = (\sqrt[3]{x})^3 - (1)^3.$)

76. $\lim\limits_{x \to 16} \dfrac{\sqrt[4]{x} - 2}{x - 16}$

77–80. Limits involving conjugates *Evaluate the following limits.*

77. $\lim\limits_{x \to 1} \dfrac{x - 1}{\sqrt{x} - 1}$

78. $\lim\limits_{x \to 1} \dfrac{x - 1}{\sqrt{4x + 5} - 3}$

79. $\lim\limits_{x \to 4} \dfrac{3(x - 4)\sqrt{x + 5}}{3 - \sqrt{x + 5}}$

80. $\lim\limits_{x \to 0} \dfrac{x}{\sqrt{cx + 1} - 1}$, where c is a nonzero constant

81. Creating functions satisfying given limit conditions Find functions f and g such that $\lim\limits_{x \to 1} f(x) = 0$ and $\lim\limits_{x \to 1} (f(x)\,g(x)) = 5$.

82. Creating functions satisfying given limit conditions Find a function f satisfying $\lim\limits_{x \to 1} \left(\dfrac{f(x)}{x - 1} \right) = 2$.

83. Finding constants Find constants b and c in the polynomial $p(x) = x^2 + bx + c$ such that $\lim\limits_{x \to 2} \dfrac{p(x)}{x - 2} = 6$. Are the constants unique?

Applications

84. A problem from relativity theory Suppose a spaceship of length L_0 travels at a high speed v relative to an observer. To the observer, the ship appears to have a smaller length given by the *Lorentz contraction formula*

$$L = L_0 \sqrt{1 - \dfrac{v^2}{c^2}},$$

where c is the speed of light.

  a. What is the observed length L of the ship if it is traveling at 50% of the speed of light?

  b. What is the observed length L of the ship if it is traveling at 75% of the speed of light?

  c. In parts (a) and (b), what happens to L as the speed of the ship increases?

  d. Find $\lim\limits_{v \to c^-} L_0 \sqrt{1 - \dfrac{v^2}{c^2}}$ and explain the significance of this limit.

85. Limit of the radius of a cylinder A right circular cylinder with a height of 10 cm and a surface area of S cm^2 has a radius given by

$$r(S) = \dfrac{1}{2}\left(\sqrt{100 + \dfrac{2S}{\pi}} - 10 \right).$$

Find $\lim\limits_{S \to 0^+} r(S)$ and interpret your result.

86. Torricelli's Law A cylindrical tank is filled with water to a depth of 9 meters. At $t = 0$, a drain in the bottom of the tank is opened and water flows out of the tank. The depth of water in the tank (measured from the bottom of the tank) t seconds after the drain is opened is approximated by $d(t) = (3 - 0.015t)^2$, for $0 \leq t \leq 200$. Evaluate and interpret $\lim\limits_{t \to 200^-} d(t)$.

87. Electric field The magnitude of the electric field at a point x meters from the midpoint of a 0.1-m line of charge is given by

$$E(x) = \dfrac{4.35}{x\sqrt{x^2 + 0.01}} \text{ (in units of newtons per coulomb, N/C).}$$

Evaluate $\lim\limits_{x \to 10} E(x)$.

Additional Exercises

88–89. Limits of composite functions

88. If $\lim\limits_{x \to 1} f(x) = 4$, find $\lim\limits_{x \to -1} f(x^2)$.

89. Suppose $g(x) = f(1 - x)$, for all x, $\lim\limits_{x \to 1^+} f(x) = 4$, and $\lim\limits_{x \to 1^-} f(x) = 6$. Find $\lim\limits_{x \to 0^+} g(x)$ and $\lim\limits_{x \to 0^-} g(x)$.

90. Two trigonometric inequalities Consider the angle θ in standard position in a unit circle, where $0 \leq \theta < \pi/2$ or $-\pi/2 < \theta < 0$ (use both figures).

   a. Show that $|AC| = |\sin \theta|$, for $-\pi/2 < \theta < \pi/2$. (*Hint:* Consider the cases $0 \leq \theta < \pi/2$ and $-\pi/2 < \theta < 0$ separately.)

   b. Show that $|\sin \theta| < |\theta|$, for $-\pi/2 < \theta < \pi/2$. (*Hint:* The length of arc AB is θ, if $0 \leq \theta < \pi/2$, and $-\theta$, if $-\pi/2 < \theta < 0$.)

   c. Conclude that $-|\theta| \leq \sin \theta \leq |\theta|$, for $-\pi/2 < \theta < \pi/2$.

   d. Show that $0 \leq 1 - \cos \theta \leq |\theta|$, for $-\pi/2 < \theta < \pi/2$.

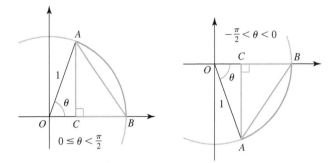

91. Theorem 2.4a Given the polynomial

$$p(x) = b_n x^n + b_{n-1} x^{n-1} + \cdots + b_1 x + b_0,$$

prove that $\lim\limits_{x \to a} p(x) = p(a)$ for any value of a.

QUICK CHECK ANSWERS

1. $0, 2$ **2.** 2 **3.** 3 **4.** 1 ◀

2.4 Infinite Limits

Two more limit scenarios are frequently encountered in calculus and are discussed in this and the following section. An *infinite limit* occurs when function values increase or decrease without bound near a point. The other type of limit, known as a *limit at infinity*, occurs when the independent variable x increases or decreases without bound. The ideas behind infinite limits and limits at infinity are quite different. Therefore, it is important to distinguish these limits and the methods used to calculate them.

An Overview

To illustrate the differences between infinite limits and limits at infinity, consider the values of $f(x) = 1/x^2$ in Table 2.6. As x approaches 0 from either side, $f(x)$ grows larger and larger. Because $f(x)$ does not approach a finite number as x approaches 0, $\lim\limits_{x \to 0} f(x)$ does not exist. Nevertheless, we use limit notation and write $\lim\limits_{x \to 0} f(x) = \infty$. The infinity symbol indicates that $f(x)$ grows arbitrarily large as x approaches 0. This is an example of an *infinite limit*; in general, the *dependent variable* becomes arbitrarily large in magnitude as the *independent variable* approaches a finite number.

Table 2.6

x	$f(x) = 1/x^2$
± 0.1	100
± 0.01	$10,000$
± 0.001	$1,000,000$
$\downarrow$	$\downarrow$
0	∞

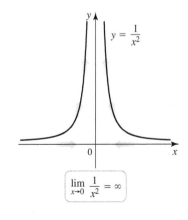

$$\lim\limits_{x \to 0} \frac{1}{x^2} = \infty$$

With *limits at infinity*, the opposite occurs: The *dependent variable* approaches a finite number as the *independent variable* becomes arbitrarily large in magnitude. In Table 2.7 we see that $f(x) = 1/x^2$ approaches 0 as x increases. In this case, we write $\lim_{x \to \infty} f(x) = 0$.

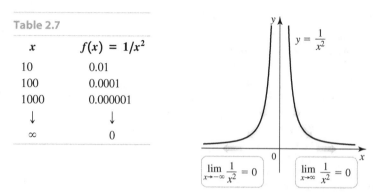

Table 2.7	
x	$f(x) = 1/x^2$
10	0.01
100	0.0001
1000	0.000001
↓	↓
∞	0

A general picture of these two limit scenarios—occurring with the same function—is shown in Figure 2.23.

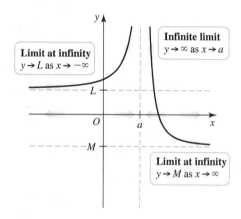

Figure 2.23

Infinite Limits

The following definition of infinite limits is informal, but it is adequate for most functions encountered in this book. A precise definition is given in Section 2.7.

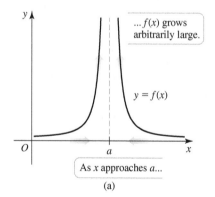

(a)

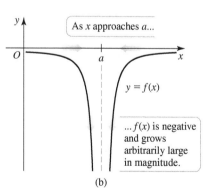

(b)

Figure 2.24

DEFINITION Infinite Limits

Suppose f is defined for all x near a. If $f(x)$ grows arbitrarily large for all x sufficiently close (but not equal) to a (Figure 2.24a), we write

$$\lim_{x \to a} f(x) = \infty$$

and say the limit of $f(x)$ as x approaches a is infinity.

If $f(x)$ is negative and grows arbitrarily large in magnitude for all x sufficiently close (but not equal) to a (Figure 2.24b), we write

$$\lim_{x \to a} f(x) = -\infty$$

and say the limit of $f(x)$ as x approaches a is negative infinity. *In both cases, the limit does not exist.*

EXAMPLE 1 **Infinite limits** Analyze $\lim\limits_{x \to 1} \dfrac{x}{(x^2 - 1)^2}$ and $\lim\limits_{x \to -1} \dfrac{x}{(x^2 - 1)^2}$ using the graph of the function.

SOLUTION The graph of $f(x) = \dfrac{x}{(x^2 - 1)^2}$ (Figure 2.25) shows that as x approaches 1 (from either side), the values of f grow arbitrarily large. Therefore, the limit does not exist and we write

$$\lim_{x \to 1} \frac{x}{(x^2 - 1)^2} = \infty.$$

As x approaches -1, the values of f are negative and grow arbitrarily large in magnitude; therefore,

$$\lim_{x \to -1} \frac{x}{(x^2 - 1)^2} = -\infty.$$

Related Exercises 7–8 ◄

Example 1 illustrates *two-sided* infinite limits. As with finite limits, we also need to work with right-sided and left-sided infinite limits.

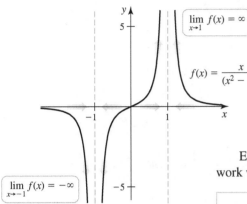

$\lim\limits_{x \to 1} f(x) = \infty$

$f(x) = \dfrac{x}{(x^2 - 1)^2}$

$\lim\limits_{x \to -1} f(x) = -\infty$

Figure 2.25

DEFINITION **One-Sided Infinite Limits**

Suppose f is defined for all x near a with $x > a$. If $f(x)$ becomes arbitrarily large for all x sufficiently close to a with $x > a$, we write $\lim\limits_{x \to a^+} f(x) = \infty$ (Figure 2.26a).

The one-sided infinite limits $\lim\limits_{x \to a^+} f(x) = -\infty$ (Figure 2.26b), $\lim\limits_{x \to a^-} f(x) = \infty$ (Figure 2.26c), and $\lim\limits_{x \to a^-} f(x) = -\infty$ (Figure 2.26d) are defined analogously.

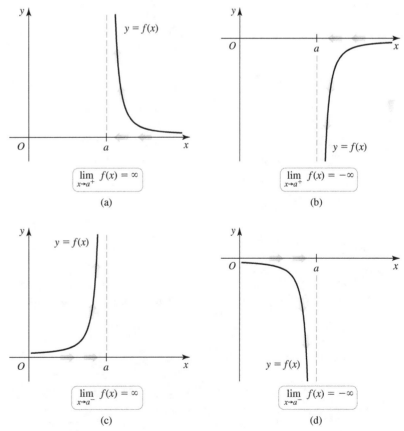

$\lim\limits_{x \to a^+} f(x) = \infty$

(a)

$\lim\limits_{x \to a^+} f(x) = -\infty$

(b)

$\lim\limits_{x \to a^-} f(x) = \infty$

(c)

$\lim\limits_{x \to a^-} f(x) = -\infty$

(d)

Figure 2.26

QUICK CHECK 1 Sketch the graph of a function and its vertical asymptote that satisfies the conditions $\lim\limits_{x \to 2^+} f(x) = -\infty$ and $\lim\limits_{x \to 2^-} f(x) = \infty$. ◄

In all the infinite limits illustrated in Figure 2.26, the line $x = a$ is called a *vertical asymptote*; it is a vertical line that is approached by the graph of f as x approaches a.

DEFINITION **Vertical Asymptote**

If $\lim\limits_{x \to a} f(x) = \pm\infty$, $\lim\limits_{x \to a^+} f(x) = \pm\infty$, or $\lim\limits_{x \to a^-} f(x) = \pm\infty$, the line $x = a$ is called a **vertical asymptote** of f.

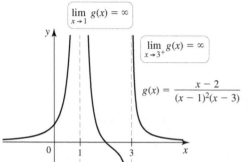

Figure 2.27

EXAMPLE 2 Determining limits graphically The vertical lines $x = 1$ and $x = 3$ are vertical asymptotes of the function $g(x) = \dfrac{x - 2}{(x - 1)^2 (x - 3)}$. Use Figure 2.27 to analyze the following limits.

a. $\lim\limits_{x \to 1} g(x)$ **b.** $\lim\limits_{x \to 3^-} g(x)$ **c.** $\lim\limits_{x \to 3} g(x)$

SOLUTION

a. The values of g grow arbitrarily large as x approaches 1 from either side. Therefore, $\lim\limits_{x \to 1} g(x) = \infty$.

b. The values of g are negative and grow arbitrarily large in magnitude as x approaches 3 from the left, so $\lim\limits_{x \to 3^-} g(x) = -\infty$.

c. Note that $\lim\limits_{x \to 3^+} g(x) = \infty$ and $\lim\limits_{x \to 3^-} g(x) = -\infty$. Because g behaves differently as $x \to 3^-$ and as $x \to 3^+$, we do not write $\lim\limits_{x \to 3} g(x) = \infty$. We simply say that the limit does not exist.

Related Exercises 9–16 ◄

Finding Infinite Limits Analytically

Many infinite limits are analyzed using a simple arithmetic property: The fraction a/b grows arbitrarily large in magnitude if b approaches 0 while a remains nonzero and relatively constant. For example, consider the fraction $(5 + x)/x$ for values of x approaching 0 from the right (Table 2.8).

We see that $\dfrac{5 + x}{x} \to \infty$ as $x \to 0^+$ because the numerator $5 + x$ approaches 5 while the denominator is positive and approaches 0. Therefore, we write $\lim\limits_{x \to 0^+} \dfrac{5 + x}{x} = \infty$. Similarly, $\lim\limits_{x \to 0^-} \dfrac{5 + x}{x} = -\infty$ because the numerator approaches 5 while the denominator approaches 0 through negative values.

Table 2.8

x	$\dfrac{5 + x}{x}$
0.01	$\dfrac{5.01}{0.01} = 501$
0.001	$\dfrac{5.001}{0.001} = 5001$
0.0001	$\dfrac{5.0001}{0.0001} = 50{,}001$
$\downarrow$	$\downarrow$
0^+	∞

EXAMPLE 3 Determining limits analytically Analyze the following limits.

a. $\lim\limits_{x \to 3^+} \dfrac{2 - 5x}{x - 3}$ **b.** $\lim\limits_{x \to 3^-} \dfrac{2 - 5x}{x - 3}$

SOLUTION

a. As $x \to 3^+$, the numerator $2 - 5x$ approaches $2 - 5(3) = -13$ while the denominator $x - 3$ is positive and approaches 0. Therefore,

$$\lim_{x \to 3^+} \frac{\overbrace{2 - 5x}^{\text{approaches } -13}}{\underbrace{x - 3}_{\text{positive and approaches } 0}} = -\infty.$$

b. As $x \to 3^-$, $2 - 5x$ approaches $2 - 5(3) = -13$ while $x - 3$ is negative and approaches 0. Therefore,

$$\lim_{x \to 3^-} \underbrace{\frac{\overbrace{2 - 5x}^{\text{approaches} -13}}{x - 3}}_{\substack{\text{negative and} \\ \text{approaches } 0}} = \infty.$$

QUICK CHECK 2 Analyze $\lim\limits_{x \to 0^+} \dfrac{x - 5}{x}$ and $\lim\limits_{x \to 0^-} \dfrac{x - 5}{x}$ by determining the sign of the numerator and denominator. ◀

These limits imply that the given function has a vertical asymptote at $x = 3$; they also imply that the two-sided limit $\lim\limits_{x \to 3} \dfrac{2x - 5}{x - 3}$ does not exist.

Related Exercises 17–28 ◀

EXAMPLE 4 **Determining limits analytically** Analyze $\lim\limits_{x \to -4^+} \dfrac{-x^3 + 5x^2 - 6x}{-x^3 - 4x^2}$.

➤ We can assume that $x \neq 0$ because we are considering function values near $x = -4$.

SOLUTION First we factor and simplify, assuming $x \neq 0$:

$$\frac{-x^3 + 5x^2 - 6x}{-x^3 - 4x^2} = \frac{-x(x - 2)(x - 3)}{-x^2(x + 4)} = \frac{(x - 2)(x - 3)}{x(x + 4)}.$$

As $x \to -4^+$, we find that

$$\lim_{x \to -4^+} \frac{-x^3 + 5x^2 - 6x}{-x^3 - 4x^2} = \lim_{x \to -4^+} \underbrace{\frac{\overbrace{(x - 2)(x - 3)}^{\text{approaches } 42}}{x(x + 4)}}_{\substack{\text{negative and} \\ \text{approaches } 0}} = -\infty.$$

QUICK CHECK 3 Verify that $x(x + 4) \to 0$ through negative values as $x \to -4^+$. ◀

This limit implies that the given function has a vertical asymptote at $x = -4$.

Related Exercises 17–28 ◀

➤ Example 5 illustrates that $f(x)/g(x)$ might not grow arbitrarily large in magnitude if *both* $f(x)$ and $g(x)$ approach 0. Such limits are called *indeterminate forms*; they are examined in detail in Section 4.7.

EXAMPLE 5 **Location of vertical asymptotes** Let $f(x) = \dfrac{x^2 - 4x + 3}{x^2 - 1}$. Determine the following limits and find the vertical asymptotes of f. Verify your work with a graphing utility.

a. $\lim\limits_{x \to 1} f(x)$ **b.** $\lim\limits_{x \to -1^-} f(x)$ **c.** $\lim\limits_{x \to -1^+} f(x)$

SOLUTION

a. Notice that as $x \to 1$, both the numerator and denominator of f approach 0, and the function is undefined at $x = 1$. To compute $\lim\limits_{x \to 1} f(x)$, we first factor:

➤ It is permissible to cancel the factor $x - 1$ in $\lim\limits_{x \to 1} \dfrac{(x - 1)(x - 3)}{(x - 1)(x + 1)}$ because x approaches 1 but is not equal to 1. Therefore, $x - 1 \neq 0$.

$$\begin{aligned} \lim_{x \to 1} f(x) &= \lim_{x \to 1} \frac{x^2 - 4x + 3}{x^2 - 1} \\ &= \lim_{x \to 1} \frac{(x - 1)(x - 3)}{(x - 1)(x + 1)} \quad \text{Factor.} \\ &= \lim_{x \to 1} \frac{(x - 3)}{(x + 1)} \quad \text{Cancel like factors, } x \neq 1. \\ &= \frac{1 - 3}{1 + 1} = -1. \quad \text{Substitute } x = 1. \end{aligned}$$

Therefore, $\lim\limits_{x \to 1} f(x) = -1$ (even though $f(1)$ is undefined). The line $x = 1$ is *not* a vertical asymptote of f.

b. In part (a) we showed that

$$f(x) = \frac{x^2 - 4x + 3}{x^2 - 1} = \frac{x - 3}{x + 1}, \quad \text{provided } x \neq 1.$$

We use this fact again. As x approaches -1 from the left, the one-sided limit is

$$\lim_{x \to -1^-} f(x) = \lim_{x \to -1^-} \overbrace{\frac{x - 3}{\underbrace{x + 1}_{\substack{\text{negative and} \\ \text{approaches } 0}}}}^{\text{approaches } -4} = \infty.$$

c. As x approaches -1 from the right, the one-sided limit is

$$\lim_{x \to -1^+} f(x) = \lim_{x \to -1^+} \overbrace{\frac{x - 3}{\underbrace{x + 1}_{\substack{\text{positive and} \\ \text{approaches } 0}}}}^{\text{approaches } -4} = -\infty.$$

The infinite limits $\lim\limits_{x \to -1^+} f(x) = -\infty$ and $\lim\limits_{x \to -1^-} f(x) = \infty$ each imply that the line $x = -1$ is a vertical asymptote of f. The graph of f generated by a graphing utility *may* appear as shown in Figure 2.28a. If so, two corrections must be made. A hole should appear in the graph at $(1, -1)$ because $\lim\limits_{x \to 1} f(x) = -1$, but $f(1)$ is undefined.

It is also a good idea to replace the solid vertical line with a dashed line to emphasize that the vertical asymptote is not a part of the graph of f (Figure 2.28b).

> Graphing utilities vary in how they display vertical asymptotes. The errors shown in Figure 2.28a do not occur on all graphing utilities.

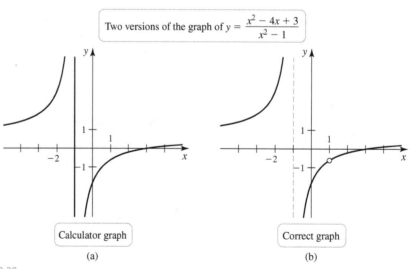

Two versions of the graph of $y = \dfrac{x^2 - 4x + 3}{x^2 - 1}$

Calculator graph
(a)

Correct graph
(b)

Figure 2.28

Related Exercises 29–34 ◀

QUICK CHECK 4 The line $x = 2$ is not a vertical asymptote of $y = \dfrac{(x - 1)(x - 2)}{x - 2}$. Why not? ◀

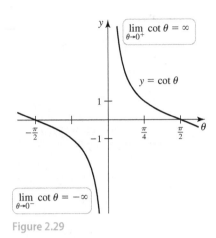

Figure 2.29

EXAMPLE 6 **Limits of trigonometric functions** Analyze the following limits.

a. $\lim_{\theta \to 0^+} \cot \theta$ **b.** $\lim_{\theta \to 0^-} \cot \theta$

SOLUTION

a. Recall that $\cot \theta = \cos \theta / \sin \theta$. Furthermore (Example 8, Section 2.3), $\lim_{\theta \to 0^+} \cos \theta = 1$ and $\sin \theta$ is positive and approaches 0 as $\theta \to 0^+$. Therefore, as $\theta \to 0^+$, $\cot \theta$ becomes arbitrarily large and positive, which means $\lim_{\theta \to 0^+} \cot \theta = \infty$. This limit is confirmed by the graph of $\cot \theta$ (Figure 2.29), which has a vertical asymptote at $\theta = 0$.

b. In this case, $\lim_{\theta \to 0^-} \cos \theta = 1$ and as $\theta \to 0^-$, $\sin \theta \to 0$ with $\sin \theta < 0$. Therefore, as $\theta \to 0^-$, $\cot \theta$ is negative and becomes arbitrarily large in magnitude. It follows that $\lim_{\theta \to 0^-} \cot \theta = -\infty$, as confirmed by the graph of $\cot \theta$.

Related Exercises 35–40 ◄

SECTION 2.4 EXERCISES

Review Questions

1. Use a graph to explain the meaning of $\lim_{x \to a^+} f(x) = -\infty$.

2. Use a graph to explain the meaning of $\lim_{x \to a} f(x) = \infty$.

3. What is a vertical asymptote?

4. Consider the function $F(x) = f(x)/g(x)$ with $g(a) = 0$. Does F necessarily have a vertical asymptote at $x = a$? Explain your reasoning.

5. Suppose $f(x) \to 100$ and $g(x) \to 0$, with $g(x) < 0$, as $x \to 2$. Determine $\lim_{x \to 2} \dfrac{f(x)}{g(x)}$.

6. Evaluate $\lim_{x \to 3^-} \dfrac{1}{x - 3}$ and $\lim_{x \to 3^+} \dfrac{1}{x - 3}$.

Basic Skills

7. **Analyzing infinite limits numerically** Compute the values of $f(x) = \dfrac{x + 1}{(x - 1)^2}$ in the following table and use them to determine $\lim_{x \to 1} f(x)$.

x	$\dfrac{x + 1}{(x - 1)^2}$	x	$\dfrac{x + 1}{(x - 1)^2}$
1.1		0.9	
1.01		0.99	
1.001		0.999	
1.0001		0.9999	

8. **Analyzing infinite limits graphically** Use the graph of $f(x) = \dfrac{x}{(x^2 - 2x - 3)^2}$ to determine $\lim_{x \to -1} f(x)$ and $\lim_{x \to 3} f(x)$.

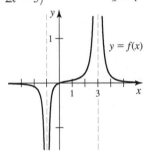

9. **Analyzing infinite limits graphically** The graph of f in the figure has vertical asymptotes at $x = 1$ and $x = 2$. Analyze the following limits.

a. $\lim_{x \to 1^-} f(x)$ **b.** $\lim_{x \to 1^+} f(x)$ **c.** $\lim_{x \to 1} f(x)$

d. $\lim_{x \to 2^-} f(x)$ **e.** $\lim_{x \to 2^+} f(x)$ **f.** $\lim_{x \to 2} f(x)$

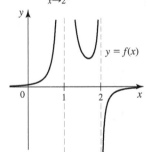

10. Analyzing infinite limits graphically The graph of g in the figure has vertical asymptotes at $x = 2$ and $x = 4$. Analyze the following limits.

a. $\lim\limits_{x \to 2^-} g(x)$ b. $\lim\limits_{x \to 2^+} g(x)$ c. $\lim\limits_{x \to 2} g(x)$

d. $\lim\limits_{x \to 4^-} g(x)$ e. $\lim\limits_{x \to 4^+} g(x)$ f. $\lim\limits_{x \to 4} g(x)$

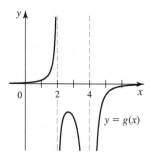

11. Analyzing infinite limits graphically The graph of h in the figure has vertical asymptotes at $x = -2$ and $x = 3$. Analyze the following limits.

a. $\lim\limits_{x \to -2^-} h(x)$ b. $\lim\limits_{x \to -2^+} h(x)$ c. $\lim\limits_{x \to -2} h(x)$

d. $\lim\limits_{x \to 3^-} h(x)$ e. $\lim\limits_{x \to 3^+} h(x)$ f. $\lim\limits_{x \to 3} h(x)$

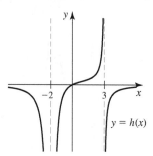

12. Analyzing infinite limits graphically The graph of p in the figure has vertical asymptotes at $x = -2$ and $x = 3$. Analyze the following limits.

a. $\lim\limits_{x \to -2^-} p(x)$ b. $\lim\limits_{x \to -2^+} p(x)$ c. $\lim\limits_{x \to -2} p(x)$

d. $\lim\limits_{x \to 3^-} p(x)$ e. $\lim\limits_{x \to 3^+} p(x)$ f. $\lim\limits_{x \to 3} p(x)$

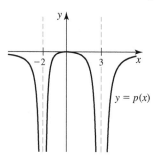

13. Analyzing infinite limits graphically Graph the function
$$f(x) = \frac{1}{x^2 - x}$$ using a graphing utility with the window $[-1, 2] \times [-10, 10]$. Use your graph to determine the following limits.

a. $\lim\limits_{x \to 0^-} f(x)$ b. $\lim\limits_{x \to 0^+} f(x)$ c. $\lim\limits_{x \to 1^-} f(x)$ d. $\lim\limits_{x \to 1^+} f(x)$

14. Analyzing infinite limits graphically Graph the function
$$f(x) = \frac{e^{-x}}{x(x + 2)^2}$$ using a graphing utility. (Experiment with your choice of a graphing window.) Use your graph to determine the following limits.

a. $\lim\limits_{x \to -2^+} f(x)$ b. $\lim\limits_{x \to -2^-} f(x)$ c. $\lim\limits_{x \to 0^-} f(x)$ d. $\lim\limits_{x \to 0^+} f(x)$

15. Sketching graphs Sketch a possible graph of a function f, together with vertical asymptotes, satisfying all the following conditions on $[0, 4]$.

$f(1) = 0, \qquad f(3)$ is undefined, $\qquad \lim\limits_{x \to 3} f(x) = 1,$

$\lim\limits_{x \to 0^+} f(x) = -\infty, \qquad \lim\limits_{x \to 2} f(x) = \infty, \qquad \lim\limits_{x \to 4^-} f(x) = \infty$

16. Sketching graphs Sketch a possible graph of a function g, together with vertical asymptotes, satisfying all the following conditions.

$g(2) = 1, \qquad g(5) = -1, \qquad \lim\limits_{x \to 4} g(x) = -\infty,$

$\lim\limits_{x \to 7^-} g(x) = \infty, \qquad \lim\limits_{x \to 7^+} g(x) = -\infty$

17–28. Determining limits analytically *Determine the following limits or state that they do not exist.*

17. a. $\lim\limits_{x \to 2^+} \dfrac{1}{x - 2}$ b. $\lim\limits_{x \to 2^-} \dfrac{1}{x - 2}$ c. $\lim\limits_{x \to 2} \dfrac{1}{x - 2}$

18. a. $\lim\limits_{x \to 3^+} \dfrac{2}{(x - 3)^3}$ b. $\lim\limits_{x \to 3^-} \dfrac{2}{(x - 3)^3}$ c. $\lim\limits_{x \to 3} \dfrac{2}{(x - 3)^3}$

19. a. $\lim\limits_{x \to 4^+} \dfrac{x - 5}{(x - 4)^2}$ b. $\lim\limits_{x \to 4^-} \dfrac{x - 5}{(x - 4)^2}$ c. $\lim\limits_{x \to 4} \dfrac{x - 5}{(x - 4)^2}$

20. a. $\lim\limits_{x \to 1^+} \dfrac{x - 2}{(x - 1)^3}$ b. $\lim\limits_{x \to 1^-} \dfrac{x - 2}{(x - 1)^3}$ c. $\lim\limits_{x \to 1} \dfrac{x - 2}{(x - 1)^3}$

21. a. $\lim\limits_{x \to 3^+} \dfrac{(x - 1)(x - 2)}{(x - 3)}$ b. $\lim\limits_{x \to 3^-} \dfrac{(x - 1)(x - 2)}{(x - 3)}$

c. $\lim\limits_{x \to 3} \dfrac{(x - 1)(x - 2)}{(x - 3)}$

22. a. $\lim\limits_{x \to -2^+} \dfrac{(x - 4)}{x(x + 2)}$ b. $\lim\limits_{x \to -2^-} \dfrac{(x - 4)}{x(x + 2)}$

c. $\lim\limits_{x \to -2} \dfrac{(x - 4)}{x(x + 2)}$

23. a. $\lim\limits_{x \to 2^+} \dfrac{x^2 - 4x + 3}{(x - 2)^2}$ b. $\lim\limits_{x \to 2^-} \dfrac{x^2 - 4x + 3}{(x - 2)^2}$

c. $\lim\limits_{x \to 2} \dfrac{x^2 - 4x + 3}{(x - 2)^2}$

24. a. $\lim\limits_{x \to -2^+} \dfrac{x^3 - 5x^2 + 6x}{x^4 - 4x^2}$ b. $\lim\limits_{x \to -2^-} \dfrac{x^3 - 5x^2 + 6x}{x^4 - 4x^2}$

c. $\lim\limits_{x \to -2} \dfrac{x^3 - 5x^2 + 6x}{x^4 - 4x^2}$ d. $\lim\limits_{x \to 2} \dfrac{x^3 - 5x^2 + 6x}{x^4 - 4x^2}$

25. $\lim\limits_{x\to 0} \dfrac{x^3 - 5x^2}{x^2}$

26. $\lim\limits_{t\to 5} \dfrac{4t^2 - 100}{t - 5}$

27. $\lim\limits_{x\to 1^+} \dfrac{x^2 - 5x + 6}{x - 1}$

28. $\lim\limits_{z\to 4} \dfrac{z - 5}{(z^2 - 10z + 24)^2}$

29. Location of vertical asymptotes Analyze the following limits and find the vertical asymptotes of $f(x) = \dfrac{x - 5}{x^2 - 25}$.

  a. $\lim\limits_{x\to 5} f(x)$ **b.** $\lim\limits_{x\to -5^-} f(x)$ **c.** $\lim\limits_{x\to -5^+} f(x)$

30. Location of vertical asymptotes Analyze the following limits and find the vertical asymptotes of $f(x) = \dfrac{x + 7}{x^4 - 49x^2}$.

  a. $\lim\limits_{x\to 7^-} f(x)$ **b.** $\lim\limits_{x\to 7^+} f(x)$ **c.** $\lim\limits_{x\to -7} f(x)$ **d.** $\lim\limits_{x\to 0} f(x)$

31–34. Finding vertical asymptotes *Find all vertical asymptotes $x = a$ of the following functions. For each value of a, determine* $\lim\limits_{x\to a^+} f(x)$, $\lim\limits_{x\to a^-} f(x)$, *and* $\lim\limits_{x\to a} f(x)$.

31. $f(x) = \dfrac{x^2 - 9x + 14}{x^2 - 5x + 6}$

32. $f(x) = \dfrac{\cos x}{x^2 + 2x}$

33. $f(x) = \dfrac{x + 1}{x^3 - 4x^2 + 4x}$

34. $f(x) = \dfrac{x^3 - 10x^2 + 16x}{x^2 - 8x}$

35–38. Trigonometric limits *Determine the following limits.*

35. $\lim\limits_{\theta\to 0^+} \csc \theta$

36. $\lim\limits_{x\to 0^-} \csc x$

37. $\lim\limits_{x\to 0^+} (-10 \cot x)$

38. $\lim\limits_{\theta\to \pi/2^+} \dfrac{1}{3} \tan \theta$

⊤ 39. Analyzing infinite limits graphically Graph the function $y = \tan x$ with the window $[-\pi, \pi] \times [-10, 10]$. Use the graph to analyze the following limits.

  a. $\lim\limits_{x\to \pi/2^+} \tan x$ **b.** $\lim\limits_{x\to \pi/2^-} \tan x$

  c. $\lim\limits_{x\to -\pi/2^+} \tan x$ **d.** $\lim\limits_{x\to -\pi/2^-} \tan x$

⊤ 40. Analyzing infinite limits graphically Graph the function $y = \sec x \tan x$ with the window $[-\pi, \pi] \times [-10, 10]$. Use the graph to analyze the following limits.

  a. $\lim\limits_{x\to \pi/2^+} \sec x \tan x$ **b.** $\lim\limits_{x\to \pi/2^-} \sec x \tan x$

  c. $\lim\limits_{x\to -\pi/2^+} \sec x \tan x$ **d.** $\lim\limits_{x\to -\pi/2^-} \sec x \tan x$

Further Explorations

41. Explain why or why not Determine whether the following statements are true and give an explanation or counterexample.

  a. The line $x = 1$ is a vertical asymptote of the function $f(x) = \dfrac{x^2 - 7x + 6}{x^2 - 1}$.

  b. The line $x = -1$ is a vertical asymptote of the function $f(x) = \dfrac{x^2 - 7x + 6}{x^2 - 1}$.

  c. If g has a vertical asymptote at $x = 1$ and $\lim\limits_{x\to 1^+} g(x) = \infty$, then $\lim\limits_{x\to 1^-} g(x) = \infty$.

42. Finding a function with vertical asymptotes Find polynomials p and q such that $f = p/q$ is undefined at 1 and 2, but f has a vertical asymptote only at 2. Sketch a graph of your function.

43. Finding a function with infinite limits Give a formula for a function f that satisfies $\lim\limits_{x\to 6^+} f(x) = \infty$ and $\lim\limits_{x\to 6^-} f(x) = -\infty$.

44. Matching Match functions a–f with graphs A–F in the figure without using a graphing utility.

  a. $f(x) = \dfrac{x}{x^2 + 1}$ **b.** $f(x) = \dfrac{x}{x^2 - 1}$

  c. $f(x) = \dfrac{1}{x^2 - 1}$ **d.** $f(x) = \dfrac{x}{(x - 1)^2}$

  e. $f(x) = \dfrac{1}{(x - 1)^2}$ **f.** $f(x) = \dfrac{x}{x + 1}$

A.

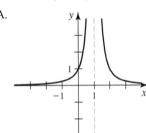

B.

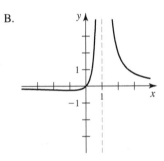

C.

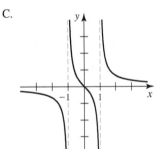

D.

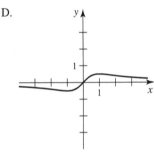

E.

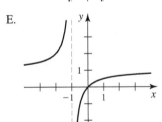

F.

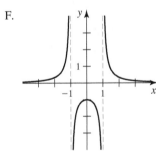

⊤ 45–52. Asymptotes *Use analytical methods and/or a graphing utility to identify the vertical asymptotes (if any) of the following functions.*

45. $f(x) = \dfrac{x^2 - 3x + 2}{x^{10} - x^9}$

46. $g(x) = 2 - \ln x^2$

47. $h(x) = \dfrac{e^x}{(x + 1)^3}$

48. $p(x) = \sec\left(\dfrac{\pi x}{2}\right)$, for $|x| < 2$

49. $g(\theta) = \tan \dfrac{\pi\theta}{10}$ **50.** $q(s) = \dfrac{\pi}{s - \sin s}$

51. $f(x) = \dfrac{1}{\sqrt{x}\, \sec x}$ **52.** $g(x) = e^{1/x}$

Additional Exercises

53. Limits with a parameter Let $f(x) = \dfrac{x^2 - 7x + 12}{x - a}$.

a. For what values of a, if any, does $\lim\limits_{x \to a^+} f(x)$ equal a finite number?

b. For what values of a, if any, does $\lim\limits_{x \to a^+} f(x) = \infty$?

c. For what values of a, if any, does $\lim\limits_{x \to a^+} f(x) = -\infty$?

54–55. Steep secant lines

a. Given the graph of f in the following figures, find the slope of the secant line that passes through $(0, 0)$ and $(h, f(h))$ in terms of h, for $h > 0$ and $h < 0$.

b. Analyze the limit of the slope of the secant line found in part (a) as $h \to 0^+$ and $h \to 0^-$. What does this tell you about the line tangent to the curve at $(0, 0)$?

54. $f(x) = x^{1/3}$ **55.** $f(x) = x^{2/3}$

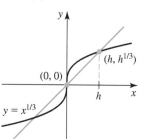

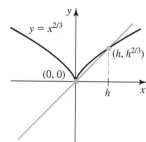

QUICK CHECK ANSWERS

1. Answers will vary, but all graphs should have a vertical asymptote at $x = 2$.   **2.** $-\infty$; ∞ **3.** As $x \to -4^+$, $x < 0$ and $(x + 4) > 0$, so $x(x + 4) \to 0$ through negative values.   **4.** $\lim\limits_{x \to 2} \dfrac{(x - 1)(x - 2)}{x - 2} = \lim\limits_{x \to 2} (x - 1) = 1$, which is not an infinite limit, so $x = 2$ is not a vertical asymptote. ◄

2.5 Limits at Infinity

Limits at infinity—as opposed to infinite limits—occur when the independent variable becomes large in magnitude. For this reason, limits at infinity determine what is called the *end behavior* of a function. An application of these limits is to determine whether a system (such as an ecosystem or a large oscillating structure) reaches a steady state as time increases.

Limits at Infinity and Horizontal Asymptotes

Figure 2.30 shows the graph of $y = \tan x$ (black curve) with vertical asymptotes at $x = \pm\dfrac{\pi}{2}$. Recall from Section 1.3 that on the interval $\left(-\dfrac{\pi}{2}, \dfrac{\pi}{2}\right)$, the graph of $\tan^{-1} x$ is obtained by reflecting the graph of $\tan x$ across the line $y = x$. Notice that when we do this reflection across the line $y = x$, the vertical asymptotes of $\tan x$ become the horizontal lines $y = \pm\dfrac{\pi}{2}$, which are associated with the graph of $y = \tan^{-1} x$ (blue curve). The

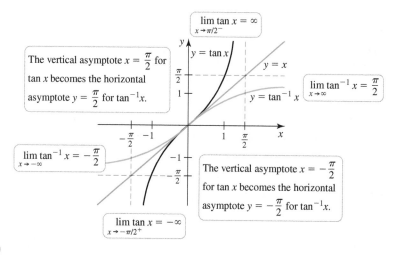

Figure 2.30

figure shows that as x becomes arbitrarily large (denoted $x \to \infty$), the graph of $\tan^{-1} x$ approaches the horizontal line $y = \dfrac{\pi}{2}$, and as x becomes arbitrarily large in magnitude and negative (denoted $x \to -\infty$), the graph of $\tan^{-1} x$ approaches the horizontal line $y = -\dfrac{\pi}{2}$. Observe that the limits for $\tan^{-1} x$ as $x \to \pm \infty$ correspond perfectly with the one-sided limits for $\tan x$ as $x \to \pm \dfrac{\pi}{2}$. We use limit notation to summarize the behavior of these two functions concisely:

$$\lim_{x \to \infty} \tan^{-1} x = \frac{\pi}{2} \quad \text{corresponds to} \quad \lim_{x \to \pi/2^-} \tan x = \infty \text{ and}$$

$$\lim_{x \to -\infty} \tan^{-1} x = -\frac{\pi}{2} \quad \text{corresponds to} \quad \lim_{x \to -\pi/2^+} \tan x = -\infty.$$

The one-sided limits for $\tan x$ are infinite limits from Section 2.4; they indicate vertical asymptotes. The limits we have written for $\tan^{-1} x$ are called *limits at infinity*, and the horizontal lines $y = \pm \dfrac{\pi}{2}$ approached by the graph of $\tan^{-1} x$ are *horizontal asymptotes*.

DEFINITION Limits at Infinity and Horizontal Asymptotes

If $f(x)$ becomes arbitrarily close to a finite number L for all sufficiently large and positive x, then we write

$$\lim_{x \to \infty} f(x) = L.$$

We say the limit of $f(x)$ as x approaches infinity is L. In this case, the line $y = L$ is a **horizontal asymptote** of f (Figure 2.31). The limit at negative infinity, $\lim\limits_{x \to -\infty} f(x) = M$, is defined analogously. When this limit exists, $y = M$ is a horizontal asymptote.

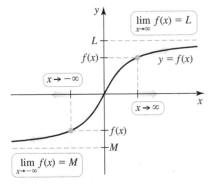

$\lim\limits_{x \to \infty} f(x) = L$

$y = f(x)$

$x \to -\infty$

$x \to \infty$

$f(x)$

$\lim\limits_{x \to -\infty} f(x) = M$

Figure 2.31

QUICK CHECK 1 Evaluate $x/(x+1)$ for $x = 10, 100,$ and 1000. What is $\lim\limits_{x \to \infty} \dfrac{x}{x+1}$? ◄

▶ The limit laws of Theorem 2.3 and the Squeeze Theorem apply if $x \to a$ is replaced with $x \to \infty$ or $x \to -\infty$.

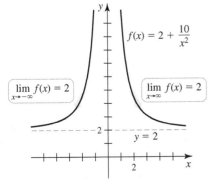

$f(x) = 2 + \dfrac{10}{x^2}$

$\lim\limits_{x \to -\infty} f(x) = 2$

$\lim\limits_{x \to \infty} f(x) = 2$

$y = 2$

Figure 2.32

EXAMPLE 1 Limits at infinity Evaluate the following limits.

a. $\displaystyle\lim_{x \to -\infty} \left(2 + \frac{10}{x^2} \right)$ **b.** $\displaystyle\lim_{x \to \infty} \left(5 + \frac{\sin x}{\sqrt{x}} \right)$

SOLUTION

a. As x becomes large and negative, x^2 becomes large and positive; in turn, $10/x^2$ approaches 0. By the limit laws of Theorem 2.3,

$$\lim_{x \to -\infty} \left(2 + \frac{10}{x^2} \right) = \underbrace{\lim_{x \to -\infty} 2}_{\text{equals 2}} + \underbrace{\lim_{x \to -\infty} \left(\frac{10}{x^2} \right)}_{\text{equals 0}} = 2 + 0 = 2.$$

Therefore, the graph of $y = 2 + 10/x^2$ approaches the horizontal asymptote $y = 2$ as $x \to -\infty$ (Figure 2.32). Notice that $\lim\limits_{x \to \infty} \left(2 + \dfrac{10}{x^2} \right)$ is also equal to 2, which implies that the graph has a single horizontal asymptote.

b. The numerator of $\sin x / \sqrt{x}$ is bounded between -1 and 1; therefore, for $x > 0$,

$$-\frac{1}{\sqrt{x}} \le \frac{\sin x}{\sqrt{x}} \le \frac{1}{\sqrt{x}}.$$

As $x \to \infty$, $\sqrt{x}$ becomes arbitrarily large, which means that

$$\lim_{x \to \infty} \frac{-1}{\sqrt{x}} = \lim_{x \to \infty} \frac{1}{\sqrt{x}} = 0.$$

It follows by the Squeeze Theorem (Theorem 2.5) that $\lim\limits_{x \to \infty} \dfrac{\sin x}{\sqrt{x}} = 0.$

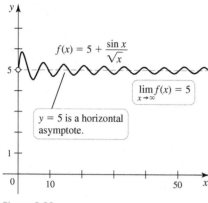

Figure 2.33

Using the limit laws of Theorem 2.3,

$$\lim_{x \to \infty} \left(5 + \frac{\sin x}{\sqrt{x}} \right) = \underbrace{\lim_{x \to \infty} 5}_{\text{equals 5}} + \underbrace{\lim_{x \to \infty} \frac{\sin x}{\sqrt{x}}}_{\text{equals 0}} = 5.$$

The graph of $y = 5 + \dfrac{\sin x}{\sqrt{x}}$ approaches the horizontal asymptote $y = 5$ as x becomes large (Figure 2.33). Note that the curve intersects its asymptote infinitely many times.

Related Exercises 9–14 ◄

Infinite Limits at Infinity

It is possible for a limit to be *both* an infinite limit and a limit at infinity. This type of limit occurs if $f(x)$ becomes arbitrarily large in magnitude as x becomes arbitrarily large in magnitude. Such a limit is called an *infinite limit at infinity* and is illustrated by the function $f(x) = x^3$ (Figure 2.34).

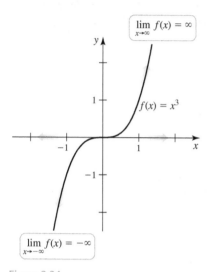

Figure 2.34

> **DEFINITION Infinite Limits at Infinity**
>
> If $f(x)$ becomes arbitrarily large as x becomes arbitrarily large, then we write
>
> $$\lim_{x \to \infty} f(x) = \infty.$$
>
> The limits $\lim_{x \to \infty} f(x) = -\infty$, $\lim_{x \to -\infty} f(x) = \infty$, and $\lim_{x \to -\infty} f(x) = -\infty$ are defined similarly.

Infinite limits at infinity tell us about the behavior of polynomials for large-magnitude values of x. First, consider power functions $f(x) = x^n$, where n is a positive integer. Figure 2.35 shows that when n is even, $\lim_{x \to \pm\infty} x^n = \infty$, and when n is odd, $\lim_{x \to \infty} x^n = \infty$ and $\lim_{x \to -\infty} x^n = -\infty$.

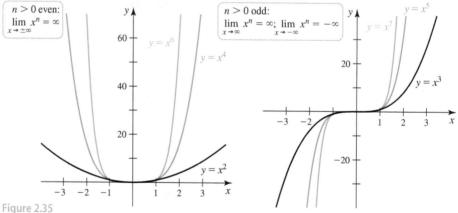

Figure 2.35

It follows that reciprocals of power functions $f(x) = 1/x^n = x^{-n}$, where n is a positive integer, behave as follows:

$$\lim_{x \to \infty} \frac{1}{x^n} = \lim_{x \to \infty} x^{-n} = 0 \quad \text{and} \quad \lim_{x \to -\infty} \frac{1}{x^n} = \lim_{x \to -\infty} x^{-n} = 0.$$

QUICK CHECK 2 Describe the behavior of $p(x) = -3x^3$ as $x \to \infty$ and as $x \to -\infty$. ◄

From here, it is a short step to finding the behavior of any polynomial as $x \to \pm\infty$. Let $p(x) = a_n x^n + a_{n-1} x^{n-1} + \cdots + a_2 x^2 + a_1 x + a_0$. We now write p in the equivalent form

$$p(x) = x^n \left(a_n + \underbrace{\frac{a_{n-1}}{x}}_{\to 0} + \underbrace{\frac{a_{n-2}}{x^2}}_{\to 0} + \cdots + \underbrace{\frac{a_0}{x^n}}_{\to 0} \right).$$

Notice that as x becomes large in magnitude, all the terms in p except the first term approach zero. Therefore, as $x \to \pm\infty$, we see that $p(x) \approx a_n x^n$. This means that as $x \to \pm\infty$, the behavior of p is determined by the term $a_n x^n$ with the highest power of x.

> **THEOREM 2.6   Limits at Infinity of Powers and Polynomials**
> Let n be a positive integer and let p be the polynomial
> $p(x) = a_n x^n + a_{n-1} x^{n-1} + \cdots + a_2 x^2 + a_1 x + a_0$, where $a_n \neq 0$.
>
> 1. $\displaystyle \lim_{x \to \pm\infty} x^n = \infty$ when n is even.
>
> 2. $\displaystyle \lim_{x \to \infty} x^n = \infty$ and $\displaystyle \lim_{x \to -\infty} x^n = -\infty$ when n is odd.
>
> 3. $\displaystyle \lim_{x \to \pm\infty} \frac{1}{x^n} = \lim_{x \to \pm\infty} x^{-n} = 0.$
>
> 4. $\displaystyle \lim_{x \to \pm\infty} p(x) = \lim_{x \to \pm\infty} a_n x^n = \pm\infty$, depending on the degree of the polynomial and the sign of the leading coefficient a_n.

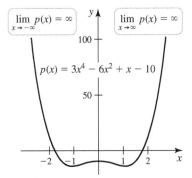

$\displaystyle \lim_{x \to -\infty} p(x) = \infty$ $\displaystyle \lim_{x \to \infty} p(x) = \infty$

$p(x) = 3x^4 - 6x^2 + x - 10$

Figure 2.36

EXAMPLE 2   Limits at infinity Evaluate the limits as $x \to \pm\infty$ of the following functions.

a. $p(x) = 3x^4 - 6x^2 + x - 10$ **b.** $q(x) = -2x^3 + 3x^2 - 12$

SOLUTION

a. We use the fact that the limit is determined by the behavior of the leading term:

$$\lim_{x \to \infty} (3x^4 - 6x^2 + x - 10) = \lim_{x \to \infty} 3\underset{\to \, \infty}{\underline{x^4}} = \infty.$$

Similarly,

$$\lim_{x \to -\infty} (3x^4 - 6x^2 + x - 10) = \lim_{x \to -\infty} 3\underset{\to \, \infty}{\underline{x^4}} = \infty.$$

Figure 2.36 illustrates these limits.

b. Noting that the leading coefficient is negative, we have

$$\lim_{x \to \infty} (-2x^3 + 3x^2 - 12) = \lim_{x \to \infty} (-2\underset{\to \, \infty}{\underline{x^3}}) = -\infty$$

$$\lim_{x \to -\infty} (-2x^3 + 3x^2 - 12) = \lim_{x \to -\infty} (-2\underset{\to \, -\infty}{\underline{x^3}}) = \infty.$$

The graph of q (Figure 2.37) confirms these results.

Related Exercises 15–24 ◀

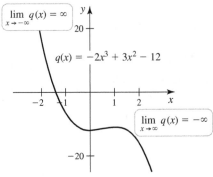

$\displaystyle \lim_{x \to -\infty} q(x) = \infty$

$q(x) = -2x^3 + 3x^2 - 12$

$\displaystyle \lim_{x \to \infty} q(x) = -\infty$

Figure 2.37

End Behavior

The behavior of polynomials as $x \to \pm\infty$ is an example of what is often called *end behavior*. Having treated polynomials, we now turn to the end behavior of rational, algebraic, and transcendental functions.

EXAMPLE 3   End behavior of rational functions Determine the end behavior for the following rational functions.

a. $f(x) = \dfrac{3x + 2}{x^2 - 1}$ **b.** $g(x) = \dfrac{40x^4 + 4x^2 - 1}{10x^4 + 8x^2 + 1}$ **c.** $h(x) = \dfrac{x^3 - 2x + 1}{2x + 4}$

SOLUTION

a. An effective approach for determining limits of rational functions at infinity is to divide both the numerator and denominator by x^n, where n is the degree of the

▶ Recall that the *degree* of a polynomial is the highest power of x that appears.

polynomial in the denominator. This strategy forces the terms corresponding to lower powers of x to approach 0 in the limit. In this case, we divide by x^2:

$$\lim_{x\to\infty}\frac{3x+2}{x^2-1}=\lim_{x\to\infty}\frac{\dfrac{3x+2}{x^2}}{\dfrac{x^2-1}{x^2}}=\lim_{x\to\infty}\frac{\overbrace{\dfrac{3}{x}+\dfrac{2}{x^2}}^{\text{approaches 0}}}{\underbrace{1-\dfrac{1}{x^2}}_{\text{approaches 0}}}=\frac{0}{1}=0.$$

A similar calculation gives $\lim_{x\to-\infty}\dfrac{3x+2}{x^2-1}=0$; therefore, the graph of f has the horizontal asymptote $y=0$. You should confirm that the zeros of the denominator are -1 and 1, which correspond to vertical asymptotes (Figure 2.38). In this example, the degree of the polynomial in the numerator is *less than* the degree of the polynomial in the denominator.

b. Again we divide both the numerator and denominator by the largest power appearing in the denominator, which is x^4:

$$\lim_{x\to\infty}\frac{40x^4+4x^2-1}{10x^4+8x^2+1}=\lim_{x\to\infty}\frac{\dfrac{40x^4}{x^4}+\dfrac{4x^2}{x^4}-\dfrac{1}{x^4}}{\dfrac{10x^4}{x^4}+\dfrac{8x^2}{x^4}+\dfrac{1}{x^4}}\qquad\text{Divide the numerator and denominator by } x^4.$$

$$=\lim_{x\to\infty}\frac{40+\overbrace{\dfrac{4}{x^2}}^{\text{approaches 0}}-\overbrace{\dfrac{1}{x^4}}^{\text{approaches 0}}}{10+\underbrace{\dfrac{8}{x^2}}_{\text{approaches 0}}+\underbrace{\dfrac{1}{x^4}}_{\text{approaches 0}}}\qquad\text{Simplify.}$$

$$=\frac{40+0+0}{10+0+0}=4.\qquad\text{Evaluate limits.}$$

Using the same steps (dividing each term by x^4), it can be shown that $\lim_{x\to-\infty}\dfrac{40x^4+4x^2-1}{10x^4+8x^2+1}=4$. This function has the horizontal asymptote $y=4$ (Figure 2.39). Notice that the degree of the polynomial in the numerator *equals* the degree of the polynomial in the denominator.

c. We divide the numerator and denominator by the largest power of x appearing in the denominator, which is x, and then take the limit:

$$\lim_{x\to\infty}\frac{x^3-2x+1}{2x+4}=\lim_{x\to\infty}\frac{\dfrac{x^3}{x}-\dfrac{2x}{x}+\dfrac{1}{x}}{\dfrac{2x}{x}+\dfrac{4}{x}}\qquad\text{Divide the numerator and denominator by } x.$$

$$=\lim_{x\to\infty}\frac{\overbrace{x^2}^{\text{arbitrarily large}}-\overbrace{2}^{\text{constant}}+\overbrace{\dfrac{1}{x}}^{\text{approaches 0}}}{\underbrace{2}_{\text{constant}}+\underbrace{\dfrac{4}{x}}_{\text{approaches 0}}}\qquad\text{Simplify.}$$

$$=\infty.\qquad\text{Take limits.}$$

As $x\to\infty$, all the terms in this function either approach zero or are constant—except the x^2-term in the numerator, which becomes arbitrarily large. Therefore, the limit of the function does not exist. Using a similar analysis, we find that $\lim_{x\to-\infty}\dfrac{x^3-2x+1}{2x+4}=\infty$. These limits are not finite, so the graph of the function has no horizontal asymptote (Figure 2.40).

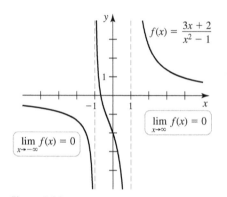

$f(x)=\dfrac{3x+2}{x^2-1}$

$\lim_{x\to\infty} f(x)=0$

$\lim_{x\to-\infty} f(x)=0$

Figure 2.38

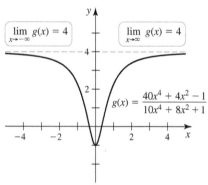

$\lim_{x\to-\infty} g(x)=4$

$\lim_{x\to\infty} g(x)=4$

$g(x)=\dfrac{40x^4+4x^2-1}{10x^4+8x^2+1}$

Figure 2.39

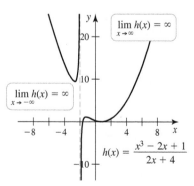

$\lim_{x\to\infty} h(x)=\infty$

$\lim_{x\to-\infty} h(x)=\infty$

$h(x)=\dfrac{x^3-2x+1}{2x+4}$

Figure 2.40

There is, however, a vertical asymptote due to the fact that $x = -2$ is a zero of the denominator. In this case, the degree of the polynomial in the numerator is *greater than* the degree of the polynomial in the denominator.

Related Exercises 25–34 ◄

A special case of end behavior arises with rational functions. As shown in the next example, if the graph of a function f approaches a line (with finite and nonzero slope) as $x \to \pm\infty$, then that line is a **slant asymptote**, or **oblique asymptote**, of f.

EXAMPLE 4   Slant asymptotes Determine the end behavior of the function

$$f(x) = \frac{2x^2 + 6x - 2}{x + 1}.$$

SOLUTION We first divide the numerator and denominator by the largest power of x appearing in the denominator, which is x:

$$\lim_{x \to \infty} \frac{2x^2 + 6x - 2}{x + 1} = \lim_{x \to \infty} \frac{\dfrac{2x^2}{x} + \dfrac{6x}{x} - \dfrac{2}{x}}{\dfrac{x}{x} + \dfrac{1}{x}}$$

Divide the numerator and denominator by x.

$$= \lim_{x \to \infty} \frac{\overbrace{2x}^{\text{arbitrarily large}} + \overbrace{6}^{\text{constant}} - \overbrace{\dfrac{2}{x}}^{\text{approaches 0}}}{\underbrace{1}_{\text{constant}} + \underbrace{\dfrac{1}{x}}_{\text{approaches 0}}}$$

Simplify.

$$= \infty.$$

Take limits.

A similar analysis shows that $\displaystyle\lim_{x \to -\infty} \frac{2x^2 + 6x - 2}{x + 1} = -\infty$. Because these limits are not finite, f has no horizontal asymptote.

However, there is more to be learned about the end behavior of this function. Using long division, the function f is written

$$f(x) = \frac{2x^2 + 6x - 2}{x + 1} = \underbrace{2x + 4}_{\ell(x)} - \underbrace{\frac{6}{x + 1}}_{\substack{\text{approaches 0 as} \\ x \to \infty}}.$$

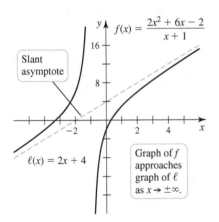

$f(x) = \dfrac{2x^2 + 6x - 2}{x + 1}$

Slant asymptote

$\ell(x) = 2x + 4$

Graph of f approaches graph of ℓ as $x \to \pm\infty$.

Figure 2.41

▶ More generally, a line $y = \ell(x)$ (with finite and nonzero slope) is a slant asymptote of a function f if $\displaystyle\lim_{x \to \infty} (f(x) - \ell(x)) = 0$ or $\displaystyle\lim_{x \to -\infty} (f(x) - \ell(x)) = 0$.

As $x \to \infty$, the term $6/(x + 1)$ approaches 0, and we see that the function f behaves like the linear function $\ell(x) = 2x + 4$. For this reason, the graphs of f and ℓ approach each other as $x \to \infty$ (Figure 2.41). A similar argument shows that the graphs of f and ℓ also approach each other as $x \to -\infty$. The line described by ℓ is a slant asymptote; it occurs with rational functions only when the degree of the polynomial in the numerator exceeds the degree of the polynomial in the denominator by exactly 1.

Related Exercises 35–40 ◄

The conclusions reached in Examples 3 and 4 can be generalized for all rational functions. These results are summarized in Theorem 2.7 (Exercise 80).

QUICK CHECK 3 Use Theorem 2.7 to find the vertical and horizontal asymptotes of $y = \dfrac{10x}{3x - 1}$. ◄

THEOREM 2.7   End Behavior and Asymptotes of Rational Functions

Suppose $f(x) = \dfrac{p(x)}{q(x)}$ is a rational function, where

$$p(x) = a_m x^m + a_{m-1} x^{m-1} + \cdots + a_2 x^2 + a_1 x + a_0 \quad \text{and}$$
$$q(x) = b_n x^n + b_{n-1} x^{n-1} + \cdots + b_2 x^2 + b_1 x + b_0,$$

with $a_m \neq 0$ and $b_n \neq 0$.

a. Degree of numerator less than degree of denominator If $m < n$, then $\displaystyle\lim_{x \to \pm\infty} f(x) = 0$ and $y = 0$ is a horizontal asymptote of f.

b. Degree of numerator equals degree of denominator If $m = n$, then $\lim\limits_{x \to \pm\infty} f(x) = a_m/b_n$ and $y = a_m/b_n$ is a horizontal asymptote of f.

c. Degree of numerator greater than degree of denominator If $m > n$, then $\lim\limits_{x \to \pm\infty} f(x) = \infty$ or $-\infty$ and f has no horizontal asymptote.

d. Slant asymptote If $m = n + 1$, then $\lim\limits_{x \to \pm\infty} f(x) = \infty$ or $-\infty$, f has no horizontal asymptote, but f has a slant asymptote.

e. Vertical asymptotes Assuming that f is in reduced form (p and q share no common factors), vertical asymptotes occur at the zeros of q.

Although it isn't stated explicitly, Theorem 2.7 implies that a rational function can have at most one horizontal asymptote, and whenever there is a horizontal asymptote, $\lim\limits_{x \to \infty} \dfrac{p(x)}{q(x)} = \lim\limits_{x \to -\infty} \dfrac{p(x)}{q(x)}$. The same cannot be said of other functions, as the next examples show.

EXAMPLE 5   End behavior of an algebraic function Determine the end behavior of
$$f(x) = \frac{10x^3 - 3x^2 + 8}{\sqrt{25x^6 + x^4 + 2}}.$$

SOLUTION The square root in the denominator forces us to revise the strategy used with rational functions. First, consider the limit as $x \to \infty$. The highest power of the polynomial in the denominator is 6. However, the polynomial is under a square root, so effectively, the term with the highest power in the denominator is $\sqrt{x^6} = x^3$. Dividing the numerator and denominator by x^3, for $x > 0$, the limit becomes

$$\lim_{x \to \infty} \frac{10x^3 - 3x^2 + 8}{\sqrt{25x^6 + x^4 + 2}} = \lim_{x \to \infty} \frac{\dfrac{10x^3}{x^3} - \dfrac{3x^2}{x^3} + \dfrac{8}{x^3}}{\sqrt{\dfrac{25x^6}{x^6} + \dfrac{x^4}{x^6} + \dfrac{2}{x^6}}} \qquad \text{Divide by } \sqrt{x^6} = x^3.$$

$$= \lim_{x \to \infty} \frac{10 - \overbrace{\dfrac{3}{x}}^{\text{approaches } 0} + \overbrace{\dfrac{8}{x^3}}^{\text{approaches } 0}}{\sqrt{25 + \underbrace{\dfrac{1}{x^2}}_{\text{approaches } 0} + \underbrace{\dfrac{2}{x^6}}_{\text{approaches } 0}}} \qquad \text{Simplify.}$$

$$= \frac{10}{\sqrt{25}} = 2. \qquad \text{Evaluate limits.}$$

▶ Recall that
$$\sqrt{x^2} = |x| = \begin{cases} x & \text{if } x \ge 0 \\ -x & \text{if } x < 0. \end{cases}$$

Therefore,
$$\sqrt{x^6} = |x^3| = \begin{cases} x^3 & \text{if } x \ge 0 \\ -x^3 & \text{if } x < 0. \end{cases}$$

Because x is negative as $x \to -\infty$, we have $\sqrt{x^6} = -x^3$.

As $x \to -\infty$, x^3 is negative, so we divide the numerator and denominator by $\sqrt{x^6} = -x^3$ (which is positive):

$$\lim_{x \to -\infty} \frac{10x^3 - 3x^2 + 8}{\sqrt{25x^6 + x^4 + 2}} = \lim_{x \to -\infty} \frac{\dfrac{10x^3}{-x^3} - \dfrac{3x^2}{-x^3} + \dfrac{8}{-x^3}}{\sqrt{\dfrac{25x^6}{x^6} + \dfrac{x^4}{x^6} + \dfrac{2}{x^6}}} \qquad \text{Divide by } \sqrt{x^6} = -x^3 > 0.$$

$$= \lim_{x \to -\infty} \frac{-10 + \overbrace{\dfrac{3}{x}}^{\text{approaches } 0} - \overbrace{\dfrac{8}{x^3}}^{\text{approaches } 0}}{\sqrt{25 + \underbrace{\dfrac{1}{x^2}}_{\text{approaches } 0} + \underbrace{\dfrac{2}{x^6}}_{\text{approaches } 0}}} \qquad \text{Simplify.}$$

$$= -\frac{10}{\sqrt{25}} = -2. \qquad \text{Evaluate limits.}$$

The limits reveal two asymptotes, $y = 2$ and $y = -2$. Observe that the graph crosses both horizontal asymptotes (Figure 2.42).

Related Exercises 41–44 ◄

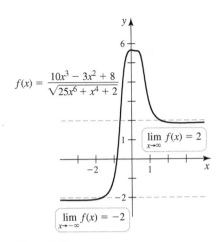

$$f(x) = \frac{10x^3 - 3x^2 + 8}{\sqrt{25x^6 + x^4 + 2}}$$

$$\lim_{x \to \infty} f(x) = 2$$

$$\lim_{x \to -\infty} f(x) = -2$$

Figure 2.42

EXAMPLE 6 **End behavior of transcendental functions** Determine the end behavior of the following transcendental functions.

a. $f(x) = e^x$ and $g(x) = e^{-x}$ **b.** $h(x) = \ln x$ **c.** $f(x) = \cos x$

SOLUTION

a. The graph of $f(x) = e^x$ (Figure 2.43) makes it clear that as $x \to \infty$, e^x increases without bound. All exponential functions b^x with $b > 1$ behave this way, because raising a number greater than 1 to ever-larger powers produces numbers that increase without bound. The figure also suggests that as $x \to -\infty$, the graph of e^x approaches the horizontal asymptote $y = 0$. This claim is confirmed analytically by recognizing that

$$\lim_{x \to -\infty} e^x = \lim_{x \to \infty} e^{-x} = \lim_{x \to \infty} \frac{1}{e^x} = 0.$$

Therefore, $\lim_{x \to \infty} e^x = \infty$ and $\lim_{x \to -\infty} e^x = 0$. Because $e^{-x} = 1/e^x$, it follows that

$$\lim_{x \to \infty} e^{-x} = 0 \text{ and } \lim_{x \to -\infty} e^{-x} = \infty.$$

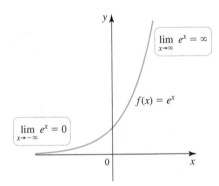

$$\lim_{x \to \infty} e^x = \infty$$

$$f(x) = e^x$$

$$\lim_{x \to -\infty} e^x = 0$$

Figure 2.43

b. The domain of $\ln x$ is $\{x : x > 0\}$, so we evaluate $\lim_{x \to 0^+} \ln x$ and $\lim_{x \to \infty} \ln x$ to determine end behavior. For the first limit, recall that $\ln x$ is the inverse of e^x (Figure 2.44), and the graph of $\ln x$ is a reflection of the graph of e^x across the line $y = x$. The horizontal asymptote ($y = 0$) of e^x is also reflected across $y = x$, becoming a vertical asymptote ($x = 0$) for $\ln x$. These observations imply that $\lim_{x \to 0^+} \ln x = -\infty$.

It is not obvious whether the graph of $\ln x$ approaches a horizontal asymptote or whether the function grows without bound as $x \to \infty$. Furthermore, the numerical evidence (Table 2.9) is inconclusive because $\ln x$ increases very slowly. The inverse relation between e^x and $\ln x$ is again useful. The fact that the *domain* of e^x is $(-\infty, \infty)$ implies that the *range* of $\ln x$ is also $(-\infty, \infty)$. Therefore, the values of $\ln x$ lie in the interval $(-\infty, \infty)$, and it follows that $\lim_{x \to \infty} \ln x = \infty$.

c. The cosine function oscillates between -1 and 1 as $x \to \infty$ (Figure 2.45). Therefore, $\lim_{x \to \infty} \cos x$ does not exist. For the same reason, $\lim_{x \to -\infty} \cos x$ does not exist.

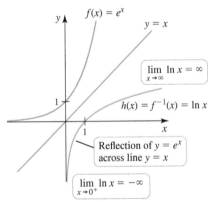

$$f(x) = e^x$$
$$y = x$$

$$\lim_{x \to \infty} \ln x = \infty$$

$$h(x) = f^{-1}(x) = \ln x$$

Reflection of $y = e^x$ across line $y = x$

$$\lim_{x \to 0^+} \ln x = -\infty$$

Figure 2.44

Table 2.9

x	$\ln x$
10	2.303
10^5	11.513
10^{10}	23.026
10^{50}	115.129
10^{99}	227.956
↓	↓
∞	???

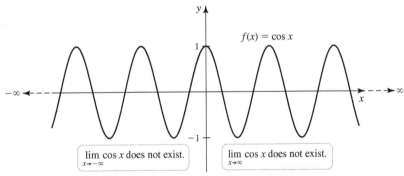

$$f(x) = \cos x$$

$\lim_{x \to -\infty} \cos x$ does not exist. $\lim_{x \to \infty} \cos x$ does not exist.

Figure 2.45

Related Exercises 45–50 ◄

The end behavior of exponential and logarithmic functions is important. We summarize these results in the following theorem.

THEOREM 2.8   **End Behavior of e^x, e^{-x}, and $\ln x$**
The end behavior for e^x and e^{-x} on $(-\infty, \infty)$ and $\ln x$ on $(0, \infty)$ is given by the following limits:

$$\lim_{x \to \infty} e^x = \infty \qquad \text{and} \qquad \lim_{x \to -\infty} e^x = 0,$$

$$\lim_{x \to \infty} e^{-x} = 0 \qquad \text{and} \qquad \lim_{x \to -\infty} e^{-x} = \infty,$$

$$\lim_{x \to 0^+} \ln x = -\infty \qquad \text{and} \qquad \lim_{x \to \infty} \ln x = \infty.$$

QUICK CHECK 4 How do the functions e^{10x} and e^{-10x} behave as $x \to \infty$ and as $x \to -\infty$? ◄

SECTION 2.5 EXERCISES

Review Questions

1. Explain the meaning of $\lim_{x \to -\infty} f(x) = 10$.

2. What is a horizontal asymptote?

3. Determine $\lim_{x \to \infty} \dfrac{f(x)}{g(x)}$ if $f(x) \to 100,000$ and $g(x) \to \infty$ as $x \to \infty$.

4. Describe the end behavior of $g(x) = e^{-2x}$.

5. Describe the end behavior of $f(x) = -2x^3$.

6. The text describes four cases that arise when examining the end behavior of a rational function $f(x) = p(x)/q(x)$. Describe the end behavior associated with each case.

7. Evaluate $\lim_{x \to \infty} e^x$, $\lim_{x \to -\infty} e^x$, and $\lim_{x \to \infty} e^{-x}$.

8. Use a sketch to find the end behavior of $f(x) = \ln x$.

Basic Skills

9–14. Limits at infinity *Evaluate the following limits.*

9. $\displaystyle\lim_{x \to \infty} \left(3 + \dfrac{10}{x^2}\right)$

10. $\displaystyle\lim_{x \to \infty} \left(5 + \dfrac{1}{x} + \dfrac{10}{x^2}\right)$

11. $\displaystyle\lim_{\theta \to \infty} \dfrac{\cos \theta}{\theta^2}$

12. $\displaystyle\lim_{x \to \infty} \dfrac{3 + 2x + 4x^2}{x^2}$

13. $\displaystyle\lim_{x \to \infty} \dfrac{\cos x^5}{\sqrt{x}}$

14. $\displaystyle\lim_{x \to -\infty} \left(5 + \dfrac{100}{x} + \dfrac{\sin^4 x^3}{x^2}\right)$

15–24. Infinite limits at infinity *Determine the following limits.*

15. $\displaystyle\lim_{x \to \infty} x^{12}$

16. $\displaystyle\lim_{x \to -\infty} 3\,x^{11}$

17. $\displaystyle\lim_{x \to \infty} x^{-6}$

18. $\displaystyle\lim_{x \to -\infty} x^{-11}$

19. $\displaystyle\lim_{x \to \infty} (3x^{12} - 9x^7)$

20. $\displaystyle\lim_{x \to -\infty} (3x^7 + x^2)$

21. $\displaystyle\lim_{x \to -\infty} (-3x^{16} + 2)$

22. $\displaystyle\lim_{x \to -\infty} 2x^{-8}$

23. $\displaystyle\lim_{x \to \infty} (-12x^{-5})$

24. $\displaystyle\lim_{x \to -\infty} (2x^{-8} + 4x^3)$

25–34. Rational functions *Determine $\lim_{x \to \infty} f(x)$ and $\lim_{x \to -\infty} f(x)$ for the following rational functions. Then give the horizontal asymptote of f (if any).*

25. $f(x) = \dfrac{4x}{20x + 1}$

26. $f(x) = \dfrac{3x^2 - 7}{x^2 + 5x}$

27. $f(x) = \dfrac{6x^2 - 9x + 8}{3x^2 + 2}$

28. $f(x) = \dfrac{4x^2 - 7}{8x^2 + 5x + 2}$

29. $f(x) = \dfrac{3x^3 - 7}{x^4 + 5x^2}$

30. $f(x) = \dfrac{x^4 + 7}{x^5 + x^2 - x}$

31. $f(x) = \dfrac{2x + 1}{3x^4 - 2}$

32. $f(x) = \dfrac{12x^8 - 3}{3x^8 - 2x^7}$

33. $f(x) = \dfrac{40x^5 + x^2}{16x^4 - 2x}$

34. $f(x) = \dfrac{-x^3 + 1}{2x + 8}$

35–40. Slant (oblique) asymptotes *Complete the following steps for the given functions.*

a. *Use polynomial long division to find the slant asymptote of f.*

b. *Find the vertical asymptotes of f.*

c. *Graph f and all its asymptotes with a graphing utility. Then sketch a graph of the function by hand, correcting any errors appearing in the computer-generated graph.*

35. $f(x) = \dfrac{x^2 - 3}{x + 6}$

36. $f(x) = \dfrac{x^2 - 1}{x + 2}$

37. $f(x) = \dfrac{x^2 - 2x + 5}{3x - 2}$

38. $f(x) = \dfrac{3x^2 - 2x + 7}{2x - 5}$

39. $f(x) = \dfrac{4x^3 + 4x^2 + 7x + 4}{1 + x^2}$

40. $f(x) = \dfrac{3x^2 - 2x + 5}{3x + 4}$

41–44. Algebraic functions *Determine $\lim_{x \to \infty} f(x)$ and $\lim_{x \to -\infty} f(x)$ for the following functions. Then give the horizontal asymptote(s) of f (if any).*

41. $f(x) = \dfrac{4x^3 + 1}{2x^3 + \sqrt{16x^6 + 1}}$

42. $f(x) = \dfrac{\sqrt{x^2 + 1}}{2x + 1}$

43. $f(x) = \dfrac{\sqrt[3]{x^6 + 8}}{4x^2 + \sqrt{3x^4 + 1}}$

44. $f(x) = 4x(3x - \sqrt{9x^2 + 1})$

45–50. Transcendental functions *Determine the end behavior of the following transcendental functions by analyzing appropriate limits. Then provide a simple sketch of the associated graph, showing asymptotes if they exist.*

45. $f(x) = -3e^{-x}$

46. $f(x) = 2^x$

47. $f(x) = 1 - \ln x$

48. $f(x) = |\ln x|$

49. $f(x) = \sin x$

50. $f(x) = \dfrac{50}{e^{2x}}$

Further Explorations

51. Explain why or why not Determine whether the following statements are true and give an explanation or counterexample.

   a. The graph of a function never crosses one of its horizontal asymptotes.

   b. A rational function f has both $\lim\limits_{x\to\infty} f(x) = L$ (where L is finite) and $\lim\limits_{x\to-\infty} f(x) = \infty$.

   c. The graph of a function can have at most two horizontal asymptotes.

52–61. Horizontal and vertical asymptotes

a. Analyze $\lim\limits_{x\to\infty} f(x)$ *and* $\lim\limits_{x\to-\infty} f(x)$, *and then identify any horizontal asymptotes.*

b. Find the vertical asymptotes. For each vertical asymptote $x = a$, analyze $\lim\limits_{x\to a^-} f(x)$ *and* $\lim\limits_{x\to a^+} f(x)$.

52. $f(x) = \dfrac{x^2 - 4x + 3}{x - 1}$ **53.** $f(x) = \dfrac{2x^3 + 10x^2 + 12x}{x^3 + 2x^2}$

54. $f(x) = \dfrac{\sqrt{16x^4 + 64x^2} + x^2}{2x^2 - 4}$

55. $f(x) = \dfrac{3x^4 + 3x^3 - 36x^2}{x^4 - 25x^2 + 144}$

56. $f(x) = 16x^2\left(4x^2 - \sqrt{16x^4 + 1}\right)$

57. $f(x) = \dfrac{x^2 - 9}{x(x - 3)}$

58. $f(x) = \dfrac{x - 1}{x^{2/3} - 1}$

59. $f(x) = \dfrac{\sqrt{x^2 + 2x + 6} - 3}{x - 1}$

60. $f(x) = \dfrac{|1 - x^2|}{x(x + 1)}$

61. $f(x) = \sqrt{|x|} - \sqrt{|x - 1|}$

62–65. End behavior for transcendental functions

62. The central branch of $f(x) = \tan x$ is shown in the figure.

   a. Analyze $\lim\limits_{x\to\pi/2^-} \tan x$ and $\lim\limits_{x\to-\pi/2^+} \tan x$. Are these infinite limits or limits at infinity?

   b. Sketch a graph of $g(x) = \tan^{-1}x$ by reflecting the graph of f over the line $y = x$ and use it to evaluate $\lim\limits_{x\to\infty} \tan^{-1}x$ and $\lim\limits_{x\to-\infty} \tan^{-1} x$.

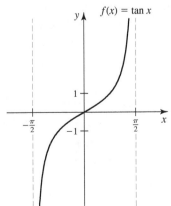

$f(x) = \tan x$

63. Consider the graph $y = \sec^{-1} x$ (see Section 1.4) and evaluate the following limits using the graph. Assume the domain is $\{x\colon |x| \geq 1\}$.

   a. $\lim\limits_{x\to\infty} \sec^{-1} x$ **b.** $\lim\limits_{x\to-\infty} \sec^{-1} x$

64. The **hyperbolic cosine function**, denoted $\cosh x$, is used to model the shape of a hanging cable (a telephone wire, for example). It is defined as $\cosh x = \dfrac{e^x + e^{-x}}{2}$.

   a. Determine its end behavior by analyzing $\lim\limits_{x\to\infty} \cosh x$ and $\lim\limits_{x\to-\infty} \cosh x$.

   b. Evaluate $\cosh 0$. Use symmetry and part (a) to sketch a plausible graph for $y = \cosh x$.

65. The **hyperbolic sine function** is defined as $\sinh x = \dfrac{e^x - e^{-x}}{2}$.

   a. Determine its end behavior by analyzing $\lim\limits_{x\to\infty} \sinh x$ and $\lim\limits_{x\to-\infty} \sinh x$.

   b. Evaluate $\sinh 0$. Use symmetry and part (a) to sketch a plausible graph for $y = \sinh x$.

66–67. Sketching graphs *Sketch a possible graph of a function f that satisfies all the given conditions. Be sure to identify all vertical and horizontal asymptotes.*

66. $f(-1) = -2$, $f(1) = 2$, $f(0) = 0$, $\lim\limits_{x\to\infty} f(x) = 1$, $\lim\limits_{x\to-\infty} f(x) = -1$

67. $\lim\limits_{x\to0^+} f(x) = \infty$, $\lim\limits_{x\to0^-} f(x) = -\infty$, $\lim\limits_{x\to\infty} f(x) = 1$, $\lim\limits_{x\to-\infty} f(x) = -2$

68. Asymptotes Find the vertical and horizontal asymptotes of $f(x) = e^{1/x}$.

69. Asymptotes Find the vertical and horizontal asymptotes of $f(x) = \dfrac{\cos x + 2\sqrt{x}}{\sqrt{x}}$.

Applications

70–75. Steady states *If a function f represents a system that varies in time, the existence of $\lim\limits_{t\to\infty} f(t)$ means that the system reaches a steady state (or equilibrium). For the following systems, determine whether a steady state exists and give the steady-state value.*

70. The population of a bacteria culture is given by $p(t) = \dfrac{2500}{t + 1}$.

71. The population of a culture of tumor cells is given by $p(t) = \dfrac{3500t}{t + 1}$.

72. The amount of drug (in milligrams) in the blood after an IV tube is inserted is $m(t) = 200(1 - 2^{-t})$.

73. The value of an investment in dollars is given by $v(t) = 1000e^{0.065t}$.

74. The population of a colony of squirrels is given by $p(t) = \dfrac{1500}{3 + 2e^{-0.1t}}$.

75. The amplitude of an oscillator is given by $a(t) = 2\left(\dfrac{t + \sin t}{t}\right)$.

76–79. Looking ahead to sequences *A sequence is an infinite, ordered list of numbers that is often defined by a function. For example, the sequence* $\{2, 4, 6, 8, \dots\}$ *is specified by the function* $f(n) = 2n$, *where* $n = 1, 2, 3, \dots$ *. The limit of such a sequence is* $\lim_{n \to \infty} f(n)$, *provided the limit exists. All the limit laws for limits at infinity may be applied to limits of sequences. Find the limit of the following sequences or state that the limit does not exist.*

76. $\left\{4, 2, \dfrac{4}{3}, 1, \dfrac{4}{5}, \dfrac{2}{3}, \dots \right\}$, which is defined by $f(n) = \dfrac{4}{n}$, for $n = 1, 2, 3, \dots$

77. $\left\{0, \dfrac{1}{2}, \dfrac{2}{3}, \dfrac{3}{4}, \dots \right\}$, which is defined by $f(n) = \dfrac{n-1}{n}$, for $n = 1, 2, 3, \dots$

78. $\left\{\dfrac{1}{2}, \dfrac{4}{3}, \dfrac{9}{4}, \dfrac{16}{5}, \dots \right\}$, which is defined by $f(n) = \dfrac{n^2}{n+1}$, for $n = 1, 2, 3, \dots$

79. $\left\{2, \dfrac{3}{4}, \dfrac{4}{9}, \dfrac{5}{16}, \dots \right\}$, which is defined by $f(n) = \dfrac{n+1}{n^2}$, for $n = 1, 2, 3, \dots$

Additional Exercises

80. End behavior of a rational function Suppose $f(x) = \dfrac{p(x)}{q(x)}$ is a rational function, where
$$p(x) = a_m x^m + a_{m-1} x^{m-1} + \cdots + a_2 x^2 + a_1 x + a_0,$$
$$q(x) = b_n x^n + b_{n-1} x^{n-1} + \cdots + b_2 x^2 + b_1 x + b_0, a_m \neq 0,$$
and $b_n \neq 0$.

a. Prove that if $m = n$, then $\lim_{x \to \pm\infty} f(x) = \dfrac{a_m}{b_n}$.

b. Prove that if $m < n$, then $\lim_{x \to \pm\infty} f(x) = 0$.

81. Horizontal and slant asymptotes

a. Is it possible for a rational function to have both slant and horizontal asymptotes? Explain.

b. Is it possible for an algebraic function to have two distinct slant asymptotes? Explain or give an example.

82. End behavior of exponentials Use the following instructions to determine the end behavior of $f(x) = \dfrac{e^x + e^{2x}}{e^{2x} + e^{3x}}$.

a. Evaluate $\lim_{x \to \infty} f(x)$ by first dividing the numerator and denominator by e^{3x}.

b. Evaluate $\lim_{x \to -\infty} f(x)$ by first dividing the numerator and denominator by e^{2x}.

c. Give the horizontal asymptote(s).

d. Graph f to confirm your work in parts (a)–(c).

83–84. Limits of exponentials *Evaluate* $\lim_{x \to \infty} f(x)$ *and* $\lim_{x \to -\infty} f(x)$. *Then state the horizontal asymptote(s) of f. Confirm your findings by plotting f.*

83. $f(x) = \dfrac{2e^x + 3e^{2x}}{e^{2x} + e^{3x}}$ **84.** $f(x) = \dfrac{3e^x + e^{-x}}{e^x + e^{-x}}$

85. Subtle asymptotes Use analytical methods to identify all the asymptotes of $f(x) = \dfrac{\ln(9 - x^2)}{2e^x - e^{-x}}$. Then confirm your results by locating the asymptotes with a graphing utility.

QUICK CHECK ANSWERS

1. $10/11, 100/101, 1000/1001, 1$ **2.** $p(x) \to -\infty$ as $x \to \infty$ and $p(x) \to \infty$ as $x \to -\infty$ **3.** Horizontal asymptote is $y = \frac{10}{3}$; vertical asymptote is $x = \frac{1}{3}$.
4. $\lim_{x \to \infty} e^{10x} = \infty$, $\lim_{x \to -\infty} e^{10x} = 0$, $\lim_{x \to \infty} e^{-10x} = 0$, $\lim_{x \to -\infty} e^{-10x} = \infty$ ◄

2.6 Continuity

The graphs of many functions encountered in this text contain no holes, jumps, or breaks. For example, if $L = f(t)$ represents the length of a fish t years after it is hatched, then the length of the fish changes gradually as t increases. Consequently, the graph of $L = f(t)$ contains no breaks (Figure 2.46a). Some functions, however, do contain abrupt changes in their values. Consider a parking meter that accepts only quarters and each quarter buys 15 minutes of parking. Letting $c(t)$ be the cost (in dollars) of parking for t minutes, the graph of c has breaks at integer multiples of 15 minutes (Figure 2.46b).

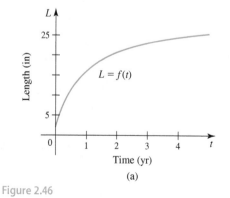

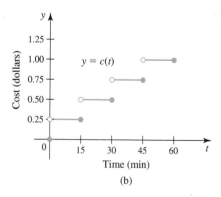

Figure 2.46

QUICK CHECK 1 For what values of t in $(0, 60)$ does the graph of $y = c(t)$ in Figure 2.46b have a discontinuity?◄

Informally, we say that a function f is *continuous* at a if the graph of f does not have a hole or break at a (that is, if the graph near a can be drawn without lifting the pencil). If a function is not continuous at a, then a is a *point of discontinuity*.

Continuity at a Point

This informal description of continuity is sufficient for determining the continuity of simple functions, but it is not precise enough to deal with more complicated functions such as

$$h(x) = \begin{cases} x \sin \dfrac{1}{x} & \text{if } x \neq 0 \\ 0 & \text{if } x = 0. \end{cases}$$

It is difficult to determine whether the graph of h has a break at 0 because it oscillates rapidly as x approaches 0 (Figure 2.47). We need a better definition.

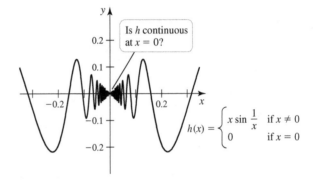

Figure 2.47

DEFINITION Continuity at a Point

A function f is **continuous** at a if $\lim\limits_{x \to a} f(x) = f(a)$. If f is not continuous at a, then a is a **point of discontinuity**.

There is more to this definition than first appears. If $\lim\limits_{x \to a} f(x) = f(a)$, then $f(a)$ and $\lim\limits_{x \to a} f(x)$ must both exist, and they must be equal. The following checklist is helpful in determining whether a function is continuous at a.

Continuity Checklist

In order for f to be continuous at a, the following three conditions must hold.

1. $f(a)$ is defined (a is in the domain of f).
2. $\lim\limits_{x \to a} f(x)$ exists.
3. $\lim\limits_{x \to a} f(x) = f(a)$ (the value of f equals the limit of f at a).

If *any* item in the continuity checklist fails to hold, the function fails to be continuous at a. From this definition, we see that continuity has an important practical consequence:

> *If f is continuous at a, then $\lim\limits_{x \to a} f(x) = f(a)$, and direct substitution may be used to evaluate $\lim\limits_{x \to a} f(x)$.*

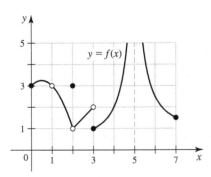

Figure 2.48

EXAMPLE 1 Points of discontinuity Use the graph of f in Figure 2.48 to identify values of x on the interval $(0, 7)$ at which f has a discontinuity.

> In Example 1, the discontinuities at $x = 1$ and $x = 2$ are called **removable discontinuities** because they can be removed by redefining the function at these points (in this case, $f(1) = 3$ and $f(2) = 1$). The discontinuity at $x = 3$ is called a **jump discontinuity**. The discontinuity at $x = 5$ is called an **infinite discontinuity**. These terms are discussed in Exercises 95–101.

SOLUTION The function f has discontinuities at $x = 1, 2, 3,$ and 5 because the graph contains holes or breaks at these locations. The continuity checklist tells us why f is not continuous at these points.

- $f(1)$ is not defined.
- $f(2) = 3$ and $\lim_{x \to 2} f(x) = 1$. Therefore, $f(2)$ and $\lim_{x \to 2} f(x)$ exist but are not equal.
- $\lim_{x \to 3} f(x)$ does not exist because the left-sided limit $\lim_{x \to 3^-} f(x) = 2$ differs from the right-sided limit $\lim_{x \to 3^+} f(x) = 1$.
- Neither $\lim_{x \to 5} f(x)$ nor $f(5)$ exists.   *Related Exercises 9–12* ◄

EXAMPLE 2 **Identifying discontinuities** Determine whether the following functions are continuous at a. Justify each answer using the continuity checklist.

a. $f(x) = \dfrac{3x^2 + 2x + 1}{x - 1}; \quad a = 1$

b. $g(x) = \dfrac{3x^2 + 2x + 1}{x - 1}; \quad a = 2$

c. $h(x) = \begin{cases} x \sin \dfrac{1}{x} & \text{if } x \neq 0 \\ 0 & \text{if } x = 0 \end{cases}; a = 0$

SOLUTION

a. The function f is not continuous at 1 because $f(1)$ is undefined.

b. Because g is a rational function and the denominator is nonzero at 2, it follows by Theorem 2.3 that $\lim_{x \to 2} g(x) = g(2) = 17$. Therefore, g is continuous at 2.

c. By definition, $h(0) = 0$. In Exercise 55 of Section 2.3, we used the Squeeze Theorem to show that $\lim_{x \to 0} x \sin \dfrac{1}{x} = 0$. Therefore, $\lim_{x \to 0} h(x) = h(0)$, which implies that h is continuous at 0.   *Related Exercises 13–20* ◄

The following theorems make it easier to test various combinations of functions for continuity at a point.

THEOREM 2.9   Continuity Rules

If f and g are continuous at a, then the following functions are also continuous at a. Assume c is a constant and $n > 0$ is an integer.

a. $f + g$ **b.** $f - g$
c. cf **d.** fg
e. f/g, provided $g(a) \neq 0$ **f.** $(f(x))^n$

To prove the first result, note that if f and g are continuous at a, then $\lim_{x \to a} f(x) = f(a)$ and $\lim_{x \to a} g(x) = g(a)$. From the limit laws of Theorem 2.3, it follows that

$$\lim_{x \to a} (f(x) + g(x)) = f(a) + g(a).$$

Therefore, $f + g$ is continuous at a. Similar arguments lead to the continuity of differences, products, quotients, and powers of continuous functions. The next theorem is a direct consequence of Theorem 2.9.

> **THEOREM 2.10   Polynomial and Rational Functions**
>
> **a.** A polynomial function is continuous for all x.
>
> **b.** A rational function (a function of the form $\dfrac{p}{q}$, where p and q are polynomials) is continuous for all x for which $q(x) \neq 0$.

EXAMPLE 3   Applying the continuity theorems For what values of x is the function

$$f(x) = \frac{x}{x^2 - 7x + 12}$$ continuous?

SOLUTION

a. Because f is rational, Theorem 2.10b implies it is continuous for all x at which the denominator is nonzero. The denominator factors as $(x - 3)(x - 4)$, so it is zero at $x = 3$ and $x = 4$. Therefore, f is continuous for all x except $x = 3$ and $x = 4$ (Figure 2.49).   *Related Exercises 21–26* ◀

The following theorem allows us to determine when a composition of two functions is continuous at a point. Its proof is informative and is outlined in Exercise 102.

> **THEOREM 2.11   Continuity of Composite Functions at a Point**
> If g is continuous at a and f is continuous at $g(a)$, then the composite function $f \circ g$ is continuous at a.

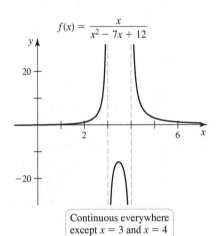

$$f(x) = \frac{x}{x^2 - 7x + 12}$$

Continuous everywhere except $x = 3$ and $x = 4$

Figure 2.49

QUICK CHECK 2 Evaluate $\lim\limits_{x \to 4} \sqrt{x^2 + 9}$ and $\sqrt{\lim\limits_{x \to 4} (x^2 + 9)}$. How do these results illustrate that the order of a function evaluation and a limit may be switched for continuous functions? ◀

Theorem 2.11 is useful because it allows us to conclude that the composition of two continuous functions is continuous at a point. For example, the composite function $\left(\dfrac{x}{x-1}\right)^3$ is continuous for all $x \neq 1$. Furthermore, under the stated conditions on f and g, the limit of $f \circ g$ is evaluated by direct substitution; that is,

$$\lim_{x \to a} f(g(x)) = f(g(a)).$$

EXAMPLE 4   Limit of a composition Evaluate $\lim\limits_{x \to 0} \left(\dfrac{x^4 - 2x + 2}{x^6 + 2x^4 + 1}\right)^{10}$.

SOLUTION The rational function $\dfrac{x^4 - 2x + 2}{x^6 + 2x^4 + 1}$ is continuous for all x because its

denominator is always positive (Theorem 2.10b). Therefore, $\left(\dfrac{x^4 - 2x + 2}{x^6 + 2x^4 + 1}\right)^{10}$, which is the composition of the continuous function $f(x) = x^{10}$ and a continuous rational function, is continuous for all x by Theorem 2.11. By direct substitution,

$$\lim_{x \to 0} \left(\frac{x^4 - 2x + 2}{x^6 + 2x^4 + 1}\right)^{10} = \left(\frac{0^4 - 2 \cdot 0 + 2}{0^6 + 2 \cdot 0^4 + 1}\right)^{10} = 2^{10} = 1024.$$

Related Exercises 27–30 ◀

Closely related to Theorem 2.11 are two useful results dealing with limits of composite functions. We present these results—one a more general version of the other—in a single theorem.

> **THEOREM 2.12** **Limits of Composite Functions**
>
> **1.** If g is continuous at a and f is continuous at $g(a)$, then
> $$\lim_{x \to a} f(g(x)) = f\left(\lim_{x \to a} g(x)\right).$$
>
> **2.** If $\lim_{x \to a} g(x) = L$ and f is continuous at L, then
> $$\lim_{x \to a} f(g(x)) = f\left(\lim_{x \to a} g(x)\right).$$

Proof: The first statement follows directly from Theorem 2.11, which states that $\lim_{x \to a} f(g(x)) = f(g(a))$. If g is continuous at a, then $\lim_{x \to a} g(x) = g(a)$, and it follows that

$$\lim_{x \to a} f(g(x)) = f(\underbrace{g(a)}_{\lim_{x \to a} g(x)}) = f\left(\lim_{x \to a} g(x)\right).$$

The proof of the second statement relies on the formal definition of a limit, which is discussed in Section 2.7. ◄

Both statements of Theorem 2.12 justify interchanging the order of a limit and a function evaluation. By the second statement, the inner function of the composition needn't be continuous at the point of interest, but it must have a limit at that point. Note also that $\lim_{x \to a}$ can be replaced with $\lim_{x \to a^+}$ or $\lim_{x \to a^-}$ in Theorem 2.12, provided g is right- or left-continuous at a, respectively, in statement (1). In statement (2), $\lim_{x \to a}$ can be replaced with $\lim_{x \to \infty}$ or $\lim_{x \to -\infty}$.

EXAMPLE 5 **Limits of a composite functions** Evaluate the following limits.

a. $\lim\limits_{x \to -1} \sqrt{2x^2 - 1}$　　　　**b.** $\lim\limits_{x \to 2} \cos\left(\dfrac{x^2 - 4}{x - 2}\right)$

SOLUTION

a. We show later in this section that $\sqrt{x}$ is continuous for $x \geq 0$. The inner function of the composite function $\sqrt{2x^2 - 1}$ is $2x^2 - 1$; it is continuous and positive at -1. By the first statement of Theorem 2.12,

$$\lim_{x \to -1} \sqrt{2x^2 - 1} = \sqrt{\underbrace{\lim_{x \to -1} (2x^2 - 1)}_{1}} = \sqrt{1} = 1.$$

b. We show later in this section that $\cos x$ is continuous at all points of its domain. The inner function of the composite function $\cos\left(\dfrac{x^2 - 4}{x - 2}\right)$ is $\dfrac{x^2 - 4}{x - 2}$, which is not continuous at 2. However,

$$\lim_{x \to 2} \frac{x^2 - 4}{x - 2} = \lim_{x \to 2} \frac{(x - 2)(x + 2)}{x - 2} = \lim_{x \to 2} (x + 2) = 4.$$

Therefore, by the second statement of Theorem 2.12,

$$\lim_{x \to 2} \cos\left(\frac{x^2 - 4}{x - 2}\right) = \cos\left(\underbrace{\lim_{x \to 2} \frac{x^2 - 4}{x - 2}}_{4}\right) = \cos 4 \approx -0.654.$$

Related Exercises 31–34 ◄

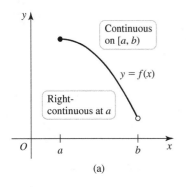

(a)

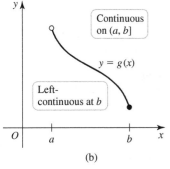

(b)

Figure 2.50

Continuity on an Interval

A function is *continuous on an interval* if it is continuous at every point in that interval. Consider the functions f and g whose graphs are shown in Figure 2.50. Both these functions are continuous for all x in (a, b), but what about the endpoints? To answer this question, we introduce the ideas of *left-continuity* and *right-continuity*.

> **DEFINITION Continuity at Endpoints**
>
> A function f is **continuous from the left** (or **left-continuous**) at a if $\lim_{x \to a^-} f(x) = f(a)$, and f is **continuous from the right** (or **right-continuous**) at a if $\lim_{x \to a^+} f(x) = f(a)$.

Combining the definitions of left-continuous and right-continuous with the definition of continuity at a point, we define what it means for a function to be continuous on an interval.

> **DEFINITION Continuity on an Interval**
>
> A function f is **continuous on an interval** I if it is continuous at all points of I. If I contains its endpoints, continuity on I means continuous from the right or left at the endpoints.

To illustrate these definitions, consider again the functions in Figure 2.50. In Figure 2.50a, f is continuous from the right at a because $\lim_{x \to a^+} f(x) = f(a)$, but it is not continuous from the left at b because $f(b)$ is not defined. Therefore, f is continuous on the interval $[a, b)$. The behavior of the function g in Figure 2.50b is the opposite: It is continuous from the left at b, but it is not continuous from the right at a. Therefore, g is continuous on $(a, b]$.

QUICK CHECK 3 Modify the graphs of the functions f and g in Figure 2.50 to obtain functions that are continuous on $[a, b]$. ◄

EXAMPLE 6 Intervals of continuity Determine the intervals of continuity for
$$f(x) = \begin{cases} x^2 + 1 & \text{if } x \le 0 \\ 3x + 5 & \text{if } x > 0. \end{cases}$$

SOLUTION This piecewise function consists of two polynomials that describe a parabola and a line (Figure 2.51). By Theorem 2.10, f is continuous for all $x \ne 0$. From its graph, it appears that f is left-continuous at 0. This observation is verified by noting that
$$\lim_{x \to 0^-} f(x) = \lim_{x \to 0^-} (x^2 + 1) = 1,$$
which means that $\lim_{x \to 0^-} f(x) = f(0)$. However, because
$$\lim_{x \to 0^+} f(x) = \lim_{x \to 0^+} (3x + 5) = 5 \ne f(0),$$
we see that f is not right-continuous at 0. Therefore, f is continuous on $(-\infty, 0]$ and on $(0, \infty)$.
Related Exercises 35–40 ◄

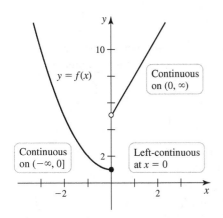

Figure 2.51

Functions Involving Roots

Recall that Limit Law 7 of Theorem 2.3 states

$$\lim_{x \to a} (f(x))^{n/m} = \left(\lim_{x \to a} f(x) \right)^{n/m},$$

provided $f(x) \ge 0$, for x near a, if m is even and n/m is reduced. Therefore, if m is odd and f is continuous at a, then $[f(x)]^{n/m}$ is continuous at a, because

$$\lim_{x \to a} (f(x))^{n/m} = \left(\lim_{x \to a} f(x) \right)^{n/m} = (f(a))^{n/m}.$$

When m is even, the continuity of $(f(x))^{n/m}$ must be handled more carefully because this function is defined only when $f(x) \ge 0$. Exercise 59 of Section 2.7 establishes an important fact:

If f is continuous at a and $f(a) > 0$, then $f(x) > 0$ for all values of x in the domain of f and in some interval containing a.

Combining this fact with Theorem 2.11 (the continuity of composite functions), it follows that $(f(x))^{n/m}$ is continuous at a provided $f(a) > 0$. At points where $f(a) = 0$, the behavior of $(f(x))^{n/m}$ varies. Often we find that $(f(x))^{n/m}$ is left- or right-continuous at that point, or it may be continuous from both sides.

> **THEOREM 2.13   Continuity of Functions with Roots**
> Assume that m and n are positive integers with no common factors. If m is an odd integer, then $(f(x))^{n/m}$ is continuous at all points at which f is continuous.
> If m is even, then $(f(x))^{n/m}$ is continuous at all points a at which f is continuous and $f(a) > 0$.

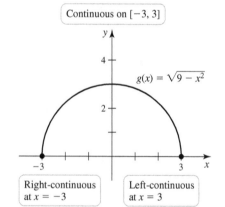

Continuous on $[-3, 3]$

$g(x) = \sqrt{9 - x^2}$

Right-continuous at $x = -3$

Left-continuous at $x = 3$

Figure 2.52

EXAMPLE 7   Continuity with roots For what values of x are the following functions continuous?

a. $g(x) = \sqrt{9 - x^2}$ 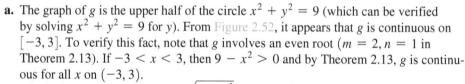 **b.** $f(x) = (x^2 - 2x + 4)^{2/3}$

SOLUTION

a. The graph of g is the upper half of the circle $x^2 + y^2 = 9$ (which can be verified by solving $x^2 + y^2 = 9$ for y). From Figure 2.52, it appears that g is continuous on $[-3, 3]$. To verify this fact, note that g involves an even root ($m = 2, n = 1$ in Theorem 2.13). If $-3 < x < 3$, then $9 - x^2 > 0$ and by Theorem 2.13, g is continuous for all x on $(-3, 3)$.

   At the right endpoint, $\lim_{x \to 3^-} \sqrt{9 - x^2} = 0 = g(3)$ by Limit Law 7, which implies that g is left-continuous at 3. Similarly, g is right-continuous at -3 because $\lim_{x \to -3^+} \sqrt{9 - x^2} = 0 = g(-3)$. Therefore, g is continuous on $[-3, 3]$.

QUICK CHECK 4 On what interval is $f(x) = x^{1/4}$ continuous? On what interval is $f(x) = x^{2/5}$ continuous? ◄

b. The polynomial $x^2 - 2x + 4$ is continuous for all x by Theorem 2.10a. Because f involves an odd root ($m = 3, n = 2$ in Theorem 2.13), f is continuous for all x.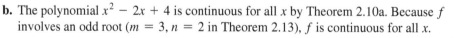

Related Exercises 41–50 ◄

Continuity of Transcendental Functions

The understanding of continuity that we have developed with algebraic functions may now be applied to transcendental functions.

Trigonometric Functions   In Example 8 of Section 2.3, we used the Squeeze Theorem to show that $\lim\limits_{x \to 0} \sin x = 0$ and $\lim\limits_{x \to 0} \cos x = 1$. Because $\sin 0 = 0$ and $\cos 0 = 1$, these limits imply that $\sin x$ and $\cos x$ are continuous at 0. The graph of $y = \sin x$ (Figure 2.53) suggests that $\lim\limits_{x \to a} \sin x = \sin a$ for any value of a, which means that $\sin x$ is continuous on $(-\infty, \infty)$. The graph of $y = \cos x$ also indicates that $\cos x$ is continuous for all x. Exercise 105 outlines a proof of these results.

With these facts in hand, we appeal to Theorem 2.9e to discover that the remaining trigonometric functions are continuous on their domains. For example, because $\sec x = 1/\cos x$, the secant function is continuous for all x for which $\cos x \neq 0$ (for all x except odd multiples of $\pi/2$) (Figure 2.54). Likewise, the tangent, cotangent, and cosecant functions are continuous at all points of their domains.

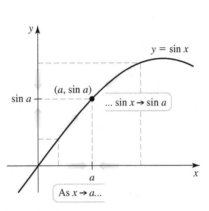

Figure 2.53

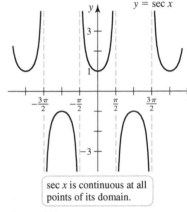

sec x is continuous at all points of its domain.

Figure 2.54

Exponential Functions   The continuity of exponential functions of the form $f(x) = b^x$, with $0 < b < 1$ or $b > 1$, raises an important question. Consider the function $f(x) = 4^x$ (Figure 2.55). Evaluating f is routine if x is rational:

$$4^3 = 4 \cdot 4 \cdot 4 = 64; \quad 4^{-2} = \frac{1}{4^2} = \frac{1}{16}; \quad 4^{3/2} = \sqrt{4^3} = 8; \quad \text{and} \quad 4^{-1/3} = \frac{1}{\sqrt[3]{4}}.$$

But what is meant by 4^x when x is an irrational number, such as $\sqrt{2}$? In order for $f(x) = 4^x$ to be continuous for all real numbers, it must also be defined when x is an irrational number. Providing a working definition for an expression such as $4^{\sqrt{2}}$ requires mathematical results that don't appear until Chapter 6. Until then, we assume without proof that the domain of $f(x) = b^x$ is the set of all real numbers and that f is continuous at all points of its domain.

Inverse Functions   Suppose a function f is continuous and one-to-one on an interval I. Reflecting the graph of f through the line $y = x$ generates the graph of f^{-1}. The reflection process introduces no discontinuities in the graph of f^{-1}, so it is plausible (and indeed true) that f^{-1} is continuous on the interval corresponding to I. We state this fact without a formal proof.

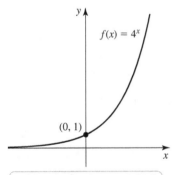

Exponential functions are defined for all real numbers and are continuous on $(-\infty, \infty)$, as shown in Chapter 6

Figure 2.55

> **THEOREM 2.14   Continuity of Inverse Functions**
> If a function f is continuous on an interval I and has an inverse on I, then its inverse f^{-1} is also continuous (on the interval consisting of the points $f(x)$, where x is in I).

Because all the trigonometric functions are continuous on their domains, they are also continuous when their domains are restricted for the purpose of defining inverse functions. Therefore, by Theorem 2.14, the inverse trigonometric functions are continuous at all points of their domains.

Logarithmic functions of the form $f(x) = \log_b x$ are continuous at all points of their domains for the same reason: They are inverses of exponential functions, which are one-to-one and continuous. Collecting all these facts, we have the following theorem.

THEOREM 2.15 Continuity of Transcendental Functions
The following functions are continuous at all points of their domains.

Trigonometric		**Inverse Trigonometric**		**Exponential**	
$\sin x$	$\cos x$	$\sin^{-1} x$	$\cos^{-1} x$	b^x	e^x
$\tan x$	$\cot x$	$\tan^{-1} x$	$\cot^{-1} x$	**Logarithmic**	
$\sec x$	$\csc x$	$\sec^{-1} x$	$\csc^{-1} x$	$\log_b x$	$\ln x$

For each function listed in Theorem 2.15, we have $\lim\limits_{x \to a} f(x) = f(a)$, provided a is in the domain of the function. This means that limits of these functions may be evaluated by direct substitution at points in the domain.

EXAMPLE 8 Limits involving transcendental functions Analyze the following limits after determining the continuity of the functions involved.

a. $\lim\limits_{x \to 0} \dfrac{\cos^2 x - 1}{\cos x - 1}$
     b. $\lim\limits_{x \to 1} \left(\sqrt[4]{\ln x} + \tan^{-1} x \right)$

SOLUTION

> Limits like the one in Example 8a are denoted 0/0 and are known as *indeterminate forms*, to be studied further in Section 4.7.

a. Both $\cos^2 x - 1$ and $\cos x - 1$ are continuous for all x by Theorems 2.9 and 2.15. However, the ratio of these functions is continuous only when $\cos x - 1 \neq 0$, which occurs when x is not an integer multiple of 2π. Note that both the numerator and denominator of $\dfrac{\cos^2 x - 1}{\cos x - 1}$ approach 0 as $x \to 0$. To evaluate the limit, we factor and simplify:

$$\lim\limits_{x \to 0} \frac{\cos^2 x - 1}{\cos x - 1} = \lim\limits_{x \to 0} \frac{(\cos x - 1)(\cos x + 1)}{\cos x - 1} = \lim\limits_{x \to 0} (\cos x + 1)$$

(where $\cos x - 1$ may be canceled because it is nonzero as x approaches 0). The limit on the right is now evaluated using direct substitution:

$$\lim\limits_{x \to 0} (\cos x + 1) = \cos 0 + 1 = 2.$$

QUICK CHECK 5 Show that $f(x) = \sqrt[4]{\ln x}$ is right-continuous at $x = 1$. ◄

b. By Theorem 2.15, $\ln x$ is continuous on its domain $(0, \infty)$. However, $\ln x > 0$ only when $x > 1$, so Theorem 2.13 implies that $\sqrt[4]{\ln x}$ is continuous on $(1, \infty)$. At $x = 1$, $\sqrt[4]{\ln x}$ is right-continuous (Quick Check 5). The domain of $\tan^{-1} x$ is all real numbers, and it is continuous on $(-\infty, \infty)$. Therefore, $f(x) = \sqrt[4]{\ln x} + \tan^{-1} x$ is continuous on $[1, \infty)$. Because the domain of f does not include points with $x < 1$, $\lim\limits_{x \to 1^-} \left(\sqrt[4]{\ln x} + \tan^{-1} x \right)$ does not exist, which implies that $\lim\limits_{x \to 1} \left(\sqrt[4]{\ln x} + \tan^{-1} x \right)$ does not exist.
Related Exercises 51–56 ◄

We close this section with an important theorem that has both practical and theoretical uses.

The Intermediate Value Theorem

A common problem in mathematics is finding solutions to equations of the form $f(x) = L$. Before attempting to find values of x satisfying this equation, it is worthwhile to determine whether a solution exists.

The existence of solutions is often established using a result known as the *Intermediate Value Theorem*. Given a function f and a constant L, we assume L lies strictly between $f(a)$ and $f(b)$. The Intermediate Value Theorem says that if f is continuous on $[a, b]$, then the graph of f must cross the horizontal line $y = L$ at least once (Figure 2.56). Although this theorem is easily illustrated, its proof is beyond the scope of this text.

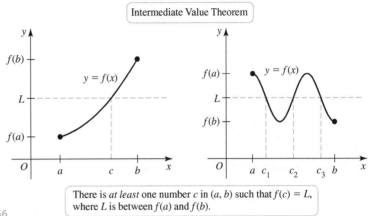

There is *at least* one number c in (a, b) such that $f(c) = L$, where L is between $f(a)$ and $f(b)$.

Figure 2.56

> **THEOREM 2.16   The Intermediate Value Theorem**
>
> Suppose f is continuous on the interval $[a, b]$ and L is a number strictly between $f(a)$ and $f(b)$. Then there exists at least one number c in (a, b) satisfying $f(c) = L$.

The importance of continuity in Theorem 2.16 is illustrated in Figure 2.57, where we see a function f that is not continuous on $[a, b]$. For the value of L shown in the figure, there is no value of c in (a, b) satisfying $f(c) = L$. The next example illustrates a practical application of the Intermediate Value Theorem.

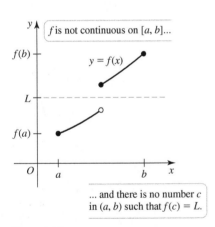

f is not continuous on $[a, b]$...

... and there is no number c in (a, b) such that $f(c) = L$.

Figure 2.57

QUICK CHECK 6 Does the equation $f(x) = x^3 + x + 1 = 0$ have a solution on the interval $[-1, 1]$? Explain. ◄

EXAMPLE 9   Finding an interest rate Suppose you invest $1000 in a special 5-year savings account with a fixed annual interest rate r, with monthly compounding. The amount of money A in the account after 5 years (60 months) is

$A(r) = 1000\left(1 + \dfrac{r}{12}\right)^{60}$. Your goal is to have $1400 in the account after 5 years.

a. Use the Intermediate Value Theorem to show there is a value of r in $(0, 0.08)$—that is, an interest rate between 0% and 8%—for which $A(r) = 1400$.

b. Use a graphing utility to illustrate your explanation in part (a) and then estimate the interest rate required to reach your goal.

SOLUTION

a. As a polynomial in r (of degree 60), $A(r) = 1000\left(1 + \dfrac{r}{12}\right)^{60}$ is continuous for all r.

Evaluating $A(r)$ at the endpoints of the interval $[0, 0.08]$, we have $A(0) = 1000$ and $A(0.08) \approx 1489.85$. Therefore,

$$A(0) < 1400 < A(0.08),$$

and it follows, by the Intermediate Value Theorem, that there is a value of r in $(0, 0.08)$ for which $A(r) = 1400$.

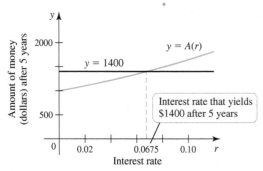

Figure 2.58

b. The graphs of $y = A(r)$ and the horizontal line $y = 1400$ are shown in Figure 2.58; it is evident that they intersect between $r = 0$ and $r = 0.08$. Solving $A(r) = 1400$ algebraically or using a root finder reveals that the curve and line intersect at $r \approx 0.0675$. Therefore, an interest rate of approximately 6.75% is required for the investment to be worth $1400 after 5 years. *Related Exercises 57–64* ◄

SECTION 2.6 EXERCISES

Review Questions

1. Which of the following functions are continuous for all values in their domain? Justify your answers.

   a. $a(t) = $ altitude of a skydiver t seconds after jumping from a plane

   b. $n(t) = $ number of quarters needed to park legally in a metered parking space for t minutes

   c. $T(t) = $ temperature t minutes after midnight in Chicago on January 1

   d. $p(t) = $ number of points scored by a basketball player after t minutes of a basketball game

2. Give the three conditions that must be satisfied by a function to be continuous at a point.

3. What does it mean for a function to be continuous on an interval?

4. We informally describe a function f to be continuous at a if its graph contains no holes or breaks at a. Explain why this is not an adequate definition of continuity.

5. Complete the following sentences.

   a. A function is continuous from the left at a if _____.

   b. A function is continuous from the right at a if _____.

6. Describe the points (if any) at which a rational function fails to be continuous.

7. What is the domain of $f(x) = e^x/x$ and where is f continuous?

8. Explain the Intermediate Value Theorem using words and pictures.

Basic Skills

9–12. Discontinuities from a graph *Determine the points at which the following functions f have discontinuities. At each point of discontinuity, state the conditions in the continuity checklist that are violated.*

9.

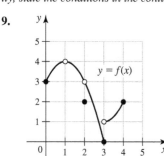

10.

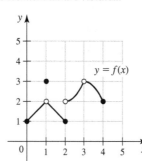

11.

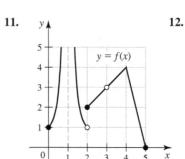

12.

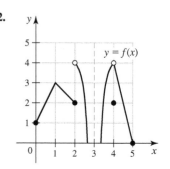

13–20. Continuity at a point *Determine whether the following functions are continuous at a. Use the continuity checklist to justify your answer.*

13. $f(x) = \dfrac{2x^2 + 3x + 1}{x^2 + 5x}$; $a = 5$

14. $f(x) = \dfrac{2x^2 + 3x + 1}{x^2 + 5x}$; $a = -5$

15. $f(x) = \sqrt{x - 2}$; $a = 1$

16. $g(x) = \dfrac{1}{x - 3}$; $a = 3$

17. $f(x) = \begin{cases} \dfrac{x^2 - 1}{x - 1} & \text{if } x \neq 1 \\ 3 & \text{if } x = 1 \end{cases}$; $a = 1$

18. $f(x) = \begin{cases} \dfrac{x^2 - 4x + 3}{x - 3} & \text{if } x \neq 3 \\ 2 & \text{if } x = 3 \end{cases}$; $a = 3$

19. $f(x) = \dfrac{5x - 2}{x^2 - 9x + 20}$; $a = 4$

20. $f(x) = \begin{cases} \dfrac{x^2 + x}{x + 1} & \text{if } x \neq -1 \\ 2 & \text{if } x = -1 \end{cases}$; $a = -1$

21–26. Continuity on intervals *Use Theorem 2.10 to determine the intervals on which the following functions are continuous.*

21. $p(x) = 4x^5 - 3x^2 + 1$

22. $g(x) = \dfrac{3x^2 - 6x + 7}{x^2 + x + 1}$

23. $f(x) = \dfrac{x^5 + 6x + 17}{x^2 - 9}$

24. $s(x) = \dfrac{x^2 - 4x + 3}{x^2 - 1}$

25. $f(x) = \dfrac{1}{x^2 - 4}$

26. $f(t) = \dfrac{t + 2}{t^2 - 4}$

27–30. Limits of compositions *Evaluate each limit and justify your answer.*

27. $\lim\limits_{x \to 0} (x^8 - 3x^6 - 1)^{40}$

28. $\lim\limits_{x \to 2} \left(\dfrac{3}{2x^5 - 4x^2 - 50} \right)^4$

29. $\lim\limits_{x \to 1} \left(\dfrac{x + 5}{x + 2} \right)^4$

30. $\lim\limits_{x \to \infty} \left(\dfrac{2x + 1}{x} \right)^3$

31–34. Limits of composite functions *Evaluate each limit and justify your answer.*

31. $\lim\limits_{x \to 4} \sqrt{\dfrac{x^3 - 2x^2 - 8x}{x - 4}}$

32. $\lim\limits_{x \to 4} \tan \dfrac{t - 4}{\sqrt{t} - 2}$

33. $\lim\limits_{x \to 0} \ln \dfrac{2 \sin x}{x}$

34. $\lim\limits_{x \to 0} \left(\dfrac{x}{\sqrt{16x + 1} - 1} \right)^{1/3}$

35–38. Intervals of continuity *Determine the intervals of continuity for the following functions.*

35. The graph of Exercise 9

36. The graph of Exercise 10

37. The graph of Exercise 11

38. The graph of Exercise 12

39. Intervals of continuity Let

$$f(x) = \begin{cases} 2x & \text{if } x < 1 \\ x^2 + 3x & \text{if } x \geq 1. \end{cases}$$

a. Use the continuity checklist to show that f is not continuous at 1.

b. Is f continuous from the left or right at 1?

c. State the interval(s) of continuity.

40. Intervals of continuity Let

$$f(x) = \begin{cases} x^3 + 4x + 1 & \text{if } x \leq 0 \\ 2x^3 & \text{if } x > 0. \end{cases}$$

a. Use the continuity checklist to show that f is not continuous at 0.

b. Is f continuous from the left or right at 0?

c. State the interval(s) of continuity.

41–46. Functions with roots *Determine the interval(s) on which the following functions are continuous. Be sure to consider right- and left-continuity at the endpoints.*

41. $f(x) = \sqrt{2x^2 - 16}$

42. $g(x) = \sqrt{x^4 - 1}$

43. $f(x) = \sqrt[3]{x^2 - 2x - 3}$

44. $f(t) = (t^2 - 1)^{3/2}$

45. $f(x) = (2x - 3)^{2/3}$

46. $f(z) = (z - 1)^{3/4}$

47–50. Limits with roots *Evaluate each limit and justify your answer.*

47. $\lim\limits_{x \to 2} \sqrt{\dfrac{4x + 10}{2x - 2}}$

48. $\lim\limits_{x \to -1} (x^2 - 4 + \sqrt[3]{x^2 - 9})$

49. $\lim\limits_{x \to 3} \sqrt{x^2 + 7}$

50. $\lim\limits_{t \to 2} \dfrac{t^2 + 5}{1 + \sqrt{t^2 + 5}}$

51–56. Continuity and limits with transcendental functions *Determine the interval(s) on which the following functions are continuous; then analyze the given limits.*

51. $f(x) = \csc x;\ \lim\limits_{x \to \pi/4} f(x);\ \lim\limits_{x \to 2\pi^-} f(x)$

52. $f(x) = e^{\sqrt{x}};\ \lim\limits_{x \to 4} f(x);\ \lim\limits_{x \to 0^+} f(x)$

53. $f(x) = \dfrac{1 + \sin x}{\cos x};\ \lim\limits_{x \to \pi/2^-} f(x);\ \lim\limits_{x \to 4\pi/3} f(x)$

54. $f(x) = \dfrac{\ln x}{\sin^{-1} x};\ \lim\limits_{x \to 1^-} f(x)$

55. $f(x) = \dfrac{e^x}{1 - e^x};\ \lim\limits_{x \to 0^-} f(x);\ \lim\limits_{x \to 0^+} f(x)$

56. $f(x) = \dfrac{e^{2x} - 1}{e^x - 1};\ \lim\limits_{x \to 0} f(x)$

T 57. Intermediate Value Theorem and interest rates Suppose $5000 is invested in a savings account for 10 years (120 months), with an annual interest rate of r, compounded monthly. The amount of money in the account after 10 years is $A(r) = 5000(1 + r/12)^{120}$.

a. Use the Intermediate Value Theorem to show there is a value of r in $(0, 0.08)$—an interest rate between 0% and 8%—that allows you to reach your savings goal of $7000 in 10 years.

b. Use a graph to illustrate your explanation in part (a); then approximate the interest rate required to reach your goal.

T 58. Intermediate Value Theorem and mortgage payments You are shopping for a $150,000, 30-year (360-month) loan to buy a house. The monthly payment is

$$m(r) = \dfrac{150{,}000(r/12)}{1 - (1 + r/12)^{-360}},$$

where r is the annual interest rate. Suppose banks are currently offering interest rates between 6% and 8%.

a. Use the Intermediate Value Theorem to show there is a value of r in $(0.06, 0.08)$—an interest rate between 6% and 8%—that allows you to make monthly payments of $1000 per month.

b. Use a graph to illustrate your explanation to part (a). Then determine the interest rate you need for monthly payments of $1000.

T 59–64. Applying the Intermediate Value Theorem

a. *Use the Intermediate Value Theorem to show that the following equations have a solution on the given interval.*

b. *Use a graphing utility to find all the solutions to the equation on the given interval.*

c. *Illustrate your answers with an appropriate graph.*

59. $2x^3 + x - 2 = 0;\ (-1, 1)$

60. $\sqrt{x^4 + 25x^3 + 10} = 5;\ (0, 1)$

61. $x^3 - 5x^2 + 2x = -1;\ (-1, 5)$

62. $-x^5 - 4x^2 + 2\sqrt{x} + 5 = 0;\ (0, 3)$

63. $x + e^x = 0;\ (-1, 0)$

64. $x \ln x - 1 = 0;\ (1, e)$

Further Explorations

65. Explain why or why not Determine whether the following statements are true and give an explanation or counterexample.

  a. If a function is left-continuous and right-continuous at a, then it is continuous at a.

  b. If a function is continuous at a, then it is left-continuous and right-continuous at a.

  c. If $a < b$ and $f(a) \leq L \leq f(b)$, then there is some value of c in (a, b) for which $f(c) = L$.

  d. Suppose f is continuous on $[a, b]$. Then there is a point c in (a, b) such that $f(c) = (f(a) + f(b))/2$.

66. Continuity of the absolute value function Prove that the absolute value function $|x|$ is continuous for all values of x. (*Hint:* Using the definition of the absolute value function, compute $\lim_{x \to 0^-} |x|$ and $\lim_{x \to 0^+} |x|$.)

67–70. Continuity of functions with absolute values *Use the continuity of the absolute value function (Exercise 66) to determine the interval(s) on which the following functions are continuous.*

67. $f(x) = |x^2 + 3x - 18|$ **68.** $g(x) = \left| \dfrac{x + 4}{x^2 - 4} \right|$

69. $h(x) = \left| \dfrac{1}{\sqrt{x} - 4} \right|$ **70.** $h(x) = |x^2 + 2x + 5| + \sqrt{x}$

71–80. Miscellaneous limits *Evaluate the following limits or state that they do not exist.*

71. $\displaystyle \lim_{x \to \pi} \frac{\cos^2 x + 3\cos x + 2}{\cos x + 1}$ **72.** $\displaystyle \lim_{x \to 3\pi/2} \frac{\sin^2 x + 6\sin x + 5}{\sin^2 x - 1}$

73. $\displaystyle \lim_{x \to \pi/2} \frac{\sin x - 1}{\sqrt{\sin x} - 1}$ **74.** $\displaystyle \lim_{\theta \to 0} \frac{\dfrac{1}{2 + \sin \theta} - \dfrac{1}{2}}{\sin \theta}$

75. $\displaystyle \lim_{x \to 0} \frac{\cos x - 1}{\sin^2 x}$ **76.** $\displaystyle \lim_{x \to 0^+} \frac{1 - \cos^2 x}{\sin x}$

77. $\displaystyle \lim_{x \to \infty} \frac{\tan^{-1} x}{x}$ **78.** $\displaystyle \lim_{t \to \infty} \frac{\cos t}{e^{3t}}$

79. $\displaystyle \lim_{x \to 1^-} \frac{x}{\ln x}$ **80.** $\displaystyle \lim_{x \to 0^+} \frac{x}{\ln x}$

81. Pitfalls using technology The graph of the *sawtooth function* $y = x - \lfloor x \rfloor$, where $\lfloor x \rfloor$ is the greatest integer function or floor function (Exercise 37, Section 2.2), was obtained using a graphing utility (see figure). Identify any inaccuracies appearing in the graph and then plot an accurate graph by hand.

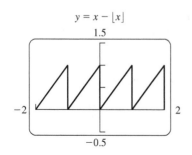

$$y = x - \lfloor x \rfloor$$

82. Pitfalls using technology Graph the function $f(x) = \dfrac{\sin x}{x}$ using a graphing window of $[-\pi, \pi] \times [0, 2]$.

  a. Sketch a copy of the graph obtained with your graphing device and describe any inaccuracies appearing in the graph.

  b. Sketch an accurate graph of the function. Is f continuous at 0?

  c. What is the value of $\displaystyle \lim_{x \to 0} \frac{\sin x}{x}$?

83. Sketching functions

  a. Sketch the graph of a function that is not continuous at 1, but is defined at 1.

  b. Sketch the graph of a function that is not continuous at 1, but has a limit at 1.

84. An unknown constant Determine the value of the constant a for which the function

$$f(x) = \begin{cases} \dfrac{x^2 + 3x + 2}{x + 1} & \text{if } x \neq -1 \\ a & \text{if } x = -1 \end{cases}$$

is continuous at -1.

85. An unknown constant Let

$$g(x) = \begin{cases} x^2 + x & \text{if } x < 1 \\ a & \text{if } x = 1 \\ 3x + 5 & \text{if } x > 1. \end{cases}$$

  a. Determine the value of a for which g is continuous from the left at 1.

  b. Determine the value of a for which g is continuous from the right at 1.

  c. Is there a value of a for which g is continuous at 1? Explain.

86. Asymptotes of a function containing exponentials Let $f(x) = \dfrac{2e^x + 5e^{3x}}{e^{2x} - e^{3x}}$. Analyze $\displaystyle \lim_{x \to 0^-} f(x)$, $\displaystyle \lim_{x \to 0^+} f(x)$, $\displaystyle \lim_{x \to -\infty} f(x)$, and $\displaystyle \lim_{x \to \infty} f(x)$. Then give the horizontal and vertical asymptotes of f. Plot f to verify your results.

87. Asymptotes of a function containing exponentials Let $f(x) = \dfrac{2e^x + 10e^{-x}}{e^x + e^{-x}}$. Analyze $\displaystyle \lim_{x \to 0} f(x)$, $\displaystyle \lim_{x \to -\infty} f(x)$, and $\displaystyle \lim_{x \to \infty} f(x)$. Then give the horizontal and vertical asymptotes of f. Plot f to verify your results.

88–89. Applying the Intermediate Value Theorem *Use the Intermediate Value Theorem to verify that the following equations have three solutions on the given interval. Use a graphing utility to find the approximate roots.*

88. $x^3 + 10x^2 - 100x + 50 = 0$; $(-20, 10)$

89. $70x^3 - 87x^2 + 32x - 3 = 0$; $(0, 1)$

Applications

90. Parking costs Determine the intervals of continuity for the parking cost function c introduced at the outset of this section (see figure). Consider $0 \le t \le 60$.

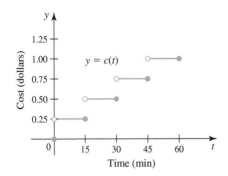

T 91. Investment problem Assume you invest $250 at the end of each year for 10 years at an annual interest rate of r. The amount of money in your account after 10 years is

$$A = \frac{250((1 + r)^{10} - 1)}{r}.$$ Assume your goal is to have $3500 in your account after 10 years.

a. Use the Intermediate Value Theorem to show that there is an interest rate r in the interval $(0.01, 0.10)$—between 1% and 10%—that allows you to reach your financial goal.

b. Use a calculator to estimate the interest rate required to reach your financial goal.

92. Applying the Intermediate Value Theorem Suppose you park your car at a trailhead in a national park and begin a 2-hr hike to a lake at 7 A.M. on a Friday morning. On Sunday morning, you leave the lake at 7 A.M. and start the 2-hr hike back to your car. Assume the lake is 3 mi from your car. Let $f(t)$ be your distance from the car t hours after 7 A.M. on Friday morning and let $g(t)$ be your distance from the car t hours after 7 A.M. on Sunday morning.

a. Evaluate $f(0), f(2), g(0)$, and $g(2)$.

b. Let $h(t) = f(t) - g(t)$. Find $h(0)$ and $h(2)$.

c. Use the Intermediate Value Theorem to show that there is some point along the trail that you will pass at exactly the same time of morning on both days.

93. The monk and the mountain A monk set out from a monastery in the valley at dawn. He walked all day up a winding path, stopping for lunch and taking a nap along the way. At dusk, he arrived at a temple on the mountaintop. The next day the monk made the return walk to the valley, leaving the temple at dawn, walking the same path for the entire day, and arriving at the monastery in the evening. Must there be one point along the path that the monk occupied at the same time of day on both the ascent and descent? (*Hint:* The question can be answered without the Intermediate Value Theorem.) (*Source:* Arthur Koestler, *The Act of Creation.*)

Additional Exercises

94. Does continuity of $|f|$ imply continuity of f? Let

$$g(x) = \begin{cases} 1 & \text{if } x \ge 0 \\ -1 & \text{if } x < 0. \end{cases}$$

a. Write a formula for $|g(x)|$.

b. Is g continuous at $x = 0$? Explain.

c. Is $|g|$ continuous at $x = 0$? Explain.

d. For any function f, if $|f|$ is continuous at a, does it necessarily follow that f is continuous at a? Explain.

95–96. Classifying discontinuities *The discontinuities in graphs (a) and (b) are* **removable discontinuities** *because they disappear if we define or redefine f at a so that $f(a) = \lim_{x \to a} f(x)$. The function in graph (c) has a* **jump discontinuity** *because left and right limits exist at a but are unequal. The discontinuity in graph (d) is an* **infinite discontinuity** *because the function has a vertical asymptote at a.*

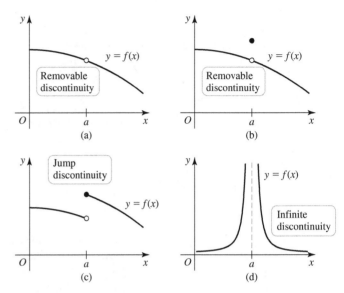

95. Is the discontinuity at a in graph (c) removable? Explain.

96. Is the discontinuity at a in graph (d) removable? Explain.

97–98. Removable discontinuities *Show that the following functions have a removable discontinuity at the given point. See Exercises 95–96.*

97. $f(x) = \dfrac{x^2 - 7x + 10}{x - 2}; x = 2$

98. $g(x) = \begin{cases} \dfrac{x^2 - 1}{1 - x} & \text{if } x \ne 1 \\ 3 & \text{if } x = 1 \end{cases}; x = 1$

99. Do removable discontinuities exist? See Exercises 95–96.

a. Does the function $f(x) = x \sin(1/x)$ have a removable discontinuity at $x = 0$?

b. Does the function $g(x) = \sin(1/x)$ have a removable discontinuity at $x = 0$?

T 100–101. Classifying discontinuities *Classify the discontinuities in the following functions at the given points. See Exercises 95–96.*

100. $f(x) = \dfrac{|x - 2|}{x - 2}; x = 2$

101. $h(x) = \dfrac{x^3 - 4x^2 + 4x}{x(x - 1)}; x = 0$ and $x = 1$

102. Continuity of composite functions Prove Theorem 2.11: If g is continuous at a and f is continuous at $g(a)$, then the composition $f \circ g$ is continuous at a. (*Hint:* Write the definition of continuity for f and g separately; then combine them to form the definition of continuity for $f \circ g$.)

103. Continuity of compositions

a. Find functions f and g such that each function is continuous at 0 but $f \circ g$ is not continuous at 0.

b. Explain why examples satisfying part (a) do not contradict Theorem 2.12.

104. Violation of the Intermediate Value Theorem? Let $f(x) = \dfrac{|x|}{x}$. Then $f(-2) = -1$ and $f(2) = 1$. Therefore, $f(-2) < 0 < f(2)$, but there is no value of c between -2 and 2 for which $f(c) = 0$. Does this fact violate the Intermediate Value Theorem? Explain.

105. Continuity of $\sin x$ and $\cos x$

   a. Use the identity $\sin(a + h) = \sin a \cos h + \cos a \sin h$ with the fact that $\lim\limits_{x \to 0} \sin x = 0$ to prove that $\lim\limits_{x \to a} \sin x = \sin a$, thereby establishing that $\sin x$ is continuous for all x. (*Hint:* Let $h = x - a$ so that $x = a + h$ and note that $h \to 0$ as $x \to a$.)

   b. Use the identity $\cos(a + h) = \cos a \cos h - \sin a \sin h$ with the fact that $\lim\limits_{x \to 0} \cos x = 1$ to prove that $\lim\limits_{x \to a} \cos x = \cos a$.

QUICK CHECK ANSWERS

1. $t = 15, 30, 45$ **2.** Both expressions have a value of 5, showing that $\lim\limits_{x \to a} f(g(x)) = f(\lim\limits_{x \to a} g(x))$.   **3.** Fill in the endpoints.   **4.** $[0, \infty)$; $(-\infty, \infty)$ **5.** Note that $\lim\limits_{x \to 1^+} \sqrt[4]{\ln x} = \sqrt[4]{\lim\limits_{x \to 1^+} \ln x} = 0$ and $f(1) = \sqrt[4]{\ln 1} = 0$. Because the limit from the right and the value of the function at $x = 1$ are equal, the function is right-continuous at $x = 1$.   **6.** The equation has a solution on the interval $[-1, 1]$ because f is continuous on $[-1, 1]$ and $f(-1) < 0 < f(1)$. ◄

2.7 Precise Definitions of Limits

The limit definitions already encountered in this chapter are adequate for most elementary limits. However, some of the terminology used, such as *sufficiently close* and *arbitrarily large*, needs clarification. The goal of this section is to give limits a solid mathematical foundation by transforming the previous limit definitions into precise mathematical statements.

Moving Toward a Precise Definition

> The phrase *for all x near a* means for all x in an open interval containing a.

> The Greek letters δ (delta) and ε (epsilon) represent small positive numbers in the discussion of limits.

> The two conditions $|x - a| < \delta$ and $x \neq a$ are written concisely as $0 < |x - a| < \delta$.

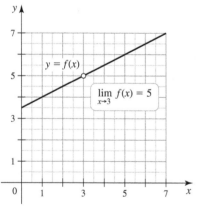

Figure 2.59

> The founders of calculus, Isaac Newton (1642–1727) and Gottfried Leibniz (1646–1716), developed the core ideas of calculus without using a precise definition of a limit. It was not until the 19th century that a rigorous definition was introduced by Augustin-Louis Cauchy (1789–1857) and later refined by Karl Weierstrass (1815–1897).

Assume the function f is defined for all x near a, except possibly at a. Recall that $\lim\limits_{x \to a} f(x) = L$ means that $f(x)$ is arbitrarily close to L for all x sufficiently close (but not equal) to a. This limit definition is made precise by observing that the distance between $f(x)$ and L is $|f(x) - L|$ and that the distance between x and a is $|x - a|$. Therefore, we write $\lim\limits_{x \to a} f(x) = L$ if we can make $|f(x) - L|$ arbitrarily small for any x, distinct from a, with $|x - a|$ sufficiently small. For instance, if we want $|f(x) - L|$ to be less than 0.1, then we must find a number $\delta > 0$ such that

$$|f(x) - L| < 0.1 \quad \text{whenever} \quad |x - a| < \delta \quad \text{and} \quad x \neq a.$$

If, instead, we want $|f(x) - L|$ to be less than 0.001, then we must find *another* number $\delta > 0$ such that

$$|f(x) - L| < 0.001 \quad \text{whenever} \quad 0 < |x - a| < \delta.$$

For the limit to exist, it must be true that for *any* $\varepsilon > 0$, we can always find a $\delta > 0$ such that

$$|f(x) - L| < \varepsilon \quad \text{whenever} \quad 0 < |x - a| < \delta.$$

EXAMPLE 1   **Determining values of δ from a graph**   Figure 2.59 shows the graph of a linear function f with $\lim\limits_{x \to 3} f(x) = 5$. For each value of $\varepsilon > 0$, determine a value of $\delta > 0$ satisfying the statement

$$|f(x) - 5| < \varepsilon \quad \text{whenever} \quad 0 < |x - 3| < \delta.$$

   a. $\varepsilon = 1$ **b.** $\varepsilon = \frac{1}{2}$

SOLUTION

   a. With $\varepsilon = 1$, we want $f(x)$ to be less than 1 unit from 5, which means $f(x)$ is between 4 and 6. To determine a corresponding value of δ, draw the horizontal lines $y = 4$ and $y = 6$ (Figure 2.60a). Then sketch vertical lines passing through the points where the horizontal lines and the graph of f intersect (Figure 2.60b). We see that the vertical

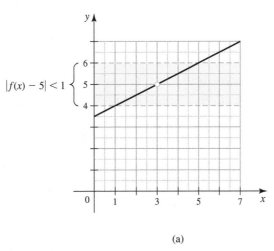

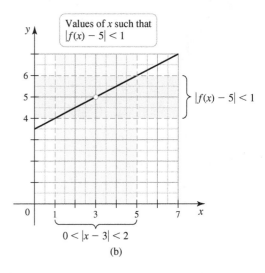

Figure 2.60

(a)

(b)

lines intersect the x-axis at $x = 1$ and $x = 5$. Note that $f(x)$ is less than 1 unit from 5 on the y-axis if x is within 2 units of 3 on the x-axis. So for $\varepsilon = 1$, we let $\delta = 2$ or any smaller positive value.

▶ Once an acceptable value of δ is found satisfying the statement

$$|f(x) - L| < \varepsilon \quad \text{whenever}$$

$$0 < |x - a| < \delta,$$

any smaller positive value of δ also works.

b. With $\varepsilon = \frac{1}{2}$, we want $f(x)$ to lie within a half-unit of 5, or equivalently, $f(x)$ must lie between 4.5 and 5.5. Proceeding as in part (a), we see that $f(x)$ is within a half-unit of 5 on the y-axis (Figure 2.61a) if x is less than 1 unit from 3 (Figure 2.61b). So for $\varepsilon = \frac{1}{2}$, we let $\delta = 1$ or any smaller positive number.

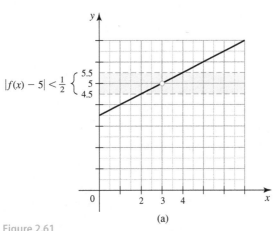

Figure 2.61

(a)

(b)

Related Exercises 9–12 ◀

The idea of a limit, as illustrated in Example 1, may be described in terms of a contest between two people named Epp and Del. First, Epp picks a particular number $\varepsilon > 0$; then he challenges Del to find a corresponding value of $\delta > 0$ such that

$$|f(x) - 5| < \varepsilon \quad \text{whenever} \quad 0 < |x - 3| < \delta. \tag{1}$$

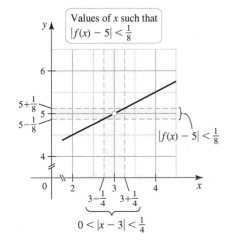

Figure 2.62

To illustrate, suppose Epp chooses $\varepsilon = 1$. From Example 1, we know that Del will satisfy (1) by choosing $0 < \delta \le 2$. If Epp chooses $\varepsilon = \frac{1}{2}$, then (by Example 1) Del responds by letting $0 < \delta \le 1$. If Epp lets $\varepsilon = \frac{1}{8}$, then Del chooses $0 < \delta \le \frac{1}{4}$ (Figure 2.62). In fact, there is a pattern: For *any* $\varepsilon > 0$ that Epp chooses, no matter how small, Del will satisfy (1) by choosing a positive value of δ satisfying $0 < \delta \le 2\varepsilon$. Del has discovered a mathematical relationship: If $0 < \delta \le 2\varepsilon$ and $0 < |x - 3| < \delta$, then $|f(x) - 5| < \varepsilon$, for *any* $\varepsilon > 0$. This conversation illustrates the general procedure for proving that $\lim_{x \to a} f(x) = L$.

QUICK CHECK 1 In Example 1, find a positive number δ satisfying the statement

$$|f(x) - 5| < \frac{1}{100} \quad \text{whenever} \quad 0 < |x - 3| < \delta. ◄$$

A Precise Definition

Example 1 dealt with a linear function, but it points the way to a precise definition of a limit for any function. As shown in Figure 2.63, $\lim_{x \to a} f(x) = L$ means that for *any* positive number ε, there is another positive number δ such that

$$|f(x) - L| < \varepsilon \quad \text{whenever} \quad 0 < |x - a| < \delta.$$

In all limit proofs, the goal is to find a relationship between ε and δ that gives an admissible value of δ, in terms of ε only. This relationship must work for any positive value of ε.

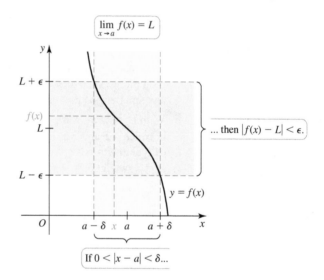

Figure 2.63

> The value of δ in the precise definition of a limit depends only on ε.

> Definitions of the one-sided limits $\lim_{x \to a^+} f(x) = L$ and $\lim_{x \to a^-} f(x) = L$ are discussed in Exercises 39–43.

DEFINITION **Limit of a Function**

Assume that $f(x)$ exists for all x in some open interval containing a, except possibly at a. We say **the limit of $f(x)$ as x approaches a is L**, written

$$\lim_{x \to a} f(x) = L,$$

if for *any* number $\varepsilon > 0$ there is a corresponding number $\delta > 0$ such that

$$|f(x) - L| < \varepsilon \quad \text{whenever} \quad 0 < |x - a| < \delta.$$

EXAMPLE 2 **Finding δ for a given ε using a graphing utility** Let $f(x) = x^3 - 6x^2 + 12x - 5$ and demonstrate that $\lim_{x \to 2} f(x) = 3$ as follows. For the given values of ε, use a graphing utility to find a value of $\delta > 0$ such that

$$|f(x) - 3| < \varepsilon \quad \text{whenever} \quad 0 < |x - 2| < \delta.$$

a. $\varepsilon = 1$ **b.** $\varepsilon = \frac{1}{2}$

SOLUTION

a. The condition $|f(x) - 3| < \varepsilon = 1$ implies that $f(x)$ lies between 2 and 4. Using a graphing utility, we graph f and the lines $y = 2$ and $y = 4$ (Figure 2.64). These lines intersect the graph of f at $x = 1$ and at $x = 3$. We now sketch the vertical lines $x = 1$ and $x = 3$ and observe that $f(x)$ is within 1 unit of 3 whenever x is within 1 unit of 2 on the x-axis (Figure 2.64). Therefore, with $\varepsilon = 1$, we can choose any δ with $0 < \delta \leq 1$.

b. The condition $|f(x) - 3| < \varepsilon = \frac{1}{2}$ implies that $f(x)$ lies between 2.5 and 3.5 on the y-axis. We now find that the lines $y = 2.5$ and $y = 3.5$ intersect the graph of f at $x \approx 1.21$ and $x \approx 2.79$ (Figure 2.65). Observe that if x is less than 0.79 unit from 2 on the x-axis, then $f(x)$ is less than a half unit from 3 on the y-axis. Therefore, with $\varepsilon = \frac{1}{2}$ we can choose any δ with $0 < \delta \leq 0.79$.

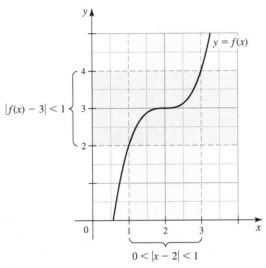

Figure 2.64

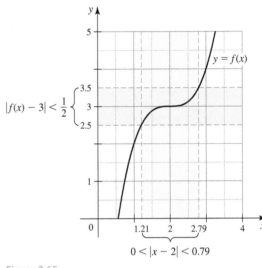

Figure 2.65

This procedure could be repeated for smaller and smaller values of $\varepsilon > 0$. For each value of ε, there exists a corresponding value of δ, proving that the limit exists.

Related Exercises 13–14 ◄

QUICK CHECK 2 For the function f given in Example 2, estimate a value of $\delta > 0$ satisfying $|f(x) - 3| < 0.25$ whenever $0 < |x - 2| < \delta$. ◄

The inequality $0 < |x - a| < \delta$ means that x lies between $a - \delta$ and $a + \delta$ with $x \neq a$. We say that the interval $(a - \delta, a + \delta)$ is **symmetric about** a because a is the midpoint of the interval. Symmetric intervals are convenient, but Example 3 demonstrates that we don't always get symmetric intervals without a bit of extra work.

EXAMPLE 3 **Finding a symmetric interval** Figure 2.66 shows the graph of g with $\lim\limits_{x \to 2} g(x) = 3$. For each value of ε, find the corresponding values of $\delta > 0$ that satisfy the condition

$$|g(x) - 3| < \varepsilon \quad \text{whenever} \quad 0 < |x - 2| < \delta.$$

a. $\varepsilon = 2$

b. $\varepsilon = 1$

c. For any given value of ε, make a conjecture about the corresponding values of δ that satisfy the limit condition.

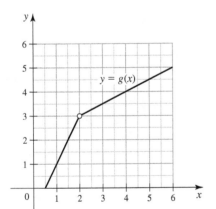

Figure 2.66

SOLUTION

a. With $\varepsilon = 2$, we need a value of $\delta > 0$ such that $g(x)$ is within 2 units of 3, which means between 1 and 5, whenever x is less than δ units from 2. The horizontal lines $y = 1$ and $y = 5$ intersect the graph of g at $x = 1$ and $x = 6$. Therefore, $|g(x) - 3| < 2$ if x lies in the interval $(1, 6)$ with $x \neq 2$ (Figure 2.67a). However, we want x to lie in an interval that is *symmetric* about 2. We can guarantee that $|g(x) - 3| < 2$ only if x is less than 1 unit away from 2, on either side of 2 (Figure 2.67b). Therefore, with $\varepsilon = 2$, we take $\delta = 1$ or any smaller positive number.

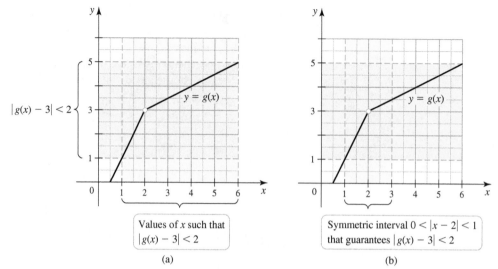

Figure 2.67

b. With $\varepsilon = 1$, $g(x)$ must lie between 2 and 4 (Figure 2.68a). This implies that x must be within a half unit to the left of 2 and within 2 units to the right of 2. Therefore, $|g(x) - 3| < 1$ provided x lies in the interval $(1.5, 4)$. To obtain a symmetric interval about 2, we take $\delta = \frac{1}{2}$ or any smaller positive number. Then we are guaranteed that $|g(x) - 3| < 1$ when $0 < |x - 2| < \frac{1}{2}$ (Figure 2.68b).

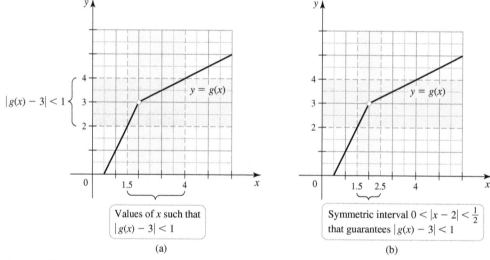

Figure 2.68

c. From parts (a) and (b), it appears that if we choose $\delta \le \varepsilon/2$, the limit condition is satisfied for any $\varepsilon > 0$.

Related Exercises 15–18 ◄

In Examples 2 and 3, we showed that a limit exists by discovering a relationship between ε and δ that satisfies the limit condition. We now generalize this procedure.

Limit Proofs

We use the following two-step process to prove that $\lim_{x \to a} f(x) = L$.

> The first step of the limit-proving process is the preliminary work of finding a candidate for δ. The second step verifies that the δ found in the first step actually works.

Steps for proving that $\lim_{x \to a} f(x) = L$

1. **Find δ.** Let ε be an arbitrary positive number. Use the inequality $|f(x) - L| < \varepsilon$ to find a condition of the form $|x - a| < \delta$, where δ depends only on the value of ε.

2. **Write a proof.** For any $\varepsilon > 0$, assume $0 < |x - a| < \delta$ and use the relationship between ε and δ found in Step 1 to prove that $|f(x) - L| < \varepsilon$.

EXAMPLE 4 Limit of a linear function Prove that $\lim_{x \to 4} (4x - 15) = 1$ using the precise definition of a limit.

SOLUTION

Step 1: *Find δ.* In this case, $a = 4$ and $L = 1$. Assuming $\varepsilon > 0$ is given, we use $|(4x - 15) - 1| < \varepsilon$ to find an inequality of the form $|x - 4| < \delta$. If $|(4x - 15) - 1| < \varepsilon$, then

$$|4x - 16| < \varepsilon$$

$$4|x - 4| < \varepsilon \qquad \text{Factor } 4x - 16.$$

$$|x - 4| < \frac{\varepsilon}{4}. \qquad \text{Divide by 4 and identify } \delta = \varepsilon/4.$$

We have shown that $|(4x - 15) - 1| < \varepsilon$ implies that $|x - 4| < \varepsilon/4$. Therefore, a plausible relationship between δ and ε is $\delta = \varepsilon/4$. We now write the actual proof.

Step 2: *Write a proof.* Let $\varepsilon > 0$ be given and assume $0 < |x - 4| < \delta$ where $\delta = \varepsilon/4$. The aim is to show that $|(4x - 15) - 1| < \varepsilon$ for all x such that $0 < |x - 4| < \delta$. We simplify $|(4x - 15) - 1|$ and isolate the $|x - 4|$ term:

$$|(4x - 15) - 1| = |4x - 16|$$

$$= 4 \underbrace{|x - 4|}_{\text{less than } \delta = \varepsilon/4}$$

$$< 4\left(\frac{\varepsilon}{4}\right) = \varepsilon.$$

We have shown that for any $\varepsilon > 0$,

$$|f(x) - L| = |(4x - 15) - 1| < \varepsilon \quad \text{whenever} \quad 0 < |x - 4| < \delta,$$

provided $0 < \delta \le \varepsilon/4$. Therefore, $\lim_{x \to 4} (4x - 15) = 1$.

Related Exercises 19–24 ◄

Justifying Limit Laws

The precise definition of a limit is used to prove the limit laws in Theorem 2.3. Essential in several of these proofs is the **triangle inequality**, which states that

$$|x + y| \le |x| + |y|, \quad \text{for all real numbers } x \text{ and } y.$$

EXAMPLE 5 Proof of Limit Law 1 Prove that if $\lim_{x \to a} f(x)$ and $\lim_{x \to a} g(x)$ exist, then

$$\lim_{x \to a} (f(x) + g(x)) = \lim_{x \to a} f(x) + \lim_{x \to a} g(x).$$

> Because $\lim_{x \to a} f(x)$ exists, if there exists a $\delta > 0$ for any given $\varepsilon > 0$, then there also exists a $\delta > 0$ for any given $\frac{\varepsilon}{2}$.

SOLUTION Assume that $\varepsilon > 0$ is given. Let $\lim_{x \to a} f(x) = L$, which implies that there exists a $\delta_1 > 0$ such that

$$|f(x) - L| < \frac{\varepsilon}{2} \quad \text{whenever} \quad 0 < |x - a| < \delta_1.$$

Similarly, let $\lim_{x \to a} g(x) = M$, which implies there exists a $\delta_2 > 0$ such that

$$|g(x) - M| < \frac{\varepsilon}{2} \quad \text{whenever} \quad 0 < |x - a| < \delta_2.$$

> The minimum value of a and b is denoted $\min\{a, b\}$. If $x = \min\{a, b\}$, then x is the smaller of a and b. If $a = b$, then x equals the common value of a and b. In either case, $x \le a$ and $x \le b$.

Let $\delta = \min\{\delta_1, \delta_2\}$ and suppose $0 < |x - a| < \delta$. Because $\delta \le \delta_1$, it follows that $0 < |x - a| < \delta_1$ and $|f(x) - L| < \varepsilon/2$. Similarly, because $\delta \le \delta_2$, it follows that $0 < |x - a| < \delta_2$ and $|g(x) - M| < \varepsilon/2$. Therefore,

$$
\begin{aligned}
|(f(x) + g(x)) - (L + M)| &= |(f(x) - L) + (g(x) - M)| \quad \text{\small Rearrange terms.} \\
&\le |f(x) - L| + |g(x) - M| \quad \text{\small Triangle inequality} \\
&< \frac{\varepsilon}{2} + \frac{\varepsilon}{2} = \varepsilon.
\end{aligned}
$$

> Proofs of other limit laws are outlined in Exercises 25–26.

We have shown that given any $\varepsilon > 0$, if $0 < |x - a| < \delta$, then $|(f(x) + g(x)) - (L + M)| < \varepsilon$, which implies that $\lim_{x \to a}(f(x) + g(x)) = L + M = \lim_{x \to a} f(x) + \lim_{x \to a} g(x)$.

Related Exercises 25–28 ◄

Infinite Limits

> Notice that for infinite limits, N plays the role that ε plays for regular limits. It sets a tolerance or bound for the function values $f(x)$.

In Section 2.4, we stated that $\lim_{x \to a} f(x) = \infty$ if $f(x)$ grows *arbitrarily large* as x approaches a. More precisely, this means that for any positive number N (no matter how large), $f(x)$ is larger than N if x is sufficiently close to a but not equal to a.

DEFINITION Two-Sided Infinite Limit

The **infinite limit** $\lim_{x \to a} f(x) = \infty$ means that for any positive number N, there exists a corresponding $\delta > 0$ such that

$$f(x) > N \quad \text{whenever} \quad 0 < |x - a| < \delta.$$

As shown in Figure 2.69, to prove that $\lim_{x \to a} f(x) = \infty$, we let N represent *any* positive number. Then we find a value of $\delta > 0$, depending only on N, such that

$$f(x) > N \quad \text{whenever} \quad 0 < |x - a| < \delta.$$

This process is similar to the two-step process for finite limits.

> Precise definitions for $\lim_{x \to a} f(x) = -\infty$, $\lim_{x \to a^+} f(x) = -\infty$, $\lim_{x \to a^+} f(x) = \infty$, $\lim_{x \to a^-} f(x) = -\infty$, and $\lim_{x \to a^-} f(x) = \infty$ are given in Exercises 45–49.

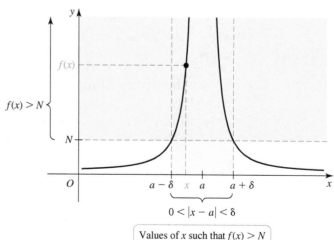

Figure 2.69

> **Steps for proving that $\lim\limits_{x \to a} f(x) = \infty$**
>
> 1. **Find δ.** Let N be an arbitrary positive number. Use the statement $f(x) > N$ to find an inequality of the form $|x - a| < \delta$, where δ depends only on N.
> 2. **Write a proof.** For any $N > 0$, assume $0 < |x - a| < \delta$ and use the relationship between N and δ found in Step 1 to prove that $f(x) > N$.

EXAMPLE 6   An Infinite Limit Proof Let $f(x) = \dfrac{1}{(x-2)^2}$. Prove that $\lim\limits_{x \to 2} f(x) = \infty$.

SOLUTION

Step 1: Find $\delta > 0$. Assuming $N > 0$, we use the inequality $\dfrac{1}{(x-2)^2} > N$ to find δ, where δ depends only on N. Taking reciprocals of this inequality, it follows that

$$(x-2)^2 < \frac{1}{N}$$

$$|x - 2| < \frac{1}{\sqrt{N}}. \quad \text{Take the square root of both sides.}$$

▶ Recall that $\sqrt{x^2} = |x|$.

The inequality $|x - 2| < \dfrac{1}{\sqrt{N}}$ has the form $|x - 2| < \delta$ if we let $\delta = \dfrac{1}{\sqrt{N}}$. We now write a proof based on this relationship between δ and N.

Step 2: Write a proof. Suppose $N > 0$ is given. Let $\delta = \dfrac{1}{\sqrt{N}}$ and assume $0 < |x - 2| < \delta = \dfrac{1}{\sqrt{N}}$. Squaring both sides of the inequality $|x - 2| < \dfrac{1}{\sqrt{N}}$ and taking reciprocals, we have

$$(x-2)^2 < \frac{1}{N} \quad \text{Square both sides.}$$

$$\frac{1}{(x-2)^2} > N. \quad \text{Take reciprocals of both sides.}$$

QUICK CHECK 3 In Example 6, if N is increased by a factor of 100, how must δ change? ◀

We see that for any positive N, if $0 < |x - 2| < \delta = \dfrac{1}{\sqrt{N}}$, then $f(x) = \dfrac{1}{(x-2)^2} > N$. It follows that $\lim\limits_{x \to 2} \dfrac{1}{(x-2)^2} = \infty$. Note that because $\delta = \dfrac{1}{\sqrt{N}}$, δ decreases as N increases.

Related Exercises 29–32 ◀

Limits at Infinity

Precise definitions can also be written for the limits at infinity $\lim\limits_{x \to \infty} f(x) = L$ and $\lim\limits_{x \to -\infty} f(x) = L$. For discussion and examples, see Exercises 50–51.

SECTION 2.7 EXERCISES

Review Questions

1. Suppose x lies in the interval $(1, 3)$ with $x \neq 2$. Find the smallest positive value of δ such that the inequality $0 < |x - 2| < \delta$ is true.

2. Suppose $f(x)$ lies in the interval $(2, 6)$. What is the smallest value of ε such that $|f(x) - 4| < \varepsilon$?

3. Which one of the following intervals is not symmetric about $x = 5$?

   a. $(1, 9)$ **b.** $(4, 6)$ **c.** $(3, 8)$ **d.** $(4.5, 5.5)$

4. Does the set $\{x: 0 < |x - a| < \delta\}$ include the point $x = a$? Explain.

5. State the precise definition of $\lim\limits_{x \to a} f(x) = L$.

6. Interpret $|f(x) - L| < \varepsilon$ in words.

7. Suppose $|f(x) - 5| < 0.1$ whenever $0 < x < 5$. Find all values of $\delta > 0$ such that $|f(x) - 5| < 0.1$ whenever $0 < |x - 2| < \delta$.

8. Give the definition of $\lim\limits_{x \to a} f(x) = \infty$ and interpret it using pictures.

Basic Skills

9. **Determining values of δ from a graph** The function f in the figure satisfies $\lim\limits_{x \to 2} f(x) = 5$. Determine the largest value of $\delta > 0$ satisfying each statement.

   a. If $0 < |x - 2| < \delta$, then $|f(x) - 5| < 2$.
   b. If $0 < |x - 2| < \delta$, then $|f(x) - 5| < 1$.

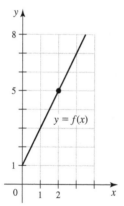

10. **Determining values of δ from a graph** The function f in the figure satisfies $\lim\limits_{x \to 2} f(x) = 4$. Determine the largest value of $\delta > 0$ satisfying each statement.

    a. If $0 < |x - 2| < \delta$, then $|f(x) - 4| < 1$.
    b. If $0 < |x - 2| < \delta$, then $|f(x) - 4| < 1/2$.

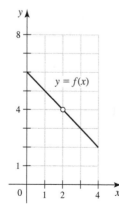

11. **Determining values of δ from a graph** The function f in the figure satisfies $\lim\limits_{x \to 3} f(x) = 6$. Determine the largest value of $\delta > 0$ satisfying each statement.

    a. If $0 < |x - 3| < \delta$, then $|f(x) - 6| < 3$.
    b. If $0 < |x - 3| < \delta$, then $|f(x) - 6| < 1$.

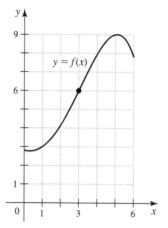

12. **Determining values of δ from a graph** The function f in the figure satisfies $\lim\limits_{x \to 4} f(x) = 5$. Determine the largest value of $\delta > 0$ satisfying each statement.

    a. If $0 < |x - 4| < \delta$, then $|f(x) - 5| < 1$.
    b. If $0 < |x - 4| < \delta$, then $|f(x) - 5| < 0.5$.

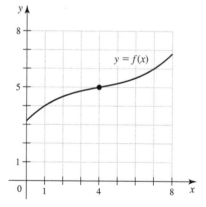

13. **Finding δ for a given ε using a graph** Let $f(x) = x^3 + 3$ and note that $\lim\limits_{x \to 0} f(x) = 3$. For each value of ε, use a graphing utility to find all values of $\delta > 0$ such that $|f(x) - 3| < \varepsilon$ whenever $0 < |x - 0| < \delta$. Sketch graphs illustrating your work.

    a. $\varepsilon = 1$ **b.** $\varepsilon = 0.5$

14. **Finding δ for a given ε using a graph** Let $g(x) = 2x^3 - 12x^2 + 26x + 4$ and note that $\lim\limits_{x \to 2} g(x) = 24$. For each value of ε, use a graphing utility to find all values of $\delta > 0$ such that $|g(x) - 24| < \varepsilon$ whenever $0 < |x - 2| < \delta$. Sketch graphs illustrating your work.

    a. $\varepsilon = 1$ **b.** $\varepsilon = 0.5$

15. **Finding a symmetric interval** The function f in the figure satisfies $\lim\limits_{x \to 2} f(x) = 3$. For each value of ε, find all values of $\delta > 0$ such that

$$|f(x) - 3| < \varepsilon \quad \text{whenever} \quad 0 < |x - 2| < \delta. \quad (2)$$

a. $\varepsilon = 1$

b. $\varepsilon = \frac{1}{2}$

c. For any $\varepsilon > 0$, make a conjecture about the corresponding value of δ satisfying (2).

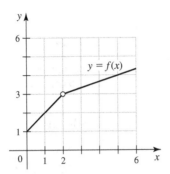

16. **Finding a symmetric interval** The function f in the figure satisfies $\lim_{x \to 4} f(x) = 5$. For each value of ε, find all values of $\delta > 0$ such that

$$|f(x) - 5| < \varepsilon \quad \text{whenever} \quad 0 < |x - 4| < \delta. \quad (3)$$

a. $\varepsilon = 2$ **b.** $\varepsilon = 1$

c. For any $\varepsilon > 0$, make a conjecture about the corresponding value of δ satisfying (3).

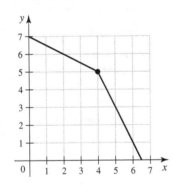

T 17. **Finding a symmetric interval** Let $f(x) = \dfrac{2x^2 - 2}{x - 1}$ and note that $\lim_{x \to 1} f(x) = 4$. For each value of ε, use a graphing utility to find all values of $\delta > 0$ such that $|f(x) - 4| < \varepsilon$ whenever $0 < |x - 1| < \delta$.

a. $\varepsilon = 2$ **b.** $\varepsilon = 1$

c. For any $\varepsilon > 0$, make a conjecture about the value of δ that satisfies the preceding inequality.

T 18. **Finding a symmetric interval** Let $f(x) = \begin{cases} \frac{1}{3}x + 1 & \text{if } x \le 3 \\ \frac{1}{2}x + \frac{1}{2} & \text{if } x > 3 \end{cases}$ and note that $\lim_{x \to 3} f(x) = 2$. For each value of ε, use a graphing utility to find all values of $\delta > 0$ such that $|f(x) - 2| < \varepsilon$ whenever $0 < |x - 3| < \delta$.

a. $\varepsilon = \frac{1}{2}$ **b.** $\varepsilon = \frac{1}{4}$

c. For any $\varepsilon > 0$, make a conjecture about the value of δ that satisfies the preceding inequality.

19–24. Limit proofs *Use the precise definition of a limit to prove the following limits.*

19. $\lim_{x \to 1} (8x + 5) = 13$

20. $\lim_{x \to 3} (-2x + 8) = 2$

21. $\lim_{x \to 4} \dfrac{x^2 - 16}{x - 4} = 8$ (*Hint:* Factor and simplify.)

22. $\lim_{x \to 3} \dfrac{x^2 - 7x + 12}{x - 3} = -1$

23. $\lim_{x \to 0} x^2 = 0$ (*Hint:* Use the identity $\sqrt{x^2} = |x|$.)

24. $\lim_{x \to 3} (x - 3)^2 = 0$ (*Hint:* Use the identity $\sqrt{x^2} = |x|$.)

25. **Proof of Limit Law 2** Suppose $\lim_{x \to a} f(x) = L$ and $\lim_{x \to a} g(x) = M$. Prove that $\lim_{x \to a} (f(x) - g(x)) = L - M$.

26. **Proof of Limit Law 3** Suppose $\lim_{x \to a} f(x) = L$. Prove that $\lim_{x \to a} [cf(x)] = cL$, where c is a constant.

27. **Limit of a constant function and $f(x) = x$** Give proofs of the following theorems.

a. $\lim_{x \to a} c = c$ for any constant c

b. $\lim_{x \to a} x = a$ for any constant a

28. **Continuity of linear functions** Prove Theorem 2.2: If $f(x) = mx + b$, then $\lim_{x \to a} f(x) = ma + b$ for constants $m \ne 0$ and b (the case $m = 0$ is considered in Exercise 27a). (*Hint:* For a given $\varepsilon > 0$, let $\delta = \varepsilon / |m|$.) Explain why this result implies that linear functions are continuous.

29–32. Limit proofs for infinite limits *Use the precise definition of infinite limits to prove the following limits.*

29. $\lim_{x \to 4} \dfrac{1}{(x - 4)^2} = \infty$

30. $\lim_{x \to -1} \dfrac{1}{(x + 1)^4} = \infty$

31. $\lim_{x \to 0} \left(\dfrac{1}{x^2} + 1\right) = \infty$

32. $\lim_{x \to 0} \left(\dfrac{1}{x^4} - \sin x\right) = \infty$

Further Explorations

33. **Explain why or why not** Determine whether the following statements are true and give an explanation or counterexample. Assume a and L are finite numbers and assume $\lim_{x \to a} f(x) = L$.

a. For a given $\varepsilon > 0$, there is one value of $\delta > 0$ for which $|f(x) - L| < \varepsilon$ whenever $0 < |x - a| < \delta$.

b. The limit $\lim_{x \to a} f(x) = L$ means that given an arbitrary $\delta > 0$, we can always find an $\varepsilon > 0$ such that $|f(x) - L| < \varepsilon$ whenever $0 < |x - a| < \delta$.

c. The limit $\lim_{x \to a} f(x) = L$ means that for any arbitrary $\varepsilon > 0$, we can always find a $\delta > 0$ such that $|f(x) - L| < \varepsilon$ whenever $0 < |x - a| < \delta$.

d. If $|x - a| < \delta$, then $a - \delta < x < a + \delta$.

34. **Finding δ algebraically** Let $f(x) = x^2 - 2x + 3$.

a. For $\varepsilon = 0.25$, find the largest value of $\delta > 0$ satisfying the statement

$$|f(x) - 2| < \varepsilon \quad \text{whenever} \quad 0 < |x - 1| < \delta.$$

b. Verify that $\lim_{x \to 1} f(x) = 2$ as follows. For any $\varepsilon > 0$, find the largest value of $\delta > 0$ satisfying the statement

$$|f(x) - 2| < \varepsilon \quad \text{whenever} \quad 0 < |x - 1| < \delta.$$

35–38. Challenging limit proofs *Use the definition of a limit to prove the following results.*

35. $\lim_{x \to 3} \dfrac{1}{x} = \dfrac{1}{3}$ (*Hint:* As $x \to 3$, eventually the distance between x and 3 is less than 1. Start by assuming $|x - 3| < 1$ and show $\dfrac{1}{|x|} < \dfrac{1}{2}$.)

36. $\lim\limits_{x\to 4}\dfrac{x-4}{\sqrt{x}-2}=4$ (*Hint:* Multiply the numerator and denominator by $\sqrt{x}+2$.)

37. $\lim\limits_{x\to 1/10}\dfrac{1}{x}=10$ (*Hint:* To find δ, you need to bound x away from 0. So let $\left|x-\dfrac{1}{10}\right|<\dfrac{1}{20}$.)

38. $\lim\limits_{x\to 5}\dfrac{1}{x^2}=\dfrac{1}{25}$

39–43. Precise definitions for left- and right-sided limits
Use the following definitions.

*Assume f exists for all x near a with $x>a$. We say **the limit of $f(x)$ as x approaches a from the right of a is L** and write $\lim\limits_{x\to a^+}f(x)=L$, if for any $\varepsilon>0$ there exists $\delta>0$ such that*
$$|f(x)-L|<\varepsilon \quad\text{whenever}\quad 0<x-a<\delta.$$

*Assume f exists for all x near a with $x<a$. We say **the limit of $f(x)$ as x approaches a from the left of a is L** and write $\lim\limits_{x\to a^-}f(x)=L$, if for any $\varepsilon>0$ there exists $\delta>0$ such that*
$$|f(x)-L|<\varepsilon \quad\text{whenever}\quad 0<a-x<\delta.$$

39. Comparing definitions Why is the last inequality in the definition of $\lim\limits_{x\to a}f(x)=L$, namely, $0<|x-a|<\delta$, replaced with $0<x-a<\delta$ in the definition of $\lim\limits_{x\to a^+}f(x)=L$?

40. Comparing definitions Why is the last inequality in the definition of $\lim\limits_{x\to a}f(x)=L$, namely, $0<|x-a|<\delta$, replaced with $0<a-x<\delta$ in the definition of $\lim\limits_{x\to a^-}f(x)=L$?

41. One-sided limit proofs Prove the following limits for
$$f(x)=\begin{cases}3x-4 & \text{if } x<0\\ 2x-4 & \text{if } x\ge 0.\end{cases}$$

   a. $\lim\limits_{x\to 0^+}f(x)=-4$ **b.** $\lim\limits_{x\to 0^-}f(x)=-4$
   c. $\lim\limits_{x\to 0}f(x)=-4$

42. Determining values of δ from a graph The function f in the figure satisfies $\lim\limits_{x\to 2^+}f(x)=0$ and $\lim\limits_{x\to 2^-}f(x)=1$. Determine all values of $\delta>0$ that satisfy each statement.

   a. $|f(x)-0|<2$ whenever $0<x-2<\delta$
   b. $|f(x)-0|<1$ whenever $0<x-2<\delta$
   c. $|f(x)-1|<2$ whenever $0<2-x<\delta$
   d. $|f(x)-1|<1$ whenever $0<2-x<\delta$

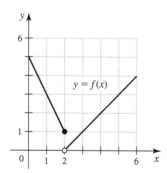

43. One-sided limit proof Prove that $\lim\limits_{x\to 0^+}\sqrt{x}=0$.

Additional Exercises

44. The relationship between one-sided and two-sided limits Prove the following statements to establish the fact that $\lim\limits_{x\to a}f(x)=L$ if and only if $\lim\limits_{x\to a^-}f(x)=L$ and $\lim\limits_{x\to a^+}f(x)=L$.

   a. If $\lim\limits_{x\to a^-}f(x)=L$ and $\lim\limits_{x\to a^+}f(x)=L$, then $\lim\limits_{x\to a}f(x)=L$.
   b. If $\lim\limits_{x\to a}f(x)=L$, then $\lim\limits_{x\to a^-}f(x)=L$ and $\lim\limits_{x\to a^+}f(x)=L$.

45. Definition of one-sided infinite limits We write $\lim\limits_{x\to a^+}f(x)=-\infty$ if for any negative number N there exists $\delta>0$ such that
$$f(x)<N \quad\text{whenever}\quad 0<x-a<\delta.$$

   a. Write an analogous formal definition for $\lim\limits_{x\to a^+}f(x)=\infty$.
   b. Write an analogous formal definition for $\lim\limits_{x\to a^-}f(x)=-\infty$.
   c. Write an analogous formal definition for $\lim\limits_{x\to a^-}f(x)=\infty$.

46–47. One-sided infinite limits *Use the definitions given in Exercise 45 to prove the following infinite limits.*

46. $\lim\limits_{x\to 1^+}\dfrac{1}{1-x}=-\infty$ **47.** $\lim\limits_{x\to 1^-}\dfrac{1}{1-x}=\infty$

48–49. Definition of an infinite limit *We write $\lim\limits_{x\to a}f(x)=-\infty$ if for any negative number M there exists $\delta>0$ such that*
$$f(x)<M \quad\text{whenever}\quad 0<|x-a|<\delta.$$

Use this definition to prove the following statements.

48. $\lim\limits_{x\to 1}\dfrac{-2}{(x-1)^2}=-\infty$ **49.** $\lim\limits_{x\to -2}\dfrac{-10}{(x+2)^4}=-\infty$

50–51. Definition of a limit at infinity *The limit at infinity $\lim\limits_{x\to\infty}f(x)=L$ means that for any $\varepsilon>0$ there exists $N>0$ such that*
$$|f(x)-L|<\varepsilon \quad\text{whenever}\quad x>N.$$

Use this definition to prove the following statements.

50. $\lim\limits_{x\to\infty}\dfrac{10}{x}=0$ **51.** $\lim\limits_{x\to\infty}\dfrac{2x+1}{x}=2$

52–53. Definition of infinite limits at infinity *We write $\lim\limits_{x\to\infty}f(x)=\infty$ if for any positive number M there is a corresponding $N>0$ such that*
$$f(x)>M \quad\text{whenever}\quad x>N.$$

Use this definition to prove the following statements.

52. $\lim\limits_{x\to\infty}\dfrac{x}{100}=\infty$ **53.** $\lim\limits_{x\to\infty}\dfrac{x^2+x}{x}=\infty$

54. Proof of the Squeeze Theorem Assume the functions f, g, and h satisfy the inequality $f(x)\le g(x)\le h(x)$ for all values of x near a, except possibly at a. Prove that if $\lim\limits_{x\to a}f(x)=\lim\limits_{x\to a}h(x)=L$, then $\lim\limits_{x\to a}g(x)=L$.

55. Limit proof Suppose f is defined for all values of x near a, except possibly at a. Assume for any integer $N>0$ there is another integer $M>0$ such that $|f(x)-L|<1/N$ whenever $|x-a|<1/M$. Prove that $\lim\limits_{x\to a}f(x)=L$ using the precise definition of a limit.

56–58. Proving that $\lim\limits_{x \to a} f(x) \neq L$ *Use the following definition for the* nonexistence *of a limit. Assume f is defined for all values of x near a, except possibly at a. We write $\lim\limits_{x \to a} f(x) \neq L$ if for some $\varepsilon > 0$, there is no value of $\delta > 0$ satisfying the condition*

$$|f(x) - L| < \varepsilon \quad \text{whenever} \quad 0 < |x - a| < \delta.$$

56. For the following function, note that $\lim\limits_{x \to 2} f(x) \neq 3$. Find all values of $\varepsilon > 0$ for which the preceding condition for nonexistence is satisfied.

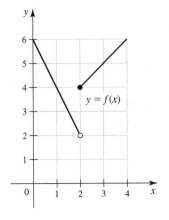

57. Prove that $\lim\limits_{x \to 0} \dfrac{|x|}{x}$ does not exist.

58. Let

$$f(x) = \begin{cases} 0 & \text{if } x \text{ is rational} \\ 1 & \text{if } x \text{ is irrational.} \end{cases}$$

Prove that $\lim\limits_{x \to a} f(x)$ does not exist for any value of a. (*Hint:* Assume $\lim\limits_{x \to a} f(x) = L$ for some values of a and L and let $\varepsilon = \frac{1}{2}$.)

59. A continuity proof Suppose f is continuous at a and assume $f(a) > 0$. Show that there is a positive number $\delta > 0$ for which $f(x) > 0$ for all values of x in $(a - \delta, a + \delta)$. (In other words, f is positive for all values of x in the domain of f and in some interval containing a.)

QUICK CHECK ANSWERS

1. $\delta = \frac{1}{50}$ or smaller   **2.** $\delta = 0.62$ or smaller   **3.** δ must decrease by a factor of $\sqrt{100} = 10$ (at least). ◄

 CHAPTER 2   REVIEW EXERCISES

1. **Explain why or why not** Determine whether the following statements are true and give an explanation or counterexample.

   a. The rational function $\dfrac{x - 1}{x^2 - 1}$ has vertical asymptotes at $x = -1$ and $x = 1$.

   b. Numerical or graphical methods always produce good estimates of $\lim\limits_{x \to a} f(x)$.

   c. The value of $\lim\limits_{x \to a} f(x)$, if it exists, is found by calculating $f(a)$.

   d. If $\lim\limits_{x \to a} f(x) = \infty$ or $\lim\limits_{x \to a} f(x) = -\infty$, then $\lim\limits_{x \to a} f(x)$ does not exist.

   e. If $\lim\limits_{x \to a} f(x)$ does not exist, then either $\lim\limits_{x \to a} f(x) = \infty$ or $\lim\limits_{x \to a} f(x) = -\infty$.

   f. The line $y = 2x + 1$ is a slant asymptote of the function

   $$f(x) = \frac{2x^2 + x}{x - 3}.$$

   g. If a function is continuous on the intervals (a, b) and $[b, c)$, where $a < b < c$, then the function is also continuous on (a, c).

   h. If $\lim\limits_{x \to a} f(x)$ can be calculated by direct substitution, then f is continuous at $x = a$.

2. **Estimating limits graphically** Use the graph of f in the figure to find the following values, or state that they do not exist.

   a. $f(-1)$ **b.** $\lim\limits_{x \to -1^-} f(x)$ **c.** $\lim\limits_{x \to -1^+} f(x)$ **d.** $\lim\limits_{x \to -1} f(x)$

   e. $f(1)$ **f.** $\lim\limits_{x \to 1} f(x)$ **g.** $\lim\limits_{x \to 2} f(x)$ **h.** $\lim\limits_{x \to 3^-} f(x)$

   i. $\lim\limits_{x \to 3^+} f(x)$ **j.** $\lim\limits_{x \to 3} f(x)$

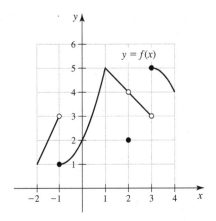

3. **Points of discontinuity** Use the graph of f in the figure to determine the values of x in the interval $(-3, 5)$ at which f fails to be continuous. Justify your answers using the continuity checklist.

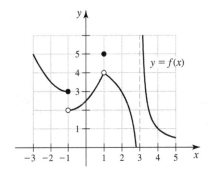

4. Computing a limit graphically and analytically

a. Graph $y = \dfrac{\sin 2\theta}{\sin \theta}$ with a graphing utility. Comment on any inaccuracies in the graph and then sketch an accurate graph of the function.

b. Estimate $\displaystyle\lim_{\theta \to 0} \dfrac{\sin 2\theta}{\sin \theta}$ using the graph in part (a).

c. Verify your answer to part (b) by finding the value of $\displaystyle\lim_{\theta \to 0} \dfrac{\sin 2\theta}{\sin \theta}$ analytically using the trigonometric identity $\sin 2\theta = 2 \sin \theta \cos \theta$.

5. Computing a limit numerically and analytically

a. Estimate $\displaystyle\lim_{x \to \pi/4} \dfrac{\cos 2x}{\cos x - \sin x}$ by making a table of values of $\dfrac{\cos 2x}{\cos x - \sin x}$ for values of x approaching $\pi/4$. Round your estimate to four digits.

b. Use analytic methods to find the value of $\displaystyle\lim_{x \to \pi/4} \dfrac{\cos 2x}{\cos x - \sin x}$.

6. Snowboard rental Suppose the rental cost for a snowboard is $25 for the first day (or any part of the first day) plus $15 for each additional day (or any part of a day).

a. Graph the function $c = f(t)$ that gives the cost of renting a snowboard for t days, for $0 \le t \le 5$.

b. Evaluate $\displaystyle\lim_{t \to 2.9} f(t)$.

c. Evaluate $\displaystyle\lim_{t \to 3^-} f(t)$ and $\displaystyle\lim_{t \to 3^+} f(t)$.

d. Interpret the meaning of the limits in part (c).

e. For what values of t is f continuous? Explain.

7. Sketching a graph Sketch the graph of a function f with all the following properties.

$$\lim_{x \to -2^-} f(x) = \infty \qquad \lim_{x \to -2^+} f(x) = -\infty \qquad \lim_{x \to 0} f(x) = \infty$$

$$\lim_{x \to 3^-} f(x) = 2 \qquad \lim_{x \to 3^+} f(x) = 4 \qquad f(3) = 1$$

8–21. Evaluating limits *Determine the following limits analytically.*

8. $\displaystyle\lim_{x \to 1000} 18\pi^2$

9. $\displaystyle\lim_{x \to 1} \sqrt{5x + 6}$

10. $\displaystyle\lim_{h \to 0} \dfrac{\sqrt{5x + 5h} - \sqrt{5x}}{h}$, where x is constant

11. $\displaystyle\lim_{x \to 1} \dfrac{x^3 - 7x^2 + 12x}{4 - x}$

12. $\displaystyle\lim_{x \to 4} \dfrac{x^3 - 7x^2 + 12x}{4 - x}$

13. $\displaystyle\lim_{x \to 1} \dfrac{1 - x^2}{x^2 - 8x + 7}$

14. $\displaystyle\lim_{x \to 3} \dfrac{\sqrt{3x + 16} - 5}{x - 3}$

15. $\displaystyle\lim_{x \to 3} \dfrac{1}{x - 3}\left(\dfrac{1}{\sqrt{x + 1}} - \dfrac{1}{2}\right)$

16. $\displaystyle\lim_{t \to 1/3} \dfrac{t - 1/3}{(3t - 1)^2}$

17. $\displaystyle\lim_{x \to 3} \dfrac{x^4 - 81}{x - 3}$

18. $\displaystyle\lim_{p \to 1} \dfrac{p^5 - 1}{p - 1}$

19. $\displaystyle\lim_{x \to 81} \dfrac{\sqrt[4]{x} - 3}{x - 81}$

20. $\displaystyle\lim_{\theta \to \pi/4} \dfrac{\sin^2 \theta - \cos^2 \theta}{\sin \theta - \cos \theta}$

21. $\displaystyle\lim_{x \to \pi/2} \dfrac{\dfrac{1}{\sqrt{\sin x}} - 1}{x + \pi/2}$

22. **One-sided limits** Analyze $\displaystyle\lim_{x \to 1^+} \sqrt{\dfrac{x - 1}{x - 3}}$ and $\displaystyle\lim_{x \to 1^-} \sqrt{\dfrac{x - 1}{x - 3}}$.

23. Applying the Squeeze Theorem

a. Use a graphing utility to illustrate the inequalities

$$\cos x \le \dfrac{\sin x}{x} \le \dfrac{1}{\cos x}$$

on $[-1, 1]$.

b. Use part (a) and the Squeeze Theorem to explain why

$$\lim_{x \to 0} \dfrac{\sin x}{x} = 1.$$

24. Applying the Squeeze Theorem Assume the function g satisfies the inequality $1 \le g(x) \le \sin^2 x + 1$, for x near 0. Use the Squeeze Theorem to find $\displaystyle\lim_{x \to 0} g(x)$.

25–29. Finding infinite limits *Analyze the following limits.*

25. $\displaystyle\lim_{x \to 5} \dfrac{x - 7}{x(x - 5)^2}$

26. $\displaystyle\lim_{x \to -5^+} \dfrac{x - 5}{x + 5}$

27. $\displaystyle\lim_{x \to 3^-} \dfrac{x - 4}{x^2 - 3x}$

28. $\displaystyle\lim_{u \to 0^+} \dfrac{u - 1}{\sin u}$

29. $\displaystyle\lim_{x \to 0^-} \dfrac{2}{\tan x}$

30. Finding vertical asymptotes Let $f(x) = \dfrac{x^2 - 5x + 6}{x^2 - 2x}$.

a. Analyze $\displaystyle\lim_{x \to 0^-} f(x)$, $\displaystyle\lim_{x \to 0^+} f(x)$, $\displaystyle\lim_{x \to 2^-} f(x)$, and $\displaystyle\lim_{x \to 2^+} f(x)$.

b. Does the graph of f have any vertical asymptotes? Explain.

c. Graph f and then sketch the graph with paper and pencil, correcting any errors obtained with the graphing utility.

31–36. Limits at infinity *Evaluate the following limits or state that they do not exist.*

31. $\displaystyle\lim_{x \to \infty} \dfrac{2x - 3}{4x + 10}$

32. $\displaystyle\lim_{x \to \infty} \dfrac{x^4 - 1}{x^5 + 2}$

33. $\displaystyle\lim_{x \to -\infty} (-3x^3 + 5)$

34. $\displaystyle\lim_{z \to \infty} \left(e^{-2z} + \dfrac{2}{z}\right)$

35. $\displaystyle\lim_{x \to \infty} (3 \tan^{-1} x + 2)$

36. $\displaystyle\lim_{r \to \infty} \dfrac{1}{\ln r + 1}$

37–40. End behavior *Determine the end behavior of the following functions.*

37. $f(x) = \dfrac{4x^3 + 1}{1 - x^3}$

38. $f(x) = \dfrac{x + 1}{\sqrt{9x^2 + x}}$

39. $f(x) = 1 - e^{-2x}$

40. $f(x) = \dfrac{1}{\ln x^2}$

41–42. Vertical and horizontal asymptotes *Find all vertical and horizontal asymptotes of the following functions.*

41. $f(x) = \dfrac{1}{\tan^{-1} x}$

42. $f(x) = \dfrac{2x^2 + 6}{2x^2 + 3x - 2}$

43–46. Slant asymptotes

a. Analyze $\lim\limits_{x \to \infty} f(x)$ and $\lim\limits_{x \to -\infty} f(x)$ for each function.

b. Determine whether f has a slant asymptote. If so, write the equation of the slant asymptote.

43. $f(x) = \dfrac{3x^2 + 2x - 1}{4x + 1}$

44. $f(x) = \dfrac{9x^2 + 4}{(2x - 1)^2}$

45. $f(x) = \dfrac{1 + x - 2x^2 - x^3}{x^2 + 1}$

46. $f(x) = \dfrac{x(x + 2)^3}{3x^2 - 4x}$

47–50. Continuity at a point Determine whether the following functions are continuous at a. Use the continuity checklist to justify your answers.

47. $f(x) = \dfrac{1}{x - 5}$; $a = 5$

48. $g(x) = \begin{cases} \dfrac{x^2 - 16}{x - 4} & \text{if } x \neq 4 \\ 9 & \text{if } x = 4 \end{cases}$; $a = 4$

49. $h(x) = \sqrt{x^2 - 9}$; $a = 3$

50. $g(x) = \begin{cases} \dfrac{x^2 - 16}{x - 4} & \text{if } x \neq 4 \\ 8 & \text{if } x = 4 \end{cases}$; $a = 4$

51–54. Continuity on intervals Find the intervals on which the following functions are continuous. Specify right- or left-continuity at the endpoints.

51. $f(x) = \sqrt{x^2 - 5}$

52. $g(x) = e^{\sqrt{x - 2}}$

53. $h(x) = \dfrac{2x}{x^3 - 25x}$

54. $g(x) = \cos e^x$

55. **Determining unknown constants** Let

$$g(x) = \begin{cases} 5x - 2 & \text{if } x < 1 \\ a & \text{if } x = 1 \\ ax^2 + bx & \text{if } x > 1. \end{cases}$$

Determine values of the constants a and b for which g is continuous at $x = 1$.

56. **Left- and right-continuity**

a. Is $h(x) = \sqrt{x^2 - 9}$ left-continuous at $x = 3$? Explain.

b. Is $h(x) = \sqrt{x^2 - 9}$ right-continuous at $x = 3$? Explain.

57. **Sketching a graph** Sketch the graph of a function that is continuous on $(0, 1]$ and continuous on $(1, 2)$ but is not continuous on $(0, 2)$.

58. **Intermediate Value Theorem**

a. Use the Intermediate Value Theorem to show that the equation $x^5 + 7x + 5 = 0$ has a solution in the interval $(-1, 0)$.

b. Estimate a solution to $x^5 + 7x + 5 = 0$ in $(-1, 0)$ using a root finder.

59. **Antibiotic dosing** The amount of an antibiotic (in mg) in the blood t hours after an intravenous line is opened is given by

$$m(t) = 100(e^{-0.1t} - e^{-0.3t}).$$

a. Use the Intermediate Value Theorem to show the amount of drug is 30 mg at some time in the interval $[0, 5]$ and again at some time in the interval $[5, 15]$.

b. Estimate the times at which $m = 30$ mg.

c. Is the amount of drug in the blood ever 50 mg?

60. **Limit proof** Give a formal proof that $\lim\limits_{x \to 1} (5x - 2) = 3$.

61. **Limit proof** Give a formal proof that $\lim\limits_{x \to 5} \dfrac{x^2 - 25}{x - 5} = 10$.

62. **Limit proofs**

a. Assume $|f(x)| \leq L$ for all x near a and $\lim\limits_{x \to a} g(x) = 0$. Give a formal proof that $\lim\limits_{x \to a} (f(x)g(x)) = 0$.

b. Find a function f for which $\lim\limits_{x \to 2} (f(x)(x - 2)) \neq 0$. Why doesn't this violate the result stated in (a)?

c. The Heaviside function is defined as

$$H(x) = \begin{cases} 0 & \text{if } x < 0 \\ 1 & \text{if } x \geq 0. \end{cases}$$

Explain why $\lim\limits_{x \to 0} [xH(x)] = 0$.

63. **Infinite limit proof** Give a formal proof that $\lim\limits_{x \to 2} \dfrac{1}{(x - 2)^4} = \infty$.

Chapter 2 Guided Projects

Applications of the material in this chapter and related topics can be found in the following Guided Projects. For additional information, see the Preface.

- Fixed-point iteration

- Local linearity

3

Derivatives

Chapter Preview Now that you are familiar with limits, the door to calculus stands open. The first task is to introduce the fundamental concept of the *derivative*. Suppose a function f represents a quantity of interest; for example, the variable cost of manufacturing an item, the population of a country, or the position of an orbiting satellite. The derivative of f is another function, denoted f', that gives the slope of the curve $y = f(x)$ as it changes with respect to x. Equivalently, the derivative of f gives the *instantaneous rate of change* of f with respect to the independent variable. We use limits not only to define the derivative but also to develop efficient rules for finding derivatives. The applications of the derivative—which we introduce along the way—are endless because almost everything around us is in a state of change, and derivatives describe change.

3.1 Introducing the Derivative

In this section, we return to the problem of finding the slope of a line tangent to a curve, introduced at the beginning of Chapter 2. This problem is important for several reasons.

- We identify the slope of the tangent line with the *instantaneous rate of change* of a function (Figure 3.1).

- The slopes of the tangent lines as they change along a curve are the values of a new function called the *derivative*.

- Looking farther ahead, if a curve represents the trajectory of a moving object, the tangent line at a point on the curve indicates the direction of motion at that point (Figure 3.2).

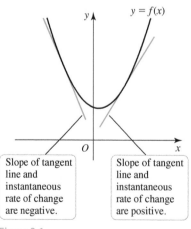

Slope of tangent line and instantaneous rate of change are negative.

Slope of tangent line and instantaneous rate of change are positive.

Figure 3.1

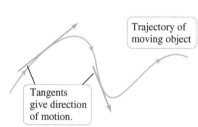

Trajectory of moving object

Tangents give direction of motion.

Figure 3.2

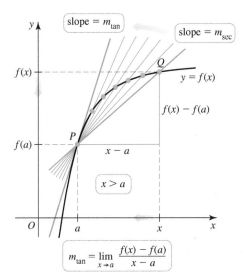

Figure 3.3

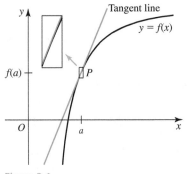

Figure 3.4

> The definition of m_{sec} involves a *difference quotient*, introduced in Section 1.1.

In Section 2.1, we gave an intuitive definition of a tangent line and used numerical evidence to estimate its slope. We now make these ideas precise.

Tangent Lines and Rates of Change

Consider the curve $y = f(x)$ and a secant line intersecting the curve at the points $P(a, f(a))$ and $Q(x, f(x))$ (Figure 3.3). The difference $f(x) - f(a)$ is the change in the value of f on the interval $[a, x]$, while $x - a$ is the change in x. As discussed in Chapters 1 and 2, the slope of the secant line $\overleftrightarrow{PQ}$ is

$$m_{sec} = \frac{f(x) - f(a)}{x - a},$$

and it gives the *average rate of change* in f on the interval $[a, x]$.

Figure 3.3 also shows what happens as the variable point x approaches the fixed point a. If the curve is smooth at $P(a, f(a))$—it has no kinks or corners—the secant lines approach a *unique* line that intersects the curve at P; this line is the *tangent line* at P. As x approaches a, the slopes m_{sec} of the secant lines approach a unique number m_{tan} that we call the *slope of the tangent line*; that is,

$$m_{tan} = \lim_{x \to a} \frac{f(x) - f(a)}{x - a}.$$

The slope of the tangent line at P is also called the *instantaneous rate of change* in f at a because it measures how quickly f changes at a.

The tangent line has another geometric interpretation. As discussed in Section 2.1, if the curve $y = f(x)$ is smooth at a point $P(a, f(a))$, then the curve looks more like a line as we zoom in on P. The line that is approached as we zoom in on P is the tangent line (Figure 3.4). A smooth curve has the property of *local linearity*, which means that if we look at a point on the curve locally (by zooming in), then the curve appears linear.

DEFINITION Rate of Change and the Slope of the Tangent Line

The **average rate of change** in f on the interval $[a, x]$ is the slope of the corresponding secant line:

$$m_{sec} = \frac{f(x) - f(a)}{x - a}.$$

The **instantaneous rate of change** in f at a is

$$m_{tan} = \lim_{x \to a} \frac{f(x) - f(a)}{x - a}, \tag{1}$$

which is also the **slope of the tangent line** at $(a, f(a))$, provided this limit exists. The **tangent line** is the unique line through $(a, f(a))$ with slope m_{tan}. Its equation is

$$y - f(a) = m_{tan}(x - a).$$

QUICK CHECK 1 Sketch the graph of a function f near a point a. As in Figure 3.3, draw a secant line that passes through $(a, f(a))$ and a neighboring point $(x, f(x))$ with $x < a$. Use arrows to show how the secant lines approach the tangent line as x approaches a. ◄

> If x and y have physical units, then the average and instantaneous rates of change have units of (units of y)/(units of x). For example, if y has units of meters and x has units of seconds, the units of the rate of change are meters/second (m/s).

EXAMPLE 1 Equation of a tangent line Let $f(x) = -16x^2 + 96x$ (the position function examined in Section 2.1) and consider the point $P(1, 80)$ on the curve.

a. Find the slope of the line tangent to the graph of f at P.

b. Find an equation of the tangent line in part (a).

SOLUTION

a. We use the definition of the slope of the tangent line with $a = 1$:

$$m_{\tan} = \lim_{x \to 1} \frac{f(x) - f(1)}{x - 1} \qquad \text{Definition of slope of tangent line}$$

$$= \lim_{x \to 1} \frac{(-16x^2 + 96x) - 80}{x - 1} \qquad f(x) = -16x^2 + 96x; f(1) = 80$$

$$= \lim_{x \to 1} \frac{-16(x - 5)(x - 1)}{x - 1} \qquad \text{Factor the numerator.}$$

$$= -16 \underbrace{\lim_{x \to 1} (x - 5)}_{-4} = 64. \qquad \text{Cancel factors } (x \neq 1) \text{ and evaluate the limit.}$$

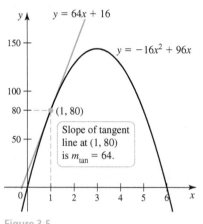

Figure 3.5

These calculations confirm the conjecture made in Section 2.1: The slope of the line tangent to the graph of $f(x) = -16x^2 + 96x$ at $(1, 80)$ is 64.

b. An equation of the line passing through $(1, 80)$ with slope $m_{\tan} = 64$ is $y - 80 = 64(x - 1)$ or $y = 64x + 16$. The graph of f and the tangent line at $(1, 80)$ are shown in Figure 3.5.

Related Exercises 9–14 ◄

QUICK CHECK 2 In Example 1, is the slope of the tangent line at $(2, 128)$ greater than or less than the slope at $(1, 80)$? ◄

An alternative formula for the slope of the tangent line is helpful for future work. Consider again the curve $y = f(x)$ and the secant line intersecting the curve at the points P and Q. We now let $(a, f(a))$ and $(a + h, f(a + h))$ be the coordinates of P and Q, respectively (Figure 3.6). The difference in the x-coordinates of P and Q is $(a + h) - a = h$. Note that Q is located to the right of P if $h > 0$ and to the left of P if $h < 0$.

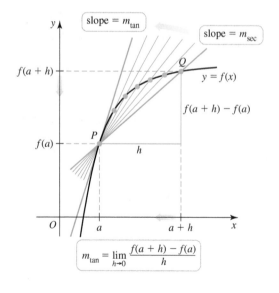

Figure 3.6

The slope of the secant line $\overleftrightarrow{PQ}$ using the new notation is $m_{\sec} = \dfrac{f(a + h) - f(a)}{h}$.

As h approaches 0, the variable point Q approaches P and the slopes of the secant lines approach the slope of the tangent line. Therefore, the slope of the tangent line at $(a, f(a))$, which is also the instantaneous rate of change of f at a, is

$$m_{\tan} = \lim_{h \to 0} \frac{f(a + h) - f(a)}{h}.$$

ALTERNATIVE DEFINITION   **Rate of Change and the Slope of the Tangent Line**

The **average rate of change** in f on the interval $[a, a + h]$ is the slope of the corresponding secant line:

$$m_{\text{sec}} = \frac{f(a + h) - f(a)}{h}.$$

The **instantaneous rate of change** in f at a is

$$m_{\text{tan}} = \lim_{h \to 0} \frac{f(a + h) - f(a)}{h}, \tag{2}$$

which is also the **slope of the tangent line** at $(a, f(a))$, provided this limit exists.

EXAMPLE 2   Equation of a tangent line Find an equation of the line tangent to the graph of $f(x) = x^3 + 4x$ at $(1, 5)$.

SOLUTION We let $a = 1$ in definition (2) and first find $f(1 + h)$. After expanding and collecting terms, we have

$$f(1 + h) = (1 + h)^3 + 4(1 + h) = h^3 + 3h^2 + 7h + 5.$$

Substituting $f(1 + h)$ and $f(1) = 5$, the slope of the tangent line is

$$
\begin{aligned}
m_{\text{tan}} &= \lim_{h \to 0} \frac{f(1 + h) - f(1)}{h} && \text{Definition of } m_{\text{tan}} \\
&= \lim_{h \to 0} \frac{(h^3 + 3h^2 + 7h + 5) - 5}{h} && \text{Substitute } f(1 + h) \text{ and } f(1) = 5. \\
&= \lim_{h \to 0} \frac{h(h^2 + 3h + 7)}{h} && \text{Simplify.} \\
&= \lim_{h \to 0} (h^2 + 3h + 7) && \text{Cancel } h, \text{ noting } h \neq 0. \\
&= 7. && \text{Evaluate the limit.}
\end{aligned}
$$

The tangent line has slope $m_{\text{tan}} = 7$ and passes through the point $(1, 5)$ (Figure 3.7); its equation is $y - 5 = 7(x - 1)$ or $y = 7x - 2$. We could also say that the instantaneous rate of change of f at $x = 1$ is 7.

Related Exercises 15–26 ◄

> ▶ By the definition of the limit as $h \to 0$, notice that h approaches 0 but $h \neq 0$. Therefore, it is permissible to cancel h from the numerator and denominator of $\dfrac{h(h^2 + 3h + 7)}{h}$.

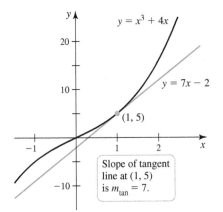

Figure 3.7

QUICK CHECK 3 Set up the calculation in Example 2 using definition (1) for the slope of the tangent line rather than definition (2). Does the calculation appear more difficult using definition (1)? ◄

The Derivative Function

So far we have computed the slope of the tangent line at one fixed point on a curve. If this point is moved along the curve, the tangent line also moves, and, in general, its slope changes (Figure 3.8). For this reason, the slope of the tangent line for the function f is itself a function, called the *derivative* of f.

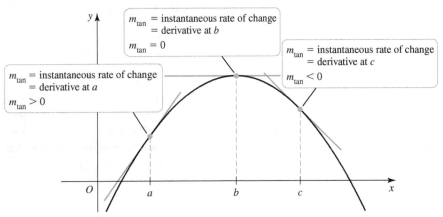

Figure 3.8

We let f' (read f *prime*) denote the derivative function for f, which means that $f'(a)$, when it exists, is the slope of the line tangent to the graph of f at $(a, f(a))$. Using definition (2) for the slope of the tangent line, we have

$$f'(a) = m_{\tan} = \lim_{h \to 0} \frac{f(a + h) - f(a)}{h}.$$

We now take an important step. The derivative is a special function, but it works just like any other function. For example, if the graph of f is smooth and 2 is in the domain of f, then $f'(2)$ is the slope of the line tangent to the graph of f at the point $(2, f(2))$. Similarly, if -2 is in the domain of f, then $f'(-2)$ is the slope of the tangent line at the point $(-2, f(-2))$. In fact, if x is *any* point in the domain of f, then $f'(x)$ is the slope of the tangent line at the point $(x, f(x))$. When we introduce a variable point x, the expression $f'(x)$ becomes the *derivative function*.

> ► To emphasize an important point, $f'(2)$ or $f'(-2)$ or $f'(a)$, for a real number a, are real numbers, whereas f' or $f'(x)$ refer to the derivative *function*.

> ► The process of finding f' is called *differentiation*, and to *differentiate* f means to find f'.

> ► Just as we have two definitions for the slope of the tangent line, we may also use the following definition for the derivative of f at a:
> $$f'(a) = \lim_{x \to a} \frac{f(x) - f(a)}{x - a}.$$

DEFINITION The Derivative Function

The **derivative** of f is the function

$$f'(x) = \lim_{h \to 0} \frac{f(x + h) - f(x)}{h},$$

provided the limit exists and x is the domain of f. If $f'(x)$ exists, we say that f is **differentiable** at x. If f is differentiable at every point of an open interval I, we say that f is differentiable on I.

Notice that the definition of f' applies only at points in the domain of f. Therefore, the domain of f' is no larger than the domain of f. If the limit in the definition of f' fails to exist at some points, then the domain of f' is a subset of the domain of f. Let's use this definition to compute a derivative function.

EXAMPLE 3 Computing a derivative Consider once again the function $f(x) = -16x^2 + 96x$ of Example 1 and find its derivative.

SOLUTION

> ► Notice that this argument applies for $h > 0$ and for $h < 0$; that is, the limit as $h \to 0^+$ and the limit as $h \to 0^-$ are equal.

$$f'(x) = \lim_{h \to 0} \frac{f(x + h) - f(x)}{h} \qquad \text{Definition of } f'(x)$$

$$= \lim_{h \to 0} \frac{\overbrace{-16(x + h)^2 + 96(x + h)}^{f(x+h)} - \overbrace{(-16x^2 + 96x)}^{f(x)}}{h} \qquad \text{Substitute.}$$

$$= \lim_{h \to 0} \frac{-16(x^2 + 2xh + h^2) + 96x + 96h + 16x^2 - 96x}{h} \qquad \text{Expand the numerator.}$$

$$= \lim_{h \to 0} \frac{h(-32x + 96 - 16h)}{h} \qquad \text{Simplify and factor out } h.$$

$$= \lim_{h \to 0} (-32x + 96 - 16h) = -32x + 96 \qquad \text{Cancel } h \text{ and evaluate the limit.}$$

The derivative is $f'(x) = -32x + 96$, which gives the slope of the tangent line (equivalently, the instantaneous rate of change) at *any* point on the curve. For example, at the point $(1, 80)$, the slope of the tangent line is $f'(1) = -32(1) + 96 = 64$, confirming the calculation in Example 1. The slope of the tangent line at $(3, 144)$ is $f'(3) = -32(3) + 96 = 0$, which means the tangent line is horizontal at that point (Figure 3.9).

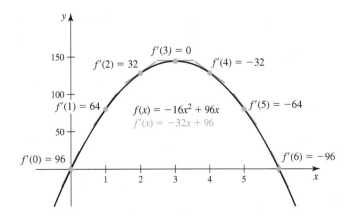

Figure 3.9

Related Exercises 27–40 ◄

QUICK CHECK 4 In Example 3, determine the slope of the tangent line at $x = 2$. ◄

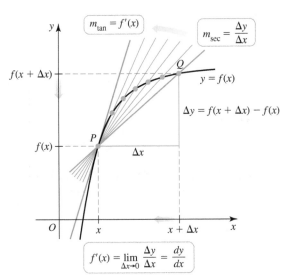

Figure 3.10

▶ The notation $\dfrac{dy}{dx}$ is read *the derivative of y with respect to x* or *dy dx*. It does not mean dy divided by dx, but it is a reminder of the limit of the quotient $\Delta y / \Delta x$.

▶ The derivative notation dy/dx was introduced by Gottfried Wilhelm von Leibniz (1646–1716), one of the coinventors of calculus. His notation is used today in its original form. The notation used by Sir Isaac Newton (1642–1727), the other coinventor of calculus, is used less frequently.

Derivative Notation

For historical and practical reasons, several notations for the derivative are used. To see the origin of one notation, recall that the slope of the secant line through two points $P(x, f(x))$ and $Q(x + h, f(x + h))$ on the curve $y = f(x)$ is $\dfrac{f(x + h) - f(x)}{h}$. The quantity h is the change in the x-coordinate in moving from P to Q. A standard notation for change is the symbol Δ (uppercase Greek letter delta). So we replace h with Δx to represent the change in x. Similarly, $f(x + h) - f(x) = f(x + \Delta x) - f(x)$ is the change in y, denoted Δy (Figure 3.10). Therefore, the slope of the secant line is

$$m_{\text{sec}} = \frac{f(x + \Delta x) - f(x)}{\Delta x} = \frac{\Delta y}{\Delta x}.$$

By letting $\Delta x \to 0$, the slope of the tangent line at $(x, f(x))$ is

$$f'(x) = \lim_{\Delta x \to 0} \frac{f(x + \Delta x) - f(x)}{\Delta x} = \lim_{\Delta x \to 0} \frac{\Delta y}{\Delta x} = \frac{dy}{dx}.$$

The new notation for the derivative is $\dfrac{dy}{dx}$; it reminds us that $f'(x)$ is the limit of $\dfrac{\Delta y}{\Delta x}$ as $\Delta x \to 0$.

In addition to the notation $f'(x)$ and $\dfrac{dy}{dx}$, other common ways of writing the derivative include

$$\frac{df}{dx}, \qquad \frac{d}{dx}(f(x)), \qquad D_x(f(x)), \quad \text{and} \quad y'(x).$$

The following notations represents the derivative of f evaluated at a.

$$f'(a), \qquad y'(a), \qquad \frac{df}{dx}\bigg|_{x=a}, \quad \text{and} \quad \frac{dy}{dx}\bigg|_{x=a}$$

QUICK CHECK 5 What are some other ways to write $f'(3)$, where $y = f(x)$? ◄

► Example 4 gives the first of many derivative formulas to be presented in the text:

$$\frac{d}{dx}(\sqrt{x}) = \frac{1}{2\sqrt{x}}.$$

Remember this result. It will be used often.

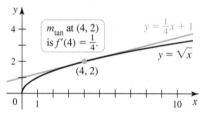

Figure 3.11

QUICK CHECK 6 In Example 4, do the slopes of the tangent lines increase or decrease as x increases? Explain. ◄

QUICK CHECK 7 Express the derivative of $p = q(r)$ in three ways. ◄

EXAMPLE 4   A derivative calculation Let $y = f(x) = \sqrt{x}$.

a. Compute $\dfrac{dy}{dx}$.

b. Find an equation of the line tangent to the graph of f at $(4, 2)$.

SOLUTION

a.
$$\frac{dy}{dx} = \lim_{h \to 0} \frac{f(x+h) - f(x)}{h} \qquad \text{Definition of } \frac{dy}{dx} = f'(x)$$

$$= \lim_{h \to 0} \frac{\sqrt{x+h} - \sqrt{x}}{h} \qquad \text{Substitute } f(x) = \sqrt{x}.$$

$$= \lim_{h \to 0} \frac{(\sqrt{x+h} - \sqrt{x})}{h} \frac{(\sqrt{x+h} + \sqrt{x})}{(\sqrt{x+h} + \sqrt{x})} \qquad \begin{array}{l}\text{Multiply the numerator and}\\ \text{denominator by } \sqrt{x+h} + \sqrt{x}.\end{array}$$

$$= \lim_{h \to 0} \frac{1}{\sqrt{x+h} + \sqrt{x}} = \frac{1}{2\sqrt{x}} \qquad \text{Simplify and evaluate the limit.}$$

b. The slope of the tangent line at $(4, 2)$ is

$$\left.\frac{dy}{dx}\right|_{x=4} = \frac{1}{2\sqrt{4}} = \frac{1}{4}.$$

Therefore, an equation of the tangent line (Figure 3.11) is

$$y - 2 = \frac{1}{4}(x - 4) \quad \text{or} \quad y = \frac{1}{4}x + 1.$$

Related Exercises 41–42 ◄

If a function is given in terms of variables other than x and y, we make an adjustment to the derivative definition. For example, if $y = g(t)$, we replace f with g and x with t to obtain the *derivative of g with respect to t*:

$$g'(t) = \lim_{h \to 0} \frac{g(t+h) - g(t)}{h}.$$

Other notations for $g'(t)$ include $\dfrac{dg}{dt}, \dfrac{d}{dt}(g(t)), D_t(g(t)),$ and $y'(t)$.

EXAMPLE 5   Another derivative calculation Let $g(t) = 1/t^2$ and compute $g'(t)$.

SOLUTION

$$g'(t) = \lim_{h \to 0} \frac{g(t+h) - g(t)}{h} \qquad \text{Definition of } g'$$

$$= \lim_{h \to 0} \frac{1}{h}\left(\frac{1}{(t+h)^2} - \frac{1}{t^2}\right) \qquad \text{Substitute } g(t) = 1/t^2.$$

$$= \lim_{h \to 0} \frac{1}{h}\left(\frac{t^2 - (t+h)^2}{t^2(t+h)^2}\right) \qquad \text{Common denominator}$$

$$= \lim_{h \to 0} \frac{1}{h}\left(\frac{-2ht - h^2}{t^2(t+h)^2}\right) \qquad \text{Expand the numerator and simplify.}$$

$$= \lim_{h \to 0} \left(\frac{-2t - h}{t^2(t+h)^2}\right) \qquad h \neq 0; \text{ cancel } h.$$

$$= -\frac{2}{t^3} \qquad \text{Evaluate the limit.}$$

Related Exercises 43–46 ◄

SECTION 3.1 EXERCISES

Review Questions

1. Use definition (1) (p. 127) for the slope of a tangent line to explain how slopes of secant lines approach the slope of the tangent line at a point.

2. Explain why the slope of a secant line can be interpreted as an average rate of change.

3. Explain why the slope of the tangent line can be interpreted as an instantaneous rate of change.

4. For a given function f, what does f' represent?

5. Given a function f and a point a in its domain, what does $f'(a)$ represent?

6. Explain the relationships among the slope of a tangent line, the instantaneous rate of change, and the value of the derivative at a point.

7. Why is the notation $\dfrac{dy}{dx}$ used to represent the derivative?

8. Give three different notations for the derivative of f with respect to x.

Basic Skills

9–14. Equations of tangent lines by definition (1)

a. Use definition (1) (p. 127) to find the slope of the line tangent to the graph of f at P.

b. Determine an equation of the tangent line at P.

c. Plot the graph of f and the tangent line at P.

9. $f(x) = x^2 - 5;\ P(3, 4)$

10. $f(x) = -3x^2 - 5x + 1;\ P(1, -7)$

11. $f(x) = -5x + 1;\ P(1, -4)$ 12. $f(x) = 5;\ P(1, 5)$

13. $f(x) = \dfrac{1}{x};\ P(-1, -1)$ 14. $f(x) = \dfrac{4}{x^2};\ P(-1, 4)$

15–26. Equations of tangent lines by definition (2)

a. Use definition (2) (p. 129) to find the slope of the line tangent to the graph of f at P.

b. Determine an equation of the tangent line at P.

15. $f(x) = 2x + 1;\ P(0, 1)$ 16. $f(x) = 3x^2 - 4x;\ P(1, -1)$

17. $f(x) = -7x;\ P(-1, 7)$ 18. $f(x) = 8 - 2x^2;\ P(0, 8)$

19. $f(x) = x^2 - 4;\ P(2, 0)$ 20. $f(x) = 1/x;\ P(1, 1)$

21. $f(x) = x^3;\ P(1, 1)$ 22. $f(x) = \dfrac{1}{2x + 1};\ P(0, 1)$

23. $f(x) = \dfrac{1}{3 - 2x};\ P\left(-1, \dfrac{1}{5}\right)$ 24. $f(x) = \sqrt{x - 1};\ P(2, 1)$

25. $f(x) = \sqrt{x + 3};\ P(1, 2)$ 26. $f(x) = \dfrac{x}{x + 1};\ P(-2, 2)$

27–36. Derivatives and tangent lines

a. For the following functions and values of a, find $f'(a)$.

b. Determine an equation of the line tangent to the graph of f at the point $(a, f(a))$ for the given value of a.

27. $f(x) = 8x;\ a = -3$ 28. $f(x) = x^2;\ a = 3$

29. $f(x) = 4x^2 + 2x;\ a = -2$ 30. $f(x) = 2x^3;\ a = 10$

31. $f(x) = \dfrac{1}{\sqrt{x}};\ a = \dfrac{1}{4}$ 32. $f(x) = \dfrac{1}{x^2};\ a = 1$

33. $f(x) = \sqrt{2x + 1};\ a = 4$ 34. $f(x) = \sqrt{3x};\ a = 12$

35. $f(x) = \dfrac{1}{x + 5};\ a = 5$ 36. $f(x) = \dfrac{1}{3x - 1};\ a = 2$

37–40. Lines tangent to parabolas

a. Find the derivative function f' for the following functions f.

b. Find an equation of the line tangent to the graph of f at $(a, f(a))$ for the given value of a.

c. Graph f and the tangent line.

37. $f(x) = 3x^2 + 2x - 10;\ a = 1$

38. $f(x) = 3x^2;\ a = 0$

39. $f(x) = 5x^2 - 6x + 1;\ a = 2$

40. $f(x) = 1 - x^2;\ a = -1$

41. A derivative formula

a. Use the definition of the derivative to determine
$$\dfrac{d}{dx}(ax^2 + bx + c),$$ where a, b, and c are constants.

b. Let $f(x) = 4x^2 - 3x + 10$ and use part (a) to find $f'(x)$.

c. Use part (b) to find $f'(1)$.

42. A derivative formula

a. Use the definition of the derivative to determine
$$\dfrac{d}{dx}(\sqrt{ax + b}),$$ where a and b are constants.

b. Let $f(x) = \sqrt{5x + 9}$ and use part (a) to find $f'(x)$.

c. Use part (b) to find $f'(-1)$.

43–46. Derivative calculations *Evaluate the derivative of the following functions at the given point.*

43. $y = 1/(t + 1);\ t = 1$ 44. $y = t - t^2;\ t = 2$

45. $c = 2\sqrt{s} - 1;\ s = 25$ 46. $A = \pi r^2;\ r = 3$

Further Explorations

47. **Explain why or why not** Determine whether the following statements are true and give an explanation or counterexample.

   a. For linear functions, the slope of any secant line always equals the slope of any tangent line.

   b. The slope of the secant line passing through the points P and Q is less than the slope of the tangent line at P.

   c. Consider the graph of the parabola $f(x) = x^2$. For $x > 0$ and $h > 0$, the secant line through $(x, f(x))$ and $(x + h, f(x + h))$ always has a greater slope than the tangent line at $(x, f(x))$.

48. **Slope of a line** Consider the line $f(x) = mx + b$, where m and b are constants. Show that $f'(x) = m$ for all x. Interpret this result.

49–52. Calculating derivatives

a. For the following functions, find f' using the definition.

b. Determine an equation of the line tangent to the graph of f at $(a, f(a))$ for the given value of a.

49. $f(x) = \sqrt{3x + 1};\ a = 8$ 50. $f(x) = \sqrt{x + 2};\ a = 7$

51. $f(x) = \dfrac{2}{3x + 1};\ a = -1$ 52. $f(x) = \dfrac{1}{x};\ a = -5$

53–54. Analyzing slopes *Use the points A, B, C, D, and E in the following graphs to answer these questions.*

a. *At which points is the slope of the curve negative?*
b. *At which points is the slope of the curve positive?*
c. *Using A–E, list the slopes in decreasing order.*

Year	1950	1960	1970	1980	1990	2000	2010
t	0	10	20	30	40	50	60
$p(t)$	59,900	139,126	304,744	528,000	852,737	1,563,282	1,951,269

(*Source:* U.S. Bureau of Census)

53.

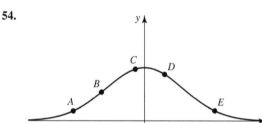

54.

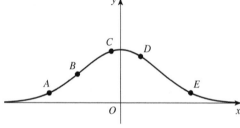

Applications

T 55. Power and energy Energy is the capacity to do work, and power is the rate at which energy is used or consumed. Therefore, if $E(t)$ is the energy function for a system, then $P(t) = E'(t)$ is the power function. A unit of energy is the kilowatt-hour (1 kWh is the amount of energy needed to light ten 100-W lightbulbs for an hour); the corresponding units for power are kilowatts. The following figure shows the energy consumed by a small community over a 25-hour period.

a. Estimate the power at $t = 10$ and $t = 20$ hr. Be sure to include units in your calculation.
b. At what times on the interval $[0, 25]$ is the power zero?
c. At what times on the interval $[0, 25]$ is the power a maximum?

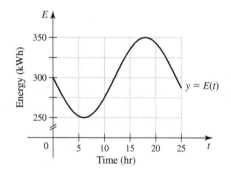

T 56. Population of Las Vegas Let $p(t)$ represent the population of the Las Vegas metropolitan area t years after 1950, as shown in the table and figure.

a. Compute the average rate of growth of Las Vegas from 1970 to 1980.
b. Explain why the average rate of growth calculated in part (a) is a good estimate of the instantaneous rate of growth of Las Vegas in 1975.
c. Compute the average rate of growth of Las Vegas from 1990 to 2000. Is the average rate of growth an overestimate or underestimate of the instantaneous rate of growth of Las Vegas in 2000? Approximate the growth rate in 2000.

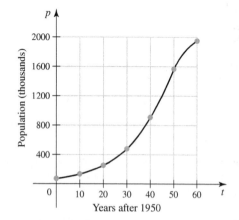

Years after 1950

57–60. Find the function *The following limits represent the slope of a curve $y = f(x)$ at the point $(a, f(a))$. Determine a possible function f and number a; then calculate the limit.*

57. $\displaystyle \lim_{x \to 2} \frac{\frac{1}{x+1} - \frac{1}{3}}{x-2}$

58. $\displaystyle \lim_{h \to 0} \frac{\sqrt{2+h} - \sqrt{2}}{h}$

59. $\displaystyle \lim_{h \to 0} \frac{(2+h)^4 - 16}{h}$

60. $\displaystyle \lim_{x \to 1} \frac{3x^2 + 4x - 7}{x-1}$

61. Is it differentiable? Is $f(x) = \dfrac{x^2 - 5x + 6}{x - 2}$ differentiable at $x = 2$? Justify your answer.

62. Looking ahead: Derivative of x^n Use the definition
$$f'(x) = \lim_{h \to 0} \frac{f(x+h) - f(x)}{h}$$ to find $f'(x)$ for the following functions.

a. $f(x) = x^2$
b. $f(x) = x^3$
c. $f(x) = x^4$
d. Based on your answers to parts (a)–(c), propose a formula for $f'(x)$ if $f(x) = x^n$, where n is a positive integer.

63. Determining the unknown constant Let
$$f(x) = \begin{cases} 2x^2 & \text{if } x \le 1 \\ ax - 2 & \text{if } x > 1. \end{cases}$$

Determine a value of a (if possible) for which f' is continuous at $x = 1$.

64–67. Approximating derivatives *Assuming the limit exists, the definition of the derivative $f'(a) = \displaystyle\lim_{h \to 0} \frac{f(a+h) - f(a)}{h}$ implies that if h is small, then an approximation to $f'(a)$ is given by*
$$f'(a) \approx \frac{f(a+h) - f(a)}{h}.$$

*If $h > 0$, then this approximation is called a **forward difference quotient**; if $h < 0$, it is a **backward difference quotient**. As shown in the following exercises, these formulas are used to approximate f' at a point when f is a complicated function or when f is represented by a set of data points.*

64. Let $f(x) = \sqrt{x}$.

    a. Find the exact value of $f'(4)$.

    b. Show that $f'(4) \approx \dfrac{f(4 + h) - f(4)}{h} = \dfrac{\sqrt{4 + h} - 2}{h}$.

    c. Complete columns 2 and 5 of the following table and describe how $\dfrac{\sqrt{4 + h} - 2}{h}$ behaves as h approaches 0.

h	$\dfrac{\sqrt{4 + h} - 2}{h}$	**Error**	h	$\dfrac{\sqrt{4 + h} - 2}{h}$	**Error**
0.1			-0.1		
0.01			-0.01		
0.001			-0.001		
0.0001			-0.0001		

    d. The accuracy of an approximation is measured by

$$\text{error} = |\text{exact value} - \text{approximate value}|.$$

    Use the exact value of $f'(4)$ in part (a) to complete columns 3 and 6 in the table. Describe the behavior of the errors as h approaches 0.

65. Another way to approximate derivatives is to use the **centered difference quotient**:

$$f'(a) \approx \dfrac{f(a + h) - f(a - h)}{2h}.$$

Again, consider $f(x) = \sqrt{x}$.

    a. Graph f near the point $(4, 2)$ and let $h = \frac{1}{2}$ in the centered difference quotient. Draw the line whose slope is computed by the centered difference quotient and explain why the centered difference quotient approximates $f'(4)$.

    b. Use the centered difference quotient to approximate $f'(4)$ by completing the following table.

h	**Approximation**	**Error**
0.1		
0.01		
0.001		

    c. Explain why it is not necessary to use negative values of h in the table in part (b).

    d. Compare the accuracy of the derivative estimates in part (b) with those found in Exercise 64.

66. The following table gives the distance $f(t)$ fallen by a smoke jumper t seconds after she opens her chute.

    a. Use the forward difference quotient with $h = 0.5$ to estimate the velocity of the smoke jumper at $t = 2$ seconds.

    b. Repeat part (a) using the centered difference quotient.

t (seconds)	$f(t)$ (feet)
0	0
0.5	4
1.0	15
1.5	33
2.0	55
2.5	81
3.0	109
3.5	138
4.0	169

67. The *error function* (denoted erf (x)) is an important function in statistics because it is related to the normal distribution. Its graph is shown in the figure, and values at several points are shown in the table.

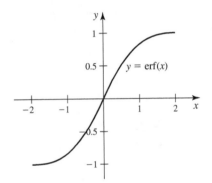

x	erf (x)	x	erf (x)
0.75	0.711156	1.05	0.862436
0.8	0.742101	1.1	0.880205
0.85	0.770668	1.15	0.896124
0.9	0.796908	1.2	0.910314
0.95	0.820891	1.25	0.922900
1.0	0.842701	1.3	0.934008

    a. Use forward and centered difference quotients to find approximations to $\dfrac{d}{dx}(\text{erf}\,(x))\Big|_{x=1}$.

    b. Given that $\dfrac{d}{dx}(\text{erf}\,(x))\Big|_{x=1} = \dfrac{2}{e\sqrt{\pi}}$, compute the error in the approximations in part (a).

QUICK CHECK ANSWERS

2. The slope is less at $x = 2$.   **3.** Definition (1) requires factoring the numerator or long division to cancel $(x - 1)$.   **4.** 32   **5.** $\dfrac{df}{dx}\Big|_{x=3}, \dfrac{dy}{dx}\Big|_{x=3}, y'(3)$

6. The slopes of the tangent lines decrease as x increases. The values of $f'(x) = \dfrac{1}{2\sqrt{x}}$ also decrease as x increases.

7. $\dfrac{dq}{dr}, \dfrac{dp}{dr}, D_r(q(r)), q'(r), p'(r)$ ◄

3.2 Working with Derivatives

Having defined the derivative, we now spend some time becoming acquainted with this new and important function. In this section, we explore how the graphs of a function and its derivative are related, and we explain the important relationship between continuity and differentiability.

Graphs of Derivatives

The function f' is called the derivative of f because it is *derived* from f. The following examples illustrate how to *derive* the graph of f' from the graph of f.

EXAMPLE 1 **Graph of the derivative** Sketch the graph of f' from the graph of f (Figure 3.12).

SOLUTION The graph of f consists of line segments, which are their own tangent lines. Therefore, the slope of the curve $y = f(x)$, for $x < -2$, is -1; that is, $f'(x) = -1$, for $x < -2$. Similarly, $f'(x) = 1$, for $-2 < x < 0$, and $f'(x) = -\frac{1}{2}$, for $x > 0$. Figure 3.13 shows the graph of f in black and the graph of f' in red.

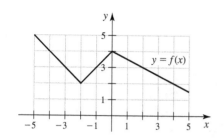

Figure 3.12

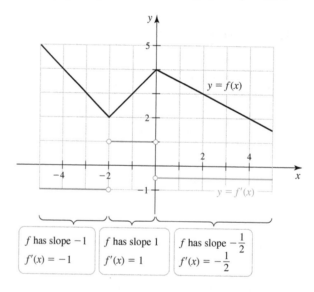

Figure 3.13

> In terms of limits at $x = -2$, we can write
> $$\lim_{h \to 0^-} \frac{f(-2 + h) - f(-2)}{h} = -1 \text{ and}$$
> $$\lim_{h \to 0^+} \frac{f(-2 + h) - f(-2)}{h} = 1. \text{ Because}$$
> the one-sided limits are not equal, $f'(-2)$ does not exist. The analogous one-sided limits at $x = 0$ are also unequal.

QUICK CHECK 1 In Example 1, why is f' not continuous at $x = -2$ and at $x = 0$? ◄

Notice that the slopes of the tangent lines change abruptly at $x = -2$ and $x = 0$. As a result, $f'(-2)$ and $f'(0)$ are undefined and the graph of the derivative has a discontinuity at these points.

Related Exercises 5–12 ◄

EXAMPLE 2 **Graph of the derivative** Sketch the graph of g' using the graph of g (Figure 3.14).

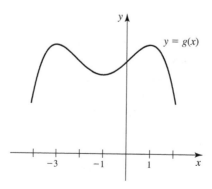

Figure 3.14

SOLUTION Without an equation for g, the best we can do is to find the general shape of the graph of g'. Here are the key observations.

1. Note that the lines tangent to the graph of g at $x = -3, -1$, and 1 have a slope of 0. Therefore,

$$g'(-3) = g'(-1) = g'(1) = 0,$$

which means the graph of g' has x-intercepts at these points (Figure 3.15a).

2. For $x < -3$, the slopes of the tangent lines are positive and decrease to 0 as x approaches -3 from the left. Therefore, $g'(x)$ is positive for $x < -3$ and decreases to 0 as x approaches -3.

3. For $-3 < x < -1$, $g'(x)$ is negative; it initially decreases as x increases and then increases to 0 at $x = -1$. For $-1 < x < 1$, $g'(x)$ is positive; it initially increases as x increases and then returns to 0 at $x = 1$.

4. Finally, $g'(x)$ is negative and decreasing for $x > 1$. Because the slope of g changes gradually, the graph of g' is continuous with no jumps or breaks (Figure 3.15b).

QUICK CHECK 2 Is it true that if $f(x) > 0$ at a point, then $f'(x) > 0$ at that point? Is it true that if $f'(x) > 0$ at a point, then $f(x) > 0$ at that point? Explain. ◄

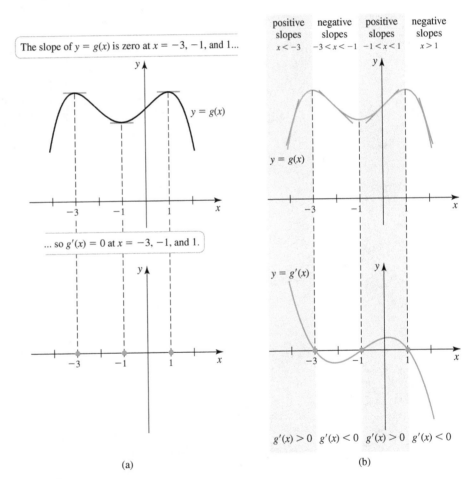

The slope of $y = g(x)$ is zero at $x = -3, -1$, and 1...

... so $g'(x) = 0$ at $x = -3, -1$, and 1.

positive slopes $x < -3$ negative slopes $-3 < x < -1$ positive slopes $-1 < x < 1$ negative slopes $x > 1$

$y = g(x)$

$y = g'(x)$

$g'(x) > 0$ $g'(x) < 0$ $g'(x) > 0$ $g'(x) < 0$

(a)   (b)

Figure 3.15

Related Exercises 5–12 ◄

EXAMPLE 3 Graphing the derivative with asymptotes The graph of the function f is shown in Figure 3.16. Sketch a graph of its derivative.

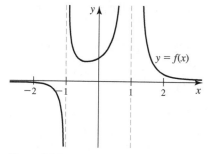

Figure 3.16

▶ Although it is the case in Example 3, a function and its derivative do not always share the same vertical asymptotes.

SOLUTION Identifying intervals on which the slopes of tangent lines are zero, positive, and negative, we make the following observations:

- A horizontal tangent line occurs at approximately $\left(-\frac{1}{3}, f\left(-\frac{1}{3}\right)\right)$. Therefore, $f'\left(-\frac{1}{3}\right) = 0$.
- On the interval $(-\infty, -1)$, slopes of tangent lines are negative and increase in magnitude without bound as we approach -1 from the left.
- On the interval $\left(-1, -\frac{1}{3}\right)$, slopes of tangent lines are negative and increase to zero at $-\frac{1}{3}$.
- On the interval $\left(-\frac{1}{3}, 1\right)$, slopes of tangent lines are positive and increase without bound as we approach 1 from the left.
- On the interval $(1, \infty)$, slopes of tangent lines are negative and increase to zero.

Assembling all this information, we obtain a graph of f' shown in Figure 3.17. Notice that f and f' have the same vertical asymptotes. However, as we pass through -1, the sign of f changes, but the sign of f' does not change. As we pass through 1, the sign of f does not change, but the sign of f' does change.

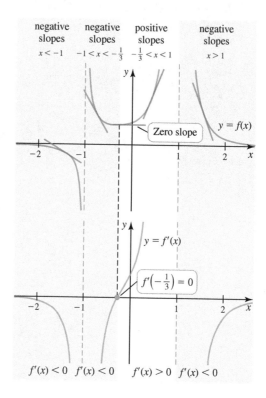

Figure 3.17

Related Exercises 13–14 ◀

Continuity

We now return to the discussion of continuity (Section 2.6) and investigate the relationship between continuity and differentiability. Specifically, we show that if a function is differentiable at a point, then it is also continuous at that point.

THEOREM 3.1   Differentiable Implies Continuous
If f is differentiable at a, then f is continuous at a.

Proof: Because f is differentiable at a point a, we know that

$$f'(a) = \lim_{x \to a} \frac{f(x) - f(a)}{x - a}$$

exists. To show that f is continuous at a, we must show that $\lim_{x \to a} f(x) = f(a)$. The key is the identity

> ▶ Expression (1) is an identity because it holds for all $x \neq a$, which can be seen by canceling $x - a$ and simplifying.

$$f(x) = \frac{f(x) - f(a)}{x - a}(x - a) + f(a), \quad \text{for } x \neq a. \tag{1}$$

Taking the limit as x approaches a on both sides of (1) and simplifying, we have

$$
\begin{aligned}
\lim_{x \to a} f(x) &= \lim_{x \to a}\left(\frac{f(x) - f(a)}{x - a}(x - a) + f(a)\right) && \text{Use identity.}\\
&= \underbrace{\lim_{x \to a}\left(\frac{f(x) - f(a)}{x - a}\right)}_{f'(a)} \underbrace{\lim_{x \to a}(x - a)}_{0} + \underbrace{\lim_{x \to a} f(a)}_{f(a)} && \text{Theorem 2.3}\\
&= f'(a) \cdot 0 + f(a) && \text{Evaluate limits.}\\
&= f(a). && \text{Simplify.}
\end{aligned}
$$

Therefore, $\lim_{x \to a} f(x) = f(a)$, which means that f is continuous at a. ◄

QUICK CHECK 3 Verify that the right-hand side of (1) equals $f(x)$ if $x \neq a$. ◄

Theorem 3.1 tells us that if f is differentiable at a point, then it is necessarily continuous at that point. Therefore, if f is *not* continuous at a point, then f is *not* differentiable there (Figure 3.18). So Theorem 3.1 can be stated in another way.

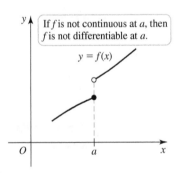

Figure 3.18

> ▶ The alternative version of Theorem 3.1 is called the *contrapositive* of the first statement of Theorem 3.1. A statement and its contrapositive are two equivalent ways of expressing the same statement. For example, the statement
>
> *If I live in Denver, then I live in Colorado*
> is logically equivalent to its contrapositive:
>
> *If I do not live in Colorado, then I do not live in Denver.*

> ▶ To avoid confusion about continuity and differentiability, it helps to think about the function $f(x) = |x|$: It is continuous everywhere but not differentiable at 0.

THEOREM 3.1 (ALTERNATIVE VERSION)   Not Continuous Implies Not Differentiable
If f is not continuous at a, then f is not differentiable at a.

It is tempting to read more into Theorem 3.1 than what it actually states. If f is continuous at a point, f is *not* necessarily differentiable at that point. For example, consider the continuous function in Figure 3.19 and note the **corner point** at a. Ignoring the portion of the graph for $x > a$, we might be tempted to conclude that ℓ_1 is the line tangent to the curve at a. Ignoring the part of the graph for $x < a$, we might incorrectly conclude that ℓ_2 is the line tangent to the curve at a. The slopes of ℓ_1 and ℓ_2 are not equal. Because of the abrupt change in the slope of the curve at a, f is not differentiable at a: The limit that defines f' does not exist at a.

▶ Continuity requires that
$$\lim_{x \to a} (f(x) - f(a)) = 0.$$
Differentiability requires more:
$$\lim_{x \to a} \frac{f(x) - f(a)}{x - a} \text{ must exist.}$$

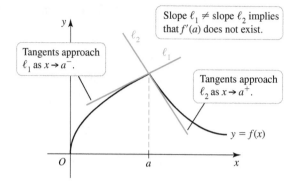

Figure 3.19

▶ See Exercises 33–36 for a formal definition of a vertical tangent line.

Another common situation occurs when the graph of a function f has a vertical tangent line at a. In this case, $f'(a)$ is undefined because the slope of a vertical line is undefined. A vertical tangent line may occur at a sharp point on the curve called a **cusp** (for example, the function $f(x) = \sqrt{|x|}$ in Figure 3.20a). In other cases, a vertical tangent line may occur without a cusp (for example, the function $f(x) = \sqrt[3]{x}$ in Figure 3.20b).

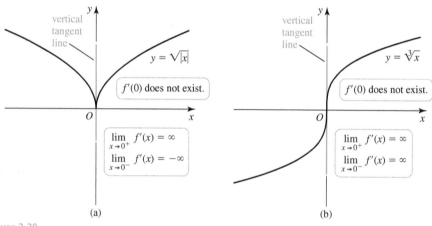

Figure 3.20

When Is a Function Not Differentiable at a Point?

A function f is *not* differentiable at a if at least one of the following conditions holds:

a. f is not continuous at a (Figure 3.18).

b. f has a corner at a (Figure 3.19).

c. f has a vertical tangent at a (Figure 3.20).

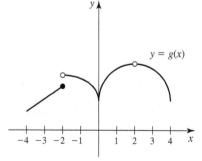

Figure 3.21

EXAMPLE 4 Continuous and differentiable Consider the graph of g in Figure 3.21.

a. Find the values of x in the interval $(-4, 4)$ at which g is not continuous.

b. Find the values of x in the interval $(-4, 4)$ at which g is not differentiable.

c. Sketch a graph of the derivative of g.

SOLUTION

a. The function g fails to be continuous at -2 (where the one-sided limits are not equal) and at 2 (where g is not defined).

b. Because it is not continuous at ± 2, g is not differentiable at those points. Furthermore, g is not differentiable at 0, because the graph has a cusp at that point.

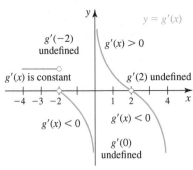

Figure 3.22

c. A sketch of the derivative (Figure 3.22) has the following features:

- $g'(x) > 0$, for $-4 < x < -2$ and $0 < x < 2$
- $g'(x) < 0$, for $-2 < x < 0$ and $2 < x < 4$
- $g'(x)$ approaches $-\infty$ as $x \to 0^-$ and as $x \to 4^-$, and $g'(x)$ approaches ∞ as $x \to 0^+$
- $g'(x)$ approaches 0 as $x \to 2$ from either side, although $g'(2)$ does not exist.

Related Exercises 15–16 ◄

SECTION 3.2 EXERCISES

Review Questions

1. Explain why $f'(x)$ could be positive or negative at a point where $f(x) > 0$.

2. Explain why $f(x)$ could be positive or negative at a point where $f'(x) < 0$.

3. If f is differentiable at a, must f be continuous at a?

4. If f is continuous at a, must f be differentiable at a?

Basic Skills

5–6. Derivatives from graphs *Use the graph of f to sketch a graph of f'.*

5.
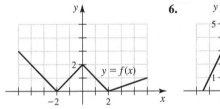

6.
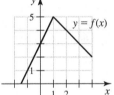

7. **Matching functions with derivatives** Match graphs a–d of functions with graphs A–C of their derivatives.

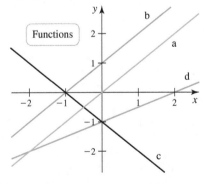

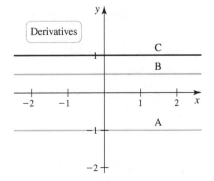

8. **Matching derivatives with functions** Match graphs a–d of derivative functions with possible graphs A–D of the corresponding functions.

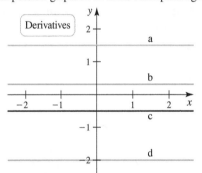

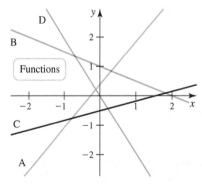

9. **Matching functions with derivatives** Match the functions a–d in the first set of figures with the derivative functions A–D in the next set of figures

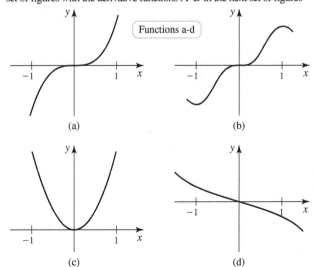

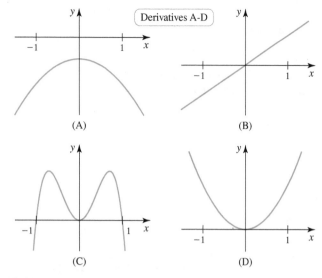

Derivatives A-D

(A)

(B)

(C)

(D)

10–12. Sketching derivatives *Reproduce the graph of f and then plot a graph of f′ on the same set of axes.*

10.

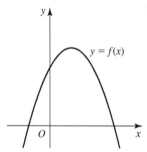

y = f(x)

11.

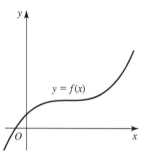

y = f(x)

12.

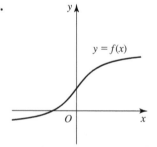

y = f(x)

13–14. Graphing the derivative with asymptotes *Sketch a graph of the derivative of the functions f shown in the figures.*

13.

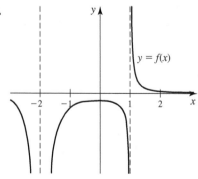

y = f(x)

14.

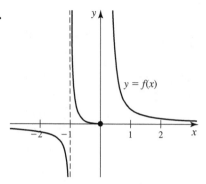

y = f(x)

15. Where is the function continuous? Differentiable? Use the graph of *f* in the figure to do the following.

  a. Find the values of *x* in $(0, 3)$ at which *f* is not continuous.
  b. Find the values of *x* in $(0, 3)$ at which *f* is not differentiable.
  c. Sketch a graph of *f′*.

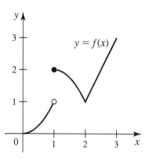

y = f(x)

16. Where is the function continuous? Differentiable? Use the graph of *g* in the figure to do the following.

  a. Find the values of *x* in $(0, 4)$ at which *g* is not continuous.
  b. Find the values of *x* in $(0, 4)$ at which *g* is not differentiable.
  c. Sketch a graph of *g′*.

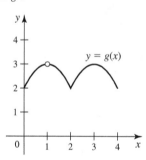

y = g(x)

Further Explorations

17. Explain why or why not Determine whether the following statements are true and give an explanation or counterexample.

  a. If the function *f* is differentiable for all values of *x*, then *f* is continuous for all values of *x*.
  b. The function $f(x) = |x + 1|$ is continuous for all *x*, but not differentiable for all *x*.
  c. It is possible for the domain of *f* to be (a, b) and the domain of *f′* to be $[a, b]$.

18. Finding *f* from *f′* Sketch the graph of $f′(x) = 2$. Then sketch three possible graphs of *f*.

19. Finding *f* from *f′* Sketch the graph of $f′(x) = x$. Then sketch a possible graph of *f*. Is more than one graph possible?

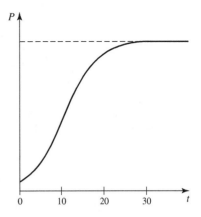

20. Finding f from f' Create the graph of a continuous function f such that

$$f'(x) = \begin{cases} 1 & \text{if } x < 0 \\ 0 & \text{if } 0 < x < 1 \\ -1 & \text{if } x > 1. \end{cases}$$

Is more than one graph possible?

21–24. Normal lines *A line perpendicular to another line or to a tangent line is called a **normal line**. Find an equation of the line perpendicular to the line that is tangent to the following curves at the given point P.*

21. $y = 3x - 4$; $P(1, -1)$

22. $y = \sqrt{x}$; $P(4, 2)$

23. $y = \dfrac{2}{x}$; $P(1, 2)$

24. $y = x^2 - 3x$; $P(3, 0)$

25–28. Aiming a tangent line *Given the function f and the point Q, find all points P on the graph of f such that the line tangent to f at P passes though Q. Check your work by graphing f and the tangent lines.*

25. $f(x) = x^2 + 1$; $Q(3, 6)$

26. $f(x) = -x^2 + 4x - 3$; $Q(0, 6)$

27. $f(x) = \dfrac{1}{x}$; $Q(-2, 4)$

T 28. $f(x) = e^{-x}$; $Q(1, -4)$

Applications

29. Voltage on a capacitor A capacitor is a device in an electrical circuit that stores charge. In one particular circuit, the charge on the capacitor Q varies in time as shown in the figure.

a. At what time is the rate of change of the charge Q' the greatest?
b. Is Q' positive or negative for $t \geq 0$?
c. Is Q' an increasing or decreasing function of time (or neither)?
d. Sketch the graph of Q'. You do not need a scale on the vertical axis.

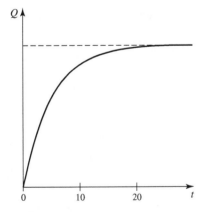

30. Logistic growth A common model for population growth uses the logistic (or sigmoid) curve. Consider the logistic curve in the figure, where $P(t)$ is the population at time $t \geq 0$.

a. At approximately what time is the rate of growth P' the greatest?
b. Is P' positive or negative for $t \geq 0$?
c. Is P' an increasing or decreasing function of time (or neither)?
d. Sketch the graph of P'. You do not need a scale on the vertical axis.

Additional Exercises

31–32. One-sided derivatives *The **right-sided** and **left-sided** derivatives of a function at a point a are given by*

$$f_+'(a) = \lim_{h \to 0^+} \frac{f(a + h) - f(a)}{h} \text{ and } f_-'(a) = \lim_{h \to 0^-} \frac{f(a + h) - f(a)}{h},$$

respectively, provided these limits exist. The derivative $f'(a)$ exists if and only if $f_+'(a) = f_-'(a)$.

a. Sketch the following functions.
b. Compute $f_+'(a)$ and $f_-'(a)$ at the given point a.
c. Is f continuous at a? Is f differentiable at a?

31. $f(x) = |x - 2|$; $a = 2$

32. $f(x) = \begin{cases} 4 - x^2 & \text{if } x \leq 1 \\ 2x + 1 & \text{if } x > 1 \end{cases}$; $a = 1$

33–36. Vertical tangent lines *If a function f is continuous at a and $\lim_{x \to a} |f'(x)| = \infty$, then the curve $y = f(x)$ has a vertical tangent line at a and the equation of the tangent line is $x = a$. If a is an endpoint of a domain, then the appropriate one-sided derivative (Exercises 31–32) is used. Use this information to answer the following questions.*

T 33. Graph the following functions and determine the location of the vertical tangent lines.
a. $f(x) = (x - 2)^{1/3}$ **b.** $f(x) = (x + 1)^{2/3}$
c. $f(x) = \sqrt{|x - 4|}$ **d.** $f(x) = x^{5/3} - 2x^{1/3}$

34. The preceding definition of a vertical tangent line includes four cases: $\lim_{x \to a^+} f'(x) = \pm \infty$ combined with $\lim_{x \to a^-} f'(x) = \pm \infty$ (for example, one case is $\lim_{x \to a^+} f'(x) = -\infty$ and $\lim_{x \to a^-} f'(x) = \infty$). Sketch a continuous function that has a vertical tangent line at a in each of the four cases.

35. Verify that $f(x) = x^{1/3}$ has a vertical tangent line at $x = 0$.

T 36. Graph the following curves and determine the location of any vertical tangent lines.
a. $x^2 + y^2 = 9$ **b.** $x^2 + y^2 + 2x = 0$

37. Continuity is necessary for differentiability
a. Graph the function $f(x) = \begin{cases} x & \text{for } x \leq 0 \\ x + 1 & \text{for } x > 0. \end{cases}$
b. For $x < 0$, what is $f'(x)$?
c. For $x > 0$, what is $f'(x)$?
d. Graph f' on its domain.
e. Is f differentiable at 0? Explain.

QUICK CHECK ANSWERS

1. The slopes of the tangent lines change abruptly at $x = -2$ and 0. **2.** No; no ◄

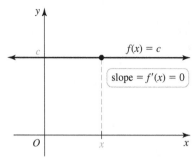

Figure 3.23

> We expect the derivative of a constant function to be 0 at every point because the values of a constant function do not change. This means the instantaneous rate of change is 0 at every point.

QUICK CHECK 1 Find the values of $\dfrac{d}{dx}(5)$ and $\dfrac{d}{dx}(\pi)$. ◄

> You will see several versions of the Power Rule as we progress. It is extended in exactly the same form given in Theorem 3.3—first to negative integer powers, then to rational powers, and finally to real powers.

> Note that this factoring formula agrees with familiar factoring formulas for differences of perfect squares and cubes:
> $$x^2 - a^2 = (x - a)(x + a)$$
> $$x^3 - a^3 = (x - a)(x^2 + ax + a^2).$$

3.3 Rules of Differentiation

If you always had to use limits to evaluate derivatives, as we did in Section 3.1, calculus would be a tedious affair. The goal of this chapter is to establish rules and formulas for quickly evaluating derivatives—not just for individual functions but for entire families of functions. By the end of the chapter, you will have learned many derivative rules and formulas, all of which are listed in the endpapers of the book.

The Constant and Power Rules for Derivatives

The graph of the **constant function** $f(x) = c$ is a horizontal line with a slope of 0 at every point (Figure 3.23). It follows that $f'(x) = 0$ or, equivalently, $\dfrac{d}{dx}(c) = 0$ (Exercise 74). This observation leads to the *Constant Rule* for derivatives.

THEOREM 3.2   Constant Rule

If c is a real number, then $\dfrac{d}{dx}(c) = 0$.

Next, consider power functions of the form $f(x) = x^n$, where n is a nonnegative integer. If you completed Exercise 62 in Section 3.1, you used the limit definition of the derivative to discover that

$$\frac{d}{dx}(x^2) = 2x, \qquad \frac{d}{dx}(x^3) = 3x^2, \quad \text{and} \quad \frac{d}{dx}(x^4) = 4x^3.$$

In each case, the derivative of x^n could be evaluated by placing the exponent n in front of x as a coefficient and decreasing the exponent by 1. Based on these observations, we state and prove the following theorem.

THEOREM 3.3   Power Rule

If n is a nonnegative integer, then $\dfrac{d}{dx}(x^n) = nx^{n-1}$.

Proof: We let $f(x) = x^n$ and use the definition of the derivative in the form

$$f'(a) = \lim_{x \to a} \frac{f(x) - f(a)}{x - a}.$$

With $n = 1$ and $f(x) = x$, we have

$$f'(a) = \lim_{x \to a} \frac{f(x) - f(a)}{x - a} = \lim_{x \to a} \frac{x - a}{x - a} = 1,$$

as given by the Power Rule.

With $n \geq 2$ and $f(x) = x^n$, note that $f(x) - f(a) = x^n - a^n$. A factoring formula gives

$$x^n - a^n = (x - a)(x^{n-1} + x^{n-2}a + \cdots + xa^{n-2} + a^{n-1}).$$

Therefore,

$$f'(a) = \lim_{x \to a} \frac{x^n - a^n}{x - a}$$ Definition of $f'(a)$

$$= \lim_{x \to a} \frac{(x - a)(x^{n-1} + x^{n-2}a + \cdots + xa^{n-2} + a^{n-1})}{x - a}$$ Factor $x^n - a^n$.

$$= \lim_{x \to a} (x^{n-1} + x^{n-2}a + \cdots + xa^{n-2} + a^{n-1})$$ Cancel common factors.

$$= \underbrace{a^{n-1} + a^{n-2} \cdot a + \cdots + a \cdot a^{n-2} + a^{n-1}}_{n \text{ terms}} = na^{n-1}.$$ Evaluate the limit.

Replacing a with the variable x in $f'(a) = na^{n-1}$, we obtain the result given in the Power Rule for $n \geq 2$. Finally, note that the Constant Rule is consistent with the Power Rule with $n = 0$.   ◄

EXAMPLE 1   Derivatives of power and constant functions Evaluate the following derivatives.

a. $\dfrac{d}{dx}(x^9)$ **b.** $\dfrac{d}{dx}(x)$ **c.** $\dfrac{d}{dx}(2^8)$

SOLUTION

a. $\dfrac{d}{dx}(x^9) = 9x^{9-1} = 9x^8$ Power Rule

b. $\dfrac{d}{dx}(x) = \dfrac{d}{dx}(x^1) = 1x^0 = 1$ Power Rule

QUICK CHECK 2 Use the graph of $y = x$ to give a geometric explanation of why $\dfrac{d}{dx}(x) = 1$. ◄

c. You might be tempted to use the Power Rule here, but $2^8 = 256$ is a constant. So by the Constant Rule, $\dfrac{d}{dx}(2^8) = 0$.   *Related Exercises 7–12* ◄

Constant Multiple Rule

Consider the problem of finding the derivative of a constant c multiplied by a function f (assuming that f' exists). We apply the definition of the derivative in the form

$$f'(x) = \lim_{h \to 0} \frac{f(x + h) - f(x)}{h}$$

to the function cf:

$$\frac{d}{dx}(cf(x)) = \lim_{h \to 0} \frac{cf(x + h) - cf(x)}{h}$$ Definition of the derivative of cf

$$= \lim_{h \to 0} \frac{c(f(x + h) - f(x))}{h}$$ Factor out c.

$$= c \lim_{h \to 0} \frac{f(x + h) - f(x)}{h}$$ Theorem 2.3

$$= cf'(x).$$ Definition of $f'(x)$

This calculation leads to the *Constant Multiple Rule* for derivatives.

▶ Theorem 3.4 says that the derivative of a constant multiplied by a function is the constant multiplied by the derivative of the function.

THEOREM 3.4   Constant Multiple Rule
If f is differentiable at x and c is a constant, then

$$\frac{d}{dx}(cf(x)) = cf'(x).$$

EXAMPLE 2 **Derivatives of constant multiples of functions** Evaluate the following derivatives.

a. $\dfrac{d}{dx}\left(-\dfrac{7x^{11}}{8}\right)$ **b.** $\dfrac{d}{dt}\left(\dfrac{3}{8}\sqrt{t}\right)$

SOLUTION

a.
$$\dfrac{d}{dx}\left(-\dfrac{7x^{11}}{8}\right) = -\dfrac{7}{8}\cdot\dfrac{d}{dx}(x^{11}) \quad \text{Constant Multiple Rule}$$

$$= -\dfrac{7}{8}\cdot 11x^{10} \quad \text{Power Rule}$$

$$= -\dfrac{77}{8}x^{10} \quad \text{Simplify.}$$

> In Example 4 of Section 3.1, we proved that $\dfrac{d}{dt}(\sqrt{t}) = \dfrac{1}{2\sqrt{t}}$.

b.
$$\dfrac{d}{dt}\left(\dfrac{3}{8}\sqrt{t}\right) = \dfrac{3}{8}\cdot\dfrac{d}{dt}(\sqrt{t}) \quad \text{Constant Multiple Rule}$$

$$= \dfrac{3}{8}\cdot\dfrac{1}{2\sqrt{t}} \quad \text{Replace } \dfrac{d}{dt}(\sqrt{t}) \text{ with } \dfrac{1}{2\sqrt{t}}.$$

$$= \dfrac{3}{16\sqrt{t}}$$

Related Exercises 13–18 ◄

Sum Rule

Many functions are sums of simpler functions. Therefore, it is useful to establish a rule for calculating the derivative of the sum of two or more functions.

> In words, Theorem 3.5 states that the derivative of a sum is the sum of the derivatives.

THEOREM 3.5 **Sum Rule**
If f and g are differentiable at x, then

$$\dfrac{d}{dx}(f(x) + g(x)) = f'(x) + g'(x).$$

Proof: Let $F = f + g$, where f and g are differentiable at x, and use the definition of the derivative:

$$\dfrac{d}{dx}(f(x) + g(x)) = F'(x)$$

$$= \lim_{h\to 0}\dfrac{F(x + h) - F(x)}{h} \quad \text{Definition of derivative}$$

$$= \lim_{h\to 0}\dfrac{(f(x + h) + g(x + h)) - (f(x) + g(x))}{h} \quad \text{Replace } F \text{ with } f + g.$$

$$= \lim_{h\to 0}\left[\dfrac{f(x + h) - f(x)}{h} + \dfrac{g(x + h) - g(x)}{h}\right] \quad \text{Regroup.}$$

$$= \lim_{h\to 0}\dfrac{f(x + h) - f(x)}{h} + \lim_{h\to 0}\dfrac{g(x + h) - g(x)}{h} \quad \text{Theorem 2.3}$$

$$= f'(x) + g'(x). \quad \text{Definition of } f' \text{ and } g'$$
◄

QUICK CHECK 3 If $f(x) = x^2$ and $g(x) = 2x$, what is the derivative of $f(x) + g(x)$? ◄

The Sum Rule can be extended to three or more differentiable functions, $f_1, f_2, \ldots, f_n$, to obtain the **Generalized Sum Rule**:

$$\dfrac{d}{dx}(f_1(x) + f_2(x) + \cdots + f_n(x)) = f_1'(x) + f_2'(x) + \cdots + f_n'(x).$$

The difference of two functions $f - g$ can be rewritten as the sum $f + (-g)$. By combining the Sum Rule with the Constant Multiple Rule, the **Difference Rule** is established:

$$\frac{d}{dx}(f(x) - g(x)) = f'(x) - g'(x).$$

Let's put the Sum and Difference Rules to work on one of the more common problems: differentiating polynomials.

EXAMPLE 3   Derivative of a polynomial Determine $\dfrac{d}{dw}(2w^3 + 9w^2 - 6w + 4)$.

SOLUTION

$$\frac{d}{dw}(2w^3 + 9w^2 - 6w + 4)$$

$$= \frac{d}{dw}(2w^3) + \frac{d}{dw}(9w^2) - \frac{d}{dw}(6w) + \frac{d}{dw}(4) \qquad \text{Generalized Sum Rule and Difference Rule}$$

$$= 2\frac{d}{dw}(w^3) + 9\frac{d}{dw}(w^2) - 6\frac{d}{dw}(w) + \frac{d}{dw}(4) \qquad \text{Constant Multiple Rule}$$

$$= 2 \cdot 3w^2 + 9 \cdot 2w - 6 \cdot 1 + 0 \qquad \text{Power Rule and Constant Rule}$$

$$= 6w^2 + 18w - 6 \qquad \text{Simplify.}$$

Related Exercises 19–34 ◄

The technique used to differentiate the polynomial in Example 3 may be used for *any* polynomial. Much of the remainder of this chapter is devoted to discovering differentiation rules for the families of functions introduced in Chapter 1: rational, exponential, logarithmic, algebraic, and trigonometric functions.

The Derivative of the Natural Exponential Function

The exponential function $f(x) = b^x$ was introduced in Chapter 1. Let's begin by looking at the graphs of two members of this family, $y = 2^x$ and $y = 3^x$ (Figure 3.24). The slope of the line tangent to the graph of $f(x) = b^x$ at $x = 0$ is given by

$$f'(0) = \lim_{h \to 0} \frac{f(0 + h) - f(0)}{h} = \lim_{h \to 0} \frac{b^h - b^0}{h} = \lim_{h \to 0} \frac{b^h - 1}{h}.$$

We investigate this limit numerically for $b = 2$ and $b = 3$. Table 3.1 shows values of $\dfrac{2^h - 1}{h}$ and $\dfrac{3^h - 1}{h}$ (which are slopes of secant lines) for values of h approaching 0 from the right.

➤ The limit $\lim_{h \to 0} \dfrac{2^h - 1}{h}$ was explored in Example 7 of Section 2.3.

Table 3.1

h	$\dfrac{2^h - 1}{h}$	$\dfrac{3^h - 1}{h}$
1.0	1.000000	2.000000
0.1	0.717735	1.161232
0.01	0.695555	1.104669
0.001	0.693387	1.099216
0.0001	0.693171	1.098673
0.00001	0.693150	1.098618

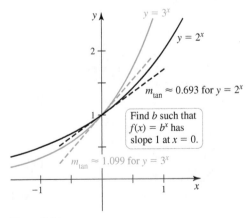

Figure 3.24

Exercise 64 gives similar approximations for the limit as h approaches 0 from the left. These numerical values suggest that

$$\lim_{h \to 0} \frac{2^h - 1}{h} \approx 0.693 \quad \text{Less than 1}$$

$$\lim_{h \to 0} \frac{3^h - 1}{h} \approx 1.099. \quad \text{Greater than 1}$$

These two facts, together with the graphs in Figure 3.24, suggest that there is a number b with $2 < b < 3$ such that the graph of $y = b^x$ has a tangent line with slope 1 at $x = 0$. This number b has the property that

$$\lim_{h \to 0} \frac{b^h - 1}{h} = 1.$$

It can be shown that, indeed, such a number b exists. In fact, it is the number $e = 2.718281828459\ldots$ that was introduced in Chapter 1. Therefore, the exponential function whose tangent line has slope 1 at $x = 0$ is the *natural exponential function* $f(x) = e^x$ (Figure 3.25).

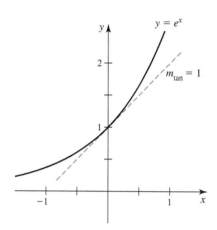

Figure 3.25

▶ The constant e was identified and named by the Swiss mathematician Leonhard Euler (1707–1783) (pronounced "oiler").

DEFINITION The Number e

The number $e = 2.718281828459\ldots$ satisfies

$$\lim_{h \to 0} \frac{e^h - 1}{h} = 1.$$

It is the base of the natural exponential function $f(x) = e^x$.

With the preceding facts in mind, the derivative of $f(x) = e^x$ is computed as follows:

$$\frac{d}{dx}(e^x) = \lim_{h \to 0} \frac{e^{x+h} - e^x}{h} \quad \text{Definition of the derivative}$$

$$= \lim_{h \to 0} \frac{e^x \cdot e^h - e^x}{h} \quad \text{Property of exponents}$$

$$= \lim_{h \to 0} \frac{e^x(e^h - 1)}{h} \quad \text{Factor out } e^x.$$

$$= e^x \cdot \underbrace{\lim_{h \to 0} \frac{e^h - 1}{h}}_{1} \quad e^x \text{ is constant as } h \to 0; \text{ definition of } e.$$

$$= e^x \cdot 1 = e^x.$$

We have proved a remarkable fact: The derivative of the exponential function is itself; it is the only function (other than constant multiples of e^x and $f(x) = 0$) with this property.

▶ The Power Rule *cannot* be applied to exponential functions; that is, $\frac{d}{dx}(e^x) \neq xe^{x-1}$. Also note that $\frac{d}{dx}(e^{10}) \neq e^{10}$. Instead, $\frac{d}{dx}(e^c) = 0$, for any real number c, because e^c is a constant.

THEOREM 3.6   The Derivative of e^x

The function $f(x) = e^x$ is differentiable for all real numbers x, and

$$\frac{d}{dx}(e^x) = e^x.$$

QUICK CHECK 4 Find the derivative of $f(x) = 4e^x - 3x^2$. ◀

Slopes of Tangent Lines

The derivative rules presented in this section allow us to determine slopes of tangent lines and rates of change for many functions.

EXAMPLE 4   Finding tangent lines

a. Write an equation of the line tangent to the graph of $f(x) = 2x - \dfrac{e^x}{2}$ at the point $(0, -\tfrac{1}{2})$.

b. Find the point(s) on the graph of f at which the tangent line is horizontal.

SOLUTION

a. To find the slope of the tangent line at $(0, -\tfrac{1}{2})$, we first calculate $f'(x)$:

$$f'(x) = \frac{d}{dx}\left(2x - \frac{e^x}{2}\right)$$

$$= \frac{d}{dx}(2x) - \frac{d}{dx}\left(\frac{1}{2}e^x\right) \quad \text{Difference Rule}$$

$$= 2\frac{d}{dx}(x) - \frac{1}{2}\cdot\frac{d}{dx}(e^x) \quad \text{Constant Multiple Rule}$$

$$\underbrace{\phantom{2\frac{d}{dx}(x)}}_{1} \quad \underbrace{\phantom{\frac{d}{dx}(e^x)}}_{e^x}$$

$$= 2 - \frac{1}{2}e^x. \quad \text{Evaluate derivatives.}$$

It follows that the slope of the tangent line at $(0, -\tfrac{1}{2})$ is

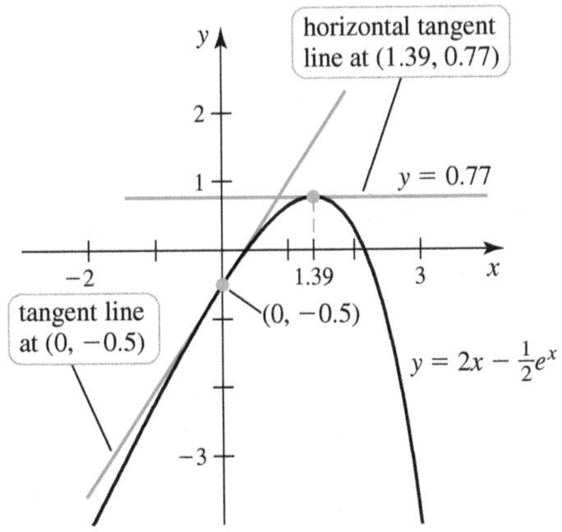

$$f'(0) = 2 - \frac{1}{2}e^0 = \frac{3}{2}.$$

Figure 3.26 shows the tangent line passing through $(0, -\tfrac{1}{2})$; it has the equation

$$y - \left(-\frac{1}{2}\right) = \frac{3}{2}(x - 0) \quad \text{or} \quad y = \frac{3}{2}x - \frac{1}{2}.$$

horizontal tangent line at (1.39, 0.77)

$y = 0.77$

tangent line at $(0, -0.5)$

$(0, -0.5)$

$y = 2x - \tfrac{1}{2}e^x$

Figure 3.26

▶ Observe that the function has a maximum value of approximately 0.77 at the point where the tangent line has a slope of 0. We explore the importance of horizontal tangent lines in Chapter 4.

b. Because the slope of a horizontal tangent line is 0, our goal is to solve $f'(x) = 2 - \tfrac{1}{2}e^x = 0$. Multiplying both sides of this equation by 2 and rearranging gives the equation $e^x = 4$. Taking the natural logarithm of both sides, we find that $x = \ln 4$. Therefore, $f'(x) = 0$ at $x = \ln 4 \approx 1.39$, and f has a horizontal tangent at $(\ln 4, f(\ln 4)) \approx (1.39, 0.77)$ (Figure 3.26).

Related Exercises 35–43 ◄

EXAMPLE 5   Slope of a tangent line

Let $f(x) = 2x^3 - 15x^2 + 24x$. For what values of x does the line tangent to the graph of f have a slope of 6?

SOLUTION The tangent line has a slope of 6 when

$$f'(x) = 6x^2 - 30x + 24 = 6.$$

Subtracting 6 from both sides of the equation and factoring, we have

$$6(x^2 - 5x + 3) = 0.$$

Using the quadratic formula, the roots are

$$x = \frac{5 - \sqrt{13}}{2} \approx 0.697 \quad \text{and} \quad x = \frac{5 + \sqrt{13}}{2} \approx 4.303.$$

Therefore, the slope of the curve at these points is 6 (Figure 3.27).

Related Exercises 35–43 ◄

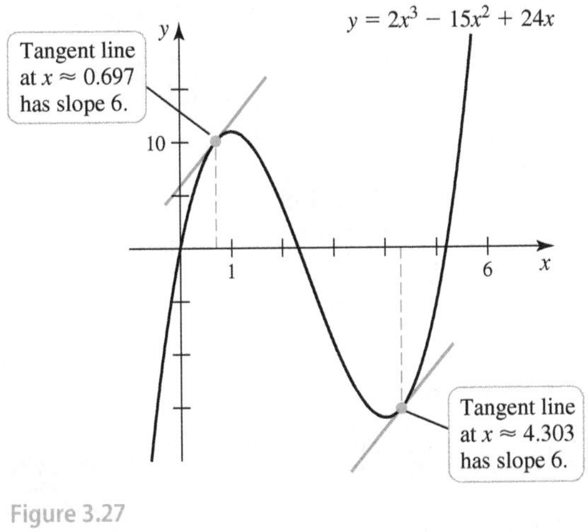

$y = 2x^3 - 15x^2 + 24x$

Tangent line at $x \approx 0.697$ has slope 6.

Tangent line at $x \approx 4.303$ has slope 6.

Figure 3.27

QUICK CHECK 5 Determine the point(s) at which $f(x) = x^3 - 12x$ has a horizontal tangent line. ◄

Higher-Order Derivatives

▶ The prime notation, f', f'', and f''', is typically used only for the first, second, and third derivatives.

Because the derivative of a function f is a function in its own right, we can take the derivative of f'. The result is the *second derivative of f*, denoted f'' (read f *double prime*). The derivative of the second derivative is the *third derivative of f*, denoted f''' or (read f *triple prime*). In general, derivatives of order $n \geq 2$ are called *higher-order derivatives*.

> **DEFINITION Higher-Order Derivatives**
>
> Assuming $y = f(x)$ can be differentiated as often as necessary, the **second derivative** of f is
>
> $$f''(x) = \frac{d}{dx}(f'(x)).$$
>
> For integers $n \geq 2$, the **nth derivative** of f is
>
> $$f^{(n)}(x) = \frac{d}{dx}(f^{(n-1)}(x)).$$

▶ Parentheses are placed around n to distinguish a derivative from a power. Therefore, $f^{(n)}$ is the nth derivative of f and f^n is the function f raised to the nth power.

▶ The notation $\dfrac{d^2f}{dx^2}$ comes from $\dfrac{d}{dx}\left(\dfrac{df}{dx}\right)$ and is read $d\,2\,f\,dx$ *squared*.

Other common notations for the second derivative of $y = f(x)$ include $\dfrac{d^2y}{dx^2}$ and $\dfrac{d^2f}{dx^2}$; the notations $\dfrac{d^ny}{dx^n}$, $\dfrac{d^nf}{dx^n}$, and $y^{(n)}$ are used for the nth derivative of f.

EXAMPLE 6 Finding higher-order derivatives Find the third derivative of the following functions.

a. $f(x) = 3x^3 - 5x + 12$ **b.** $y = 3t + 2e^t$

SOLUTION

a.
$$f'(x) = 9x^2 - 5$$
$$f''(x) = \frac{d}{dx}(9x^2 - 5) = 18x$$
$$f'''(x) = 18$$

▶ In Example 6a, note that $f^{(4)}(x) = 0$, which means that all successive derivatives are also 0. In general, the nth derivative of an nth-degree polynomial is a constant, which implies that derivatives of order $k > n$ are 0.

b. Here we use an alternative notation for higher-order derivatives:

$$\frac{dy}{dt} = \frac{d}{dt}(3t + 2e^t) = 3 + 2e^t$$
$$\frac{d^2y}{dt^2} = \frac{d}{dt}(3 + 2e^t) = 2e^t$$
$$\frac{d^3y}{dt^3} = \frac{d}{dt}(2e^t) = 2e^t.$$

QUICK CHECK 6 With $f(x) = x^5$, find $f^{(5)}(x)$ and $f^{(6)}(x)$. With $g(x) = e^x$, find $g^{(100)}(x)$. ◀

In this case, $\dfrac{d^ny}{dt^n} = 2e^t$, for $n \geq 2$.

Related Exercises 44–48 ◀

SECTION 3.3 EXERCISES

Review Questions

Assume the derivatives of f and g exist in Exercises 1–6.

1. If the limit definition of a derivative can be used to find f', then what is the purpose of using other rules to find f'?

2. In this section, we showed that the rule $\dfrac{d}{dx}(x^n) = nx^{n-1}$ is valid for what values of n?

3. Give a nonzero function that is its own derivative.

4. How do you find the derivative of the sum of two functions $f + g$?

5. How do you find the derivative of a constant multiplied by a function?

6. How do you find the fifth derivative of a function?

Basic Skills

7–12. Derivatives of power and constant functions *Find the derivative of the following functions.*

7. $y = x^5$

8. $f(t) = t^{11}$

9. $f(x) = 5$

10. $g(x) = e^3$

11. $h(t) = t$

12. $f(v) = v^{100}$

13–18. Derivatives of constant multiples of functions *Find the derivative of the following functions. See Example 4 of Section 3.1 for the derivative of $\sqrt{x}$.*

13. $f(x) = 5x^3$

14. $g(w) = \frac{5}{6}w^{12}$

15. $p(x) = 8x$

16. $g(t) = 6\sqrt{t}$

17. $g(t) = 100t^2$

18. $f(s) = \dfrac{\sqrt{s}}{4}$

19–24. Derivatives of the sum of functions *Find the derivative of the following functions.*

19. $f(x) = 3x^4 + 7x$

20. $g(x) = 6x^5 - x$

21. $f(x) = 10x^4 - 32x + e^2$

22. $f(t) = 6\sqrt{t} - 4t^3 + 9$

23. $g(w) = 2w^3 + 3w^2 + 10w$

24. $s(t) = 4\sqrt{t} - \frac{1}{4}t^4 + t + 1$

25–28. Derivatives of products *Find the derivative of the following functions by first expanding the expression. Simplify your answers.*

25. $f(x) = (2x + 1)(3x^2 + 2)$

26. $g(r) = (5r^3 + 3r + 1)(r^2 + 3)$

27. $h(x) = (x^2 + 1)^2$

28. $h(x) = \sqrt{x}(\sqrt{x} - 1)$

29–34. Derivatives of quotients *Find the derivative of the following functions by first simplifying the expression.*

29. $f(w) = \dfrac{w^3 - w}{w}$

30. $y = \dfrac{12s^3 - 8s^2 + 12s}{4s}$

31. $g(x) = \dfrac{x^2 - 1}{x - 1}$

32. $h(x) = \dfrac{x^3 - 6x^2 + 8x}{x^2 - 2x}$

33. $y = \dfrac{x - a}{\sqrt{x} - \sqrt{a}}$; a is a positive constant.

34. $y = \dfrac{x^2 - 2ax + a^2}{x - a}$; a is a constant.

⊞ 35–38. Equations of tangent lines

a. Find an equation of the line tangent to the given curve at a.
b. Use a graphing utility to graph the curve and the tangent line on the same set of axes.

35. $y = -3x^2 + 2$; $a = 1$

36. $y = x^3 - 4x^2 + 2x - 1$; $a = 2$

37. $y = e^x$; $a = \ln 3$

38. $y = \dfrac{e^x}{4} - x$; $a = 0$

39. Finding slope locations Let $f(x) = x^2 - 6x + 5$.

  a. Find the values of x for which the slope of the curve $y = f(x)$ is 0.
  b. Find the values of x for which the slope of the curve $y = f(x)$ is 2.

40. Finding slope locations Let $f(t) = t^3 - 27t + 5$.

  a. Find the values of t for which the slope of the curve $y = f(t)$ is 0.
  b. Find the values of t for which the slope of the curve $y = f(t)$ is 21.

41. Finding slope locations Let $f(x) = 2x^3 - 3x^2 - 12x + 4$.

  a. Find all points on the graph of f at which the tangent line is horizontal.
  b. Find all points on the graph of f at which the tangent line has slope 60.

42. Finding slope locations Let $f(x) = 2e^x - 6x$.

  a. Find all points on the graph of f at which the tangent line is horizontal.
  b. Find all points on the graph of f at which the tangent line has slope 12.

43. Finding slope locations Let $f(x) = 4\sqrt{x} - x$.

  a. Find all points on the graph of f at which the tangent line is horizontal.
  b. Find all points on the graph of f at which the tangent line has slope $-\frac{1}{2}$.

44–48. Higher-order derivatives *Find $f'(x)$, $f''(x)$, and $f'''(x)$ for the following functions.*

44. $f(x) = 3x^3 + 5x^2 + 6x$

45. $f(x) = 5x^4 + 10x^3 + 3x + 6$

46. $f(x) = 3x^2 + 5e^x$

47. $f(x) = \dfrac{x^2 - 7x - 8}{x + 1}$

48. $f(x) = 10e^x$

Further Explorations

49. Explain why or why not Determine whether the following statements are true and give an explanation or counterexample.

  a. $\dfrac{d}{dx}(10^5) = 5 \cdot 10^4$.
  b. The slope of a line tangent to $f(x) = e^x$ is never 0.
  c. $\dfrac{d}{dx}(e^3) = e^3$.
  d. $\dfrac{d}{dx}(e^x) = xe^{x-1}$.
  e. $\dfrac{d^n}{dx^n}(5x^3 + 2x + 5) = 0$, for any integer $n \geq 3$.

50. Tangent lines Suppose $f(3) = 1$ and $f'(3) = 4$. Let $g(x) = x^2 + f(x)$ and $h(x) = 3f(x)$.

  a. Find an equation of the line tangent to $y = g(x)$ at $x = 3$.
  b. Find an equation of the line tangent to $y = h(x)$ at $x = 3$.

51. Derivatives from tangent lines Suppose the line tangent to the graph of f at $x = 2$ is $y = 4x + 1$ and suppose the line tangent to the graph of g at $x = 2$ has slope 3 and passes through $(0, -2)$. Find an equation of the line tangent to the following curves at $x = 2$.

  a. $y = f(x) + g(x)$
  b. $y = f(x) - 2g(x)$
  c. $y = 4f(x)$

52. Tangent line Find the equation of the line tangent to the curve $y = x + \sqrt{x}$ that has slope 2.

53. Tangent line given Determine the constants b and c such that the line tangent to $f(x) = x^2 + bx + c$ at $x = 1$ is $y = 4x + 2$.

54–57. Derivatives from a graph *Let $F = f + g$ and $G = 3f - g$, where the graphs of f and g are shown in the figure. Find the following derivatives.*

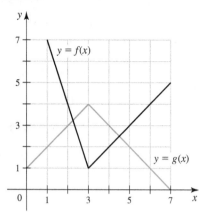

54. $F'(2)$ **55.** $G'(2)$ **56.** $F'(5)$ **57.** $G'(5)$

58–60. Derivatives from a table *Use the table to find the following derivatives.*

x	1	2	3	4	5
$f'(x)$	3	5	2	1	4
$g'(x)$	2	4	3	1	5

58. $\dfrac{d}{dx}\,(f(x) + g(x))\Big|_{x=1}$ **59.** $\dfrac{d}{dx}\,(1.5f(x))\Big|_{x=2}$

60. $\dfrac{d}{dx}\,(2x - 3g(x))\Big|_{x=4}$

61–63. Derivatives from limits *The following limits represent $f'(a)$ for some function f and some real number a.*

a. *Find a possible function f and number a.*
b. *Evaluate the limit by computing $f'(a)$.*

61. $\displaystyle\lim_{h \to 0} \frac{\sqrt{9 + h} - \sqrt{9}}{h}$

62. $\displaystyle\lim_{h \to 0} \frac{(1 + h)^8 + (1 + h)^3 - 2}{h}$

63. $\displaystyle\lim_{x \to 1} \frac{x^{100} - 1}{x - 1}$

64. Important limits Complete the following table and give approximations for $\displaystyle\lim_{h \to 0^-} \frac{2^h - 1}{h}$ and $\displaystyle\lim_{h \to 0^-} \frac{3^h - 1}{h}$.

h	$\dfrac{2^h - 1}{h}$	$\dfrac{3^h - 1}{h}$
-1.0		
-0.1		
-0.01		
-0.001		
-0.0001		
-0.00001		

65–68. Calculator limits *Use a calculator to approximate the following limits.*

65. $\displaystyle\lim_{x \to 0} \frac{e^{3x} - 1}{x}$ **66.** $\displaystyle\lim_{n \to \infty} \left(1 + \frac{1}{n}\right)^n$

67. $\displaystyle\lim_{x \to 0^+} x^x$ **68.** $\displaystyle\lim_{x \to 0^+} \left(\frac{1}{x}\right)^x$

69. Calculating limits exactly The limit $\displaystyle\lim_{x \to 0} \frac{e^x - 1}{x}$ is the derivative of a function f at a point a. Find one possible f and a, and evaluate the limit.

Applications

70. Projectile trajectory The position of a small rocket that is launched vertically upward is given by $s(t) = -5t^2 + 40t + 100$, for $0 \le t \le 10$, where t is measured in seconds and s is measured in meters above the ground.

a. Find the rate of change in the position (instantaneous velocity) of the rocket, for $0 \le t \le 10$.
b. At what time is the instantaneous velocity zero?
c. At what time does the instantaneous velocity have the greatest magnitude, for $0 \le t \le 10$?
d. Graph the position and instantaneous velocity, for $0 \le t \le 10$.

71. Height estimate The distance an object falls (when released from rest, under the influence of Earth's gravity, and with no air resistance) is given by $d(t) = 16t^2$, where d is measured in feet and t is measured in seconds. A rock climber sits on a ledge on a vertical wall and carefully observes the time it takes a small stone to fall from the ledge to the ground.

a. Compute $d'(t)$. What units are associated with the derivative and what does it measure? Interpret the derivative.
b. If it takes 6 s for a stone to fall to the ground, how high is the ledge? How fast is the stone moving when it strikes the ground (in mi/hr)?

72. Cell growth When observations begin at $t = 0$, a cell culture has 1200 cells and continues to grow according to the function $p(t) = 1200\,e^t$, where p is the number of cells and t is measured in days.

a. Compute $p'(t)$. What units are associated with the derivative and what does it measure?
b. On the interval $[0, 4]$, when is the growth rate $p'(t)$ the least? When is it the greatest?

73. City urbanization City planners model the size of their city using the function $A(t) = -\frac{1}{50}t^2 + 2t + 20$, for $0 \le t \le 50$, where A is measured in square miles and t is the number of years after 2010.

a. Compute $A'(t)$. What units are associated with this derivative and what does the derivative measure?
b. How fast will the city be growing when it reaches a size of 38 mi²?
c. Suppose that the population density of the city remains constant from year to year at 1000 people/mi². Determine the growth rate of the population in 2030.

Additional Exercises

74. Constant Rule proof For the constant function $f(x) = c$, use the definition of the derivative to show that $f'(x) = 0$.

75. Alternative proof of the Power Rule The Binomial Theorem states that for any positive integer n,

$$(a + b)^n = a^n + na^{n-1}b + \frac{n(n-1)}{2 \cdot 1} a^{n-2}b^2$$

$$+ \frac{n(n-1)(n-2)}{3 \cdot 2 \cdot 1} a^{n-3}b^3 + \cdots + nab^{n-1} + b^n.$$

Use this formula and the definition

$$f'(x) = \lim_{h \to 0} \frac{f(x+h) - f(x)}{h}$$ to show that $\frac{d}{dx}(x^n) = nx^{n-1}$, for any positive integer n.

76. Looking ahead: Power Rule for negative integers Suppose n is a negative integer and $f(x) = x^n$. Use the following steps to prove that $f'(a) = na^{n-1}$, which means the Power Rule for positive integers extends to all integers. This result is proved in Section 3.4 by a different method.

a. Assume that $m = -n$, so that $m > 0$. Use the definition

$$f'(a) = \lim_{x \to a} \frac{x^n - a^n}{x - a} = \lim_{x \to a} \frac{x^{-m} - a^{-m}}{x - a}.$$

Simplify using the factoring rule (which is valid for $n > 0$)
$$x^n - a^n = (x - a)(x^{n-1} + x^{n-2}a + \cdots + xa^{n-2} + a^{n-1})$$
until it is possible to take the limit.

b. Use this result to find $\frac{d}{dx}(x^{-7})$ and $\frac{d}{dx}\left(\frac{1}{x^{10}}\right)$.

77. Extending the Power Rule to $n = \frac{1}{2}, \frac{3}{2}$ and $\frac{5}{2}$ With Theorem 3.3 and Exercise 76, we have shown that the Power Rule,

$\frac{d}{dx}(x^n) = nx^{n-1}$, applies to any integer n. Later in the chapter, we extend this rule so that it applies to any rational number n.

a. Explain why the Power Rule is consistent with the formula
$$\frac{d}{dx}(\sqrt{x}) = \frac{1}{2\sqrt{x}}.$$

b. Prove that the Power Rule holds for $n = \frac{3}{2}$. (*Hint:* Use the definition of the derivative: $\frac{d}{dx}(x^{3/2}) = \lim_{h \to 0} \frac{(x+h)^{3/2} - x^{3/2}}{h}$.)

c. Prove that the Power Rule holds for $n = \frac{5}{2}$.

d. Propose a formula for $\frac{d}{dx}(x^{n/2})$, for any positive integer n.

78. Computing the derivative of $f(x) = e^{-x}$

a. Use the definition of the derivative to show that
$$\frac{d}{dx}(e^{-x}) = e^{-x} \cdot \lim_{h \to 0} \frac{e^{-h} - 1}{h}.$$

b. Show that the limit in part (a) is equal to -1. (*Hint:* Use the facts that $\lim_{h \to 0} \frac{e^h - 1}{h} = 1$ and e^x is continuous for all x.)

c. Use parts (a) and (b) to find the derivative of $f(x) = e^{-x}$.

79. Computing the derivative of $f(x) = e^{2x}$

a. Use the definition of the derivative to show that
$$\frac{d}{dx}(e^{2x}) = e^{2x} \cdot \lim_{h \to 0} \frac{e^{2h} - 1}{h}.$$

b. Show that the limit in part (a) is equal to 2. (*Hint:* Factor $e^{2h} - 1$.)

c. Use parts (a) and (b) to find the derivative of $f(x) = e^{2x}$.

80. Computing the derivative of $f(x) = x^2 e^x$

a. Use the definition of the derivative to show that
$$\frac{d}{dx}(x^2 e^x) = e^x \cdot \lim_{h \to 0} \frac{(x^2 + 2xh + h^2)e^h - x^2}{h}.$$

b. Manipulate the limit in part (a) to arrive at $f'(x) = e^x(x^2 + 2x)$. (*Hint:* Use the fact that $\lim_{h \to 0} \frac{e^h - 1}{h} = 1$.)

QUICK CHECK ANSWERS

1. $\frac{d}{dx}(5) = 0$ and $\frac{d}{dx}(\pi) = 0$ because 5 and π are constants.
2. The slope of the curve $y = x$ is 1 at any point; therefore, $\frac{d}{dx}(x) = 1$.   3. $2x + 2$ 4. $f'(x) = 4e^x - 6x$
5. $x = 2$ and $x = -2$ 6. $f^{(5)}(x) = 120, f^{(6)}(x) = 0$, $g^{(100)}(x) = e^x$ ◄

3.4 The Product and Quotient Rules

The derivative of a sum of functions is the sum of the derivatives. So you might assume that the derivative of a product of functions is the product of the derivatives. Consider, however, the functions $f(x) = x^3$ and $g(x) = x^4$. In this case, $\frac{d}{dx}(f(x)g(x)) = \frac{d}{dx}(x^7) = 7x^6$,

but $f'(x)g'(x) = 3x^2 \cdot 4x^3 = 12x^5$. Therefore, $\frac{d}{dx}(f \cdot g) \neq f' \cdot g'$. Similarly, the derivative of a quotient is *not* the quotient of the derivatives. The purpose of this section is to develop rules for differentiating products and quotients of functions.

Product Rule

Here is an anecdote that suggests the formula for the Product Rule. Imagine running along a road at a constant speed. Your speed is determined by two factors: the length of your stride and the number of strides you take each second. Therefore,

$$\text{running speed} = \text{stride length} \cdot \text{stride rate}.$$

For example, if your stride length is 3 ft per stride and you take 2 strides/s, then your speed is 6 ft/s.

Now suppose your stride length increases by 0.5 ft, from 3 to 3.5 ft. Then the change in speed is calculated as follows:

$$\begin{aligned}
\textit{change} \text{ in speed} &= \text{change in stride length} \cdot \text{stride rate} \\
&= 0.5 \cdot 2 = 1 \text{ ft/s}.
\end{aligned}$$

Alternatively, suppose your stride length remains constant but your stride rate increases by 0.25 strides/s, from 2 to 2.25 strides/s. Then

$$\begin{aligned}
\textit{change} \text{ in speed} &= \text{stride length} \cdot \text{change in stride rate} \\
&= 3 \cdot 0.25 = 0.75 \text{ ft/s}.
\end{aligned}$$

If both your stride rate and stride length change simultaneously, we expect two contributions to the change in your running speed:

$$\begin{aligned}
\textit{change} \text{ in speed} &= (\text{change in stride length} \cdot \text{stride rate}) \\
&\quad + (\text{stride length} \cdot \text{change in stride rate}) \\
&= 1 \text{ ft/s} + 0.75 \text{ ft/s} = 1.75 \text{ ft/s}.
\end{aligned}$$

This argument correctly suggests that the derivative (or rate of change) of a product of two functions has *two components*, as shown by the following rule.

> ► In words, Theorem 3.7 states that the derivative of the product of two functions equals the derivative of the first function multiplied by the second function plus the first function multiplied by the derivative of the second function.

THEOREM 3.7 Product Rule

If f and g are differentiable at x, then

$$\frac{d}{dx}(f(x)g(x)) = f'(x)g(x) + f(x)g'(x).$$

Proof: We apply the definition of the derivative to the function fg:

$$\frac{d}{dx}(f(x)g(x)) = \lim_{h \to 0} \frac{f(x+h)g(x+h) - f(x)g(x)}{h}.$$

A useful tactic is to add $-f(x)g(x+h) + f(x)g(x+h)$ (which equals 0) to the numerator, so that

$$\frac{d}{dx}(f(x)g(x)) = \lim_{h \to 0} \frac{f(x+h)g(x+h) - f(x)g(x+h) + f(x)g(x+h) - f(x)g(x)}{h}.$$

The fraction is now split and the numerators are factored:

$$\frac{d}{dx}(f(x)g(x))$$

$$= \lim_{h \to 0} \frac{f(x+h)g(x+h) - f(x)g(x+h)}{h} + \lim_{h \to 0} \frac{f(x)g(x+h) - f(x)g(x)}{h}$$

> ► As $h \to 0$, $f(x)$ does not change in value because it is independent of h.

$$= \lim_{h \to 0} \left(\underbrace{\frac{f(x+h) - f(x)}{h}}_{\substack{\text{approaches } f'(x) \text{ as} \\ h \to 0}} \cdot \underbrace{g(x+h)}_{\substack{\text{approaches} \\ g(x) \\ \text{as } h \to 0}} \right) + \lim_{h \to 0} \left(\underbrace{f(x)}_{\substack{\text{equals} \\ f(x) \text{ as} \\ h \to 0}} \cdot \underbrace{\frac{g(x+h) - g(x)}{h}}_{\substack{\text{approaches } g'(x) \\ \text{as } h \to 0}} \right)$$

$$= f'(x) \cdot g(x) + f(x) \cdot g'(x).$$

The continuity of g is used to conclude that $\lim_{h \to 0} g(x+h) = g(x)$.   ◄

EXAMPLE 1 Using the Product Rule Find and simplify the following derivatives.

a. $\dfrac{d}{dv}(v^2(2\sqrt{v}+1))$ **b.** $\dfrac{d}{dx}(x^2e^x)$

> In Example 4 of Section 3.1, we proved that $\dfrac{d}{dv}(\sqrt{v}) = \dfrac{1}{2\sqrt{v}}$.

SOLUTION

a. $\dfrac{d}{dv}(v^2(2\sqrt{v}+1)) = \left(\dfrac{d}{dv}(v^2)\right)(2\sqrt{v}+1) + v^2\left(\dfrac{d}{dv}(2\sqrt{v}+1)\right)$ Product Rule

$\qquad\qquad\qquad\qquad = 2v(2\sqrt{v}+1) + v^2\left(2\cdot\dfrac{1}{2\sqrt{v}}\right)$ Evaluate the derivatives.

$\qquad\qquad\qquad\qquad = 4v^{3/2} + 2v + v^{3/2} = 5v^{3/2} + 2v$ Simplify.

b. $\dfrac{d}{dx}(x^2e^x) = \underbrace{2x}_{\frac{d}{dx}(x^2)}\cdot e^x + x^2\cdot\underbrace{e^x}_{\frac{d}{dx}(e^x)} = xe^x(2+x)$

Related Exercises 7–18 ◄

QUICK CHECK 1 Find the derivative of $f(x) = x^5$. Then find the same derivative using the Product Rule with $f(x) = x^2x^3$. ◄

Quotient Rule

Consider the quotient $q(x) = \dfrac{f(x)}{g(x)}$ and note that $f(x) = g(x)q(x)$. By the Product Rule, we have

$$f'(x) = g'(x)q(x) + g(x)q'(x).$$

Solving for $q'(x)$, we find that

$$q'(x) = \dfrac{f'(x) - g'(x)q(x)}{g(x)}.$$

Substituting $q(x) = \dfrac{f(x)}{g(x)}$ produces a rule for finding $q'(x)$:

$$q'(x) = \dfrac{f'(x) - g'(x)\dfrac{f(x)}{g(x)}}{g(x)}$$ Replace $q(x)$ with $\dfrac{f(x)}{g(x)}$.

$$\qquad = \dfrac{g(x)\left(f'(x) - g'(x)\dfrac{f(x)}{g(x)}\right)}{g(x)\cdot g(x)}$$ Multiply numerator and denominator by $g(x)$.

$$\qquad = \dfrac{g(x)f'(x) - f(x)g'(x)}{(g(x))^2}.$$ Simplify.

This calculation produces the correct result for the derivative of a quotient. However, there is one subtle point: How do we know that the derivative of f/g exists in the first place? A complete proof of the Quotient Rule is outlined in Exercise 86.

> In words, Theorem 3.8 states that the derivative of the quotient of two functions equals the denominator multiplied by the derivative of the numerator minus the numerator multiplied by the derivative of the denominator, all divided by the denominator squared. An easy way to remember the Quotient Rule is with
>
> $$\dfrac{LoD(Hi) - HiD(Lo)}{(Lo)^2}.$$

THEOREM 3.8 Quotient Rule

If f and g are differentiable at x and $g(x) \neq 0$, then the derivative of f/g at x exists and

$$\dfrac{d}{dx}\left(\dfrac{f(x)}{g(x)}\right) = \dfrac{g(x)f'(x) - f(x)g'(x)}{(g(x))^2}.$$

EXAMPLE 2 Using the Quotient Rule Find and simplify the following derivatives.

a. $\dfrac{d}{dx}\left(\dfrac{x^2 + 3x + 4}{x^2 - 1}\right)$ **b.** $\dfrac{d}{dx}(e^{-x})$

> The Product and Quotient Rules are used on a regular basis throughout this text. It is a good idea to memorize these rules (along with the other derivative rules and formulas presented in this chapter) so that you can evaluate derivatives quickly.

SOLUTION

a.

$$\frac{d}{dx}\left(\frac{x^2 + 3x + 4}{x^2 - 1}\right) = \frac{\overbrace{(x^2 - 1)(2x + 3)}^{\substack{(x^2 - 1)\cdot\text{the derivative} \\ \text{of } (x^2 + 3x + 4)}} - \overbrace{(x^2 + 3x + 4)2x}^{\substack{(x^2 + 3x + 4)\cdot\text{the} \\ \text{derivative of } (x^2 - 1)}}}{\underbrace{(x^2 - 1)^2}_{\substack{\text{the denominator} \\ (x^2 - 1)\text{ squared}}}} \qquad \text{Quotient Rule}$$

$$= \frac{2x^3 - 2x + 3x^2 - 3 - 2x^3 - 6x^2 - 8x}{(x^2 - 1)^2} \qquad \text{Expand.}$$

$$= \frac{-3x^2 - 10x - 3}{(x^2 - 1)^2} \qquad \text{Simplify.}$$

b. We rewrite e^{-x} as $\dfrac{1}{e^x}$ and use the Quotient Rule:

$$\frac{d}{dx}\left(\frac{1}{e^x}\right) = \frac{e^x \cdot 0 - 1 \cdot e^x}{(e^x)^2} = -\frac{1}{e^x} = -e^{-x}.$$

Related Exercises 19–32 ◄

QUICK CHECK 2 Find the derivative of $f(x) = x^5$. Then find the same derivative using the Quotient Rule with $f(x) = x^8/x^3$. ◄

EXAMPLE 3 Finding tangent lines Find an equation of the line tangent to the graph of $f(x) = \dfrac{x^2 + 1}{x^2 - 4}$ at the point $(3, 2)$. Plot the curve and tangent line.

SOLUTION To find the slope of the tangent line, we compute f' using the Quotient Rule:

$$f'(x) = \frac{(x^2 - 4)\, 2x - (x^2 + 1)\, 2x}{(x^2 - 4)^2} \qquad \text{Quotient Rule}$$

$$= \frac{2x^3 - 8x - 2x^3 - 2x}{(x^2 - 4)^2} = -\frac{10x}{(x^2 - 4)^2}. \qquad \text{Simplify.}$$

The slope of the tangent line at $(3, 2)$ is

$$m_{\text{tan}} = f'(3) = -\frac{10(3)}{(3^2 - 4)^2} = -\frac{6}{5}.$$

Therefore, an equation of the tangent line is

$$y - 2 = -\frac{6}{5}(x - 3), \quad \text{or} \quad y = -\frac{6}{5}x + \frac{28}{5}.$$

The graphs of f and the tangent line are shown in Figure 3.28.

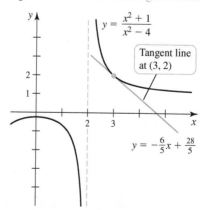

Figure 3.28

Related Exercises 33–36 ◄

Extending the Power Rule to Negative Integers

The Power Rule in Section 3.3 says that $\dfrac{d}{dx}(x^n) = nx^{n-1}$, for nonnegative integers n.

Using the Quotient Rule, we show that the Power Rule also holds if n is a negative integer. Assume n is a negative integer and let $m = -n$, so that $m > 0$. Then

$$\frac{d}{dx}(x^n) = \frac{d}{dx}\left(\frac{1}{x^m}\right) \qquad\qquad x^n = \frac{1}{x^{-n}} = \frac{1}{x^m}$$

$$= \frac{x^m\overbrace{\left(\dfrac{d}{dx}(1)\right)}^{\substack{\text{derivative of a}\\\text{constant is }0}} - 1\overbrace{\left(\dfrac{d}{dx}x^m\right)}^{\substack{\text{equals}\\ mx^{m-1}}}}{(x^m)^2} \qquad \text{Quotient Rule}$$

$$= -\frac{mx^{m-1}}{x^{2m}} \qquad\qquad \text{Simplify.}$$

$$= -mx^{-m-1} \qquad\qquad \frac{x^{m-1}}{x^{2m}} = x^{m-1-2m}$$

$$= nx^{n-1}. \qquad\qquad \text{Replace } -m \text{ with } n.$$

This calculation leads to the first extension of the Power Rule; the rule now applies to all integers.

> **THEOREM 3.9 Extended Power Rule**
> If n is any integer, then
> $$\frac{d}{dx}(x^n) = nx^{n-1}.$$

QUICK CHECK 3 Find the derivative of $f(x) = 1/x^5$ in two different ways: using the Extended Power Rule and using the Quotient Rule. ◄

EXAMPLE 4   Using the Extended Power Rule Find the following derivatives.

a. $\dfrac{d}{dx}\left(\dfrac{9}{x^5}\right)$ **b.** $\dfrac{d}{dt}\left(\dfrac{3t^{16} - 4}{t^6}\right)$

SOLUTION

a. $\dfrac{d}{dx}\left(\dfrac{9}{x^5}\right) = \dfrac{d}{dx}(9x^{-5}) = 9(-5x^{-6}) = -45x^{-6} = -\dfrac{45}{x^6}$

b. The derivative of $\dfrac{3t^{16} - 4}{t^6}$ can be evaluated by the Quotient Rule, but an alternative method is to rewrite the expression using negative powers:

$$\frac{3t^{16} - 4}{t^6} = \frac{3t^{16}}{t^6} - \frac{4}{t^6} = 3t^{10} - 4t^{-6}.$$

We now differentiate using the Extended Power Rule:

$$\frac{d}{dt}\left(\frac{3t^{16} - 4}{t^6}\right) = \frac{d}{dt}(3t^{10} - 4t^{-6}) = 30t^9 + 24t^{-7}.$$

Related Exercises 37–42 ◄

The Derivative of e^{kx}

Consider the composite function $y = e^{2x}$, for which we presently have no differentiation rule. We rewrite the function and apply the Product Rule:

$$\frac{d}{dx}(e^{2x}) = \frac{d}{dx}(e^x \cdot e^x)$$ $e^{2x} = e^x \cdot e^x$

$$= \frac{d}{dx}(e^x) \cdot e^x + e^x \cdot \frac{d}{dx}(e^x)$$ Product Rule

$$= e^x \cdot e^x + e^x \cdot e^x = 2e^{2x}.$$ Evaluate derivatives.

In a similar fashion, $y = e^{3x}$ is differentiated by writing it as the product $y = e^x \cdot e^{2x}$. You should verify that $\frac{d}{dx}(e^{3x}) = 3e^{3x}$. Extending this strategy, it can be shown that $\frac{d}{dx}(e^{kx}) = ke^{kx}$, for positive integers k (Exercise 88 illustrates a proof by induction). The Quotient Rule is used to show that the rule holds for negative integers k (Exercise 89). Finally, we prove in Section 3.7 (Exercise 94) that the rule holds for all real numbers k.

THEOREM 3.10   The derivative of e^{kx}
For real numbers k,

$$\frac{d}{dx}(e^{kx}) = ke^{kx}.$$

EXAMPLE 5   Exponential derivatives Compute dy/dx for the following functions.

a. $y = xe^{5x}$ **b.** $y = 1000e^{0.07x}$

SOLUTION

a. We use the Product Rule and the fact that $\frac{d}{dx}(e^{kx}) = ke^{kx}$:

$$\frac{dy}{dx} = \underbrace{1}_{\frac{d}{dx}(x) = 1} \cdot e^{5x} + x \cdot \underbrace{5e^{5x}}_{\frac{d}{dx}(e^{5x}) = 5e^{5x}} = (1 + 5x)e^{5x}.$$

b. Here we use the Constant Multiple Rule:

$$\frac{dy}{dx} = 1000 \cdot \frac{d}{dx}(e^{0.07x}) = 1000 \cdot 0.07e^{0.07x} = 70e^{0.07x}.$$

Related Exercises 43–50 ◄

QUICK CHECK 4 Find the derivative of $f(x) = 4e^{0.5x}$. ◄

Rates of Change

Remember that the derivative has multiple uses and interpretations. The following example illustrates the derivative as a rate of change of a population. Specifically, the derivative tells us when the population is growing most rapidly and how the population behaves in the long run.

EXAMPLE 6   Population growth rates The population of a culture of cells increases and approaches a constant level (often called a *steady state* or a *carrying capacity*). The population is modeled by the function $p(t) = \dfrac{400}{1 + 3e^{-0.5t}}$, where $t \geq 0$ is measured in hours (Figure 3.29).

a. Compute and graph the instantaneous growth rate of the population, for any $t \geq 0$.

b. At approximately what time is the instantaneous growth rate the greatest?

c. What is the steady-state population?

SOLUTION

a. The instantaneous growth rate is given by the derivative of the population function:

$$p'(t) = \frac{d}{dt}\left(\frac{400}{1 + 3e^{-0.5t}}\right)$$

$$= \frac{(1 + 3e^{-0.5t}) \cdot \overbrace{\frac{d}{dt}(400)}^{\text{equals } 0} - 400\frac{d}{dt}(1 + 3e^{-0.5t})}{(1 + 3e^{-0.5t})^2} \qquad \text{Quotient Rule}$$

$$= \frac{-400(-1.5e^{-0.5t})}{(1 + 3e^{-0.5t})^2} = \frac{600e^{-0.5t}}{(1 + 3e^{-0.5t})^2}. \qquad \text{Simplify.}$$

The growth rate has units of cells per hour; its graph is shown in Figure 3.29.

▶ Methods for determining exactly when the growth rate is a maximum are discussed in Chapter 4.

b. The growth rate $p'(t)$ has a maximum at the point at which the population curve is steepest. Using a graphing utility, this point corresponds to $t \approx 2.2$ hr and the growth rate has a value of $p'(2.2) \approx 50\,\text{cells/hr}$.

c. To determine whether the population approaches a fixed value after a long period of time (the steady-state population), we must investigate the limit of the population function as $t \to \infty$. In this case, the steady-state population exists and is

$$\lim_{t \to \infty} p(t) = \lim_{t \to \infty} \frac{400}{1 + 3\underbrace{e^{-0.5t}}_{\text{approaches } 0}} = 400,$$

which is confirmed by the population curve in Figure 3.29. Notice that as the population approaches its steady state, the growth rate p' approaches zero. *Related Exercises 51–56* ◀

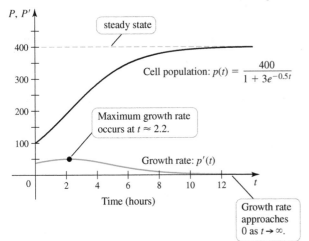

Figure 3.29

Combining Derivative Rules

Some situations call for the use of multiple differentiation rules. This section concludes with one such example.

EXAMPLE 7 Combining derivative rules Find the derivative of

$$y = \frac{4xe^x}{x^2 + 1}.$$

SOLUTION In this case, we have the quotient of two functions, with a product $(4x\,e^x)$ in the numerator.

$$\frac{dy}{dx} = \frac{(x^2 + 1) \cdot \frac{d}{dx}(4xe^x) - (4xe^x) \cdot \frac{d}{dx}(x^2 + 1)}{(x^2 + 1)^2} \qquad \text{Quotient Rule}$$

$$= \frac{(x^2 + 1)(4e^x + 4xe^x) - (4xe^x)(2x)}{(x^2 + 1)^2} \qquad \begin{array}{l}\frac{d}{dx}(4xe^x) = 4e^x + 4xe^x \\ \text{by the Product Rule}\end{array}$$

$$= \frac{4e^x(x^3 - x^2 + x + 1)}{(x^2 + 1)^2} \qquad \text{Simplify.}$$

Related Exercises 57–60 ◀

SECTION 3.4 EXERCISES

Review Questions

1. How do you find the derivative of the product of two functions that are differentiable at a point?

2. How do you find the derivative of the quotient of two functions that are differentiable at a point?

3. State the Extended Power Rule for differentiating x^n. For what values of n does the rule apply?

4. Show two ways to differentiate $f(x) = 1/x^{10}$.

5. What is the derivative of $y = e^{kx}$? For what values of k does this rule apply?

6. Show two ways to differentiate $f(x) = (x - 3)(x^2 + 4)$.

Basic Skills

7–14. Derivatives of products *Find the derivative of the following functions.*

7. $f(x) = 3x^4(2x^2 - 1)$ 8. $g(x) = 6x - 2xe^x$

9. $f(t) = t^5 e^t$ 10. $g(w) = e^w(5w^2 + 3w + 1)$

11. $h(x) = (x - 1)(x^3 + x^2 + x + 1)$

12. $f(x) = \left(1 + \dfrac{1}{x^2}\right)(x^2 + 1)$

13. $g(w) = e^w(w^3 - 1)$ 14. $s(t) = 4e^t\sqrt{t}$

15–18. Derivatives by two different methods

a. *Use the Product Rule to find the derivative of the given function. Simplify your result.*

b. *Find the derivative by expanding the product first. Verify that your answer agrees with part (a).*

15. $f(x) = (x - 1)(3x + 4)$

16. $y = (t^2 + 7t)(3t - 4)$

17. $g(y) = (3y^4 - y^2)(y^2 - 4)$

18. $h(z) = (z^3 + 4z^2 + z)(z - 1)$

19–28. Derivatives of quotients *Find the derivative of the following functions.*

19. $f(x) = \dfrac{x}{x + 1}$ 20. $f(x) = \dfrac{x^3 - 4x^2 + x}{x - 2}$

21. $f(x) = \dfrac{e^x}{e^x + 1}$ 22. $f(x) = \dfrac{2e^x - 1}{2e^x + 1}$

23. $f(x) = xe^{-x}$ 24. $f(x) = e^{-x}\sqrt{x}$

25. $y = (3t - 1)(2t - 2)^{-1}$ 26. $h(w) = \dfrac{w^2 - 1}{w^2 + 1}$

27. $g(x) = \dfrac{e^x}{x^2 - 1}$ 28. $y = (2\sqrt{x} - 1)(4x + 1)^{-1}$

29–32. Derivatives by two different methods

a. *Use the Quotient Rule to find the derivative of the given function. Simplify your result.*

b. *Find the derivative by first simplifying the function. Verify that your answer agrees with part (a).*

29. $f(w) = \dfrac{w^3 - w}{w}$ 30. $y = \dfrac{4s^3 - 8s^2 + 4s}{4s}$

31. $y = \dfrac{x^2 - a^2}{x - a}$, where a is a constant.

32. $y = \dfrac{x^2 - 2ax + a^2}{x - a}$, where a is a constant.

⊤ 33–36. Equations of tangent lines

a. *Find an equation of the line tangent to the given curve at a.*

b. *Use a graphing utility to graph the curve and the tangent line on the same set of axes.*

33. $y = \dfrac{x + 5}{x - 1}$; $a = 3$ 34. $y = \dfrac{2x^2}{3x - 1}$; $a = 1$

35. $y = 1 + 2x + xe^x$; $a = 0$

36. $y = \dfrac{e^x}{x}$; $a = 1$

37–42. Extended Power Rule *Find the derivative of the following functions.*

37. $f(x) = 3x^{-9}$ 38. $y = \dfrac{4}{p^3}$

39. $g(t) = 3t^2 + \dfrac{6}{t^7}$ 40. $y = \dfrac{w^4 + 5w^2 + w}{w^2}$

41. $g(t) = \dfrac{t^3 + 3t^2 + t}{t^3}$ 42. $p(x) = \dfrac{4x^3 + 3x + 1}{2x^5}$

43–50. Derivatives with exponentials *Compute the derivative of the following functions.*

43. $f(x) = xe^{7x}$ 44. $g(t) = 2te^{t/2}$

45. $f(x) = 15e^{3x}$ 46. $y = 3x^2 - 2x + e^{-2x}$

47. $g(x) = \dfrac{x}{e^{3x}}$ 48. $f(x) = (1 - 2x)e^{-x}$

49. $y = \dfrac{2e^x + 3e^{-x}}{3}$ 50. $A = 2500e^{0.075t}$

⊤ 51–52. Population growth *Consider the following population functions.*

a. *Find the instantaneous growth rate of the population, for $t \geq 0$.*

b. *What is the instantaneous growth rate at $t = 5$?*

c. *Estimate the time when the instantaneous growth rate is the greatest.*

d. *Evaluate and interpret $\lim\limits_{t \to \infty} p'(t)$.*

e. *Use a graphing utility to graph the population and its growth rate.*

51. $p(t) = \dfrac{200t}{t + 2}$ 52. $p(t) = \dfrac{800}{1 + 7e^{-0.2t}}$

53. **Antibiotic decay** The half-life of an antibiotic in the bloodstream is 10 hours. If an initial dose of 20 milligrams is administered, the quantity left after t hours is modeled by $Q(t) = 20e^{-0.0693t}$, for $t \geq 0$.

    a. Find the instantaneous rate of change of the amount of antibiotic in the bloodstream, for $t \geq 0$.

b. How fast is the amount of antibiotic changing at $t = 0$? At $t = 2$?

c. Evaluate and interpret $\lim\limits_{t \to \infty} Q(t)$ and $\lim\limits_{t \to \infty} Q'(t)$.

54. Bank account A \$200 investment in a savings account grows according to $A(t) = 200e^{0.0398t}$, for $t \geq 0$, where t is measured in years.

  a. Find the balance of the account after 10 years.

  b. How fast is the account growing (in dollars/year) at $t = 10$?

  c. Use your answers to parts (a) and (b) to write the equation of the line tangent to the curve $A = 200e^{0.0398t}$ at the point $(10, A(10))$.

55. Finding slope locations Let $f(x) = xe^{2x}$.

  a. Find the values of x for which the slope of the curve $y = f(x)$ is 0.

  b. Explain the meaning of your answer to part (a) in terms of the graph of f.

56. Finding slope locations Let $f(t) = 100e^{-0.05t}$.

  a. Find the values of t for which the slope of the curve $y = f(t)$ is -5.

  b. Does the graph of f have a horizontal tangent line?

57–60. Combining rules *Compute the derivative of the following functions.*

57. $g(x) = \dfrac{(x + 1)e^x}{x - 2}$

58. $h(x) = \dfrac{(x - 1)(2x^2 - 1)}{x^3 - 1}$

59. $h(x) = \dfrac{xe^x}{x + 1}$

60. $h(x) = \dfrac{x + 1}{x^2 e^x}$

Further Explorations

61. Explain why or why not Determine whether the following statements are true and give an explanation or counterexample.

  a. $\dfrac{d}{dx}(e^5) = 5e^4$.

  b. The Quotient Rule must be used to evaluate $\dfrac{d}{dx}\left(\dfrac{x^2 + 3x + 2}{x}\right)$.

  c. $\dfrac{d}{dx}\left(\dfrac{1}{x^5}\right) = \dfrac{1}{5x^4}$.

  d. $\dfrac{d^n}{dx^n}(e^{3x}) = 3^n e^{3x}$, for any integer $n \geq 1$.

62–63. Higher-order derivatives *Find $f'(x)$, $f''(x)$, and $f'''(x)$.*

62. $f(x) = \dfrac{1}{x}$

63. $f(x) = x^2 e^{3x}$

64–65. First and second derivatives *Find $f'(x)$ and $f''(x)$.*

64. $f(x) = \dfrac{x}{x + 2}$

65. $f(x) = \dfrac{x^2 - 7x}{x + 1}$

66–71. Choose your method *Use any method to evaluate the derivative of the following functions.*

66. $f(x) = \dfrac{4 - x^2}{x - 2}$

67. $f(x) = 4x^2 - \dfrac{2x}{5x + 1}$

68. $f(z) = z^2(e^{3z} + 4) - \dfrac{2z}{z^2 + 1}$

69. $h(r) = \dfrac{2 - r - \sqrt{r}}{r + 1}$

70. $y = \dfrac{x - a}{\sqrt{x} - \sqrt{a}}$, where a is a positive constant.

71. $h(x) = (5x^7 + 5x)(6x^3 + 3x^2 + 3)$

72. Tangent lines Suppose $f(2) = 2$ and $f'(2) = 3$. Let $g(x) = x^2 \cdot f(x)$ and $h(x) = \dfrac{f(x)}{x - 3}$.

  a. Find an equation of the line tangent to $y = g(x)$ at $x = 2$.

  b. Find an equation of the line tangent to $y = h(x)$ at $x = 2$.

73. The Witch of Agnesi The graph of $y = \dfrac{a^3}{x^2 + a^2}$, where a is a constant, is called the *witch of Agnesi* (named after the 18th-century Italian mathematician Maria Agnesi).

  a. Let $a = 3$ and find an equation of the line tangent to
  $$y = \dfrac{27}{x^2 + 9} \text{ at } x = 2.$$

  b. Plot the function and the tangent line found in part (a).

74–79. Derivatives from a table *Use the following table to find the given derivatives.*

x	1	2	3	4
$f(x)$	5	4	3	2
$f'(x)$	3	5	2	1
$g(x)$	4	2	5	3
$g'(x)$	2	4	3	1

74. $\dfrac{d}{dx}(f(x)g(x))\Big|_{x=1}$

75. $\dfrac{d}{dx}\left(\dfrac{f(x)}{g(x)}\right)\Big|_{x=2}$

76. $\dfrac{d}{dx}(xf(x))\Big|_{x=3}$

77. $\dfrac{d}{dx}\left(\dfrac{f(x)}{x + 2}\right)\Big|_{x=4}$

78. $\dfrac{d}{dx}\left(\dfrac{xf(x)}{g(x)}\right)\Big|_{x=4}$

79. $\dfrac{d}{dx}\left(\dfrac{f(x)g(x)}{x}\right)\Big|_{x=4}$

80. Derivatives from tangent lines Suppose the line tangent to the graph of f at $x = 2$ is $y = 4x + 1$ and suppose $y = 3x - 2$ is the line tangent to the graph of g at $x = 2$. Find an equation of the line tangent to the following curves at $x = 2$.

  a. $y = f(x)g(x)$

  b. $y = \dfrac{f(x)}{g(x)}$

Applications

81. Electrostatic force The magnitude of the electrostatic force between two point charges Q and q of the same sign is given by $F(x) = \dfrac{kQq}{x^2}$, where x is the distance (measured in meters) between the charges and $k = 9 \times 10^9$ N-m^2/C^2 is a physical constant (C stands for coulomb, the unit of charge; N stands for newton, the unit of force).

  a. Find the instantaneous rate of change of the force with respect to the distance between the charges.

b. For two identical charges with $Q = q = 1$ C, what is the instantaneous rate of change of the force at a separation of $x = 0.001$ m?

c. Does the magnitude of the instantaneous rate of change of the force increase or decrease with the separation? Explain.

82. Gravitational force The magnitude of the gravitational force between two objects of mass M and m is given by $F(x) = -\dfrac{GMm}{x^2}$, where x is the distance between the centers of mass of the objects and $G = 6.7 \times 10^{-11}$ N-m²/kg² is the gravitational constant (N stands for newton, the unit of force; the negative sign indicates an attractive force).

a. Find the instantaneous rate of change of the force with respect to the distance between the objects.

b. For two identical objects of mass $M = m = 0.1$ kg, what is the instantaneous rate of change of the force at a separation of $x = 0.01$ m?

c. Does the instantaneous rate of change of the force increase or decrease with the separation? Explain.

Additional Exercises

83. Special Product Rule In general, the derivative of a product is not the product of the derivatives. Find nonconstant functions f and g such that the derivative of fg equals $f'g'$.

84. Special Quotient Rule In general, the derivative of a quotient is not the quotient of the derivatives. Find nonconstant functions f and g such that the derivative of f/g equals f'/g'.

85. Means and tangents Suppose f is differentiable on an interval containing a and b, and let $P(a, f(a))$ and $Q(b, f(b))$ be distinct points on the graph of f. Let c be the x-coordinate of the point at which the lines tangent to the curve at P and Q intersect, assuming that the tangent lines are not parallel (see figure).

a. If $f(x) = x^2$, show that $c = (a + b)/2$, the arithmetic mean of a and b, for real numbers a and b.

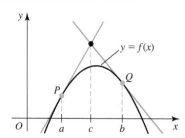

b. If $f(x) = \sqrt{x}$, show that $c = \sqrt{ab}$, the geometric mean of a and b, for $a > 0$ and $b > 0$.

c. If $f(x) = 1/x$, show that $c = 2ab/(a + b)$, the harmonic mean of a and b, for $a > 0$ and $b > 0$.

d. Find an expression for c in terms of a and b for any (differentiable) function f whenever c exists.

86. Proof of the Quotient Rule Let $F = f/g$ be the quotient of two functions that are differentiable at x.

a. Use the definition of F' to show that
$$\frac{d}{dx}\left(\frac{f(x)}{g(x)}\right) = \lim_{h \to 0} \frac{f(x + h)g(x) - f(x)g(x + h)}{hg(x + h)g(x)}.$$

b. Now add $-f(x)g(x) + f(x)g(x)$ (which equals 0) to the numerator in the preceding limit to obtain
$$\lim_{h \to 0} \frac{f(x + h)g(x) - f(x)g(x) + f(x)g(x) - f(x)g(x + h)}{hg(x + h)g(x)}.$$

Use this limit to obtain the Quotient Rule.

c. Explain why $F' = (f/g)'$ exists, whenever $g(x) \neq 0$.

87. Product Rule for the second derivative Assuming the first and second derivatives of f and g exist at x, find a formula for
$$\frac{d^2}{dx^2}(f(x)g(x)).$$

88. Proof by induction: derivative of e^{kx} for positive integers k Proof by induction is a method in which one begins by showing that a statement, which involves positive integers, is true for a particular value (usually $k = 1$). In the second step, the statement is assumed to be true for $k = n$, and the statement is proved for $k = n + 1$, which concludes the proof.

a. Show that $\dfrac{d}{dx}(e^{kx}) = ke^{kx}$, for $k = 1$.

b. Assume the rule is true for $k = n$ (that is, assume $\dfrac{d}{dx}(e^{nx}) = ne^{nx}$), and show this assumption implies that the rule is true for $k = n + 1$. (*Hint:* Write $e^{(n+1)x}$ as the product of two functions and use the Product Rule.)

89. Derivative of e^{kx} for negative integers k Use the Quotient Rule and Exercise 88 to show that $\dfrac{d}{dx}(e^{kx}) = ke^{kx}$, for negative integers k.

90. Quotient Rule for the second derivative Assuming the first and second derivatives of f and g exist at x, find a formula for
$$\frac{d^2}{dx^2}\left(\frac{f(x)}{g(x)}\right).$$

91. Product Rule for three functions Assume that f, g, and h are differentiable at x.

a. Use the Product Rule (twice) to find a formula for
$$\frac{d}{dx}(f(x)g(x)h(x)).$$

b. Use the formula in (a) to find $\dfrac{d}{dx}(e^{2x}(x - 1)(x + 3))$.

92. One of the Leibniz Rules One of several Leibniz Rules in calculus deals with higher-order derivatives of products. Let $(fg)^{(n)}$ denote the nth derivative of the product fg, for $n \geq 1$.

a. Prove that $(fg)^{(2)} = f''g + 2f'g' + fg''$.

b. Prove that, in general,
$$(fg)^{(n)} = \sum_{k=0}^{n}\binom{n}{k}f^{(k)}g^{(n-k)},$$

where $\dbinom{n}{k} = \dfrac{n!}{k!(n - k)!}$ are the binomial coefficients.

c. Compare the result of (b) to the expansion of $(a + b)^n$.

QUICK CHECK ANSWERS

1. $f'(x) = 5x^4$ by either method   2. $f'(x) = 5x^4$ by either method   3. $f'(x) = -5x^{-6}$ by either method   4. $f'(x) = 2e^{0.5x}$ ◄

3.5 Derivatives of Trigonometric Functions

> Results stated in this section assume that angles are measured in *radians*.

From variations in market trends and ocean temperatures to daily fluctuations in tides and hormone levels, change is often cyclical or periodic. Trigonometric functions are well suited for describing such cyclical behavior. In this section, we investigate the derivatives of trigonometric functions and their many uses.

Two Special Limits

Our principal goal is to determine derivative formulas for $\sin x$ and $\cos x$. To do this, we use two special limits.

THEOREM 3.11 Trigonometric Limits

$$\lim_{x \to 0} \frac{\sin x}{x} = 1 \qquad \lim_{x \to 0} \frac{\cos x - 1}{x} = 0$$

Note that these limits cannot be evaluated by direct substitution because in both cases, the numerator and denominator approach zero as $x \to 0$. We first examine numerical and graphical evidence supporting Theorem 3.11, and then we offer an analytic proof.

The values of $\dfrac{\sin x}{x}$, rounded to 10 digits, appear in Table 3.2. As x approaches zero from both sides, it appears that $\dfrac{\sin x}{x}$ approaches 1. Figure 3.30 shows a graph of $y = \dfrac{\sin x}{x}$, with a hole at $x = 0$, where the function is undefined. The graphical evidence also strongly suggests (but does not prove) that $\lim\limits_{x \to 0} \dfrac{\sin x}{x} = 1$. Similar evidence indicates that $\dfrac{\cos x - 1}{x}$ approaches 0 as x approaches 0.

Using a geometric argument and the methods of Chapter 2, we now prove that $\lim\limits_{x \to 0} \dfrac{\sin x}{x} = 1$. The proof that $\lim\limits_{x \to 0} \dfrac{\cos x - 1}{x} = 0$ is found in Exercise 73.

Proof: Consider Figure 3.31, in which $\triangle OAD$, $\triangle OBC$, and the sector OAC of the unit circle (with central angle x) are shown. Observe that with $0 < x < \pi/2$,

$$\text{area of } \triangle OAD < \text{area of sector } OAC < \text{area of } \triangle OBC. \tag{1}$$

Because the circle in Figure 3.31 is a *unit* circle, $OA = OC = 1$. It follows that $\sin x = \dfrac{AD}{OA} = AD$, $\cos x = \dfrac{OD}{OA} = OD$, and $\tan x = \dfrac{BC}{OC} = BC$. From these observations, we conclude that

- the area of $\triangle OAD = \dfrac{1}{2}(OD)(AD) = \dfrac{1}{2}\cos x \sin x$,

- the area of sector $OAC = \dfrac{1}{2} \cdot 1^2 \cdot x = \dfrac{x}{2}$, and

- the area of $\triangle OBC = \dfrac{1}{2}(OC)(BC) = \dfrac{1}{2}\tan x$.

Substituting these results into (1), we have

$$\frac{1}{2}\cos x \sin x < \frac{x}{2} < \frac{1}{2}\tan x.$$

Table 3.2

x	$\dfrac{\sin x}{x}$
± 0.1	0.9983341665
± 0.01	0.9999833334
± 0.001	0.9999998333

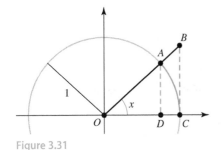

The graph of $y = \dfrac{\sin x}{x}$ suggests that $\lim\limits_{x \to 0} \dfrac{\sin x}{x} = 1$.

Figure 3.30

Figure 3.31

> Area of a sector of a circle of radius r formed by a central angle θ:

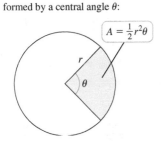

$$A = \tfrac{1}{2}r^2\theta$$

Replacing $\tan x$ with $\dfrac{\sin x}{\cos x}$ and multiplying the inequalities by $\dfrac{2}{\sin x}$ (which is positive) leads to the inequalities

$$\cos x < \frac{x}{\sin x} < \frac{1}{\cos x}.$$

When we take reciprocals and reverse the inequalities, we have

$$\cos x < \frac{\sin x}{x} < \frac{1}{\cos x}, \tag{2}$$

for $0 < x < \pi/2$.

A similar argument shows that the inequalities in (2) also hold for $-\pi/2 < x < 0$. Taking the limit as $x \to 0$ in (2), we find that

$$\underbrace{\lim_{x\to 0} \cos x}_{1} < \lim_{x\to 0} \frac{\sin x}{x} < \underbrace{\lim_{x\to 0} \frac{1}{\cos x}}_{1}.$$

➤ $\lim_{x\to 0} \dfrac{\sin x}{x} = 1$ implies that if $|x|$ is

small, then $\sin x \approx x$.

The Squeeze Theorem (Theorem 2.5) now implies that $\lim_{x\to 0} \dfrac{\sin x}{x} = 1$.   ◀

EXAMPLE 1   **Calculating trigonometric limits**   Evaluate the following limits.

a. $\lim_{x\to 0} \dfrac{\sin 4x}{x}$ **b.** $\lim_{x\to 0} \dfrac{\sin 3x}{\sin 5x}$

SOLUTION

a. To use the fact that $\lim_{x\to 0} \dfrac{\sin x}{x} = 1$, the argument of the sine function in the numerator must be the same as the denominator. Multiplying and dividing $\dfrac{\sin 4x}{x}$ by 4, we evaluate the limit as follows:

$$\lim_{x\to 0} \frac{\sin 4x}{x} = \lim_{x\to 0} \frac{4\sin 4x}{4x} \qquad \text{Multiply and divide by 4.}$$

$$= 4\lim_{t\to 0} \underbrace{\frac{\sin t}{t}}_{1} \qquad \text{Factor out 4 and let } t = 4x; \, t \to 0 \text{ as } x \to 0.$$

$$= 4(1) = 4. \qquad \text{Theorem 3.11}$$

b. The first step is to divide the numerator and denominator of $\dfrac{\sin 3x}{\sin 5x}$ by x:

$$\frac{\sin 3x}{\sin 5x} = \frac{(\sin 3x)/x}{(\sin 5x)/x}.$$

As in part (a), we now divide and multiply $\dfrac{\sin 3x}{x}$ by 3 and divide and multiply $\dfrac{\sin 5x}{x}$ by 5. In the numerator, we let $t = 3x$, and in the denominator, we let $u = 5x$. In each case, $t \to 0$ and $u \to 0$ as $x \to 0$. Therefore,

$$\lim_{x \to 0} \frac{\sin 3x}{\sin 5x} = \lim_{x \to 0} \frac{\dfrac{3 \sin 3x}{3x}}{\dfrac{5 \sin 5x}{5x}} \qquad \text{Multiply and divide by 3 and 5.}$$

$$= \frac{3}{5} \frac{\lim\limits_{t \to 0} (\sin t)/t}{\lim\limits_{u \to 0} (\sin u)/u} \qquad \text{Let } t = 3x \text{ in numerator and } u = 5x \text{ in denominator.}$$

$$= \frac{3}{5} \cdot \frac{1}{1} = \frac{3}{5}. \qquad \text{Both limits equal 1.} \qquad \textit{Related Exercises 7–16} \blacktriangleleft$$

QUICK CHECK 1 Evaluate $\lim\limits_{x \to 0} \dfrac{\tan 2x}{x}$. ◄

We now use the important limits of Theorem 3.11 to establish the derivatives of $\sin x$ and $\cos x$.

Derivatives of Sine and Cosine Functions

We start with the definition of the derivative,

$$f'(x) = \lim_{h \to 0} \frac{f(x + h) - f(x)}{h},$$

with $f(x) = \sin x$, and then appeal to the sine addition identity

$$\sin (x + h) = \sin x \cos h + \cos x \sin h.$$

The derivative is

$$f'(x) = \lim_{h \to 0} \frac{\sin (x + h) - \sin x}{h} \qquad \text{Definition of derivative}$$

$$= \lim_{h \to 0} \frac{\sin x \cos h + \cos x \sin h - \sin x}{h} \qquad \text{Sine addition identity}$$

$$= \lim_{h \to 0} \frac{\sin x (\cos h - 1) + \cos x \sin h}{h} \qquad \text{Factor } \sin x.$$

$$= \lim_{h \to 0} \frac{\sin x (\cos h - 1)}{h} + \lim_{h \to 0} \frac{\cos x \sin h}{h} \qquad \text{Theorem 2.3}$$

$$= \sin x \left(\underbrace{\lim_{h \to 0} \frac{\cos h - 1}{h}}_{0} \right) + \cos x \left(\underbrace{\lim_{h \to 0} \frac{\sin h}{h}}_{1} \right) \qquad \begin{array}{l} \text{Both } \sin x \text{ and } \cos x \text{ are} \\ \text{independent of } h. \end{array}$$

$$= (\sin x)(0) + \cos x (1) \qquad \text{Theorem 3.11}$$

$$= \cos x. \qquad \text{Simplify.}$$

We have proved the important result that $\dfrac{d}{dx}(\sin x) = \cos x$.

The fact that $\dfrac{d}{dx}(\cos x) = -\sin x$ is proved in a similar way using a cosine addition identity (Exercise 75).

THEOREM 3.12 **Derivatives of Sine and Cosine**

$$\frac{d}{dx}(\sin x) = \cos x \qquad \frac{d}{dx}(\cos x) = -\sin x$$

From a geometric point of view, these derivative formulas make sense. Because $f(x) = \sin x$ is a periodic function, we expect its derivative to be periodic. Observe that the horizontal tangent lines on the graph of $f(x) = \sin x$ (Figure 3.32a) occur at the zeros of $f'(x) = \cos x$. Similarly, the horizontal tangent lines on the graph of $f(x) = \cos x$ occur at the zeros of $f'(x) = -\sin x$ (Figure 3.32b).

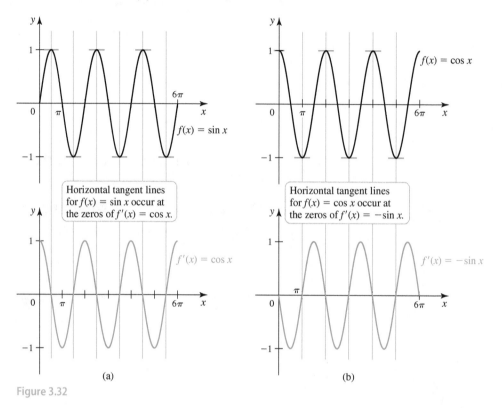

Figure 3.32

QUICK CHECK 2 At what points on the interval $[0, 2\pi]$ does the graph of $f(x) = \sin x$ have tangent lines with positive slopes? At what points on the interval $[0, 2\pi]$ is $\cos x > 0$? Explain the connection. ◄

EXAMPLE 2   Derivatives involving trigonometric functions Calculate dy/dx for the following functions.

a. $y = e^{2x} \cos x$ **b.** $y = \sin x - x \cos x$ **c.** $y = \dfrac{1 + \sin x}{1 - \sin x}$

SOLUTION

a.
$$\frac{dy}{dx} = \frac{d}{dx}(e^{2x} \cos x) = \overbrace{2e^{2x} \cos x}^{\substack{e^{2x}\cdot\text{ derivative}\\ \text{of } e^{2x}\cdot\cos x}} + \overbrace{e^{2x}(-\sin x)}^{\substack{e^{2x}\cdot\text{ derivative}\\ \text{of }\cos x}} \qquad \text{Product Rule}$$

$$= e^{2x}(2 \cos x - \sin x) \qquad \text{Simplify.}$$

b.
$$\frac{dy}{dx} = \frac{d}{dx}(\sin x) - \frac{d}{dx}(x \cos x) \qquad \text{Difference Rule}$$

$$= \cos x - (\underbrace{(1) \cos x}_{\substack{\text{derivative of } x\\ \cdot \cos x}} + \underbrace{x(-\sin x)}_{\substack{x\cdot \text{ derivative}\\ \text{of } \cos x}}) \qquad \text{Product Rule}$$

$$= x \sin x \qquad \text{Simplify.}$$

$$\text{c.} \quad \frac{dy}{dx} = \frac{\overbrace{(1 - \sin x)}^{\text{derivative of}}(\cos x) - (1 + \sin x)\overbrace{(-\cos x)}^{\text{derivative of}}}{(1 - \sin x)^2} \quad \text{Quotient Rule}$$

$$= \frac{\cos x - \cos x \sin x + \cos x + \sin x \cos x}{(1 - \sin x)^2} \quad \text{Expand.}$$

$$= \frac{2\cos x}{(1 - \sin x)^2} \quad \text{Simplify.}$$

Related Exercises 17–28 ◄

Derivatives of Other Trigonometric Functions

The derivatives of $\tan x$, $\cot x$, $\sec x$, and $\csc x$ are obtained using the derivatives of $\sin x$ and $\cos x$ together with the Quotient Rule and trigonometric identities.

EXAMPLE 3   **Derivative of the tangent function**   Calculate $\dfrac{d}{dx}(\tan x)$.

> Recall that $\tan x = \dfrac{\sin x}{\cos x}$, $\cot x = \dfrac{\cos x}{\sin x}$, $\sec x = \dfrac{1}{\cos x}$, and $\csc x = \dfrac{1}{\sin x}$.

SOLUTION   Using the identity $\tan x = \dfrac{\sin x}{\cos x}$ and the Quotient Rule, we have

$$\frac{d}{dx}(\tan x) = \frac{d}{dx}\left(\frac{\sin x}{\cos x}\right)$$

$$= \frac{\cos x \overbrace{\cos x}^{\text{derivative of } \sin x} - \sin x \overbrace{(-\sin x)}^{\text{derivative of } \cos x}}{\cos^2 x} \quad \text{Quotient Rule}$$

$$= \frac{\cos^2 x + \sin^2 x}{\cos^2 x} \quad \text{Simplify numerator.}$$

$$= \frac{1}{\cos^2 x} = \sec^2 x. \quad \cos^2 x + \sin^2 x = 1$$

Therefore, $\dfrac{d}{dx}(\tan x) = \sec^2 x.$ *Related Exercises 29–31* ◄

The derivatives of $\cot x$, $\sec x$, and $\csc x$ are given in Theorem 3.13 (Exercises 29–31).

> One way to remember Theorem 3.13 is to learn the derivatives of the sine, tangent, and secant functions. Then replace each function with its corresponding **cofunction** and put a negative sign on the right-hand side of the new derivative formula.
>
> $$\frac{d}{dx}(\sin x) = \cos x \quad \leftrightarrow$$
>
> $$\frac{d}{dx}(\cos x) = -\sin x$$
>
> $$\frac{d}{dx}(\tan x) = \sec^2 x \quad \leftrightarrow$$
>
> $$\frac{d}{dx}(\cot x) = -\csc^2 x$$
>
> $$\frac{d}{dx}(\sec x) = \sec x \tan x \quad \leftrightarrow$$
>
> $$\frac{d}{dx}(\csc x) = -\csc x \cot x$$

THEOREM 3.13   **Derivatives of the Trigonometric Functions**

$$\frac{d}{dx}(\sin x) = \cos x \qquad\qquad \frac{d}{dx}(\cos x) = -\sin x$$

$$\frac{d}{dx}(\tan x) = \sec^2 x \qquad\qquad \frac{d}{dx}(\cot x) = -\csc^2 x$$

$$\frac{d}{dx}(\sec x) = \sec x \tan x \qquad\qquad \frac{d}{dx}(\csc x) = -\csc x \cot x$$

QUICK CHECK 3   The formulas for $\dfrac{d}{dx}(\cot x)$, $\dfrac{d}{dx}(\sec x)$, and $\dfrac{d}{dx}(\csc x)$ can be determined using the Quotient Rule. Why? ◄

EXAMPLE 4 **Derivatives involving sec x and csc x** Find the derivative of $y = \sec x \csc x$.

SOLUTION

$$\frac{dy}{dx} = \frac{d}{dx}(\sec x \cdot \csc x)$$

$$= \underbrace{\sec x \tan x \csc x}_{\text{derivative of sec } x} + \sec x \underbrace{(-\csc x \cot x)}_{\text{derivative of csc } x} \qquad \text{Product Rule}$$

$$= \underbrace{\frac{1}{\cos x}}_{\sec x} \cdot \underbrace{\frac{\sin x}{\cos x}}_{\tan x} \cdot \underbrace{\frac{1}{\sin x}}_{\csc x} - \underbrace{\frac{1}{\cos x}}_{\sec x} \cdot \underbrace{\frac{1}{\sin x}}_{\csc x} \cdot \underbrace{\frac{\cos x}{\sin x}}_{\cot x} \qquad \begin{array}{l}\text{Write functions in terms of}\\ \sin x \text{ and } \cos x.\end{array}$$

$$= \frac{1}{\cos^2 x} - \frac{1}{\sin^2 x} \qquad \text{Cancel and simplify.}$$

$$= \sec^2 x - \csc^2 x \qquad \text{Definition of sec } x \text{ and csc } x$$

Related Exercises 32–40 ◄

QUICK CHECK 4 Why is the derivative of $\sec x \csc x$ equal to the derivative of $\dfrac{1}{\cos x \sin x}$? ◄

Higher-Order Trigonometric Derivatives

Higher-order derivatives of the sine and cosine functions are important in many applications, particularly in problems that involve oscillations, vibrations, or waves. A few higher-order derivatives of $y = \sin x$ reveal a pattern.

$$\frac{dy}{dx} = \cos x \qquad\qquad \frac{d^2 y}{dx^2} = \frac{d}{dx}(\cos x) = -\sin x$$

$$\frac{d^3 y}{dx^3} = \frac{d}{dx}(-\sin x) = -\cos x \qquad \frac{d^4 y}{dx^4} = \frac{d}{dx}(-\cos x) = \sin x$$

We see that the higher-order derivatives of $\sin x$ cycle back periodically to $\pm \sin x$. In general, it can be shown that $\dfrac{d^{2n} y}{dx^{2n}} = (-1)^n \sin x$, with a similar result for $\cos x$ (Exercise 80). This cyclic behavior in the derivatives of $\sin x$ and $\cos x$ does not occur with the other trigonometric functions.

QUICK CHECK 5 Find $\dfrac{d^2 y}{dx^2}$ and $\dfrac{d^4 y}{dx^4}$ when $y = \cos x$. Find $\dfrac{d^{40} y}{dx^{40}}$ and $\dfrac{d^{42} y}{dx^{42}}$ when $y = \sin x$. ◄

EXAMPLE 5 **Second-order derivatives** Find the second derivative of $y = \csc x$.

SOLUTION By Theorem 3.13, $\dfrac{dy}{dx} = -\csc x \cot x$.

Applying the Product Rule gives the second derivative:

$$\frac{d^2 y}{dx^2} = \frac{d}{dx}(-\csc x \cot x)$$

$$= \left(\frac{d}{dx}(-\csc x)\right)\cot x - \csc x \frac{d}{dx}(\cot x) \qquad \text{Product Rule}$$

$$= (\csc x \cot x)\cot x - \csc x (-\csc^2 x) \qquad \text{Calculate derivatives.}$$

$$= \csc x (\cot^2 x + \csc^2 x). \qquad \text{Factor.}$$

Related Exercises 41–48 ◄

SECTION 3.5 EXERCISES

Review Questions

1. Why is it not possible to evaluate $\lim\limits_{x\to 0}\dfrac{\sin x}{x}$ by direct substitution?

2. How is $\lim\limits_{x\to 0}\dfrac{\sin x}{x}$ used in this section?

3. Explain why the Quotient Rule is used to determine the derivative of $\tan x$ and $\cot x$.

4. How can you use the derivatives $\dfrac{d}{dx}(\sin x) = \cos x$,

   $\dfrac{d}{dx}(\tan x) = \sec^2 x$, and $\dfrac{d}{dx}(\sec x) = \sec x \tan x$ to remember the derivatives of $\cos x$, $\cot x$, and $\csc x$?

5. Let $f(x) = \sin x$. What is the value of $f'(\pi)$?

6. Where does the graph of $\sin x$ have a horizontal tangent line? Where does $\cos x$ have a value of zero? Explain the connection between these two observations.

Basic Skills

7–16. Trigonometric limits *Use Theorem 3.11 to evaluate the following limits.*

7. $\lim\limits_{x\to 0}\dfrac{\sin 3x}{x}$

8. $\lim\limits_{x\to 0}\dfrac{\sin 5x}{3x}$

9. $\lim\limits_{x\to 0}\dfrac{\sin 7x}{\sin 3x}$

10. $\lim\limits_{x\to 0}\dfrac{\sin 3x}{\tan 4x}$

11. $\lim\limits_{x\to 0}\dfrac{\tan 5x}{x}$

12. $\lim\limits_{\theta\to 0}\dfrac{\cos^2\theta - 1}{\theta}$

13. $\lim\limits_{x\to 0}\dfrac{\tan 7x}{\sin x}$

14. $\lim\limits_{\theta\to 0}\dfrac{\sec\theta - 1}{\theta}$

15. $\lim\limits_{x\to 2}\dfrac{\sin(x - 2)}{x^2 - 4}$

16. $\lim\limits_{x\to -3}\dfrac{\sin(x + 3)}{x^2 + 8x + 15}$

17–28. Calculating derivatives *Find dy/dx for the following functions.*

17. $y = \sin x + \cos x$

18. $y = 5x^2 + \cos x$

19. $y = e^{-x}\sin x$

20. $y = \sin x + 4e^{0.5x}$

21. $y = x \sin x$

22. $y = e^{6x}\sin x$

23. $y = \dfrac{\cos x}{\sin x + 1}$

24. $y = \dfrac{1 - \sin x}{1 + \sin x}$

25. $y = \sin x \cos x$

26. $y = \dfrac{(x^2 - 1)\sin x}{\sin x + 1}$

27. $y = \cos^2 x$

28. $y = \dfrac{x \sin x}{1 + \cos x}$

29–31. Derivatives of other trigonometric functions *Verify the following derivative formulas using the Quotient Rule.*

29. $\dfrac{d}{dx}(\cot x) = -\csc^2 x$

30. $\dfrac{d}{dx}(\sec x) = \sec x \tan x$

31. $\dfrac{d}{dx}(\csc x) = -\csc x \cot x$

32–40. Derivatives involving other trigonometric functions *Find the derivative of the following functions.*

32. $y = \tan x + \cot x$

33. $y = \sec x + \csc x$

34. $y = \sec x \tan x$

35. $y = e^{5x}\csc x$

36. $y = \dfrac{\tan w}{1 + \tan w}$

37. $y = \dfrac{\cot x}{1 + \csc x}$

38. $y = \dfrac{\tan t}{1 + \sec t}$

39. $y = \dfrac{1}{\sec z \csc z}$

40. $y = \csc^2\theta - 1$

41–48. Second-order derivatives *Find y'' for the following functions.*

41. $y = x \sin x$

42. $y = \cos x$

43. $y = e^x \sin x$

44. $y = \dfrac{1}{2}e^x \cos x$

45. $y = \cot x$

46. $y = \tan x$

47. $y = \sec x \csc x$

48. $y = \cos\theta \sin\theta$

Further Explorations

49. **Explain why or why not** Determine whether the following statements are true and give an explanation or counterexample.

   a. $\dfrac{d}{dx}(\sin^2 x) = \cos^2 x$.

   b. $\dfrac{d^2}{dx^2}(\sin x) = \sin x$.

   c. $\dfrac{d^4}{dx^4}(\cos x) = \cos x$.

   d. The function $\sec x$ is not differentiable at $x = \pi/2$.

50–55. Trigonometric limits *Evaluate the following limits or state that they do not exist.*

50. $\lim\limits_{x\to 0}\dfrac{\sin ax}{bx}$, where a and b are constants with $b \neq 0$

51. $\lim\limits_{x\to 0}\dfrac{\sin ax}{\sin bx}$, where a and b are constants with $b \neq 0$

52. $\lim\limits_{x\to \pi/2}\dfrac{\cos x}{x - (\pi/2)}$

53. $\lim\limits_{x\to 0}\dfrac{3\sec^5 x}{x^2 + 4}$

54. $\lim\limits_{x\to \infty}\dfrac{\cos x}{x}$

55. $\lim\limits_{x\to \pi/4} 3\csc 2x \cot 2x$

56–61. Calculating derivatives *Find dy/dx for the following functions.*

56. $y = \dfrac{\sin x}{1 + \cos x}$

57. $y = x \cos x \sin x$

58. $y = \dfrac{1}{2 + \sin x}$

59. $y = \dfrac{\sin x}{\sin x - \cos x}$

60. $y = \dfrac{x \cos x}{1 + x^3}$

61. $y = \dfrac{1 - \cos x}{1 + \cos x}$

62–65. Equations of tangent lines

a. *Find an equation of the line tangent to the following curves at the given value of x.*
b. *Use a graphing utility to plot the curve and the tangent line.*

62. $y = 4 \sin x \cos x; \; x = \dfrac{\pi}{3}$

63. $y = 1 + 2 \sin x; \; x = \dfrac{\pi}{6}$

64. $y = \csc x; \; x = \dfrac{\pi}{4}$

65. $y = \dfrac{\cos x}{1 - \cos x}; \; x = \dfrac{\pi}{3}$

66. Locations of tangent lines

a. For what values of x does $g(x) = x - \sin x$ have a horizontal tangent line?
b. For what values of x does $g(x) = x - \sin x$ have a slope of 1?

67. Locations of horizontal tangent lines For what values of x does $f(x) = x - 2 \cos x$ have a horizontal tangent line?

68. Matching Match the graphs of the functions in a–d with the graphs of their derivatives in A–D.

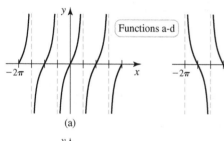

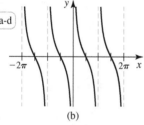

(a)   (b)

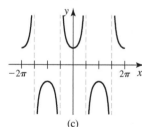

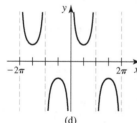

(c)   (d)

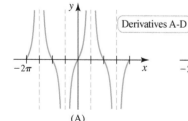

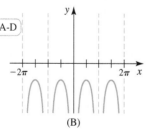

(A)   (B)

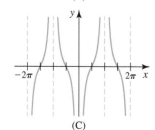

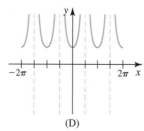

(C)   (D)

Applications

69. Velocity of an oscillator An object oscillates along a vertical line, and its position in centimeters is given by $y(t) = 30 (\sin t - 1)$, where $t \geq 0$ is measured in seconds and y is positive in the upward direction.

a. Graph the position function, for $0 \leq t \leq 10$.
b. Find the velocity of the oscillator, $v(t) = y'(t)$.
c. Graph the velocity function, for $0 \leq t \leq 10$.
d. At what times and positions is the velocity zero?
e. At what times and positions is the velocity a maximum?
f. The acceleration of the oscillator is $a(t) = v'(t)$. Find and graph the acceleration function.

70. Damped sine wave The graph of $f(t) = e^{-kt} \sin t$ with $k > 0$ is called a *damped* sine wave; it is used in a variety of applications, such as modeling the vibrations of a shock absorber.

a. Use a graphing utility to graph f for $k = 1, \frac{1}{2}$, and $\frac{1}{10}$ to understand why these curves are called damped sine waves. What effect does k have on the behavior of the graph?
b. Compute $f'(t)$ for $k = 1$ and use it to determine where the graph of f has a horizontal tangent.
c. Evaluate $\displaystyle\lim_{t \to \infty} e^{-t} \sin t$ by using the Squeeze Theorem. What does the result say about the oscillations of a damped sine wave?

71. A differential equation A differential equation is an equation involving an unknown function and its derivatives. Consider the differential equation $y''(t) + y(t) = 0$ (see Chapter 8).

a. Show that $y = A \sin t$ satisfies the equation for any constant A.
b. Show that $y = B \cos t$ satisfies the equation for any constant B.
c. Show that $y = A \sin t + B \cos t$ satisfies the equation for any constants A and B.

Additional Exercises

72. Using identities Use the identity $\sin 2x = 2 \sin x \cos x$ to find $\dfrac{d}{dx} (\sin 2x)$. Then use the identity $\cos 2x = \cos^2 x - \sin^2 x$ to express the derivative of $\sin 2x$ in terms of $\cos 2x$.

73. Proof of $\displaystyle\lim_{x \to 0} \dfrac{\cos x - 1}{x} = 0$ Use the trigonometric identity $\cos^2 x + \sin^2 x = 1$ to prove that $\displaystyle\lim_{x \to 0} \dfrac{\cos x - 1}{x} = 0$. (*Hint:* Begin by multiplying the numerator and denominator by $\cos x + 1$.)

74. Another method for proving $\displaystyle\lim_{x \to 0} \dfrac{\cos x - 1}{x} = 0$ Use the half-angle formula $\sin^2 x = \dfrac{1 - \cos 2x}{2}$ to prove that $\displaystyle\lim_{x \to 0} \dfrac{\cos x - 1}{x} = 0$.

75. Proof of $\dfrac{d}{dx} (\cos x) = -\sin x$ Use the definition of the derivative and the trigonometric identity

$$\cos (x + h) = \cos x \cos h - \sin x \sin h$$

to prove that $\dfrac{d}{dx} (\cos x) = -\sin x$.

76. Continuity of a piecewise function Let

$$f(x) = \begin{cases} \dfrac{3 \sin x}{x} & \text{if } x \neq 0 \\ a & \text{if } x = 0. \end{cases}$$

For what values of a is f continuous?

77. Continuity of a piecewise function Let

$$g(x) = \begin{cases} \dfrac{1 - \cos x}{2x} & \text{if } x \neq 0 \\ a & \text{if } x = 0. \end{cases}$$

For what values of a is g continuous?

78. Computing limits with angles in degrees Suppose your graphing calculator has two functions, one called sin x, which calculates the sine of x when x is in radians, and the other called $s(x)$, which calculates the sine of x when x is in degrees.

a. Explain why $s(x) = \sin\left(\dfrac{\pi}{180} x\right)$.

b. Evaluate $\lim\limits_{x \to 0} \dfrac{s(x)}{x}$. Verify your answer by estimating the limit on your calculator.

79. Derivatives of $\sin^n x$ Calculate the following derivatives using the Product Rule.

a. $\dfrac{d}{dx}(\sin^2 x)$ **b.** $\dfrac{d}{dx}(\sin^3 x)$ **c.** $\dfrac{d}{dx}(\sin^4 x)$

d. Based on your answers to parts (a)–(c), make a conjecture about $\dfrac{d}{dx}(\sin^n x)$, where n is a positive integer. Then prove the result by induction.

80. Higher-order derivatives of $\sin x$ and $\cos x$ Prove that

$$\dfrac{d^{2n}}{dx^{2n}}(\sin x) = (-1)^n \sin x \text{ and } \dfrac{d^{2n}}{dx^{2n}}(\cos x) = (-1)^n \cos x.$$

81–84. Identifying derivatives from limits *The following limits equal the derivative of a function f at a point a.*

a. *Find one possible f and a.*
b. *Evaluate the limit.*

81. $\lim\limits_{h \to 0} \dfrac{\sin\left(\frac{\pi}{6} + h\right) - \frac{1}{2}}{h}$ **82.** $\lim\limits_{h \to 0} \dfrac{\cos\left(\frac{\pi}{6} + h\right) - \frac{\sqrt{3}}{2}}{h}$

83. $\lim\limits_{x \to \pi/4} \dfrac{\cot x - 1}{x - \frac{\pi}{4}}$ **84.** $\lim\limits_{h \to 0} \dfrac{\tan\left(\frac{5\pi}{6} + h\right) + \frac{1}{\sqrt{3}}}{h}$

85–86. Difference quotients *Suppose that f is differentiable for all x and consider the function*

$$D(x) = \dfrac{f(x + 0.01) - f(x)}{0.01}.$$

For the following functions, graph D on the given interval, and explain why the graph appears as it does. What is the relationship between the functions f and D?

85. $f(x) = \sin x$ on $[-\pi, \pi]$

86. $f(x) = \dfrac{x^3}{3} + 1$ on $[-2, 2]$

QUICK CHECK ANSWERS

1. 2 **2.** $0 < x < \frac{\pi}{2}$ and $\frac{3\pi}{2} < x < 2\pi$. The value of $\cos x$ is the slope of the line tangent to the curve $y = \sin x$.
3. The Quotient Rule is used because each function is a quotient when written in terms of the sine and cosine functions.
4. $\dfrac{1}{\cos x \sin x} = \dfrac{1}{\cos x} \cdot \dfrac{1}{\sin x} = \sec x \csc x$
5. $\dfrac{d^2 y}{dx^2} = -\cos x, \dfrac{d^4 y}{dx^4} = \cos x, \dfrac{d^{40}}{dx^{40}}(\sin x) = \sin x,$
$\dfrac{d^{42}}{dx^{42}}(\sin x) = -\sin x$ ◄

3.6 Derivatives as Rates of Change

The theme of this section is the *derivative as a rate of change*. Observing the world around us, we see that almost everything is in a state of change: The size of the Internet is increasing; your blood pressure fluctuates; as supply increases, prices decrease; and the universe is expanding. This section explores a few of the many applications of this idea and demonstrates why calculus is called the mathematics of change.

One-Dimensional Motion

Describing the motion of objects such as projectiles and planets was one of the challenges that led to the development of calculus in the 17th century. We begin by considering the motion of an object confined to one dimension; that is, the object moves along a line. This motion could be horizontal (for example, a car moving along a straight highway), or it could be vertical (such as a projectile launched vertically into the air).

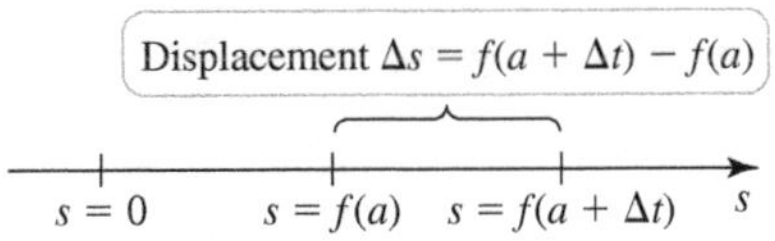

▶ When describing the motion of objects, it is customary to use t as the independent variable to represent time. Generally, motion is assumed to begin at $t = 0$.

Position and Velocity   Suppose an object moves along a straight line and its location at time t is given by the **position function** $s = f(t)$. All positions are measured relative to a reference point $s = 0$. The **displacement** of the object between $t = a$ and $t = a + \Delta t$ is $\Delta s = f(a + \Delta t) - f(a)$, where the elapsed time is Δt units (Figure 3.33).

Displacement $\Delta s = f(a + \Delta t) - f(a)$

$s = 0$ $s = f(a)$ $s = f(a + \Delta t)$ s

Figure 3.33

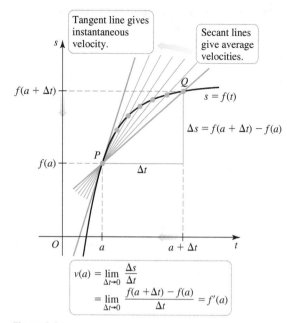

Figure 3.34

Recall from Section 2.1 that the *average velocity* of the object over the interval $[a, a + \Delta t]$ is the displacement Δs of the object divided by the elapsed time Δt:

$$v_{av} = \frac{\Delta s}{\Delta t} = \frac{f(a + \Delta t) - f(a)}{\Delta t}.$$

The average velocity is the slope of the secant line passing through the points $P(a, f(a))$ and $Q(a + \Delta t, f(a + \Delta t))$ (Figure 3.34).

As Δt approaches 0, the average velocity is calculated over smaller and smaller time intervals, and the limiting value of these average velocities, when it exists, is the *instantaneous velocity* at a. This is the same argument used to arrive at the derivative. The conclusion is that the instantaneous velocity at time a, denoted $v(a)$, is the derivative of the position function evaluated at a:

$$v(a) = \lim_{\Delta t \to 0} \frac{f(a + \Delta t) - f(a)}{\Delta t} = f'(a).$$

Equivalently, the instantaneous velocity at a is the rate of change in the position function at a; it also equals the slope of the line tangent to the curve $s = f(t)$ at $P(a, f(a))$.

> ➤ Using the various derivative notations, the velocity is also written $v(t) = s'(t) = ds/dt$. If *average* or *instantaneous* is not specified, *velocity* is understood to mean instantaneous velocity.

DEFINITION Average and Instantaneous Velocity

Let $s = f(t)$ be the position function of an object moving along a line. The **average velocity** of the object over the time interval $[a, a + \Delta t]$ is the slope of the secant line between $(a, f(a))$ and $(a + \Delta t, f(a + \Delta t))$:

$$v_{av} = \frac{f(a + \Delta t) - f(a)}{\Delta t}.$$

The **instantaneous velocity** at a is the slope of the line tangent to the position curve, which is the derivative of the position function:

$$v(a) = \lim_{\Delta t \to 0} \frac{f(a + \Delta t) - f(a)}{\Delta t} = f'(a).$$

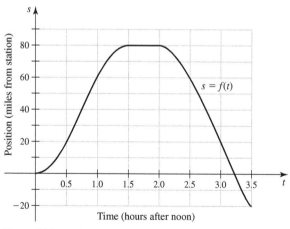

Figure 3.35

QUICK CHECK 1 Does the speedometer in your car measure average or instantaneous velocity? ◄

EXAMPLE 1   Position and velocity of a patrol car Assume a police station is located along a straight east-west freeway. At noon ($t = 0$), a patrol car leaves the station heading east. The position function of the car $s = f(t)$ gives the location of the car in miles east ($s > 0$) or west ($s < 0$) of the station t hours after noon (Figure 3.35).

a. Describe the location of the patrol car during the first 3.5 hr of the trip.

b. Calculate the displacement and average velocity of the car between 2:00 P.M. and 3:30 P.M. ($2 \le t \le 3.5$).

c. At what time(s) is the instantaneous velocity greatest *as the car travels east*?

SOLUTION

a. The graph of the position function indicates the car travels 80 miles east between $t = 0$ (noon) and $t = 1.5$ (1:30 P.M.). The car is at rest and its position does not change from $t = 1.5$ to $t = 2$ (that is, from 1:30 P.M. to 2:00 P.M.). Starting at $t = 2$, the car's distance from the station decreases, which means the car travels west, eventually ending up 20 miles west of the station at $t = 3.5$ (3:30 P.M.) (Figure 3.36).

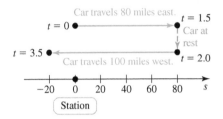

Figure 3.36

b. The position of the car at 3:30 P.M. is $f(3.5) = -20$ (Figure 3.35; the negative sign indicates the car is 20 miles *west* of the station), and the position of the car at 2:00 P.M. is $f(2) = 80$. Therefore, the displacement is

$$\Delta s = f(3.5) - f(2) = -20 \text{ mi} - 80 \text{ mi} = -100 \text{ mi}$$

during an elapsed time of $\Delta t = 3.5 - 2 = 1.5$ hr (the *negative* displacement indicates that the car moved 100 miles *west*). The average velocity is

$$v_{av} = \frac{\Delta s}{\Delta t} = \frac{-100 \text{ mi}}{1.5 \text{ hr}} \approx -66.7 \text{ mi/hr}.$$

c. The greatest eastward instantaneous velocity corresponds to points at which the graph of the position function has the greatest positive slope. The greatest slope occurs between $t = 0.5$ and $t = 1$. During this time interval, the car also has a nearly constant velocity because the curve is approximately linear. We conclude that the eastward velocity is largest from 12:30 P.M. to 1:00 P.M.   *Related Exercises 9–10* ◄

Speed and Acceleration   When only the magnitude of the velocity is of interest, we use *speed*, which is the absolute value of the velocity:

$$\text{speed} = |v|.$$

For example, a car with an instantaneous velocity of -30 mi/hr has a speed of 30 mi/hr.

A more complete description of an object moving along a line includes its *acceleration*, which is the rate of change of the velocity; that is, acceleration is the derivative of the velocity function with respect to time t. If the acceleration is positive, the object's velocity increases; if it is negative, the object's velocity decreases. Because velocity is the derivative of the position function, acceleration is the second derivative of the position. Therefore,

$$a = \frac{dv}{dt} = \frac{d^2s}{dt^2}.$$

> ► Newton's First Law of Motion says that in the absence of external forces, a moving object has no acceleration, which means the magnitude and direction of the velocity are constant.

DEFINITION   Velocity, Speed, and Acceleration

Suppose an object moves along a line with position $s = f(t)$. Then

the **velocity** at time t is $v = \dfrac{ds}{dt} = f'(t),$

the **speed** at time t is $|v| = |f'(t)|,$ and

the **acceleration** at time t is $a = \dfrac{dv}{dt} = \dfrac{d^2s}{dt^2} = f''(t).$

> The units of derivatives are consistent with the notation. If s is measured in meters and t is measured in seconds, the units of the velocity $\dfrac{ds}{dt}$ are m/s. The units of the acceleration $\dfrac{d^2s}{dt^2}$ are m/s^2.

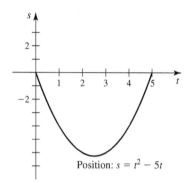

Figure 3.37

Position: $s = t^2 - 5t$

> Figure 3.37 gives the graph of the position function, not the path of the object. The motion is along a horizontal line.

QUICK CHECK 2 For an object moving along a line, is it possible for its velocity to increase while its speed decreases? Is it possible for its velocity to decrease while its speed increases? Give an example to support your answers. ◄

EXAMPLE 2   Velocity and acceleration Suppose the position (in feet) of an object moving horizontally at time t (in seconds) is $s = t^2 - 5t$, for $0 \le t \le 5$ (Figure 3.37). Assume that positive values of s correspond to positions to the right of $s = 0$.

a. Graph the velocity function on the interval $0 \le t \le 5$ and determine when the object is stationary, moving to the left, and moving to the right.

b. Graph the acceleration function on the interval $0 \le t \le 5$.

c. Describe the motion of the object.

SOLUTION

a. The velocity is $v = s'(t) = 2t - 5$. The object is stationary when $v = 2t - 5 = 0$, or at $t = 2.5$. Solving $v = 2t - 5 > 0$, the velocity is positive (motion to the right) for $\frac{5}{2} < t \le 5$. Similarly, the velocity is negative (motion to the left) for $0 \le t < \frac{5}{2}$. Though the velocity of the object is increasing at all times, its speed is decreasing for $0 \le t < \frac{5}{2}$, and then increasing for $\frac{5}{2} < t \le 5$. The graph of the velocity function (Figure 3.38) confirms these observations.

b. The acceleration is the derivative of the velocity or $a = v'(t) = s''(t) = 2$. This means that the acceleration is 2 ft/s^2, for $0 \le t \le 5$ (Figure 3.39).

c. Starting at an initial position of $s(0) = 0$, the object moves in the negative direction (to the left) with decreasing speed until it comes to rest momentarily at $s\left(\frac{5}{2}\right) = -\frac{25}{4}$. The object then moves in the positive direction (to the right) with increasing speed, reaching its initial position at $t = 5$. During this time interval, the acceleration is constant.

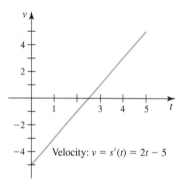

Figure 3.38

Velocity: $v = s'(t) = 2t - 5$

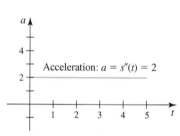

Figure 3.39

Acceleration: $a = s''(t) = 2$

Related Exercises 11–16 ◄

QUICK CHECK 3 Describe the velocity of an object that has a positive constant acceleration. Could an object have a positive acceleration and a decreasing speed? ◄

> The acceleration due to Earth's gravitational field is denoted g. In metric units, $g \approx 9.8$ m/s^2 on the surface of Earth; in the U.S. Customary System (USCS), $g \approx 32$ ft/s^2.

Free Fall We now consider a problem in which an object moves vertically in Earth's gravitational field, assuming that no other forces (such as air resistance) are at work.

EXAMPLE 3   Motion in a gravitational field Suppose a stone is thrown vertically upward with an initial velocity of 64 ft/s from a bridge 96 ft above a river. By Newton's laws of motion, the position of the stone (measured as the height above the river) after t seconds is

$$s(t) = -16t^2 + 64t + 96,$$

> The position function in Example 3 is derived in Section 6.1. Once again we mention that the graph of the position function is not the path of the stone.

where $s = 0$ is the level of the river (Figure 3.40a).

a. Find the velocity and acceleration functions.

b. What is the highest point above the river reached by the stone?

c. With what velocity will the stone strike the river?

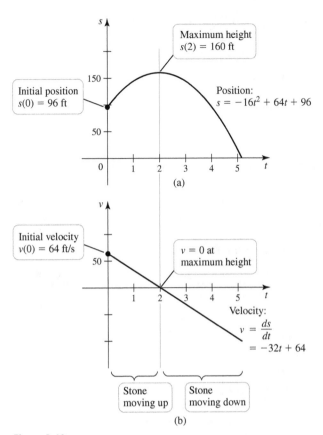

Initial position
$s(0) = 96$ ft

Maximum height
$s(2) = 160$ ft

Position:
$s = -16t^2 + 64t + 96$

(a)

Initial velocity
$v(0) = 64$ ft/s

$v = 0$ at
maximum height

Velocity:
$v = \dfrac{ds}{dt}$
$= -32t + 64$

Stone
moving up

Stone
moving down

(b)

Figure 3.40

SOLUTION

a. The velocity of the stone is the derivative of the position function, and its acceleration is the derivative of the velocity function. Therefore,

$$v = \frac{ds}{dt} = -32t + 64 \quad \text{and} \quad a = \frac{dv}{dt} = -32.$$

b. When the stone reaches its high point, its velocity is zero (Figure 3.40b). Solving $v(t) = -32t + 64 = 0$ yields $t = 2$; therefore, the stone reaches its maximum height 2 seconds after it is thrown. Its height (in feet) at that instant is

$$s(2) = -16(2)^2 + 64(2) + 96 = 160.$$

c. To determine the velocity at which the stone strikes the river, we first determine *when* it reaches the river. The stone strikes the river when $s(t) = -16t^2 + 64t + 96 = 0$. Dividing both sides of the equation by -16, we obtain $t^2 - 4t - 6 = 0$. Using the quadratic formula, the solutions are $t \approx 5.16$ or $t \approx -1.16$. Because the stone is thrown at $t = 0$, only positive values of t are of interest; therefore, the relevant root is $t \approx 5.16$. The velocity of the stone (in ft/s) when it strikes the river is approximately

$$v(5.16) = -32(5.16) + 64 = -101.12.$$

Related Exercises 17–18 ◄

QUICK CHECK 4 In Example 3, does the rock have a greater speed at $t = 1$ or $t = 3$? ◄

Growth Models

Much of the change in the world around us can be classified as *growth*: Populations, prices, and computer networks all tend to increase in size. Modeling growth is important because it often leads to an understanding of underlying processes and allows for predictions.

We let $p = f(t)$ be the measure of a quantity of interest (for example, the population of a species or the consumer price index), where $t \geq 0$ represents time. The average growth rate of p between time $t = a$ and a later time $t = a + \Delta t$ is the change Δp divided by elapsed time Δt. Therefore, the **average growth rate** of p on the interval $[a, a + \Delta t]$ is

$$\frac{\Delta p}{\Delta t} = \frac{f(a + \Delta t) - f(a)}{\Delta t}.$$

If we now let $\Delta t \to 0$, then $\dfrac{\Delta p}{\Delta t}$ approaches the derivative $\dfrac{dp}{dt}$, which is the **instantaneous growth rate** (or simply **growth rate**) of p with respect to time:

$$\frac{dp}{dt} = \lim_{\Delta t \to 0} \frac{\Delta p}{\Delta t}.$$

Once again, we see the derivative appearing as an instantaneous rate of change. In the next example, a growth function and its derivative are approximated using real data.

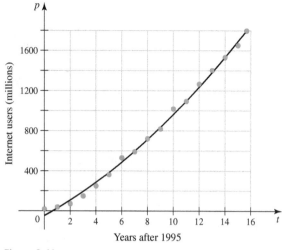

Figure 3.41

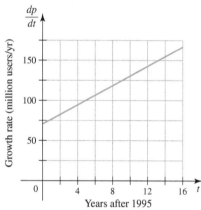

Figure 3.42

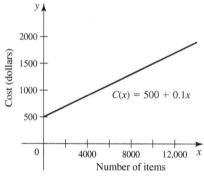

Figure 3.43

▶ Although x is a whole number of units, we treat it as a continuous variable, which is reasonable if x is large.

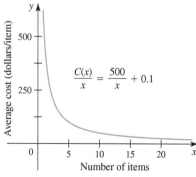

Figure 3.44

EXAMPLE 4 Internet growth The number of worldwide Internet users between 1995 and 2011 is shown in Figure 3.41. A reasonable fit to the data is given by the function $p(t) = 3.0t^2 + 70.8t - 45.8$, where t measures years after 1995.

a. Use the function p to approximate the average growth rate of Internet users from 2000 ($t = 5$) to 2005 ($t = 10$).

b. What was the instantaneous growth rate of the Internet in 2006?

c. Use a graphing utility to plot the growth rate dp/dt. What does the graph tell you about the growth rate between 1995 and 2011?

d. Assuming that the growth function can be extended beyond 2011, what is the predicted number of Internet users in 2015 ($t = 20$)?

SOLUTION

a. The average growth rate over the interval $[5, 10]$ is

$$\frac{\Delta p}{\Delta t} = \frac{p(10) - p(5)}{10 - 5} \approx \frac{962 - 383}{5} \approx 116 \text{ million users/year.}$$

b. The growth rate at time t is $p'(t) = 6.0t + 70.8$. In 2006 ($t = 11$), the growth rate was $p'(11) \approx 137$ million users/year.

c. The graph of p', for $0 \le t \le 16$, is shown in Figure 3.42. We see that the growth rate is positive and increasing, for $t \ge 0$.

d. A projection of the number of Internet users in 2015 is $p(20) \approx 2570$ million users, or about 2.6 billion users. This figure represents roughly one-third of the world's population, assuming a projected population of 7.2 billion people in 2015.

Related Exercises 19–20 ◀

QUICK CHECK 5 Using the growth function in Example 4, compare the growth rates in 1996 and 2010. ◀

Economics and Business

Our final examples illustrate how derivatives arise in economics and business. As you will see, the mathematics of derivatives is the same as it is in other applications. However, the vocabulary and interpretation are quite different.

Average and Marginal Cost   Imagine a company that manufactures large quantities of a product such as mousetraps, DVD players, or snowboards. Associated with the manufacturing process is a *cost function* $C(x)$ that gives the cost of manufacturing the first x items of the product. A simple cost function might have the form $y = C(x) = 500 + 0.1x$, as shown in Figure 3.43. It includes a **fixed cost** of $500 (setup costs and overhead) that is independent of the number of items produced. It also includes a **unit cost**, or **variable cost**, of $0.10 per item produced. For example, the cost of producing the first 1000 items is $C(1000) = \$600$.

If the company produces x items at a cost of $C(x)$, then the *average cost* is $\dfrac{C(x)}{x}$ per item. For the cost function $C(x) = 500 + 0.1x$, the average cost is

$$\frac{C(x)}{x} = \frac{500 + 0.1x}{x} = \frac{500}{x} + 0.1.$$

For example, the average cost of manufacturing the first 1000 items is

$$\frac{C(1000)}{1000} = \frac{\$600}{1000} = \$0.60/\text{unit.}$$

Plotting $C(x)/x$, we see that the average cost decreases as the number of items produced increases (Figure 3.44).

The average cost gives the cost of items already produced. But what about the cost of producing additional items? Having produced x items, the cost of producing another Δx items is $C(x + \Delta x) - C(x)$. Therefore, the average cost per item of producing those Δx additional items is

$$\frac{C(x + \Delta x) - C(x)}{\Delta x} = \frac{\Delta C}{\Delta x}.$$

If we let $\Delta x \to 0$, we see that

$$\lim_{\Delta x \to 0} \frac{\Delta C}{\Delta x} = C'(x),$$

which is called the *marginal cost*. In reality, we cannot let $\Delta x \to 0$ because Δx represents whole numbers of items.

Here is a useful interpretation of the marginal cost. Suppose $\Delta x = 1$. Then $\Delta C = C(x + 1) - C(x)$ is the cost to produce *one* additional item. In this case, we write

$$\frac{\Delta C}{\Delta x} = \frac{C(x + 1) - C(x)}{1}.$$

If the *slope* of the cost curve does not vary significantly near the point x, then—as shown in Figure 3.45—we have

$$\frac{\Delta C}{\Delta x} \approx \lim_{\Delta x \to 0} \frac{\Delta C}{\Delta x} = C'(x).$$

Therefore, the cost of producing one additional item, having already produced x items, is approximated by the marginal cost $C'(x)$. In the preceding example, we have $C'(x) = 0.1$; so if $x = 1000$ items have been produced, then the cost of producing the 1001st item is approximately $C'(1000) = \$0.10$. With this simple linear cost function, the marginal cost tells us what we already know: The cost of producing one additional item is the variable cost of $\$0.10$. With more realistic cost functions, the marginal cost may be variable.

> The average describes the past; the marginal describes the future.
> —Old saying

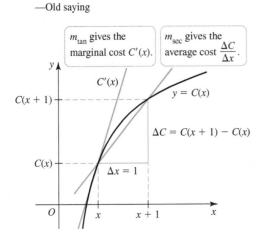

Figure 3.45

> The approximation $\Delta C / \Delta x \approx C'(x)$ says that the slope of the secant line between $(x, C(x))$ and $(x + 1, C(x + 1))$ is approximately equal to the slope of the tangent line at $(x, C(x))$. This approximation is good if the cost curve is nearly linear over a 1-unit interval.

DEFINITION Average and Marginal Cost

The **cost function** $C(x)$ gives the cost to produce the first x items in a manufacturing process. The **average cost** to produce x items is $\overline{C}(x) = C(x)/x$. The **marginal cost** $C'(x)$ is the approximate cost to produce one additional item after producing x items.

EXAMPLE 5 Average and marginal costs Suppose the cost of producing x items is given by the function (Figure 3.46)

$$C(x) = -0.02x^2 + 50x + 100, \quad \text{for} \quad 0 \le x \le 1000.$$

a. Determine the average and marginal cost functions.

b. Determine the average and marginal cost for the first 100 tems and interpret these values.

c. Determine the average and marginal cost for the first 900 items and interpret these values.

SOLUTION

a. The average cost is

$$\overline{C}(x) = \frac{C(x)}{x} = \frac{-0.02x^2 + 50x + 100}{x} = -0.02x + 50 + \frac{100}{x}$$

and the marginal cost is

$$\frac{dC}{dx} = -0.04x + 50.$$

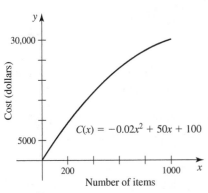

Figure 3.46

The average cost decreases as the number of items produced increases (Figure 3.47a). The marginal cost decreases linearly with a slope of -0.04 (Figure 3.47b).

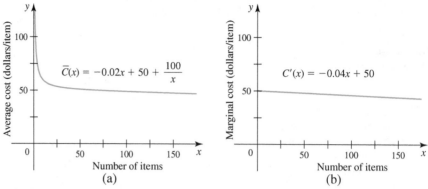

Figure 3.47

b. To produce $x = 100$ items, the average cost is

$$\overline{C}(100) = \frac{C(100)}{100} = \frac{-0.02(100)^2 + 50(100) + 100}{100} = \$49/\text{item}$$

and the marginal cost is

$$C'(100) = -0.04(100) + 50 = \$46/\text{item}.$$

These results mean that the average cost of producing the first 100 items is $49 per item, but the cost of producing one additional item (the 101st item) is approximately $46. Therefore, producing one more item is less expensive than the average cost of producing the first 100 items.

c. To produce $x = 900$ items, the average cost is

$$\overline{C}(900) = \frac{C(900)}{900} = \frac{-0.02(900)^2 + 50(900) + 100}{900} \approx \$32/\text{item}$$

and the marginal cost is

$$C'(900) = -0.04(900) + 50 = \$14/\text{item}.$$

The comparison with part (b) is revealing. The average cost of producing 900 items has dropped to $32 per item. More striking is that the marginal cost (the cost of producing the 901st item) has dropped to $14.   *Related Exercises 21–24* ◄

QUICK CHECK 6 In Example 5, what happens to the average cost as the number of items produced increases from $x = 1$ to $x = 100$? ◄

Elasticity in Economics   Economists apply the term *elasticity* to prices, income, capital, labor, and other variables in systems with input and output. Elasticity describes how changes in the input to a system are related to changes in the output. Because elasticity involves change, it also involves derivatives.

A general rule is that as the price p of an item increases, the number of sales of that item decreases. This relationship is expressed in a demand function. For example, suppose sales at a gas station have the linear demand function $D(p) = 1200 - 200p$ (Figure 3.48), where $D(p)$ is the number of gallons sold per day at a price p (measured in dollars). According to this function, if gas sells at $3.60/gal, then the owner can expect to sell $D(3.6) = 480$ gallons. If the price is increased, sales decrease.

Suppose the price of a gallon of gasoline increases from $3.60 to $3.96 per gallon; call this change $\Delta p = \$0.36$. The resulting change in the number of gallons sold is $\Delta D = D(3.96) - D(3.60) = -72$. (The change is a decrease, so it is negative.) Comparisons of the variables are more meaningful if we work with percentages. Increasing the price from \$3.60 to \$3.96 per gallon is a percentage change of $\dfrac{\Delta p}{p} = \dfrac{\$0.36}{\$3.60} = 10\%$. Similarly, the corresponding percentage change in the gallons sold is $\dfrac{\Delta D}{D} = \dfrac{-72}{480} = -15\%$.

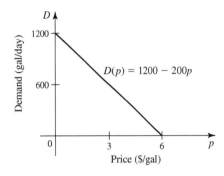

Figure 3.48

The *price elasticity of the demand* (or simply, *elasticity*) is the ratio of the percentage change in demand to the percentage change in price; that is, $E = \dfrac{\Delta D/D}{\Delta p/p}$. In the case of the gas demand function, the elasticity of this particular price change is $\dfrac{-15\%}{10\%} = -1.5$.

The elasticity is more useful when it is expressed as a function of the price. To do this, we consider small changes in p and assume the corresponding changes in D are also small. Using the definition of the derivative, the elasticity *function* is

$$E(p) = \lim_{\Delta p \to 0} \frac{\Delta D/D}{\Delta p/p} = \lim_{\Delta p \to 0} \frac{\Delta D}{\Delta p}\left(\frac{p}{D}\right) = \frac{dD}{dp}\frac{p}{D}.$$

Applying this definition to the gas demand function, we find that

$$
\begin{aligned}
E(p) &= \frac{dD}{dp}\frac{p}{D} \\[2mm]
&= \underbrace{\frac{d}{dp}(1200 - 200p)}_{D}\underbrace{\frac{p}{1200 - 200p}}_{D} && \text{Substitute } D = 1200 - 200p. \\[2mm]
&= -200\left(\frac{p}{1200 - 200p}\right) && \text{Differentiate.} \\[2mm]
&= \frac{p}{p - 6}. && \text{Simplify.}
\end{aligned}
$$

Given a particular price, the elasticity is interpreted as the percentage change in the demand that results for every 1% change in the price. For example, in the gas demand case, with $p = \$3.60$, the elasticity is $E(3.6) = -1.5$; therefore, a 2% increase in the price results in a change of $-1.5 \cdot 2\% = -3\%$ (a decrease) in the number of gallons sold.

▶ Some books define the elasticity as
$$E(p) = -\frac{dD}{dp}\frac{p}{D}$$ to make $E(p)$ positive.

DEFINITION Elasticity

If the demand for a product varies with the price according the function $D = f(p)$, then the **price elasticity of the demand** is $E(p) = \dfrac{dD}{dp}\dfrac{p}{D}.$

EXAMPLE 6   Elasticity in pork prices The demand for processed pork in Canada is described by the function $D(p) = 286 - 20p$. (*Source: Microeconomics*, J. Perloff, Addison Wesley, 2012)

a. Compute and graph the price elasticity of the demand.

b. When $-\infty < E < -1$, the demand is said to be **elastic**. When $-1 < E < 0$, the demand is said to be **inelastic**. Interpret these terms.

c. For what prices is the demand for pork elastic? Inelastic?

SOLUTION

a. Substituting the demand function into the definition of elasticity, we find that

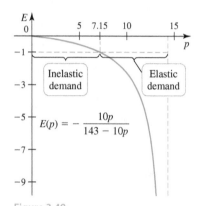

Figure 3.49

▸ When $E(p) = 0$, the demand for a good is said to be *perfectly inelastic*. In Example 6, this case occurs when $p = 0$.

$$E(p) = \frac{dD}{dp}\frac{p}{D}$$

$$= \frac{d}{dp}\underbrace{(286 - 20p)}_{D}\frac{p}{\underbrace{286 - 20p}_{D}} \qquad \text{Substitute } D = 286 - 20p.$$

$$= -20\left(\frac{p}{286 - 20p}\right) \qquad \text{Differentiate.}$$

$$= -\frac{10p}{143 - 10p}. \qquad \text{Simplify.}$$

Notice that the elasticity is undefined at $p = 14.3$, which is the price at which the demand reaches zero. (According to the model, no pork can be sold at prices above \$14.30.) Therefore, the domain of the elasticity function is $[0, 14.3)$, and on the interval $(0, 14.3)$, the elasticity is negative (Figure 3.49).

b. For prices with an elasticity in the interval $-\infty < E(p) < -1$, a $P\%$ increase in the price results in *more* than a $P\%$ decrease in the demand; this is the case of elastic (sensitive) demand. If a price has an elasticity in the interval $-1 < E(p) < 0$, a $P\%$ increase in the price results in *less* than a $P\%$ decrease in the demand; this is the case of inelastic (insensitive) demand.

c. Solving $E(p) = -\frac{10p}{143 - 10p} = -1$, we find that $E(p) < -1$, for $p > 7.15$. For prices in this interval, the demand is elastic (Figure 3.49). For prices with $0 < p < 7.15$, the demand is inelastic.   *Related Exercises 25–28* ◄

SECTION 3.6 EXERCISES

Review Questions

1. Explain the difference between the average rate of change and the instantaneous rate of change of a function f.

2. Complete the following statement. If $\dfrac{dy}{dx}$ is large, then small changes in x result in relatively _____ changes in the value of y.

3. Complete the following statement: If $\dfrac{dy}{dx}$ is small, then small changes in x result in relatively _____ changes in the value of y.

4. What is the difference between the *velocity* and *speed* of an object moving in a straight line?

5. Define the acceleration of an object moving in a straight line.

6. An object moving along a line has a constant negative acceleration. Describe the velocity of the object.

7. Suppose the average cost of producing 200 gas stoves is \$70 per stove and the marginal cost at $x = 200$ is \$65 per stove. Interpret these costs.

8. Explain why a decreasing demand function has a negative elasticity function.

Basic Skills

9. **Highway travel** A state patrol station is located on a straight north-south freeway. A patrol car leaves the station at 9:00 A.M. heading north with position function $s = f(t)$ that gives its location in miles t hours after 9:00 A.M. (see figure). Assume s is positive when the car is north of the patrol station.

a. Determine the average velocity of the car during the first 45 minutes of the trip.

b. Find the average velocity of the car over the interval $[0.25, 0.75]$. Is the average velocity a good estimate of the velocity at 9:30 A.M.?

c. Find the average velocity of the car over the interval $[1.75, 2.25]$. Estimate the velocity of the car at 11:00 A.M. and determine the direction in which the patrol car is moving.

d. Describe the motion of the patrol car relative to the patrol station between 9:00 A.M. and noon.

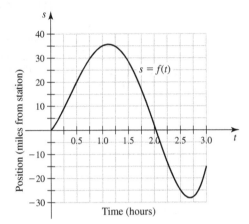

Time (hours)

10. **Airline travel** The following figure shows the position function of an airliner on an out-and-back trip from Seattle to Minneapolis, where $s = f(t)$ is the number of ground miles from Seattle t hours after take-off at 6:00 A.M. The plane returns to Seattle 8.5 hours later at 2:30 P.M.

a. Calculate the average velocity of the airliner during the first 1.5 hours of the trip $(0 \le t \le 1.5)$.

b. Calculate the average velocity of the airliner between 1:30 P.M. and 2:30 P.M. $(7.5 \le t \le 8.5)$.

c. At what time(s) is the velocity 0? Give a plausible explanation.

d. Determine the velocity of the airliner at noon $(t = 6)$ and explain why the velocity is negative.

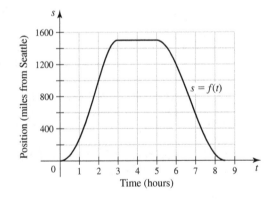

Time (hours)

11–16. Position, velocity, and acceleration *Suppose the position of an object moving horizontally after t seconds is given by the following functions $s = f(t)$, where s is measured in feet, with $s > 0$ corresponding to positions right of the origin.*

a. *Graph the position function.*

b. *Find and graph the velocity function. When is the object stationary, moving to the right, and moving to the left?*

c. *Determine the velocity and acceleration of the object at $t = 1$.*

d. *Determine the acceleration of the object when its velocity is zero.*

e. *On what intervals is the speed increasing?*

11. $f(t) = t^2 - 4t;\ 0 \le t \le 5$

12. $f(t) = -t^2 + 4t - 3;\ 0 \le t \le 5$

13. $f(t) = 2t^2 - 9t + 12;\ 0 \le t \le 3$

14. $f(t) = 18t - 3t^2;\ 0 \le t \le 8$

15. $f(t) = 2t^3 - 21t^2 + 60t;\ 0 \le t \le 6$

16. $f(t) = -6t^3 + 36t^2 - 54t;\ 0 \le t \le 4$

17. **A stone thrown vertically** Suppose a stone is thrown vertically upward from the edge of a cliff with an initial velocity of 64 ft/s from a height of 32 ft above the ground. The height s (in ft) of the stone above the ground t seconds after it is thrown is $s = -16t^2 + 64t + 32$.

a. Determine the velocity v of the stone after t seconds.

b. When does the stone reach its highest point?

c. What is the height of the stone at the highest point?

d. When does the stone strike the ground?

e. With what velocity does the stone strike the ground?

f. On what intervals is the speed increasing?

18. **A stone thrown vertically on Mars** Suppose a stone is thrown vertically upward from the edge of a cliff on Mars (where the acceleration due to gravity is only about 12 ft/s^2) with an initial velocity of 64 ft/s from a height of 192 ft above the ground. The height s of the stone above the ground after t seconds is given by $s = -6t^2 + 64t + 192$.

a. Determine the velocity v of the stone after t seconds.

b. When does the stone reach its highest point?

c. What is the height of the stone at the highest point?

d. When does the stone strike the ground?

e. With what velocity does the stone strike the ground?

19. **Population growth in Georgia** The population of the state of Georgia (in thousands) from 1995 $(t = 0)$ to 2005 $(t = 10)$ is modeled by the polynomial $p(t) = -0.27t^2 + 101t + 7055$.

a. Determine the average growth rate from 1995 to 2005.

b. What was the growth rate for Georgia in 1997 $(t = 2)$ and 2005 $(t = 10)$?

c. Use a graphing utility to graph p', for $0 \le t \le 10$. What does this graph tell you about population growth in Georgia during the period of time from 1995 to 2005?

20. **Consumer price index** The U.S. consumer price index (CPI) measures the cost of living based on a value of 100 in the years 1982–1984. The CPI for the years 1995–2012 (see figure) is modeled by the function $c(t) = 151e^{0.026t}$, where t represents years after 1995.

a. Was the average growth rate of the CPI greater between the years 1995 and 2000 or between 2005 and 2010?

b. Was the growth rate of the CPI greater in 2000 $(t = 5)$ or 2005 $(t = 10)$?

c. Use a graphing utility to graph the growth rate, for $0 \le t \le 15$. What does the graph tell you about growth in the cost of living during this time period?

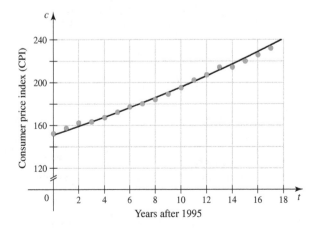

Years after 1995

21–24. Average and marginal cost *Consider the following cost functions.*

a. *Find the average cost and marginal cost functions.*
b. *Determine the average and marginal cost when x = a.*
c. *Interpret the values obtained in part (b).*

21. $C(x) = 1000 + 0.1x, \ 0 \le x \le 5000, \ a = 2000$

22. $C(x) = 500 + 0.02x, \ 0 \le x \le 2000, \ a = 1000$

23. $C(x) = -0.01x^2 + 40x + 100, \ 0 \le x \le 1500, \ a = 1000$

24. $C(x) = -0.04x^2 + 100x + 800, \ 0 \le x \le 1000, \ a = 500$

25. Demand and elasticity Based on sales data over the past year, the owner of a DVD store devises the demand function $D(p) = 40 - 2p$, where $D(p)$ is the number of DVDs that can be sold in one day at a price of p dollars.

   a. According to the model, how many DVDs can be sold in a day at price of $10?
   b. According to the model, what is the maximum price that can be charged (above which no DVDs can be sold)?
   c. Find the elasticity function for this demand function.
   d. For what prices is the demand elastic? Inelastic?
   e. If the price of DVDs is raised from $10.00 to $10.25, what is the exact percentage decrease in demand (using the demand function)?
   f. If the price of DVDs is raised from $10.00 to $10.25, what is the approximate percentage decrease in demand (using the elasticity function)?

26. Demand and elasticity The economic advisor of a large tire store proposes the demand function $D(p) = \dfrac{1800}{p - 40}$, where $D(p)$ is the number of tires of one brand and size that can be sold in one day at a price p.

   a. Recalling that the demand must be positive, what is the domain of this function?
   b. According to the model, how many tires can be sold in a day at a price of $60 per tire?
   c. Find the elasticity function on the domain of the demand function.
   d. For what prices is the demand elastic? Inelastic?
   e. If the price of tires is raised from $60 to $62, what is the approximate percentage decrease in demand (using the elasticity function)?

27. Exponential demand function Compute the elasticity for the exponential demand function $D(p) = ae^{-bp}$, where a and b are positive real numbers. For what prices is the demand elastic? Inelastic?

28. Power demand function Show that the demand function $D(p) = a/p^b$, where a and b are positive real numbers, has a constant elasticity for all positive prices.

Further Explorations

29. Explain why or why not Determine whether the following statements are true and give an explanation or counterexample.

   a. If the acceleration of an object remains constant, then its velocity is constant.
   b. If the acceleration of an object moving along a line is always 0, then its velocity is constant.
   c. It is impossible for the instantaneous velocity at all times $a \le t \le b$ to equal the average velocity over the interval $a \le t \le b$.
   d. A moving object can have negative acceleration and increasing speed.

30. A feather dropped on the moon On the moon, a feather will fall to the ground at the same rate as a heavy stone. Suppose a feather is dropped from a height of 40 m above the surface of the moon. Then its height s (in meters) above the ground after t seconds is $s = 40 - 0.8t^2$. Determine the velocity and acceleration of the feather the moment it strikes the surface of the moon.

31. Comparing velocities A stone is thrown vertically into the air at an initial velocity of 96 ft/s. On Mars, the height s (in feet) of the stone above the ground after t seconds is $s = 96t - 6t^2$ and on Earth it is $s = 96t - 16t^2$. How much higher will the stone travel on Mars than on Earth?

32. Comparing velocities Two stones are thrown vertically upward with matching initial velocities of 48 ft/s at time $t = 0$. One stone is thrown from the edge of a bridge that is 32 ft above the ground and the other stone is thrown from ground level. The height of the stone thrown from the bridge after t seconds is $f(t) = -16t^2 + 48t + 32$, and the height of the stone thrown from the ground after t seconds is $g(t) = -16t^2 + 48t$.

   a. Show that the stones reach their high points at the same time.
   b. How much higher does the stone thrown from the bridge go than the stone thrown from the ground?
   c. When do the stones strike the ground and with what velocities?

33. Matching heights A stone is thrown from the edge of a bridge that is 48 ft above the ground with an initial velocity of 32 ft/s. The height of this stone above the ground t seconds after it is thrown is $f(t) = -16t^2 + 32t + 48$. If a second stone is thrown from the ground, then its height above the ground after t seconds is given by $g(t) = -16t^2 + v_0 t$, where v_0 is the initial velocity of the second stone. Determine the value of v_0 such that both stones reach the same high point.

34. Velocity of a car The graph shows the position $s = f(t)$ of a car t hours after 5:00 P.M. relative to its starting point $s = 0$, where s is measured in miles.

   a. Describe the velocity of the car. Specifically, when is it speeding up and when is it slowing down?
   b. At approximately what time is the car traveling the fastest? The slowest?
   c. What is the approximate maximum velocity of the car? The approximate minimum velocity?

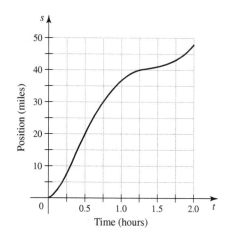

35. Velocity from position The graph of $s = f(t)$ represents the position of an object moving along a line at time $t \geq 0$.

   a. Assume the velocity of the object is 0 when $t = 0$. For what other values of t is the velocity of the object zero?

   b. When is the object moving in the positive direction and when is it moving in the negative direction?

   c. Sketch a graph of the velocity function.

   d. On what intervals is the speed increasing?

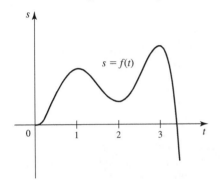

36. Fish length Assume the length L (in cm) of a particular species of fish after t years is modeled by the following graph.

   a. What does dL/dt represent and what happens to this derivative as t increases?

   b. What does the derivative tell you about how this species of fish grows?

   c. Sketch a graph of L' and L''.

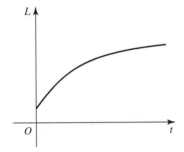

37–40. Average and marginal profit *Let $C(x)$ represent the cost of producing x items and $p(x)$ be the sale price per item if x items are sold. The profit $P(x)$ of selling x items is $P(x) = x\,p(x) - C(x)$ (revenue minus costs). The **average profit per item** when x items are sold is $P(x)/x$ and the **marginal profit** is dP/dx. The marginal profit approximates the profit obtained by selling one more item given that x items have already been sold. Consider the following cost functions C and price functions p.*

a. Find the profit function P.

b. Find the average profit function and marginal profit function.

c. Find the average profit and marginal profit if $x = a$ units are sold.

d. Interpret the meaning of the values obtained in part (c).

37. $C(x) = -0.02x^2 + 50x + 100$, $p(x) = 100$, $a = 500$

38. $C(x) = -0.02x^2 + 50x + 100$, $p(x) = 100 - 0.1x$, $a = 500$

39. $C(x) = -0.04x^2 + 100x + 800$, $p(x) = 200$, $a = 1000$

40. $C(x) = -0.04x^2 + 100x + 800$, $p(x) = 200 - 0.1x$, $a = 1000$

Applications

41. Population growth of the United States Suppose $p(t)$ represents the population of the United States (in millions) t years after the year 1900. The graph of the growth rate p' is shown in the figure.

   a. Approximately when (in what year) was the U.S. population growing most slowly between 1900 to 1990? Estimate the growth rate in that year.

   b. Approximately when (in what year) was the U.S. population growing most rapidly between 1900 and 1990? Estimate the growth rate in that year.

   c. In what years, if any, was p decreasing?

   d. In what years was the population growth rate increasing?

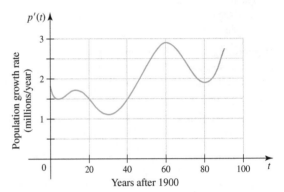

42. Average and marginal production Economists use *production functions* to describe how the output of a system varies with respect to another variable such as labor or capital. For example, the production function $P(L) = 200L + 10L^2 - L^3$ gives the output of a system as a function of the number of laborers L. The *average product* $A(L)$ is the average output per laborer when L laborers are working; that is $A(L) = P(L)/L$. The *marginal product* $M(L)$ is the approximate change in output when one additional laborer is added to L laborers; that is, $M(L) = \dfrac{dP}{dL}$.

   a. For the given production function, compute and graph P, A, and M.

   b. Suppose the peak of the average product curve occurs at $L = L_0$, so that $A'(L_0) = 0$. Show that for a general production function, $M(L_0) = A(L_0)$.

43. Velocity of a marble The position (in meters) of a marble rolling up a long incline is given by $s = \dfrac{100t}{t + 1}$, where t is measured in seconds and $s = 0$ is the starting point.

   a. Graph the position function.

   b. Find the velocity function for the marble.

   c. Graph the velocity function and give a description of the motion of the marble.

   d. At what time is the marble 80 m from its starting point?

   e. At what time is the velocity 50 m/s?

44. Tree growth Let b represent the base diameter of a conifer tree and let h represent the height of the tree, where b is measured in centimeters and h is measured in meters. Assume the height is related to the base diameter by the function $h = 5.67 + 0.70b + 0.0067b^2$.

   a. Graph the height function.

   b. Plot and interpret the meaning of $\dfrac{dh}{db}$.

45. A different interpretation of marginal cost Suppose a large company makes 25,000 gadgets per year in batches of x items at a time. After analyzing setup costs to produce each batch and taking into account storage costs, it has been determined that the total cost $C(x)$ of producing 25,000 gadgets in batches of x items at a time is given by

$$C(x) = 1,250,000 + \frac{125,000,000}{x} + 1.5x.$$

a. Determine the marginal cost and average cost functions. Graph and interpret these functions.
b. Determine the average cost and marginal cost when $x = 5000$.
c. The meaning of average cost and marginal cost here is different from earlier examples and exercises. Interpret the meaning of your answer in part (b).

46. Diminishing returns A cost function of the form $C(x) = \frac{1}{2}x^2$ reflects *diminishing returns to scale*. Find and graph the cost, average cost, and marginal cost functions. Interpret the graphs and explain the idea of diminishing returns.

47. Revenue function A store manager estimates that the demand for an energy drink decreases with increasing price according to the function $d(p) = \frac{100}{p^2 + 1}$, which means that at price p (in dollars), $d(p)$ units can be sold. The revenue generated at price p is $R(p) = p \cdot d(p)$ (price multiplied by number of units).

a. Find and graph the revenue function.
b. Find and graph the marginal revenue $R'(p)$.
c. From the graphs of R and R', estimate the price that should be charged to maximize the revenue.

48. Fuel economy Suppose you own a fuel-efficient hybrid automobile with a monitor on the dashboard that displays the mileage and gas consumption. The number of miles you can drive with g gallons of gas remaining in the tank on a particular stretch of highway is given by $m(g) = 50g - 25.8g^2 + 12.5g^3 - 1.6g^4$, for $0 \le g \le 4$.

a. Graph and interpret the mileage function.
b. Graph and interpret the gas mileage $m(g)/g$.
c. Graph and interpret dm/dg.

49. Spring oscillations A spring hangs from the ceiling at equilibrium with a mass attached to its end. Suppose you pull downward on the mass and release it 10 inches below its equilibrium position with an upward push. The distance x (in inches) of the mass from its equilibrium position after t seconds is given by the function $x(t) = 10 \sin t - 10 \cos t$, where x is positive when the mass is above the equilibrium position.

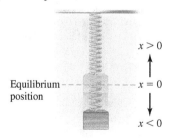

a. Graph and interpret this function.
b. Find $\frac{dx}{dt}$ and interpret the meaning of this derivative.
c. At what times is the velocity of the mass zero?
d. The function given here is a model for the motion of an object on a spring. In what ways is this model unrealistic?

50. Pressure and altitude Earth's atmospheric pressure decreases with altitude from a sea level pressure of 1000 millibars (a unit of pressure used by meteorologists). Letting z be the height above Earth's surface (sea level) in km, the atmospheric pressure is modeled by $p(z) = 1000e^{-z/10}$.

a. Compute the pressure at the summit of Mt. Everest which has an elevation of roughly 10 km. Compare the pressure on Mt. Everest to the pressure at sea level.
b. Compute the average change in pressure in the first 5 km above Earth's surface.
c. Compute the rate of change of the pressure at an elevation of 5 km.
d. Does $p'(z)$ increase or decrease with z? Explain.
e. What is the meaning of $\lim_{z \to \infty} p(z) = 0$?

51. A race Jean and Juan run a one-lap race on a circular track. Their angular positions on the track during the race are given by the functions $\theta(t)$ and $\varphi(t)$, respectively, where $0 \le t \le 4$ and t is measured in minutes (see figure). These angles are measured in radians, where $\theta = \varphi = 0$ represent the starting position and $\theta = \varphi = 2\pi$ represent the finish position. The angular velocities of the runners are $\theta'(t)$ and $\varphi'(t)$.

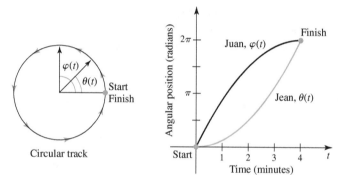

Circular track

a. Compare in words the angular velocity of the two runners and the progress of the race.
b. Which runner has the greater average angular velocity?
c. Who wins the race?
d. Jean's position is given by $\theta(t) = \pi t^2/8$. What is her angular velocity at $t = 2$ and at what time is her angular velocity the greatest?
e. Juan's position is given by $\varphi(t) = \pi t(8 - t)/8$. What is his angular velocity at $t = 2$ and at what time is his angular velocity the greatest?

52. Power and energy Power and energy are often used interchangeably, but they are quite different. **Energy** is what makes matter move or heat up. It is measured in units of **joules** or **Calories**, where 1 Cal = 4184 J. One hour of walking consumes roughly 10^6 J, or 240 Cal. On the other hand, **power** is the rate at which energy is used, which is measured in **watts**, where 1 W = 1 J/s. Other useful units of power are **kilowatts** (1 kW = 10^3 W) and **megawatts** (1 MW = 10^6 W). If energy is used at a rate of 1 kW for one hour, the total amount of energy used is 1 **kilowatt-hour** (1 kWh = 3.6×10^6 J). Suppose the cumulative energy used in a large building over a 24-hr period is given by $E(t) = 100t + 4t^2 - \frac{t^3}{9}$ kWh, where $t = 0$ corresponds to midnight.

a. Graph the energy function.
b. The power is the rate of energy consumption; that is, $P(t) = E'(t)$. Find the power over the interval $0 \le t \le 24$.
c. Graph the power function and interpret the graph. What are the units of power in this case?

T **53. Flow from a tank** A cylindrical tank is full at time $t = 0$ when a valve in the bottom of the tank is opened. By Torricelli's Law, the volume of water in the tank after t hours is $V = 100(200 - t)^2$, measured in cubic meters.

a. Graph the volume function. What is the volume of water in the tank before the valve is opened?
b. How long does it take the tank to empty?
c. Find the rate at which water flows from the tank and plot the flow rate function.
d. At what time is the magnitude of the flow rate a minimum? A maximum?

T **54. Cell population** The population of a culture of cells after t days is approximated by the function $P(t) = \dfrac{1600}{1 + 7e^{-0.02t}}$, for $t \geq 0$.

a. Graph the population function.
b. What is the average growth rate during the first 10 days?
c. Looking at the graph, when does the growth rate appear to be a maximum?
d. Differentiate the population function to determine the growth rate function $P'(t)$.
e. Graph the growth rate. When is it a maximum and what is the population at the time that the growth rate is a maximum?

T **55. Bungee jumper** A woman attached to a bungee cord jumps from a bridge that is 30 m above a river. Her height in meters above the river t seconds after the jump is $y(t) = 15(1 + e^{-t} \cos t)$, for $t \geq 0$.

a. Determine her velocity at $t = 1$ and $t = 3$.
b. Use a graphing utility to determine when she is moving downward and when she is moving upward during the first 10 s.
c. Use a graphing utility to estimate the maximum upward velocity.

T **56. Spring runoff** The flow of a small stream is monitored for 90 days between May 1 and August 1. The total water that flows past a gauging station is given by

$$V(t) = \begin{cases} \dfrac{4}{5}t^2 & \text{if } 0 \leq t < 45 \\ -\dfrac{4}{5}(t^2 - 180t + 4050) & \text{if } 45 \leq t < 90, \end{cases}$$

where V is measured in cubic feet and t is measured in days, with $t = 0$ corresponding to May 1.

a. Graph the volume function.
b. Find the flow rate function $V'(t)$ and graph it. What are the units of the flow rate?
c. Describe the flow of the stream over the 3-month period. Specifically, when is the flow rate a maximum?

57. Temperature distribution A thin copper rod, 4 meters in length, is heated at its midpoint, and the ends are held at a constant temperature of $0°$. When the temperature reaches equilibrium, the temperature profile is given by $T(x) = 40x(4 - x)$, where $0 \leq x \leq 4$ is the position along the rod. The **heat flux** at a point on the rod equals $-kT'(x)$, where $k > 0$ is a constant. If the heat flux is positive at a point, heat moves in the positive x-direction at that point, and if the heat flux is negative, heat moves in the negative x-direction.

a. With $k = 1$, what is the heat flux at $x = 1$? At $x = 3$?
b. For what values of x is the heat flux negative? Positive?
c. Explain the statement that heat flows out of the rod at its ends.

QUICK CHECK ANSWERS

1. Instantaneous velocity   **2.** Yes; yes   **3.** If an object has positive acceleration, then its velocity is increasing. If the velocity is negative but increasing, then the acceleration is positive and the speed is decreasing. For example, the velocity may increase from -2 m/s to -1 m/s to 0 m/s.   **4.** $v(1) = 32$ ft/s and $v(3) = -32$ ft/s, so the speed is 32 ft/s at both times.   **5.** The growth rate in 1996 $(t = 1)$ is approximately 77 million users/year. It is less than half of the growth rate in 2010 $(t = 15)$, which is approximately 161 million users/year.   **6.** As x increases from 1 to 100, the average cost decreases from \$150/item to \$49/item. ◄

3.7 The Chain Rule

The differentiation rules presented so far allow us to find derivatives of many functions. However, these rules are inadequate for finding the derivatives of most *composite functions*. Here is a typical situation. If $f(x) = x^3$ and $g(x) = 5x + 4$, then their composition is $f(g(x)) = (5x + 4)^3$. One way to find the derivative is by expanding $(5x + 4)^3$ and differentiating the resulting polynomial. Unfortunately, this strategy becomes prohibitive for functions such as $(5x + 4)^{100}$. We need a better approach.

QUICK CHECK 1 Explain why it is not practical to calculate $\dfrac{d}{dx}(5x + 4)^{100}$ by first expanding $(5x + 4)^{100}$. ◄

Chain Rule Formulas

An efficient method for differentiating composite functions, called the *Chain Rule*, is motivated by the following example. Suppose Yancey, Uri, and Xan pick apples. Let y, u, and x represent the number of apples picked in some period of time by Yancey, Uri, and Xan, respectively. Yancey picks apples three times faster than Uri, which means the rate at which Yancey picks apples with respect to Uri is $\dfrac{dy}{du} = 3$. Uri picks apples twice as fast

➤ Expressions such as dy/dx should not be treated as fractions. Nevertheless, you can check symbolically that you have written the Chain Rule correctly by noting that du appears in the "numerator" and "denominator." If it were "canceled," the Chain Rule would have dy/dx on both sides.

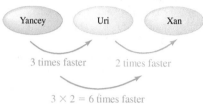

3 times faster   2 times faster

$3 \times 2 = 6$ times faster

Figure 3.50

as Xan, so $\dfrac{du}{dx} = 2$. Therefore, Yancey picks apples at a rate that is $3 \cdot 2 = 6$ times greater than Xan's rate, which means that $\dfrac{dy}{dx} = 6$ (Figure 3.50). Observe that

$$\frac{dy}{dx} = \frac{dy}{du} \cdot \frac{du}{dx} = 3 \cdot 2 = 6.$$

The equation $\dfrac{dy}{dx} = \dfrac{dy}{du} \cdot \dfrac{du}{dx}$ is one form of the Chain Rule. It is referred to as Version 1 of the Chain Rule in this text.

Alternatively, the Chain Rule may be expressed in terms of composite functions. Let $y = f(u)$ and $u = g(x)$, which means y is related to x through the composite function $y = f(u) = f(g(x))$. The derivative $\dfrac{dy}{dx}$ is now expressed as the product

$$\underbrace{\frac{d}{dx}\big(f(g(x))\big)}_{\substack{dy \\ \overline{dx}}} = \underbrace{f'(u)}_{\substack{dy \\ \overline{du}}} \cdot \underbrace{g'(x)}_{\substack{du \\ \overline{dx}}}.$$

Replacing u with $g(x)$ results in

$$\frac{d}{dx}\big(f(g(x))\big) = f'(g(x)) \cdot g'(x),$$

which we refer to as Version 2 of the Chain Rule.

➤ The two versions of the Chain Rule differ only in notation. Mathematically, they are identical. Version 2 of the Chain Rule states that the derivative of $y = f(g(x))$ is the derivative of f evaluated at $g(x)$ multiplied by the derivative of g evaluated at x.

THEOREM 3.14   The Chain Rule

Suppose $y = f(u)$ is differentiable at $u = g(x)$ and $u = g(x)$ is differentiable at x. The composite function $y = f(g(x))$ is differentiable at x, and its derivative can be expressed in two equivalent ways.

Version 1 $\dfrac{dy}{dx} = \dfrac{dy}{du} \cdot \dfrac{du}{dx}$

Version 2 $\dfrac{d}{dx}\big(f(g(x))\big) = f'(g(x)) \cdot g'(x)$

➤ There may be several ways to choose an inner function $u = g(x)$ and an outer function $y = f(u)$. Nevertheless, we often refer to *the* inner and *the* outer function for the most obvious choices.

A proof of the Chain Rule is given at the end of this section. For now, it's important to learn how to use it. With the composite function $f(g(x))$, we refer to g as the *inner function* and f as the *outer function* of the composition. The key to using the Chain Rule is identifying the inner and outer functions. The following four steps outline the differentiation process, although you will soon find that the procedure can be streamlined.

PROCEDURE   Using the Chain Rule

Assume the differentiable function $y = f(g(x))$ is given.

1. Identify an outer function f and an inner function g, and let $u = g(x)$.
2. Replace $g(x)$ with u to express y in terms of u:

$$y = f(\underbrace{g(x)}_{u}) \Rightarrow y = f(u).$$

3. Calculate the product $\dfrac{dy}{du} \cdot \dfrac{du}{dx}$.

4. Replace u with $g(x)$ in $\dfrac{dy}{du}$ to obtain $\dfrac{dy}{dx}$.

QUICK CHECK 2 Identify an inner function (call it g) of $y = (5x + 4)^3$. Let $u = g(x)$ and express the outer function f in terms of u. ◄

EXAMPLE 1 **Version 1 of the Chain Rule** For each of the following composite functions, find the inner function $u = g(x)$ and the outer function $y = f(u)$. Use Version 1 of the Chain Rule to find $\dfrac{dy}{dx}$.

a. $y = (5x + 4)^3$ **b.** $y = \sin^3 x$ **c.** $y = \sin x^3$

SOLUTION

a. The inner function of $y = (5x + 4)^3$ is $u = 5x + 4$, and the outer function is $y = u^3$. By Version 1 of the Chain Rule, we have

$$\frac{dy}{dx} = \frac{dy}{du} \cdot \frac{du}{dx} \qquad \text{Version 1}$$

$$= 3u^2 \cdot 5 \qquad y = u^3 \Rightarrow \frac{dy}{du} = 3u^2$$

$$u = 5x + 4 \Rightarrow \frac{du}{dx} = 5$$

$$= 3(5x + 4)^2 \cdot 5 \quad \text{Replace } u \text{ with } 5x + 4.$$

$$= 15(5x + 4)^2.$$

> When using trigonometric functions, expressions such as $\sin^n (x)$ always mean $(\sin x)^n$, except when $n = -1$. In Example 1, $\sin^3 x = (\sin x)^3$.

b. Replacing the shorthand form $y = \sin^3 x$ with $y = (\sin x)^3$, we identify the inner function as $u = \sin x$. Letting $y = u^3$, we have

$$\frac{dy}{dx} = \frac{dy}{du} \cdot \frac{du}{dx} = \underbrace{3u^2}_{3u^2} \cdot \cos x = \underbrace{3 \sin^2 x \cos x}.$$

QUICK CHECK 3 In Example 1a, we showed that

$$\frac{d}{dx}((5x + 4)^3) = 15(5x + 4)^2.$$

Verify this result by expanding $(5x + 4)^3$ and differentiating. ◄

c. Although $y = \sin x^3$ appears to be similar to the function $y = \sin^3 x$ in part (b), the inner function in this case is $u = x^3$ and the outer function is $y = \sin u$. Therefore,

$$\frac{dy}{dx} = \frac{dy}{du} \cdot \frac{du}{dx} = (\cos u) \cdot 3x^2 = 3x^2 \cos x^3.$$

Related Exercises 7–18 ◄

Version 2 of the Chain Rule, $\dfrac{d}{dx}\big(f(g(x))\big) = f'(g(x)) \cdot g'(x)$, is equivalent to Version 1; it just uses different derivative notation. With Version 2, we identify an outer function $y = f(u)$ and an inner function $u = g(x)$. Then $\dfrac{d}{dx}\big(f(g(x))\big)$ is the product of $f'(u)$ evaluated at $u = g(x)$ and $g'(x)$.

EXAMPLE 2 **Version 2 of the Chain Rule** Use Version 2 of the Chain Rule to calculate the derivatives of the following functions.

a. $(6x^3 + 3x + 1)^{10}$ **b.** $\sqrt{5x^2 + 1}$ **c.** $\left(\dfrac{5t^2}{3t^2 + 2}\right)^3$

SOLUTION

a. The inner function of $(6x^3 + 3x + 1)^{10}$ is $g(x) = 6x^3 + 3x + 1$, and the outer function is $f(u) = u^{10}$. The derivative of the outer function is $f'(u) = 10u^9$, which, when evaluated at $g(x)$, is $10(6x^3 + 3x + 1)^9$. The derivative of the inner function is $g'(x) = 18x^2 + 3$. Multiplying the derivatives of the outer and inner functions, we have

$$\frac{d}{dx}((6x^3 + 3x + 1)^{10}) = \underbrace{10(6x^3 + 3x + 1)^9}_{f'(u) \text{ evaluated at } g(x)} \cdot \underbrace{(18x^2 + 3)}_{g'(x)}$$

$$= 30(6x^2 + 1)(6x^3 + 3x + 1)^9. \qquad \text{Factor and simplify.}$$

b. The inner function of $\sqrt{5x^2 + 1}$ is $g(x) = 5x^2 + 1$, and the outer function is $f(u) = \sqrt{u}$. The derivatives of these functions are $f'(u) = \dfrac{1}{2\sqrt{u}}$ and $g'(x) = 10x$. Therefore,

$$\frac{d}{dx}\sqrt{5x^2 + 1} = \underbrace{\frac{1}{2\sqrt{5x^2 + 1}}}_{\substack{f'(u)\text{ evaluated}\\ \text{at }g(x)}} \cdot \underbrace{10x}_{g'(x)} = \frac{5x}{\sqrt{5x^2 + 1}}.$$

c. The inner function of $\left(\dfrac{5t^2}{3t^2 + 2}\right)^3$ is $g(t) = \dfrac{5t^2}{3t^2 + 2}$. The outer function is $f(u) = u^3$, whose derivative is $f'(u) = 3u^2$. The derivative of the inner function requires the Quotient Rule. Applying the Chain Rule, we have

$$\frac{d}{dt}\left(\frac{5t^2}{3t^2 + 2}\right)^3 = \underbrace{3\left(\frac{5t^2}{3t^2 + 2}\right)^2}_{\substack{f'(u)\text{ evaluated}\\ \text{at }g(t)}} \cdot \underbrace{\frac{(3t^2 + 2)10t - 5t^2(6t)}{(3t^2 + 2)^2}}_{g'(t)\text{ by the Quotient Rule}} = \frac{1500t^5}{(3t^2 + 2)^4}.$$

Related Exercises 19–36 ◄

The Chain Rule is also used to calculate the derivative of a composite function for a specific value of the variable. If $h(x) = f(g(x))$ and a is a real number, then $h'(a) = f'(g(a))g'(a)$, provided the necessary derivatives exist. Therefore, $h'(a)$ is the derivative of f evaluated at $g(a)$ multiplied by the derivative of g evaluated at a.

Table 3.3

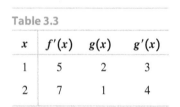

x	$f'(x)$	$g(x)$	$g'(x)$
1	5	2	3
2	7	1	4

EXAMPLE 3 Calculating derivatives at a point Let $h(x) = f(g(x))$. Use the values in Table 3.3 to calculate $h'(1)$ and $h'(2)$.

SOLUTION We use $h'(a) = f'(g(a))g'(a)$ with $a = 1$:

$$h'(1) = f'(g(1))g'(1) = f'(2)g'(1) = 7 \cdot 3 = 21.$$

With $a = 2$, we have

$$h'(2) = f'(g(2))g'(2) = f'(1)g'(2) = 5 \cdot 4 = 20.$$

Related Exercises 37–38 ◄

EXAMPLE 4 Applying the Chain Rule A trail runner programs her GPS unit to record her altitude a (in feet) every 10 minutes during a training run in the mountains; the resulting data are shown in Table 3.4. Meanwhile, at a nearby weather station, a weather probe records the atmospheric pressure p (in hectopascals, or hPa) at various altitudes, shown in Table 3.5.

Table 3.4

t (minutes)	0	10	20	30	40	50	60	70	80
$a(t)$ (altitude)	10,000	10,220	10,510	10,980	11,660	12,330	12,710	13,330	13,440

Table 3.5

a (altitude)	5485	7795	10,260	11,330	12,330	13,330	14,330	15,830	16,230
$p(a)$ (pressure)	1000	925	840	821	793	765	738	700	690

Use the Chain Rule to estimate the rate of change in pressure per unit time experienced by the trail runner when she is 50 minutes into her run.

SOLUTION We seek the rate of change in the pressure $\dfrac{dp}{dt}$, which is given by the Chain Rule:

$$\frac{dp}{dt} = \frac{dp}{da}\frac{da}{dt}.$$

> The difference quotient $\dfrac{p(a+h) - p(a)}{h}$ is a *forward difference quotient* when $h > 0$ (see Exercises 64–67 in Section 3.1).

The runner is at an altitude of 12,330 feet 50 minutes into her run, so we must compute dp/da when $a = 12{,}330$ and da/dt when $t = 50$. These derivatives can be approximated using the following forward difference quotients.

$$\left.\frac{dp}{da}\right|_{a=12{,}330} \approx \frac{p(12{,}330 + 1000) - p(12{,}330)}{1000} \qquad \left.\frac{da}{dt}\right|_{t=50} \approx \frac{a(50 + 10) - a(50)}{10}$$

$$= \frac{765 - 793}{1000} \qquad\qquad\qquad\qquad = \frac{12{,}710 - 12{,}330}{10}$$

$$= -0.028\frac{\text{hPa}}{\text{ft}} \qquad\qquad\qquad\qquad\quad = 38.0\frac{\text{ft}}{\text{min}}$$

We now compute the rate of change of the pressure with respect to time:

$$\frac{dp}{dt} = \frac{dp}{da}\frac{da}{dt}$$

$$\approx -0.028\frac{\text{hPa}}{\text{ft}} \cdot 38.0\frac{\text{ft}}{\text{min}} = -1.06\frac{\text{hPa}}{\text{min}}.$$

As expected, dp/dt is negative because the pressure decreases with increasing altitude (Table 3.5) as the runner ascends the trail. Note also that the units are consistent.

Related Exercises 39–40 ◄

Chain Rule for Powers

The Chain Rule leads to a general derivative rule for powers of differentiable functions. In fact, we have already used it in several examples. Consider the function $f(x) = (g(x))^n$, where n is an integer. Letting $f(u) = u^n$ be the outer function and $u = g(x)$ be the inner function, we obtain the Chain Rule for powers of functions.

> In Section 3.9, Theorem 3.15 is generalized to all real numbers n.

THEOREM 3.15   Chain Rule for Powers

If g is differentiable for all x in its domain and n is an integer, then

$$\frac{d}{dx}\left((g(x))^n\right) = n(g(x))^{n-1}g'(x).$$

EXAMPLE 5   Chain Rule for powers   Find $\dfrac{d}{dx}(\tan x + 10)^{21}$.

SOLUTION With $g(x) = \tan x + 10$, the Chain Rule gives

$$\frac{d}{dx}(\tan x + 10)^{21} = 21(\tan x + 10)^{20}\frac{d}{dx}(\tan x + 10)$$

$$= 21(\tan x + 10)^{20}\sec^2 x.$$

Related Exercises 41–44 ◄

The Composition of Three or More Functions

We can differentiate the composition of three or more functions by applying the Chain Rule repeatedly, as shown in the following example.

▶ Before dismissing the function in Example 6 as merely a tool to teach the Chain Rule, consider the graph of a related function, $y = \sin(e^{1.3\cos x}) + 1$ (Figure 3.51). This periodic function has two peaks per cycle and could be used as a simple model of traffic flow (two rush hours followed by light traffic in the middle of the night), tides (high tide, medium tide, high tide, low tide, . . .), or the presence of certain allergens in the air (peaks in the spring and fall).

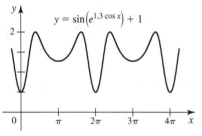

Figure 3.51

EXAMPLE 6   Composition of three functions Calculate the derivative of $\sin(e^{\cos x})$.

SOLUTION The inner function of $\sin(e^{\cos x})$ is $e^{\cos x}$. Because $e^{\cos x}$ is also a composition of two functions, the Chain Rule is used again to calculate $\dfrac{d}{dx}(e^{\cos x})$, where $\cos x$ is the inner function:

$$\frac{d}{dx}\underbrace{(\sin(\overbrace{e^{\cos x}}^{\text{inner}}))}_{\text{outer}} = \cos(e^{\cos x})\frac{d}{dx}(e^{\cos x}) \qquad \text{Chain Rule}$$

$$= \cos(e^{\cos x})\,\underbrace{e^{\cos x}\cdot\frac{d}{dx}(\cos x)}_{\frac{d}{dx}(e^{\cos x})} \qquad \text{Chain Rule}$$

$$= \cos(e^{\cos x})\cdot e^{\cos x}\,(-\sin x) \qquad \text{Differentiate } \cos x.$$

$$= -\sin x\cdot e^{\cos x}\cdot\cos(e^{\cos x}). \qquad \text{Simplify.}$$

Related Exercises 45–56 ◀

QUICK CHECK 4 Let $y = \tan^{10}(x^5)$. Find f, g, and h such that $y = f(u)$, where $u = g(v)$ and $v = h(x)$. ◀

The Chain Rule is often used together with other derivative rules. Example 7 illustrates how several differentiation rules are combined.

EXAMPLE 7   Combining rules Find $\dfrac{d}{dx}(x^2\sqrt{x^2 + 1})$.

SOLUTION The given function is the product of x^2 and $\sqrt{x^2 + 1}$, and $\sqrt{x^2 + 1}$ is a composite function. We apply the Product Rule and then the Chain Rule:

$$\frac{d}{dx}(x^2\sqrt{x^2+1}) = \underbrace{\frac{d}{dx}(x^2)}_{2x}\cdot\sqrt{x^2+1} + x^2\cdot\underbrace{\frac{d}{dx}(\sqrt{x^2+1})}_{\text{Use Chain Rule}} \qquad \text{Product Rule}$$

$$= 2x\sqrt{x^2+1} + x^2\cdot\frac{1}{2\sqrt{x^2+1}}\cdot 2x \qquad \text{Chain Rule}$$

$$= 2x\sqrt{x^2+1} + \frac{x^3}{\sqrt{x^2+1}} \qquad \text{Simplify.}$$

$$= \frac{3x^3 + 2x}{\sqrt{x^2+1}}. \qquad \text{Simplify.}$$

Related Exercises 57–68 ◀

Proof of the Chain Rule

Suppose f is differentiable at $u = g(a)$, g is differentiable at a, and $h(x) = f(g(x))$. By the definition of the derivative of h,

$$h'(a) = \lim_{x\to a}\frac{h(x) - h(a)}{x - a} = \lim_{x\to a}\frac{f(g(x)) - f(g(a))}{x - a}. \qquad (1)$$

We assume that $g(a) \neq g(x)$ for values of x near a but not equal to a. This assumption holds for most, but not all, functions encountered in this text. For a proof of the Chain Rule without this assumption, see Exercise 103.

We multiply the right side of equation (1) by $\dfrac{g(x) - g(a)}{g(x) - g(a)}$, which equals 1, and let $v = g(x)$ and $u = g(a)$. The result is

$$h'(a) = \lim_{x \to a} \frac{f(g(x)) - f(g(a))}{g(x) - g(a)} \cdot \frac{g(x) - g(a)}{x - a}$$

$$= \lim_{x \to a} \frac{f(v) - f(u)}{v - u} \cdot \frac{g(x) - g(a)}{x - a}.$$

By assumption, g is differentiable at a; therefore, it is continuous at a. This means that $\lim_{x \to a} g(x) = g(a)$, so $v \to u$ as $x \to a$. Consequently,

$$h'(a) = \underbrace{\lim_{v \to u} \frac{f(v) - f(u)}{v - u}}_{f'(u)} \cdot \underbrace{\lim_{x \to a} \frac{g(x) - g(a)}{x - a}}_{g'(a)} = f'(u)g'(a).$$

Because f and g are differentiable at u and a, respectively, the two limits in this expression exist; therefore, $h'(a)$ exists. Noting that $u = g(a)$, we have $h'(a) = f'(g(a))g'(a)$. Replacing a with the variable x gives the Chain Rule: $h'(x) = f'(g(x))g'(x)$. ◀

SECTION 3.7 EXERCISES

Review Questions

1. Two equivalent forms of the Chain Rule for calculating the derivative of $y = f(g(x))$ are presented in this section. State both forms.

2. Let $h(x) = f(g(x))$, where f and g are differentiable on their domains. If $g(1) = 3$ and $g'(1) = 5$, what else do you need to know to calculate $h'(1)$?

3. Fill in the blanks. The derivative of $f(g(x))$ equals f' evaluated at _____ multiplied by g' evaluated at _____.

4. Identify the inner and outer functions in the composition $\cos^4 x$.

5. Identify the inner and outer functions in the composition $(x^2 + 10)^{-5}$.

6. Express $Q(x) = \cos^4(x^2 + 1)$ as the composition of three functions; that is, identify f, g, and h so that $Q(x) = f(g(h(x)))$.

Basic Skills

7–18. Version 1 of the Chain Rule *Use Version 1 of the Chain Rule to calculate $\dfrac{dy}{dx}$.*

7. $y = (3x + 7)^{10}$ 8. $y = (5x^2 + 11x)^{20}$ 9. $y = \sin^5 x$

10. $y = \cos x^5$ 11. $y = e^{5x-7}$ 12. $y = \sqrt{7x - 1}$

13. $y = \sqrt{x^2 + 1}$ 14. $y = e^{\sqrt{x}}$ 15. $y = \tan 5x^2$

16. $y = \sin \dfrac{x}{4}$ 17. $y = \sec e^x$ 18. $y = e^{-x^2}$

19–34. Version 2 of the Chain Rule *Use Version 2 of the Chain Rule to calculate the derivatives of the following functions.*

19. $y = (3x^2 + 7x)^{10}$ 20. $y = (x^2 + 2x + 7)^8$

21. $y = \sqrt{10x + 1}$ 22. $y = \sqrt{x^2 + 9}$

23. $y = 5(7x^3 + 1)^{-3}$ 24. $y = \cos 5t$

25. $y = \sec(3x + 1)$ 26. $y = \csc e^x$

27. $y = \tan e^x$ 28. $y = e^{\tan t}$

29. $y = \sin(4x^3 + 3x + 1)$ 30. $y = \csc(t^2 + t)$

31. $y = \sin(2\sqrt{x})$ 32. $y = \cos^4 \theta + \sin^4 \theta$

33. $y = (\sec x + \tan x)^5$ 34. $y = \sin(4 \cos z)$

35–36. Similar-looking composite functions *Two composite functions are given that look similar, but in fact are quite different. Identify the inner function $u = g(x)$ and the outer function $y = f(u)$; then evaluate $\dfrac{dy}{dx}$ using the Chain Rule.*

35. a. $y = \cos^3 x$
    b. $y = \cos x^3$

36. a. $y = (e^x)^3$
    b. $y = e^{(x^3)}$

37. **Chain Rule using a table** Let $h(x) = f(g(x))$ and $p(x) = g(f(x))$. Use the table to compute the following derivatives.

a. $h'(3)$ b. $h'(2)$ c. $p'(4)$
d. $p'(2)$ e. $h'(5)$

x	1	2	3	4	5
$f(x)$	0	3	5	1	0
$f'(x)$	5	2	-5	-8	-10
$g(x)$	4	5	1	3	2
$g'(x)$	2	10	20	15	20

38. Chain Rule using a table Let $h(x) = f(g(x))$ and $k(x) = g(g(x))$. Use the table to compute the following derivatives.

    a. $h'(1)$ **b.** $h'(2)$ **c.** $h'(3)$ **d.** $k'(3)$
    e. $k'(1)$ **f.** $k'(5)$

x	1	2	3	4	5
$f'(x)$	−6	−3	8	7	2
$g(x)$	4	1	5	2	3
$g'(x)$	9	7	3	−1	−5

39. Applying the Chain Rule Use the data in Tables 3.4 and 3.5 of Example 4 to estimate the rate of change in pressure with respect to time experienced by the runner when she is at an altitude of 13,330 ft. Make use of a forward difference quotient when estimating the required derivatives.

40. Changing temperature The *lapse rate* is the rate at which the temperature in Earth's atmosphere decreases with altitude. For example, a lapse rate of 6.5° Celsius/km means the temperature *decreases* at a rate of 6.5°C per kilometer of altitude. The lapse rate varies with location and with other variables such as humidity. However, at a given time and location, the lapse rate is often nearly constant in the first 10 kilometers of the atmosphere. A radiosonde (weather balloon) is released from Earth's surface, and its altitude (measured in km above sea level) at various times (measured in hours) is given in the table below.

Time (hr)	0	0.5	1	1.5	2	2.5
Altitude (km)	0.5	1.2	1.7	2.1	2.5	2.9

    a. Assuming a lapse rate of 6.5° C/km, what is the approximate rate of change of the temperature with respect to time as the balloon rises 1.5 hours into the flight? Specify the units of your result, and use a forward difference quotient when estimating the required derivative.
    b. How does an increase in lapse rate change your answer in part (a)?
    c. Is it necessary to know the actual temperature to carry out the calculation in part (a)? Explain.

41–44. Chain Rule for powers *Use the Chain Rule to find the derivative of the following functions.*

41. $y = (2x^6 - 3x^3 + 3)^{25}$ **42.** $y = (\cos x + 2\sin x)^8$

43. $y = (1 + 2\tan x)^{15}$ **44.** $y = (1 - e^x)^4$

45–56. Repeated use of the Chain Rule *Calculate the derivative of the following functions.*

45. $y = \sqrt{1 + \cot^2 x}$ **46.** $y = \sqrt{(3x - 4)^2 + 3x}$

47. $y = \sin(\sin(e^x))$ **48.** $y = \sin^2(e^{3x+1})$

49. $y = \sin^5(\cos 3x)$ **50.** $y = \cos^4(7x^3)$

51. $y = \tan(e^{\sqrt{3x}})$ **52.** $y = (1 - e^{-0.05x})^{-1}$

53. $y = \sqrt{x + \sqrt{x}}$ **54.** $y = \sqrt{x + \sqrt{x + \sqrt{x}}}$

55. $y = f(g(x^2))$, where f and g are differentiable for all real numbers

56. $y = \left(f(g(x^m))\right)^n$, where f and g are differentiable for all real numbers, and m and n are integers

57–68. Combining rules *Use the Chain Rule combined with other differentiation rules to find the derivative of the following functions.*

57. $y = \left(\dfrac{x}{x + 1}\right)^5$ **58.** $y = \left(\dfrac{e^x}{x + 1}\right)^8$

59. $y = e^{x^2+1}\sin x^3$ **60.** $y = \tan(x e^x)$

61. $y = \theta^2\sec 5\theta$ **62.** $y = \left(\dfrac{3x}{4x + 2}\right)^5$

63. $y = ((x + 2)(x^2 + 1))^4$ **64.** $y = e^{2x}(2x - 7)^5$

65. $y = \sqrt{x^4 + \cos 2x}$ **66.** $y = \dfrac{te^t}{t + 1}$

67. $y = (p + \pi)^2\sin p^2$ **68.** $y = (z + 4)^3\tan z$

Further Explorations

69. Explain why or why not Determine whether the following statements are true and give an explanation or counterexample.

    a. The function $x \sin x$ can be differentiated without using the Chain Rule.
    b. The function $e^{\sqrt{x+1}}$ should be differentiated using the Chain Rule.
    c. The derivative of a product is *not* the product of the derivatives, but the derivative of a composition is a product of derivatives.
    d. $\dfrac{d}{dx}P(Q(x)) = P'(x)Q'(x)$.

70–73. Second derivatives *Find $\dfrac{d^2y}{dx^2}$ for the following functions.*

70. $y = x\cos x^2$ **71.** $y = \sin x^2$

72. $y = \sqrt{x^2 + 2}$ **73.** $y = e^{-2x^2}$

74. Derivatives by different methods

    a. Calculate $\dfrac{d}{dx}(x^2 + x)^2$ using the Chain Rule. Simplify your answer.
    b. Expand $(x^2 + x)^2$ first and then calculate the derivative. Verify that your answer agrees with part (a).

75–76. Square root derivatives *Find the derivative of the following functions.*

75. $y = \sqrt{f(x)}$, where f is differentiable and nonnegative at x

76. $y = \sqrt{f(x)g(x)}$, where f and g are differentiable and nonnegative at x

77. Tangent lines Determine an equation of the line tangent to the graph of $y = \dfrac{(x^2 - 1)^2}{x^3 - 6x - 1}$ at the point $(3, 8)$. Graph the function and the tangent line.

78. Tangent lines Determine equations of the lines tangent to the graph of $y = x\sqrt{5 - x^2}$ at the points $(1, 2)$ and $(-2, -2)$. Graph the function and the tangent lines.

79. Tangent lines Assume f and g are differentiable on their domains with $h(x) = f(g(x))$. Suppose the equation of the line tangent to the graph of g at the point $(4, 7)$ is $y = 3x - 5$ and the equation of the line tangent to the graph of f at $(7, 9)$ is $y = -2x + 23$.

    a. Calculate $h(4)$ and $h'(4)$.
    b. Determine an equation of the line tangent to the graph of h at the point on the graph where $x = 4$.

80. Tangent lines Assume f is a differentiable function whose graph passes through the point $(1, 4)$. Suppose $g(x) = f(x^2)$ and the line tangent to the graph of f at $(1, 4)$ is $y = 3x + 1$. Determine each of the following.

    a. $g(1)$ **b.** $g'(x)$ **c.** $g'(1)$

    d. An equation of the line tangent to the graph of g when $x = 1$

81. Tangent lines Find the equation of the line tangent to $y = e^{2x}$ at $x = \frac{1}{2} \ln 3$. Graph the function and the tangent line.

82. Composition containing $\sin x$ Suppose f is differentiable on $[-2, 2]$ with $f'(0) = 3$ and $f'(1) = 5$. Let $g(x) = f(\sin x)$. Evaluate the following expressions.

    a. $g'(0)$ **b.** $g'\left(\dfrac{\pi}{2}\right)$ **c.** $g'(\pi)$

83. Composition containing $\sin x$ Suppose f is differentiable for all real numbers with $f(0) = -3$, $f(1) = 3$, $f'(0) = 3$, and $f'(1) = 5$. Let $g(x) = \sin(\pi f(x))$. Evaluate the following expressions.

    a. $g'(0)$ **b.** $g'(1)$

Applications

84–86. Vibrations of a spring *Suppose an object of mass m is attached to the end of a spring hanging from the ceiling. The mass is at its equilibrium position $y = 0$ when the mass hangs at rest. Suppose you push the mass to a position y_0 units above its equilibrium position and release it. As the mass oscillates up and down (neglecting any friction in the system), the position y of the mass after t seconds is*

$$y = y_0 \cos\left(t\sqrt{\frac{k}{m}}\right), \tag{2}$$

where $k > 0$ is a constant measuring the stiffness of the spring (the larger the value of k, the stiffer the spring) and y is positive in the upward direction.

84. Use equation (2) to answer the following questions.

    a. Find $\dfrac{dy}{dt}$, the velocity of the mass. Assume k and m are constant.

    b. How would the velocity be affected if the experiment were repeated with four times the mass on the end of the spring?

    c. How would the velocity be affected if the experiment were repeated with a spring having four times the stiffness (k is increased by a factor of 4)?

    d. Assume that y has units of meters, t has units of seconds, m has units of kg, and k has units of kg/s². Show that the units of the velocity in part (a) are consistent.

85. Use equation (2) to answer the following questions.

    a. Find the second derivative $\dfrac{d^2 y}{dt^2}$.

    b. Verify that $\dfrac{d^2 y}{dt^2} = -\dfrac{k}{m} y$.

86. Use equation (2) to answer the following questions.

    a. The *period* T is the time required by the mass to complete one oscillation. Show that $T = 2\pi\sqrt{\dfrac{m}{k}}$.

    b. Assume k is constant and calculate $\dfrac{dT}{dm}$.

    c. Give a physical explanation of why $\dfrac{dT}{dm}$ is positive.

87. A damped oscillator The displacement of a mass on a spring suspended from the ceiling is given by $y = 10 e^{-t/2} \cos \dfrac{\pi t}{8}$.

    a. Graph the displacement function.

    b. Compute and graph the velocity of the mass, $v(t) = y'(t)$.

    c. Verify that the velocity is zero when the mass reaches the high and low points of its oscillation.

88. Oscillator equation A mechanical oscillator (such as a mass on a spring or a pendulum) subject to frictional forces satisfies the equation (called a differential equation)

$$y''(t) + 2y'(t) + 5y(t) = 0,$$

where y is the displacement of the oscillator from its equilibrium position. Verify by substitution that the function $y(t) = e^{-t}(\sin 2t - 2\cos 2t)$ satisfies this equation.

89. Hours of daylight The number of hours of daylight at any point on Earth fluctuates throughout the year. In the northern hemisphere, the shortest day is on the winter solstice and the longest day is on the summer solstice. At 40° north latitude, the length of a day is approximated by

$$D(t) = 12 - 3\cos\left(\frac{2\pi(t + 10)}{365}\right),$$

where D is measured in hours and $0 \le t \le 365$ is measured in days, with $t = 0$ corresponding to January 1.

    a. Approximately how much daylight is there on March 1 ($t = 59$)?

    b. Find the rate at which the daylight function changes.

    c. Find the rate at which the daylight function changes on March 1. Convert your answer to units of min/day and explain what this result means.

    d. Graph the function $y = D'(t)$ using a graphing utility.

    e. At what times of year is the length of day changing most rapidly? Least rapidly?

90. A mixing tank A 500-liter (L) tank is filled with pure water. At time $t = 0$, a salt solution begins flowing into the tank at a rate of 5 L/min. At the same time, the (fully mixed) solution flows out of the tank at a rate of 5.5 L/min. The mass of salt in grams in the tank at any time $t \ge 0$ is given by

$$M(t) = 250(1000 - t)(1 - 10^{-30}(1000 - t)^{10})$$

and the volume of solution in the tank (in liters) is given by $V(t) = 500 - 0.5t$.

    a. Graph the mass function and verify that $M(0) = 0$.

    b. Graph the volume function and verify that the tank is empty when $t = 1000$ min.

    c. The concentration of the salt solution in the tank (in g/L) is given by $C(t) = M(t)/V(t)$. Graph the concentration function and comment on its properties. Specifically, what are $C(0)$ and $\lim\limits_{t \to 1000^-} C(t)$?

    d. Find the rate of change of the mass $M'(t)$, for $0 \le t \le 1000$.

    e. Find the rate of change of the concentration $C'(t)$, for $0 \le t \le 1000$.

    f. For what times is the concentration of the solution increasing? Decreasing?

91. Power and energy The total energy in megawatt-hr (MWh) used by a town is given by

$$E(t) = 400t + \frac{2400}{\pi} \sin \frac{\pi t}{12},$$

where $t \geq 0$ is measured in hours, with $t = 0$ corresponding to noon.

a. Find the power, or rate of energy consumption, $P(t) = E'(t)$ in units of megawatts (MW).
b. At what time of day is the rate of energy consumption a maximum? What is the power at that time of day?
c. At what time of day is the rate of energy consumption a minimum? What is the power at that time of day?
d. Sketch a graph of the power function reflecting the times at which energy use is a minimum or maximum.

Additional Exercises

92. Deriving trigonometric identities

a. Differentiate both sides of the identity $\cos 2t = \cos^2 t - \sin^2 t$ to prove that $\sin 2t = 2 \sin t \cos t$.
b. Verify that you obtain the same identity for $\sin 2t$ as in part (a) if you differentiate the identity $\cos 2t = 2 \cos^2 t - 1$.
c. Differentiate both sides of the identity $\sin 2t = 2 \sin t \cos t$ to prove that $\cos 2t = \cos^2 t - \sin^2 t$.

93. Proof of $\cos^2 x + \sin^2 x = 1$ Let $f(x) = \cos^2 x + \sin^2 x$.

a. Use the Chain Rule to show that $f'(x) = 0$.
b. Assume that if $f' = 0$, then f is a constant function. Calculate $f(0)$ and use it with part (a) to explain why $\cos^2 x + \sin^2 x = 1$.

94. Using the Chain Rule to prove that $\dfrac{d}{dx}(e^{kx}) = ke^{kx}$

a. Identify the inner function g and the outer function f for the composition $f(g(x)) = e^{kx}$, where k is a real number.
b. Use the Chain Rule to show that $\dfrac{d}{dx}(e^{kx}) = ke^{kx}$.

95. Deriving the Quotient Rule using the Product Rule and Chain Rule Suppose you forgot the Quotient Rule for calculating $\dfrac{d}{dx}\left(\dfrac{f(x)}{g(x)}\right)$. Use the Chain Rule and Product Rule with the identity $\dfrac{f(x)}{g(x)} = f(x)(g(x))^{-1}$ to derive the Quotient Rule.

96. The Chain Rule for second derivatives

a. Derive a formula for the second derivative, $\dfrac{d^2}{dx^2}\big(f(g(x))\big)$.
b. Use the formula in part (a) to calculate $\dfrac{d^2}{dx^2}(\sin(3x^4 + 5x^2 + 2))$.

97–100. Calculating limits *The following limits are the derivatives of a composite function h at a point a.*

a. *Find a possible function h and number a.*
b. *Use the Chain Rule to find each limit. Verify your answer using a calculator.*

97. $\displaystyle \lim_{x \to 2} \frac{(x^2 - 3)^5 - 1}{x - 2}$

98. $\displaystyle \lim_{x \to 0} \frac{\sqrt{4 + \sin x} - 2}{x}$

99. $\displaystyle \lim_{h \to 0} \frac{\sin(\pi/2 + h)^2 - \sin(\pi^2/4)}{h}$

100. $\displaystyle \lim_{h \to 0} \frac{\dfrac{1}{3((1 + h)^5 + 7)^{10}} - \dfrac{1}{3(8)^{10}}}{h}$

101. Limit of a difference quotient Assuming that f is differentiable for all x, simplify $\displaystyle \lim_{x \to 5} \frac{f(x^2) - f(25)}{x - 5}$.

102. Derivatives of even and odd functions Recall that f is even if $f(-x) = f(x)$, for all x in the domain of f, and f is odd if $f(-x) = -f(x)$, for all x in the domain of f.

a. If f is a differentiable, even function on its domain, determine whether f' is even, odd, or neither.
b. If f is a differentiable, odd function on its domain, determine whether f' is even, odd, or neither.

103. A general proof of the Chain Rule Let f and g be differentiable functions with $h(x) = f(g(x))$. For a given constant a, let $u = g(a)$ and $v = g(x)$, and define

$$H(v) = \begin{cases} \dfrac{f(v) - f(u)}{v - u} - f'(u) & \text{if } v \neq u \\ 0 & \text{if } v = u. \end{cases}$$

a. Show that $\displaystyle \lim_{v \to u} H(v) = 0$.
b. For any value of u show that
$$f(v) - f(u) = (H(v) + f'(u))(v - u).$$
c. Show that
$$h'(a) = \lim_{x \to a} \left((H(g(x)) + f'(g(a))) \cdot \frac{g(x) - g(a)}{x - a} \right).$$
d. Show that $h'(a) = f'(g(a))g'(a)$.

QUICK CHECK ANSWERS

1. The expansion of $(5x + 4)^{100}$ contains 101 terms. It would take too much time to calculate the expansion and the derivative. **2.** The inner function is $u = 5x + 4$, and the outer function is $y = u^3$. **4.** $f(u) = u^{10}$; $u = g(v) = \tan v$; $v = h(x) = x^5$ ◄

3.8 Implicit Differentiation

This chapter has been devoted to calculating derivatives of functions of the form $y = f(x)$, where y is defined *explicitly* as a function of x. However, relations between variables are often expressed *implicitly*. For example, the equation of the unit circle $x^2 + y^2 = 1$ does not specify y directly, but rather defines y implicitly. This equation does not represent a single function because its graph fails the vertical line test (Figure 3.52a). If, however, the equation $x^2 + y^2 = 1$ is solved for y, then *two* functions emerge: $y = -\sqrt{1 - x^2}$ and $y = \sqrt{1 - x^2}$ (Figure 3.52b). Having identified two explicit functions that describe the circle, their derivatives are found using the Chain Rule.

$$\text{If } y = \sqrt{1 - x^2}, \text{ then } \frac{dy}{dx} = -\frac{x}{\sqrt{1 - x^2}}. \tag{1}$$

$$\text{If } y = -\sqrt{1 - x^2}, \text{ then } \frac{dy}{dx} = \frac{x}{\sqrt{1 - x^2}}. \tag{2}$$

We use equation (1) to find the slope of the curve at any point on the upper half of the unit circle and equation (2) to find the slope of the curve at any point on the lower half of the circle.

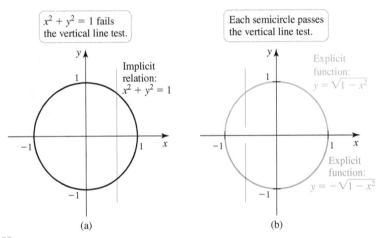

$x^2 + y^2 = 1$ fails the vertical line test.

Implicit relation: $x^2 + y^2 = 1$

Each semicircle passes the vertical line test.

Explicit function: $y = \sqrt{1 - x^2}$

Explicit function: $y = -\sqrt{1 - x^2}$

(a)   (b)

Figure 3.52

QUICK CHECK 1 The equation $x - y^2 = 0$ implicitly defines what two functions? ◄

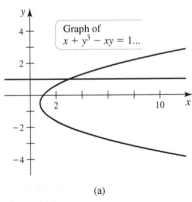

Graph of $x + y^3 - xy = 1...$

(a)

Figure 3.53

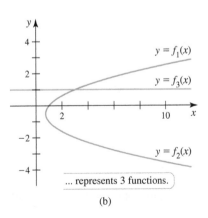

$y = f_1(x)$

$y = f_3(x)$

$y = f_2(x)$

... represents 3 functions.

(b)

While it is straightforward to solve some implicit equations for y (such as $x^2 + y^2 = 1$ or $x - y^2 = 0$), it is difficult or impossible to solve other equations for y. For example, the graph of $x + y^3 - xy = 1$ (Figure 3.53a) represents three functions: the upper half of a parabola $y = f_1(x)$, the lower half of a parabola $y = f_2(x)$, and the horizontal line $y = f_3(x)$ (Figure 3.53b). Solving for y to obtain these three functions is challenging (Exercise 61), and even after solving for y, derivatives for each of the three functions must be calculated separately. The goal of this section is to find a *single* expression for the derivative *directly* from an equation without first solving for y. This technique, called **implicit differentiation**, is demonstrated through examples.

EXAMPLE 1   Implicit differentiation

a. Calculate $\dfrac{dy}{dx}$ directly from the equation for the unit circle $x^2 + y^2 = 1$.

b. Find the slope of the unit circle at $\left(\dfrac{1}{2}, \dfrac{\sqrt{3}}{2}\right)$ and $\left(\dfrac{1}{2}, -\dfrac{\sqrt{3}}{2}\right)$.

SOLUTION

a. To indicate the choice of x as the independent variable, it is helpful to replace the variable y with $y(x)$:

$$x^2 + (y(x))^2 = 1. \quad \text{Replace } y \text{ with } y(x).$$

We now take the derivative of each term in the equation *with respect to x*:

$$\underbrace{\frac{d}{dx}(x^2)}_{2x} + \underbrace{\frac{d}{dx}(y(x))^2}_{\text{Use the Chain Rule}} = \underbrace{\frac{d}{dx}(1)}_{0}.$$

By the Chain Rule, $\dfrac{d}{dx}(y(x))^2 = 2y(x)y'(x)$, or $\dfrac{d}{dx}(y^2) = 2y\dfrac{dy}{dx}$. Substituting this result, we have

$$2x + 2y\frac{dy}{dx} = 0.$$

The last step is to solve for $\dfrac{dy}{dx}$:

$$2y\frac{dy}{dx} = -2x \quad \text{Subtract } 2x \text{ from both sides.}$$

$$\frac{dy}{dx} = -\frac{x}{y}. \quad \text{Divide by } 2y \text{ and simplify.}$$

This result holds provided $y \neq 0$. At the points $(1, 0)$ and $(-1, 0)$, the circle has vertical tangent lines.

b. Notice that the derivative $\dfrac{dy}{dx} = -\dfrac{x}{y}$ depends on *both* x and y. Therefore, to find the slope of the circle at $\left(\dfrac{1}{2}, \dfrac{\sqrt{3}}{2}\right)$, we substitute both $x = 1/2$ and $y = \sqrt{3}/2$ into the derivative formula. The result is

$$\frac{dy}{dx}\bigg|_{\left(\frac{1}{2}, \frac{\sqrt{3}}{2}\right)} = -\frac{1/2}{\sqrt{3}/2} = -\frac{1}{\sqrt{3}}.$$

The slope of the curve at $\left(\dfrac{1}{2}, -\dfrac{\sqrt{3}}{2}\right)$ is

$$\frac{dy}{dx}\bigg|_{\left(\frac{1}{2}, -\frac{\sqrt{3}}{2}\right)} = -\frac{1/2}{-\sqrt{3}/2} = \frac{1}{\sqrt{3}}.$$

The curve and tangent lines are shown in Figure 3.54.   *Related Exercises 5–12* ◄

Example 1 illustrates the technique of implicit differentiation. It is done without solving for y, and it produces $\dfrac{dy}{dx}$ in terms of both x and y. The derivative obtained in Example 1 is consistent with the derivatives calculated explicitly in equations (1) and (2). For the upper half of the circle, substituting $y = \sqrt{1 - x^2}$ into the implicit derivative $\dfrac{dy}{dx} = -\dfrac{x}{y}$ gives

$$\frac{dy}{dx} = -\frac{x}{y} = -\frac{x}{\sqrt{1 - x^2}},$$

> Implicit differentiation usually produces an expression for dy/dx in terms of both x and y. The notation $\dfrac{dy}{dx}\bigg|_{(a, b)}$ tells us to replace x with a and y with b in the expression for dy/dx.

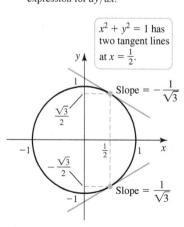

Figure 3.54

which agrees with equation (1). For the lower half of the circle, substituting $y = -\sqrt{1 - x^2}$ into $\dfrac{dy}{dx} = -\dfrac{x}{y}$ gives

$$\frac{dy}{dx} = -\frac{x}{y} = \frac{x}{\sqrt{1 - x^2}},$$

which is consistent with equation (2). Therefore, implicit differentiation gives a single unified derivative $\dfrac{dy}{dx} = -\dfrac{x}{y}$.

EXAMPLE 2   Implicit differentiation Find $y'(x)$ when $\sin xy = x^2 + y$.

SOLUTION It is impossible to solve this equation for y in terms of x, so we differentiate implicitly. Differentiating both sides of the equation with respect to x, using the Chain Rule and the Product Rule on the left side, gives

$$(\cos xy)(y + xy') = 2x + y'.$$

We now solve for y':

$$\begin{aligned}
xy'\cos xy - y' &= 2x - y \cos xy &&\text{Rearrange terms.}\\
y'(x \cos xy - 1) &= 2x - y \cos xy &&\text{Factor on left side.}\\
y' &= \frac{2x - y \cos xy}{x \cos xy - 1}. &&\text{Solve for } y'.
\end{aligned}$$

Notice that the final result gives y' in terms of both x and y.   *Related Exercises 13–24* ◄

QUICK CHECK 2 Use implicit differentiation to find $\dfrac{dy}{dx}$ for $x - y^2 = 3$. ◄

Slopes of Tangent Lines

Derivatives obtained by implicit differentiation typically depend on x and y. Therefore, the slope of a curve at a particular point (a, b) requires both the x- and y-coordinates of the point. These coordinates are also needed to find an equation of the tangent line at that point.

QUICK CHECK 3 If a function is defined explicitly in the form $y = f(x)$, which coordinates are needed to find the slope of a tangent line—the x-coordinate, the y-coordinate, or both? ◄

> Because y is a function of x, we have
>
> $$\frac{d}{dx}(x) = 1 \quad \text{and}$$
>
> $$\frac{d}{dx}(y) = y'.$$
>
> To differentiate y^3 with respect to x, we need the Chain Rule.

EXAMPLE 3   Finding tangent lines with implicit functions Find an equation of the line tangent to the curve $x^2 + xy - y^3 = 7$ at $(3, 2)$.

SOLUTION We calculate the derivative of each term of the equation $x^2 + xy - y^3 = 7$ with respect to x:

$$\begin{aligned}
\frac{d}{dx}(x^2) + \frac{d}{dx}(xy) - \frac{d}{dx}(y^3) &= \frac{d}{dx}(7) &&\text{Differentiate each term.}\\
2x + \underbrace{y + xy'}_{\text{Product Rule}} - \underbrace{3y^2 y'}_{\text{Chain Rule}} &= 0 &&\text{Calculate the derivatives.}\\
3y^2 y' - xy' &= 2x + y &&\text{Group the terms containing } y'.\\
y' &= \frac{2x + y}{3y^2 - x}. &&\text{Factor and solve for } y'.
\end{aligned}$$

To find the slope of the tangent line at $(3, 2)$, we substitute $x = 3$ and $y = 2$ into the derivative formula:

$$\left.\frac{dy}{dx}\right|_{(3, 2)} = \left.\frac{2x + y}{3y^2 - x}\right|_{(3, 2)} = \frac{8}{9}.$$

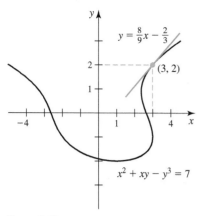

$y = \frac{8}{9}x - \frac{2}{3}$

(3, 2)

$x^2 + xy - y^3 = 7$

Figure 3.55

An equation of the line passing through $(3, 2)$ with slope $\frac{8}{9}$ is

$$y - 2 = \frac{8}{9}(x - 3) \quad \text{or} \quad y = \frac{8}{9}x - \frac{2}{3}.$$

Figure 3.55 shows the graphs of the curve $x^2 + xy - y^3 = 7$ and the tangent line.

Related Exercises 25–30 ◄

Higher-Order Derivatives of Implicit Functions

In previous sections of this chapter, we found higher-order derivatives $\dfrac{d^n y}{dx^n}$ by first calculating $\dfrac{dy}{dx}, \dfrac{d^2 y}{dx^2}, \dots,$ and $\dfrac{d^{n-1} y}{dx^{n-1}}$. The same approach is used with implicit differentiation.

EXAMPLE 4   A second derivative Find $\dfrac{d^2 y}{dx^2}$ if $x^2 + y^2 = 1$.

SOLUTION The first derivative $\dfrac{dy}{dx} = -\dfrac{x}{y}$ was computed in Example 1.

We now calculate the derivative of each side of this equation and simplify the right side:

$$\frac{d}{dx}\left(\frac{dy}{dx}\right) = \frac{d}{dx}\left(-\frac{x}{y}\right) \qquad \text{Take derivatives with respect to } x.$$

$$\frac{d^2 y}{dx^2} = -\frac{y \cdot 1 - x\dfrac{dy}{dx}}{y^2} \qquad \text{Quotient Rule}$$

$$= -\frac{y - x\left(-\dfrac{x}{y}\right)}{y^2} \qquad \text{Substitute for } \frac{dy}{dx}.$$

$$= -\frac{x^2 + y^2}{y^3} \qquad \text{Simplify.}$$

$$= -\frac{1}{y^3}. \qquad x^2 + y^2 = 1$$

Related Exercises 31–36 ◄

The Power Rule for Rational Exponents

The Extended Power Rule (Section 3.4) states that $\dfrac{d}{dx}(x^n) = nx^{n-1}$, if n is an integer. Using implicit differentiation, this rule can be further extended to rational values of n such as $\frac{1}{2}$ or $-\frac{5}{3}$. Assume p and q are integers with $q \neq 0$ and let $y = x^{p/q}$, where $x \geq 0$ when q is even. By raising each side of $y = x^{p/q}$ to the power q, we obtain $y^q = x^p$. Assuming that y is a differentiable function of x on its domain, both sides of $y^q = x^p$ are differentiated with respect to x:

$$qy^{q-1}\frac{dy}{dx} = px^{p-1}.$$

We now divide both sides by qy^{q-1} and simplify to obtain

$$\frac{dy}{dx} = \frac{p}{q} \cdot \frac{x^{p-1}}{y^{q-1}} = \frac{p}{q} \cdot \frac{x^{p-1}}{(x^{p/q})^{q-1}} \qquad \text{Substitute } x^{p/q} \text{ for } y.$$

$$= \frac{p}{q} \cdot \frac{x^{p-1}}{x^{p-p/q}} \qquad \text{Multiply exponents in the denominator.}$$

$$= \frac{p}{q} \cdot x^{p/q-1}. \qquad \text{Simplify by combining exponents.}$$

If we let $n = \dfrac{p}{q}$, then $\dfrac{d}{dx}(x^n) = nx^{n-1}$. So the Power Rule for rational exponents is the same as the Power Rule for integer exponents.

> ▶ The assumption that $y = x^{p/q}$ is differentiable on its domain is proved in Section 3.9, where the Power Rule is proved for all real powers; that is, we prove that $\dfrac{d}{dx}(x^n) = nx^{n-1}$ holds for any real number n.

THEOREM 3.16   Power Rule for Rational Exponents
Assume p and q are integers with $q \neq 0$. Then

$$\frac{d}{dx}(x^{p/q}) = \frac{p}{q}x^{p/q-1},$$

provided $x > 0$ when q is even.

EXAMPLE 5   Rational exponent Calculate $\dfrac{dy}{dx}$ for the following functions.

a. $y = \dfrac{1}{\sqrt{x}}$ **b.** $y = (x^6 + 3x)^{2/3}$

QUICK CHECK 4 Verify the derivative formula $\dfrac{d}{dx}(\sqrt{x}) = \dfrac{1}{2\sqrt{x}}$ (first encountered in Example 4 of Section 3.1) by using Theorem 3.16. ◄

SOLUTION

a. $\dfrac{dy}{dx} = \dfrac{d}{dx}(x^{-1/2}) = -\dfrac{1}{2}x^{-3/2} = -\dfrac{1}{2x^{3/2}}$

b. We apply the Chain Rule, where the outer function is $u^{2/3}$ and the inner function is $x^6 + 3x$:

$$\frac{dy}{dx} = \frac{d}{dx}((x^6 + 3x)^{2/3}) = \underbrace{\frac{2}{3}(x^6 + 3x)^{-1/3}}_{\text{derivative of outer function}} \underbrace{(6x^5 + 3)}_{\text{derivative of inner function}}$$

$$= \frac{2(2x^5 + 1)}{(x^6 + 3x)^{1/3}}.$$

Related Exercises 37–44 ◄

EXAMPLE 6   Implicit differentiation with rational exponents Find the slope of the curve $2(x + y)^{1/3} = y$ at the point $(4, 4)$.

SOLUTION We begin by differentiating both sides of the given equation:

$$\frac{2}{3}(x + y)^{-2/3}\left(1 + \frac{dy}{dx}\right) = \frac{dy}{dx} \qquad \text{Implicit differentiation, Chain Rule, Theorem 3.16}$$

$$\frac{2}{3}(x + y)^{-2/3} = \frac{dy}{dx} - \frac{2}{3}(x + y)^{-2/3}\frac{dy}{dx} \qquad \text{Expand and collect like terms.}$$

$$\frac{2}{3}(x + y)^{-2/3} = \frac{dy}{dx}\left(1 - \frac{2}{3}(x + y)^{-2/3}\right). \qquad \text{Factor out } \frac{dy}{dx}.$$

Solving for dy/dx, we find that

$$\frac{dy}{dx} = \frac{\dfrac{2}{3}(x + y)^{-2/3}}{1 - \dfrac{2}{3}(x + y)^{-2/3}} \qquad \text{Divide by } 1 - \frac{2}{3}(x + y)^{-2/3}.$$

$$\frac{dy}{dx} = \frac{2}{3(x + y)^{2/3} - 2}. \qquad \text{Multiply by } 3(x + y)^{2/3} \text{ and simplify.}$$

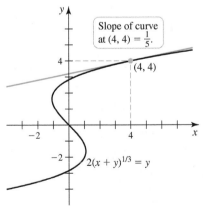

Slope of curve at $(4, 4) = \frac{1}{5}$.

$(4, 4)$

$2(x + y)^{1/3} = y$

Figure 3.56

Note that the point $(4, 4)$ *does* lie on the curve (Figure 3.56). The slope of the curve at $(4, 4)$ is found by substituting $x = 4$ and $y = 4$ into the formula for $\dfrac{dy}{dx}$:

$$\left.\frac{dy}{dx}\right|_{(4, 4)} = \frac{2}{3(8)^{2/3} - 2} = \frac{1}{5}.$$

Related Exercises 45–50 ◄

SECTION 3.8 EXERCISES

Review Questions

1. For some equations, such as $x^2 + y^2 = 1$ or $x - y^2 = 0$, it is possible to solve for y and then calculate $\dfrac{dy}{dx}$. Even in these cases, explain why implicit differentiation is usually a more efficient method for calculating the derivative.

2. Explain the differences between computing the derivatives of functions that are defined implicitly and explicitly.

3. Why are both the x-coordinate and the y-coordinate generally needed to find the slope of the tangent line at a point for an implicitly defined function?

4. In this section, for what values of n did we prove that
$$\frac{d}{dx}(x^n) = nx^{n-1}?$$

Basic Skills

5–12. Implicit differentiation *Carry out the following steps.*

a. Use implicit differentiation to find $\dfrac{dy}{dx}$.

b. Find the slope of the curve at the given point.

5. $x^4 + y^4 = 2$; $(1, -1)$
6. $x = e^y$; $(2, \ln 2)$

7. $y^2 = 4x$; $(1, 2)$
8. $y^2 + 3x = 8$; $(1, \sqrt{5})$

9. $\sin y = 5x^4 - 5$; $(1, \pi)$
10. $\sqrt{x} - 2\sqrt{y} = 0$; $(4, 1)$

11. $\cos y = x$; $\left(0, \dfrac{\pi}{2}\right)$
12. $\tan xy = x + y$; $(0, 0)$

13–24. Implicit differentiation *Use implicit differentiation to find $\dfrac{dy}{dx}$.*

13. $\sin xy = x + y$
14. $e^{xy} = 2y$

15. $x + y = \cos y$
16. $x + 2y = \sqrt{y}$

17. $\cos y^2 + x = e^y$
18. $y = \dfrac{x + 1}{y - 1}$

19. $x^3 = \dfrac{x + y}{x - y}$
20. $(xy + 1)^3 = x - y^2 + 8$

21. $6x^3 + 7y^3 = 13xy$
22. $\sin x \cos y = \sin x + \cos y$

23. $\sqrt{x^4 + y^2} = 5x + 2y^3$
24. $\sqrt{x + y^2} = \sin y$

25–30. Tangent lines *Carry out the following steps.*

a. Verify that the given point lies on the curve.
b. Determine an equation of the line tangent to the curve at the given point.

25. $x^2 + xy + y^2 = 7$; $(2, 1)$
26. $x^4 - x^2y + y^4 = 1$; $(-1, 1)$

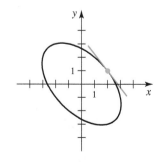
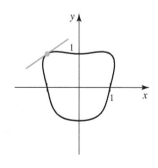

27. $\sin y + 5x = y^2$; $\left(\dfrac{\pi^2}{5}, \pi\right)$
28. $x^3 + y^3 = 2xy$; $(1, 1)$

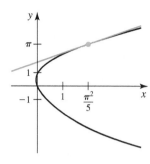
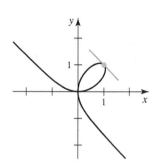

29. $\cos(x - y) + \sin y = \sqrt{2}$; $\left(\dfrac{\pi}{2}, \dfrac{\pi}{4}\right)$

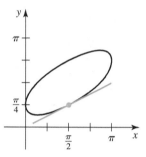

30. $(x^2 + y^2)^2 = \dfrac{25}{4}xy^2$; $(1, 2)$

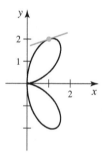

31–36. Second derivatives *Find $\dfrac{d^2y}{dx^2}$.*

31. $x + y^2 = 1$
32. $2x^2 + y^2 = 4$

33. $x + y = \sin y$
34. $x^4 + y^4 = 64$

35. $e^{2y} + x = y$
36. $\sin x + x^2y = 10$

37–44. Derivatives of functions with rational exponents *Find $\dfrac{dy}{dx}$.*

37. $y = x^{5/4}$
38. $y = \sqrt[3]{x^2 - x + 1}$

39. $y = (5x + 1)^{2/3}$
40. $y = e^x\sqrt{x^3}$

41. $y = \sqrt[4]{\dfrac{2x}{4x - 3}}$
42. $y = x(x + 1)^{1/3}$

43. $y = \sqrt[3]{(1 + x^{1/3})^2}$
44. $y = \dfrac{x}{\sqrt[5]{x} + x}$

45–50. Implicit differentiation with rational exponents *Determine the slope of the following curves at the given point.*

45. $\sqrt[3]{x} + \sqrt[3]{y^4} = 2$; $(1, 1)$
46. $x^{2/3} + y^{2/3} = 2$; $(1, 1)$

47. $x\sqrt[3]{y} + y = 10$; $(1, 8)$
48. $(x + y)^{2/3} = y$; $(4, 4)$

49. $xy + x^{3/2}y^{-1/2} = 2$; $(1, 1)$
50. $xy^{5/2} + x^{3/2}y = 12$; $(4, 1)$

Further Explorations

51. Explain why or why not Determine whether the following statements are true and give an explanation or counterexample.

    a. For any equation containing the variables x and y, the derivative dy/dx can be found by first using algebra to rewrite the equation in the form $y = f(x)$.

    b. For the equation of a circle of radius r, $x^2 + y^2 = r^2$, we have $\dfrac{dy}{dx} = -\dfrac{x}{y}$, for $y \neq 0$ and any real number $r > 0$.

    c. If $x = 1$, then by implicit differentiation, $1 = 0$.

    d. If $xy = 1$, then $y' = 1/x$.

52–54. Multiple tangent lines *Complete the following steps.*

    a. *Find equations of all lines tangent to the curve at the given value of x.*

    b. *Graph the tangent lines on the given graph.*

52. $x + y^3 - y = 1$; $x = 1$ **53.** $x + y^2 - y = 1$; $x = 1$

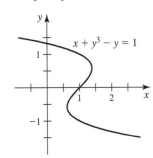

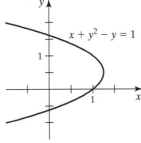

54. $4x^3 = y^2(4 - x)$; $x = 2$
(cissoid of Diocles)

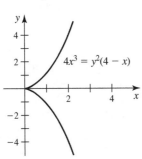

55. Witch of Agnesi Let $y(x^2 + 4) = 8$ (see figure).

    a. Use implicit differentiation to find $\dfrac{dy}{dx}$.

    b. Find equations of all lines tangent to the curve $y(x^2 + 4) = 8$ when $y = 1$.

    c. Solve the equation $y(x^2 + 4) = 8$ for y to find an explicit expression for y and then calculate $\dfrac{dy}{dx}$.

    d. Verify that the results of parts (a) and (c) are consistent.

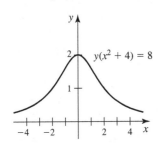

56. Vertical tangent lines

    a. Determine the points at which the curve $x + y^3 - y = 1$ has a vertical tangent line (see Exercise 52).

    b. Does the curve have any horizontal tangent lines? Explain.

57. Vertical tangent lines

    a. Determine the points where the curve $x + y^2 - y = 1$ has a vertical tangent line (see Exercise 53).

    b. Does the curve have any horizontal tangent lines? Explain.

58–59. Tangent lines for ellipses *Find the equations of the vertical and horizontal tangent lines of the following ellipses.*

58. $x^2 + 4y^2 + 2xy = 12$

59. $9x^2 + y^2 - 36x + 6y + 36 = 0$

60–64. Identifying functions from an equation *The following equations implicitly define one or more functions.*

    a. *Find $\dfrac{dy}{dx}$ using implicit differentiation.*

    b. *Solve the given equation for y to identify the implicitly defined functions $y = f_1(x), y = f_2(x), \ldots$.*

    c. *Use the functions found in part (b) to graph the given equation.*

60. $y^3 = ax^2$ (Neile's semicubical parabola)

61. $x + y^3 - xy = 1$ (*Hint:* Rewrite as $y^3 - 1 = xy - x$ and then factor both sides.)

62. $y^2 = \dfrac{x^2(4 - x)}{4 + x}$ (right strophoid)

63. $x^4 = 2(x^2 - y^2)$ (eight curve)

64. $y^2(x + 2) = x^2(6 - x)$ (trisectrix)

65–70. Normal lines *A normal line at a point P on a curve passes through P and is perpendicular to the line tangent to the curve at P (see figure). Use the following equations and graphs to determine an equation of the normal line at the given point. Illustrate your work by graphing the curve with the normal line.*

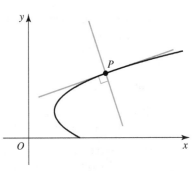

65. Exercise 25   **66.** Exercise 26   **67.** Exercise 27

68. Exercise 28   **69.** Exercise 29   **70.** Exercise 30

71–74. Visualizing tangent and normal lines

    a. *Determine an equation of the tangent line and normal line at the given point (x_0, y_0) on the following curves. (See instructions for Exercises 65–70.)*

    b. *Graph the tangent and normal lines on the given graph.*

71. $3x^3 + 7y^3 = 10y$; $(x_0, y_0) = (1, 1)$

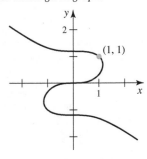

72. $x^4 = 2x^2 + 2y^2$;
$(x_0, y_0) = (2, 2)$
(kampyle of Eudoxus)

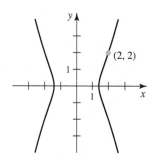

73. $(x^2 + y^2 - 2x)^2 = 2(x^2 + y^2)$;
$(x_0, y_0) = (2, 2)$
(limaçon of Pascal)

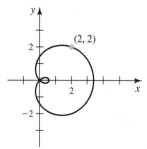

74. $(x^2 + y^2)^2 = \dfrac{25}{3}(x^2 - y^2)$;
$(x_0, y_0) = (2, -1)$
(lemniscate of Bernoulli)

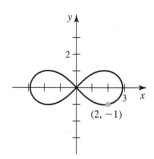

Applications

75. Cobb-Douglas production function The output of an economic system Q, subject to two inputs, such as labor L and capital K, is often modeled by the Cobb-Douglas production function $Q = cL^aK^b$. When $a + b = 1$, the case is called *constant returns to scale*. Suppose $Q = 1280$, $a = \dfrac{1}{3}$, $b = \dfrac{2}{3}$, and $c = 40$.

  a. Find the rate of change of capital with respect to labor, dK/dL.
  b. Evaluate the derivative in part (a) with $L = 8$ and $K = 64$.

76. Surface area of a cone The lateral surface area of a cone of radius r and height h (the surface area excluding the base) is $A = \pi r \sqrt{r^2 + h^2}$.

  a. Find dr/dh for a cone with a lateral surface area of $A = 1500\pi$.
  b. Evaluate this derivative when $r = 30$ and $h = 40$.

77. Volume of a spherical cap Imagine slicing through a sphere with a plane (sheet of paper). The smaller piece produced is called a spherical cap. Its volume is $V = \pi h^2(3r - h)/3$, where r is the radius of the sphere and h is the thickness of the cap.

  a. Find dr/dh for a sphere with a volume of $5\pi/3$.
  b. Evaluate this derivative when $r = 2$ and $h = 1$.

78. Volume of a torus The volume of a torus (doughnut or bagel) with an inner radius of a and an outer radius of b is $V = \pi^2(b + a)(b - a)^2/4$.

  a. Find db/da for a torus with a volume of $64\pi^2$.
  b. Evaluate this derivative when $a = 6$ and $b = 10$.

Additional Exercises

79–81. Orthogonal trajectories *Two curves are* **orthogonal** *to each other if their tangent lines are perpendicular at each point of intersection (recall that two lines are perpendicular to each other if their slopes are negative reciprocals). A family of curves forms* **orthogonal trajectories** *with another family of curves if each curve in one family is orthogonal to each curve in the other family. For example, the parabolas $y = cx^2$ form orthogonal trajectories with the family of ellipses $x^2 + 2y^2 = k$, where c and k are constants (see figure).*

Find dy/dx for each equation of the following pairs. Use the derivatives to explain why the families of curves form orthogonal trajectories.

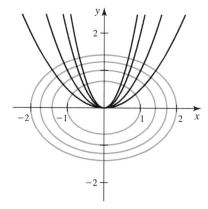

79. $y = mx$; $x^2 + y^2 = a^2$, where m and a are constants

80. $y = cx^2$; $x^2 + 2y^2 = k$, where c and k are constants

81. $xy = a$; $x^2 - y^2 = b$, where a and b are constants

82. Finding slope Find the slope of the curve $5\sqrt{x} - 10\sqrt{y} = \sin x$ at the point $(4\pi, \pi)$.

83. A challenging derivative Find $\dfrac{dy}{dx}$, where $(x^2 + y^2)(x^2 + y^2 + x) = 8xy^2$.

84. A challenging derivative Find $\dfrac{dy}{dx}$, where $\sqrt{3x^7 + y^2} = \sin^2 y + 100xy$.

85. A challenging second derivative Find $\dfrac{d^2y}{dx^2}$, where $\sqrt{y} + xy = 1$.

🔢 **86–89. Work carefully** *Proceed with caution when using implicit differentiation to find points at which a curve has a specified slope. For the following curves, find the points on the curve (if they exist) at which the tangent line is horizontal or vertical. Once you have found possible points, make sure they actually lie on the curve. Confirm your results with a graph.*

86. $y^2 - 3xy = 2$ **87.** $x^2(3y^2 - 2y^3) = 4$

88. $x^2(y - 2) - e^y = 0$ **89.** $x(1 - y^2) + y^3 = 0$

QUICK CHECK ANSWERS

1. $y = \sqrt{x}$ and $y = -\sqrt{x}$ **2.** $\dfrac{dy}{dx} = \dfrac{1}{2y}$

3. Only the x-coordinate is needed.

4. $\dfrac{d}{dx}(\sqrt{x}) = \dfrac{d}{dx}(x^{1/2}) = \dfrac{1}{2}x^{-1/2} = \dfrac{1}{2\sqrt{x}}$ ◄

3.9 Derivatives of Logarithmic and Exponential Functions

We return now to the major theme of this chapter: developing rules of differentiation for the standard families of functions. First, we discover how to differentiate the natural logarithmic function. From there, we treat general exponential and logarithmic functions.

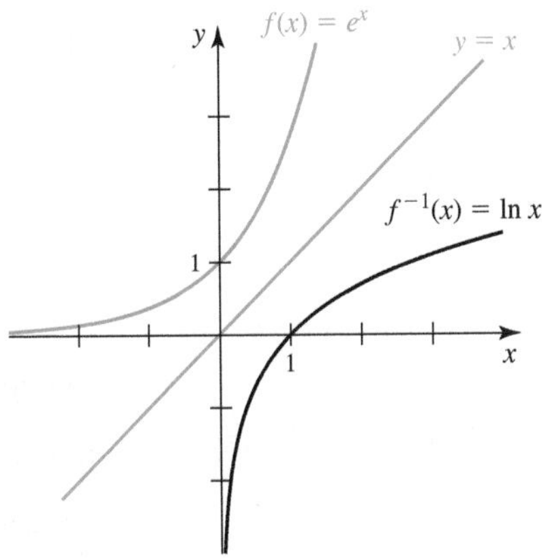

The Derivative of $y = \ln x$

Recall from Section 1.3 that the natural exponential function $f(x) = e^x$ is a one-to-one function on the interval $(-\infty, \infty)$. Therefore, it has an inverse, which is the natural logarithmic function $f^{-1}(x) = \ln x$. The domain of f^{-1} is the range of f, which is $(0, \infty)$. The graphs of f and f^{-1} are symmetric about the line $y = x$ (Figure 3.57). This inverse relationship has several important consequences, summarized as follows.

> **Inverse Properties for e^x and $\ln x$**
>
> **1.** $e^{\ln x} = x$, for $x > 0$, and $\ln(e^x) = x$, for all x.
>
> **2.** $y = \ln x$ if and only if $x = e^y$.
>
> **3.** For real numbers x and $b > 0$, $b^x = e^{\ln b^x} = e^{x \ln b}$.

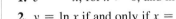

Figure 3.57

▶ A careful development of property (3) is given in Section 6.8.

QUICK CHECK 1 Simplify $e^{2 \ln x}$. Express 5^x using the base e. ◀

▶ Figure 3.57 also provides evidence that $\ln x$ is differentiable for $x > 0$: Its graph is smooth with no jumps or cusps.

With these preliminary observations, we now determine the derivative of $\ln x$. A theorem we prove in Section 3.10 says that because e^x is differentiable on its domain, its inverse $\ln x$ is also differentiable on its domain.

To find the derivative of $y = \ln x$, we begin with inverse property (2) and write $x = e^y$, where $x > 0$. The key step is to compute dy/dx with implicit differentiation. Using the Chain Rule to differentiate both sides of $x = e^y$ with respect to x, we have

$$x = e^y \qquad \text{\small $y = \ln x$ if and only if $x = e^y$}$$

$$1 = e^y \cdot \frac{dy}{dx} \qquad \text{\small Differentiate both sides with respect to x.}$$

$$\frac{dy}{dx} = \frac{1}{e^y} = \frac{1}{x}. \qquad \text{\small Solve for dy/dx and use $x = e^y$.}$$

Therefore,

$$\frac{d}{dx}(\ln x) = \frac{1}{x}.$$

Because the domain of the natural logarithm is $(0, \infty)$, this rule is limited to positive values of x (Figure 3.58a).

An important extension is obtained by considering the function $\ln |x|$, which is defined for all $x \neq 0$. By the definition of the absolute value,

▶ Recall that
$$|x| = \begin{cases} x & \text{if } x \geq 0 \\ -x & \text{if } x < 0. \end{cases}$$

$$\ln |x| = \begin{cases} \ln x & \text{if } x > 0 \\ \ln(-x) & \text{if } x < 0. \end{cases}$$

For $x > 0$, it follows immediately that

$$\frac{d}{dx}(\ln |x|) = \frac{d}{dx}(\ln x) = \frac{1}{x}.$$

When $x < 0$, a similar calculation using the Chain Rule reveals that

$$\frac{d}{dx}(\ln|x|) = \frac{d}{dx}(\ln(-x)) = \frac{1}{(-x)}(-1) = \frac{1}{x}.$$

Therefore, we have the result that the derivative of $\ln|x|$ is $\frac{1}{x}$, for $x \neq 0$ (Figure 3.58b).

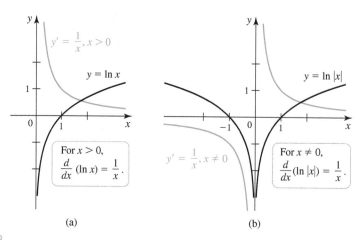

For $x > 0$,
$$\frac{d}{dx}(\ln x) = \frac{1}{x}.$$

For $x \neq 0$,
$$\frac{d}{dx}(\ln|x|) = \frac{1}{x}.$$

(a)   (b)

Figure 3.58

Taking these results one step further and using the Chain Rule to differentiate $\ln|u(x)|$, we obtain the following theorem.

> **THEOREM 3.17 Derivative of ln x**
>
> $$\frac{d}{dx}(\ln x) = \frac{1}{x}, \text{ for } x > 0 \qquad \frac{d}{dx}(\ln|x|) = \frac{1}{x}, \text{ for } x \neq 0$$
>
> If u is differentiable at x and $u(x) \neq 0$, then
>
> $$\frac{d}{dx}(\ln|u(x)|) = \frac{u'(x)}{u(x)}.$$

EXAMPLE 1 Derivatives involving ln x Find $\dfrac{dy}{dx}$ for the following functions.

a. $y = \ln 4x$ **b.** $y = x\ln x$ **c.** $y = \ln|\sec x|$ **d.** $y = \dfrac{\ln x^2}{x^2}$

SOLUTION

a. Using the Chain Rule,

$$\frac{dy}{dx} = \frac{d}{dx}(\ln 4x) = \frac{1}{4x} \cdot 4 = \frac{1}{x}.$$

An alternative method uses a property of logarithms before differentiating:

$$\frac{d}{dx}(\ln 4x) = \frac{d}{dx}(\ln 4 + \ln x) \quad \text{\small ln } xy = \text{\small ln } x + \text{\small ln } y$$

$$= 0 + \frac{1}{x} = \frac{1}{x}. \quad \text{\small ln 4 is a constant.}$$

▶ Because $\ln x$ and $\ln 4x$ differ by an additive constant ($\ln 4x = \ln x + \ln 4$), the derivatives of $\ln x$ and $\ln 4x$ are equal.

b. By the Product Rule,

$$\frac{dy}{dx} = \frac{d}{dx}(x\ln x) = 1 \cdot \ln x + x \cdot \frac{1}{x} = \ln x + 1.$$

c. Using the Chain Rule and the second part of Theorem 3.17,

$$\frac{dy}{dx} = \frac{1}{\sec x}\left(\frac{d}{dx}(\sec x)\right) = \frac{1}{\sec x}(\sec x \tan x) = \tan x.$$

d. The Quotient Rule and Chain Rule give

$$\frac{dy}{dx} = \frac{x^2\left(\dfrac{1}{x^2}\cdot 2x\right) - (\ln x^2)\,2x}{(x^2)^2} = \frac{2x - 2x\ln x^2}{x^4} = \frac{2(1 - \ln x^2)}{x^3}.$$

Related Exercises 9–22 ◄

QUICK CHECK 2 Find $\dfrac{d}{dx}(\ln x^p)$, where $x > 0$ and p is a rational number, in two ways: (1) using the Chain Rule and (2) by first using a property of logarithms. ◄

The Derivative of b^x

A rule similar to $\dfrac{d}{dx}(e^x) = e^x$ exists for computing the derivative of b^x, where $b > 0$. Because $b^x = e^{x \ln b}$ by inverse property (3), its derivative is

$$\frac{d}{dx}(b^x) = \frac{d}{dx}(e^{x\ln b}) = \underbrace{e^{x\ln b}}_{b^x}\cdot\ln b. \qquad \text{Chain Rule with } \frac{d}{dx}(x\ln b) = \ln b$$

Noting that $e^{x\ln b} = b^x$ results in the following theorem.

➤ Check that when $b = e$, Theorem 3.18 becomes

$$\frac{d}{dx}(e^x) = e^x.$$

> **THEOREM 3.18   Derivative of b^x**
> If $b > 0$ and $b \neq 1$, then for all x,
> $$\frac{d}{dx}(b^x) = b^x \ln b.$$

Notice that when $b > 1$, $\ln b > 0$ and the graph of $y = b^x$ has tangent lines with positive slopes for all x. When $0 < b < 1$, $\ln b < 0$ and the graph of $y = b^x$ has tangent lines with negative slopes for all x. In either case, the tangent line at $(0, 1)$ has slope $\ln b$ (Figure 3.59).

EXAMPLE 2   Derivatives with b^x Find the derivative of the following functions.

a. $f(x) = 3^x$ **b.** $g(t) = 108 \cdot 2^{t/12}$

SOLUTION

a. Using Theorem 3.18, $f'(x) = 3^x \ln 3$.

b.
$$g'(t) = 108\,\frac{d}{dt}(2^{t/12}) \qquad \text{Constant Multiple Rule}$$

$$= 108 \cdot \ln 2 \cdot 2^{t/12}\underbrace{\frac{d}{dt}\left(\frac{t}{12}\right)}_{1/12} \qquad \text{Chain Rule}$$

$$= 9\ln 2 \cdot 2^{t/12} \qquad \text{Simplify.}$$

Related Exercises 23–30 ◄

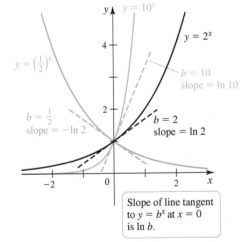

$y = 10^x$

$y = 2^x$

$b = 10$
slope $= \ln 10$

$y = \left(\frac{1}{2}\right)^x$

$b = \frac{1}{2}$
slope $= -\ln 2$

$b = 2$
slope $= \ln 2$

Slope of line tangent to $y = b^x$ at $x = 0$ is $\ln b$.

Figure 3.59

Table 3.6

Mother's Age	Incidence of Down Syndrome	Decimal Equivalent
30	1 in 900	0.00111
35	1 in 400	0.00250
36	1 in 300	0.00333
37	1 in 230	0.00435
38	1 in 180	0.00556
39	1 in 135	0.00741
40	1 in 105	0.00952
42	1 in 60	0.01667
44	1 in 35	0.02875
46	1 in 20	0.05000
48	1 in 16	0.06250
49	1 in 12	0.08333

(*Source:* E.G. Hook and A. Lindsjo, *The American Journal of Human Genetics*, 30, Jan 1978)

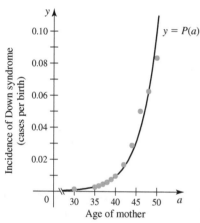

Figure 3.60

▷ The model in Example 3 was created using a method called *exponential regression*. The parameters A and B are chosen so that the function $P(a) = AB^a$ fits the data as closely as possible.

EXAMPLE 3   An exponential model Table 3.6 and Figure 3.60 show how the incidence of Down syndrome in newborn infants increases with the age of the mother. The data can be modeled with the exponential function $P(a) = \dfrac{1}{1{,}613{,}000} 1.2733^a$, where a is the age of the mother (in years) and $P(a)$ is the incidence (number of Down syndrome children per total births).

a. According to the model, at what age is the incidence of Down syndrome equal to 0.01 (that is, 1 in 100)?

b. Compute $P'(a)$.

c. Find $P'(35)$ and $P'(46)$, and interpret each.

SOLUTION

a. We let $P(a) = 0.01$ and solve for a:

$$0.01 = \frac{1}{1{,}613{,}000} 1.2733^a$$

$$\ln 16{,}130 = \ln\left(1.2733^a\right) \qquad \text{Multiply both sides by 1,613,000 and take logarithms of both sides.}$$

$$\ln 16{,}130 = a \ln 1.2733 \qquad \text{Property of logarithms}$$

$$a = \frac{\ln 16{,}130}{\ln 1.2733} \approx 40 \text{ (years old)}. \qquad \text{Solve for } a.$$

b. $P'(a) = \dfrac{1}{1{,}613{,}000} \dfrac{d}{da}(1.2733^a)$

$$= \frac{1}{1{,}613{,}000} 1.2733^a \ln 1.2733$$

$$\approx \frac{1}{6{,}676{,}000} 1.2733^a$$

c. The derivative measures the rate of change of the incidence with respect to age. For a 35-year-old woman,

$$P'(35) = \frac{1}{6{,}676{,}000} 1.2733^{35} \approx 0.0007,$$

which means the incidence increases at a rate of about 0.0007/year. By age 46, the rate of change is

$$P'(46) = \frac{1}{6{,}676{,}000} 1.2733^{46} \approx 0.01,$$

which is a significant increase over the rate of change of the incidence at age 35.

Related Exercises 31–33 ◀

QUICK CHECK 3 Suppose $A = 500(1.045)^t$. Compute $\dfrac{dA}{dt}$. ◀

The General Power Rule

As it stands now, the Power Rule for derivatives says that $\dfrac{d}{dx}(x^p) = px^{p-1}$, for rational powers p. The rule is now extended to all real powers.

> **THEOREM 3.19 General Power Rule**
> For real numbers p and for $x > 0$,
>
> $$\frac{d}{dx}(x^p) = px^{p-1}.$$
>
> Furthermore, if u is a positive differentiable function on its domain, then
>
> $$\frac{d}{dx}(u(x)^p) = p(u(x))^{p-1} \cdot u'(x).$$

Proof: For $x > 0$ and real numbers p, we have $x^p = e^{p \ln x}$ by inverse property (3). Therefore, the derivative of x^p is computed as follows:

$$\frac{d}{dx}(x^p) = \frac{d}{dx}(e^{p \ln x}) \qquad \text{Inverse property (3)}$$

$$= e^{p \ln x} \cdot \frac{p}{x} \qquad \text{Chain Rule, } \frac{d}{dx}(p \ln x) = \frac{p}{x}$$

$$= x^p \cdot \frac{p}{x} \qquad e^{p \ln x} = x^p$$

$$= px^{p-1}. \qquad \text{Simplify.}$$

We see that $\frac{d}{dx}(x^p) = px^{p-1}$ for all real powers p. The second part of the General Power Rule follows from the Chain Rule. ◄

EXAMPLE 4 Computing derivatives Find the derivative of the following functions.

a. $y = x^{\pi}$ **b.** $y = \pi^x$ **c.** $y = (x^2 + 4)^e$

SOLUTION

> ▶ Recall that power functions have the variable in the base, while exponential functions have the variable in the exponent.

a. With $y = x^{\pi}$, we have a power function with an irrational exponent; by the General Power Rule,

$$\frac{dy}{dx} = \pi x^{\pi - 1}, \text{ for } x > 0.$$

b. Here we have an exponential function with base $b = \pi$. By Theorem 3.18,

$$\frac{dy}{dx} = \pi^x \ln \pi.$$

c. The Chain Rule and General Power Rule are required:

$$\frac{dy}{dx} = e(x^2 + 4)^{e-1} \cdot 2x = 2ex\,(x^2 + 4)^{e-1}.$$

Because $x^2 + 4 > 0$, for all x, the result is valid for all x.

Related Exercises 34–44 ◄

Functions of the form $f(x) = (g(x))^{h(x)}$, where both g and h are nonconstant functions, are neither exponential functions nor power functions (they are sometimes called *tower functions*). To compute their derivatives, we use the identity $b^x = e^{x \ln b}$ to rewrite f with base e:

$$f(x) = (g(x))^{h(x)} = e^{h(x) \ln g(x)}.$$

This function carries the restriction $g(x) > 0$. The derivative of f is then computed using the methods developed in this section. A specific case is illustrated in the following example.

EXAMPLE 5 **General exponential functions** Let $f(x) = x^{\sin x}$, for $x \geq 0$.

a. Find $f'(x)$.   **b.** Evaluate $f'\left(\dfrac{\pi}{2}\right)$.

SOLUTION

a. The key step is to use $b^x = e^{x \ln b}$ to write f in the form

$$f(x) = x^{\sin x} = e^{(\sin x) \ln x}.$$

We now differentiate:

$$f'(x) = e^{(\sin x) \ln x} \frac{d}{dx}((\sin x) \ln x) \qquad \text{Chain Rule}$$

$$= \underbrace{e^{(\sin x) \ln x}}_{x^{\sin x}}\left((\cos x) \ln x + \frac{\sin x}{x}\right) \qquad \text{Product Rule}$$

$$= x^{\sin x}\left((\cos x) \ln x + \frac{\sin x}{x}\right).$$

b. Letting $x = \dfrac{\pi}{2}$, we find that

$$f'\left(\frac{\pi}{2}\right) = \left(\frac{\pi}{2}\right)^{\sin (\pi/2)}\left(\underbrace{\left(\cos \frac{\pi}{2}\right)}_{0} \ln \frac{\pi}{2} + \underbrace{\frac{\sin (\pi/2)}{\pi/2}}_{2/\pi}\right) \qquad \text{Substitute } x = \frac{\pi}{2}.$$

$$= \frac{\pi}{2}\left(0 + \frac{2}{\pi}\right) = 1.$$

Related Exercises 45–50 ◀

EXAMPLE 6 **Finding a horizontal tangent line** Determine whether the graph of $f(x) = x^x$, for $x > 0$, has any horizontal tangent lines.

SOLUTION A horizontal tangent occurs when $f'(x) = 0$. To find the derivative, we first write $f(x) = x^x = e^{x \ln x}$:

$$\frac{d}{dx}(x^x) = \frac{d}{dx}(e^{x \ln x})$$

$$= \underbrace{e^{x \ln x}}_{x^x}\left(1 \cdot \ln x + x \cdot \frac{1}{x}\right) \qquad \text{Chain Rule; Product Rule}$$

$$= x^x(\ln x + 1). \qquad \text{Simplify; } e^{x \ln x} = x^x.$$

The equation $f'(x) = 0$ implies that $x^x = 0$ or $\ln x + 1 = 0$. The first equation has no solution because $x^x = e^{x \ln x} > 0$, for all $x > 0$. We solve the second equation, $\ln x + 1 = 0$, as follows:

$$\ln x = -1$$
$$e^{\ln x} = e^{-1} \qquad \text{Exponentiate both sides.}$$
$$x = \frac{1}{e}. \qquad e^{\ln x} = x$$

Therefore, the graph of $f(x) = x^x$ (Figure 3.61) has a single horizontal tangent at $(e^{-1}, f(e^{-1})) \approx (0.368, 0.692)$.

Related Exercises 51–54 ◀

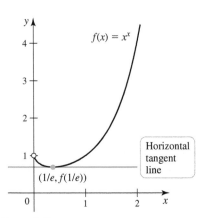

Figure 3.61

Derivatives of General Logarithmic Functions

The general exponential function $f(x) = b^x$ is one-to-one when $b > 0$ with $b \neq 1$. The inverse function $f^{-1}(x) = \log_b x$ is the logarithmic function with base b. The technique used to differentiate the natural logarithm applies to the general logarithmic function. We begin with the inverse relationship

$$y = \log_b x \Longleftrightarrow x = b^y, \text{ where } x > 0.$$

Differentiating both sides of $x = b^y$ with respect to x, we obtain

> An alternative proof of Theorem 3.20 uses the change-of-base formula $\log_b x = \dfrac{\ln x}{\ln b}$ (Section 1.3). Differentiating both sides of this equation gives the same result.

$$1 = b^y \ln b \cdot \frac{dy}{dx} \quad \text{Implicit differentiation}$$

$$\frac{dy}{dx} = \frac{1}{b^y \ln b} \quad \text{Solve for } \frac{dy}{dx}.$$

$$\frac{dy}{dx} = \frac{1}{x \ln b}. \quad b^y = x.$$

A similar argument applied to $y = \log_b |x|$ with $x < 0$ leads to the following theorem.

QUICK CHECK 4 Compute dy/dx for $y = \log_3 x.$ ◄

> **THEOREM 3.20   Derivative of $\log_b x$**
> If $b > 0$ and $b \neq 1$, then
>
> $$\frac{d}{dx}(\log_b x) = \frac{1}{x \ln b}, \text{ for } x > 0 \quad \text{and} \quad \frac{d}{dx}(\log_b |x|) = \frac{1}{x \ln b}, \text{ for } x \neq 0.$$

EXAMPLE 7   Derivatives with general logarithms Compute the derivative of the following functions.

a. $f(x) = \log_5 (2x + 1)$ **b.** $T(n) = n \log_2 n$

SOLUTION

a. We use Theorem 3.20 with the Chain Rule assuming $2x + 1 > 0$:

$$f'(x) = \frac{1}{(2x + 1) \ln 5} \cdot 2 = \frac{2}{\ln 5} \cdot \frac{1}{2x + 1}. \quad \text{Chain Rule}$$

> The function in Example 7b is used in computer science as an estimate of the computing time needed to carry out a *sorting algorithm* on a list of n items.

b. $$T'(n) = \log_2 n + n \cdot \frac{1}{n \ln 2} = \log_2 n + \frac{1}{\ln 2} \quad \text{Product Rule}$$

We can change bases and write the result in base e:

$$T'(n) = \frac{\ln n}{\ln 2} + \frac{1}{\ln 2} = \frac{\ln n + 1}{\ln 2}.$$

Related Exercises 55–60 ◄

QUICK CHECK 5 Show that the derivative computed in Example 7b can be expressed in base 2 as $T'(n) = \log_2 (en).$ ◄

Logarithmic Differentiation

Products, quotients, and powers of functions are usually differentiated using the derivative rules of the same name (perhaps combined with the Chain Rule). There are times, however, when the direct computation of a derivative is very tedious. Consider the function

> The properties of logarithms needed for logarithmic differentiation (where $x > 0$ and $y > 0$):
>
> **1.** $\ln xy = \ln x + \ln y$
>
> **2.** $\ln (x/y) = \ln x - \ln y$
>
> **3.** $\ln x^y = y \ln x$
>
> All three properties are used in Example 8.

$$f(x) = \frac{(x^3 - 1)^4 \sqrt{3x - 1}}{x^2 + 4}.$$

We would need the Quotient, Product, and Chain Rules just to compute $f'(x)$, and simplifying the result would require additional work. The properties of logarithms reviewed in Section 1.3 are useful for differentiating such functions.

EXAMPLE 8   Logarithmic differentiation Let $f(x) = \dfrac{(x^3 - 1)^4\sqrt{3x - 1}}{x^2 + 4}$ and compute $f'(x)$.

SOLUTION We begin by taking the natural logarithm of both sides and simplifying the result:

> In the event that $f \leq 0$ for some values of x, $\ln f(x)$ is not defined. In that case, we generally find the derivative of $|y| = |f(x)|$.

$$\ln (f(x)) = \ln \left(\frac{(x^3 - 1)^4\sqrt{3x - 1}}{x^2 + 4} \right)$$

$$= \ln (x^3 - 1)^4 + \ln \sqrt{3x - 1} - \ln (x^2 + 4) \qquad \log xy = \log x + \log y$$

$$= 4 \ln (x^3 - 1) + \tfrac{1}{2} \ln (3x - 1) - \ln (x^2 + 4). \qquad \log x^y = y \log x$$

We now differentiate both sides using the Chain Rule; specifically, the derivative of the left side is $\dfrac{d}{dx} (\ln f(x)) = \dfrac{f'(x)}{f(x)}$. Therefore,

$$\frac{f'(x)}{f(x)} = 4 \cdot \frac{1}{x^3 - 1} \cdot 3x^2 + \frac{1}{2} \cdot \frac{1}{3x - 1} \cdot 3 - \frac{1}{x^2 + 4} \cdot 2x.$$

Solving for $f'(x)$, we have

$$f'(x) = f(x)\left(\frac{12x^2}{x^3 - 1} + \frac{3}{2(3x - 1)} - \frac{2x}{x^2 + 4} \right).$$

Finally, we replace $f(x)$ with the original function:

$$f'(x) = \frac{(x^3 - 1)^4\sqrt{3x - 1}}{x^2 + 4} \left(\frac{12x^2}{x^3 - 1} + \frac{3}{2(3x - 1)} - \frac{2x}{x^2 + 4} \right).$$

Related Exercises 61–68 ◄

Logarithmic differentiation also provides an alternative method for finding derivatives of functions of the form $g(x)^{h(x)}$. The derivative of $f(x) = x^x$ (Example 6) is computed as follows, assuming $x > 0$:

$$f(x) = x^x$$

$$\ln (f(x)) = \ln (x^x) = x \ln x \qquad \text{Take logarithms of both sides; use properties.}$$

$$\frac{1}{f(x)} f'(x) = 1 \cdot \ln x + x \cdot \frac{1}{x} \qquad \text{Differentiate both sides.}$$

$$f'(x) = f(x)(\ln x + 1) \qquad \text{Solve for } f'(x) \text{ and simplify.}$$

$$f'(x) = x^x (\ln x + 1). \qquad \text{Replace } f(x) \text{ with } x^x.$$

This result agrees with Example 6. The decision about which method to use is largely one of preference.

SECTION 3.9 EXERCISES

Review Questions

1. Use $x = e^y$ to explain why $\dfrac{d}{dx} (\ln x) = \dfrac{1}{x}$, for $x > 0$.

2. Sketch the graph of $f(x) = \ln |x|$ and explain how the graph shows that $f'(x) = \dfrac{1}{x}$.

3. Show that $\dfrac{d}{dx} (\ln kx) = \dfrac{d}{dx} (\ln x)$, where $x > 0$ and k is a positive real number.

4. State the derivative rule for the exponential function $f(x) = b^x$. How does it differ from the derivative formula for e^x?

5. State the derivative rule for the logarithmic function $f(x) = \log_b x$. How does it differ from the derivative formula for $\ln x$?

6. Explain why $b^x = e^{x \ln b}$.

7. Express the function $f(x) = g(x)^{h(x)}$ in terms of the natural logarithmic and natural exponential functions (base e).

8. Explain the general procedure of logarithmic differentiation.

Basic Skills

9–22. Derivatives involving ln x *Find the following derivatives.*

9. $\dfrac{d}{dx}(\ln 7x)$ **10.** $\dfrac{d}{dx}(x^2 \ln x)$ **11.** $\dfrac{d}{dx}(\ln x^2)$

12. $\dfrac{d}{dx}(\ln 2x^8)$ **13.** $\dfrac{d}{dx}(\ln|\sin x|)$ **14.** $\dfrac{d}{dx}\left(\dfrac{\ln x^2}{x}\right)$

15. $\dfrac{d}{dx}\left(\ln\left(\dfrac{x+1}{x-1}\right)\right)$ **16.** $\dfrac{d}{dx}(e^x \ln x)$ **17.** $\dfrac{d}{dx}((x^2+1)\ln x)$

18. $\dfrac{d}{dx}(\ln|x^2-1|)$ **19.** $\dfrac{d}{dx}(\ln(\ln x))$ **20.** $\dfrac{d}{dx}(\ln(\cos^2 x))$

21. $\dfrac{d}{dx}\left(\dfrac{\ln x}{\ln x + 1}\right)$ **22.** $\dfrac{d}{dx}(\ln(e^x + e^{-x}))$

23–30. Derivatives of b^x *Find the derivatives of the following functions.*

23. $y = 8^x$ **24.** $y = 5^{3t}$ **25.** $y = 5 \cdot 4^x$

26. $y = 4^{-x}\sin x$ **27.** $y = x^3 \cdot 3^x$ **28.** $P = \dfrac{40}{1 + 2^{-t}}$

29. $A = 250(1.045)^{4t}$ **30.** $y = \ln 10^x$

31. Exponential model The following table shows the *time of useful consciousness* at various altitudes in the situation where a pressurized airplane suddenly loses pressure. The change in pressure drastically reduces available oxygen, and hypoxia sets in. The upper value of each time interval is roughly modeled by $T = 10 \cdot 2^{-0.274a}$, where T measures time in minutes and a is the altitude over 22,000 in thousands of feet ($a = 0$ corresponds to 22,000 ft).

Altitude (in ft)	Time of Useful Consciousness
22,000	5 to 10 min
25,000	3 to 5 min
28,000	2.5 to 3 min
30,000	1 to 2 min
35,000	30 to 60 s
40,000	15 to 20 s
45,000	9 to 15 s

a. A Learjet flying at 38,000 ft ($a = 16$) suddenly loses pressure when the seal on a window fails. According to this model, how long do the pilot and passengers have to deploy oxygen masks before they become incapacitated?

b. What is the average rate of change of T with respect to a over the interval from 24,000 to 30,000 ft (include units)?

c. Find the instantaneous rate of change dT/da, compute it at 30,000 ft, and interpret its meaning.

32. Magnitude of an earthquake The energy (in joules) released by an earthquake of magnitude M is given by the equation $E = 25,000 \cdot 10^{1.5M}$. (This equation can be solved for M to define the magnitude of a given earthquake; it is a refinement of the original Richter scale created by Charles Richter in 1935.)

a. Compute the energy released by earthquakes of magnitude 1, 2, 3, 4, and 5. Plot the points on a graph and join them with a smooth curve.

b. Compute dE/dM and evaluate it for $M = 3$. What does this derivative mean? (M has no units, so the units of the derivative are J per change in magnitude.)

33. Diagnostic scanning Iodine-123 is a radioactive isotope used in medicine to test the function of the thyroid gland. If a 350-microcurie (μCi) dose of iodine-123 is administered to a patient, the quantity Q left in the body after t hours is approximately $Q = 350\left(\frac{1}{2}\right)^{t/13.1}$.

a. How long does it take for the level of iodine-123 to drop to 10 μCi?

b. Find the rate of change of the quantity of iodine-123 at 12 hr, 1 day, and 2 days. What do your answers say about the rate at which iodine decreases as time increases?

34–44. General Power Rule *Use the General Power Rule where appropriate to find the derivative of the following functions.*

34. $f(x) = x^e$ **35.** $f(x) = 2^x$ **36.** $f(x) = 2x^{\sqrt{2}}$

37. $g(y) = e^y \cdot y^e$ **38.** $s(t) = \cos 2^t$

39. $r = e^{2\theta}$ **40.** $y = \ln(x^3 + 1)^\pi$

41. $f(x) = (2x - 3)x^{3/2}$ **42.** $y = \tan(x^{0.74})$

43. $f(x) = \dfrac{2^x}{2^x + 1}$ **44.** $f(x) = (2^x + 1)^\pi$

45–50. Derivatives of General Exponential Function (or g^h) *Find the derivative of each function and evaluate the derivative at the given value of a.*

45. $f(x) = x^{\cos x}$; $a = \pi/2$

46. $g(x) = x^{\ln x}$; $a = e$

47. $h(x) = x^{\sqrt{x}}$; $a = 4$

48. $f(x) = (x^2 + 1)^x$; $a = 1$

49. $f(x) = (\sin x)^{\ln x}$; $a = \pi/2$

50. $f(x) = (\tan x)^{x-1}$; $a = \pi/4$

51–54. Tangent lines and general exponential functions

51. Find an equation of the line tangent to $y = x^{\sin x}$ at the point $x = 1$.

52. Determine whether the graph of $y = x^{\sqrt{x}}$ has any horizontal tangent lines.

53. The graph of $y = (x^2)^x$ has two horizontal tangent lines. Find equations for both of them.

54. The graph of $y = x^{\ln x}$ has one horizontal tangent line. Find an equation for it.

55–60. Derivatives of logarithmic functions *Calculate the derivative of the following functions.*

55. $y = 4\log_3(x^2 - 1)$

56. $y = \log_{10} x$

57. $y = \cos x \ln(\cos^2 x)$

58. $y = \log_8 |\tan x|$

59. $y = \dfrac{1}{\log_4 x}$

60. $y = \log_2(\log_2 x)$

61–68. Logarithmic differentiation *Use logarithmic differentiation to evaluate $f'(x)$.*

61. $f(x) = \dfrac{(x + 1)^{10}}{(2x - 4)^8}$

62. $f(x) = x^2 \cos x$

63. $f(x) = x^{\ln x}$

64. $f(x) = \dfrac{\tan^{10} x}{(5x + 3)^6}$

65. $f(x) = \dfrac{(x + 1)^{3/2} (x - 4)^{5/2}}{(5x + 3)^{2/3}}$

66. $f(x) = \dfrac{x^8 \cos^3 x}{\sqrt{x - 1}}$

67. $f(x) = (\sin x)^{\tan x}$

68. $f(x) = \left(1 + \dfrac{1}{x}\right)^{2x}$

Further Explorations

69. Explain why or why not Determine whether the following statements are true and give an explanation or counterexample.

   a. The derivative of $\log_2 9 = 1/(9 \ln 2)$.

   b. $\ln (x + 1) + \ln (x - 1) = \ln (x^2 - 1)$, for all x.

   c. The exponential function 2^{x+1} can be written in base e as $e^{2 \ln (x+1)}$.

   d. $\dfrac{d}{dx} (\sqrt{2}^x) = x\sqrt{2}^{x-1}$.

   e. $\dfrac{d}{dx} (x^{\sqrt{2}}) = \sqrt{2}\, x^{\sqrt{2}-1}$.

70–73. Higher-order derivatives *Find the following higher-order derivatives.*

70. $\dfrac{d^3}{dx^3} (x^{4.2}) \Big|_{x=1}$

71. $\dfrac{d^2}{dx^2} (\log_{10} x)$

72. $\dfrac{d^n}{dx^n} (2^x)$

73. $\dfrac{d^3}{dx^3} (x^2 \ln x)$

74–76. Derivatives by different methods *Calculate the derivative of the following functions (i) using the fact that $b^x = e^{x \ln b}$ and (ii) by using logarithmic differentiation. Verify that both answers are the same.*

74. $y = (x^2 + 1)^x$ **75.** $y = 3^x$ **76.** $y = g(x)^{h(x)}$

77–82. Derivatives of logarithmic functions *Use the properties of logarithms to simplify the following functions before computing $f'(x)$.*

77. $f(x) = \ln (3x + 1)^4$

78. $f(x) = \ln \dfrac{2x}{(x^2 + 1)^3}$

79. $f(x) = \ln \sqrt{10x}$

80. $f(x) = \log_2 \dfrac{8}{\sqrt{x + 1}}$

81. $f(x) = \ln \dfrac{(2x - 1)(x + 2)^3}{(1 - 4x)^2}$

82. $f(x) = \ln (\sec^4 x \tan^2 x)$

⊞ 83. Tangent lines Find the equation of the line tangent to $y = 2^{\sin x}$ at $x = \pi/2$. Graph the function and the tangent line.

⊞ 84. Horizontal tangents The graph of $y = \cos x \cdot \ln \cos^2 x$ has seven horizontal tangent lines on the interval $[0, 2\pi]$. Find the approximate x-coordinates of all points at which these tangent lines occur.

85–92. General logarithmic and exponential derivatives *Compute the following derivatives. Use logarithmic differentiation where appropriate.*

85. $\dfrac{d}{dx} (x^{10x})$ **86.** $\dfrac{d}{dx} (2x)^{2x}$ **87.** $\dfrac{d}{dx} (x^{\cos x})$

88. $\dfrac{d}{dx} (x^\pi + \pi^x)$ **89.** $\dfrac{d}{dx} \left(1 + \dfrac{1}{x}\right)^x$ **90.** $\dfrac{d}{dx} (1 + x^2)^{\sin x}$

91. $\dfrac{d}{dx} (x^{(x^{10})})$ **92.** $\dfrac{d}{dx} (\ln x)^{x^2}$

Applications

93–96. Logistic growth *Scientists often use the logistic growth function* $P(t) = \dfrac{P_0 K}{P_0 + (K - P_0)e^{-r_0 t}}$ *to model population growth, where P_0 is the initial population at time $t = 0$, K is the **carrying capacity**, and r_0 is the base growth rate. The carrying capacity is a theoretical upper bound on the total population that the surrounding environment can support. The figure shows the sigmoid (S-shaped) curve associated with a typical logistic model.*

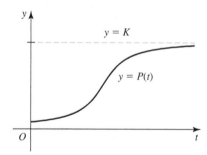

⊞ 93. Gone fishing When a reservoir is created by a new dam, 50 fish are introduced into the reservoir, which has an estimated carrying capacity of 8000 fish. A logistic model of the fish population is $P(t) = \dfrac{400{,}000}{50 + 7950e^{-0.5t}}$, where t is measured in years.

   a. Graph P using a graphing utility. Experiment with different windows until you produce an S-shaped curve characteristic of the logistic model. What window works well for this function?

   b. How long does it take the population to reach 5000 fish? How long does it take the population to reach 90% of the carrying capacity?

   c. How fast (in fish per year) is the population growing at $t = 0$? At $t = 5$?

   d. Graph P' and use the graph to estimate the year in which the population is growing fastest.

94. World population (part 1) The population of the world reached 6 billion in 1999 ($t = 0$). Assume Earth's carrying capacity is 15 billion and the base growth rate is $r_0 = 0.025$ per year.

    a. Write a logistic growth function for the world's population (in billions) and graph your equation on the interval $0 \le t \le 200$ using a graphing utility.

    b. What will the population be in the year 2020? When will it reach 12 billion?

95. World population (part 2) The *relative growth rate r* of a function f measures the rate of change of the function compared to its value at a particular point. It is computed as $r(t) = f'(t)/f(t)$.

    a. Confirm that the relative growth rate in 1999 ($t = 0$) for the logistic model in Exercise 94 is $r(0) = P'(0)/P(0) = 0.015$. This means the world's population was growing at 1.5% per year in 1999.

    b. Compute the relative growth rate of the world's population in 2010 and 2020. What appears to be happening to the relative growth rate as time increases?

    c. Evaluate $\lim\limits_{t\to\infty} r(t) = \lim\limits_{t\to\infty} \dfrac{P'(t)}{P(t)}$, where $P(t)$ is the logistic growth function from Exercise 94. What does your answer say about populations that follow a logistic growth pattern?

96. Population crash The logistic model can be used for situations in which the initial population P_0 is above the carrying capacity K. For example, consider a deer population of 1500 on an island where a fire has reduced the carrying capacity to 1000 deer.

    a. Assuming a base growth rate of $r_0 = 0.1$ and an initial population of $P(0) = 1500$, write a logistic growth function for the deer population and graph it. Based on the graph, what happens to the deer population in the long run?

    b. How fast (in deer per year) is the population declining immediately after the fire at $t = 0$?

    c. How long does it take the deer population to decline to 1200 deer?

97. Savings plan Beginning at age 30, a self-employed plumber saves $250 per month in a retirement account until he reaches age 65. The account offers 6% interest, compounded monthly. The balance in the account after t years is given by $A(t) = 50{,}000(1.005^{12t} - 1)$.

    a. Compute the balance in the account after 5, 15, 25, and 35 years. What is the average rate of change in the value of the account over the intervals $[5, 15]$, $[15, 25]$, and $[25, 35]$?

    b. Suppose the plumber started saving at age 25 instead of age 30. Find the balance at age 65 (after 40 years of investing).

    c. Use the derivative dA/dt to explain the surprising result in part (b) and to explain this advice: Start saving for retirement as early as possible.

Additional Exercises

98. Tangency question It is easily verified that the graphs of $y = x^2$ and $y = e^x$ have no points of intersection (for $x > 0$), and the graphs of $y = x^3$ and $y = e^x$ have two points of intersection. It follows that for some real number $2 < p < 3$, the graphs of $y = x^p$ and $y = e^x$ have exactly one point of intersection (for $x > 0$). Using analytical and/or graphical methods, determine p and the coordinates of the single point of intersection.

99. Tangency question It is easily verified that the graphs of $y = 1.1^x$ and $y = x$ have two points of intersection, and the graphs of $y = 2^x$ and $y = x$ have no points of intersection. It follows that for some real number $1 < p < 2$, the graphs of $y = p^x$ and $y = x$ have exactly one point of intersection. Using analytical and/or graphical methods, determine p and the coordinates of the single point of intersection.

100. Triple intersection Graph the functions $f(x) = x^3$, $g(x) = 3^x$, and $h(x) = x^x$ and find their common intersection point (exactly).

101–104. Calculating limits exactly *Use the definition of the derivative to evaluate the following limits.*

101. $\lim\limits_{x\to e} \dfrac{\ln x - 1}{x - e}$

102. $\lim\limits_{h\to 0} \dfrac{\ln(e^8 + h) - 8}{h}$

103. $\lim\limits_{h\to 0} \dfrac{(3 + h)^{3+h} - 27}{h}$

104. $\lim\limits_{x\to 2} \dfrac{5^x - 25}{x - 2}$

105. Derivative of $u(x)^{v(x)}$ Use logarithmic differentiation to prove that

$$\frac{d}{dx}\left(u(x)^{v(x)}\right) = u(x)^{v(x)}\left(\frac{dv}{dx}\ln u(x) + \frac{v(x)}{u(x)}\frac{du}{dx}\right).$$

106. Tangent lines and exponentials. Assume b is given with $b > 0$ and $b \ne 1$. Find the y-coordinate of the point on the curve $y = b^x$ at which the tangent line passes through the origin. (*Source: The College Mathematics Journal*, 28, Mar 1997)

QUICK CHECK ANSWERS

1. x^2 (for $x > 0$); $e^{x\ln 5}$ **2.** Either way, $\dfrac{d}{dx}(\ln x^p) = \dfrac{p}{x}$.

3. $\dfrac{dA}{dt} = 500(1.045)^t \cdot \ln 1.045 \approx 22(1.045)^t$ **4.** $\dfrac{dy}{dx} = \dfrac{1}{x\ln 3}$

5. $T'(n) = \log_2 n + \dfrac{1}{\ln 2} = \log_2 n + \dfrac{1}{\dfrac{\log_2 2}{\log_2 e}} =$

$\log_2 n + \log_2 e = \log_2(en)$ ◄

3.10 Derivatives of Inverse Trigonometric Functions

The inverse trigonometric functions, introduced in Section 1.4, are major players in calculus. In this section, we develop the derivatives of the six inverse trigonometric functions and begin an exploration of their many applications. The method for differentiating the inverses of more general functions is also presented.

Inverse Sine and Its Derivative

Recall from Section 1.4 that $y = \sin^{-1} x$ is the value of y such that $x = \sin y$, where $-\pi/2 \leq y \leq \pi/2$. The domain of $\sin^{-1} x$ is $\{x: -1 \leq x \leq 1\}$ (Figure 3.62). The derivative of $y = \sin^{-1} x$ follows by differentiating both sides of $x = \sin y$ with respect to x, simplifying, and solving for dy/dx:

$$x = \sin y \qquad \quad y = \sin^{-1} x \iff x = \sin y$$

$$\frac{d}{dx}(x) = \frac{d}{dx}(\sin y) \qquad \text{Differentiate with respect to } x.$$

$$1 = (\cos y)\frac{dy}{dx} \qquad \text{Chain Rule on the right side}$$

$$\frac{dy}{dx} = \frac{1}{\cos y}. \qquad \text{Solve for } \frac{dy}{dx}.$$

The identity $\sin^2 y + \cos^2 y = 1$ is used to express this derivative in terms of x. Solving for $\cos y$ yields

$$\cos y = \pm\sqrt{1 - \underbrace{\sin^2 y}_{x^2}} \quad x = \sin y \implies x^2 = \sin^2 y$$

$$= \pm\sqrt{1 - x^2}.$$

Because y is restricted to the interval $-\pi/2 \leq y \leq \pi/2$, we have $\cos y \geq 0$. Therefore, we choose the positive branch of the square root, and it follows that

$$\frac{dy}{dx} = \frac{d}{dx}(\sin^{-1} x) = \frac{1}{\sqrt{1 - x^2}}.$$

This result is consistent with the graph of $f(x) = \sin^{-1} x$ (Figure 3.63).

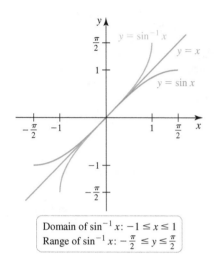

Domain of $\sin^{-1} x$: $-1 \leq x \leq 1$
Range of $\sin^{-1} x$: $-\frac{\pi}{2} \leq y \leq \frac{\pi}{2}$

Figure 3.62

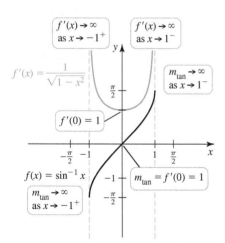

Figure 3.63

THEOREM 3.21   Derivative of Inverse Sine

$$\frac{d}{dx}(\sin^{-1} x) = \frac{1}{\sqrt{1 - x^2}}, \text{ for } -1 < x < 1$$

QUICK CHECK 1 Is $f(x) = \sin^{-1} x$ an even or odd function? Is $f'(x)$ an even or odd function? ◄

EXAMPLE 1   Derivatives involving the inverse sine Compute the following derivatives.

a. $\dfrac{d}{dx}(\sin^{-1}(x^2 - 1))$ **b.** $\dfrac{d}{dx}(\cos(\sin^{-1} x))$

SOLUTION We apply the Chain Rule for both derivatives.

a. $\dfrac{d}{dx}(\sin^{-1}\underbrace{(x^2 - 1)}_{u}) = \underbrace{\dfrac{1}{\sqrt{1 - (x^2 - 1)^2}}}_{\text{derivative of } \sin^{-1} u \text{ evaluated at } u = x^2 - 1} \cdot \underbrace{2x}_{u'(x)} = \dfrac{2x}{\sqrt{2x^2 - x^4}}$

b. $\dfrac{d}{dx}\left(\cos\left(\sin^{-1}x\right)\right) = \underbrace{-\sin\left(\sin^{-1}x\right)}_{\substack{\text{derivative of the}\\\text{outer function }\cos u\\\text{evaluated at }u=\sin^{-1}x}}\cdot\underbrace{\dfrac{1}{\sqrt{1-x^2}}}_{\substack{\text{derivative of the}\\\text{inner function }\sin^{-1}x}} = -\dfrac{x}{\sqrt{1-x^2}}$

where $u = \sin^{-1}x$

This result is valid for $-1 < x < 1$, where $\sin\left(\sin^{-1}x\right) = x$. *Related Exercises 7–12* ◄

Derivatives of Inverse Tangent and Secant

The derivatives of the inverse tangent and inverse secant are derived using a method similar to that used for the inverse sine. Once these three derivative results are known, the derivatives of the inverse cosine, cotangent, and cosecant follow immediately.

Inverse Tangent Recall from Section 1.4 that $y = \tan^{-1}x$ is the value of y such that $x = \tan y$, where $-\pi/2 < y < \pi/2$. The domain of $y = \tan^{-1}x$ is $\{x: -\infty < x < \infty\}$ (Figure 3.64). To find $\dfrac{dy}{dx}$, we differentiate both sides of $x = \tan y$ with respect to x and simplify:

$$x = \tan y \qquad {\scriptstyle y=\tan^{-1}x \;\Leftrightarrow\; x=\tan y}$$

$$\frac{d}{dx}(x) = \frac{d}{dx}(\tan y) \qquad {\scriptstyle \text{Differentiate with respect to }x.}$$

$$1 = \sec^2 y\cdot\frac{dy}{dx} \qquad {\scriptstyle \text{Chain Rule}}$$

$$\frac{dy}{dx} = \frac{1}{\sec^2 y}. \qquad {\scriptstyle \text{Solve for }\frac{dy}{dx}.}$$

To express this derivative in terms of x, we combine the trigonometric identity $\sec^2 y = 1 + \tan^2 y$ with $x = \tan y$ to obtain $\sec^2 y = 1 + x^2$. Substituting this result into the expression for dy/dx, it follows that

$$\frac{dy}{dx} = \frac{d}{dx}\left(\tan^{-1}x\right) = \frac{1}{1+x^2}.$$

The graphs of the inverse tangent and its derivative (Figure 3.65) are informative. Letting $f(x) = \tan^{-1}x$ and $f'(x) = \dfrac{1}{1+x^2}$, we see that $f'(0) = 1$, which is the maximum value of the derivative; that is, $\tan^{-1}x$ has its maximum slope at $x = 0$. As $x \to \infty$, $f'(x)$ approaches zero; likewise, as $x \to -\infty$, $f'(x)$ approaches zero.

> The result in Example 1b can also be obtained by noting that $\cos\left(\sin^{-1}x\right) = \sqrt{1-x^2}$ and differentiating this expression (Exercise 75).

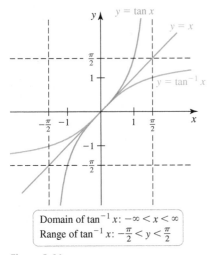

Domain of $\tan^{-1}x$: $-\infty < x < \infty$
Range of $\tan^{-1}x$: $-\frac{\pi}{2} < y < \frac{\pi}{2}$

Figure 3.64

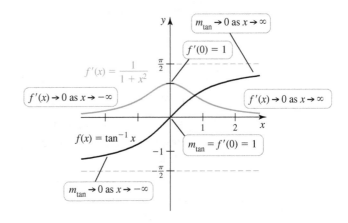

Figure 3.65

QUICK CHECK 2 How do the slopes of the lines tangent to the graph of $y = \tan^{-1}x$ behave as $x \to \infty$? ◄

Inverse Secant   Recall from Section 1.4 that $y = \sec^{-1} x$ is the value of y such that $x = \sec y$, where $0 \le y \le \pi$, with $y \ne \pi/2$. The domain of $y = \sec^{-1} x$ is $\{x: |x| \ge 1\}$ (Figure 3.66).

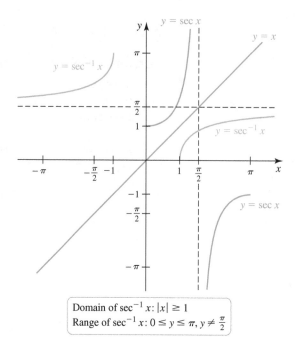

Domain of $\sec^{-1} x$: $|x| \ge 1$

Range of $\sec^{-1} x$: $0 \le y \le \pi$, $y \ne \dfrac{\pi}{2}$

Figure 3.66

The derivative of the inverse secant presents a new twist. Let $y = \sec^{-1} x$, or $x = \sec y$, and then differentiate both sides of $x = \sec y$ with respect to x:

$$1 = \sec y \tan y \frac{dy}{dx}.$$

Solving for $\dfrac{dy}{dx}$ produces

$$\frac{dy}{dx} = \frac{d}{dx}(\sec^{-1} x) = \frac{1}{\sec y \tan y}.$$

The final step is to express $\sec y \tan y$ in terms of x by using the identity $\sec^2 y = 1 + \tan^2 y$. Solving this equation for $\tan y$, we have

$$\tan y = \pm \sqrt{\underbrace{\sec^2 y}_{x^2} - 1} = \pm \sqrt{x^2 - 1}.$$

Two cases must be examined to resolve the sign on the square root:

• By the definition of $y = \sec^{-1} x$, if $x \ge 1$, then $0 \le y < \pi/2$ and $\tan y > 0$. In this case, we choose the positive branch and take $\tan y = \sqrt{x^2 - 1}$.

• However, if $x \le -1$, then $\pi/2 < y \le \pi$ and $\tan y < 0$. Now we choose the negative branch.

This argument accounts for the $\tan y$ factor in the derivative. For the $\sec y$ factor, we have $\sec y = x$. Therefore, the derivative of the inverse secant is

$$\frac{d}{dx}(\sec^{-1} x) = \begin{cases} \dfrac{1}{x\sqrt{x^2 - 1}} & \text{if } x > 1 \\[4mm] -\dfrac{1}{x\sqrt{x^2 - 1}} & \text{if } x < -1, \end{cases}$$

which is an awkward result. The absolute value helps here: Recall that $|x| = x$, if $x > 0$, and $|x| = -x$, if $x < 0$. It follows that

$$\frac{d}{dx}(\sec^{-1} x) = \frac{1}{|x|\sqrt{x^2 - 1}}, \text{ for } |x| > 1.$$

We see that the slope of the inverse secant function is always positive, which is consistent with this derivative result (Figure 3.66).

Derivatives of Other Inverse Trigonometric Functions The hard work is complete. The derivative of the inverse cosine results from the identity

$$\cos^{-1} x + \sin^{-1} x = \frac{\pi}{2}.$$

> This identity was proved in Example 5 of Section 1.4.

Differentiating both sides of this equation with respect to x, we find that

$$\frac{d}{dx}(\cos^{-1} x) + \underbrace{\frac{d}{dx}(\sin^{-1} x)}_{1/\sqrt{1 - x^2}} = \underbrace{\frac{d}{dx}\left(\frac{\pi}{2}\right)}_{0}.$$

Solving for $\frac{d}{dx}(\cos^{-1} x)$, the required derivative is

$$\frac{d}{dx}(\cos^{-1} x) = -\frac{1}{\sqrt{1 - x^2}}.$$

In a similar manner, the analogous identities

$$\cot^{-1} x + \tan^{-1} x = \frac{\pi}{2} \quad \text{and} \quad \csc^{-1} x + \sec^{-1} x = \frac{\pi}{2}$$

are used to show that the derivatives of $\cot^{-1} x$ and $\csc^{-1} x$ are the negative of the derivatives of $\tan^{-1} x$ and $\sec^{-1} x$, respectively (Exercise 73).

QUICK CHECK 3 Summarize how the derivatives of inverse trigonometric functions are related to the derivatives of the corresponding inverse cofunctions (for example, inverse tangent and inverse cotangent). ◄

> **THEOREM 3.22** **Derivatives of Inverse Trigonometric Functions**
>
> $$\frac{d}{dx}(\sin^{-1} x) = \frac{1}{\sqrt{1 - x^2}} \qquad \frac{d}{dx}(\cos^{-1} x) = -\frac{1}{\sqrt{1 - x^2}}, \text{ for } -1 < x < 1$$
>
> $$\frac{d}{dx}(\tan^{-1} x) = \frac{1}{1 + x^2} \qquad \frac{d}{dx}(\cot^{-1} x) = -\frac{1}{1 + x^2}, \text{ for } -\infty < x < \infty$$
>
> $$\frac{d}{dx}(\sec^{-1} x) = \frac{1}{|x|\sqrt{x^2 - 1}} \qquad \frac{d}{dx}(\csc^{-1} x) = -\frac{1}{|x|\sqrt{x^2 - 1}}, \text{ for } |x| > 1$$

EXAMPLE 2 **Derivatives of inverse trigonometric functions**

a. Evaluate $f'(2\sqrt{3})$, where $f(x) = x \tan^{-1}(x/2)$.

b. Find an equation of the line tangent to the graph of $g(x) = \sec^{-1} 2x$ at the point $(1, \pi/3)$.

SOLUTION

a. $f'(x) = 1 \cdot \tan^{-1}\frac{x}{2} + x\underbrace{\frac{1}{1 + (x/2)^2} \cdot \frac{1}{2}}_{\frac{d}{dx}(\tan^{-1}(x/2))}$ Product Rule and Chain Rule

$$= \tan^{-1}\frac{x}{2} + \frac{2x}{4 + x^2}$$ Simplify.

We evaluate f' at $x = 2\sqrt{3}$ and note that $\tan^{-1}\sqrt{3} = \pi/3$:

$$f'(2\sqrt{3}) = \tan^{-1}\sqrt{3} + \frac{2(2\sqrt{3})}{4 + (2\sqrt{3})^2} = \frac{\pi}{3} + \frac{\sqrt{3}}{4}.$$

b. The slope of the tangent line at $(1, \pi/3)$ is $g'(1)$. Using the Chain Rule, we have

$$g'(x) = \frac{d}{dx}(\sec^{-1} 2x) = \frac{2}{|2x|\sqrt{4x^2 - 1}} = \frac{1}{|x|\sqrt{4x^2 - 1}}.$$

It follows that $g'(1) = 1/\sqrt{3}$. An equation of the tangent line is

$$y - \frac{\pi}{3} = \frac{1}{\sqrt{3}}(x - 1) \quad \text{or} \quad y = \frac{1}{\sqrt{3}}x + \frac{\pi}{3} - \frac{1}{\sqrt{3}}.$$

Related Exercises 13–34 ◄

EXAMPLE 3   Shadows in a ballpark As the sun descends behind the 150-ft grandstand of a baseball stadium, the shadow of the stadium moves across the field (Figure 3.67). Let ℓ be the line segment between the edge of the shadow and the sun, and let θ be the angle of elevation of the sun—the angle between ℓ and the horizontal. The length of the shadow s is the distance between the edge of the shadow and the base of the grandstand.

a. Express θ as a function of the shadow length s.

b. Compute $d\theta/ds$ when $s = 200$ ft and explain what this rate of change measures.

SOLUTION

a. The tangent of θ is

$$\tan \theta = \frac{150}{s},$$

where $s > 0$. Taking the inverse tangent of both sides of this equation, we find that

$$\theta = \tan^{-1}\frac{150}{s}.$$

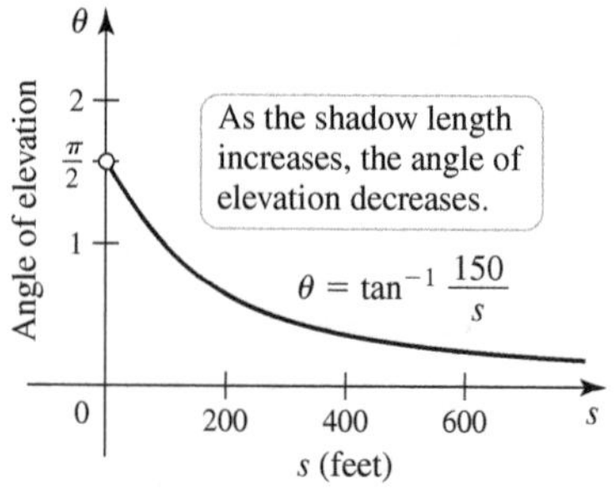

As shown in Figure 3.68, as the shadow length approaches zero, the sun's angle of elevation θ approaches $\pi/2$ ($\theta = \pi/2$ means the sun is overhead). As the shadow length increases, θ decreases and approaches zero.

b. Using the Chain Rule, we have

$$\frac{d\theta}{ds} = \frac{1}{1 + (150/s)^2}\frac{d}{ds}\left(\frac{150}{s}\right) \qquad \text{Chain Rule: } \frac{d}{du}(\tan^{-1} u) = \frac{1}{1 + u^2}$$

$$= \frac{1}{1 + (150/s)^2}\left(-\frac{150}{s^2}\right) \qquad \text{Evaluate the derivative.}$$

$$= -\frac{150}{s^2 + 22{,}500}. \qquad \text{Simplify.}$$

Notice that $d\theta/ds$ is negative for all values of s, which means longer shadows are associated with smaller angles of elevation (Figure 3.68). At $s = 200$ ft, we have

$$\left.\frac{d\theta}{ds}\right|_{s=200} = -\frac{150}{200^2 + 150^2} = -0.0024 \frac{\text{rad}}{\text{ft}}.$$

When the length of the shadow is $s = 200$ ft, the angle of elevation is changing at a rate of -0.0024 rad/ft, or $-0.138°/$ft.

Related Exercises 35–36 ◄

QUICK CHECK 4 Example 3 makes the claim that $d\theta/ds = -0.0024$ rad/ft is equivalent to $-0.138°/$ft. Verify this claim. ◄

Figure 3.67

As the shadow length increases, the angle of elevation decreases.

$\theta = \tan^{-1}\dfrac{150}{s}$

Figure 3.68

Derivatives of Inverse Functions in General

We found the derivatives of the inverse trigonometric functions using implicit differentiation. However, this approach does not always work. For example, suppose we know only f and its derivative f' and want to evaluate the derivative of f^{-1}. The key to finding the derivative of the inverse function lies in the symmetry of the graphs of f and f^{-1}.

EXAMPLE 4   **Linear functions, inverses, and derivatives**   Consider the general linear function $y = f(x) = mx + b$, where $m \neq 0$ and b are constants.

a. Write the inverse of f in the form $y = f^{-1}(x)$.

b. Find the derivative of the inverse $\dfrac{d}{dx}(f^{-1}(x))$.

c. Consider the specific case $f(x) = 2x - 6$. Graph f and f^{-1}, and find the slope of each line.

SOLUTION

a. Solving $y = mx + b$ for x, we find that $mx = y - b$, or

$$x = \frac{y}{m} - \frac{b}{m}.$$

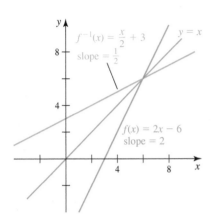

Figure 3.69

Writing this function in the form $y = f^{-1}(x)$ (by reversing the roles of x and y), we have

$$y = f^{-1}(x) = \frac{x}{m} - \frac{b}{m},$$

which describes a line with slope $1/m$.

b. The derivative of f^{-1} is

$$(f^{-1})'(x) = \frac{1}{m} = \frac{1}{f'(x)}.$$

Notice that $f'(x) = m$, so the derivative of f^{-1} is the reciprocal of f'.

c. In the case that $f(x) = 2x - 6$, we have $f^{-1}(x) = x/2 + 3$. The graphs of these two lines are symmetric about the line $y = x$ (Figure 3.69). Furthermore, the slope of the line $y = f(x)$ is 2 and the slope of $y = f^{-1}(x)$ is $\frac{1}{2}$; that is, the slopes (and, therefore, the derivatives) are reciprocals of each other.

Related Exercises 37–39 ◄

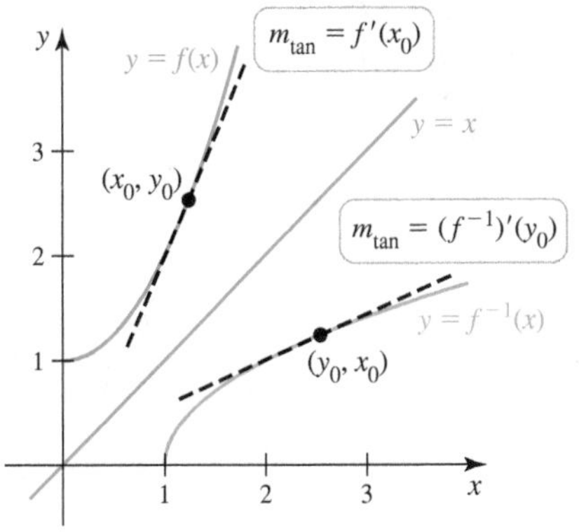

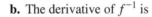

The reciprocal property obeyed by f' and $(f^{-1})'$ in Example 4 holds for all functions with inverses. Figure 3.70 shows the graphs of a typical one-to-one function and its inverse. It also shows a pair of symmetric points—(x_0, y_0) on the graph of f and (y_0, x_0) on the graph of f^{-1}—along with the tangent lines at these points. Notice that as the lines tangent to the graph of f get steeper (as x increases), the corresponding lines tangent to the graph of f^{-1} get less steep. The next theorem makes this relationship precise.

Figure 3.70

▶ The result of Theorem 3.23 is also written in the form

$$(f^{-1})'(f(x_0)) = \frac{1}{f'(x_0)}$$

or

$$(f^{-1})'(y_0) = \frac{1}{f'(f^{-1}(y_0))}.$$

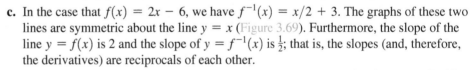

THEOREM 3.23   **Derivative of the Inverse Function**

Let f be differentiable and have an inverse on an interval I. If x_0 is a point of I at which $f'(x_0) \neq 0$, then f^{-1} is differentiable at $y_0 = f(x_0)$ and

$$(f^{-1})'(y_0) = \frac{1}{f'(x_0)}, \text{ where } y_0 = f(x_0).$$

To understand this theorem, suppose that (x_0, y_0) is a point on the graph of f, which means that (y_0, x_0) is the corresponding point on the graph of f^{-1}. Then the slope of the line tangent to the graph of f^{-1} at the point (y_0, x_0) is the reciprocal of the slope of the line tangent to the graph of f at the point (x_0, y_0). Importantly, the theorem says that we can evaluate the derivative of the inverse function without finding the inverse function itself.

Proof: Before doing a short calculation, we note two facts:

• At a point x_0 where f is differentiable, $y_0 = f(x_0)$ and $x_0 = f^{-1}(y_0)$.
• As a differentiable function, f is continuous at x_0 (Theorem 3.1), which implies that f^{-1} is continuous at y_0 (Theorem 2.14). Therefore, as $y \to y_0$, $x \to x_0$.

Using the definition of the derivative, we have

$$(f^{-1})'(y_0) = \lim_{y \to y_0} \frac{f^{-1}(y) - f^{-1}(y_0)}{y - y_0} \qquad \text{Definition of derivative of } f^{-1}$$

$$= \lim_{x \to x_0} \frac{x - x_0}{f(x) - f(x_0)} \qquad y = f(x) \text{ and } x = f^{-1}(y); \ x \to x_0 \text{ as } y \to y_0$$

$$= \lim_{x \to x_0} \frac{1}{\dfrac{f(x) - f(x_0)}{x - x_0}} \qquad \frac{a}{b} = \frac{1}{b/a}$$

$$= \frac{1}{f'(x_0)}. \qquad \text{Definition of derivative of } f$$

QUICK CHECK 5 Sketch the graphs of $y = \sin x$ and $y = \sin^{-1} x$. Then verify that Theorem 3.23 holds at the point $(0, 0)$. ◄

We have shown that $(f^{-1})'(y_0)$ exists (f^{-1} is differentiable at y_0) and that it equals the reciprocal of $f'(x_0)$. ◄

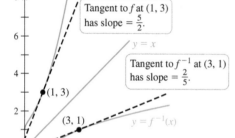

Figure 3.71

EXAMPLE 5   Derivative of an inverse function The function $f(x) = \sqrt{x} + x^2 + 1$ is one-to-one, for $x \geq 0$, and has an inverse on that interval. Find the slope of the curve $y = f^{-1}(x)$ at the point $(3, 1)$.

SOLUTION The point $(1, 3)$ is on the graph of f; therefore, $(3, 1)$ is on the graph of f^{-1}. In this case, the slope of the curve $y = f^{-1}(x)$ at the point $(3, 1)$ is the reciprocal of the slope of the curve $y = f(x)$ at $(1, 3)$ (Figure 3.71). Note that $f'(x) = \dfrac{1}{2\sqrt{x}} + 2x$, which means that $f'(1) = \dfrac{1}{2} + 2 = \dfrac{5}{2}$. Therefore,

$$(f^{-1})'(3) = \frac{1}{f'(1)} = \frac{1}{5/2} = \frac{2}{5}.$$

Observe that it is not necessary to find a formula for f^{-1} to evaluate its derivative at a point.

Related Exercises 40–50 ◄

EXAMPLE 6   Derivatives of an inverse function Use the values of a one-to-one differentiable function f in Table 3.7 to compute the indicated derivatives or state that the derivative cannot be determined.

Table 3.7

x	-1	0	1	2	3
$f(x)$	2	3	5	6	7
$f'(x)$	$1/2$	2	$3/2$	1	$2/3$

a. $(f^{-1})'(5)$ **b.** $(f^{-1})'(2)$ **c.** $(f^{-1})'(1)$

SOLUTION We use the realtionship $(f^{-1})'(y_0) = \dfrac{1}{f'(x_0)}$, where $y_0 = f(x_0)$.

a. In this case, $y_0 = f(x_0) = 5$. Using Table 3.7, we see that $x_0 = 1$ and $f'(1) = \dfrac{3}{2}$. Therefore, $(f^{-1})'(5) = \dfrac{1}{f'(1)} = \dfrac{2}{3}$.

b. In this case, $y_0 = f(x_0) = 2$, which implies that $x_0 = -1$ and $f'(-1) = \dfrac{1}{2}$.
Therefore, $(f^{-1})'(2) = \dfrac{1}{f'(-1)} = 2$.

c. With $y_0 = f(x_0) = 1$, Table 3.7 does not supply a value of x_0. Therefore, neither $f'(x_0)$ nor $(f^{-1})'(1)$ can be determined.

Related Exercises 51–52 ◄

SECTION 3.10 EXERCISES

Review Questions

1. State the derivative formulas for $\sin^{-1} x$, $\tan^{-1} x$, and $\sec^{-1} x$.

2. What is the slope of the line tangent to the graph of $y = \sin^{-1} x$ at $x = 0$?

3. What is the slope of the line tangent to the graph of $y = \tan^{-1} x$ at $x = -2$?

4. How are the derivatives of $\sin^{-1} x$ and $\cos^{-1} x$ related?

5. Suppose f is a one-to-one function with $f(2) = 8$ and $f'(2) = 4$. What is the value of $(f^{-1})'(8)$?

6. Explain how to find $(f^{-1})'(y_0)$, given that $y_0 = f(x_0)$.

Basic Skills

7–12. Derivatives of inverse sine *Evaluate the derivatives of the following functions.*

7. $f(x) = \sin^{-1} 2x$

8. $f(x) = x \sin^{-1} x$

9. $f(w) = \cos(\sin^{-1} 2w)$

10. $f(x) = \sin^{-1}(\ln x)$

11. $f(x) = \sin^{-1}(e^{-2x})$

12. $f(x) = \sin^{-1}(e^{\sin x})$

13–30. Derivatives *Evaluate the derivatives of the following functions.*

13. $f(x) = \tan^{-1} 10x$

14. $f(x) = x \cot^{-1}(x/3)$

15. $f(y) = \tan^{-1}(2y^2 - 4)$

16. $g(z) = \tan^{-1}(1/z)$

17. $f(z) = \cot^{-1} \sqrt{z}$

18. $f(x) = \sec^{-1} \sqrt{x}$

19. $f(x) = \cos^{-1}(1/x)$

20. $f(t) = (\cos^{-1} t)^2$

21. $f(u) = \csc^{-1}(2u + 1)$

22. $f(t) = \ln(\tan^{-1} t)$

23. $f(y) = \cot^{-1}(1/(y^2 + 1))$

24. $f(w) = \sin(\sec^{-1} 2w)$

25. $f(x) = \sec^{-1}(\ln x)$

26. $f(x) = \tan^{-1}(e^{4x})$

27. $f(x) = \csc^{-1}(\tan e^x)$

28. $f(x) = \sin(\tan^{-1}(\ln x))$

29. $f(s) = \cot^{-1}(e^s)$

30. $f(x) = 1/\tan^{-1}(x^2 + 4)$

31–34. Tangent lines *Find an equation of the line tangent to the graph of f at the given point.*

31. $f(x) = \tan^{-1} 2x$; $(1/2, \pi/4)$

32. $f(x) = \sin^{-1}(x/4)$; $(2, \pi/6)$

33. $f(x) = \cos^{-1} x^2$; $(1/\sqrt{2}, \pi/3)$

34. $f(x) = \sec^{-1}(e^x)$; $(\ln 2, \pi/3)$

ℹ 35. Angular size A boat sails directly toward a 150-meter skyscraper that stands on the edge of a harbor. The angular size θ of the building is the angle formed by lines from the top and bottom of the building to the observer (see figure).

a. What is the rate of change of the angular size $d\theta/dx$ when the boat is $x = 500$ m from the building?

b. Graph $d\theta/dx$ as a function of x and determine the point at which the angular size changes most rapidly.

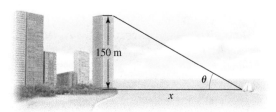

ℹ 36. Angle of elevation A small plane, moving at 70 m/s, flies horizontally on a line 400 meters directly above an observer. Let θ be the angle of elevation of the plane (see figure).

a. What is the rate of change of the angle of elevation $d\theta/dx$ when the plane is $x = 500$ m past the observer?

b. Graph $d\theta/dx$ as a function of x and determine the point at which θ changes most rapidly.

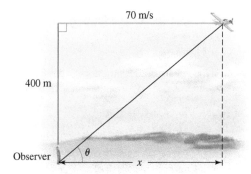

37–42. Derivatives of inverse functions at a point *Find the derivative of the inverse of the following functions at the specified point on the graph of the inverse function. You do not need to find f^{-1}.*

37. $f(x) = 3x + 4$; $(16, 4)$

38. $f(x) = \frac{1}{2}x + 8$; $(10, 4)$

39. $f(x) = -5x + 4$; $(-1, 1)$

40. $f(x) = x^2 + 1$, for $x \geq 0$; $(5, 2)$

41. $f(x) = \tan x;\ (1, \pi/4)$

42. $f(x) = x^2 - 2x - 3,$ for $x \le 1;\ (12, -3)$

43–46. Slopes of tangent lines *Given the function f, find the slope of the line tangent to the graph of f^{-1} at the specified point on the graph of f^{-1}.*

43. $f(x) = \sqrt{x};\ (2, 4)$

44. $f(x) = x^3;\ (8, 2)$

45. $f(x) = (x + 2)^2;\ (36, 4)$

46. $f(x) = -x^2 + 8;\ (7, 1)$

47–50. Derivatives and inverse functions

47. Find $(f^{-1})'(3)$ if $f(x) = x^3 + x + 1$.

48. Find the slope of the curve $y = f^{-1}(x)$ at $(4, 7)$ if the slope of the curve $y = f(x)$ at $(7, 4)$ is $\frac{2}{3}$.

49. Suppose the slope of the curve $y = f^{-1}(x)$ at $(4, 7)$ is $\frac{4}{5}$. Find $f'(7)$.

50. Suppose the slope of the curve $y = f(x)$ at $(4, 7)$ is $\frac{1}{5}$. Find $(f^{-1})'(7)$.

51–52. Derivatives of inverse functions from a table *Use the following tables to determine the indicated derivatives or state that the derivative cannot be determined.*

51.

x	-2	-1	0	1	2
$f(x)$	2	3	4	6	7
$f'(x)$	1	1/2	2	3/2	1

a. $(f^{-1})'(4)$ **b.** $(f^{-1})'(6)$ **c.** $(f^{-1})'(1)$ **d.** $f'(1)$

52.

x	-4	-2	0	2	4
$f(x)$	0	1	2	3	4
$f'(x)$	5	4	3	2	1

a. $f'(f(0))$ **b.** $(f^{-1})'(0)$
c. $(f^{-1})'(1)$ **d.** $(f^{-1})'(f(4))$

Further Explorations

53. Explain why or why not Determine whether the following statements are true and give an explanation or counterexample.

a. $\dfrac{d}{dx}(\sin^{-1} x + \cos^{-1} x) = 0$.

b. $\dfrac{d}{dx}(\tan^{-1} x) = \sec^2 x$.

c. The lines tangent to the graph of $y = \sin^{-1} x$ on the interval $[-1, 1]$ have a minimum slope of 1.

d. The lines tangent to the graph of $y = \sin x$ on the interval $[-\pi/2, \pi/2]$ have a maximum slope of 1.

e. If $f(x) = 1/x$, then $(f^{-1})'(x) = -1/x^2$.

54–57. Graphing f and f'
a. *Graph f with a graphing utility.*
b. *Compute and graph f'.*
c. *Verify that the zeros of f' correspond to points at which f has a horizontal tangent line.*

54. $f(x) = (x - 1)\sin^{-1} x$ on $[-1, 1]$

55. $f(x) = (x^2 - 1)\sin^{-1} x$ on $[-1, 1]$

56. $f(x) = (\sec^{-1} x)/x$ on $[1, \infty)$

57. $f(x) = e^{-x}\tan^{-1} x$ on $[0, \infty)$

58. Graphing with inverse trigonometric functions

a. Graph the function $f(x) = \dfrac{\tan^{-1} x}{x^2 + 1}$.

b. Compute and graph f' and determine (perhaps approximately) the points at which $f'(x) = 0$.

c. Verify that the zeros of f' correspond to points at which f has a horizontal tangent line.

59–66. Derivatives of inverse functions *Consider the following functions (on the given interval, if specified). Find the inverse function, express it as a function of x, and find the derivative of the inverse function.*

59. $f(x) = 3x - 4$

60. $f(x) = |x + 2|,$ for $x \le -2$

61. $f(x) = x^2 - 4,$ for $x > 0$

62. $f(x) = \dfrac{x}{x + 5}$

63. $f(x) = \sqrt{x + 2},$ for $x \ge -2$

64. $f(x) = x^{2/3},$ for $x > 0$

65. $f(x) = x^{-1/2},$ for $x > 0$

66. $f(x) = x^3 + 3$

Applications

67. Towing a boat A boat is towed toward a dock by a cable attached to a winch that stands 10 feet above the water level (see figure). Let θ be the angle of elevation of the winch and let ℓ be the length of the cable as the boat is towed toward the dock.

a. Show that the rate of change of θ with respect to ℓ is
$$\frac{d\theta}{d\ell} = \frac{-10}{\ell\sqrt{\ell^2 - 100}}.$$

b. Compute $\dfrac{d\theta}{d\ell}$ when $\ell = 50, 20,$ and 11 ft.

c. Find $\lim\limits_{\ell \to 10^+} \dfrac{d\theta}{d\ell}$ and explain what happens as the last foot of cable is reeled in (note that the boat is at the dock when $\ell = 10$).

d. It is evident from the figure that θ increases as the boat is towed to the dock. Why, then, is $d\theta/d\ell$ negative?

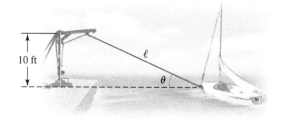

68. Tracking a dive A biologist standing at the bottom of an 80-foot vertical cliff watches a peregrine falcon dive from the top of the cliff at a 45° angle from the horizontal (see figure).

    a. Express the angle of elevation θ from the biologist to the falcon as a function of the height h of the bird above the ground. (*Hint:* The vertical distance between the top of the cliff and the falcon is $80 - h$.)

    b. What is the rate of change of θ with respect to the bird's height when it is 60 feet above the ground?

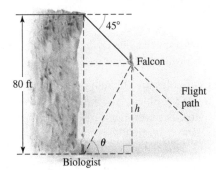

69. Angle to a particle, part I A particle travels clockwise on a circular path of diameter D, monitored by a sensor on the circle at point P; the other endpoint of the diameter on which the sensor lies is Q (see figure). Let θ be the angle between the diameter PQ and the line from the sensor to the particle. Let c be the length of the chord from the particle's position to Q.

    a. Calculate $d\theta/dc$.

    b. Evaluate $\left.\dfrac{d\theta}{dc}\right|_{c=0}$.

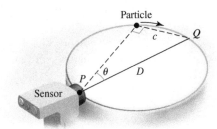

70. Angle to a particle, part II The figure in Exercise 69 shows the particle traveling away from the sensor, which may have influenced your solution (we expect you used the inverse sine function). Suppose instead that the particle approaches the sensor (see figure). How would this change the solution? Explain the differences in the two answers.

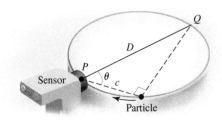

Additional Exercises

71. Derivative of the inverse sine Find the derivative of the inverse sine function using Theorem 3.23.

72. Derivative of the inverse cosine Find the derivative of the inverse cosine function in the following two ways.

    a. Using Theorem 3.23

    b. Using the identity $\sin^{-1} x + \cos^{-1} x = \pi/2$

73. Derivative of $\cot^{-1} x$ and $\csc^{-1} x$ Use a trigonometric identity to show that the derivatives of the inverse cotangent and inverse cosecant differ from the derivatives of the inverse tangent and inverse secant, respectively, by a multiplicative factor of -1.

74. Tangents and inverses Suppose $y = L(x) = ax + b$ (with $a \neq 0$) is the equation of the line tangent to the graph of a one-to-one function f at (x_0, y_0). Also, suppose that $y = M(x) = cx + d$ is the equation of the line tangent to the graph of f^{-1} at (y_0, x_0).

    a. Express a and b in terms of x_0 and y_0.

    b. Express c in terms of a, and d in terms of a, x_0, and y_0.

    c. Prove that $L^{-1}(x) = M(x)$.

75–78. Identity proofs *Prove the following identities and give the values of x for which they are true.*

75. $\cos\left(\sin^{-1} x\right) = \sqrt{1 - x^2}$

76. $\cos\left(2 \sin^{-1} x\right) = 1 - 2x^2$

77. $\tan\left(2 \tan^{-1} x\right) = \dfrac{2x}{1 - x^2}$

78. $\sin\left(2 \sin^{-1} x\right) = 2x\sqrt{1 - x^2}$

79. An inverse tangent identity

    a. Use derivatives to show that $\tan^{-1} \dfrac{2}{n^2}$ and $\tan^{-1}(n + 1) - \tan^{-1}(n - 1)$ differ by a constant.

    b. Prove that $\tan^{-1} \dfrac{2}{n^2} = \tan^{-1}(n + 1) - \tan^{-1}(n - 1)$.

(*Source: The College Mathematics Journal*, 32, 4, Sep 2001)

QUICK CHECK ANSWERS

1. $f(x) = \sin^{-1} x$ is odd and $f'(x) = 1/\sqrt{1 - x^2}$ is even.
2. The slopes of the tangent lines approach 0.
3. One is the negative of the other.   **4.** Recall that $1° = \pi/180$ rad. So 0.0024 rad/ft is equivalent to 0.138°/ft.
5. Both curves have a slope of 1 at $(0, 0)$. ◀

3.11 Related Rates

We now return to the theme of derivatives as rates of change in problems in which the variables change with respect to *time*. The essential feature of these problems is that two or more variables, which are related in a known way, are themselves changing in time. Here are two examples illustrating this type of problem.

- An oil rig springs a leak and the oil spreads in a (roughly) circular patch around the rig. If the radius of the oil patch increases at a known rate, how fast is the area of the patch changing (Example 1)?
- Two airliners approach an airport with known speeds, one flying west and one flying north. How fast is the distance between the airliners changing (Example 2)?

In the first problem, the two related variables are the radius and the area of the oil patch. Both are changing in time. The second problem has three related variables: the positions of the two airliners and the distance between them. Again, the three variables change in time. The goal in both problems is to determine the rate of change of one of the variables at a specific moment of time—hence the name *related rates*.

We present a progression of examples in this section. After the first example, a general procedure is given for solving related-rate problems.

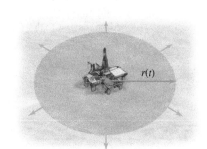

Figure 3.72

EXAMPLE 1   Spreading oil An oil rig springs a leak in calm seas, and the oil spreads in a circular patch around the rig. If the radius of the oil patch increases at a rate of 30 m/hr, how fast is the area of the patch increasing when the patch has a radius of 100 meters (Figure 3.72)?

SOLUTION Two variables change simultaneously: the radius of the circle and its area. The key relationship between the radius and area is $A = \pi r^2$. It helps to rewrite the basic relationship showing explicitly which quantities vary in time. In this case, we rewrite A and r as $A(t)$ and $r(t)$ to emphasize that they change with respect to t (time). The general expression relating the radius and area at any time t is $A(t) = \pi r(t)^2$.

The goal is to find the rate of change of the area of the circle, which is $A'(t)$, given that $r'(t) = 30$ m/hr. To introduce derivatives into the problem, we differentiate the area relation $A(t) = \pi r(t)^2$ with respect to t:

$$A'(t) = \frac{d}{dt}(\pi r(t)^2)$$

$$= \pi \frac{d}{dt}(r(t)^2)$$

$$= \pi (2r(t)) r'(t) \quad \text{Chain Rule}$$

$$= 2\pi r(t) r'(t). \quad \text{Simplify.}$$

Substituting the given values $r(t) = 100$ m and $r'(t) = 30$ m/hr, we have (including units)

$$A'(t) = 2\pi r(t) r'(t)$$

$$= 2\pi(100 \text{ m})\left(30 \frac{\text{m}}{\text{hr}}\right)$$

$$= 6000\pi \frac{\text{m}^2}{\text{hr}}.$$

> It is important to remember that substitution of specific values of the variables occurs *after* differentiating.

We see that the area of the oil spill increases at a rate of $6000\pi \approx 18{,}850$ m²/hr. Including units is a simple way to check your work. In this case, we expect an answer with units of area per unit time, so m²/hr makes sense.

Notice that the rate of change of the area depends on the radius of the spill. As the radius increases, the rate of change of the area also increases.

QUICK CHECK 1 In Example 1, what is the rate of change of the area when the radius is 200 m? 300 m? ◄

Related Exercises 5–19 ◄

Using Example 1 as a template, we offer a set of guidelines for solving related-rate problems. There are always variations that arise for individual problems, but here is a general procedure.

PROCEDURE **Steps for Related-Rate Problems**

1. Read the problem carefully, making a sketch to organize the given information. Identify the rates that are given and the rate that is to be determined.

2. Write one or more equations that express the basic relationships among the variables.

3. Introduce rates of change by differentiating the appropriate equation(s) with respect to time t.

4. Substitute known values and solve for the desired quantity.

5. Check that units are consistent and the answer is reasonable. (For example, does it have the correct sign?)

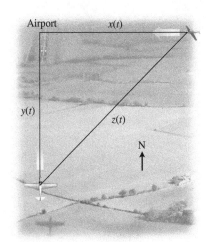

Figure 3.73

➤ In Example 1, we replaced A and r with $A(t)$ and $r(t)$, respectively, to remind us of the independent variable. After some practice, this replacement is not necessary.

➤ One could solve the equation $z^2 = x^2 + y^2$ for z, with the result

$$z = \sqrt{x^2 + y^2},$$

and then differentiate. However, it is easier to differentiate implicitly as shown in the example.

EXAMPLE 2 **Converging airplanes** Two small planes approach an airport, one flying due west at 120 mi/hr and the other flying due north at 150 mi/hr. Assuming they fly at the same constant elevation, how fast is the distance between the planes changing when the westbound plane is 180 miles from the airport and the northbound plane is 225 miles from the airport?

SOLUTION A sketch such as Figure 3.73 helps us visualize the problem and organize the information. Let $x(t)$ and $y(t)$ denote the distance from the airport to the westbound and northbound planes, respectively. The paths of the two planes form the legs of a right triangle, and the distance between them, denoted $z(t)$, is the hypotenuse. By the Pythagorean theorem, $z^2 = x^2 + y^2$.

Our aim is to find dz/dt, the rate of change of the distance between the planes. We first differentiate both sides of $z^2 = x^2 + y^2$ with respect to t:

$$\frac{d}{dt}(z^2) = \frac{d}{dt}(x^2 + y^2) \implies 2z\frac{dz}{dt} = 2x\frac{dx}{dt} + 2y\frac{dy}{dt}.$$

Notice that the Chain Rule is needed because x, y, and z are functions of t. Solving for dz/dt results in

$$\frac{dz}{dt} = \frac{2x\frac{dx}{dt} + 2y\frac{dy}{dt}}{2z} = \frac{x\frac{dx}{dt} + y\frac{dy}{dt}}{z}.$$

This equation relates the unknown rate dz/dt to the known quantities x, y, z, dx/dt, and dy/dt. For the westbound plane, $dx/dt = -120$ mi/hr (negative because the distance is decreasing), and for the northbound plane, $dy/dt = -150$ mi/hr. At the moment of interest, when $x = 180$ mi and $y = 225$ mi, the distance between the planes is

$$z = \sqrt{x^2 + y^2} = \sqrt{180^2 + 225^2} \approx 288 \text{ mi}.$$

Substituting these values gives

$$\frac{dz}{dt} = \frac{x\frac{dx}{dt} + y\frac{dy}{dt}}{z} \approx \frac{(180 \text{ mi})(-120 \text{ mi/hr}) + (225 \text{ mi})(-150 \text{ mi/hr})}{288 \text{ mi}}$$

$$\approx -192 \text{ mi/hr}.$$

Notice that $dz/dt < 0$, which means the distance between the planes is *decreasing* at a rate of about 192 mi/hr.   *Related Exercises 20–26* ◄

QUICK CHECK 2 Assuming the same plane speeds as in Example 2, how fast is the distance between the planes changing if $x = 60$ mi and $y = 75$ mi? ◄

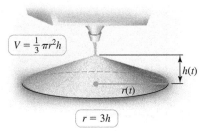

$$V = \frac{1}{3}\pi r^2 h$$

$h(t)$

$r(t)$

$r = 3h$

Figure 3.74

EXAMPLE 3   Sandpile Sand falls from an overhead bin, accumulating in a conical pile with a radius that is always three times its height. If the sand falls from the bin at a rate of $120 \text{ ft}^3/\text{min}$, how fast is the height of the sandpile changing when the pile is 10 ft high?

SOLUTION A sketch of the problem (Figure 3.74) shows the three relevant variables: the volume V, the radius r, and the height h of the sandpile. The aim is to find the rate of change of the height dh/dt at the instant that $h = 10$ ft, given that $dV/dt = 120 \text{ ft}^3/\text{min}$. The basic relationship among the variables is the formula for the volume of a cone, $V = \frac{1}{3}\pi r^2 h$. We now use the given fact that the radius is always three times the height. Substituting $r = 3h$ into the volume relationship gives V in terms of h:

$$V = \frac{1}{3}\pi r^2 h = \frac{1}{3}\pi(3h)^2 h = 3\pi h^3.$$

Rates of change are introduced by differentiating both sides of $V = 3\pi h^3$ with respect to t. Using the Chain Rule, we have

$$\frac{dV}{dt} = 9\pi h^2 \frac{dh}{dt}.$$

Now we find dh/dt at the instant that $h = 10$ ft, given that $dV/dt = 120 \text{ ft}^3/\text{min}$. Solving for dh/dt and substituting these values, we have

$$\frac{dh}{dt} = \frac{dV/dt}{9\pi h^2} \qquad \text{Solve for } \frac{dh}{dt}.$$

$$= \frac{120 \text{ ft}^3/\text{min}}{9\pi(10 \text{ ft})^2} \approx 0.042 \ \frac{\text{ft}}{\text{min}}. \quad \text{Substitute for } \frac{dV}{dt} \text{ and } h.$$

At the instant that the sandpile is 10 ft high, the height is changing at a rate of 0.042 ft/min. Notice how the units work out consistently.

Related Exercises 27–33 ◄

QUICK CHECK 3 In Example 3, what is the rate of change of the height when $h = 2$ ft? Does the rate of change of the height increase or decrease with increasing height? ◄

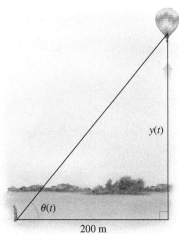

$y(t)$

$\theta(t)$

200 m

Figure 3.75

EXAMPLE 4   Observing a launch An observer stands 200 meters from the launch site of a hot-air balloon. The balloon rises vertically at a constant rate of 4 m/s. How fast is the angle of elevation of the balloon increasing 30 seconds after the launch? (The angle of elevation is the angle between the ground and the observer's line of sight to the balloon.)

SOLUTION Figure 3.75 shows the geometry of the launch. As the balloon rises, its distance from the ground y and its angle of elevation θ change simultaneously. An equation expressing the relationship between these variables is $\tan\theta = y/200$. To find $d\theta/dt$, we differentiate both sides of this relationship using the Chain Rule:

$$\sec^2\theta \frac{d\theta}{dt} = \frac{1}{200}\frac{dy}{dt}.$$

Next we solve for $\frac{d\theta}{dt}$:

$$\frac{d\theta}{dt} = \frac{dy/dt}{200\sec^2\theta} = \frac{(dy/dt)\cdot\cos^2\theta}{200}.$$

The rate of change of the angle of elevation depends on the angle of elevation and the speed of the balloon. Thirty seconds after the launch, the balloon has risen $y = (4 \text{ m/s})(30 \text{ s}) = 120$ m. To complete the problem, we need the value of $\cos\theta$. Note that when $y = 120$ m, the distance between the observer and the balloon is

$$d = \sqrt{120^2 + 200^2} \approx 233.24 \text{ m}.$$

➤ The solution to Example 4 is reported in units of rad/s. Where did radians come from? Because a radian has no physical dimension (it is the ratio of an arc length and a radius), no unit appears. We write rad/s for clarity because $d\theta/dt$ is the rate of change of an angle.

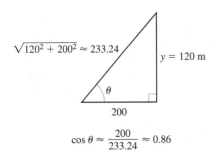

$\sqrt{120^2 + 200^2} \approx 233.24$

$y = 120$ m

θ

200

$\cos \theta \approx \dfrac{200}{233.24} \approx 0.86$

Figure 3.76

▶ Recall that to convert radians to degrees, we use

$$\text{degrees} = \frac{180}{\pi} \cdot \text{radians}.$$

Therefore, $\cos \theta \approx 200/233.24 \approx 0.86$ (Figure 3.76), and the rate of change of the angle of elevation is

$$\frac{d\theta}{dt} = \frac{(dy/dt) \cdot \cos^2 \theta}{200} \approx \frac{(4 \text{ m/s})(0.86^2)}{200 \text{ m}} = 0.015 \text{ rad/s}.$$

At this instant, the balloon is rising at an angular rate of 0.015 rad/s, or slightly less than $1°/\text{s}$, as seen by the observer.

Related Exercises 34–39 ◄

QUICK CHECK 4 In Example 4, notice that as the balloon rises (as θ increases), the rate of change of the angle of elevation decreases to zero. When does the maximum value of $\theta'(t)$ occur, and what is it? ◄

SECTION 3.11 EXERCISES

Review Questions

1. Give an example in which one dimension of a geometric figure changes and produces a corresponding change in the area or volume of the figure.

2. Explain how implicit differentiation can simplify the work in a related-rates problem.

3. If two opposite sides of a rectangle increase in length, how must the other two opposite sides change if the area of the rectangle is to remain constant?

4. Explain why the term *related rates* describes the problems of this section.

Basic Skills

5. **Expanding square** The sides of a square increase in length at a rate of 2 m/s.

   a. At what rate is the area of the square changing when the sides are 10 m long?
   b. At what rate is the area of the square changing when the sides are 20 m long?
   c. Draw a graph that shows how the rate of change of the area varies with the side length.

6. **Shrinking square** The sides of a square decrease in length at a rate of 1 m/s.

   a. At what rate is the area of the square changing when the sides are 5 m long?
   b. At what rate are the lengths of the diagonals of the square changing?

7. **Expanding isosceles triangle** The legs of an isosceles right triangle increase in length at a rate of 2 m/s.

   a. At what rate is the area of the triangle changing when the legs are 2 m long?
   b. At what rate is the area of the triangle changing when the hypotenuse is 1 m long?
   c. At what rate is the length of the hypotenuse changing?

8. **Shrinking isosceles triangle** The hypotenuse of an isosceles right triangle decreases in length at a rate of 4 m/s.

   a. At what rate is the area of the triangle changing when the legs are 5 m long?
   b. At what rate are the lengths of the legs of the triangle changing?
   c. At what rate is the area of the triangle changing when the area is 4 m²?

9. **Expanding circle** The area of a circle increases at a rate of 1 cm²/s.

   a. How fast is the radius changing when the radius is 2 cm?
   b. How fast is the radius changing when the circumference is 2 cm?

10. **Expanding cube** The edges of a cube increase at a rate of 2 cm/s. How fast is the volume changing when the length of each edge is 50 cm?

11. **Shrinking circle** A circle has an initial radius of 50 ft when the radius begins decreasing at a rate of 2 ft/min. What is the rate of change of the area at the instant the radius is 10 ft?

12. **Shrinking cube** The volume of a cube decreases at a rate of 0.5 ft³/min. What is the rate of change of the side length when the side lengths are 12 ft?

13. **Balloons** A spherical balloon is inflated and its volume increases at a rate of 15 in³/min. What is the rate of change of its radius when the radius is 10 in?

14. **Piston compression** A piston is seated at the top of a cylindrical chamber with radius 5 cm when it starts moving into the chamber at a constant speed of 3 cm/s (see figure). What is the rate of change of the volume of the cylinder when the piston is 2 cm from the base of the chamber?

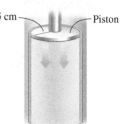

5 cm — Piston

15. **Melting snowball** A spherical snowball melts at a rate proportional to its surface area. Show that the rate of change of the radius is constant. (*Hint:* Surface area $= 4\pi r^2$.)

16. Bug on a parabola A bug is moving along the right side of the parabola $y = x^2$ at a rate such that its distance from the origin is increasing at 1 cm/min. At what rates are the x- and y-coordinates of the bug increasing when the bug is at the point $(2, 4)$?

17. Another bug on a parabola A bug is moving along the parabola $y = x^2$. At what point on the parabola are the x- and y-coordinates changing at the same rate? (*Source: Calculus*, Tom M. Apostol, Vol. 1, John Wiley & Sons, New York, 1967.)

18. Expanding rectangle A rectangle initially has dimensions 2 cm by 4 cm. All sides begin increasing in length at a rate of 1 cm/s. At what rate is the area of the rectangle increasing after 20 s?

19. Filling a pool A swimming pool is 50 m long and 20 m wide. Its depth decreases linearly along the length from 3 m to 1 m (see figure). It is initially empty and is filled at a rate of 1 m³/min. How fast is the water level rising 250 min after the filling begins? How long will it take to fill the pool?

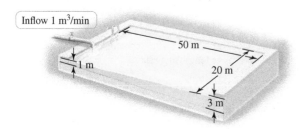

20. Altitude of a jet A jet ascends at a 10° angle from the horizontal with an airspeed of 550 mi/hr (its speed along its line of flight is 550 mi/hr). How fast is the altitude of the jet increasing? If the sun is directly overhead, how fast is the shadow of the jet moving on the ground?

21. Rate of dive of a submarine A surface ship is moving (horizontally) in a straight line at 10 km/hr. At the same time, an enemy submarine maintains a position directly below the ship while diving at an angle that is 20° below the horizontal. How fast is the submarine's altitude decreasing?

22. Divergent paths Two boats leave a port at the same time; one travels west at 20 mi/hr and the other travels south at 15 mi/hr. At what rate is the distance between them changing 30 minutes after they leave the port?

23. Ladder against the wall A 13-foot ladder is leaning against a vertical wall (see figure) when Jack begins pulling the foot of the ladder away from the wall at a rate of 0.5 ft/s. How fast is the top of the ladder sliding down the wall when the foot of the ladder is 5 ft from the wall?

24. Ladder against the wall again A 12-foot ladder is leaning against a vertical wall when Jack begins pulling the foot of the ladder away from the wall at a rate of 0.2 ft/s. What is the configuration of the ladder at the instant that the vertical speed of the top of the ladder equals the horizontal speed of the foot of the ladder?

25. Moving shadow A 5-foot-tall woman walks at 8 ft/s toward a streetlight that is 20 ft above the ground. What is the rate of change of the length of her shadow when she is 15 ft from the streetlight? At what rate is the tip of her shadow moving?

26. Baseball runners Runners stand at first and second base in a baseball game. At the moment a ball is hit, the runner at first base runs to second base at 18 ft/s; simultaneously, the runner on second runs to third base at 20 ft/s. How fast is the distance between the runners changing 1 second after the ball is hit (see figure)? (*Hint:* The distance between consecutive bases is 90 ft and the bases lie at the corners of a square.)

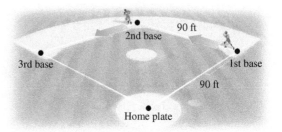

27. Growing sandpile Sand falls from an overhead bin and accumulates in a conical pile with a radius that is always three times its height. Suppose the height of the pile increases at a rate of 2 cm/s when the pile is 12 cm high. At what rate is the sand leaving the bin at that instant?

28. Draining a water heater A water heater that has the shape of a right cylindrical tank with a radius of 1 ft and a height of 4 ft is being drained. How fast is water draining out of the tank (in ft³/min) if the water level is dropping at 6 in/min?

29. Draining a tank An inverted conical water tank with a height of 12 ft and a radius of 6 ft is drained through a hole in the vertex at a rate of 2 ft³/s (see figure). What is the rate of change of the water depth when the water depth is 3 ft? (*Hint:* Use similar triangles.)

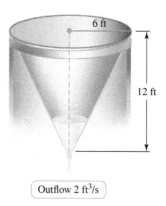

30. Drinking a soda At what rate is soda being sucked out of a cylindrical glass that is 6 in tall and has a radius of 2 in? The depth of the soda decreases at a constant rate of 0.25 in/s.

31. **Draining a cone** Water is drained out of an inverted cone having the same dimensions as the cone depicted in Exercise 29. If the water level drops at 1 ft/min, at what rate is water (in ft³/min) draining from the tank when the water depth is 6 ft?

32. **Filling a hemispherical tank** A hemispherical tank with a radius of 10 m is filled from an inflow pipe at a rate of 3 m³/min (see figure). How fast is the water level rising when the water level is 5 m from the bottom of the tank? (*Hint:* The volume of a cap of thickness h sliced from a sphere of radius r is $\pi h^2(3r - h)/3$.)

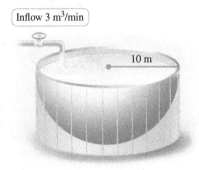

Inflow 3 m³/min

10 m

33. **Surface area of hemispherical tank** For the situation described in Exercise 32, what is the rate of change of the area of the exposed surface of the water when the water is 5 m deep?

34. **Observing a launch** An observer stands 300 ft from the launch site of a hot-air balloon. The balloon is launched vertically and maintains a constant upward velocity of 20 ft/s. What is the rate of change of the angle of elevation of the balloon when it is 400 ft from the ground? The angle of elevation is the angle θ between the observer's line of sight to the balloon and the ground.

35. **Another balloon story** A hot-air balloon is 150 ft above the ground when a motorcycle (traveling in a straight line on a horizontal road) passes directly beneath it going 40 mi/hr (58.67 ft/s). If the balloon rises vertically at a rate of 10 ft/s, what is the rate of change of the distance between the motorcycle and the balloon 10 seconds later?

36. **Fishing story** An angler hooks a trout and begins turning her circular reel at 1.5 rev/s. If the radius of the reel (and the fishing line on it) is 2 in, how fast is she reeling in her fishing line?

37. **Another fishing story** An angler hooks a trout and reels in his line at 4 in/s. Assume the tip of the fishing rod is 12 ft above the water and directly above the angler, and the fish is pulled horizontally directly toward the angler (see figure). Find the horizontal speed of the fish when it is 20 ft from the angler.

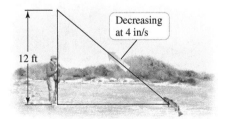

Decreasing at 4 in/s

12 ft

38. **Flying a kite** Once Kate's kite reaches a height of 50 ft (above her hands), it rises no higher but drifts due east in a wind blowing 5 ft/s. How fast is the string running through Kate's hands at the moment that she has released 120 ft of string?

39. **Rope on a boat** A rope passing through a capstan on a dock is attached to a boat offshore. The rope is pulled in at a constant rate of 3 ft/s, and the capstan is 5 ft vertically above the water. How fast is the boat traveling when it is 10 ft from the dock?

Further Explorations

40. **Parabolic motion** An arrow is shot into the air and moves along the parabolic path $y = x(50 - x)$ (see figure). The horizontal component of velocity is always 30 ft/s. What is the vertical component of velocity when (i) $x = 10$ and (ii) $x = 40$?

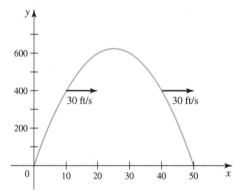

41. **Time-lagged flights** An airliner passes over an airport at noon traveling 500 mi/hr due west. At 1:00 P.M., another airliner passes over the same airport at the same elevation traveling due north at 550 mi/hr. Assuming both airliners maintain their (equal) elevations, how fast is the distance between them changing at 2:30 P.M.?

42. **Disappearing triangle** An equilateral triangle initially has sides of length 20 ft when each vertex moves toward the midpoint of the opposite side at a rate of 1.5 ft/min. Assuming the triangle remains equilateral, what is the rate of change of the area of the triangle at the instant the triangle disappears?

43. **Clock hands** The hands of the clock in the tower of the Houses of Parliament in London are approximately 3 m and 2.5 m in length. How fast is the distance between the tips of the hands changing at 9:00? (*Hint:* Use the Law of Cosines.)

44. **Filling two pools** Two cylindrical swimming pools are being filled simultaneously at the same rate (in m³/min; see figure). The smaller pool has a radius of 5 m, and the water level rises at a rate of 0.5 m/min. The larger pool has a radius of 8 m. How fast is the water level rising in the larger pool?

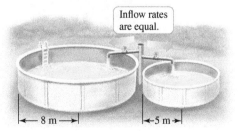

Inflow rates are equal.

8 m   5 m

45. Filming a race A camera is set up at the starting line of a drag race 50 ft from a dragster at the starting line (camera 1 in the figure). Two seconds after the start of the race, the dragster has traveled 100 ft and the camera is turning at 0.75 rad/s while filming the dragster.

   a. What is the speed of the dragster at this point?

   b. A second camera (camera 2 in the figure) filming the dragster is located on the starting line 100 ft away from the dragster at the start of the race. How fast is this camera turning 2 seconds after the start of the race?

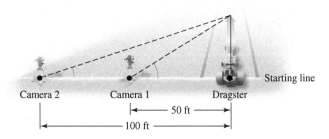

46. Two tanks A conical tank with an upper radius of 4 m and a height of 5 m drains into a cylindrical tank with a radius of 4 m and a height of 5 m (see figure). If the water level in the conical tank drops at a rate of 0.5 m/min, at what rate does the water level in the cylindrical tank rise when the water level in the conical tank is 3 m? 1 m?

47. Oblique tracking A port and a radar station are 2 mi apart on a straight shore running east and west (see figure). A ship leaves the port at noon traveling northeast at a rate of 15 mi/hr. If the ship maintains its speed and course, what is the rate of change of the tracking angle θ between the shore and the line between the radar station and the ship at 12:30 P.M.? (*Hint:* Use the Law of Sines.)

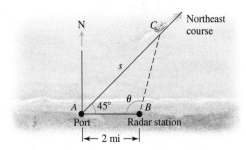

48. Oblique tracking A ship leaves port traveling southwest at a rate of 12 mi/hr. At noon, the ship reaches its closest approach to a radar station, which is on the shore 1.5 mi from the port. If the ship maintains its speed and course, what is the rate of change of the tracking angle θ between the radar station and the ship at 1:30 P.M. (see figure)? (*Hint:* Use the Law of Sines.)

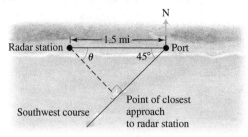

49. Watching an elevator An observer is 20 m above the ground floor of a large hotel atrium looking at a glass-enclosed elevator shaft that is 20 m horizontally from the observer (see figure). The angle of elevation of the elevator is the angle that the observer's line of sight makes with the horizontal (it may be positive or negative). Assuming that the elevator rises at a rate of 5 m/s, what is the rate of change of the angle of elevation when the elevator is 10 m above the ground? When the elevator is 40 m above the ground?

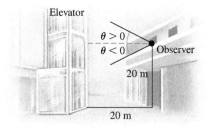

50. A lighthouse problem A lighthouse stands 500 m off a straight shore and the focused beam of its light revolves four times each minute. As shown in the figure, P is the point on shore closest to the lighthouse and Q is a point on the shore 200 m from P. What is the speed of the beam along the shore when it strikes the point Q? Describe how the speed of the beam along the shore varies with the distance between P and Q. Neglect the height of the lighthouse.

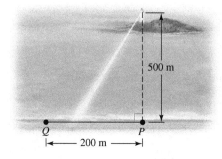

51. Navigation A boat leaves a port traveling due east at 12 mi/hr. At the same time, another boat leaves the same port traveling northeast at 15 mi/hr. The angle θ of the line between the boats is measured relative to due north (see figure). What is the rate of change of this angle 30 min after the boats leave the port? 2 hr after the boats leave the port?

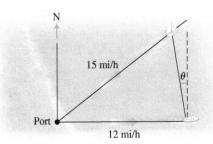

52. Watching a Ferris wheel An observer stands 20 m from the bottom of a 10-m-tall Ferris wheel on a line that is perpendicular to the face of the Ferris wheel. The wheel revolves at a rate of π rad/min, and the observer's line of sight with a specific seat on the wheel makes an angle θ with the ground (see figure). Forty seconds after that seat leaves the lowest point on the wheel, what is the rate of change of θ? Assume the observer's eyes are level with the bottom of the wheel.

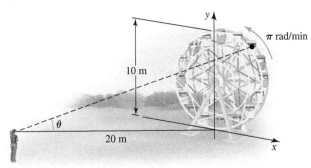

53. Viewing angle The bottom of a large theater screen is 3 ft above your eye level and the top of the screen is 10 ft above your eye level. Assume you walk away from the screen (perpendicular to the screen) at a rate of 3 ft/s while looking at the screen. What is the rate of change of the viewing angle θ when you are 30 ft from the wall on which the screen hangs, assuming the floor is horizontal (see figure)?

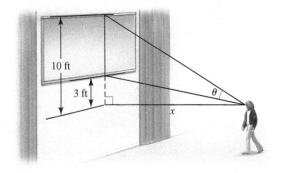

54. Searchlight—wide beam A revolving searchlight, which is 100 m from the nearest point on a straight highway, casts a horizontal beam along a highway (see figure). The beam leaves the spotlight at an angle of $\pi/16$ rad and revolves at a rate of $\pi/6$ rad/s. Let w be the width of the beam as it sweeps along the highway and θ be the angle that the center of the beam makes with the perpendicular to the highway. What is the rate of change of w when $\theta = \pi/3$? Neglect the height of the searchlight.

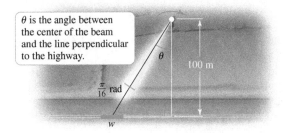

55. Draining a trough A trough in the shape of a half cylinder has length 5 m and radius 1 m. The trough is full of water when a valve is opened, and water flows out of the bottom of the trough at a rate of 1.5 m³/hr (see figure). (*Hint:* The area of a sector of a circle of a radius r subtended by an angle θ is $r^2\theta/2$.)

  a. How fast is the water level changing when the water level is 0.5 m from the bottom of the trough?

  b. What is the rate of change of the surface area of the water when the water is 0.5 m deep?

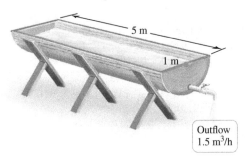

56. Divergent paths Two boats leave a port at the same time, one traveling west at 20 mi/hr and the other traveling southwest at 15 mi/hr. At what rate is the distance between them changing 30 min after they leave the port?

QUICK CHECK ANSWERS

1. $12{,}000\pi$ m²/hr, $18{,}000\pi$ m²/hr   **2.** -192 mi/hr
3. 1.1 ft/min; decreases with height   **4.** $t = 0, \theta = 0$,
$\theta'(0) = 0.02$ rad/s ◄

CHAPTER 3   REVIEW EXERCISES

1. **Explain why or why not** Determine whether the following statements are true and give an explanation or counterexample.

   a. The function $f(x) = |2x + 1|$ is continuous for all x; therefore, it is differentiable for all x.

   b. If $\dfrac{d}{dx}(f(x)) = \dfrac{d}{dx}(g(x))$, then $f = g$.

   c. For any function f, $\dfrac{d}{dx}|f(x)| = |f'(x)|$.

   d. The value of $f'(a)$ fails to exist only if the curve $y = f(x)$ has a vertical tangent line at $x = a$.

   e. An object can have negative acceleration and increasing speed.

2–5. Slopes and tangent lines from the definition

   a. *Use either definition of the derivative to determine the slope of the curve $y = f(x)$ at the given point P.*

   b. *Find an equation of the line tangent to the curve $y = f(x)$ at P; then graph the curve and the tangent line.*

2. $f(x) = 4x^2 - 7x + 5$; $P(2, 7)$

3. $f(x) = 5x^3 + x$; $P(1, 6)$

4. $f(x) = \dfrac{x + 3}{2x + 1}$; $P(0, 3)$

5. $f(x) = \dfrac{1}{2\sqrt{3x + 1}}$; $P\left(0, \dfrac{1}{2}\right)$

6. **Calculating average and instantaneous velocities** Suppose the height s of an object (in m) above the ground after t seconds is approximated by the function $s = -4.9t^2 + 25t + 1$.

   a. Make a table showing the average velocities of the object from time $t = 1$ to $t = 1 + h$, for $h = 0.01, 0.001, 0.0001$, and 0.00001.

   b. Use the table in part (a) to estimate the instantaneous velocity of the object at $t = 1$.

   c. Use limits to verify your estimate in part (b).

7. **Population of the United States** The population of the United States (in millions) by decade is given in the table, where t is the number of years after 1900. These data are plotted and fitted with a smooth curve $y = p(t)$ in the figure.

   a. Compute the average rate of population growth from 1950 to 1960.

   b. Explain why the average rate of growth from 1950 to 1960 is a good approximation to the (instantaneous) rate of growth in 1955.

   c. Estimate the instantaneous rate of growth in 1985.

Year	1900	1910	1920	1930	1940	1950
t	0	10	20	30	40	50
$p(t)$	76.21	92.23	106.02	123.2	132.16	152.32

Year	1960	1970	1980	1990	2000	2010
t	60	70	80	90	100	110
$p(t)$	179.32	203.30	226.54	248.71	281.42	308.94

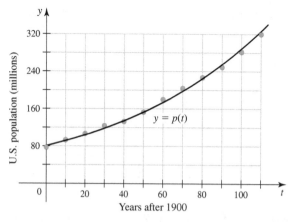

8. **Growth rate of bacteria** Suppose the following graph represents the number of bacteria in a culture t hours after the start of an experiment.

   a. At approximately what time is the instantaneous growth rate the greatest, for $0 \le t \le 36$? Estimate the growth rate at this time.

   b. At approximately what time in the interval $0 \le t \le 36$ is the instantaneous growth rate the least? Estimate the instantaneous growth rate at this time.

   c. What is the average growth rate over the interval $0 \le t \le 36$?

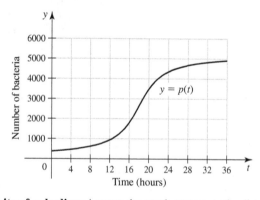

9. **Velocity of a skydiver** Assume the graph represents the distance (in m) fallen by a skydiver t seconds after jumping out of a plane.

   a. Estimate the velocity of the skydiver at $t = 15$.

   b. Estimate the velocity of the skydiver at $t = 70$.

   c. Estimate the average velocity of the skydiver between $t = 20$ and $t = 90$.

   d. Sketch a graph of the velocity function, for $0 \le t \le 120$.

   e. What significant event occurred at $t = 30$?

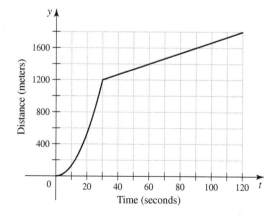

10–11. Using the definition of the derivative *Use the definition of the derivative to do the following.*

10. Verify that $f'(x) = 4x - 3$, where $f(x) = 2x^2 - 3x + 1$.

11. Verify that $g'(x) = \dfrac{1}{\sqrt{2x - 3}}$, where $g(x) = \sqrt{2x - 3}$.

12. Sketching a derivative graph Sketch a graph of f' for the function f shown in the figure.

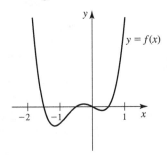

13. Sketching a derivative graph Sketch a graph of g' for the function g shown in the figure.

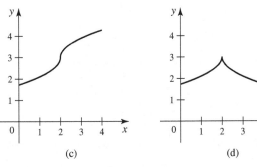

14. Matching functions and derivatives Match the functions in a–d with the derivatives in A–D.

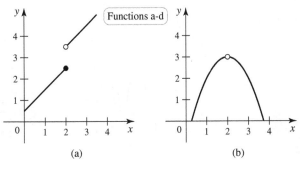

(a)

(b)

(c)

(d)

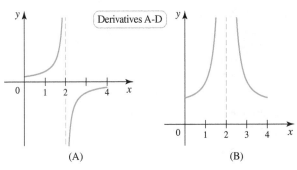

(A)

(B)

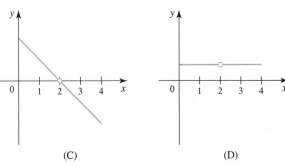

(C)

(D)

15–36. Evaluating derivatives *Evaluate and simplify the following derivatives.*

15. $\dfrac{d}{dx}\left(\dfrac{2}{3}x^3 + \pi x^2 + 7x + 1\right)$

16. $\dfrac{d}{dx}\left(2x\sqrt{x^2 - 2x + 2}\right)$

17. $\dfrac{d}{dt}(5t^2 \sin t)$

18. $\dfrac{d}{dx}(5x + \sin^3 x + \sin x^3)$

19. $\dfrac{d}{d\theta}(4 \tan(\theta^2 + 3\theta + 2))$

20. $\dfrac{d}{dx}(\csc^5 3x)$

21. $\dfrac{d}{du}\left(\dfrac{4u^2 + u}{8u + 1}\right)$

22. $\dfrac{d}{dt}\left(\dfrac{3t^2 - 1}{3t^2 + 1}\right)^{-3}$

23. $\dfrac{d}{d\theta}(\tan(\sin \theta))$

24. $\dfrac{d}{dv}\left(\dfrac{v}{3v^2 + 2v + 1}\right)^{1/3}$

25. $\dfrac{d}{dx}(2x(\sin x)\sqrt{3x - 1})$

26. $\dfrac{d}{dx}(xe^{-10x})$

27. $\dfrac{d}{dx}(x \ln^2 x)$

28. $\dfrac{d}{dw}(e^{-w} \ln w)$

29. $\dfrac{d}{dx}(2^{x^2 - x})$

30. $\dfrac{d}{dx}(\log_3(x + 8))$

31. $\dfrac{d}{dx}\left(\sin^{-1}\dfrac{1}{x}\right)$

32. $\dfrac{d}{dx}(x^{\sin x})$

33. $f'(1)$ when $f(x) = x^{1/x}$

34. $f'(1)$ when $f(x) = \tan^{-1}(4x^2)$

35. $\dfrac{d}{dx}(x \sec^{-1} x)\Big|_{x = \frac{2}{\sqrt{3}}}$

36. $\dfrac{d}{dx}(\tan^{-1} e^{-x})\Big|_{x = 0}$

37–39. Implicit differentiation *Calculate $y'(x)$ for the following relations.*

37. $y = \dfrac{e^y}{1 + \sin x}$

38. $\sin x \cos(y - 1) = \dfrac{1}{2}$

39. $y\sqrt{x^2 + y^2} = 15$

40. Quadratic functions

   a. Show that if $(a, f(a))$ is any point on the graph of $f(x) = x^2$, then the slope of the tangent line at that point is $m = 2a$.

   b. Show that if $(a, f(a))$ is any point on the graph of $f(x) = bx^2 + cx + d$, then the slope of the tangent line at that point is $m = 2ab + c$.

41–44. Tangent lines *Find an equation of the line tangent to the following curves at the given point.*

41. $y = 3x^3 + \sin x;\ (0, 0)$

42. $y = \dfrac{4x}{x^2 + 3};\ (3, 1)$

43. $y + \sqrt{xy} = 6;\ (1, 4)$

44. $x^2 y + y^3 = 75;\ (4, 3)$

45. Horizontal/vertical tangent lines For what value(s) of x is the line tangent to the curve $y = x\sqrt{6 - x}$ horizontal? Vertical?

46. A parabola property Let $f(x) = x^2$.

   a. Show that $\dfrac{f(x) - f(y)}{x - y} = f'\left(\dfrac{x + y}{2}\right)$, for all $x \neq y$.

   b. Is this property true for $f(x) = ax^2$, where a is a nonzero real number?

   c. Give a geometrical interpretation of this property.

   d. Is this property true for $f(x) = ax^3$?

47–48. Higher-order derivatives *Find y', y'', and y''' for the following functions.*

47. $y = \sin \sqrt{x}$

48. $y = (x - 3)\sqrt{x + 2}$

49–52. Derivative formulas *Evaluate the following derivatives. Express your answers in terms of f, g, f', and g'.*

49. $\dfrac{d}{dx}(x^2 f(x))$

50. $\dfrac{d}{dx}\sqrt{\dfrac{f(x)}{g(x)}}$

51. $\dfrac{d}{dx}\left(\dfrac{x f(x)}{g(x)}\right)$

52. $\dfrac{d}{dx} f(\sqrt{g(x)}),\ g(x) \geq 0$

53. Finding derivatives from a table Find the values of the following derivatives using the table.

x	1	3	5	7	9
$f(x)$	3	1	9	7	5
$f'(x)$	7	9	5	1	3
$g(x)$	9	7	5	3	1
$g'(x)$	5	9	3	1	7

   a. $\dfrac{d}{dx}(f(x) + 2g(x))\Big|_{x=3}$

   b. $\dfrac{d}{dx}\left(\dfrac{x f(x)}{g(x)}\right)\Big|_{x=1}$

   c. $\dfrac{d}{dx} f(g(x^2))\Big|_{x=3}$

   d. $\dfrac{d}{dx}(f(x)^3)\Big|_{x=5}$

   e. $(g^{-1})'(7)$

54–55. Limits *The following limits represent the derivative of a function f at a point a. Find a possible f and a, and then evaluate the limit.*

54. $\displaystyle\lim_{h \to 0} \dfrac{\sin^2\left(\dfrac{\pi}{4} + h\right) - \dfrac{1}{2}}{h}$

55. $\displaystyle\lim_{x \to 5} \dfrac{\tan(\pi\sqrt{3x - 11})}{x - 5}$

56–57. Derivative of the inverse at a point *Consider the following functions. In each case, without finding the inverse, evaluate the derivative of the inverse at the given point.*

56. $f(x) = 1/(x + 1)$ at $f(0)$

57. $y = \sqrt{x^3 + x - 1}$ at $y = 3$

58–59. Derivative of the inverse *Find the derivative of the inverse of the following functions. Express the result with x as the independent variable.*

58. $f(x) = 12x - 16$

59. $f(x) = x^{-1/3}$

60. A function and its inverse function The function $f(x) = \dfrac{x}{x + 1}$ is one-to-one for $x > -1$ and has an inverse on that interval.

   a. Graph f, for $x > -1$.

   b. Find the inverse function f^{-1} corresponding to the function graphed in part (a). Graph f^{-1} on the same set of axes as in part (a).

   c. Evaluate the derivative of f^{-1} at the point $\left(\frac{1}{2}, 1\right)$.

   d. Sketch the tangent lines on the graphs of f and f^{-1} at $\left(1, \frac{1}{2}\right)$ and $\left(\frac{1}{2}, 1\right)$, respectively.

61. Derivative of the inverse in two ways Let $f(x) = \sin x$, $f^{-1}(x) = \sin^{-1} x$, and $(x_0, y_0) = (\pi/4, 1/\sqrt{2})$.

   a. Evaluate $(f^{-1})'(1/\sqrt{2})$ using Theorem 3.23.

   b. Evaluate $(f^{-1})'(1/\sqrt{2})$ directly by differentiating f^{-1}. Check for agreement with part (a).

62–63. Derivatives from a graph *If possible, evaluate the following derivatives using the graphs of f and f'.*

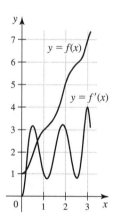

62. a. $\dfrac{d}{dx}(x f(x))\Big|_{x=2}$ **b.** $\dfrac{d}{dx}(f(x^2))\Big|_{x=1}$ **c.** $\dfrac{d}{dx}(f(f(x)))\Big|_{x=1}$

63. a. $(f^{-1})'(7)$ **b.** $(f^{-1})'(3)$ **c.** $(f^{-1})'(f(2))$

64. Velocity of a probe A small probe is launched vertically from the ground. After it reaches its high point, a parachute deploys and the probe descends to Earth. The height of the probe above the ground is $s(t) = \dfrac{300t - 50t^2}{t^3 + 2}$, for $0 \leq t \leq 6$.

   a. Graph the height function and describe the motion of the probe.

   b. Find the velocity of the probe.

   c. Graph the velocity function and determine the approximate time at which the velocity is a maximum.

65. Marginal and average cost Suppose the cost of producing x lawn mowers is $C(x) = -0.02x^2 + 400x + 5000$.

    a. Determine the average and marginal costs for $x = 3000$ lawn mowers.

    b. Interpret the meaning of your results in part (a).

66. Marginal and average cost Suppose a company produces fly rods. Assume $C(x) = -0.0001x^3 + 0.05x^2 + 60x + 800$ represents the cost of making x fly rods.

    a. Determine the average and marginal costs for $x = 400$ fly rods.

    b. Interpret the meaning of your results in part (a).

67. Population growth Suppose $p(t) = -1.7t^3 + 72t^2 + 7200t + 80{,}000$ is the population of a city t years after 1950.

    a. Determine the average rate of growth of the city from 1950 to 2000.

    b. What was the rate of growth of the city in 1990?

68. Position of a piston The distance between the head of a piston and the end of a cylindrical chamber is given by $x(t) = \dfrac{8t}{t+1}$ cm, for $t \geq 0$ (measured in seconds). The radius of the cylinder is 4 cm.

    a. Find the volume of the chamber, for $t \geq 0$.

    b. Find the rate of change of the volume $V'(t)$, for $t \geq 0$.

    c. Graph the derivative of the volume function. On what intervals is the volume increasing? Decreasing?

69. Boat rates Two boats leave a dock at the same time. One boat travels south at 30 mi/hr and the other travels east at 40 mi/hr. After half an hour, how fast is the distance between the boats increasing?

70. Rate of inflation of a balloon A spherical balloon is inflated at a rate of $10 \text{ cm}^3/\text{min}$. At what rate is the diameter of the balloon increasing when the balloon has a diameter of 5 cm?

71. Rate of descent of a hot-air balloon A rope is attached to the bottom of a hot-air balloon that is floating above a flat field. If the angle of the rope to the ground remains $65°$ and the rope is pulled in at 5 ft/s, how quickly is the elevation of the balloon changing?

72. Filling a tank Water flows into a conical tank at a rate of $2 \text{ ft}^3/\text{min}$. If the radius of the top of the tank is 4 ft and the height is 6 ft, determine how quickly the water level is rising when the water is 2 ft deep in the tank.

73. Angle of elevation A jet flies horizontally 500 ft directly above a spectator at an air show at 450 mi/hr. How quickly is the angle of elevation (between the ground and the line from the spectator to the jet) changing 2 seconds later?

74. Viewing angle A man whose eye level is 6 ft above the ground walks toward a billboard at a rate of 2 ft/s. The bottom of the billboard is 10 ft above the ground, and it is 15 ft high. The man's viewing angle is the angle formed by the lines between the man's eyes and the top and bottom of the billboard. At what rate is the viewing angle changing when the man is 30 ft from the billboard?

Chapter 3 Guided Projects

Applications of the material in this chapter and related topics can be found in the following Guided Projects. For additional information, see the Preface.

- Numerical differentiation
- Enzyme kinetics
- Elasticity in economics
- Pharmacokinetics—drug metabolism

4

Applications of the Derivative

Chapter Preview   Much of the previous chapter was devoted to the basic mechanics of derivatives: evaluating them and interpreting them as rates of change. We now apply derivatives to a variety of mathematical questions, many of which concern the properties of functions and their graphs. One outcome of this work is a set of analytical curve-sketching methods that produce accurate graphs of functions. Equally important, derivatives allow us to formulate and solve a wealth of practical problems. For example, an asteroid passes perilously close to Earth: At what point along their trajectories is the distance separating them smallest, and what is the minimum distance? An economist has a mathematical model that relates the demand for a product to its price: What price maximizes the revenue? In this chapter, we develop the tools needed to answer such questions. In addition, we begin an ongoing discussion about approximating functions, we present an important result called the Mean Value Theorem, and we work with a powerful method that enables us to evaluate a new kind of limit. The chapter concludes with two important topics: a numerical approach to approximating roots of functions, called Newton's method, and a preview of integral calculus, which is the subject of Chapter 5.

4.1 Maxima and Minima

With a working understanding of derivatives, we now undertake one of the fundamental tasks of calculus: analyzing the behavior and producing accurate graphs of functions. An important question associated with any function concerns its maximum and minimum values: On a given interval (perhaps the entire domain), where does the function assume its largest and smallest values? Questions about maximum and minimum values take on added significance when a function represents a practical quantity, such as the profits of a company, the surface area of a container, or the speed of a space vehicle.

Absolute Maxima and Minima

Imagine taking a long hike through varying terrain from west to east. Your elevation changes as you walk over hills, through valleys, and across plains, and you reach several high and low points along the journey. Analogously, when we examine a function f over an interval on the x-axis, its values increase and decrease, reaching high points and low points (Figure 4.1). You can view our study of functions in this chapter as an exploratory hike along the x-axis.

> **DEFINITION** **Absolute Maximum and Minimum**
>
> Let f be defined on a set D containing c. If $f(c) \geq f(x)$ for every x in D, then $f(c)$ is an **absolute maximum** value of f on D. If $f(c) \leq f(x)$ for every x in D, then $f(c)$ is an **absolute minimum** value of f on D. An **absolute extreme value** is either an absolute maximum or an absolute minimum value.

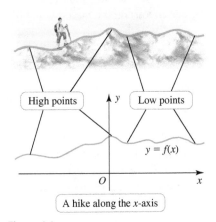

High points

Low points

$y = f(x)$

A hike along the x-axis

Figure 4.1

▶ Absolute maximum and minimum values are also called *global* maximum and minimum values. The plural of maximum is maxima; the plural of minimum is minima.

The existence and location of absolute extreme values depend on both the function and the interval of interest. Figure 4.2 shows various cases for the function $f(x) = x^2$. Notice that if the interval of interest is not closed, a function might not attain absolute extreme values (Figure 4.2a, c, and d).

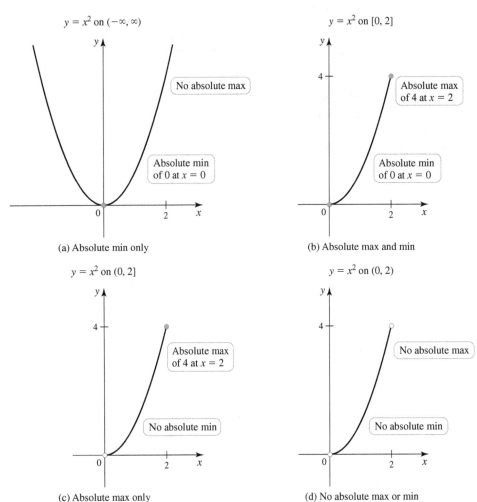

$y = x^2$ on $(-\infty, \infty)$

No absolute max

Absolute min of 0 at $x = 0$

(a) Absolute min only

$y = x^2$ on $[0, 2]$

Absolute max of 4 at $x = 2$

Absolute min of 0 at $x = 0$

(b) Absolute max and min

$y = x^2$ on $(0, 2]$

Absolute max of 4 at $x = 2$

No absolute min

(c) Absolute max only

$y = x^2$ on $(0, 2)$

No absolute max

No absolute min

(d) No absolute max or min

Figure 4.2

However, defining a function on a closed interval is not enough to guarantee the existence of absolute extreme values. Both functions in Figure 4.3 are defined at every point of a closed interval, but neither function attains an absolute maximum—the discontinuity in each function prevents it from happening.

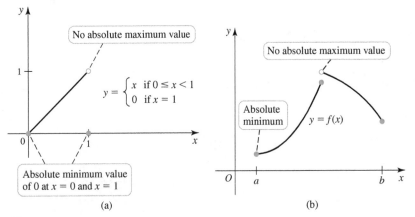

No absolute maximum value

$y = \begin{cases} x & \text{if } 0 \le x < 1 \\ 0 & \text{if } x = 1 \end{cases}$

Absolute minimum value of 0 at $x = 0$ and $x = 1$

(a)

No absolute maximum value

Absolute minimum

$y = f(x)$

(b)

Figure 4.3

It turns out that *two* conditions ensure the existence of absolute maximum and minimum values on an interval: The function must be continuous on the interval, and the interval must be closed and bounded.

> ▶ The proof of the Extreme Value Theorem relies on properties of the real numbers, found in advanced books.

THEOREM 4.1   Extreme Value Theorem

A function that is continuous on a closed interval $[a, b]$ has an absolute maximum value and an absolute minimum value on that interval.

QUICK CHECK 1 Sketch the graph of a function that is continuous on an interval but does not have an absolute minimum value. Sketch the graph of a function that is defined on a closed interval but does not have an absolute minimum value. ◄

EXAMPLE 1   Locating absolute maximum and minimum values For the functions in Figure 4.4, identify the location of the absolute maximum value and the absolute minimum value on the interval $[a, b]$. Do the functions meet the conditions of the Extreme Value Theorem?

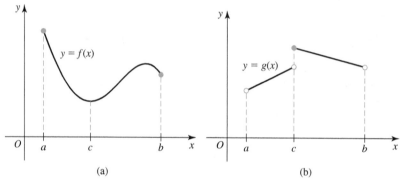

(a)   (b)

Figure 4.4

SOLUTION

a. The function f is continuous on the closed interval $[a, b]$, so the Extreme Value Theorem guarantees an absolute maximum (which occurs at a) and an absolute minimum (which occurs at c).

b. The function g does not satisfy the conditions of the Extreme Value Theorem because it is not continuous, and it is defined only on the open interval (a, b). It does not have an absolute minimum value. It does, however, have an absolute maximum at c. Therefore, a function may violate the conditions of the Extreme Value Theorem and still have an absolute maximum or minimum (or both).

Related Exercises 11–14 ◄

Local Maxima and Minima

Figure 4.5 shows a function defined on the interval $[a, b]$. It has an absolute minimum at the endpoint a and an absolute maximum at the interior point e. In addition, the function

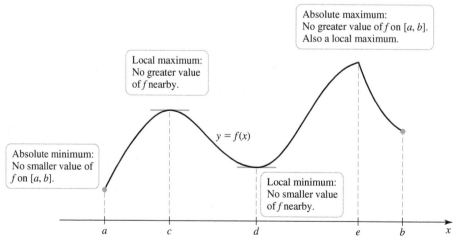

Absolute maximum:
No greater value of f on $[a, b]$.
Also a local maximum.

Local maximum:
No greater value of f nearby.

Absolute minimum:
No smaller value of f on $[a, b]$.

Local minimum:
No smaller value of f nearby.

$y = f(x)$

Figure 4.5

has special behavior at c, where its value is greatest *among values at nearby points*, and at d, where its value is least *among values at nearby points*. A point at which a function takes on the maximum or minimum value among values at nearby points is important.

> Local maximum and minimum values are also called *relative maximum* and *minimum values*. Local extrema (plural) and *local extremum* (singular) refer to either local maxima or local minima.

DEFINITION Local Maximum and Minimum Values

Suppose c is an interior point of some interval I on which f is defined. If $f(c) \geq f(x)$ for all x in I, then $f(c)$ is a **local maximum** value of f. If $f(c) \leq f(x)$ for all x in I, then $f(c)$ is a **local minimum** value of f.

In this book, we adopt the convention that local maximum values and local minimum values occur only at interior points of the interval(s) of interest. For example, in Figure 4.5, the minimum value that occurs at the endpoint a is not a local minimum. However, it is the absolute minimum of the function on $[a, b]$.

EXAMPLE 2   Locating various maxima and minima   Figure 4.6 shows the graph of a function defined on $[a, b]$. Identify the location of the various maxima and minima using the terms *absolute* and *local*.

SOLUTION   The function f is continuous on a closed interval; by Theorem 4.1, it has absolute maximum and minimum values on $[a, b]$. The function has a local minimum value and its absolute minimum value at p. It has another local minimum value at r. The absolute maximum value of f occurs at both q and s (which also correspond to local maximum values).

Related Exercises 15–22 ◀

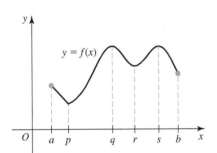

Figure 4.6

Critical Points   Another look at Figure 4.6 shows that local maxima and minima occur at points in the open interval (a, b) where the derivative is zero ($x = q, r$, and s) and at points where the derivative fails to exist ($x = p$). We now make this observation precise.

Figure 4.7 illustrates a function that is differentiable at c with a local maximum at c. For x near c with $x < c$, the secant lines through $(x, f(x))$ and $(c, f(c))$ have nonnegative slopes. For x near c with $x > c$, the secant lines through $(x, f(x))$ and $(c, f(c))$ have nonpositive slopes. As $x \to c$, the slopes of these secant lines approach the slope of the tangent line at $(c, f(c))$. These observations imply that the slope of the tangent line must be both nonnegative and nonpositive, which happens only if $f'(c) = 0$. Similar reasoning leads to the same conclusion for a function with a local minimum at c: $f'(c)$ must be zero. This argument is an outline of the proof (Exercise 83) of the following theorem.

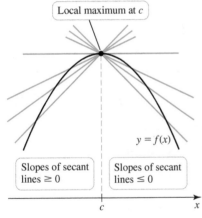

Figure 4.7

THEOREM 4.2   Local Extreme Value Theorem

If f has a local maximum or minimum value at c and $f'(c)$ exists, then $f'(c) = 0$.

> Theorem 4.2, often attributed to Fermat, is one of the clearest examples in mathematics of a necessary, but not sufficient, condition. A local maximum (or minimum) at c necessarily implies a critical point at c, but a critical point at c is not sufficient to imply a local maximum (or minimum) there.

Local extrema can also occur at points c where $f'(c)$ does not exist. Figure 4.8 shows two such cases, one in which c is a point of discontinuity and one in which f has a corner point at c. Because local extrema may occur at points c where $f'(c) = 0$ *and* where $f'(c)$ does not exist, we make the following definition.

DEFINITION Critical Point

An interior point c of the domain of f at which $f'(c) = 0$ or $f'(c)$ fails to exist is called a **critical point** of f.

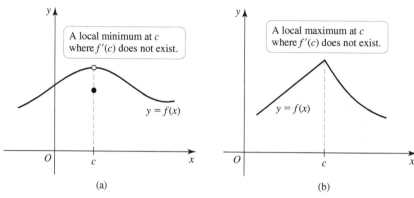

Figure 4.8

Note that the converse of Theorem 4.2 is not necessarily true. It is possible that $f'(c) = 0$ at a point without a local maximum or local minimum value occurring there (Figure 4.9a). It is also possible that $f'(c)$ fails to exist, with no local extreme value occurring at c (Figure 4.9b). Therefore, critical points are *candidates* for the location of local extreme values, but you must determine whether they actually correspond to local maxima or minima. This procedure is discussed in Section 4.2.

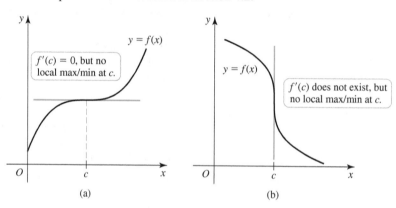

Figure 4.9

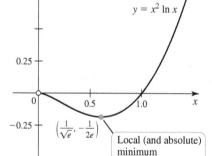

Figure 4.10

EXAMPLE 3   Locating critical points Find the critical points of $f(x) = x^2 \ln x$.

SOLUTION Note that f is differentiable on its domain, which is $(0, \infty)$. By the Product Rule,

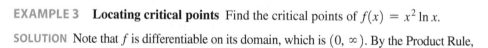

$$f'(x) = 2x \cdot \ln x + x^2 \cdot \frac{1}{x} = x(2 \ln x + 1).$$

Setting $f'(x) = 0$ gives $x(2 \ln x + 1) = 0$, which has the solution $x = e^{-1/2} = 1/\sqrt{e}$. Because $x = 0$ is not in the domain of f, it is not a critical point. Therefore, the only critical point is $x = 1/\sqrt{e} \approx 0.61$. A graph of f (Figure 4.10) reveals that a local (and, indeed, absolute) minimum value occurs at $1/\sqrt{e}$, where the value of the function is $-1/(2e)$.

Related Exercises 23–36 ◄

QUICK CHECK 2 Consider the function $f(x) = x^3$. Where is the critical point of f? Does f have a local maximum or minimum at the critical point? ◄

Locating Absolute Maxima and Minima

Theorem 4.1 guarantees the existence of absolute extreme values of a continuous function on a closed interval $[a, b]$, but it doesn't say where these values are located. Two observations lead to a procedure for locating absolute extreme values.

• An absolute extreme value in the interior of an interval is also a local extreme value, and we know that local extreme values occur at the critical points of f.

• Absolute extreme values may also occur at the endpoints of the interval of interest.

These two facts suggest the following procedure for locating the absolute extreme values of a function continuous on a closed interval.

> **PROCEDURE**   **Locating Absolute Extreme Values on a Closed Interval**
> Assume the function f is continuous on the closed interval $[a, b]$.
>
> 1. Locate the critical points c in (a, b), where $f'(c) = 0$ or $f'(c)$ does not exist. These points are candidates for absolute maxima and minima.
> 2. Evaluate f at the critical points and at the endpoints of $[a, b]$.
> 3. Choose the largest and smallest values of f from Step 2 for the absolute maximum and minimum values, respectively.

Note that the preceding procedure box does not address the case in which f is continuous on an open interval. If the interval of interest is an open interval, then absolute extreme values—if they exist—occur at interior points.

EXAMPLE 4   **Absolute extreme values** Find the absolute maximum and minimum values of the following functions.

a. $f(x) = x^4 - 2x^3$ on the interval $[-2, 2]$

b. $g(x) = x^{2/3}(2 - x)$ on the interval $[-1, 2]$

SOLUTION

a. Because f is a polynomial, its derivative exists everywhere. So if f has critical points, they are points at which $f'(x) = 0$. Computing f' and setting it equal to zero, we have

$$f'(x) = 4x^3 - 6x^2 = 2x^2(2x - 3) = 0.$$

Solving this equation gives the critical points $x = 0$ and $x = \frac{3}{2}$, both of which lie in the interval $[-2, 2]$; these points and the endpoints are *candidates* for the location of absolute extrema. Evaluating f at each of these points, we have

$$f(-2) = 32, \quad f(0) = 0, \quad f\left(\tfrac{3}{2}\right) = -\tfrac{27}{16}, \quad \text{and} \quad f(2) = 0.$$

The largest of these function values is $f(-2) = 32$, which is the absolute maximum of f on $[-2, 2]$. The smallest of these values is $f\left(\frac{3}{2}\right) = -\frac{27}{16}$, which is the absolute minimum of f on $[-2, 2]$. The graph of f (Figure 4.11) shows that the critical point $x = 0$ corresponds to neither a local maximum nor a local minimum.

b. Differentiating $g(x) = x^{2/3}(2 - x) = 2x^{2/3} - x^{5/3}$, we have

$$g'(x) = \frac{4}{3}x^{-1/3} - \frac{5}{3}x^{2/3} = \frac{4 - 5x}{3x^{1/3}}.$$

Because $g'(0)$ is undefined and 0 is in the domain of g, $x = 0$ is a critical point. In addition, $g'(x) = 0$ when $4 - 5x = 0$, so $x = \frac{4}{5}$ is also a critical point. These two critical points and the endpoints are *candidates* for the location of absolute extrema. The next step is to evaluate g at the critical points and endpoints:

$$g(-1) = 3, \quad g(0) = 0, \quad g\left(\tfrac{4}{5}\right) \approx 1.03, \quad \text{and} \quad g(2) = 0.$$

The largest of these function values is $g(-1) = 3$, which is the absolute maximum value of g on $[-1, 2]$. The least of these values is 0, which occurs twice. Therefore, g has its absolute minimum value on $[-1, 2]$ at the critical point $x = 0$ and the endpoint $x = 2$ (Figure 4.12).   *Related Exercises 37–50* ◄

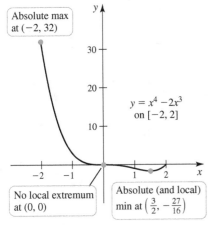

Absolute max at (−2, 32)

$y = x^4 - 2x^3$ on $[-2, 2]$

No local extremum at (0, 0)

Absolute (and local) min at $\left(\frac{3}{2}, -\frac{27}{16}\right)$

Figure 4.11

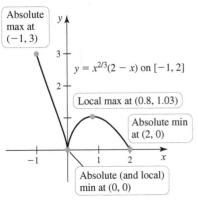

Absolute max at (−1, 3)

$y = x^{2/3}(2 - x)$ on $[-1, 2]$

Local max at (0.8, 1.03)

Absolute min at (2, 0)

Absolute (and local) min at (0, 0)

Figure 4.12

We now apply these ideas to a practical situation.

EXAMPLE 5   **Trajectory high point** A stone is launched vertically upward from a bridge 80 ft above the ground at a speed of 64 ft/s. Its height above the ground t seconds after the launch is given by

$$f(t) = -16t^2 + 64t + 80, \quad \text{for } 0 \le t \le 5.$$

When does the stone reach its maximum height?

➤ The derivation of the position function for an object moving in a gravitational field is given in Section 6.1.

SOLUTION We must evaluate the height function at the critical points and at the endpoints. The critical points satisfy the equation

$$f'(t) = -32t + 64 = -32(t - 2) = 0,$$

so the only critical point is $t = 2$. We now evaluate f at the endpoints and at the critical point:

$$f(0) = 80, \quad f(2) = 144, \quad \text{and} \quad f(5) = 0.$$

On the interval $[0, 5]$, the absolute maximum occurs at $t = 2$, at which time the stone reaches a height of 144 ft. Because $f'(t)$ is the velocity of the stone, the maximum height occurs at the instant the velocity is zero.

Related Exercises 51–54 ◄

SECTION 4.1 EXERCISES

Review Questions

1. What does it mean for a function to have an absolute extreme value at a point c of an interval $[a, b]$?

2. What are local maximum and minimum values of a function?

3. What conditions must be met to ensure that a function has an absolute maximum value and an absolute minimum value on an interval?

4. Sketch the graph of a function that is continuous on an open interval (a, b) but has neither an absolute maximum nor an absolute minimum value on (a, b).

5. Sketch the graph of a function that has an absolute maximum, a local minimum, but no absolute minimum on $[0, 3]$.

6. What is a critical point of a function?

7. Sketch the graph of a function f that has a local maximum value at a point c where $f'(c) = 0$.

8. Sketch the graph of a function f that has a local minimum value at a point c where $f'(c)$ is undefined.

9. How do you determine the absolute maximum and minimum values of a continuous function on a closed interval?

10. Explain how a function can have an absolute minimum value at an endpoint of an interval.

Basic Skills

11–14. Absolute maximum/minimum values *Use the following graphs to identify the points (if any) on the interval $[a, b]$ at which the function has an absolute maximum value or an absolute minimum value.*

11.

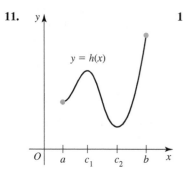

12.

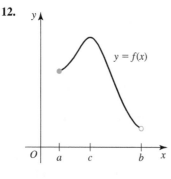

13.

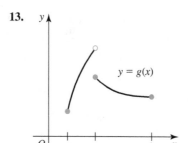

14.

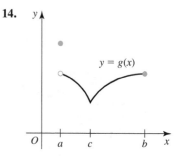

15–18. Local and absolute extreme values *Use the following graphs to identify the points on the interval $[a, b]$ at which local and absolute extreme values occur.*

15.

16.

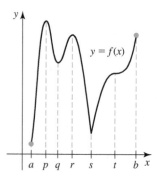

17.

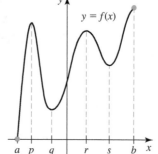

18.

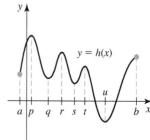

19–22. Designing a function *Sketch a graph of a function f continuous on $[0, 4]$ satisfying the given properties.*

19. $f'(x) = 0$ for $x = 1$ and 2; f has an absolute maximum at $x = 4$; f has an absolute minimum at $x = 0$; and f has a local minimum at $x = 2$.

20. $f'(x) = 0$ for $x = 1, 2,$ and 3; f has an absolute minimum at $x = 1$; f has no local extremum at $x = 2$; and f has an absolute maximum at $x = 3$.

21. $f'(1)$ and $f'(3)$ are undefined; $f'(2) = 0$; f has a local maximum at $x = 1$; f has a local minimum at $x = 2$; f has an absolute maximum at $x = 3$; and f has an absolute minimum at $x = 4$.

22. $f'(x) = 0$ at $x = 1$ and 3; $f'(2)$ is undefined; f has an absolute maximum at $x = 2$; f has neither a local maximum nor a local minimum at $x = 1$; and f has an absolute minimum at $x = 3$.

23–36. Locating critical points

  a. *Find the critical points of the following functions on the domain or on the given interval.*

  b. *Use a graphing utility to determine whether each critical point corresponds to a local maximum, local minimum, or neither.*

23. $f(x) = 3x^2 - 4x + 2$ **24.** $f(x) = \dfrac{1}{8}x^3 - \dfrac{1}{2}x$ on $[-1, 3]$

25. $f(x) = \dfrac{x^3}{3} - 9x$ on $[-7, 7]$

26. $f(x) = \dfrac{x^4}{4} - \dfrac{x^3}{3} - 3x^2 + 10$ on $[-4, 4]$

27. $f(x) = 3x^3 + \dfrac{3x^2}{2} - 2x$ on $[-1, 1]$

28. $f(x) = \dfrac{4x^5}{5} - 3x^3 + 5$ on $[-2, 2]$

29. $f(x) = x/(x^2 + 1)$ **30.** $f(x) = 12x^5 - 20x^3$ on $[-2, 2]$

31. $f(x) = (e^x + e^{-x})/2$ **32.** $f(x) = \sin x \cos x$ on $[0, 2\pi]$

33. $f(x) = 1/x + \ln x$ **34.** $f(x) = x^2 - 2\ln(x^2 + 1)$

35. $f(x) = x^2\sqrt{x + 1}$ on $[-1, 1]$

36. $f(x) = (\sin^{-1} x)(\cos^{-1} x)$ on $[0, 1]$

37–50. Absolute maxima and minima

  a. *Find the critical points of f on the given interval.*

  b. *Determine the absolute extreme values of f on the given interval when they exist.*

  c. *Use a graphing utility to confirm your conclusions.*

37. $f(x) = x^2 - 10$ on $[-2, 3]$

38. $f(x) = (x + 1)^{4/3}$ on $[-9, 7]$

39. $f(x) = \cos^2 x$ on $[0, \pi]$

40. $f(x) = x/(x^2 + 3)^2$ on $[-2, 2]$

41. $f(x) = \sin 3x$ on $[-\pi/4, \pi/3]$

42. $f(x) = x^{2/3}$ on $[-8, 8]$

43. $f(x) = (2x)^x$ on $[0.1, 1]$

44. $f(x) = xe^{1-x/2}$ on $[0, 5]$

45. $f(x) = x^2 + \cos^{-1} x$ on $[-1, 1]$

46. $f(x) = x\sqrt{2 - x^2}$ on $[-\sqrt{2}, \sqrt{2}]$

47. $f(x) = 2x^3 - 15x^2 + 24x$ on $[0, 5]$

48. $f(x) = |2x - x^2|$ on $[-2, 3]$

49. $f(x) = \dfrac{4x^3}{3} + 5x^2 - 6x$ on $[-4, 1]$

50. $f(x) = 2x^6 - 15x^4 + 24x^2$ on $[-2, 2]$

51. Trajectory high point A stone is launched vertically upward from a cliff 192 feet above the ground at a speed of 64 ft/s. Its height above the ground t seconds after the launch is given by $s = -16t^2 + 64t + 192$, for $0 \le t \le 6$. When does the stone reach its maximum height?

52. Maximizing revenue A sales analyst determines that the revenue from sales of fruit smoothies is given by $R(x) = -60x^2 + 300x$, where x is the price in dollars charged per item, for $0 \le x \le 5$.

  a. Find the critical points of the revenue function.

  b. Determine the absolute maximum value of the revenue function and the price that maximizes the revenue.

53. Maximizing profit Suppose a tour guide has a bus that holds a maximum of 100 people. Assume his profit (in dollars) for taking n people on a city tour is $P(n) = n(50 - 0.5n) - 100$. (Although P is defined only for positive integers, treat it as a continuous function.)

  a. How many people should the guide take on a tour to maximize the profit?

  b. Suppose the bus holds a maximum of 45 people. How many people should be taken on a tour to maximize the profit?

54. Maximizing rectangle perimeters All rectangles with an area of 64 have a perimeter given by $P(x) = 2x + 128/x$, where x is the length of one side of the rectangle. Find the absolute minimum value of the perimeter function on the interval $(0, \infty)$. What are the dimensions of the rectangle with minimum perimeter?

Further Explorations

55. Explain why or why not Determine whether the following statements are true and give an explanation or counterexample.

  a. The function $f(x) = \sqrt{x}$ has a local maximum on the interval $[0, \infty)$.

  b. If a function has an absolute maximum on a closed interval, then the function must be continuous on that interval.

  c. A function f has the property that $f'(2) = 0$. Therefore, f has a local extreme value at $x = 2$.

  d. Absolute extreme values of a function on a closed interval always occur at a critical point or an endpoint of the interval.

56–63. Absolute maxima and minima

  a. *Find the critical points of f on the given interval.*

  b. *Determine the absolute extreme values of f on the given interval.*

  c. *Use a graphing utility to confirm your conclusions.*

56. $f(x) = (x - 2)^{1/2}$ on $[2, 6]$

57. $f(x) = 2^x \sin x$ on $[-2, 6]$

58. $f(x) = x^{1/2}(x^2/5 - 4)$ on $[0, 4]$

59. $f(x) = \sec x$ on $[-\pi/4, \pi/4]$

60. $f(x) = x^{1/3}(x + 4)$ on $[-27, 27]$

61. $f(x) = x^3 e^{-x}$ on $[-1, 5]$

62. $f(x) = x \ln(x/5)$ on $[0.1, 5]$

63. $f(x) = x/\sqrt{x - 4}$ on $[6, 12]$

64–67. Critical points of functions with unknown parameters *Find the critical points of f. Assume a is a constant.*

64. $f(x) = x/\sqrt{x - a}$ **65.** $f(x) = x\sqrt{x - a}$

66. $f(x) = x^3 - 3ax^2 + 3a^2x - a^3$

67. $f(x) = \dfrac{1}{5}x^5 - a^4x$

68–73. Critical points and extreme values

a. *Find the critical points of the following functions on the given interval.*

b. *Use a graphing utility to determine whether the critical points correspond to local maxima, local minima, or neither.*

c. *Find the absolute maximum and minimum values on the given interval when they exist.*

68. $f(x) = 6x^4 - 16x^3 - 45x^2 + 54x + 23$ on $[-5, 5]$

69. $f(\theta) = 2 \sin \theta + \cos \theta$ on $[-2\pi, 2\pi]$

70. $f(x) = x^{2/3}(4 - x^2)$ on $[-3, 4]$

71. $g(x) = (x - 3)^{5/3}(x + 2)$ on $[-4, 4]$

72. $f(t) = 3t/(t^2 + 1)$ on $[-2, 2]$

73. $h(x) = (5 - x)/(x^2 + 2x - 3)$ on $[-10, 10]$

74–75. Absolute value functions *Graph the following functions and determine the local and absolute extreme values on the given interval.*

74. $f(x) = |x - 3| + |x + 2|$ on $[-4, 4]$

75. $g(x) = |x - 3| - 2|x + 1|$ on $[-2, 3]$

Applications

76. Minimum surface area box All boxes with a square base and a volume of 50 ft^3 have a surface area given by $S(x) = 2x^2 + 200/x$, where x is the length of the sides of the base. Find the absolute minimum of the surface area function on the interval $(0, \infty)$. What are the dimensions of the box with minimum surface area?

77. Every second counts You must get from a point P on the straight shore of a lake to a stranded swimmer who is 50 m from a point Q on the shore that is 50 m from you (see figure). If you can swim at a speed of 2 m/s and run at a speed of 4 m/s, at what point along the shore, x meters from Q, should you stop running and start swimming if you want to reach the swimmer in the minimum time?

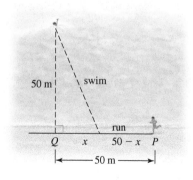

a. Find the function T that gives the travel time as a function of x, where $0 \le x \le 50$.

b. Find the critical point of T on $(0, 50)$.

c. Evaluate T at the critical point and the endpoints ($x = 0$ and $x = 50$) to verify that the critical point corresponds to an absolute minimum. What is the minimum travel time?

d. Graph the function T to check your work.

78. Dancing on a parabola Two people, A and B, walk along the parabola $y = x^2$ in such a way that the line segment L between them is always perpendicular to the line tangent to the parabola at A's position. What are the positions of A and B when L has minimum length?

a. Assume that A's position is (a, a^2), where $a > 0$. Find the slope of the line tangent to the parabola at A and find the slope of the line that is perpendicular to the tangent line at A.

b. Find the equation of the line joining A and B when A is at (a, a^2).

c. Find the position of B on the parabola when A is at (a, a^2).

d. Write the function $F(a)$ that gives the *square* of the distance between A and B as it varies with a. (The square of the distance is minimized at the same point that the distance is minimized; it is easier to work with the square of the distance.)

e. Find the critical point of F on the interval $a > 0$.

f. Evaluate F at the critical point and verify that it corresponds to an absolute minimum. What are the positions of A and B that minimize the length of L? What is the minimum length?

g. Graph the function F to check your work.

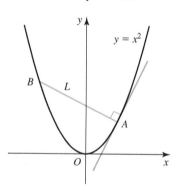

Additional Exercises

79. Values of related functions Suppose f is differentiable on $(-\infty, \infty)$ and assume it has a local extreme value at the point $x = 2$, where $f(2) = 0$. Let $g(x) = xf(x) + 1$ and let $h(x) = xf(x) + x + 1$, for all values of x.

a. Evaluate $g(2), h(2), g'(2)$, and $h'(2)$.

b. Does either g or h have a local extreme value at $x = 2$? Explain.

80. Extreme values of parabolas Consider the function $f(x) = ax^2 + bx + c$, with $a \ne 0$. Explain geometrically why f has exactly one absolute extreme value on $(-\infty, \infty)$. Find the critical point to determine the value of x at which f has an extreme value.

81. Even and odd functions

   a. Suppose a nonconstant even function f has a local minimum at c. Does f have a local maximum or minimum at $-c$? Explain. (An even function satisfies $f(-x) = f(x)$.)

   b. Suppose a nonconstant odd function f has a local minimum at c. Does f have a local maximum or minimum at $-c$? Explain. (An odd function satisfies $f(-x) = -f(x)$.)

82. A family of double-humped functions Consider the functions $f(x) = x/(x^2 + 1)^n$, where n is a positive integer.

   a. Show that these functions are odd for all positive integers n.

   b. Show that the critical points of these functions are
$$x = \pm \frac{1}{\sqrt{2n - 1}},$$ for all positive integers n. (Start with the special cases $n = 1$ and $n = 2$.)

   c. Show that as n increases, the absolute maximum values of these functions decrease.

   d. Use a graphing utility to verify your conclusions.

83. Proof of the Local Extreme Value Theorem Prove Theorem 4.2 for a local maximum: If f has a local maximum value at the point c and $f'(c)$ exists, then $f'(c) = 0$. Use the following steps.

   a. Suppose f has a local maximum at c. What is the sign of $f(x) - f(c)$ if x is near c and $x > c$? What is the sign of $f(x) - f(c)$ if x is near c and $x < c$?

   b. If $f'(c)$ exists, then it is defined by $\lim\limits_{x \to c} \dfrac{f(x) - f(c)}{x - c}$. Examine this limit as $x \to c^+$ and conclude that $f'(c) \le 0$.

   c. Examine the limit in part (b) as $x \to c^-$ and conclude that $f'(c) \ge 0$.

   d. Combine parts (b) and (c) to conclude that $f'(c) = 0$.

QUICK CHECK ANSWERS

1. The continuous function $f(x) = x$ does not have an absolute minimum on the open interval $(0, 1)$. The function $f(x) = -x$ on $\left[0, \frac{1}{2}\right)$ and $f(x) = 0$ on $\left[\frac{1}{2}, 1\right]$ does not have an absolute minimum on $[0, 1]$.   **2.** The critical point is $x = 0$. Although $f'(0) = 0$, the function has neither a local maximum nor minimum at $x = 0$. ◄

4.2 What Derivatives Tell Us

In the previous section, we saw that the derivative is a tool for finding critical points, which are related to local maxima and minima. As we show in this section, derivatives (first *and* second derivatives) tell us much more about the behavior of functions.

Increasing and Decreasing Functions

We have used the terms *increasing* and *decreasing* informally in earlier sections to describe a function or its graph. For example, the graph in Figure 4.13a rises as x increases, so the corresponding function is increasing. In Figure 4.13b, the graph falls as x increases, so the corresponding function is decreasing. The following definition makes these ideas precise.

> ▶ A function is called **monotonic** if it is either increasing or decreasing. We can make a further distinction by defining **nondecreasing** ($f(x_2) \ge f(x_1)$ whenever $x_2 > x_1$) and **nonincreasing** ($f(x_2) \le f(x_1)$ whenever $x_2 > x_1$).

DEFINITION Increasing and Decreasing Functions

Suppose a function f is defined on an interval I. We say that f is **increasing** on I if $f(x_2) > f(x_1)$ whenever x_1 and x_2 are in I and $x_2 > x_1$. We say that f is **decreasing** on I if $f(x_2) < f(x_1)$ whenever x_1 and x_2 are in I and $x_2 > x_1$.

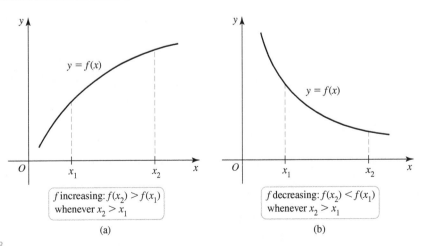

f increasing: $f(x_2) > f(x_1)$ whenever $x_2 > x_1$

(a)

f decreasing: $f(x_2) < f(x_1)$ whenever $x_2 > x_1$

(b)

Figure 4.13

Intervals of Increase and Decrease   The graph of a function f gives us an idea of the intervals on which f is increasing and decreasing. But how do we determine those intervals precisely? This question is answered by making a connection to the derivative.

Recall that the derivative of a function gives the slopes of tangent lines. If the derivative is positive on an interval, the tangent lines on that interval have positive slopes, and the function is increasing on the interval (Figure 4.14a). Said differently, positive derivatives on an interval imply positive rates of change on the interval, which, in turn, indicate an increase in function values.

Similarly, if the derivative is negative on an interval, the tangent lines on that interval have negative slopes, and the function is decreasing on that interval (Figure 4.14b). These observations are proved in Section 4.6 using a result called the Mean Value Theorem.

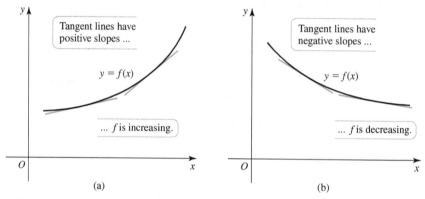

Figure 4.14

▶ The converse of Theorem 4.3 may not be true. According to the definition, $f(x) = x^3$ is increasing on $(-\infty, \infty)$ but it is not true that $f'(x) > 0$ on $(-\infty, \infty)$ (because $f'(0) = 0$).

THEOREM 4.3   Test for Intervals of Increase and Decrease
Suppose f is continuous on an interval I and differentiable at all interior points of I. If $f'(x) > 0$ at all interior points of I, then f is increasing on I. If $f'(x) < 0$ at all interior points of I, then f is decreasing on I.

QUICK CHECK 1 Explain why a positive derivative on an interval implies that the function is increasing on the interval. ◀

EXAMPLE 1   Sketching a function   Sketch a graph of a function f that is continuous on $(-\infty, \infty)$ and satisfies the following conditions.

1. $f' > 0$ on $(-\infty, 0), (4, 6)$, and $(6, \infty)$.
2. $f' < 0$ on $(0, 4)$.
3. $f'(0)$ is undefined.
4. $f'(4) = f'(6) = 0$.

SOLUTION By condition (1), f is increasing on the intervals $(-\infty, 0), (4, 6)$, and $(6, \infty)$. By condition (2), f is decreasing on $(0, 4)$. Continuity of f and condition (3) imply that f has a cusp or corner at $x = 0$, and by condition (4), the graph has a horizontal tangent line at $x = 4$ and $x = 6$. It is useful to summarize these results using a *sign graph* (Figure 4.15).

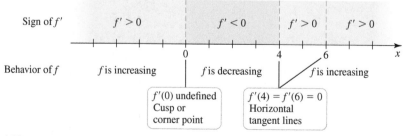

Figure 4.15

One possible graph satisfying these conditions is shown in Figure 4.16. Notice that the graph has a cusp at $x = 0$. Furthermore, although $f'(4) = f'(6) = 0$, f has a local minimum at $x = 4$ but no local extremum at $x = 6$.

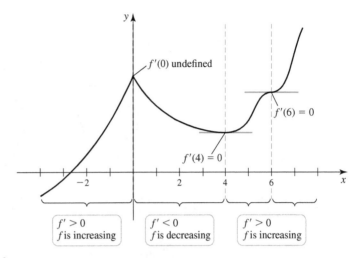

$f'(0)$ undefined

$f'(6) = 0$

$f'(4) = 0$

| $f' > 0$ | $f' < 0$ | $f' > 0$ |
| f is increasing | f is decreasing | f is increasing |

Figure 4.16

Related Exercises 11–16 ◄

EXAMPLE 2 **Intervals of increase and decrease** Find the intervals on which the following functions are increasing and decreasing.

a. $f(x) = xe^{-x}$ **b.** $f(x) = 2x^3 + 3x^2 + 1$

SOLUTION

a. By the Product Rule, $f'(x) = e^{-x} + x(-e^{-x}) = (1 - x)e^{-x}$. Solving $f'(x) = 0$ and noting that $e^{-x} \neq 0$ for all x, the sole critical point is $x = 1$. Therefore, if f' changes sign, then it does so at $x = 1$ and nowhere else, which implies f' has the same sign throughout each of the intervals $(-\infty, 1)$ and $(1, \infty)$. We determine the sign of f' on each interval by evaluating f' at selected points in each interval:

- At $x = 0$, $f'(0) = 1 > 0$. So $f' > 0$ on $(-\infty, 1)$, which means that f is increasing on $(-\infty, 1)$.
- At $x = 2$, $f'(2) = -e^{-2} < 0$. So $f' < 0$ on $(1, \infty)$, which means that f is decreasing on $(1, \infty)$.

Note also that the graph of f has a horizontal tangent line at $x = 1$. We verify these conclusions by plotting f and f' (Figure 4.17).

b. In this case, $f'(x) = 6x^2 + 6x = 6x(x + 1)$. To find the intervals of increase, we first solve $6x(x + 1) = 0$ and determine that the critical points are $x = 0$ and $x = -1$. If f' changes sign, then it does so at these points and nowhere else; that is, f' has the same sign throughout each of the intervals $(-\infty, -1)$, $(-1, 0)$, and $(0, \infty)$. Evaluating f' at selected points of each interval determines the sign of f' on that interval.

- At $x = -2$, $f'(-2) = 12 > 0$, so $f' > 0$ and f is increasing on $(-\infty, -1)$.
- At $x = -\frac{1}{2}$, $f'(-\frac{1}{2}) = -\frac{3}{2} < 0$, so $f' < 0$ and f is decreasing on $(-1, 0)$.
- At $x = 1$, $f'(1) = 12 > 0$, so $f' > 0$ and f is increasing on $(0, \infty)$.

The graph of f has a horizontal tangent line at $x = -1$ and $x = 0$. Figure 4.18 shows the graph of f superimposed on the graph of f', confirming our conclusions.

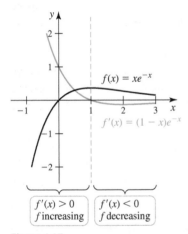

$f(x) = xe^{-x}$

$f'(x) = (1 - x)e^{-x}$

| $f'(x) > 0$ | $f'(x) < 0$ |
| f increasing | f decreasing |

Figure 4.17

➤ Appendix A shows how to solve inequalities using test values.

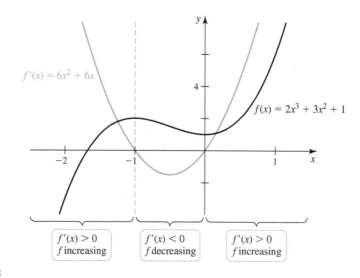

Figure 4.18

Related Exercises 17–38 ◄

Identifying Local Maxima and Minima

Using what we know about increasing and decreasing functions, we can now identify local extrema. Suppose $x = c$ is a critical point of f, where $f'(c) = 0$. Suppose also that f' changes sign at c with $f'(x) < 0$ on an interval (a, c) to the left of c and $f'(x) > 0$ on an interval (c, b) to the right of c. In this case f' is decreasing to the left of c and increasing to the right of c, which means that f has a local minimum at c, as shown in Figure 4.19a.

Similarly, suppose f' changes sign at c with $f'(x) > 0$ on an interval (a, c) to the left of c and $f'(x) < 0$ on an interval (c, b) to the right of c. Then f is increasing to the left of c and decreasing to the right of c, so f has a local maximum at c, as shown in Figure 4.19b.

Figure 4.20 shows typical features of a function on an interval $[a, b]$. At local maxima or minima (c_2, c_3, and c_4), f' changes sign. Although c_1 and c_5 are critical points, the sign of f' is the same on both sides near these points, so there is no local maximum or minimum at these points. As emphasized earlier, *critical points do not always correspond to local extreme values.*

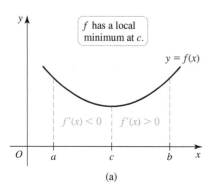

Figure 4.19

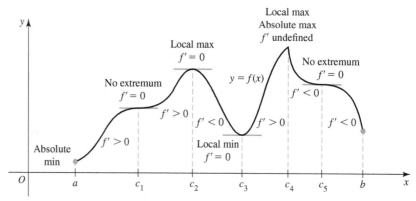

Figure 4.20

QUICK CHECK 2 Sketch a function f that is differentiable on $(-\infty, \infty)$ with the following properties: (i) $x = 0$ and $x = 2$ are critical points; (ii) f is increasing on $(-\infty, 2)$; (iii) f is decreasing on $(2, \infty)$. ◄

First Derivative Test   The observations used to interpret Figure 4.20 are summarized in a powerful test for identifying local maxima and minima.

> **THEOREM 4.4   First Derivative Test**
> Suppose that f is continuous on an interval that contains a critical point c and assume f is differentiable on an interval containing c, except perhaps at c itself.
>
> • If f' changes sign from positive to negative as x increases through c, then f has a **local maximum** at c.
>
> • If f' changes sign from negative to positive as x increases through c, then f has a **local minimum** at c.
>
> • If f' is positive on both sides near c or negative on both sides near c, then f has no local extreme value at c.

Proof: Suppose that $f'(x) > 0$ on an interval (a, c). By Theorem 4.3, we know that f is increasing on (a, c), which implies that $f(x) < f(c)$ for all x in (a, c). Similarly, suppose that $f'(x) < 0$ on an interval (c, b). This time Theorem 4.3 says that f is decreasing on (c, b), which implies that $f(x) < f(c)$ for all x in (c, b). Therefore, $f(x) \leq f(c)$ for all x in (a, b) and f has a local maximum at c. The proofs of the other two cases are similar.   ◄

EXAMPLE 3   Using the First Derivative Test Consider the function
$$f(x) = 3x^4 - 4x^3 - 6x^2 + 12x + 1.$$

a. Find the intervals on which f is increasing and decreasing.

b. Identify the local extrema of f.

SOLUTION

a. Differentiating f, we find that
$$\begin{aligned} f'(x) &= 12x^3 - 12x^2 - 12x + 12 \\ &= 12(x^3 - x^2 - x + 1) \\ &= 12(x + 1)(x - 1)^2. \end{aligned}$$

Solving $f'(x) = 0$ gives the critical points $x = -1$ and $x = 1$. The critical points determine the intervals $(-\infty, -1)$, $(-1, 1)$, and $(1, \infty)$ on which f' does not change sign. Choosing a test point in each interval, a sign graph of f' is constructed (Figure 4.21) that summarizes the behavior of f.

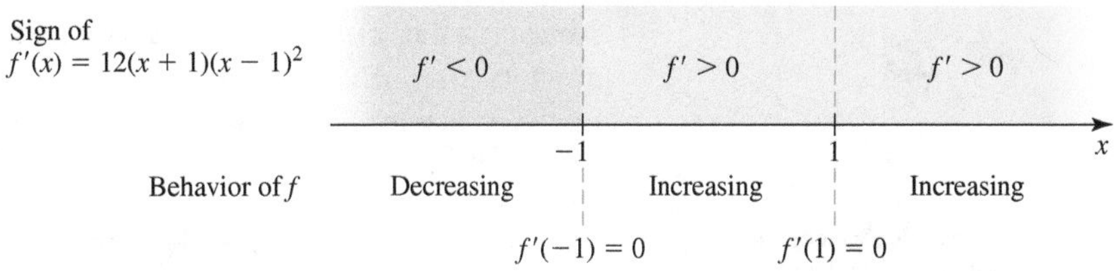

Sign of $f'(x) = 12(x + 1)(x - 1)^2$	$f' < 0$	$f' > 0$	$f' > 0$
		-1	1
Behavior of f	Decreasing	Increasing	Increasing
		$f'(-1) = 0$	$f'(1) = 0$

Figure 4.21

b. Note that f is a polynomial, so it is continuous on $(-\infty, \infty)$. Because f' changes sign from negative to positive as x passes through the critical point $x = -1$, it follows by the First Derivative Test that f has a local minimum value of $f(-1) = -10$ at $x = -1$. Observe that f' is positive on both sides near $x = 1$, so f does not have a local extreme value at $x = 1$ (Figure 4.22).

Related Exercises 39–48 ◄

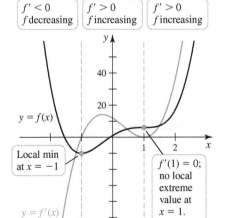

$f' < 0$	$f' > 0$	$f' > 0$
f decreasing	f increasing	f increasing

$y = f(x)$

Local min at $x = -1$

$f'(1) = 0$; no local extreme value at $x = 1$.

$y = f'(x)$

Figure 4.22

EXAMPLE 4   Extreme values   Find the local extrema of the function
$g(x) = x^{2/3}(2 - x)$.

SOLUTION   In Example 4b of Section 4.1, we found that

$$g'(x) = \frac{4}{3}x^{-1/3} - \frac{5}{3}x^{2/3} = \frac{4 - 5x}{3x^{1/3}}$$

and that the critical points of g are $x = 0$ and $x = \frac{4}{5}$. These two critical points are *candidates* for local extrema, and Theorem 4.4 is used to classify each as a local maximum, local minimum, or neither.

On the interval $(-\infty, 0)$, the numerator of g' is positive and the denominator is negative (Figure 4.23). Therefore, $g'(x) < 0$ on $(-\infty, 0)$. On the interval $(0, \frac{4}{5})$, the numerator of g' is positive, as is the denominator. Therefore, $g'(x) > 0$ on $(0, \frac{4}{5})$. We see that as x passes through 0, g' changes sign from negative to positive, which means g has a local minimum at 0. A similar argument shows that g' changes sign from positive to negative as x passes through $\frac{4}{5}$, so g has a local maximum at $\frac{4}{5}$. These observations are confirmed by the graphs of g and g' (Figure 4.24).

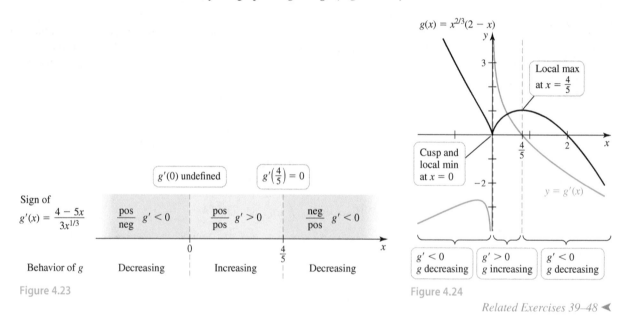

Sign of
$g'(x) = \dfrac{4 - 5x}{3x^{1/3}}$ $\dfrac{\text{pos}}{\text{neg}}\ g' < 0$ $\dfrac{\text{pos}}{\text{pos}}\ g' > 0$ $\dfrac{\text{neg}}{\text{pos}}\ g' < 0$

Behavior of g Decreasing   Increasing   Decreasing

Figure 4.23

Figure 4.24

Related Exercises 39–48 ◄

QUICK CHECK 3   Explain how the First Derivative Test determines whether $f(x) = x^2$ has a local maximum or local minimum at the critical point $x = 0$. ◄

Absolute Extreme Values on Any Interval   Theorem 4.1 guarantees the existence of absolute extreme values only on closed intervals. What can be said about absolute extrema on intervals that are not closed? The following theorem provides a valuable test.

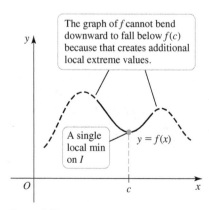

The graph of f cannot bend downward to fall below $f(c)$ because that creates additional local extreme values.

A single local min on I

$y = f(x)$

Figure 4.25

> **THEOREM 4.5   One Local Extremum Implies Absolute Extremum**
> Suppose f is continuous on an interval I that contains exactly one local extremum at c.
>
> • If a local maximum occurs at c, then $f(c)$ is the absolute maximum of f on I.
> • If a local minimum occurs at c, then $f(c)$ is the absolute minimum of f on I.

The proof of Theorem 4.5 is beyond the scope of this text, although Figure 4.25 illustrates why the theorem is plausible. Assume f has exactly one local minimum on I at c. Notice that there is no other point on the graph at which f has a value less than $f(c)$. If such a point did exist, the graph would have to bend downward to drop below $f(c)$. Because f is continuous, this cannot happen as it implies additional local extreme values on I. A similar argument applies to a solitary local maximum.

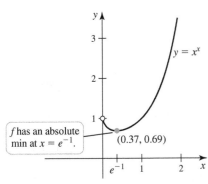

f has an absolute min at $x = e^{-1}$.

(0.37, 0.69)

Figure 4.26

EXAMPLE 5 **Finding an absolute extremum** Verify that $f(x) = x^x$ has an absolute extreme value on its domain.

SOLUTION First note that f is continuous on its domain $(0, \infty)$. Because $f(x) = x^x = e^{x \ln x}$, it follows that

$$f'(x) = e^{x \ln x}(1 + \ln x) = x^x(1 + \ln x).$$

Solving $f'(x) = 0$ gives a single critical point $x = e^{-1}$; there is no point in the domain at which $f'(x)$ does not exist. The critical point splits the domain of f into the intervals $(0, e^{-1})$ and (e^{-1}, ∞). Evaluating the sign of f' on each interval gives $f'(x) < 0$ on $(0, e^{-1})$ and $f'(x) > 0$ on (e^{-1}, ∞); therefore, by the First Derivative Test, a local minimum occurs at $x = e^{-1}$. Because it is the only local extremum on $(0, \infty)$, it follows from Theorem 4.5 that the absolute minimum of f occurs at $x = e^{-1}$ (Figure 4.26). Its value is $f(e^{-1}) \approx 0.69$.

Related Exercises 49–52 ◄

Concavity and Inflection Points

Just as the first derivative is related to the slope of tangent lines, the second derivative also has geometric meaning. Consider $f(x) = x^3$, shown in Figure 4.27. Its graph bends upward for $x > 0$, reflecting the fact that the tangent lines get steeper as x increases. It follows that the first derivative is increasing for $x > 0$. A function with the property that f' is increasing on an interval is *concave up* on that interval.

Similarly, $f(x) = x^3$ bends downward for $x < 0$ because it has a decreasing first derivative on that interval. A function with the property that f' is decreasing as x increases on an interval is *concave down* on that interval.

Here is another useful characterization of concavity. If a function is concave up at a point (any point $x > 0$ in Figure 4.27), then its graph near that point lies *above* the tangent line at that point. Similarly, if a function is concave down at a point (any point $x < 0$ in Figure 4.27), then its graph near that point lies *below* the tangent line at that point (Exercise 104).

Finally, imagine a function f that changes concavity (from up to down, or vice versa) at a point c in the domain of f. For example, $f(x) = x^3$ in Figure 4.27 changes from concave down to concave up as x passes through $x = 0$. A point on the graph of f at which f changes concavity is called an *inflection point*.

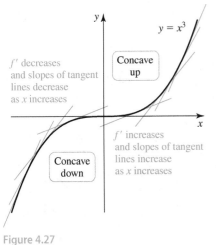

f' decreases and slopes of tangent lines decrease as x increases

Concave up

Concave down

f' increases and slopes of tangent lines increase as x increases

Figure 4.27

DEFINITION **Concavity and Inflection Point**

Let f be differentiable on an open interval I. If f' is increasing on I, then f is **concave up** on I. If f' is decreasing on I, then f is **concave down** on I.

If f is continuous at c and f changes concavity at c (from up to down, or vice versa), then f has an **inflection point** at c.

Applying Theorem 4.3 to f' leads to a test for concavity in terms of the second derivative. Specifically, if $f'' > 0$ on an interval I, then f' is increasing on I and f is concave up on I. Similarly, if $f'' < 0$ on I, then f is concave down on I. In addition, if the values of f'' change sign at a point c (from positive to negative, or vice versa), then the concavity of f changes at c and f has an inflection point at c (Figure 4.28a). We now have a useful interpretation of the second derivative: It measures *concavity*.

> **THEOREM 4.6** **Test for Concavity**
> Suppose that f'' exists on an open interval I.
>
> - If $f'' > 0$ on I, then f is concave up on I.
> - If $f'' < 0$ on I, then f is concave down on I.
> - If c is a point of I at which f'' changes sign at c (from positive to negative, or vice versa), then f has an inflection point at c.

There are a few important but subtle points here. The fact that $f''(c) = 0$ does not necessarily imply that f has an inflection point at c. A good example is $f(x) = x^4$. Although $f''(0) = 0$, the concavity does not change at $x = 0$ (a similar function is shown in Figure 4.28b).

Typically, if f has an inflection point at c, then $f''(c) = 0$, reflecting the smooth change in concavity. However, an inflection point may also occur at a point where f'' does not exist. For example, the function $f(x) = x^{1/3}$ has a vertical tangent line and an inflection point at $x = 0$ (a similar function is shown in Figure 4.28c). Finally, note that the function shown in Figure 4.28d, with behavior similar to that of $f(x) = x^{2/3}$, does not have an inflection point at c despite the fact that $f''(c)$ does not exist. In summary, if $f''(c) = 0$ or $f''(c)$ does not exist, then $(c, f(c))$ is a candidate for an inflection point. To be certain an inflection point occurs at c, we must show that the concavity of f changes at c.

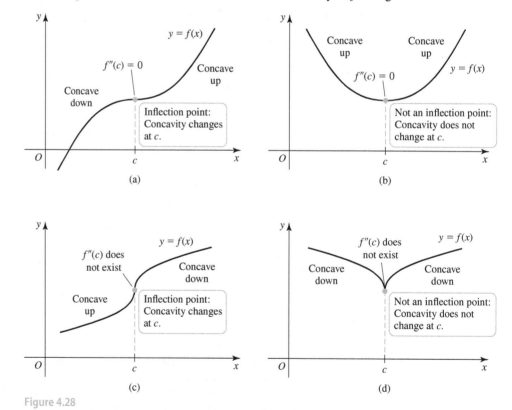

Figure 4.28

QUICK CHECK 4 Verify that the function $f(x) = x^4$ is concave up for $x > 0$ and for $x < 0$. Is $x = 0$ an inflection point? Explain. ◄

EXAMPLE 6 **Interpreting concavity** Sketch a function satisfying each set of conditions on some interval.

a. $f'(t) > 0$ and $f''(t) > 0$ **b.** $g'(t) > 0$ and $g''(t) < 0$

c. Which of the functions, f or g, could describe a population that increases and approaches a steady state as $t \to \infty$?

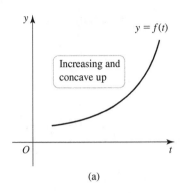

Increasing and concave up

$y = f(t)$

(a)

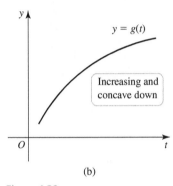

$y = g(t)$

Increasing and concave down

(b)

Figure 4.29

SOLUTION

a. Figure 4.29a shows the graph of a function that is increasing ($f'(t) > 0$) and concave up ($f''(t) > 0$).

b. Figure 4.29b shows the graph of a function that is increasing ($g'(t) > 0$) and concave down ($g''(t) < 0$).

c. Because f increases at an *increasing* rate, the graph of f could not approach a horizontal asymptote, so f could not describe a population that approaches a steady state. On the other hand, g increases at a *decreasing* rate, so its graph could approach a horizontal asymptote, depending on the rate at which g increases.

Related Exercises 53–56 ◀

EXAMPLE 7   Detecting concavity Identify the intervals on which the following functions are concave up or concave down. Then locate the inflection points.

a. $f(x) = 3x^4 - 4x^3 - 6x^2 + 12x + 1$

b. $f(x) = \sin^{-1} x$ on $(-1, 1)$

SOLUTION

a. This function was considered in Example 3, where we found that

$$f'(x) = 12(x + 1)(x - 1)^2.$$

It follows that

$$f''(x) = 12(x - 1)(3x + 1).$$

We see that $f''(x) = 0$ at $x = 1$ and $x = -\frac{1}{3}$. These points are *candidates* for inflection points; to be certain that they are inflection points, we must determine whether the concavity changes at these points. The sign graph in Figure 4.30 shows the following:

• $f''(x) > 0$ and f is concave up on $(-\infty, -\frac{1}{3})$ and $(1, \infty)$.

• $f''(x) < 0$ and f is concave down on $(-\frac{1}{3}, 1)$.

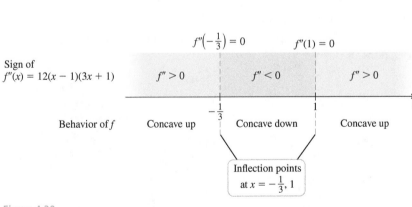

$f''\left(-\frac{1}{3}\right) = 0$ $f''(1) = 0$

Sign of
$f''(x) = 12(x - 1)(3x + 1)$ $f'' > 0$ $f'' < 0$ $f'' > 0$

Behavior of f Concave up $-\frac{1}{3}$ Concave down 1 Concave up

Inflection points
at $x = -\frac{1}{3}, 1$

Figure 4.30

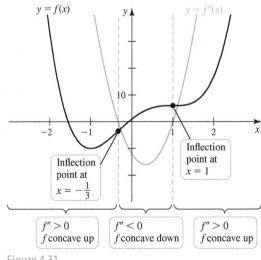

$y = f(x)$ $y = f''(x)$

Inflection point at $x = -\frac{1}{3}$

Inflection point at $x = 1$

$f'' > 0$
f concave up

$f'' < 0$
f concave down

$f'' > 0$
f concave up

Figure 4.31

We see that the sign of f'' changes at $x = -\frac{1}{3}$ and at $x = 1$, so the concavity of f also changes at these points. Therefore, inflection points occur at $x = -\frac{1}{3}$ and $x = 1$. The graphs of f and f'' (Figure 4.31) show that the concavity of f changes at the zeros of f''.

b. The first derivative of $f(x) = \sin^{-1} x$ is $f'(x) = 1/\sqrt{1 - x^2}$. We use the Chain Rule to compute the second derivative:

$$f''(x) = -\frac{1}{2}(1 - x^2)^{-3/2} \cdot (-2x) = \frac{x}{(1 - x^2)^{3/2}}.$$

The only zero of f'' is $x = 0$, and because its denominator is positive on $(-1, 1)$, f'' changes sign at $x = 0$ from negative to positive. Therefore, f is concave down on $(-1, 0)$ and concave up on $(0, 1)$, with an inflection point at $x = 0$ (Figure 4.32).

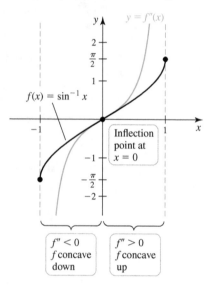

Figure 4.32

Related Exercises 57–70 ◄

Second Derivative Test   It is now a short step to a test that uses the second derivative to identify local maxima and minima.

> ➤ In the inconclusive case of Theorem 4.7 in which $f''(c) = 0$, it is usually best to use the First Derivative Test.

THEOREM 4.7   Second Derivative Test for Local Extrema
Suppose that f'' is continuous on an open interval containing c with $f'(c) = 0$.

• If $f''(c) > 0$, then f has a local minimum at c (Figure 4.33a).

• If $f''(c) < 0$, then f has a local maximum at c (Figure 4.33b).

• If $f''(c) = 0$, then the test is inconclusive; f may have a local maximum, local minimum, or neither at c.

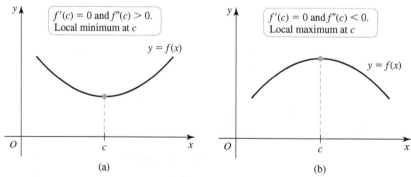

Figure 4.33

Proof: Assume $f''(c) > 0$. Because f'' is continuous on an interval containing c, it follows that $f'' > 0$ on some open interval I containing c and that f' is increasing on I. Because $f'(c) = 0$, it follows that f' changes sign at c from negative to positive, which, by the First Derivative Test, implies that f has a local minimum at c. The proofs of the second and third statements are similar. ◄

QUICK CHECK 5 Sketch a graph of a function with $f'(x) > 0$ and $f''(x) > 0$ on an interval. Sketch a graph of a function with $f'(x) < 0$ and $f''(x) < 0$ on an interval. ◄

EXAMPLE 8 **The Second Derivative Test** Use the Second Derivative Test to locate the local extrema of the following functions.

a. $f(x) = 3x^4 - 4x^3 - 6x^2 + 12x + 1$ on $[-2, 2]$ **b.** $f(x) = \sin^2 x$

SOLUTION

a. This function was considered in Examples 3 and 7, where we found that

$$f'(x) = 12(x + 1)(x - 1)^2 \quad \text{and} \quad f''(x) = 12(x - 1)(3x + 1).$$

Therefore, the critical points of f are $x = -1$ and $x = 1$. Evaluating f'' at the critical points, we find that $f''(-1) = 48 > 0$. By the Second Derivative Test, f has a local minimum at $x = -1$. At the other critical point, $f''(1) = 0$, so the test is inconclusive. You can check that the first derivative does not change sign at $x = 1$, which means f does not have a local maximum or minimum at $x = 1$ (Figure 4.34).

b. Using the Chain Rule and a trigonometric identity, we have $f'(x) = 2 \sin x \cos x = \sin 2x$ and $f''(x) = 2 \cos 2x$. The critical points occur when $f'(x) = \sin 2x = 0$, or when $x = 0, \pm \pi/2, \pm \pi, \ldots$. To apply the Second Derivative Test, we evaluate f'' at the critical points:

- $f''(0) = 2 > 0$, so f has a local minimum at $x = 0$.
- $f''(\pm \pi/2) = -2 < 0$, so f has a local maximum at $x = \pm \pi/2$.
- $f''(\pm \pi) = 2 > 0$, so f has a local minimum at $x = \pm \pi$.

This pattern continues, and we see that f has alternating local maxima and minima, evenly spaced every $\pi/2$ units (Figure 4.35).

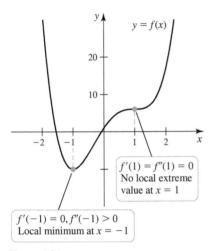

$f'(1) = f''(1) = 0$
No local extreme value at $x = 1$

$f'(-1) = 0, f''(-1) > 0$
Local minimum at $x = -1$

Figure 4.34

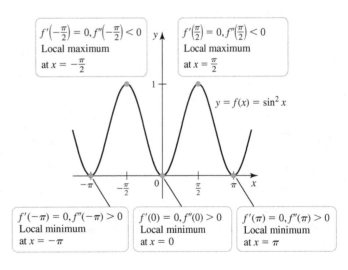

$f'\left(-\frac{\pi}{2}\right) = 0, f''\left(-\frac{\pi}{2}\right) < 0$
Local maximum at $x = -\frac{\pi}{2}$

$f'\left(\frac{\pi}{2}\right) = 0, f''\left(\frac{\pi}{2}\right) < 0$
Local maximum at $x = \frac{\pi}{2}$

$y = f(x) = \sin^2 x$

$f'(-\pi) = 0, f''(-\pi) > 0$
Local minimum at $x = -\pi$

$f'(0) = 0, f''(0) > 0$
Local minimum at $x = 0$

$f'(\pi) = 0, f''(\pi) > 0$
Local minimum at $x = \pi$

Figure 4.35

Related Exercises 71–82 ◄

Recap of Derivative Properties

This section has demonstrated that the first and second derivatives of a function provide valuable information about its graph. The relationships among a function's derivatives and its extreme values and concavity are summarized in Figure 4.36.

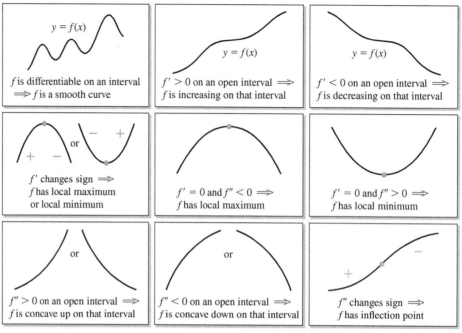

Figure 4.36

SECTION 4.2 EXERCISES

Review Questions

1. Explain how the first derivative of a function determines where the function is increasing and decreasing.

2. Explain how to apply the First Derivative Test.

3. Sketch the graph of a function that has neither a local maximum nor a local minimum at a point where $f'(x) = 0$.

4. Explain how to apply the Second Derivative Test.

5. Suppose f'' exists and is positive on an interval I. Describe the relationship between the graph of f and its tangent lines on the interval I.

6. Sketch a function that changes from concave up to concave down as x increases. Describe how the second derivative of this function changes.

7. What is an inflection point?

8. Give a function that does not have an inflection point at a point where $f''(x) = 0$.

9. Is it possible for a function to satisfy $f(x) > 0, f'(x) > 0$, and $f''(x) < 0$ on an interval? Explain.

10. Suppose f is continuous on an interval containing a critical point c and $f''(c) = 0$. How do you determine whether f has a local extreme value at $x = c$?

Basic Skills

11–14. Sketches from properties *Sketch a graph of a function that is continuous on $(-\infty, \infty)$ and has the following properties. Use a sign graph to summarize information about the function.*

11. $f'(x) < 0$ on $(-\infty, 2); f'(x) > 0$ on $(2, 5); f'(x) < 0$ on $(5, \infty)$

12. $f'(-1)$ is undefined; $f'(x) > 0$ on $(-\infty, -1); f'(x) < 0$ on $(-1, \infty)$

13. $f(0) = f(4) = f'(0) = f'(2) = f'(4) = 0; f(x) \geq 0$ on $(-\infty, \infty)$

14. $f'(-2) = f'(2) = f'(6) = 0; f'(x) \geq 0$ on $(-\infty, \infty)$

15–16. Functions from derivatives *The following figures give the graph of the derivative of a continuous function f that passes through the origin. Sketch a possible graph of f on the same set of axes.*

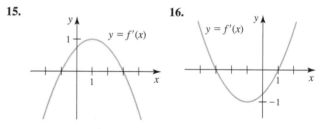

17–26. Increasing and decreasing functions *Find the intervals on which f is increasing and decreasing. Superimpose the graphs of f and f' to verify your work.*

17. $f(x) = 4 - x^2$

18. $f(x) = x^2 - 16$

19. $f(x) = (x - 1)^2$

20. $f(x) = x^3 + 4x$

21. $f(x) = 12 + x - x^2$

22. $f(x) = x^4 - 4x^3 + 4x^2$

23. $f(x) = -\dfrac{x^4}{4} + x^3 - x^2$

24. $f(x) = 2x^5 - \dfrac{15x^4}{4} + \dfrac{5x^3}{3}$

25. $f(x) = x^2 \ln x^2 + 1$

26. $f(x) = \dfrac{e^x}{e^{2x} + 1}$

27–38. Increasing and decreasing functions *Find the intervals on which f is increasing and decreasing.*

27. $f(x) = 3 \cos 3x$ on $[-\pi, \pi]$

28. $f(x) = \cos^2 x$ on $[-\pi, \pi]$

29. $f(x) = x^{2/3}(x^2 - 4)$

30. $f(x) = x^2\sqrt{9 - x^2}$ on $(-3, 3)$

31. $f(x) = \tan^{-1} x$

32. $f(x) = \ln |x|$

33. $f(x) = -12x^5 + 75x^4 - 80x^3$

34. $f(x) = x^2 - 2\ln x$

35. $f(x) = -2x^4 + x^2 + 10$

36. $f(x) = \dfrac{x^4}{4} - \dfrac{8x^3}{3} + \dfrac{15x^2}{2} + 8$

37. $f(x) = xe^{-x^2/2}$

38. $f(x) = \tan^{-1}\left(\dfrac{x}{x^2 + 2}\right)$

39–48. First Derivative Test

a. *Locate the critical points of f.*
b. *Use the First Derivative Test to locate the local maximum and minimum values.*
c. *Identify the absolute maximum and minimum values of the function on the given interval (when they exist).*

39. $f(x) = x^2 + 3$ on $[-3, 2]$

40. $f(x) = -x^2 - x + 2$ on $[-4, 4]$

41. $f(x) = x\sqrt{4 - x^2}$ on $[-2, 2]$

42. $f(x) = 2x^3 + 3x^2 - 12x + 1$ on $[-2, 4]$

43. $f(x) = -x^3 + 9x$ on $[-4, 3]$

44. $f(x) = 2x^5 - 5x^4 - 10x^3 + 4$ on $[-2, 4]$

45. $f(x) = x^{2/3}(x - 5)$ on $[-5, 5]$

46. $f(x) = \dfrac{x^2}{x^2 - 1}$ on $[-4, 4]$

47. $f(x) = \sqrt{x}\ln x$ on $(0, \infty)$

48. $f(x) = \tan^{-1} x - x^3$ on $[-1, 1]$

49–52. Absolute extreme values *Verify that the following functions satisfy the conditions of Theorem 4.5 on their domains. Then find the location and value of the absolute extremum guaranteed by the theorem.*

49. $f(x) = xe^{-x}$

50. $f(x) = 4x + 1/\sqrt{x}$

51. $A(r) = 24/r + 2\pi r^2, r > 0$

52. $f(x) = x\sqrt{3 - x}$

53–56. Sketching curves *Sketch a graph of a function f that is continuous on $(-\infty, \infty)$ and has the following properties.*

53. $f'(x) > 0, f''(x) > 0$

54. $f'(x) < 0$ and $f''(x) > 0$ on $(-\infty, 0); f'(x) > 0$ and $f''(x) > 0$ on $(0, \infty)$

55. $f'(x) < 0$ and $f''(x) < 0$ on $(-\infty, 0); f'(x) < 0$ and $f''(x) > 0$ on $(0, \infty)$

56. $f'(x) < 0$ and $f''(x) > 0$ on $(-\infty, 0); f'(x) < 0$ and $f''(x) < 0$ on $(0, \infty)$

57–70. Concavity *Determine the intervals on which the following functions are concave up or concave down. Identify any inflection points.*

57. $f(x) = x^4 - 2x^3 + 1$

58. $f(x) = -x^4 - 2x^3 + 12x^2$

59. $f(x) = 5x^4 - 20x^3 + 10$

60. $f(x) = \dfrac{1}{1 + x^2}$

61. $f(x) = e^x(x - 3)$

62. $f(x) = 2x^2 \ln x - 5x^2$

63. $g(t) = \ln(3t^2 + 1)$

64. $g(x) = \sqrt[3]{x - 4}$

65. $f(x) = e^{-x^2/2}$

66. $f(x) = \tan^{-1} x$

67. $f(x) = \sqrt{x}\ln x$

68. $h(t) = 2 + \cos 2t$, for $-\pi \le t \le \pi$

69. $g(t) = 3t^5 - 30t^4 + 80t^3 + 100$

70. $f(x) = 2x^4 + 8x^3 + 12x^2 - x - 2$

71–82. Second Derivative Test *Locate the critical points of the following functions. Then use the Second Derivative Test to determine (if possible) whether they correspond to local maxima or local minima.*

71. $f(x) = x^3 - 3x^2$

72. $f(x) = 6x^2 - x^3$

73. $f(x) = 4 - x^2$

74. $g(x) = x^3 - 6$

75. $f(x) = e^x(x - 7)$

76. $f(x) = e^x(x^2 - 7x - 12)$

77. $f(x) = 2x^3 - 3x^2 + 12$

78. $p(x) = x^4 e^{-x}$

79. $f(x) = x^2 e^{-x}$

80. $g(x) = \dfrac{x^4}{2 - 12x^2}$

81. $f(x) = 2x^2 \ln x - 11x^2$

82. $f(x) = \sqrt{x}\left(\dfrac{12}{7}x^3 - 4x^2\right)$

Further Explorations

83. **Explain why or why not** Determine whether the following statements are true and give an explanation or counterexample.

a. If $f'(x) > 0$ and $f''(x) < 0$ on an interval, then f is increasing at a decreasing rate on the interval.

b. If $f'(c) > 0$ and $f''(c) = 0$, then f has a local maximum at c.

c. Two functions that differ by an additive constant both increase and decrease on the same intervals.

d. If f and g increase on an interval, then the product fg also increases on that interval.

e. There exists a function f that is continuous on $(-\infty, \infty)$ with exactly three critical points, all of which correspond to local maxima.

84–85. Functions from derivatives *Consider the following graphs of f' and f''. On the same set of axes, sketch the graph of a possible function f. The graphs of f are not unique.*

84.

85.

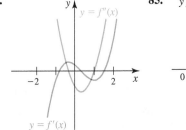

86. **Is it possible?** Determine whether the following properties can be satisfied by a function that is continuous on $(-\infty, \infty)$. If such a function is possible, provide an example or a sketch of the function. If such a function is not possible, explain why.

a. A function f is concave down and positive everywhere.
b. A function f is increasing and concave down everywhere.
c. A function f has exactly two local extrema and three inflection points.
d. A function f has exactly four zeros and two local extrema.

87. Matching derivatives and functions The following figures show the graphs of three functions (graphs a–c). Match each function with its first derivative (graphs d–f) *and* its second derivative (graphs g–i).

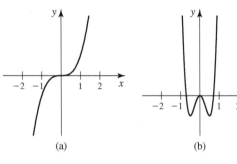

(a)   (b)

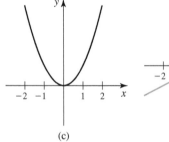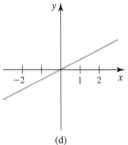

(c)   (d)

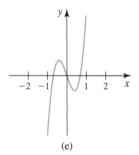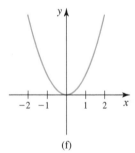

(e)   (f)

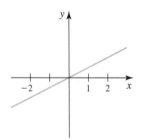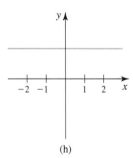

(g)   (h)

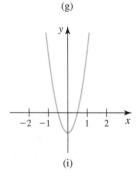

(i)

88. Graphical analysis The figure shows the graphs of f, f', and f''. Which curve is which?

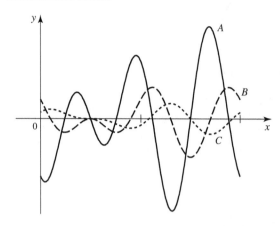

89. Sketching graphs Sketch the graph of a function f continuous on $[a, b]$ such that f, f', and f'' have the signs indicated in the following table on $[a, b]$. There are eight different cases lettered A–H and eight different graphs.

Case	A	B	C	D	E	F	G	H
f	+	+	+	+	−	−	−	−
f'	+	+	−	−	+	+	−	−
f''	+	−	+	−	+	−	+	−

90–93. Designer functions *Sketch the graph of a function that is continuous on $(-\infty, \infty)$ and satisfies the following sets of conditions.*

90. $f''(x) > 0$ on $(-\infty, -2); f''(-2) = 0; f'(-1) = f'(1) = 0;$ $f''(2) = 0; f'(3) = 0; f''(x) > 0$ on $(4, \infty)$

91. $f(-2) = f''(-1) = 0; f'(-\frac{3}{2}) = 0; f(0) = f'(0) = 0;$ $f(1) = f'(1) = 0$

92. $f'(x) > 0$, for all x in the domain of $f'; f'(-2)$ and $f'(1)$ do not exist; $f''(0) = 0$

93. $f''(x) > 0$ on $(-\infty, -2); f''(x) < 0$ on $(-2, 1); f''(x) > 0$ on $(1, 3); f''(x) < 0$ on $(3, \infty)$

94. Graph carefully Graph the function $f(x) = 60x^5 - 901x^3 + 27x$ in the window $[-4, 4] \times [-10000, 10000]$. How many extreme values do you see? Locate *all* the extreme values by analyzing f'.

95. Interpreting the derivative The graph of f' on the interval $[-3, 2]$ is shown in the figure.

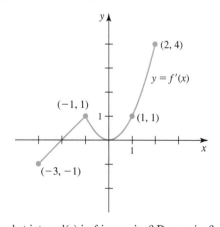

a. On what interval(s) is f increasing? Decreasing?
b. Find the critical points of f. Which critical points correspond to local maxima? Local minima? Neither?

c. At what point(s) does f have an inflection point?

d. On what interval(s) is f concave up? Concave down?

e. Sketch the graph of f''.

f. Sketch one possible graph of f.

96–99. Second Derivative Test *Locate the critical points of the following functions and use the Second Derivative Test to determine (if possible) whether they correspond to local maxima or local minima.*

96. $p(t) = 2t^3 + 3t^2 - 36t$

T 97. $f(x) = \dfrac{x^4}{4} - \dfrac{5x^3}{3} - 4x^2 + 48x$

98. $h(x) = (x + a)^4$; a constant

99. $f(x) = x^3 + 2x^2 + 4x - 1$

100. Concavity of parabolas Consider the general parabola described by the function $f(x) = ax^2 + bx + c$. For what values of $a, b,$ and c is f concave up? For what values of $a, b,$ and c is f concave down?

Applications

T 101. Demand functions and elasticity Economists use *demand functions* to describe how much of a commodity can be sold at varying prices. For example, the demand function $D(p) = 500 - 10p$ says that at a price of $p = 10$, a quantity of $D(10) = 400$ units of the commodity can be sold. The elasticity $E = \dfrac{dD}{dp} \dfrac{p}{D}$ of the demand gives the approximate percent change in the demand for every 1% change in the price. (See Section 3.5 or the Guided Project *Elasticity in Economics* for more on demand functions and elasticity.)

a. Compute the elasticity of the demand function $D(p) = 500 - 10p$.

b. If the price is \$12 and increases by 4.5%, what is the approximate percent change in the demand?

c. Show that for the linear demand function $D(p) = a - bp$, where a and b are positive real numbers, the elasticity is a decreasing function, for $p \geq 0$ and $p \neq a/b$.

d. Show that the demand function $D(p) = a/p^b$, where a and b are positive real numbers, has a constant elasticity for all positive prices.

102. Population models A typical population curve is shown in the figure. The population is small at $t = 0$ and increases toward a steady-state level called the *carrying capacity*. Explain why the maximum growth rate occurs at an inflection point of the population curve.

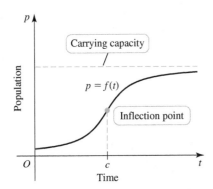

103. Population models The population of a species is given by the function $P(t) = \dfrac{Kt^2}{t^2 + b}$, where $t \geq 0$ is measured in years and K and b are positive real numbers.

a. With $K = 300$ and $b = 30$, what is $\lim\limits_{t \to \infty} P(t)$, the carrying capacity of the population?

b. With $K = 300$ and $b = 30$, when does the maximum growth rate occur?

c. For arbitrary positive values of K and b, when does the maximum growth rate occur (in terms of K and b)?

Additional Exercises

104. Tangent lines and concavity Give an argument to support the claim that if a function is concave up at a point, then the tangent line at that point lies below the curve near that point.

105. Symmetry of cubics Consider the general cubic polynomial $f(x) = x^3 + ax^2 + bx + c$, where $a, b,$ and c are real numbers.

a. Show that f has exactly one inflection point and it occurs at $x^* = -a/3$.

b. Show that f is an odd function with respect to the inflection point $(x^*, f(x^*))$. This means that $f(x^*) - f(x^* + x) = f(x^* - x) - f(x^*)$, for all x.

106. Properties of cubics Consider the general cubic polynomial $f(x) = x^3 + ax^2 + bx + c$, where $a, b,$ and c are real numbers.

a. Prove that f has exactly one local maximum and one local minimum provided that $a^2 > 3b$.

b. Prove that f has no extreme values if $a^2 < 3b$.

T 107. A family of single-humped functions Consider the functions $f(x) = \dfrac{1}{x^{2n} + 1}$, where n is a positive integer.

a. Show that these functions are even.

b. Show that the graphs of these functions intersect at the points $(\pm 1, \frac{1}{2})$, for all positive values of n.

c. Show that the inflection points of these functions occur at $x = \pm \sqrt[2n]{\dfrac{2n - 1}{2n + 1}}$, for all positive values of n.

d. Use a graphing utility to verify your conclusions.

e. Describe how the inflection points and the shape of the graphs change as n increases.

108. Even quartics Consider the quartic (fourth-degree) polynomial $f(x) = x^4 + bx^2 + d$ consisting only of even-powered terms.

a. Show that the graph of f is symmetric about the y-axis.

b. Show that if $b \geq 0$, then f has one critical point and no inflection points.

c. Show that if $b < 0$, then f has three critical points and two inflection points. Find the critical points and inflection points, and show that they alternate along the x-axis. Explain why one critical point is always $x = 0$.

d. Prove that the number of distinct real roots of f depends on the values of the coefficients b and d, as shown in the figure. The curve that divides the plane is the parabola $d = b^2/4$.

e. Find the number of real roots when $b = 0$ or $d = 0$ or $d = b^2/4$.

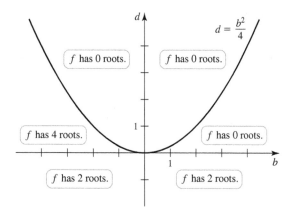

109. General quartic Show that the general quartic (fourth-degree) polynomial $f(x) = x^4 + ax^3 + bx^2 + cx + d$ has either zero or two inflection points, and that the latter case occurs provided that $b < 3a^2/8$.

110. First Derivative Test is not exhaustive Sketch the graph of a (simple) nonconstant function f that has a local maximum at $x = 1$, with $f'(1) = 0$, where f' does not change sign from positive to negative as x increases through 1. Why can't the First Derivative Test be used to classify the critical point at $x = 1$ as a local maximum? How could the test be rephrased to account for such a critical point?

QUICK CHECK ANSWERS

1. Positive derivatives on an interval mean the curve is rising on the interval, which means the function is increasing on the interval.   **2.**

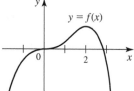

3. $f'(x) < 0$ on $(-\infty, 0)$ and $f'(x) > 0$ on $(0, \infty)$. Therefore, f has a local minimum at $x = 0$ by the First Derivative Test.   **4.** $f''(x) = 12x^2$, so $f''(x) > 0$ for $x < 0$ and for $x > 0$. There is no inflection point at $x = 0$ because the second derivative does not change sign.   **5.** The first curve should be rising and concave up. The second curve should be falling and concave down.

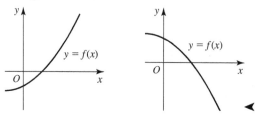

4.3 Graphing Functions

We have now collected the tools required for a comprehensive approach to graphing functions. These *analytical methods* are indispensable, even with the availability of powerful graphing utilities, as illustrated by the following example.

Calculators and Analysis

Suppose you want to graph the harmless-looking function $f(x) = x^3/3 - 400x$. The result of plotting f using a graphing calculator with a default window of $[-10, 10] \times [-10, 10]$ is shown in Figure 4.37a; one vertical line appears on the screen. Zooming out to the window $[-100, 100] \times [-100, 100]$ produces three vertical lines (Figure 4.37b); it is still difficult to understand the behavior of the function using only this graph. Expanding the window even more to $[-1000, 1000] \times [-1000, 1000]$ is no better. So what do we do?

QUICK CHECK 1 Graph $f(x) = x^3/3 - 400x$ using various windows on a graphing calculator. Find a window that gives a better graph of f than those in Figure 4.37. ◄

The function $f(x) = x^3/3 - 400x$ has a reasonable graph, but it cannot be found automatically by letting technology do all the work. Here is the message of this section: Graphing utilities are valuable for exploring functions, producing preliminary graphs, and checking your work. But they should not be relied on exclusively because they cannot explain *why* a graph has its shape. Rather, graphing utilities should be used in an interactive way with the analytical methods presented in this chapter.

Graphing Guidelines

The following set of guidelines need not be followed exactly for every function, and you will find that several steps can often be done at once. Depending on the specific problem,

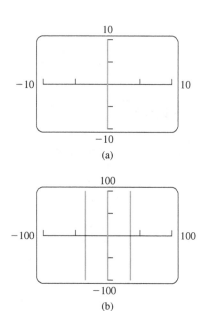

Figure 4.37

some of the steps are best done analytically, while other steps can be done with a graphing utility. Experiment with both approaches and try to find a good balance. We also present a schematic record-keeping procedure to keep track of discoveries as they are made.

> The precise order of these steps may vary from one problem to another.

Graphing Guidelines for $y = f(x)$

1. **Identify the domain or interval of interest.** On what interval(s) should the function be graphed? It may be the domain of the function or some subset of the domain.

2. **Exploit symmetry.** Take advantage of symmetry. For example, is the function *even* $(f(-x) = f(x))$, *odd* $(f(-x) = -f(x))$, or neither?

3. **Find the first and second derivatives.** They are needed to determine extreme values, concavity, inflection points, and intervals of increase and decrease. Computing derivatives—particularly second derivatives—may not be practical, so some functions may need to be graphed without complete derivative information.

4. **Find critical points and possible inflection points.** Determine points at which $f'(x) = 0$ or f' is undefined. Determine points at which $f''(x) = 0$ or f'' is undefined.

5. **Find intervals on which the function is increasing/decreasing and concave up/down.** The first derivative determines the intervals of increase and decrease. The second derivative determines the intervals on which the function is concave up or concave down.

6. **Identify extreme values and inflection points.** Use either the First or Second Derivative Test to classify the critical points. Both x- and y-coordinates of maxima, minima, and inflection points are needed for graphing.

7. **Locate all asymptotes and determine end behavior.** Vertical asymptotes often occur at zeros of denominators. Horizontal asymptotes require examining limits as $x \to \pm \infty$; these limits determine end behavior.

8. **Find the intercepts.** The y-intercept of the graph is found by setting $x = 0$. The x-intercepts are found by setting $y = 0$; they are the real zeros (or roots) of f (those values of x that satisfy $f(x) = 0$).

9. **Choose an appropriate graphing window and plot a graph.** Use the results of the previous steps to graph the function. If you use graphing software, check for consistency with your analytical work. Is your graph *complete*—that is, does it show all the essential details of the function?

EXAMPLE 1   A warm-up Given the following information about the first and second derivatives of a function f that is continuous on $(-\infty, \infty)$, summarize the information using a sign graph, and then sketch a possible graph of f.

$$f' < 0, f'' > 0 \text{ on } (-\infty, 0) \quad f' > 0, f'' > 0 \text{ on } (0, 1) \quad f' > 0, f'' < 0 \text{ on } (1, 2)$$
$$f' < 0, f'' < 0 \text{ on } (2, 3) \qquad f' < 0, f'' > 0 \text{ on } (3, 4) \quad f' > 0, f'' > 0 \text{ on } (4, \infty)$$

SOLUTION Figure 4.38 uses the given information to determine the behavior of f and its graph. For example, on the interval $(-\infty, 0), f$ is decreasing and concave up; so we sketch a segment of a curve with these properties on this interval. Continuing in this manner, we obtain a useful summary of the properties of f.

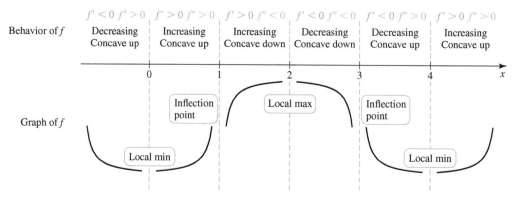

Figure 4.38

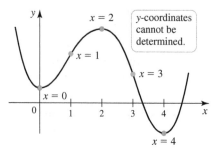

Figure 4.39

Assembling the information shown in Figure 4.38, a possible graph of f is produced (Figure 4.39). Notice that derivative information is not sufficient to determine the y-coordinates of points on the curve.

Related Exercises 7–8 ◄

QUICK CHECK 2 Explain why the function f and $f + C$, where C is a constant, have the same derivative properties. ◄

EXAMPLE 2   A deceptive polynomial Use the graphing guidelines to graph $f(x) = \dfrac{x^3}{3} - 400x$ on its domain.

SOLUTION

1. **Domain** The domain of any polynomial is $(-\infty, \infty)$.
2. **Symmetry** Because f consists of odd powers of the variable, it is an odd function. Its graph is symmetric about the origin.
3. **Derivatives** The derivatives of f are

$$f'(x) = x^2 - 400 \quad \text{and} \quad f''(x) = 2x.$$

> Notice that the first derivative of an odd polynomial is an even polynomial and the second derivative is an odd polynomial (assuming the original polynomial is of degree 3 or greater).

4. **Critical points and possible inflection points** Solving $f'(x) = 0$, we find that the critical points are $x = \pm 20$. Solving $f''(x) = 0$, we see that a possible inflection point occurs at $x = 0$.

> See Appendix A for solving inequalities using test values.

5. **Increasing/decreasing and concavity** Note that

$$f'(x) = x^2 - 400 = (x - 20)(x + 20).$$

Solving the inequality $f'(x) < 0$, we find that f is decreasing on the interval $(-20, 20)$. Solving the inequality $f'(x) > 0$ reveals that f is increasing on the intervals $(-\infty, -20)$ and $(20, \infty)$ (Figure 4.40). By the First Derivative Test, we have enough information to conclude that f has a local maximum at $x = -20$ and a local minimum at $x = 20$.

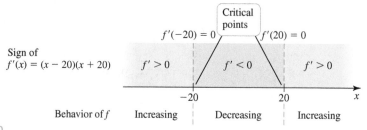

Figure 4.40

Furthermore, $f''(x) = 2x < 0$ on $(-\infty, 0)$, so f is concave down on this interval. Also, $f''(x) > 0$ on $(0, \infty)$, so f is concave up on $(0, \infty)$ (Figure 4.41).

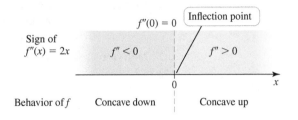

Figure 4.41

The evidence obtained so far is summarized in Figure 4.42.

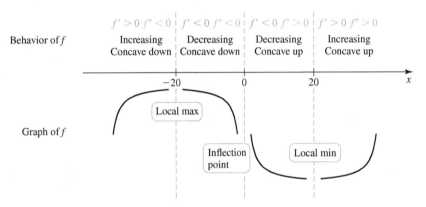

Figure 4.42

6. **Extreme values and inflection points** In this case, the Second Derivative Test is easily applied and it confirms what we have already learned. Because $f''(-20) < 0$ and $f''(20) > 0$, f has a local maximum at $x = -20$ and a local minimum at $x = 20$. The corresponding function values are $f(-20) = 16{,}000/3 = 5333\frac{1}{3}$ and $f(20) = -f(-20) = -5333\frac{1}{3}$. Finally, we see that f'' changes sign at $x = 0$, making $(0, 0)$ an inflection point.

7. **Asymptotes and end behavior** Polynomials have neither vertical nor horizontal asymptotes. Because the highest-power term in the polynomial is x^3 (an odd power) and the leading coefficient is positive, we have the end behavior

$$\lim_{x \to \infty} f(x) = \infty \quad \text{and} \quad \lim_{x \to -\infty} f(x) = -\infty.$$

8. **Intercepts** The y-intercept is $(0, 0)$. We solve the equation $f(x) = 0$ to find the x-intercepts:

$$\frac{x^3}{3} - 400x = x\left(\frac{x^2}{3} - 400\right) = 0.$$

The roots of this equation are $x = 0$ and $x = \pm\sqrt{1200} \approx \pm 34.6$.

9. **Graph the function** Using the information found in Steps 1–8, we choose the graphing window $[-40, 40] \times [-6000, 6000]$ and produce the graph shown in Figure 4.43. Notice that the symmetry detected in Step 2 is evident in this graph.

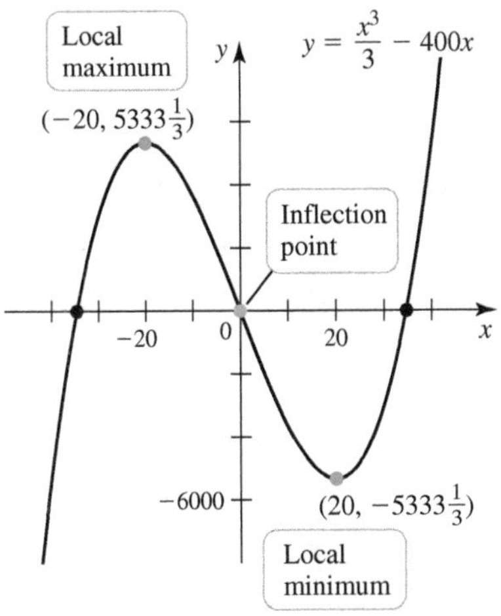

Related Exercises 9–14 ◄

EXAMPLE 3 **The surprises of a rational function** Use the graphing guidelines to graph $f(x) = \dfrac{10x^3}{x^2 - 1}$ on its domain.

Figure 4.43

SOLUTION

1. **Domain** The zeros of the denominator are $x = \pm 1$, so the domain is $\{x : x \neq \pm 1\}$.

2. **Symmetry** This function consists of an odd function divided by an even function. The product or quotient of an even function and an odd function is odd. Therefore, the graph is symmetric about the origin.

3. **Derivatives** The Quotient Rule is used to find the first and second derivatives:

$$f'(x) = \frac{10x^2(x^2 - 3)}{(x^2 - 1)^2} \quad \text{and} \quad f''(x) = \frac{20x(x^2 + 3)}{(x^2 - 1)^3}.$$

4. **Critical points and possible inflection points** The solutions of $f'(x) = 0$ occur where the numerator equals 0, provided the denominator is nonzero at those points. Solving $10x^2(x^2 - 3) = 0$ gives the critical points $x = 0$ and $x = \pm\sqrt{3}$. The solutions of $f''(x) = 0$ are found by solving $20x(x^2 + 3) = 0$; we see that the only possible inflection point occurs at $x = 0$.

5. **Increasing/decreasing and concavity** To find the sign of f', first note that the denominator of f' is nonnegative, as is the factor $10x^2$ in the numerator. So the sign of f' is determined by the sign of the factor $x^2 - 3$, which is negative on $(-\sqrt{3}, \sqrt{3})$ (excluding $x = \pm 1$) and positive on $(-\infty, -\sqrt{3})$ and $(\sqrt{3}, \infty)$. Therefore, f is decreasing on $(-\sqrt{3}, \sqrt{3})$ (excluding $x = \pm 1$) and increasing on $(-\infty, -\sqrt{3})$ and $(\sqrt{3}, \infty)$.

   The sign of f'' is a bit trickier. Because $x^2 + 3$ is positive, the sign of f'' is determined by the sign of $20x$ in the numerator and $(x^2 - 1)^3$ in the denominator. When $20x$ and $(x^2 - 1)^3$ have the same sign, $f''(x) > 0$; when $20x$ and $(x^2 - 1)^3$ have opposite signs, $f''(x) < 0$ (Table 4.1). The results of this analysis are shown in Figure 4.44.

> Sign charts and sign graphs (Table 4.1 and Figure 4.44) must be constructed carefully when vertical asymptotes are involved: The sign of f' and f'' may or may not change at an asymptote.

Table 4.1

	$20x$	$x^2 + 3$	$(x^2 - 1)^3$	**Sign of f''**
$(-\infty, -1)$	$-$	$+$	$+$	$-$
$(-1, 0)$	$-$	$+$	$-$	$+$
$(0, 1)$	$+$	$+$	$-$	$-$
$(1, \infty)$	$+$	$+$	$+$	$+$

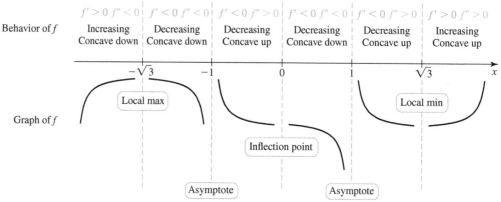

Figure 4.44

6. **Extreme values and inflection points** The First Derivative Test is easily applied by looking at Figure 4.44. The function is increasing on $(-\infty, -\sqrt{3})$ and decreasing on $(-\sqrt{3}, -1)$; therefore, f has a local maximum at $x = -\sqrt{3}$, where $f(-\sqrt{3}) = -15\sqrt{3}$. Similarly, f has a local minimum at $x = \sqrt{3}$, where $f(\sqrt{3}) = 15\sqrt{3}$. (These results could also be obtained with the Second Derivative Test.) There is no local extreme value at the critical point $x = 0$, only a horizontal tangent line.

Using Table 4.1 from Step 5, we see that f'' changes sign at $x = \pm 1$ and at $x = 0$. The points $x = \pm 1$ are not in the domain of f, so they cannot correspond to inflection points. However, there is an inflection point at $(0, 0)$.

7. **Asymptotes and end behavior** Recall from Section 2.4 that zeros of the denominator, which in this case are $x = \pm 1$, are candidates for vertical asymptotes. Checking the behavior of f on either side of $x = \pm 1$, we find

$$\lim_{x \to -1^-} f(x) = -\infty, \qquad \lim_{x \to -1^+} f(x) = \infty.$$

$$\lim_{x \to 1^-} f(x) = -\infty, \qquad \lim_{x \to 1^+} f(x) = \infty.$$

It follows that f has vertical asymptotes at $x = \pm 1$. The degree of the numerator is greater than the degree of the denominator, so there is no horizontal asymptote. Using long division, it can be shown that

$$f(x) = 10x + \frac{10x}{x^2 - 1}.$$

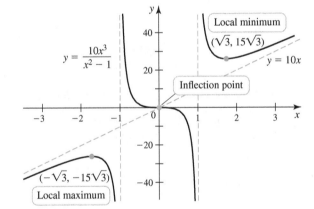

$$y = \frac{10x^3}{x^2 - 1}$$

Local minimum
$(\sqrt{3}, 15\sqrt{3})$

$y = 10x$

Inflection point

$(-\sqrt{3}, -15\sqrt{3})$

Local maximum

Figure 4.45

Therefore, as $x \to \pm\infty$, the graph of f approaches the line $y = 10x$. This line is a slant asymptote (Section 2.5).

8. **Intercepts** The zeros of a rational function coincide with the zeros of the numerator, provided that those points are not also zeros of the denominator. In this case, the zeros of f satisfy $10x^3 = 0$, or $x = 0$ (which is not a zero of the denominator). Therefore, $(0, 0)$ is both the x- and y-intercept.

9. **Graphing** We now assemble an accurate graph of f, as shown in Figure 4.45. A window of $[-3, 3] \times [-40, 40]$ gives a complete graph of the function. Notice that the symmetry about the origin deduced in Step 2 is apparent in the graph.

Related Exercises 15–20 ◄

QUICK CHECK 3 Verify that the function f in Example 3 is symmetric about the origin by showing that $f(-x) = -f(x)$. ◄

In the next two examples, we show how the guidelines may be streamlined to some extent.

▶ The function $f(x) = e^{-x^2}$ and the family of functions $f(x) = ce^{-ax^2}$ are central to the study of statistics. They have bell-shaped graphs and describe Gaussian or normal distributions.

EXAMPLE 4 **The normal distribution** Analyze the function $f(x) = e^{-x^2}$ and draw its graph.

SOLUTION The domain of f is all real numbers, and $f(x) > 0$ for all x. Because $f(-x) = f(x)$, f is an even function and its graph is symmetric about the y-axis.

Extreme values and inflection points follow from the derivatives of f. Using the Chain Rule, we have $f'(x) = -2xe^{-x^2}$. The critical points satisfy $f'(x) = 0$, which has the single root $x = 0$ (because $e^{-x^2} > 0$ for all x). It now follows that

• $f'(x) > 0$, for $x < 0$, so f is increasing on $(-\infty, 0)$.

• $f'(x) < 0$, for $x > 0$, so f is decreasing on $(0, \infty)$.

By the First Derivative Test, we see that f has a local maximum (and an absolute maximum by Theorem 4.5) at $x = 0$ where $f(0) = 1$.

Differentiating $f'(x) = -2xe^{-x^2}$ with the Product Rule yields

$$f''(x) = e^{-x^2}(-2) + (-2x)(-2xe^{-x^2}) \quad \text{Product Rule}$$
$$= 2e^{-x^2}(2x^2 - 1). \quad \text{Simplify.}$$

Again using the fact that $e^{-x^2} > 0$, for all x, we see that $f''(x) = 0$ when $2x^2 - 1 = 0$ or when $x = \pm 1/\sqrt{2}$; these values are candidates for inflection points. Observe that $f''(x) > 0$ and f is concave up on $(-\infty, -1/\sqrt{2})$ and $(1/\sqrt{2}, \infty)$, while $f''(x) < 0$ and f is concave down on $(-1/\sqrt{2}, 1/\sqrt{2})$. Because f'' changes sign at $x = \pm 1/\sqrt{2}$, we have inflection points at $(\pm 1/\sqrt{2}, 1/\sqrt{e})$ (Figure 4.46).

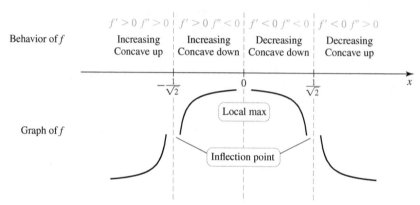

Figure 4.46

To determine the end behavior, notice that $\lim\limits_{x \to \pm\infty} e^{-x^2} = 0$, so $y = 0$ is a horizontal asymptote of f. Assembling all of these facts, an accurate graph can now be drawn (Figure 4.47).   *Related Exercises 21–42* ◄

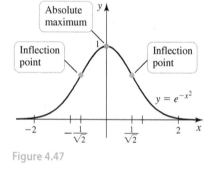

Figure 4.47

EXAMPLE 5   Roots and cusps Graph $f(x) = \frac{1}{8}x^{2/3}(9x^2 - 8x - 16)$ on its domain.

SOLUTION The domain of f is $(-\infty, \infty)$. The polynomial factor in f consists of both even and odd powers, so f has no special symmetry. Computing the first derivative is straightforward if you first expand f as a sum of three terms:

$$f'(x) = \frac{d}{dx}\left(\frac{9x^{8/3}}{8} - x^{5/3} - 2x^{2/3}\right) \quad \text{Expand } f.$$
$$= 3x^{5/3} - \frac{5}{3}x^{2/3} - \frac{4}{3}x^{-1/3} \quad \text{Differentiate.}$$
$$= \frac{(x - 1)(9x + 4)}{3x^{1/3}}. \quad \text{Simplify.}$$

The critical points are now identified: f' is undefined at $x = 0$ (because $x^{-1/3}$ is undefined there) and $f'(x) = 0$ at $x = 1$ and $x = -\frac{4}{9}$. So we have three critical points to analyze. Table 4.2 tracks the signs of the factors in the numerator and denominator of f', and shows the sign of f' on the relevant intervals; this information is recorded in Figure 4.48.

Table 4.2

	$3x^{1/3}$	$9x + 4$	$x - 1$	Sign of f'
$(-\infty, -\frac{4}{9})$	−	−	−	−
$(-\frac{4}{9}, 0)$	−	+	−	+
$(0, 1)$	+	+	−	−
$(1, \infty)$	+	+	+	+

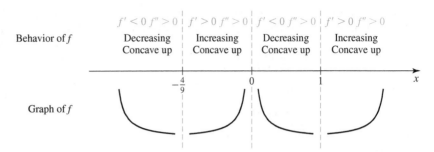

Figure 4.48

We use the second line in the calculation of f' to compute the second derivative:

$$f''(x) = \frac{d}{dx}\left(3x^{5/3} - \frac{5}{3}x^{2/3} - \frac{4}{3}x^{-1/3}\right)$$

$$= 5x^{2/3} - \frac{10}{9}x^{-1/3} + \frac{4}{9}x^{-4/3} \qquad \text{Differentiate.}$$

$$= \frac{45x^2 - 10x + 4}{9x^{4/3}}. \qquad \text{Simplify.}$$

▶ To show that $f''(x) > 0$ (for $x \neq 0$), analyze its numerator and denominator.

- The graph of $45x^2 - 10x + 4$ is a parabola that opens upward (its leading coefficient is positive) with no x-intercepts (verified by the quadratic formula). Therefore, the numerator is always positive.
- The denominator is nonnegative because $9x^{4/3} = 9(x^{1/3})^4$ (even powers are nonnegative).

Solving $f''(x) = 0$, we discover that $f''(x) > 0$, for all x except $x = 0$, where it is undefined. Therefore, f is concave up on $(-\infty, 0)$ and $(0, \infty)$ (Figure 4.48).

By the Second Derivative Test, because $f''(x) > 0$, for $x \neq 0$, the critical points $x = -\frac{4}{9}$ and $x = 1$ correspond to local minima; their y-coordinates are $f\left(-\frac{4}{9}\right) \approx -0.78$ and $f(1) = -\frac{15}{8} = -1.875$.

What about the third critical point $x = 0$? Note that $f(0) = 0$, and f is increasing just to the left of 0 and decreasing just to the right. By the First Derivative Test, f has a local maximum at $x = 0$. Furthermore, $f'(x) \to \infty$ as $x \to 0^-$ and $f'(x) \to -\infty$ as $x \to 0^+$, so the graph of f has a cusp at $x = 0$.

As $x \to \pm\infty$, f is dominated by its highest-power term, which is $9x^{8/3}/8$. This term becomes large and positive as $x \to \pm\infty$; therefore, f has no absolute maximum. Its absolute minimum occurs at $x = 1$ because, comparing the two local minima, $f(1) < f\left(-\frac{4}{9}\right)$.

The roots of f satisfy $\frac{1}{8}x^{2/3}(9x^2 - 8x - 16) = 0$, which gives $x = 0$ and

$$x = \frac{4}{9}(1 \pm \sqrt{10}) \approx -0.96 \quad \text{and} \quad 1.85. \qquad \text{Use the quadratic formula.}$$

With the information gathered in this analysis, we obtain the graph shown in Figure 4.49.

Related Exercises 21–42 ◀

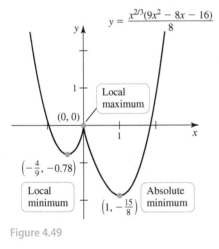

$$y = \frac{x^{2/3}(9x^2 - 8x - 16)}{8}$$

Local maximum

$(0, 0)$

$\left(-\frac{4}{9}, -0.78\right)$

Local minimum

$\left(1, -\frac{15}{8}\right)$

Absolute minimum

Figure 4.49

SECTION 4.3 EXERCISES

Review Questions

1. Why is it important to determine the domain of f before graphing f?

2. Explain why it is useful to know about symmetry in a function.

3. Can the graph of a polynomial have vertical or horizontal asymptotes? Explain.

4. Where are the vertical asymptotes of a rational function located?

5. How do you find the absolute maximum and minimum values of a function that is continuous on a closed interval?

6. Describe the possible end behavior of a polynomial.

Basic Skills

7–8. Shape of the curve *Sketch a curve with the following properties.*

7. $f' < 0$ and $f'' < 0$, for $x < 3$
   $f' < 0$ and $f'' > 0$, for $x > 3$

8. $f' < 0$ and $f'' < 0$, for $x < -1$
   $f' < 0$ and $f'' > 0$, for $-1 < x < 2$
   $f' > 0$ and $f'' > 0$, for $2 < x < 8$
   $f' > 0$ and $f'' < 0$, for $8 < x < 10$
   $f' > 0$ and $f'' > 0$, for $x > 10$

9–14. Graphing polynomials *Sketch a graph of the following polynomials. Identify local extrema, inflection points, and x- and y-intercepts when they exist.*

9. $f(x) = x^3 - 6x^2 + 9x$ **10.** $f(x) = 3x - x^3$

11. $f(x) = x^4 - 6x^2$ **12.** $f(x) = 2x^6 - 3x^4$

13. $f(x) = (x - 6)(x + 6)^2$ **14.** $f(x) = 27(x - 2)^2(x + 2)$

15–20. Graphing rational functions *Use the guidelines of this section to make a complete graph of f.*

15. $f(x) = \dfrac{x^2}{x - 2}$ **16.** $f(x) = \dfrac{x^2}{x^2 - 4}$

17. $f(x) = \dfrac{3x}{x^2 - 1}$ **18.** $f(x) = \dfrac{2x - 3}{2x - 8}$

19. $f(x) = \dfrac{x^2 + 12}{2x + 1}$ **20.** $f(x) = \dfrac{4x + 4}{x^2 + 3}$

21–36. More graphing *Make a complete graph of the following functions. If an interval is not specified, graph the function on its domain. Use a graphing utility to check your work.*

21. $f(x) = \tan^{-1} x^2$ **22.** $f(x) = \ln(x^2 + 1)$

23. $f(x) = x + 2\cos x$ on $[-2\pi, 2\pi]$

24. $f(x) = x - 3x^{2/3}$ **25.** $f(x) = x - 3x^{1/3}$

26. $f(x) = 2 - x^{2/3} + x^{4/3}$ **27.** $f(x) = \sin x - x$ on $[0, 2\pi]$

28. $f(x) = x\sqrt{x + 3}$ **29.** $g(t) = e^{-t}\sin t$ on $[-\pi, \pi]$

30. $g(x) = x^2 \ln x$

31. $f(x) = x + \tan x$ on $\left(-\dfrac{3\pi}{2}, \dfrac{3\pi}{2}\right)$

32. $f(x) = (\ln x)/x^2$ **33.** $f(x) = x \ln x$

34. $g(x) = e^{-x^2/2}$ **35.** $p(x) = xe^{-x^2}$

36. $g(x) = 1/(e^{-x} - 1)$

37–42. Graphing with technology *Make a complete graph of the following functions. A graphing utility is useful in locating intercepts, local extreme values, and inflection points.*

37. $f(x) = \dfrac{1}{3}x^3 - 2x^2 - 5x + 2$

38. $f(x) = \dfrac{1}{15}x^3 - x + 1$

39. $f(x) = 3x^4 + 4x^3 - 12x^2$

40. $f(x) = x^3 - 33x^2 + 216x - 2$

41. $f(x) = \dfrac{3x - 5}{x^2 - 1}$

42. $f(x) = x^{1/3}(x - 2)^2$

Further Explorations

43. Explain why or why not Determine whether the following statements are true and give an explanation or counterexample.

a. If the zeros of f' are -3, 1, and 4, then the local extrema of f are located at these points.

b. If the zeros of f'' are -2 and 4, then the inflection points of f are located at these points.

c. If the zeros of the denominator of f are -3 and 4, then f has vertical asymptotes at these points.

d. If a rational function has a finite limit as $x \to \infty$, then it must have a finite limit as $x \to -\infty$.

44–47. Functions from derivatives *Use the derivative f' to determine the x-coordinates of the local maxima and minima of f, and the intervals of increase and decrease. Sketch a possible graph of f (f is not unique).*

44. $f'(x) = (x - 1)(x + 2)(x + 4)$

45. $f'(x) = 10\sin 2x$ on $[-2\pi, 2\pi]$

46. $f'(x) = \dfrac{1}{6}(x + 1)(x - 2)^2(x - 3)$

47. $f'(x) = x^2(x + 2)(x - 1)$

48–49. Functions from graphs *Use the graphs of f' and f'' to find the critical points and inflection points of f, the intervals on which f is increasing and decreasing, and the intervals of concavity. Then graph f assuming $f(0) = 0$.*

48.

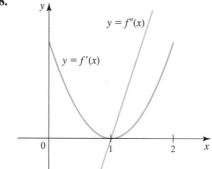

49.

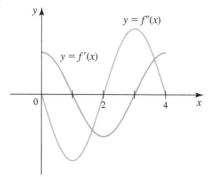

50–53. Nice cubics and quartics *The following third- and fourth-degree polynomials have a property that makes them relatively easy to graph. Make a complete graph and describe the property.*

50. $f(x) = x^4 + 8x^3 - 270x^2 + 1$

51. $f(x) = x^3 - 6x^2 - 135x$

52. $f(x) = x^3 - 147x + 286$

53. $f(x) = x^3 - 3x^2 - 144x - 140$

54. Oscillations Consider the function $f(x) = \cos(\ln x)$, for $x > 0$. Use analytical techniques and a graphing utility.

a. Locate all local extrema on the interval $(0, 4]$.

b. Identify the inflection points on the interval $(0, 4]$.

c. Locate the three smallest zeros of f on the interval $(0.1, \infty)$.

d. Sketch the graph of f.

55. Local max/min of $x^{1/x}$ Use analytical methods to find all local extrema of the function $f(x) = x^{1/x}$, for $x > 0$. Verify your work using a graphing utility.

56. Local max/min of x^x Use analytical methods to find all local extrema of the function $f(x) = x^x$, for $x > 0$. Verify your work using a graphing utility.

57–60. Designer functions *Sketch a continuous function f on some interval that has the properties described.*

57. The function f has one inflection point but no local extrema.

58. The function f has three real zeros and exactly two local minima.

59. The function f satisfies $f'(-2) = 2, f'(0) = 0, f'(1) = -3,$ and $f'(4) = 1$.

60. The function f has the same finite limit as $x \to \pm\infty$ and has exactly one absolute minimum and one absolute maximum.

61–68. More graphing *Sketch a complete graph of the following functions. Use analytical methods and a graphing utility together in a complementary way.*

61. $f(x) = \dfrac{-x\sqrt{x^2 - 4}}{x - 2}$

62. $f(x) = 3\sqrt[4]{x} - \sqrt{x} - 2$

63. $f(x) = 3x^4 - 44x^3 + 60x^2$ (*Hint:* Two different graphing windows may be needed.)

64. $f(x) = \dfrac{1}{1 + \cos \pi x}$ on $(1, 3)$

65. $f(x) = 10x^6 - 36x^5 - 75x^4 + 300x^3 + 120x^2 - 720x$

66. $f(x) = \dfrac{\sin \pi x}{1 + \sin \pi x}$ on $[0, 2]$

67. $f(x) = \dfrac{x\sqrt{|x^2 - 1|}}{x^4 + 1}$

68. $f(x) = \sin(3\pi \cos x)$ on $[-\pi/2, \pi/2]$

69. Hidden oscillations Use analytical methods together with a graphing utility to graph the following functions on the interval $[-2\pi, 2\pi]$. Define f at $x = 0$ so that it is continuous there. Be sure to uncover all relevant features of the graph.

a. $f(x) = \dfrac{1 - \cos^3 x}{x^2}$ **b.** $f(x) = \dfrac{1 - \cos^5 x}{x^2}$

70. Cubic with parameters Locate all local maxima and minima of $f(x) = x^3 - 3bx^2 + 3a^2x + 23$, where a and b are constants, in the following cases.

a. $|a| < |b|$ **b.** $|a| > |b|$ **c.** $|a| = |b|$

Applications

71. Height functions The figure shows six containers, each of which is filled from the top. Assume that water is poured into the containers at a constant rate and each container is filled in 10 seconds. Assume also that the horizontal cross sections of the containers are always circles. Let $h(t)$ be the depth of water in the container at time t, for $0 \le t \le 10$.

a. For each container, sketch a graph of the function $y = h(t)$, for $0 \le t \le 10$.

b. Explain why h is an increasing function.

c. Describe the concavity of the function. Identify inflection points when they occur.

d. For each container, where does h' (the derivative of h) have an absolute maximum on $[0, 10]$?

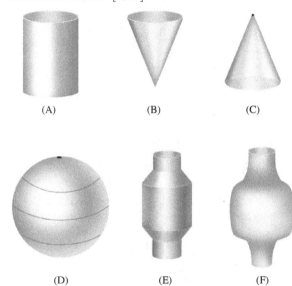

(A)   (B)   (C)

(D)   (E)   (F)

72. A pursuit curve A man is stands 1 mi east of a crossroads. At noon, a dog starts walking north from the crossroads at 1 mi/hr (see figure). At the same instant, the man starts walking and at all times walks directly toward the dog at $s > 1$ mi/hr. The path in the xy plane followed by the man as he pursues his dog is given by the function

$$y = f(x) = \frac{s}{2}\left(\frac{x^{(s+1)/s}}{s + 1} - \frac{x^{(s-1)/s}}{s - 1}\right) + \frac{s}{s^2 - 1}.$$

Select various values of $s > 1$ and graph this pursuit curve. Comment on the changes in the curve as s increases.

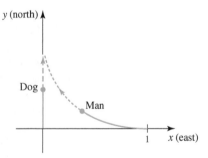

Additional Exercises

73. Derivative information Suppose a continuous function f is concave up on $(-\infty, 0)$ and $(0, \infty)$. Assume f has a local maximum at $x = 0$. What, if anything, do you know about $f'(0)$? Explain with an illustration.

74. $e^\pi > \pi^e$ Prove that $e^\pi > \pi^e$ by first finding the maximum value of $f(x) = \ln x/x$.

T 75–81. Special curves *The following classical curves have been studied by generations of mathematicians. Use analytical methods (including implicit differentiation) and a graphing utility to graph the curves. Include as much detail as possible.*

75. $x^{2/3} + y^{2/3} = 1$ (Astroid or hypocycloid with four cusps)

76. $y = \dfrac{8}{x^2 + 4}$ (Witch of Agnesi)

77. $x^3 + y^3 = 3xy$ (Folium of Descartes)

78. $y^2 = \dfrac{x^3}{2 - x}$ (Cissoid of Diocles)

79. $y^4 - x^4 - 4y^2 + 5x^2 = 0$ (Devil's curve)

80. $y^2 = x^3(1 - x)$ (Pear curve)

81. $x^4 - x^2 + y^2 = 0$ (Figure-8 curve)

T 82. Elliptic curves The equation $y^2 = x^3 - ax + 3$, where a is a parameter, defines a well-known family of *elliptic curves*.

a. Verify that if $a = 3$, the graph consists of a single curve.
b. Verify that if $a = 4$, the graph consists of two distinct curves.
c. By experimentation, determine the value of a ($3 < a < 4$) at which the graph separates into two curves.

T 83. Lamé curves The equation $|y/a|^n + |x/a|^n = 1$, where n and a are positive real numbers, defines the family of Lamé curves. Make a complete graph of this function with $a = 1$, for $n = \frac{2}{3}, 1, 2, 3$. Describe the progression that you observe as n increases.

T 84. An exotic curve (Putnam Exam 1942) Find the coordinates of four local maxima of the function $f(x) = \dfrac{x}{1 + x^6 \sin^2 x}$ and graph the function, for $0 \le x \le 10$.

T 85. A family of superexponential functions Let $f(x) = (a - x)^x$, where $a > 0$.

a. What is the domain of f (in terms of a)?
b. Describe the end behavior of f (near the boundary of its domain).
c. Compute f'. Then graph f and f' for $a = 0.5, 1, 2$, and 3.
d. Show that f has a single local maximum at the point z that satisfies $z = (a - z) \ln (a - z)$.
e. Describe how z (found in part (d)) varies as a increases. Describe how $f(z)$ varies as a increases.

86. x^y **versus** y^x Consider positive real numbers x and y. Notice that $4^3 < 3^4$, while $3^2 > 2^3$ and $4^2 = 2^4$. Describe the regions in the first quadrant of the xy-plane in which $x^y > y^x$ and $x^y < y^x$.

T 87–90. Combining technology with analytical methods *Use a graphing utility together with analytical methods to create a complete graph of the following functions. Be sure to find and label the intercepts, local extrema, inflection points, asymptotes, intervals where the function is increasing/decreasing, and intervals of concavity.*

87. $f(x) = \dfrac{\tan^{-1} x}{x^2 + 1}$

88. $f(x) = \dfrac{\sqrt{4x^2 + 1}}{x^2 + 1}$

89. $f(x) = \dfrac{x \sin x}{x^2 + 1}$ on $[-2\pi, 2\pi]$

90. $f(x) = x/\ln x$

QUICK CHECK ANSWERS

1. Make the window larger in the y-direction.
2. Notice that f and $f + C$ have the same derivatives.
3. $f(-x) = \dfrac{10(-x)^3}{(-x)^2 - 1} = -\dfrac{10x^3}{x^2 - 1} = -f(x)$ ◄

4.4 Optimization Problems

The theme of this section is *optimization*, a topic arising in many disciplines that rely on mathematics. A structural engineer may seek the dimensions of a beam that maximize strength for a specified cost. A packaging designer may seek the dimensions of a container that maximize the volume of the container for a given surface area. Airline strategists need to find the best allocation of airliners among several hubs to minimize fuel costs and maximize passenger miles. In all these examples, the challenge is to find an *efficient* way to carry out a task, where "efficient" could mean least expensive, most profitable, least time consuming, or, as you will see, many other measures.

To introduce the ideas behind optimization problems, think about pairs of nonnegative real numbers x and y between 0 and 20 with the property that their sum is 20, that is, $x + y = 20$. Of all possible pairs, which has the greatest product?

Table 4.3 displays a few cases showing how the product of two nonnegative numbers varies while their sum remains constant. The condition that $x + y = 20$ is called a **constraint**: It tells us to consider only (nonnegative) values of x and y satisfying this equation.

The quantity that we wish to maximize (or minimize in other cases) is called the **objective function**; in this case, the objective function is the product $P = xy$. From

Table 4.3

x	y	$x + y$	$P = xy$
1	19	20	19
5.5	14.5	20	79.75
9	11	20	99
13	7	20	91
18	2	20	36

Table 4.3, it appears that the product is greatest if both x and y are near the middle of the interval $[0, 20]$.

This simple problem has all the essential features of optimization problems. At their heart, optimization problems take the following form:

What is the maximum (minimum) value of an objective function subject to the given constraint(s)?

> In this problem, it is just as easy to eliminate x as y. In other problems, eliminating one variable may result in less work than eliminating other variables.

For the problem at hand, this question would be stated as, "What pair of nonnegative numbers maximizes $P = xy$ subject to the constraint $x + y = 20$?" The first step is to use the constraint to express the objective function $P = xy$ in terms of a single variable. In this case, the constraint is

$$x + y = 20, \quad \text{or} \quad y = 20 - x.$$

Substituting for y, the objective function becomes

$$P = xy = x(20 - x) = 20x - x^2,$$

which is a function of the single variable x. Notice that the values of x lie in the interval $0 \le x \le 20$ with $P(0) = P(20) = 0$.

To maximize P, we first find the critical points by solving

$$P'(x) = 20 - 2x = 0$$

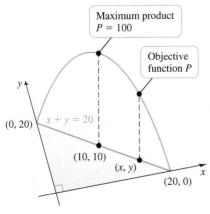

Figure 4.50

to obtain the solution $x = 10$. To find the absolute maximum value of P on the interval $[0, 20]$, we check the endpoints and the critical points. Because $P(0) = P(20) = 0$ and $P(10) = 100$, we conclude that P has its absolute maximum value at $x = 10$. By the constraint $x + y = 20$, the numbers with the greatest product are $x = y = 10$, and their product is $P = 100$.

Figure 4.50 summarizes this problem. We see the constraint line $x + y = 20$ in the xy-plane. Above the line is the objective function $P = xy$. As x and y vary along the constraint line, the objective function changes, reaching a maximum value of 100 when $x = y = 10$.

QUICK CHECK 1 Verify that in the previous example, the same result is obtained if the constraint $x + y = 20$ is used to eliminate x rather than y. ◄

Most optimization problems have the same basic structure as the preceding example: There is an objective function, which may involve several variables, and one or more constraints. The methods of calculus (Sections 4.1 and 4.2) are used to find the minimum or maximum values of the objective function.

EXAMPLE 1 Rancher's dilemma A rancher has 400 ft of fence for constructing a rectangular corral. One side of the corral will be formed by a barn and requires no fence. Three exterior fences and two interior fences partition the corral into three rectangular regions as shown in Figure 4.51. What are the dimensions of the corral that maximize the enclosed area? What is the area of that corral?

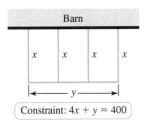

Figure 4.51

SOLUTION We first sketch the corral (Figure 4.51), where $x \ge 0$ is the width and $y \ge 0$ is the length of the corral. The amount of fence required is $4x + y$, so the constraint is $4x + y = 400$, or $y = 400 - 4x$.

The objective function to be maximized is the area of the corral, $A = xy$. Using $y = 400 - 4x$, we eliminate y and express A as a function of x:

$$A = xy = x(400 - 4x) = 400x - 4x^2.$$

> Recall from Section 4.1 that the absolute extreme values occur at critical points or endpoints.

Notice that the width of the corral must be at least $x = 0$, and it cannot exceed $x = 100$ (because 400 ft of fence are available). Therefore, we maximize $A(x) = 400x - 4x^2$, for $0 \le x \le 100$. The critical points of the objective function satisfy

$$A'(x) = 400 - 8x = 0,$$

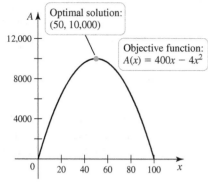

Figure 4.52

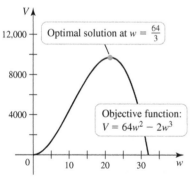

Objective function: $V = w^2h$
Constraint: $2w + h = 64$

Figure 4.53

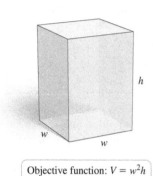

Figure 4.54

which has the solution $x = 50$. To find the absolute maximum value of A, we check the endpoints of $[0, 100]$ and the critical point $x = 50$. Because $A(0) = A(100) = 0$ and $A(50) = 10,000$, the absolute maximum value of A occurs when $x = 50$. Using the constraint, the optimal length of the corral is $y = 400 - 4(50) = 200$. Therefore, the maximum area of 10,000 ft^2 is achieved with dimensions $x = 50$ ft and $y = 200$ ft. The objective function A is shown in Figure 4.52.

Related Exercises 5–14 ◄

QUICK CHECK 2 Find the objective function in Example 1 (in terms of x) (i) if there is no interior fence and (ii) if there is one interior fence that forms a right angle with the barn, as in Figure 4.51. ◄

EXAMPLE 2   Airline regulations Suppose an airline policy states that all baggage must be box-shaped with a sum of length, width, and height not exceeding 64 in. What are the dimensions and volume of a square-based box with the greatest volume under these conditions?

SOLUTION We sketch a square-based box whose length and width are w and whose height is h (Figure 4.53). By the airline policy, the constraint is $2w + h = 64$. The objective function is the volume, $V = w^2h$. Either w or h may be eliminated from the objective function; the constraint $h = 64 - 2w$ implies that the volume is

$$V = w^2h = w^2(64 - 2w) = 64w^2 - 2w^3.$$

The objective function has now been expressed in terms of a single variable. Notice that w is nonnegative and cannot exceed 32, so the domain of V is $0 \le w \le 32$. The critical points satisfy

$$V'(w) = 128w - 6w^2 = 2w(64 - 3w) = 0,$$

which has roots $w = 0$ and $w = \frac{64}{3}$. By the First (or Second) Derivative Test, $w = \frac{64}{3}$ corresponds to a local maximum. At the endpoints, $V(0) = V(32) = 0$. Therefore, the volume function has an absolute maximum of $V(64/3) \approx 9709$ in^3. The dimensions of the optimal box are $w = 64/3$ in and $h = 64 - 2w = 64/3$ in, so the optimal box is a cube. A graph of the volume function is shown in Figure 4.54.

Related Exercises 15–17 ◄

QUICK CHECK 3 Find the objective function in Example 2 (in terms of w) if the constraint is that the sum of length and width and height cannot exceed 108 in. ◄

Optimization Guidelines   With two examples providing some insight, we present a procedure for solving optimization problems. These guidelines provide a general framework, but the details may vary depending on the problem.

Guidelines for Optimization Problems

1. Read the problem carefully, identify the variables, and organize the given information with a picture.

2. Identify the objective function (the function to be optimized). Write it in terms of the variables of the problem.

3. Identify the constraint(s). Write them in terms of the variables of the problem.

4. Use the constraint(s) to eliminate all but one independent variable of the objective function.

5. With the objective function expressed in terms of a single variable, find the interval of interest for that variable.

6. Use methods of calculus to find the absolute maximum or minimum value of the objective function on the interval of interest. If necessary, check the endpoints.

EXAMPLE 3 Walking and swimming Suppose you are standing on the shore of a circular pond with a radius of 1 mile and you want to get to a point on the shore directly opposite your position (on the other end of a diameter). You plan to swim at 2 mi/hr from your current position to another point P on the shore and then walk at 3 mi/hr along the shore to the terminal point (Figure 4.55). How should you choose P to minimize the total time for the trip?

SOLUTION As shown in Figure 4.55, the initial point is chosen arbitrarily, and the terminal point is at the other end of a diameter. The easiest way to describe the transition point P is to refer to the central angle θ. If $\theta = 0$, then the entire trip is done by walking; if $\theta = \pi$, the entire trip is done by swimming. So the interval of interest is $0 \le \theta \le \pi$.

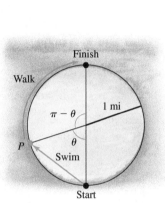

Figure 4.55

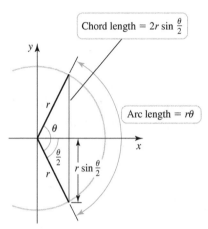

Figure 4.56

The objective function is the total travel time as it varies with θ. For each leg of the trip (swim and walk), the travel time is the distance traveled divided by the speed. We need a few facts from circular geometry. The length of the swimming leg is the length of the chord of the circle corresponding to the angle θ. For a circle of radius r, this chord length is given by $2r \sin (\theta/2)$ (Figure 4.56). So the time for the swimming leg (with $r = 1$ and a speed of 2 mi/hr) is

> To show that the chord length of a circle is $2r \sin (\theta/2)$, draw a line from the center of the circle to the midpoint of the chord. This line bisects the angle θ. Using a right triangle, half the length of the chord is $r \sin (\theta/2)$.

$$\text{time} = \frac{\text{distance}}{\text{rate}} = \frac{2 \sin (\theta/2)}{2} = \sin \frac{\theta}{2}.$$

The length of the walking leg is the length of the arc of the circle corresponding to the angle $\pi - \theta$. For a circle of radius r, the arc length corresponding to an angle θ is $r\theta$ (Figure 4.56). Therefore, the time for the walking leg (with an angle $\pi - \theta$, $r = 1$, and a speed of 3 mi/hr) is

$$\text{time} = \frac{\text{distance}}{\text{rate}} = \frac{\pi - \theta}{3}.$$

The total travel time for the trip (in hours) is the objective function

$$T(\theta) = \sin \frac{\theta}{2} + \frac{\pi - \theta}{3}, \quad \text{for} \quad 0 \le \theta \le \pi.$$

> You can check two special cases: If the entire trip is done walking, the travel time is $(\pi \text{ mi})/(3 \text{ mi/hr}) \approx 1.05$ hr. If the entire trip is done swimming, the travel time is $(2 \text{ mi})/(2 \text{ mi/hr}) = 1$ hr.

We now analyze the objective function. The critical points of T satisfy

$$\frac{dT}{d\theta} = \frac{1}{2} \cos \frac{\theta}{2} - \frac{1}{3} = 0 \quad \text{or} \quad \cos \frac{\theta}{2} = \frac{2}{3}.$$

Using a calculator, the only solution in the interval $[0, \pi]$ is $\theta = 2 \cos^{-1} \left(\frac{2}{3}\right) \approx 1.68$ rad $\approx 96°$, which is the critical point.

Evaluating the objective function at the critical point and at the endpoints, we find that $T(1.68) \approx 1.23$ hr, $T(0) = \pi/3 \approx 1.05$ hr, and $T(\pi) = 1$ hr. We conclude that the minimum travel time is $T(\pi) = 1$ hr when the entire trip is done swimming. The *maximum* travel time, corresponding to $\theta \approx 96°$, is $T \approx 1.23$ hr.

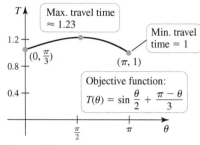

Figure 4.57

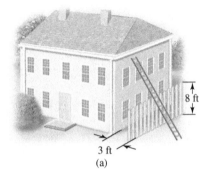

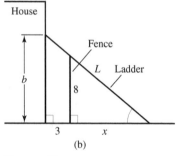

Figure 4.58

The objective function is shown in Figure 4.57. In general, the maximum and minimum travel times depend on the walking and swimming speeds (Exercise 18).

Related Exercises 18–21 ◄

EXAMPLE 4   Ladder over the fence   An 8-foot-tall fence runs parallel to the side of a house 3 feet away (Figure 4.58a). What is the length of the shortest ladder that clears the fence and reaches the house? Assume that the vertical wall of the house and the horizontal ground have infinite extent (see Exercise 23 for more realistic assumptions).

SOLUTION   Let's first ask why we expect a minimum ladder length. You could put the foot of the ladder far from the fence, so it clears the fence at a shallow angle; but the ladder would be long. Or you could put the foot of the ladder close to the fence, so it clears the fence at a steep angle; but again, the ladder would be long. Somewhere between these extremes, there is a ladder position that minimizes the ladder length.

The objective function in this problem is the ladder length L. The position of the ladder is specified by x, the distance between the foot of the ladder and the fence (Figure 4.58b). The goal is to express L as a function of x, where $x > 0$.

The Pythagorean theorem gives the relationship

$$L^2 = (x + 3)^2 + b^2,$$

where b is the height of the top of the ladder above the ground. Similar triangles give the constraint $8/x = b/(3 + x)$. We now solve the constraint equation for b and substitute to express L^2 in terms of x:

$$L^2 = (x + 3)^2 + \underbrace{\left(\frac{8(x + 3)}{x}\right)^2}_{b} = (x + 3)^2\left(1 + \frac{64}{x^2}\right).$$

At this juncture, we could find the critical points of L by first solving the preceding equation for L and then solving $L' = 0$. However, the solution is simplified considerably if we note that L is a nonnegative function. Therefore, L and L^2 have local extrema at the same points, so we choose to minimize L^2. The derivative of L^2 is

$$\frac{d}{dx}\left[(x + 3)^2\left(1 + \frac{64}{x^2}\right)\right] = 2(x + 3)\left(1 + \frac{64}{x^2}\right) + (x + 3)^2\left(-\frac{128}{x^3}\right) \quad \text{Chain Rule and Product Rule}$$

$$= 2(x + 3)\left(1 + \frac{64}{x^2} - (x + 3)\frac{64}{x^3}\right) \quad \text{Factor.}$$

$$= \frac{2(x + 3)(x^3 - 192)}{x^3}. \quad \text{Simplify.}$$

Because $x > 0$, we have $x + 3 \neq 0$; therefore, the condition $\frac{d}{dx}(L^2) = 0$ becomes $x^3 - 192 = 0$, or $x = 4\sqrt[3]{3} \approx 5.77$. By the First Derivative Test, this critical point corresponds to a local minimum. By Theorem 4.5, this solitary local minimum is also the absolute minimum on the interval $(0, \infty)$. Therefore, the minimum ladder length occurs when the foot of the ladder is approximately 5.77 ft from the fence. We find that $L^2(5.77) \approx 224.77$ and the minimum ladder length is $\sqrt{224.77} \approx 15$ ft.

Related Exercises 22–23 ◄

SECTION 4.4 EXERCISES

Review Questions

1. Fill in the blanks: The goal of an optimization problem is to find the maximum or minimum value of the _____ function subject to the _____.

2. If the objective function involves more than one independent variable, how are the extra variables eliminated?

3. Suppose the objective function is $Q = x^2 y$ and you know that $x + y = 10$. Write the objective function first in terms of x and then in terms of y.

4. Suppose you wish to minimize a continuous objective function on a closed interval, but you find that it has only a single local maximum. Where should you look for the solution to the problem?

Basic Skills

5. **Maximum area rectangles** Of all rectangles with a perimeter of 10, which one has the maximum area? (Give the dimensions.)

6. **Maximum area rectangles** Of all rectangles with a fixed perimeter of P, which one has the maximum area? (Give the dimensions in terms of P.)

7. **Minimum perimeter rectangles** Of all rectangles of area 100, which one has the minimum perimeter?

8. **Minimum perimeter rectangles** Of all rectangles with a fixed area A, which one has the minimum perimeter? (Give the dimensions in terms of A.)

9. **Maximum product** What two nonnegative real numbers with a sum of 23 have the largest possible product?

10. **Sum of squares** What two nonnegative real numbers a and b whose sum is 23 maximize $a^2 + b^2$? Minimize $a^2 + b^2$?

11. **Minimum sum** What two positive real numbers whose product is 50 have the smallest possible sum?

12. **Maximum product** Find numbers x and y satisfying the equation $3x + y = 12$ such that the product of x and y is as large as possible.

13. **Minimum sum** Find positive numbers x and y satisfying the equation $xy = 12$ such that the sum $2x + y$ is as small as possible.

14. **Pen problems**
    a. A rectangular pen is built with one side against a barn. Two hundred meters of fencing are used for the other three sides of the pen. What dimensions maximize the area of the pen?
    b. A rancher plans to make four identical and adjacent rectangular pens against a barn, each with an area of 100 m² (see figure). What are the dimensions of each pen that minimize the amount of fence that must be used?

Barn			
100	100	100	100

15. **Minimum-surface-area box** Of all boxes with a square base and a volume of 100 m³, which one has the minimum surface area? (Give its dimensions.)

16. **Maximum-volume box** Suppose an airline policy states that all baggage must be box-shaped with a sum of length, width, and height not exceeding 108 in. What are the dimensions and volume of a square-based box with the greatest volume under these conditions?

17. **Shipping crates** A square-based, box-shaped shipping crate is designed to have a volume of 16 ft³. The material used to make the base costs twice as much (per square foot) as the material in the sides, and the material used to make the top costs half as much (per square foot) as the material in the sides. What are the dimensions of the crate that minimize the cost of materials?

18. **Walking and swimming** A man wishes to get from an initial point on the shore of a circular lake with radius 1 mi to a point on the shore directly opposite (on the other end of the diameter). He plans to swim from the initial point to another point on the shore and then walk along the shore to the terminal point.
    a. If he swims at 2 mi/hr and walks at 4 mi/hr, what are the minimum and maximum times for the trip?
    b. If he swims at 2 mi/hr and walks at 1.5 mi/hr, what are the minimum and maximum times for the trip?
    c. If he swims at 2 mi/hr, what is the minimum walking speed for which it is quickest to walk the entire distance?

19. **Minimum distance** Find the point P on the line $y = 3x$ that is closest to the point $(50, 0)$. What is the least distance between P and $(50, 0)$?

20. **Minimum distance** Find the point P on the curve $y = x^2$ that is closet to the point $(18, 0)$. What is the least distance between P and $(18, 0)$?

21. **Walking and rowing** A boat on the ocean is 4 mi from the nearest point on a straight shoreline; that point is 6 mi from a restaurant on the shore. A woman plans to row the boat straight to a point on the shore and then walk along the shore to the restaurant.

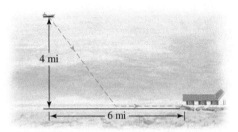

    a. If she walks at 3 mi/hr and rows at 2 mi/hr, at which point on the shore should she land to minimize the total travel time?
    b. If she walks at 3 mi/hr, what is the minimum speed at which she must row so that the quickest way to the restaurant is to row directly (with no walking)?

22. **Shortest ladder** A 10-ft-tall fence runs parallel to the wall of a house at a distance of 4 ft. Find the length of the shortest ladder that extends from the ground to the house without touching the fence. Assume the vertical wall of the house and the horizontal ground have infinite extent.

23. **Shortest ladder—more realistic** An 8-ft-tall fence runs parallel to the wall of a house at a distance of 5 ft. Find the length of the shortest ladder that extends from the ground to the house without touching the fence. Assume that the vertical wall of the house is 20 ft high and the horizontal ground extends 20 ft from the fence.

Further Explorations and Applications

24. **Rectangles beneath a parabola** A rectangle is constructed with its base on the x-axis and two of its vertices on the parabola $y = 16 - x^2$. What are the dimensions of the rectangle with the maximum area? What is that area?

25. **Rectangles beneath a semicircle** A rectangle is constructed with its base on the diameter of a semicircle with radius 5 and its two other vertices on the semicircle. What are the dimensions of the rectangle with maximum area?

26. **Circle and square** A piece of wire of length 60 is cut, and the resulting two pieces are formed to make a circle and a square. Where should the wire be cut to (a) minimize and (b) maximize the combined area of the circle and the square?

27. **Maximum-volume cone** A cone is constructed by cutting a sector from a circular sheet of metal with radius 20. The cut sheet is then folded up and welded (see figure). Find the radius and height of the cone with maximum volume that can be formed in this way.

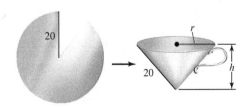

28. Covering a marble Imagine a flat-bottomed cylindrical pot with a circular cross section of radius 4. A marble with radius $0 < r < 4$ is placed in the bottom of the pot. What is the radius of the marble that requires the most water to cover it completely?

29. Optimal garden A rectangular flower garden with an area of 30 m² is surrounded by a grass border 1 m wide on two sides and 2 m wide on the other two sides (see figure). What dimensions of the garden minimize the combined area of the garden and borders?

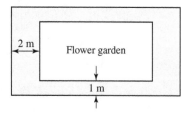

30. Rectangles beneath a line

a. A rectangle is constructed with one side on the positive x-axis, one side on the positive y-axis, and the vertex opposite the origin on the line $y = 10 - 2x$. What dimensions maximize the area of the rectangle? What is the maximum area?

b. Is it possible to construct a rectangle with a greater area than that found in part (a) by placing one side of the rectangle on the line $y = 10 - 2x$ and the two vertices not on that line on the positive x- and y-axes? Find the dimensions of the rectangle of maximum area that can be constructed in this way.

31. Kepler's wine barrel Several mathematical stories originated with the second wedding of the mathematician and astronomer Johannes Kepler. Here is one: While shopping for wine for his wedding, Kepler noticed that the price of a barrel of wine (here assumed to be a cylinder) was determined solely by the length d of a dipstick that was inserted diagonally through a centered hole in the top of the barrel to the edge of the base of the barrel (see figure). Kepler realized that this measurement does not determine the volume of the barrel and that for a fixed value of d, the volume varies with the radius r and height h of the barrel. For a fixed value of d, what is the ratio r/h that maximizes the volume of the barrel?

32. Folded boxes

a. Squares with sides of length x are cut out of each corner of a rectangular piece of cardboard measuring 3 ft by 4 ft. The resulting piece of cardboard is then folded into a box without a lid. Find the volume of the largest box that can be formed in this way.

b. Suppose that in part (a) the original piece of cardboard is a square with sides of length ℓ. Find the volume of the largest box that can be formed in this way.

c. Suppose that in part (a) the original piece of cardboard is a rectangle with sides of length ℓ and L. Holding ℓ fixed, find the size of the corner squares x that maximizes the volume of the box as $L \to \infty$. (*Source: Mathematics Teacher*, Nov 2002)

33. Making silos A grain silo consists of a cylindrical concrete tower surmounted by a metal hemispherical dome. The metal in the dome costs 1.5 times as much as the concrete (per unit of surface area). If the volume of the silo is 750 m³, what are the dimensions of the silo (radius and height of the cylindrical tower) that minimize the cost of the materials? Assume the silo has no floor and no flat ceiling under the dome.

34. Suspension system A load must be suspended 6 m below a high ceiling using cables attached to two supports that are 2 m apart (see figure). How far below the ceiling (x in the figure) should the cables be joined to minimize the total length of cable used?

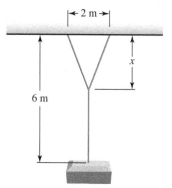

35. Light sources The intensity of a light source at a distance is directly proportional to the strength of the source and inversely proportional to the square of the distance from the source. Two light sources, one twice as strong as the other, are 12 m apart. At what point on the line segment joining the sources is the intensity the weakest?

36. Crease-length problem A rectangular sheet of paper of width a and length b, where $0 < a < b$, is folded by taking one corner of the sheet and placing it at a point P on the opposite long side of the sheet (see figure). The fold is then flattened to form a crease across the sheet. Assuming that the fold is made so that there is no flap extending beyond the original sheet, find the point P that produces the crease of minimum length. What is the length of that crease?

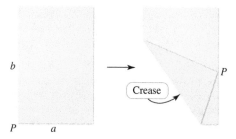

37. Laying cable An island is 3.5 mi from the nearest point on a straight shoreline; that point is 8 mi from a power station (see figure). A utility company plans to lay electrical cable underwater from the island to the shore and then underground along the shore to the power station. Assume that it costs \$2400/mi to lay underwater cable and \$1200/mi to lay underground cable. At what point should the underwater cable meet the shore to minimize the cost of the project?

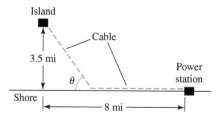

38. Laying cable again Solve the problem in Exercise 37, but this time minimize the cost with respect to the smaller angle θ between the underwater cable and the shore. (You should get the same answer.)

39. Sum of isosceles distances

  a. An isosceles triangle has a base of length 4 and two sides of length $2\sqrt{2}$. Let P be a point on the perpendicular bisector of the base. Find the location P that minimizes the sum of the distances between P and the three vertices.

  b. Assume in part (a) that the height of the isosceles triangle is $h > 0$ and its base has length 4. Show that the location of P that gives a minimum solution is independent of h for

$$h \geq \frac{2}{\sqrt{3}}.$$

40. Circle in a triangle What are the radius and area of the circle of maximum area that can be inscribed in an isosceles triangle whose two equal sides have length 1?

41. Slant height and cones Among all right circular cones with a slant height of 3, what are the dimensions (radius and height) that maximize the volume of the cone? The slant height of a cone is the distance from the outer edge of the base to the vertex.

42. Blood testing Suppose that a blood test for a disease is given to a population of N people, where N is large. At most, N individual blood tests must be done. The following strategy reduces the number of tests. Suppose 100 people are selected from the population and their blood samples are pooled. One test determines whether any of the 100 people test positive. If the test is positive, those 100 people are tested individually, making 101 tests necessary. However, if the pooled sample tests negative, then 100 people have been tested with one test. This procedure is then repeated. Probability theory shows that if the group size is x (for example, $x = 100$, as described here), then the average number of blood tests required to test N people is $N(1 - q^x + 1/x)$, where q is the probability that any one person tests negative. What group size x minimizes the average number of tests in the case that $N = 10,000$ and $q = 0.95$? Assume that x is a nonnegative real number.

43. Crankshaft A crank of radius r rotates with an angular frequency ω. It is connected to a piston by a connecting rod of length L (see figure). The acceleration of the piston varies with the position of the crank according to the function

$$a(\theta) = \omega^2 r\left(\cos\theta + \frac{r\cos 2\theta}{L}\right).$$

For fixed ω and r, find the values of θ, with $0 \leq \theta \leq 2\pi$, for which the acceleration of the piston is a maximum and minimum.

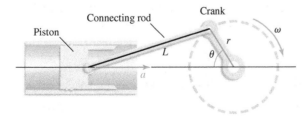

44. Metal rain gutters A rain gutter is made from sheets of metal 9 in wide. The gutters have a 3-in base and two 3-in sides, folded up at an angle θ (see figure). What angle θ maximizes the cross-sectional area of the gutter?

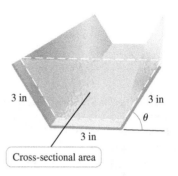

Cross-sectional area

45. Optimal soda can

  a. Classical problem Find the radius and height of a cylindrical soda can with a volume of 354 cm³ that minimize the surface area.

  b. Real problem Compare your answer in part (a) to a real soda can, which has a volume of 354 cm³, a radius of 3.1 cm, and a height of 12.0 cm, to conclude that real soda cans do not seem to have an optimal design. Then use the fact that real soda cans have a double thickness in their top and bottom surfaces to find the radius and height that minimizes the surface area of a real can (the surface areas of the top and bottom are now twice their values in part (a)). Are these dimensions closer to the dimensions of a real soda can?

46. Cylinder and cones (Putnam Exam 1938) Right circular cones of height h and radius r are attached to each end of a right circular cylinder of height h and radius r, forming a double-pointed object. For a given surface area A, what are the dimensions r and h that maximize the volume of the object?

47. Viewing angles An auditorium with a flat floor has a large screen on one wall. The lower edge of the screen is 3 ft above eye level, and the upper edge of the screen is 10 ft above eye level (see figure). How far from the screen should you stand to maximize your viewing angle θ?

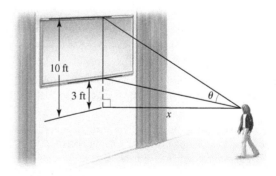

48. Searchlight problem—narrow beam A searchlight is 100 m from the nearest point on a straight highway (see figure). As it rotates, the searchlight casts a horizontal beam that intersects the highway in a point. If the light revolves at a rate of $\pi/6$ rad/s, find the rate at which the beam sweeps along the highway as a function of θ. For what value of θ is this rate maximized?

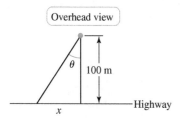

49. **Watching a Ferris wheel** An observer stands 20 m from the bottom of a Ferris wheel on a line that is perpendicular to the face of the wheel, with her eyes at the level of the bottom of the wheel. The wheel revolves at a rate of π rad/min, and the observer's line of sight with a specific seat on the Ferris wheel makes an angle θ with the horizontal (see figure). At what time during a full revolution is θ changing most rapidly?

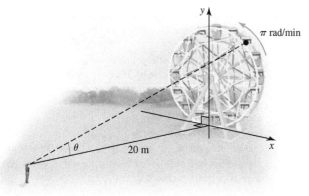

50. **Maximum angle** Find the value of x that maximizes θ in the figure.

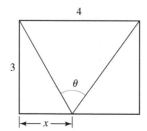

51. **Maximum-volume cylinder in a sphere** Find the dimensions of the right circular cylinder of maximum volume that can be placed inside a sphere of radius R.

52. **Rectangles in triangles** Find the dimensions and area of the rectangle of maximum area that can be inscribed in the following figures.

   a. A right triangle with a given hypotenuse length L
   b. An equilateral triangle with a given side length L
   c. A right triangle with a given area A
   d. An arbitrary triangle with a given area A (The result applies to any triangle, but first consider triangles for which all the angles are less than or equal to 90°.)

53. **Cylinder in a cone** A right circular cylinder is placed inside a cone of radius R and height H so that the base of the cylinder lies on the base of the cone.

   a. Find the dimensions of the cylinder with maximum volume. Specifically, show that the volume of the maximum-volume cylinder is $\frac{4}{9}$ the volume of the cone.

   b. Find the dimensions of the cylinder with maximum lateral surface area (area of the curved surface).

54. **Maximizing profit** Suppose you own a tour bus and you book groups of 20 to 70 people for a day tour. The cost per person is $30 minus $0.25 for every ticket sold. If gas and other miscellaneous costs are $200, how many tickets should you sell to maximize your profit? Treat the number of tickets as a nonnegative real number.

55. **Cone in a cone** A right circular cone is inscribed inside a larger right circular cone with a volume of 150 cm³. The axes of the cones coincide and the vertex of the inner cone touches the center of the base of the outer cone. Find the ratio of the heights of the cones that maximizes the volume of the inner cone.

56. **Another pen problem** A rancher is building a horse pen on the corner of her property using 1000 ft of fencing. Because of the unusual shape of her property, the pen must be built in the shape of a trapezoid (see figure).

   a. Determine the lengths of the sides that maximize the area of the pen.
   b. Suppose there is already a fence along the side of the property opposite the side of length y. Find the lengths of the sides that maximize the area of the pen, using 1000 ft of fencing.

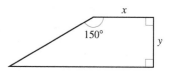

57. **Minimum-length roads** A house is located at each corner of a square with side lengths of 1 mi. What is the length of the shortest road system with straight roads that connects all of the houses by roads (that is, a road system that allows one to drive from any house to any other house)? (*Hint:* Place two points inside the square at which roads meet.) (*Source: Problems for Mathematicians Young and Old*, P. Halmos, MAA, 1991)

58. **Light transmission** A window consists of a rectangular pane of clear glass surmounted by a semicircular pane of tinted glass. The clear glass transmits twice as much light per unit of surface area as the tinted glass. Of all such windows with a fixed perimeter P, what are the dimensions of the window that transmits the most light?

59. **Slowest shortcut** Suppose you are standing in a field near a straight section of railroad tracks just as the locomotive of a train passes the point nearest to you, which is $\frac{1}{4}$ mi away. The train, with length $\frac{1}{3}$ mi, is traveling at 20 mi/hr. If you start running in a straight line across the field, how slowly can you run and still catch the train? In which direction should you run?

60. **The arbelos** An arbelos is the region enclosed by three mutually tangent semicircles; it is the region inside the larger semicircle and outside the two smaller semicircles (see figure).

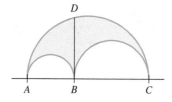

a. Given an arbelos in which the diameter of the largest circle is 1, what positions of point B maximize the area of the arbelos?

b. Show that the area of the arbelos is the area of a circle whose diameter is the distance BD in the figure.

61. Proximity questions

a. What point on the line $y = 3x + 4$ is closest to the origin?

b. What point on the parabola $y = 1 - x^2$ is closest to the point $(1, 1)$?

c. Find the point on the graph of $y = \sqrt{x}$ that is nearest the point $(p, 0)$ if (i) $p > \frac{1}{2}$; and (ii) $0 < p < \frac{1}{2}$. Express the answer in terms of p.

62. Turning a corner with a pole

a. What is the length of the longest pole that can be carried horizontally around a corner at which a 3-ft corridor and a 4-ft corridor meet at right angles?

b. What is the length of the longest pole that can be carried horizontally around a corner at which a corridor that is a feet wide and a corridor that is b feet wide meet at right angles?

c. What is the length of the longest pole that can be carried horizontally around a corner at which a corridor that is $a = 5$ ft wide and a corridor that is $b = 5$ ft wide meet at an angle of 120°?

d. What is the length of the longest pole that can be carried around a corner at which a corridor that is a feet wide and a corridor that is b feet wide meet at right angles, assuming there is an 8-ft ceiling and that you may tilt the pole at any angle?

63. Travel costs A simple model for travel costs involves the cost of gasoline and the cost of a driver. Specifically, assume that gasoline costs $\$ p$/gallon and the vehicle gets g miles per gallon. Also assume that the driver earns $\$ w$/hour.

a. A plausible function to describe how gas mileage (in mi/gal) varies with speed v is $g(v) = v(85 - v)/60$. Evaluate $g(0)$, $g(40)$, and $g(60)$ and explain why these values are reasonable.

b. At what speed does the gas mileage function have its maximum?

c. Explain why the formula $C(v) = Lp/g(v) + Lw/v$ gives the cost of the trip in dollars, where L is the length of the trip and v is the constant speed. Show that the dimensions are consistent.

d. Let $L = 400$ mi, $p = \$4$/gal, and $w = \$20$/hr. At what (constant) speed should the vehicle be driven to minimize the cost of the trip?

e. Should the optimal speed be increased or decreased (compared with part (d)) if L is increased from 400 mi to 500 mi? Explain.

f. Should the optimal speed be increased or decreased (compared with part (d)) if p is increased from $\$4$/gal to $\$4.20$/gal? Explain.

g. Should the optimal speed be increased or decreased (compared with part (d)) if w is decreased from $\$20$/hr to $\$15$/hr? Explain.

64. Do dogs know calculus? A mathematician stands on a beach with his dog at point A. He throws a tennis ball so that it hits the water at point B. The dog, wanting to get to the tennis ball as quickly as possible, runs along the straight beach line to point D and then swims from point D to point B to retrieve his ball. Assume C is the point on the edge of the beach closest to the tennis ball (see figure).

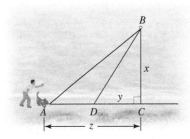

a. Assume the dog runs at speed r and swims at speed s, where $r > s$ and both are measured in meters/second. Also assume the lengths of BC, CD, and AC are x, y, and z, respectively. Find a function $T(y)$ representing the total time it takes the dog to get to the ball.

b. Verify that the value of y that minimizes the time it takes to retrieve the ball is $y = \dfrac{x}{\sqrt{r/s + 1}\sqrt{r/s - 1}}$.

c. If the dog runs at 8 m/s and swims at 1 m/s, what ratio y/x produces the fastest retrieving time?

d. A dog named Elvis who runs at 6.4 m/s and swims at 0.910 m/s was found to use an average ratio y/x of 0.144 to retrieve his ball. Does Elvis appear to know calculus? (*Source: Do Dogs Know Calculus?* T. Pennings, *The College Mathematics Journal*, 34, 3, May 2003)

65. Fermat's Principle

a. Two poles of heights m and n are separated by a horizontal distance d. A rope is stretched from the top of one pole to the ground and then to the top of the other pole. Show that the configuration that requires the least amount of rope occurs when $\theta_1 = \theta_2$ (see figure).

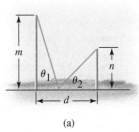

(a)

b. Fermat's Principle states that when light travels between two points in the same medium (at a constant speed), it travels on the path that minimizes the travel time. Show that when light from a source A reflects off a surface and is received at point B, the angle of incidence equals the angle of reflection, or $\theta_1 = \theta_2$ (see figure).

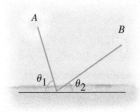

(b)

66. Snell's Law Suppose that a light source at A is in a medium in which light travels at speed v_1 and the point B is in a medium in which light travels at speed v_2 (see figure). Using Fermat's Principle, which states that light travels along the path that requires the minimum travel time (Exercise 65), show that the path taken between points A and B satisfies $(\sin\theta_1)/v_1 = (\sin\theta_2)/v_2$.

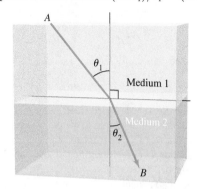

67. Tree notch (Putnam Exam 1938, rephrased) A notch is cut in a cylindrical vertical tree trunk. The notch penetrates to the axis of the cylinder and is bounded by two half-planes that intersect on a diameter D of the tree. The angle between the two half-planes is θ. Prove that for a given tree and fixed angle θ, the volume of the notch is minimized by taking the bounding planes at equal angles to the horizontal plane that also passes through D.

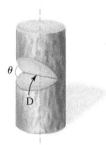

T 68. Gliding mammals Many species of small mammals (such as flying squirrels and marsupial gliders) have the ability to walk and glide. Recent research suggests that these animals choose the most energy-efficient means of travel. According to one empirical model, the energy required for a glider with body mass m to walk a horizontal distance D is $8.46\,Dm^{2/3}$ (where m is measured in grams, D is measured in meters, and energy is measured in microliters of oxygen consumed in respiration). The energy cost of climbing to a height $D\tan\theta$ and gliding a distance D at an angle θ below the horizontal is modeled by $1.36\,m\,D\tan\theta$ (where $\theta = 0$ represents horizontal flight and $\theta > 45°$ represents controlled falling). Therefore, the function

$$S(m,\theta) = 8.46m^{2/3} - 1.36m\tan\theta$$

gives the energy difference per horizontal meter traveled between walking and gliding: If $S > 0$ for given values of m and θ, then it is more costly to walk than glide.

a. For what glide angles is it more efficient for a 200-gram animal to glide rather that walk?

b. Find the threshold function $\theta = g(m)$ that gives the curve along which walking and gliding are equally efficient. Is it an increasing or decreasing function of body mass?

c. To make gliding more efficient than walking, do larger gliders have a larger or smaller selection of glide angles than smaller gliders?

d. Let $\theta = 25°$ (a typical glide angle). Graph S as a function of m, for $0 \le m \le 3000$. For what values of m is gliding more efficient?

e. For $\theta = 25°$, what value of m (call it m^*) maximizes S?

f. Does m^*, as defined in part (e), increase or decrease with increasing θ? That is, as a glider reduces its glide angle, does its optimal size become larger or smaller?

g. Assuming Dumbo is a gliding elephant whose weight is 1 metric ton (10^6 g), what glide angle would Dumbo use to be more efficient at gliding than walking?

(*Source: Energetic savings and the body size distribution of gliding mammals*, R. Dial, *Evolutionary Ecology Research* 5, 2003)

69. A challenging pen problem Two triangular pens are built against a barn. Two hundred meters of fencing are to be used for the three sides and the diagonal dividing fence (see figure). What dimensions maximize the area of the pen?

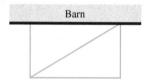

70. Minimizing related functions Find the values of x that minimize each function.

a. $f(x) = (x-1)^2 + (x-5)^2$

b. $f(x) = (x-a)^2 + (x-b)^2$, for constants a and b

c. $f(x) = \sum_{k=1}^{n}(x-a_k)^2$, for a positive integer n and constants $a_1, a_2, \ldots, a_n$.

(*Source: Calculus*, Vol. 1, T. Apostol, John Wiley and Sons, 1967)

QUICK CHECK ANSWERS

2. (i) $A = 400x - 2x^2$ (ii) $A = 400x - 3x^2$
3. $V = 108w^2 - 2w^3$ ◄

4.5 Linear Approximation and Differentials

Imagine plotting a smooth curve with a graphing utility. Now pick a point P on the curve, draw the line tangent to the curve at P, and zoom in on it several times. As you successively enlarge the curve near P, it looks more and more like the tangent line (Figure 4.59a). This fundamental observation—that smooth curves appear straighter on smaller scales—is called *local linearity*; it is the basis of many important mathematical ideas, one of which is *linear approximation*.

Now consider a curve with a corner or cusp at a point Q (Figure 4.59b). No amount of magnification "straightens out" the curve or removes the corner at Q. The different behavior at P and Q is related to the idea of differentiability: The function in Figure 4.59a is differentiable at P, whereas the function in Figure 4.59b is not differentiable at Q. One of the requirements for the techniques presented in this section is that the function be differentiable at the point in question.

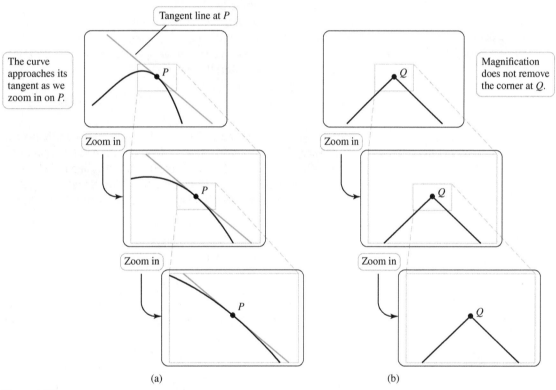

(a)   (b)

Figure 4.59

Linear Approximation

Figure 4.59a suggests that when we zoom in on the graph of a smooth function at a point P, the curve approaches its tangent line at P. This fact is the key to understanding linear approximation. The idea is to use the line tangent to the curve at P to approximate the value of the function at points near P. Here's how it works.

Assume f is differentiable on an interval containing the point a. The slope of the line tangent to the curve at the point $(a, f(a))$ is $f'(a)$. Therefore, an equation of the tangent line is

$$y - f(a) = f'(a)(x - a) \quad \text{or} \quad y = \underbrace{f(a) + f'(a)(x - a)}_{L(x)}.$$

This tangent line represents a new function L that we call the *linear approximation* to f at the point a (Figure 4.60). If f and f' are easy to evaluate at a, then the value of f at points near a is easily approximated using the linear approximation L. That is,

$$f(x) \approx L(x) = f(a) + f'(a)(x - a).$$

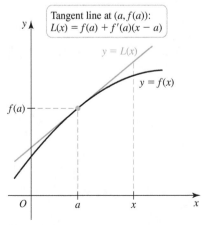

Figure 4.60

This approximation improves as x approaches a.

DEFINITION **Linear Approximation to f at a**

Suppose f is differentiable on an interval I containing the point a. The **linear approximation** to f at a is the linear function

$$L(x) = f(a) + f'(a)(x - a), \quad \text{for } x \text{ in } I.$$

QUICK CHECK 1 Sketch the graph of a function f that is concave up on an interval containing the point a. Sketch the linear approximation to f at a. Is the graph of the linear approximation above or below the graph of f? ◄

EXAMPLE 1   **Useful driving math** Suppose you are driving along a highway at a nearly constant speed and you record the number of seconds it takes to travel between two consecutive mile markers. If it takes 60 seconds, to travel one mile, then your average speed is 1 mi/60 s or 60 mi/hr. Now suppose that you travel one mile in $60 + x$ seconds; for example, if it takes 62 seconds, then $x = 2$, and if it takes 57 seconds, then $x = -3$. In this case, your average speed over one mile is 1 mi/$(60 + x)$s. Because there are 3600 s in 1 hr, the function

> In Example 1, notice that when x is positive, you are driving slower than 60 mi/hr; when x is negative, you are driving faster than 60 mi/hr.

$$s(x) = \frac{3600}{60 + x} = 3600(60 + x)^{-1}$$

gives your average speed in mi/hr if you travel one mile in x seconds more or less than 60 seconds. For example, if you travel one mile in 62 seconds, then $x = 2$ and your average speed is $s(2) \approx 58.06$ mi/hr. If you travel one mile in 57 seconds, then $x = -3$ and your average speed is $s(-3) \approx 63.16$ mi/hr. Because you don't want to use a calculator while driving, you need an easy approximation to this function. Use linear approximation to derive such a formula.

SOLUTION The idea is to find the linear approximation to s at the point 0. We first use the Chain Rule to compute

$$s'(x) = -3600(60 + x)^{-2},$$

and then note that $s(0) = 60$ and $s'(0) = -3600 \cdot 60^{-2} = -1$. Using the linear approximation formula, we find that

$$s(x) \approx L(x) = s(0) + s'(0)(x - 0) = 60 - x.$$

For example, if you travel one mile in 62 seconds, then $x = 2$ and your average speed is approximately $L(2) = 58$ mi/hr, which is very close to the exact value given previously. If you travel one mile in 57 seconds, then $x = -3$ and your average speed is approximately $L(-3) = 63$ mi/hr, which again is close to the exact value.

Related Exercises 7–12 ◄

QUICK CHECK 2 In Example 1, suppose you travel one mile in 75 seconds. What is the average speed given by the linear approximation formula? What is the exact average speed? Explain the discrepancy between the two values. ◄

EXAMPLE 2   **Linear approximations and errors**

a. Find the linear approximation to $f(x) = \sqrt{x}$ at $x = 1$ and use it to approximate $\sqrt{1.1}$.
b. Use linear approximation to estimate the value of $\sqrt{0.1}$.

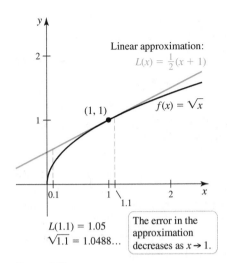

Figure 4.61

$L(1.1) = 1.05$
$\sqrt{1.1} = 1.0488\ldots$

The error in the approximation decreases as $x \to 1$.

Table 4.4

x	$L(x)$	Exact $\sqrt{x}$	Error
1.2	1.1	$1.0954\ldots$	4.6×10^{-3}
1.1	1.05	$1.0488\ldots$	1.2×10^{-3}
1.01	1.005	$1.0049\ldots$	1.2×10^{-5}
1.001	1.0005	$1.0005\ldots$	1.2×10^{-7}

▶ We choose $a = \frac{9}{100}$ because it is close to 0.1 and its square root is easy to evaluate.

SOLUTION

a. We construct the linear approximation

$$L(x) = f(a) + f'(a)(x - a),$$

where $f(x) = \sqrt{x}$, $f'(x) = 1/(2\sqrt{x})$, and $a = 1$. Noting that $f(a) = f(1) = 1$ and $f'(a) = f'(1) = \frac{1}{2}$, we have

$$L(x) = 1 + \frac{1}{2}(x - 1) = \frac{1}{2}(x + 1),$$

which is an equation of the line tangent to the curve at the point $(1, 1)$ (Figure 4.61). Because $x = 1.1$ is near $x = 1$, we approximate $\sqrt{1.1}$ by $L(1.1)$:

$$\sqrt{1.1} \approx L(1.1) = \frac{1}{2}(1.1 + 1) = 1.05.$$

The exact value is $f(1.1) = \sqrt{1.1} = 1.0488\ldots$; therefore, the linear approximation has an error of about 0.0012. Furthermore, our approximation is an *overestimate* because the tangent line lies above the graph of f. In Table 4.4, we see several approximations to $\sqrt{x}$ for x near 1 and the associated errors $|L(x) - \sqrt{x}|$. Clearly, the errors decrease as x approaches 1.

b. If the linear approximation $L(x) = \frac{1}{2}(x + 1)$ obtained in part (a) is used to approximate $\sqrt{0.1}$, we have

$$\sqrt{0.1} \approx L(0.1) = \frac{1}{2}(0.1 + 1) = 0.55.$$

A calculator gives $\sqrt{0.1} = 0.3162\ldots$, which shows that the approximation is well off the mark. The error arises because the tangent line through $(1, 1)$ is not close to the curve at $x = 0.1$ (Figure 4.61). For this reason, we seek a different value of a, with the requirement that it is near $x = 0.1$, and both $f(a)$ and $f'(a)$ are easily computed. It is tempting to try $a = 0$, but $f'(0)$ is undefined. One choice that works well is $a = \frac{9}{100} = 0.09$. Using the linear approximation $L(x) = f(a) + f'(a)(x - a)$, we have

$$\sqrt{0.1} \approx L(0.1) = \underbrace{\sqrt{\frac{9}{100}}}_{f(a)} + \underbrace{\frac{1}{2\sqrt{9/100}}}_{f'(a)} \underbrace{\left(\frac{1}{10} - \frac{9}{100}\right)}_{(x-a)}$$

$$= \frac{3}{10} + \frac{10}{6}\left(\frac{1}{100}\right)$$

$$= \frac{19}{60} \approx 0.3167.$$

This approximation agrees with the exact value to three decimal places.

Related Exercises 13–20 ◀

QUICK CHECK 3 Suppose you want to use linear approximation to estimate $\sqrt{0.18}$. What is a good choice for a? ◀

EXAMPLE 3 Linear approximation for the sine function Find the linear approximation to $f(x) = \sin x$ at $x = 0$ and use it to approximate $\sin 2.5°$.

SOLUTION We first construct a linear approximation $L(x) = f(a) + f'(a)(x - a)$, where $f(x) = \sin x$ and $a = 0$. Noting that $f(0) = 0$ and $f'(0) = \cos(0) = 1$, we have

$$L(x) = 0 + 1(x - 0) = x.$$

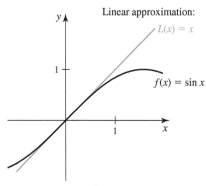

Linear approximation:

$L(x) = x$

$f(x) = \sin x$

Figure 4.62

Again, the linear approximation is the line tangent to the curve at the point $(0, 2)$ (Figure 4.62). Before using $L(x)$ to approximate $\sin 2.5°$, we convert to radian measure (the derivative formulas for trigonometric functions require angles in radians):

$$2.5° = 2.5°\left(\frac{\pi}{180°}\right) = \frac{\pi}{72} \approx 0.04363 \text{ rad.}$$

Therefore, $\sin 2.5° \approx L(0.04363) = 0.04363$. A calculator gives $\sin 2.5° \approx 0.04362$, so the approximation is accurate to four decimal places.

Related Exercises 21–30 ◄

In Examples 2 and 3, we used a calculator to check the accuracy of our approximations. This raises the question: Why bother with linear approximation when a calculator does a better job? There are some good answers to that question.

Linear approximation is actually just the first step in the process of *polynomial approximation*. While linear approximation does a decent job of estimating function values when x is near a, we can generally do better with higher-degree polynomials. These ideas are explored further in Chapter 9.

Linear approximation also allows us to discover simple approximations to complicated functions. In Example 3, we found the *small-angle approximation to the sine function*: $\sin x \approx x$ for x near 0.

QUICK CHECK 4 Explain why the linear approximation to $f(x) = \cos x$ at $x = 0$ is $L(x) = 1$. ◄

Linear Approximation and Concavity

Additional insight into linear approximation is gained by bringing concavity into the picture. Figure 4.63a shows the graph of a function f and its linear approximation (tangent line) at the point $(a, f(a))$. In this particular case, f is concave up on an interval containing a, and the graph of L lies below the graph of f near a. As a result, the linear approximation evaluated at a point near a is less than the exact value of f at that point. In other words, the linear approximation *underestimates* values of f near a.

The contrasting case is shown in Figure 4.63b, where we see graphs of f and L when f is concave down on an interval containing a. Now the graph of L lies above the graph of f, which means the linear approximation *overestimates* values of f near a.

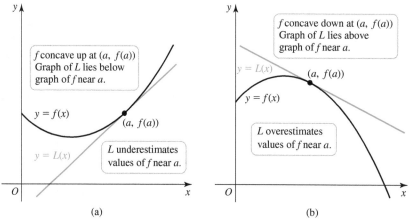

(a)   (b)

Figure 4.63

We can make another observation related to the degree of concavity (also called *curvature*). A large value of $|f''(a)|$ (large curvature) means that near $(a, f(a))$, the slope of the curve changes rapidly and the graph of f separates quickly from the tangent line. A small value of $|f''(a)|$ (small curvature) means the slope of the curve changes slowly and the curve is relatively flat near $(a, f(a))$; therefore, the curve remains close to the tangent line. As a result, absolute errors in linear approximation are larger when $|f''(a)|$ is large.

EXAMPLE 4   Linear approximation and concavity

a. Find the linear approximation to $f(x) = x^{1/3}$ at $x = 1$ and $x = 27$.

b. Use the linear approximations of part (a) to approximate $\sqrt[3]{2}$ and $\sqrt[3]{26}$

c. Are the approximations in part (b) overestimates or underestimates?

d. Compute the error in the approximations of part (b). Which error is greater? Explain.

SOLUTION

a. Note that

$$f(1) = 1, \quad f(27) = 3, \quad f'(x) = \frac{1}{3x^{2/3}}, \quad f'(1) = \frac{1}{3}, \quad \text{and} \quad f'(27) = \frac{1}{27}.$$

Therefore, the linear approximation at $x = 1$ is

$$L_1(x) = 1 + \frac{1}{3}(x - 1) = \frac{1}{3}x + \frac{2}{3},$$

and the linear approximation at $x = 27$ is

$$L_2(x) = 3 + \frac{1}{27}(x - 27) = \frac{1}{27}x + 2.$$

b. Using the results of part (a), we find that

$$\sqrt[3]{2} \approx L_1(2) = \frac{1}{3} \cdot 2 + \frac{2}{3} = \frac{4}{3} \approx 1.333$$

and

$$\sqrt[3]{26} \approx L_2(26) = \frac{1}{27} \cdot 26 + 2 \approx 2.963.$$

c. Figure 4.64 shows the graphs of f and the linear approximations L_1 and L_2 at $x = 1$ and $x = 27$, respectively (note the different scales on the x-axes). We see that f is concave down at both points, which is confirmed by the fact that

$$f''(x) = -\frac{2}{9}x^{-5/3} < 0, \quad \text{for} \quad x > 0.$$

As a result, the linear approximations lie above the graph of f and both approximations are overestimates.

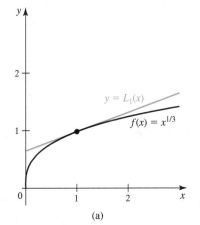
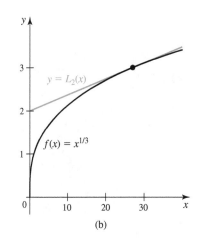

(a)   (b)

Figure 4.64

d. The error in the two linear approximations are

$$\left| L_1(2) - 2^{1/3} \right| \approx 0.073 \quad \text{and} \quad \left| L_2(26) - 26^{1/3} \right| \approx 0.00047.$$

Because $|f''(1)| \approx 0.22$ and $|f''(27)| \approx 0.00091$, the curvature of f is much greater at $x = 1$ than at $x = 27$, explaining why the approximation of $\sqrt[3]{26}$ is more accurate than the approximation of $\sqrt[3]{2}$.

Related Exercises 31–34 ◄

A Variation on Linear Approximation   Linear approximation says that a function f can be approximated as

$$f(x) \approx f(a) + f'(a)(x - a),$$

where a is fixed and x is a nearby point. We first rewrite this expression as

$$\underbrace{f(x) - f(a)}_{\Delta y} \approx f'(a)\underbrace{(x - a)}_{\Delta x}.$$

It is customary to use the notation Δ (capital Greek delta) to denote a change. The factor $x - a$ is the change in the x-coordinate between a and a nearby point x. Similarly, $f(x) - f(a)$ is the corresponding change in the y-coordinate (Figure 4.65). So we write this approximation as

$$\Delta y \approx f'(a)\, \Delta x.$$

In other words, a change in y (the function value) can be approximated by the corresponding change in x magnified or diminished by a factor of $f'(a)$. This interpretation states the familiar fact that $f'(a)$ is the rate of change of y with respect to x.

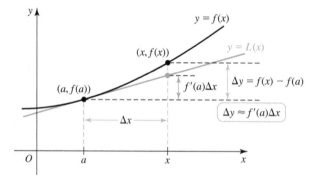

Figure 4.65

Relationship Between Δx and Δy

Suppose f is differentiable on an interval I containing the point a. The change in the value of f between two points a and $a + \Delta x$ is approximately

$$\Delta y \approx f'(a)\, \Delta x,$$

where $a + \Delta x$ is in I.

EXAMPLE 5   Estimating changes with linear approximations

a. Approximate the change in $y = f(x) = x^9 - 2x + 1$ when x changes from 1.00 to 1.05.

b. Approximate the change in the surface area of a spherical hot-air balloon when the radius decreases from 4 m to 3.9 m.

SOLUTION

a. The change in y is $\Delta y \approx f'(a)\, \Delta x$, where $a = 1$, $\Delta x = 0.05$, and $f'(x) = 9x^8 - 2$. Substituting these values, we find that

$$\Delta y \approx f'(a)\, \Delta x = f'(1) \cdot 0.05 = 7 \cdot 0.05 = 0.35.$$

If x increases from 1.00 to 1.05, then y increases by approximately 0.35.

> Notice that the units in these calculations are consistent. If r has units of meters (m), S' has units of $m^2/m = m$, so ΔS has units of m^2, as it should.

QUICK CHECK 5 Given that the volume of a sphere is $V = 4\pi r^3/3$, find an expression for the approximate change in the volume when the radius changes from a to $a + \Delta r$. ◄

b. The surface area of a sphere is $S = 4\pi r^2$, so the change in the surface area when the radius changes by Δr is $\Delta S \approx S'(a) \, \Delta r$. Substituting $S'(r) = 8\pi r$, $a = 4$, and $\Delta r = -0.1$, the approximate change in the surface area is

$$\Delta S \approx S'(a) \, \Delta r = S'(4) \cdot (-0.1) = 32\pi \cdot (-0.1) \approx -10.05.$$

The change in surface area is approximately -10.05 m^2; it is negative, reflecting a decrease.

Related Exercises 35–40 ◄

SUMMARY **Uses of Linear Approximation**

• To approximate f near $x = a$, use

$$f(x) \approx L(x) = f(a) + f'(a)(x - a).$$

• To approximate the change Δy in the dependent variable when x changes from a to $a + \Delta x$, use

$$\Delta y \approx f'(a) \, \Delta x.$$

Differentials

We now introduce an important concept that allows us to distinguish two related quantities:

• the change in the function $y = f(x)$ as x changes from a to $a + \Delta x$ (which we call Δy, as before), and

• the change in the linear approximation $y = L(x)$ as x changes from a to $a + \Delta x$ (which we call the *differential dy*).

Consider a function $y = f(x)$ differentiable on an interval containing a. If the x-coordinate changes from a to $a + \Delta x$, the corresponding change in the function is *exactly*

$$\Delta y = f(a + \Delta x) - f(a).$$

Using the linear approximation $L(x) = f(a) + f'(a)(x - a)$, the change in L as x changes from a to $a + \Delta x$ is

$$
\begin{aligned}
\Delta L &= L(a + \Delta x) - L(a) \\
&= \underbrace{(f(a) + f'(a)(a + \Delta x - a))}_{L(a + \Delta x)} - \underbrace{(f(a) + f'(a)(a - a))}_{L(a)} \\
&= f'(a) \, \Delta x.
\end{aligned}
$$

To distinguish Δy and ΔL, we define two new variables called *differentials*. The differential dx is simply Δx; the differential dy is the change in the linear approximation, which is $\Delta L = f'(a) \, \Delta x$. Using this notation,

$$\Delta L = \underbrace{dy}_{\substack{\text{same} \\ \text{as } \Delta L}} = f'(a) \, \Delta x = f'(a) \, \underbrace{dx}_{\substack{\text{same} \\ \text{as } \Delta x}}.$$

Therefore, at the point a, we have $dy = f'(a) \, dx$. More generally, we replace the fixed point a by a variable point x and write

$$dy = f'(x) \, dx.$$

DEFINITION **Differentials**

Let f be differentiable on an interval containing x. A small change in x is denoted by the **differential** dx. The corresponding change in f is approximated by the **differential** $dy = f'(x) \, dx$; that is,

$$\Delta y = f(x + dx) - f(x) \approx dy = f'(x) \, dx.$$

> Of the two coinventors of calculus, Gottfried Leibniz relied on the idea of differentials in his development of calculus. Leibniz's notation for differentials is essentially the same as the notation we use today. An Irish philosopher of the day, Bishop Berkeley, called differentials "the ghost of departed quantities."

Figure 4.66 shows that if $\Delta x = dx$ is small, then the change in f, which is Δy, is well approximated by the change in the linear approximation, which is dy. Furthermore, the approximation $\Delta y \approx dy$ improves as dx approaches 0. The notation for differentials is consistent with the notation for the derivative: If we divide both sides of $dy = f'(x)\, dx$ by dx, we have

$$\frac{dy}{dx} = \frac{f'(x)\, dx}{dx} = f'(x).$$

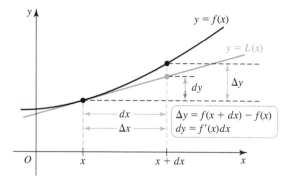

Figure 4.66

EXAMPLE 6 **Differentials as change** Use the notation of differentials to write the approximate change in $f(x) = 3\cos^2 x$ given a small change dx.

SOLUTION With $f(x) = 3\cos^2 x$, we have $f'(x) = -6\cos x \sin x = -3\sin 2x$. Therefore,

> Recall that $\sin 2x = 2\sin x \cos x$.

$$dy = f'(x)\, dx = -3\sin 2x\, dx.$$

The interpretation is that a small change dx in the independent variable x produces an approximate change in the dependent variable of $dy = -3\sin 2x\, dx$ in y. For example, if x increases from $x = \pi/4$ to $x = \pi/4 + 0.1$, then $dx = 0.1$ and

$$dy = -3\sin(\pi/2)(0.1) = -0.3.$$

The approximate change in the function is -0.3, which means a decrease of approximately 0.3.

Related Exercises 41–50 ◄

SECTION 4.5 EXERCISES

Review Questions

1. Sketch the graph of a smooth function f and label a point $P(a, (f(a))$ on the curve. Draw the line that represents the linear approximation to f at P.

2. Suppose you find the linear approximation to a differentiable function at a local maximum of that function. Describe the graph of the linear approximation.

3. How is linear approximation used to approximate the value of a function f near a point at which f and f' are easily evaluated?

4. How can linear approximation be used to approximate the change in $y = f(x)$ given a change in x?

5. Given a function f that is differentiable on its domain, write and explain the relationship between the differentials dx and dy.

6. Does the differential dy represent the change in f or the change in the linear approximation to f? Explain.

Basic Skills

7–8. Estimating speed *Use the linear approximation given in Example 1 to answer the following questions.*

7. If you travel one mile in 59 seconds, what is your approximate average speed? What is your exact speed?

8. If you travel one mile in 63 seconds, what is your approximate average speed? What is your exact speed?

9–12. Estimating time *Suppose you want to travel D miles at a constant speed of $(60 + x)$ mi/hr, where x could be positive or negative. The time in minutes required to travel D miles is $T(x) = 60D(60 + x)^{-1}$.*

9. Show that the linear approximation to T at the point $x = 0$ is

$$T(x) \approx L(x) = D\left(1 - \frac{x}{60}\right).$$

10. Use the result of Exercise 9 to approximate the amount of time it takes to drive 45 miles at 62 mi/hr. What is the exact time required?

11. Use the result of Exercise 9 to approximate the amount of time it takes to drive 80 miles at 57 mi/hr. What is the exact time required?

12. Use the result of Exercise 9 to approximate the amount of time it takes to drive 93 miles at 63 mi/hr. What is the exact time required?

T 13–20. Linear approximation

a. *Write the equation of the line that represents the linear approximation to the following functions at the given point a.*
b. *Graph the function and the linear approximation at a.*
c. *Use the linear approximation to estimate the given function value.*
d. *Compute the percent error in your approximation,*
   $100 \, |\text{approximation} - \text{exact}| / |\text{exact}|$, *where the exact value is given by a calculator.*

13. $f(x) = 12 - x^2; a = 2; f(2.1)$

14. $f(x) = \sin x; a = \pi/4; f(0.75)$

15. $f(x) = \ln(1 + x); a = 0; f(0.9)$

16. $f(x) = x/(x + 1); a = 1; f(1.1)$

17. $f(x) = \cos x; a = 0; f(-0.01)$

18. $f(x) = e^x; a = 0; f(0.05)$

19. $f(x) = (8 + x)^{-1/3}; a = 0; f(-0.1)$

20. $f(x) = \sqrt[4]{x}; a = 81; f(85)$

21–30. Estimations with linear approximation *Use linear approximations to estimate the following quantities. Choose a value of a that produces a small error.*

21. $1/203$ 22. $\tan 3°$ 23. $\sqrt{146}$ 24. $\sqrt[3]{65}$

25. $\ln(1.05)$ 26. $\sqrt{5/29}$ 27. $e^{0.06}$ 28. $1/\sqrt{119}$

29. $1/\sqrt[3]{510}$ 30. $\cos 31°$

31–34. Linear approximation and concavity *Carry out the following steps for the given functions f and points a.*

a. *Find the linear approximation L to the function f at the point a.*
b. *Graph f and L on the same set of axes.*
c. *Based on the graphs in part (a), state whether linear approximations to f near a are underestimates or overestimates.*
d. *Compute $f''(a)$ to confirm your conclusion in part (c).*

31. $f(x) = \dfrac{2}{x}, a = 1$ 32. $f(x) = 5 - x^2, a = 2$

33. $f(x) = e^{-x}, a = \ln 2$ 34. $f(x) = \sqrt{2} \cos x, a = \dfrac{\pi}{4}$

35–40. Approximating changes

35. Approximate the change in the volume of a sphere when its radius changes from $r = 5$ ft to $r = 5.1$ ft $(V(r) = \frac{4}{3}\pi r^3)$.

36. Approximate the change in the atmospheric pressure when the altitude increases from $z = 2$ km to $z = 2.01$ km $(P(z) = 1000 \, e^{-z/10})$.

37. Approximate the change in the volume of a right circular cylinder of fixed radius $r = 20$ cm when its height decreases from $h = 12$ cm to $h = 11.9$ cm $(V(h) = \pi r^2 h)$.

38. Approximate the change in the volume of a right circular cone of fixed height $h = 4$ m when its radius increases from $r = 3$ m to $r = 3.05$ m $(V(r) = \pi r^2 h/3)$.

39. Approximate the change in the lateral surface area (excluding the area of the base) of a right circular cone with fixed height $h = 6$ m when its radius decreases from $r = 10$ m to $r = 9.9$ m $(S = \pi r \sqrt{r^2 + h^2})$.

40. Approximate the change in the magnitude of the electrostatic force between two charges when the distance between them increases from $r = 20$ m to $r = 21$ m $(F(r) = 0.01/r^2)$.

41–50. Differentials *Consider the following functions and express the relationship between a small change in x and the corresponding change in y in the form $dy = f'(x) \, dx$.*

41. $f(x) = 2x + 1$ 42. $f(x) = \sin^2 x$

43. $f(x) = 1/x^3$ 44. $f(x) = e^{2x}$

45. $f(x) = 2 - a \cos x$, a constant

46. $f(x) = (4 + x)/(4 - x)$

47. $f(x) = 3x^3 - 4x$ 48. $f(x) = \sin^{-1} x$

49. $f(x) = \tan x$ 50. $f(x) = \ln(1 - x)$

Further Explorations

51. **Explain why or why not** Determine whether the following statements are true and give an explanation or counterexample.

    a. The linear approximation to $f(x) = x^2$ at $x = 0$ is $L(x) = 0$.
    b. Linear approximation at $x = 0$ provides a good approximation to $f(x) = |x|$.
    c. If $f(x) = mx + b$, then the linear approximation to f at any point is $L(x) = f(x)$.
    d. When linear approximation is used to estimate values of $\ln x$ near $x = e$, the approximations are overestimates of the true values.

52. **Linear approximation** Estimate $f(5.1)$ given that $f(5) = 10$ and $f'(5) = -2$.

53. **Linear approximation** Estimate $f(3.85)$ given that $f(4) = 3$ and $f'(4) = 2$.

T 54–57. Linear approximation

a. *Write an equation of the line that represents the linear approximation to the following functions at a.*
b. *Graph the function and the linear approximation at a.*
c. *Use the linear approximation to estimate the given quantity.*
d. *Compute the percent error in your approximation.*

54. $f(x) = \tan x; a = 0; \tan 3°$

55. $f(x) = 1/(x + 1); a = 0; 1/1.1$

56. $f(x) = \cos x; a = \pi/4; \cos 0.8$

57. $f(x) = e^{-x}; a = 0; e^{-0.03}$

Applications

58. **Ideal Gas Law** The pressure P, temperature T, and volume V of an ideal gas are related by $PV = nRT$, where n is the number of moles of the gas and R is the universal gas constant. For the purposes of this exercise, let $nR = 1$; therefore $P = T/V$.

    a. Suppose that the volume is held constant and the temperature increases by $\Delta T = 0.05$. What is the approximate change in the pressure? Does the pressure increase or decrease?
    b. Suppose that the temperature is held constant and the volume increases by $\Delta V = 0.1$. What is the approximate change in the pressure? Does the pressure increase or decrease?

c. Suppose that the pressure is held constant and the volume increases by $\Delta V = 0.1$. What is the approximate change in the temperature? Does the temperature increase or decrease?

T 59. Error in driving speed Consider again the average speed $s(x)$ and its linear approximation $L(x)$ discussed in Example 1. The error in using $L(x)$ to approximates $s(x)$ is given by $E(x) = |L(x) - s(x)|$. Use a graphing utility to determine the (approximate) values of x for which $E(x) \le 1$. What does your answer say about the accuracy of the average speeds estimated by $L(x)$ over this interval?

60. Time function Show that the function $T(x) = 60\,D(60 + x)^{-1}$ gives the time in minutes required to drive D miles at $60 + x$ miles per hour.

T 61. Errors in approximations Suppose $f(x) = \sqrt[3]{x}$ is to be approximated near $x = 8$. Find the linear approximation to f at 8. Then complete the following table, showing the errors in various approximations. Use a calculator to obtain the exact values. The percent error is $100\,|\text{approximation} - \text{exact}|/|\text{exact}|$. Comment on the behavior of the errors as x approaches 8.

x	Linear approx.	Exact value	Percent error
8.1			
8.01			
8.001			
8.0001			
7.9999			
7.999			
7.99			
7.9			

T 62. Errors in approximations Suppose $f(x) = 1/(1 + x)$ is to be approximated near $x = 0$. Find the linear approximation to f at 0. Then complete the following table showing the errors in various approximations. Use a calculator to obtain the exact values. The percent error is $100\,|\text{approximation} - \text{exact}|/|\text{exact}|$. Comment on the behavior of the errors as x approaches 0.

x	Linear approx.	Exact value	Percent error
0.1			
0.01			
0.001			
0.0001			
−0.0001			
−0.001			
−0.01			
−0.1			

Additional Exercises

63. Linear approximation and the second derivative Draw the graph of a function f such that $f(1) = f'(1) = f''(1) = 1$. Draw the linear approximation to the function at the point $(1, 1)$. Now draw the graph of another function g such that $g(1) = g'(1) = 1$ and $g''(1) = 10$. (It is not possible to represent the second derivative exactly, but your graphs should reflect the fact that $f''(1)$ is relatively small and $g''(1)$ is relatively large.) Now suppose that linear approximations are used to approximate $f(1.1)$ and $g(1.1)$.

a. Which function value has the more accurate linear approximation near $x = 1$ and why?

b. Explain why the error in the linear approximation to f near a point a is proportional to the magnitude of $f''(a)$.

QUICK CHECK ANSWERS

1. The linear approximation lies below the graph of f for x near a. **2.** $L(15) = 45$, $s(15) = 48$; $x = 15$ is not close to 0. **3.** $a = 0.16$ **4.** Note that $f(0) = 1$ and $f'(0) = 0$, so $L(x) = 1$ (this is the line tangent to $y = \cos x$ at $(0, 1)$). **5.** $\Delta V \approx 4\pi a^2\,\Delta r$ ◀

4.6 Mean Value Theorem

▶ Michel Rolle (1652–1719) is one of the less celebrated mathematicians whose name is nevertheless attached to a theorem. He worked in Paris most of his life as a scribe and published his theorem in 1691.

The *Mean Value Theorem* is a cornerstone in the theoretical framework of calculus. Several critical theorems (some stated in previous sections) rely on the Mean Value Theorem; this theorem also appears in practical applications. We begin with a preliminary result known as Rolle's Theorem.

Rolle's Theorem

Consider a function f that is continuous on a closed interval $[a, b]$ and differentiable on the open interval (a, b). Furthermore, assume f has the special property that $f(a) = f(b)$ (Figure 4.67). The statement of Rolle's Theorem is not surprising: It says that somewhere between a and b, there is at least one point at which f has a horizontal tangent line.

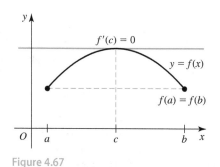

Figure 4.67

> **THEOREM 4.8   Rolle's Theorem**
> Let f be continuous on a closed interval $[a, b]$ and differentiable on (a, b) with $f(a) = f(b)$. There is at least one point c in (a, b) such that $f'(c) = 0$.

Proof: The function f satisfies the conditions of Theorem 4.1 (Extreme Value Theorem); therefore, it attains its absolute maximum and minimum values on $[a, b]$. Those values are attained either at an endpoint or at an interior point c.

Case 1: First suppose that f attains both its absolute maximum and minimum values at the endpoints. Because $f(a) = f(b)$, the maximum and minimum values are equal, and it follows that f is a constant function on $[a, b]$. Therefore, $f'(x) = 0$ for all x in (a, b), and the conclusion of the theorem holds.

Case 2: Assume at least one of the absolute extreme values of f does not occur at an endpoint. Then f must attain an absolute extreme value at an interior point of $[a, b]$; therefore, f must have either a local maximum or a local minimum at a point c in (a, b). We know from Theorem 4.2 that at a local extremum, the derivative is zero. Therefore, $f'(c) = 0$ for at least one point c of (a, b), and again the conclusion of the theorem holds. ◄

Why does Rolle's Theorem require continuity? A function that is not continuous on $[a, b]$ may have identical values at both endpoints and still not have a horizontal tangent line at any point on the interval (Figure 4.68a). Similarly, a function that is continuous on $[a, b]$ but not differentiable at a point of (a, b) may also fail to have a horizontal tangent line (Figure 4.68b).

> ► The Extreme Value Theorem, discussed in Section 4.1, states that a function that is continuous on a closed bounded interval attains its absolute maximum and minimum values on that interval.

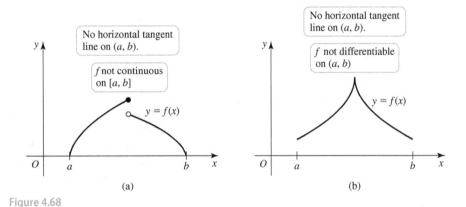

Figure 4.68

QUICK CHECK 1 Where on the interval $[0, 4]$ does $f(x) = 4x - x^2$ have a horizontal tangent line? ◄

EXAMPLE 1 **Verifying Rolle's Theorem** Find an interval I on which Rolle's Theorem applies to $f(x) = x^3 - 7x^2 + 10x$. Then find all points c in I at which $f'(c) = 0$.

SOLUTION Because f is a polynomial, it is everywhere continuous and differentiable. We need an interval $[a, b]$ with the property that $f(a) = f(b)$. Noting that $f(x) = x(x - 2)(x - 5)$, we choose the interval $[0, 5]$, because $f(0) = f(5) = 0$ (other intervals are possible). The goal is to find points c in the interval $(0, 5)$ at which $f'(c) = 0$, which amounts to the familiar task of finding the critical points of f. The critical points satisfy

$$f'(x) = 3x^2 - 14x + 10 = 0.$$

Using the quadratic formula, the roots are

$$x = \frac{7 \pm \sqrt{19}}{3}, \quad \text{or} \quad x \approx 0.88 \quad \text{and} \quad x \approx 3.79.$$

As shown in Figure 4.69, the graph of f has two points at which the tangent line is horizontal.

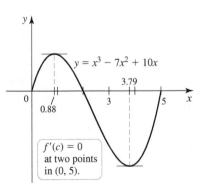

Figure 4.69

Related Exercises 7–14 ◄

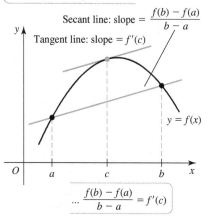

Figure 4.70

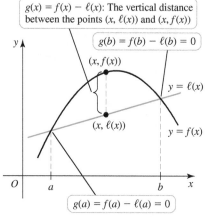

Figure 4.71

► The proofs of Rolle's Theorem and the Mean Value Theorem are nonconstructive: The theorems claim that a certain point exists, but their proofs do not say how to find it.

Mean Value Theorem

The Mean Value Theorem is easily understood with the aid of a picture. Figure 4.70 shows a function f differentiable on (a, b) with a secant line passing through $(a, f(a))$ and $(b, f(b))$; the slope of the secant line is the average rate of change of f over $[a, b]$. The Mean Value Theorem claims that there exists a point c in (a, b) at which the slope of the tangent line at c is equal to the slope of the secant line. In other words, we can find a point on the graph of f where the tangent line is parallel to the secant line.

THEOREM 4.9 Mean Value Theorem

If f is continuous on the closed interval $[a, b]$ and differentiable on (a, b), then there is at least one point c in (a, b) such that

$$\frac{f(b) - f(a)}{b - a} = f'(c).$$

Proof: The strategy of the proof is to use the function f of the Mean Value Theorem to form a new function g that satisfies Rolle's Theorem. Notice that the continuity and differentiability conditions of Rolle's Theorem and the Mean Value Theorem are the same. We devise g so that it satisfies the conditions $g(a) = g(b) = 0$.

As shown in Figure 4.71, the secant line passing through $(a, f(a))$ and $(b, f(b))$ is described by a function ℓ. We now define a new function g that measures the vertical distance between the given function f and the line ℓ. This function is simply $g(x) = f(x) - \ell(x)$. Because f and ℓ are continuous on $[a, b]$ and differentiable on (a, b), it follows that g is also continuous on $[a, b]$ and differentiable on (a, b). Furthermore, because the graphs of f and ℓ intersect at $x = a$ and $x = b$, we have $g(a) = f(a) - \ell(a) = 0$ and $g(b) = f(b) - \ell(b) = 0$.

We now have a function g that satisfies the conditions of Rolle's Theorem. By that theorem, we are guaranteed the existence of at least one point c in the interval (a, b) such that $g'(c) = 0$. By the definition of g, this condition implies that $f'(c) - \ell'(c) = 0$, or $f'(c) = \ell'(c)$.

We are almost finished. What is $\ell'(c)$? It is just the slope of the secant line, which is

$$\frac{f(b) - f(a)}{b - a}.$$

Therefore, $f'(c) = \ell'(c)$ implies that

$$\frac{f(b) - f(a)}{b - a} = f'(c). \qquad \triangleleft$$

QUICK CHECK 2 Sketch the graph of a function that illustrates why the continuity condition of the Mean Value Theorem is needed. Sketch the graph of a function that illustrates why the differentiability condition of the Mean Value Theorem is needed. ◄

The following situation offers an interpretation of the Mean Value Theorem. Imagine driving for 2 hours to a town 100 miles away. While your average speed is $100\,\text{mi}/2\,\text{hr} = 50\,\text{mi}/\text{hr}$, your instantaneous speed (measured by the speedometer) almost certainly varies. The Mean Value Theorem says that at some point during the trip, your instantaneous speed equals your average speed, which is 50 mi/hr. In Example 2, we apply these ideas to the science of weather forecasting.

EXAMPLE 2 Mean Value Theorem in action The *lapse rate* is the rate at which the temperature T decreases in the atmosphere with respect to increasing altitude z. It is typically reported in units of °C/km and is defined by $\gamma = -dT/dz$. When the lapse rate rises above 7°C/km in a certain layer of the atmosphere, it indicates favorable conditions for thunderstorm and tornado formation, provided other atmospheric conditions are also present.

Suppose the temperature at $z = 2.9$ km is $T = 7.6°C$ and the temperature at $z = 5.6$ km is $T = -14.3°C$. Assume also that the temperature function is continuous and differentiable at all altitudes of interest. What can a meteorologist conclude from these data?

SOLUTION Figure 4.72 shows the two data points plotted on a graph of altitude and temperature. The slope of the line joining these points is

$$\frac{-14.3°C - 7.6°C}{5.6 \text{ km} - 2.9 \text{ km}} = -8.1°C/\text{km},$$

which means, on average, the temperature is decreasing at 8.1°C/km in the layer of air between 2.9 km and 5.6 km. With only two data points, we cannot know the entire temperature profile. The Mean Value Theorem, however, guarantees that there is at least one altitude at which $dT/dz = -8.1°C/\text{km}$. At each such altitude, the lapse rate is $\gamma = -dT/dz = 8.1°C/\text{km}$. Because this lapse rate is above the 7°C/km threshold associated with unstable weather, the meteorologist might expect an increased likelihood of severe storms.

> ▶ Meteorologists look for "steep" lapse rates in the layer of the atmosphere where the pressure is between 700 and 500 hPa (hectopascals). This range of pressure typically corresponds to altitudes between 3 km and 5.5 km. The data in Example 2 were recorded in Denver at nearly the same time a tornado struck 50 mi to the north.

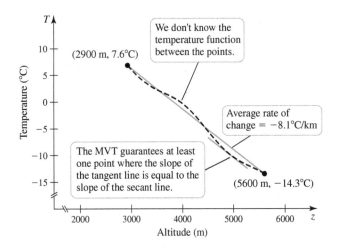

Figure 4.72

Related Exercises 15–16 ◀

EXAMPLE 3 **Verifying the Mean Value Theorem** Determine whether the function $f(x) = 2x^3 - 3x + 1$ satisfies the conditions of the Mean Value Theorem on the interval $[-2, 2]$. If so, find the point(s) guaranteed to exist by the theorem.

SOLUTION The polynomial f is everywhere continuous and differentiable, so it satisfies the conditions of the Mean Value Theorem. The average rate of change of the function on the interval $[-2, 2]$ is

$$\frac{f(2) - f(-2)}{2 - (-2)} = \frac{11 - (-9)}{4} = 5.$$

The goal is to find points in $(-2, 2)$ at which the line tangent to the curve has a slope of 5—that is, to find points at which $f'(x) = 5$. Differentiating f, this condition becomes

$$f'(x) = 6x^2 - 3 = 5 \quad \text{or} \quad x^2 = \frac{4}{3}.$$

Therefore, the points guaranteed to exist by the Mean Value Theorem are $x = \pm 2/\sqrt{3} \approx \pm 1.15$. The tangent lines have slope 5 at the corresponding points on the curve (Figure 4.73).

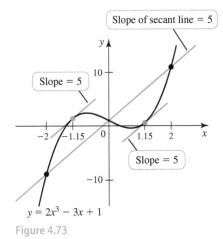

Figure 4.73

Related Exercises 17–24 ◀

Consequences of the Mean Value Theorem

We close with several results—some postponed from previous sections—that follow from the Mean Value Theorem.

We already know that the derivative of a constant function is zero; that is, if $f(x) = C$, then $f'(x) = 0$ (Theorem 3.2). Theorem 4.10 states the converse of this result.

> **THEOREM 4.10   Zero Derivative Implies Constant Function**
> If f is differentiable and $f'(x) = 0$ at all points of an interval I, then f is a constant function on I.

Proof: Suppose $f'(x) = 0$ on $[a, b]$, where a and b are distinct points of I. By the Mean Value Theorem, there exists a point c in (a, b) such that

$$\frac{f(b) - f(a)}{b - a} = \underbrace{f'(c) = 0.}_{\substack{f'(x) = 0 \text{ for} \\ \text{all } x \text{ in } I}}$$

Multiplying both sides of this equation by $b - a \neq 0$, it follows that $f(b) = f(a)$, and this is true for every pair of points a and b in I. If $f(b) = f(a)$ for every pair of points in an interval, then f is a constant function on that interval.   ◄

Theorem 4.11 builds on the conclusion of Theorem 4.10.

> **THEOREM 4.11   Functions with Equal Derivatives Differ by a Constant**
> If two functions have the property that $f'(x) = g'(x)$, for all x of an interval I, then $f(x) - g(x) = C$ on I, where C is a constant; that is, f and g differ by a constant.

Proof: The fact that $f'(x) = g'(x)$ on I implies that $f'(x) - g'(x) = 0$ on I. Recall that the derivative of a difference of two functions equals the difference of the derivatives, so we can write

$$f'(x) - g'(x) = (f - g)'(x) = 0.$$

QUICK CHECK 3 Give two distinct linear functions f and g that satisfy $f'(x) = g'(x)$; that is, the lines have equal slopes. Show that f and g differ by a constant. ◄

Now we have a function $f - g$ whose derivative is zero on I. By Theorem 4.10, $f(x) - g(x) = C$, for all x in I, where C is a constant; that is, f and g differ by a constant.   ◄

In Section 4.2, we stated and gave an argument to support the test for intervals of increase and decrease. With the Mean Value Theorem, we can prove this important result.

> **THEOREM 4.12   Intervals of Increase and Decrease**
> Suppose f is continuous on an interval I and differentiable at all interior points of I. If $f'(x) > 0$ at all interior points of I, then f is increasing on I. If $f'(x) < 0$ at all interior points of I, then f is decreasing on I.

Proof: Let a and b be any two distinct points in the interval I with $b > a$. By the Mean Value Theorem,

$$\frac{f(b) - f(a)}{b - a} = f'(c),$$

for some c between a and b. Equivalently,

$$f(b) - f(a) = f'(c)(b - a).$$

Notice that $b - a > 0$ by assumption. So if $f'(c) > 0$, then $f(b) - f(a) > 0$. Therefore, for all a and b in I with $b > a$, we have $f(b) > f(a)$, which implies that f is increasing on I. Similarly, if $f'(c) < 0$, then $f(b) - f(a) < 0$ or $f(b) < f(a)$. It follows that f is decreasing on I.   ◄

SECTION 4.6 EXERCISES

Review Questions

1. Explain Rolle's Theorem with a sketch.

2. Draw the graph of a function for which the conclusion of Rolle's Theorem does not hold.

3. Explain why Rolle's Theorem cannot be applied to the function $f(x) = |x|$ on the interval $[-a, a]$, for any $a > 0$.

4. Explain the Mean Value Theorem with a sketch.

5. Draw the graph of a function for which the conclusion of the Mean Value Theorem does not hold.

6. At what points c does the conclusion of the Mean Value Theorem hold for $f(x) = x^3$ on the interval $[-10, 10]$?

Basic Skills

7–14. Rolle's Theorem *Determine whether Rolle's Theorem applies to the following functions on the given interval. If so, find the point(s) that are guaranteed to exist by Rolle's Theorem.*

7. $f(x) = x(x - 1)^2$; $[0, 1]$ 8. $f(x) = \sin 2x$; $[0, \pi/2]$

9. $f(x) = \cos 4x$; $[\pi/8, 3\pi/8]$ 10. $f(x) = 1 - |x|$; $[-1, 1]$

11. $f(x) = 1 - x^{2/3}$; $[-1, 1]$

12. $f(x) = x^3 - 2x^2 - 8x$; $[-2, 4]$

13. $g(x) = x^3 - x^2 - 5x - 3$; $[-1, 3]$

14. $h(x) = e^{-x^2}$; $[-a, a]$, where $a > 0$

15. **Lapse rates in the atmosphere** Concurrent measurements indicate that at an elevation of 6.1 km, the temperature is $-10.3°C$, and at an elevation of 3.2 km, the temperature is $8.0°C$. Based on the Mean Value Theorem, can you conclude that the lapse rate exceeds the threshold value of $7°C/km$ at some intermediate elevation? Explain.

16. **Drag racer acceleration** The fastest drag racers can reach a speed of 330 mi/hr over a quarter-mile strip in 4.45 seconds (from a standing start). Complete the following sentence about such a drag racer: At some point during the race, the maximum acceleration of the drag racer is at least _____ mi/hr/s.

17–24. Mean Value Theorem

a. *Determine whether the Mean Value Theorem applies to the following functions on the given interval $[a, b]$.*

b. *If so, find the point(s) that are guaranteed to exist by the Mean Value Theorem.*

c. *For those cases in which the Mean Value Theorem applies, make a sketch of the function and the line that passes through $(a, f(a))$ and $(b, f(b))$. Mark the points P at which the slope of the function equals the slope of the secant line. Then sketch the tangent line at P.*

17. $f(x) = 7 - x^2$; $[-1, 2]$ 18. $f(x) = 3 \sin 2x$; $[0, \pi/4]$

19. $f(x) = e^x$; $[0, \ln 4]$ 20. $f(x) = \ln 2x$; $[1, e]$

21. $f(x) = \sin^{-1} x$; $[0, 1/2]$ 22. $f(x) = x + 1/x$; $[1, 3]$

23. $f(x) = 2x^{1/3}$; $[-8, 8]$ 24. $f(x) = x/(x + 2)$; $[-1, 2]$

Further Explorations

25. **Explain why or why not** Determine whether the following statements are true and give an explanation or counterexample.

   a. The continuous function $f(x) = 1 - |x|$ satisfies the conditions of the Mean Value Theorem on the interval $[-1, 1]$.
   b. Two differentiable functions that differ by a constant always have the same derivative.
   c. If $f'(x) = 0$, then $f(x) = 10$.

26–28. Questions about derivatives

26. Without evaluating derivatives, which of the functions $f(x) = \ln x$, $g(x) = \ln 2x$, $h(x) = \ln x^2$, and $p(x) = \ln 10x^2$ have the same derivative?

27. Without evaluating derivatives, which of the functions $g(x) = 2x^{10}$, $h(x) = x^{10} + 2$, and $p(x) = x^{10} - \ln 2$ have the same derivative as $f(x) = x^{10}$?

28. Find all functions f whose derivative is $f'(x) = x + 1$.

29. **Mean Value Theorem and graphs** By visual inspection, locate all points on the interval $[-4, 4]$ at which the slope of the tangent line equals the average rate of change of the function on the interval $[-4, 4]$.

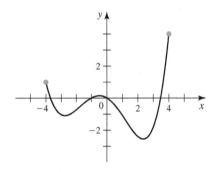

30–31. Mean Value Theorem and graphs *Find all points on the interval $(1, 3)$ at which the slope of the tangent line equals the average rate of change of f on $[1, 3]$. Reconcile your results with the Mean Value Theorem.*

30.

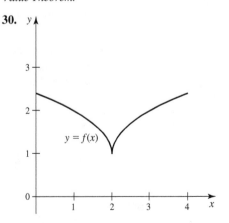

31.

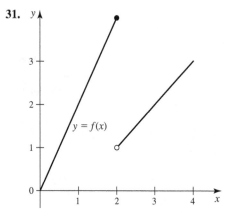

Applications

32. Avalanche forecasting Avalanche forecasters measure the *temperature gradient* dT/dh, which is the rate at which the temperature in a snowpack T changes with respect to its depth h. A large temperature gradient may lead to a weak layer in the snowpack. When these weak layers collapse, avalanches occur. Avalanche forecasters use the following rule of thumb: If dT/dh exceeds 10°C/m anywhere in the snowpack, conditions are favorable for weak-layer formation, and the risk of avalanche increases. Assume the temperature function is continuous and differentiable.

   a. An avalanche forecaster digs a snow pit and takes two temperature measurements. At the surface ($h = 0$), the temperature is −12°C. At a depth of 1.1 m, the temperature is 2°C. Using the Mean Value Theorem, what can he conclude about the temperature gradient? Is the formation of a weak layer likely?

   b. One mile away, a skier finds that the temperature at a depth of 1.4 m is −1°C, and at the surface, it is −12°C. What can be concluded about the temperature gradient? Is the formation of a weak layer in her location likely?

   c. Because snow is an excellent insulator, the temperature of snow-covered ground is often near 0°C. Furthermore, the surface temperature of snow in a particular area does not vary much from one location to the next. Explain why a weak layer is more likely to form in places where the snowpack is not too deep.

   d. The term *isothermal* is used to describe the situation where all layers of the snowpack are at the same temperature (typically near the freezing point). Is a weak layer likely to form in isothermal snow? Explain.

33. Mean Value Theorem and the police A state patrol officer saw a car start from rest at a highway on-ramp. She radioed ahead to a patrol officer 30 mi along the highway. When the car reached the location of the second officer 28 min later, it was clocked going 60 mi/hr. The driver of the car was given a ticket for exceeding the 60-mi/hr speed limit. Why can the officer conclude that the driver exceeded the speed limit?

34. Mean Value Theorem and the police again Compare carefully to Exercise 33. A state patrol officer saw a car start from rest at a highway on-ramp. She radioed ahead to another officer 30 mi along the highway. When the car reached the location of the second officer 30 min later, it was clocked going 60 mi/hr. Can the patrol officer conclude that the driver exceeded the speed limit?

35. Running pace Explain why if a runner completes a 6.2-mi (10-km) race in 32 min, then he must have been running at exactly 11 mi/hr at least twice in the race. Assume the runner's speed at the finish line is zero.

Additional Exercises

36. Mean Value Theorem for linear functions Interpret the Mean Value Theorem when it is applied to any linear function.

37. Mean Value Theorem for quadratic functions Consider the quadratic function $f(x) = Ax^2 + Bx + C$, where A, B, and C are real numbers with $A \neq 0$. Show that when the Mean Value Theorem is applied to f on the interval $[a, b]$, the number c guaranteed by the theorem is the midpoint of the interval.

38. Means

   a. Show that the point c guaranteed to exist by the Mean Value Theorem for $f(x) = x^2$ on $[a, b]$ is the arithmetic mean of a and b; that is, $c = (a + b)/2$.

   b. Show that the point c guaranteed to exist by the Mean Value Theorem for $f(x) = 1/x$ on $[a, b]$, where $0 < a < b$, is the geometric mean of a and b; that is, $c = \sqrt{ab}$.

39. Equal derivatives Verify that the functions $f(x) = \tan^2 x$ and $g(x) = \sec^2 x$ have the same derivative. What can you say about the difference $f - g$? Explain.

40. Equal derivatives Verify that the functions $f(x) = \sin^2 x$ and $g(x) = -\cos^2 x$ have the same derivative. What can you say about the difference $f - g$? Explain.

41. 100-m speed The Jamaican sprinter Usain Bolt set a world record of 9.58 s in the 100-m dash in the summer of 2009. Did his speed ever exceed 37 km/hr during the race? Explain.

42. Condition for nondifferentiability Suppose $f'(x) < 0 < f''(x)$, for $x < a$, and $f'(x) > 0 > f''(x)$, for $x > a$. Prove that f is not differentiable at a. (*Hint:* Assume f is differentiable at a and apply the Mean Value Theorem to f'.) More generally, show that if f' and f'' change sign at the same point, then f is not differentiable at that point.

43. Generalized Mean Value Theorem Suppose the functions f and g are continuous on $[a, b]$ and differentiable on (a, b), where $g(a) \neq g(b)$. Then there is a point c in (a, b) at which

$$\frac{f(b) - f(a)}{g(b) - g(a)} = \frac{f'(c)}{g'(c)}.$$

This result is known as the **Generalized (or Cauchy's) Mean Value Theorem**.

   a. If $g(x) = x$, then show that the Generalized Mean Value Theorem reduces to the Mean Value Theorem.

   b. Suppose $f(x) = x^2 - 1$, $g(x) = 4x + 2$, and $[a, b] = [0, 1]$. Find a value of c satisfying the Generalized Mean Value Theorem.

QUICK CHECK ANSWERS

1. $x = 2$ **2.** The functions shown in Figure 4.68 provide examples. **3.** The graphs of $f(x) = 3x$ and $g(x) = 3x + 2$ have the same slope. Note that $f(x) - g(x) = -2$, a constant. ◀

4.7 L'Hôpital's Rule

The study of limits in Chapter 2 was thorough but not exhaustive. Some limits, called *indeterminate forms*, cannot generally be evaluated using the techniques presented in Chapter 2. These limits tend to be the more interesting limits that arise in practice. A powerful result called *l'Hôpital's Rule* enables us to evaluate such limits with relative ease.

Here is how indeterminate forms arise. If f is a *continuous* function at a point a, then we know that $\lim_{x \to a} f(x) = f(a)$, allowing the limit to be evaluated by computing $f(a)$. But there are many limits that cannot be evaluated by substitution. In fact, we encountered such a limit in Section 3.4:

$$\lim_{x \to 0} \frac{\sin x}{x} = 1.$$

If we attempt to substitute $x = 0$ into $(\sin x)/x$, we get $0/0$, which has no meaning. Yet we proved that $(\sin x)/x$ has the limit 1 at $x = 0$ (Theorem 3.11). This limit is an example of an *indeterminate form*; specifically, $\lim_{x \to 0} \frac{\sin x}{x}$ has the form $0/0$ because the numerator and denominator both approach 0 as $x \to 0$.

The meaning of an *indeterminate form* is further illustrated by $\lim_{x \to \infty} \frac{ax}{x + 1}$, where $a \neq 0$. This limit has the indeterminate form ∞ / ∞ (meaning that the numerator and denominator become arbitrarily large in magnitude as $x \to \infty$), but the actual value of the limit is

$$\lim_{x \to \infty} \frac{ax}{x + 1} = a \lim_{x \to \infty} \frac{x}{x + 1} = a, \text{ where } a \text{ is any nonzero real number. In general, a limit}$$

with the form ∞ / ∞ or $0/0$ can have *any* value—which is why these limits must be handled carefully.

> ▶ The notations $0/0$ and ∞ / ∞ are merely symbols used to describe various types of indeterminate forms. The notation $0/0$ does not imply division by 0.

L'Hôpital's Rule for the Form 0/0

Consider a function of the form $f(x)/g(x)$ and assume that $\lim_{x \to a} f(x) = \lim_{x \to a} g(x) = 0$.

Then the limit $\lim_{x \to a} \frac{f(x)}{g(x)}$ has the indeterminate form $0/0$. We first state l'Hôpital's Rule and then prove a special case.

> ▶ Guillaume François l'Hôpital (lo-pee-tal) (1661–1704) is credited with writing the first calculus textbook. Much of the material in his book, including l'Hôpital's Rule, was provided by the Swiss mathematician Johann Bernoulli (1667–1748).

THEOREM 4.13   L'Hôpital's Rule

Suppose f and g are differentiable on an open interval I containing a with $g'(x) \neq 0$ on I when $x \neq a$. If $\lim_{x \to a} f(x) = \lim_{x \to a} g(x) = 0$, then

$$\lim_{x \to a} \frac{f(x)}{g(x)} = \lim_{x \to a} \frac{f'(x)}{g'(x)},$$

provided the limit on the right exists (or is $\pm \infty$). The rule also applies if $x \to a$ is replaced with $x \to \pm \infty$, $x \to a^+$, or $x \to a^-$.

Proof (special case): The proof of this theorem relies on the Generalized Mean Value Theorem (Exercise 43 of Section 4.6). We prove a special case of the theorem in which we assume that f' and g' are continuous at a, $f(a) = g(a) = 0$, and $g'(a) \neq 0$. We have

$$\lim_{x \to a} \frac{f'(x)}{g'(x)} = \frac{f'(a)}{g'(a)} \qquad \text{Continuity of } f' \text{ and } g'$$

$$= \frac{\lim\limits_{x \to a} \dfrac{f(x) - f(a)}{x - a}}{\lim\limits_{x \to a} \dfrac{g(x) - g(a)}{x - a}} \qquad \text{Definition of } f'(a) \text{ and } g'(a)$$

▶ The definition of the derivative provides an example of an indeterminate form. Assuming f is differentiable at x,

$$f'(x) = \lim_{h \to 0} \frac{f(x + h) - f(x)}{h}$$

has the form $0/0$.

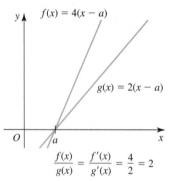

$$f(x) = 4(x - a)$$

$$g(x) = 2(x - a)$$

$$\frac{f(x)}{g(x)} = \frac{f'(x)}{g'(x)} = \frac{4}{2} = 2$$

Figure 4.74

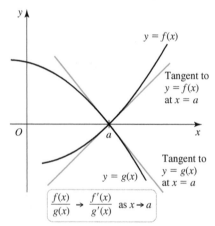

$y = f(x)$

Tangent to
$y = f(x)$
at $x = a$

$y = g(x)$

Tangent to
$y = g(x)$
at $x = a$

$\frac{f(x)}{g(x)} \to \frac{f'(x)}{g'(x)}$ as $x \to a$

Figure 4.75

QUICK CHECK 1 Which of the following functions lead to an indeterminate form as $x \to 0$: $f(x) = x^2/(x + 2)$, $g(x) = (\tan 3x)/x$, or $h(x) = (1 - \cos x)/x^2$? ◀

▶ The limit in part (a) can also be evaluated by factoring the numerator and canceling $(x - 1)$:

$$\lim_{x \to 1} \frac{x^3 + x^2 - 2x}{x - 1}$$

$$= \lim_{x \to 1} \frac{x(x - 1)(x + 2)}{x - 1}$$

$$= \lim_{x \to 1} x(x + 2) = 3.$$

$$= \lim_{x \to a} \frac{\dfrac{f(x) - f(a)}{x - a}}{\dfrac{g(x) - g(a)}{x - a}} \qquad \text{Limit of a quotient, } g'(a) \neq 0$$

$$= \lim_{x \to a} \frac{f(x) - f(a)}{g(x) - g(a)} \qquad \text{Cancel } x - a.$$

$$= \lim_{x \to a} \frac{f(x)}{g(x)}. \qquad f(a) = g(a) = 0 \qquad \blacktriangleleft$$

The geometry of l'Hôpital's Rule offers some insight. First consider two *linear* functions, f and g, whose graphs both pass through the point $(a, 0)$ with slopes 4 and 2, respectively; this means that

$$f(x) = 4(x - a) \quad \text{and} \quad g(x) = 2(x - a).$$

Furthermore, $f(a) = g(a) = 0, f'(x) = 4$, and $g'(x) = 2$ (Figure 4.74).
Looking at the quotient f/g, we see that

$$\frac{f(x)}{g(x)} = \frac{4(x - a)}{2(x - a)} = \frac{4}{2} = \frac{f'(x)}{g'(x)}. \qquad \text{Exactly}$$

This argument may be generalized, and we find that for any linear functions f and g with $f(a) = g(a) = 0$,

$$\lim_{x \to a} \frac{f(x)}{g(x)} = \lim_{x \to a} \frac{f'(x)}{g'(x)},$$

provided $g'(a) \neq 0$.

If f and g are not linear functions, we replace them with their linear approximations at a (Figure 4.75). Zooming in on the point a, the curves are close to their respective tangent lines $y = f'(a)(x - a)$ and $y = g'(a)(x - a)$, which have slopes $f'(a)$ and $g'(a) \neq 0$, respectively. Near $x = a$, we have

$$\frac{f(x)}{g(x)} \approx \frac{f'(a)(x - a)}{g'(a)(x - a)} = \frac{f'(a)}{g'(a)}.$$

Therefore, the ratio of the functions is well approximated by the ratio of the derivatives. In the limit as $x \to a$, we again have

$$\lim_{x \to a} \frac{f(x)}{g(x)} = \lim_{x \to a} \frac{f'(x)}{g'(x)}.$$

EXAMPLE 1 Using l'Hôpital's Rule Evaluate the following limits.

a. $\displaystyle \lim_{x \to 1} \frac{x^3 + x^2 - 2x}{x - 1}$ **b.** $\displaystyle \lim_{x \to 0} \frac{\sqrt{9 + 3x} - 3}{x}$

SOLUTION

a. Direct substitution of $x = 1$ into $\dfrac{x^3 + x^2 - 2x}{x - 1}$ produces the indeterminate form $0/0$.

Applying l'Hôpital's Rule with $f(x) = x^3 + x^2 - 2x$ and $g(x) = x - 1$ gives

$$\lim_{x \to 1} \frac{x^3 + x^2 - 2x}{x - 1} = \lim_{x \to 1} \frac{f'(x)}{g'(x)} = \lim_{x \to 1} \frac{3x^2 + 2x - 2}{1} = 3.$$

b. Substituting $x = 0$ into this function produces the indeterminate form $0/0$. Let $f(x) = \sqrt{9 + 3x} - 3$ and $g(x) = x$, and note that $f'(x) = \dfrac{3}{2\sqrt{9 + 3x}}$ and $g'(x) = 1$. Applying l'Hôpital's Rule, we have

$$\underbrace{\lim_{x\to 0} \frac{\sqrt{9 + 3x} - 3}{x}}_{f/g} = \underbrace{\lim_{x\to 0} \frac{\dfrac{3}{2\sqrt{9 + 3x}}}{1}}_{f'/g'} = \frac{1}{2}.$$

Related Exercises 13–22 ◄

L'Hôpital's Rule requires evaluating $\lim\limits_{x\to a} f'(x)/g'(x)$. It may happen that this second limit is another indeterminate form to which l'Hôpital's Rule may again be applied.

EXAMPLE 2   **L'Hôpital's Rule repeated**   Evaluate the following limits.

a. $\lim\limits_{x\to 0} \dfrac{e^x - x - 1}{x^2}$ **b.** $\lim\limits_{x\to 2} \dfrac{x^3 - 3x^2 + 4}{x^4 - 4x^3 + 7x^2 - 12x + 12}$

SOLUTION

a. This limit has the indeterminate form $0/0$. Applying l'Hôpital's Rule, we have

$$\lim_{x\to 0} \frac{e^x - x - 1}{x^2} = \lim_{x\to 0} \frac{e^x - 1}{2x},$$

which is another limit of the form $0/0$. Therefore, we apply l'Hôpital's Rule again:

$$\lim_{x\to 0} \frac{e^x - x - 1}{x^2} = \lim_{x\to 0} \frac{e^x - 1}{2x} \qquad \text{L'Hôpital's Rule}$$

$$= \lim_{x\to 0} \frac{e^x}{2} \qquad \text{L'Hôpital's Rule again}$$

$$= \frac{1}{2}. \qquad \text{Evaluate limit.}$$

b. Evaluating the numerator and denominator at $x = 2$, we see that this limit has the form $0/0$. Applying l'Hôpital's Rule twice, we have

$$\lim_{x\to 2} \frac{x^3 - 3x^2 + 4}{x^4 - 4x^3 + 7x^2 - 12x + 12} = \underbrace{\lim_{x\to 2} \frac{3x^2 - 6x}{4x^3 - 12x^2 + 14x - 12}}_{\text{limit of the form } 0/0} \qquad \text{L'Hôpital's Rule}$$

$$= \lim_{x\to 2} \frac{6x - 6}{12x^2 - 24x + 14} \qquad \begin{array}{l}\text{L'Hôpital's Rule}\\ \text{again}\end{array}$$

$$= \frac{3}{7}. \qquad \text{Evaluate limit.}$$

It is easy to overlook a crucial step in this computation: After applying l'Hôpital's Rule the first time, you *must* establish that the new limit is an indeterminate form before applying l'Hôpital's Rule a second time.

Related Exercises 23–36 ◄

Indeterminate Form ∞/∞

L'Hôpital's Rule also applies directly to limits of the form $\lim\limits_{x\to a} f(x)/g(x)$, where $\lim\limits_{x\to a} f(x) = \pm\infty$ and $\lim\limits_{x\to a} g(x) = \pm\infty$; this indeterminate form is denoted ∞/∞. The proof of this result is found in advanced books.

THEOREM 4.14 L'Hôpital's Rule (∞/∞)

Suppose that f and g are differentiable on an open interval I containing a, with $g'(x) \neq 0$ on I when $x \neq a$. If $\lim\limits_{x\to a} f(x) = \pm\infty$ and $\lim\limits_{x\to a} g(x) = \pm\infty$, then

$$\lim_{x\to a} \frac{f(x)}{g(x)} = \lim_{x\to a} \frac{f'(x)}{g'(x)},$$

provided the limit on the right exists (or is $\pm\infty$). The rule also applies for $x \to \pm\infty$, $x \to a^+$, or $x \to a^-$.

QUICK CHECK 2 Which of the following functions lead to an indeterminate form as $x \to \infty$: $f(x) = \sin x / x$, $g(x) = 2^x / x^2$, or $h(x) = (3x^2 + 4)/x^2$? ◄

EXAMPLE 3   **L'Hôpital's Rule for ∞/∞** Evaluate the following limits.

a. $\lim\limits_{x\to\infty} \dfrac{4x^3 - 6x^2 + 1}{2x^3 - 10x + 3}$ **b.** $\lim\limits_{x\to\pi/2^-} \dfrac{1 + \tan x}{\sec x}$

SOLUTION

> As shown in Section 2.5, the limit in Example 3a could also be evaluated by first dividing the numerator and denominator by x^3 or by using Theorem 2.7.

a. This limit has the indeterminate form ∞/∞ because both the numerator and the denominator approach ∞ as $x \to \infty$. Applying l'Hôpital's Rule three times, we have

$$\underbrace{\lim_{x\to\infty} \frac{4x^3 - 6x^2 + 1}{2x^3 - 10x + 3}}_{\infty/\infty} = \underbrace{\lim_{x\to\infty} \frac{12x^2 - 12x}{6x^2 - 10}}_{\infty/\infty} = \underbrace{\lim_{x\to\infty} \frac{24x - 12}{12x}}_{\infty/\infty} = \lim_{x\to\infty} \frac{24}{12} = 2.$$

b. In this limit, both the numerator and denominator approach ∞ as $x \to \pi/2^-$. L'Hôpital's Rule gives us

> In Exercise 3b, notice that we simplify $\sec^2 x/(\sec x \tan x)$ before taking the final limit. This step is important.

$$\lim_{x\to\pi/2^-} \frac{1 + \tan x}{\sec x} = \lim_{x\to\pi/2^-} \frac{\sec^2 x}{\sec x \tan x} \quad \text{L'Hôpital's Rule}$$

$$= \lim_{x\to\pi/2^-} \frac{1}{\sin x} \quad \text{Simplify.}$$

$$= 1. \quad \text{Evaluate limit.}$$

Related Exercises 37–44 ◄

Related Indeterminate Forms: $0 \cdot \infty$ and $\infty - \infty$

We now consider limits of the form $\lim\limits_{x\to a} f(x)g(x)$, where $\lim\limits_{x\to a} f(x) = 0$ and $\lim\limits_{x\to a} g(x) = \pm\infty$; such limits are denoted $0 \cdot \infty$. *L'Hôpital's Rule cannot be directly applied to limits of this form.* Furthermore, it's risky to jump to conclusions about such limits. Suppose $f(x) = x$ and $g(x) = \dfrac{1}{x^2}$, in which case $\lim\limits_{x\to 0} f(x) = 0$, $\lim\limits_{x\to 0} g(x) = \infty$, and $\lim\limits_{x\to 0} f(x)g(x) = \lim\limits_{x\to 0} \dfrac{1}{x}$ does not exist. On the other hand, if $f(x) = x$ and $g(x) = \dfrac{1}{\sqrt{x}}$, we have $\lim\limits_{x\to 0^+} f(x) = 0$, $\lim\limits_{x\to 0^+} g(x) = \infty$, and $\lim\limits_{x\to 0^+} f(x)g(x) = \lim\limits_{x\to 0^+} \sqrt{x} = 0$. So a limit of the form $0 \cdot \infty$, in which the two functions compete with each other, may have any value or may not exist. The following example illustrates how this indeterminate form can be recast in the form $0/0$ or ∞/∞.

EXAMPLE 4 L'Hôpital's Rule for $0 \cdot \infty$ Evaluate $\lim\limits_{x \to \infty} x^2 \sin\left(\dfrac{1}{4x^2}\right)$.

SOLUTION This limit has the form $0 \cdot \infty$. A common technique that converts this form to either $0/0$ or ∞/∞ is to *divide by the reciprocal*. We rewrite the limit and apply l'Hôpital's Rule:

$$\underbrace{\lim_{x \to \infty} x^2 \sin\left(\frac{1}{4x^2}\right)}_{0 \cdot \infty \text{ form}} = \underbrace{\lim_{x \to \infty} \frac{\sin\left(\dfrac{1}{4x^2}\right)}{\dfrac{1}{x^2}}}_{\text{recast in } 0/0 \text{ form}} \qquad x^2 = \frac{1}{1/x^2}$$

$$= \lim_{x \to \infty} \frac{\cos\left(\dfrac{1}{4x^2}\right)\dfrac{1}{4}(-2x^{-3})}{-2x^{-3}} \qquad \text{L'Hôpital's Rule}$$

$$= \frac{1}{4} \lim_{x \to \infty} \cos\left(\frac{1}{4x^2}\right) \qquad \text{Simplify.}$$

$$= \frac{1}{4}. \qquad \frac{1}{4x^2} \to 0, \cos 0 = 1$$

Related Exercises 45–50 ◄

QUICK CHECK 3 What is the form of the limit $\lim\limits_{x \to \pi/2^-} (x - \pi/2)(\tan x)$? Write it in the form $0/0$. ◄

Limits of the form $\lim\limits_{x \to a} (f(x) - g(x))$, where $\lim\limits_{x \to a} f(x) = \infty$ and $\lim\limits_{x \to a} g(x) = \infty$, are indeterminate forms that we denote $\infty - \infty$. L'Hôpital's Rule cannot be applied directly to an $\infty - \infty$ form. It must first be expressed in the form $0/0$ or ∞/∞. With the $\infty - \infty$ form, it is easy to reach erroneous conclusions. For example, if $f(x) = 3x + 5$ and $g(x) = 3x$, then

$$\lim_{x \to \infty} ((3x + 5) - (3x)) = 5.$$

However, if $f(x) = 3x$ and $g(x) = 2x$, then

$$\lim_{x \to \infty} (3x - 2x) = \lim_{x \to \infty} x = \infty.$$

These examples show again why indeterminate forms are deceptive. Before proceeding, we introduce another useful technique.

Occasionally, it helps to convert a limit as $x \to \infty$ to a limit as $t \to 0^+$ (or vice versa) by a *change of variables*. To evaluate $\lim\limits_{x \to \infty} f(x)$, we define $t = 1/x$ and note that as $x \to \infty$, $t \to 0^+$. Then

$$\lim_{x \to \infty} f(x) = \lim_{t \to 0^+} f\left(\frac{1}{t}\right).$$

This idea is illustrated in the next example.

EXAMPLE 5   L'Hôpital's Rule for ∞ − ∞ Evaluate $\lim\limits_{x\to\infty} (x - \sqrt{x^2 - 3x})$.

SOLUTION As $x \to \infty$, both terms in the difference $x - \sqrt{x^2 - 3x}$ approach ∞ and this limit has the form $\infty - \infty$. We first factor x from the expression and form a quotient:

$$\lim_{x\to\infty} (x - \sqrt{x^2 - 3x}) = \lim_{x\to\infty} (x - \sqrt{x^2(1 - 3/x)}) \quad \text{Factor } x^2 \text{ under square root.}$$

$$= \lim_{x\to\infty} x(1 - \sqrt{1 - 3/x}) \quad x > 0, \text{ so } \sqrt{x^2} = x$$

$$= \lim_{x\to\infty} \frac{1 - \sqrt{1 - 3/x}}{1/x}. \quad \begin{array}{l}\text{Write } 0 \cdot \infty \text{ form as } 0/0 \\ \text{form; } x = \dfrac{1}{1/x}.\end{array}$$

This new limit has the form $0/0$, and l'Hôpital's Rule may be applied. One way to proceed is to use the change of variables $t = 1/x$:

$$\lim_{x\to\infty} \frac{1 - \sqrt{1 - 3/x}}{1/x} = \lim_{t\to 0^+} \frac{1 - \sqrt{1 - 3t}}{t} \quad \text{Let } t = 1/x; \text{ replace } \lim_{x\to\infty} \text{ with } \lim_{t\to 0^+}.$$

$$= \lim_{t\to 0^+} \frac{\dfrac{3}{2\sqrt{1 - 3t}}}{1} \quad \text{L'Hôpital's Rule}$$

$$= \frac{3}{2}. \quad \text{Evaluate limit.}$$

Related Exercises 51–54 ◄

Indeterminate Forms 1^∞, 0^0, and ∞^0

The indeterminate forms 1^∞, 0^0, and ∞^0 all arise in limits of the form $\lim\limits_{x\to a} f(x)^{g(x)}$, where $x \to a$ could be replaced with $x \to a^{\pm}$ or $x \to \pm\infty$. L'Hôpital's Rule cannot be applied directly to the indeterminate forms 1^∞, 0^0, and ∞^0. They must first be expressed in the form $0/0$ or ∞/∞. Here is how we proceed.

The inverse relationship between $\ln x$ and e^x says that $f^g = e^{g \ln f}$, so we first write

$$\lim_{x\to a} f(x)^{g(x)} = \lim_{x\to a} e^{g(x) \ln f(x)}.$$

By the continuity of the exponential function, we switch the order of the limit and the exponential function (Theorem 2.12); therefore,

$$\lim_{x\to a} f(x)^{g(x)} = \lim_{x\to a} e^{g(x) \ln f(x)} = e^{\lim_{x\to a} g(x) \ln f(x)},$$

provided $\lim\limits_{x\to a} g(x) \ln f(x)$ exists. Therefore, $\lim\limits_{x\to a} f(x)^{g(x)}$ is evaluated using the following two steps.

> Notice the following:
> • For 1^∞, L has the form $\infty \cdot \ln 1 = \infty \cdot 0$.
> • For 0^0, L has the form $0 \cdot \ln 0 = 0 \cdot -\infty$.
> • For ∞^0, L has the form $0 \cdot \ln \infty = 0 \cdot \infty$.

PROCEDURE   Indeterminate forms 1^∞, 0^0, and ∞^0

Assume $\lim\limits_{x\to a} f(x)^{g(x)}$ has the indeterminate form 1^∞, 0^0, or ∞^0.

1. Analyze $L = \lim\limits_{x\to a} g(x) \ln f(x)$. This limit can be put in the form $0/0$ or ∞/∞, both of which are handled by l'Hôpital's Rule.

2. When L is finite, $\lim\limits_{x\to a} f(x)^{g(x)} = e^L$. If $L = \infty$ or $-\infty$, then $\lim\limits_{x\to a} f(x)^{g(x)} = \infty$ or $\lim\limits_{x\to a} f(x)^{g(x)} = 0$, respectively.

QUICK CHECK 4 Explain why a limit of the form 0^∞ is not an indeterminate form. ◄

EXAMPLE 6 **Indeterminate forms 0^0 and 1^∞** Evaluate the following limits.

a. $\displaystyle\lim_{x\to 0^+} x^x$ **b.** $\displaystyle\lim_{x\to\infty}\left(1+\frac{1}{x}\right)^x$

SOLUTION

a. This limit has the form 0^0. Using the given two-step procedure, we note that $x^x = e^{x\ln x}$ and first evaluate

$$L = \lim_{x\to 0^+} x\ln x.$$

This limit has the form $0\cdot\infty$, which may be put in the form ∞/∞ so that l'Hôpital's Rule can be applied:

$$L = \lim_{x\to 0^+} x\ln x = \lim_{x\to 0^+}\frac{\ln x}{1/x} \qquad x = \frac{1}{1/x}$$

$$= \lim_{x\to 0^+}\frac{1/x}{-1/x^2} \qquad \text{L'Hôpital's Rule for } \infty/\infty \text{ form}$$

$$= \lim_{x\to 0^+}(-x) = 0. \qquad \text{Simplify and evaluate the limit.}$$

The second step is to exponentiate the limit:

$$\lim_{x\to 0^+} x^x = e^L = e^0 = 1.$$

We conclude that $\displaystyle\lim_{x\to 0^+} x^x = 1$ (Figure 4.76).

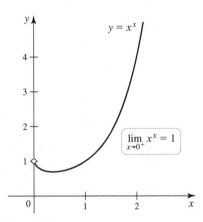

Figure 4.76

$y = x^x$

$\displaystyle\lim_{x\to 0^+} x^x = 1$

▶ The limit in Example 6b is often given as a definition of e. It is a special case of the more general limit

$$\lim_{x\to\infty}\left(1+\frac{a}{x}\right)^x = e^a.$$

See Exercise 119.

b. This limit has the form 1^∞. Noting that $(1+1/x)^x = e^{x\ln(1+1/x)}$, the first step is to evaluate

$$L = \lim_{x\to\infty} x\ln\left(1+\frac{1}{x}\right),$$

which has the form $0\cdot\infty$. Proceeding as in part (a), we have

$$L = \lim_{x\to\infty} x\ln\left(1+\frac{1}{x}\right) = \lim_{x\to\infty}\frac{\ln(1+1/x)}{1/x} \qquad x = \frac{1}{1/x}$$

$$= \lim_{x\to\infty}\frac{\dfrac{1}{1+1/x}\cdot\left(-\dfrac{1}{x^2}\right)}{\left(-\dfrac{1}{x^2}\right)} \qquad \text{L'Hôpital's Rule for } 0/0 \text{ form}$$

$$= \lim_{x\to\infty}\frac{1}{1+1/x} = 1. \qquad \text{Simplify and evaluate.}$$

The second step is to exponentiate the limit:

$$\lim_{x\to\infty}\left(1+\frac{1}{x}\right)^x = e^L = e^1 = e.$$

The function $y = (1+1/x)^x$ (Figure 4.77) has a horizontal asymptote $y = e \approx 2.71828$.

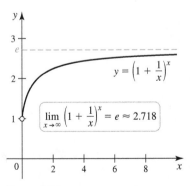

Figure 4.77

$y = \left(1+\dfrac{1}{x}\right)^x$

$\displaystyle\lim_{x\to\infty}\left(1+\frac{1}{x}\right)^x = e \approx 2.718$

Related Exercises 55–68 ◀

Growth Rates of Functions

An important use of l'Hôpital's Rule is to compare the growth rates of functions. Here are two questions—one practical and one theoretical—that demonstrate the importance of comparative growth rates of functions.

> ► Models of epidemics produce more complicated functions than the one given here, but they have the same general features.

- A particular theory for modeling the spread of an epidemic predicts that the number of infected people t days after the start of the epidemic is given by the function

$$N(t) = 2.5t^2 e^{-0.01t} = 2.5 \frac{t^2}{e^{0.01t}}.$$

Question: In the long run (as $t \to \infty$), does the epidemic spread or does it die out?

> ► The Prime Number Theorem was proved simultaneously (two different proofs) in 1896 by Jacques Hadamard and Charles de la Vallée Poussin, relying on fundamental ideas contributed by Riemann.

- A prime number is an integer $p \geq 2$ that has only two divisors, 1 and itself. The first few prime numbers are 2, 3, 5, 7, and 11. A celebrated theorem states that the number of prime numbers less than x is approximately

$$P(x) = \frac{x}{\ln x}, \quad \text{for large values of } x.$$

Question: According to this theorem, is the number of prime numbers infinite?

These two questions involve a comparison of two functions. In the first question, if t^2 grows faster than $e^{0.01t}$ as $t \to \infty$, then $\lim_{t \to \infty} N(t) = \infty$ and the epidemic grows. If $e^{0.01t}$ grows faster than t^2 as $t \to \infty$, then $\lim_{t \to \infty} N(t) = 0$ and the epidemic dies out. We will explain what is meant by *grows faster than* in a moment.

In the second question, the comparison is between x and $\ln x$. If x grows faster than $\ln x$ as $x \to \infty$, then $\lim_{x \to \infty} P(x) = \infty$ and the number of prime numbers is infinite.

Our goal is to obtain a ranking of the following families of functions based on their growth rates:

> ► Another function with a large growth rate is the factorial function, defined for integers as $f(n) = n! = n(n-1) \cdots 2 \cdot 1$. See Exercise 116.

- mx, where $m > 0$ (represents linear functions)
- x^p, where $p > 0$ (represents polynomials and algebraic functions)
- x^x (sometimes called a *superexponential* or *tower function*)
- $\ln x$ (represents logarithmic functions)
- $\ln^q x$, where $q > 0$ (represents powers of logarithmic functions)
- $x^p \ln x$, where $p > 0$ (a combination of powers and logarithms)
- e^x (represents exponential functions).

QUICK CHECK 5 Before proceeding, use your intuition and rank these classes of functions in order of their growth rates. ◄

We need to be precise about growth rates and what it means for f to grow faster than g as $x \to \infty$. We work with the following definitions.

DEFINITION Growth Rates of Functions (as $x \to \infty$)

Suppose f and g are functions with $\lim_{x \to \infty} f(x) = \lim_{x \to \infty} g(x) = \infty$. Then f **grows faster than** g as $x \to \infty$ if

$$\lim_{x \to \infty} \frac{g(x)}{f(x)} = 0 \quad \text{or, equivalently, if} \quad \lim_{x \to \infty} \frac{f(x)}{g(x)} = \infty.$$

The functions f and g have **comparable growth rates** if

$$\lim_{x \to \infty} \frac{f(x)}{g(x)} = M,$$

where $0 < M < \infty$ (M is nonzero and finite).

The idea of growth rates is illustrated nicely with graphs. Figure 4.78 shows a family of linear functions of the form $y = mx$, where $m > 0$, and powers of x of the form $y = x^p$, where $p > 1$. We see that powers of x grow faster (their curves rise at a greater rate) than the linear functions as $x \to \infty$.

Figure 4.79 shows that exponential functions of the form $y = b^x$, where $b > 1$, grow faster than powers of x of the form $y = x^p$, where $p > 0$, as $x \to \infty$ (Example 8).

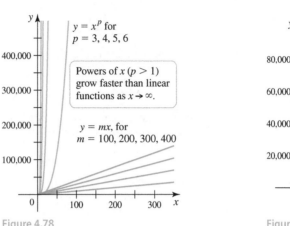

Figure 4.78

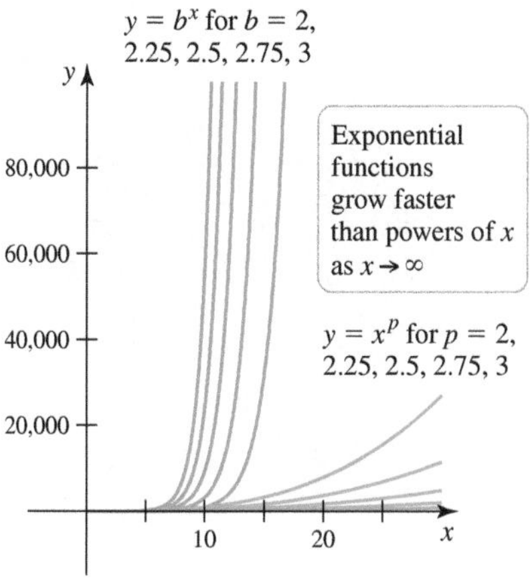

Figure 4.79

QUICK CHECK 6 Compare the growth rates of $f(x) = x^2$ and $g(x) = x^3$ as $x \to \infty$. Compare the growth rates of $f(x) = x^2$ and $g(x) = 10x^2$ as $x \to \infty$. ◄

We now begin a systematic comparison of growth rates. Note that a growth rate limit involves an indeterminate form ∞ / ∞, so l'Hôpital's Rule is always in the picture.

EXAMPLE 7 **Powers of x vs. powers of ln x** Compare the growth rates as $x \to \infty$ of the following pairs of functions.

a. $f(x) = \ln x$ and $g(x) = x^p$, where $p > 0$
b. $f(x) = \ln^q x$ and $g(x) = x^p$, where $p > 0$ and $q > 0$

SOLUTION

a. The limit of the ratio of the two functions is

$$\lim_{x \to \infty} \frac{\ln x}{x^p} = \lim_{x \to \infty} \frac{1/x}{px^{p-1}} \quad \text{L'Hôpital's Rule}$$

$$= \lim_{x \to \infty} \frac{1}{px^p} \quad \text{Simplify.}$$

$$= 0. \quad \text{Evaluate the limit.}$$

We see that any positive power of x grows faster than $\ln x$.

b. We compare $\ln^q x$ and x^p by observing that

$$\lim_{x \to \infty} \frac{\ln^q x}{x^p} = \lim_{x \to \infty} \left(\frac{\ln x}{x^{p/q}} \right)^q = \left(\underbrace{\lim_{x \to \infty} \frac{\ln x}{x^{p/q}}}_{0} \right)^q.$$

By part (a), $\displaystyle\lim_{x \to \infty} \frac{\ln x}{x^{p/q}} = 0$ (because $p/q > 0$). Therefore, $\displaystyle\lim_{x \to \infty} \frac{\ln^q x}{x^p} = 0$ (because $q > 0$). We conclude that any positive power of x grows faster than any positive power of $\ln x$.

Related Exercises 69–80 ◄

EXAMPLE 8 Powers of x vs. exponentials Compare the rates of growth of $f(x) = x^p$ and $g(x) = e^x$ as $x \to \infty$, where p is a positive real number.

SOLUTION The goal is to evaluate $\lim\limits_{x \to \infty} \dfrac{x^p}{e^x}$, for $p > 0$. This comparison is most easily done using Example 7 and a change of variables. We let $x = \ln t$ and note that as $x \to \infty$, we also have $t \to \infty$. With this substitution, $x^p = \ln^p t$ and $e^x = e^{\ln t} = t$. Therefore,

$$\lim_{x \to \infty} \frac{x^p}{e^x} = \lim_{t \to \infty} \frac{\ln^p t}{t} = 0. \quad \text{Example 7}$$

We see that increasing exponential functions grow faster than positive powers of x (Figure 4.79).

Related Exercises 69–80 ◄

These examples, together with the comparison of exponential functions b^x and the superexponential x^x (Exercise 120), establish a ranking of growth rates.

THEOREM 4.15 Ranking Growth Rates as $x \to \infty$

Let $f \ll g$ mean that g grows faster than f as $x \to \infty$. With positive real numbers $p, q, r,$ and s and $b > 1$,

$$\ln^q x \ll x^p \ll x^p \ln^r x \ll x^{p+s} \ll b^x \ll x^x.$$

You should try to build these relative growth rates into your intuition. They are useful in future chapters (Chapter 8 on sequences, in particular), and they can be used to evaluate limits at infinity quickly.

Pitfalls in Using l'Hôpital's Rule

We close with a list of common pitfalls when using l'Hôpital's Rule.

1. L'Hôpital's Rule says $\lim\limits_{x \to a} \dfrac{f(x)}{g(x)} = \lim\limits_{x \to a} \dfrac{f'(x)}{g'(x)}$, not

$$\lim_{x \to a} \frac{f(x)}{g(x)} = \lim_{x \to a} \left(\frac{f(x)}{g(x)} \right)' \quad \text{or} \quad \lim_{x \to a} \frac{f(x)}{g(x)} = \lim_{x \to a} \left(\frac{1}{g(x)} \right)' f'(x).$$

In other words, you should evaluate $f'(x)$ and $g'(x)$, form their quotient, and then take the limit. Don't confuse l'Hôpital's Rule with the Quotient Rule.

2. Be sure that the given limit involves the indeterminate form $0/0$ or ∞ / ∞ before applying l'Hôpital's Rule. For example, consider the following erroneous use of l'Hôpital's Rule:

$$\lim_{x \to 0} \frac{1 - \sin x}{\cos x} = \lim_{x \to 0} \frac{-\cos x}{\sin x},$$

which does not exist. The original limit is not an indeterminate form in the first place. This limit should be evaluated by direct substitution:

$$\lim_{x \to 0} \frac{1 - \sin x}{\cos x} = \frac{1 - \sin 0}{1} = 1.$$

3. When using l'Hôpital's Rule repeatedly, be sure to simplify expressions as much as possible at each step and evaluate the limit as soon as the new limit is no longer an indeterminate form.

4. Repeated use of l'Hôpital's Rule occasionally leads to unending cycles, in which case other methods must be used. For example, limits of the form $\lim\limits_{x \to \infty} \dfrac{\sqrt{ax + 1}}{\sqrt{bx + 1}}$, where a and b are real numbers, lead to such behavior (Exercise 111).

5. Be sure that the limit produced by l'Hôpital's Rule exists. Consider $\lim\limits_{x\to\infty} \dfrac{3x + \cos x}{x}$, which has the form ∞/∞. Applying l'Hôpital's Rule, we have

$$\lim_{x\to\infty} \frac{3x + \cos x}{x} = \lim_{x\to\infty} \frac{3 - \sin x}{1}.$$

It is tempting to conclude that because the limit on the right side does not exist, the original limit also does not exist. In fact, the original limit has a value of 3 (divide numerator and denominator by x). To reach a conclusion from l'Hôpital's Rule, the limit produced by l'Hôpital's Rule must exist (or be $\pm\infty$).

SECTION 4.7 EXERCISES

Review Questions

1. Explain with examples what is meant by the indeterminate form $0/0$.

2. Why are special methods, such as l'Hôpital's Rule, needed to evaluate indeterminate forms (as opposed to substitution)?

3. Explain the steps used to apply l'Hôpital's Rule to a limit of the form $0/0$.

4. To which indeterminate forms does l'Hôpital's Rule apply *directly*?

5. Explain how to convert a limit of the form $0 \cdot \infty$ to a limit of the form $0/0$ or ∞/∞.

6. Give an example of a limit of the form ∞/∞ as $x \to 0$.

7. Explain why the form 1^∞ is indeterminate and cannot be evaluated by substitution. Explain how the competing functions behave.

8. Give the two-step method for attacking an indeterminate limit of the form $\lim\limits_{x\to a} f(x)^{g(x)}$.

9. In terms of limits, what does it mean for f to grow faster than g as $x \to \infty$?

10. In terms of limits, what does it mean for the rates of growth of f and g to be comparable as $x \to \infty$?

11. Rank the functions x^3, $\ln x$, x^x, and 2^x in order of increasing growth rates as $x \to \infty$.

12. Rank the functions x^{100}, $\ln x^{10}$, x^x, and 10^x in order of increasing growth rates as $x \to \infty$.

Basic Skills

13–22. 0/0 form *Evaluate the following limits using l'Hôpital's Rule.*

13. $\lim\limits_{x\to 2} \dfrac{x^2 - 2x}{8 - 6x + x^2}$

14. $\lim\limits_{x\to -1} \dfrac{x^4 + x^3 + 2x + 2}{x + 1}$

15. $\lim\limits_{x\to 1} \dfrac{\ln x}{4x - x^2 - 3}$

16. $\lim\limits_{x\to 0} \dfrac{e^x - 1}{x^2 + 3x}$

17. $\lim\limits_{x\to e} \dfrac{\ln x - 1}{x - e}$

18. $\lim\limits_{x\to 1} \dfrac{4\tan^{-1} x - \pi}{x - 1}$

19. $\lim\limits_{x\to 0} \dfrac{3\sin 4x}{5x}$

20. $\lim\limits_{x\to 2\pi} \dfrac{x\sin x + x^2 - 4\pi^2}{x - 2\pi}$

21. $\lim\limits_{u\to \pi/4} \dfrac{\tan u - \cot u}{u - \pi/4}$

22. $\lim\limits_{z\to 0} \dfrac{\tan 4z}{\tan 7z}$

23–36. 0/0 form *Evaluate the following limits.*

23. $\lim\limits_{x\to 0} \dfrac{1 - \cos 3x}{8x^2}$

24. $\lim\limits_{x\to 0} \dfrac{\sin^2 3x}{x^2}$

25. $\lim\limits_{x\to \pi} \dfrac{\cos x + 1}{(x - \pi)^2}$

26. $\lim\limits_{x\to 0} \dfrac{e^x - x - 1}{5x^2}$

27. $\lim\limits_{x\to 0} \dfrac{e^x - \sin x - 1}{x^4 + 8x^3 + 12x^2}$

28. $\lim\limits_{x\to 0} \dfrac{\sin x - x}{7x^3}$

29. $\lim\limits_{x\to \infty} \dfrac{e^{1/x} - 1}{1/x}$

30. $\lim\limits_{x\to \infty} \dfrac{\tan^{-1} x - \pi/2}{1/x}$

31. $\lim\limits_{x\to -1} \dfrac{x^3 - x^2 - 5x - 3}{x^4 + 2x^3 - x^2 - 4x - 2}$

32. $\lim\limits_{x\to 1} \dfrac{x^n - 1}{x - 1}$, n is a positive integer

33. $\lim\limits_{v\to 3} \dfrac{v - 1 - \sqrt{v^2 - 5}}{v - 3}$

34. $\lim\limits_{y\to 2} \dfrac{y^2 + y - 6}{\sqrt{8 - y^2} - y}$

35. $\lim\limits_{x\to 2} \dfrac{x^2 - 4x + 4}{\sin^2(\pi x)}$

36. $\lim\limits_{x\to 2} \dfrac{\sqrt[3]{3x + 2} - 2}{x - 2}$

37–44. ∞/∞ form *Evaluate the following limits.*

37. $\lim\limits_{x\to \infty} \dfrac{3x^4 - x^2}{6x^4 + 12}$

38. $\lim\limits_{x\to \infty} \dfrac{4x^3 - 2x^2 + 6}{\pi x^3 + 4}$

39. $\lim\limits_{x\to \pi/2^-} \dfrac{\tan x}{3/(2x - \pi)}$

40. $\lim\limits_{x\to \infty} \dfrac{e^{3x}}{3e^{3x} + 5}$

41. $\lim\limits_{x\to \infty} \dfrac{\ln(3x + 5)}{\ln(7x + 3) + 1}$

42. $\lim\limits_{x\to \infty} \dfrac{\ln(3x + 5e^x)}{\ln(7x + 3e^{2x})}$

43. $\lim\limits_{x\to \infty} \dfrac{x^2 - \ln(2/x)}{3x^2 + 2x}$

44. $\lim\limits_{x\to \pi/2} \dfrac{2\tan x}{\sec^2 x}$

45–50. $0 \cdot \infty$ form *Evaluate the following limits.*

45. $\lim\limits_{x\to 0} x \csc x$

46. $\lim\limits_{x\to 1^-} (1 - x)\tan\left(\dfrac{\pi x}{2}\right)$

47. $\lim\limits_{x\to 0} \csc 6x \sin 7x$

48. $\lim\limits_{x\to \infty} \left(\csc(1/x)(e^{1/x} - 1)\right)$

49. $\lim\limits_{x\to \pi/2^-} \left(\dfrac{\pi}{2} - x\right)\sec x$

50. $\lim\limits_{x\to 0^+} (\sin x)\sqrt{\dfrac{1 - x}{x}}$

51–54. $\infty - \infty$ form *Evaluate the following limits.*

51. $\lim\limits_{x \to 0^+} \left(\cot x - \dfrac{1}{x} \right)$

52. $\lim\limits_{x \to \infty} (x - \sqrt{x^2 + 1})$

53. $\lim\limits_{\theta \to \pi/2^-} (\tan \theta - \sec \theta)$

54. $\lim\limits_{x \to \infty} (x - \sqrt{x^2 + 4x})$

55–68. $1^\infty, 0^0, \infty^0$ forms *Evaluate the following limits or explain why they do not exist. Check your results by graphing.*

55. $\lim\limits_{x \to 0^+} x^{2x}$

56. $\lim\limits_{x \to 0} (1 + 4x)^{3/x}$

57. $\lim\limits_{\theta \to \pi/2^-} (\tan \theta)^{\cos \theta}$

58. $\lim\limits_{\theta \to 0^+} (\sin \theta)^{\tan \theta}$

59. $\lim\limits_{x \to 0^+} (1 + x)^{\cot x}$

60. $\lim\limits_{x \to \infty} \left(1 + \dfrac{1}{x} \right)^{\ln x}$

61. $\lim\limits_{x \to \infty} \left(1 + \dfrac{a}{x} \right)^x$, for a constant a

62. $\lim\limits_{x \to 0} (e^{5x} + x)^{1/x}$

63. $\lim\limits_{x \to 0} (e^{ax} + x)^{1/x}$, for a constant a

64. $\lim\limits_{x \to 0} (2^{ax} + x)^{1/x}$, for a constant a

65. $\lim\limits_{x \to 0^+} (\tan x)^x$

66. $\lim\limits_{z \to \infty} \left(1 + \dfrac{10}{z^2} \right)^{z^2}$

67. $\lim\limits_{x \to 0} (x + \cos x)^{1/x}$

68. $\lim\limits_{x \to 0^+} \left(\dfrac{1}{3} \cdot 3^x + \dfrac{2}{3} \cdot 2^x \right)^{1/x}$

69–80. Comparing growth rates *Use limit methods to determine which of the two given functions grows faster or state that they have comparable growth rates.*

69. x^{10}; $e^{0.01x}$

70. $x^2 \ln x$; $\ln^2 x$

71. $\ln x^{20}$; $\ln x$

72. $\ln x$; $\ln(\ln x)$

73. 100^x; x^x

74. $x^2 \ln x$; x^3

75. x^{20}; 1.00001^x

76. $x^{10} \ln^{10} x$; x^{11}

77. x^x; $(x/2)^x$

78. $\ln \sqrt{x}$; $\ln^2 x$

79. e^{x^2}; e^{10x}

80. e^{x^2}; $x^{x/10}$

Further Explorations

81. Explain why or why not Determine whether the following statements are true and give an explanation or counterexample.

 a. By l'Hôpital's Rule, $\lim\limits_{x \to 2} \dfrac{x - 2}{x^2 - 1} = \lim\limits_{x \to 2} \dfrac{1}{2x} = \dfrac{1}{4}$.

 b. $\lim\limits_{x \to 0} (x \sin x) = \lim\limits_{x \to 0} f(x)g(x) =$
  $\lim\limits_{x \to 0} f'(x) \lim\limits_{x \to 0} g'(x) = (\lim\limits_{x \to 0} 1)(\lim\limits_{x \to 0} \cos x) = 1.$

 c. $\lim\limits_{x \to 0^+} x^{1/x}$ is an indeterminate form.

 d. The number 1 raised to any fixed power is 1. Therefore, because $(1 + x) \to 1$ as $x \to 0$, $(1 + x)^{1/x} \to 1$ as $x \to 0$.

 e. The functions $\ln x^{100}$ and $\ln x$ have comparable growth rates as $x \to \infty$.

 f. The function e^x grows faster than 2^x as $x \to \infty$.

82–83. Two methods *Evaluate the following limits in two different ways: Use the methods of Chapter 2 and use l'Hôpital's Rule.*

82. $\lim\limits_{x \to \infty} \dfrac{100x^3 - 3}{x^4 - 2}$

83. $\lim\limits_{x \to \infty} \dfrac{2x^3 - x^2 + 1}{5x^3 + 2x}$

84. L'Hôpital's example Evaluate one of the limits l'Hôpital used in his own textbook in about 1700:

$$\lim\limits_{x \to a} \dfrac{\sqrt{2a^3x - x^4} - a\sqrt[3]{a^2 x}}{a - \sqrt[4]{ax^3}}, \text{ where } a \text{ is a real number.}$$

85–102. Miscellaneous limits by any means *Use analytical methods to evaluate the following limits.*

85. $\lim\limits_{x \to 6} \dfrac{\sqrt[5]{5x + 2} - 2}{1/x - 1/6}$

86. $\lim\limits_{x \to \infty} x^2 \ln\left(\cos \dfrac{1}{x} \right)$

87. $\lim\limits_{x \to \infty} (\sqrt{x - 2} - \sqrt{x - 4})$

88. $\lim\limits_{x \to \pi/2} (\pi - 2x) \tan x$

89. $\lim\limits_{x \to \infty} x^3 \left(\dfrac{1}{x} - \sin \dfrac{1}{x} \right)$

90. $\lim\limits_{x \to \infty} (x^2 e^{1/x} - x^2 - x)$

91. $\lim\limits_{x \to 1^+} \left(\dfrac{1}{x - 1} - \dfrac{1}{\sqrt{x - 1}} \right)$

92. $\lim\limits_{x \to 0^+} x^{1/\ln x}$

93. $\lim\limits_{x \to \infty} \dfrac{\log_2 x}{\log_3 x}$

94. $\lim\limits_{x \to \infty} (\log_2 x - \log_3 x)$

95. $\lim\limits_{n \to \infty} \dfrac{1 + 2 + \cdots + n}{n^2}$

 (*Hint: Use* $1 + 2 + \cdots + n = \dfrac{n(n + 1)}{2}.$)

96. $\lim\limits_{x \to 0} \left(\dfrac{\sin x}{x} \right)^{1/x^2}$

97. $\lim\limits_{x \to 1} \dfrac{x \ln x - x + 1}{x \ln^2 x}$

98. $\lim\limits_{x \to 1} \dfrac{x \ln x + \ln x - 2x + 2}{x^2 \ln^3 x}$

99. $\lim\limits_{x \to 0^+} x^{1/(1 + \ln x)}$

100. $\lim\limits_{n \to \infty} \left(\cot \dfrac{1}{n} - n \right)$

101. $\lim\limits_{n \to \infty} \left(n \cot \dfrac{1}{n} - n^2 \right)$

102. $\lim\limits_{n \to \infty} n^2 \ln\left(n \sin \dfrac{1}{n} \right)$

103. It may take time The ranking of growth rates given in the text applies for $x \to \infty$. However, these rates may not be evident for small values of x. For example, an exponential grows faster than any power of x. However, for $1 < x < 19{,}800$, x^2 is greater than $e^{x/1000}$. For the following pairs of functions, estimate the point at which the faster-growing function overtakes the slower-growing function (for the last time).

 a. $\ln^3 x$ and $x^{0.3}$
 b. $2^{x/100}$ and x^3
 c. $x^{x/100}$ and e^x
 d. $\ln^{10} x$ and $e^{x/10}$

104–107. Limits with parameters *Evaluate the following limits in terms of the parameters a and b, which are positive real numbers. In each case, graph the function for specific values of the parameters to check your results.*

104. $\lim\limits_{x \to 0} (1 + ax)^{b/x}$

105. $\lim\limits_{x \to 0^+} (a^x - b^x)^x, a > b > 0$

106. $\lim\limits_{x \to 0^+} (a^x - b^x)^{1/x}, a > b > 0$

107. $\lim\limits_{x \to 0} \dfrac{a^x - b^x}{x}$

Applications

108. An optics limit The theory of interference of coherent oscillators requires the limit $\lim\limits_{\delta \to 2m\pi} \dfrac{\sin^2 (N\delta/2)}{\sin^2 (\delta/2)}$, where N is a positive integer and m is any integer. Show that the value of this limit is N^2.

109. Compound interest Suppose you make a deposit of $\$P$ into a savings account that earns interest at a rate of 100 r% per year.

   a. Show that if interest is compounded once per year, then the balance after t years is $B(t) = P(1 + r)^t$.

   b. If interest is compounded m times per year, then the balance after t years is $B(t) = P(1 + r/m)^{mt}$. For example, $m = 12$ corresponds to monthly compounding, and the interest rate for each month is $r/12$. In the limit $m \to \infty$, the compounding is said to be *continuous*. Show that with continuous compounding, the balance after t years is $B(t) = Pe^{rt}$.

110. Algorithm complexity The complexity of a computer algorithm is the number of operations or steps the algorithm needs to complete its task assuming there are n pieces of input (for example, the number of steps needed to put n numbers in ascending order). Four algorithms for doing the same task have complexities of A: $n^{3/2}$, B: $n \log_2 n$, C: $n(\log_2 n)^2$, and D: $\sqrt{n} \log_2 n$. Rank the algorithms in order of increasing efficiency for large values of n. Graph the complexities as they vary with n and comment on your observations.

Additional Exercises

111. L'Hôpital loops Consider the limit $\lim\limits_{x \to \infty} \dfrac{\sqrt{ax + b}}{\sqrt{cx + d}}$, where a, b, c, and d are positive real numbers. Show that l'Hôpital's Rule fails for this limit. Find the limit using another method.

112. General $\infty - \infty$ result Let a and b be positive real numbers. Evaluate $\lim\limits_{x \to \infty} (ax - \sqrt{a^2x^2 - bx})$ in terms of a and b.

113. Exponential functions and powers Show that any exponential function b^x, for $b > 1$, grows faster than x^p, for $p > 0$.

114. Exponentials with different bases Show that $f(x) = a^x$ grows faster than $g(x) = b^x$ as $x \to \infty$ if $1 < b < a$.

115. Logs with different bases Show that $f(x) = \log_a x$ and $g(x) = \log_b x$, where $a > 1$ and $b > 1$, grow at a comparable rate as $x \to \infty$.

116. Factorial growth rate The factorial function is defined for positive integers as $n! = n(n - 1)(n - 2) \cdots 3 \cdot 2 \cdot 1$. For example, $5! = 5 \cdot 4 \cdot 3 \cdot 2 \cdot 1 = 120$. A valuable result that gives good approximations to $n!$ for large values of n is *Stirling's formula*, $n! \approx \sqrt{2\pi n}\, n^n e^{-n}$. Use this formula and a calculator to determine where the factorial function appears in the ranking of growth rates given in Theorem 4.15. (See the Guided Project *Stirling's Formula*.)

117. A geometric limit Let $f(\theta)$ be the area of the triangle ABP (see figure) and let $g(\theta)$ be the area of the region between the chord PB and the arc PB. Evaluate $\lim\limits_{\theta \to 0} g(\theta)/f(\theta)$.

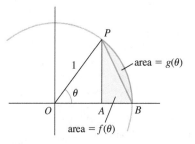

118. A fascinating function Consider the function $f(x) = (ab^x + (1 - a)c^x)^{1/x}$, where a, b, and c are positive real numbers with $0 < a < 1$.

   a. Graph f for several sets of (a, b, c). Verify that in all cases f is an increasing function with a single inflection point, for all x.

   b. Use analytical methods to determine $\lim\limits_{x \to 0} f(x)$ in terms of a, b, and c.

   c. Show that $\lim\limits_{x \to \infty} f(x) = \max \{b, c\}$ and $\lim\limits_{x \to -\infty} f(x) = \min \{b, c\}$, for any $0 < a < 1$.

   d. Estimate the location of the inflection point of f.

119. Exponential limit Prove that $\lim\limits_{x \to \infty} \left(1 + \dfrac{a}{x}\right)^x = e^a$, for $a \neq 0$.

120. Exponentials vs. super exponentials Show that x^x grows faster than b^x as $x \to \infty$, for $b > 1$.

121. Exponential growth rates

   a. For what values of $b > 0$ does b^x grow faster than e^x as $x \to \infty$?

   b. Compare the growth rates of e^x and e^{ax} as $x \to \infty$, for $a > 0$.

QUICK CHECK ANSWERS

1. g and h **2.** g and h **3.** $0 \cdot \infty$; $(x - \pi/2)/\cot x$
4. The form 0^∞ (for example, $\lim\limits_{x \to 0^+} x^{1/x}$) is not indeterminate, because as the base goes to zero, raising it to larger and larger powers drives the entire function to zero.   **6.** x^3 grows faster than x^2 as $x \to \infty$, whereas x^2 and $10x^2$ have comparable growth rates as $x \to \infty$. ◄

4.8 Newton's Method

A common problem that arises in mathematics is finding the *roots*, or *zeros*, of a function. The roots of a function are the values of x that satisfy the equation $f(x) = 0$. Equivalently, they correspond to the x-intercepts of the graph of f. You have already seen an important example of a root-finding problem. To find the critical points of a function f, we must solve the equation $f'(x) = 0$; that is, we find the roots of f'. Newton's method, which we discuss in this section, is one of the most effective methods for *approximating* the roots of a function.

> Newton's method is attributed to Sir Isaac Newton, who devised the method in 1669. However, similar methods were known prior to Newton's time. A special case of Newton's method for approximating square roots is called the Babylonian method and was probably invented by Greek mathematicians.

Why Approximate?

A little background about roots of functions explains why a method is needed to approximate roots. If you are given a linear function, such as $f(x) = 2x - 9$, you know how to use algebraic methods to solve $f(x) = 0$ and find the single root $x = \frac{9}{2}$. Similarly, given the quadratic function $f(x) = x^2 - 6x - 72$, you know how to factor or use the quadratic formula to discover that the roots are $x = 12$ and $x = -6$. It turns out that formulas also exist for finding the roots of cubic (third-degree) and quartic (fourth-degree) polynomials. Methods such as factoring and algebra are called *analytical methods*; when they work, they give the roots of a function *exactly* in terms of arithmetic operations and radicals.

Here is an important fact: Apart from the functions we have listed—polynomials of degree four or less—analytical methods do not give the roots of most functions. To be sure, there are special cases in which analytical methods work. For example, you should verify that the single real root of $f(x) = e^{2x} + 2e^x - 3$ is $x = 0$ and that the two real roots of $f(x) = x^{10} - 1$ are $x = 1$ and $x = -1$. But in general, the roots of even relatively simple functions such as $f(x) = e^{-x} - x$ cannot be found exactly using analytical methods.

When analytical methods do not work, which is the majority of cases, we need another approach. That approach is to approximate roots using *numerical methods*, such as Newton's method.

Deriving Newton's Method

Newton's method is most easily derived geometrically. Assume that r is a root of f that we wish to approximate; this means that $f(r) = 0$. We also assume that f is differentiable on some interval containing r. Suppose x_0 is an initial approximation to r that is generally obtained by some preliminary analysis. A better approximation to r is often obtained by carrying out the following two steps:

• A line tangent to the curve $y = f(x)$ at the point $(x_0, f(x_0))$ is drawn.

• The point $(x_1, 0)$ at which the tangent line intersects the x-axis is found and x_1 becomes the new approximation to r.

For the curve shown in Figure 4.80a, x_1 is a better approximation to the root r than x_0.

> Sequences are the subject of Chapter 8. An ordered set of numbers
> $$\{x_1, x_2, x_3, \dots\}$$
> is a sequence, and if its values approach a number r, we say that the sequence *converges* to r. If a sequence fails to approach a single number, the sequence *diverges*.

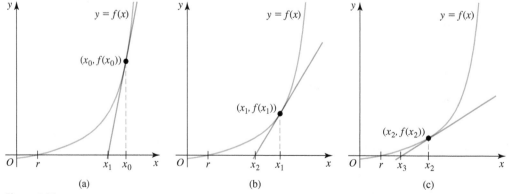

Figure 4.80

To improve the approximation x_1, we repeat the two-step process, using x_1 to determine the next estimate x_2 (Figure 4.80b). Then x_2 is used to obtain x_3 (Figure 4.80c), and so forth. Continuing in this fashion, we obtain a *sequence* of approximations $\{x_1, x_2, x_3, \dots\}$

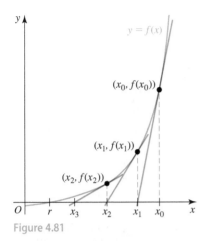

Figure 4.81

▶ Recall that the point-slope form of the equation of a line with slope m passing through (x_n, y_n) is

$$y - y_n = m(x - x_n).$$

that ideally get closer and closer, or *converge*, to the root r. Several steps of Newton's method and the convergence of the approximations to the root are shown in Figure 4.81.

All that remains is to find a formula that captures the process just described. Assume that we have computed the nth approximation x_n to the root r and we want to obtain the next approximation x_{n+1}. We first draw the line tangent to the curve at the point $(x_n, f(x_n))$; its slope is $m = f'(x_n)$. Using the point-slope form of the equation of a line, an equation of the tangent line at the point $(x_n, f(x_n))$ is

$$y - f(x_n) = \underbrace{f'(x_n)}_{m}(x - x_n).$$

We find the point at which this line intersects the x-axis by setting $y = 0$ in the equation of the line and solving for x. This value of x becomes the new approximation x_{n+1}:

$$0 - f(x_n) = f'(x_n)(x - \underbrace{x_n}_{\text{becomes } x_{n+1}}).$$
$$\underset{\text{set } y \text{ to } 0}{}$$

Solving for x and calling it x_{n+1}, we find that

$$\underbrace{x_{n+1}}_{\substack{\text{new} \\ \text{approximation}}} = \underbrace{x_n}_{\substack{\text{current} \\ \text{approximation}}} - \frac{f(x_n)}{f'(x_n)}, \quad \text{provided } f'(x_n) \neq 0.$$

We have derived the general step of Newton's method for approximating roots of a function f. This step is repeated for $n = 0, 1, 2, \ldots$, until a termination condition is met (to be discussed).

PROCEDURE   **Newton's Method for Approximating Roots of $f(x) = 0$**

1. Choose an initial approximation x_0 as close to a root as possible.
2. For $n = 0, 1, 2, \ldots$

$$x_{n+1} = x_n - \frac{f(x_n)}{f'(x_n)},$$

provided $f'(x_n) \neq 0$.
3. End the calculations when a termination condition is met.

▶ Newton's method is an example of a repetitive loop calculation called an *iteration*. The most efficient way to implement the method is with a calculator or computer. The method is also included in many software packages.

QUICK CHECK 1 Verify that setting $y = 0$ in the equation $y - f(x_n) = f'(x_n)(x - x_n)$ and solving for x gives the formula for Newton's method. ◄

EXAMPLE 1   Applying Newton's method Approximate the roots of $f(x) = x^3 - 5x + 1$ (Figure 4.82) using seven steps of Newton's method. Use $x_0 = -3$, $x_0 = 1$, and $x_0 = 4$ as initial approximations.

SOLUTION Noting that $f'(x) = 3x^2 - 5$, Newton's method takes the form

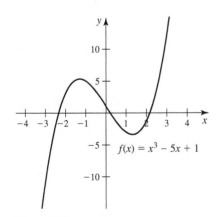

Figure 4.82

$$x_{n+1} = x_n - \frac{\overbrace{x_n^3 - 5x_n + 1}^{f(x_n)}}{\underbrace{3x_n^2 - 5}_{f'(x_n)}} = \frac{2x_n^3 - 1}{3x_n^2 - 5},$$

where $n = 0, 1, 2, \ldots$, and x_0 is specified. With an initial approximation of $x_0 = -3$, the first approximation is

$$x_1 = \frac{2x_0^3 - 1}{3x_0^2 - 5} = \frac{2(-3)^3 - 1}{3(-3)^2 - 5} = -2.5.$$

Table 4.5

n	x_n	x_n	x_n
0	-3	1	4
1	-2.500000	-0.500000	2.953488
2	-2.345455	0.294118	2.386813
3	-2.330203	0.200215	2.166534
4	-2.330059	0.201639	2.129453
5	-2.330059	0.201640	2.128420
6	-2.330059	0.201640	2.128419
7	-2.330059	0.201640	2.128419

➤ The numbers in Table 4.5 were computed with 16 decimal digits of precision. The results are displayed with 6 digits to the right of the decimal point.

QUICK CHECK 2 What happens if you apply Newton's method to the function $f(x) = x$? ◄

The second approximation is

$$x_2 = \frac{2x_1^3 - 1}{3x_1^2 - 5} = \frac{2(-2.5)^3 - 1}{3(-2.5)^2 - 5} \approx -2.345455.$$

Continuing in this fashion, we generate the first seven approximations shown in Table 4.5. The approximations generated from the initial approximations $x_0 = 1$ and $x_0 = 4$ are also shown in the table.

Notice that with the initial approximation $x_0 = -3$ (second column), the resulting sequence of approximations settles on the value -2.330059 after four iterations, and then there are no further changes in these digits. A similar behavior is seen with the initial approximations $x_0 = 1$ and $x_0 = 4$. Based on this evidence, we conclude that -2.330059, 0.201640, and 2.128419 are approximations to the roots of f with at least six digits (to the right of the decimal point) of accuracy.

A graph of f (Figure 4.83) confirms that f has three real roots and that the Newton approximations to the three roots are reasonable. The figure also shows the first three Newton approximations at each root.   *Related Exercises 5–14* ◄

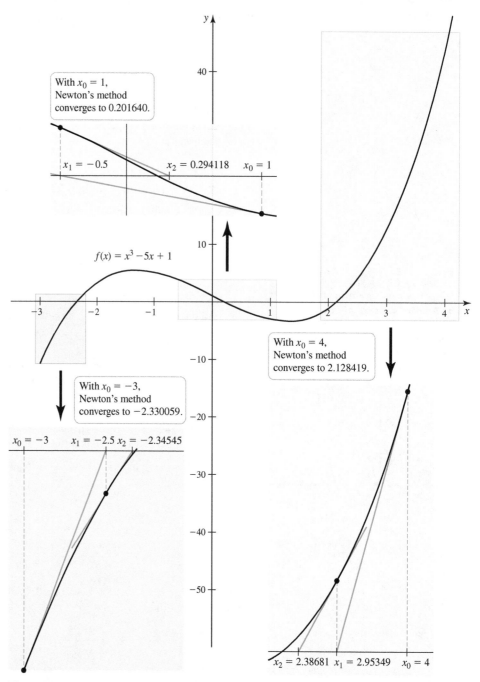

With $x_0 = 1$, Newton's method converges to 0.201640.

$x_1 = -0.5$ $x_2 = 0.294118$ $x_0 = 1$

$f(x) = x^3 - 5x + 1$

With $x_0 = -3$, Newton's method converges to -2.330059.

$x_0 = -3$ $x_1 = -2.5$ $x_2 = -2.34545$

With $x_0 = 4$, Newton's method converges to 2.128419.

$x_2 = 2.38681$ $x_1 = 2.95349$ $x_0 = 4$

Figure 4.83

> If you write a program for Newton's method, it is a good idea to specify a maximum number of iterations as an escape clause in case the method does not converge.

> Small residuals do not always imply small errors: The function shown below has a zero at $x = 0$. An approximation such as 0.5 has a small residual but a large error.

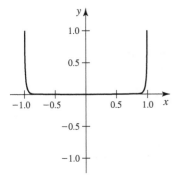

When Do You Stop?

Example 1 raises an important question and gives a practical answer: How many Newton approximations should you compute? Ideally, we would like to compute the **error** in x_n as an approximation to the root r, which is the quantity $|x_n - r|$. Unfortunately, we don't know r in practice; it is the quantity that we are trying to approximate. So we need a practical way to estimate the error.

In the second column of Table 4.5, we see that x_4 and x_5 agree in their seven digits, -2.330059. A general rule of thumb is that if two successive approximations agree to, say, seven digits, then those common digits are accurate (as an approximation to the root). So if you want p digits of accuracy in your approximation, you should compute until either two successive approximations agree to p digits or until some maximum number of iterations is exceeded (in which case Newton's method has failed to find an approximation of the root with the desired accuracy).

There is another practical way to gauge the accuracy of approximations. Because Newton's method generates approximations to a root of f, it follows that as the approximations x_n approach the root, $f(x_n)$ should approach zero. The quantity $f(x_n)$ is called a **residual**, and small residuals usually (but not always) suggest that the approximations have small errors. In Example 1, we find that for the approximations in the second column, $f(x_7) = -1.8 \times 10^{-15}$; for the approximations in the third column, $f(x_7) = 1.1 \times 10^{-16}$; and for the approximations in the fourth column, $f(x_7) = -1.8 \times 10^{-15}$. All these residuals (computed in full precision) are small in magnitude, giving additional confidence that the approximations have small errors.

EXAMPLE 2   Finding intersection points Find the points at which the curves $y = \cos x$ and $y = x$ intersect.

SOLUTION The graphs of two functions g and h intersect at points whose x-coordinates satisfy $g(x) = h(x)$, or, equivalently, where

$$f(x) = g(x) - h(x) = 0.$$

We see that finding intersection points is a root-finding problem. In this case, the intersection points of the curves $y = \cos x$ and $y = x$ satisfy

$$f(x) = \cos x - x = 0.$$

A preliminary graph is advisable to determine the number of intersection points and good initial approximations. From Figure 4.84a, we see that the two curves have one intersection point, and its x-coordinate is between 0 and 1. Equivalently, the function f has a zero between 0 and 1 (Figure 4.84b). A reasonable initial approximation is $x_0 = 0.5$.

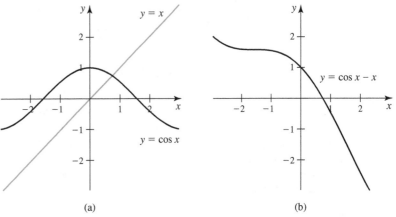

(a)   (b)

Figure 4.84

Newton's method takes the form

$$x_{n+1} = x_n - \frac{\overbrace{\cos x_n - x_n}^{f(x_n)}}{\underbrace{-\sin x_n - 1}_{f'(x_n)}} = \frac{x_n \sin x_n + \cos x_n}{\sin x_n + 1}.$$

The results of Newton's method, using an initial approximation of $x_0 = 0.5$, are shown in Table 4.6.

Table 4.6

n	x_n	Residual
0	0.5	0.377583
1	0.755222	−0.0271033
2	0.739142	−0.0000946154
3	0.739085	−1.18098 × 10^{-9}
4	0.739085	0
5	0.739085	0

We see that after four iterations, the approximations agree to six digits; so we take 0.739085 as the approximation to the root. Furthermore, the residuals, shown in the last column and computed with full precision, are essentially zero, which confirms the accuracy of the approximation. Therefore, the intersection point is approximately (0.739085, 0.739085) (because the point lies on the line $y = x$).

Related Exercises 15–20 ◄

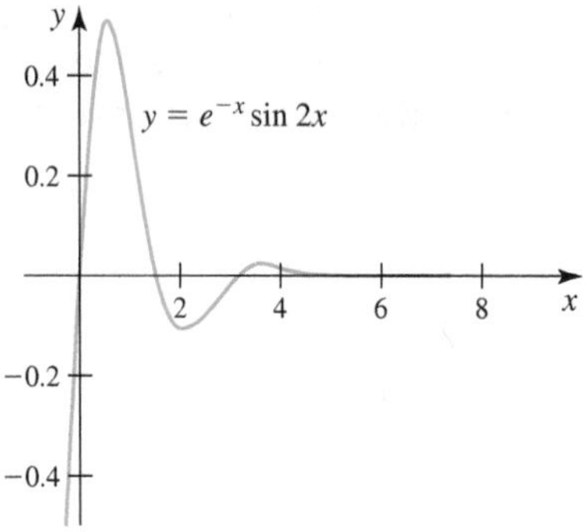

EXAMPLE 3 **Finding local extrema** Find the x-coordinate of the first local maximum and the first local minimum of the function $f(x) = e^{-x} \sin 2x$ on the interval $(0, \infty)$.

SOLUTION A graph of the function provides some guidance. Figure 4.85 shows that f has an infinite number of local extrema for $x > 0$. The first local maximum occurs on the interval $[0, 1]$, and the first local minimum occurs on the interval $[2, 3]$.

To locate the local extrema, we must find the critical points by solving

$$f'(x) = e^{-x}(2 \cos 2x - \sin 2x) = 0.$$

To this equation, we apply Newton's method. The results of the calculations, using initial approximations of $x_0 = 0.2$ and $x_0 = 2.5$, are shown in Table 4.7.

Newton's method finds the two critical points quickly, and they are consistent with the graph of f. We conclude that the first local maximum occurs at $x \approx 0.553574$ and the first local minimum occurs at $x \approx 2.124371$.

Related Exercises 21–24 ◄

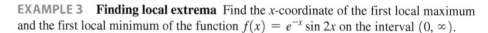

$y = e^{-x} \sin 2x$

Figure 4.85

Table 4.7

n	x_n	x_n
0	0.200000	2.500000
1	0.499372	1.623915
2	0.550979	2.062202
3	0.553568	2.121018
4	0.553574	2.124360
5	0.553574	2.124371
6	0.553574	2.124371

> ➤ A more thorough analysis of the rate at which Newton's method converges and the ways in which it fails to converge is presented in a course in numerical analysis.
>
> Newton's method is widely used because in general, it has a remarkable rate of convergence; the number of digits of accuracy roughly doubles with each iteration.

Pitfalls of Newton's Method

Given a good initial approximation, Newton's method usually converges to a root. In addition, when the method converges, it usually does so quickly. However, when Newton's method fails, it does so in curious and spectacular ways. The formula for Newton's method suggests one way in which the method could encounter difficulties: The term $f'(x_n)$ appears in a denominator, so if at any step $f'(x_n) = 0$, then the method breaks down. Furthermore, if $f'(x_n)$ is close to zero at any step, then the method may converge slowly or may fail to converge. The following example shows three ways in which Newton's method may go awry.

EXAMPLE 4   **Difficulties with Newton's method** Find the root of $f(x) = \dfrac{8x^2}{3x^2 + 1}$

using Newton's method with initial approximations of $x_0 = 1$, $x_0 = 0.15$, and $x_0 = 1.1$.

SOLUTION Notice that f has the single root $x = 0$. So the point of the example is not to find the root, but to investigate the performance of Newton's method. Computing f' and doing a few steps of algebra show that the formula for Newton's method is

$$x_{n+1} = x_n - \frac{f(x_n)}{f'(x_n)} = \frac{x_n}{2}(1 - 3x_n^2).$$

The results of five iterations of Newton's method are displayed in Table 4.8, and they tell three different stories.

Table 4.8

n	x_n	x_n	x_n
0	1	0.15	1.1
1	-1	0.0699375	-1.4465
2	1	0.0344556	3.81665
3	-1	0.0171665	-81.4865
4	1	0.00857564	8.11572×10^5
5	-1	0.00428687	-8.01692×10^{17}

The approximations generated using $x_0 = 1$ (second column) get stuck in a cycle that alternates between $+1$ and -1. The geometry underlying this rare occurrence is illustrated in Figure 4.86.

The approximations generated using $x_0 = 0.15$ (third column) actually converge to the root 0, but they converge slowly (Figure 4.87). Notice that the error is reduced by a factor of approximately 2 with each step. Newton's method usually has a faster rate of error reduction. The slow convergence is due to the fact that both f and f' have zeros at 0. As mentioned earlier, if the approximations x_n approach a zero of f', the rate of convergence is often compromised.

The approximations generated using $x_0 = 1.1$ (fourth column) increase in magnitude quickly and do not converge to a finite value, even though this initial approximation seems reasonable. The geometry of this case is shown in Figure 4.88.

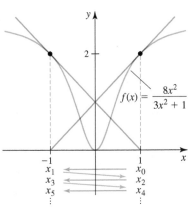

Figure 4.86

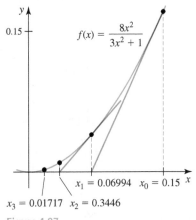

Figure 4.87

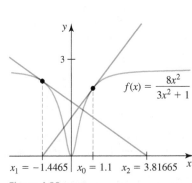

Figure 4.88

The three cases in this example illustrate several ways that Newton's method may fail to converge at its usual rate: The approximations may cycle or wander, they may converge slowly, or they may diverge (often at a rapid rate).

Related Exercises 25–26 ◄

SECTION 4.8 EXERCISES

Review Questions

1. Give a geometric explanation of Newton's method.

2. Explain how the iteration formula for Newton's method works.

3. How do you decide when to terminate Newton's method?

4. Give the formula for Newton's method for the function $f(x) = x^2 - 5$.

Basic Skills

5–8. Formulating Newton's method *Write the formula for Newton's method and use the given initial approximation to compute the approximations x_1 and x_2.*

5. $f(x) = x^2 - 6; x_0 = 3$

6. $f(x) = x^2 - 2x - 3; x_0 = 2$

7. $f(x) = e^{-x} - x; x_0 = \ln 2$

8. $f(x) = x^3 - 2; x_0 = 2$

9–14. Finding roots with Newton's method *Use a calculator or program to compute the first 10 iterations of Newton's method when it is applied to the following functions with the given initial approximation. Make a table similar to that in Example 1.*

9. $f(x) = x^2 - 10; x_0 = 4$

10. $f(x) = x^3 + x^2 + 1; x_0 = -2$

11. $f(x) = \sin x + x - 1; x_0 = 1.5$

12. $f(x) = e^x - 5; x_0 = 2$

13. $f(x) = \tan x - 2x; x_0 = 1.5$

14. $f(x) = \ln(x + 1) - 1; x_0 = 1.7$

15–20. Finding intersection points *Use Newton's method to approximate all the intersection points of the following pairs of curves. Some preliminary graphing or analysis may help in choosing good initial approximations.*

15. $y = \sin x$ and $y = \dfrac{x}{2}$

16. $y = e^x$ and $y = x^3$

17. $y = \dfrac{1}{x}$ and $y = 4 - x^2$

18. $y = x^3$ and $y = x^2 + 1$

19. $y = 4\sqrt{x}$ and $y = x^2 + 1$

20. $y = \ln x$ and $y = x^3 - 2$

21–24. Newton's method and curve sketching *Use Newton's method to find approximate answers to the following questions.*

21. Where is the first local minimum of $f(x) = \dfrac{\cos x}{x}$ on the interval $(0, \infty)$ located?

22. Where are all the local extrema of $f(x) = 3x^4 + 8x^3 + 12x^2 + 48x$ located?

23. Where are the inflection points of $f(x) = \dfrac{9}{5}x^5 - \dfrac{15}{2}x^4 + \dfrac{7}{3}x^3 + 30x^2 + 1$ located?

24. Where is the local extremum of $f(x) = \dfrac{e^x}{x}$ located? (Use Newton's method.)

25–26. Slow convergence

25. The functions $f(x) = (x - 1)^2$ and $g(x) = x^2 - 1$ both have a root at $x = 1$. Apply Newton's method to both functions with an initial approximation $x_0 = 2$. Compare the rate at which the method converges in each case and give an explanation.

26. Consider the function $f(x) = x^5 + 4x^4 + x^3 - 10x^2 - 4x + 8$, which has zeros at $x = 1$ and $x = -2$. Apply Newton's method to this function with initial approximations of $x_0 = -1$, $x_0 = -0.2$, $x_0 = 0.2$, and $x_0 = 2$. Discuss and compare the results of the calculations.

Further Explorations

27. **Explain why or why not** Determine whether the following statements are true and give an explanation or counterexample.

   a. Newton's method is an example of a numerical method for approximating the roots of a function.

   b. Newton's method gives a better approximation to the roots of a quadratic equation than the quadratic formula.

   c. Newton's method always finds an approximate root of a function.

28–31. Fixed points *An important question about many functions concerns the existence and location of fixed points. A **fixed point** of f is a value of x that satisfies the equation $f(x) = x$; it corresponds to a point at which the graph of f intersects the line $y = x$. Find all the fixed points of the following functions. Use preliminary analysis and graphing to determine good initial approximations.*

28. $f(x) = 5 - x^2$

29. $f(x) = \dfrac{x^3}{10} + 1$

30. $f(x) = \tan\dfrac{x}{2}$ on $(-\pi, \pi)$

31. $f(x) = 2x \cos x$ on $[0, 2]$

32–38. More root finding *Find all the roots of the following functions. Use preliminary analysis and graphing to determine good initial approximations.*

32. $f(x) = \cos x - \dfrac{x}{7}$

33. $f(x) = \cos 2x - x^2 + 2x$

34. $f(x) = \dfrac{x}{6} - \sec x$ on $[0, 8]$

35. $f(x) = e^{-x} - \dfrac{x + 4}{5}$

36. $f(x) = \dfrac{x^5}{5} - \dfrac{x^3}{4} - \dfrac{1}{20}$

37. $f(x) = \ln x - x^2 + 3x - 1$

38. $f(x) = x^2(x - 100) + 1$

☐ 39. Residuals and errors Approximate the root of $f(x) = x^{10}$ at $x = 0$ using Newton's method with an initial approximation of $x_0 = 0.5$. Make a table showing the first 10 approximations, the error in these approximations (which is $|x_n - 0| = |x_n|$), and the residual of these approximations (which is $f(x_n)$). Comment on the relative size of the errors and the residuals and give an explanation.

☐ 40. A tangent question Verify by graphing that the graphs of $y = \sin x$ and $y = x/2$ have one point of intersection, for $x > 0$, whereas the graphs of $y = \sin x$ and $y = x/9$ have three points of intersection, for $x > 0$. Approximate the value of a such that the graphs of $y = \sin x$ and $y = x/a$ have exactly two points of intersection, for $x > 0$.

☐ 41. A tangent question Verify by graphing that the graphs of $y = e^x$ and $y = x$ have no points of intersection, whereas the graphs of $y = e^{x/3}$ and $y = x$ have two points of intersection. Approximate the value of $a > 0$ such that the graphs of $y = e^{x/a}$ and $y = x$ have exactly one point of intersection.

☐ 42. Approximating square roots Let $a > 0$ be given and suppose we want to approximate $\sqrt{a}$ using Newton's method.

   a. Explain why the square root problem is equivalent to finding the positive root of $f(x) = x^2 - a$.

   b. Show that Newton's method applied to this function takes the form (sometimes called the *Babylonian method*)
$$x_{n+1} = \frac{1}{2}\left(x_n + \frac{a}{x_n}\right), \text{ for } n = 0, 1, 2, \ldots.$$

   c. How would you choose initial approximations to approximate $\sqrt{13}$ and $\sqrt{73}$?

   d. Approximate $\sqrt{13}$ and $\sqrt{73}$ with at least 10 significant digits.

☐ 43. Approximating reciprocals To approximate the reciprocal of a number a without using division, we can apply Newton's method to the function $f(x) = \dfrac{1}{x} - a$.

   a. Verify that Newton's method gives the formula $x_{n+1} = (2 - ax_n)x_n$.

   b. Apply Newton's method with $a = 7$ using a starting value of your choice. Compute an approximation with eight digits of accuracy. What number does Newton's method approximate in this case?

☐ 44. Modified Newton's method The function f has a root of *multiplicity* 2 at r if $f(r) = f'(r) = 0$ and $f''(r) \neq 0$. In this case, a slight modification of Newton's method, known as the *modified* (or *accelerated*) Newton's method, is given by the formula
$$x_{n+1} = x_n - \frac{2f(x_n)}{f'(x_n)}, \text{ for } n = 0, 1, 2, \ldots.$$
This modified form generally increases the rate of convergence.

   a. Verify that 0 is a root of multiplicity 2 of the function $f(x) = e^{2\sin x} - 2x - 1$.

   b. Apply Newton's method and the modified Newton's method using $x_0 = 0.1$ to find the value of x_3 in each case. Compare the accuracy of each value of x_3.

   c. Consider the function $f(x) = \dfrac{8x^2}{3x^2 + 1}$ given in Example 4. Use the modified Newton's method to find the value of x_3 using $x_0 = 0.15$. Compare this value to the value of x_3 found in Example 4 with $x_0 = 0.15$.

Applications

☐ 45. A damped oscillator The displacement of a particular object as it bounces vertically up and down on a spring is given by $y(t) = 2.5e^{-t}\cos 2t$, where the initial displacement is $y(0) = 2.5$ and $y = 0$ corresponds to the rest position (see figure).

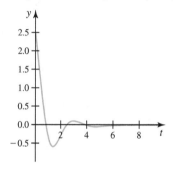

   a. Find the time at which the object first passes the rest position, $y = 0$.

   b. Find the time and the displacement when the object reaches its lowest point.

   c. Find the time at which the object passes the rest position for the second time.

   d. Find the time and the displacement when the object reaches its high point for the second time.

☐ 46. The sinc function The sinc function, $\operatorname{sinc}(x) = \dfrac{\sin x}{x}$ for $x \neq 0$, $\operatorname{sinc}(0) = 1$, appears frequently in signal-processing applications.

   a. Graph the sinc function on $[-2\pi, 2\pi]$.

   b. Locate the first local minimum and the first local maximum of $\operatorname{sinc}(x)$, for $x > 0$.

☐ 47. An eigenvalue problem A certain kind of differential equation (see Section 7.9) leads to the root-finding problem $\tan \pi\lambda = \lambda$, where the roots λ are called **eigenvalues**. Find the first three positive eigenvalues of this problem.

Additional Exercises

☐ 48. Fixed points of quadratics and quartics Let $f(x) = ax(1 - x)$, where a is a real number and $0 \leq x \leq 1$. Recall that the fixed point of a function is a value of x such that $f(x) = x$ (Exercises 28–31).

   a. Without using a calculator, find the values of a, with $0 < a \leq 4$, such that f has a fixed point. Give the fixed point in terms of a.

   b. Consider the polynomial $g(x) = f(f(x))$. Write g in terms of a and powers of x. What is its degree?

   c. Graph g for $a = 2, 3,$ and 4.

   d. Find the number and location of the fixed points of g for $a = 2, 3,$ and 4 on the interval $0 \leq x \leq 1$.

49. Basins of attraction Suppose f has a real root r and Newton's method is used to approximate r with an initial approximation x_0. The **basin of attraction** of r is the set of initial approximations that produce a sequence that converges to r. Points near r are often in the basin of attraction of r—but not always. Sometimes an initial approximation x_0 may produce a sequence that doesn't converge, and sometimes an initial approximation x_0 may produce a sequence that converges to a distant root. Let $f(x) = (x + 2)(x + 1)(x - 3)$, which has roots $x = -2, -1$, and 3. Use Newton's method with initial approximations on the interval $[-4, 4]$ to determine (approximately) the basin of each root.

QUICK CHECK ANSWERS

1. $0 - f(x_n) = f'(x_n)(x - x_n) \implies -\dfrac{f(x_n)}{f'(x_n)} = x - x_n \implies$

$x = x_n - \dfrac{f(x_n)}{f'(x_n)}$ **2.** Newton's method will find the root $x = 0$ exactly in one step. ◄

4.9 Antiderivatives

The goal of differentiation is to find the derivative f' of a given function f. The reverse process, called *antidifferentiation*, is equally important: Given a function f, we look for an *antiderivative* function F whose derivative is f; that is, a function F such that $F' = f$.

DEFINITION Antiderivative

A function F is an **antiderivative** of f on an interval I provided $F'(x) = f(x)$, for all x in I.

In this section, we revisit derivative formulas developed in previous chapters to discover corresponding antiderivative formulas.

Thinking Backward

Consider the derivative formula $\dfrac{d}{dx}(x) = 1$. It implies that an antiderivative of $f(x) = 1$ is $F(x) = x$ because $F'(x) = f(x)$. Using the same logic, we can write

QUICK CHECK 1 Verify by differentiation that x^3 is an antiderivative of $3x^2$ and $-\cos x$ is an antiderivative of $\sin x$. ◄

$$\frac{d}{dx}(x^2) = 2x \quad \implies \quad \text{an antiderivative of } f(x) = 2x \text{ is } F(x) = x^2 \text{ and}$$

$$\frac{d}{dx}(\sin x) = \cos x \quad \implies \quad \text{an antiderivative of } f(x) = \cos x \text{ is } F(x) = \sin x.$$

Each of these proposed antiderivative formulas is easily checked by showing that $F' = f$.

An immediate question arises: Does a function have more than one antiderivative? To answer this question, let's focus on $f(x) = 1$ and the antiderivative $F(x) = x$. Because the derivative of a constant C is zero, we see that $F(x) = x + C$ is also an antiderivative of $f(x) = 1$, which is easy to check:

$$F'(x) = \frac{d}{dx}(x + C) = 1 = f(x).$$

Therefore, $f(x) = 1$ actually has an infinite number of antiderivatives. For the same reason, any function of the form $F(x) = x^2 + C$ is an antiderivative of $f(x) = 2x$, and any function of the form $F(x) = \sin x + C$ is an antiderivative of $f(x) = \cos x$, where C is an arbitrary constant.

We might ask whether there are still *more* antiderivatives of a given function. The following theorem provides the answer.

THEOREM 4.16   The Family of Antiderivatives

Let F be any antiderivative of f on an interval I. Then *all* the antiderivatives of f on I have the form $F + C$, where C is an arbitrary constant.

Proof: Suppose that F and G are antiderivatives of f on an interval I. Then $F' = f$ and $G' = f$, which implies that $F' = G'$ on I. Theorem 4.11 states that functions with equal derivatives differ by a constant. Therefore, $G = F + C$, and all antiderivatives of f have the form $F + C$, where C is an arbitrary constant.   ◄

Theorem 4.16 says that while there are infinitely many antiderivatives of a function, they are all of one family, namely, those functions of the form $F + C$. Because the antiderivatives of a particular function differ by a constant, the antiderivatives are vertical translations of one another (Figure 4.89).

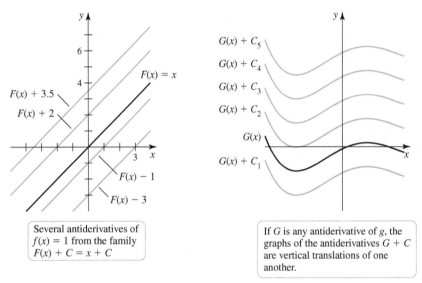

Several antiderivatives of $f(x) = 1$ from the family $F(x) + C = x + C$

If G is any antiderivative of g, the graphs of the antiderivatives $G + C$ are vertical translations of one another.

Figure 4.89

EXAMPLE 1   Finding antiderivatives Use what you know about derivatives to find all antiderivatives of the following functions.

a. $f(x) = 3x^2$ **b.** $f(x) = \dfrac{1}{1 + x^2}$ **c.** $f(t) = \sin t$

SOLUTION

a. Note that $\dfrac{d}{dx}(x^3) = 3x^2$. Therefore, an antiderivative of $f(x) = 3x^2$ is x^3. By Theorem 4.16, the complete family of antiderivatives is $F(x) = x^3 + C$, where C is an arbitrary constant.

b. Because $\dfrac{d}{dx}(\tan^{-1} x) = \dfrac{1}{1 + x^2}$, all antiderivatives of f are of the form $F(x) = \tan^{-1} x + C$, where C is an arbitrary constant.

c. Recall that $\dfrac{d}{dt}(\cos t) = -\sin t$. We seek a function whose derivative is $\sin t$, not $-\sin t$. Observing that $\dfrac{d}{dt}(-\cos t) = \sin t$, it follows that the antiderivatives of $\sin t$ are $F(t) = -\cos t + C$, where C is an arbitrary constant.

Related Exercises 11–22 ◄

QUICK CHECK 2 Find the family of antiderivatives for each of $f(x) = e^x$, $g(x) = 4x^3$, and $h(x) = \sec^2 x$. ◄

Indefinite Integrals

The notation $\dfrac{d}{dx}(f(x))$ means *take the derivative of $f(x)$* with respect to x. We need analogous notation for antiderivatives. For historical reasons that become apparent in the next chapter, the notation that means *find the antiderivatives of f* is the **indefinite integral** $\int f(x)\,dx$. Every time an indefinite integral sign $\int$ appears, it is followed by a function called the **integrand**, which in turn is followed by the differential dx. For now, dx simply means that x is the independent variable, or the **variable of integration**. The notation $\int f(x)\,dx$ represents *all* the antiderivatives of f. When the integrand is a function of a variable different from x—say, $g(t)$—then we write $\int g(t)\,dt$ to represent the antiderivatives of g.

Using this new notation, the three results of Example 1 are written

$$\int 3x^2\,dx = x^3 + C, \quad \int \frac{1}{1 + x^2}\,dx = \tan^{-1} x + C, \quad \text{and} \quad \int \sin t\,dt = -\cos t + C,$$

where C is an arbitrary constant called a **constant of integration**. The derivative formulas presented earlier in the text may be written in terms of indefinite integrals. We begin with the Power Rule.

> ► Notice that if $p = -1$ in Theorem 4.17, then $F(x)$ is undefined. The antiderivative of $f(x) = x^{-1}$ is discussed in Example 5. The case $p = 0$ says that $\int 1\,dx = x + C$.

THEOREM 4.17   Power Rule for Indefinite Integrals

$$\int x^p\,dx = \frac{x^{p+1}}{p + 1} + C,$$

where $p \neq -1$ is a real number and C is an arbitrary constant.

Proof: The theorem says that the antiderivatives of $f(x) = x^p$ have the form $F(x) = \dfrac{x^{p+1}}{p+1} + C$. Differentiating F, we verify that $F'(x) = f(x)$, provided $p \neq -1$:

$$F'(x) = \frac{d}{dx}\left(\frac{x^{p+1}}{p+1} + C\right)$$

$$= \frac{d}{dx}\left(\frac{x^{p+1}}{p+1}\right) + \underbrace{\frac{d}{dx}(C)}_{0}$$

$$= \frac{(p+1)x^{(p+1)-1}}{p+1} + 0 = x^p. \qquad ◄$$

> ► Any indefinite integral calculation can be checked by differentiation: The derivative of the alleged indefinite integral must equal the integrand.

Theorems 3.4 and 3.5 (Section 3.2) state the Constant Multiple and Sum Rules for derivatives. Here are the corresponding antiderivative rules, which are proved by differentiation.

THEOREM 4.18   Constant Multiple and Sum Rules

Constant Multiple Rule: $\displaystyle\int cf(x)\,dx = c\int f(x)\,dx$, for real numbers c

Sum Rule: $\displaystyle\int (f(x) + g(x))\,dx = \int f(x)\,dx + \int g(x)\,dx$

The following example shows how Theorems 4.17 and 4.18 are used.

EXAMPLE 2 **Indefinite integrals** Determine the following indefinite integrals.

a. $\displaystyle\int (3x^5 + 2 - 5\sqrt{x})\, dx$ **b.** $\displaystyle\int \left(\frac{4x^{19} - 5x^{-8}}{x^2}\right) dx$ **c.** $\displaystyle\int (z^2 + 1)(2z - 5)\, dz$

SOLUTION

> $\int dx$ means $\int 1\, dx$, which is the indefinite integral of the constant function $f(x) = 1$, so $\int dx = x + C$.

a. $\displaystyle\int (3x^5 + 2 - 5\sqrt{x})\, dx = \int 3x^5\, dx + \int 2\, dx - \int 5x^{1/2}\, dx$ Sum Rule

$$= 3\int x^5\, dx + 2\int dx - 5\int x^{1/2}\, dx$$ Constant Multiple Rule

> Each indefinite integral in Example 2a produces an arbitrary constant, all of which may be combined in one arbitrary constant called C.

$$= 3\cdot\frac{x^6}{6} + 2\cdot x - 5\cdot\frac{x^{3/2}}{3/2} + C$$ Power Rule

$$= \frac{x^6}{2} + 2x - \frac{10}{3}x^{3/2} + C$$ Simplify.

b. $\displaystyle\int \left(\frac{4x^{19} - 5x^{-8}}{x^2}\right) dx = \int (4x^{17} - 5x^{-10})\, dx$ Simplify the integrand.

$$= 4\int x^{17}\, dx - 5\int x^{-10}\, dx$$ Sum and Constant Multiple Rules

$$= 4\cdot\frac{x^{18}}{18} - 5\cdot\frac{x^{-9}}{-9} + C$$ Power Rule

$$= \frac{2x^{18}}{9} + \frac{5x^{-9}}{9} + C$$ Simplify.

> Examples 2b and 2c show that in general, the indefinite integral of a product or quotient is not the product or quotient of indefinite integrals.

c. $\displaystyle\int (z^2 + 1)(2z - 5)\, dz = \int (2z^3 - 5z^2 + 2z - 5)\, dz$ Expand integrand.

$$= \frac{1}{2}z^4 - \frac{5}{3}z^3 + z^2 - 5z + C$$ Integrate each term.

All these results should be checked by differentiation.

Related Exercises 23–36 ◄

Indefinite Integrals of Trigonometric Functions

In this section, we have two goals that can be accomplished at the same time. The first goal is to write the familiar derivative results for trigonometric functions as indefinite integrals. The second goal is to show how these results are generalized using the Chain Rule. The following example illustrates the key ideas.

EXAMPLE 3 **Indefinite integrals of trigonometric functions** Evaluate the following indefinite integrals.

a. $\displaystyle\int \sec^2 x\, dx$ **b.** $\displaystyle\int \sin 3x\, dx$

c. $\displaystyle\int \sec ax \tan ax\, dx$, where $a \neq 0$ is a real number

> Remember the words that go with antiderivatives and indefinite integrals. The statement $\dfrac{d}{dx}(\tan x) = \sec^2 x$ says that $\tan x$ can be differentiated to get $\sec^2 x$. Therefore,
> $$\int \sec^2 x\, dx = \tan x + C.$$

SOLUTION

a. The derivative result $\dfrac{d}{dx}(\tan x) = \sec^2 x$ is reversed to produce the indefinite integral

$$\int \sec^2 x\, dx = \tan x + C.$$

> The statement $\dfrac{d}{dx}(\cos 3x) = -3 \sin 3x$ says that $\cos 3x$ can be differentiated to get $-3 \sin 3x$. Therefore,
>
> $\int (-3 \sin 3x)\, dx = \cos 3x + C.$

b. From Example 1c, we know that $\int \sin x\, dx = -\cos x + C$. The complication in the given integral is the factor of 3 in $\sin 3x$. Here is the thinking that allows us to handle this factor. A derivative result that appears related to the given indefinite integral is $\dfrac{d}{dx}(\cos 3x) = -3 \sin 3x$, which is obtained using the Chain Rule. We write this derivative result as the indefinite integral

$$\int (-3 \sin 3x)\, dx = \cos 3x + C, \quad \text{or} \quad -3 \int \sin 3x\, dx = \cos 3x + C.$$

Dividing both sides of this equation by -3 gives the desired result,

$$\int \sin 3x\, dx = -\frac{1}{3} \cos 3x + C,$$

> If C is an arbitrary constant and $a \neq 0$ is a real number, then C/a is also an arbitrary constant and we continue to call it C.

which can be checked by differentiation. Notice that 3 could be replaced in this example with any constant $a \neq 0$ to produce the more general result

$$\int \sin ax\, dx = -\frac{1}{a} \cos ax + C.$$

c. A derivative result that appears related to this indefinite integral is $\dfrac{d}{dx}(\sec x) = \sec x \tan x$, or more generally, using the Chain Rule,

$$\frac{d}{dx}(\sec ax) = a \sec ax \tan ax.$$

Writing this derivative result as an indefinite integral, we have

$$\int a \sec ax \tan ax\, dx = \sec ax + C.$$

After dividing through by a, we have

$$\int \sec ax \tan ax\, dx = \frac{1}{a} \sec ax + C.$$

Related Exercises 37–46 ◀

The technique used in Example 3 of writing a Chain Rule result as an indefinite integral can be used to obtain the integrals in Table 4.9. We assume that $a \neq 0$ is a real number and that C is an arbitrary constant.

> In Section 5.5, we show how to derive the results in Tables 4.9 and 4.10 using the Substitution Rule.

Table 4.9 Indefinite Integrals of Trigonometric Functions

1. $\dfrac{d}{dx}(\sin ax) = a \cos ax \implies \int \cos ax\, dx = \dfrac{1}{a} \sin ax + C$

2. $\dfrac{d}{dx}(\cos ax) = -a \sin ax \implies \int \sin ax\, dx = -\dfrac{1}{a} \cos ax + C$

3. $\dfrac{d}{dx}(\tan ax) = a \sec^2 ax \implies \int \sec^2 ax\, dx = \dfrac{1}{a} \tan ax + C$

4. $\dfrac{d}{dx}(\cot ax) = -a \csc^2 ax \implies \int \csc^2 ax\, dx = -\dfrac{1}{a} \cot ax + C$

5. $\dfrac{d}{dx}(\sec ax) = a \sec ax \tan ax \implies \int \sec ax \tan ax\, dx = \dfrac{1}{a} \sec ax + C$

6. $\dfrac{d}{dx}(\csc ax) = -a \csc ax \cot ax \implies \int \csc ax \cot ax\, dx = -\dfrac{1}{a} \csc ax + C$

QUICK CHECK 3 Use differentiation to verify that $\int \sin 2x\, dx = -\dfrac{1}{2} \cos 2x + C$. ◀

EXAMPLE 4 Indefinite integrals of trigonometric functions Determine the following indefinite integrals.

a. $\displaystyle\int \sec^2 3x \, dx$ **b.** $\displaystyle\int \cos \frac{x}{2} \, dx$

SOLUTION These integrals follow directly from Table 4.9 and can be verified by differentiation.

a. Letting $a = 3$ in result (3) of Table 4.9, we have

$$\int \sec^2 3x \, dx = \frac{\tan 3x}{3} + C.$$

b. We let $a = \frac{1}{2}$ in result (1) of Table 4.9, which says that

$$\int \cos \frac{x}{2} \, dx = \frac{\sin (x/2)}{1/2} + C = 2 \sin \frac{x}{2} + C.$$

Related Exercises 37–46 ◀

Other Indefinite Integrals

We now continue the process of rewriting familiar derivative results as indefinite integrals. As in Example 3, we generally begin with a derivative based on the Chain Rule and then express it as an indefinite integral.

EXAMPLE 5 Additional indefinite integrals Evaluate the following indefinite integrals. Assume a is a nonzero real number.

a. $\displaystyle\int \frac{dx}{x}$ **b.** $\displaystyle\int e^{ax} \, dx$ **c.** $\displaystyle\int \frac{dx}{a^2 + x^2}$

SOLUTION

a. In this case, we know that $\dfrac{d}{dx}(\ln|x|) = \dfrac{1}{x}$, for $x \neq 0$. The corresponding indefinite integral follows immediately:

$$\int \frac{dx}{x} = \ln|x| + C.$$

This result fills the gap in the Power Rule for the case $p = -1$.

b. By the Chain Rule, we know that $\dfrac{d}{dx}(e^{ax}) = ae^{ax}$. Written as an indefinite integral, this result is equivalent to $\displaystyle\int ae^{ax} \, dx = e^{ax} + C$. We divide through by a to obtain

$$\int e^{ax} \, dx = \frac{1}{a} e^{ax} + C,$$

which can be verified by differentiation.

c. The integrand $\dfrac{1}{a^2 + x^2}$ looks familiar (see Example 1b); it suggests that we begin with the derivative formula $\dfrac{d}{dx}(\tan^{-1} x) = \dfrac{1}{1 + x^2}$. As before, we call on the Chain Rule to generalize this result and write

$$\frac{d}{dx}\left(\tan^{-1} \frac{x}{a}\right) = \frac{1/a}{1 + \left(\dfrac{x}{a}\right)^2} = \frac{a}{a^2 + x^2}.$$

▶ In Example 5c, we could have applied the Chain Rule to $\tan^{-1} ax$ and derived a useful indefinite integral. However, working with $\tan^{-1} \dfrac{x}{a}$ produces a more common form of the integral.

Expressed as an indefinite integral, we find that

$$\int \frac{a}{a^2 + x^2} \, dx = \tan^{-1} \frac{x}{a} + C.$$

Dividing through by a gives

$$\int \frac{dx}{a^2 + x^2} = \frac{1}{a} \tan^{-1} \frac{x}{a} + C.$$

Related Exercises 47–58 ◄

The ideas used in Example 5 lead to the results in Table 4.10, where $a \neq 0$ is a real number and C is an arbitrary constant.

➤ Tables 4.9 and 4.10 are subsets of the table of integrals at the end of the book.

Table 4.10 Other Indefinite Integrals

7. $\dfrac{d}{dx}(e^{ax}) = ae^{ax} \implies \displaystyle\int e^{ax} \, dx = \dfrac{1}{a} e^{ax} + C$

8. $\dfrac{d}{dx}(b^x) = b^x \ln b \implies \displaystyle\int b^x \, dx = \dfrac{1}{\ln b} b^x + C, b > 0, b \neq 1$

9. $\dfrac{d}{dx}(\ln |x|) = \dfrac{1}{x} \implies \displaystyle\int \dfrac{dx}{x} = \ln |x| + C$

10. $\dfrac{d}{dx}\left(\sin^{-1} \dfrac{x}{a}\right) = \dfrac{1}{\sqrt{a^2 - x^2}} \implies \displaystyle\int \dfrac{dx}{\sqrt{a^2 - x^2}} = \sin^{-1} \dfrac{x}{a} + C$

11. $\dfrac{d}{dx}\left(\tan^{-1} \dfrac{x}{a}\right) = \dfrac{a}{a^2 + x^2} \implies \displaystyle\int \dfrac{dx}{a^2 + x^2} = \dfrac{1}{a} \tan^{-1} \dfrac{x}{a} + C$

12. $\dfrac{d}{dx}\left(\sec^{-1} \left|\dfrac{x}{a}\right|\right) = \dfrac{a}{x\sqrt{x^2 - a^2}} \implies \displaystyle\int \dfrac{dx}{x\sqrt{x^2 - a^2}} = \dfrac{1}{a} \sec^{-1} \left|\dfrac{x}{a}\right| + C, a > 0$

EXAMPLE 6   Indefinite integrals Determine the following indefinite integrals.

a. $\displaystyle\int e^{-10t} \, dt$ **b.** $\displaystyle\int \frac{4}{\sqrt{9 - x^2}} \, dx$ **c.** $\displaystyle\int \frac{dx}{16x^2 + 1}$

SOLUTION

➤ The results in Tables 4.9 and 4.10 apply regardless of what we call the variable of integration.

a. Setting $a = -10$ in result (7) of Table 4.10, we find that

$$\int e^{-10t} \, dt = -\frac{1}{10} e^{-10t} + C.$$

b. Setting $a = 3$ in result (10) of Table 4.10, we have

$$\int \frac{4}{\sqrt{9 - x^2}} \, dx = 4 \int \frac{dx}{\sqrt{3^2 - x^2}} = 4 \sin^{-1} \frac{x}{3} + C.$$

c. An algebra step is needed to put this integral in a form that matches Table 4.10. We first write

$$\int \frac{dx}{16x^2 + 1} = \frac{1}{16} \int \frac{dx}{x^2 + \frac{1}{16}} = \frac{1}{16} \int \frac{dx}{x^2 + \left(\frac{1}{4}\right)^2}.$$

Setting $a = \frac{1}{4}$ in result (11) of Table 4.10 gives

$$\int \frac{dx}{16x^2 + 1} = \frac{1}{16} \int \frac{dx}{x^2 + \left(\frac{1}{4}\right)^2} = \frac{1}{16} \cdot 4 \tan^{-1} 4x + C = \frac{1}{4} \tan^{-1} 4x + C.$$

Related Exercises 47–58 ◄

Introduction to Differential Equations

An equation involving an unknown function and its derivatives is called a **differential equation**. Here is an example to get us started.

Suppose you know that the derivative of a function f satisfies the equation

$$f'(x) = 2x + 10.$$

QUICK CHECK 4 Explain why an antiderivative of f' is f. ◀

To find a function f that satisfies this equation, we note that the solutions are antiderivatives of $2x + 10$, which are $x^2 + 10x + C$, where C is an arbitrary constant. So we have found an infinite number of solutions, all of the form $f(x) = x^2 + 10x + C$.

Now consider a more general differential equation of the form $f'(x) = g(x)$, where g is given and f is unknown. The solution f consists of the antiderivatives of g, which involve an arbitrary constant. In most practical cases, the differential equation is accompanied by an **initial condition** that allows us to determine the arbitrary constant. Therefore, we consider problems of the form

$$f'(x) = g(x), \quad \text{where } g \text{ is given, and} \qquad \text{Differential equation}$$

$$f(a) = b, \quad \text{where } a \text{ and } b \text{ are given.} \qquad \text{Initial condition}$$

A differential equation coupled with an initial condition is called an **initial value problem**.

EXAMPLE 7 An initial value problem Solve the initial value problem $f'(x) = x^2 - 2x$ with $f(1) = \frac{1}{3}$.

SOLUTION The solution f is an antiderivative of $x^2 - 2x$. Therefore,

$$f(x) = \frac{x^3}{3} - x^2 + C,$$

where C is an arbitrary constant. We have determined that the solution is a member of a family of functions, all of which differ by a constant. This family of functions, called the **general solution**, is shown in Figure 4.90, where we see curves for various choices of C.

Using the initial condition $f(1) = \frac{1}{3}$, we must find the particular function in the general solution whose graph passes through the point $\left(1, \frac{1}{3}\right)$. Imposing the condition $f(1) = \frac{1}{3}$, we reason as follows:

$$f(x) = \frac{x^3}{3} - x^2 + C \qquad \text{General solution}$$

$$f(1) = \frac{1}{3} - 1 + C \qquad \text{Substitute } x = 1.$$

$$\frac{1}{3} = \frac{1}{3} - 1 + C \qquad f(1) = \frac{1}{3}$$

$$C = 1. \qquad \text{Solve for } C.$$

Therefore, the solution to the initial value problem is

$$f(x) = \frac{x^3}{3} - x^2 + 1,$$

which is just one of the curves in the family shown in Figure 4.90.

Related Exercises 59–82 ◀

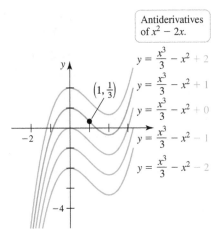

Antiderivatives of $x^2 - 2x$.

$$y = \frac{x^3}{3} - x^2 + 2$$
$$y = \frac{x^3}{3} - x^2 + 1$$
$$y = \frac{x^3}{3} - x^2 + 0$$
$$y = \frac{x^3}{3} - x^2 - 1$$
$$y = \frac{x^3}{3} - x^2 - 2$$

Figure 4.90

▶ It is advisable to check that the solution satisfies the original problem: $f'(x) = x^2 - 2x$ and $f(1) = \frac{1}{3} - 1 + 1 = \frac{1}{3}$.

QUICK CHECK 5 Position is an antiderivative of velocity. But there are infinitely many antiderivatives that differ by a constant. Explain how two objects can have the same velocity function but two different position functions. ◀

Motion Problems Revisited

Antiderivatives allow us to revisit the topic of one-dimensional motion introduced in Section 3.6. Suppose the position of an object that moves along a line relative to an origin is $s(t)$, where $t \geq 0$ measures elapsed time. The velocity of the object is $v(t) = s'(t)$, which may now be read in terms of antiderivatives: *The position function is an antiderivative of the velocity.* If we are given the velocity function of an object and its position at a particular time, we can determine its position at all future times by solving an initial value problem.

> The convention with motion problems is to assume that motion begins at $t = 0$. This means that initial conditions are specified at $t = 0$.

We also know that the acceleration $a(t)$ of an object moving in one dimension is the rate of change of the velocity, which means $a(t) = v'(t)$. In antiderivative terms, this says that the velocity is an antiderivative of the acceleration. Therefore, if we are given the acceleration of an object and its velocity at a particular time, we can determine its velocity at all times. These ideas lie at the heart of modeling the motion of objects.

Initial Value Problems for Velocity and Position

Suppose an object moves along a line with a (known) velocity $v(t)$, for $t \geq 0$. Then its position is found by solving the initial value problem

$$s'(t) = v(t), \quad s(0) = s_0, \quad \text{where } s_0 \text{ is the (known) initial position.}$$

If the (known) acceleration of the object $a(t)$ is given, then its velocity is found by solving the initial value problem

$$v'(t) = a(t), \quad v(0) = v_0, \quad \text{where } v_0 \text{ is the (known) initial velocity.}$$

EXAMPLE 8   A race Runner A begins at the point $s(0) = 0$ and runs with velocity $v(t) = 2t$. Runner B begins with a head start at the point $S(0) = 8$ and runs with velocity $V(t) = 2$. Find the positions of the runners for $t \geq 0$ and determine who is ahead at $t = 6$ time units.

SOLUTION Let the position of Runner A be $s(t)$, with an initial position $s(0) = 0$. Then the position function satisfies the initial value problem

$$s'(t) = 2t, \quad s(0) = 0.$$

The solution is an antiderivative of $s'(t) = 2t$, which has the form $s(t) = t^2 + C$. Substituting $s(0) = 0$, we find that $C = 0$. Therefore, the position of Runner A is given by $s(t) = t^2$, for $t \geq 0$.

Let the position of Runner B be $S(t)$, with an initial position $S(0) = 8$. This position function satisfies the initial value problem

$$S'(t) = 2, \quad S(0) = 8.$$

The antiderivatives of $S'(t) = 2$ are $S(t) = 2t + C$. Substituting $S(0) = 8$ implies that $C = 8$. Therefore, the position of Runner B is given by $S(t) = 2t + 8$, for $t \geq 0$.

The graphs of the position functions are shown in Figure 4.91. Runner B begins with a head start but is overtaken when $s(t) = S(t)$, or when $t^2 = 2t + 8$. The solutions of this equation are $t = 4$ and $t = -2$. Only the positive solution is relevant because the race takes place for $t \geq 0$, so Runner A overtakes Runner B at $t = 4$, when $s = S = 16$. When $t = 6$, Runner A has the lead.

Related Exercises 83–96 ◄

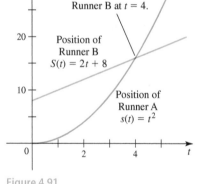

Figure 4.91

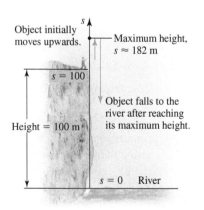

Figure 4.92

EXAMPLE 9   Motion with gravity Neglecting air resistance, the motion of an object moving vertically near Earth's surface is determined by the acceleration due to gravity, which is approximately 9.8 m/s^2. Suppose a stone is thrown vertically upward at $t = 0$ with a velocity of 40 m/s from the edge of a cliff that is 100 m above a river.

a. Find the velocity $v(t)$ of the object, for $t \geq 0$.

b. Find the position $s(t)$ of the object, for $t \geq 0$.

c. Find the maximum height of the object above the river.

d. With what speed does the object strike the river?

SOLUTION We establish a coordinate system in which the positive s-axis points vertically upward with $s = 0$ corresponding to the river (Figure 4.92). Let $s(t)$ be the position of the stone measured relative to the river, for $t \geq 0$. The initial velocity of the stone is $v(0) = 40 \text{ m/s}$ and the initial position of the stone is $s(0) = 100 \text{ m}$.

▶ The acceleration due to gravity at Earth's surface is approximately $g = 9.8 \text{ m/s}^2$, or $g = 32 \text{ ft/s}^2$. It varies even at sea level from about 9.8640 at the poles to 9.7982 at the equator. The equation $v'(t) = -g$ is an instance of Newton's Second Law of Motion and assumes no other forces (such as air resistance) are present.

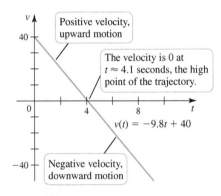

Positive velocity, upward motion

The velocity is 0 at $t \approx 4.1$ seconds, the high point of the trajectory.

$v(t) = -9.8t + 40$

Negative velocity, downward motion

Figure 4.93

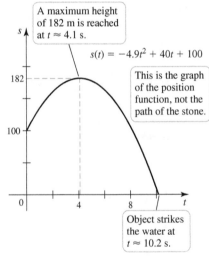

A maximum height of 182 m is reached at $t \approx 4.1$ s.

$s(t) = -4.9t^2 + 40t + 100$

This is the graph of the position function, not the path of the stone.

Object strikes the water at $t \approx 10.2$ s.

Figure 4.94

a. The acceleration due to gravity points in the *negative s*-direction. Therefore, the initial value problem governing the motion of the object is

$$\text{acceleration} = v'(t) = -9.8, \; v(0) = 40.$$

The antiderivatives of -9.8 are $v(t) = -9.8t + C$. The initial condition $v(0) = 40$ gives $C = 40$. Therefore, the velocity of the stone is

$$v(t) = -9.8t + 40.$$

As shown in Figure 4.93, the velocity decreases from its initial value $v(0) = 40$ until it reaches zero at the high point of the trajectory. This point is reached when

$$v(t) = -9.8t + 40 = 0$$

or when $t \approx 4.1$ s. For $t > 4.1$, the velocity is negative and increases in magnitude as the stone falls to Earth.

b. Knowing the velocity function of the stone, we can determine its position. The position function satisfies the initial value problem

$$v(t) = s'(t) = -9.8t + 40, \; s(0) = 100.$$

The antiderivatives of $-9.8t + 40$ are

$$s(t) = -4.9t^2 + 40t + C.$$

The initial condition $s(0) = 100$ implies $C = 100$, so the position function of the stone is

$$s(t) = -4.9t^2 + 40t + 100,$$

as shown in Figure 4.94. The parabolic graph of the position function is not the actual trajectory of the stone; the stone moves vertically along the s-axis.

c. The position function of the stone increases for $0 < t < 4.1$. At $t \approx 4.1$, the stone reaches a high point of $s(4.1) \approx 182$ m.

d. For $t > 4.1$, the position function decreases, and the stone strikes the river when $s(t) = 0$. The roots of this equation are $t \approx 10.2$ and $t \approx -2.0$. Only the first root is relevant because the motion starts at $t = 0$. Therefore, the stone strikes the ground at $t \approx 10.2$ s. Its speed (in m/s) at this instant is $|v(10.2)| \approx |-60| = 60$.

Related Exercises 97–100 ◀

SECTION 4.9 EXERCISES

Review Questions

1. Fill in the blanks with either of the words *the derivative* or *an antiderivative*: If $F'(x) = f(x)$, then f is _____ of F and F is _____ of f.

2. Describe the set of antiderivatives of $f(x) = 0$.

3. Describe the set of antiderivatives of $f(x) = 1$.

4. Why do two different antiderivatives of a function differ by a constant?

5. Give the antiderivatives of x^p. For what values of p does your answer apply?

6. Give the antiderivatives of e^{-x}.

7. Give the antiderivatives of $1/x$.

8. Evaluate $\int \cos ax \, dx$ and $\int \sin ax \, dx$, where a is a constant.

9. If $F(x) = x^2 - 3x + C$ and $F(-1) = 4$, what is the value of C?

10. For a given function f, explain the steps used to solve the initial value problem $F'(t) = f(t), F(0) = 10$.

Basic Skills

11–22. Finding antiderivatives *Find all the antiderivatives of the following functions. Check your work by taking derivatives.*

11. $f(x) = 5x^4$

12. $g(x) = 11x^{10}$

13. $f(x) = \sin 2x$

14. $g(x) = -4 \cos 4x$

15. $P(x) = 3 \sec^2 x$

16. $Q(s) = \csc^2 s$

17. $f(y) = -2/y^3$

18. $H(z) = -6z^{-7}$

19. $f(x) = e^x$

20. $h(y) = y^{-1}$

21. $G(s) = \dfrac{1}{s^2 + 1}$

22. $F(t) = \pi$

23–36. Indefinite integrals *Determine the following indefinite integrals. Check your work by differentiation.*

23. $\int (3x^5 - 5x^9)\, dx$

24. $\int (3u^{-2} - 4u^2 + 1)\, du$

25. $\int \left(4\sqrt{x} - \dfrac{4}{\sqrt{x}}\right) dx$

26. $\int \left(\dfrac{5}{t^2} + 4t^2\right) dt$

27. $\int (5s + 3)^2\, ds$

28. $\int 5m(12m^3 - 10m)\, dm$

29. $\int (3x^{1/3} + 4x^{-1/3} + 6)\, dx$ **30.** $\int 6\sqrt[3]{x}\, dx$

31. $\int (3x + 1)(4 - x)\, dx$ **32.** $\int (4z^{1/3} - z^{-1/3})\, dz$

33. $\int \left(\dfrac{3}{x^4} + 2 - \dfrac{3}{x^2}\right) dx$ **34.** $\int \sqrt[5]{r^2}\, dr$

35. $\int \dfrac{4x^4 - 6x^2}{x}\, dx$ **36.** $\int \dfrac{12t^8 - t}{t^3}\, dt$

37–46. Indefinite integrals involving trigonometric functions
Determine the following indefinite integrals. Check your work by differentiation.

37. $\int (\sin 2y + \cos 3y)\, dy$ **38.** $\int \left(\sin 4t - \sin \dfrac{t}{4}\right) dt$

39. $\int (\sec^2 x - 1)\, dx$ **40.** $\int 2\sec^2 2v\, dv$

41. $\int (\sec^2 \theta + \sec \theta \tan \theta)\, d\theta$ **42.** $\int \dfrac{\sin \theta - 1}{\cos^2 \theta}\, d\theta$

43. $\int (3t^2 + \sec^2 2t)\, dt$ **44.** $\int \csc 3\varphi \cot 3\varphi\, d\varphi$

45. $\int \sec 4\theta \tan 4\theta\, d\theta$ **46.** $\int \csc^2 6x\, dx$

47–58. Other indefinite integrals *Determine the following indefinite integrals. Check your work by differentiation.*

47. $\int \dfrac{1}{2y}\, dy$ **48.** $\int (e^{2t} + 2\sqrt{t})\, dt$

49. $\int \dfrac{6}{\sqrt{25 - x^2}}\, dx$ **50.** $\int \dfrac{3}{4 + v^2}\, dv$

51. $\int \dfrac{dx}{x\sqrt{x^2 - 100}}$ **52.** $\int \dfrac{2}{16z^2 + 25}\, dz$

53. $\int \dfrac{1}{x\sqrt{x^2 - 25}}\, dx$ **54.** $\int (49 - x^2)^{-1/2}\, dx$

55. $\int \dfrac{t + 1}{t}\, dt$ **56.** $\int (22x^{10} - 24\, e^{12x})\, dx$

57. $\int e^{x+2}\, dx$ **58.** $\int \dfrac{10t^5 - 3}{t}\, dt$

59–66. Particular antiderivatives *For the following functions f, find the antiderivative F that satisfies the given condition.*

59. $f(x) = x^5 - 2x^{-2} + 1;\ F(1) = 0$

60. $f(t) = \sec^2 t;\ F(\pi/4) = 1$

61. $f(v) = \sec v \tan v;\ F(0) = 2$

62. $f(x) = (4\sqrt{x} + 6/\sqrt{x})/x^2;\ F(1) = 4$

63. $f(x) = 8x^3 - 2x^{-2};\ F(1) = 5$

64. $f(u) = 2e^u + 3;\ F(0) = 8$

65. $f(y) = \dfrac{3y^3 + 5}{y};\ F(1) = 3$

66. $f(\theta) = 2\sin 2\theta - 4\cos 4\theta;\ F\left(\dfrac{\pi}{4}\right) = 2$

67–76. Solving initial value problems *Find the solution of the following initial value problems.*

67. $f'(x) = 2x - 3;\ f(0) = 4$

68. $g'(x) = 7x^6 - 4x^3 + 12;\ g(1) = 24$

69. $g'(x) = 7x\left(x^6 - \dfrac{1}{7}\right);\ g(1) = 2$

70. $h'(t) = 6\sin 3t;\ h(\pi/6) = 6$

71. $f'(u) = 4(\cos u - \sin 2u);\ f(\pi/6) = 0$

72. $p'(t) = 10e^{-t};\ p(0) = 100$

73. $y'(t) = \dfrac{3}{t} + 6;\ y(1) = 8$

74. $u'(x) = \dfrac{e^{2x} + 4e^{-x}}{e^x};\ u(\ln 2) = 2$

75. $y'(\theta) = \dfrac{\sqrt{2}\cos^3 \theta + 1}{\cos^2 \theta};\ y\left(\dfrac{\pi}{4}\right) = 3$

76. $v'(x) = 4x^{1/3} + 2x^{-1/3};\ v(8) = 40$

77–82. Graphing general solutions *Graph several functions that satisfy the following differential equations. Then find and graph the particular function that satisfies the given initial condition.*

77. $f'(x) = 2x - 5;\ f(0) = 4$

78. $f'(x) = 3x^2 - 1;\ f(1) = 2$

79. $f'(x) = 3x + \sin \pi x;\ f(2) = 3$

80. $f'(s) = 4\sec s \tan s;\ f(\pi/4) = 1$

81. $f'(t) = 1/t;\ f(1) = 4$

82. $f'(x) = 2\cos 2x;\ f(0) = 1$

83–88. Velocity to position *Given the following velocity functions of an object moving along a line, find the position function with the given initial position. Then graph both the velocity and position functions.*

83. $v(t) = 2t + 4;\ s(0) = 0$

84. $v(t) = e^{-2t} + 4;\ s(0) = 2$

85. $v(t) = 2\sqrt{t};\ s(0) = 1$

86. $v(t) = 2\cos t;\ s(0) = 0$

87. $v(t) = 6t^2 + 4t - 10;\ s(0) = 0$

88. $v(t) = 2\sin 2t;\ s(0) = 0$

89–94. Acceleration to position *Given the following acceleration functions of an object moving along a line, find the position function with the given initial velocity and position.*

89. $a(t) = -32;\ v(0) = 20, s(0) = 0$

90. $a(t) = 4;\ v(0) = -3, s(0) = 2$

91. $a(t) = 0.2\, t;\ v(0) = 0, s(0) = 1$

92. $a(t) = 2 \cos t; \ v(0) = 1, s(0) = 0$

93. $a(t) = 3 \sin 2t; \ v(0) = 1, s(0) = 10$

94. $a(t) = 2e^{-t/6}; \ v(0) = 1, s(0) = 0$

95–96. Races *The velocity function and initial position of Runners A and B are given. Analyze the race that results by graphing the position functions of the runners and finding the time and positions (if any) at which they first pass each other.*

95. A: $v(t) = \sin t, \ s(0) = 0;$ B: $V(t) = \cos t, \ S(0) = 0$

96. A: $v(t) = 2e^{-t}, \ s(0) = 0;$ B: $V(t) = 4e^{-4t}, \ S(0) = 10$

97–100. Motion with gravity *Consider the following descriptions of the vertical motion of an object subject only to the acceleration due to gravity. Begin with the acceleration equation $a(t) = v'(t) = g$, where $g = -9.8 \, m/s^2$.*

a. *Find the velocity of the object for all relevant times.*
b. *Find the position of the object for all relevant times.*
c. *Find the time when the object reaches its highest point. What is the height?*
d. *Find the time when the object strikes the ground.*

97. A softball is popped up vertically (from the ground) with a velocity of 30 m/s.

98. A stone is thrown vertically upward with a velocity of 30 m/s from the edge of a cliff 200 m above a river.

99. A payload is released at an elevation of 400 m from a hot-air balloon that is rising at a rate of 10 m/s.

100. A payload is dropped at an elevation of 400 m from a hot-air balloon that is descending at a rate of 10 m/s.

Further Explorations

101. Explain why or why not Determine whether the following statements are true and give an explanation or counterexample.

a. $F(x) = x^3 - 4x + 100$ and $G(x) = x^3 - 4x - 100$ are antiderivatives of the same function.
b. If $F'(x) = f(x)$, then f is an antiderivative of F.
c. If $F'(x) = f(x)$, then $\int f(x) \, dx = F(x) + C$.
d. $f(x) = x^3 + 3$ and $g(x) = x^3 - 4$ are derivatives of the same function.
e. If $F'(x) = G'(x)$, then $F(x) = G(x)$.

102–109. Miscellaneous indefinite integrals Determine the following indefinite integrals. Check your work by differentiation.

102. $\int \left(\sqrt[3]{x^2} + \sqrt{x^3} \right) dx$

103. $\int \dfrac{e^{2x} - e^{-2x}}{2} \, dx$

104. $\int (4 \cos 4w - 3 \sin 3w) \, dw$

105. $\int (\csc^2 \theta + 2\theta^2 - 3\theta) \, d\theta$

106. $\int (\csc^2 \theta + 1) \, d\theta$

107. $\int \dfrac{1 + \sqrt{x}}{x} \, dx$

108. $\int \dfrac{2 + x^2}{1 + x^2} \, dx$

109. $\int \sqrt{x} \left(2x^6 - 4 \sqrt[3]{x} \right) dx$

110–113. Functions from higher derivatives *Find the function F that satisfies the following differential equations and initial conditions.*

110. $F''(x) = 1, F'(0) = 3, F(0) = 4$

111. $F''(x) = \cos x, F'(0) = 3, F(\pi) = 4$

112. $F'''(x) = 4x, F''(0) = 0, F'(0) = 1, F(0) = 3$

113. $F'''(x) = 672x^5 + 24x, F''(0) = 0, F'(0) = 2, F(0) = 1$

Applications

114. Mass on a spring A mass oscillates up and down on the end of a spring. Find its position s relative to the equilibrium position if its acceleration is $a(t) = \sin \pi t$ and its initial velocity and position are $v(0) = 3$ and $s(0) = 0$, respectively.

115. Flow rate A large tank is filled with water when an outflow valve is opened at $t = 0$. Water flows out at a rate, in gal/min, given by $Q'(t) = 0.1(100 - t^2)$, for $0 \le t \le 10$.

a. Find the amount of water $Q(t)$ that has flowed out of the tank after t minutes, given the initial condition $Q(0) = 0$.
b. Graph the flow function Q, for $0 \le t \le 10$.
c. How much water flows out of the tank in 10 min?

116. General headstart problem Suppose that object A is located at $s = 0$ at time $t = 0$ and starts moving along the s-axis with a velocity given by $v(t) = 2at$, where $a > 0$. Object B is located at $s = c > 0$ at $t = 0$ and starts moving along the s-axis with a constant velocity given by $V(t) = b > 0$. Show that A always overtakes B at time

$$t = \frac{b + \sqrt{b^2 + 4ac}}{2a}.$$

Additional Exercises

117. Using identities Use the identities $\sin^2 x = (1 - \cos 2x)/2$ and $\cos^2 x = (1 + \cos 2x)/2$ to find $\int \sin^2 x \, dx$ and $\int \cos^2 x \, dx$.

118–121. Verifying indefinite integrals *Verify the following indefinite integrals by differentiation. These integrals are derived in later chapters.*

118. $\int \dfrac{\cos \sqrt{x}}{\sqrt{x}} \, dx = 2 \sin \sqrt{x} + C$

119. $\int \dfrac{x}{\sqrt{x^2 + 1}} \, dx = \sqrt{x^2 + 1} + C$

120. $\int x^2 \cos x^3 \, dx = \dfrac{1}{3} \sin x^3 + C$

121. $\int \dfrac{x}{(x^2 - 1)^2} \, dx = -\dfrac{1}{2(x^2 - 1)} + C$

QUICK CHECK ANSWERS

1. $d/dx(x^3) = 3x^2$ and $d/dx(-\cos x) = \sin x$
2. $e^x + C, x^4 + C, \tan x + C$
3. $d/dx(-(\cos 2x)/2 + C) = \sin 2x$ **4.** One function that can be differentiated to get f' is f. Therefore, f is an antiderivative of f'.   **5.** The two position functions involve two different initial positions; they differ by a constant. ◄

CHAPTER 4   REVIEW EXERCISES

1. **Explain why or why not** Determine whether the following statements are true and give an explanation or counterexample.

    a. If $f'(c) = 0$, then f has a local maximum or minimum at c.
    b. If $f''(c) = 0$, then f has an inflection point at c.
    c. $F(x) = x^2 + 10$ and $G(x) = x^2 - 100$ are antiderivatives of the same function.
    d. Between two local minima of a function continuous on $(-\infty, \infty)$, there must be a local maximum.
    e. The linear approximation to $f(x) = \sin x$ at $x = 0$ is $L(x) = x$.
    f. If $\lim\limits_{x \to \infty} f(x) = \infty$ and $\lim\limits_{x \to \infty} g(x) = \infty$, then
    $$\lim\limits_{x \to \infty} (f(x) - g(x)) = 0.$$

2. **Locating extrema** Consider the graph of a function f on the interval $[-3, 3]$.

    a. Give the approximate coordinates of the local maxima and minima of f.
    b. Give the approximate coordinates of the absolute maximum and minimum of f (if they exist).
    c. Give the approximate coordinates of the inflection point(s) of f.
    d. Give the approximate coordinates of the zero(s) of f.
    e. On what intervals (approximately) is f concave up?
    f. On what intervals (approximately) is f concave down?

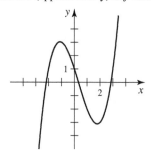

3–4. Designer functions *Sketch the graph of a function continuous on the given interval that satisfies the following conditions.*

3. f is continuous on the interval $[-4, 4]$; $f'(x) = 0$ for $x = -2$, 0, and 3; f has an absolute minimum at $x = 3$; f has a local minimum at $x = -2$; f has a local maximum at $x = 0$; f has an absolute maximum at $x = -4$.

4. f is continuous on $(-\infty, \infty)$; $f'(x) < 0$ and $f''(x) < 0$ on $(-\infty, 0)$; $f'(x) > 0$ and $f''(x) > 0$ on $(0, \infty)$.

5. **Functions from derivatives** Given the graphs of f' and f'', sketch a possible graph of f.

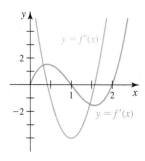

6–10. Critical points *Find the critical points of the following functions on the given intervals. Identify the absolute maximum and minimum values (if they exist). Graph the function to confirm your conclusions.*

6. $f(x) = \sin 2x + 3$ on $[-\pi, \pi]$

7. $f(x) = 2x^3 - 3x^2 - 36x + 12$ on $(-\infty, \infty)$

8. $f(x) = 4x^{1/2} - x^{5/2}$ on $[0, 4]$

9. $f(x) = 2x \ln x + 10$ on $(0, 4)$

10. $g(x) = x \sin^{-1} x$ on $[-1, 1]$

11. **Absolute values** Consider the function
    $f(x) = |x - 2| + |x + 3|$ on $[-4, 4]$. Graph f, identify the critical points, and give the coordinates of the local and absolute extreme values.

12. **Inflection points** Does $f(x) = 2x^5 - 10x^4 + 20x^3 + x + 1$ have any inflection points? If so, identify them.

13–20. Curve sketching *Use the guidelines given in Section 4.3 to make a complete graph of the following functions on their domains or on the given interval. Use a graphing utility to check your work.*

13. $f(x) = x^4/2 - 3x^2 + 4x + 1$

14. $f(x) = \dfrac{3x}{x^2 + 3}$

15. $f(x) = 4 \cos (\pi(x - 1))$ on $[0, 2]$

16. $f(x) = \dfrac{x^2 + x}{4 - x^2}$

17. $f(x) = \sqrt[3]{x} - \sqrt{x} + 2$

18. $f(x) = \dfrac{\cos \pi x}{1 + x^2}$ on $[-2, 2]$

19. $f(x) = x^{2/3} + (x + 2)^{1/3}$

20. $f(x) = x(x - 1) e^{-x}$

21. **Optimization** A right triangle has legs of length h and r, and a hypotenuse of length 4 (see figure). It is revolved about the leg of length h to sweep out a right circular cone. What values of h and r maximize the volume of the cone? (Volume of a cone $= \pi r^2 h/3$.)

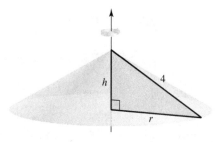

22. **Rectangles beneath a curve** A rectangle is constructed with one side on the positive x-axis, one side on the positive y-axis, and the vertex opposite the origin on the curve $y = \cos x$, for $0 < x < \pi/2$. Approximate the dimensions of the rectangle that maximize the area of the rectangle. What is the area?

23. Maximum printable area A rectangular page in a textbook (with width x and length y) has an area of 98 in^2, top and bottom margins set at 1 in, and left and right margins set at $\frac{1}{2}$ in. The printable area of the page is the rectangle that lies within the margins. What are the dimensions of the page that maximize the printable area?

24. Nearest point What point on the graph of $f(x) = \frac{5}{2} - x^2$ is closest to the origin? (*Hint*: You can minimize the square of the distance.)

25. Maximum area A line segment of length 10 joins the points $(0, p)$ and $(q, 0)$ to form a triangle in the first quadrant. Find the values of p and q that maximize the area of the triangle.

26. Minimum painting surface A metal cistern in the shape of a right circular cylinder with volume $V = 50 \text{ m}^3$ needs to be painted each year to reduce corrosion. The paint is applied only to surfaces exposed to the elements (the outside cylinder wall and the circular top). Find the dimensions r and h of the cylinder that minimize the area of the painted surfaces.

27–28. Linear approximation

a. Find the linear approximation to f at the given point a.
b. Use your answer from part (a) to estimate the given function value. Does your approximation underestimate or overestimate the exact function value?

27. $f(x) = x^{2/3}$; $a = 27$; $f(29)$

28. $f(x) = \sin^{-1} x$; $a = 1/2$; $f(0.48)$

29–30. Estimations with linear approximation *Use linear approximation to estimate the following quantities. Choose a value of a to produce a small error.*

29. $1/4.2^2$

30. $\tan^{-1} 1.05$

31. Change in elevation The elevation h (in feet above the ground) of a stone dropped from a height of 1000 ft is modeled by the equation $h(t) = 1000 - 16t^2$, where t is measured in seconds and air resistance is neglected. Approximate the change in elevation over the interval $5 \le t \le 5.7$ (recall that $\Delta h \approx h'(a) \Delta t$).

32. Change in energy The energy E (in joules) released by an earthquake of magnitude M is modeled by the equation $E(M) = 25{,}000 \cdot 10^{1.5\,M}$. Approximate the change in energy released when the magnitude changes from 7.0 to 7.5 (recall that $\Delta E \approx E'(a) \Delta M$).

33. Mean Value Theorem The population of a culture of cells grows according to the function $P(t) = \dfrac{100t}{t + 1}$, where $t \ge 0$ is measured in weeks.

  a. What is the average rate of change in the population over the interval $[0, 8]$?
  b. At what point of the interval $[0, 8]$ is the instantaneous rate of change equal to the average rate of change?

34. Growth rate of bamboo Bamboo belongs to the grass family and is one of the fastest-growing plants in the world.

  a. A bamboo shoot was 500 cm tall at 10.00 A.M. and 515 cm at 3:00 P.M. Compute the average growth rate of the bamboo shoot in cm/hr over the period of time from 10:00 A.M. to 3:00 P.M.

  b. Based on the Mean Value Theorem, what can you conclude about the instantaneous growth rate of bamboo measured in *millimeters per second* between 10:00 A.M. and 3:00 P.M.?

T 35. Newton's method Use Newton's method to approximate the roots of $f(x) = 3x^3 - 4x^2 + 1$ to six digits.

T 36. Newton's method Use Newton's method to approximate the roots of $f(x) = e^{-2x} + 2e^x - 6$ to six digits. Make a table showing the first five approximations for each root using an initial estimate of your choice.

T 37. Newton's method Use Newton's method to approximate the x-coordinate of the inflection points of $f(x) = 2x^5 - 6x^3 - 4x + 2$ to six digits.

38–51. Limits *Evaluate the following limits. Use l'Hôpital's Rule when needed.*

38. $\displaystyle \lim_{t \to 2} \frac{t^3 - t^2 - 2t}{t^2 - 4}$

39. $\displaystyle \lim_{t \to 0} \frac{1 - \cos 6t}{2t}$

40. $\displaystyle \lim_{x \to \infty} \frac{5x^2 + 2x - 5}{\sqrt{x^4 - 1}}$

41. $\displaystyle \lim_{\theta \to 0} \frac{3 \sin^2 2\theta}{\theta^2}$

42. $\displaystyle \lim_{x \to \infty} \left(\sqrt{x^2 + x + 1} - \sqrt{x^2 - x} \right)$

43. $\displaystyle \lim_{\theta \to 0} 2\theta \cot 3\theta$

44. $\displaystyle \lim_{x \to 0} \frac{e^{-2x} - 1 + 2x}{x^2}$

45. $\displaystyle \lim_{y \to 0^+} \frac{\ln^{10} y}{\sqrt{y}}$

46. $\displaystyle \lim_{\theta \to 0} \frac{3 \sin 8\theta}{8 \sin 3\theta}$

47. $\displaystyle \lim_{x \to 1} \frac{x^4 - x^3 - 3x^2 + 5x - 2}{x^3 + x^2 - 5x + 3}$

48. $\displaystyle \lim_{x \to \infty} \frac{\ln x^{100}}{\sqrt{x}}$

49. $\displaystyle \lim_{x \to 0} \csc x \sin^{-1} x$

50. $\displaystyle \lim_{x \to \infty} \frac{\ln^3 x}{\sqrt{x}}$

51. $\displaystyle \lim_{x \to \infty} \ln \left(\frac{x + 1}{x - 1} \right)$

52–59. $1^\infty, 0^0, \infty^0$ forms *Evaluate the following limits. Check your results by graphing.*

52. $\displaystyle \lim_{x \to 0^+} (1 + x)^{\cot x}$

53. $\displaystyle \lim_{x \to \pi/2^-} (\sin x)^{\tan x}$

54. $\displaystyle \lim_{x \to \infty} (\sqrt{x} + 1)^{1/x}$

55. $\displaystyle \lim_{x \to 0^+} |\ln x|^x$

56. $\displaystyle \lim_{x \to \infty} x^{1/x}$

57. $\displaystyle \lim_{x \to \infty} \left(1 - \frac{3}{x} \right)^x$

58. $\displaystyle \lim_{x \to \infty} \left(\frac{2}{\pi} \tan^{-1} x \right)^x$

59. $\displaystyle \lim_{x \to 1} (x - 1)^{\sin \pi x}$

60–67. Comparing growth rates *Determine which of the two functions grows faster or state that they have comparable growth rates.*

60. x^{100} and 1.1^x

61. $x^{1/2}$ and $x^{1/3}$

62. $\ln x$ and $\log_{10} x$

63. $\sqrt{x}$ and $\ln^{10} x$

64. $10x$ and $\ln x^2$

65. e^x and 3^x

66. $\sqrt{x^6 + 10}$ and x^3

67. 2^x and $4^{x/2}$

68–81. Indefinite integrals *Determine the following indefinite integrals.*

68. $\displaystyle\int (x^8 - 3x^3 + 1)\, dx$

69. $\displaystyle\int (2x + 1)^2 dx$

70. $\displaystyle\int \frac{x + 1}{x}\, dx$

71. $\displaystyle\int \left(\frac{1}{x^2} - \frac{2}{x^{5/2}} \right) dx$

72. $\displaystyle\int \frac{x^4 - 2\sqrt{x} + 2}{x^2}\, dx$

73. $\displaystyle\int (1 + \cos 3\theta)\, d\theta$

74. $\displaystyle\int 2 \sec^2 \theta\, d\theta$

75. $\displaystyle\int \sec 2x \tan 2x\, dx$

76. $\displaystyle\int 2e^{2x}\, dx$

77. $\displaystyle\int \frac{12}{x}\, dx$

78. $\displaystyle\int \frac{dx}{\sqrt{1 - x^2}}$

79. $\displaystyle\int \frac{dx}{x^2 + 1}$

80. $\displaystyle\int \frac{1 + \tan \theta}{\sec \theta}\, d\theta$

81. $\displaystyle\int (\sqrt[4]{x^3} + \sqrt{x^5})\, dx$

82–85. Functions from derivatives *Find the function with the following properties.*

82. $f'(x) = 3x^2 - 1$ and $f(0) = 10$

83. $f'(t) = \sin t + 2t$ and $f(0) = 5$

84. $g'(t) = t^2 + t^{-2}$ and $g(1) = 1$

85. $h'(x) = \sin^2 x$ and $h(1) = 1$ (*Hint:* $\sin^2 x = (1 - \cos 2x)/2$.)

86. Motion along a line Two objects move along the x-axis with position functions $x_1(t) = 2 \sin t$ and $x_2(t) = \sin (t - \pi/2)$. At what times on the interval $[0, 2\pi]$ are the objects closest to each other and farthest from each other?

87. Vertical motion with gravity A rocket is launched vertically upward with an initial velocity of 120 m/s from a platform that is 125 m above the ground. Assume that the only force at work is gravity. Determine and graph the velocity and position functions of the rocket, for $t \geq 0$. Then describe the motion in words.

88. Logs of logs Compare the growth rates of $\ln x$, $\ln (\ln x)$, and $\ln (\ln (\ln x))$.

89. Two limits with exponentials Evaluate

$$\lim_{x \to 0^+} \frac{x}{\sqrt{1 - e^{-x^2}}} \quad \text{and} \quad \lim_{x \to 0^+} \frac{x^2}{1 - e^{-x^2}} \quad \text{and confirm}$$

your result by graphing.

90. Geometric mean Prove that $\displaystyle\lim_{r \to 0} \left(\frac{a^r + b^r + c^r}{3} \right)^{1/r} = \sqrt[3]{abc}$,

where a, b, and c are positive real numbers.

91–92. Two methods *Evaluate the following limits in two different ways: Use the methods of Chapter 2 and use l'Hôpital's Rule.*

91. $\displaystyle\lim_{x \to \infty} \frac{2x^5 - x + 1}{5x^6 + x}$

92. $\displaystyle\lim_{x \to \infty} \frac{4x^4 - \sqrt{x}}{2x^4 + x^{-1}}$

93. Towers of exponents The functions

$$f(x) = (x^x)^x \quad \text{and} \quad g(x) = x^{(x^x)}$$

are different functions. For example, $f(3) = 19{,}683$ and $g(3) \approx 7.6 \times 10^{12}$. Determine whether $\displaystyle\lim_{x \to 0^+} f(x)$ and $\displaystyle\lim_{x \to 0^+} g(x)$ are indeterminate forms and evaluate the limits.

94. Cosine limits Let n be a positive integer. Use graphical and/or analytical methods to verify the following limits.

a. $\displaystyle\lim_{x \to 0} \frac{1 - \cos x^n}{x^{2n}} = \frac{1}{2}$

b. $\displaystyle\lim_{x \to 0} \frac{1 - \cos^n x}{x^2} = \frac{n}{2}$

95. Limits for e Consider the function $g(x) = (1 + 1/x)^{x+a}$. Show that if $0 \leq a < \frac{1}{2}$, then $g(x) \to e$ from *below* as $x \to \infty$; if $\frac{1}{2} \leq a < 1$, then $g(x) \to e$ from *above* as $x \to \infty$.

96. A family of super-exponential functions Let $f(x) = (a + x)^x$, where $a > 0$.

a. What is the domain of f (in terms of a)?

b. Describe the end behavior of f (near the left boundary of its domain and as $x \to \infty$).

c. Compute f'. Then graph f and f', for $a = 0.5, 1, 2,$ and 3.

d. Show that f has a single local minimum at the point z that satisfies $(z + a) \ln (z + a) + z = 0$.

e. Describe how z (found in part (d)) varies as a increases. Describe how $f(z)$ varies as a increases.

Chapter 4 Guided Projects

Applications of the material in this chapter and related topics can be found in the following Guided Projects. For additional information, see the Preface.

- Oscillators
- Ice cream, geometry, and calculus
- Newton's method

9

Power Series

Chapter Preview   Until now, you have worked with infinite series consisting of real numbers. In this chapter, we make a seemingly small, but significant, change by considering infinite series whose terms include powers of a variable. With this change, an infinite series becomes a *power series*. One of the most fundamental ideas in all of calculus is that functions can be represented by power series. As a first step toward this result, we look at approximating functions using polynomials. The transition from polynomials to power series is then straightforward, and we learn how to represent the familiar functions of mathematics in terms of power series called *Taylor series*. The remainder of the chapter is devoted to the properties and many uses of Taylor series.

9.1 Approximating Functions with Polynomials

Power series provide a way to represent familiar functions and to define new functions. For this reason, power series—like sets and functions—are among the most fundamental entities in mathematics.

What Is a Power Series?

A *power series* is an infinite series of the form

$$\sum_{k=0}^{\infty} c_k x^k = \underbrace{c_0 + c_1 x + c_2 x^2 + \cdots + c_n x^n}_{n\text{th-degree polynomial}} + \underbrace{c_{n+1} x^{n+1} + \cdots}_{\text{terms continue}},$$

or, more generally,

$$\sum_{k=0}^{\infty} c_k (x - a)^k = \underbrace{c_0 + c_1 (x - a) + \cdots + c_n (x - a)^n}_{n\text{th-degree polynomial}} + \underbrace{c_{n+1}(x - a)^{n+1} + \cdots}_{\text{terms continue}},$$

where the *center* of the series a and the coefficients c_k are constants. This type of series is called a power series because it consists of powers of x or $(x - a)$.

Viewed another way, a power series is built up from polynomials of increasing degree, as shown in the following progression.

$$\left.\begin{aligned}
&\text{Degree 0: } c_0 \\
&\text{Degree 1: } c_0 + c_1 x \\
&\text{Degree 2: } c_0 + c_1 x + c_2 x^2 \\
&\qquad \vdots \qquad \vdots \qquad \vdots \\
&\text{Degree } n: c_0 + c_1 x + c_2 x^2 + \cdots + c_n x^n = \sum_{k=0}^{n} c_k x^k
\end{aligned}\right\} \text{Polynomials}$$

$$\left.\begin{aligned}
&\qquad \vdots \qquad \vdots \qquad \vdots \\
&c_0 + c_1 x + c_2 x^2 + \cdots + c_n x^n + \cdots = \sum_{k=0}^{\infty} c_k x^k
\end{aligned}\right\} \text{Power series}$$

According to this perspective, a power series is a "super-polynomial." Therefore, we begin our exploration of power series by using polynomials to approximate functions.

Polynomial Approximation

An important observation motivates our work. To evaluate a polynomial $\left(\text{say, } f(x) = x^8 - 4x^5 + \frac{1}{2}\right)$, all we need is arithmetic—addition, subtraction, multiplication, and division. However, algebraic functions $\left(\text{say, } f(x) = \sqrt[3]{x^4 - 1}\right)$ and the trigonometric, logarithmic, and exponential functions usually cannot be evaluated exactly using arithmetic. Therefore, it makes practical sense to use the simplest of functions, polynomials, to approximate more complicated functions.

Linear and Quadratic Approximation

In Section 4.5, you learned that if a function f is differentiable at a point a, then it can be approximated near a by its tangent line, which is the linear approximation to f at the point a. The linear approximation at a is given by

$$y - f(a) = f'(a)(x - a) \quad \text{or} \quad y = f(a) + f'(a)(x - a).$$

Because the linear approximation is a first-degree polynomial, we name it p_1:

$$p_1(x) = f(a) + f'(a)(x - a).$$

This polynomial has some important properties: It matches f in *value* and in *slope* at a. In other words (Figure 9.1),

$$p_1(a) = f(a) \quad \text{and} \quad p_1'(a) = f'(a).$$

Linear approximation works well if f has a fairly constant slope near a. However, if f has a lot of curvature near a, then the tangent line may not provide an accurate approximation. To remedy this situation, we create a quadratic approximating polynomial by adding one new term to the linear polynomial. Denoting this new polynomial p_2, we let

$$p_2(x) = \underbrace{f(a) + f'(a)(x - a)}_{p_1(x)} + \underbrace{c_2(x - a)^2}_{\text{quadratic term}}.$$

The new term consists of a coefficient c_2 that must be determined and a quadratic factor $(x - a)^2$.

To determine c_2 and to ensure that p_2 is a good approximation to f near the point a, we require that p_2 agree with f in value, slope, and concavity at a; that is, p_2 must satisfy the matching conditions

$$p_2(a) = f(a), \quad p_2'(a) = f'(a), \quad \text{and} \quad p_2''(a) = f''(a),$$

where we assume that f and its first and second derivatives exist at a (Figure 9.2).

Substituting $x = a$ into p_2, we see immediately that $p_2(a) = f(a)$, so the first matching condition is met. Differentiating p_2 once, we have

$$p_2'(x) = f'(a) + 2c_2(x - a).$$

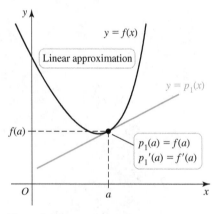

Figure 9.1

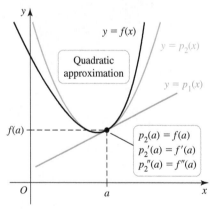

Figure 9.2

▶ Matching concavity (second derivatives) ensures that the graph of p_2 bends in the same direction as the graph of f at a.

So $p_2'(a) = f'(a)$, and the second matching condition is also met. Because $p_2''(a) = 2c_2$, the third matching condition is

$$p_2''(a) = 2c_2 = f''(a).$$

It follows that $c_2 = \frac{1}{2}f''(a)$; therefore, the quadratic approximating polynomial is

$$p_2(x) = \underbrace{f(a) + f'(a)(x - a)}_{p_1(x)} + \frac{f''(a)}{2}(x - a)^2.$$

EXAMPLE 1   Linear and quadratic approximations for $\ln x$

a. Find the linear approximation to $f(x) = \ln x$ at $x = 1$.

b. Find the quadratic approximation to $f(x) = \ln x$ at $x = 1$.

c. Use these approximations to estimate $\ln 1.05$.

SOLUTION

a. Note that $f(1) = 0$, $f'(x) = 1/x$, and $f'(1) = 1$. Therefore, the linear approximation to $f(x) = \ln x$ at $x = 1$ is

$$p_1(x) = f(1) + f'(1)(x - 1) = 0 + 1(x - 1) = x - 1.$$

As shown in Figure 9.3, p_1 matches f in value ($p_1(1) = f(1)$) and in slope ($p_1'(1) = f'(1)$) at $x = 1$.

b. We first compute $f''(x) = -1/x^2$ and $f''(1) = -1$. Building on the linear approximation found in part (a), the quadratic approximation is

$$p_2(x) = \underbrace{x - 1}_{p_1(x)} + \underbrace{\frac{1}{2}f''(1)(x - 1)^2}_{c_2}$$

$$= (x - 1) - \frac{1}{2}(x - 1)^2.$$

Because p_2 matches f in value, slope, and concavity at $x = 1$, it provides a better approximation to f near $x = 1$ (Figure 9.3).

c. To approximate $\ln 1.05$, we substitute $x = 1.05$ into each polynomial approximation:

$$p_1(1.05) = 1.05 - 1 = 0.05 \text{ and} \qquad \text{Linear approximation}$$

$$p_2(1.05) = (1.05 - 1) - \frac{1}{2}(1.05 - 1)^2 = 0.04875. \quad \text{Quadratic approximation}$$

The value of $\ln 1.05$ given by a calculator, rounded to five decimal places, is 0.04879, showing the improvement in quadratic approximation over linear approximation.

Related Exercises 7–14 ◄

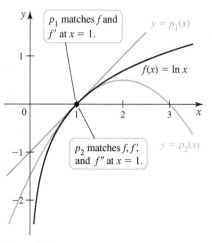

Figure 9.3

We now extend the idea of linear and quadratic approximation to obtain higher-degree polynomials that generally provide better approximations.

Taylor Polynomials

> Building on ideas that were already circulating in the early 18th century, Brook Taylor (1685–1731) published Taylor's Theorem in 1715. He is also credited with discovering integration by parts.

Assume that f and its first n derivatives exist at a; our goal is to find an nth-degree polynomial that approximates the values of f near a. The first step is to use p_2 to obtain a cubic polynomial p_3 of the form

$$p_3(x) = p_2(x) + c_3(x - a)^3$$

that satisfies the four matching conditions

$$p_3(a) = f(a), \quad p_3'(a) = f'(a), \quad p_3''(a) = f''(a), \quad \text{and} \quad p_3'''(a) = f'''(a).$$

Because p_3 is built "on top of " p_2, the first three matching conditions are met. The last condition, $p_3'''(a) = f'''(a)$, is used to determine c_3. A short calculation shows that $p_3'''(x) = 3 \cdot 2c_3 = 3!c_3$, so the last matching condition is $p_3'''(a) = 3!c_3 = f'''(a)$. Solving for c_3, we have $c_3 = \dfrac{f'''(a)}{3!}$. Therefore, the cubic approximating polynomial is

$$p_3(x) = \underbrace{f(a) + f'(a)(x - a) + \frac{f''(a)}{2!}(x - a)^2}_{p_2(x)} + \frac{f'''(a)}{3!}(x - a)^3.$$

> Recall that $2! = 2 \cdot 1$, $3! = 3 \cdot 2 \cdot 1$, $k! = k \cdot (k-1)!$, and by definition, $0! = 1$.

QUICK CHECK 1 Verify that p_3 satisfies $p_3{}^{(k)}(a) = f^{(k)}(a)$, for $k = 0, 1, 2$, and 3. ◄

Continuing in this fashion (Exercise 74), building each new polynomial on the previous polynomial, the nth approximating polynomial for f at a is

$$p_n(x) = f(a) + f'(a)(x - a) + \frac{f''(a)}{2!}(x - a)^2 + \cdots + \frac{f^{(n)}(a)}{n!}(x - a)^n.$$

It satisfies the $n + 1$ matching conditions

$$p_n(a) = f(a), \quad p_n{}'(a) = f'(a), \quad p_n{}''(a) = f''(a), \ldots, p_n^{(n)}(a) = f^{(n)}(a).$$

These conditions ensure that the graph of p_n conforms as closely as possible to the graph of f near a (Figure 9.4).

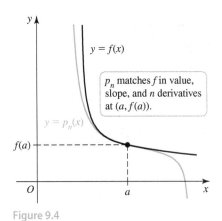

$y = f(x)$

p_n matches f in value, slope, and n derivatives at $(a, f(a))$.

$y = p_n(x)$

$f(a)$

O a x

Figure 9.4

> Recall that $f^{(n)}$ denotes the nth derivative of f. By convention, the zeroth derivative $f^{(0)}$ is f itself.

DEFINITION Taylor Polynomials

Let f be a function with f', f'', $\ldots$, and $f^{(n)}$ defined at a. The **nth-order Taylor polynomial** for f with its **center** at a, denoted p_n, has the property that it matches f in value, slope, and all derivatives up to the nth derivative at a; that is,

$$p_n(a) = f(a), p_n{}'(a) = f'(a), \ldots, \text{and } p_n^{(n)}(a) = f^{(n)}(a).$$

The nth-order Taylor polynomial centered at a is

$$p_n(x) = f(a) + f'(a)(x - a) + \frac{f''(a)}{2!}(x - a)^2 + \cdots + \frac{f^{(n)}(a)}{n!}(x - a)^n.$$

More compactly, $p_n(x) = \displaystyle\sum_{k=0}^{n} c_k(x - a)^k$, where the **coefficients** are

$$c_k = \frac{f^{(k)}(a)}{k!}, \quad \text{for } k = 0, 1, 2, \ldots, n.$$

EXAMPLE 2   Taylor polynomials for $\sin x$ Find the Taylor polynomials $p_1, \ldots, p_7$ centered at $x = 0$ for $f(x) = \sin x$.

SOLUTION We begin by differentiating f repeatedly and evaluating the derivatives at 0; these calculations allow us to compute c_k, for $k = 0, 1, \ldots, 7$. Notice that a pattern emerges:

$$f(x) = \sin x \Rightarrow f(0) = 0$$
$$f'(x) = \cos x \Rightarrow f'(0) = 1$$
$$f''(x) = -\sin x \Rightarrow f''(0) = 0$$
$$f'''(x) = -\cos x \Rightarrow f'''(0) = -1$$
$$f^{(4)}(x) = \sin x \Rightarrow f^{(4)}(0) = 0.$$

The derivatives of $\sin x$ at 0 cycle through the values $\{0, 1, 0, -1\}$. Therefore, $f^{(5)}(0) = 1$, $f^{(6)}(0) = 0$, and $f^{(7)}(0) = -1$.

We now construct the Taylor polynomials that approximate $f(x) = \sin x$ near 0, beginning with the linear polynomial. The polynomial of order $n = 1$ is

$$p_1(x) = f(0) + f'(0)(x - 0) = x,$$

whose graph is the line through the origin with slope 1 (Figure 9.5). Notice that f and p_1 agree in value ($f(0) = p_1(0) = 0$) and in slope ($f'(0) = p_1'(0) = 1$) at 0. We see that p_1 provides a good fit to f near 0, but the graphs diverge visibly for $|x| > 0.5$.

The polynomial of order $n = 2$ is

$$p_2(x) = \underbrace{f(0)}_{0} + \underbrace{f'(0)x}_{1} + \underbrace{\frac{f''(0)}{2!}x^2}_{0} = x,$$

so p_2 is the same as p_1.

The polynomial of order $n = 3$ is

$$p_3(x) = \underbrace{f(0) + f'(0)x + \frac{f''(0)}{2!}x^2}_{p_2(x)\,=\,x} + \underbrace{\frac{f'''(0)}{3!}x^3}_{-1/3!} = x - \frac{x^3}{6}.$$

We have designed p_3 to agree with f in value, slope, concavity, and third derivative at 0 (Figure 9.6). Consequently, p_3 provides a better approximation to f over a larger interval than p_1.

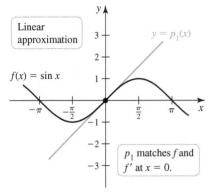

Linear approximation

$f(x) = \sin x$

$y = p_1(x)$

p_1 matches f and f' at $x = 0$.

Figure 9.5

> It is worth repeating that the next polynomial in the sequence is obtained by adding one new term to the previous polynomial. For example,
>
> $$p_3(x) = p_2(x) + \frac{f'''(a)}{3!}(x - a)^3.$$

QUICK CHECK 2 Verify the following properties for $f(x) = \sin x$ and $p_3(x) = x - x^3/6$:

$$f(0) = p_3(0),$$
$$f'(0) = p_3'(0),$$
$$f''(0) = p_3''(0), \text{ and}$$
$$f'''(0) = p_3'''(0). \quad \blacktriangleleft$$

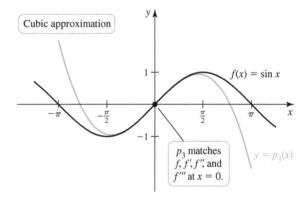

Cubic approximation

$f(x) = \sin x$

p_3 matches f, f', f'', and f''' at $x = 0$.

$y = p_3(x)$

Figure 9.6

The procedure for finding Taylor polynomials may be extended to polynomials of any order. Because the even derivatives of $f(x) = \sin x$ are zero at $x = 0$, $p_4(x) = p_3(x)$. For the same reason, $p_6(x) = p_5(x)$:

$$p_6(x) = p_5(x) = x - \frac{x^3}{3!} + \frac{x^5}{5!}. \quad c_5 = \frac{f^{(5)}(0)}{5!} = \frac{1}{5!}$$

Finally, the Taylor polynomial of order $n = 7$ is

$$p_7(x) = x - \frac{x^3}{3!} + \frac{x^5}{5!} - \frac{x^7}{7!}. \quad c_7 = \frac{f^{(7)}(0)}{7!} = -\frac{1}{7!}$$

From Figure 9.7 we see that as the order of the Taylor polynomials increases, more accurate approximations to $f(x) = \sin x$ are obtained over larger intervals centered at 0. For example, p_7 is a good fit to $f(x) = \sin x$ over the interval $[-\pi, \pi]$. Notice that $\sin x$ and its Taylor polynomials (centered at 0) are all odd functions.

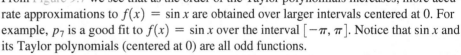

Related Exercises 15–22 ◄

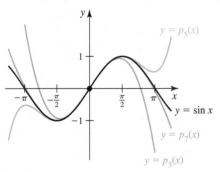

$y = p_5(x)$

$y = \sin x$

$y = p_7(x)$

$y = p_3(x)$

Figure 9.7

QUICK CHECK 3 Why do the Taylor polynomials for $\sin x$ centered at 0 consist only of odd powers of x? ◄

Approximations with Taylor Polynomials

Taylor polynomials find widespread use in approximating functions, as illustrated in the following examples.

EXAMPLE 3   Taylor polynomials for e^x

a. Find the Taylor polynomials of order $n = 0, 1, 2$, and 3 for $f(x) = e^x$ centered at 0. Graph f and the polynomials.

> Recall that if c is an approximation to x, the absolute error in c is $|x - c|$ and the relative error in c is $|x - c|/|x|$. We use *error* to refer to *absolute error*.

b. Use the polynomials in part (a) to approximate $e^{0.1}$ and $e^{-0.25}$. Find the absolute errors, $|f(x) - p_n(x)|$, in the approximations. Use calculator values for the exact values of f.

SOLUTION

a. Recall that the coefficients for the Taylor polynomials centered at 0 are

$$c_k = \frac{f^{(k)}(0)}{k!}, \qquad \text{for } k = 0, 1, 2, \ldots, n.$$

With $f(x) = e^x$, we have $f^{(k)}(x) = e^x$, $f^{(k)}(0) = 1$, and $c_k = 1/k!$, for $k = 0, 1, 2, 3 \ldots$. The first four polynomials are

$$p_0(x) = f(0) = 1,$$
$$p_1(x) = f(0) + f'(0)x = 1 + x,$$
$$\underbrace{p_1(x) = 1}_{} \quad \underbrace{1}_{}$$

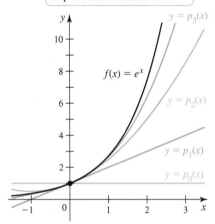

Taylor polynomials for $f(x) = e^x$ centered at 0. Approximations improve as n increases.

$$p_2(x) = f(0) + f'(0)x + \frac{f''(0)}{2!}x^2 = 1 + x + \frac{x^2}{2}, \text{ and}$$
$$\underbrace{p_1(x) = 1 + x}_{} \qquad \underbrace{1/2}_{}$$

$$p_3(x) = f(0) + f'(0)x + \frac{f''(0)}{2!}x^2 + \frac{f^{(3)}(0)}{3!}x^3 = 1 + x + \frac{x^2}{2} + \frac{x^3}{6}.$$
$$\underbrace{p_2(x) = 1 + x + x^2/2}_{} \qquad \underbrace{1/6}_{}$$

Notice that each successive polynomial provides a better fit to $f(x) = e^x$ near 0 (Figure 9.8). Continuing the pattern in these polynomials, the nth-order Taylor polynomial for e^x centered at 0 is

$$p_n(x) = 1 + x + \frac{x^2}{2!} + \frac{x^3}{3!} + \cdots + \frac{x^n}{n!} = \sum_{k=0}^{n} \frac{x^k}{k!}.$$

Figure 9.8

b. We evaluate $p_n(0.1)$ and $p_n(-0.25)$, for $n = 0, 1, 2$, and 3, and compare these values to the calculator values of $e^{0.1} \approx 1.1051709$ and $e^{-0.25} \approx 0.77880078$. The results are shown in Table 9.1. Observe that the errors in the approximations decrease as n increases. In addition, the errors in approximating $e^{0.1}$ are smaller in magnitude than the errors in approximating $e^{-0.25}$ because $x = 0.1$ is closer to the center of the polynomials than $x = -0.25$. Reasonable approximations based on these calculations are $e^{0.1} \approx 1.105$ and $e^{-0.25} \approx 0.78$.

> A rule of thumb in finding estimates based on several approximations: Keep all the digits that are common to the last two approximations after rounding.

Table 9.1

n	Approximation $p_n(0.1)$	Absolute Error $\lvert e^{0.1} - p_n(0.1) \rvert$	Approximation $p_n(-0.25)$	Absolute Error $\lvert e^{-0.25} - p_n(-0.25) \rvert$
0	1	1.1×10^{-1}	1	2.2×10^{-1}
1	1.1	5.2×10^{-3}	0.75	2.9×10^{-2}
2	1.105	1.7×10^{-4}	0.78125	2.4×10^{-3}
3	1.105167	4.3×10^{-6}	0.778646	1.5×10^{-4}

QUICK CHECK 4 Write out the next two Taylor polynomials p_4 and p_5 for $f(x) = e^x$ in Example 3. ◄

Related Exercises 23–28 ◄

EXAMPLE 4 **Approximating a real number using Taylor polynomials** Use polynomials of order $n = 0, 1, 2,$ and 3 to approximate $\sqrt{18}$.

SOLUTION Letting $f(x) = \sqrt{x}$, we choose the center $a = 16$ because it is near 18, and f and its derivatives are easy to evaluate at 16. The Taylor polynomials have the form

$$p_n(x) = f(16) + f'(16)(x - 16) + \frac{f''(16)}{2!}(x - 16)^2 + \cdots + \frac{f^{(n)}(16)}{n!}(x - 16)^n.$$

We now evaluate the required derivatives:

$$f(x) = \sqrt{x} \Rightarrow f(16) = 4,$$

$$f'(x) = \frac{1}{2}x^{-1/2} \Rightarrow f'(16) = \frac{1}{8},$$

$$f''(x) = -\frac{1}{4}x^{-3/2} \Rightarrow f''(16) = -\frac{1}{256}, \text{ and}$$

$$f'''(x) = \frac{3}{8}x^{-5/2} \Rightarrow f'''(16) = \frac{3}{8192}.$$

Therefore, the polynomial p_3 (which includes p_0, p_1, and p_2) is

$$p_3(x) = \underbrace{\underbrace{\underbrace{4}_{p_0(x)} + \frac{1}{8}(x - 16)}_{p_1(x)} - \frac{1}{512}(x - 16)^2}_{p_2(x)} + \frac{1}{16{,}384}(x - 16)^3.$$

The Taylor polynomials (Figure 9.9) give better approximations to f as the order of the approximation increases.

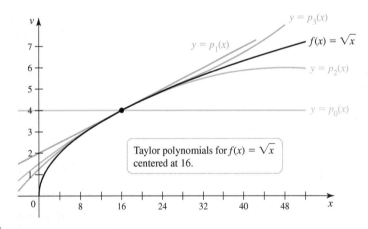

Figure 9.9

Letting $x = 18$, we obtain the approximations to $\sqrt{18}$ and the associated absolute errors shown in Table 9.2. (A calculator is used for the value of $\sqrt{18}$.) As expected, the errors decrease as n increases. Based on these calculations, a reasonable approximation is $\sqrt{18} \approx 4.24$.

Table 9.2

n	Approximation $p_n(18)$	Absolute Error $\lvert \sqrt{18} - p_n(18) \rvert$
0	4	2.4×10^{-1}
1	4.25	7.4×10^{-3}
2	4.242188	4.5×10^{-4}
3	4.242676	3.5×10^{-5}

QUICK CHECK 5 At what point would you center the Taylor polynomials for $\sqrt{x}$ and $\sqrt[4]{x}$ to approximate $\sqrt{51}$ and $\sqrt[4]{15}$, respectively? ◄

Related Exercises 29–48 ◄

Remainder in a Taylor Polynomial

Taylor polynomials provide good approximations to functions near a specific point. But how accurate are the approximations? To answer this question we define the *remainder* in a Taylor polynomial. If p_n is the Taylor polynomial for f of order n, then the remainder at the point x is

$$R_n(x) = f(x) - p_n(x).$$

The absolute value of the remainder is the error made in approximating $f(x)$ by $p_n(x)$. Equivalently, we have $f(x) = p_n(x) + R_n(x)$, which says that f consists of two components: the polynomial approximation and the associated remainder.

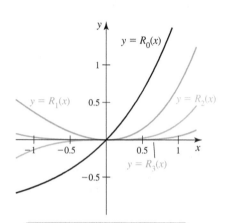

Remainders increase in magnitude as $|x|$ increases. Remainders decrease in magnitude to zero as n increases.

Figure 9.10

> The remainder R_n for a Taylor polynomial can be expressed in several different forms. The form stated in Theorem 9.1 is called the *Lagrange form* of the remainder.

> **DEFINITION Remainder in a Taylor Polynomial**
>
> Let p_n be the Taylor polynomial of order n for f. The **remainder** in using p_n to approximate f at the point x is
>
> $$R_n(x) = f(x) - p_n(x).$$

The idea of a remainder is illustrated in Figure 9.10, where we see the remainders associated with various Taylor polynomials for $f(x) = e^x$ centered at 0 (Example 3). For fixed order n, the remainders tend to increase in magnitude as x moves farther from the center of the polynomials (in this case 0). And for fixed x, remainders decrease in magnitude to zero with increasing n.

The remainder for a Taylor polynomial may be written quite concisely, which enables us to estimate remainders. The following result is known as *Taylor's Theorem* (or the *Remainder Theorem*).

> **THEOREM 9.1 Taylor's Theorem (Remainder Theorem)**
>
> Let f have continuous derivatives up to $f^{(n+1)}$ on an open interval I containing a. For all x in I,
>
> $$f(x) = p_n(x) + R_n(x),$$
>
> where p_n is the nth-order Taylor polynomial for f centered at a and the remainder is
>
> $$R_n(x) = \frac{f^{(n+1)}(c)}{(n + 1)!} (x - a)^{n+1},$$
>
> for some point c between x and a.

Discussion: We make two observations about Theorem 9.1 and outline a proof in Exercise 92. First, the case $n = 0$ is the Mean Value Theorem (Section 4.6), which states that

$$\frac{f(x) - f(a)}{x - a} = f'(c),$$

where c is a point between x and a. Rearranging this expression, we have

$$f(x) = \underbrace{f(a)}_{p_0(x)} + \underbrace{f'(c)(x - a)}_{R_0(x)}$$

$$= p_0(x) + R_0(x),$$

which is Taylor's Theorem with $n = 0$. Not surprisingly, the term $f^{(n+1)}(c)$ in Taylor's Theorem comes from a Mean Value Theorem argument.

The second observation makes the remainder easier to remember. If you write the $(n + 1)$st Taylor polynomial p_{n+1}, the highest-degree term is $\dfrac{f^{(n+1)}(a)}{(n + 1)!} (x - a)^{n+1}$.

Replacing $f^{(n+1)}(a)$ with $f^{(n+1)}(c)$ results in the remainder for p_n.

Estimating the Remainder

The remainder has both practical and theoretical importance. We deal with practical matters now and theoretical matters in Section 9.3. The remainder is used to estimate errors in approximations and to determine the number of terms of a Taylor polynomial needed to achieve a prescribed accuracy.

Because c is generally unknown, the difficulty in estimating the remainder is finding a bound for $|f^{(n+1)}(c)|$. Assuming this can be done, the following theorem gives a standard estimate for the remainder term.

THEOREM 9.2 **Estimate of the Remainder**

Let n be a fixed positive integer. Suppose there exists a number M such that $|f^{(n+1)}(c)| \leq M$, for all c between a and x inclusive. The remainder in the nth-order Taylor polynomial for f centered at a satisfies

$$|R_n(x)| = |f(x) - p_n(x)| \leq M \frac{|x - a|^{n+1}}{(n+1)!}.$$

Proof: The proof requires taking the absolute value of the remainder in Theorem 9.1, replacing $|f^{(n+1)}(c)|$ with a larger quantity M, and forming an inequality. ◀

We now give three examples that demonstrate how the remainder is computed and used in different ways.

EXAMPLE 5 **Estimating the remainder for $\cos x$** Find a bound for the magnitude of the remainder for the Taylor polynomials of $f(x) = \cos x$ centered at 0.

SOLUTION According to Theorem 9.1 with $a = 0$, we have

$$R_n(x) = \frac{f^{(n+1)}(c)}{(n+1)!} x^{n+1},$$

where c is a point between 0 and x. Notice that $f^{(n+1)}(c) = \pm \sin c$ or $f^{(n+1)}(c) = \pm \cos c$ depending on the value of n. In all cases, $|f^{(n+1)}(c)| \leq 1$. Therefore, we take $M = 1$ in Theorem 9.2, and the absolute value of the remainder can be bounded as

$$|R_n(x)| = \left| \frac{f^{(n+1)}(c)}{(n+1)!} x^{n+1} \right| \leq \frac{|x|^{n+1}}{(n+1)!}.$$

For example, if we approximate $\cos 0.1$ using the Taylor polynomial p_{10}, the remainder satisfies

$$|R_{10}(0.1)| \leq \frac{0.1^{11}}{11!} \approx 2.5 \times 10^{-19}.$$

Related Exercises 49–54 ◀

EXAMPLE 6 **Estimating a remainder** Consider again Example 4 in which we approximated $\sqrt{18}$ using the Taylor polynomial

$$p_3(x) = 4 + \frac{1}{8}(x - 16) - \frac{1}{512}(x - 16)^2 + \frac{1}{16,384}(x - 16)^3.$$

In that example, we computed the error in the approximation knowing the exact value of $\sqrt{18}$ (obtained with a calculator). In the more realistic case in which we do not know the exact value, Theorem 9.2 allows us to estimate remainders (or errors). Applying this theorem with $n = 3$, $a = 16$, and $x = 18$, we find that the remainder in approximating $\sqrt{18}$ by $p_3(18)$ satisfies the bound

$$|R_3(18)| \leq M \frac{(18 - 16)^4}{4!} = \frac{2}{3} M,$$

where M is a number that satisfies $\left|f^{(4)}(c)\right| \leq M$, for all c between 16 and 18 inclusive. In this particular problem, we find that $f^{(4)}(c) = -\dfrac{15}{16}c^{-7/2}$, so M must be chosen (as small as possible) such that $\left|f^{(4)}(c)\right| = \dfrac{15}{16}c^{-7/2} = \dfrac{15}{16c^{7/2}} \leq M$, for $16 \leq c \leq 18$.

You can verify that $\dfrac{15}{16c^{7/2}}$ is a decreasing function of c on $[16, 18]$ and has a maximum value of approximately 5.7×10^{-5} at $c = 16$ (Figure 9.11). Therefore, a bound on the remainder is

$$\left|R_3(18)\right| \leq \frac{2}{3}M \approx \frac{2}{3}\cdot 5.7 \times 10^{-5} \approx 3.8 \times 10^{-5}.$$

Notice that the actual error computed in Example 4 (Table 9.2) is 3.5×10^{-5}, which is less than the bound on the remainder—as it should be.

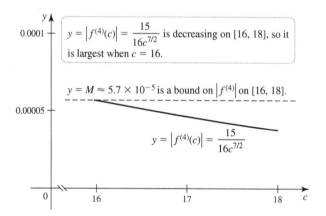

Figure 9.11

Related Exercises 55–60 ◄

EXAMPLE 7 **Estimating the remainder for e^x** Find a bound on the remainder in approximating $e^{0.45}$ using the Taylor polynomial of order $n = 6$ for $f(x) = e^x$ centered at 0.

SOLUTION Using Theorem 9.2, a bound on the remainder is given by

$$\left|R_n(x)\right| \leq M\frac{\left|x - a\right|^{n+1}}{(n + 1)!},$$

where M is chosen such that $\left|f^{(n+1)}(c)\right| \leq M$, for all c between a and x inclusive. Notice that $f(x) = e^x$ implies that $f^{(k)}(x) = e^x$, for $k = 0, 1, 2, \ldots$. In this particular problem, we have $n = 6$, $a = 0$, and $x = 0.45$, so the bound on the remainder takes the form

$$\left|R_6(0.45)\right| \leq M\frac{\left|0.45 - 0\right|^7}{7!} \approx 7.4 \times 10^{-7}\,M,$$

where M is chosen such that $\left|f^{(7)}(c)\right| = e^c \leq M$, for all c in the interval $[0, 0.45]$. Because e^c is an increasing function of c, its maximum value on the interval $[0, 0.45]$ occurs at $c = 0.45$ and is $e^{0.45}$. However, $e^{0.45}$ cannot be evaluated exactly (it is the number we are approximating), so we must find a number M such that $e^{0.45} \leq M$. Here is one of many ways to obtain a bound: We observe that $e^{0.45} < e^{1/2} < 4^{1/2} = 2$ and take $M = 2$ (Figure 9.12). Therefore, a bound on the remainder is

$$\left|R_6(0.45)\right| \leq 7.4 \times 10^{-7}\,M \approx 1.5 \times 10^{-6}.$$

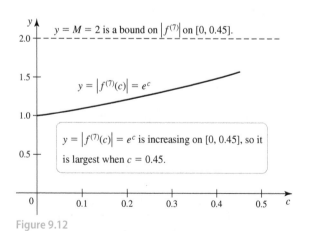

Figure 9.12

▶ Recall that if $f(x) = e^x$, then

$$p_n(x) = \sum_{k=0}^{n} \frac{x^k}{k!}.$$

QUICK CHECK 6 In Example 7, find an approximate upper bound for $R_7(0.45)$. ◀

Using the Taylor polynomial derived in Example 3 with $n = 6$, the resulting approximation to $e^{0.45}$ is

$$p_6(0.45) = \sum_{k=0}^{6} \frac{0.45^k}{k!} \approx 1.5683114;$$

it has an error that does not exceed 1.5×10^{-6}.

Related Exercises 55–60 ◀

EXAMPLE 8   Working with the remainder The nth-order Taylor polynomial for $f(x) = \ln(1 - x)$ centered at 0 is

$$p_n(x) = -\sum_{k=1}^{n} \frac{x^k}{k} = -x - \frac{x^2}{2} - \frac{x^3}{3} - \cdots - \frac{x^n}{n}.$$

a. Find a bound on the error in approximating $\ln(1 - x)$ by $p_3(x)$ for values of x in the interval $\left[-\frac{1}{2}, \frac{1}{2}\right]$.

b. How many terms of the Taylor polynomial are needed to approximate values of $f(x) = \ln(1 - x)$ with an error less than 10^{-3} on the interval $\left[-\frac{1}{2}, \frac{1}{2}\right]$?

SOLUTION

a. The remainder for the Taylor polynomial p_3 is $R_3(x) = \dfrac{f^{(4)}(c)}{4!} x^4$, where c is

between 0 and x. Computing four derivatives of f, we find that $f^{(4)}(x) = -\dfrac{6}{(1 - x)^4}$.

On the interval $\left[-\frac{1}{2}, \frac{1}{2}\right]$, the maximum magnitude of this derivative occurs at $x = \frac{1}{2}$ (because the denominator is smallest at $x = \frac{1}{2}$) and is $6/\left(\frac{1}{2}\right)^4 = 96$. Similarly, the factor x^4 has its maximum magnitude at $x = \pm\frac{1}{2}$ and it is $\left(\frac{1}{2}\right)^4 = \frac{1}{16}$. Therefore,

$$|R_3(x)| \leq \frac{96}{4!}\left(\frac{1}{16}\right) = 0.25 \text{ on the interval } \left[-\frac{1}{2}, \frac{1}{2}\right]. \text{ The error in approximating } f(x)$$

by $p_3(x)$, for $-\frac{1}{2} \leq x \leq \frac{1}{2}$, does not exceed 0.25.

b. For any positive integer n, the remainder is $R_n(x) = \dfrac{f^{(n+1)}(c)}{(n + 1)!} x^{n+1}$. Differentiating f several times reveals that

$$f^{(n+1)}(x) = -\frac{n!}{(1 - x)^{n+1}}.$$

On the interval $\left[-\frac{1}{2}, \frac{1}{2}\right]$, the maximum magnitude of this derivative occurs at $x = \frac{1}{2}$ and is $n!/\left(\frac{1}{2}\right)^{n+1}$. Similarly, x^{n+1} has its maximum magnitude at $x = \pm\frac{1}{2}$, and it is $\left(\frac{1}{2}\right)^{n+1}$. Therefore, a bound on the remainder is

$$|R_n(x)| = \frac{1}{(n + 1)!} \cdot \underbrace{|f^{(n+1)}(c)|}_{\leq\, n!2^{n+1}} \cdot \underbrace{|x|^{n+1}}_{\leq\, \left(\frac{1}{2}\right)^{n+1}}$$

$$\leq \frac{1}{(n + 1)!} \cdot n!2^{n+1} \cdot \frac{1}{2^{n+1}}$$

$$= \frac{1}{n + 1}. \qquad\qquad \frac{n!}{n + 1!} = \frac{1}{n + 1}$$

To ensure that the error is less than 10^{-3} on the entire interval $\left[-\frac{1}{2}, \frac{1}{2}\right]$, n must satisfy $|R_n| \leq \dfrac{1}{n + 1} < 10^{-3}$ or $n > 999$. The error is likely to be significantly less than 10^{-3} if x is near 0.

Related Exercises 61–72 ◀

SECTION 9.1 EXERCISES

Review Questions

1. Suppose you use a second-order Taylor polynomial centered at 0 to approximate a function f. What matching conditions are satisfied by the polynomial?

2. Does the accuracy of an approximation given by a Taylor polynomial generally increase or decrease with the order of the approximation? Explain.

3. The first three Taylor polynomials for $f(x) = \sqrt{1 + x}$ centered at 0 are $p_0(x) = 1$, $p_1(x) = 1 + \dfrac{x}{2}$, and $p_2(x) = 1 + \dfrac{x}{2} - \dfrac{x^2}{8}$. Find three approximations to $\sqrt{1.1}$.

4. In general, how many terms do the Taylor polynomials p_2 and p_3 have in common?

5. How is the remainder $R_n(x)$ in a Taylor polynomial defined?

6. Explain how to estimate the remainder in an approximation given by a Taylor polynomial.

Basic Skills

7–14. Linear and quadratic approximation

a. Find the linear approximating polynomial for the following functions centered at the given point a.
b. Find the quadratic approximating polynomial for the following functions centered at the given point a.
c. Use the polynomials obtained in parts (a) and (b) to approximate the given quantity.

7. $f(x) = 8x^{3/2}$, $a = 1$; approximate $8 \cdot 1.1^{3/2}$.

8. $f(x) = \dfrac{1}{x}$, $a = 1$; approximate $\dfrac{1}{1.05}$.

9. $f(x) = e^{-x}$, $a = 0$; approximate $e^{-0.2}$.

10. $f(x) = \sqrt{x}$, $a = 4$; approximate $\sqrt{3.9}$.

11. $f(x) = (1 + x)^{-1}$, $a = 0$; approximate $\dfrac{1}{1.05}$.

12. $f(x) = \cos x$, $a = \pi/4$; approximate $\cos(0.24\pi)$.

13. $f(x) = x^{1/3}$, $a = 8$; approximate $7.5^{1/3}$.

14. $f(x) = \tan^{-1} x$, $a = 0$; approximate $\tan^{-1} 0.1$.

15–22. Taylor polynomials

a. Find the nth-order Taylor polynomials of the given function centered at 0, for $n = 0, 1,$ and 2.
b. Graph the Taylor polynomials and the function.

15. $f(x) = \cos x$

16. $f(x) = e^{-x}$

17. $f(x) = \ln(1 - x)$

18. $f(x) = (1 + x)^{-1/2}$

19. $f(x) = \tan x$

20. $f(x) = (1 + x)^{-2}$

21. $f(x) = (1 + x)^{-3}$

22. $f(x) = \sin^{-1} x$

23–28. Approximations with Taylor polynomials

a. Use the given Taylor polynomial p_2 to approximate the given quantity.
b. Compute the absolute error in the approximation assuming the exact value is given by a calculator.

23. Approximate $\sqrt{1.05}$ using $f(x) = \sqrt{1 + x}$ and $p_2(x) = 1 + x/2 - x^2/8$.

24. Approximate $\sqrt[3]{1.1}$ using $f(x) = \sqrt[3]{1 + x}$ and $p_2(x) = 1 + x/3 - x^2/9$.

25. Approximate $\dfrac{1}{\sqrt{1.08}}$ using $f(x) = \dfrac{1}{\sqrt{1 + x}}$ and $p_2(x) = 1 - x/2 + 3x^2/8$.

26. Approximate $\ln 1.06$ using $f(x) = \ln(1 + x)$ and $p_2(x) = x - x^2/2$.

27. Approximate $e^{-0.15}$ using $f(x) = e^{-x}$ and $p_2(x) = 1 - x + x^2/2$.

28. Approximate $\dfrac{1}{1.12^3}$ using $f(x) = \dfrac{1}{(1 + x)^3}$ and $p_2(x) = 1 - 3x + 6x^2$.

29–38. Taylor polynomials centered at $a \neq 0$

a. Find the nth-order Taylor polynomials for the following functions centered at the given point a, for $n = 0, 1,$ and 2.
b. Graph the Taylor polynomials and the function.

29. $f(x) = x^3$, $a = 1$

30. $f(x) = 8\sqrt{x}$, $a = 1$

31. $f(x) = \sin x$, $a = \pi/4$

32. $f(x) = \cos x$, $a = \pi/6$

33. $f(x) = \sqrt{x}$, $a = 9$

34. $f(x) = \sqrt[3]{x}$, $a = 8$

35. $f(x) = \ln x$, $a = e$

36. $f(x) = \sqrt[4]{x}$, $a = 16$

37. $f(x) = \tan^{-1} x + x^2 + 1$, $a = 1$

38. $f(x) = e^x$, $a = \ln 2$

39–48. Approximations with Taylor polynomials

a. Approximate the given quantities using Taylor polynomials with $n = 3$.
b. Compute the absolute error in the approximation assuming the exact value is given by a calculator.

39. $e^{0.12}$

40. $\cos(-0.2)$

41. $\tan(-0.1)$

42. $\ln 1.05$

43. $\sqrt{1.06}$

44. $\sqrt[4]{79}$

45. $\sqrt{101}$

46. $\sqrt[3]{126}$

47. $\sinh 0.5$

48. $\tanh 0.5$

49–54. Remainders
Find the remainder R_n for the nth-order Taylor polynomial centered at a for the given functions. Express the result for a general value of n.

49. $f(x) = \sin x$, $a = 0$

50. $f(x) = \cos 2x$, $a = 0$

51. $f(x) = e^{-x}$, $a = 0$

52. $f(x) = \cos x$, $a = \pi/2$

53. $f(x) = \sin x$, $a = \pi/2$

54. $f(x) = 1/(1 - x)$, $a = 0$

55–60. Estimating errors
Use the remainder to find a bound on the error in approximating the following quantities with the nth-order Taylor polynomial centered at 0. Estimates are not unique.

55. $\sin 0.3$, $n = 4$

56. $\cos 0.45$, $n = 3$

57. $e^{0.25}$, $n = 4$

58. $\tan 0.3$, $n = 2$

59. $e^{-0.5}$, $n = 4$

60. $\ln 1.04$, $n = 3$

61–66. Error bounds *Use the remainder to find a bound on the error in the following approximations on the given interval. Error bounds are not unique.*

61. $\sin x \approx x - x^3/6$ on $[-\pi/4, \pi/4]$

62. $\cos x \approx 1 - x^2/2$ on $[-\pi/4, \pi/4]$

63. $e^x \approx 1 + x + x^2/2$ on $\left[-\frac{1}{2}, \frac{1}{2}\right]$

64. $\tan x \approx x$ on $[-\pi/6, \pi/6]$

65. $\ln(1 + x) \approx x - x^2/2$ on $[-0.2, 0.2]$

66. $\sqrt{1 + x} \approx 1 + x/2$ on $[-0.1, 0.1]$

67–72. Number of terms *What is the minimum order of the Taylor polynomial required to approximate the following quantities with an absolute error no greater than 10^{-3}? (The answer depends on your choice of a center.)*

67. $e^{-0.5}$ **68.** $\sin 0.2$ **69.** $\cos(-0.25)$

70. $\ln 0.85$ **71.** $\sqrt{1.06}$ **72.** $1/\sqrt{0.85}$

Further Explorations

73. Explain why or why not Determine whether the following statements are true and give an explanation or counterexample.

 a. Only even powers of x appear in the Taylor polynomials for $f(x) = e^{-2x}$ centered at 0.
 b. Let $f(x) = x^5 - 1$. The Taylor polynomial for f of order 10 centered at 0 is f itself.
 c. Only even powers of x appear in the nth-order Taylor polynomial for $f(x) = \sqrt{1 + x^2}$ centered at 0.
 d. Suppose f'' is continuous on an interval that contains a, where f has an inflection point at a. Then the second-order Taylor polynomial for f at a is linear.

74. Taylor coefficients for $x = a$ Follow the procedure in the text to show that the nth-order Taylor polynomial that matches f and its derivatives up to order n at a has coefficients

$$c_k = \frac{f^{(k)}(a)}{k!}, \text{ for } k = 0, 1, 2, \ldots, n.$$

75. Matching functions with polynomials Match functions a–f with Taylor polynomials A–F (all centered at 0). Give reasons for your choices.

 a. $\sqrt{1 + 2x}$ **A.** $p_2(x) = 1 + 2x + 2x^2$

 b. $\dfrac{1}{\sqrt{1 + 2x}}$ **B.** $p_2(x) = 1 - 6x + 24x^2$

 c. e^{2x} **C.** $p_2(x) = 1 + x - \dfrac{x^2}{2}$

 d. $\dfrac{1}{1 + 2x}$ **D.** $p_2(x) = 1 - 2x + 4x^2$

 e. $\dfrac{1}{(1 + 2x)^3}$ **E.** $p_2(x) = 1 - x + \dfrac{3}{2}x^2$

 f. e^{-2x} **F.** $p_2(x) = 1 - 2x + 2x^2$

76. Dependence of errors on x Consider $f(x) = \ln(1 - x)$ and its Taylor polynomials given in Example 8.

 a. Graph $y = |f(x) - p_2(x)|$ and $y = |f(x) - p_3(x)|$ on the interval $\left[-\frac{1}{2}, \frac{1}{2}\right]$ (two curves).
 b. At what points of $\left[-\frac{1}{2}, \frac{1}{2}\right]$ is the error largest? Smallest?
 c. Are these results consistent with the theoretical error bounds obtained in Example 8?

Applications

77–84. Small argument approximations *Consider the following common approximations when x is near zero.*

 a. Estimate $f(0.1)$ and give a bound on the error in the approximation.
 b. Estimate $f(0.2)$ and give a bound on the error in the approximation.

77. $f(x) = \sin x \approx x$ **78.** $f(x) = \tan x \approx x$

79. $f(x) = \cos x \approx 1 - x^2/2$ **80.** $f(x) = \tan^{-1}x \approx x$

81. $f(x) = \sqrt{1 + x} \approx 1 + x/2$

82. $f(x) = \ln(1 + x) \approx x - x^2/2$

83. $f(x) = e^x \approx 1 + x$ **84.** $f(x) = \sin^{-1}x \approx x$

85. Errors in approximations Suppose you approximate $f(x) = \sec x$ at the points $x = -0.2, -0.1, 0.0, 0.1,$ and 0.2 using the Taylor polynomials $p_2(x) = 1 + x^2/2$ and $p_4(x) = 1 + x^2/2 + 5x^4/24$. Assume that the exact value of $\sec x$ is given by a calculator.

 a. Complete the table showing the absolute errors in the approximations at each point. Show two significant digits.

x	$|\sec x - p_2(x)|$	$|\sec x - p_4(x)|$
-0.2		
-0.1		
0.0		
0.1		
0.2		

 b. In each error column, how do the errors vary with x? For what values of x are the errors largest and smallest in magnitude?

86–89. Errors in approximations *Carry out the procedure described in Exercise 85 with the following functions and Taylor polynomials.*

86. $f(x) = \cos x$, $p_2(x) = 1 - \dfrac{x^2}{2}$, $p_4(x) = 1 - \dfrac{x^2}{2} + \dfrac{x^4}{24}$

87. $f(x) = e^{-x}$, $p_1(x) = 1 - x$, $p_2(x) = 1 - x + \dfrac{x^2}{2}$

88. $f(x) = \ln(1 + x)$, $p_1(x) = x$, $p_2(x) = x - \dfrac{x^2}{2}$

89. $f(x) = \tan x$, $p_1(x) = x$, $p_3(x) = x + \dfrac{x^3}{3}$

90. Best expansion point Suppose you wish to approximate $\cos(\pi/12)$ using Taylor polynomials. Is the approximation more accurate if you use Taylor polynomials centered at 0 or $\pi/6$? Use a calculator for numerical experiments and check for consistency with Theorem 9.2. Does the answer depend on the order of the polynomial?

91. Best expansion point Suppose you wish to approximate $e^{0.35}$ using Taylor polynomials. Is the approximation more accurate if you use Taylor polynomials centered at 0 or $\ln 2$? Use a calculator for numerical experiments and check for consistency with Theorem 9.2. Does the answer depend on the order of the polynomial?

Additional Exercises

92. Proof of Taylor's Theorem There are several proofs of Taylor's Theorem, which lead to various forms of the remainder. The following proof is instructive because it leads to two different forms of the remainder and it relies on the Fundamental Theorem of Calculus, integration by parts, and the Mean Value Theorem for Integrals. Assume that f has at least $n + 1$ continuous derivatives on an interval containing a.

a. Show that the Fundamental Theorem of Calculus can be written in the form

$$f(x) = f(a) + \int_a^x f'(t)\, dt.$$

b. Use integration by parts ($u = f'(t)$, $dv = dt$) to show that

$$f(x) = f(a) + (x - a)f'(a) + \int_a^x (x - t)f''(t)\, dt.$$

c. Show that n integrations by parts gives

$$f(x) = f(a) + \frac{f'(a)}{1!}(x - a) + \frac{f''(a)}{2!}(x - a)^2 + \cdots$$
$$+ \underbrace{\frac{f^{(n)}(a)}{n!}(x - a)^n + \int_a^x \frac{f^{(n+1)}(t)}{n!}(x - t)^n\, dt.}_{R_n(x)}$$

d. *Challenge:* The result in part (c) looks like $f(x) = p_n(x) + R_n(x)$, where p_n is the nth-order Taylor polynomial and R_n is a new form of the remainder, known as the integral form of the remainder. Use the Mean Value Theorem for Integrals (Section 5.4) to show that R_n can be expressed in the form

$$R_n(x) = \frac{f^{(n+1)}(c)}{(n + 1)!}(x - a)^{n+1},$$

where c is between a and x.

93. Tangent line is p_1 Let f be differentiable at $x = a$.

a. Find the equation of the line tangent to the curve $y = f(x)$ at $(a, f(a))$.

b. Verify that the Taylor polynomial p_1 centered at a describes the tangent line found in part (a).

94. Local extreme points and inflection points Suppose f has continuous first and second derivatives at a.

a. Show that if f has a local maximum at a, then the Taylor polynomial p_2 centered at a also has a local maximum at a.

b. Show that if f has a local minimum at a, then the Taylor polynomial p_2 centered at a also has a local minimum at a.

c. Is it true that if f has an inflection point at a, then the Taylor polynomial p_2 centered at a also has an inflection point at a?

d. Are the converses in parts (a) and (b) true? If p_2 has a local extreme point at a, does f have the same type of point at a?

95. Approximating sin x Let $f(x) = \sin x$ and let p_n and q_n be nth-order Taylor polynomials for f centered at 0 and π, respectively.

a. Find p_5 and q_5.

b. Graph f, p_5, and q_5 on the interval $[-\pi, 2\pi]$. On what interval is p_5 a better approximation to f than q_5? On what interval is q_5 a better approximation to f than p_5?

c. Complete the following table showing the errors in the approximations given by p_5 and q_5 at selected points.

x	$|\sin x - p_5(x)|$	$|\sin x - q_5(x)|$
$\pi/4$		
$\pi/2$		
$3\pi/4$		
$5\pi/4$		
$7\pi/4$		

d. At which points in the table is p_5 a better approximation to f than q_5? At which points do p_5 and q_5 give comparable approximations to f? Explain your observations.

96. Approximating ln x Let $f(x) = \ln x$ and let p_n and q_n be the nth-order Taylor polynomials for f centered at 1 and e, respectively.

a. Find p_3 and q_3.

b. Graph f, p_3, and q_3 on the interval $(0, 4]$.

c. Complete the following table showing the errors in the approximations given by p_3 and q_3 at selected points.

x	$|\ln x - p_3(x)|$	$|\ln x - q_3(x)|$
0.5		
1.0		
1.5		
2		
2.5		
3		
3.5		

d. At which points in the table is p_3 a better approximation to f than q_3? Explain your observations.

97. Approximating square roots Let p_1 and q_1 be the first-order Taylor polynomials for $f(x) = \sqrt{x}$ centered at 36 and 49, respectively.

a. Find p_1 and q_1.

b. Complete the following table showing the errors when using p_1 and q_1 to approximate $f(x)$ at $x = 37, 39, 41, 43, 45,$ and 47. Use a calculator to obtain an exact value of $f(x)$.

x	$|\sqrt{x} - p_1(x)|$	$|\sqrt{x} - q_1(x)|$
37		
39		
41		
43		
45		
47		

c. At which points in the table is p_1 a better approximation to f than q_1? Explain this result.

98. A different kind of approximation When approximating a function f using a Taylor polynomial, we use information about f and its derivatives at one point. An alternative approach (called *interpolation*) uses information about f at several different points. Suppose we wish to approximate $f(x) = \sin x$ on the interval $[0, \pi]$.

a. Write the (quadratic) Taylor polynomial p_2 for f centered at $\frac{\pi}{2}$.

b. Now consider a quadratic interpolating polynomial $q(x) = ax^2 + bx + c$. The coefficients a, b, and c are chosen such that the following conditions are satisfied:

$$q(0) = f(0), q\left(\frac{\pi}{2}\right) = f\left(\frac{\pi}{2}\right), \text{ and } q(\pi) = f(\pi).$$

Show that $q(x) = -\frac{4}{\pi^2}x^2 + \frac{4}{\pi}x.$

c. Graph f, p_2, and q on $[0, \pi]$.

d. Find the error in approximating $f(x) = \sin x$ at the points $\frac{\pi}{4}, \frac{\pi}{2}, \frac{3\pi}{4}$, and π using p_2 and q.

e. Which function, p_2 or q, is a better approximation to f on $[0, \pi]$? Explain.

QUICK CHECK ANSWERS

3. $f(x) = \sin x$ is an odd function, and its even-ordered derivatives are zero at 0, so its Taylor polynomials are also odd functions. **4.** $p_4(x) = p_3(x) + \frac{x^4}{4!}; p_5(x) = p_4(x) + \frac{x^5}{5!}$

5. $x = 49$ and $x = 16$ are good choices. **6.** Because $e^{0.45} < 2, |R_7(0.45)| < 2\frac{0.45^8}{8!} \approx 8.3 \times 10^{-8}.$ ◄

9.2 Properties of Power Series

The preceding section demonstrated that Taylor polynomials provide accurate approximations to many functions and that, in general, the approximations improve as the degree of the polynomials increases. In this section, we take the next step and let the degree of the Taylor polynomials increase without bound to produce a *power series*.

Geometric Series as Power Series

A good way to become familiar with power series is to return to *geometric series*, first encountered in Section 8.3. Recall that for a fixed number r,

$$\sum_{k=0}^{\infty} r^k = 1 + r + r^2 + \cdots = \frac{1}{1 - r}, \quad \text{provided } |r| < 1.$$

It's a small change to replace the real number r with the variable x. In doing so, the geometric series becomes a new representation of a familiar function:

$$\sum_{k=0}^{\infty} x^k = 1 + x + x^2 + \cdots = \frac{1}{1 - x}, \quad \text{provided } |x| < 1.$$

This infinite series is a power series and it is a representation of the function $1/(1 - x)$ that is valid on the interval $|x| < 1$.

In general, power series are used to represent familiar functions such as trigonometric, exponential, and logarithmic functions. They are also used to define new functions. For example, consider the function defined by

$$g(x) = \sum_{k=1}^{\infty} \frac{(-1)^k k}{4^k} x^{2k}.$$

The term *function* is used advisedly because it's not yet clear whether g really is a function. If so, is it continuous? Does it have a derivative? Judging by its graph (Figure 9.13), g appears to be an ordinary continuous and differentiable function on $(-2, 2)$ (which is identified at the end of the chapter). In fact, power series satisfy the defining property of all functions: For each admissible value of x, a power series has at most one value. For this reason, we refer to a power series as a function, although the domain, properties, and identity of the function may need to be discovered.

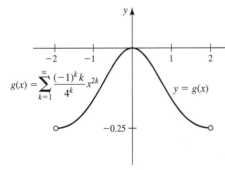

$$g(x) = \sum_{k=1}^{\infty} \frac{(-1)^k k}{4^k} x^{2k}$$

$$y = g(x)$$

Figure 9.13

▶ Figure 9.13 shows an approximation to the graph of g made by summing the first 500 terms of the power series at selected values of x on the interval $(-2, 2)$.

QUICK CHECK 1 By substituting $x = 0$ in the power series for g, evaluate $g(0)$ for the function in Figure 9.13. ◄

Convergence of Power Series

First let's establish some terminology associated with power series.

DEFINITION **Power Series**

A **power series** has the general form

$$\sum_{k=0}^{\infty} c_k (x - a)^k,$$

where a and c_k are real numbers, and x is a variable. The c_k's are the **coefficients** of the power series and a is the **center** of the power series. The set of values of x for which the series converges is its **interval of convergence**. The **radius of convergence** of the power series, denoted R, is the distance from the center of the series to the boundary of the interval of convergence (Figure 9.14).

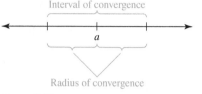

Interval of convergence

a

Radius of convergence

Figure 9.14

How do we determine the interval of convergence for a given power series? The presence of the terms x^k or $(x - a)^k$ in a power series suggests using the Ratio Test or the Root Test. Because these terms could be positive or negative, we test a power series for absolute convergence (remember that the Ratio and Root Tests apply only to series with positive terms). By Theorem 8.21, if we determine the values of x for which the series converges absolutely, we have a set of values for which the series converges.

Before turning to examples, we point out some important facts. Suppose we test the series $\sum a_k$ for absolute convergence using the Ratio Test. If

$$r = \lim_{k \to \infty} \left| \frac{a_{k+1}}{a_k} \right| < 1,$$

it follows that $\sum |a_k|$ converges, which in turn implies that $\sum a_k$ converges (Theorem 8.21). On the other hand, if $r > 1$, then for large k we have $|a_{k+1}| > |a_k|$, which means the terms of the sequence $\{a_k\}$ grow in magnitude as $k \to \infty$. Therefore, $\lim_{k \to \infty} a_k \neq 0$, and we conclude that $\sum a_k$ diverges by the Divergence Test (recall that the Divergence Test applies to *arbitrary* series). If $r = 1$, the Ratio Test is inconclusive, and we use other tests to determine convergence.

A similar argument can be made when using the Root Test to determine the interval of convergence. We first test the series for absolute convergence. When $\rho < 1$, the series converges absolutely (and therefore converges), but when $\rho > 1$, the terms of the series do not tend to 0, so the series diverges by the Divergence Test. If $\rho = 1$, the test is inconclusive, and other tests must be used.

The following examples illustrate how the Ratio and Root Tests are used to determine the interval and radius of convergence.

EXAMPLE 1 **Interval and radius of convergence** Find the interval and radius of convergence for each power series.

a. $\displaystyle\sum_{k=0}^{\infty} \frac{x^k}{k!}$ **b.** $\displaystyle\sum_{k=0}^{\infty} \frac{(-1)^k(x - 2)^k}{4^k}$ **c.** $\displaystyle\sum_{k=1}^{\infty} k!\, x^k$

SOLUTION

a. The center of the power series is 0 and the terms of the series are $x^k/k!$. Due to the presence of the factor $k!$, we test the series for absolute convergence using the Ratio Test:

$$r = \lim_{k \to \infty} \frac{\left| x^{k+1}/(k + 1)! \right|}{\left| x^k/k! \right|} \qquad \text{Ratio Test for absolute convergence}$$

$$= \lim_{k \to \infty} \frac{|x|^{k+1}}{|x|^k} \cdot \frac{k!}{(k + 1)!} \qquad \text{Invert and multiply.}$$

$$= |x| \lim_{k \to \infty} \frac{1}{k + 1} = 0. \qquad \text{Simplify and take the limit with } x \text{ fixed.}$$

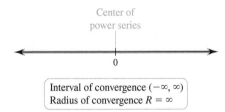

Interval of convergence $(-\infty, \infty)$
Radius of convergence $R = \infty$

Figure 9.15

Notice that in taking the limit as $k \to \infty$, x is held fixed. Because $r = 0$ for all real numbers x, the series converges absolutely for all x. Using Theorem 8.21, we conclude that the series converges for all x. Therefore, the interval of convergence is $(-\infty, \infty)$ (Figure 9.15) and the radius of convergence is $R = \infty$.

b. We test for absolute convergence using the Root Test:

$$\rho = \lim_{k \to \infty} \sqrt[k]{\left| \frac{(-1)^k(x-2)^k}{4^k} \right|} = \frac{|x-2|}{4}.$$

In this case, ρ depends on the value of x. For absolute convergence, x must satisfy

$$\rho = \frac{|x-2|}{4} < 1,$$

which implies that $|x-2| < 4$. Using standard techniques for solving inequalities, the solution set is $-4 < x - 2 < 4$, or $-2 < x < 6$. We conclude that the series converges on $(-2, 6)$ (by Theorem 8.21, absolute convergence implies convergence). When $-\infty < x < -2$ or $6 < x < \infty$, we have $\rho > 1$, so the series diverges on these intervals (the terms of the series do not approach 0 as $k \to \infty$ and the Divergence Test applies).

▶ Either the Ratio Test or the Root Test works for the power series in Example 1b.

The Root Test does not give information about convergence at the endpoints $x = -2$ and $x = 6$, because at these points, the Root Test results in $\rho = 1$. To test for convergence at the endpoints, we substitute each endpoint into the series and carry out separate tests. At $x = -2$, the power series becomes

$$\sum_{k=0}^{\infty} \frac{(-1)^k(x-2)^k}{4^k} = \sum_{k=0}^{\infty} \frac{4^k}{4^k} \quad \text{Substitute } x = -2 \text{ and simplify.}$$

$$= \sum_{k=0}^{\infty} 1. \quad \text{Diverges by Divergence Test}$$

▶ The Ratio and Root Tests determine the radius of convergence conclusively. However, the interval of convergence is not determined until the endpoints are tested.

The series clearly diverges at the left endpoint. At $x = 6$, the power series is

$$\sum_{k=0}^{\infty} \frac{(-1)^k(x-2)^k}{4^k} = \sum_{k=0}^{\infty} (-1)^k \frac{4^k}{4^k} \quad \text{Substitute } x = 6 \text{ and simplify.}$$

$$= \sum_{k=0}^{\infty} (-1)^k. \quad \text{Diverges by Divergence Test}$$

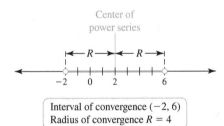

Interval of convergence $(-2, 6)$
Radius of convergence $R = 4$

Figure 9.16

This series also diverges at the right endpoint. Therefore, the interval of convergence is $(-2, 6)$, excluding the endpoints (Figure 9.16), and the radius of convergence is $R = 4$.

c. In this case, the Ratio Test is preferable:

$$r = \lim_{k \to \infty} \frac{|(k+1)! \, x^{k+1}|}{|k! \, x^k|} \quad \text{Ratio Test for absolute convergence}$$

$$= |x| \lim_{k \to \infty} \frac{(k+1)!}{k!} \quad \text{Simplify.}$$

$$= |x| \lim_{k \to \infty} (k+1) \quad \text{Simplify.}$$

$$= \infty. \quad \text{If } x \neq 0$$

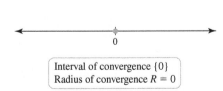

Interval of convergence $\{0\}$
Radius of convergence $R = 0$

Figure 9.17

We see that $r > 1$ for all $x \neq 0$, so the series diverges on $(-\infty, 0)$ and $(0, \infty)$.

The only way to satisfy $r < 1$ is to take $x = 0$, in which case the power series has a value of 0. The interval of convergence of the power series consists of the single point $x = 0$ (Figure 9.17), and the radius of convergence is $R = 0$.

Related Exercises 9–28 ◀

Example 1 illustrates the three common types of intervals of convergence, which are summarized in the following theorem (see Appendix B for a proof).

▶ Theorem 9.3 implies that the interval of convergence is symmetric about the center of the series; the radius of convergence R is determined by analyzing r from the Ratio Test (or ρ from the Root Test). The theorem says nothing about convergence at the endpoints. For example, the intervals of convergence $(2, 6)$, $(2, 6], [2, 6)$, and $[2, 6]$ all have a radius of convergence of $R = 2$.

> **THEOREM 9.3 Convergence of Power Series**
>
> A power series $\sum_{k=0}^{\infty} c_k(x - a)^k$ centered at a converges in one of three ways:
>
> 1. The series converges for all x, in which case the interval of convergence is $(-\infty, \infty)$ and the radius of convergence is $R = \infty$.
>
> 2. There is a real number $R > 0$ such that the series converges for $|x - a| < R$ and diverges for $|x - a| > R$, in which case the radius of convergence is R.
>
> 3. The series converges only at a, in which case the radius of convergence is $R = 0$.

QUICK CHECK 2 What are the interval and radius of convergence of the geometric series $\sum x^k$? ◀

EXAMPLE 2 Interval and radius of convergence Use the Ratio Test to find the radius and interval of convergence of $\sum_{k=1}^{\infty} \dfrac{(x - 2)^k}{\sqrt{k}}$.

▶ The power series in Example 2 could also be analyzed using the Root Test.

SOLUTION

$$
\begin{aligned}
r &= \lim_{k \to \infty} \frac{|(x - 2)^{k+1}/\sqrt{k + 1}|}{|(x - 2)^k/\sqrt{k}|} && \text{Ratio Test for absolute convergence} \\[2mm]
&= |x - 2| \lim_{k \to \infty} \sqrt{\frac{k}{k + 1}} && \text{Simplify.} \\[2mm]
&= |x - 2| \sqrt{\underbrace{\lim_{k \to \infty} \frac{k}{k + 1}}_{1}} && \text{Limit Law} \\[2mm]
&= |x - 2| && \text{Limit equals 1.}
\end{aligned}
$$

The series converges absolutely (and therefore converges) for all x such that $r < 1$, which implies $|x - 2| < 1$, or $1 < x < 3$. On the intervals $-\infty < x < 1$ and $3 < x < \infty$, we have $r > 1$ and the series diverges.

We now test the endpoints. Substituting $x = 1$ gives the series

$$
\sum_{k=1}^{\infty} \frac{(x - 2)^k}{\sqrt{k}} = \sum_{k=1}^{\infty} \frac{(-1)^k}{\sqrt{k}}.
$$

This series converges by the Alternating Series Test (the terms of the series decrease in magnitude and approach 0 as $k \to \infty$). Substituting $x = 3$ gives the series

$$
\sum_{k=1}^{\infty} \frac{(x - 2)^k}{\sqrt{k}} = \sum_{k=1}^{\infty} \frac{1}{\sqrt{k}},
$$

which is a divergent p-series. We conclude that the interval of convergence is $1 \le x < 3$ and the radius of convergence is $R = 1$ (Figure 9.18).

Related Exercises 9–28 ◀

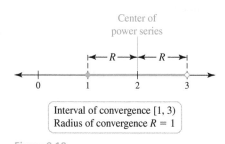

Center of
power series

Interval of convergence $[1, 3)$
Radius of convergence $R = 1$

Figure 9.18

Combining Power Series

A power series defines a function on its interval of convergence. When power series are combined algebraically, new functions are defined. The following theorem, stated without proof, gives three common ways to combine power series.

> ➤ New power series can also be defined as the product and quotient of power series. The calculation of the coefficients of such series is more challenging (Exercise 75).

> ➤ Theorem 9.4 also applies to power series centered at points other than $x = 0$. Property 1 applies directly; Properties 2 and 3 apply with slight modifications.

THEOREM 9.4   Combining Power Series

Suppose the power series $\sum c_k x^k$ and $\sum d_k x^k$ converge to $f(x)$ and $g(x)$, respectively, on an interval I.

1. **Sum and difference:** The power series $\sum (c_k \pm d_k)x^k$ converges to $f(x) \pm g(x)$ on I.

2. **Multiplication by a power:** Suppose m is an integer such that $k + m \geq 0$ for all terms of the power series $x^m \sum c_k x^k = \sum c_k x^{k+m}$. This series converges to $x^m f(x)$ for all $x \neq 0$ in I. When $x = 0$, the series converges to $\lim_{x \to 0} x^m f(x)$.

3. **Composition:** If $h(x) = bx^m$, where m is a positive integer and b is a nonzero real number, the power series $\sum c_k (h(x))^k$ converges to the composite function $f(h(x))$, for all x such that $h(x)$ is in I.

EXAMPLE 3   Combining power series Given the geometric series

$$\frac{1}{1-x} = \sum_{k=0}^{\infty} x^k = 1 + x + x^2 + x^3 + \cdots, \qquad \text{for } |x| < 1,$$

find the power series and interval of convergence for the following functions.

a. $\dfrac{x^5}{1-x}$ **b.** $\dfrac{1}{1-2x}$ **c.** $\dfrac{1}{1+x^2}$

SOLUTION

a.
$$\frac{x^5}{1-x} = x^5 \left(1 + x + x^2 + \cdots \right) \qquad \text{Theorem 9.4, Property 2}$$

$$= x^5 + x^6 + x^7 + \cdots$$

$$= \sum_{k=0}^{\infty} x^{k+5}$$

This geometric series has a ratio $r = x$ and converges when $|r| = |x| < 1$. The interval of convergence is $|x| < 1$.

b. We substitute $2x$ for x in the power series for $\dfrac{1}{1-x}$:

$$\frac{1}{1-2x} = 1 + (2x) + (2x)^2 + \cdots \qquad \text{Theorem 9.4, Property 3}$$

$$= \sum_{k=0}^{\infty} (2x)^k.$$

This geometric series has a ratio $r = 2x$ and converges provided $|r| = |2x| < 1$ or $|x| < \frac{1}{2}$. The interval of convergence is $|x| < \frac{1}{2}$.

c. We substitute $-x^2$ for x in the power series for $\dfrac{1}{1-x}$:

$$\frac{1}{1+x^2} = 1 + (-x^2) + (-x^2)^2 + \cdots \qquad \text{Theorem 9.4, Property 3}$$

$$= 1 - x^2 + x^4 - \cdots$$

$$= \sum_{k=0}^{\infty} (-1)^k x^{2k}.$$

This geometric series has a ratio of $r = -x^2$ and converges provided $|r| = |-x^2| = |x^2| < 1$ or $|x| < 1$.

Related Exercises 29–40 ◀

Differentiating and Integrating Power Series

Some properties of polynomials carry over to power series, but others do not. For example, a polynomial is defined for all values of x, whereas a power series is defined only on its interval of convergence. In general, the properties of polynomials carry over to power series when the power series is restricted to its interval of convergence. The following result illustrates this principle.

> ➤ Theorem 9.5 makes no claim about the convergence of the differentiated or integrated series at the endpoints of the interval of convergence.

THEOREM 9.5   Differentiating and Integrating Power Series

Suppose the power series $\sum c_k(x - a)^k$ converges for $|x - a| < R$ and defines a function f on that interval.

1. Then f is differentiable (which implies continuous) for $|x - a| < R$, and f' is found by differentiating the power series for f term by term; that is,

$$f'(x) = \sum k c_k(x - a)^{k-1},$$

for $|x - a| < R$.

2. The indefinite integral of f is found by integrating the power series for f term by term; that is,

$$\int f(x)\,dx = \sum c_k \frac{(x - a)^{k+1}}{k + 1} + C,$$

for $|x - a| < R$, where C is an arbitrary constant.

The proof of this theorem requires advanced ideas and is omitted. However, some discussion is in order before turning to examples. The statements in Theorem 9.5 about term-by-term differentiation and integration say two things. First, the differentiated and integrated power series converge, provided x belongs to the interior of the interval of convergence. But the theorem claims more than convergence. According to the theorem, the differentiated and integrated power series converge to the derivative and indefinite integral of f, respectively, on the interior of the interval of convergence. Let's use this theorem to develop new power series.

EXAMPLE 4   Differentiating and integrating power series   Consider the geometric series

$$f(x) = \frac{1}{1 - x} = \sum_{k=0}^{\infty} x^k = 1 + x + x^2 + x^3 + \cdots, \quad \text{for } |x| < 1.$$

a. Differentiate this series term by term to find the power series for f' and identify the function it represents.

b. Integrate this series term by term and identify the function it represents.

SOLUTION

a. We know that $f'(x) = (1 - x)^{-2}$. Differentiating the series, we find that

$$f'(x) = \frac{d}{dx}(1 + x + x^2 + x^3 + \cdots) \quad \text{Differentiate the power series for } f.$$

$$= 1 + 2x + 3x^2 + \cdots \quad \text{Differentiate term by term.}$$

$$= \sum_{k=0}^{\infty} (k + 1)\, x^k. \quad \text{Summation notation}$$

Therefore, on the interval $|x| < 1$,

$$f'(x) = (1 - x)^{-2} = \sum_{k=0}^{\infty} (k + 1)\, x^k.$$

Theorem 9.5 makes no claim about convergence of the differentiated series to f' at the endpoints. In this case, substituting $x = \pm 1$ into the power series for f' reveals that the series diverges at both endpoints.

b. Integrating f and integrating the power series term by term, we have

$$\int \frac{dx}{1-x} = \int (1 + x + x^2 + x^3 + \cdots) \, dx,$$

which implies that

$$-\ln|1-x| = x + \frac{x^2}{2} + \frac{x^3}{3} + \frac{x^4}{4} + \cdots + C,$$

where C is an arbitrary constant. Notice that the left side is 0 when $x = 0$. The right side is 0 when $x = 0$ provided we choose $C = 0$. Because $|x| < 1$, the absolute value sign on the left side may be removed. Multiplying both sides by -1, we have a series representation for $\ln(1-x)$:

$$\ln(1-x) = -x - \frac{x^2}{2} - \frac{x^3}{3} - \frac{x^4}{4} - \cdots = -\sum_{k=1}^{\infty} \frac{x^k}{k}.$$

It is interesting to test the endpoints of the interval $|x| < 1$. When $x = 1$, the series is (a multiple of) the divergent harmonic series, and when $x = -1$, the series is the convergent alternating harmonic series (Section 8.6). So the interval of convergence is $-1 \le x < 1$. Although we know the series converges at $x = -1$, Theorem 9.5 guarantees convergence to $\ln(1-x)$ only at the interior points. We cannot use Theorem 9.5 to claim that the series converges to $\ln 2$ at $x = -1$. In fact, it does, as shown in Section 9.3.

Related Exercises 41–46 ◄

QUICK CHECK 3 Use the result of Example 4 to write a series representation for $\ln \frac{1}{2} = -\ln 2$. ◄

EXAMPLE 5 **Functions to power series** Find power series representations centered at 0 for the following functions and give their intervals of convergence.

a. $\tan^{-1} x$ **b.** $\ln\left(\dfrac{1+x}{1-x}\right)$

SOLUTION In both cases, we work with known power series and use differentiation, integration, and other combinations.

a. The key is to recall that

$$\int \frac{dx}{1+x^2} = \tan^{-1} x + C$$

and that, by Example 3c,

$$\frac{1}{1+x^2} = 1 - x^2 + x^4 - \cdots, \qquad \text{provided } |x| < 1.$$

We now integrate both sides of this last expression:

$$\int \frac{dx}{1+x^2} = \int (1 - x^2 + x^4 - \cdots) \, dx,$$

which implies that

$$\tan^{-1} x = x - \frac{x^3}{3} + \frac{x^5}{5} - \cdots + C.$$

Substituting $x = 0$ and noting that $\tan^{-1} 0 = 0$, the two sides of this equation agree provided we choose $C = 0$. Therefore,

$$\tan^{-1} x = x - \frac{x^3}{3} + \frac{x^5}{5} - \cdots = \sum_{k=0}^{\infty} \frac{(-1)^k x^{2k+1}}{2k+1}.$$

▶ Again, Theorem 9.5 does not guarantee that the power series in Example 5a converges to $\tan^{-1} x$ at $x = \pm 1$. In fact, it does.

By Theorem 9.5, this power series converges to $\tan^{-1} x$ for $|x| < 1$. Testing the endpoints separately, we find that it also converges at $x = \pm 1$. Therefore, the interval of convergence is $[-1, 1]$.

b. We have already seen (Example 4) that

$$\ln(1 - x) = -x - \frac{x^2}{2} - \frac{x^3}{3} - \cdots.$$

▶ Nicolaus Mercator (1620–1687) and Sir Isaac Newton (1642–1727) independently derived the power series for $\ln(1 + x)$, which is called the *Mercator series*.

Replacing x with $-x$ (Property 3 of Theorem 9.4), we have

$$\ln(1 - (-x)) = \ln(1 + x) = x - \frac{x^2}{2} + \frac{x^3}{3} - \cdots.$$

Subtracting these two power series gives

$$\ln\left(\frac{1+x}{1-x}\right) = \ln(1+x) - \ln(1-x) \quad \text{Properties of logarithms}$$

$$= \underbrace{\left(x - \frac{x^2}{2} + \frac{x^3}{3} - \cdots\right)}_{\ln(1+x)} - \underbrace{\left(-x - \frac{x^2}{2} - \frac{x^3}{3} - \cdots\right)}_{\ln(1-x)}, \quad \text{for } |x| < 1$$

$$= 2\left(x + \frac{x^3}{3} + \frac{x^5}{5} + \cdots\right) \quad \text{Combine; use Property 1 of Theorem 9.4.}$$

$$= 2\sum_{k=0}^{\infty} \frac{x^{2k+1}}{2k+1}. \quad \text{Summation notation}$$

This power series is the difference of two power series, both of which converge on the interval $|x| < 1$. Therefore, by Theorem 9.4, the new series also converges on $|x| < 1$.

Related Exercises 47–52 ◀

QUICK CHECK 4 Verify that the power series in Example 5b does not converge at the endpoints $x = \pm 1$. ◀

If you look carefully, every example in this section is ultimately based on the geometric series. Using this single series, we were able to develop power series for many other functions. Imagine what we could do with a few more basic power series. The following section accomplishes precisely that end. There, we discover power series for many of the standard functions of calculus.

SECTION 9.2 EXERCISES

Review Questions

1. Write the first four terms of a power series with coefficients $c_0, c_1, c_2,$ and c_3 centered at 0.

2. Write the first four terms of a power series with coefficients $c_0, c_1, c_2,$ and c_3 centered at 3.

3. What tests are used to determine the radius of convergence of a power series?

4. Explain why a power series is tested for *absolute* convergence.

5. Do the interval and radius of convergence of a power series change when the series is differentiated or integrated? Explain.

6. What is the radius of convergence of the power series $\sum c_k (x/2)^k$ if the radius of convergence of $\sum c_k x^k$ is R?

7. What is the interval of convergence of the power series $\sum (4x)^k$?

8. How are the radii of convergence of the power series $\sum c_k x^k$ and $\sum (-1)^k c_k x^k$ related?

Basic Skills

9–28. Interval and radius of convergence *Determine the radius of convergence of the following power series. Then test the endpoints to determine the interval of convergence.*

9. $\sum (2x)^k$

10. $\sum \dfrac{(2x)^k}{k!}$

11. $\sum \dfrac{(x-1)^k}{k}$

12. $\sum \dfrac{(x-1)^k}{k!}$

13. $\sum (kx)^k$

14. $\sum k!\,(x-10)^k$

15. $\sum \sin^k\!\left(\dfrac{1}{k}\right)x^k$

16. $\sum \dfrac{2^k(x-3)^k}{k}$

17. $\sum \left(\dfrac{x}{3}\right)^k$

18. $\sum (-1)^k \dfrac{x^k}{5^k}$

19. $\sum \dfrac{x^k}{k^k}$

20. $\sum (-1)^k \dfrac{k(x-4)^k}{2^k}$

21. $\sum \dfrac{k^2 x^{2k}}{k!}$

22. $\sum k\,(x-1)^k$

23. $\sum \dfrac{x^{2k+1}}{3^{k-1}}$

24. $\sum \left(-\dfrac{x}{10}\right)^{2k}$

25. $\sum \dfrac{(x-1)^k k^k}{(k+1)^k}$

26. $\sum \dfrac{(-2)^k (x+3)^k}{3^{k+1}}$

27. $\sum \dfrac{k^{20} x^k}{(2k+1)!}$

28. $\sum (-1)^k \dfrac{x^{3k}}{27^k}$

29–34. Combining power series *Use the geometric series*

$$f(x) = \frac{1}{1-x} = \sum_{k=0}^{\infty} x^k, \quad \text{for } |x| < 1,$$

to find the power series representation for the following functions (centered at 0). Give the interval of convergence of the new series.

29. $f(3x) = \dfrac{1}{1-3x}$

30. $g(x) = \dfrac{x^3}{1-x}$

31. $h(x) = \dfrac{2x^3}{1-x}$

32. $f(x^3) = \dfrac{1}{1-x^3}$

33. $p(x) = \dfrac{4x^{12}}{1-x}$

34. $f(-4x) = \dfrac{1}{1+4x}$

35–40. Combining power series *Use the power series representation*

$$f(x) = \ln(1-x) = -\sum_{k=1}^{\infty} \frac{x^k}{k}, \quad \text{for } -1 \le x < 1,$$

to find the power series for the following functions (centered at 0). Give the interval of convergence of the new series.

35. $f(3x) = \ln(1-3x)$

36. $g(x) = x^3 \ln(1-x)$

37. $h(x) = x \ln(1-x)$

38. $f(x^3) = \ln(1-x^3)$

39. $p(x) = 2x^6 \ln(1-x)$

40. $f(-4x) = \ln(1+4x)$

41–46. Differentiating and integrating power series *Find the power series representation for g centered at 0 by differentiating or integrating the power series for f (perhaps more than once). Give the interval of convergence for the resulting series.*

41. $g(x) = \dfrac{2}{(1-2x)^2}$ using $f(x) = \dfrac{1}{1-2x}$

42. $g(x) = \dfrac{1}{(1-x)^3}$ using $f(x) = \dfrac{1}{1-x}$

43. $g(x) = \dfrac{1}{(1-x)^4}$ using $f(x) = \dfrac{1}{1-x}$

44. $g(x) = \dfrac{x}{(1+x^2)^2}$ using $f(x) = \dfrac{1}{1+x^2}$

45. $g(x) = \ln(1-3x)$ using $f(x) = \dfrac{1}{1-3x}$

46. $g(x) = \ln(1+x^2)$ using $f(x) = \dfrac{x}{1+x^2}$

47–52. Functions to power series *Find power series representations centered at 0 for the following functions using known power series. Give the interval of convergence for the resulting series.*

47. $f(x) = \dfrac{1}{1+x^2}$

48. $f(x) = \dfrac{1}{1-x^4}$

49. $f(x) = \dfrac{3}{3+x}$

50. $f(x) = \ln\sqrt{1-x^2}$

51. $f(x) = \ln\sqrt{4-x^2}$

52. $f(x) = \tan^{-1}(4x^2)$

Further Explorations

53. Explain why or why not Determine whether the following statements are true and give an explanation or counterexample.

  a. The interval of convergence of the power series $\sum c_k (x-3)^k$ could be $(-2, 8)$.

  b. The series $\sum (-2x)^k$ converges on the interval $-\frac{1}{2} < x \le \frac{1}{2}$.

  c. If $f(x) = \sum c_k x^k$ on the interval $|x| < 1$, then $f(x^2) = \sum c_k x^{2k}$ on the interval $|x| < 1$.

  d. If $f(x) = \sum c_k x^k = 0$, for all x on an interval $(-a, a)$, then $c_k = 0$, for all k.

54. Radius of convergence Find the radius of convergence of

$$\sum \left(1 + \frac{1}{k}\right)^{k^2} x^k.$$

55. Radius of convergence Find the radius of convergence of

$$\sum \frac{k!\,x^k}{k^k}.$$

56–59. Summation notation *Write the following power series in summation (sigma) notation.*

56. $1 + \dfrac{x}{2} + \dfrac{x^2}{4} + \dfrac{x^3}{6} + \cdots$

57. $1 - \dfrac{x}{2} + \dfrac{x^2}{3} - \dfrac{x^3}{4} + \cdots$

58. $x - \dfrac{x^3}{4} + \dfrac{x^5}{9} - \dfrac{x^7}{16} + \cdots$

59. $-\dfrac{x^2}{1!} + \dfrac{x^4}{2!} - \dfrac{x^6}{3!} + \dfrac{x^8}{4!} - \cdots$

60. Scaling power series If the power series $f(x) = \sum c_k x^k$ has an interval of convergence of $|x| < R$, what is the interval of convergence of the power series for $f(ax)$, where $a \ne 0$ is a real number?

61. Shifting power series If the power series $f(x) = \sum c_k x^k$ has an interval of convergence of $|x| < R$, what is the interval of convergence of the power series for $f(x - a)$, where $a \ne 0$ is a real number?

62–67. Series to functions *Find the function represented by the following series and find the interval of convergence of the series. (Not all these series are power series.)*

62. $\sum\limits_{k=0}^{\infty} (x^2 + 1)^{2k}$

63. $\sum\limits_{k=0}^{\infty} (\sqrt{x} - 2)^k$

64. $\sum\limits_{k=1}^{\infty} \dfrac{x^{2k}}{4k}$

65. $\sum\limits_{k=0}^{\infty} e^{-kx}$

66. $\sum\limits_{k=1}^{\infty} \dfrac{(x-2)^k}{3^{2k}}$

67. $\sum\limits_{k=0}^{\infty} \left(\dfrac{x^2-1}{3}\right)^k$

68. A useful substitution Replace x with $x - 1$ in the series

$$\ln(1 + x) = \sum_{k=1}^{\infty} \frac{(-1)^{k+1} x^k}{k}$$ to obtain a power series for $\ln x$

centered at $x = 1$. What is the interval of convergence for the new power series?

69–72. Exponential function *In Section 9.3, we show that the power series for the exponential function centered at 0 is*

$$e^x = \sum_{k=0}^{\infty} \frac{x^k}{k!}, \quad \text{for } -\infty < x < \infty.$$

Use the methods of this section to find the power series for the following functions. Give the interval of convergence for the resulting series.

69. $f(x) = e^{-x}$ **70.** $f(x) = e^{2x}$

71. $f(x) = e^{-3x}$ **72.** $f(x) = x^2 e^x$

Additional Exercises

73. Powers of x multiplied by a power series Prove that if

$$f(x) = \sum_{k=0}^{\infty} c_k x^k$$ converges with radius of convergence R, then

the power series for $x^m f(x)$ also converges with radius of convergence R, for positive integers m.

⊤ 74. Remainders Let

$$f(x) = \sum_{k=0}^{\infty} x^k = \frac{1}{1-x} \quad \text{and} \quad S_n(x) = \sum_{k=0}^{n-1} x^k.$$

The remainder in truncating the power series after n terms is $R_n(x) = f(x) - S_n(x)$, which depends on x.

a. Show that $R_n(x) = x^n/(1-x)$.

b. Graph the remainder function on the interval $|x| < 1$ for $n = 1, 2, 3$. Discuss and interpret the graph. Where on the interval is $|R_n(x)|$ largest? Smallest?

c. For fixed n, minimize $|R_n(x)|$ with respect to x. Does the result agree with the observations in part (b)?

d. Let $N(x)$ be the number of terms required to reduce $|R_n(x)|$ to less than 10^{-6}. Graph the function $N(x)$ on the interval $|x| < 1$. Discuss and interpret the graph.

75. Product of power series Let

$$f(x) = \sum_{k=0}^{\infty} c_k x^k \quad \text{and} \quad g(x) = \sum_{k=0}^{\infty} d_k x^k.$$

a. Multiply the power series together as if they were polynomials, collecting all terms that are multiples of 1, x, and x^2. Write the first three terms of the product $f(x)g(x)$.

b. Find a general expression for the coefficient of x^n in the product series, for $n = 0, 1, 2, \ldots$.

76. Inverse sine Given the power series

$$\frac{1}{\sqrt{1-x^2}} = 1 + \frac{1}{2}x^2 + \frac{1 \cdot 3}{2 \cdot 4}x^4 + \frac{1 \cdot 3 \cdot 5}{2 \cdot 4 \cdot 6}x^6 + \cdots,$$

for $-1 < x < 1$, find the power series for $f(x) = \sin^{-1} x$ centered at 0.

⊤ 77. Computing with power series Consider the following function and its power series:

$$f(x) = \frac{1}{(1-x)^2} = \sum_{k=1}^{\infty} kx^{k-1}, \quad \text{for } -1 < x < 1.$$

a. Let $S_n(x)$ be the sum of the first n terms of the series. With $n = 5$ and $n = 10$, graph $f(x)$ and $S_n(x)$ at the sample points $x = -0.9, -0.8, \ldots, -0.1, 0, 0.1, \ldots, 0.8, 0.9$ (two graphs). Where is the difference in the graphs the greatest?

b. What value of n is needed to guarantee that $|f(x) - S_n(x)| < 0.01$ at all of the sample points?

QUICK CHECK ANSWERS

1. $g(0) = 0$ **2.** $|x| < 1, R = 1$ **3.** Substituting

$x = 1/2, \ln(1/2) = -\ln 2 = -\sum_{k=1}^{\infty} \frac{1}{2^k k}$ ◄

9.3 Taylor Series

In the preceding section, we saw that a power series represents a function on its interval of convergence. This section explores the opposite question: Given a function, what is its power series representation? We have already made significant progress in answering this question because we know how Taylor polynomials are used to approximate functions. We now extend Taylor polynomials to produce power series—called *Taylor series*—that provide series representations for functions.

Taylor Series for a Function

Suppose a function f has derivatives $f^{(k)}(a)$ of *all* orders at the point a. If we write the nth-order Taylor polynomial for f centered at a and allow n to increase indefinitely, a power series is obtained:

$$\underbrace{c_0 + c_1(x - a) + c_2(x - a)^2 + \cdots + c_n(x - a)^n}_{\text{Taylor polynomial of order } n} + \cdots \xrightarrow{n \to \infty} \sum_{k=0}^{\infty} c_k(x - a)^k.$$

The coefficients of the Taylor polynomial are given by

$$c_k = \frac{f^{(k)}(a)}{k!}, \quad \text{for } k = 0, 1, 2, \dots.$$

These coefficients are also the coefficients of the power series, which is called the *Taylor series for f centered at a*. It is the natural extension of the set of Taylor polynomials for f at a. The special case of a Taylor series centered at 0 is called a *Maclaurin series*.

> Maclaurin series are named after the Scottish mathematician Colin Maclaurin (1698–1746), who described them (with credit to Taylor) in a textbook in 1742.

DEFINITION Taylor/Maclaurin Series for a Function

Suppose the function f has derivatives of all orders on an interval centered at the point a. The **Taylor series for f centered at a** is

$$f(a) + f'(a)(x - a) + \frac{f'(a)}{2!}(x - a)^2 + \frac{f^{(3)}(a)}{3!}(x - a)^3 + \cdots$$

$$= \sum_{k=0}^{\infty} \frac{f^{(k)}(a)}{k!}(x - a)^k.$$

A Taylor series centered at 0 is called a **Maclaurin series**.

For the Taylor series to be useful, we need to know two things:

- the values of x for which the Taylor series converges, and
- the values of x for which the Taylor series for f *equals* f.

> There are unusual cases in which the Taylor series for a function converges to a different function (Exercise 90).

The second question is subtle and is postponed for a few pages. For now, we find the Taylor series for f centered at a point, but we refrain from saying $f(x)$ equals the power series.

QUICK CHECK 1 Verify that if the Taylor series for f centered at a is evaluated at $x = a$, then the Taylor series equals $f(a)$. ◄

EXAMPLE 1   Maclaurin series and convergence Find the Maclaurin series (which is the Taylor series centered at 0) for the following functions. Find the interval of convergence.

a. $f(x) = \cos x$ **b.** $f(x) = \dfrac{1}{1 - x}$

SOLUTION The procedure for finding the coefficients of a Taylor series is the same as for Taylor polynomials; most of the work is computing the derivatives of f.

a. The Maclaurin series has the form

$$\sum_{k=0}^{\infty} c_k x^k, \quad \text{where } c_k = \frac{f^{(k)}(0)}{k!}, \quad \text{for } k = 0, 1, 2, \dots.$$

We evaluate derivatives of $f(x) = \cos x$ at $x = 0$.

$$f(x) = \cos x \implies f(0) = 1$$
$$f'(x) = -\sin x \implies f'(0) = 0$$
$$f''(x) = -\cos x \implies f''(0) = -1$$
$$f'''(x) = \sin x \implies f'''(0) = 0$$
$$f^{(4)}(x) = \cos x \implies f^{(4)}(0) = 1$$
$$\vdots \qquad\qquad \vdots$$

> In Example 1a, we note that both cos x and its Maclaurin series are even functions. Be cautions with this observation. A Taylor series for an even function centered at a point different from 0 may be even, odd, or neither. A similar behavior occurs with odd functions.

Because the odd-order derivatives are zero, $c_k = \dfrac{f^{(k)}(0)}{k!} = 0$ when k is odd. Using the even-order derivatives, we have

$$c_0 = f(0) = 1, \qquad c_2 = \frac{f^{(2)}(0)}{2!} = -\frac{1}{2!},$$

$$c_4 = \frac{f^{(4)}(0)}{4!} = \frac{1}{4!}, \qquad c_6 = \frac{f^{(6)}(0)}{6!} = -\frac{1}{6!},$$

and in general, $c_{2k} = \dfrac{(-1)^k}{(2k)!}$. Therefore, the Maclaurin series for f is

$$1 - \frac{x^2}{2!} + \frac{x^4}{4!} - \frac{x^6}{6!} + \cdots = \sum_{k=0}^{\infty} \frac{(-1)^k}{(2k)!} x^{2k}.$$

Notice that this series contains all the Taylor polynomials. In this case, it consists only of even powers of x, reflecting the fact that cos x is an even function.

For what values of x does the series converge? As discussed in Section 9.2, we apply the Ratio Test to $\displaystyle\sum_{k=0}^{\infty} \left| \frac{(-1)^k}{(2k)!} x^{2k} \right|$ to test for absolute convergence:

$$r = \lim_{k \to \infty} \left| \frac{(-1)^{k+1} x^{2(k+1)}/(2(k+1))!}{(-1)^k x^{2k}/(2k)!} \right| \qquad r = \lim_{k \to \infty} \left| \frac{a_{k+1}}{a_k} \right|$$

$$= \lim_{k \to \infty} \left| \frac{x^2}{(2k+2)(2k+1)} \right| = 0. \qquad \text{Simplify and take the limit with } x \text{ fixed.}$$

> Recall that
>
> $$(2k + 2)! = (2k + 2)(2k + 1)(2k)!.$$
>
> Therefore, $\dfrac{(2k)!}{(2k + 2)!} = \dfrac{1}{(2k + 2)(2k + 1)}.$

In this case, $r < 1$ for all x, so the Maclaurin series converges absolutely for all x, which implies (by Theorem 8.21) that the series converges for all x. We conclude that the interval of convergence is $-\infty < x < \infty$.

b. We proceed in a similar way with $f(x) = 1/(1 - x)$ by evaluating the derivatives of f at 0:

$$f(x) = \frac{1}{1 - x} \implies f(0) = 1,$$

$$f'(x) = \frac{1}{(1 - x)^2} \implies f'(0) = 1,$$

$$f''(x) = \frac{2}{(1 - x)^3} \implies f''(0) = 2!,$$

$$f'''(x) = \frac{3 \cdot 2}{(1 - x)^4} \implies f'''(0) = 3!,$$

$$f^{(4)}(x) = \frac{4 \cdot 3 \cdot 2}{(1 - x)^5} \implies f^{(4)}(0) = 4!,$$

and in general, $f^{(k)}(0) = k!$. Therefore, the Maclaurin series coefficients are $c_k = \dfrac{f^{(k)}(0)}{k!} = \dfrac{k!}{k!} = 1$, for $k = 0, 1, 2, \dots$. The series for f centered at 0 is

$$1 + x + x^2 + x^3 + \cdots = \sum_{k=0}^{\infty} x^k.$$

This power series is familiar! The Maclaurin series for $f(x) = 1/(1 - x)$ is a geometric series. We could apply the Ratio Test, but we have already demonstrated that this series converges for $|x| < 1$.

Related Exercises 9–20 ◄

QUICK CHECK 2 Based on Example 1b, what is the Taylor series for $f(x) = (1 + x)^{-1}$? ◄

The preceding example has an important lesson. *There is only one power series representation for a given function about a given point; however, there may be several ways to find it.*

EXAMPLE 2   **Center other than 0** Find the first four nonzero terms of the Taylor series for $f(x) = \sqrt[3]{x}$ centered at 8.

SOLUTION Notice that f has derivatives of all orders at $x = 8$. The Taylor series centered at 8 has the form

$$\sum_{k=0}^{\infty} c_k(x - 8)^k, \quad \text{where } c_k = \frac{f^{(k)}(8)}{k!}.$$

Next, we evaluate derivatives:

$$f(x) = x^{1/3} \Rightarrow f(8) = 2,$$

$$f'(x) = \frac{1}{3}x^{-2/3} \Rightarrow f'(8) = \frac{1}{12},$$

$$f''(x) = -\frac{2}{9}x^{-5/3} \Rightarrow f''(8) = -\frac{1}{144}, \text{ and}$$

$$f'''(x) = \frac{10}{27}x^{-8/3} \Rightarrow f'''(8) = \frac{5}{3456}.$$

We now assemble the power series:

$$2 + \frac{1}{12}(x - 8) + \frac{1}{2!}\left(-\frac{1}{144}\right)(x - 8)^2 + \frac{1}{3!}\left(\frac{5}{3456}\right)(x - 8)^3 + \cdots$$

$$= 2 + \frac{1}{12}(x - 8) - \frac{1}{288}(x - 8)^2 + \frac{5}{20,736}(x - 8)^3 + \cdots.$$

Related Exercises 21–28 ◄

EXAMPLE 3   **Manipulating Maclaurin series** Let $f(x) = e^x$.

a. Find the Maclaurin series for f.

b. Find its interval of convergence.

c. Use the Maclaurin series for e^x to find the Maclaurin series for the functions $x^4 e^x$, e^{-2x}, and e^{-x^2}.

SOLUTION

a. The coefficients of the Taylor polynomials for $f(x) = e^x$ centered at 0 are $c_k = 1/k!$ (Example 3, Section 9.1). They are also the coefficients of the Maclaurin series. Therefore, the Maclaurin series for e^x is

$$1 + \frac{x}{1!} + \frac{x^2}{2!} + \cdots + \frac{x^n}{n!} + \cdots = \sum_{k=0}^{\infty} \frac{x^k}{k!}.$$

b. By the Ratio Test,

$$r = \lim_{k \to \infty} \left| \frac{x^{k+1}/(k + 1)!}{x^k/k!} \right| \quad \text{Substitute } (k + 1)\text{st and } k\text{th terms.}$$

$$= \lim_{k \to \infty} \left| \frac{x}{k + 1} \right| = 0. \quad \text{Simplify; take the limit with } x \text{ fixed.}$$

Because $r < 1$ for all x, the interval of convergence is $-\infty < x < \infty$.

c. As stated in Theorem 9.4, power series may be added, multiplied by powers of x, or composed with functions on their intervals of convergence. Therefore, the Maclaurin series for $x^4 e^x$ is

$$x^4 \sum_{k=0}^{\infty} \frac{x^k}{k!} = \sum_{k=0}^{\infty} \frac{x^{k+4}}{k!} = x^4 + \frac{x^5}{1!} + \frac{x^6}{2!} + \cdots + \frac{x^{k+4}}{k!} + \cdots.$$

Similarly, e^{-2x} is the composition $f(-2x)$. Replacing x with $-2x$ in the Maclaurin series for f, the series representation for e^{-2x} is

$$\sum_{k=0}^{\infty} \frac{(-2x)^k}{k!} = \sum_{k=0}^{\infty} \frac{(-1)^k (2x)^k}{k!} = 1 - 2x + 2x^2 - \frac{4}{3}x^3 + \cdots.$$

The Maclaurin series for e^{-x^2} is obtained by replacing x with $-x^2$ in the power series for f. The resulting series is

$$\sum_{k=0}^{\infty} \frac{(-x^2)^k}{k!} = \sum_{k=0}^{\infty} \frac{(-1)^k x^{2k}}{k!} = 1 - x^2 + \frac{x^4}{2!} - \frac{x^6}{3!} + \cdots.$$

QUICK CHECK 3 Find the first three terms of the Maclaurin series for $2xe^x$ and e^{-x}. ◄

Because the interval of convergence of $f(x) = e^x$ is $-\infty < x < \infty$, the manipulations used to obtain the series for $x^4 e^x$, e^{-2x}, or e^{-x^2} do not change the interval of convergence. If in doubt about the interval of convergence of a new series, apply the Ratio Test.

Related Exercises 29–38 ◄

The Binomial Series

We know from algebra that if p is a positive integer, then $(1 + x)^p$ is a polynomial of degree p. In fact,

$$(1 + x)^p = \binom{p}{0} + \binom{p}{1}x + \binom{p}{2}x^2 + \cdots + \binom{p}{p}x^p,$$

> ▶ For nonnegative integers p and k with $0 \le k \le p$, the binomial coefficients may also be defined as
> $$\binom{p}{k} = \frac{p!}{k!(p-k)!},$$ where $0! = 1$. The coefficients form the rows of Pascal's triangle. The coefficients of $(1 + x)^5$ form the sixth row of the triangle.
>
> $$1$$
> $$1 \quad 1$$
> $$1 \quad 2 \quad 1$$
> $$1 \quad 3 \quad 3 \quad 1$$
> $$1 \quad 4 \quad 6 \quad 4 \quad 1$$
> $$1 \quad 5 \quad 10 \quad 10 \quad 5 \quad 1$$

where the binomial coefficients $\binom{p}{k}$ are defined as follows.

DEFINITION Binomial Coefficients

For real numbers p and integers $k \ge 1$,

$$\binom{p}{k} = \frac{p(p-1)(p-2)\cdots(p-k+1)}{k!}, \qquad \binom{p}{0} = 1.$$

For example,

$$(1 + x)^5 = \underbrace{\binom{5}{0}}_{1} + \underbrace{\binom{5}{1}}_{5}x + \underbrace{\binom{5}{2}}_{10}x^2 + \underbrace{\binom{5}{3}}_{10}x^3 + \underbrace{\binom{5}{4}}_{5}x^4 + \underbrace{\binom{5}{5}}_{1}x^5$$

$$= 1 + 5x + 10x^2 + 10x^3 + 5x^4 + x^5.$$

QUICK CHECK 4 Evaluate the binomial coefficients $\binom{-3}{2}$ and $\binom{\frac{1}{2}}{3}$. ◄

Our goal is to extend this idea to the functions $f(x) = (1 + x)^p$, where $p \neq 0$ is a real number. The result is a Taylor series called the *binomial series*.

> **THEOREM 9.6 Binomial Series**
> For real numbers $p \neq 0$, the Taylor series for $f(x) = (1 + x)^p$ centered at 0 is the **binomial series**
>
> $$\sum_{k=0}^{\infty} \binom{p}{k} x^k = 1 + \sum_{k=1}^{\infty} \frac{p(p-1)(p-2)\cdots(p-k+1)}{k!} x^k$$
>
> $$= 1 + px + \frac{p(p-1)}{2!} x^2 + \frac{p(p-1)(p-2)}{3!} x^3 + \cdots.$$
>
> The series converges for $|x| < 1$ (and possibly at the endpoints, depending on p). If p is a nonnegative integer, the series terminates and results in a polynomial of degree p.

Proof: We seek a power series centered at 0 of the form

$$\sum_{k=0}^{\infty} c_k x^k, \quad \text{where } c_k = \frac{f^{(k)}(0)}{k!}, \quad \text{for } k = 0, 1, 2, \ldots.$$

> To evaluate $\binom{p}{k}$, start with p and successively subtract 1 until k factors are obtained; then take the product of these k factors and divide by $k!$. Recall that $\binom{p}{0} = 1$.

The job is to evaluate the derivatives of f at 0:

$$f(x) = (1 + x)^p \Rightarrow f(0) = 1,$$
$$f'(x) = p(1 + x)^{p-1} \Rightarrow f'(0) = p,$$
$$f''(x) = p(p-1)(1 + x)^{p-2} \Rightarrow f''(0) = p(p-1), \text{ and}$$
$$f'''(x) = p(p-1)(p-2)(1 + x)^{p-3} \Rightarrow f'''(0) = p(p-1)(p-2).$$

A pattern emerges: The kth derivative $f^{(k)}(0)$ involves the k factors $p(p-1)(p-2)\cdots(p-k+1)$. In general, we have

$$f^{(k)}(0) = p(p-1)(p-2)\cdots(p-k+1).$$

Therefore,

$$c_k = \frac{f^{(k)}(0)}{k!} = \frac{p(p-1)(p-2)\cdots(p-k+1)}{k!} = \binom{p}{k}, \quad \text{for } k = 0, 1, 2, \ldots.$$

The Taylor series for $f(x) = (1 + x)^p$ centered at 0 is

$$\binom{p}{0} + \binom{p}{1} x + \binom{p}{2} x^2 + \binom{p}{3} x^3 + \cdots = \sum_{k=0}^{\infty} \binom{p}{k} x^k.$$

This series has the same general form for all values of p. When p is a nonnegative integer, the series terminates and it is a polynomial of degree p.

The interval of convergence for the binomial series is determined by the Ratio Test. Holding p and x fixed, the relevant limit is

$$r = \lim_{k \to \infty} \left| \frac{x^{k+1} p(p-1)\cdots(p-k+1)(p-k)/(k+1)!}{x^k p(p-1)\cdots(p-k+1)/k!} \right| \quad \text{Ratio of } (k+1)\text{st to } k\text{th term}$$

$$= |x| \lim_{k \to \infty} \underbrace{\left| \frac{p-k}{k+1} \right|}_{\text{approaches } 1} \quad \text{Cancel factors and simplify.}$$

$$= |x|. \quad \text{With } p \text{ fixed, } \lim_{k \to \infty} \left| \frac{(p-k)}{k+1} \right| = 1.$$

> In Theorem 9.6, it can be shown that the interval of convergence for the binomial series is
> - $(-1, 1)$ if $p \leq -1$,
> - $(-1, 1]$ if $-1 < p < 0$, and
> - $[-1, 1]$ if $p > 0$ and not an integer.

Absolute convergence requires that $r = |x| < 1$. Therefore, the series converges for $|x| < 1$. Depending on the value of p, the interval of convergence may include the endpoints; see margin note. ◄

➤ A binomial series is a Taylor series. Because the series in Example 4 is centered at 0, it is also a Maclaurin series.

EXAMPLE 4   Binomial series Consider the function $f(x) = \sqrt{1 + x}$.

a. Find the first four terms of the binomial series for f centered at 0.

b. Approximate $\sqrt{1.15}$ to three decimal places. Assume the series for f converges to f on its interval of convergence, which is $[-1, 1]$.

SOLUTION

a. We use the formula for the binomial coefficients with $p = \frac{1}{2}$ to compute the first four coefficients:

$$c_0 = 1, \qquad c_1 = \binom{\frac{1}{2}}{1} = \frac{\left(\frac{1}{2}\right)}{1!} = \frac{1}{2},$$

$$c_2 = \binom{\frac{1}{2}}{2} = \frac{\frac{1}{2}\left(-\frac{1}{2}\right)}{2!} = -\frac{1}{8}, \quad c_3 = \binom{\frac{1}{2}}{3} = \frac{\frac{1}{2}\left(-\frac{1}{2}\right)\left(-\frac{3}{2}\right)}{3!} = \frac{1}{16}.$$

The leading terms of the binomial series are

$$1 + \frac{1}{2}x - \frac{1}{8}x^2 + \frac{1}{16}x^3 - \cdots.$$

Table 9.3

n	Approximation $p_n(0.15)$
0	1.0
1	1.075
2	1.0721875
3	1.072398438

➤ The remainder theorem for alternating series (Section 8.6) could be used in Example 4 to estimate the number of terms of the Maclaurin series needed to achieve a desired accuracy.

b. Truncating the binomial series in part (a) produces Taylor polynomials p_n that may be used to approximate $f(0.15) = \sqrt{1.15}$. With $x = 0.15$, we find the polynomial approximations shown in Table 9.3. Four terms of the power series ($n = 3$) give $\sqrt{1.15} \approx 1.072$. Because the approximations with $n = 2$ and $n = 3$ agree to three decimal places, when rounded, the approximation 1.072 is accurate to three decimal places.

Related Exercises 39–44 ◄

QUICK CHECK 5 Use two and three terms of the binomial series in Example 4 to approximate $\sqrt{1.1}$. ◄

EXAMPLE 5   Working with binomial series Consider the functions

$$f(x) = \sqrt[3]{1 + x} \quad \text{and} \quad g(x) = \sqrt[3]{c + x}, \text{ where } c > 0 \text{ is a constant.}$$

a. Find the first four terms of the binomial series for f centered at 0.

b. Use part (a) to find the first four terms of the binomial series for g centered at 0.

c. Use part (b) to approximate $\sqrt[3]{23}, \sqrt[3]{24}, \ldots, \sqrt[3]{31}$. Assume the series for g converges to g on its interval of convergence.

SOLUTION

a. Because $f(x) = (1 + x)^{1/3}$, we find the binomial coefficients with $p = \frac{1}{3}$.

$$c_0 = \binom{\frac{1}{3}}{0} = 1, \qquad c_1 = \binom{\frac{1}{3}}{1} = \frac{\left(\frac{1}{3}\right)}{1!} = \frac{1}{3},$$

$$c_2 = \binom{\frac{1}{3}}{2} = \frac{\left(\frac{1}{3}\right)\left(\frac{1}{3} - 1\right)}{2!} = -\frac{1}{9}, \quad c_3 = \binom{\frac{1}{3}}{3} = \frac{\left(\frac{1}{3}\right)\left(\frac{1}{3} - 1\right)\left(\frac{1}{3} - 2\right)}{3!} = \frac{5}{81} \cdots$$

The first four terms of the binomial series are

$$1 + \frac{1}{3}x - \frac{1}{9}x^2 + \frac{5}{81}x^3 - \cdots.$$

b. To avoid deriving a new series for $g(x) = \sqrt[3]{c + x}$, a few steps of algebra allow us to use part (a). Note that

$$g(x) = \sqrt[3]{c + x} = \sqrt[3]{c\left(1 + \frac{x}{c}\right)} = \sqrt[3]{c} \cdot \sqrt[3]{1 + \frac{x}{c}} = \sqrt[3]{c} \cdot f\left(\frac{x}{c}\right).$$

In other words, g can be expressed in terms of f, for which we already have a binomial series. The binomial series for g is obtained by substituting x/c into the binomial series for f and multiplying by $\sqrt[3]{c}$:

$$g(x) = \sqrt[3]{c}\underbrace{\left(1 + \frac{1}{3}\left(\frac{x}{c}\right) - \frac{1}{9}\left(\frac{x}{c}\right)^2 + \frac{5}{81}\left(\frac{x}{c}\right)^3 - \cdots\right)}_{f(x/c)}.$$

It can be shown that the series for f in part (a) converges to $f(x)$ for $|x| \le 1$. Therefore, the series for $f(x/c)$ converges to $f(x/c)$ provided $|x/c| \le 1$, or, equivalently, for $|x| \le c$.

c. The series of part (b) may be truncated after four terms to approximate cube roots. For example, note that $\sqrt[3]{29} = \sqrt[3]{\underset{c}{27} + \underset{x}{2}}$, so we take $c = 27$ and $x = 2$.

The choice $c = 27$ is made because 29 is near 27 and $\sqrt[3]{c} = \sqrt[3]{27} = 3$ is easy to evaluate. Substituting $c = 27$ and $x = 2$, we find that

$$\sqrt[3]{29} \approx \sqrt[3]{27}\left(1 + \frac{1}{3}\left(\frac{2}{27}\right) - \frac{1}{9}\left(\frac{2}{27}\right)^2 + \frac{5}{81}\left(\frac{2}{27}\right)^3\right) \approx 3.0723.$$

The same method is used to approximate the cube roots of 23, 24, ..., 30, 31 (Table 9.4). The absolute error is the difference between the approximation and the value given by a calculator. Notice that the errors increase as we move away from 27.

Table 9.4

	Approximation	Absolute Error
$\sqrt[3]{23}$	2.8439	6.7×10^{-5}
$\sqrt[3]{24}$	2.8845	2.0×10^{-5}
$\sqrt[3]{25}$	2.9240	3.9×10^{-6}
$\sqrt[3]{26}$	2.9625	2.4×10^{-7}
$\sqrt[3]{27}$	3	0
$\sqrt[3]{28}$	3.0366	2.3×10^{-7}
$\sqrt[3]{29}$	3.0723	3.5×10^{-6}
$\sqrt[3]{30}$	3.1072	1.7×10^{-5}
$\sqrt[3]{31}$	3.1414	5.4×10^{-5}

Related Exercises 45–56 ◄

Convergence of Taylor Series

It may seem that the story of Taylor series is over. But there is a technical point that is easily overlooked. Given a function f, we know how to write its Taylor series centered at a point a, and we know how to find its interval of convergence. We still do not know that the series actually converges to f. The remaining task is to determine when the Taylor series for f actually converges to f on its interval of convergence. Fortunately, the necessary tools have already been presented in Taylor's Theorem (Theorem 9.1), which gives the remainder for Taylor polynomials.

Assume f has derivatives of *all* orders on an open interval containing the point a. Taylor's Theorem tells us that

$$f(x) = p_n(x) + R_n(x),$$

where p_n is the nth-order Taylor polynomial for f centered at a,

$$R_n(x) = \frac{f^{(n+1)}(c)}{(n+1)!}(x - a)^{n+1}$$

is the remainder, and c is a point between x and a. We see that the remainder, $R_n(x) = f(x) - p_n(x)$, measures the difference between f and the approximating polynomial p_n.

When we say the Taylor series converges to f at a point x, we mean the value of the Taylor series at x equals $f(x)$; that is, $\lim_{n \to \infty} p_n(x) = f(x)$. The following theorem makes these ideas precise.

THEOREM 9.7   Convergence of Taylor Series

Let f have derivatives of all orders on an open interval I containing a. The Taylor series for f centered at a converges to f, for all x in I, if and only if $\lim_{n \to \infty} R_n(x) = 0$, for all x in I, where

$$R_n(x) = \frac{f^{(n+1)}(c)}{(n+1)!}(x-a)^{n+1}$$

is the remainder at x (with c between x and a).

Proof: The theorem requires derivatives of *all* orders. Therefore, by Taylor's Theorem (Theorem 9.1), the remainder exists in the given form for all n. Let p_n denote the nth-order Taylor polynomial and note that $\lim_{n \to \infty} p_n(x)$ is the Taylor series for f centered at a, evaluated at a point x in I.

First, assume that $\lim_{n \to \infty} R_n(x) = 0$ on the interval I and recall that $p_n(x) = f(x) - R_n(x)$. Taking limits of both sides, we have

$$\underbrace{\lim_{n \to \infty} p_n(x)}_{\text{Taylor series}} = \lim_{n \to \infty} (f(x) - R_n(x)) = \underbrace{\lim_{n \to \infty} f(x)}_{f(x)} - \underbrace{\lim_{n \to \infty} R_n(x)}_{0} = f(x).$$

We conclude that the Taylor series $\lim_{n \to \infty} p_n(x)$ equals $f(x)$, for all x in I.

Conversely, if the Taylor series converges to f, then $f(x) = \lim_{n \to \infty} p_n(x)$ and

$$0 = f(x) - \lim_{n \to \infty} p_n(x) = \underbrace{\lim_{n \to \infty} (f(x) - p_n(x))}_{R_n(x)} = \lim_{n \to \infty} R_n(x).$$

It follows that $\lim_{n \to \infty} R_n(x) = 0$, for all x in I.   ◄

Even with an expression for the remainder, it may be difficult to show that $\lim_{n \to \infty} R_n(x) = 0$. The following examples illustrate cases in which it is possible.

EXAMPLE 6   Remainder in the Maclaurin series for e^x Show that the Maclaurin series for $f(x) = e^x$ converges to $f(x)$, for $-\infty < x < \infty$.

SOLUTION As shown in Example 3, the Maclaurin series for $f(x) = e^x$ is

$$\sum_{k=0}^{\infty} \frac{x^k}{k!} = 1 + x + \frac{x^2}{2!} + \cdots + \frac{x^n}{n!} + \cdots,$$

which converges for $-\infty < x < \infty$. In Example 7 of Section 9.1 it was shown that the remainder is

$$R_n(x) = \frac{e^c}{(n+1)!} x^{n+1},$$

where c is between 0 and x. Notice that the intermediate point c varies with n, but it is always between 0 and x. Therefore, e^c is between $e^0 = 1$ and e^x; in fact, $e^c \leq e^{|x|}$, for all n. It follows that

$$|R_n(x)| \leq \frac{e^{|x|}}{(n+1)!} |x|^{n+1}.$$

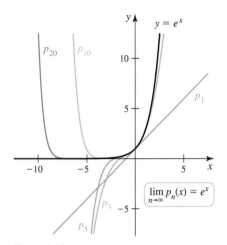

Figure 9.19

Holding x fixed, we have

$$\lim_{n \to \infty} |R_n(x)| = \lim_{n \to \infty} \frac{e^{|x|}}{(n+1)!} |x|^{n+1} = e^{|x|} \lim_{n \to \infty} \frac{|x|^{n+1}}{(n+1)!} = 0,$$

where we used the fact that $\lim_{n \to \infty} x^n/n! = 0$, for $-\infty < x < \infty$ (Section 8.2). Because $\lim_{n \to \infty} |R_n(x)| = 0$, it follows that for all real numbers x, the Taylor series converges to e^x, or

$$e^x = \sum_{k=0}^{\infty} \frac{x^k}{k!} = 1 + x + \frac{x^2}{2!} + \cdots + \frac{x^n}{n!} + \cdots.$$

The convergence of the Taylor series to e^x is illustrated in Figure 9.19, where Taylor polynomials of increasing degree are graphed together with e^x.

Related Exercises 57–60 ◄

EXAMPLE 7   **Maclaurin series convergence for cos x**   Show that the Maclaurin series for $\cos x$,

$$1 - \frac{x^2}{2!} + \frac{x^4}{4!} - \frac{x^6}{6!} + \cdots = \sum_{k=0}^{\infty} (-1)^k \frac{x^{2k}}{(2k)!},$$

converges to $f(x) = \cos x$, for $-\infty < x < \infty$.

SOLUTION   To show that the power series converges to f, we must show that $\lim_{n \to \infty} |R_n(x)| = 0$, for $-\infty < x < \infty$. According to Taylor's Theorem with $a = 0$,

$$R_n(x) = \frac{f^{(n+1)}(c)}{(n+1)!} x^{n+1},$$

where c is between 0 and x. Notice that $f^{(n+1)}(c) = \pm \sin c$ or $f^{(n+1)}(c) = \pm \cos c$. In all cases, $|f^{(n+1)}(c)| \le 1$. Therefore, the absolute value of the remainder term is bounded as

$$|R_n(x)| = \left| \frac{f^{(n+1)}(c)}{(n+1)!} x^{n+1} \right| \le \frac{|x|^{n+1}}{(n+1)!}.$$

Holding x fixed and using $\lim_{n \to \infty} x^n/n! = 0$, we see that $\lim_{n \to \infty} R_n(x) = 0$ for all x. Therefore, the given power series converges to $f(x) = \cos x$, for all x; that is, $\cos x = \sum_{k=0}^{\infty} \frac{(-1)^k x^{2k}}{(2k)!}$. The convergence of the Taylor series to $\cos x$ is illustrated in Figure 9.20.

Related Exercises 57–60 ◄

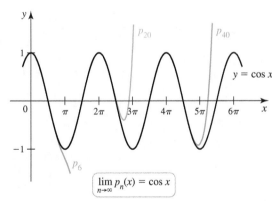

Figure 9.20

The procedure used in Examples 6 and 7 can be carried out for all the Taylor series we have worked with so far (with varying degrees of difficulty). In each case, the Taylor series converges to the function it represents on the interval of convergence. Table 9.5 summarizes commonly used Taylor series centered at 0 and the functions to which they converge.

▶ Table 9.5 asserts, without proof, that in several cases, the Taylor series for f converges to f at the endpoints of the interval of convergence. Proving convergence at the endpoints generally requires advanced techniques. It may also be done using the following theorem:

Suppose the Taylor series for f centered at 0 converges to f on the interval $(-R, R)$. If the series converges at $x = R$, then it converges to $\lim\limits_{x \to R^-} f(x)$. If the series converges at $x = -R$, then it converges to $\lim\limits_{x \to -R^+} f(x)$.

For example, this theorem would allow us to conclude that the series for $\ln(1 + x)$ converges to $\ln 2$ at $x = 1$.

Table 9.5

$$\frac{1}{1 - x} = 1 + x + x^2 + \cdots + x^k + \cdots = \sum_{k=0}^{\infty} x^k, \quad \text{for } |x| < 1$$

$$\frac{1}{1 + x} = 1 - x + x^2 - \cdots + (-1)^k x^k + \cdots = \sum_{k=0}^{\infty} (-1)^k x^k, \quad \text{for } |x| < 1$$

$$e^x = 1 + x + \frac{x^2}{2!} + \cdots + \frac{x^k}{k!} + \cdots = \sum_{k=0}^{\infty} \frac{x^k}{k!}, \quad \text{for } |x| < \infty$$

$$\sin x = x - \frac{x^3}{3!} + \frac{x^5}{5!} - \cdots + \frac{(-1)^k x^{2k+1}}{(2k+1)!} + \cdots = \sum_{k=0}^{\infty} \frac{(-1)^k x^{2k+1}}{(2k+1)!}, \quad \text{for } |x| < \infty$$

$$\cos x = 1 - \frac{x^2}{2!} + \frac{x^4}{4!} - \cdots + \frac{(-1)^k x^{2k}}{(2k)!} + \cdots = \sum_{k=0}^{\infty} \frac{(-1)^k x^{2k}}{(2k)!}, \quad \text{for } |x| < \infty$$

$$\ln(1 + x) = x - \frac{x^2}{2} + \frac{x^3}{3} - \cdots + \frac{(-1)^{k+1} x^k}{k} + \cdots = \sum_{k=1}^{\infty} \frac{(-1)^{k+1} x^k}{k}, \quad \text{for } -1 < x \le 1$$

$$-\ln(1 - x) = x + \frac{x^2}{2} + \frac{x^3}{3} + \cdots + \frac{x^k}{k} + \cdots = \sum_{k=1}^{\infty} \frac{x^k}{k}, \quad \text{for } -1 \le x < 1$$

$$\tan^{-1} x = x - \frac{x^3}{3} + \frac{x^5}{5} - \cdots + \frac{(-1)^k x^{2k+1}}{2k+1} + \cdots = \sum_{k=0}^{\infty} \frac{(-1)^k x^{2k+1}}{2k+1}, \quad \text{for } |x| \le 1$$

$$\sinh x = x + \frac{x^3}{3!} + \frac{x^5}{5!} + \cdots + \frac{x^{2k+1}}{(2k+1)!} + \cdots = \sum_{k=0}^{\infty} \frac{x^{2k+1}}{(2k+1)!}, \quad \text{for } |x| < \infty$$

$$\cosh x = 1 + \frac{x^2}{2!} + \frac{x^4}{4!} + \cdots + \frac{x^{2k}}{(2k)!} + \cdots = \sum_{k=0}^{\infty} \frac{x^{2k}}{(2k)!}, \quad \text{for } |x| < \infty$$

▶ As noted on p. 689, the binomial series may converge to $(1 + x)^p$ at $x = \pm 1$, depending on the value of p.

$$(1 + x)^p = \sum_{k=0}^{\infty} \binom{p}{k} x^k, \text{ for } |x| < 1 \text{ and } \binom{p}{k} = \frac{p(p-1)(p-2)\cdots(p-k+1)}{k!}, \binom{p}{0} = 1$$

SECTION 9.3 EXERCISES

Review Questions

1. How are the Taylor polynomials for a function f centered at a related to the Taylor series for the function f centered at a?

2. What conditions must be satisfied by a function f to have a Taylor series centered at a?

3. How do you find the coefficients of the Taylor series for f centered at a?

4. How do you find the interval of convergence of a Taylor series?

5. Suppose you know the Maclaurin series for f and it converges for $|x| < 1$. How do you find the Maclaurin series for $f(x^2)$ and where does it converge?

6. For what values of p does the Taylor series for $f(x) = (1 + x)^p$ centered at 0 terminate?

7. In terms of the remainder, what does it mean for a Taylor series for a function f to converge to f?

8. Write the Maclaurin series for e^{2x}.

Basic Skills

9–20. Maclaurin series

a. Find the first four nonzero terms of the Maclaurin series for the given function.

b. Write the power series using summation notation.

c. Determine the interval of convergence of the series.

9. $f(x) = e^{-x}$

10. $f(x) = \cos 2x$

11. $f(x) = (1 + x^2)^{-1}$

12. $f(x) = \ln(1 + 4x)$

13. $f(x) = e^{2x}$

14. $f(x) = (1 + 2x)^{-1}$

15. $f(x) = \tan^{-1} \dfrac{x}{2}$

16. $f(x) = \sin 3x$

17. $f(x) = 3^x$

18. $f(x) = \log_3(x + 1)$

19. $f(x) = \cosh 3x$

20. $f(x) = \sinh 2x$

21–28. Taylor series centered at $a \neq 0$

a. Find the first four nonzero terms of the Taylor series for the given function centered at a.

b. Write the power series using summation notation.

21. $f(x) = \sin x, a = \pi/2$ **22.** $f(x) = \cos x, a = \pi$

23. $f(x) = 1/x, a = 1$ **24.** $f(x) = 1/x, a = 2$

25. $f(x) = \ln x, a = 3$ **26.** $f(x) = e^x, a = \ln 2$

27. $f(x) = 2^x, a = 1$ **28.** $f(x) = 10^x, a = 2$

29–38. Manipulating Taylor series *Use the Taylor series in Table 9.5 to find the first four nonzero terms of the Taylor series for the following functions centered at 0.*

29. $\ln(1 + x^2)$ **30.** $\sin x^2$

31. $\dfrac{1}{1 - 2x}$ **32.** $\ln(1 + 2x)$

33. $\begin{cases} \dfrac{e^x - 1}{x} & \text{if } x \neq 0 \\ 1 & \text{if } x = 0 \end{cases}$ **34.** $\cos x^3$

35. $(1 + x^4)^{-1}$ **36.** $x \tan^{-1} x^2$

37. $\sinh x^2$ **38.** $\cosh 3x$

⊤ 39–44. Binomial series

a. Find the first four nonzero terms of the binomial series centered at 0 for the given function.

b. Use the first four nonzero terms of the series to approximate the given quantity.

39. $f(x) = (1 + x)^{-2}$; approximate $1/1.21 = 1/1.1^2$.

40. $f(x) = \sqrt{1 + x}$; approximate $\sqrt{1.06}$.

41. $f(x) = \sqrt[4]{1 + x}$; approximate $\sqrt[4]{1.12}$.

42. $f(x) = (1 + x)^{-3}$; approximate $1/1.331 = 1/1.1^3$.

43. $f(x) = (1 + x)^{-2/3}$; approximate $1.18^{-2/3}$.

44. $f(x) = (1 + x)^{2/3}$; approximate $1.02^{2/3}$.

45–50. Working with binomial series *Use properties of power series, substitution, and factoring to find the first four nonzero terms of the Maclaurin series for the following functions. Give the interval of convergence for the new series (Theorem 9.4 is useful). Use the Maclaurin series*

$$\sqrt{1 + x} = 1 + \frac{x}{2} - \frac{x^2}{8} + \frac{x^3}{16} - \cdots, \quad \text{for } -1 \leq x \leq 1.$$

45. $\sqrt{1 + x^2}$ **46.** $\sqrt{4 + x}$

47. $\sqrt{9 - 9x}$ **48.** $\sqrt{1 - 4x}$

49. $\sqrt{a^2 + x^2}, a > 0$ **50.** $\sqrt{4 - 16x^2}$

51–56. Working with binomial series *Use properties of power series, substitution, and factoring of constants to find the first four nonzero terms of the Maclaurin series for the following functions. Use the Maclaurin series*

$$(1 + x)^{-2} = 1 - 2x + 3x^2 - 4x^3 + \cdots, \quad \text{for } -1 < x < 1.$$

51. $(1 + 4x)^{-2}$ **52.** $\dfrac{1}{(1 - 4x)^2}$

53. $\dfrac{1}{(4 + x^2)^2}$ **54.** $(x^2 - 4x + 5)^{-2}$

55. $\dfrac{1}{(3 + 4x)^2}$ **56.** $\dfrac{1}{(1 + 4x^2)^2}$

57–60. Remainders *Find the remainder in the Taylor series centered at the point a for the following functions. Then show that $\lim_{n \to \infty} R_n(x) = 0$ for all x in the interval of convergence.*

57. $f(x) = \sin x, a = 0$ **58.** $f(x) = \cos 2x, a = 0$

59. $f(x) = e^{-x}, a = 0$ **60.** $f(x) = \cos x, a = \pi/2$

Further Explorations

61. Explain why or why not Determine whether the following statements are true and give an explanation or counterexample.

  a. The function $f(x) = \sqrt{x}$ has a Taylor series centered at 0.

  b. The function $f(x) = \csc x$ has a Taylor series centered at $\pi/2$.

  c. If f has a Taylor series that converges only on $(-2, 2)$, then $f(x^2)$ has a Taylor series that also converges only on $(-2, 2)$.

  d. If $p(x)$ is the Taylor series for f centered at 0, then $p(x - 1)$ is the Taylor series for f centered at 1.

  e. The Taylor series for an even function about 0 has only even powers of x.

62–69. Any method

a. Use any analytical method to find the first four nonzero terms of the Taylor series centered at 0 for the following functions. You do not need to use the definition of the Taylor series coefficients.

b. Determine the radius of convergence of the series.

62. $f(x) = \cos 2x + 2 \sin x$

63. $f(x) = \dfrac{e^x + e^{-x}}{2}$

64. $f(x) = \begin{cases} \dfrac{\sin x}{x} & \text{if } x \neq 0 \\ 1 & \text{if } x = 0 \end{cases}$

65. $f(x) = (1 + x^2)^{-2/3}$

66. $f(x) = x^2 \cos x^2$

67. $f(x) = \sqrt{1 - x^2}$

68. $f(x) = b^x$, for $b > 0, b \neq 1$

69. $f(x) = \dfrac{1}{x^4 + 2x^2 + 1}$

⊤ 70–73. Approximating powers *Compute the coefficients for the Taylor series for the following functions about the given point a and then use the first four terms of the series to approximate the given number.*

70. $f(x) = \sqrt{x}$ with $a = 36$; approximate $\sqrt{39}$.

71. $f(x) = \sqrt[3]{x}$ with $a = 64$; approximate $\sqrt[3]{60}$.

72. $f(x) = 1/\sqrt{x}$ with $a = 4$; approximate $1/\sqrt{3}$.

73. $f(x) = \sqrt[4]{x}$ with $a = 16$; approximate $\sqrt[4]{13}$.

74. Geometric/binomial series Recall that the Taylor series for $f(x) = 1/(1 - x)$ about 0 is the geometric series $\sum_{k=0}^{\infty} x^k$. Show that this series can also be found as a binomial series.

75. Integer coefficients Show that the first five nonzero coefficients of the Taylor series (binomial series) for $f(x) = \sqrt{1 + 4x}$ about 0 are integers. (In fact, *all* the coefficients are integers.)

76. Choosing a good center Suppose you want to approximate $\sqrt{72}$ using four terms of a Taylor series. Compare the accuracy of the approximations obtained using Taylor series for $\sqrt{x}$ centered at 64 and 81.

77. Alternative means By comparing the first four terms, show that the Maclaurin series for $\sin^2 x$ can be found (a) by squaring the Maclaurin series for $\sin x$, (b) by using the identity $\sin^2 x = (1 - \cos 2x)/2$, or (c) by computing the coefficients using the definition.

78. Alternative means By comparing the first four terms, show that the Maclaurin series for $\cos^2 x$ can be found (a) by squaring the Maclaurin series for $\cos x$, (b) by using the identity $\cos^2 x = (1 + \cos 2x)/2$, or (c) by computing the coefficients using the definition.

79. Designer series Find a power series that has $(2, 6)$ as an interval of convergence.

80–81. Patterns in coefficients *Find the next two terms of the following Taylor series.*

80. $\sqrt{1 + x}$: $1 + \dfrac{1}{2}x - \dfrac{1}{2 \cdot 4}x^2 + \dfrac{1 \cdot 3}{2 \cdot 4 \cdot 6}x^3 - \cdots$.

81. $\dfrac{1}{\sqrt{1 + x}}$: $1 - \dfrac{1}{2}x + \dfrac{1 \cdot 3}{2 \cdot 4}x^2 - \dfrac{1 \cdot 3 \cdot 5}{2 \cdot 4 \cdot 6}x^3 + \cdots$.

82. Composition of series Use composition of series to find the first three terms of the Maclaurin series for the following functions.

    a. $e^{\sin x}$ **b.** $e^{\tan x}$ **c.** $\sqrt{1 + \sin^2 x}$

Applications

83–86. Approximations *Choose a Taylor series and center point to approximate the following quantities with an error of 10^{-4} or less.*

83. $\cos 40°$ **84.** $\sin (0.98\pi)$

85. $\sqrt[3]{83}$ **86.** $1/\sqrt[4]{17}$

87. Different approximation strategies Suppose you want to approximate $\sqrt[3]{128}$ to within 10^{-4} of the exact value.

    a. Use a Taylor polynomial for $f(x) = (125 + x)^{1/3}$ centered at 0.

    b. Use a Taylor polynomial for $f(x) = x^{1/3}$ centered at 125.

    c. Compare the two approaches. Are they equivalent?

Additional Exercises

88. Mean Value Theorem Explain why the Mean Value Theorem (Theorem 4.9 of Section 4.6) is a special case of Taylor's Theorem.

89. Version of the Second Derivative Test Assume that f has at least two continuous derivatives on an interval containing a with $f'(a) = 0$. Use Taylor's Theorem to prove the following version of the Second Derivative Test.

    a. If $f''(x) > 0$ on some interval containing a, then f has a local minimum at a.

    b. If $f''(x) < 0$ on some interval containing a, then f has a local maximum at a.

90. Nonconvergence to f Consider the function

$$f(x) = \begin{cases} e^{-1/x^2} & \text{if } x \neq 0 \\ 0 & \text{if } x = 0. \end{cases}$$

    a. Use the definition of the derivative to show that $f'(0) = 0$.

    b. Assume the fact that $f^{(k)}(0) = 0$, for $k = 1, 2, 3, \ldots$. (You can write a proof using the definition of the derivative.) Write the Taylor series for f centered at 0.

    c. Explain why the Taylor series for f does not converge to f for $x \neq 0$.

QUICK CHECK ANSWERS

1. When evaluated at $x = a$, all terms of the series are zero except the first term, which is $f(a)$. Therefore, the series equals $f(a)$ at this point.   **2.** $1 - x + x^2 - x^3 + x^4 - \cdots$ **3.** $2x + 2x^2 + x^3$; $1 - x + x^2/2$ **4.** $6, 1/16$ **5.** $1.05, 1.04875$ ◄

9.4 Working with Taylor Series

We now know the Taylor series for many familiar functions, and we have tools for working with power series. The goal of this final section is to illustrate additional techniques associated with power series. As you will see, power series cover the entire landscape of calculus from limits and derivatives to integrals and approximation. We present five different topics that you can explore selectively.

Limits by Taylor Series

An important use of Taylor series is evaluating limits. Two examples illustrate the essential ideas.

> ▶ L'Hôpital's Rule may be impractical when it must be used more than once on the same limit or when derivatives are difficult to compute.

EXAMPLE 1   A limit by Taylor series Evaluate $\lim\limits_{x \to 0} \dfrac{x^2 + 2 \cos x - 2}{3x^4}$.

SOLUTION Because the limit has the indeterminate form $0/0$, l'Hôpital's Rule can be used, which requires four applications of the rule. Alternatively, because the limit involves values of x near 0, we substitute the Maclaurin series for $\cos x$. Recalling that

$$\cos x = 1 - \frac{x^2}{2} + \frac{x^4}{24} - \frac{x^6}{720} + \cdots, \quad \text{Table 9.5, page 694}$$

we have

> ▶ In using series to evaluate limits, it is often not obvious how many terms of the Taylor series to use. When in doubt, include extra (higher-order) terms. The dots in the calculation stand for powers of x greater than the last power that appears.

$$\lim_{x \to 0} \frac{x^2 + 2 \cos x - 2}{3x^4} = \lim_{x \to 0} \frac{x^2 + 2\left(1 - \dfrac{x^2}{2} + \dfrac{x^4}{24} - \dfrac{x^6}{720} + \cdots\right) - 2}{3x^4} \quad \text{Substitute for } \cos x.$$

$$= \lim_{x \to 0} \frac{x^2 + \left(2 - x^2 + \dfrac{x^4}{12} - \dfrac{x^6}{360} + \cdots\right) - 2}{3x^4} \quad \text{Simplify.}$$

$$= \lim_{x \to 0} \frac{\dfrac{x^4}{12} - \dfrac{x^6}{360} + \cdots}{3x^4} \quad \text{Simplify.}$$

$$= \lim_{x \to 0} \left(\frac{1}{36} - \frac{x^2}{1080} + \cdots\right) = \frac{1}{36}. \quad \begin{array}{l}\text{Use Theorem 9.4,}\\ \text{Property 2;}\\ \text{evaluate limit.}\end{array}$$

Related Exercises 7–24 ◀

QUICK CHECK 1 Use the Taylor series $\sin x = x - x^3/6 + \cdots$ to verify that $\lim\limits_{x \to 0} (\sin x)/x = 1$. ◀

EXAMPLE 2   A limit by Taylor series Evaluate

$$\lim_{x \to \infty} \left(6x^5 \sin \frac{1}{x} - 6x^4 + x^2\right).$$

SOLUTION A Taylor series may be centered at any finite point in the domain of the function, but we don't have the tools needed to expand a function about $x = \infty$. Using a technique introduced earlier, we replace x with $1/t$ and note that as $x \to \infty$, $t \to 0^+$. The new limit becomes

$$\lim_{x \to \infty} \left(6x^5 \sin \frac{1}{x} - 6x^4 + x^2\right) = \lim_{t \to 0^+} \left(\frac{6 \sin t}{t^5} - \frac{6}{t^4} + \frac{1}{t^2}\right) \quad \text{Replace } x \text{ with } 1/t.$$

$$= \lim_{t \to 0^+} \left(\frac{6 \sin t - 6t + t^3}{t^5}\right). \quad \text{Common denominator}$$

This limit has the indeterminate form $0/0$. We now expand $\sin t$ in a Taylor series centered at $t = 0$. Because

$$\sin t = t - \frac{t^3}{6} + \frac{t^5}{120} - \frac{t^7}{5040} + \cdots, \quad \text{Table 9.5, page 694}$$

the value of the original limit is

$$\lim_{t \to 0^+} \left(\frac{6 \sin t - 6t + t^3}{t^5} \right)$$

$$= \lim_{t \to 0^+} \left(\frac{6\left(t - \frac{t^3}{6} + \frac{t^5}{120} - \frac{t^7}{5040} + \cdots \right) - 6t + t^3}{t^5} \right) \quad \text{Substitute for } \sin t.$$

$$= \lim_{t \to 0^+} \left(\frac{\frac{t^5}{20} - \frac{t^7}{840} + \cdots}{t^5} \right) \quad \text{Simplify.}$$

$$= \lim_{t \to 0^+} \left(\frac{1}{20} - \frac{t^2}{840} + \cdots \right) = \frac{1}{20}. \quad \text{Use Theorem 9.4,}$$
Property 2; evaluate limit.

Related Exercises 7–24 ◄

Differentiating Power Series

The following examples illustrate ways in which term-by-term differentiation (Theorem 9.5) may be used.

EXAMPLE 3 Power series for derivatives Differentiate the Maclaurin series for $f(x) = \sin x$ to verify that $\dfrac{d}{dx}(\sin x) = \cos x$.

SOLUTION The Maclaurin series for $f(x) = \sin x$ is

$$\sin x = x - \frac{x^3}{3!} + \frac{x^5}{5!} - \frac{x^7}{7!} + \cdots,$$

and it converges for $-\infty < x < \infty$. By Theorem 9.5, the differentiated series also converges for $-\infty < x < \infty$ and it converges to $f'(x)$. Differentiating, we have

$$\frac{d}{dx}\left(x - \frac{x^3}{3!} + \frac{x^5}{5!} - \frac{x^7}{7!} + \cdots \right) = 1 - \frac{x^2}{2!} + \frac{x^4}{4!} - \frac{x^6}{6!} + \cdots = \cos x.$$

QUICK CHECK 2 Differentiate the power series for $\cos x$ (given in Example 3) and identify the result. ◄

The differentiated series is the Maclaurin series for $\cos x$, confirming that $f'(x) = \cos x$.

Related Exercises 25–32 ◄

EXAMPLE 4 A differential equation Find a power series solution of the differential equation $y'(t) = y + 2$, subject to the initial condition $y(0) = 6$. Identify the function represented by the power series.

SOLUTION Because the initial condition is given at $t = 0$, we assume the solution has a Taylor series centered at 0 of the form $y(t) = \displaystyle\sum_{k=0}^{\infty} c_k t^k$, where the coefficients c_k must be determined. Recall that the coefficients of the Taylor series are given by

$$c_k = \frac{y^{(k)}(0)}{k!}, \quad \text{for } k = 0, 1, 2, \ldots.$$

If we can determine $y^{(k)}(0)$, for $k = 0, 1, 2, \ldots$, the coefficients of the series are also determined.

Substituting the initial condition $t = 0$ and $y = 6$ into the power series

$$y(t) = c_0 + c_1 t + c_2 t^2 + \cdots,$$

we find that

$$6 = c_0 + c_1 (0) + c_2 (0)^2 + \cdots.$$

It follows that $c_0 = 6$. To determine $y'(0)$, we substitute $t = 0$ into the differential equation; the result is $y'(0) = y(0) + 2 = 6 + 2 = 8$. Therefore, $c_1 = y'(0)/1! = 8$.

The remaining derivatives are obtained by successively differentiating the differential equation and substituting $t = 0$. We find that $y''(0) = y'(0) = 8$, $y'''(0) = y''(0) = 8$, and in general, $y^{(k)}(0) = 8$, for $k = 2, 3, 4, \ldots$. Therefore,

$$c_k = \frac{y^{(k)}(0)}{k!} = \frac{8}{k!}, \quad \text{for } k = 1, 2, 3, \ldots,$$

and the Taylor series for the solution is

$$y(t) = c_0 + c_1 t + c_2 t^2 + \cdots$$

$$= 6 + \frac{8}{1!}t + \frac{8}{2!}t^2 + \frac{8}{3!}t^3 + \cdots.$$

To identify the function represented by this series, we write

$$y(t) = \underbrace{-2 + 8}_{6} + \frac{8}{1!}t + \frac{8}{2!}t^2 + \frac{8}{3!}t^3 + \cdots$$

$$= -2 + 8\underbrace{\left(1 + t + \frac{t^2}{2!} + \frac{t^3}{3!} + \cdots\right)}_{e^t}.$$

The power series that appears is the Taylor series for e^t. Therefore, the solution is $y = -2 + 8e^t$.

> You should check that $y(t) = -2 + 8e^t$ satisfies $y'(t) = y + 2$ and $y(0) = 6$.

Related Exercises 33–36 ◄

Integrating Power Series

The following example illustrates the use of power series in approximating integrals that cannot be evaluated by analytical methods.

EXAMPLE 5 Approximating a definite integral Approximate the value of the integral $\int_0^1 e^{-x^2}\, dx$ with an error no greater than 5×10^{-4}.

SOLUTION The antiderivative of e^{-x^2} cannot be expressed in terms of familiar functions. The strategy is to write the Maclaurin series for e^{-x^2} and integrate it term by term. Recall that integration of a power series is valid within its interval of convergence (Theorem 9.5). Beginning with the Maclaurin series

$$e^x = 1 + x + \frac{x^2}{2!} + \frac{x^3}{3!} + \cdots + \frac{x^n}{n!} + \cdots,$$

which converges for $-\infty < x < \infty$, we replace x with $-x^2$ to obtain

$$e^{-x^2} = 1 - x^2 + \frac{x^4}{2!} - \frac{x^6}{3!} + \cdots + \frac{(-1)^n x^{2n}}{n!} + \cdots,$$

which also converges for $-\infty < x < \infty$. By the Fundamental Theorem of Calculus,

$$\int_0^1 e^{-x^2}\, dx = \left(x - \frac{x^3}{3} + \frac{x^5}{5\cdot 2!} - \frac{x^7}{7\cdot 3!} + \cdots + \frac{(-1)^n x^{2n+1}}{(2n+1)n!} + \cdots\right)\Bigg|_0^1$$

$$= 1 - \frac{1}{3} + \frac{1}{5\cdot 2!} - \frac{1}{7\cdot 3!} + \cdots + \frac{(-1)^n}{(2n+1)n!} + \cdots.$$

> The integral in Example 5 is important in statistics and probability theory because of its relationship to the *normal distribution*.

Because the definite integral is expressed as an alternating series, the magnitude of the remainder in truncating the series after n terms is less than the magnitude of the first neglected term, which is $\left|\dfrac{(-1)^{n+1}}{(2n+3)(n+1)!}\right|$. By trial and error, we find that the magnitude of

this term is less than 5×10^{-4} if $n \geq 5$ (with $n = 5$, we have $\dfrac{1}{13 \cdot 6!} \approx 1.07 \times 10^{-4}$).
The sum of the terms of the series up to $n = 5$ gives the approximation

$$\int_0^1 e^{-x^2}\, dx \approx 1 - \frac{1}{3} + \frac{1}{5 \cdot 2!} - \frac{1}{7 \cdot 3!} + \frac{1}{9 \cdot 4!} - \frac{1}{11 \cdot 5!} \approx 0.747.$$

Related Exercises 37–44 ◄

Representing Real Numbers

When values of x are substituted into a convergent power series, the result may be a series representation of a familiar real number. The following example illustrates some techniques.

EXAMPLE 6   Evaluating infinite series

a. Use the Maclaurin series for $f(x) = \tan^{-1} x$ to evaluate

$$1 - \frac{1}{3} + \frac{1}{5} - \cdots = \sum_{k=0}^{\infty} \frac{(-1)^k}{2k + 1}.$$

b. Let $f(x) = (e^x - 1)/x$, for $x \neq 0$, and $f(0) = 1$. Use the Maclaurin series for f to evaluate $f'(1)$ and $\displaystyle\sum_{k=1}^{\infty} \frac{k}{(k + 1)!}$.

SOLUTION

> ► The series in Example 6a (known as the *Gregory series*) is one of a multitude of series representations of π. Because this series converges slowly, it does not provide an efficient way to approximate π.

a. From Table 9.5 (page 694), we see that for $|x| \leq 1$,

$$\tan^{-1} x = x - \frac{x^3}{3} + \frac{x^5}{5} - \cdots + \frac{(-1)^k x^{2k+1}}{2k + 1} + \cdots = \sum_{k=0}^{\infty} \frac{(-1)^k x^{2k+1}}{2k + 1}.$$

Substituting $x = 1$, we have

$$\tan^{-1} 1 = 1 - \frac{1^3}{3} + \frac{1^5}{5} - \cdots = \sum_{k=0}^{\infty} \frac{(-1)^k}{2k + 1}.$$

Because $\tan^{-1} 1 = \pi/4$, the value of the series is $\pi/4$.

b. Using the Maclaurin series for e^x, the series for $f(x) = (e^x - 1)/x$ is

$$f(x) = \frac{e^x - 1}{x} = \frac{1}{x}\left(\left(1 + x + \frac{x^2}{2!} + \frac{x^3}{3!} + \cdots\right) - 1\right) \quad \text{Substitute series for } e^x.$$

$$= 1 + \frac{x}{2!} + \frac{x^2}{3!} + \frac{x^3}{4!} + \cdots = \sum_{k=1}^{\infty} \frac{x^{k-1}}{k!}, \quad \text{Theorem 9.4, Property 2}$$

which converges for $-\infty < x < \infty$. By the Quotient Rule,

$$f'(x) = \frac{xe^x - (e^x - 1)}{x^2}.$$

Differentiating the series for f term by term (Theorem 9.5), we find that

$$f'(x) = \frac{d}{dx}\left(1 + \frac{x}{2!} + \frac{x^2}{3!} + \frac{x^3}{4!} + \cdots\right)$$

$$= \frac{1}{2!} + \frac{2x}{3!} + \frac{3x^2}{4!} + \cdots = \sum_{k=1}^{\infty} \frac{kx^{k-1}}{(k + 1)!}.$$

We now have two expressions for f'; they are evaluated at $x = 1$ to show that

> **QUICK CHECK 3** What value of x would you substitute into the Maclaurin series for $\tan^{-1} x$ to obtain a series representation for $\pi/6$? ◄

$$f'(1) = 1 = \sum_{k=1}^{\infty} \frac{k}{(k + 1)!}.$$

Related Exercises 45–54 ◄

Representing Functions as Power Series

Power series have a fundamental role in mathematics in defining functions and providing alternative representations of familiar functions. As an overall review, we close this chapter with two examples that use many techniques for working with power series.

EXAMPLE 7 **Identify the series** Identify the function represented by the power series $\sum_{k=0}^{\infty} \frac{(1-2x)^k}{k!}$ and give its interval of convergence.

SOLUTION The Maclaurin series for the exponential function,

$$e^x = \sum_{k=0}^{\infty} \frac{x^k}{k!},$$

converges for $-\infty < x < \infty$. Replacing x with $1-2x$ produces the given series:

$$\sum_{k=0}^{\infty} \frac{(1-2x)^k}{k!} = e^{1-2x}.$$

This replacement is allowed because $1-2x$ is within the interval of convergence of the series for e^x; that is, $-\infty < 1-2x < \infty$, for all x. Therefore, the given series represents e^{1-2x}, for $-\infty < x < \infty$. *Related Exercises 55–64* ◄

EXAMPLE 8 **Mystery series** The power series $\sum_{k=1}^{\infty} \frac{(-1)^k k}{4^k} x^{2k}$ appeared in the opening of Section 9.2. Determine the interval of convergence of the power series and find the function it represents on this interval.

SOLUTION Applying the Ratio Test to the series, we determine that it converges when $|x^2/4| < 1$, which implies that $|x| < 2$. A quick check of the endpoints of the original series confirms that it diverges at $x = \pm 2$. Therefore, the interval of convergence is $|x| < 2$.

To find the function represented by the series, we apply several maneuvers until we obtain a geometric series. First note that

$$\sum_{k=1}^{\infty} \frac{(-1)^k k}{4^k} x^{2k} = \sum_{k=1}^{\infty} k\left(-\frac{1}{4}\right)^k x^{2k}.$$

The series on the right is not a geometric series because of the presence of the factor k. The key is to realize that k could appear in this way through differentiation; specifically, something like $\frac{d}{dx}(x^{2k}) = 2kx^{2k-1}$. To achieve terms of this form, we write

$$\underbrace{\sum_{k=1}^{\infty} \frac{(-1)^k k}{4^k} x^{2k}}_{\text{original series}} = \sum_{k=1}^{\infty} k\left(-\frac{1}{4}\right)^k x^{2k}$$

$$= \frac{1}{2}\sum_{k=1}^{\infty} 2k\left(-\frac{1}{4}\right)^k x^{2k} \quad \text{Multiply and divide by 2.}$$

$$= \frac{x}{2}\sum_{k=1}^{\infty} 2k\left(-\frac{1}{4}\right)^k x^{2k-1}. \quad \text{Remove } x \text{ from the series.}$$

Now we identify the last series as the derivative of another series:

$$\underbrace{\sum_{k=1}^{\infty} \frac{(-1)^k k}{4^k} x^{2k}}_{\text{original series}} = \frac{x}{2}\sum_{k=1}^{\infty}\left(-\frac{1}{4}\right)^k \underbrace{2kx^{2k-1}}_{\frac{d}{dx}(x^{2k})}$$

$$= \frac{x}{2}\sum_{k=1}^{\infty}\left(-\frac{1}{4}\right)^k \frac{d}{dx}(x^{2k}) \quad \text{Identify a derivative.}$$

$$= \frac{x}{2}\frac{d}{dx}\left(\sum_{k=1}^{\infty}\left(-\frac{x^2}{4}\right)^k\right). \quad \text{Combine factors; differentiate term by term.}$$

This last series is a geometric series with a ratio $r = -x^2/4$ and first term $-x^2/4$; therefore, its value is $\dfrac{-x^2/4}{1 + (x^2/4)}$, provided $\left|\dfrac{x^2}{4}\right| < 1$, or $|x| < 2$. We now have

$$\underbrace{\sum_{k=1}^{\infty} \frac{(-1)^k k}{4^k} x^{2k}}_{\text{original series}} = \frac{x}{2} \frac{d}{dx}\left(\sum_{k=1}^{\infty}\left(-\frac{x^2}{4}\right)^k\right)$$

$$= \frac{x}{2} \frac{d}{dx}\left(\frac{-x^2/4}{1 + (x^2/4)}\right) \qquad \text{Sum of geometric series}$$

$$= \frac{x}{2} \frac{d}{dx}\left(\frac{-x^2}{4 + x^2}\right) \qquad \text{Simplify.}$$

$$= -\frac{4x^2}{(4 + x^2)^2}. \qquad \text{Differentiate and simplify.}$$

Therefore, the function represented by the power series on $(-2, 2)$ has been uncovered; it is

$$f(x) = -\frac{4x^2}{(4 + x^2)^2}.$$

Notice that f is defined for $-\infty < x < \infty$ (Figure 9.21), but its power series centered at 0 converges to f only on $(-2, 2)$.

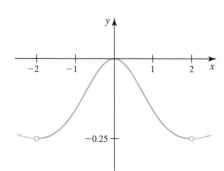

$$\sum_{k=1}^{\infty} \frac{(-1)^k k}{4^k} x^{2k} = -\frac{4x^2}{(4 + x^2)^2} \text{ on } (-2, 2)$$

Figure 9.21

Related Exercises 55–64 ◀

SECTION 9.4 EXERCISES

Review Questions

1. Explain the strategy presented in this section for evaluating a limit of the form $\lim\limits_{x \to a} f(x)/g(x)$, where f and g have Taylor series centered at a.

2. Explain the method presented in this section for approximating $\int_a^b f(x)\,dx$, where f has a Taylor series with an interval of convergence centered at a that includes b.

3. How would you approximate $e^{-0.6}$ using the Taylor series for e^x?

4. Suggest a Taylor series and a method for approximating π.

5. If $f(x) = \sum\limits_{k=0}^{\infty} c_k x^k$ and the series converges for $|x| < b$, what is the power series for $f'(x)$?

6. What condition must be met by a function f for it to have a Taylor series centered at a?

Basic Skills

7–24. Limits *Evaluate the following limits using Taylor series.*

7. $\lim\limits_{x \to 0} \dfrac{e^x - 1}{x}$

8. $\lim\limits_{x \to 0} \dfrac{\tan^{-1} x - x}{x^3}$

9. $\lim\limits_{x \to 0} \dfrac{-x - \ln(1 - x)}{x^2}$

10. $\lim\limits_{x \to 0} \dfrac{\sin 2x}{x}$

11. $\lim\limits_{x \to 0} \dfrac{e^x - e^{-x}}{x}$

12. $\lim\limits_{x \to 0} \dfrac{1 + x - e^x}{4x^2}$

13. $\lim\limits_{x \to 0} \dfrac{2 \cos 2x - 2 + 4x^2}{2x^4}$

14. $\lim\limits_{x \to \infty} x \sin \dfrac{1}{x}$

15. $\lim\limits_{x \to 0} \dfrac{\ln(1 + x) - x + x^2/2}{x^3}$

16. $\lim\limits_{x \to 4} \dfrac{x^2 - 16}{\ln(x - 3)}$

17. $\lim\limits_{x \to 0} \dfrac{3 \tan^{-1} x - 3x + x^3}{x^5}$

18. $\lim\limits_{x \to 0} \dfrac{\sqrt{1 + x} - 1 - (x/2)}{4x^2}$

19. $\lim\limits_{x \to 0} \dfrac{12x - 8x^3 - 6 \sin 2x}{x^5}$

20. $\lim\limits_{x \to 1} \dfrac{x - 1}{\ln x}$

21. $\lim\limits_{x \to 2} \dfrac{x - 2}{\ln(x - 1)}$

22. $\lim\limits_{x \to \infty} x(e^{1/x} - 1)$

23. $\lim\limits_{x \to 0} \dfrac{e^{-2x} - 4e^{-x/2} + 3}{2x^2}$

24. $\lim\limits_{x \to 0} \dfrac{(1 - 2x)^{-1/2} - e^x}{8x^2}$

25–32. Power series for derivatives

a. *Differentiate the Taylor series about 0 for the following functions.*
b. *Identify the function represented by the differentiated series.*
c. *Give the interval of convergence of the power series for the derivative.*

25. $f(x) = e^x$

26. $f(x) = \cos x$

27. $f(x) = \ln(1 + x)$

28. $f(x) = \sin x^2$

29. $f(x) = e^{-2x}$

30. $f(x) = (1 - x)^{-1}$

31. $f(x) = \tan^{-1} x$

32. $f(x) = -\ln(1 - x)$

33–36. Differential equations

a. *Find a power series for the solution of the following differential equations, subject to the given initial condition.*
b. *Identify the function represented by the power series.*

33. $y'(t) - y = 0$, $y(0) = 2$

34. $y'(t) + 4y = 8$, $y(0) = 0$

35. $y'(t) - 3y = 10$, $y(0) = 2$

36. $y'(t) = 6y + 9$, $y(0) = 2$

■ **37–44. Approximating definite integrals** *Use a Taylor series to approximate the following definite integrals. Retain as many terms as needed to ensure the error is less than* 10^{-4}.

37. $\displaystyle\int_0^{0.25} e^{-x^2}\, dx$

38. $\displaystyle\int_0^{0.2} \sin x^2\, dx$

39. $\displaystyle\int_{-0.35}^{0.35} \cos 2x^2\, dx$

40. $\displaystyle\int_0^{0.2} \sqrt{1 + x^4}\, dx$

41. $\displaystyle\int_0^{0.35} \tan^{-1} x\, dx$

42. $\displaystyle\int_0^{0.4} \ln(1 + x^2)\, dx$

43. $\displaystyle\int_0^{0.5} \frac{dx}{\sqrt{1 + x^6}}$

44. $\displaystyle\int_0^{0.2} \frac{\ln(1 + t)}{t}\, dt$

45–50. Approximating real numbers *Use an appropriate Taylor series to find the first four nonzero terms of an infinite series that is equal to the following numbers.*

45. e^2

46. $\sqrt{e}$

47. $\cos 2$

48. $\sin 1$

49. $\ln \frac{3}{2}$

50. $\tan^{-1} \frac{1}{2}$

51. Evaluating an infinite series Let $f(x) = (e^x - 1)/x$, for $x \neq 0$, and $f(0) = 1$. Use the Taylor series for f about 0 and evaluate $f(1)$ to find the value of $\displaystyle\sum_{k=0}^{\infty} \frac{1}{(k + 1)!}$.

52. Evaluating an infinite series Let $f(x) = (e^x - 1)/x$, for $x \neq 0$, and $f(0) = 1$. Use the Taylor series for f and f' about 0 to evaluate $f'(2)$ to find the value of $\displaystyle\sum_{k=1}^{\infty} \frac{k\, 2^{k-1}}{(k + 1)!}$.

53. Evaluating an infinite series Write the Taylor series for $f(x) = \ln(1 + x)$ about 0 and find its interval of convergence. Assume the Taylor series converges to f on the interval of convergence. Evaluate $f(1)$ to find the value of $\displaystyle\sum_{k=1}^{\infty} \frac{(-1)^{k+1}}{k}$ (the alternating harmonic series).

54. Evaluating an infinite series Write the Maclaurin series for $f(x) = \ln(1 + x)$ and find the interval of convergence. Evaluate $f(-\frac{1}{2})$ to find the value of $\displaystyle\sum_{k=1}^{\infty} \frac{1}{k \cdot 2^k}$.

55–64. Representing functions by power series *Identify the functions represented by the following power series.*

55. $\displaystyle\sum_{k=0}^{\infty} \frac{x^k}{2^k}$

56. $\displaystyle\sum_{k=0}^{\infty} (-1)^k \frac{x^k}{3^k}$

57. $\displaystyle\sum_{k=0}^{\infty} (-1)^k \frac{x^{2k}}{4^k}$

58. $\displaystyle\sum_{k=0}^{\infty} 2^k x^{2k+1}$

59. $\displaystyle\sum_{k=1}^{\infty} \frac{x^k}{k}$

60. $\displaystyle\sum_{k=0}^{\infty} \frac{(-1)^k x^{k+1}}{4^k}$

61. $\displaystyle\sum_{k=1}^{\infty} (-1)^k \frac{k x^{k+1}}{3^k}$

62. $\displaystyle\sum_{k=1}^{\infty} \frac{x^{2k}}{k}$

63. $\displaystyle\sum_{k=2}^{\infty} \frac{k(k - 1) x^k}{3^k}$

64. $\displaystyle\sum_{k=2}^{\infty} \frac{x^k}{k(k - 1)}$

Further Explorations

65. Explain why or why not Determine whether the following statements are true and give an explanation or counterexample.

    a. To evaluate $\displaystyle\int_0^2 \frac{dx}{1 - x}$, one could expand the integrand in a Taylor series and integrate term by term.

    b. To approximate $\pi/3$, one could substitute $x = \sqrt{3}$ into the Taylor series for $\tan^{-1} x$.

    c. $\displaystyle\sum_{k=0}^{\infty} \frac{(\ln 2)^k}{k!} = 2$.

66–68. Limits with a parameter *Use Taylor series to evaluate the following limits. Express the result in terms of the parameter(s).*

66. $\displaystyle\lim_{x \to 0} \frac{e^{ax} - 1}{x}$

67. $\displaystyle\lim_{x \to 0} \frac{\sin ax}{\sin bx}$

68. $\displaystyle\lim_{x \to 0} \frac{\sin ax - \tan^{-1} ax}{bx^3}$

69. A limit by Taylor series Use Taylor series to evaluate $\displaystyle\lim_{x \to 0} \left(\frac{\sin x}{x}\right)^{1/x^2}$.

70. Inverse hyperbolic sine The *inverse hyperbolic sine* is defined in several ways; among them are

$$\sinh^{-1} x = \ln\left(x + \sqrt{x^2 + 1}\right) = \int_0^x \frac{dt}{\sqrt{1 + t^2}}.$$

Find the first four terms of the Taylor series for $\sinh^{-1} x$ using these two definitions (and be sure they agree).

71–74. Derivative trick *Here is an alternative way to evaluate higher derivatives of a function f that may save time. Suppose you can find the Taylor series for f centered at the point a without evaluating derivatives (for example, from a known series). Explain why $f^{(k)}(a) = k!$ multiplied by the coefficient of $(x - a)^k$. Use this idea to evaluate $f^{(3)}(0)$ and $f^{(4)}(0)$ for the following functions. Use known series and do not evaluate derivatives.*

71. $f(x) = e^{\cos x}$

72. $f(x) = \dfrac{x^2 + 1}{\sqrt[3]{1 + x}}$

73. $f(x) = \displaystyle\int_0^x \sin t^2\, dt$

74. $f(x) = \displaystyle\int_0^x \frac{1}{1 + t^4}\, dt$

Applications

75. Probability: tossing for a head The expected (average) number of tosses of a fair coin required to obtain the first head is $\displaystyle\sum_{k=1}^{\infty} k(\frac{1}{2})^k$. Evaluate this series and determine the expected number of tosses. (*Hint:* Differentiate a geometric series.)

76. Probability: sudden death playoff Teams A and B go into sudden death overtime after playing to a tie. The teams alternate possession of the ball, and the first team to score wins. Each team has a $\frac{1}{6}$ chance of scoring when it has the ball, with Team A having the ball first.

    a. The probability that Team A ultimately wins is $\displaystyle\sum_{k=0}^{\infty} \frac{1}{6}(\frac{5}{6})^{2k}$. Evaluate this series.

    b. The expected number of rounds (possessions by either team) required for the overtime to end is $\displaystyle\frac{1}{6}\sum_{k=1}^{\infty} k(\frac{5}{6})^{k-1}$. Evaluate this series.

■ **77. Elliptic integrals** The period of a pendulum is given by

$$T = 4\sqrt{\frac{\ell}{g}} \int_0^{\pi/2} \frac{d\theta}{\sqrt{1 - k^2 \sin^2 \theta}} = 4\sqrt{\frac{\ell}{g}}\, F(k),$$

where ℓ is the length of the pendulum, $g \approx 9.8 \text{ m/s}^2$ is the acceleration due to gravity, $k = \sin(\theta_0/2)$, and θ_0 is the initial angular displacement of the pendulum (in radians). The integral in this formula $F(k)$ is called an *elliptic integral*, and it cannot be evaluated analytically.

a. Approximate $F(0.1)$ by expanding the integrand in a Taylor (binomial) series and integrating term by term.
b. How many terms of the Taylor series do you suggest using to obtain an approximation to $F(0.1)$ with an error less than 10^{-3}?
c. Would you expect to use fewer or more terms (than in part (b)) to approximate $F(0.2)$ to the same accuracy? Explain.

78. Sine integral function The function $\text{Si}(x) = \int_0^x \frac{\sin t}{t}\,dt$ is called the *sine integral function*.

a. Expand the integrand in a Taylor series about 0.
b. Integrate the series to find a Taylor series for Si.
c. Approximate $\text{Si}(0.5)$ and $\text{Si}(1)$. Use enough terms of the series so the error in the approximation does not exceed 10^{-3}.

79. Fresnel integrals The theory of optics gives rise to the two *Fresnel integrals*

$$S(x) = \int_0^x \sin t^2\,dt \quad \text{and} \quad C(x) = \int_0^x \cos t^2\,dt.$$

a. Compute $S'(x)$ and $C'(x)$.
b. Expand $\sin t^2$ and $\cos t^2$ in a Maclaurin series and then integrate to find the first four nonzero terms of the Maclaurin series for S and C.
c. Use the polynomials in part (b) to approximate $S(0.05)$ and $C(-0.25)$.
d. How many terms of the Maclaurin series are required to approximate $S(0.05)$ with an error no greater than 10^{-4}?
e. How many terms of the Maclaurin series are required to approximate $C(-0.25)$ with an error no greater than 10^{-6}?

80. Error function An essential function in statistics and the study of the normal distribution is the *error function*

$$\text{erf}(x) = \frac{2}{\sqrt{\pi}} \int_0^x e^{-t^2}\,dt.$$

a. Compute the derivative of $\text{erf}(x)$.
b. Expand e^{-t^2} in a Maclaurin series; then integrate to find the first four nonzero terms of the Maclaurin series for erf.
c. Use the polynomial in part (b) to approximate $\text{erf}(0.15)$ and $\text{erf}(-0.09)$.
d. Estimate the error in the approximations of part (c).

81. Bessel functions Bessel functions arise in the study of wave propagation in circular geometries (for example, waves on a circular drum head). They are conveniently defined as power series. One of an infinite family of Bessel functions is

$$J_0(x) = \sum_{k=0}^{\infty} \frac{(-1)^k}{2^{2k}(k!)^2} x^{2k}.$$

a. Write out the first four terms of J_0.
b. Find the radius and interval of convergence of the power series for J_0.
c. Differentiate J_0 twice and show (by keeping terms through x^6) that J_0 satisfies the equation $x^2 y''(x) + x y'(x) + x^2 y(x) = 0$.

Additional Exercises

82. Power series for sec x Use the identity $\sec x = \dfrac{1}{\cos x}$ and long division to find the first three terms of the Maclaurin series for $\sec x$.

83. Symmetry

a. Use infinite series to show that $\cos x$ is an even function. That is, show $\cos(-x) = \cos x$.
b. Use infinite series to show that $\sin x$ is an odd function. That is, show $\sin(-x) = -\sin x$.

84. Behavior of csc x We know that $\lim\limits_{x \to 0^+} \csc x = \infty$. Use long division to determine exactly how $\csc x$ grows as $x \to 0^+$. Specifically, find a, b, and c (all positive) in the following sentence: As $x \to 0^+$, $\csc x \approx \dfrac{a}{x^b} + cx$.

85. L'Hôpital's Rule by Taylor series Suppose f and g have Taylor series about the point a.

a. If $f(a) = g(a) = 0$ and $g'(a) \neq 0$, evaluate $\lim\limits_{x \to a} f(x)/g(x)$ by expanding f and g in their Taylor series. Show that the result is consistent with l'Hôpital's Rule.
b. If $f(a) = g(a) = f'(a) = g'(a) = 0$ and $g''(a) \neq 0$, evaluate $\lim\limits_{x \to a} \dfrac{f(x)}{g(x)}$ by expanding f and g in their Taylor series. Show that the result is consistent with two applications of l'Hôpital's Rule.

86. Newton's derivation of the sine and arcsine series Newton discovered the binomial series and then used it ingeniously to obtain many more results. Here is a case in point.

a. Referring to the figure, show that $x = \sin s$ or $s = \sin^{-1} x$.
b. The area of a circular sector of radius r subtended by an angle θ is $\frac{1}{2} r^2 \theta$. Show that the area of the circular sector APE is $s/2$, which implies that

$$s = 2 \int_0^x \sqrt{1 - t^2}\,dt - x\sqrt{1 - x^2}.$$

c. Use the binomial series for $f(x) = \sqrt{1 - x^2}$ to obtain the first few terms of the Taylor series for $s = \sin^{-1} x$.
d. Newton next inverted the series in part (c) to obtain the Taylor series for $x = \sin s$. He did this by assuming that $\sin s = \sum a_k s^k$ and solving $x = \sin(\sin^{-1} x)$ for the coefficients a_k. Find the first few terms of the Taylor series for $\sin s$ using this idea (a computer algebra system might be helpful as well).

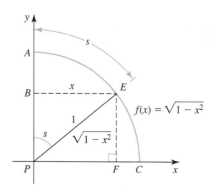

1. $\dfrac{\sin x}{x} = \dfrac{x - x^3/3! + \cdots}{x} = 1 - \dfrac{x^2}{3!} + \cdots \to 1$ as $x \to 0$

2. The result is the power series for $-\sin x$.   3. $x = 1/\sqrt{3}$ (which lies in the interval of convergence) ◄

CHAPTER 9   REVIEW EXERCISES

1. **Explain why or why not** Determine whether the following statements are true and give an explanation or counterexample.

   a. Let p_n be the nth-order Taylor polynomial for f centered at 2. The approximation $p_3(2.1) \approx f(2.1)$ is likely to be more accurate than the approximation $p_2(2.2) \approx f(2.2)$.

   b. If the Taylor series for f centered at 3 has a radius of convergence of 6, then the interval of convergence is $[-3, 9]$.

   c. The interval of convergence of the power series $\sum c_k x^k$ could be $\left(-\frac{7}{3}, \frac{7}{3}\right)$.

   d. The Maclaurin series for $f(x) = (1 + x)^{12}$ has a finite number of nonzero terms.

2–9. Taylor polynomials *Find the nth-order Taylor polynomial for the following functions centered at the given point a.*

2. $f(x) = \sin 2x, n = 3, a = 0$

3. $f(x) = \cos x^2, n = 2, a = 0$

4. $f(x) = e^{-x}, n = 2, a = 0$

5. $f(x) = \ln(1 + x), n = 3, a = 0$

6. $f(x) = \cos x, n = 2, a = \pi/4$

7. $f(x) = \ln x, n = 2, a = 1$

8. $f(x) = \sinh 2x, n = 4, a = 0$

9. $f(x) = \cosh x, n = 3, a = \ln 2$

10–13. Approximations

   a. Find the Taylor polynomials of order $n = 0, 1,$ and 2 for the given functions centered at the given point a.

   b. Make a table showing the approximations and the absolute error in these approximations using a calculator for the exact function value.

10. $f(x) = \cos x, a = 0$; approximate $\cos(-0.08)$.

11. $f(x) = e^x, a = 0$; approximate $e^{-0.08}$.

12. $f(x) = \sqrt{1 + x}, a = 0$; approximate $\sqrt{1.08}$.

13. $f(x) = \sin x, a = \pi/4$; approximate $\sin(\pi/5)$.

14–16. Estimating remainders *Find the remainder term $R_n(x)$ for the Taylor series centered at 0 for the following functions. Find an upper bound for the magnitude of the remainder on the given interval for the given value of n. (The bound is not unique.)*

14. $f(x) = e^x$; bound $R_3(x)$, for $|x| < 1$.

15. $f(x) = \sin x$; bound $R_3(x)$, for $|x| < \pi$.

16. $f(x) = \ln(1 - x)$; bound $R_3(x)$, for $|x| < 1/2$.

17–24. Radius and interval of convergence *Use the Ratio or Root Test to determine the radius of convergence of the following power series. Test the endpoints to determine the interval of convergence, when appropriate.*

17. $\sum \dfrac{k^2 x^k}{k!}$

18. $\sum \dfrac{x^{4k}}{k^2}$

19. $\sum (-1)^k \dfrac{(x + 1)^{2k}}{k!}$

20. $\sum \dfrac{(x - 1)^k}{k \cdot 5^k}$

21. $\sum \left(\dfrac{x}{9}\right)^{3k}$

22. $\sum \dfrac{(x + 2)^k}{\sqrt{k}}$

23. $\sum \dfrac{(x + 2)^k}{2^k \ln k}$

24. $x + \dfrac{x^3}{3} + \dfrac{x^5}{5} + \dfrac{x^7}{7} + \cdots$

25–30. Power series from the geometric series *Use the geometric series $\sum\limits_{k=0}^{\infty} x^k = \dfrac{1}{1 - x}$, for $|x| < 1$, to determine the Maclaurin series and the interval of convergence for the following functions.*

25. $f(x) = \dfrac{1}{1 - x^2}$

26. $f(x) = \dfrac{1}{1 + x^3}$

27. $f(x) = \dfrac{1}{1 + 5x}$

28. $f(x) = \dfrac{10x}{1 + x}$

29. $f(x) = \dfrac{1}{(1 - 10x)^2}$

30. $f(x) = \ln(1 - 4x)$

31–38. Taylor series *Write out the first three nonzero terms of the Taylor series for the following functions centered at the given point a. Then write the series using summation notation.*

31. $f(x) = e^{3x}, a = 0$

32. $f(x) = 1/x, a = 1$

33. $f(x) = \cos x, a = \pi/2$

34. $f(x) = \dfrac{x^2}{1 + x}, a = 0$

35. $f(x) = \tan^{-1} 4x, a = 0$

36. $f(x) = \sin 2x, a = -\pi/2$

37. $f(x) = \cosh 3x, a = 0$

38. $f(x) = \dfrac{1}{4 + x^2}, a = 0$

39–42. Binomial series *Write out the first three terms of the Maclaurin series for the following functions.*

39. $f(x) = (1 + x)^{1/3}$

40. $f(x) = (1 + x)^{-1/2}$

41. $f(x) = (1 + x/2)^{-3}$

42. $f(x) = (1 + 2x)^{-5}$

43–46. Convergence *Write the remainder term $R_n(x)$ for the Taylor series for the following functions centered at the given point a. Then show that $\lim\limits_{n \to \infty} |R_n(x)| = 0$, for all x in the given interval.*

43. $f(x) = e^{-x}, a = 0, -\infty < x < \infty$

44. $f(x) = \sin x, a = 0, -\infty < x < \infty$

45. $f(x) = \ln(1 + x), a = 0, -\frac{1}{2} \le x \le \frac{1}{2}$

46. $f(x) = \sqrt{1 + x}, a = 0, -\frac{1}{2} \le x \le \frac{1}{2}$

47–52. Limits by power series *Use Taylor series to evaluate the following limits.*

47. $\lim\limits_{x \to 0} \dfrac{x^2/2 - 1 + \cos x}{x^4}$

48. $\lim\limits_{x \to 0} \dfrac{2 \sin x - \tan^{-1} x - x}{2x^5}$

49. $\lim\limits_{x \to 4} \dfrac{\ln(x - 3)}{x^2 - 16}$

50. $\displaystyle\lim_{x\to 0}\frac{\sqrt{1+2x}-1-x}{x^2}$

51. $\displaystyle\lim_{x\to 0}\frac{\sec x-\cos x-x^2}{x^4}$ $\left(\textit{Hint: The Maclaurin series for } \sec x \textit{ is}\right.$
$\left.1+\dfrac{x^2}{2}+\dfrac{5x^4}{24}+\dfrac{61x^6}{720}+\cdots.\right)$

52. $\displaystyle\lim_{x\to 0}\frac{(1+x)^{-2}-\sqrt[3]{1-6x}}{2x^2}$

■ 53–56. Definite integrals by power series *Use a Taylor series to approximate the following definite integrals. Retain as many terms as necessary to ensure the error is less than* 10^{-3}.

53. $\displaystyle\int_0^{1/2} e^{-x^2}\,dx$ **54.** $\displaystyle\int_0^{1/2}\tan^{-1}x\,dx$

55. $\displaystyle\int_0^1 x\cos x\,dx$ **56.** $\displaystyle\int_0^{1/2}x^2\tan^{-1}x\,dx$

■ 57–60. Approximating real numbers *Use an appropriate Taylor series to find the first four nonzero terms of an infinite series that is equal to the following numbers. There is more than one way to choose the center of the series.*

57. $\sqrt{119}$ **58.** $\sin 20°$

59. $\tan^{-1}\left(-\frac{1}{3}\right)$ **60.** $\sinh(-1)$

61. A differential equation Find a power series solution of the differential equation $y'(x)-4y+12=0$, subject to the condition $y(0)=4$. Identify the solution in terms of known functions.

■ 62. Rejected quarters The probability that a random quarter is *not* rejected by a vending machine is given by the integral

$11.4\int_0^{0.14}e^{-102x^2}\,dx$ (assuming that the weights of quarters are normally distributed with a mean of 5.670 g and a standard deviation of 0.07 g). Expand the integrand in $n=2$ and $n=3$ terms of a Taylor series and integrate to find two estimates of the probability. Check for agreement between the two estimates.

■ 63. Approximating ln 2 Consider the following three ways to approximate ln 2.

a. Use the Taylor series for $\ln(1+x)$ centered at 0 and evaluate it at $x=1$ (convergence was asserted in Table 9.5). Write the resulting infinite series.

b. Use the Taylor series for $\ln(1-x)$ centered at 0 and the identity $\ln 2=-\ln\dfrac{1}{2}$. Write the resulting infinite series.

c. Use the property $\ln(a/b)=\ln a-\ln b$ and the series of parts (a) and (b) to find the Taylor series for $f(x)=\ln\left(\dfrac{1+x}{1-x}\right)$ centered at 0.

d. At what value of x should the series in part (c) be evaluated to approximate ln 2? Write the resulting infinite series for ln 2.

e. Using four terms of the series, which of the three series derived in parts (a)–(d) gives the best approximation to ln 2? Can you explain why?

■ 64. Graphing Taylor polynomials Consider the function $f(x)=(1+x)^{-4}$.

a. Find the Taylor polynomials p_0, p_1, p_2, and p_3 centered at 0.

b. Use a graphing utility to plot the Taylor polynomials and f, for $-1<x<1$.

c. For each Taylor polynomial, give the interval on which its graph appears indistinguishable from the graph of f.

Chapter 9 Guided Projects

Applications of the material in this chapter and related topics can be found in the following Guided Projects. For additional information, see the Preface.

• Series approximations to π
• Euler's formula (Taylor series with complex numbers)
• Stirling's formula and $n!$

• Three-sigma quality control
• Fourier series

A

Appendix

The goal of this appendix is to establish the essential notation, terminology, and algebraic skills that are used throughout the book.

Algebra

EXAMPLE 1 Algebra review

a. Evaluate $(-32)^{2/5}$.

b. Simplify $\dfrac{1}{x-2} - \dfrac{1}{x+2}$.

c. Solve the equation $\dfrac{x^4 - 5x^2 + 4}{x-1} = 0$.

SOLUTION

a. Recall that $(-32)^{2/5} = ((-32)^{1/5})^2$. Because $(-32)^{1/5} = \sqrt[5]{-32} = -2$, we have $(-32)^{2/5} = (-2)^2 = 4$.

   Another option is to write $(-32)^{2/5} = ((-32)^2)^{1/5} = 1024^{1/5} = 4$.

b. Finding a common denominator and simplifying leads to

$$\frac{1}{x-2} - \frac{1}{x+2} = \frac{(x+2)-(x-2)}{(x-2)(x+2)} = \frac{4}{x^2-4}.$$

c. Notice that $x = 1$ cannot be a solution of the equation because the left side of the equation is undefined at $x = 1$. Because $x - 1 \neq 0$, both sides of the equation can be multiplied by $x - 1$ to produce $x^4 - 5x^2 + 4 = 0$. After factoring, this equation becomes $(x^2 - 4)(x^2 - 1) = 0$, which implies $x^2 - 4 = (x - 2)(x + 2) = 0$ or $x^2 - 1 = (x - 1)(x + 1) = 0$. The roots of $x^2 - 4 = 0$ are $x = \pm 2$, and the roots of $x^2 - 1 = 0$ are $x = \pm 1$. Excluding $x = 1$, the roots of the original equation are $x = -1$ and $x = \pm 2$.

Related Exercises 15–26 ◄

Sets of Real Numbers

Figure A.1 shows the notation for **open intervals**, **closed intervals**, and various **bounded** and **unbounded intervals**. Notice that either interval notation or set notation may be used.

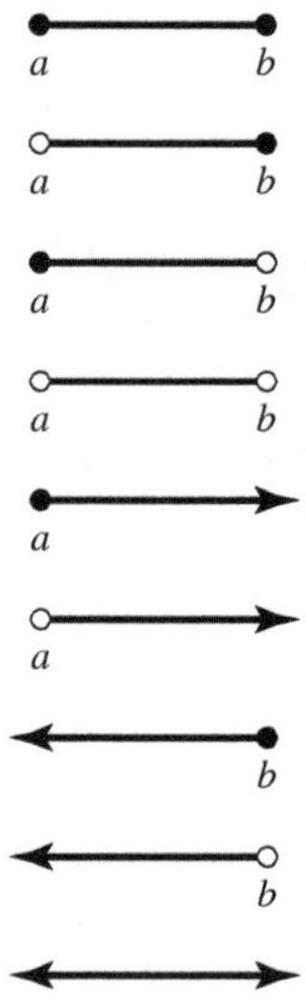

	$[a, b] = \{x: a \le x \le b\}$	Closed, bounded interval
	$(a, b] = \{x: a < x \le b\}$	Bounded interval
	$[a, b) = \{x: a \le x < b\}$	Bounded interval
	$(a, b) = \{x: a < x < b\}$	Open, bounded interval
	$[a, \infty) = \{x: x \ge a\}$	Unbounded interval
	$(a, \infty) = \{x: x > a\}$	Unbounded interval
	$(-\infty, b] = \{x: x \le b\}$	Unbounded interval
	$(-\infty, b) = \{x: x < b\}$	Unbounded interval
	$(-\infty, \infty) = \{x: -\infty < x < \infty\}$	Unbounded interval

Figure A.1

EXAMPLE 2 **Solving inequalities** Solve the following inequalities.

a. $-x^2 + 5x - 6 < 0$ **b.** $\dfrac{x^2 - x - 2}{x - 3} \le 0$

SOLUTION

a. We multiply by -1, reverse the inequality, and then factor:

$$x^2 - 5x + 6 > 0 \quad \text{Multiply by } -1.$$
$$(x - 2)(x - 3) > 0. \quad \text{Factor.}$$

The roots of the corresponding equation $(x - 2)(x - 3) = 0$ are $x = 2$ and $x = 3$. These roots partition the number line (Figure A.2) into three intervals: $(-\infty, 2)$, $(2, 3)$, and $(3, \infty)$. On each interval, the product $(x - 2)(x - 3)$ does not change sign. To determine the sign of the product on a given interval, a **test value** x is selected and the sign of $(x - 2)(x - 3)$ is determined at x.

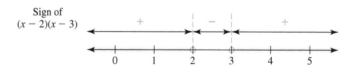

Figure A.2

A convenient choice for x in $(-\infty, 2)$ is $x = 0$. At this test value,

$$(x - 2)(x - 3) = (-2)(-3) > 0.$$

Using a test value of $x = 2.5$ in the interval $(2, 3)$, we have

$$(x - 2)(x - 3) = (0.5)(-0.5) < 0.$$

A test value of $x = 4$ in $(3, \infty)$ gives

$$(x - 2)(x - 3) = (2)(1) > 0.$$

> The set of numbers $\{x: x \text{ is in } (-\infty, 2)$ or $(3, \infty)\}$ may also be expressed using the union symbol:
>
> $(-\infty, 2) \cup (3, \infty)$.

Therefore, $(x - 2)(x - 3) > 0$ on $(-\infty, 2)$ and $(3, \infty)$. We conclude that the inequality $-x^2 + 5x - 6 < 0$ is satisfied for all x in either $(-\infty, 2)$ or $(3, \infty)$ (Figure A.2).

b. The expression $\dfrac{x^2 - x - 2}{x - 3}$ can change sign only at points where the numerator or denominator of $\dfrac{x^2 - x - 2}{x - 3}$ equals 0. Because

$$\frac{x^2 - x - 2}{x - 3} = \frac{(x + 1)(x - 2)}{x - 3},$$

the numerator is 0 when $x = -1$ or $x = 2$, and the denominator is 0 at $x = 3$. Therefore, we examine the sign of $\dfrac{(x + 1)(x - 2)}{x - 3}$ on the intervals $(-\infty, -1)$, $(-1, 2), (2, 3),$ and $(3, \infty)$.

Using test values on these intervals, we see that $\dfrac{(x + 1)(x - 2)}{x - 3} < 0$ on $(-\infty, -1)$ and $(2, 3)$. Furthermore, the expression is 0 when $x = -1$ and $x = 2$. Therefore, $\dfrac{x^2 - x - 2}{x - 3} \le 0$ for all values of x in either $(-\infty, -1]$ or $[2, 3)$ (Figure A.3).

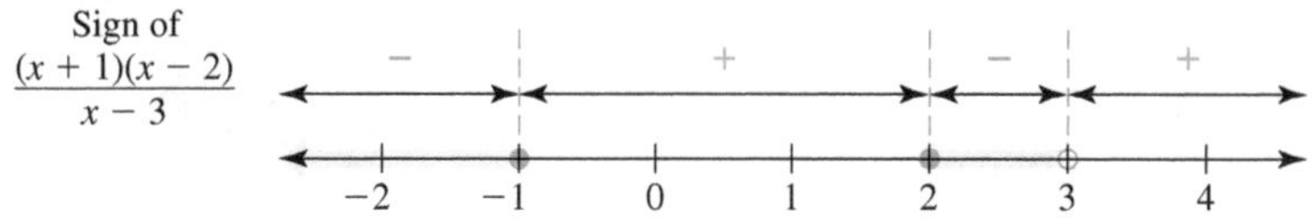

Test Value	$x + 1$	$x - 2$	$x - 3$	Result
-2	$-$	$-$	$-$	$-$
0	$+$	$-$	$-$	$+$
2.5	$+$	$+$	$-$	$-$
4	$+$	$+$	$+$	$+$

Sign of
$\dfrac{(x + 1)(x - 2)}{x - 3}$

Figure A.3

Related Exercises 27–30 ◄

Absolute Value

The **absolute value** of a real number x, denoted $|x|$, is the distance between x and the origin on the number line (Figure A.4). More generally, $|x - y|$ is the distance between the points x and y on the number line. The absolute value has the following definition and properties.

> The absolute value is useful in simplifying square roots. Because $\sqrt{a}$ is nonnegative, we have $\sqrt{a^2} = |a|$. For example, $\sqrt{3^2} = 3$ and $\sqrt{(-3)^2} = \sqrt{9} = 3$. Note that the solutions of $x^2 = 9$ are $|x| = 3$ or $x = \pm 3$.

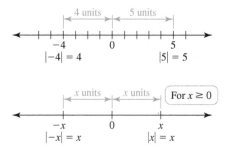

Figure A.4

Definition and Properties of the Absolute Value

The absolute value of a real number x is defined as

$$|x| = \begin{cases} x & \text{if } x \ge 0 \\ -x & \text{if } x < 0. \end{cases}$$

Let a be a positive real number.

1. $|x| = a \Leftrightarrow x = \pm a$ 　　　 **2.** $|x| < a \Leftrightarrow -a < x < a$

3. $|x| > a \Leftrightarrow x > a$ or $x < -a$ **4.** $|x| \le a \Leftrightarrow -a \le x \le a$

5. $|x| \ge a \Leftrightarrow x \ge a$ or $x \le -a$ **6.** $|x + y| \le |x| + |y|$

> Property 6 is called the **triangle inequality**.

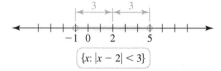

$\{x: |x - 2| < 3\}$

Figure A.5

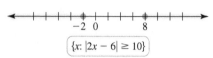

$\{x: |2x - 6| \geq 10\}$

Figure A.6

EXAMPLE 3   Inequalities with absolute values Solve the following inequalities. Then sketch the solution on the number line and express it in interval notation.

a. $|x - 2| < 3$ **b.** $|2x - 6| \geq 10$

SOLUTION

a. Using property 2 of the absolute value, $|x - 2| < 3$ is written as

$$-3 < x - 2 < 3.$$

Adding 2 to each term of these inequalities results in $-1 < x < 5$ (Figure A.5). This set of numbers is written as $(-1, 5)$ in interval notation.

b. Using property 5, the inequality $|2x - 6| \geq 10$ implies that

$$2x - 6 \geq 10 \quad \text{or} \quad 2x - 6 \leq -10.$$

We add 6 to both sides of the first inequality to obtain $2x \geq 16$, which implies $x \geq 8$. Similarly, the second inequality yields $x \leq -2$ (Figure A.6). In interval notation, the solution is $(-\infty, -2]$ or $[8, \infty)$.

Related Exercises 31–34 ◄

Cartesian Coordinate System

The conventions of the **Cartesian coordinate system** or ***xy*-coordinate system** are illustrated in Figure A.7. The set of real numbers is often denoted $\mathbb{R}$. The set of all ordered pairs of real numbers, which comprise the *xy*-plane, is often denoted $\mathbb{R}^2$.

➤ The familiar (x, y) coordinate system is named after René Descartes (1596–1650). However, it was introduced independently and simultaneously by Pierre de Fermat (1601–1665).

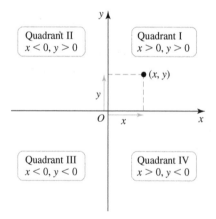

Figure A.7

Distance Formula and Circles

By the Pythagorean theorem (Figure A.8), we have the following formula for the distance between two points $P_1(x_1, y_1)$ and $P_2(x_2, y_2)$.

Distance Formula

The distance between the points $P_1(x_1, y_1)$ and $P_2(x_2, y_2)$ is

$$|P_1 P_2| = \sqrt{(x_2 - x_1)^2 + (y_2 - y_1)^2}.$$

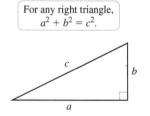

For any right triangle, $a^2 + b^2 = c^2$.

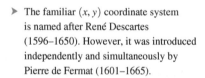

Figure A.8

A **circle** is the set of points in the plane whose distance from a fixed point (the **center**) is constant (the **radius**). This definition leads to the following equations that describe a circle.

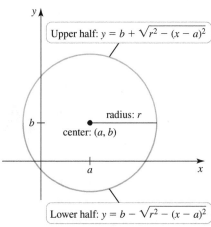

Figure A.9

Equation of a Circle

The equation of a circle centered at (a, b) with radius r is

$$(x - a)^2 + (y - b)^2 = r^2.$$

Solving for y, the equations of the upper and lower halves of the circle (Figure A.9) are

$$y = b + \sqrt{r^2 - (x - a)^2} \quad \text{Upper half of the circle}$$
$$y = b - \sqrt{r^2 - (x - a)^2}. \quad \text{Lower half of the circle}$$

EXAMPLE 4 Sets involving circles

a. Find the equation of the circle with center $(2, 4)$ passing through $(-2, 1)$.

b. Describe the set of points satisfying $x^2 + y^2 - 4x - 6y < 12$.

SOLUTION

a. The radius of the circle equals the length of the line segment between the center $(2, 4)$ and the point on the circle $(-2, 1)$, which is

$$\sqrt{(2 - (-2))^2 + (4 - 1)^2} = 5.$$

Therefore, the equation of the circle is

$$(x - 2)^2 + (y - 4)^2 = 25.$$

> Recall that the procedure shown here for completing the square works when the coefficient on the quadratic term is 1. When the coefficient is not 1, it must be factored out before completing the square.

b. To put this inequality in a recognizable form, we complete the square on the left side of the inequality:

$$x^2 + y^2 - 4x - 6y = x^2 - 4x \underbrace{+ 4 - 4}_{} + y^2 - 6y \underbrace{+ 9 - 9}_{}$$

Add and subtract the square of half the coefficient of x. Add and subtract the square of half the coefficient of y.

$$= \underbrace{x^2 - 4x + 4}_{(x - 2)^2} + \underbrace{y^2 - 6y + 9}_{(y - 3)^2} - 4 - 9$$

$$= (x - 2)^2 + (y - 3)^2 - 13.$$

Therefore, the original inequality becomes

$$(x - 2)^2 + (y - 3)^2 - 13 < 12, \quad \text{or} \quad (x - 2)^2 + (y - 3)^2 < 25.$$

> A **circle** is the set of all points whose distance from a fixed point is a constant. A **disk** is the set of all points within and possibly on a circle.

This inequality describes those points that lie within the circle centered at $(2, 3)$ with radius 5 (Figure A.10). Note that a dashed curve is used to indicate that the circle itself is not part of the solution.

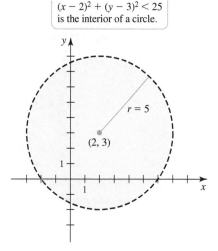

The solution to $(x - 2)^2 + (y - 3)^2 < 25$ is the interior of a circle.

Figure A.10

Related Exercises 35–36 ◄

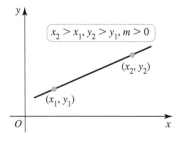

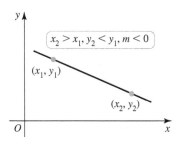

Figure A.11

> Given a particular line, we often talk about *the* equation of a line. But the equation of a specific line is not unique. Having found one equation, we can multiply it by any nonzero constant to produce another equation of the same line.

Equations of Lines

The **slope** m of the line passing through the points $P_1(x_1, y_1)$ and $P_2(x_2, y_2)$ is the *rise over run* (Figure A.11), computed as

$$m = \frac{\text{change in vertical coordinate}}{\text{change in horizontal coordinate}} = \frac{y_2 - y_1}{x_2 - x_1}.$$

Equations of a Line

Point-slope form The equation of the line with slope m passing through the point (x_1, y_1) is $y - y_1 = m(x - x_1)$.

Slope-intercept form The equation of the line with slope m and y-intercept $(0, b)$ is $y = mx + b$ (Figure A.12a).

General linear equation The equation $Ax + By + C = 0$ describes a line in the plane, provided A and B are not both zero.

Vertical and horizontal lines The vertical line that passes through $(a, 0)$ has an equation $x = a$; its slope is undefined. The horizontal line through $(0, b)$ has an equation $y = b$, with slope equal to 0 (Figure A.12b).

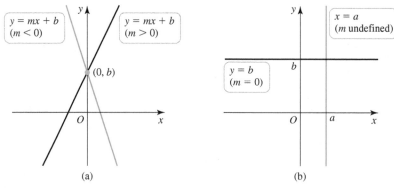

Figure A.12

EXAMPLE 5   Working with linear equations Find an equation of the line passing through the points $(1, -2)$ and $(-4, 5)$.

SOLUTION The slope of the line through the points $(1, -2)$ and $(-4, 5)$ is

$$m = \frac{5 - (-2)}{-4 - 1} = \frac{7}{-5} = -\frac{7}{5}.$$

Using the point $(1, -2)$, the point-slope form of the equation is

$$y - (-2) = -\frac{7}{5}(x - 1).$$

> Because both points $(1, -2)$ and $(-4, 5)$ lie on the line and must satisfy the equation of the line, either point can be used to determine an equation of the line.

Solving for y yields the slope-intercept form of the equation:

$$y = -\frac{7}{5}x - \frac{3}{5}.$$

Related Exercises 37–40 ◄

Parallel and Perpendicular Lines

Two lines in the plane may have either of two special relationships to each other: They may be parallel or perpendicular.

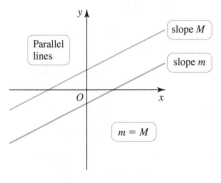

Parallel Lines

Two distinct nonvertical lines are **parallel** if they have the same slope; that is, the lines with equations $y = mx + b$ and $y = Mx + B$ are parallel if and only if $m = M$. Two distinct vertical lines are parallel.

EXAMPLE 6   Parallel lines   Find an equation of the line parallel to $3x - 6y + 12 = 0$ that intersects the x-axis at $(4, 0)$.

SOLUTION   Solving the equation $3x - 6y + 12 = 0$ for y, we have

$$y = \frac{1}{2}x + 2.$$

This line has a slope of $\frac{1}{2}$ and any line parallel to it has a slope of $\frac{1}{2}$. Therefore, the line that passes through $(4, 0)$ with slope $\frac{1}{2}$ has the point-slope equation $y - 0 = \frac{1}{2}(x - 4)$. After simplifying, an equation of the line is

$$y = \frac{1}{2}x - 2.$$

Notice that the slopes of the two lines are the same; only the y-intercepts differ.

Related Exercises 41–42 ◄

▶ The slopes of perpendicular lines are *negative reciprocals* of each other.

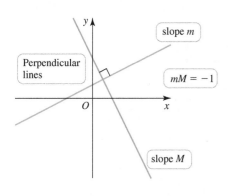

Perpendicular Lines

Two lines with slopes $m \neq 0$ and $M \neq 0$ are **perpendicular** if and only if $mM = -1$, or equivalently, $m = -1/M$.

EXAMPLE 7   Perpendicular lines   Find an equation of the line passing through the point $(-2, 5)$ perpendicular to the line $\ell: 4x - 2y + 7 = 0$.

SOLUTION   The equation of ℓ can be written $y = 2x + \frac{7}{2}$, which reveals that its slope is 2. Therefore, the slope of any line perpendicular to ℓ is $-\frac{1}{2}$. The line with slope $-\frac{1}{2}$ passing through the point $(-2, 5)$ is

$$y - 5 = -\frac{1}{2}(x + 2), \quad \text{or} \quad y = -\frac{x}{2} + 4.$$

Related Exercises 43–44 ◄

APPENDIX A EXERCISES

Review Questions

1. State the meaning of $\{x: -4 < x \leq 10\}$. Express the set $\{x: -4 < x \leq 10\}$ using interval notation and draw it on a number line.

2. Write the interval $(-\infty, 2)$ in set notation and draw it on a number line.

3. Give the definition of $|x|$.

4. Write the inequality $|x - 2| \leq 3$ without absolute value symbols.

5. Write the inequality $|2x - 4| \geq 3$ without absolute value symbols.

6. Write an equation of the set of all points that are a distance 5 units from the point $(2, 3)$.

7. Explain how to find the distance between two points whose coordinates are known.

8. Sketch the set of points $\{(x, y): x^2 + (y - 2)^2 > 16\}$.

9. Give an equation of the upper half of the circle centered at the origin with radius 6.

10. What are the possible solution sets of the equation $x^2 + y^2 + Cx + Dy + E = 0$?

11. Give an equation of the line with slope m that passes through the point $(4, -2)$.

12. Give an equation of the line with slope m and y-intercept $(0, 6)$.

13. What is the relationship between the slopes of two parallel lines?

14. What is the relationship between the slopes of two perpendicular lines?

Basic Skills

15–20. Algebra review *Simplify or evaluate the following expressions without a calculator.*

15. $(1/8)^{-2/3}$

16. $\sqrt[3]{-125} + \sqrt{1/25}$

17. $(u + v)^2 - (u - v)^2$

18. $\dfrac{(a + h)^2 - a^2}{h}$

19. $\dfrac{1}{x + h} - \dfrac{1}{x}$

20. $\dfrac{2}{x + 3} - \dfrac{2}{x - 3}$

21–26. Algebra review

21. Factor $y^2 - y^{-2}$.

22. Solve $x^3 - 9x = 0$.

23. Solve $u^4 - 11u^2 + 18 = 0$.

24. Solve $4^x - 6(2^x) = -8$.

25. Simplify $\dfrac{(x + h)^3 - x^3}{h}$, for $h \neq 0$.

26. Rewrite $\dfrac{\sqrt{x + h} - \sqrt{x}}{h}$, where $h \neq 0$, without square roots in the numerator.

27–30. Solving inequalities *Solve the following inequalities and draw the solution on a number line.*

27. $x^2 - 6x + 5 < 0$

28. $\dfrac{x + 1}{x + 2} < 6$

29. $\dfrac{x^2 - 9x + 20}{x - 6} \leq 0$

30. $x\sqrt{x - 1} > 0$

31–34. Inequalities with absolute values *Solve the following inequalities. Then draw the solution on a number line and express it using interval notation.*

31. $|3x - 4| > 8$

32. $1 \leq |x| \leq 10$

33. $3 < |2x - 1| < 5$

34. $2 < |\frac{x}{2} - 5| < 6$

35–36. Circle calculations *Solve the following problems.*

35. Find the equation of the lower half of the circle with center $(-1, 2)$ and radius 3.

36. Describe the set of points that satisfy $x^2 + y^2 + 6x + 8y \geq 25$.

37–40. Working with linear equations *Find an equation of the line ℓ that satisfies the given condition. Then draw the graph of ℓ.*

37. ℓ has slope $5/3$ and y-intercept $(0, 4)$.

38. ℓ has undefined slope and passes through $(0, 5)$.

39. ℓ has y-intercept $(0, -4)$ and x-intercept $(5, 0)$.

40. ℓ is parallel to the x-axis and passes through the point $(2, 3)$.

41–42. Parallel lines *Find an equation of the following lines and draw their graphs.*

41. The line with y-intercept $(0, 12)$ parallel to the line $x + 2y = 8$

42. The line with x-intercept $(-6, 0)$ parallel to the line $2x - 5 = 0$

43–44. Perpendicular lines *Find an equation of the following lines.*

43. The line passing through $(3, -6)$ perpendicular to the line $y = -3x + 2$

44. The perpendicular bisector of the line joining the points $(-9, 2)$ and $(3, -5)$

Further Explorations

45. Explain why or why not State whether the following statements are true and give an explanation or counterexample.

    a. $\sqrt{16} = \pm 4$.

    b. $\sqrt{4^2} = \sqrt{(-4)^2}$.

    c. There are two real numbers that satisfy the condition $|x| = -2$.

    d. $|\pi^2 - 9| < 0$.

    e. The point $(1, 1)$ is inside the circle of radius 1 centered at the origin.

    f. $\sqrt{x^4} = x^2$ for all real numbers x.

    g. $\sqrt{a^2} < \sqrt{b^2}$ implies $a < b$ for all real numbers a and b.

46–48. Intervals to sets *Express the following intervals in set notation. Use absolute value notation when possible.*

46. $(-\infty, 12)$

47. $(-\infty, -2]$ or $[4, \infty)$

48. $(2, 3]$ or $[4, 5)$

49–50. Sets in the plane *Graph each set in the xy-plane.*

49. $\{(x, y): |x - y| = 0\}$

50. $\{(x, y): |x| = |y|\}$

Answers

CHAPTER 1

Section 1.1 Exercises, pp. 9–12

1. A function is a rule that assigns to each value of the independent variable in the domain a unique value of the dependent variable in the range. **3.** A graph is that of a function provided no vertical line intersects the graph at more than one point. **5.** The first statement **7.** 2; −2
9. $f(-x) = f(x)$

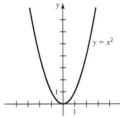

11. B **13.** $D = \mathbb{R}, R = [-10, \infty)$ **15.** $D = [-2, 2], R = [0, 2]$
17. $D = \mathbb{R}, R = \mathbb{R}$ **19.** $D = [-3, 3]; R = [0, 27]$ **21.** The independent variable is t; the dependent variable is d; $D = [0, 8]$. **23.** The independent variable is h; the dependent variable is V; $D = [0, 50]$.

25. 96 **27.** $1/z^3$ **29.** $1/(y^3 - 3)$ **31.** $(u^2 - 4)^3$ **33.** $\dfrac{x - 3}{10 - 3x}$

35. x **37.** $g(x) = x^3 - 5, f(x) = x^{10}; D = \mathbb{R}$
39. $g(x) = x^4 + 2, f(x) = \sqrt{x}; D = \mathbb{R}$
41. $(f \circ g)(x) = |x^2 - 4|; D = \mathbb{R}$

43. $(f \circ G)(x) = \dfrac{1}{|x - 2|}; D = \{x : x \neq 2\}$

45. $(G \circ g \circ f)(x) = \dfrac{1}{x^2 - 6}; D = \{x : x \neq \sqrt{6}, -\sqrt{6}\}$

47. $x^4 - 8x^2 + 12$ **49.** $f(x) = x - 3$ **51.** $f(x) = x^2$
53. $f(x) = x^2$ **55. a.** 4 **b.** 1 **c.** 3 **d.** 3 **e.** 8 **f.** 1 **57.** $2x + h$

59. $-\dfrac{2}{x(x + h)}$ **61.** $\dfrac{1}{(x + h + 1)(x + 1)}$ **63.** $x^2 + ax + a^2 - 2$

65. $\dfrac{4(x + a)}{a^2 x^2}$ **67. a.**

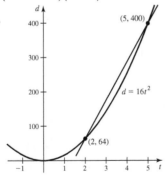

b. $m_{\text{sec}} = 112$ ft/s; the object falls at an average rate of 112 ft/s.

69. a.

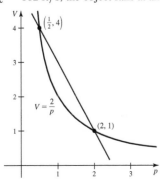

b. $m_{\text{sec}} = -2$ cm³/atmosphere; the volume decreases at an average rate of 2 cm³/atmosphere over the interval $0.5 \leq p \leq 2$.

71. y-axis **73.** No symmetry **75.** x-axis, y-axis, origin **77.** Origin
79. A is even, B is odd, and C is even. **81. a.** True **b.** False
c. True **d.** False **e.** False **f.** True **g.** True **h.** False **i.** True
83.

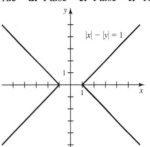

85. $f(x) = 3x - 2$ or $f(x) = -3x + 4$ **87.** $f(x) = x^2 - 6$

89. $\dfrac{1}{\sqrt{x + h} + \sqrt{x}}; \dfrac{1}{\sqrt{x} + \sqrt{a}}$

91. $\dfrac{3}{\sqrt{x}(x + h) + x\sqrt{x + h}}; \dfrac{3}{x\sqrt{a} + a\sqrt{x}}$

93. a. $[0, 3 + \sqrt{14}]$
b.

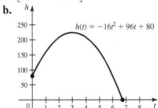

At time $t = 3$, the maximum height is 224 ft.

95. None **97.** Symmetry about the origin **99.** y-axis **101.** y-axis
103. a. 4 **b.** 1 **c.** 3 **d.** −2 **e.** −1 **f.** 7

Section 1.2 Exercises, pp. 21–26

1. A formula, a graph, a table, words **3.** $\mathbb{R}$ except points at which the denominator is zero
5.

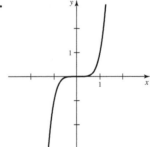

7. Shift the graph to the left 2 units. **9.** Compress the graph horizontally by a factor of 3. **11.** $y = -\frac{2}{3}x - 1$
13. $y = 2x + 1$

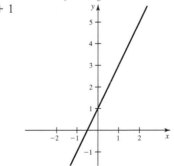

15. $d = -3p/50 + 27; D = [0, 450]$

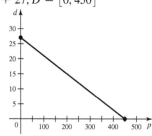

17. $p(t) = 24t + 500; 860$

19. $y = \begin{cases} x + 3 & \text{if } x < 0 \\ -\frac{1}{2}x + 3 & \text{if } x \geq 0 \end{cases}$

21. $c(t) = \begin{cases} 0.05t & \text{if } 0 \leq t \leq 60 \\ 1.2 + 0.03t & \text{if } 60 < t \leq 120 \end{cases}$

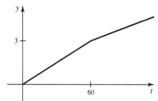

23.

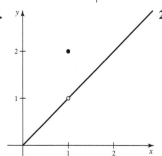

25.

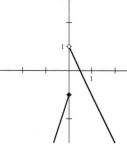

27.

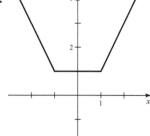

29. a.

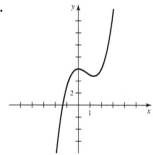

b. $D = \mathbb{R}$

c. One peak near $x = 0$; one valley near $x = 4/3$; x-intercept approx. $(-1.3, 0)$, y-intercept $(0, 6)$

31. a.

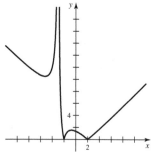

b. $D = \{x : x \neq -3\}$ **c.** Undefined at $x = -3$; a valley near $x = -5.2$; x-intercepts (and valleys) at $(-2, 0)$ and $(2, 0)$; a peak near $x = -0.8$; y-intercept $(0, \frac{4}{3})$

33. a.

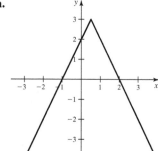

b. $D = (-\infty, \infty)$ **c.** One peak at $x = \frac{1}{2}$; x-intercepts $(-1, 0)$ and $(2, 0)$; y-intercept $(0, 2)$ **35.** $s(x) = 2$

37. $s(x) = \begin{cases} 1 & \text{if } x < 0 \\ -\frac{1}{2} & \text{if } x > 0 \end{cases}$

39. a. 12 **b.** 36 **c.** $A(x) = 6x$ **41. a.** 12 **b.** 21

c. $A(x) = \begin{cases} 8x - x^2 & \text{if } 0 \leq x \leq 3 \\ 2x + 9 & \text{if } x > 3 \end{cases}$

43. $f(x) = |x - 2| + 3; g(x) = -|x + 2| - 1$

45. a. Shift 3 units to the right.

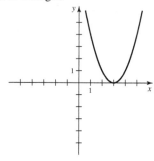

b. Horizontal scaling by a factor of 2, then shift 2 units to the right.

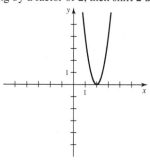

c. Shift to the right 2 units, vertical scaling by a factor of 3 and flip, shift up 4 units.

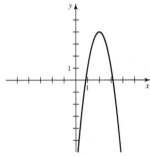

d. Horizontal scaling by a factor of $\frac{1}{3}$, horizontal shift right 2 units, vertical scaling by a factor of 6, vertical shift up 1 unit

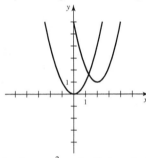

47. Shift the graph of $y = x^2$ right 2 units and up 1 unit.

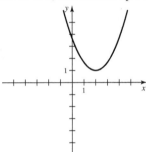

49. Stretch the graph of $y = x^2$ vertically by a factor of 3 and reflect across the x-axis.   **51.** Shift the graph of $y = x^2$ left 3 units and stretch vertically by a factor of 2.   **53.** Shift the graph of $y = x^2$ to the left $\frac{1}{2}$ unit, stretch vertically by a factor of 4, reflect across the x-axis, and then shift up 13 units to obtain the graph of h.   **55. a.** True **b.** False **c.** True **d.** False   **57.** $(0, 0)$ and $(4, 16)$ **59.** $y = \sqrt{x} - 1$
61. $s(t) = 30\sqrt{5}t$; $D = [0, 4]$

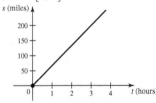

63. $y = 3200/x$; $D = (0, 5]$

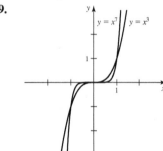

65.

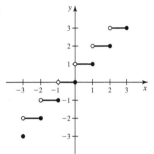

67.

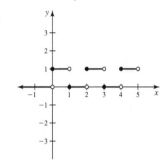

69.

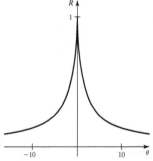

71. a. A, D, F, I **b.** E **c.** B, H **d.** I **e.** A
73. a.

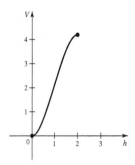

b. $\theta = 0$; vision is sharpest when we look straight ahead. **c.** $|\theta| \leq 0.19°$ (less than $\frac{1}{5}$ of a degree) **75. a.** $p(t) = 328.3t + 1875$ **b.** 4830
77. a. $f(m) = 350m + 1200$ **b.** Buy
79. $0 \leq h \leq 2$

81. a. $S(x) = x^2 + \dfrac{500}{x}$ **b.** Approximately 6.3 ft

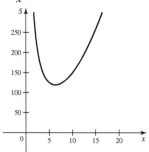

85. a.

n	1	2	3	4	5
$f(n)$	1	2	6	24	120

b.   **c.** 10

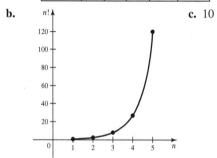

87. a.

n	1	2	3	4	5	6	7	8	9	10
$T(n)$	1	5	14	30	55	91	140	204	285	385

b. $D = \{n: n \text{ is a positive integer}\}$ **c.** 14

Section 1.3 Exercises, pp. 35–38

1. $D = \mathbb{R}$; $R = (0, \infty)$ **3.** If a function f is not one-to-one, then there are domain values, x_1 and x_2, such that $x_1 \neq x_2$ but $f(x_1) = f(x_2)$. If f^{-1} exists, by definition, $f^{-1}(f(x_1)) = x_1$ and $f^{-1}(f(x_2)) = x_2$ so that f^{-1} assigns two different range values to the single domain value of $f(x_1)$.

5.

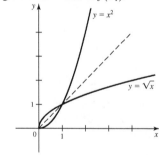

7. The expression $\log_b x$ represents the power to which b must be raised to obtain x.   **9.** $D = (0, \infty)$; $R = \mathbb{R}$
11. $(-\infty, -1], [-1, 1], [1, \infty)$

13.

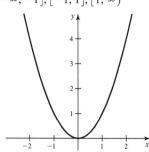

15. $(-\infty, \infty)$ **17.** $(-\infty, 5), (5, \infty)$ **19.** $(-\infty, 0), (0, \infty)$

21. a. $f^{-1}(x) = \frac{1}{2}x$ **23. a.** $f^{-1}(x) = -\frac{1}{4}x + \frac{3}{2}$
25. a. $f^{-1}(x) = \frac{1}{3}x - \frac{5}{3}$ **27. a.** $f^{-1}(x) = x^2 - 2, x \geq 0$
29. a. $f_1(x) = \sqrt{1 - x^2}$; $0 \leq x \leq 1$
$f_2(x) = \sqrt{1 - x^2}$; $-1 \leq x \leq 0$
$f_3(x) = -\sqrt{1 - x^2}$; $-1 \leq x \leq 0$
$f_4(x) = -\sqrt{1 - x^2}$; $0 \leq x \leq 1$
b. $f_1^{-1}(x) = \sqrt{1 - x^2}$; $0 \leq x \leq 1$
$f_2^{-1}(x) = -\sqrt{1 - x^2}$; $0 \leq x \leq 1$
$f_3^{-1}(x) = -\sqrt{1 - x^2}$; $-1 \leq x \leq 0$
$f_4^{-1}(x) = \sqrt{1 - x^2}$; $-1 \leq x \leq 0$
31. $f^{-1}(x) = -\dfrac{1}{4}x + 2$ **33.** $f^{-1}(x) = x^2, x \geq 0$

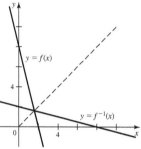

35. $f^{-1}(x) = \sqrt[4]{x - 4}, x \geq 4$ **37.** $f^{-1}(x) = \sqrt{x - 5} + 1, x \geq 5$

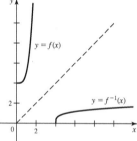
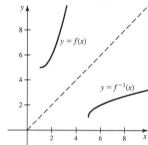

39.

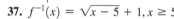

41. 1000   **43.** 2   **45.** $1/e$ **47.** -0.2 **49.** 1.19   **51.** $-0.09\overline{6}$
53. $\ln 21/\ln 7$ **55.** $\ln 5/(3 \ln 3) + 5/3$ **57.** 451 years
59. $\ln 15/\ln 2$ **61.** $\ln 40/\ln 4$ **63.** $e^{x \ln 2}$
65. $\log_5 |x|/\log_5 e$ **67.** e **69. a.** False   **b.** False   **c.** False
d. True   **e.** False   **f.** False   **g.** True   **71.** A is $y = \log_2 x$; B is $y = \log_4 x$; C is $y = \log_{10} x$.

73.

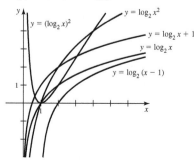

75. $f^{-1}(x) = \sqrt[3]{x} - 1, D = \mathbb{R}$
77. $f_1^{-1}(x) = \sqrt{2/x - 2}, D_1 = (0, 1]; f_2^{-1}(x) = -\sqrt{2/x - 2},$
$D_2 = (0, 1]$ **79. b.** $\dfrac{p(t + 12)}{p(t)} = 2$ **c.** 38,400   **d.** 19.0 hr
e. 72.7 hr   **81. a.** No   **b.** $f^{-1}(h) = 2 - \dfrac{1}{4}\sqrt{64 - h}$
c. $f^{-1}(h) = 2 + \dfrac{1}{4}\sqrt{64 - h}$ **d.** 0.542 s   **e.** 3.837 s
83. Let $y = \log_b x$. Then $b^y = x$ and $(1/b)^y = 1/x$. Therefore,
$y = -\log_{1/b} x$. Thus, $\log_{1/b} x = -y = -\log_b x$.
87. a.

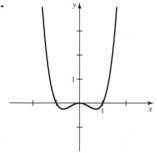

f is one-to-one
on the intervals
$(-\infty, -1/\sqrt{2}], [-1/\sqrt{2}, 0],$
$[0, 1/\sqrt{2}], [1/\sqrt{2}, \infty)$

b. $x = \sqrt{\dfrac{1 \pm \sqrt{4y + 1}}{2}}, -\sqrt{\dfrac{1 \pm \sqrt{4y + 1}}{2}}$

Section 1.4 Exercises, pp. 47–51

1. $\sin\theta = \text{opp/hyp}; \cos\theta = \text{adj/hyp}; \tan\theta = \text{opp/adj};$
$\cot\theta = \text{adj/opp}; \sec\theta = \text{hyp/adj}; \csc\theta = \text{hyp/opp}$
3. The radian measure of an angle θ is the length s of an arc
on the unit circle associated with θ.   **5.** $\sin^2\theta + \cos^2\theta = 1$,
$1 + \cot^2\theta = \csc^2\theta, \tan^2\theta + 1 = \sec^2\theta$
7. $\{x: x \text{ is an odd multiple of } \pi/2\}$ **9.** Sine is not one-to-
one on its domain.   **11.** Yes; no   **13.** Vertical asymptotes at
$x = \pi/2$ and $x = -\pi/2$ **15.** $-\frac{1}{2}$ **17.** 1   **19.** $-1/\sqrt{3}$
21. $1/\sqrt{3}$ **23.** 1   **25.** -1 **27.** Undefined
29. $\sec\theta = \dfrac{r}{x} = \dfrac{1}{x/r} = \dfrac{1}{\cos\theta}$ **31.** Dividing both sides of
$\cos^2\theta + \sin^2\theta = 1$ by $\cos^2\theta$ gives $1 + \tan^2\theta = \sec^2\theta$.
33. Because $\cos(\pi/2 - \theta) = \sin\theta$, for all θ,
$1/\cos(\pi/2 - \theta) = 1/\sin\theta$, excluding integer multiples of π, and
$\sec(\pi/2 - \theta) = \csc\theta$.   **35.** $\dfrac{\sqrt{2 + \sqrt{3}}}{2}$ or $\dfrac{\sqrt{6} + \sqrt{2}}{4}$
37. $\pi/4 + n\pi, n = 0, \pm 1, \pm 2, \ldots$
39. $\pi/6, 5\pi/6, 7\pi/6, 11\pi/6$
41. $\pi/4 + 2n\pi, 3\pi/4 + 2n\pi, n = 0, \pm 1, \pm 2, \ldots$
43. $\pi/12, 5\pi/12, 3\pi/4, 13\pi/12, 17\pi/12, 7\pi/4$
45. $0, \pi/2, \pi, 3\pi/2$ **47.** $\pi/2$ **49.** $\pi/4$ **51.** $\pi/3$ **53.** $2\pi/3$
55. -1 **57.** $\sqrt{1 - x^2}$ **59.** $\dfrac{\sqrt{4 - x^2}}{2}$ **61.** $2x\sqrt{1 - x^2}$
63. $\cos^{-1}x + \cos^{-1}(-x) = \theta + (\pi - \theta) = \pi$

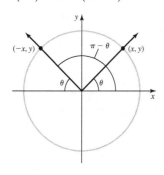

65. The functions are equal.   **67.** $\pi/3$ **69.** $\pi/3$ **71.** $\pi/4$
73. $\pi/2 - 2$ **75.** $\dfrac{1}{\sqrt{x^2 + 1}}$ **77.** $1/x$ **79.** $x/\sqrt{x^2 + 16}$
81. $\sin^{-1}\dfrac{x}{6} = \tan^{-1}\left(\dfrac{x}{\sqrt{36 - x^2}}\right) = \sec^{-1}\left(\dfrac{6}{\sqrt{36 - x^2}}\right)$
83. a. False   **b.** False   **c.** False   **d.** False   **e.** True
f. False   **g.** True   **h.** False   **85.** $\sin\theta = \frac{12}{13}; \tan\theta = \frac{12}{5}; \sec\theta = \frac{13}{5};$
$\csc\theta = \frac{13}{12}; \cot\theta = \frac{5}{12}$ **87.** $\sin\theta = \frac{12}{13}; \cos\theta = \frac{5}{13}; \tan\theta = \frac{12}{5};$
$\sec\theta = \frac{13}{5}; \cot\theta = \frac{5}{12}$ **89.** Amp = 3; period = 6π
91. Amp = 3.6; period = 48   **93.** Stretch the graph of $y = \cos x$
horizontally by a factor of 3, stretch vertically by a factor of 2, and reflect across the x-axis.

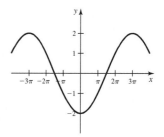

95. Stretch the graph of $y = \cos x$ horizontally by a factor of $24/\pi$;
then stretch it vertically by a factor of 3.6 and shift it up 2 units.

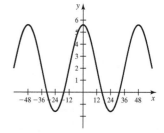

97. $y = 3\sin(\pi x/12 - 3\pi/4) + 13$ **99.** About 6 ft
101. $d(t) = 10\cos(4\pi t/3)$ **103.** h
105. $s(t) = 117.5 - 87.5\sin\left(\dfrac{\pi}{182.5}(t - 95)\right)$
$S(t) = 844.5 + 87.5\sin\left(\dfrac{\pi}{182.5}(t - 67)\right)$

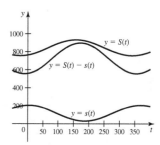

107. Area of circle is πr^2; $\theta/(2\pi)$ represents the proportion of area
swept out by a central angle θ. Thus, the area of such a sector is
$(\theta/2\pi)\pi r^2 = r^2\theta/2$.

Chapter 1 Review Exercises, pp. 51–53

1. a. True **b.** False **c.** False **d.** True
e. False **f.** False **g.** True
3. a.

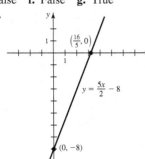

b.

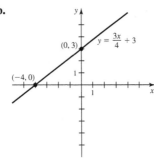

c.

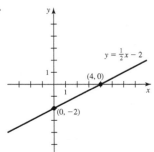

5. $f(x) = \begin{cases} 0 & \text{if } x \geq 0 \\ 4x & \text{if } x < 0 \end{cases}$

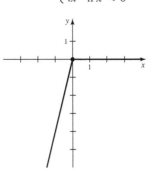

7. a.

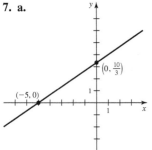

b.

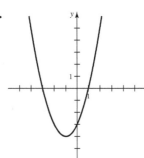

c.

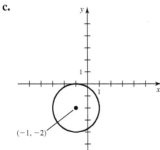

d.

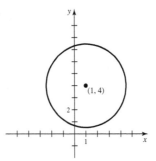

9. $D_f = \mathbb{R}, R_f = \mathbb{R}; D_g = [0, \infty), R_g = [0, \infty)$

11. $B = -\dfrac{1}{500}a + 212$

13. a.

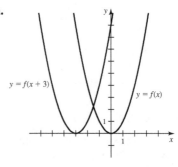

b.

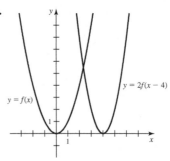

c.

d.

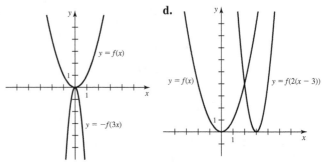

15. a. 1 **b.** $\sqrt{x^3}$ **c.** $\sin^3 \sqrt{x}$ **d.** $\mathbb{R}$ **e.** $[-1, 1]$
17. $2x + h - 2; x + a - 2$ **19.** $3x^2 + 3xh + h^2; x^2 + ax + a^2$
21. a. y-axis **b.** y-axis **c.** x-axis, y-axis, origin **23.** $x = 2$;
base does not matter **25.** $(-\infty, 0], [0, 2],$ and $[2, \infty)$
27. $f^{-1}(x) = 2 + \sqrt{x - 1}$

29. a. $3\pi/4$ **b.** $144°$ **c.** $40\pi/3$ **31. a.** $f(t) = -2\cos\dfrac{\pi t}{3}$
b. $f(t) = 5\sin\dfrac{\pi t}{12} + 15$ **33. a.** F **b.** E **c.** D **d.** B
e. C **f.** A **35.** $(7\pi/6, -1/2); (11\pi/6, -1/2)$ **37.** $\pi/6$
39. $-\pi/2$ **41.** x **43.** $\cos\theta = \frac{5}{13}; \tan\theta = \frac{12}{5}; \cot\theta = \frac{5}{12};$
$\sec\theta = \frac{13}{5}; \csc\theta = \frac{13}{12}$ **45.** $\dfrac{\sqrt{4 - x^2}}{2}$ **47.** $\pi/2 - \theta$ **49.** 0
51. $1 - 2x^2$

CHAPTER 2

Section 2.1 Exercises, pp. 59–60

1. $\dfrac{s(b) - s(a)}{b - a}$ **3.** $\dfrac{f(b) - f(a)}{b - a}$ **5.** The instantaneous velocity at $t = a$ is the slope of the line tangent to the position curve at $t = a$.
7. 20 **9. a.** 48 **b.** 64 **c.** 80 **d.** $16(6 - h)$ **11. a.** 36 **b.** 44
c. 52 **d.** 60 **13.** $m_{\text{sec}} = 60$; the slope is the average velocity of the object over the interval $[0.5, 2]$.

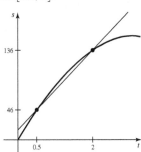

15.

Time interval	Average velocity
$[1, 2]$	80
$[1, 1.5]$	88
$[1, 1.1]$	94.4
$[1, 1.01]$	95.84
$[1, 1.001]$	95.984
$v_{\text{inst}} = 96$	

17. 47.84, 47.984, 47.9984; instantaneous velocity appears to be 48

19.

Time interval	Average velocity
$[2, 3]$	20
$[2.9, 3]$	5.60
$[2.99, 3]$	4.16
$[2.999, 3]$	4.016
$[2.9999, 3]$	4.002
$v_{\text{inst}} = 4$	

21.

Time interval	Average velocity
$[3, 3.5]$	-24
$[3, 3.1]$	-17.6
$[3, 3.01]$	-16.16
$[3, 3.001]$	-16.016
$[3, 3.0001]$	-16.002
$v_{\text{inst}} = -16$	

23.

Time interval	Average velocity
$[0, 1]$	36.372
$[0, 0.5]$	67.318
$[0, 0.1]$	79.468
$[0, 0.01]$	79.995
$[0, 0.001]$	80.000
$v_{\text{inst}} = 80$	

25.

Interval	Slope of secant line
$[1, 2]$	6
$[1.5, 2]$	7
$[1.9, 2]$	7.8
$[1.99, 2]$	7.98
$[1.999, 2]$	7.998
$m_{\text{tan}} = 8$	

27.

Interval	Slope of secant line
$[0, 1]$	1.718
$[0, 0.5]$	1.297
$[0, 0.1]$	1.052
$[0, 0.01]$	1.005
$[0, 0.001]$	1.001
$m_{\text{tan}} = 1$	

29. a.

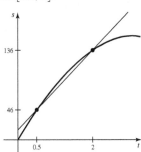

b. $(2, -1)$

c.

Interval	Slope of secant line
$[2, 2.5]$	0.5
$[2, 2.1]$	0.1
$[2, 2.01]$	0.01
$[2, 2.001]$	0.001
$[2, 2.0001]$	0.0001
$m_{\text{tan}} = 0$	

31. a.

b. $t = 4$

c.

Interval	Average velocity
$[4, 4.5]$	-8
$[4, 4.1]$	-1.6
$[4, 4.01]$	-0.16
$[4, 4.001]$	-0.016
$[4, 4.0001]$	-0.0016
$v_{\text{inst}} = 0$	

d. $0 \le t < 4$ **e.** $4 < t \le 9$ **33.** 0.6366, 0.9589, 0.9996, 1

Section 2.2 Exercises, pp. 65–68

1. As x approaches a from either side, the values of $f(x)$ approach L.
3. As x approaches a from the right, the values of $f(x)$ approach L.
5. $L = M$ **7. a.** 5   **b.** 3   **c.** Does not exist   **d.** 1   **e.** 2
9. a. -1 **b.** 1   **c.** 2   **d.** 2
11. a.

x	$f(x)$	x	$f(x)$
1.9	3.9	2.1	4.1
1.99	3.99	2.01	4.01
1.999	3.999	2.001	4.001
1.9999	3.9999	2.0001	4.0001

b. 4

13. a.

t	$g(t)$	t	$g(t)$
8.9	5.983287	9.1	6.016621
8.99	5.998333	9.01	6.001666
8.999	5.999833	9.001	6.000167

b. 6

15. From the graph and table, the limit appears to be 0.

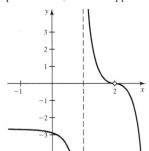

x	1.99	1.999	1.9999	2.0001	2.001	2.01
$f(x)$	0.0021715	0.00014476	0.000010857	-0.000010857	-0.00014476	-0.0021715

17. From the graph and table, the limit appears to be 2.

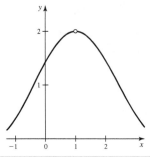

x	0.9	0.99	0.999	1.001	1.01	1.1
$f(x)$	1.993342	1.999933	1.999999	1.999999	1.999933	1.993342

19. $\lim\limits_{x \to 5^+} f(x) = 10$; $\lim\limits_{x \to 5^-} f(x) = 10$; $\lim\limits_{x \to 5} f(x) = 10$

21. a. 0   **b.** 1   **c.** 0   **d.** Does not exist; $\lim\limits_{x \to 1^-} f(x) \neq \lim\limits_{x \to 1^+} f(x)$

23. a. 3   **b.** 2   **c.** 2   **d.** 2   **e.** 2   **f.** 4   **g.** 1   **h.** Does not exist
i. 3   **j.** 3   **k.** 3   **l.** 3

25. a.

x	$\sin(1/x)$
$2/\pi$	1
$2/(3\pi)$	-1
$2/(5\pi)$	1
$2/(7\pi)$	-1
$2/(9\pi)$	1
$2/(11\pi)$	-1

The value alternates between 1 and -1.

b. The function alternates between 1 and -1 infinitely many times on the interval $(0, h)$ no matter how small $h > 0$ becomes.
c. Does not exist.   **27. a.** False   **b.** False   **c.** False
d. False   **e.** True
29.

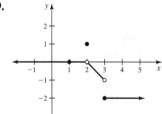

31.

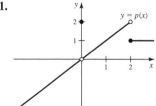

33. Approximately 403.4   **35.** 1   **37. a.** $-2, -1, 1, 2$ **b.** $2, 2, 2$
c. $\lim\limits_{x \to a^-} \lfloor x \rfloor = a - 1$ and $\lim\limits_{x \to a^+} \lfloor x \rfloor = a$, if a is an integer
d. $\lim\limits_{x \to a^-} \lfloor x \rfloor = \lfloor a \rfloor$ and $\lim\limits_{x \to a^+} \lfloor x \rfloor = \lfloor a \rfloor$, if a is not an integer
e. Limit exists provided a is not an integer   **39.** 0   **41.** 16

43. a.

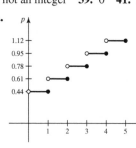

b. \$0.95

c. $\lim\limits_{x \to 1^+} f(w) = 0.61$ is the cost of a letter that weighs just over 1 oz;
$\lim\limits_{x \to 1^-} f(w) = 0.44$ is the cost of a letter that weighs just under 1 oz.
d. No; $\lim\limits_{x \to 4^+} f(w) \neq \lim\limits_{x \to 4^-} f(w)$ **45. a.** 8   **b.** 5   **47. a.** 2; 3; 4
b. p **49.** $\dfrac{p}{q}$

Section 2.3 Exercises, pp. 76–79

1. $\lim\limits_{x \to a} f(x) = f(a)$ **3.** Those values of a for which the denominator
is not zero   **5.** $\dfrac{x^2 - 7x + 12}{x - 3} = x - 4$, for $x \neq 3$ **7.** 20   **9.** 4
11. 5   **13.** -45 **15.** 4   **17.** 32; Constant Multiple Law   **19.** 5;
Difference Law   **21.** 12; Quotient and Product Laws   **23.** 32; Power
Law   **25.** 8   **27.** 3   **29.** 3   **31.** -5 **33. a.** 2   **b.** 0   **c.** Does
not exist   **35. a.** 0   **b.** $\sqrt{x - 2}$ is undefined for $x < 2$.
37. $\lim\limits_{x \to 0^-} |x| = \lim\limits_{x \to 0^-} (-x) = 0$ and $\lim\limits_{x \to 0^+} |x| = \lim\limits_{x \to 0^+} x = 0$ **39.** 2
41. -8 **43.** -1 **45.** -12 **47.** $\frac{1}{6}$ **49.** $2\sqrt{a}$ **51.** $\frac{1}{8}$

53. a. 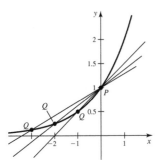   **b.** $\dfrac{2^x - 1}{x}$

c.

x	$\dfrac{2^x - 1}{x}$
-1	0.5
-0.1	0.6697
-0.01	0.6908
-0.001	0.6929
-0.0001	0.6931
-0.00001	0.6931
Limit $\approx$ 0.693	

55. a. Because $\left| \sin\dfrac{1}{x} \right| \le 1$ for all $x \ne 0$, we have that

$$|x| \left| \sin\dfrac{1}{x} \right| \le |x|.$$

That is, $\left| x \sin\dfrac{1}{x} \right| \le |x|$, so that $-|x| \le x \sin\dfrac{1}{x} \le |x|$ for all $x \ne 0$.

b.

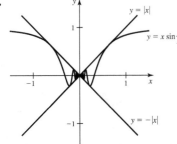

c. $\lim\limits_{x \to 0} -|x| = 0$ and $\lim\limits_{x \to 0} |x| = 0$; by part (a) and the Squeeze

Theorem, $\lim\limits_{x \to 0} x \sin\dfrac{1}{x} = 0$

57. a.

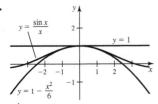

b. $\lim\limits_{x \to 0} \dfrac{\sin x}{x} = 1$ **59. a.** False   **b.** False   **c.** False   **d.** False

e. False   **61.** 8   **63.** 5   **65.** 10   **67.** -3 **69.** $a = -13$;

$\lim\limits_{x \to -1} g(x) = 6$ **71.** 6   **73.** $5a^4$ **75.** $\dfrac{1}{3}$ **77.** 2   **79.** -54

81. $f(x) = x - 1, g(x) = \dfrac{5}{x - 1}$ **83.** $b = 2$ and $c = -8$; yes

85. $\lim\limits_{S \to 0^+} r(S) = 0$; the radius of the cylinder approaches 0 as the surface area of the cylinder approaches 0.   **87.** 0.0435 N/C   **89.** 6; 4

Section 2.4 Exercises, pp. 85–88

1. $\lim\limits_{x \to a^+} f(x) = -\infty$ means that as x approaches a from the right, the values of $f(x)$ are negative and become arbitrarily large in magnitude.
3. A vertical asymptote for a function f is a vertical line $x = a$ where one (or more) of the following is true:

$$\lim\limits_{x \to a^-} f(x) = \pm\infty; \quad \lim\limits_{x \to a^+} f(x) = \pm\infty.$$

5. $-\infty$ **7.** ∞ **9. a.** ∞ **b.** ∞ **c.** ∞ **d.** ∞ **e.** $-\infty$ **f.** Does not exist   **11. a.** $-\infty$ **b.** $-\infty$ **c.** $-\infty$ **d.** ∞ **e.** $-\infty$ **f.** Does not exist   **13. a.** ∞ **b.** $-\infty$ **c.** $-\infty$ **d.** ∞
15.

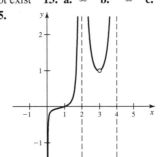

17. a. ∞ **b.** $-\infty$ **c.** Does not exist   **19. a.** $-\infty$
b. $-\infty$ **c.** $-\infty$ **21. a.** ∞ **b.** $-\infty$ **c.** Does not exist
23. a. $-\infty$ **b.** $-\infty$ **c.** $-\infty$ **25.** -5 **27.** ∞
29. a. $1/10$ **b.** $-\infty$ **c.** ∞; vertical asymptote: $x = -5$
31. $x = 3$; $\lim\limits_{x \to 3^+} f(x) = -\infty$; $\lim\limits_{x \to 3^-} f(x) = \infty$; $\lim\limits_{x \to 3} f(x)$ does not exist   **33.** $x = 0$ and $x = 2$; $\lim\limits_{x \to 0^+} f(x) = \infty$; $\lim\limits_{x \to 0^-} f(x) = -\infty$;
$\lim\limits_{x \to 0} f(x)$ does not exist; $\lim\limits_{x \to 2^+} f(x) = \infty$; $\lim\limits_{x \to 2^-} f(x) = \infty$;
$\lim\limits_{x \to 2} f(x) = \infty$ **35.** ∞ **37.** $-\infty$ **39. a.** $-\infty$ **b.** ∞ **c.** $-\infty$
d. ∞ **41. a.** False   **b.** True   **c.** False   **43.** $f(x) = \dfrac{1}{x - 6}$
45. $x = 0$ **47.** $x = -1$ **49.** $\theta = 10k + 5$, for any integer k
51. $x = 0$ **53. a.** $a = 4$ or $a = 3$ **b.** Either $a > 4$ or $a < 3$
c. $3 < a < 4$ **55. a.** $\dfrac{1}{\sqrt[3]{h}}$, regardless of the sign of h **b.** $\lim\limits_{h \to 0^+}$
$\dfrac{1}{\sqrt[3]{h}} = \infty$; $\lim\limits_{h \to 0^-} \dfrac{1}{\sqrt[3]{h}} = -\infty$; the tangent line at $(0, 0)$ is vertical.

Section 2.5 Exercises, pp. 96–98

1. As $x < 0$ becomes arbitrarily large in magnitude, the corresponding values of f approach 10.   **3.** 0   **5.** $\lim\limits_{x \to \infty} f(x) = -\infty$; $\lim\limits_{x \to -\infty} f(x) = \infty$
7. ∞; 0; 0   **9.** 3   **11.** 0   **13.** 0   **15.** ∞ **17.** 0   **19.** ∞ **21.** $-\infty$
23. 0   **25.** $\lim\limits_{x \to \infty} f(x) = \lim\limits_{x \to -\infty} f(x) = \frac{1}{5}; y = \frac{1}{5}$
27. $\lim\limits_{x \to \infty} f(x) = 2$; $\lim\limits_{x \to -\infty} f(x) = 2; y = 2$
29. $\lim\limits_{x \to \infty} f(x) = \lim\limits_{x \to -\infty} f(x) = 0; y = 0$
31. $\lim\limits_{x \to \infty} f(x) = \lim\limits_{x \to -\infty} f(x) = 0; y = 0$ **33.** $\lim\limits_{x \to \infty} f(x) = \infty$;
$\lim\limits_{x \to -\infty} f(x) = -\infty$; none   **35. a.** $y = x - 6$ **b.** $x = -6$
c.

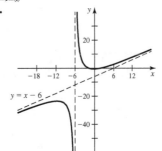

37. a. $y = \frac{1}{3}x - \frac{4}{9}$ **b.** $x = \frac{2}{3}$

c.

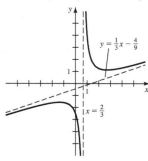

39. a. $y = 4x + 4$ **b.** No vertical asymptote

c.

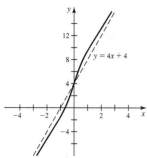

41. $\lim\limits_{x \to \infty} f(x) = \frac{2}{3}$; $\lim\limits_{x \to -\infty} f(x) = -2$; $y = \frac{2}{3}$; $y = -2$

43. $\lim\limits_{x \to \infty} f(x) = \lim\limits_{x \to -\infty} f(x) = \dfrac{1}{4 + \sqrt{3}}$; $y = \dfrac{1}{4 + \sqrt{3}}$

45. $\lim\limits_{x \to \infty} (-3e^{-x}) = 0$; $\lim\limits_{x \to -\infty} (-3e^{-x}) = -\infty$

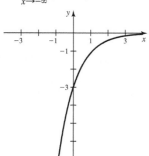

47. $\lim\limits_{x \to \infty} (1 - \ln x) = -\infty$; $\lim\limits_{x \to 0^+} (1 - \ln x) = \infty$

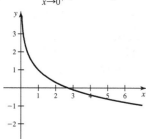

49. $\lim\limits_{x \to \infty} \sin x$ does not exist; $\lim\limits_{x \to -\infty} \sin x$ does not exist

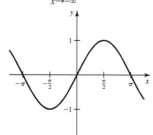

51. a. False **b.** False **c.** True

53. a. $\lim\limits_{x \to \infty} f(x) = 2$; $\lim\limits_{x \to -\infty} f(x) = 2$; $y = 2$

b. $x = 0$; $\lim\limits_{x \to 0^+} f(x) = \infty$; $\lim\limits_{x \to 0^-} f(x) = -\infty$

55. a. $\lim\limits_{x \to \infty} f(x) = 3$; $\lim\limits_{x \to -\infty} f(x) = 3$; $y = 3$

b. $x = -3$ and $x = 4$; $\lim\limits_{x \to -3^-} f(x) = \infty$; $\lim\limits_{x \to -3^+} f(x) = -\infty$;

$\lim\limits_{x \to 4^-} f(x) = -\infty$; $\lim\limits_{x \to 4^+} f(x) = \infty$

57. a. $\lim\limits_{x \to \infty} f(x) = 1$; $\lim\limits_{x \to -\infty} f(x) = 1$; $y = 1$

b. $x = 0$; $\lim\limits_{x \to 0^+} f(x) = \infty$; $\lim\limits_{x \to 0^-} f(x) = -\infty$

59. a. $\lim\limits_{x \to \infty} f(x) = 1$; $\lim\limits_{x \to -\infty} f(x) = -1$; $y = 1$ and $y = -1$

b. No vertical asymptote **61. a.** $\lim\limits_{x \to \infty} f(x) = 0$; $\lim\limits_{x \to -\infty} f(x) = 0$;

$y = 0$ **b.** No vertical asymptote **63. a.** $\dfrac{\pi}{2}$ **b.** $\dfrac{\pi}{2}$

65. a. $\lim\limits_{x \to \infty} \sinh x = \infty$; $\lim\limits_{x \to -\infty} \sinh x = -\infty$

b. $\sinh 0 = 0$

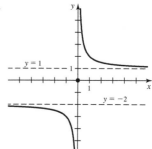

67.

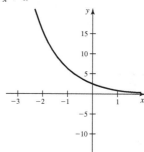

69. $x = 0$; $y = 2$ **71.** 3500 **73.** No steady state **75.** 2 **77.** 1

79. 0 **81. a.** No; f has a horizontal asymptote if $m = n$ and it has a slant asymptote if $m = n + 1$. **b.** Yes; $f(x) = x^4/\sqrt{x^6 + 1}$

83. $\lim\limits_{x \to \infty} f(x) = 0$; $\lim\limits_{x \to -\infty} f(x) = \infty$; $y = 0$

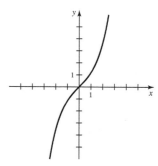

85. $x = \pm 3, x = -\dfrac{1}{2}\ln 2 \approx -0.347$

Section 2.6 Exercises, pp. 108–112

1. a, c   **3.** A function is continuous on an interval if it is continuous at each point of the interval. If the interval contains endpoints, then the function must be right- or left-continuous at those points.

5. a. $\lim\limits_{x \to a^-} f(x) = f(a)$ **b.** $\lim\limits_{x \to a^+} f(x) = f(a)$

7. $\{x: x \neq 0\}, \{x: x \neq 0\}$ **9.** $a = 2$, item 3; $a = 3$, item 2; $a = 1$, item 1   **11.** $a = 1$, item 1; $a = 2$, item 2; $a = 3$, item 1

13. Yes; $\lim\limits_{x \to 5} f(x) = f(5)$.   **15.** No; $f(1)$ is undefined.   **17.** No; $\lim\limits_{x \to 1} f(x) = 2$ but $f(1) = 3$.   **19.** No; $f(4)$ is undefined.

21. $(-\infty, \infty)$ **23.** $(-\infty, -3), (-3, 3), (3, \infty)$

25. $(-\infty, -2), (-2, 2), (2, \infty)$ **27.** 1   **29.** 16   **31.** $2\sqrt{6}$

33. $\ln 2$ **35.** $[0, 1), (1, 2), (2, 3], (3, 4]$

37. $[0, 1), (1, 2), [2, 3), (3, 5]$ **39. a.** $\lim\limits_{x \to 1} f(x)$ does not exist.
b. Continuous from the right   **c.** $(-\infty, 1), [1, \infty)$

41. $(-\infty, -2\sqrt{2}], [2\sqrt{2}, \infty)$ **43.** $(-\infty, \infty)$ **45.** $(-\infty, \infty)$ **47.** 3

49. 4   **51.** $(n\pi, (n + 1)\pi)$, where n is an integer; $\sqrt{2}; -\infty$

53. $\left(\dfrac{n\pi}{2}, \left(\dfrac{n}{2} + 1 \right) \dfrac{\pi}{2} \right)$, where n is an odd integer; $\infty; \sqrt{3} - 2$

55. $(-\infty, 0), (0, \infty); \infty; -\infty$

57. a. A is continuous on $[0, 0.08]$, and 7000 is between $A(0) = 5000$ and $A(0.08) = 11{,}098.20$. By the Intermediate Value Theorem, there is at least one c in $(0, 0.08)$ such that $A(c) = 7000$.
b.

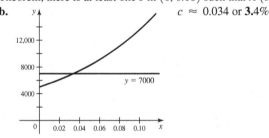

$c \approx 0.034$ or **3.4%**

59. b. $x \approx 0.835$ **61. b.** $x \approx -0.285; x \approx 0.778; x \approx 4.507$
63. b. -0.567 **65. a.** True   **b.** True   **c.** False   **d.** False
67. $(-\infty, \infty)$ **69.** $[0, 16), (16, \infty)$ **71.** 1   **73.** 2   **75.** $-\frac{1}{2}$
77. 0   **79.** $-\infty$
81. The vertical line segments should not appear.

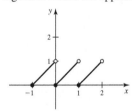

83. a, b.

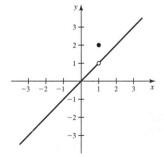

85. a. 2   **b.** 8   **c.** No; $\lim\limits_{x \to 1^-} g(x) = 2$ and $\lim\limits_{x \to 1^+} g(x) = 8$.

87. $\lim\limits_{x \to 0} f(x) = 6, \ \lim\limits_{x \to -\infty} f(x) = 10$, and $\lim\limits_{x \to \infty} f(x) = 2$; no vertical asymptote; $y = 2$ and $y = 10$ are the horizontal asymptotes.

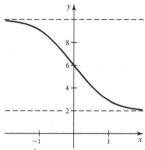

89. $x_1 = \frac{1}{7}; x_2 = \frac{1}{2}; x_3 = \frac{3}{5}$ **91. a.** $A(r)$ is continuous on $[0.01, 0.10]$ and $A(0.01) = 2615.55$, while $A(0.10) = 3984.36$. Therefore, $A(0.01) < 3500 < A(0.10)$. By the Intermediate Value Theorem, there exists c in $(0.01, 0.10)$ such that $A(c) = 3500$. Therefore, c is the desired interest rate.   **b.** $r \approx 7.28\%$ **93.** Yes. Imagine there is a clone of the monk who walks down the path at the same time the monk walks up the path. The monk and his clone must cross paths at some time between dawn and dusk.   **95.** No; f cannot be made continuous at $x = a$ by redefining $f(a)$.   **97.** $\lim\limits_{x \to 2} f(x) = -3$; define $f(2)$ to be -3.   **99. a.** Yes   **b.** No
101. $a = 0$ removable discontinuity; $a = 1$ infinite discontinuity
103. a. For example, $f(x) = 1/(x - 1), g(x) = x + 1$
b. For continuity, g must be continuous at 0 and f must be continuous at $g(0)$.

Section 2.7 Exercises, pp. 120–123

1. 1   **3.** c   **5.** Given any $\varepsilon > 0$ there exists a $\delta > 0$ such that $|f(x) - L| < \varepsilon$ whenever $0 < |x - a| < \delta$.   **7.** $0 < \delta \leq 2$
9. a. $\delta = 1$ **b.** $\delta = \frac{1}{2}$ **11. a.** $\delta = 2$ **b.** $\delta = \frac{1}{2}$
13. a. $0 < \delta \leq 1$ **b.** $0 < \delta \leq 0.79$
15. a. $0 < \delta \leq 1$ **b.** $0 < \delta \leq \frac{1}{2}$ **c.** $0 < \delta \leq \varepsilon$
17. a. $0 < \delta \leq 1$ **b.** $0 < \delta \leq \frac{1}{2}$ **c.** $0 < \delta \leq \frac{\varepsilon}{2}$
19. $\delta = \varepsilon/8$ **21.** $\delta = \varepsilon$ **23.** $\delta = \sqrt{\varepsilon}$ **27. a.** Use any $\delta > 0$
b. $\delta = \varepsilon$ **29.** $\delta = 1/\sqrt{N}$ **31.** $\delta = 1/\sqrt{N - 1}$ **33. a.** False
b. False   **c.** True   **d.** True   **35.** $\delta = \min\{1, 6\varepsilon\}$
37. $\delta = \min\{1/20, \varepsilon/200\}$ **39.** For $x > a$, $|x - a| = x - a$.
41. a. $\delta = \varepsilon/2$ **b.** $\delta = \varepsilon/3$ **c.** Because $\lim\limits_{x \to 0^+} f(x) = \lim\limits_{x \to 0^-} f(x) = -4$, $\lim\limits_{x \to 0} f(x) = -4$.   **43.** $\delta = \varepsilon^2$
45. a. For each $N > 0$ there exists $\delta > 0$ such that $f(x) > N$ whenever $0 < x - a < \delta$.   **b.** For each $N < 0$ there exists $\delta > 0$ such that $f(x) < N$ whenever $0 < a - x < \delta$.   **c.** For each $N > 0$ there exists $\delta > 0$ such that $f(x) > N$ whenever $0 < a - x < \delta$.   **47.** $\delta = 1/N$ **49.** $\delta = (-10/M)^{1/4}$
51. $N = 1/\varepsilon$ **53.** $N = M - 1$

Chapter 2 Review Exercises, pp. 123–125

1. a. False   **b.** False   **c.** False   **d.** True   **e.** False   **f.** False
g. False   **h.** True   **3.** $x = -1$; $\lim\limits_{x \to -1} f(x)$ does not exist; $x = 1$; $\lim\limits_{x \to 1} f(x) \neq f(1)$; $x = 3$; $f(3)$ is undefined.   **5. a.** 1.414   **b.** $\sqrt{2}$
7.

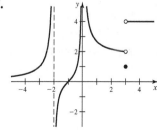

9. $\sqrt{11}$ **11.** 2   **13.** $\frac{1}{3}$ **15.** $-\frac{1}{16}$ **17.** 108   **19.** $\frac{1}{108}$ **21.** 0
23. a.

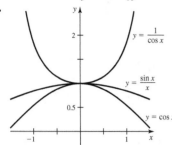

b. $\lim\limits_{x\to 0}\cos x \le \lim\limits_{x\to 0}\dfrac{\sin x}{x} \le \lim\limits_{x\to 0}\dfrac{1}{\cos x};$

$$1 \le \lim_{x\to 0}\frac{\sin x}{x} \le 1;$$

$$\lim_{x\to 0}\frac{\sin x}{x} = 1$$

25. $-\infty$ **27.** ∞ **29.** $-\infty$ **31.** $\frac{1}{2}$ **33.** ∞

35. $3\pi/2 + 2$ **37.** $\lim\limits_{x\to\infty} f(x) = -4$; $\lim\limits_{x\to-\infty} f(x) = -4$
39. $\lim\limits_{x\to\infty} f(x) = 1$; $\lim\limits_{x\to-\infty} f(x) = -\infty$ **41.** Horizontal asymptotes
at $y = 2/\pi$ and $y = -2/\pi$; vertical asymptote at $x = 0$

43. a. ∞; $-\infty$ **b.** $y = \dfrac{3x}{4} + \dfrac{5}{16}$ is the slant asymptote.
45. a. $-\infty$; ∞ **b.** $y = -x - 2$ is the slant asymptote.   **47.** No;
$f(5)$ does not exist.   **49.** No; $\lim\limits_{x\to 3^-} h(x)$ does not exist, which implies
$\lim\limits_{x\to 3} h(x)$ does not exist.   **51.** $(-\infty, -\sqrt{5}]$ and $[\sqrt{5}, \infty)$; left-
continuous at $-\sqrt{5}$ and right-continuous at $\sqrt{5}$ **53.** $(-\infty, -5)$,
$(-5, 0), (0, 5)$, and $(5, \infty)$ **55.** $a = 3, b = 0$
57.

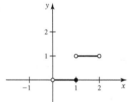

59. a. $m(0) < 30 < m(5)$ and $m(5) > 30 > m(15)$.   **b.** $m = 30$
when $t \approx 2.4$ and $t \approx 10.8$.   **c.** No; the maximum amount is
approximately $m(5.5) \approx 38.5$.   **61.** $\delta = \varepsilon$ **63.** $\delta = 1/\sqrt[4]{N}$

CHAPTER 3

Section 3.1 Exercises, pp. 133–135

1. Given the point $(a, f(a))$ and any point $(x, f(x))$ near $(a, f(a))$,
the slope of the secant line joining these points is $\dfrac{f(x) - f(a)}{x - a}$. The
limit of this quotient as x approaches a is the slope of the tangent line
at the point.   **3.** The average rate of change over the interval $[a, x]$ is
$\dfrac{f(x) - f(a)}{x - a}$. The value of $\lim\limits_{x\to a}\dfrac{f(x) - f(a)}{x - a}$ is the slope of the tangent
line; it is also the limit of average rates of change, which is the instan-
taneous rate of change at $x = a$.   **5.** $f'(a)$ is the slope of the tangent
line at $(a, f(a))$ or the instantaneous rate of change of f at a.   **7.** $\dfrac{dy}{dx}$
is the limit of $\dfrac{\Delta y}{\Delta x}$ and is the rate of change of y with respect to x.

9. a. 6   **b.** $y = 6x - 14$
c.

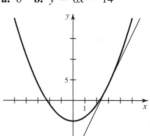

11. a. -5 **b.** $y = -5x + 1$
c.

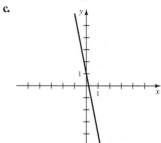

13. a. -1 **b.** $y = -x - 2$ **15. a.** 2   **b.** $y = 2x + 1$
c.

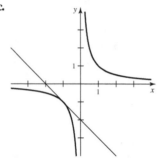

17. a. -7 **b.** $y = -7x$ **19. a.** 4   **b.** $y = 4x - 8$ **21. a.** 3
b. $y = 3x - 2$ **23. a.** $\frac{2}{25}$ **b.** $y = \frac{2}{25}x + \frac{7}{25}$ **25. a.** $\frac{1}{4}$
b. $y = \frac{1}{4}x + \frac{7}{4}$ **27. a.** $f'(-3) = 8$ **b.** $y = 8x$
29. a. $f'(-2) = -14$ **b.** $y = -14x - 16$ **31. a.** $f'(\frac{1}{4}) = -4$
b. $y = -4x + 3$ **33. a.** $\frac{1}{3}$ **b.** $y = \frac{1}{3}x + \frac{5}{3}$ **35. a.** $-\frac{1}{100}$
b. $y = -\frac{x}{100} + \frac{3}{20}$ **37. a.** $f'(x) = 6x + 2$ **b.** $y = 8x - 13$
c.

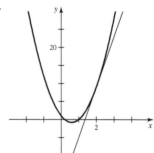

39. a. $f'(x) = 10x - 6$ **b.** $y = 14x - 19$
c.

41. a. $2ax + b$ **b.** $8x - 3$ **c.** 5   **43.** $-\frac{1}{4}$ **45.** $\frac{1}{5}$ **47. a.** True
b. False   **c.** True   **49. a.** $f'(x) = \dfrac{3}{2\sqrt{3x + 1}}$ **b.** $y = 3x/10 + 13/5$
51. a. $f'(x) = -\dfrac{6}{(3x + 1)^2}$ **b.** $y = -3x/2 - 5/2$ **53. a.** C, D
b. A, B, E **c.** A, B, E, D, C **55. a.** Approximately 10 kW;
approximately -5 kW   **b.** $t = 6$ and $t = 18$ **c.** $t = 12$

57. $f(x) = \dfrac{1}{x+1}$; $a = 2$; $-\dfrac{1}{9}$ **59.** $f(x) = x^4$; $a = 2$; 32

61. No; f is not defined at $x = 2$.   **63.** $a = 4$

65. a.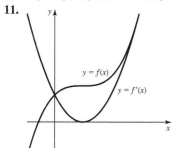

b.

h	Approximation	Error
0.1	0.25002	2.0×10^{-5}
0.01	0.25000	2.0×10^{-7}
0.001	0.25000	2.0×10^{-9}

c. Values of x on both sides of 4 are used in the formula.
d. The centered difference approximations are more accurate than
the forward and backward difference approximations.
67. a. 0.39470, 0.41545   **b.** 0.02, 0.0003

Section 3.2 Exercises, pp. 141–143

1. The slope of a curve at a point is independent of the function value
at that point.   **3.** Yes   **5.**

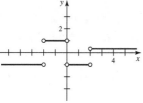

7. a–C; b–C; c–A; d–B   **9.** a–D; b–C; c–B; d–A

11.

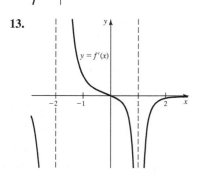

13.

15. a. $x = 1$ **b.** $x = 1, x = 2$ **c.**

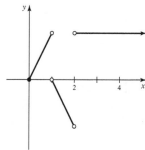

17. a. True   **b.** True   **c.** False

19. Yes

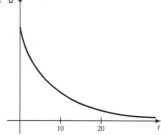

21. $y = -\dfrac{x}{3} - \dfrac{2}{3}$

23. $y = \dfrac{x}{2} + \dfrac{3}{2}$ **25.** $(1, 2), (5, 26)$ **27.** $(1, 1), \left(-\dfrac{1}{2}, -2\right)$

29. a. $t = 0$ **b.** Positive   **c.** Decreasing
d.

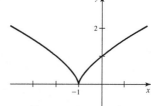

31. b. $f'_+(2) = 1, f'_-(2) = -1$ **c.** f is continuous but not differentiable at $x = 2$.
33. a.

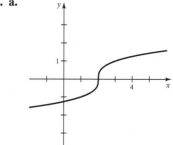

Vertical tangent line $x = 2$

b.

Vertical tangent line $x = -1$

c.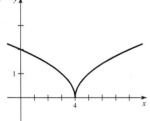

Vertical tangent line $x = 4$

d.

Vertical tangent line $x = 0$

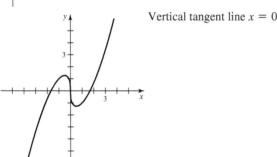

35. $f'(x) = \dfrac{1}{3}x^{-2/3}$ and $\lim\limits_{x \to 0^-} |f'(x)| = \lim\limits_{x \to 0^+} |f'(x)| = \infty$

37. a.

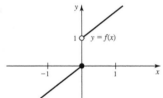

b. 1   **c.** 1   **d.**

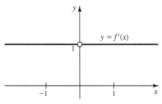

e. f is not differentiable at 0 because it is not continuous at 0.

Section 3.3 Exercises, pp. 150–153

1. Using the definition can be tedious.   **3.** $f(x) = e^x$ **5.** Take the product of the constant and the derivative of the function.   **7.** $5x^4$
9. 0   **11.** 1   **13.** $15x^2$ **15.** 8   **17.** $200t$ **19.** $12x^3 + 7$
21. $40x^3 - 32$ **23.** $6w^2 + 6w + 10$ **25.** $18x^2 + 6x + 4$

27. $4x^3 + 4x$ **29.** $2w$, for $w \neq 0$ **31.** 1, for $x \neq 1$ **33.** $\dfrac{1}{2\sqrt{x}}$, for

$x \neq a$ **35. a.** $y = -6x + 5$
b.

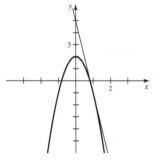

37. a. $y = 3x + 3 - 3\ln 3$ **b.**

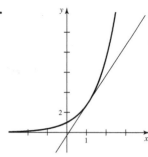

39. a. $x = 3$ **b.** $x = 4$ **41. a.** $(-1, 11), (2, -16)$ **b.** $(-3, -41)$, $(4, 36)$ **43. a.** $(4, 4)$ **b.** $(16, 0)$ **45.** $f'(x) = 20x^3 + 30x^2 + 3$; $f''(x) = 60x^2 + 60x$; $f'''(x) = 120x + 60$
47. $f'(x) = 1; f''(x) = f'''(x) = 0$, for $x \neq -1$ **49. a.** False
b. True   **c.** False   **d.** False   **e.** False   **51. a.** $y = 7x - 1$
b. $y = -2x + 5$ **c.** $y = 16x + 4$ **53.** $b = 2, c = 3$ **55.** -10

57. 4   **59.** 7.5   **61. a.** $f(x) = \sqrt{x}; a = 9$ **b.** $f'(9) = \dfrac{1}{6}$

63. a. $f(x) = x^{100}; a = 1$ **b.** $f'(1) = 100$ **65.** 3   **67.** 1
69. $f(x) = e^x; a = 0; f'(0) = 1$ **71. a.** $d'(t) = 32\,t$; ft/s; the velocity of the stone   **b.** 576 ft; approx. 131 mi/hr
73. a. $A'(t) = -\frac{1}{25}t + 2$ measures the rate at which the city grows in mi^2/yr.   **b.** 1.6 mi^2/yr   **c.** 1200 people/yr   **77. d.** $\frac{n}{2} x^{n/2-1}$
79. c. $2e^{2x}$

Section 3.4 Exercises, pp. 160–162

1. $\dfrac{d}{dx}(f(x)\,g(x)) = f'(x)\,g(x) + f(x)\,g'(x)$ **3.** $\dfrac{d}{dx}(x^n) = nx^{n-1}$, for any integer n **5.** $y' = ke^{kx}$, for any real number k
7. $36x^5 - 12x^3$ **9.** $e^t t^4 (t + 5)$ **11.** $4x^3$ **13.** $e^w(w^3 + 3w^2 - 1)$

15. a. $6x + 1$ **17. a.** $18y^5 - 52y^3 + 8y$ **19.** $\dfrac{1}{(x + 1)^2}$

21. $\dfrac{e^x}{(e^x + 1)^2}$ **23.** $e^{-x}(1 - x)$ **25.** $-\dfrac{1}{(t - 1)^2}$ **27.** $\dfrac{e^x(x^2 - 2x - 1)}{(x^2 - 1)^2}$
29. a. $2w$, for $w \neq 0$ **31.** 1, for $x \neq a$ **33. a.** $y = -3x/2 + 17/2$
b.

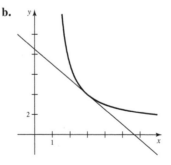

35. a. $y = 3x + 1$ **b.**

37. $-27x^{-10}$ **39.** $6t - 42/t^8$ **41.** $-3/t^2 - 2/t^3$ **43.** $e^{7x}(7x + 1)$
45. $45e^{3x}$ **47.** $e^{-3x}(1 - 3x)$ **49.** $\frac{2}{3}e^x - e^{-x}$

51. a. $p'(t) = \left(\dfrac{20}{t + 2}\right)^2$ **b.** $p'(5) \approx 8.16$ **c.** $t = 0$

d. $\lim\limits_{t \to \infty} p'(t) = 0$; the population approaches a steady state.

e.

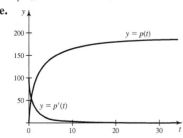

53. a. $Q'(t) = -1.386e^{-0.0693t}$ **b.** -1.386 mg/hr; -1.207 mg/hr

c. $\lim\limits_{t \to \infty} Q(t) = 0$—eventually none of the drug remains in the bloodstream; $\lim\limits_{t \to \infty} Q'(t) = 0$—the rate at which the body excretes the drug goes to zero over time. **55. a.** $x = -\frac{1}{2}$ **b.** The line tangent to the graph of $f(x)$ at $x = -\frac{1}{2}$ is horizontal. **57.** $\dfrac{e^x(x^2 - x - 5)}{(x - 2)^2}$

59. $\dfrac{e^x(x^2 + x + 1)}{(x + 1)^2}$ **61. a.** False **b.** False **c.** False **d.** True

63. $f'(x) = x e^{3x}(3x + 2)$
$f''(x) = e^{3x}(9x^2 + 12x + 2)$
$f'''(x) = 9e^{3x}(3x^2 + 6x + 2)$

65. $f'(x) = \dfrac{x^2 + 2x - 7}{(x + 1)^2}$; $f''(x) = \dfrac{16}{(x + 1)^3}$

67. $8x - \dfrac{2}{(5x + 1)^2}$ **69.** $\dfrac{r - 6\sqrt{r} - 1}{2\sqrt{r}(r + 1)^2}$

71. $300x^9 + 135x^8 + 105x^6 + 120x^3 + 45x^2 + 15$

73. a. $y = -\dfrac{108}{169}x + \dfrac{567}{169}$ **b.**

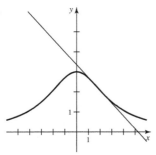

75. $-\frac{3}{2}$ **77.** $\frac{1}{9}$ **79.** $\frac{7}{8}$ **81. a.** $F'(x) = -\dfrac{1.8 \times 10^{10} \, Qq}{x^3}$ N/m

b. -1.8×10^{19} N/m **c.** $|F'(x)|$ decreases as x increases.
83. One possible pair: $f(x) = e^{ax}$ and $g(x) = e^{bx}$, where

$b = \dfrac{a}{a - 1}$, $a \neq 1$ **87.** $f''g + 2f'g' + fg''$

91. a. $f'gh + fg'h + fgh'$ **b.** $2e^{2x}(x^2 + 3x - 2)$

Section 3.5 Exercises, pp. 169–171

1. $\dfrac{\sin x}{x}$ is undefined at $x = 0$. **3.** The tangent and cotangent functions are defined as ratios of the sine and cosine functions.
5. -1 **7.** 3 **9.** $\frac{7}{3}$ **11.** 5 **13.** 7 **15.** $\frac{1}{4}$ **17.** $\cos x - \sin x$
19. $e^{-x}(\cos x - \sin x)$ **21.** $\sin x + x \cos x$ **23.** $-\dfrac{1}{1 + \sin x}$
25. $\cos^2 x - \sin^2 x = \cos 2x$ **27.** $-2 \sin x \cos x = -\sin 2x$
33. $\sec x \tan x - \csc x \cot x$ **35.** $e^{5x} \csc x(5 - \cot x)$

37. $-\dfrac{\csc x}{1 + \csc x}$ **39.** $\cos^2 z - \sin^2 z = \cos 2z$ **41.** $2 \cos x - x \sin x$

43. $2e^x \cos x$ **45.** $2 \csc^2 x \cot x$ **47.** $2\left(\sec^2 x \tan x + \csc^2 x \cot x\right)$
49. a. False **b.** False **c.** True **d.** True **51.** a/b **53.** $\frac{3}{4}$

55. 0 **57.** $x \cos 2x + \frac{1}{2} \sin 2x$ **59.** $\dfrac{1}{2 \sin x \cos x - 1}$

61. $\dfrac{2 \sin x}{(1 + \cos x)^2}$ **63. a.** $y = \sqrt{3}x + 2 - \dfrac{\pi\sqrt{3}}{6}$

b.

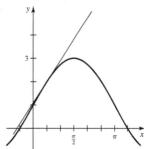

65. a. $y = -2\sqrt{3}x + \dfrac{2\sqrt{3}\pi}{3} + 1$ **b.**

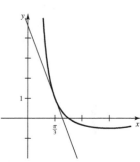

67. $x = 7\pi/6 + 2k\pi$ and $x = 11\pi/6 + 2k\pi$, where k is an integer
69. a.

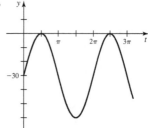

b. $v(t) = 30 \cos t$

c.

d. $v(t) = 0$, for $t = (2k + 1)\dfrac{\pi}{2}$, where k is any nonnegative

integer; the position is $y\left((2k + 1)\dfrac{\pi}{2}\right) = 0$ if k is even or

$y\left((2k + 1)\dfrac{\pi}{2}\right) = -60$ if k is odd.

e. $v(t)$ is at a maximum at $t = 2k\pi$, where k is a nonnegative integer; the position is $y(2k\pi) = -30$.

f. $a(t) = -30 \sin t$

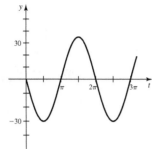

77. $a = 0$ **79. a.** $2 \sin x \cos x$ **b.** $3 \sin^2 x \cos x$ **c.** $4 \sin^3 x \cos x$
d. $n \sin^{n-1} x \cos x$; the conjecture is true for $n = 1$. If it holds

for $n = k$, then when $n = k + 1$, we have $\dfrac{d}{dx}(\sin^{k+1} x) =$

$\dfrac{d}{dx}(\sin^k x \cdot \sin x) = \sin^k x \cos x + \sin x \cdot k \sin^{k-1} x \cos x =$

$(k + 1) \sin^k x \cos x$.   **81. a.** $f(x) = \sin x$; $a = \pi/6$ **b.** $\sqrt{3}/2$
83. a. $f(x) = \cot x$; $a = \pi/4$ **b.** -2 **85.** Because D is a
difference quotient for f (and $h = 0.01$ is small), D is a good approximation to f'. Therefore, the graph of D is nearly indistinguishable
from the graph of $f'(x) = \cos x$.

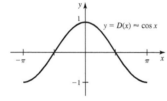

Section 3.6 Exercises, pp. 180–185

1. The average rate of change is $\dfrac{f(x + \Delta x) - f(x)}{\Delta x}$, whereas the

instantaneous rate of change is the limit as Δx goes to zero in this
quotient.   **3.** Small   **5.** If the position of the object at time t is $s(t)$,
then the acceleration at time t is $a(t) = d^2 s/dt^2$.   **7.** Each of the first
200 stoves costs, on average, \$70 to produce. When 200 stoves have
already been produced, the 201st stove costs \$65 to produce.
9. a. 40 mi/hr   **b.** 40 mi/hr; yes   **c.** -60 mi/hr; -60 mi/hr; south
d. The police car drives away from the police station going north
until about 10:08, when it turns around and heads south, toward the
police station. It continues south until it passes the police station at
about 11:02 and keeps going south until about 11:40, when it turns
around and heads north.
11. a.

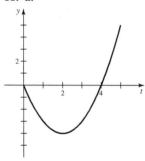

b. $v(t) = 2t - 4$; stationary at
$t = 2$, to the right on $(2, 5]$, to
the left on $[0, 2)$

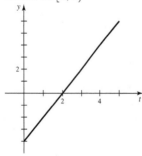

c. $v(1) = -2$ ft/s; $a(1) = 2$ ft/s^2 **d.** $a(2) = 2$ ft/s^2 **e.** $(2, 5]$
13. a.

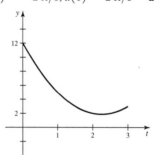

b. $v(t) = 4t - 9$; stationary at
$t = \frac{9}{4}$, to the right on $\left(\frac{9}{4}, 3\right]$, to the
left on $\left[0, \frac{9}{4}\right)$

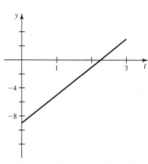

c. $v(1) = -5$ ft/s; $a(1) = 4$ ft/s^2 **d.** $a\left(\frac{9}{4}\right) = 4$ ft/s^2 **e.** $\left(\frac{9}{4}, 3\right]$
15. a.

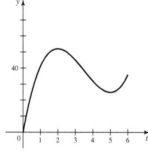

b. $v(t) = 6t^2 - 42t + 60$; stationary at $t = 2$ and $t = 5$, to the right
on $[0, 2)$ and $(5, 6]$, to the left on $(2, 5)$

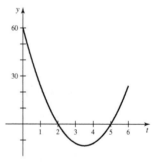

c. $v(1) = 24$ ft/s; $a(1) = -30$ ft/s^2 **d.** $a(2) = -18$ ft/s;
$a(5) = 18$ ft/s^2 **e.** $\left(2, \frac{7}{2}\right)$, $(5, 6]$ **17. a.** $v(t) = -32t + 64$
b. At $t = 2$ **c.** 96 ft   **d.** At $2 + \sqrt{6}$ **e.** $-32\sqrt{6}$ ft/s
f. $(2, 2 + \sqrt{6})$ **19. a.** 98,300 people/yr in 2005
b. 99,920 people/yr in 1997; 95,600 people/yr in 2005
c. $p'(t) = -0.54t + 101$; population increased, growth rate is
positive but decreasing
21. a. $\overline{C}(x) = \dfrac{1000}{x} + 0.1$; $C'(x) = 0.1$

b. $\overline{C}(2000) = \$0.60/$item; $C'(2000) = \$0.10/$item
c. The average cost per item when 2000 items are produced is
\$0.60/item. The cost of producing the 2001st item is \$0.10.

23. a. $\overline{C}(x) = -0.01x + 40 + 100/x; C'(x) = -0.02x + 40$
b. $\overline{C}(1000) = \$30.10/\text{item}; C'(1000) = \$20/\text{item}$
c. The average cost per item is about $30.10 when 1000 items are produced. The cost of producing the 1001st item is $20.
25. a. 20 **b.** $20 **c.** $E(p) = \frac{p}{p-20}$ **d.** Elastic for $p > 10$; inelastic for $0 < p < 10$ **e.** 2.5% **f.** 2.5% **27.** $E(p) = -bp$; elastic for $p > \frac{1}{b}$; inelastic for $0 < p < \frac{1}{b}$ **29. a.** False **b.** True
c. False **d.** True **31.** 240 ft **33.** 64 ft/s **35. a.** $t = 1, 2, 3$
b. It is moving in the positive direction for t in $(0, 1)$ and $(2, 3)$; it is moving in the negative direction for t in $(1, 2)$ and $t > 3$.
c.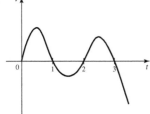
d. $(0,\frac{1}{2}), (1,\frac{3}{2}), (2,\frac{5}{2}), (3, \infty)$

37. a. $P(x) = 0.02x^2 + 50x - 100$
b. $\frac{P(x)}{x} = 0.02x + 50 - \frac{100}{x}; \frac{dP}{dx} = 0.04x + 50$
c. $\frac{P(500)}{500} = 59.8; \frac{dp}{dx}(500) = 70$
d. The profit, on average, for each of the first 500 items produced is 59.8; the profit for the 501st item produced is 70.
39. a. $P(x) = 0.04x^2 + 100x - 800$
b. $\frac{P(x)}{x} = 0.04x + 100 - \frac{800}{x}; \frac{dp}{dx} = 0.08x + 100$
c. $\frac{P(1000)}{1000} = 139.2; p'(1000) = 180$
d. The average profit per item for each of the first 1000 items produced is $139.20. The profit for the 1001st item produced is $180.
41. a. 1930, 1.1 million people/yr **b.** 1960, 2.9 million people/yr
c. The population was never decreasing.
d. (1905, 1915), (1930, 1960), (1980, 1990)
43. a. 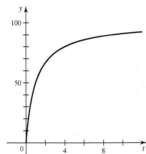   **b.** $v = \frac{100}{(t+1)^2}$
c.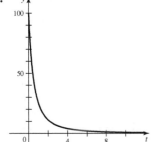

The marble moves fastest at the beginning and slows considerably over the first 5 s. It continues to slow but never actually stops.
d. $t = 4$ s **e.** $t = -1 + \sqrt{2} \approx 0.414$ s

45. a. $C'(x) = -\frac{125{,}000{,}000}{x^2} + 1.5$;
$\overline{C}(x) = \frac{C(x)}{25{,}000} = 50 + \frac{5000}{x} + 0.00006x$
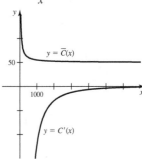
b. $C'(5000) = -3.5; \overline{C}(5000) = 51.3$ **c.** Marginal cost: If the batch size is increased from 5000 to 5001, then the cost of producing 25,000 gadgets will *decrease* by about $3.50. Average cost: When batch size is 5000, it costs $51.30 *per item* to produce all 25,000 gadgets.
47. a. $R(p) = \frac{100p}{p^2+1}$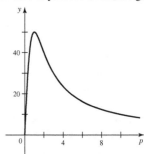
b. $R'(p) = \frac{100(1-p^2)}{(p^2+1)^2}$
c. $p = 1$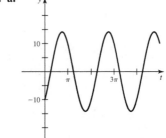
49. a.

b. $dx/dt = 10\cos t + 10\sin t$ **c.** $t = 3\pi/4 + k\pi$, where k is any positive integer **d.** The graph implies that the spring never stops oscillating. In reality, the weight would eventually come to rest.
51. a. Juan starts faster than Jean and opens up a big lead. Then Juan slows down while Jean speeds up. Jean catches up, and the race finishes in a tie. **b.** Same average velocity **c.** Tie **d.** At $t = 2$, $\theta'(2) = \pi/2$ rad/min; $\theta'(4) = \pi =$ Jean's greatest velocity
e. At $t = 2, \varphi'(2) = \pi/2$ rad/min; $\varphi'(0) = \pi =$ Juan's greatest velocity

53. a.

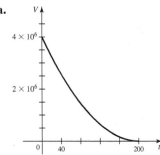 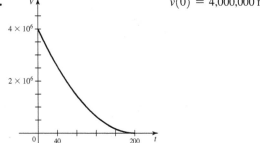

$v(0) = 4{,}000{,}000 \text{ m}^3$

b. 200 hr

c.

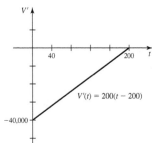

$V'(t) = 200(t - 200)$

d. The magnitude of the flow rate is greatest (most negative) at $t = 0$ and least (zero) at $t = 200$.

55. a. $v(t) = -15e^{-t}(\sin t + \cos t); v(1) \approx -7.6 \text{ m/s},$ $v(3) \approx 0.63 \text{ m/s}$ **b.** Down $(0, 2.4)$ and $(5.5, 8.6)$; up $(2.4, 5.5)$ and $(8.6, 10)$ **c.** ≈ 0.65 m/s **57. a.** $-T'(1) = -80, -T'(3) = 80$ **b.** $-T'(x) < 0$ for $0 \le x < 2; -T'(x) > 0$ for $2 < x \le 4$ **c.** Near $x = 0$, with $x > 0$, $-T'(x) < 0$, so heat flows toward the end of the rod. Similarly, near $x = 4$, with $x < 4$, $-T'(x) > 0$.

Section 3.7 Exercises, pp. 191–194

1. $\dfrac{dy}{dx} = \dfrac{dy}{du} \cdot \dfrac{du}{dx}; \dfrac{d}{dx}(f(g(x))) = f'(g(x)) \cdot g'(x)$ **3.** $g(x), x$

5. Outer: $f(x) = x^{-5}$; inner: $u = x^2 + 10$ **7.** $30(3x + 7)^9$

9. $5 \sin^4 x \cos x$ **11.** $5e^{5x-7}$ **13.** $\dfrac{x}{\sqrt{x^2 + 1}}$ **15.** $10x \sec^2(5x^2)$

17. $e^x \sec e^x \tan e^x$ **19.** $10(6x + 7)(3x^2 + 7x)^9$ **21.** $\dfrac{5}{\sqrt{10x + 1}}$

23. $-\dfrac{315x^2}{(7x^3 + 1)^4}$ **25.** $3 \sec(3x + 1) \tan(3x + 1)$ **27.** $e^x \sec^2 e^x$

29. $(12x^2 + 3) \cos(4x^3 + 3x + 1)$ **31.** $\dfrac{\cos(2\sqrt{x})}{\sqrt{x}}$

33. $5 \sec x (\sec x + \tan x)^5$ **35. a.** $u = \cos x, y = u^3;$ $\dfrac{dy}{dx} = -3 \cos^2 x \sin x$ **b.** $u = x^3, y = \cos u; \dfrac{dy}{dx} = -3x^2 \sin x^3$

37. a. 100 **b.** -100 **c.** -16 **d.** 40 **e.** 40

39. -0.297 hPa/min **41.** $y' = 25(12x^5 - 9x^2)(2x^6 - 3x^3 + 3)^{24}$

43. $y' = 30(1 + 2 \tan x)^{14} \sec^2 x$ **45.** $y' = -\dfrac{\cot x \csc^2 x}{\sqrt{1 + \cot^2 x}}$

47. $e^x \cos(\sin e^x) \cos e^x$

49. $y' = -15 \sin^4(\cos 3x)(\sin 3x)(\cos(\cos 3x))$

51. $y' = \dfrac{3e^{\sqrt{3x}}}{2\sqrt{3x}} \sec^2 e^{\sqrt{3x}}$ **53.** $y' = \dfrac{1}{2\sqrt{x + \sqrt{x}}}\left(1 + \dfrac{1}{2\sqrt{x}}\right)$

55. $y' = f'(g(x^2))g'(x^2) 2x$ **57.** $\dfrac{5x^4}{(x + 1)^6}$

59. $x e^{x^2+1}(2 \sin x^3 + 3x \cos x^3)$ **61.** $\theta \sec 5\theta(2 + 5\theta \tan 5\theta)$

63. $4((x + 2)(x^2 + 1))^3(3x + 1)(x + 1)$ **65.** $\dfrac{2x^3 - \sin 2x}{\sqrt{x^4 + \cos 2x}}$

67. $2(p + \pi)(\sin p^2 + p(p + \pi) \cos p^2)$ **69. a.** True **b.** True **c.** True **d.** False **71.** $2 \cos x^2 - 4x^2 \sin x^2$

73. $4e^{-2x^2}(4x^2 - 1)$ **75.** $y' = \dfrac{f'(x)}{2\sqrt{f(x)}}$

77. $y = -9x + 35$

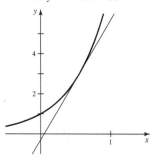

79. a. $h(4) = 9, h'(4) = -6$ **b.** $y = -6x + 33$
81. $y = 6x + 3 - 3 \ln 3$

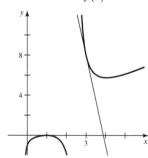

83. a. -3π **b.** -5π **85. a.** $\dfrac{d^2y}{dt^2} = \dfrac{-y_0 k}{m} \cos\left(t\sqrt{\dfrac{k}{m}}\right)$

87. a.

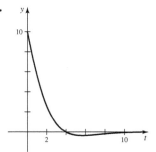

b. $v(t) = -5e^{-t/2}\left(\dfrac{\pi}{4} \sin \dfrac{\pi t}{8} + \cos \dfrac{\pi t}{8}\right)$

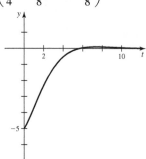

89. a. 10.88 hr **b.** $D'(t) = \frac{6\pi}{365}\sin\left(\frac{2\pi(t+10)}{365}\right)$
c. 2.87 min/day; on March 1, the length of day is increasing at a rate of about 2.87 min/day.
d.

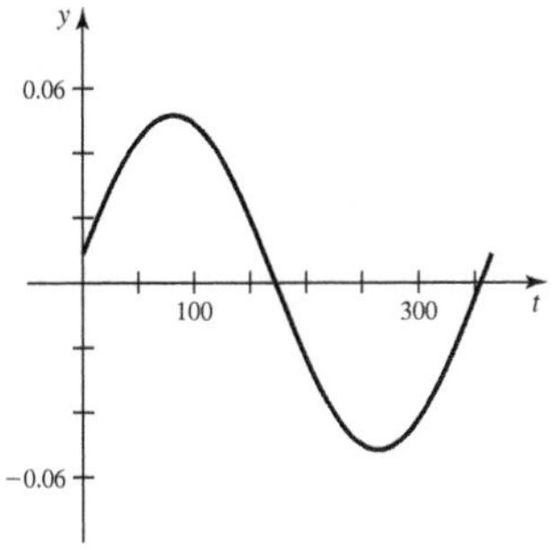

e. Most rapidly; approximately March 22 and September 22; least rapidly: approximately December 21 and June 21

91. a. $E'(t) = 400 + 200\cos\frac{\pi t}{12}$ MW **b.** At noon; $E'(0) = 600$ MW **c.** At midnight; $E'(12) = 200$ MW
d.

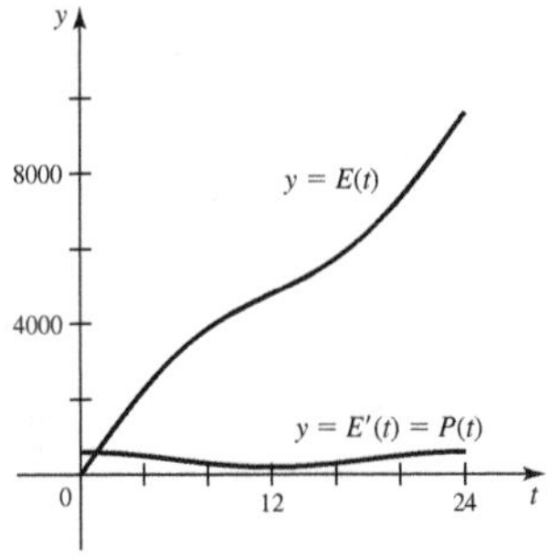

93. a. $f'(x) = -2\cos x\sin x + 2\sin x\cos x = 0$
b. $f(0) = \cos^2 0 + \sin^2 0 = 1$; $f(x) = 1$ for all x; that is, $\cos^2 x + \sin^2 x = 1$ **97. a.** $h(x) = (x^2-3)^5$; $a = 2$ **b.** 20
99. a. $h(x) = \sin x^2$; $a = \pi/2$ **b.** $\pi\cos(\pi^2/4)$ **101.** $10f'(25)$

Section 3.8 Exercises, pp. 200–202

1. There may be more than one expression for y or y'. **3.** When derived implicitly, dy/dx is usually given in terms of both x and y.
5. a. $-\frac{x^3}{y^3}$ **b.** 1 **7. a.** $\frac{2}{y}$ **b.** 1 **9. a.** $\frac{20x^3}{\cos y}$ **b.** −20
11. a. $-\frac{1}{\sin y}$ **b.** −1 **13.** $\frac{1 - y\cos xy}{x\cos xy - 1}$ **15.** $-\frac{1}{1+\sin y}$
17. $\frac{1}{2y\sin y^2 + e^y}$ **19.** $\frac{3x^2(x-y)^2 + 2y}{2x}$ **21.** $\frac{13y - 18x^2}{21y^2 - 13x}$
23. $\frac{5\sqrt{x^4+y^2} - 2x^3}{y - 6y^2\sqrt{x^4+y^2}}$ **25. a.** $2^2 + 2\cdot 1 + 1^2 = 7$
b. $y = -5x/4 + 7/2$ **27. a.** $\sin\pi + 5\left(\frac{\pi^2}{5}\right) = \pi^2$
b. $y = \frac{\pi(1+\pi)}{1+2\pi} + \frac{5}{1+2\pi}x$
29. a. $\cos\left(\frac{\pi}{2} - \frac{\pi}{4}\right) + \sin\frac{\pi}{4} = \sqrt{2}$ **b.** $y = \frac{x}{2}$
31. $-\frac{1}{4y^3}$ **33.** $\frac{\sin y}{(\cos y - 1)^3}$ **35.** $\frac{4e^{2y}}{(1-2e^{2y})^3}$ **37.** $\frac{5}{4}x^{1/4}$
39. $\frac{10}{3(5x+1)^{1/3}}$ **41.** $-\frac{3}{2^{7/4}x^{3/4}(4x-3)^{5/4}}$ **43.** $\frac{2}{9x^{2/3}\sqrt[3]{1+\sqrt[3]{x}}}$

45. $-\frac{1}{4}$ **47.** $-\frac{24}{13}$ **49.** −5 **51. a.** False **b.** True **c.** False **d.** False **53. a.** $y = x - 1$ and $y = -x + 2$
b.

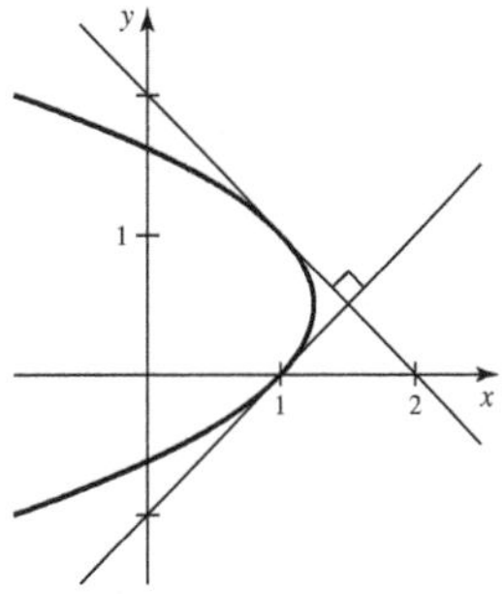

55. a. $y' = -\frac{2xy}{x^2+4}$ **b.** $y = \frac{1}{2}x + 2$, $y = -\frac{1}{2}x + 2$
c. $-\frac{16x}{(x^2+4)^2}$ **57. a.** $\left(\frac{5}{4}, \frac{1}{2}\right)$ **b.** No
59. Horizontal: $y = -6, y = 0$; vertical: $x = 1, x = 3$
61. a. $\frac{dy}{dx} = 0$ on the $y = 1$ branch; $\frac{dy}{dx} = \frac{1}{2y+1}$ on the other two branches. **b.** $f_1(x) = 1, f_2(x) = \frac{-1+\sqrt{4x-3}}{2}$, $f_3(x) = \frac{-1-\sqrt{4x-3}}{2}$
c.

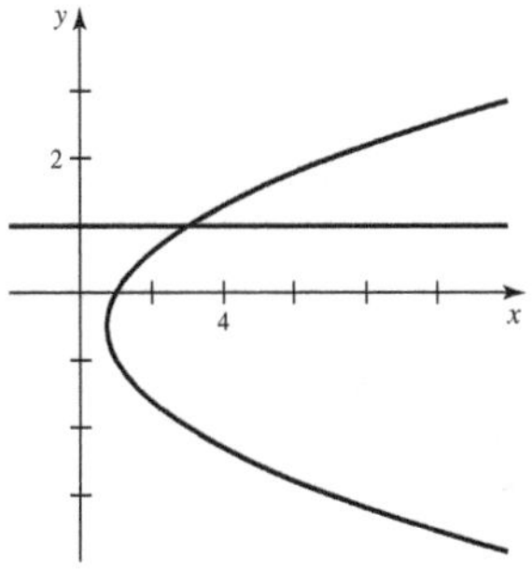

63. a. $\frac{dy}{dx} = \frac{x - x^3}{y}$ **b.** $f_1(x) = \sqrt{x^2 - \frac{x^4}{2}}$; $f_2(x) = -\sqrt{x^2 - \frac{x^4}{2}}$
c.

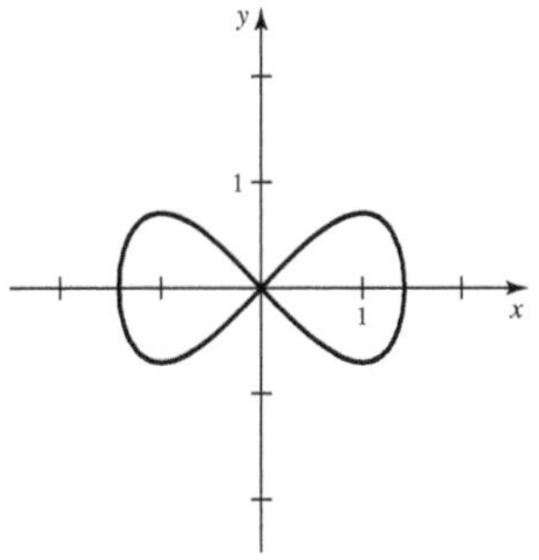

65. $y = \frac{4x}{5} - \frac{3}{5}$

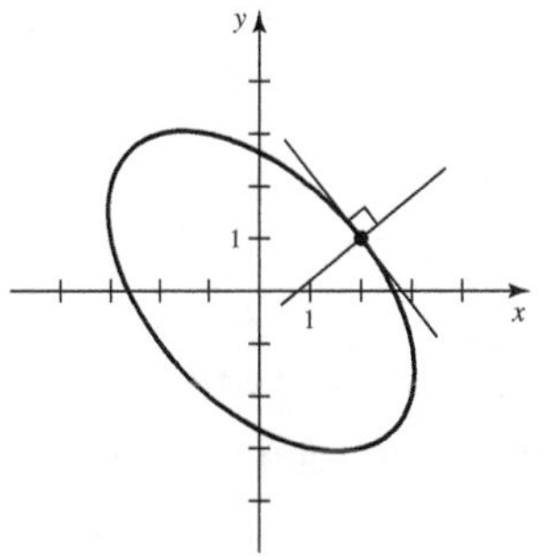

67. $y = -\dfrac{1 + 2\pi}{5}x + \pi\left(\dfrac{25 + \pi + 2\pi^2}{25}\right)$

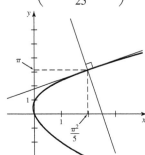

69. $y = -2x + \dfrac{5\pi}{4}$

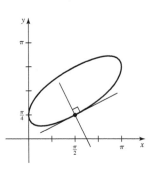

71. a. Tangent line $y = -\dfrac{9x}{11} + \dfrac{20}{11}$; normal line $y = \dfrac{11x}{9} - \dfrac{2}{9}$

b.

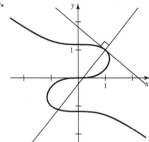

73. a. Tangent line $y = -\dfrac{x}{3} + \dfrac{8}{3}$; normal line $y = 3x - 4$

b.

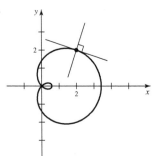

75. a. $\dfrac{dK}{dL} = -\dfrac{K}{2L}$ **b.** -4 **77.** $\dfrac{dr}{dh} = \dfrac{h - 2r}{h}; -3$

79. Note that for $y = mx$, $dy/dx = m$; for $x^2 + y^2 = a^2$, $dy/dx = -x/y$. **81.** For $xy = a$, $dy/dx = -y/x$. For $x^2 - y^2 = b$, $dy/dx = x/y$. Because $(-y/x) \cdot (x/y) = -1$, the families of curves form orthogonal trajectories. **83.** $\dfrac{7y^2 - 3x^2 - 4xy^2 - 4x^3}{2y(2x^2 + 2y^2 - 7x)}$

85. $\dfrac{2y^2(5 + 8x\sqrt{y})}{(1 + 2x\sqrt{y})^3}$ **87.** No horizontal tangent line; vertical tangent lines at $(2, 1), (-2, 1)$ **89.** No horizontal tangent line; vertical tangent lines at $(0, 0), \left(\dfrac{3\sqrt{3}}{2}, \sqrt{3}\right), \left(-\dfrac{3\sqrt{3}}{2}, -\sqrt{3}\right)$

Section 3.9 Exercises, pp. 210–213

1. $x = e^y \Rightarrow 1 = e^y y'(x) \Rightarrow y'(x) = 1/e^y = 1/x$

3. $\dfrac{d}{dx}(\ln kx) = \dfrac{d}{dx}(\ln k + \ln x) = \dfrac{d}{dx}(\ln x)$

5. $f'(x) = \dfrac{1}{x \ln b}$; if $b = e$, then $f'(x) = \dfrac{1}{x}$. **7.** $f(x) = e^{h(x)\ln g(x)}$

9. $\dfrac{1}{x}$ **11.** $2/x$ **13.** $\cot x$ **15.** $2/(1 - x^2)$ **17.** $(x^2 + 1)/x + 2x \ln x$

19. $1/(x \ln x)$ **21.** $\dfrac{1}{x(\ln x + 1)^2}$ **23.** $8^x \ln 8$ **25.** $5 \cdot 4^x \ln 4$

27. $3^x \cdot x^2(x \ln 3 + 3)$ **29.** $1000(1.045)^{4t}\ln(1.045)$

31. a. About 28.7 s **b.** -46.512 s/1000 ft **c.** $dT/da = -2.74 \cdot 2^{-0.274a} \ln 2$

At $t = 8$, $\dfrac{dT}{da} = -0.4156$ min/1000 ft

$= -24.938$ s/1000 ft.

If a plane travels at 30,000 feet and increases its altitude by 1,000 feet, the time of useful consciousness decreases by about 25 seconds. **33. a.** About 67.19 hr

b. $Q'(12) = -9.815$ μCi/hr
$Q'(24) = -5.201$ μCi/hr
$Q'(48) = -1.461$ μCi/hr

The rate at which iodine-123 leaves the body decreases with time.

35. $2^x \ln 2$ **37.** $e^y y e^{-1}(y + e)$ **39.** $2e^{2\theta}$ **41.** $\dfrac{\sqrt{x}}{2}(10x - 9)$

43. $\dfrac{2^x \ln 2}{(2^x + 1)^2}$ **45.** $x^{\cos x - 1}(\cos x - x \ln x \sin x); -\ln(\pi/2)$

47. $x^{\sqrt{x}}\left(\dfrac{2 + \ln x}{2\sqrt{x}}\right); 4(2 + \ln 4)$

49. $\dfrac{(\sin x)^{\ln x}(\ln(\sin x) + x(\ln x)\cot x)}{x}; 0$

51. $y = x \sin 1 + 1 - \sin 1$ **53.** $y = e^{2/e}$ and $y = e^{-2/e}$

55. $\dfrac{8x}{(x^2 - 1)\ln 3}$ **57.** $-\sin x(\ln(\cos^2 x) + 2)$ **59.** $-\dfrac{\ln 4}{x \ln^2 x}$

61. $\dfrac{(x + 1)^{10}}{(2x - 4)^8}\left(\dfrac{10}{x + 1} - \dfrac{8}{x - 2}\right)$ **63.** $2x^{\ln x - 1}\ln x$

65. $\dfrac{(x + 1)^{3/2}(x - 4)^{5/2}}{(5x + 3)^{2/3}}\left(\dfrac{3}{2(x + 1)} + \dfrac{5}{2(x - 4)} - \dfrac{10}{3(5x + 3)}\right)$

67. $(\sin x)^{\tan x}(1 + (\sec^2 x)\ln \sin x)$ **69. a.** False **b.** False

c. False **d.** False **e.** True **71.** $-\dfrac{1}{x^2 \ln 10}$ **73.** $\frac{2}{x}$

75. $3^x \ln 3$ **77.** $\frac{12}{(3x + 1)}$ **79.** $\frac{1}{2x}$

81. $\dfrac{2}{2x - 1} + \dfrac{3}{x + 2} + \dfrac{8}{1 - 4x}$

83. $y = 2$

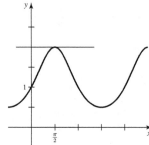

85. $10x^{10x}(1 + \ln x)$ **87.** $x^{\cos x}\left(\dfrac{\cos x}{x} - (\ln x)\sin x\right)$

89. $\left(1 + \dfrac{1}{x}\right)^x \left(\ln\left(1 + \dfrac{1}{x}\right) - \dfrac{1}{x+1}\right)$ **91.** $x^{9+x^{10}}(1 + 10 \ln x)$

93. a.

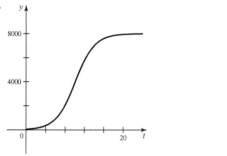

b. $t = 2 \ln 265 \approx 11.2$ years; about 14.5 years
c. $P'(0) \approx 25$ fish/year; $P'(5) \approx 264$ fish/year
d.

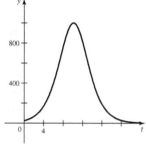

The population is growing fastest after about 10 years.
95. b. $r(11) \approx 0.0133$; $r(21) \approx 0.0118$; the relative growth rate is decreasing. **c.** $\lim\limits_{t \to \infty} r(t) = 0$; as the population gets close to carrying capacity, growth rate approaches zero.
97. a. $A(5) = \$17{,}443$
$A(15) = \$72{,}705$
$A(25) = \$173{,}248$
$A(35) = \$356{,}178$
$\$5526.20/$year, $\$10{,}054.30/$year, $\$18{,}293/$year
b. $A(40) = \$497{,}873$

c. $\dfrac{dA}{dt} = 600{,}000 \ln(1.005)\left((1.005)^{12t}\right)$

$\approx (2992.5)(1.005)^{12t}$

A increases at an increasing rate. **99.** $p = e^{1/e}$; (e, e) **101.** $1/e$
103. $27(1 + \ln 3)$

Section 3.10 Exercises, pp. 221–223

1. $\dfrac{d}{dx}(\sin^{-1} x) = \dfrac{1}{\sqrt{1 - x^2}}$; $\dfrac{d}{dx}(\tan^{-1} x) = \dfrac{1}{1 + x^2}$;

$\dfrac{d}{dx}(\sec^{-1} x) = \dfrac{1}{|x|\sqrt{x^2 - 1}}$ **3.** $\frac{1}{5}$ **5.** $\frac{1}{4}$ **7.** $\dfrac{2}{\sqrt{1 - 4x^2}}$

9. $-\dfrac{4w}{\sqrt{1 - 4w^2}}$ **11.** $-\dfrac{2e^{-2x}}{\sqrt{1 - e^{-4x}}}$ **13.** $\dfrac{10}{100x^2 + 1}$

15. $\dfrac{4y}{1 + (2y^2 - 4)^2}$ **17.** $-\dfrac{1}{2\sqrt{z}\,(1 + z)}$ **19.** $\dfrac{1}{|x|\sqrt{x^2 - 1}}$

21. $-\dfrac{1}{|2u + 1|\sqrt{u^2 + u}}$ **23.** $\dfrac{2y}{(y^2 + 1)^2 + 1}$

25. $\dfrac{1}{x|\ln x|\sqrt{(\ln x)^2 - 1}}$ **27.** $-\dfrac{e^x \sec^2 e^x}{|\tan e^x|\sqrt{\tan^2 e^x - 1}}$

29. $-\dfrac{e^s}{1 + e^{2s}}$ **31.** $y = x + \dfrac{\pi}{4} - \dfrac{1}{2}$ **33.** $y = -\dfrac{4}{\sqrt{6}}x + \dfrac{\pi}{3} + \dfrac{2}{\sqrt{3}}$

35. a. ≈ -0.00055 rad/m
b.

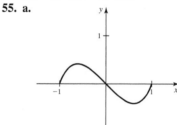

The magnitude of the change in angular size, $|d\theta/dx|$, is greatest when the boat is at the skyscraper (i.e., at $x = 0$).

37. $\frac{1}{3}$ **39.** $-\frac{1}{5}$ **41.** $\frac{1}{2}$ **43.** 4   **45.** $\frac{1}{12}$ **47.** $\frac{1}{4}$ **49.** $\frac{5}{4}$ **51. a.** $\frac{1}{2}$
b. $\frac{2}{3}$ **c.** Cannot be determined   **d.** $\frac{3}{2}$ **53. a.** True   **b.** False
c. True   **d.** True   **e.** True
55. a.

b. $f'(x) = 2x \sin^{-1} x + \dfrac{x^2 - 1}{\sqrt{1 - x^2}}$

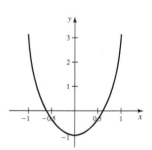

57. a.

b. $f'(x) = \dfrac{e^{-x}}{1 + x^2} - e^{-x} \tan^{-1} x$

59. $(f^{-1})'(x) = \frac{1}{3}$ **61.** $(f^{-1})'(x) = 1/(2\sqrt{x + 4})$
63. $(f^{-1})'(x) = 2x$ **65.** $(f^{-1})'(x) = -2/x^3$

67. b. $d\theta/d\ell = -0.0041, -0.0289$, and -0.1984

c. $\lim\limits_{\ell \to 10^+} d\theta/d\ell = -\infty$ **d.** The length ℓ is decreasing

69. a. $d\theta/dc = 1/\sqrt{D^2 - c^2}$ **b.** $1/D$ **73.** Use the identity $\cot^{-1} x + \tan^{-1} x = \pi/2$.

Section 3.11 Exercises, pp. 227–231

1. As the side length s of a cube changes, the surface area $6s^2$ changes as well.   **3.** The other two opposite sides decrease in length.
5. a. $40\,\text{m}^2/\text{s}$ **b.** $80\,\text{m}^2/\text{s}$

c.

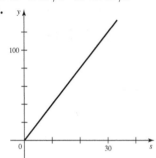

7. a. $4\,\text{m}^2/\text{s}$ **b.** $\sqrt{2}\,\text{m}^2/\text{s}$ **c.** $2\sqrt{2}\,\text{m/s}$ **9. a.** $\dfrac{1}{4\pi}\,\text{cm/s}$

b. $\dfrac{1}{2}\,\text{cm/s}$ **11.** $-40\pi\,\text{ft}^2/\text{min}$ **13.** $\dfrac{3}{80\pi}\,\text{in/min}$

17. At the point $\left(\dfrac{1}{2}, \dfrac{1}{4}\right)$ **19.** $\dfrac{1}{500}\,\text{m/min}$; 2000 min

21. $10 \tan 20° \,\text{km/hr} \approx 3.6\,\text{km/hr}$ **23.** $\dfrac{5}{24}\,\text{ft/s}$ **25.** $-\dfrac{8}{3}\,\text{ft/s}$,

$-\dfrac{32}{3}\,\text{ft/s}$ **27.** $2592\pi\,\text{cm}^3/\text{s}$ **29.** $-\dfrac{8}{9\pi}\,\text{ft/s}$ **31.** $9\pi\,\text{ft}^3/\text{min}$

33. $\dfrac{2}{5}\,\text{m}^2/\text{min}$ **35.** $57.89\,\text{ft/s}$ **37.** $4.66\,\text{in/s}$ **39.** $\dfrac{3\sqrt{5}}{2}\,\text{ft/s}$

41. $\approx 720.3\,\text{mi/hr}$ **43.** $11.06\,\text{m/hr}$ **45. a.** $187.5\,\text{ft/s}$

b. $0.938\,\text{rad/s}$ **47.** $\dfrac{d\theta}{dt} = 0.543\,\text{rad/hr}$

49. $\dfrac{d\theta}{dt} = \dfrac{1}{5}\,\text{rad/s}$, $\dfrac{d\theta}{dt} = \dfrac{1}{8}\,\text{rad/s}$ **51.** $\dfrac{d\theta}{dt} = 0\,\text{rad/s}$, for all $t \geq 0$

53. $-0.0201\,\text{rad/s}$ **55. a.** $-\dfrac{\sqrt{3}}{10}\,\text{m/hr}$ **b.** $-1\,\text{m}^2/\text{hr}$

Chapter 3 Review Exercises, pp. 232–235

1. a. False   **b.** False   **c.** False   **d.** False   **e.** True   **3. a.** 16
b. $y = 16x - 10$

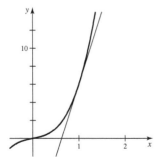

5. a. $-\dfrac{3}{4}$ **b.** $y = -\dfrac{3}{4}x + \dfrac{1}{2}$

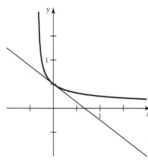

7. a. 2.70 million people/yr   **b.** The slope of the secant line through the two points is approximately equal to the slope of that tangent line at $t = 55$.   **c.** 2.217 million people/yr   **9. a.** $40\,\text{m/s}$
b. $20/3\,\text{m/s}$ **c.** $15\,\text{m/s}$ **d.**

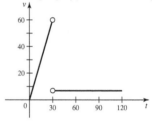

e. The skydiver deployed the parachute.
13.

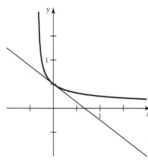

15. $2x^2 + 2\pi x + 7$ **17.** $5t^2 \cos t + 10t \sin t$

19. $(8\theta + 12) \sec^2 (\theta^2 + 3\theta + 2)$ **21.** $\dfrac{32u^2 + 8u + 1}{(8u + 1)^2}$

23. $(\sec^2 \sin \theta) \cos \theta$ **25.** $\dfrac{9x \sin x - 2 \sin x + 6x^2 \cos x - 2x \cos x}{\sqrt{3x - 1}}$

27. $(2 + \ln x) \ln x$ **29.** $(2x - 1) 2^{x^2 - x} \ln 2$ **31.** $-\dfrac{1}{|x| \sqrt{x^2 - 1}}$

33. 1   **35.** $\sqrt{3} + \pi/6$ **37.** $\dfrac{y \cos x}{e^y - 1 - \sin x}$ **39.** $-\dfrac{xy}{x^2 + 2y^2}$

41. $y = x$ **43.** $y = -\dfrac{4x}{5} + \dfrac{24}{5}$ **45.** $x = 4; x = 6$

47. $y' = \dfrac{\cos \sqrt{x}}{2\sqrt{x}}, y'' = -\dfrac{\sqrt{x} \sin \sqrt{x} + \cos \sqrt{x}}{4x^{3/2}}$,

$y''' = \dfrac{3\sqrt{x} \sin \sqrt{x} + (3 - x) \cos \sqrt{x}}{8x^{5/2}}$ **49.** $x^2 f'(x) + 2x f(x)$

51. $\dfrac{g(x)(xf'(x) + f(x)) - xf(x)g'(x)}{g^2(x)}$ **53. a.** 27   **b.** $\frac{25}{27}$ **c.** 294

d. 1215   **e.** $\frac{1}{9}$ **55.** $f(x) = \tan(\pi \sqrt{3x - 11})$, $a = 5; f'(5) = 3\pi/4$
57. $\frac{6}{13}$ **59.** $(f^{-1})'(x) = -3/x^4$ **61. a.** $(f^{-1})'(1/\sqrt{2}) = \sqrt{2}$
63. a. $\frac{1}{4}$ **b.** 1   **c.** $\frac{1}{3}$ **65. a.** $\bar{C}(3000) = \$341.67$;
$C'(3000) = \$280$ **b.** The average cost of producing the first 3000 lawn mowers is $341.67 per mower. The cost of producing the 3001st lawn mower is $280.   **67. a.** 6550 people/yr
b. $p'(40) = 4800$ people/yr   **69.** 50 mi/hr
71. $-5 \sin 65° \,\text{ft/s} \approx -4.5\,\text{ft/s}$ **73.** $0.166\,\text{rad/s}$

CHAPTER 4

Section 4.1 Exercises, pp. 242–245

1. f has an absolute maximum at c in $[a, b]$ if $f(x) \le f(c)$ for all x in $[a, b]$. f has an absolute minimum at c in $[a, b]$ if $f(x) \ge f(c)$ for all x in $[a, b]$.   **3.** The function must be continuous on a closed interval.

5. 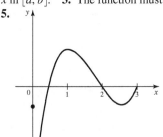   **7.**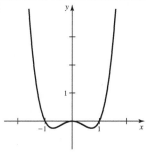

9. Evaluate the function at the critical points and at the endpoints of the interval.   **11.** Abs. min at $x = c_2$; abs. max at $x = b$
13. Abs. min at $x = a$; no abs. max   **15.** Local min at $x = q, s$; local max at $x = p, r$; abs. min at $x = a$; abs. max at $x = b$
17. Local max at $x = p$ and $x = r$; local min at $x = q$; abs. max at $x = p$; abs. min at $x = b$

19. 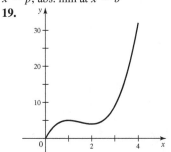   **21.**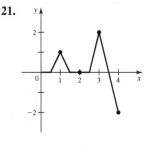

23. a. $x = \frac{2}{3}$ **b.** Local min   **25. a.** $x = \pm 3$ **b.** $x = -3$ local max, $x = 3$ local min   **27. a.** $x = -\frac{2}{3}, \frac{1}{3}$ **b.** $x = -\frac{2}{3}$ local max, $x = \frac{1}{3}$ local min   **29. a.** $x = \pm 1$ **b.** $x = -1$ local min, $x = 1$ local max   **31. a.** $x = 0$ **b.** Local min   **33. a.** $x = 1$
b. local min   **35. a.** $x = -\frac{4}{5}, 0$ **b.** $x = -\frac{4}{5}$ local max, $x = 0$ local min   **37. a.** $x = 0$ **b.** Abs. max: -1 at $x = 3$; abs. min: -10 at $x \doteq 0$ **c.**

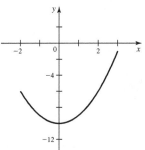

39. a. $x = \pi/2$ **b.** Abs. max: 1 at $x = 0, \pi$; abs. min: 0 at $x = \pi/2$ **c.**

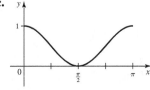

41. a. $x = \pm\pi/6$ **b.** Abs. max: 1 at $x = \pi/6$; abs. min: -1 at $x = -\pi/6$ **c.**

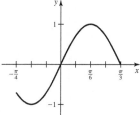

43. a. $x = 1/(2e)$ **b.** Abs. min: $(\sqrt{1/e})^{1/e}$ at $x = 1/(2e)$; abs. max: 2 at $x = 1$ **c.**

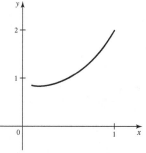

45. a. $x = 1/\sqrt{2}$ **b.** Abs. max: $1 + \pi$ at $x = -1$; abs. min: 1 at $x = 1$ **c.**

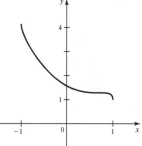

47. a. $1, 4$ **b.** Abs. max: 11 at $x = 1$; abs. min: -16 at $x = 4$
c.

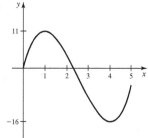

49. a. $x = -3, \frac{1}{2}$ **b.** Abs. max: 27 at $x = -3$; abs. min: $-\frac{19}{12}$ at $x = \frac{1}{2}$ **c.**

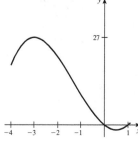

51. $t = 2$ s   **53. a.** 50   **b.** 45
55. a. False   **b.** False   **c.** False   **d.** True

57. a. $x = -0.96, 2.18, 5.32$ **b.** Abs. max: 3.72 at $x = 2.18$; abs. min: -32.80 at $x = 5.32$ **c.**

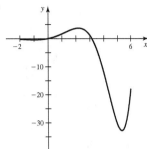

c. $T(50/\sqrt{3}) \approx 34.15$, $T(0) = 37.50$, $T(50) \approx 35.36$
d.

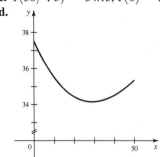

59. a. $x = 0$ **b.** Abs. max: $\sqrt{2}$ at $x = \pm\pi/4$; abs. min: 1 at $x = 0$
c.

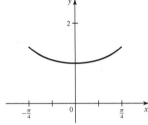

79. a. $1, 3, 0, 1$ **b.** Because $h'(2) \neq 0$, h does not have a local extreme value at $x = 2$. However, g may have a local extremum at $x = 2$ (because $g'(2) = 0$).   **81. a.** Local min at $x = -c$
b. Local max at $x = -c$ **83. a.** $f(x) - f(c) \leq 0$ for all x near c
b. $\lim\limits_{x \to c^+} \dfrac{f(x) - f(c)}{x - c} \leq 0$ **c.** $\lim\limits_{x \to c^-} \dfrac{f(x) - f(c)}{x - c} \geq 0$
d. Because $f'(c)$ exists, $\lim\limits_{x \to c^+} \dfrac{f(x) - f(c)}{x - c} = \lim\limits_{x \to c^-} \dfrac{f(x) - f(c)}{x - c}$. By parts (b) and (c), we must have that $f'(c) = 0$.

61. a. $x = 0$ and $x = 3$ **b.** Abs. max: $27/e^3$ at $x = 3$; abs. min: $-e$ at $x = -1$ **c.**

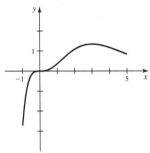

Section 4.2 Exercises, pp. 256–260

1. f is increasing on I if $f'(x) > 0$ for all x in I; f is decreasing on I if $f'(x) < 0$ for all x in I.   **3.**

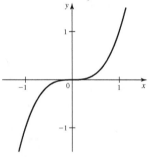

63. a. $x = 8$ **b.** Abs. max: $3\sqrt{2}$ at $x = 6$ and $x = 12$; abs. min: 4 at $x = 8$ **c.**

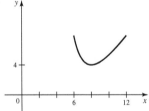

5. The tangent lines lie below the graph of f.
7. A point in the domain at which f changes concavity
9. Yes; consider the graph of $y = \sqrt{x}$ on $(0, \infty)$.
11.

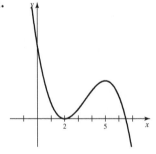

65. If $a \geq 0$, there is no critical point. If $a < 0$, $x = 2a/3$ is the only critical point.   **67.** $x = \pm a$ **69. a.** $x = \tan^{-1} 2 + k\pi$, for $k = -2, -1, 0, 1$ **b.** $x = \tan^{-1} 2 + k\pi$, for $k = -2, 0$ correspond to local max; $x = \tan^{-1} 2 + k\pi$, for $k = -1, 1$ correspond to local min.
c. Abs. max: 2.24; abs. min: -2.24 **71. a.** $x = -\frac{1}{8}$ and $x = 3$
b. $x = -\frac{1}{8}$ corresponds to a local min; $x = 3$ is neither   **c.** Abs. max: 51.23; abs. min: -12.52 **73. a.** $x = 5 - 4\sqrt{2}$ **b.** $x = 5 - 4\sqrt{2}$ corresponds to a local max.   **c.** No abs. max or min   **75.** Abs. max: 4 at $x = -1$; abs. min: -8 at $x = 3$

77. a. $T(x) = \dfrac{\sqrt{2500 + x^2}}{2} + \dfrac{50 - x}{4}$ **b.** $x = 50/\sqrt{3}$

13.

[graph]

15.

[graph with labels $y = f(x)$ and $y = f'(x)$]

17. Increasing on $(-\infty, 0)$; decreasing on $(0, \infty)$ **19.** Decreasing on $(-\infty, 1)$; increasing on $(1, \infty)$ **21.** Increasing on $(-\infty, 1/2)$; decreasing on $(1/2, \infty)$ **23.** Increasing on $(-\infty, 0), (1, 2)$; decreasing on $(0, 1), (2, \infty)$ **25.** Increasing on $\left(-\dfrac{1}{\sqrt{e}}, 0\right), \left(\dfrac{1}{\sqrt{e}}, \infty\right)$; decreasing on $\left(-\infty, -\dfrac{1}{\sqrt{e}}\right), \left(0, \dfrac{1}{\sqrt{e}}\right)$ **27.** Increasing on $(-\pi, -2\pi/3), (-\pi/3, 0), (\pi/3, 2\pi/3)$; decreasing on $(-2\pi/3, -\pi/3), (0, \pi/3), (2\pi/3, \pi)$ **29.** Decreasing on $(-\infty, -1), (0, 1)$; increasing on $(-1, 0), (1, \infty)$ **31.** Increasing on $(-\infty, \infty)$ **33.** Decreasing on $(-\infty, 1), (4, \infty)$; increasing on $(1, 4)$ **35.** Increasing on $\left(-\infty, -\frac{1}{2}\right), \left(0, \frac{1}{2}\right)$; decreasing on $\left(-\frac{1}{2}, 0\right), \left(\frac{1}{2}, \infty\right)$ **37.** Increasing on $(-1, 1)$; decreasing on $(-\infty, -1), (1, \infty)$ **39. a.** $x = 0$ **b.** Local min at $x = 0$ **c.** Abs. min: 3 at $x = 0$; abs. max: 12 at $x = -3$
41. a. $x = \pm\sqrt{2}$ **b.** Local min at $x = -\sqrt{2}$; local max at $x = \sqrt{2}$ **c.** Abs. max: 2 at $x = \sqrt{2}$; abs. min: -2 at $x = -\sqrt{2}$ **43. a.** $x = \pm\sqrt{3}$ **b.** Local min at $x = -\sqrt{3}$; local max at $x = \sqrt{3}$ **c.** Abs. max: 28 at $x = -4$; abs. min: $-6\sqrt{3}$ at $x = -\sqrt{3}$ **45. a.** $x = 2$ and $x = 0$ **b.** Local max at $x = 0$; local min at $x = 2$ **c.** Abs. min: $-10\sqrt[3]{25}$ at $x = -5$; abs. max: 0 at $x = 0, 5$ **47. a.** $x = e^{-2}$ **b.** Local min at $x = e^{-2}$ **c.** Abs. min: $-2/e$ at $x = e^{-2}$; no abs. max   **49.** Abs. max: $1/e$ at $x = 1$ **51.** Abs. min: $36\sqrt[3]{\pi/6}$ at $x = \sqrt[3]{6/\pi}$

53.
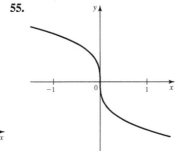

55.

57. Concave up on $(-\infty, 0), (1, \infty)$; concave down on $(0, 1)$; inflection points at $x = 0$ and $x = 1$ **59.** Concave up on $(-\infty, 0), (2, \infty)$; concave down on $(0, 2)$; inflection points at $x = 0$ and $x = 2$ **61.** Concave down on $(-\infty, 1)$; concave up on $(1, \infty)$; inflection point at $x = 1$ **63.** Concave up on $(-1/\sqrt{3}, 1/\sqrt{3})$; concave down on $(-\infty, -1/\sqrt{3}), (1/\sqrt{3}, \infty)$; inflection points at $t = \pm 1/\sqrt{3}$ **65.** Concave up on $(-\infty, -1), (1, \infty)$; concave down on $(-1, 1)$; inflection points at $x = \pm 1$ **67.** Concave up on $(0, 1)$; concave down on $(1, \infty)$; inflection point at $x = 1$ **69.** Concave up on $(0, 2), (4, \infty)$; concave down on $(-\infty, 0), (2, 4)$; inflection points at $x = 0, 2, 4$ **71.** Critical pts. $x = 0$ and $x = 2$; local max at $x = 0$, local min at $x = 2$ **73.** Critical pt. $x = 0$; local max at $x = 0$ **75.** Critical pt. $x = 6$; local min at $x = 6$ **77.** Critical pts. $x = 0$ and $x = 1$; local max at $x = 0$; local min at $x = 1$ **79.** Critical pts. $x = 0$ and $x = 2$; local min at $x = 0$; local max at $x = 2$ **81.** Critical pt. $x = e^5$; local min at $x = e^5$ **83. a.** True   **b.** False   **c.** True   **d.** False   **e.** False
85.
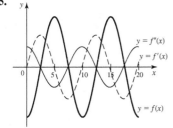

87. a–f–g, b–e–i, c–d–h

89.
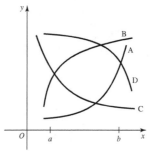
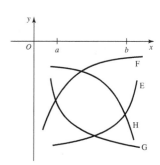

91.
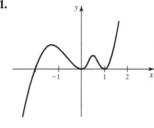

93.
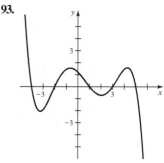

95. a. Increasing on $(-2, 2)$; decreasing on $(-3, -2)$ **b.** Critical pts. $x = -2$ and $x = 0$; local min at $x = -2$; neither a local max nor min at $x = 0$ **c.** Inflection pts. at $x = -1$ and $x = 0$
d. Concave up on $(-3, -1), (0, 2)$; concave down on $(-1, 0)$
e.
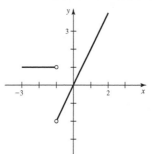

f.
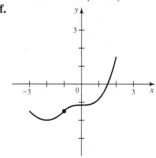

97. Critical pts. $x = -3$ and $x = 4$; local min at $x = -3$; inconclusive at $x = 4$ **99.** No critical pt.   **101. a.** $E = \dfrac{p}{p - 50}$
b. -1.4% **c.** $E'(p) = -\dfrac{ab}{(a - bp)^2} < 0$, for $p \geq 0, p \neq a/b$
d. $E(p) = -b$, for $p \geq 0$ **103. a.** 300   **b.** $t = \sqrt{10}$
c. $t = \sqrt{b/3}$ **105. a.** $f''(x) = 6x + 2a = 0$ when $x = -a/3$
b. $f(-a/3) - f(-a/3 + x) = (a^2/3)x - bx - x^3$; also,
$f(-a/3 - x) - f(-a/3) = (a^2/3)x - bx - x^3$

Section 4.3 Exercises, pp. 267–270

1. We need to know on which interval(s) to graph f.
3. No; the domain of any polynomial is $(-\infty, \infty)$; there is no vertical asymptote. Also, $\lim\limits_{x \to \pm\infty} p(x) = \pm\infty$ where p is any polynomial; there is no horizontal asymptote.   **5.** Evaluate the function at the critical points and at the endpoints. Then find the largest and smallest values among those candidates.

7.

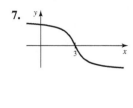

9.

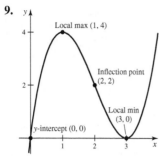

11.

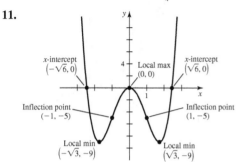

13.

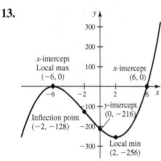

15.

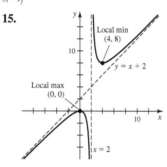

17.

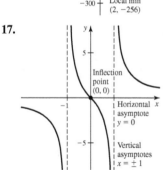

19.

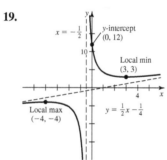

21.

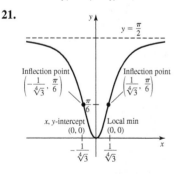

23.

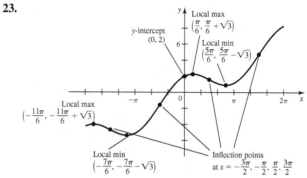

25.

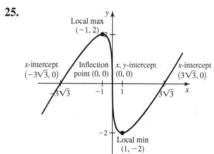

27.

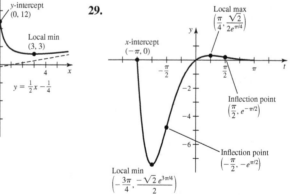

29.

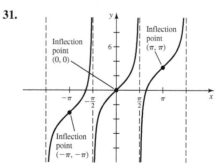

31.

33.

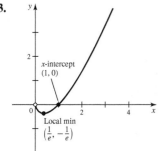

x-intercept
(1, 0)

Local min
$\left(\frac{1}{e}, -\frac{1}{e}\right)$

35.

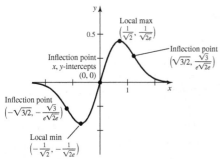

Local max
$\left(\frac{1}{\sqrt{2}}, \frac{1}{\sqrt{2e}}\right)$

Inflection point
$\left(\sqrt{3/2}, \frac{\sqrt{3}}{e\sqrt{2e}}\right)$

Inflection point
x, y-intercepts
(0, 0)

Inflection point
$\left(-\sqrt{3/2}, -\frac{\sqrt{3}}{e\sqrt{2e}}\right)$

Local min
$\left(-\frac{1}{\sqrt{2}}, -\frac{1}{\sqrt{2e}}\right)$

37.

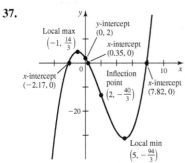

Local max
$\left(-1, \frac{14}{3}\right)$

y-intercept
(0, 2)

x-intercept
(0.35, 0)

x-intercept
(−2.17, 0)

Inflection
point
$\left(2, -\frac{40}{3}\right)$

x-intercept
(7.82, 0)

Local min
$\left(5, -\frac{94}{3}\right)$

39.

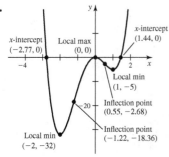

x-intercept
(−2.77, 0)

Local max
(0, 0)

x-intercept
(1.44, 0)

Local min
(1, −5)

Inflection point
(0.55, −2.68)

Inflection point
(−1.22, −18.36)

Local min
(−2, −32)

41.

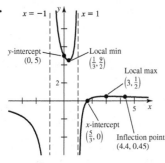

$x = -1$ $x = 1$

y-intercept
(0, 5)

Local min
$\left(\frac{1}{3}, \frac{9}{2}\right)$

Local max
$\left(3, \frac{1}{2}\right)$

x-intercept
$\left(\frac{5}{3}, 0\right)$

Inflection point
(4.4, 0.45)

43. a. False   **b.** False
c. False   **d.** True

45.

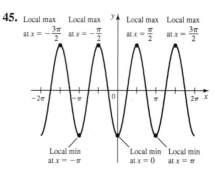

Local max
at $x = -\frac{3\pi}{2}$

Local max
at $x = -\frac{\pi}{2}$

Local max
at $x = \frac{\pi}{2}$

Local max
at $x = \frac{3\pi}{2}$

Local min
at $x = -\pi$

Local min
at $x = 0$

Local min
at $x = \pi$

47.

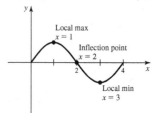

Local max
at $x = -2$

No local
extremum
at $x = 0$

Local min
at $x = 1$

49. Critical pts. at $x = 1, 3$; local max at $x = 1$; local min at $x = 3$; inflection pt. at $x = 2$; increasing on $(0, 1)$, $(3, 4)$; decreasing on $(1, 3)$; concave up on $(2, 4)$; concave down on $(0, 2)$

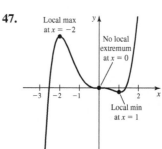

Local max
$x = 1$

Inflection point
$x = 2$

Local min
$x = 3$

51.

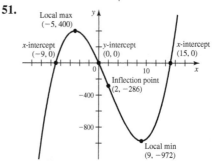

Local max
(−5, 400)

x-intercept
(−9, 0)

y-intercept
(0, 0)

x-intercept
(15, 0)

Inflection point
(2, −286)

Local min
(9, −972)

53.

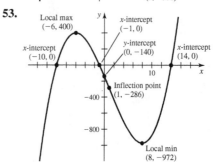

Local max
(−6, 400)

x-intercept
(−1, 0)

x-intercept
(−10, 0)

y-intercept
(0, −140)

x-intercept
(14, 0)

Inflection point
(1, −286)

Local min
(8, −972)

55. Local max of $e^{1/e}$ at $x = e$

57.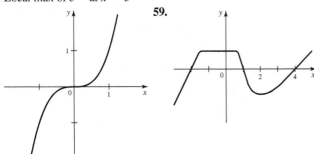

59.

61.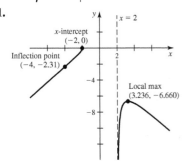

63. a.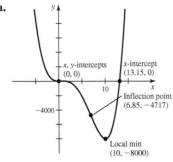

b.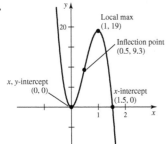

65.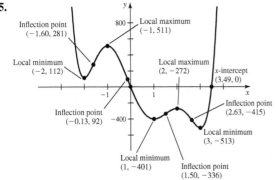

67.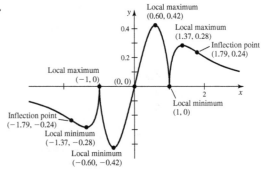

69. a.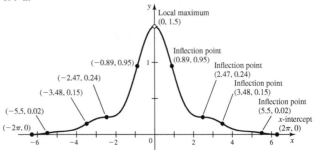

b.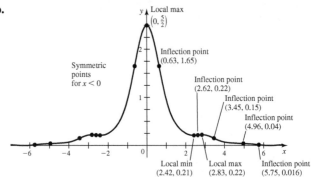

71. (A) a. 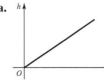   **b.** Water is being added at all times.   **c.** No concavity   **d.** h' has an abs. max at all points of $[0, 10]$.

(B) a. 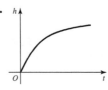   **c.** Concave down   **d.** h' has abs. max at $t = 0$.

(C) a. 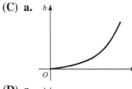   **c.** Concave up   **d.** h' has abs. max at $t = 10$.

(D) a. 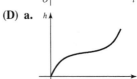   **c.** Concave up on $(0, 5)$, then concave down on $(5, 10)$; inflection pt. at $t = 5$ **d.** h' has abs. max at $t = 0$ and $t = 10$.

(E) a.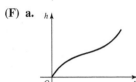

c. First, no concavity; then concave down, no concavity, concave up, and, finally, no concavity   **d.** h' has abs. max at all points of an interval $[0, a]$ and $[b, 10]$.

(F) a.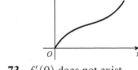

c. Concave down on $(0, 5)$; concave up on $(5, 10)$; inflection pt. at $t = 5$
d. h' has abs. max at $t = 0$ and $t = 10$.

73. $f'(0)$ does not exist.

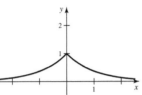

75.

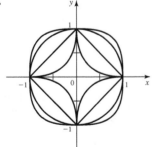

77.

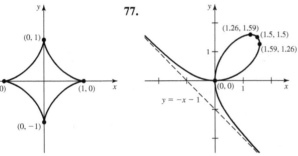

79.

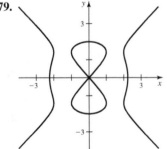

81.

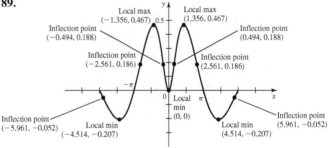

83.

85. a. $\{x : x < a\}$ **b.** $f(a) = 0$, $\lim\limits_{x \to -\infty} f(x) = 0$

c. $f'(x) = (a - x)^{x-1} ((a - x) \ln (a - x) - x)$
d. See part (c).   **e.** z and $f(z)$ increase as a increases.

87.

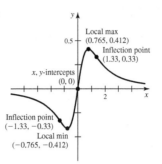

89.

Section 4.4 Exercises, pp. 274–280

1. Objective function, constraint(s)   **3.** $Q = x^2(10 - x)$;
$Q = (10 - y)^2 y$ **5.** Width $=$ length $= \frac{5}{2}$ m
7. Width $=$ length $= 10$ **9.** $\frac{23}{2}$ and $\frac{23}{2}$ **11.** $5\sqrt{2}$ and $5\sqrt{2}$
13. $x = \sqrt{6}, y = 2\sqrt{6}$ **15.** Length $=$ width $=$ height $= \sqrt[3]{100}$
17. $\dfrac{4}{\sqrt[3]{5}}$ ft by $\dfrac{4}{\sqrt[3]{5}}$ ft by $5^{2/3}$ ft   **19.** $(5, 15)$, distance ≈ 47.4
21. a. A point $8/\sqrt{5}$ mi from the point on the shore nearest the woman in the direction of the restaurant   **b.** $9/\sqrt{13}$ mi/hr
23. 18.2 ft   **25.** $\dfrac{10}{\sqrt{2}}$ cm by $\dfrac{5}{\sqrt{2}}$ cm   **27.** $h = \dfrac{20}{\sqrt{3}}$; $r = 20\sqrt{\frac{2}{3}}$
29. $\sqrt{15}$ m by $2\sqrt{15}$ m   **31.** $r/h = \sqrt{2}$ **33.** $r = h = \sqrt[3]{450/\pi}$ m
35. The point $12/(\sqrt[3]{2} + 1) \approx 5.3$ m from the weaker source
37. A point $7\sqrt{3}/6$ mi from the point on shore nearest the island, in the direction of the power station   **39. a.** $P = 2/\sqrt{3}$ units from the midpoint of the base   **41.** $r = \sqrt{6}, h = \sqrt{3}$
43. For $L \le 4r$, max at $\theta = 0$ and $\theta = 2\pi$; min at $\theta = \cos^{-1}(-L/(4r))$ and $\theta = 2\pi - \cos^{-1}(-L/(4r))$. For $L > 4r$, max at $\theta = 0$ and $\theta = 2\pi$; min at $\theta = \pi$.
45. a. $r = \sqrt[3]{177/\pi} \approx 3.83$ cm; $h = 2\sqrt[3]{177/\pi} \approx 7.67$ cm
b. $r = \sqrt[3]{177/2\pi} \approx 3.04$ cm; $h = 2\sqrt[3]{708/\pi} \approx 12.17$ cm.
Part (b) is closer to the real can.   **47.** $\sqrt{30} \approx 5.5$ ft   **49.** When the seat is at its lowest point   **51.** $r = \sqrt{2}R/\sqrt{3}$; $h = 2R/\sqrt{3}$
53. a. $r = 2R/3$; $h = \frac{1}{3}H$ **b.** $r = R/2$; $h = H/2$ **55.** 3:1
57. $(1 + \sqrt{3})$ mi ≈ 2.7 mi   **59.** You can run 12 mi/hr if you run toward the point $3/16$ mi ahead of the locomotive (when it passes the point nearest you).   **61. a.** $(-6/5, 2/5)$ **b.** Approx $(0.59, 0.65)$
c. (i) $(p - \frac{1}{2}, \sqrt{p - \frac{1}{2}})$ **(ii)** $(0, 0)$ **63. a.** $0, 30, 25$ **b.** 42.5 mi/hr
c. The units of $p/g(v)$ are \$/mi and so are the units of w/v.
Therefore, $L\left(\dfrac{p}{g(v)} + \dfrac{w}{v}\right)$ gives the total cost of a trip of L miles.
d. Approx. 62.9 mi/hr   **e.** Neither; the zeros of $C'(v)$ are independent of L.   **f.** Decreased slightly, to 62.5 mi/hr   **g.** Decreased to 60.8 mi/hr   **65. b.** Because the speed of light is constant, travel time is minimized when distance is minimized.   **67.** Let the angle of the cuts be φ_1 and φ_2, where $\varphi_1 + \varphi_2 = \theta$. The volume of the notch is proportional to $\tan \varphi_1 + \tan \varphi_2 = \tan \varphi_1 + \tan (\theta - \varphi_1)$, which is minimized when $\varphi_1 = \varphi_2 = \dfrac{\theta}{2}$.   **69.** $x \approx 38.81, y \approx 55.03$

Section 4.5 Exercises, pp. 288–290

1.

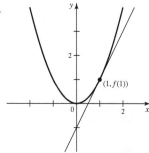

3. $f(x) \approx f(a) + f'(a)(x - a)$

5. $dy = f'(x)\, dx$ **7.** 61 mi/hr; 61.02 mi/hr

9. $L(x) = T(0) + T'(0)(x - 0) = D - (D/60)x = D(1 - x/60)$

11. 84 min; 84.21 min   **13. a.** $L(x) = -4x + 16$

b.

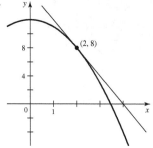

c. 7.6   **d.** 0.13% error

15. a. $L(x) = x$ **b.**

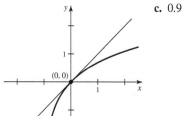

c. 0.9

d. 40% error   **17. a.** $L(x) = 1$ **b.**

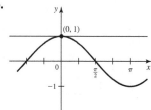

c. 1   **d.** 0.005% error   **19. a.** $y = \dfrac{1}{2} - \dfrac{x}{48}$

b.

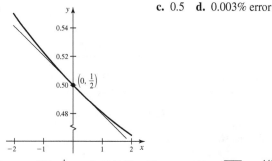

c. 0.5   **d.** 0.003% error

21. $a = 200; \frac{1}{203} \approx 0.004925$ **23.** $a = 144; \sqrt{146} \approx \frac{145}{12}$

25. $a = 1; \ln 1.05 \approx 0.05$ **27.** $a = 0; e^{0.06} \approx 1.06$

29. $a = 512; \dfrac{1}{\sqrt[3]{510}} \approx \dfrac{769}{6144} \approx 0.125$

31. a. $L(x) = -2x + 4$ **b.**

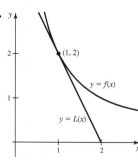

c. Underestimates   **d.** $f''(1) = 4 > 0$

33. a. $L(x) = -\dfrac{1}{2}x + \dfrac{1}{2}(1 + \ln 2)$ **b.**

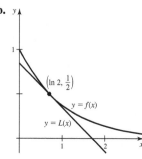

c. Underestimates   **d.** $f''(\ln 2) = \dfrac{1}{2} > 0$ **35.** $\Delta V \approx 10\pi$ ft³

37. $\Delta V \approx -40\pi$ cm³   **39.** $\Delta S \approx -\dfrac{59\pi}{5\sqrt{34}}$ m²   **41.** $dy = 2\, dx$

43. $dy = -\dfrac{3}{x^4}\, dx$ **45.** $dy = a \sin x\, dx$ **47.** $dy = (9x^2 - 4)\, dx$

49. $dy = \sec^2 x\, dx$ **51. a.** True   **b.** False   **c.** True   **d.** True

53. 2.7   **55. a.** $L(x) = 1 - x$;   **b.**

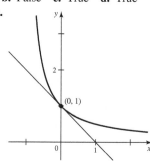

c. $1/1.1 \approx 0.9$ **d.** 1% error   **57. a.** $L(x) = 1 - x$

b.

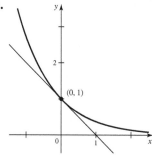

c. $e^{-0.03} \approx 0.97$ **d.** 0.05% error

59. $E(x) \le 1$ when $-7.26 \le x \le 8.26$, which corresponds to driving times for 1 mi from about 53 s to 68 s. Therefore, $L(x)$ gives approximations to $s(x)$ that are within 1 mi/hr of the true value when you drive 1 mi in t seconds, where $53 < t < 68$.

61. $L(x) = 2 + (x - 8)/12$

x	Linear approx.	Exact value	Percent error
8.1	$2.008\overline{3}$	2.00829885	1.7×10^{-3}
8.01	$2.0008\overline{3}$	2.000832986	1.7×10^{-5}
8.001	$2.00008\overline{3}$	2.00008333	1.7×10^{-7}
8.0001	$2.000008\overline{3}$	2.000008333	1.7×10^{-9}
7.9999	$1.999991\overline{6}$	1.999991667	1.7×10^{-9}
7.999	$1.999991\overline{6}$	1.999916663	1.7×10^{-7}
7.99	$1.99991\overline{6}$	1.999166319	1.7×10^{-5}
7.9	$1.9991\overline{6}$	1.991631701	1.8×10^{-3}

63. a. f; the rate at which f' is changing at 1 is smaller than the rate at which g' is changing at 1. The graph of f bends away from the linear function more slowly than the graph of g.   **b.** The larger the value of $|f''(a)|$, the greater the deviation of the curve $y = f(x)$ from the tangent line at points near $x = a$.

Section 4.6 Exercises, pp. 295–296

1. If f is a continuous function on the closed interval $[a, b]$ and is differentiable on (a, b) and the slope of the secant line that joins $(a, f(a))$ to $(b, f(b))$ is zero, then there is at least one value c in (a, b) at which the slope of the line tangent to f at $(c, f(c))$ is also zero.

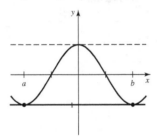

3. $f(x) = |x|$ is not differentiable at 0.
5.   **7.** $x = \frac{1}{3}$

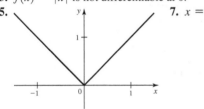

9. $x = \pi/4$ **11.** Does not apply   **13.** $x = \frac{5}{3}$ **15.** Average lapse rate $= -6.3°/\text{km}$. You cannot conclude that the lapse rate at a point exceeds the threshold value.   **17. a.** Yes   **b.** $c = \frac{1}{2}$
c.

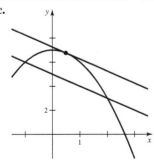

19. a. Yes   **b.** $c = \ln\left(\dfrac{3}{\ln 4}\right)$ **c.**

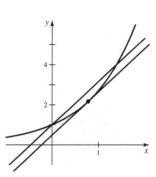

21. a. Yes   **b.** $c = \sqrt{1 - 9/\pi^2}$ **c.**

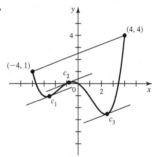

23. a. Does not apply   **25. a.** False   **b.** True   **c.** False
27. h and p **29.**

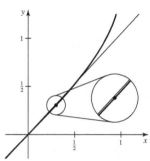

31. No such point exists; function is not continuous at 2.
33. The car's average velocity is $(30 - 0)/(28/60) = 64.3 \text{ mi/hr}$. By the MVT, the car's instantaneous velocity was 64.3 mi/hr at some time.   **35.** Average speed $= 11.6 \text{ mi/hr}$. By the MVT, the speed was exactly 11.6 mi/hr at least once. By the Intermediate Value Theorem, all speeds between 0 and 11.6 mi/hr were reached. Because the initial and final speed was 0 mi/hr, the speed of 11 mi/hr was reached at least twice.   **37.** $\dfrac{f(b) - f(a)}{b - a} = A(a + b) + B$
and $f'(x) = 2Ax + B$; $2Ax + B = A(a + b) + B$ implies that $x = \dfrac{a + b}{2}$, the midpoint of $[a, b]$.   **39.** $\tan^2 x$ and $\sec^2 x$ differ by a constant; in fact, $\tan^2 x - \sec^2 x = -1$.   **41.** Bolt's average speed was 37.58 km/hr, so he exceeded 37 km/hr during the race.
43. b. $c = \frac{1}{2}$

Section 4.7 Exercises, pp. 307–309

1. If $\lim\limits_{x \to a} f(x) = 0$ and $\lim\limits_{x \to a} g(x) = 0$, then we say $\lim\limits_{x \to a} f(x)/g(x)$ is an indeterminate form 0/0.   **3.** Take the limit of the quotient of the derivatives of the functions.   **5.** If $\lim\limits_{x \to a} f(x)g(x)$ has the indeterminate form $0 \cdot \infty$, then $\lim\limits_{x \to a}\left(\dfrac{f(x)}{1/g(x)}\right)$ has the indeterminate form 0/0 or ∞/∞.   **7.** If $\lim\limits_{x \to a} f(x) = 1$ and $\lim\limits_{x \to a} g(x) = \infty$, then $f(x)^{g(x)} \to 1^\infty$ as $x \to a$, which is meaningless; so direct substitution does not work.

9. $\lim\limits_{x\to\infty} \dfrac{g(x)}{f(x)} = 0$ **11.** $\ln x, x^3, 2^x, x^x$ **13.** -1 **15.** $1/2$ **17.** $1/e$
19. $\frac{12}{5}$ **21.** 4 **23.** $\frac{9}{16}$ **25.** $\frac{1}{2}$ **27.** $1/24$ **29.** 1 **31.** 4 **33.** $-\frac{1}{2}$
35. $1/\pi^2$ **37.** $\frac{1}{2}$ **39.** $-\frac{2}{3}$ **41.** 1 **43.** $\frac{1}{3}$ **45.** 1 **47.** $\frac{7}{6}$ **49.** 1
51. 0 **53.** 0 **55.** 1 **57.** 1 **59.** e **61.** e^a **63.** e^{a+1} **65.** 1
67. e **69.** $e^{0.01x}$ **71.** Comparable growth rates **73.** x^x
75. 1.00001^x **77.** x^x **79.** e^{x^2} **81. a.** False **b.** False **c.** False
d. False **e.** True **f.** True **83.** $\frac{2}{5}$ **85.** $-\frac{9}{4}$ **87.** 0 **89.** $\frac{1}{6}$ **91.** ∞
93. $(\ln 3)/(\ln 2)$ **95.** $\frac{1}{2}$ **97.** $\frac{1}{2}$ **99.** e **101.** $-\frac{1}{3}$
103. a. Approx. 3.43×10^{15} **b.** Approx. 3536 **c.** e^{100}
d. Approx. 163 **105.** 1 **107.** $\ln a - \ln b$

109. b. $\lim\limits_{m\to\infty} (1 + r/m)^m = \lim\limits_{m\to\infty} \left(1 + \dfrac{1}{(m/r)}\right)^{(m/r)r} = e^r$

111. $\sqrt{a/c}$ **113.** $\lim\limits_{x\to\infty} \dfrac{x^p}{b^x} = \lim\limits_{t\to\infty} \dfrac{\ln^p t}{t \ln^p b} = 0$

115. Show $\lim\limits_{x\to\infty} \dfrac{\log_a x}{\log_b x} = \dfrac{\ln b}{\ln a} \neq 0$. **117.** $1/3$

121. a. $b > e$ **b.** e^{ax} grows faster than e^x as $x \to \infty$, for $a > 1$; e^{ax}
grows slower than e^x as $x \to \infty$, for $0 < a < 1$.

Section 4.8 Exercises, pp. 316–318

1. Newton's method generates a sequence of x-intercepts of lines
tangent to the graph of f to approximate the roots of f.
3. Generally, if two successive Newton approximations agree in their
first p digits, then those approximations have p digits of accuracy. The
method is terminated when the desired accuracy is reached.
5. $x_{n+1} = x_n - \dfrac{x_n^2 - 6}{2x_n} = \dfrac{x_n^2 + 6}{2x_n}$; $x_1 = 2.5, x_2 = 2.45$

7. $x_{n+1} = x_n - \dfrac{e^{-x_n} - x_n}{e^{-x_n} - 1}$; $x_1 = 0.564382, x_2 = 0.567142$

9.

n	x_n
0	4.000000
1	3.250000
2	3.163462
3	3.162278
4	3.162278
5	3.162278
6	3.162278
7	3.162278
8	3.162278
9	3.162278
10	3.162278

11.

n	x_n
0	1.500000
1	0.101436
2	0.501114
3	0.510961
4	0.510973
5	0.510973
6	0.510973
7	0.510973
8	0.510973
9	0.510973
10	0.510973

13.

n	x_n
0	1.500000
1	1.443890
2	1.361976
3	1.268175
4	1.196179
5	1.168571
6	1.165592
7	1.165561
8	1.165561
9	1.165561
10	1.165561

15. $x \approx 0, 1.895494, -1.895494$
17. $x \approx -2.114908, 0.254102, 1.860806$
19. $x \approx 0.062997, 2.230120$
21. $x \approx 2.798386$
23. $x \approx -0.666667, 1.5, 1.666667$

25. The method converges more slowly for f, because of the double
root at $x = 1$.

n	x_n for f	x_n for g
0	2	2
1	1.5	1.25
2	1.25	1.025
3	1.125	1.0003
4	1.0625	1
5	1.03125	1
6	1.01563	1
7	1.00781	1
8	1.00391	1
9	1.00195	1
10	1.00098	1

27. a. True. **b.** False. **c.** False **29.** $x \approx 1.153467, 2.423622,$
-3.57709 **31.** $x = 0$ and $x \approx 1.047198$ **33.** $x \approx -0.335408,$
1.333057 **35.** $x \approx 0.179295$ **37.** $x \approx 0.620723, 3.03645$

39.

n	x_n	Error	Residual
0	0.5	0.5	9.8×10^{-4}
1	0.45	0.45	3.4×10^{-4}
2	0.405	0.41	1.2×10^{-4}
3	0.3645	0.36	4.1×10^{-5}
4	0.32805	0.33	1.4×10^{-5}
5	0.295245	0.30	5.0×10^{-6}
6	0.265721	0.27	1.7×10^{-6}
7	0.239148	0.24	6.1×10^{-7}
8	0.215234	0.22	2.1×10^{-7}
9	0.193710	0.19	7.4×10^{-8}
10	0.174339	0.17	2.6×10^{-8}

41. $a = e$ **43. b.** $x \approx 0.142857$ is approximately $\frac{1}{7}$.
45. a. $t = \pi/4$ **b.** $t \approx 1.33897$ **c.** $t \approx 2.35619$
d. $t \approx 2.90977$ **47.** $\lambda = 1.29011, 2.37305, 3.40918$

Section 4.9 Exercises, pp. 327–329

1. The derivative, an antiderivative **3.** $x + C$, where C is an
arbitrary constant **5.** $\dfrac{x^{p+1}}{p+1} + C$, where $p \neq -1$ **7.** $\ln|x| + C$
9. 0 **11.** $x^5 + C$ **13.** $-\frac{1}{2}\cos 2x + C$ **15.** $3\tan x + C$
17. $y^{-2} + C$ **19.** $e^x + C$ **21.** $\tan^{-1}s + C$ **23.** $\frac{1}{2}x^6 - \frac{1}{2}x^{10} + C$
25. $\frac{8}{3}x^{3/2} - 8x^{1/2} + C$ **27.** $\frac{25}{3}s^3 + 15s^2 + 9s + C$
29. $\frac{9}{4}x^{4/3} + 6x^{2/3} + 6x + C$ **31.** $-x^3 + \frac{11}{2}x^2 + 4x + C$
33. $-x^{-3} + 2x + 3x^{-1} + C$ **35.** $x^4 - 3x^2 + C$
37. $-\frac{1}{2}\cos 2y + \frac{1}{3}\sin 3y + C$ **39.** $\tan x - x + C$
41. $\tan \theta + \sec \theta + C$ **43.** $t^3 + \frac{1}{2}\tan 2t + C$ **45.** $\frac{1}{4}\sec 4\theta + C$
47. $\frac{1}{2}\ln|y| + C$ **49.** $6\sin^{-1}(x/5) + C$ **51.** $\frac{1}{10}\sec^{-1}|x/10| + C$
53. $\frac{1}{5}\sec^{-1}|\frac{x}{5}| + C$ **55.** $t + \ln|t| + C$ **57.** $e^{x+2} + C$
59. $x^6/6 + 2/x + x - 19/6$ **61.** $\sec v + 1$

63. $2x^4 + 2x^{-1} + 1$ **65.** $y^3 + 5\ln|y| + 2$

67. $f(x) = x^2 - 3x + 4$ **69.** $g(x) = \dfrac{7}{8}x^8 - \dfrac{x^2}{2} + \dfrac{13}{8}$

71. $f(u) = 4\sin u + 2\cos 2u - 3$ **73.** $y(t) = 3\ln|t| + 6t + 2$
75. $y(\theta) = \sqrt{2}\sin\theta + \tan\theta + 1$

77. $f(x) = x^2 - 5x + 4$ **79.** $f(x) = \dfrac{3x^2}{2} - \dfrac{\cos\pi x}{\pi} + \dfrac{1 - 3\pi}{\pi}$

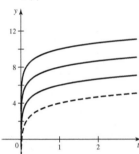
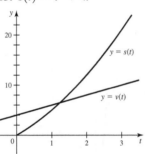

81. $f(t) = \ln t + 4$

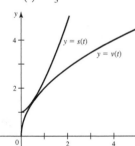

83. $s(t) = t^2 + 4t$

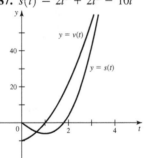

85. $s(t) = \frac{4}{3}t^{3/2} + 1$

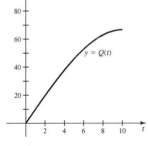

87. $s(t) = 2t^3 + 2t^2 - 10t$

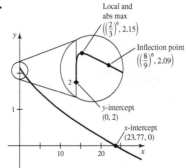

89. $-16t^2 + 20t$ **91.** $\frac{1}{30}t^3 + 1$ **93.** $-\frac{3}{2}\sin 2t + \frac{5}{2}t + 10$
95. Runner A overtakes runner B at $t = \pi/2$.
97. a. $v(t) = -9.8t + 30$ **b.** $s(t) = -4.9t^2 + 30t$
c. 45.92 m at time $t = 3.06$ **d.** $t = 6.12$
99. a. $v(t) = -9.8t + 10$ **b.** $s(t) = -4.9t^2 + 10t + 400$
c. 405.10 m at time $t = 1.02$ **d.** $t = 10.11$ **101. a.** True
b. False   **c.** True   **d.** False   **e.** False   **103.** $(e^{2x} + e^{-2x})/4 + C$
105. $-\cot\theta + 2\theta^3/3 - 3\theta^2/2 + C$ **107.** $\ln|x| + 2\sqrt{x} + C$
109. $\frac{4}{15}x^{15/2} - \frac{24}{11}x^{11/6} + C$ **111.** $F(x) = -\cos x + 3x + 3 - 3\pi$
113. $F(x) = 2x^8 + x^4 + 2x + 1$ **115. a.** $Q(t) = 10t - t^3/30$ gal
b.   **c.** $\dfrac{200}{3}$ gal

117. $\displaystyle\int \sin^2 x\,dx = x/2 - (\sin 2x)/4 + C;$

$\displaystyle\int \cos^2 x\,dx = x/2 + (\sin 2x)/4 + C$

Chapter 4 Review Exercises, pp. 330–332

1. a. False   **b.** False   **c.** True   **d.** True   **e.** True   **f.** False
3.   **5.**

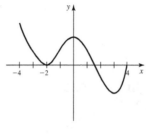
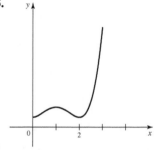

7. $x = 3$ and $x = -2$; no abs. max or min
9. $x = 1/e$; abs. min at $(1/e, 10 - 2/e)$
11.

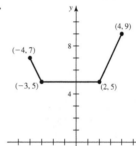

Critical pts.: all x in the interval $[-3, 2]$; abs. max at $(4, 9)$; abs. and local min at $(x, 5)$ for all x in $[-3, 2]$; local max at $(x, 5)$ for all x in $(-3, 2)$

13.

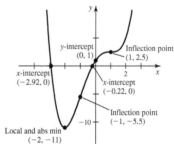

15.

17.

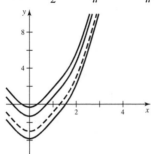

19.

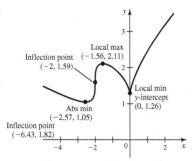

21. $r = 4\sqrt{6}/3; h = 4\sqrt{3}/3$ **23.** $x = 7, y = 14$
25. $p = q = 5\sqrt{2}$ **27. a.** $L(x) = \frac{2}{9}x + 3$
b. $\frac{85}{9} \approx 9.44$; overestimate
29. $f(x) = 1/x^2; a = 4; 1/4.2^2 \approx 9/160 = 0.05625$
31. $\Delta h \approx -112$ ft   **33. a.** $\frac{100}{9}$ cells/week   **b.** $t = 2$ weeks
35. $-0.434259, 0.767592, 1$ **37.** $0, \pm0.948683$ **39.** 0   **41.** 12
43. $\frac{2}{3}$ **45.** ∞ **47.** 0   **49.** 1   **51.** 0   **53.** 1   **55.** 1   **57.** $1/e^3$
59. 1   **61.** $x^{1/2}$ **63.** $\sqrt{x}$ **65.** 3^x **67.** Comparable growth rates
69. $\frac{4}{3}x^3 + 2x^2 + x + C$ **71.** $-\frac{1}{x} + \frac{4}{3}x^{-3/2} + C$

73. $\theta + \frac{1}{3}\sin 3\theta + C$ **75.** $\frac{1}{2}\sec 2x + C$ **77.** $12 \ln |x| + C$
79. $\tan^{-1}x + C$ **81.** $\frac{4}{7}x^{7/4} + \frac{2}{7}x^{7/2} + C$
83. $f(t) = -\cos t + t^2 + 6$

85. $h(x) = \frac{x}{2} - \frac{1}{4}\sin 2x + \frac{1}{2} + \frac{\sin 2}{4}$

87. $v(t) = -9.8t + 120; s(t) = -4.9t^2 + 120t + 125$
The rocket reaches a height of 859.69 m at time $t = 12.24$ s and
then falls to the ground, hitting at time $t = 25.49$ s.   **89.** 1; 1
91. 0   **93.** $\lim_{x \to 0^+} f(x) = 1; \lim_{x \to 0^+} g(x) = 0$

CHAPTER 9

Section 9.1 Exercises, pp. 672–675

1. $f(0) = p_2(0), f'(0) = p_2'(0),$ and $f''(0) = p_2''(0)$
3. $1, 1.05, 1.04875$ **5.** $R_n(x) = f(x) - p_n(x)$
7. a. $p_1(x) = 8 + 12(x - 1)$
b. $p_2(x) = 8 + 12(x - 1) + 3(x - 1)^2$

c. $9.2; 9.23$ **9. a.** $p_1(x) = 1 - x$ **b.** $p_2(x) = 1 - x + \frac{x^2}{2}$

c. $0.8, 0.82$ **11. a.** $p_1(x) = 1 - x$ **b.** $p_2(x) = 1 - x + x^2$
c. $0.95, 0.9525$ **13. a.** $p_1(x) = 2 + \frac{1}{12}(x - 8)$
b. $p_2(x) = 2 + \frac{1}{12}(x - 8) - \frac{1}{288}(x - 8)^2$

c. $1.958\overline{3}, 1.95747$ **15. a.** $p_0(x) = 1, p_1(x) = 1, p_2(x) = 1 - \frac{x^2}{2}$
b.

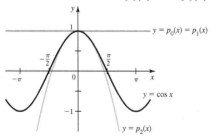

17. a. $p_0(x) = 0, p_1(x) = -x, p_2(x) = -x - \frac{x^2}{2}$

b.

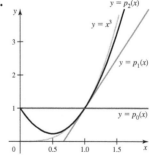

19. a. $p_0(x) = 0, p_1(x) = x, p_2(x) = x$
b.

21. a. $p_0(x) = 1, p_1(x) = 1 - 3x, p_2(x) = 1 - 3x + 6x^2$
b.

23. a. 1.0247 **b.** 7.6×10^{-6} **25. a.** 0.9624 **b.** 1.5×10^{-4}
27. a. 0.8613 **b.** 5.4×10^{-4}
29. a. $p_0(x) = 1, p_1(x) = 1 + 3(x - 1),$
$p_2(x) = 1 + 3(x - 1) + 3(x - 1)^2$
b.

31. a. $p_0(x) = \frac{\sqrt{2}}{2}, p_1(x) = \frac{\sqrt{2}}{2} + \frac{\sqrt{2}}{2}\left(x - \frac{\pi}{4}\right),$

$p_2(x) = \frac{\sqrt{2}}{2} + \frac{\sqrt{2}}{2}\left(x - \frac{\pi}{4}\right) - \frac{\sqrt{2}}{4}\left(x - \frac{\pi}{4}\right)^2$

b.

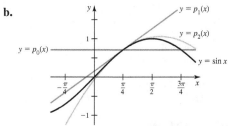

33. a. $p_0(x) = 3$, $p_1(x) = 3 + \dfrac{(x-9)}{6}$,

$p_2(x) = 3 + \dfrac{(x-9)}{6} - \dfrac{(x-9)^2}{216}$

b.

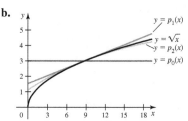

35. a. $p_0(x) = 1$, $p_1(x) = 1 + \dfrac{x-e}{e}$,

$p_2(x) = 1 + \dfrac{x-e}{e} - \dfrac{(x-e)^2}{2e^2}$

b.

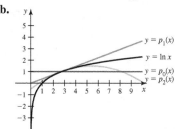

37. a. $p_0(x) = 2 + \dfrac{\pi}{4}$, $p_1(x) = 2 + \dfrac{\pi}{4} + \dfrac{5}{2}(x-1)$,

$p_2(x) = 2 + \dfrac{\pi}{4} + \dfrac{5}{2}(x-1) + \dfrac{3}{4}(x-1)^2$

b.

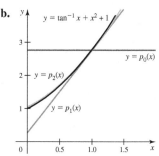

39. a. 1.12749 **b.** 8.9×10^{-6} **41. a.** -0.100333 **b.** 1.3×10^{-6}
43. a. 1.029564 **b.** 4.9×10^{-7} **45. a.** 10.04987563
b. 3.9×10^{-9} **47. a.** 0.520833 **b.** 2.6×10^{-4}

49. $R_n(x) = \dfrac{\sin^{(n+1)}(c)}{(n+1)!}x^{n+1}$, for c between x and 0.

51. $R_n(x) = \dfrac{(-1)^{n+1}e^{-c}}{(n+1)!}x^{n+1}$, for c between x and 0.

53. $R_n(x) = \dfrac{\sin^{(n+1)}(c)}{(n+1)!}\left(x - \dfrac{\pi}{2}\right)^{n+1}$, for c between x and $\dfrac{\pi}{2}$.

55. 2.0×10^{-5} **57.** 1.6×10^{-5} $(e^{0.25} < 2)$ **59.** 2.6×10^{-4}
61. With $n = 4$, $|\text{error}| \le 2.5 \times 10^{-3}$
63. With $n = 2$, $|\text{error}| \le 4.2 \times 10^{-2}$ $(e^{0.5} < 2)$
65. With $n = 2$, $|\text{error}| \le 5.4 \times 10^{-3}$
67. 4 **69.** 3 **71.** 1   **73. a.** False **b.** True **c.** True
d. True **75. a.** C **b.** E **c.** A **d.** D **e.** B **f.** F
77. a. 0.1; 1.7×10^{-4} **b.** 0.2; 1.3×10^{-3}
79. a. 0.995; 4.2×10^{-6} **b.** 0.98; 6.7×10^{-5}
81. a. 1.05; 1.3×10^{-3} **b.** 1.1; 5×10^{-3}
83. a. 1.1; 10^{-2} **b.** 1.2; 4×10^{-2}
85. a.

x	$|\sec x - p_2(x)|$	$|\sec x - p_4(x)|$
-0.2	3.4×10^{-4}	5.5×10^{-6}
-0.1	2.1×10^{-5}	8.5×10^{-8}
0.0	0	0
0.1	2.1×10^{-5}	8.5×10^{-8}
0.2	3.4×10^{-4}	5.5×10^{-6}

b. The error increases as $|x|$ increases.
87. a.

x	$|e^{-x} - p_1(x)|$	$|e^{-x} - p_2(x)|$
-0.2	2.1×10^{-2}	1.4×10^{-3}
-0.1	5.2×10^{-3}	1.7×10^{-4}
0.0	0	0
0.1	4.8×10^{-3}	1.6×10^{-4}
0.2	1.9×10^{-2}	1.3×10^{-3}

b. The error increases as $|x|$ increases.

89. a.

x	$|\tan x - p_1(x)|$	$|\tan x - p_3(x)|$
-0.2	2.7×10^{-3}	4.3×10^{-5}
-0.1	3.3×10^{-4}	1.3×10^{-6}
0.0	0	0
0.1	3.3×10^{-4}	1.3×10^{-6}
0.2	2.7×10^{-3}	4.3×10^{-5}

b. The error increases as $|x|$ increases.   **91.** Centered at $x = 0$
for all n **93. a.** $y = f(a) + f'(a)(x - a)$

95. a. $p_5(x) = x - \dfrac{x^3}{6} + \dfrac{x^5}{120}$;

$q_5(x) = -(x - \pi) + \dfrac{1}{6}(x - \pi)^3 - \dfrac{1}{120}(x - \pi)^5$

b.

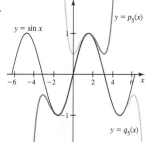

p_5 is a better approximation on $[-\pi, \pi/2]$; q_5 is a better
approximation on $(\pi/2, 2\pi]$.

c.

x	$\lvert \sin x - p_5(x) \rvert$	$\lvert \sin x - q_5(x) \rvert$
$\pi/4$	3.6×10^{-5}	7.4×10^{-2}
$\pi/2$	4.5×10^{-3}	4.5×10^{-3}
$3\pi/4$	7.4×10^{-2}	3.6×10^{-5}
$5\pi/4$	2.3	3.6×10^{-5}
$7\pi/4$	20	7.4×10^{-2}

d. p_5 is a better approximation at $x = \pi/4$; at $x = \pi/2$ the errors are equal.

97. a. $p_1(x) = 6 + \dfrac{1}{12}(x - 36);\ q_1(x) = 7 + \dfrac{1}{14}(x - 49)$

b.

x	$\lvert \sqrt{x} - p_1(x) \rvert$	$\lvert \sqrt{x} - q_1(x) \rvert$
37	5.7×10^{-4}	6.0×10^{-2}
39	5.0×10^{-3}	4.1×10^{-2}
41	1.4×10^{-2}	2.5×10^{-2}
43	2.6×10^{-2}	1.4×10^{-2}
45	4.2×10^{-2}	6.1×10^{-3}
47	6.1×10^{-2}	1.5×10^{-3}

c. p_1 is a better approximation at $x = 37, 39, 41$.

Section 9.2 Exercises, pp. 682–684

1. $c_0 + c_1 x + c_2 x^2 + c_3 x^3$ **3.** Ratio and Root Tests   **5.** The radius of convergence does not change. The interval of convergence may change.   **7.** $\lvert x \rvert < \frac{1}{4}$ **9.** $R = \frac{1}{2}; (-\frac{1}{2}, \frac{1}{2})$ **11.** $R = 1; [0, 2)$
13. $R = 0; \{x : x = 0\}$ **15.** $R = \infty; (-\infty, \infty)$
17. $R = 3; (-3, 3)$ **19.** $R = \infty; (-\infty, \infty)$ **21.** $R = \infty; (-\infty, \infty)$
23. $R = \sqrt{3}; (-\sqrt{3}, \sqrt{3})$ **25.** $R = 1; (0, 2)$
27. $R = \infty; (-\infty, \infty)$ **29.** $\displaystyle\sum_{k=0}^{\infty} (3x)^k; \left(-\frac{1}{3}, \frac{1}{3}\right)$
31. $\displaystyle 2\sum_{k=0}^{\infty} x^{k+3}; (-1, 1)$ **33.** $\displaystyle 4\sum_{k=0}^{\infty} x^{k+12}; (-1, 1)$
35. $\displaystyle -\sum_{k=1}^{\infty} \frac{(3x)^k}{k}; \left[-\frac{1}{3}, \frac{1}{3}\right)$ **37.** $\displaystyle -\sum_{k=1}^{\infty} \frac{x^{k+1}}{k}; [-1, 1)$
39. $\displaystyle -2\sum_{k=1}^{\infty} \frac{x^{k+6}}{k}; [-1, 1)$ **41.** $\displaystyle g(x) = 2\sum_{k=1}^{\infty} k(2x)^{k-1}; \left(-\frac{1}{2}, \frac{1}{2}\right)$
43. $\displaystyle g(x) = \sum_{k=3}^{\infty} \frac{k(k-1)(k-2)}{6} x^{k-3}; (-1, 1)$
45. $\displaystyle g(x) = -\sum_{k=1}^{\infty} \frac{3^k x^k}{k}; \left[-\frac{1}{3}, \frac{1}{3}\right)$ **47.** $\displaystyle \sum_{k=0}^{\infty} (-x^2)^k; (-1, 1)$
49. $\displaystyle \sum_{k=0}^{\infty} \left(-\frac{x}{3}\right)^k; (-3, 3)$ **51.** $\displaystyle \ln 2 - \frac{1}{2}\sum_{k=1}^{\infty} \frac{x^{2k}}{k4^k}; (-2, 2)$
53. a. True **b.** True **c.** True **d.** True   **55.** e
57. $\displaystyle \sum_{k=0}^{\infty} \frac{(-1)^k x^k}{k+1}$ **59.** $\displaystyle \sum_{k=1}^{\infty} \frac{(-x^2)^k}{k!}$ **61.** $\lvert x - a \rvert < R$
63. $f(x) = \dfrac{1}{3 - \sqrt{x}}; 1 < x < 9$ **65.** $f(x) = \dfrac{e^x}{e^x - 1}; 0 < x < \infty$
67. $f(x) = \dfrac{3}{4 - x^2}; -2 < x < 2$ **69.** $\displaystyle \sum_{k=0}^{\infty} \frac{(-x)^k}{k!}; -\infty < x < \infty$
71. $\displaystyle \sum_{k=0}^{\infty} \frac{(-3x)^k}{k!}; -\infty < x < \infty$

73. $\displaystyle \lim_{k \to \infty} \left\lvert \frac{c_{k+1} x^{k+1}}{c_k x^k} \right\rvert = \lim_{k \to \infty} \left\lvert \frac{c_{k+1} x^{k+m+1}}{c_k x^{k+m}} \right\rvert$, so by the Ratio Test, the two series have the same radius of convergence.
75. a. $f(x) \cdot g(x) = c_0 d_0 + (c_0 d_1 + c_1 d_0)x +$
$(c_0 d_2 + c_1 d_1 + c_2 d_0)x^2 + \cdots$.   **b.** $\displaystyle \sum_{k=0}^{n} c_k d_{n-k}$ **77. b.** $n = 112$

Section 9.3 Exercises, pp. 694–696

1. The nth Taylor polynomial is the nth partial sum of the corresponding Taylor series.   **3.** Calculate $c_k = \dfrac{f^{(k)}(a)}{k!}$ for $k = 0, 1, 2, \ldots$.

5. Replace x with x^2 in the Taylor series for $f(x)$; $\lvert x \rvert < 1$.
7. The Taylor series for a function f converges to f on an interval if, for all x in the interval, $\displaystyle \lim_{n \to \infty} R_n(x) = 0$, where $R_n(x)$ is the remainder at x.   **9. a.** $1 - x + \dfrac{x^2}{2!} - \dfrac{x^3}{3!}$ **b.** $\displaystyle \sum_{k=0}^{\infty} \frac{(-1)^k x^k}{k!}$ **c.** $(-\infty, \infty)$
11. a. $1 - x^2 + x^4 - x^6$ **b.** $\displaystyle \sum_{k=0}^{n} (-1)^k x^{2k}$ **c.** $(-1, 1)$
13. a. $1 + 2x + \dfrac{(2x)^2}{2!} + \dfrac{(2x)^3}{3!}$ **b.** $\displaystyle \sum_{k=0}^{\infty} \frac{(2x)^k}{k!}$ **c.** $(-\infty, \infty)$
15. a. $\dfrac{x}{2} - \dfrac{x^3}{3 \cdot 2^3} + \dfrac{x^5}{5 \cdot 2^5} - \dfrac{x^7}{7 \cdot 2^7}$ **b.** $\displaystyle \sum_{k=0}^{\infty} \frac{(-1)^k x^{2k+1}}{(2k+1)2^{2k+1}}$ **c.** $[-2, 2]$
17. a. $1 + (\ln 3)x + \dfrac{\ln^2 3}{2}x^2 + \dfrac{\ln^3 3}{6}x^3$ **b.** $\displaystyle \sum_{k=0}^{\infty} \frac{\ln^k 3}{k!}x^k$ **c.** $(-\infty, \infty)$
19. a. $1 + \dfrac{(3x)^2}{2} + \dfrac{(3x)^4}{24} + \dfrac{(3x)^6}{720}$ **b.** $\displaystyle \sum_{k=0}^{\infty} \frac{(3x)^{2k}}{(2k)!}$ **c.** $(-\infty, \infty)$
21. a. $1 - \dfrac{(x - \pi/2)^2}{2!} + \dfrac{(x - \pi/2)^4}{4!} - \dfrac{(x - \pi/2)^6}{6!}$
b. $\displaystyle \sum_{k=0}^{\infty} \frac{(-1)^k}{(2k)!}(x - \pi/2)^{2k}$
23. a. $1 - (x - 1) + (x - 1)^2 - (x - 1)^3$
b. $\displaystyle \sum_{k=0}^{\infty} (-1)^k (x - 1)^k$
25. a. $\ln 3 + \dfrac{(x - 3)}{3} - \dfrac{(x - 3)^2}{3^2 \cdot 2} + \dfrac{(x - 3)^3}{3^3 \cdot 3}$
b. $\ln 3 + \displaystyle \sum_{k=1}^{\infty} \frac{(-1)^{k+1}(x - 3)^k}{k3^k}$
27. a. $2 + 2(\ln 2)(x - 1) + (\ln^2 2)(x - 1)^2 + \dfrac{\ln^3 2}{3}(x - 1)^3$
b. $\displaystyle \sum_{k=0}^{\infty} \frac{2(x - 1)^k \ln^k 2}{k!}$ **29.** $x^2 - \dfrac{x^4}{2} + \dfrac{x^6}{3} - \dfrac{x^8}{4}$
31. $1 + 2x + 4x^2 + 8x^3$ **33.** $1 + \dfrac{x}{2} + \dfrac{x^2}{6} + \dfrac{x^3}{24}$
35. $1 - x^4 + x^8 - x^{12}$ **37.** $x^2 + \dfrac{x^6}{6} + \dfrac{x^{10}}{120} + \dfrac{x^{14}}{5040}$
39. a. $1 - 2x + 3x^2 - 4x^3$ **b.** 0.826
41. a. $1 + \frac{1}{4}x - \frac{3}{32}x^2 + \frac{7}{128}x^3$ **b.** 1.029
43. a. $1 - \frac{2}{3}x + \frac{5}{9}x^2 - \frac{40}{81}x^3$ **b.** 0.895
45. $1 + \dfrac{x^2}{2} - \dfrac{x^4}{8} + \dfrac{x^6}{16}; [-1, 1]$ **47.** $3 - \dfrac{3x}{2} - \dfrac{3x^2}{8} - \dfrac{3x^3}{16}; [-1, 1]$

49. $a + \dfrac{x^2}{2a} - \dfrac{x^4}{8a^3} + \dfrac{x^6}{16a^5}; \ |x| \le a$

51. $1 - 8x + 48x^2 - 256x^3$ **53.** $\dfrac{1}{16} - \dfrac{x^2}{32} + \dfrac{3x^4}{256} - \dfrac{x^6}{256}$

55. $\dfrac{1}{9} - \dfrac{2}{9}\left(\dfrac{4x}{3}\right) + \dfrac{3}{9}\left(\dfrac{4x}{3}\right)^2 - \dfrac{4}{9}\left(\dfrac{4x}{3}\right)^3$

57. $R_n(x) = \dfrac{f^{(n+1)}(c)}{(n+1)!}x^{n+1}$, where c is between 0 and x and
$f^{(n+1)}(c) = \pm\sin c$ or $\pm\cos c$. Therefore, $|R_n(x)| \le \dfrac{|x|^{n+1}}{(n+1)!} \to 0$

as $n \to \infty$, for $-\infty < x < \infty$. **59.** $R_n(x) = \dfrac{f^{(n+1)}(c)}{(n+1)!}x^{n+1}$,

where c is between 0 and x and $f^{(n+1)}(c) = (-1)^n e^{-c}$. Therefore,
$|R_n(x)| \le \dfrac{|x|^{n+1}}{e^c(n+1)!} \to 0$, as $n \to \infty$, for $-\infty < x < \infty$.

61. a. False **b.** True **c.** False **d.** False **e.** True

63. a. $1 + \dfrac{x^2}{2!} + \dfrac{x^4}{4!} + \dfrac{x^6}{6!}$ **b.** $R = \infty$

65. a. $1 - \frac{2}{3}x^2 + \frac{5}{9}x^4 - \frac{40}{81}x^6$ **b.** $R = 1$

67. a. $1 - \frac{1}{2}x^2 - \frac{1}{8}x^4 - \frac{1}{16}x^6$ **b.** $R = 1$

69. a. $1 - 2x^2 + 3x^4 - 4x^6$ **b.** $R = 1$

71. 3.9149 **73.** 1.8989 **79.** $\displaystyle\sum_{k=0}^{\infty}\left(\dfrac{x-4}{2}\right)^k$

81. $\dfrac{1 \cdot 3 \cdot 5 \cdot 7}{2 \cdot 4 \cdot 6 \cdot 8}x^4, \ \dfrac{-1 \cdot 3 \cdot 5 \cdot 7 \cdot 9}{2 \cdot 4 \cdot 6 \cdot 8 \cdot 10}x^5$ **83.** Use three terms of the

Taylor series for $\cos x$ centered at $a = \pi/4$; 0.766

85. Use six terms of the Taylor series for $\sqrt[3]{x}$ centered at $a = 64$;
4.362 **87. a.** Use three terms of the Taylor series for $\sqrt[3]{125 + x}$
centered at $a = 0$; 5.03968 **b.** Use three terms of the Taylor series
for $\sqrt[3]{x}$ centered at $a = 125$; 5.03968 **c.** Yes

Section 9.4 Exercises, pp. 702–704

1. Replace f and g with their Taylor series centered at a and evaluate the limit. **3.** Substitute $x = -0.6$ into the Taylor series for e^x
centered at 0. Because the resulting series is an alternating series, the
error can be estimated. **5.** $f'(x) = \displaystyle\sum_{k=1}^{\infty}kc_kx^{k-1}$ **7.** 1 **9.** $\frac{1}{2}$

11. 2 **13.** $\frac{2}{3}$ **15.** $\frac{1}{3}$ **17.** $\frac{3}{5}$ **19.** $-\frac{8}{5}$ **21.** 1 **23.** $\frac{3}{4}$

25. a. $1 + x + \dfrac{x^2}{2!} + \cdots + \dfrac{x^n}{n!} + \cdots$ **b.** e^x **c.** $-\infty < x < \infty$

27. a. $1 - x + x^2 - \cdots (-1)^{n-1}x^{n-1} + \cdots$ **b.** $\dfrac{1}{1+x}$ **c.** $|x| < 1$

29. a. $-2 + 4x - 8 \cdot \dfrac{x^2}{2!} + \cdots + (-2)^n \dfrac{x^{n-1}}{(n-1)!} + \cdots$

b. $-2e^{-2x}$ **c.** $-\infty < x < \infty$ **31. a.** $1 - x^2 + x^4 - \cdots$

b. $\dfrac{1}{1+x^2}$ **c.** $-1 < x < 1$

33. a. $2 + 2t + \dfrac{2t^2}{2!} + \cdots + \dfrac{2t^n}{n!} + \cdots$ **b.** $y(t) = 2e^t$

35. a. $2 + 16t + 24t^2 + 24t^3 + \cdots + \dfrac{3^{n-1} \cdot 16}{n!}t^n + \cdots$

b. $y(t) = \frac{16}{3}e^{3t} - \frac{10}{3}$ **37.** 0.2448 **39.** 0.6958

41. $\dfrac{0.35^2}{2} - \dfrac{0.35^4}{12} \approx 0.0600$ **43.** 0.4994

45. $1 + 2 + \dfrac{2^2}{2!} + \dfrac{2^3}{3!}$ **47.** $1 - 2 + \dfrac{2}{3} - \dfrac{4}{45}$ **49.** $\frac{1}{2} - \frac{1}{8} + \frac{1}{24} - \frac{1}{64}$

51. $e - 1$ **53.** $\displaystyle\sum_{k=1}^{\infty}\dfrac{(-1)^{k+1}x^k}{k}$ for $-1 < x \le 1$; ln 2

55. $\dfrac{2}{2-x}$ **57.** $\dfrac{4}{4+x^2}$ **59.** $-\ln(1-x)$ **61.** $-\dfrac{3x^2}{(3+x)^2}$

63. $\dfrac{6x^2}{(3-x)^3}$ **65. a.** False **b.** False **c.** True **67.** $\frac{a}{b}$ **69.** $e^{-1/6}$

71. $f^{(3)}(0) = 0; f^{(4)}(0) = 4e$ **73.** $f^{(3)}(0) = 2; f^{(4)}(0) = 0$

75. 2 **77. a.** 1.575 using four terms
b. At least three **c.** More terms would be needed.
79. a. $S'(x) = \sin x^2; C'(x) = \cos x^2$

b. $\dfrac{x^3}{3} - \dfrac{x^7}{7 \cdot 3!} + \dfrac{x^{11}}{11 \cdot 5!} - \dfrac{x^{15}}{15 \cdot 7!}; x - \dfrac{x^5}{5 \cdot 2!} + \dfrac{x^9}{9 \cdot 4!} - \dfrac{x^{13}}{13 \cdot 6!}$

c. $S(0.05) \approx 0.00004166664807; C(-0.25) \approx -0.2499023614$

d. 1 **e.** 2 **81. a.** $1 - \dfrac{x^2}{4} + \dfrac{x^4}{64} - \dfrac{x^6}{2304}$ **b.** $-\infty < x < \infty, R = \infty$

83. a. The Maclaurin series for $\cos x$ consists of even powers of x,
which are even functions. **b.** The Maclaurin series for $\sin x$ consists
of odd powers of x, which are odd functions.

Chapter 9 Review Exercises, pp. 705–706

1. a. True **b.** False **c.** True **d.** True **3.** $p_2(x) = 1$

5. $p_3(x) = x - \dfrac{x^2}{2} + \dfrac{x^3}{3}$ **7.** $p_2(x) = (x - 1) - \dfrac{(x-1)^2}{2}$

9. $p_3(x) = \dfrac{5}{4} + \dfrac{3}{4}(x - \ln 2) + \dfrac{5}{8}(x - \ln 2)^2 + \dfrac{1}{8}(x - \ln 2)^3$

11. a. $p_2(x) = 1 + x + \dfrac{x^2}{2}$

b.

n	$p_n(x)$	Error
0	1	7.7×10^{-2}
1	0.92	3.1×10^{-3}
2	0.9232	8.4×10^{-5}

13. a. $p_2(x) = \dfrac{\sqrt{2}}{2} + \dfrac{\sqrt{2}}{2}\left(x - \dfrac{\pi}{4}\right) - \dfrac{\sqrt{2}}{4}\left(x - \dfrac{\pi}{4}\right)^2$

b.

n	$p_n(x)$	Error
0	0.7071	1.2×10^{-1}
1	0.5960	8.2×10^{-3}
2	0.5873	4.7×10^{-4}

15. $|R_3| < \dfrac{\pi^4}{4!}$ **17.** $(-\infty, \infty), R = \infty$ **19.** $(-\infty, \infty), R = \infty$

21. $(-9, 9), R = 9$ **23.** $[-4, 0), R = 2$ **25.** $\displaystyle\sum_{k=0}^{\infty}x^{2k}; (-1, 1)$

27. $\displaystyle\sum_{k=0}^{\infty}(-5x)^k; (-\frac{1}{5}, \frac{1}{5})$ **29.** $\displaystyle\sum_{k=1}^{\infty}k(10x)^{k-1}; (-\frac{1}{10}, \frac{1}{10})$

31. $1 + 3x + \dfrac{9x^2}{2!}; \displaystyle\sum_{k=0}^{\infty}\dfrac{(3x)^k}{k!}$

33. $-(x - \pi/2) + \dfrac{(x - \pi/2)^3}{3!} - \dfrac{(x - \pi/2)^5}{5!};$

$$\sum_{k=0}^{\infty}(-1)^{k+1}\frac{(x-\pi/2)^{2k+1}}{(2k+1)!}$$

35. $4x-\dfrac{(4x)^3}{3}+\dfrac{(4x)^5}{5};\ \displaystyle\sum_{k=0}^{\infty}\dfrac{(-1)^k(4x)^{2k+1}}{2k+1}$

37. $1+\dfrac{9x^2}{2!}+\dfrac{81x^4}{4!};\ \displaystyle\sum_{k=0}^{\infty}\dfrac{(3x)^{2k}}{(2k)!}$ **39.** $1+\dfrac{x}{3}-\dfrac{x^2}{9}+\cdots$

41. $1-\dfrac{3}{2}x+\dfrac{3}{2}x^2-\cdots$ **43.** $R_n(x)=\dfrac{(-1)^{n+1}e^{-c}}{(n+1)!}x^{n+1}$, where

c is between 0 and x. $\displaystyle\lim_{n\to\infty}|R_n(x)|=\lim_{n\to\infty}\dfrac{|x^{n+1}|}{e^{|x|}}\cdot\dfrac{1}{(n+1)!}=0$ for

$-\infty<x<\infty$.   **45.** $R_n(x)=\dfrac{(-1)^n(1+c)^{-(n+1)}}{n+1}x^{n+1}$

where c is between 0 and x.

$\displaystyle\lim_{n\to\infty}|R_n(x)|=\lim_{n\to\infty}\left(\left(\dfrac{|x|}{1+c}\right)^{n+1}\cdot\dfrac{1}{n+1}\right)<\lim_{n\to\infty}\left(1^{n+1}\cdot\dfrac{1}{n+1}\right)$

$=0$, for $|x|\le\frac{1}{2}$.   **47.** $\frac{1}{24}$ **49.** $\frac{1}{8}$ **51.** $\frac{1}{6}$ **53.** 0.4615 **55.** 0.3819

57. $11-\dfrac{1}{11}-\dfrac{1}{2\cdot11^3}-\dfrac{1}{2\cdot11^5}$ **59.** $-\dfrac{1}{3}+\dfrac{1}{3\cdot3^3}-\dfrac{1}{5\cdot3^5}+\dfrac{1}{7\cdot3^7}$

61. $y=4+4x+\dfrac{4^2}{2!}x^2+\dfrac{4^3}{3!}x^3+\cdots+\dfrac{4^n}{n!}x^n+\cdots=3+e^{4x}$

63. a. $\displaystyle\sum_{k=1}^{\infty}\dfrac{(-1)^{k+1}}{k}$ **b.** $\displaystyle\sum_{k=1}^{\infty}\dfrac{1}{k2^k}$ **c.** $2\displaystyle\sum_{k=0}^{\infty}\dfrac{x^{2k+1}}{2k+1}$

d. $x=\dfrac{1}{3};\ 2\displaystyle\sum_{k=0}^{\infty}\dfrac{1}{3^{2k+1}(2k+1)}$ **e.** Series in part (d)

APPENDIX A

Exercises, pp. 1157–1158

1. The set of real numbers greater than -4 and less than or equal to 10; $(-4,10]$;

3. $|x|=\begin{cases} x & \text{if } x\ge0 \\ -x & \text{if } x<0 \end{cases}$ **5.** $2x-4\ge3$ or $2x-4\le-3$

7. Take the square root of the sum of the squares of the differences of the x- and y-coordinates.   **9.** $y=\sqrt{36-x^2}$

11. $m=\dfrac{y+2}{x-4}$ or $y=m(x-4)-2$ **13.** They are equal.

15. 4 **17.** $4uv$ **19.** $-\dfrac{h}{x(x+h)}$ **21.** $(y-y^{-1})(y+y^{-1})$

23. $u=\pm\sqrt{2},\pm3$ **25.** $3x^2+3xh+h^2$

27. $(1,5)$

29. $(-\infty,4]\cup[5,6)$

31. $\{x:x<-4/3$ or $x>4\};\ \left(-\infty,-\frac{4}{3}\right)\cup(4,\infty)$

33. $\{x:-2<x<-1$ or $2<x<3\};\ (-2,-1)\cup(2,3)$

35. $y=2-\sqrt{9-(x+1)^2}$

37. $y=\dfrac{5}{3}x+4$

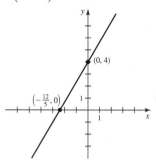

39. $y=\dfrac{4}{5}x-4$

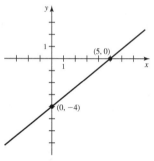

41. $x+2y=24$

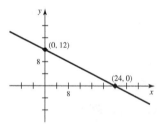

43. $y=\dfrac{1}{3}x-7$ **45. a.** False   **b.** True   **c.** False   **d.** False

e. False   **f.** True   **g.** False   **47.** $\{x:|x-1|\ge3\}$

49.

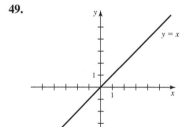

Index

Student's Solutions Manual, Single Variable

The following is taken from *Student's Solutions Manual, Single Variable* by Mark Woodward
for *Calculus: Early Transcendentals*, Second Edition by William Briggs, Lyle Cochran, and Bernard Gillett

Chapter 1

Functions

1.1 Review of Functions

1.1.1 A function is a rule which assigns each domain element to a unique range element. The independent variable is associated with the domain, while the dependent variable is associated with the range.

1.1.3 The vertical line test is used to determine whether a given graph represents a function. (Specifically, it tests whether the variable associated with the vertical axis is a function of the variable associated with the horizontal axis.) If every vertical line which intersects the graph does so in exactly one point, then the given graph represents a function. If any vertical line $x = a$ intersects the curve in more than one point, then there is more than one range value for the domain value $x = a$, so the given curve does not represent a function.

1.1.5 Item i. is true while item ii. isn't necessarily true. In the definition of function, item i. is stipulated. However, item ii. need not be true – for example, the function $f(x) = x^2$ has two different domain values associated with the one range value 4, because $f(2) = f(-2) = 4$.

1.1.7 $f(g(2)) = f(-2) = f(2) = 2$. The fact that $f(-2) = f(2)$ follows from the fact that f is an even function.

$g(f(-2)) = g(f(2)) = g(2) = -2$.

1.1.9 When f is an even function, we have $f(-x) = f(x)$ for all x in the domain of f, which ensures that the graph of the function is symmetric about the y-axis.

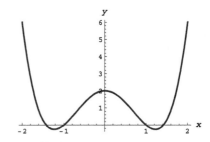

1.1.11 Graph A does not represent a function, while graph B does. Note that graph A fails the vertical line test, while graph B passes it.

1.1.13 The domain of this function is the set of a real numbers. The range is $[-10, \infty)$.

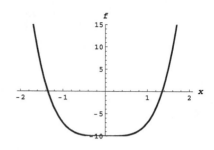

1.1.15 The domain of this function is $[-2, 2]$. The range is $[0, 2]$.

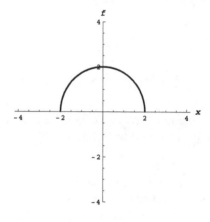

1.1.17 The domain and the range for this function are both the set of all real numbers.

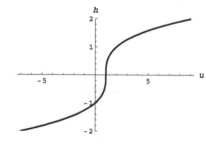

1.1.19 The domain of this function is $[-3, 3]$. The range is $[0, 27]$.

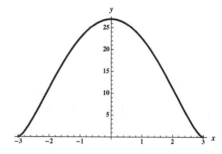

1.1.21 The independent variable t is elapsed time and the dependent variable d is distance above the ground. The domain in context is $[0, 8]$

1.1.23 The independent variable h is the height of the water in the tank and the dependent variable V is the volume of water in the tank. The domain in context is $[0, 50]$

1.1.25 $f(10) = 96$

1.1.27 $g(1/z) = (1/z)^3 = \frac{1}{z^3}$

1.1.29 $F(g(y)) = F(y^3) = \frac{1}{y^3 - 3}$

1.1.31 $g(f(u)) = g(u^2 - 4) = (u^2 - 4)^3$

1.1.33 $F(F(x)) = F\left(\frac{1}{x-3}\right) = \frac{1}{\frac{1}{x-3} - 3} = \frac{1}{\frac{1}{x-3} - \frac{3(x-3)}{x-3}} = \frac{1}{\frac{10-3x}{x-3}} = \frac{x-3}{10-3x}$

1.1.35 $f(\sqrt{x+4}) = (\sqrt{x+4})^2 - 4 = x + 4 - 4 = x.$

1.1.37 $g(x) = x^3 - 5$ and $f(x) = x^{10}$. The domain of h is the set of all real numbers.

1.1.39 $g(x) = x^4 + 2$ and $f(x) = \sqrt{x}$. The domain of h is the set of all real numbers.

1.1.41 $(f \circ g)(x) = f(g(x)) = f(x^2 - 4) = |x^2 - 4|$. The domain of this function is the set of all real numbers.

1.1.43 $(f \circ G)(x) = f(G(x)) = f\left(\frac{1}{x-2}\right) = \left|\frac{1}{x-2}\right|$. The domain of this function is the set of all real numbers except for the number 2.

1.1.45 $(G \circ g \circ f)(x) = G(g(f(x))) = G(g(|x|)) = G(x^2 - 4) = \frac{1}{x^2 - 4 - 2} = \frac{1}{x^2 - 6}$. The domain of this function is the set of all real numbers except for the numbers $\pm\sqrt{6}$.

1.1.47 $(g \circ g)(x) = g(g(x)) = g(x^2 - 4) = (x^2 - 4)^2 - 4 = x^4 - 8x^2 + 16 - 4 = x^4 - 8x^2 + 12$. The domain is the set of all real numbers.

1.1.49 Because $(x^2 + 3) - 3 = x^2$, we may choose $f(x) = x - 3$.

1.1.51 Because $(x^2 + 3)^2 = x^4 + 6x^2 + 9$, we may choose $f(x) = x^2$.

1.1.53 Because $(x^2)^2 + 3 = x^4 + 3$, this expression results from squaring x^2 and adding 3 to it. Thus we may choose $f(x) = x^2$.

1.1.55

a. $(f \circ g)(2) = f(g(2)) = f(2) = 4.$

b. $g(f(2)) = g(4) = 1.$

c. $f(g(4)) = f(1) = 3.$

d. $g(f(5)) = g(6) = 3.$

e. $f(f(8)) = f(8) = 8.$

f. $g(f(g(5))) = g(f(2)) = g(4) = 1.$

1.1.57 $\frac{f(x+h) - f(x)}{h} = \frac{(x+h)^2 - x^2}{h} = \frac{(x^2 + 2hx + h^2) - x^2}{h} = \frac{h(2x+h)}{h} = 2x + h.$

1.1.59 $\frac{f(x+h) - f(x)}{h} = \frac{\frac{2}{x+h} - \frac{2}{x}}{h} = \frac{\frac{2x - 2(x+h)}{x(x+h)}}{h} = \frac{2x - 2x - 2h}{h(x)(x+h)} = -\frac{2h}{h(x)(x+h)} = -\frac{2}{(x)(x+h)}.$

1.1.61 $\frac{f(x+h) - f(x)}{h} = \frac{\frac{x+h}{x+h+1} - \frac{x}{x+1}}{h} = \frac{\frac{(x+h)(x+1) - x(x+h+1)}{(x+1)(x+h+1)}}{h} = \frac{x^2 + x + hx + h - x^2 - xh - x}{h(x+1)(x+h+1)} = \frac{h}{h(x+1)(x+h+1)} = \frac{1}{(x+1)(x+h+1)}$

1.1.63 $\frac{f(x) - f(a)}{x-a} = \frac{x^3 - 2x - (a^3 - 2a)}{x-a} = \frac{(x^3 - a^3) - 2(x-a)}{x-a} = \frac{(x-a)(x^2 + ax + a^2) - 2(x-a)}{x-a} = \frac{(x-a)(x^2 + ax + a^2 - 2)}{x-a} = x^2 + ax + a^2 - 2.$

1.1.65 $\frac{f(x) - f(a)}{x-a} = \frac{\frac{-4}{x^2} - \frac{-4}{a^2}}{x-a} = \frac{\frac{-4a^2 + 4x^2}{a^2 x^2}}{x-a} = \frac{4(x^2 - a^2)}{(x-a)a^2 x^2} = \frac{4(x-a)(x+a)}{(x-a)a^2 x^2} = \frac{4(x+a)}{a^2 x^2}.$

1.1.67

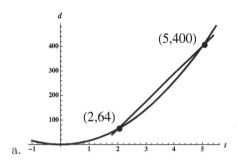

b. The slope of the secant line is given by $\frac{400-64}{5-2} = \frac{336}{3} = 112$ feet per second. The object falls at an average rate of 112 feet per second over the interval $2 \leq t \leq 5$.

a.

1.1.69

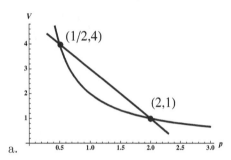

b. The slope of the secant line is given by $\frac{1-4}{2-(1/2)} = -\frac{3}{3/2} = -2$ cubic cm per atmosphere. The volume decreases at an average rate of 2 cubic cm per atmosphere over the interval $0.5 \leq p \leq 2$.

a.

1.1.71 This function is symmetric about the y-axis, because $f(-x) = (-x)^4 + 5(-x)^2 - 12 = x^4 + 5x^2 - 12 = f(x)$.

1.1.73 This function has none of the indicated symmetries. For example, note that $f(-2) = -26$, while $f(2) = 22$, so f is not symmetric about either the origin or about the y-axis, and is not symmetric about the x-axis because it is a function.

1.1.75 This curve (which is not a function) is symmetric about the x-axis, the y-axis, and the origin. Note that replacing either x by $-x$ or y by $-y$ (or both) yields the same equation. This is due to the fact that $(-x)^{2/3} = ((-x)^2)^{1/3} = (x^2)^{1/3} = x^{2/3}$, and a similar fact holds for the term involving y.

1.1.77 This function is symmetric about the origin. Note that $f(-x) = (-x)|(-x)| = -x|x| = -f(x)$.

1.1.79 Function A is symmetric about the y-axis, so is even. Function B is symmetric about the origin, so is odd. Function C is also symmetric about the y-axis, so is even.

1.1.81

a. True. A real number z corresponds to the domain element $z/2 + 19$, because $f(z/2 + 19) = 2(z/2 + 19) - 38 = z + 38 - 38 = z$.

b. False. The definition of function does not require that each range element comes from a unique domain element, rather that each domain element is paired with a unique range element.

c. True. $f(1/x) = \frac{1}{1/x} = x$, and $\frac{1}{f(x)} = \frac{1}{1/x} = x$.

d. False. For example, suppose that f is the straight line through the origin with slope 1, so that $f(x) = x$. Then $f(f(x)) = f(x) = x$, while $(f(x))^2 = x^2$.

e. False. For example, let $f(x) = x+2$ and $g(x) = 2x-1$. Then $f(g(x)) = f(2x-1) = 2x-1+2 = 2x+1$, while $g(f(x)) = g(x+2) = 2(x+2) - 1 = 2x + 3$.

f. True. This is the definition of $f \circ g$.

g. True. If f is even, then $f(-z) = f(z)$ for all z, so this is true in particular for $z = ax$. So if $g(x) = cf(ax)$, then $g(-x) = cf(-ax) = cf(ax) = g(x)$, so g is even.

h. False. For example, $f(x) = x$ is an odd function, but $h(x) = x + 1$ isn't, because $h(2) = 3$, while $h(-2) = -1$ which isn't $-h(2)$.

i. True. If $f(-x) = -f(x) = f(x)$, then in particular $-f(x) = f(x)$, so $0 = 2f(x)$, so $f(x) = 0$ for all x.

1.1.83 We will make heavy use of the fact that $|x|$ is x if $x > 0$, and is $-x$ if $x < 0$. In the first quadrant where x and y are both positive, this equation becomes $x - y = 1$ which is a straight line with slope 1 and y-intercept -1. In the second quadrant where x is negative and y is positive, this equation becomes $-x - y = 1$, which is a straight line with slope -1 and y-intercept -1. In the third quadrant where both x and y are negative, we obtain the equation $-x - (-y) = 1$, or $y = x + 1$, and in the fourth quadrant, we obtain $x + y = 1$. Graphing these lines and restricting them to the appropriate quadrants yields the following curve:

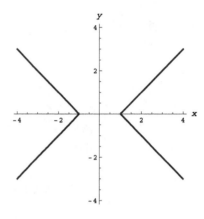

1.1.85 Because the composition of f with itself has first degree, f has first degree as well, so let $f(x) = ax + b$. Then $(f \circ f)(x) = f(ax + b) = a(ax + b) + b = a^2 x + (ab + b)$. Equating coefficients, we see that $a^2 = 9$ and $ab + b = -8$. If $a = 3$, we get that $b = -2$, while if $a = -3$ we have $b = 4$. So the two possible answers are $f(x) = 3x - 2$ and $f(x) = -3x + 4$.

1.1.87 Let $f(x) = ax^2 + bx + c$. Then $(f \circ f)(x) = f(ax^2 + bx + c) = a(ax^2 + bx + c)^2 + b(ax^2 + bx + c) + c$. Expanding this expression yields $a^3 x^4 + 2a^2 bx^3 + 2a^2 cx^2 + ab^2 x^2 + 2abcx + ac^2 + abx^2 + b^2 x + bc + c$, which simplifies to $a^3 x^4 + 2a^2 bx^3 + (2a^2 c + ab^2 + ab)x^2 + (2abc + b^2)x + (ac^2 + bc + c)$. Equating coefficients yields $a^3 = 1$, so $a = 1$. Then $2a^2 b = 0$, so $b = 0$. It then follows that $c = -6$, so the original function was $f(x) = x^2 - 6$.

1.1.89 $\frac{f(x+h) - f(x)}{h} = \frac{\sqrt{x+h} - \sqrt{x}}{h} = \frac{\sqrt{x+h} - \sqrt{x}}{h} \cdot \frac{\sqrt{x+h} + \sqrt{x}}{\sqrt{x+h} + \sqrt{x}} = \frac{(x+h) - x}{h(\sqrt{x+h} + \sqrt{x})} = \frac{1}{\sqrt{x+h} + \sqrt{x}}$.

$\frac{f(x) - f(a)}{x - a} = \frac{\sqrt{x} - \sqrt{a}}{x - a} = \frac{\sqrt{x} - \sqrt{a}}{x - a} \cdot \frac{\sqrt{x} + \sqrt{a}}{\sqrt{x} + \sqrt{a}} = \frac{x - a}{(x - a)(\sqrt{x} + \sqrt{a})} = \frac{1}{\sqrt{x} + \sqrt{a}}$.

1.1.91 $\frac{f(x+h) - f(x)}{h} = \frac{\frac{-3}{\sqrt{x+h}} - \frac{-3}{\sqrt{x}}}{h} = \frac{-3(\sqrt{x} - \sqrt{x+h})}{h\sqrt{x}\sqrt{x+h}} = \frac{-3(\sqrt{x} - \sqrt{x+h})}{h\sqrt{x}\sqrt{x+h}} \cdot \frac{\sqrt{x} + \sqrt{x+h}}{\sqrt{x} + \sqrt{x+h}} = $
$\frac{-3(x - (x+h))}{h\sqrt{x}\sqrt{x+h}(\sqrt{x} + \sqrt{x+h})} = \frac{3}{\sqrt{x}\sqrt{x+h}(\sqrt{x} + \sqrt{x+h})}$.

$\frac{f(x) - f(a)}{x - a} = \frac{\frac{-3}{\sqrt{x}} - \frac{-3}{\sqrt{a}}}{x - a} = \frac{-3\left(\frac{\sqrt{a} - \sqrt{x}}{\sqrt{a}\sqrt{x}}\right)}{x - a} = \frac{(-3)(\sqrt{a} - \sqrt{x})}{(x - a)\sqrt{a}\sqrt{x}} \cdot \frac{\sqrt{a} + \sqrt{x}}{\sqrt{a} + \sqrt{x}} = \frac{(3)(x - a)}{(x - a)(\sqrt{a}\sqrt{x})(\sqrt{a} + \sqrt{x})} = \frac{3}{\sqrt{ax}(\sqrt{a} + \sqrt{x})}$.

1.1.93

a. The formula for the height of the rocket is valid from $t = 0$ until the rocket hits the ground, which is the positive solution to $-16t^2 + 96t + 80 = 0$, which the quadratic formula reveals is $t = 3 + \sqrt{14}$. Thus, the domain is $[0, 3 + \sqrt{14}]$.

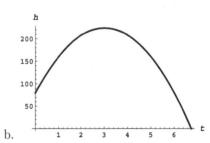

b.

The maximum appears to occur at $t = 3$. The height at that time would be 224.

1.1.95 This would not necessarily have either kind of symmetry. For example, $f(x) = x^2$ is an even function and $g(x) = x^3$ is odd, but the sum of these two is neither even nor odd.

1.1.97 This would be an odd function, so it would be symmetric about the origin. Suppose f is even and g is odd. Then $\frac{f}{g}(-x) = \frac{f(-x)}{g(-x)} = \frac{f(x)}{-g(x)} = -\frac{f}{g}(x)$.

1.1.99 This would be an even function, so it would be symmetric about the y-axis. Suppose f is even and g is even. Then $f(g(-x)) = f(g(x))$, because $g(-x) = g(x)$.

1.1.101 This would be an even function, so it would be symmetric about the y-axis. Suppose f is even and g is odd. Then $g(f(-x)) = g(f(x))$, because $f(-x) = f(x)$.

1.1.103

a. $f(g(-2)) = f(-g(2)) = f(-2) = 4$

b. $g(f(-2)) = g(f(2)) = g(4) = 1$

c. $f(g(-4)) = f(-g(4)) = f(-1) = 3$

d. $g(f(5) - 8) = g(-2) = -g(2) = -2$

e. $g(g(-7)) = g(-g(7)) = g(-4) = -1$

f. $f(1 - f(8)) = f(-7) = 7$

1.2 Representing Functions

1.2.1 Functions can be defined and represented by a formula, through a graph, via a table, and by using words.

1.2.3 The domain of a rational function $\frac{p(x)}{q(x)}$ is the set of all real numbers for which $q(x) \neq 0$.

1.2.5

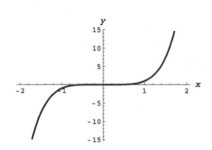

1.2.7 Compared to the graph of $f(x)$, the graph of $f(x+2)$ will be shifted 2 units to the left.

1.2.9 Compared to the graph of $f(x)$, the graph of $f(3x)$ will be scaled horizontally by a factor of 3.

1.2.11 The slope of the line shown is $m = \frac{-3-(-1)}{3-0} = -2/3$. The y-intercept is $b = -1$. Thus the function is given by $f(x) = (-2/3)x - 1$.

1.2.13

The slope is given by $\frac{5-3}{2-1} = 2$, so the equation of the line is $y - 3 = 2(x - 1)$, which can be written as $y = 2x - 2 + 3$, or $y = 2x + 1$.

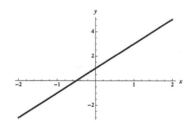

1.2.15 Using price as the independent variable p and the average number of units sold per day as the dependent variable d, we have the ordered pairs $(250, 12)$ and $(200, 15)$. The slope of the line determined by these points is $m = \frac{15-12}{200-250} = \frac{3}{-50}$. Thus the demand function has the form $d(p) = (-3/50)p + b$ for some constant b. Using the point $(200, 15)$, we find that $15 = (-3/50) \cdot 200 + b$, so $b = 27$. Thus the demand function is $d = (-3/50)p + 27$. While the domain of this linear function is the set of all real numbers, the formula is only likely to be valid for some subset of the interval $(0, 450)$, because outside of that interval either $p \leq 0$ or $d \leq 0$.

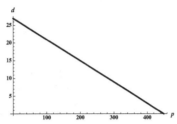

1.2.17 The slope is given by the rate of growth, which is 24. When $t = 0$ (years past 2015), the population is 500, so the point $(0, 500)$ satisfies our linear function. Thus the population is given by $p(t) = 24t + 500$. In 2030, we have $t = 15$, so the population will be approximately $p(15) = 360 + 500 = 860$.

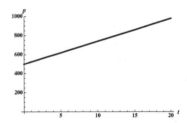

1.2.19 For $x < 0$, the graph is a line with slope 1 and y- intercept 3, while for $x > 0$, it is a line with slope $-1/2$ and y-intercept 3. Note that both of these lines contain the point $(0, 3)$. The function shown can thus be written

$$f(x) = \begin{cases} x + 3 & \text{if } x < 0; \\ -\frac{1}{2}x + 3 & \text{if } x \geq 0. \end{cases}$$

1.2.21

The cost is given by

$$c(t) = \begin{cases} 0.05t & \text{for } 0 \leq t \leq 60 \\ 1.2 + 0.03t & \text{for } 60 < t \leq 120 \end{cases}.$$

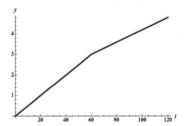

1.2.23

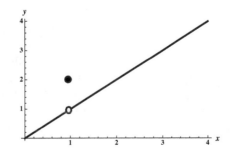

1.2.25

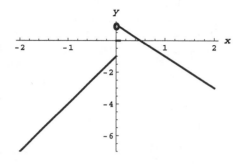

1.2.27

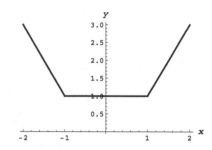

1.2.29

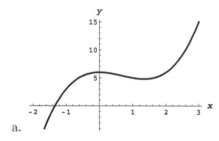

a.

b. The function is a polynomial, so its domain is the set of all real numbers.

c. It has one peak near its y-intercept of $(0, 6)$ and one valley between $x = 1$ and $x = 2$. Its x-intercept is near $x = -4/3$.

1.2.31

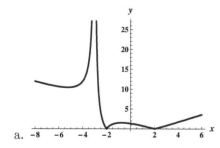

a.

b. The domain of the function is the set of all real numbers except -3.

c. There is a valley near $x = -5.2$ and a peak near $x = -0.8$. The x-intercepts are at -2 and 2, where the curve does not appear to be smooth. There is a vertical asymptote at $x = -3$. The function is never below the x-axis. The y-intercept is $(0, 4/3)$.

1.2.33

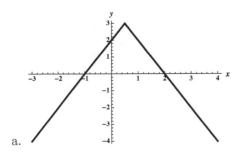

b. The domain of the function is $(-\infty, \infty)$

c. The function has a maximum of 3 at $x = 1/2$, and a y-intercept of 2.

a.

1.2.35 The slope of this line is constantly 2, so the slope function is $s(x) = 2$.

1.2.37 The slope function is given by $s(x) = \begin{cases} 1 & \text{if } x < 0; \\ -1/2 & \text{if } x > 0. \end{cases}$

1.2.39

a. Because the area under consideration is that of a rectangle with base 2 and height 6, $A(2) = 12$.

b. Because the area under consideration is that of a rectangle with base 6 and height 6, $A(6) = 36$.

c. Because the area under consideration is that of a rectangle with base x and height 6, $A(x) = 6x$.

1.2.41

a. Because the area under consideration is that of a trapezoid with base 2 and heights 8 and 4, we have $A(2) = 2 \cdot \frac{8+4}{2} = 12$.

b. Note that $A(3)$ represents the area of a trapezoid with base 3 and heights 8 and 2, so $A(3) = 3 \cdot \frac{8+2}{2} = 15$. So $A(6) = 15 + (A(6) - A(3))$, and $A(6) - A(3)$ represents the area of a triangle with base 3 and height 2. Thus $A(6) = 15 + 6 = 21$.

c. For x between 0 and 3, $A(x)$ represents the area of a trapezoid with base x, and heights 8 and $8 - 2x$. Thus the area is $x \cdot \frac{8+8-2x}{2} = 8x - x^2$. For $x > 3$, $A(x) = A(3) + A(x) - A(3) = 15 + 2(x - 3) = 2x + 9$. Thus

$$A(x) = \begin{cases} 8x - x^2 & \text{if } 0 \le x \le 3; \\ 2x + 9 & \text{if } x > 3. \end{cases}$$

1.2.43 $f(x) = |x - 2| + 3$, because the graph of f is obtained from that of $|x|$ by shifting 2 units to the right and 3 units up.

$g(x) = -|x + 2| - 1$, because the graph of g is obtained from the graph of $|x|$ by shifting 2 units to the left, then reflecting about the x-axis, and then shifting 1 unit down.

1.2.45

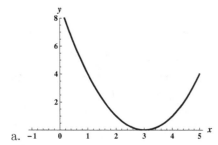

a.

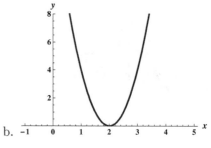

b.

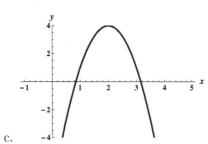

c.

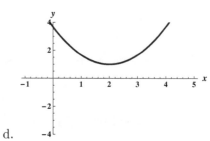

d.

1.2.47 The graph is obtained by shifting the graph of x^2 two units to the right and one unit up.

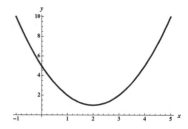

1.2.49 This function is $-3 \cdot f(x)$ where $f(x) = x^2$

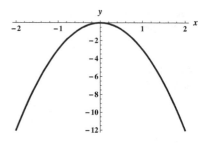

1.2.51 This function is $2 \cdot f(x + 3)$ where $f(x) = x^2$

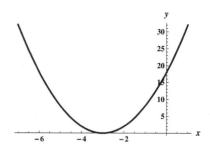

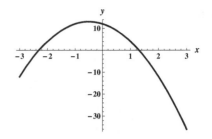

1.2.53 By completing the square, we have that $h(x) = -4(x^2 + x - 3) = -4\left(x^2 + x + \frac{1}{4} - \frac{1}{4} - 3\right) = -4(x + (1/2))^2 + 13$. So it is $-4f(x + (1/2)) + 13$ where $f(x) = x^2$.

1.2.55

a. True. A polynomial $p(x)$ can be written as the ratio of polynomials $\frac{p(x)}{1}$, so it is a rational function. However, a rational function like $\frac{1}{x}$ is not a polynomial.

b. False. For example, if $f(x) = 2x$, then $(f \circ f)(x) = f(f(x)) = f(2x) = 4x$ is linear, not quadratic.

c. True. In fact, if f is degree m and g is degree n, then the degree of the composition of f and g is $m \cdot n$, regardless of the order they are composed.

d. False. The graph would be shifted two units to the left.

1.2.57 The points of intersection are found by solving $x^2 = -x^2 + 8x$. This yields the quadratic equation $2x^2 - 8x = 0$ or $(2x)(x - 4) = 0$. So the x-values of the points of intersection are 0 and 4. The actual points of intersection are $(0, 0)$ and $(4, 16)$.

1.2.59 $y = \sqrt{x} - 1$, because the y value is always 1 less than the square root of the x value.

1.2.61 The car moving north has gone $30t$ miles after t hours and the car moving east has gone $60t$ miles. Using the Pythagorean theorem, we have $s(t) = \sqrt{(30t)^2 + (60t)^2} = \sqrt{900t^2 + 3600t^2} = \sqrt{4500t^2} = 30\sqrt{5}t$ miles. The context domain could be $[0, 4]$.

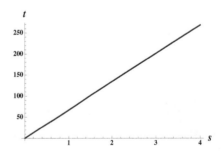

1.2.63 $y = \frac{3200}{x}$. Note that $\frac{x \text{ dollars per gallon}}{32 \text{ miles per gallon}} \cdot y \text{ miles}$ would represent the numbers of dollars, so this must be 100. So we have $\frac{xy}{32} = 100$, or $y = \frac{3200}{x}$. We certainly have $x > 0$, and a reasonable upper bound to imagine for x is \$5 (let's hope), so the context domain is $(0, 5]$.

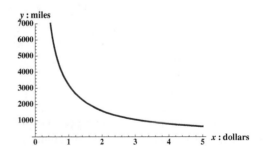

1.2.65

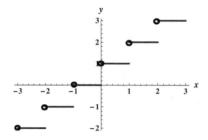

1.2.67

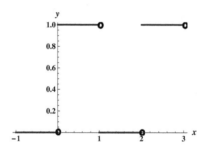

1.2.69

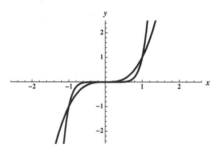

1.2.71

a. The zeros of f are the points where the graph crosses the x-axis, so these are points A, D, F, and I.

b. The only high point, or peak, of f occurs at point E, because it appears that the graph has larger and larger y values as x increases past point I and decreases past point A.

c. The only low points, or valleys, of f are at points B and H, again assuming that the graph of f continues its apparent behavior for larger values of x.

d. Past point H, the graph is rising, and is rising faster and faster as x increases. It is also rising between points B and E, but not as quickly as it is past point H. So the marked point at which it is rising most rapidly is I.

e. Before point B, the graph is falling, and falls more and more rapidly as x becomes more and more negative. It is also falling between points E and H, but not as rapidly as it is before point B. So the marked point at which it is falling most rapidly is A.

1.2.73

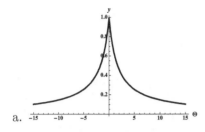

a.

b. This appears to have a maximum when $\theta = 0$. Our vision is sharpest when we look straight ahead.

c. For $|\theta| \leq .19°$. We have an extremely narrow range where our eyesight is sharp.

1.2.75

a. Using the points $(1986, 1875)$ and $(2000, 6471)$ we see that the slope is about 328.3. At $t = 0$, the value of p is 1875. Therefore a line which reasonably approximates the data is $p(t) = 328.3t + 1875$.

b. Using this line, we have that $p(9) = 4830$.

1.2.77

a. Because you are paying \$350 per month, the amount paid after m months is $y = 350m + 1200$.

b. After 4 years (48 months) you have paid $350 \cdot 48 + 1200 = 18000$ dollars. If you then buy the car for \$10,000, you will have paid a total of \$28,000 for the car instead of \$25,000. So you should buy the car instead of leasing it.

1.2.79   The function makes sense for $0 \leq h \leq 2$.

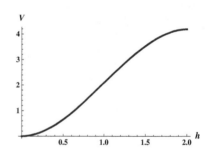

1.2.81

a. The volume of the box is $x^2 h$, but because the box has volume 125 cubic feet, we have that $x^2 h = 125$, so $h = \frac{125}{x^2}$. The surface area of the box is given by x^2 (the area of the base) plus $4 \cdot hx$, because each side has area hx. Thus $S = x^2 + 4hx = x^2 + \frac{4 \cdot 125 \cdot x}{x^2} = x^2 + \frac{500}{x}$.

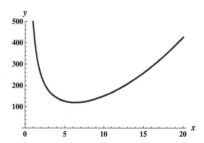

b. By inspection, it looks like the value of x which minimizes the surface area is about 6.3.

1.2.83 Suppose that the parabola f crosses the x-axis at a and b, with $a < b$. Then a and b are roots of the polynomial, so $(x - a)$ and $(x - b)$ are factors. Thus the polynomial must be $f(x) = c(x - a)(x - b)$ for some non-zero real number c. So $f(x) = cx^2 - c(a + b)x + abc$. Because the vertex always occurs at the x value which is $\frac{-\text{coefficient on } x}{2 \cdot \text{coefficient on } x^2}$ we have that the vertex occurs at $\frac{c(a+b)}{2c} = \frac{a+b}{2}$, which is halfway between a and b.

1.2.85

a.

n	1	2	3	4	5
$n!$	1	2	6	24	120

b.

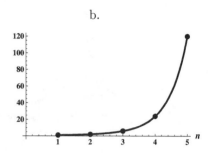

c. Using trial and error and a calculator yields that 10! is more than a million, but 9! isn't.

1.2.87

a.

n	1	2	3	4	5	6	7	8	9	10
$T(n)$	1	5	14	30	55	91	140	204	285	385

b. The domain of this function consists of the positive integers.

c. Using trial and error and a calculator yields that $T(n) > 1000$ for the first time for $n = 14$.

1.3   Inverse, Exponential and Logarithmic Functions

1.3.1 $D = \mathbb{R}, R = (0, \infty)$.

1.3.3 If a function f is not one-to-one, then there are domain values $x_1 \neq x_2$ with $f(x_1) = f(x_2)$. If f^{-1} were to exist, then $f^{-1}(f(x_1)) = f^{-1}(f(x_2))$ which would imply that $x_1 = x_2$, a contradiction.

1.3.5

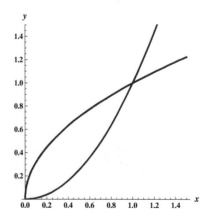

1.3.7 $\log_b x$ represents the power to which b must be raised in order to obtain x. So, $b^{\log_b x} = x$.

1.3.9 Because the domain of b^x is $\mathbb{R}$ and the range of b^x is $(0, \infty)$, and because $\log_b x$ is the inverse of b^x, the domain of $\log_b x$ is $(0, \infty)$ and the range is $\mathbb{R}$.

1.3.11 f is one-to-one on $(-\infty, -1]$, on $[-1, 1]$, and on $[1, \infty)$.

1.3.13

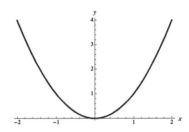

1.3.15 f is one-to-one on $\mathbb{R}$, so it has an inverse on $\mathbb{R}$.

1.3.17 f is one-to-one on its domain, which is $(-\infty, 5) \cup (5, \infty)$, so it has an inverse on that set.

1.3.19 f is one-to-one on the interval $(0, \infty)$, so it has an inverse on that interval. (Alternatively, it is one-to-one on the interval $(-\infty, 0)$, so that interval could be used as well.)

1.3.21

  a. Switching x and y, we have $x = 2y$, so $y = \frac{1}{2}x$. Thus $y = f^{-1}(x) = \frac{1}{2}x$.

  b. $f(f^{-1}(x)) = f\left(\frac{1}{2}x\right) = 2\left(\frac{1}{2}x\right) = x$. Also, $f^{-1}(f(x)) = f^{-1}(2x) = \frac{1}{2} \cdot (2x) = x$.

1.3.23

  a. Switching x and y, we have $x = 6 - 4y$. Solving for y in terms of x we have $4y = 6 - x$, so $y = f^{-1}(x) = \frac{6-x}{4}$.

  b. $f(f^{-1}(x)) = f\left(\frac{6-x}{4}\right) = 6 - 4 \cdot \left(\frac{6-x}{4}\right) = 6 - (6 - x) = x$.
  $f^{-1}(f(x)) = f^{-1}(6 - 4x) = \frac{6-(6-4x)}{4} = \frac{4x}{4} = x$.

1.3.25

  a. Switching x and y, we have $x = 3y + 5$. Solving for y in terms of x we have $y = \frac{x-5}{3}$, so $y = f^{-1}(x) = \frac{x-5}{3}$.

  b. $f(f^{-1}(x)) = f\left(\frac{x-5}{3}\right) = 3\left(\frac{x-5}{3}\right) + 5 = (x - 5) + 5 = x$.
  $f^{-1}(f(x)) = f^{-1}(3x + 5) = \frac{(3x+5)-5}{3} = \frac{3x}{3} = x$.

1.3.27

  a. Switching x and y, we have $x = \sqrt{y + 2}$. Solving for y in terms of x we have $y = f^{-1}(x) = x^2 - 2$. Note that because the range of f is $[0, \infty)$, that is also the domain of f^{-1}.

  b. $f(f^{-1}(x)) = f(x^2 - 2) = \sqrt{x^2 - 2 + 2} = |x| = x$, because x is in the domain of f^{-1} and so is nonnegative.
  $f^{-1}(f(x)) = f^{-1}(\sqrt{x + 2}) = \sqrt{x + 2}^2 - 2 = x + 2 - 2 = x$.

1.3.29 First note that because the expression is symmetric, switching x and y doesn't change the expression. Solving for y gives $|y| = \sqrt{1 - x^2}$. To get the four one-to-one functions, we restrict the domain and choose either the upper part or lower part of the circle as follows:

  a. $f_1(x) = \sqrt{1 - x^2}$, $0 \le x \le 1$
  $f_2(x) = \sqrt{1 - x^2}$, $-1 \le x \le 0$
  $f_3(x) = -\sqrt{1 - x^2}$, $-1 \le x \le 0$
  $f_4(x) = -\sqrt{1 - x^2}$, $0 \le x \le 1$

b. Reflecting these functions across the line $y = x$ yields the following:

$$f_1^{-1}(x) = \sqrt{1 - x^2},\ 0 \le x \le 1$$

$$f_2^{-1}(x) = -\sqrt{1 - x^2},\ 0 \le x \le 1$$

$$f_3^{-1}(x) = -\sqrt{1 - x^2},\ -1 \le x \le 0$$

$$f_4^{-1}(x) = \sqrt{1 - x^2},\ -1 \le x \le 0$$

1.3.31 Switching x and y gives $x = 8 - 4y$. Solving this for y yields $y = f^{-1}(x) = \frac{8-x}{4}$.

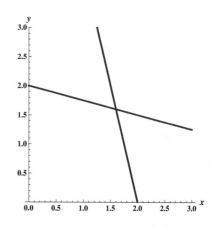

1.3.33 Switching x and y gives $x = \sqrt{y}$. Solving this for y yields $y = f^{-1}(x) = x^2$, but note that the range of f is $[0, \infty)$ so that is the domain of f^{-1}.

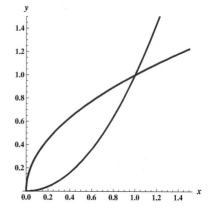

1.3.35 Switching x and y gives $x = y^4 + 4$. Solving this for y yields $y = f^{-1}(x) = \sqrt[4]{x - 4}$.

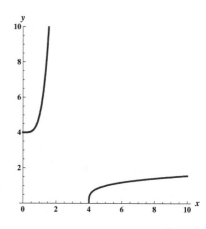

1.3.37 Begin by completing the square: $f(x) = x^2 - 2x + 6 = (x^2 - 2x + 1) + 5 = (x - 1)^2 + 5$. Switching x and y yields $x = (y - 1)^2 + 5$. Solving for y gives $|y - 1| = \sqrt{x - 5}$. Choosing the principal square root (because the original given interval has x positive) gives $y = f^{-1}(x) = \sqrt{x - 5} + 1$, $x \geq 5$.

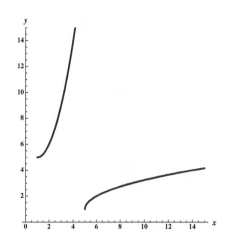

1.3.39

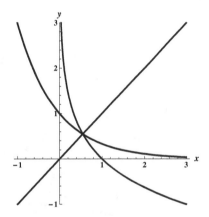

1.3.41 If $\log_{10} x = 3$, then $10^3 = x$, so $x = 1000$.

1.3.43 If $\log_8 x = 1/3$, then $x = 8^{1/3} = 2$.

1.3.45 If $\ln x = -1$, then $e^{-1} = x$, so $x = \frac{1}{e}$.

1.3.47 $\log_b \left(\frac{x}{y} \right) = \log_b x - \log_b y = .36 - .56 = -0.2$.

1.3.49 $\log_b xz = \log_b x + \log_b z = .36 + .83 = 1.19$.

1.3.51 $\log_b \frac{\sqrt{x}}{\sqrt[3]{z}} = \log_b x^{1/2} - \log_b z^{1/3} = (1/2)\log_b x - (1/3)\log_b z = (.36)/2 - (.83)/3 = -.09\overline{6}$.

1.3.53 Since $7^x = 21$, we have that $\ln 7^x = \ln 21$, so $x \ln 7 = \ln 21$, and $x = \frac{\ln 21}{\ln 7}$.

1.3.55 Since $3^{3x-4} = 15$, we have that $\ln 3^{3x-4} = \ln 15$, so $(3x - 4)\ln 3 = \ln 15$. Thus, $3x - 4 = \frac{\ln 15}{\ln 3}$, so $x = \frac{(\ln 15)/(\ln 3) + 4}{3} = \frac{\ln 15 + 4 \ln 3}{3 \ln 3} = \frac{\ln 5 + \ln 3 + 4 \ln 3}{3 \ln 3} = \frac{\ln 5}{3 \ln 3} + \frac{5}{3}$.

1.3.57 We are seeking t so that $50 = 100e^{-t/650}$. This occurs when $e^{-t/650} = \frac{1}{2}$, which is when $-\frac{t}{650} = \ln(1/2)$, so $t = 650 \ln 2 \approx 451$ years.

1.3.59 $\log_2 15 = \frac{\ln 15}{\ln 2} \approx 3.9069$.

1.3.61 $\log_4 40 = \frac{\ln 40}{\ln 4} \approx 2.6610$.

1.3.63 Let $2^x = z$. Then $\ln 2^x = \ln z$, so $x \ln 2 = \ln z$. Taking the exponential function of both sides gives $z = e^{x \ln 2}$.

1.3.65 Let $z = \ln |x|$. Then $e^z = |x|$. Taking logarithms with base 5 of both sides gives $\log_5 e^z = \log_5 |x|$, so $z \cdot \log_5 e = \log_5 |x|$, and thus $z = \frac{\log_5 |x|}{\log_5 e}$.

1.3.67 Let $z = a^{1/\ln a}$. Then $\ln z = \ln \left(a^{1/\ln a} \right) = \frac{1}{\ln a} \cdot \ln a = 1$. Thus $z = e$.

1.3.69

    a. False. For example, $3 = 3^1$, but $1 \neq \sqrt[3]{3}$.

    b. False. For example, suppose $x = y = b = 2$. Then the left-hand side of the equation is equal to 1, but the right-hand side is 0.

    c. False. $\log_5 4^6 = 6 \log_5 4 > 4 \log_5 6$.

    d. True. This follows because 10^x and $\log_{10}$ are inverses of each other.

    e. False. $\ln 2^e = e \ln 2 < 2$.

    f. False. For example $f(0) = 1$, but the alleged inverse function evaluated at 1 is not 0 (rather, it has value 1/2.)

    g. True. f is its own inverse because $f(f(x)) = f(1/x) = \frac{1}{1/x} = x$.

1.3.71

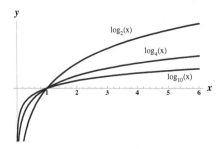

1.3.73

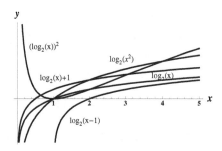

1.3.75 Note that f is one-to-one, so there is only one inverse. Switching x and y gives $x = (y + 1)^3$. Then $\sqrt[3]{x} = y + 1$, so $y = f^{-1}(x) = \sqrt[3]{x} - 1$. The domain of f^{-1} is $\mathbb{R}$.

1.3.77 Note that to get a one-to-one function, we should restrict the domain to either $[0, \infty)$ or $(-\infty, 0]$. Switching x and y yields $x = \frac{2}{y^2 + 2}$, so $y^2 + 2 = (2/x)$. So $y = \pm\sqrt{(2/x) - 2}$. So the inverse of f when the domain of f is restricted to $[0, \infty)$ is $f^{-1}(x) = \sqrt{(2/x) - 2}$, while if the domain of f is restricted to $(-\infty, 0]$ the inverse is $f^{-1}(x) = -\sqrt{(2/x) - 2}$. In either case, the domain of f^{-1} is $(0, 1]$.

1.3.79

a. $p(0) = 150(2^{0/12}) = 150$.

b. At a given time t, let the population be $z = 150(2^{t/12})$. Then 12 hours later, the time is $12 + t$, and the population is $150(2^{(t+12)/12}) = 150(2^{(t/12)+1}) = 150(2^{t/12} \cdot 2) = 2z$.

c. Since 4 days is 96 hours, we have $p(96) = 150(2^{96/12}) = 150(2^8) = 38,400$.

d. We can find the time to triple by solving $450 = 150(2^{t/12})$, which is equivalent to $3 = 2^{t/12}$. By taking logs of both sides we have $\ln 3 = \frac{t}{12} \cdot \ln 2$, so $t = \frac{12 \ln 3}{\ln 2} \approx 19.0$ hours.

e. The population will reach 10,000 when $10,000 = 150(2^{12/t})$, which is equivalent to $\frac{200}{3} = 2^{t/12}$. By taking logs of both sides we have $\ln(200/3) = \frac{t}{12} \ln 2$, so $= \frac{12 \cdot \ln(200/3)}{\ln 2} \approx 72.7$ hours.

1.3.81

a. No. The function takes on the values from 0 to 64 as t varies from 0 to 2, and then takes on the values from 64 to 0 as t varies from 2 to 4, so h is not one-to-one.

b. Solving for h in terms of t we have $h = 64t - 16t^2$, so (completing the square) we have $h - 64 = -16(t^2 - 4t + 4)$. Thus, $h - 64 = -16(t-2)^2$, and $(t-2)^2 = \frac{64-h}{16}$. Therefore $|t - 2| = \frac{\sqrt{64-h}}{4}$. When the ball is on the way up we know that $t < 2$, so the inverse of f is $f^{-1}(h) = 2 - \frac{\sqrt{64-h}}{4}$.

c. Using the work from the previous part of this problem, we have that when the ball is on the way down (when $t > 2$) we have that the inverse of f is $f^{-1}(h) = 2 + \frac{\sqrt{64-h}}{4}$.

d. On the way up, the ball is at a height of 30 ft at $2 - \frac{\sqrt{64-30}}{4} \approx 0.542$ seconds.

e. On the way down, the ball is at a height of 10 ft at $2 + \frac{\sqrt{64-10}}{4} \approx 3.837$ seconds.

1.3.83 Using the change of base formula, we have $\log_{1/b} x = \frac{\ln x}{\ln 1/b} = \frac{\ln x}{\ln 1 - \ln b} = \frac{\ln x}{-\ln b} = -\frac{\ln x}{\ln b} = -\log_b x$.

1.3.85 Using the same notation as in the previous problem, we have:
$\frac{x}{y} = \frac{b^p}{b^q} = b^{p-q}$. Thus $\log_b \frac{x}{y} = \log_b b^{p-q} = p - q = \log_b x - \log_b y$.

1.3.87

a. f is one-to-one on $(-\infty, -\sqrt{2}/2]$, on $[-\sqrt{2}/2, 0]$, on $[0, \sqrt{2}/2]$, and on $[\sqrt{2}/2, \infty)$.

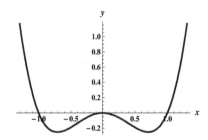

b. If $u = x^2$, then our function becomes $y = u^2 - u$. Completing the square gives $y + (1/4) = u^2 - u + (1/4) = (u - (1/2))^2$. Thus $|u - (1/2)| = \sqrt{y + (1/4)}$, so $u = (1/2) \pm \sqrt{y + (1/4)}$, with the "+" applying for $u = x^2 > (1/2)$ and the "−" applying when $u = x^2 < (1/2)$. Now letting $u = x^2$, we have $x^2 = (1/2) \pm \sqrt{y + (1/4)}$, so $x = \pm\sqrt{(1/2) \pm \sqrt{y + (1/4)}}$. Now switching the x and y gives the following inverses:

Domain of f	$(-\infty, -\sqrt{2}/2]$	$[-\sqrt{2}/2, 0]$	$[0, \sqrt{2}/2]$	$[\sqrt{2}/2, \infty)$
Range of f	$[-1/4, \infty)$	$[-1/4, 0]$	$[-1/4, 0]$	$[-1/4, \infty)$
Inverse of f	$-\sqrt{(1/2) + \sqrt{x + (1/4)}}$	$-\sqrt{(1/2) - \sqrt{x + (1/4)}}$	$\sqrt{(1/2) - \sqrt{x + (1/4)}}$	$\sqrt{(1/2) + \sqrt{x + (1/4)}}$

1.3.89 Let $y = x^3 + 2x$. This function is one-to-one, so it has an inverse. Making the suggested substitution yields $y = (z - 2/(3z))^3 + 2(z - 2/(3z))$. Expanding gives $y = z^3 - 2z + 4/(3z) - 8/(27z^3) + 2z - 4/(3z) = z^3 - 8/(27z^3)$. Thus we have $y = z^3 - 8/(27z^3)$, so $27z^3 y = 27(z^3)^2 - 8$, or $27(z^3)^2 - 27y(z^3) - 8 = 0$. Applying the quadratic formula gives $z^3 = \frac{y}{2} \pm \frac{\sqrt{3}\sqrt{32+27y^2}}{18}$ We will take the "+" part and finish solving to obtain:

$$z = \sqrt[3]{\frac{y}{2} + \frac{\sqrt{3}\sqrt{32 + 27y^2}}{18}}$$

Now

$$x = z - (2/(3z)) = \frac{3z^2 - 2}{3z} = \frac{3\left(\sqrt[3]{\frac{y}{2} + \frac{\sqrt{3}\sqrt{32+27y^2}}{18}}\right)^2 - 2}{3\sqrt[3]{\frac{y}{2} + \frac{\sqrt{3}\sqrt{32+27y^2}}{18}}}.$$

So the inverse function $f^{-1}(x)$ is now obtained by switching y and x.

1.3.91 Using the change of base formulas $\log_b c = \frac{\ln c}{\ln b}$ and $\log_c b = \frac{\ln b}{\ln c}$ we have

$$(\log_b c) \cdot (\log_c b) = \frac{\ln c}{\ln b} \cdot \frac{\ln b}{\ln c} = 1.$$

1.4 Trigonometric Functions and Their Inverses

1.4.1 Let O be the length of the side opposite the angle x, let A be length of the side adjacent to the angle x, and let H be the length of the hypotenuse. Then $\sin x = \frac{O}{H}$, $\cos x = \frac{A}{H}$, $\tan x = \frac{O}{A}$, $\csc x = \frac{H}{O}$, $\sec x = \frac{H}{A}$, and $\cot x = \frac{A}{O}$.

1.4.3 The radian measure of an angle θ is the length of the arc s on the unit circle associated with θ.

1.4.5 $\sin^2 x + \cos^2 x = 1$, $1 + \cot^2 x = \csc^2 x$, and $\tan^2 x + 1 = \sec^2 x$.

1.4.7 The tangent function is undefined where $\cos x = 0$, which is at all real numbers of the form $\frac{\pi}{2} + k\pi$, k an integer.

1.4.9 The sine function is not one-to-one over its whole domain, so in order to define an inverse, it must be restricted to an interval on which it is one-to-one.

1.4.11 $\tan(\tan^{-1}(x)) = x$ for all real numbers x. (Note that the domain of the inverse tangent is $\mathbb{R}$). However, it is not always true that $\tan^{-1}(\tan x) = x$. For example, $\tan 27\pi = 0$, and $\tan^{-1}(0) = 0$. Thus $\tan^{-1}(\tan(27\pi)) \neq 27\pi$.

1.4.13 The numbers $\pm\pi/2$ are not in the range of $\tan^{-1} x$. The range is $(-\pi/2, \pi/2)$. However, it is true that as x increases without bound, the values of $\tan^{-1} x$ get close to $\pi/2$, and as x decreases without bound, the values of $\tan^{-1} x$ get close to $-\pi/2$.

1.4.15

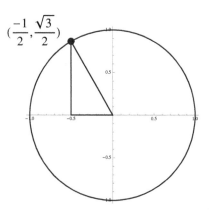

The point on the unit circle associated with $2\pi/3$ is $(-1/2, \sqrt{3}/2)$, so $\cos(2\pi/3) = -1/2$.

1.4.17

The point on the unit circle associated with $-3\pi/4$ is $(-\sqrt{2}/2, -\sqrt{2}/2)$, so $\tan(-3\pi/4) = 1$.

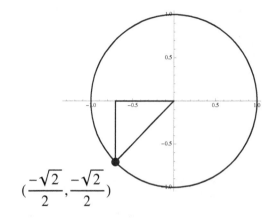

$$\left(\frac{-\sqrt{2}}{2}, \frac{-\sqrt{2}}{2}\right)$$

1.4.19

The point on the unit circle associated with $-13\pi/3$ is $(1/2, -\sqrt{3}/2)$, so $\cot(-13\pi/3) = -1/\sqrt{3} = -\sqrt{3}/3$.

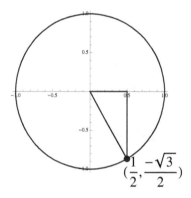

$$\left(\frac{1}{2}, \frac{-\sqrt{3}}{2}\right)$$

1.4.21

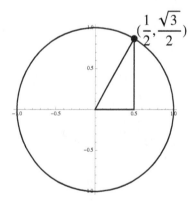

$$\left(\frac{1}{2}, \frac{\sqrt{3}}{2}\right)$$

The point on the unit circle associated with $-17\pi/3$ is $(1/2, \sqrt{3}/2)$, so $\cot(-17\pi/3) = 1/\sqrt{3} = \sqrt{3}/3$.

1.4.23 Because the point on the unit circle associated with $\theta = 0$ is the point $(1, 0)$, we have $\cos 0 = 1$.

1.4.25 Because $-\pi$ corresponds to a half circle clockwise revolution, the point on the unit circle associated with $-\pi$ is the point $(-1, 0)$. Thus $\cos(-\pi) = -1$.

1.4.27 Because $5\pi/2$ corresponds to one and a quarter counterclockwise revolutions, the point on the unit circle associated with $5\pi/2$ is the same as the point associated with $\pi/2$, which is $(0, 1)$. Thus $\sec 5\pi/2$ is undefined.

1.4.29 From our definitions of the trigonometric functions via a point $P(x, y)$ on a circle of radius $r = \sqrt{x^2 + y^2}$, we have $\sec\theta = \frac{r}{x} = \frac{1}{x/r} = \frac{1}{\cos\theta}$.

1.4.31 We have already established that $\sin^2\theta + \cos^2\theta = 1$. Dividing both sides by $\cos^2\theta$ gives $\tan^2\theta + 1 = \sec^2\theta$.

1.4.33

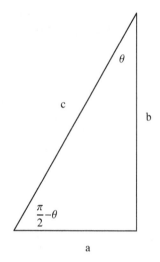

Using the triangle pictured, we see that $\sec(\pi/2 - \theta) = \frac{c}{a} = \csc\theta$.
This also follows from the sum identity $\cos(a+b) = \cos a \cos b - \sin a \sin b$ as follows: $\sec(\pi/2 - \theta) = \frac{1}{\cos(\pi/2 + (-\theta))} = \frac{1}{\cos(\pi/2)\cos(-\theta) - \sin(\pi/2)\sin(-\theta)} = \frac{1}{0 - (-\sin(\theta))} = \csc(\theta)$.

1.4.35 Using the fact that $\frac{\pi}{12} = \frac{\pi/6}{2}$ and the half-angle identity for cosine:

$$\cos^2(\pi/12) = \frac{1 + \cos(\pi/6)}{2} = \frac{1 + \sqrt{3}/2}{2} = \frac{2 + \sqrt{3}}{4}.$$

Thus, $\cos(\pi/12) = \sqrt{\frac{2+\sqrt{3}}{4}}$.

1.4.37 First note that $\tan x = 1$ when $\sin x = \cos x$. Using our knowledge of the values of the standard angles between 0 and 2π, we recognize that the sine function and the cosine function are equal at $\pi/4$. Then, because we recall that the period of the tangent function is π, we know that $\tan(\pi/4 + k\pi) = \tan(\pi/4) = 1$ for every integer value of k. Thus the solution set is $\{\pi/4 + k\pi, \text{where } k \text{ is an integer}\}$.

1.4.39 Given that $\sin^2\theta = \frac{1}{4}$, we have $|\sin\theta| = \frac{1}{2}$, so $\sin\theta = \frac{1}{2}$ or $\sin\theta = -\frac{1}{2}$. It follows that $\theta = \pi/6, 5\pi/6, 7\pi/6, 11\pi/6$.

1.4.41 The equation $\sqrt{2}\sin(x) - 1 = 0$ can be written as $\sin x = \frac{1}{\sqrt{2}} = \frac{\sqrt{2}}{2}$. Standard solutions to this equation occur at $x = \pi/4$ and $x = 3\pi/4$. Because the sine function has period 2π the set of all solutions can be written as:

$$\{\pi/4 + 2k\pi, \text{where } k \text{ is an integer}\} \cup \{3\pi/4 + 2l\pi, \text{where } l \text{ is an integer}\}.$$

1.4.43 As in the previous problem, let $u = 3x$. Then we are interested in the solutions to $\cos u = \sin u$, for $0 \leq u < 6\pi$.

This would occur for $u = 3x = \pi/4, 5\pi/4, 9\pi/4, 13\pi/4, 17\pi/4, \text{and } 21\pi/4$. Thus there are solutions for the original equation at

$$x = \pi/12, 5\pi/12, 3\pi/4, 13\pi/12, 17\pi/12, \text{and } 7\pi/4.$$

1.4.45 If $\sin\theta\cos\theta = 0$, then either $\sin\theta = 0$ or $\cos\theta = 0$. This occurs for $\theta = 0, \pi/2, \pi, 3\pi/2$.

1.4.47 Let $z = \sin^{-1}(1)$. Then $\sin z = 1$, and because $\sin\pi/2 = 1$, and $\pi/2$ is in the desired interval, $z = \pi/2$.

1.4.49 Let $z = \tan^{-1}(1)$. Then $\tan z = 1$, so $\frac{\sin z}{\cos z} = 1$, so $\sin z = \cos z$. Because $\cos \pi/4 = \sin \pi/4$, and $\pi/4$ is in the desired interval, $z = \pi/4$.

1.4.51 $\sin^{-1}(\sqrt{3}/2) = \pi/3$, because $\sin(\pi/3) = \sqrt{3}/2$.

1.4.53 $\cos^{-1}(-1/2) = 2\pi/3$, because $\cos(2\pi/3) = -1/2$.

1.4.55 $\cos(\cos^{-1}(-1)) = \cos(\pi) = -1$.

1.4.57

$$\cos(\sin^{-1}(x)) = \frac{\text{side adjacent to } \sin^{-1}(x)}{\text{hypotenuse}} = \frac{\sqrt{1-x^2}}{1} = \sqrt{1-x^2}.$$

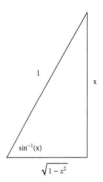

1.4.59

$$\sin(\cos^{-1}(x/2)) = \frac{\text{side opposite of } \cos^{-1}(x/2)}{\text{hypotenuse}} = \frac{\sqrt{4-x^2}}{2}.$$

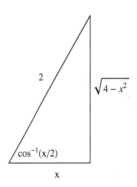

1.4.61

Using the identity given, we have $\sin(2\cos^{-1}(x)) = 2\sin(\cos^{-1}(x))\cos(\cos^{-1}(x)) = 2x\sin(\cos^{-1}(x)) = 2x\sqrt{1-x^2}$.

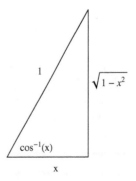

1.4.63

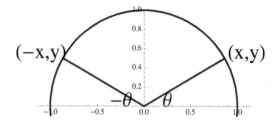

Let $\theta = \cos^{-1}(x)$, and note from the diagram that it then follows that $\cos^{-1}(-x) = \pi - \theta$. So $\cos^{-1}(x) + \cos^{-1}(-x) = \theta + \pi - \theta = \pi$.

1.4.65 The graphs appear to be identical: so $\sin^{-1} x = \pi/2 - \cos^{-1}(x)$.

1.4.67 $\tan^{-1}(\sqrt{3}) = \tan^{-1}\left(\frac{\sqrt{3}/2}{1/2}\right) = \pi/3$, because $\sin(\pi/3) = \sqrt{3}/2$ and $\cos(\pi/3) = 1/2$.

1.4.69 $\sec^{-1}(2) = \sec^{-1}\left(\frac{1}{1/2}\right) = \pi/3$, because $\sec(\pi/3) = \frac{1}{\cos(\pi/3)} = \frac{1}{1/2} = 2$.

1.4.71 $\tan^{-1}(\tan(\pi/4)) = \tan^{-1}(1) = \pi/4$.

1.4.73 Let $\csc^{-1}(\sec 2) = z$. Then $\csc z = \sec 2$, so $\sin z = \cos 2$. Now by applying the result of problem 60, we see that $z = \sin^{-1}(\cos 2) = \pi/2 - 2 = \frac{\pi - 4}{2}$.

1.4.75

$$\cos(\tan^{-1}(x)) = \frac{\text{side adjacent to } \tan^{-1}(x)}{\text{hypotenuse}} = \frac{1}{\sqrt{1 + x^2}}.$$

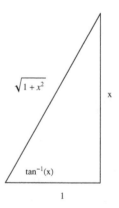

1.4.77

$$\cos(\sec^{-1}(x)) = \frac{\text{side adjacent to } \sec^{-1} x}{\text{hypotenuse}} = \frac{1}{x}.$$

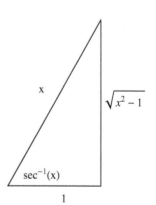

1.4.79

Assume $x > 0$. Then $\sin\left(\sec^{-1}\left(\dfrac{\sqrt{x^2+16}}{4}\right)\right) =$

$\dfrac{\text{side opposite of } \sec^{-1}\left(\frac{\sqrt{x^2+16}}{4}\right)}{\text{hypotenuse}} = \dfrac{|x|}{\sqrt{x^2+16}}$.

Note: If $x < 0$, then the expression results in a positive number, hence the necessary absolute value sign in the result.

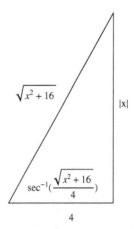

1.4.81 Because $\sin\theta = \frac{x}{6}$, $\theta = \sin^{-1}(x/6)$. Also, $\theta = \tan^{-1}\left(\frac{x}{\sqrt{36-x^2}}\right) = \sec^{-1}\left(\frac{6}{\sqrt{36-x^2}}\right)$.

1.4.83

a. False. For example, $\sin(\pi/2 + \pi/2) = \sin(\pi) = 0 \neq \sin(\pi/2) + \sin(\pi/2) = 1 + 1 = 2$.

b. False. That equation has zero solutions, because the range of the cosine function is $[-1, 1]$.

c. False. It has infinitely many solutions of the form $\pi/6 + 2k\pi$, where k is an integer (among others.)

d. False. It has period $\frac{2\pi}{\pi/12} = 24$.

e. True. The others have a range of either $[-1, 1]$ or $(-\infty, -1] \cup [1, \infty)$.

f. False. For example, suppose $x = .5$. Then $\sin^{-1}(x) = \pi/6$ and $\cos^{-1}(x) = \pi/3$, so that $\frac{\sin^{-1}(x)}{\cos^{-1}(x)} = \frac{\pi/6}{\pi/3} = .5$. However, note that $\tan^{-1}(.5) \neq .5$,

g. True. Note that the range of the inverse cosine function is $[0, \pi]$.

h. False. For example, if $x = .5$, we would have $\sin^{-1}(.5) = \pi/6 \neq 1/\sin(.5)$.

1.4.85 If $\cos\theta = 5/13$, then the Pythagorean identity gives $|\sin\theta| = 12/13$. But if $0 < \theta < \pi/2$, then the sine of θ is positive, so $\sin\theta = 12/13$. Thus $\tan\theta = 12/5$, $\cot\theta = 5/12$, $\sec\theta = 13/5$, and $\csc\theta = 13/12$.

1.4.87 If $\csc\theta = 13/12$, then $\sin\theta = 12/13$, and the Pythagorean identity gives $|\cos\theta| = 5/13$. But if $0 < \theta < \pi/2$, then the cosine of θ is positive, so $\cos\theta = 5/13$. Thus $\tan\theta = 12/5$, $\cot\theta = 5/12$, and $\sec\theta = 13/5$.

1.4.89 The amplitude is 3, and the period is $\frac{2\pi}{1/3} = 6\pi$.

1.4.91 The amplitude is 3.6, and the period is $\frac{2\pi}{\pi/24} = 48$.

1.4.93

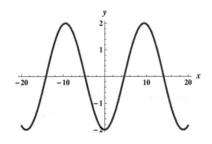

1.4.95

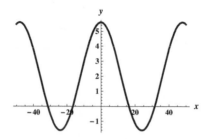

1.4.97

It is helpful to imagine first shifting the function horizontally so that the x intercept is where it should be, then stretching the function horizontally to obtain the correct period, and then stretching the function vertically to obtain the correct amplitude, and then shifting the whole graph up. Because the old x-intercept is at $x = 0$ and the new one should be at $x = 9$ (halfway between where the maximum and the minimum occur), we need to shift the function 9 units to the right. Then to get the right period, we need to multiply (before applying the sine function) by $\pi/12$ so that the new period is $\frac{2\pi}{\pi/12} = 24$. Finally, to get the right amplitude and to get the max and min at the right spots, we need to multiply on the outside by 3, and then shift the whole thing up 13 units. Thus, the desired function is:

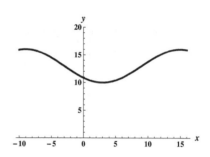

$$f(x) = 3\sin((\pi/12)(x-9))+13 = 3\sin((\pi/12)x-3\pi/4)+13.$$

1.4.99 Let C be the circumference of the earth. Then the first rope has radius $r_1 = \frac{C}{2\pi}$. The circle generated by the longer rope has circumference $C + 38$, so its radius is $r_2 = \frac{C+38}{2\pi} = \frac{C}{2\pi} + \frac{38}{2\pi} \approx r_1 + 6$, so the radius of the bigger circle is about 6 feet more than the smaller circle.

1.4.101 We are seeking a function with amplitude 10 and period 1.5, and value 10 at time 0, so it should have the form $10\cos(kt)$, where $\frac{2\pi}{k} = 1.5$. Solving for k yields $k = \frac{4\pi}{3}$, so the desired function is $d(t) = 10\cos(4\pi t/3)$.

1.4.103 Let L be the line segment connecting the tops of the ladders and let M be the horizontal line segment between the walls h feet above the ground. Now note that the triangle formed by the ladders and L is equilateral, because the angle between the ladders is 60 degrees, and the other two angles must be equal and add to 120, so they are 60 degrees as well. Now we can see that the triangle formed by L, M and the right wall is similar to the triangle formed by the left ladder, the left wall, and the ground, because they are both right triangles with one angle of 75 degrees and one of 15 degrees. Thus $M = h$ is the distance between the walls.

1.4.105

To find $s(t)$ note that we are seeking a periodic function with period 365, and with amplitude 87.5 (which is half of the number of minutes between 7:25 and 4:30). We need to shift the function 4 days plus one fourth of 365, which is about 95 days so that the max and min occur at $t = 4$ days and at half a year later. Also, to get the right value for the maximum and minimum, we need to multiply by negative one and add 117.5 (which represents 30 minutes plus half the amplitude, because $s = 0$ corresponds to 4:00 AM.) Thus we have

$$s(t) = 117.5 - 87.5 \sin\left(\frac{\pi}{182.5}(t - 95)\right).$$

A similar analysis leads to the formula

$$S(t) = 844.5 + 87.5 \sin\left(\frac{\pi}{182.5}(t - 67)\right).$$

The graph pictured shows $D(t) = S(t) - s(t)$, the length of day function, which has its max at the summer solstice which is about the 172nd day of the year, and its min at the winter solstice.

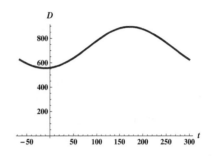

1.4.107 The area of the entire circle is πr^2. The ratio $\frac{\theta}{2\pi}$ represents the proportion of the area swept out by a central angle θ. Thus the area of a sector of a circle is this same proportion of the entire area, so it is $\frac{\theta}{2\pi} \cdot \pi r^2 = \frac{r^2\theta}{2}$.

1.4.109 Note that $\sin A = \frac{h}{c}$ and $\sin C = \frac{h}{a}$, so $h = c\sin A = a\sin C$. Thus

$$\frac{\sin A}{a} = \frac{\sin C}{c}.$$

Now drop a perpendicular from the vertex A to the line determined by $\overline{BC}$, and let h_2 be the length of this perpendicular. Then $\sin C = \frac{h_2}{b}$ and $\sin B = \frac{h_2}{C}$, so $h_2 = b\sin C = c\sin B$. Thus

$$\frac{\sin C}{c} = \frac{\sin B}{b}.$$

Putting the two displayed equations together gives

$$\frac{\sin A}{a} = \frac{\sin B}{b} = \frac{\sin C}{c}.$$

Chapter One Review

1

a. True. For example, $f(x) = x^2$ is such a function.

b. False. For example, $\cos(\pi/2 + \pi/2) = \cos(\pi) = -1 \neq \cos(\pi/2) + \cos(\pi/2) = 0 + 0 = 0$.

c. False. Consider $f(1 + 1) = f(2) = 2m + b \neq f(1) + f(1) = (m + b) + (m + b) = 2m + 2b$. (At least these aren't equal when $b \neq 0$.)

d. True. $f(f(x)) = f(1 - x) = 1 - (1 - x) = x$.

e. False. This set is the union of the disjoint intervals $(-\infty, -7)$ and $(1, \infty)$.

f. False. For example, if $x = y = 10$, then $\log_{10} xy = \log_{10} 100 = 2$, but $\log_{10} 10 \cdot \log_{10} 10 = 1 \cdot 1 = 1$.

g. True. $\sin^{-1}(\sin(2\pi)) = \sin^{-1}(0) = 0$.

3

a. This line has slope $\frac{2-(-3)}{4-2} = 5/2$. Therefore the equation of the line is $y - 2 = \frac{5}{2}(x - 4)$, so $y = \frac{5}{2}x - 8$.

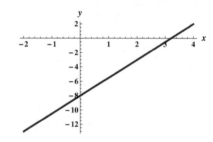

b. This line has the form $y = (3/4)x + b$, and because $(-4, 0)$ is on the line, $0 = (3/4)(-4) + b$, so $b = 3$. Thus the equation of the line is given by $y = (3/4)x + 3$.

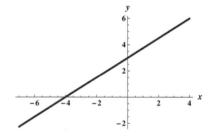

c. This line has slope $\frac{0-(-2)}{4-0} = \frac{1}{2}$, and the y-intercept is given to be -2, so the equation of this line is $y = (1/2)x - 2$.

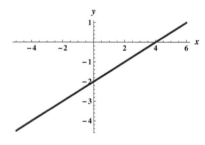

5

Because $|x| = \begin{cases} -x & \text{if } x < 0; \\ x & \text{if } x \geq 0, \end{cases}$

we have

$2(x - |x|) = \begin{cases} 2(x - (-x)) = 4x & \text{if } x < 0; \\ 2(x - x) = 0 & \text{if } x \geq 0. \end{cases}$

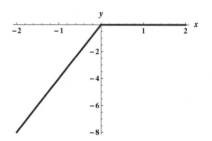

7

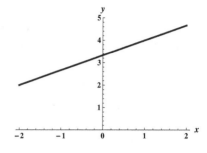

a. This is a straight line with slope 2/3 and y-intercept 10/3.

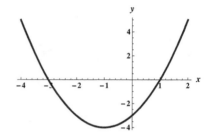

b. Completing the square gives $y = (x^2 + 2x + 1) - 4$, or $y = (x+1)^2 - 4$, so this is the standard parabola shifted one unit to the left and down 4 units.

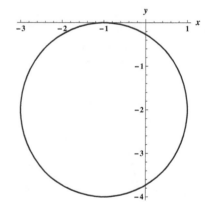

c. Completing the square, we have $x^2 + 2x + 1 + y^2 + 4y + 4 = -1 + 1 + 4$, so we have $(x+1)^2 + (y+2)^2 = 4$, a circle of radius 2 centered at $(-1, -2)$.

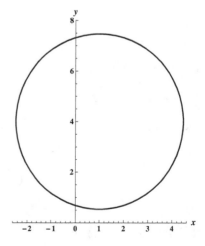

d. Completing the square, we have $x^2 - 2x + 1 + y^2 - 8y + 16 = -5 + 1 + 16$, or $(x-1)^2 + (y-4)^2 = 12$, which is a circle of radius $\sqrt{12}$ centered at $(1, 4)$.

9 The domain of $x^{1/7}$ is the set of all real numbers, as is its range. The domain of $x^{1/4}$ is the set of non-negative real numbers, as is its range.

11 We are looking for the line between the points $(0, 212)$ and $(6000, 200)$. The slope is $\frac{212-200}{0-6000} = -\frac{12}{6000} = -\frac{1}{500}$. Because the intercept is given, we deduce that the line is $B = f(a) = -\frac{1}{500}a + 212$.

13

a.

b.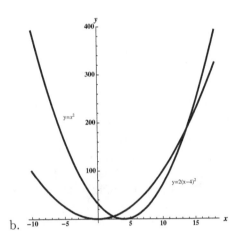

c.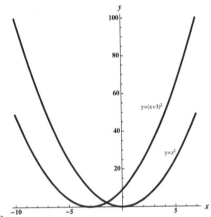

d.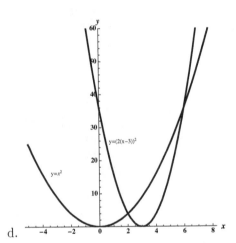

15

   a. $h(g(\pi/2)) = h(1) = 1$

   b. $h(f(x)) = h(x^3) = x^{3/2}$.

   c. $f(g(h(x))) = f(g(\sqrt{x})) = f(\sin(\sqrt{x})) = (\sin(\sqrt{x}))^3$.

   d The domain of $g(f(x))$ is $\mathbb{R}$, because the domain of both functions is the set of all real numbers.

   e. The range of $f(g(x))$ is $[-1, 1]$. This is because the range of g is $[-1, 1]$, and on the restricted domain $[-1, 1]$, the range of f is also $[-1, 1]$.

17 $\frac{f(x+h)-f(x)}{h} = \frac{(x+h)^2-2(x+h)-(x^2-2x)}{h} = \frac{x^2+2hx+h^2-2x-2h-x^2+2x}{h} = \frac{2hx+h^2-2h}{h} = 2x+h-2.$

$\frac{f(x)-f(a)}{x-a} = \frac{x^2-2x-(a^2-2a)}{x-a} = \frac{(x^2-a^2)-2(x-a)}{x-a} = \frac{(x-a)(x+a)-2(x-a)}{x-a} = x+a-2.$

19 $\frac{f(x+h)-f(x)}{h} = \frac{(x+h)^2+2-(x^3+2)}{h} = \frac{x^2+3x^2h+3xh^2+h^3+2-x^3-2}{h} = \frac{h(3x^2+3xh+h^2)}{h} = 3x^2+3xh+h^2.$

$\frac{f(x)-f(a)}{x-a} = \frac{x^3+2-(a^3+2)}{x-a} = \frac{x^3-a^3}{x-a} = \frac{(x-a)(x^2+ax+a^2)}{x-a} = x^2+ax+a^2.$

21

    a. Because $f(-x) = \cos -3x = \cos 3x = f(x)$, this is an even function, and is symmetric about the y-axis.

    b. Because $f(-x) = 3(-x)^4 - 3(-x)^2 + 1 = 3x^4 - 3x^2 + 1 = f(x)$, this is an even function, and is symmetric about the y-axis.

    c. Because replacing x by $-x$ and/or replacing y by $-y$ gives the same equation, this represents a curve which is symmetric about the y-axis and about the origin and about the x-axis.

23 If $\log x^2 + 3\log x = \log 32$, then $\log(x^2 \cdot x^3) = \log(32)$, so $x^5 = 32$ and $x = 2$. The answer does not depend on the base of the log.

25

By graphing, it is clear that this function is not one-to-one on its whole domain, but it is one-to-one on the interval $(-\infty, 0]$, on the interval $[0, 2]$, and on the interval $[2, \infty)$, so it would have an inverse if we restricted it to any of these particular intervals.

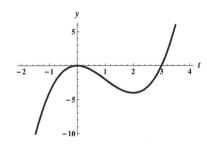

27

Completing the square gives $f(x) = x^2 - 4x + 4 + 1 = (x-2)^2 + 1$. Switching the x and y and solving for y yields $(y-2)^2 = x - 1$, so $|y-2| = \sqrt{x-1}$, and thus $y = f^{-1}(x) = 2 + \sqrt{x-1}$ (we choose the "+" rather than the "−" because the domain of f is $x > 2$, so the range of f^{-1} must also consist of numbers greater than 2.)

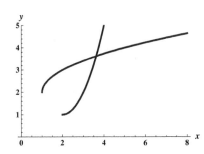

29

    a. A 135 degree angle measures $135 \cdot (\pi/180)$ radians, which is $3\pi/4$ radians.

    b. A $4\pi/5$ radian angle measues $4\pi/5 \cdot (180/\pi)$ degrees, which is 144 degrees.

    c. Because the length of the arc is the measure of the subtended angle (in radians) times the radius, this arc would be $4\pi/3 \cdot 10 = \frac{40\pi}{3}$ units long.

31

    a. We need to scale the ordinary cosine function so that its period is 6, and then shift it 3 units to the right, and multiply it by 2. So the function we seek is $y = 2\cos((\pi/3)(t-3)) = -2\cos(\pi t/3)$.

    b. We need to scale the ordinary cosine function so that its period is 24, and then shift it to the right 6 units. We then need to change the amplitude to be half the difference between the maximum and minimum, which would be 5. Then finally we need to shift the whole thing up by 15 units. The function we seek is thus $y = 15 + 5\cos((\pi/12)(t-6)) = 15 + 5\sin(\pi t/12)$.

33

    a. $-\sin x$ is pictured in F.

    b. $\cos 2x$ is pictured in E.

    c. $\tan(x/2)$ is pictured in D.

    d. $-\sec x$ is pictured in B.

    e. $\cot 2x$ is pictured in C.

    f. $\sin^2 x$ is pictured in A.

35 $\sin x = -\frac{1}{2}$ for $x = 7\pi/6$ and for $x = 11\pi/6$, so the intersection points are $(7\pi/6, -1/2)$ and $(11\pi/6, -1/2)$.

37 Because $\cos(\pi/6) = \sqrt{3}/2$, $\cos^{-1}(\sqrt{3}/2) = \pi/6$.

39 Because $\sin(-\pi/2) = -1$, $\sin^{-1}(-1) = -\pi/2$.

41 $\sin(\sin^{-1}(x)) = x$, for all x in the domain of the inverse sine function.

43 If $\theta = \sin^{-1}(12/13)$, then $0 < \theta < \pi/2$, and $\sin\theta = 12/13$. Then (using the Pythagorean identity) we can deduce that $\cos\theta = 5/13$. It must follow that $\tan\theta = 12/5$, $\cot\theta = 5/12$, $\sec\theta = 13/5$, and $\csc\theta = 13/12$.

45

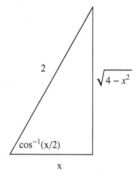

$$\sin(\cos^{-1}(x/2)) = \frac{\text{side opposite of } \cos^{-1}(x/2)}{\text{hypotenuse}} = \frac{\sqrt{4-x^2}}{2}.$$

47

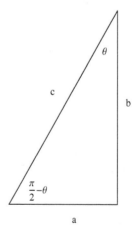

Note that

$$\tan\theta = \frac{a}{b} = \cot(\pi/2 - \theta).$$

Thus, $\cot^{-1}(\tan\theta) = \cot^{-1}(\cot(\pi/2-\theta)) = \pi/2 - \theta$.

49 Let $\theta = \sin^{-1}(x)$. Then $\sin\theta = x$ and note that then $\sin(-\theta) = -\sin\theta = -x$, so $-\theta = \sin^{-1}(-x)$. Then $\sin^{-1}(x) + \sin^{-1}(-x) = \theta + -\theta = 0$.

51 Using the hint, we have $\cos(2\sin^{-1}(x)) = \cos^2(\sin^{-1}(x)) - \sin^2(\sin^{-1}(x)) = (\sqrt{1-x^2})^2 - x^2 = 1 - 2x^2$.

Chapter 2

Limits

2.1 The Idea of Limits

2.1.1 The average velocity of the object between time $t = a$ and $t = b$ is the change in position divided by the elapsed time: $v_{av} = \frac{s(b)-s(a)}{b-a}$.

2.1.3 The slope of the secant line between points $(a, f(a))$ and $(b, f(b))$ is the ratio of the differences $f(b) - f(a)$ and $b - a$. Thus $m_{sec} = \frac{f(b)-f(a)}{b-a}$.

2.1.5 Both problems involve the same mathematics, namely finding the limit as $t \to a$ of a quotient of differences of the form $\frac{g(t)-g(a)}{t-a}$ for some function g.

2.1.7 The average velocity is $\frac{s(3)-s(2)}{3-2} = 156 - 136 = 20$.

2.1.9

   a. Over $[1, 4]$, we have $v_{av} = \frac{s(4)-s(1)}{4-1} = \frac{256-112}{3} = 48$.

   b. Over $[1, 3]$, we have $v_{av} = \frac{s(3)-s(1)}{3-1} = \frac{240-112}{2} = 64$.

   c. Over $[1, 2]$, we have $v_{av} = \frac{s(2)-s(1)}{2-1} = \frac{192-112}{1} = 80$.

   d. Over $[1, 1+h]$, we have $v_{av} = \frac{s(1+h)-s(1)}{1+h-1} = \frac{-16(1+h)^2+128(1+h)-(112)}{h} = \frac{-16h^2-32h+128h}{h} = \frac{h(-16h+96)}{h} = 96 - 16h = 16(6 - h)$.

2.1.11

   a. $\frac{s(2)-s(0)}{2-0} = \frac{72-0}{2} = 36$.

   b. $\frac{s(1.5)-s(0)}{1.5-0} = \frac{66-0}{1.5} = 44$.

   c. $\frac{s(1)-s(0)}{1-0} = \frac{52-0}{1} = 52$.

   d. $\frac{s(.5)-s(0)}{.5-0} = \frac{30-0}{.5} = 60$.

2.1.13

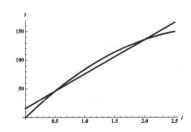

The slope of the secant line is given by $\frac{s(2)-s(.5)}{2-.5} = \frac{136-46}{1.5} = 60$. This represents the average velocity of the object over the time interval $[.5, 2]$.

2.1.15

Time Interval	[1, 2]	[1, 1.5]	[1, 1.1]	[1, 1.01]	[1, 1.001]
Average Velocity	80	88	94.4	95.84	95.984

The instantaneous velocity appears to be 96 ft/s.

2.1.17 $\frac{s(1.01)-s(1)}{.01} = 47.84$, while $\frac{s(1.001)-s(1)}{.001} = 47.984$ and $\frac{s(1.0001)-s(1)}{.0001} = 47.9984$. It appears that the instantaneous velocity at $t = 1$ is approximately 48.

2.1.19

Time Interval	[2, 3]	[2.9, 3]	[2.99, 3]	[2.999, 3]	[2.9999, 3]	[2.99999, 3]
Average Velocity	20	5.6	4.16	4.016	4.002	4.0002

The instantaneous velocity appears to be 4 ft/s.

2.1.21

Time Interval	[3, 3.1]	[3, 3.01]	[3, 3.001]	[3, 3.0001]
Average Velocity	−17.6	−16.16	−16.016	−16.002

The instantaneous velocity appears to be −16 ft/s.

2.1.23

Time Interval	[0, 0.1]	[0, 0.01]	[0, 0.001]	[0, 0.0001]
Average Velocity	79.468	79.995	80.000	80.0000

The instantaneous velocity appears to be 80 ft/s.

2.1.25

x Interval	[2, 2.1]	[2, 2.01]	[2, 2.001]	[2, 2.0001]
Slope of Secant Line	8.2	8.02	8.002	8.0002

The slope of the tangent line appears to be 8.

2.1.27

x Interval	[0, 0.1]	[0, 0.01]	[0, 0.001]	[0, 0.0001]
Slope of the Secant Line	1.05171	1.00502	1.0005	1.00005

The slope of the tangent line appears to be 1.

2.1.29

a. Note that the graph is a parabola with vertex $(2, -1)$.

b. At $(2, -1)$ the function has tangent line with slope 0.

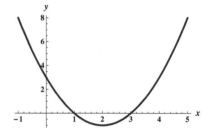

c.

x Interval	[2, 2.1]	[2, 2.01]	[2, 2.001]	[2, 2.0001]
Slope of the Secant Line	.1	.01	.001	.0001

The slope of the tangent line at $(2, -1)$ appears to be 0.

2.1.31

a. Note that the graph is a parabola with vertex $(4, 448)$.

b. At $(4, 448)$ the function has tangent line with slope 0, so $a = 4$.

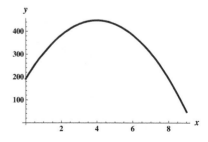

c.

x Interval	$[4, 4.1]$	$[4, 4.01]$	$[4, 4.001]$	$[4, 4.0001]$
Slope of the Secant Line	-1.6	$-.16$	$-.016$	$-.0016$

The slopes of the secant lines appear to be approaching zero.

d. On the interval $[0, 4)$ the instantaneous velocity of the projectile is positive.

e. On the interval $(4, 9]$ the instantaneous velocity of the projectile is negative.

2.1.33 For line AD, we have

$$m_{AD} = \frac{y_D - y_A}{x_D - x_A} = \frac{f(\pi) - f(\pi/2)}{\pi - (\pi/2)} = \frac{1}{\pi/2} \approx .63662.$$

For line AC, we have

$$m_{AC} = \frac{y_C - y_A}{x_C - x_A} = \frac{f(\pi/2 + .5) - f(\pi/2)}{(\pi/2 + .5) - (\pi/2)} = -\frac{\cos(\pi/2 + .5)}{.5} \approx .958851.$$

For line AB, we have

$$m_{AB} = \frac{y_B - y_A}{x_B - x_A} = \frac{f(\pi/2 + .05) - f(\pi/2)}{(\pi/2 + .05) - (\pi/2)} = -\frac{\cos(\pi/2 + .05)}{.05} \approx .999583.$$

Computing one more slope of a secant line:

$$m_{\text{sec}} = \frac{f(\pi/2 + .01) - f(\pi/2)}{(\pi/2 + .01) - (\pi/2)} = -\frac{\cos(\pi/2 + .01)}{.01} \approx .999983.$$

Conjecture: The slope of the tangent line to the graph of f at $x = \pi/2$ is 1.

2.2   Definition of a Limit

2.2.1 Suppose the function f is defined for all x near a except possibly at a. If $f(x)$ is arbitrarily close to a number L whenever x is sufficiently close to (but not equal to) a, then we write $\lim_{x \to a} f(x) = L$.

2.2.3 Suppose the function f is defined for all x near a but greater than a. If $f(x)$ is arbitrarily close to L for x sufficiently close to (but strictly greater than) a, then we write $\lim_{x \to a^+} f(x) = L$.

2.2.5 It must be true that $L = M$.

2.2.7

a. $h(2) = 5$.

b. $\lim_{x \to 2} h(x) = 3$.

c. $h(4)$ does not exist.

d. $\lim_{x \to 4} f(x) = 1$.

e. $\lim_{x \to 5} h(x) = 2$.

2.2.9

  a. $f(1) = -1$.

  b. $\lim\limits_{x \to 1} f(x) = 1$.

  c. $f(0) = 2$.

  d. $\lim\limits_{x \to 0} f(x) = 2$.

2.2.11

  a.

x	1.9	1.99	1.999	1.9999	2	2.0001	2.001	2.01	2.1
$f(x) = \frac{x^2 - 4}{x - 2}$	3.9	3.99	3.999	3.9999	undefined	4.0001	4.001	4.01	4.1

  b. $\lim\limits_{x \to 2} f(x) = 4$.

2.2.13

  a.

t	8.9	8.99	8.999	9	9.001	9.01	9.1
$g(t) = \frac{t - 9}{\sqrt{t} - 3}$	5.98329	5.99833	5.99983	undefined	6.00017	6.00167	6.01662

  b. $\lim\limits_{t \to 9} \dfrac{t - 9}{\sqrt{t} - 3} = 6$.

2.2.15

  a.

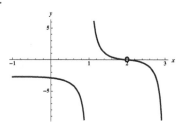

  b.

x	1.99	1.999	1.9999	2.0001	2.001	2.01
$f(x)$	.00217	.00014	.0000109	$-.0000109$	$-.00014$	$-.00217$

From both the graph and the table, the limit appears to be 0.

2.2.17

  a.

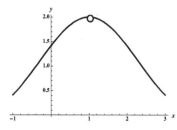

  b.

x	0.9	0.99	0.999	1.001	1.01	1.1
$f(x)$	1.993342	1.999933	1.999999	1.999999	1.999933	1.993342

From both the graph and the table, the limit appears to be 2.

2.2.19

x	4.9	4.99	4.999	4.9999	5	5.0001	5.001	5.01	5.1
$f(x) = \frac{x^2-25}{x-5}$	9.9	9.99	9.999	9.9999	undefined	10.0001	10.001	10.01	10.1

$\lim\limits_{x\to 5^+} \dfrac{x^2-25}{x-5} = 10$, $\lim\limits_{x\to 5^-} \dfrac{x^2-25}{x-5} = 10$, and thus $\lim\limits_{x\to 5} \dfrac{x^2-25}{x-5} = 10$.

2.2.21

a. $f(1) = 0$.

b. $\lim\limits_{x\to 1^-} f(x) = 1$.

c. $\lim\limits_{x\to 1^+} f(x) = 0$.

d. $\lim\limits_{x\to 1} f(x)$ does not exist, since the two one-sided limits aren't equal.

2.2.23

a. $f(1) = 3$.

b. $\lim\limits_{x\to 1^-} f(x) = 2$.

c. $\lim\limits_{x\to 1^+} f(x) = 2$.

d. $\lim\limits_{x\to 1} f(x) = 2$.

e. $f(3) = 2$.

f. $\lim\limits_{x\to 3^-} f(x) = 4$.

g. $\lim\limits_{x\to 3^+} f(x) = 1$.

h. $\lim\limits_{x\to 3} f(x)$ does not exist.

i. $f(2) = 3$.

j. $\lim\limits_{x\to 2^-} f(x) = 3$.

k. $\lim\limits_{x\to 2^+} f(x) = 3$.

l. $\lim\limits_{x\to 2} f(x) = 3$.

2.2.25

a.

x	$\frac{2}{\pi}$	$\frac{2}{3\pi}$	$\frac{2}{5\pi}$	$\frac{2}{7\pi}$	$\frac{2}{9\pi}$	$\frac{2}{11\pi}$
$f(x) = \sin(1/x)$	1	-1	1	-1	1	-1

If $x_n = \frac{2}{(2n+1)\pi}$, then $f(x_n) = (-1)^n$ where n is a non-negative integer.

b. As $x \to 0$, $1/x \to \infty$. So the values of $f(x)$ oscillate dramatically between -1 and 1.

c. $\lim\limits_{x\to 0} \sin(1/x)$ does not exist.

2.2.27

a. False. In fact $\lim\limits_{x\to 3} \dfrac{x^2-9}{x-3} = \lim\limits_{x\to 3}(x+3) = 6$.

b. False. For example, if $f(x) = \begin{cases} x^2 & \text{if } x \neq 0; \\ 5 & \text{if } x = 0 \end{cases}$ and if $a = 0$ then $f(a) = 5$ but $\lim\limits_{x\to a} f(x) = 0$.

c. False. For example, the limit in part a of this problem exists, even though the corresponding function is undefined at $a = 3$.

d. False. It is true that the limit of $\sqrt{x}$ as x approaches zero from the right is zero, but because the domain of $\sqrt{x}$ does not include any numbers to the left of zero, the two-sided limit doesn't exist.

e. True. Note that $\lim\limits_{x\to \pi/2} \cos x = 0$ and $\lim\limits_{x\to \pi/2} \sin x = 1$, so $\lim\limits_{x\to \pi/2} \dfrac{\cos x}{\sin x} = \dfrac{0}{1} = 0$.

2.2.29

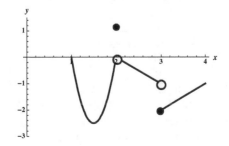

2.2.31

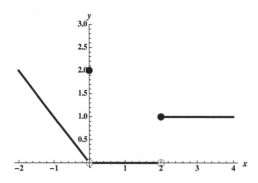

2.2.33

h	.01	.001	.0001	−.0001	−.001	−.01
$(1+3h)^{2/h}$	369.356	399.821	403.066	403.792	407.083	442.235

$\lim\limits_{h\to 0}(1+3h)^{2/h} \approx 403.4.$

2.2.35

h	.01	.001	.0001	−.0001	−.001	−.01
$\frac{\ln(1+h)}{h}$	.995033	.9995	.99995	1.00005	1.0005	1.00503

$\lim\limits_{h\to 0}\dfrac{\ln(1+h)}{h}=1.$

2.2.37

a. $\lim\limits_{x\to -1^-}\lfloor x\rfloor = -2$, $\lim\limits_{x\to -1^+}\lfloor x\rfloor = -1$, $\lim\limits_{x\to 2^-}\lfloor x\rfloor = 1$, $\lim\limits_{x\to 2^+}\lfloor x\rfloor = 2.$

b. $\lim\limits_{x\to 2.3^-}\lfloor x\rfloor = 2$, $\lim\limits_{x\to 2.3^+}\lfloor x\rfloor = 2$, $\lim\limits_{x\to 2.3}\lfloor x\rfloor = 2.$

c. In general, for an integer a, $\lim\limits_{x\to a^-}\lfloor x\rfloor = a-1$ and $\lim\limits_{x\to a^+}\lfloor x\rfloor = a.$

d. In general, if a is not an integer, $\lim\limits_{x\to a^-}\lfloor x\rfloor = \lim\limits_{x\to a^+}\lfloor x\rfloor = \lfloor a\rfloor.$

e. $\lim\limits_{x\to a}\lfloor x\rfloor$ exists and is equal to $\lfloor a\rfloor$ for non-integers a.

2.2.39 By zooming in closely, you should be able to convince yourself that the answer is 0.

2.2.41 By zooming in closely, you should be able to convince yourself that the answer is 16.

2.2.43

a. Note that the function is piecewise constant.

b. $\lim\limits_{w\to3.3} f(w) = .95$.

c. $\lim\limits_{w\to1^+} f(w) = .61$ corresponds to the fact that for any piece of mail that weighs slightly over 1 ounce, the postage will cost 61 cents. $\lim\limits_{w\to1^-} f(w) = .44$ corresponds to the fact that for any piece of mail that weighs slightly less than 1 ounce, the postage will cost 44 cents.

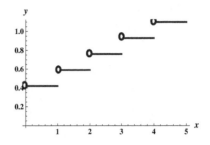

d. $\lim\limits_{w\to4} f(w)$ does not exist because the two corresponding one-side limits don't exist. (The limit from the left is .95, while the limit from the right is 1.12.)

2.2.45

a. Because of the symmetry about the y axis, we must have $\lim\limits_{x\to-2^+} f(x) = 8$.

b. Because of the symmetry about the y axis, we must have $\lim\limits_{x\to-2^-} f(x) = 5$.

2.2.47

a.

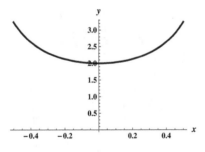

$$\lim_{x\to0} \frac{\tan 2x}{\sin x} = 2.$$

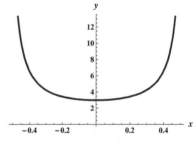

$$\lim_{x\to0} \frac{\tan 3x}{\sin x} = 3.$$

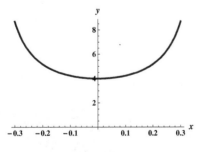

$$\lim_{x\to0} \frac{\tan 4x}{\sin x} = 4.$$

b. It appears that $\lim\limits_{x\to0} \dfrac{\tan(px)}{\sin x} = p$.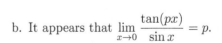

2.2.49

For $p = 8$ and $q = 2$, it appears that the limit is 4.

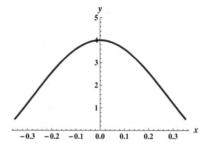

For $p = 12$ and $q = 3$, it appears that the limit is 4.

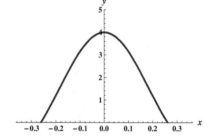

For $p = 4$ and $q = 16$, it appears that the limit is 1/4.

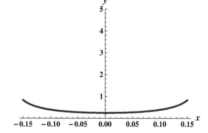

For $p = 100$ and $q = 50$, it appears that the limit is 2.

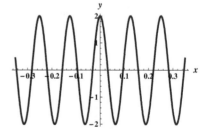

Conjecture: $\displaystyle\lim_{x \to 0} \frac{\sin px}{\sin qx} = \frac{p}{q}$.

2.3   Techniques of Computing Limits

2.3.1 If $f(x) = a_n x^n + a_{n-1} x^{n-1} + \cdots + a_1 x + a_0$, then $\lim_{x \to a} f(x) = \lim_{x \to a}(a_n x^n + a_{n-1} x^{n-1} + \cdots + a_1 x + a_0)$
$= a_n(\lim_{x \to a} x)^n + a_{n-1}(\lim_{x \to a} x)^{n-1} + \cdots + a_1 \lim_{x \to a} x + \lim_{x \to a} a_0$
$= a_n a^n + a_{n-1} a^{n-1} + \cdots + a_1 a + a_0$.

2.3.3 For a rational function $r(x)$, we have $\displaystyle\lim_{x \to a} r(x) = r(a)$ exactly for those numbers a which are in the domain of r.

2.3.5 Because $\frac{x^2-7x+12}{x-3} = \frac{(x-3)(x-4)}{x-3} = x-4$ (for $x \neq 3$), we can see that the graphs of these two functions are the same except that one is undefined at $x=3$ and the other is a straight line that is defined everywhere. Thus the function $\frac{x^2-7x+12}{x-3}$ is a straight line except that it has a "hole" at $(3,-1)$. The two functions have the same limit as $x \to 3$, namely $\lim_{x \to 3} \frac{x^2-7x+12}{x-3} = \lim_{x \to 3}(x-4) = -1$.

2.3.7 If p and q are polynomials then $\lim_{x \to 0} \frac{p(x)}{q(x)} = \frac{\lim_{x \to 0} p(x)}{\lim_{x \to 0} q(x)} = \frac{p(0)}{q(0)}$. Because this quantity is given to be equal to 10, we have $\frac{p(0)}{2} = 10$, so $p(0) = 20$.

2.3.9 $\lim_{x \to 5} \sqrt{x^2-9} = \sqrt{\lim_{x \to 5}(x^2-9)} = \sqrt{16} = 4$.

2.3.11 $\lim_{x \to 4}(3x-7) = 3\lim_{x \to 4} x - 7 = 3 \cdot 4 - 7 = 5$.

2.3.13 $\lim_{x \to -9}(5x) = 5\lim_{x \to -9} x = 5 \cdot -9 = -45$.

2.3.15 $\lim_{x \to 6} 4 = 4$.

2.3.17 $\lim_{x \to 1} 4f(x) = 4\lim_{x \to 1} f(x) = 4 \cdot 8 = 32$. This follows from the Constant Multiple Law.

2.3.19 $\lim_{x \to 1}(f(x) - g(x)) = \lim_{x \to 1} f(x) - \lim_{x \to 1} g(x) = 8 - 3 = 5$. This follows from the Difference Law.

2.3.21 $\lim_{x \to 1} \frac{f(x)g(x)}{h(x)} = \frac{\lim_{x \to 1}(f(x)g(x))}{\lim_{x \to 1} h(x)} = \frac{\lim_{x \to 1} f(x) \cdot \lim_{x \to 1} g(x)}{\lim_{x \to 1} h(x)} = \frac{8 \cdot 3}{2} = 12$. This follows from the Quotient and Product Laws.

2.3.23 $\lim_{x \to 1}(h(x))^5 = \left(\lim_{x \to 1} h(x)\right)^5 = (2)^5 = 32$. This follows from the Power Law.

2.3.25 $\lim_{x \to 1}(2x^3 - 3x^2 + 4x + 5) = \lim_{x \to 1} 2x^3 - \lim_{x \to 1} 3x^2 + \lim_{x \to 1} 4x + \lim_{x \to 1} 5 = 2(\lim_{x \to 1} x)^3 - 3(\lim_{x \to 1} x)^2 + 4(\lim_{x \to 1} x) + 5 = 2(1)^3 - 3(1)^2 + 4 \cdot 1 + 5 = 8$.

2.3.27 $\lim_{x \to 1} \frac{5x^2 + 6x + 1}{8x - 4} = \frac{\lim_{x \to 1}(5x^2 + 6x + 1)}{\lim_{x \to 1}(8x - 4)} = \frac{5(\lim_{x \to 1} x)^2 + 6\lim_{x \to 1} x + \lim_{x \to 1} 1}{8\lim_{x \to 1} x - \lim_{x \to 1} 4} = \frac{5(1)^2 + 6 \cdot 1 + 1}{8 \cdot 1 - 4} = 3$.

2.3.29 $\lim_{b \to 2} \frac{3b}{\sqrt{4b+1}-1} = \frac{\lim_{b \to 2} 3b}{\lim_{b \to 2}(\sqrt{4b+1}-1)} = \frac{3\lim_{b \to 2} b}{\lim_{b \to 2}\sqrt{4b+1} - \lim_{b \to 2} 1} = \frac{3 \cdot 2}{\sqrt{\lim_{b \to 2}(4b+1)}-1} = \frac{6}{3-1} = 3$.

2.3.31 $\lim_{x \to 3} \frac{-5x}{\sqrt{4x-3}} = \frac{\lim_{x \to 3} -5x}{\lim_{x \to 3}\sqrt{4x-3}} = \frac{-5\lim_{x \to 3} x}{\sqrt{\lim_{x \to 3}(4x-3)}} = \frac{-5 \cdot 3}{\sqrt{4\lim_{x \to 3} x - \lim_{x \to 3} 3}} = \frac{-15}{\sqrt{4 \cdot 3 - 3}} = -5$.

2.3.33

a. $\lim_{x \to -1^-} f(x) = \lim_{x \to -1^-}(x^2 + 1) = (-1)^2 + 1 = 2$.

b. $\lim_{x \to -1^+} f(x) = \lim_{x \to -1^+}\sqrt{x+1} = \sqrt{-1+1} = 0$.

c. $\lim_{x \to -1} f(x)$ does not exist.

2.3.35

a. $\lim\limits_{x\to 2^+} \sqrt{x-2} = \sqrt{2-2} = 0.$

b. The domain of $f(x) = \sqrt{x-2}$ is $[2, \infty)$. Thus, any question about this function that involves numbers less than 2 doesn't make any sense, because those numbers aren't in the domain of f.

2.3.37 Using the definition of $|x|$ given, we have $\lim\limits_{x\to 0^-} |x| = \lim\limits_{x\to 0^-} (-x) = -0 = 0$. Also, $\lim\limits_{x\to 0^+} |x| = \lim\limits_{x\to 0^+} x = 0$. Because the two one-sided limits are both 0, we also have $\lim\limits_{x\to 0} |x| = 0$.

2.3.39 $\lim\limits_{x\to 1} \dfrac{x^2-1}{x-1} = \lim\limits_{x\to 1} \dfrac{(x+1)(x-1)}{x-1} = \lim\limits_{x\to 1}(x+1) = 2.$

2.3.41 $\lim\limits_{x\to 4} \dfrac{x^2-16}{4-x} = \lim\limits_{x\to 4} \dfrac{(x+4)(x-4)}{-(x-4)} = \lim\limits_{x\to 4}[-(x+4)] = -8.$

2.3.43 $\lim\limits_{x\to b} \dfrac{(x-b)^{50} - x + b}{x-b} = \lim\limits_{x\to b} \dfrac{(x-b)^{50} - (x-b)}{x-b} = \lim\limits_{x\to b} \dfrac{(x-b)((x-b)^{49}-1)}{x-b} =$
$\lim\limits_{x\to b}[(x-b)^{49} - 1] = -1.$

2.3.45 $\lim\limits_{x\to -1} \dfrac{(2x-1)^2 - 9}{x+1} = \lim\limits_{x\to -1} \dfrac{(2x-1-3)(2x-1+3)}{x+1} = \lim\limits_{x\to -1} \dfrac{2(x-2)2(x+1)}{x+1} = \lim\limits_{x\to -1} 4(x-2) =$
$4 \cdot (-3) = -12.$

2.3.47 $\lim\limits_{x\to 9} \dfrac{\sqrt{x}-3}{x-9} = \lim\limits_{x\to 9} \dfrac{(\sqrt{x}-3)(\sqrt{x}+3)}{(x-9)(\sqrt{x}+3)} = \lim\limits_{x\to 9} \dfrac{x-9}{(x-9)(\sqrt{x}+3)} = \lim\limits_{x\to 9} \dfrac{1}{\sqrt{x}+3} = \dfrac{1}{6}.$

2.3.49 $\lim\limits_{x\to a} \dfrac{x-a}{\sqrt{x}-\sqrt{a}} = \lim\limits_{x\to a} \dfrac{x-a}{\sqrt{x}-\sqrt{a}} \cdot \dfrac{\sqrt{x}+\sqrt{a}}{\sqrt{x}+\sqrt{a}} = \lim\limits_{x\to a} \dfrac{(x-a)(\sqrt{x}+\sqrt{a})}{x-a} = \lim\limits_{x\to a}(\sqrt{x}+\sqrt{a}) = 2\sqrt{a}.$

2.3.51 $\lim\limits_{h\to 0} \dfrac{\sqrt{16+h}-4}{h} = \lim\limits_{h\to 0} \dfrac{(\sqrt{16+h}-4)(\sqrt{16+h}+4)}{h(\sqrt{16+h}+4)} = \lim\limits_{h\to 0} \dfrac{(16+h)-16}{h(\sqrt{16+h}+4)} = \lim\limits_{h\to 0} \dfrac{h}{h(\sqrt{16+h}+4)}$
$= \lim\limits_{h\to 0} \dfrac{1}{(\sqrt{16+h}+4)} = \dfrac{1}{8}.$

2.3.53

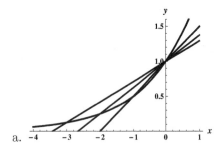

a.

b. The slope of the secant line between $(0,1)$ and $(x, 2^x)$ is $\frac{2^x-1}{x}$.

c.

x	-1	$-.1$	$-.01$	$-.001$	$-.0001$	$-.00001$
$\frac{2^x-1}{x}$	.5	.66967	.69075	.692907	.693123	.693145

It appears that $\lim\limits_{x\to 0^-} \frac{2^x-1}{x} \approx 0.693.$

2.3.55

a. The statement we are trying to prove can be stated in cases as follows: For $x > 0$, $-x \leq x \sin(1/x) \leq x$, and for $x < 0$, $x \leq x \sin(1/x) \leq -x$.

Now for all $x \neq 0$, note that $-1 \leq \sin(1/x) \leq 1$ (because the range of the sine function is $[-1, 1]$). We will consider the two cases $x > 0$ and $x < 0$ separately, but in each case, we will multiply this inequality through by x, switching the inequalities for the $x < 0$ case.

For $x > 0$ we have $-x \leq x \sin(1/x) \leq x$, and for $x < 0$ we have $-x \geq x \sin(1/x) \geq x$, which are exactly the statements we are trying to prove.

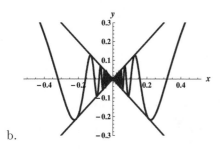

b.

c. Because $\lim\limits_{x \to 0} -|x| = \lim\limits_{x \to 0} |x| = 0$, and because $-|x| \leq x \sin(1/x) \leq |x|$, the Squeeze Theorem assures us that $\lim\limits_{x \to 0} [x \sin(1/x)] = 0$ as well.

2.3.57

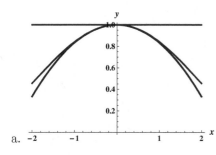

a.

b. Note that $\lim\limits_{x \to 0} \left[1 - \dfrac{x^2}{6} \right] = 1 = \lim\limits_{x \to 0} 1$. So because $1 - \frac{x^2}{6} \leq \frac{\sin x}{x} \leq 1$, the squeeze theorem assures us that $\lim\limits_{x \to 0} \dfrac{\sin x}{x} = 1$ as well.

2.3.59

a. False. For example, if $f(x) = \begin{cases} x & \text{if } x \neq 1; \\ 4 & \text{if } x = 1, \end{cases}$ then $\lim\limits_{x \to 1} f(x) = 1$ but $f(1) = 4$.

b. False. For example, if $f(x) = \begin{cases} x + 1 & \text{if } x \leq 1; \\ x - 6 & \text{if } x > 1, \end{cases}$ then $\lim\limits_{x \to 1^-} f(x) = 2$ but $\lim\limits_{x \to 1^+} f(x) = -5$.

c. False. For example, if $f(x) = \begin{cases} x & \text{if } x \neq 1; \\ 4 & \text{if } x = 1, \end{cases}$ and $g(x) = 1$, then f and g both have limit 1 as $x \to 1$, but $f(1) = 4 \neq g(1)$.

d. False. For example $\lim\limits_{x \to 2} \dfrac{x^2 - 4}{x - 2}$ exists and is equal to 4.

e. False. For example, it would be possible for the domain of f to be $[1, \infty)$, so that the one-sided limit exists but the two-sided limit doesn't even make sense. This would be true, for example, if $f(x) = x - 1$.

2.3.61 $\lim\limits_{x \to 2} (5x - 6)^{3/2} = (5 \cdot 2 - 6)^{3/2} = 4^{3/2} = 2^3 = 8$.

2.3.63 $\lim\limits_{x\to 1}\dfrac{\sqrt{10x-9}-1}{x-1}=\lim\limits_{x\to 1}\dfrac{(\sqrt{10x-9}-1)(\sqrt{10x-9}+1)}{(x-1)(\sqrt{10x-9}+1)}=\lim\limits_{x\to 1}\dfrac{(10x-9)-1}{(x-1)(\sqrt{10x-9}+1)}=$

$\lim\limits_{x\to 1}\dfrac{10(x-1)}{(x-1)(\sqrt{10x-9}+1)}=\lim\limits_{x\to 1}\dfrac{10}{(\sqrt{10x-9}+1)}=\dfrac{10}{2}=5.$

2.3.65 $\lim\limits_{h\to 0}\dfrac{(5+h)^2-25}{h}=\lim\limits_{h\to 0}\dfrac{25+10h+h^2-25}{h}=\lim\limits_{h\to 0}\dfrac{h(10+h)}{h}=\lim\limits_{h\to 0}(10+h)=10.$

2.3.67 We have

$$\lim_{w\to -k}\frac{w^2+5kw+4k^2}{w^2+kw}=\lim_{w\to -k}\frac{(w+4k)(w+k)}{(w)(w+k)}=\lim_{w\to -k}\frac{w+4k}{w}=\frac{-k+4k}{-k}=-3.$$

If $k=0$, we have $\lim\limits_{w\to -k}\dfrac{w^2+5kw+4k^2}{w^2+kw}=\lim\limits_{w\to 0}\dfrac{w^2}{w^2}=1.$

2.3.69 In order for $\lim\limits_{x\to -1}g(x)$ to exist, we need the two one-sided limits to exist and be equal. We have $\lim\limits_{x\to -1^-}g(x)=\lim\limits_{x\to -1^-}(x^2-5x)=6$, and $\lim\limits_{x\to -1^+}g(x)=\lim\limits_{x\to -1^+}(ax^3-7)=-a-7$. So we need $-a-7=6$, so we require that $a=-13$. Then $\lim\limits_{x\to -1}f(x)=6.$

2.3.71 $\lim\limits_{x\to 1}\dfrac{x^6-1}{x-1}=\lim\limits_{x\to 1}\dfrac{(x-1)(x^5+x^4+x^3+x^2+x+1)}{x-1}=\lim\limits_{x\to 1}(x^5+x^4+x^3+x^2+x+1)=6.$

2.3.73 $\lim\limits_{x\to a}\dfrac{x^5-a^5}{x-a}=\lim\limits_{x\to a}\dfrac{(x-a)(x^4+ax^3+a^2x^2+a^3x+a^4)}{x-a}=\lim\limits_{x\to a}(x^4+ax^3+a^2x^2+a^3x+a^4)=5a^4.$

2.3.75 $\lim\limits_{x\to 1}\dfrac{\sqrt[3]{x}-1}{x-1}=\lim\limits_{x\to 1}\dfrac{\sqrt[3]{x}-1}{(\sqrt[3]{x}-1)(\sqrt[3]{x^2}+\sqrt[3]{x}+1)}=\lim\limits_{x\to 1}\dfrac{1}{\sqrt[3]{x^2}+\sqrt[3]{x}+1}=\dfrac{1}{3}.$

2.3.77 $\lim\limits_{x\to 1}\dfrac{x-1}{\sqrt{x}-1}=\lim\limits_{x\to 1}\dfrac{(x-1)(\sqrt{x}+1)}{(\sqrt{x}-1)(\sqrt{x}+1)}=\lim\limits_{x\to 1}\dfrac{(x-1)(\sqrt{x}+1)}{x-1}=\lim\limits_{x\to 1}(\sqrt{x}+1)=2.$

2.3.79 $\lim\limits_{x\to 4}\dfrac{3(x-4)\sqrt{x+5}}{3-\sqrt{x+5}}=\lim\limits_{x\to 4}\dfrac{3(x-4)(\sqrt{x+5})(3+\sqrt{x+5})}{(3-\sqrt{x+5})(3+\sqrt{x+5})}=\lim\limits_{x\to 4}\dfrac{3(x-4)(\sqrt{x+5})(3+\sqrt{x+5})}{9-(x+5)}=$

$\lim\limits_{x\to 4}\dfrac{3(x-4)(\sqrt{x+5})(3+\sqrt{x+5})}{-(x-4)}=\lim\limits_{x\to 4}[-3(\sqrt{x+5})(3+\sqrt{x+5})]=(-3)(3)(3+3)=-54.$

2.3.81 Let $f(x)=x-1$ and $g(x)=\frac{5}{x-1}$. Then $\lim\limits_{x\to 1}f(x)=0$, $\lim\limits_{x\to 1}f(x)g(x)=\lim\limits_{x\to 1}\dfrac{5(x-1)}{x-1}=\lim\limits_{x\to 1}5=5.$

2.3.83 Let $p(x)=x^2+2x-8$. Then $\lim\limits_{x\to 2}\dfrac{p(x)}{x-2}=\lim\limits_{x\to 2}\dfrac{(x-2)(x+4)}{x-2}=\lim\limits_{x\to 2}(x+4)=6.$

The constants are unique. We know that 2 must be a root of p (otherwise the given limit couldn't exist), so it must have the form $p(x)=(x-2)q(x)$, and q must be a degree 1 polynomial with leading coefficient 1 (otherwise p wouldn't have leading coefficient 1.) So we have $p(x)=(x-2)(x+d)$, but because $\lim\limits_{x\to 2}\dfrac{p(x)}{x-2}=\lim\limits_{x\to 2}(x+d)=2+d=6$, we are forced to realize that $d=4$. Therefore, we have deduced that the only possibility for p is $p(x)=(x-2)(x+4)=x^2+2x-8$.

2.3.85 $\lim\limits_{S\to 0^+}r(S)=\lim\limits_{S\to 0^+}(1/2)\left(\sqrt{100+\dfrac{2S}{\pi}}-10\right)=0.$

The radius of the circular cylinder approaches zero as the surface area approaches zero.

2.3.87 $\lim\limits_{x\to 10}E(x)=\lim\limits_{x\to 10}\dfrac{4.35}{x\sqrt{x^2+0.01}}=\dfrac{4.35}{10\sqrt{100.01}}\approx .0435\text{ N/C.}$

2.3.89

a. As $x \to 0^+$, $(1-x) \to 1^-$. So $\lim\limits_{x \to 0^+} g(x) = \lim\limits_{(1-x) \to 1^-} f(1-x) = \lim\limits_{z \to 1^-} f(z) = 6$. (Where $z = 1 - x$.)

b. As $x \to 0^-$, $(1-x) \to 1^+$. So $\lim\limits_{x \to 0^-} g(x) = \lim\limits_{(1-x) \to 1^+} f(1-x) = \lim\limits_{z \to 1^+} f(z) = 4$. (Where $z = 1 - x$.)

2.3.91 $\lim\limits_{x \to a} p(x) = \lim\limits_{x \to a} (a_n x^n + a_{n-1} x^{n-1} + \cdots + a_1 x + a_0) = \lim\limits_{x \to a} (a_n x^n) + \lim\limits_{x \to a} (a_{n-1} x^{n-1}) + \cdots + \lim\limits_{x \to a} (a_1 x) +$
$\lim\limits_{x \to a} a_0 = a_n \lim\limits_{x \to a} x^n + a_{n-1} \lim\limits_{x \to a} x^{n-1} + \cdots + a_1 \lim\limits_{x \to a} x + a_0 = a_n (\lim\limits_{x \to a} x)^n + a_{n-1} (\lim\limits_{x \to a} x)^{n-1} + \cdots + a_1 (\lim\limits_{x \to a} x) + a_0 =$
$a_n a^n + a_{n-1} a^{n-1} + \cdots + a_1 a + a_0 = p(a)$.

2.4 Infinite Limits

2.4.1

$\lim\limits_{x \to a^+} f(x) = -\infty$ means that when x is very close to (but a little bigger than) a, the corresponding values for $f(x)$ are negative numbers whose absolute value is very large.

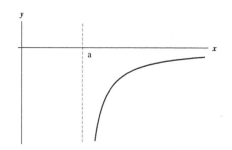

2.4.3 A vertical asymptote for a function f is a vertical line $x = a$ so that one or more of the following are true: $\lim\limits_{x \to a^-} f(x) = \pm\infty$, $\lim\limits_{x \to a^+} f(x) = \pm\infty$.

2.4.5 Because the numerator is approaching a non-zero constant while the denominator is approaching zero, the quotient of these numbers is getting big – at least the absolute value of the quotient is getting big. The quotient is actually always negative, because a number near 100 divided by a negative number is always negative. Thus $\lim\limits_{x \to 2} \dfrac{f(x)}{g(x)} = -\infty$.

2.4.7

x	$\frac{x+1}{(x-1)^2}$	x	$\frac{x+1}{(x-1)^2}$
1.1	210	.9	190
1.01	20,100	.99	19,900
1.001	2,001,000	.999	1,999,000
1.0001	200,010,000	.9999	199,990,000

From the data given, it appears that $\lim\limits_{x \to 1} f(x) = \infty$.

2.4.9

a. $\lim\limits_{x \to 1^-} f(x) = \infty$.

b. $\lim\limits_{x \to 1^+} f(x) = \infty$.

c. $\lim\limits_{x \to 1} f(x) = \infty$.

d. $\lim\limits_{x \to 2^-} f(x) = \infty$.

e. $\lim\limits_{x \to 2^+} f(x) = -\infty$.

f. $\lim\limits_{x \to 2} f(x)$ does not exist.

2.4.11

a. $\lim\limits_{x \to -2^-} h(x) = -\infty$.

b. $\lim\limits_{x \to -2^+} h(x) = -\infty$.

c. $\lim\limits_{x \to -2} h(x) = -\infty$.

d. $\lim\limits_{x \to 3^-} h(x) = \infty$.

e. $\lim\limits_{x \to 3^+} h(x) = -\infty$.

f. $\lim\limits_{x \to 3} h(x)$ does not exist.

2.4.13

    a. $\displaystyle\lim_{x\to 0^-}\frac{1}{x^2-x}=\infty$.

    b. $\displaystyle\lim_{x\to 0^+}\frac{1}{x^2-x}=-\infty$.

    c. $\displaystyle\lim_{x\to 1^-}\frac{1}{x^2-x}=-\infty$.

    d. $\displaystyle\lim_{x\to 1^+}\frac{1}{x^2-x}=\infty$.

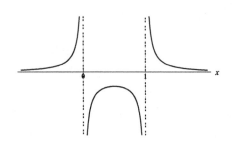

2.4.15

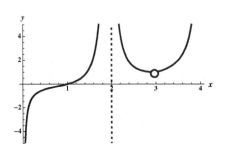

2.4.17

    a. $\displaystyle\lim_{x\to 2^+}\frac{1}{x-2}=\infty$.   b. $\displaystyle\lim_{x\to 2^-}\frac{1}{x-2}=-\infty$.   c. $\displaystyle\lim_{x\to 2}\frac{1}{x-2}$ does not exist.

2.4.19

    a. $\displaystyle\lim_{x\to 4^+}\frac{x-5}{(x-4)^2}=-\infty$.   b. $\displaystyle\lim_{x\to 4^-}\frac{x-5}{(x-4)^2}=-\infty$.   c. $\displaystyle\lim_{x\to 4}\frac{x-5}{(x-4)^2}=-\infty$.

2.4.21

    a. $\displaystyle\lim_{x\to 3^+}\frac{(x-1)(x-2)}{(x-3)}=\infty$. b. $\displaystyle\lim_{x\to 3^-}\frac{(x-1)(x-2)}{(x-3)}=-\infty$. c. $\displaystyle\lim_{x\to 3}\frac{(x-1)(x-2)}{(x-3)}$ does not exist.

2.4.23

    a. $\displaystyle\lim_{x\to 2^+}\frac{x^2-4x+3}{(x-2)^2}=-\infty$.   b. $\displaystyle\lim_{x\to 2^-}\frac{x^2-4x+3}{(x-2)^2}=-\infty$.   c. $\displaystyle\lim_{x\to 2}\frac{x^2-4x+3}{(x-2)^2}=-\infty$.

2.4.25 $\displaystyle\lim_{x\to 0}\frac{x^3-5x^2}{x^2}=\lim_{x\to 0}\frac{x^2(x-5)}{x^2}=\lim_{x\to 0}(x-5)=-5$.

2.4.27 $\displaystyle\lim_{x\to 1^+}\frac{x^2-5x+6}{x-1}=\lim_{x\to 1^+}\frac{(x-2)(x-3)}{x-1}=\infty$. (Note that as $x\to 1^+$, the numerator is near 2, while the denominator is near zero, but is positive. So the quotient is positive and large.)

2.4.29

    a. $\displaystyle\lim_{x\to 5}\frac{x-5}{x^2-25}=\lim_{x\to 5}\frac{1}{x+5}=\frac{1}{10}$, so there isn't a vertical asymptote at $x=5$.

    b. $\displaystyle\lim_{x\to -5^-}\frac{x-5}{x^2-25}=\lim_{x\to -5^-}\frac{1}{x+5}=-\infty$, so there is a vertical asymptote at $x=-5$.

c. $\displaystyle\lim_{x\to-5^+}\frac{x-5}{x^2-25} = \lim_{x\to-5^+}\frac{1}{x+5} = \infty$. This also implies that $x = -5$ is a vertical asymptote, as we already noted in part b.

2.4.31 $f(x) = \frac{x^2-9x+14}{x^2-5x+6} = \frac{(x-2)(x-7)}{(x-2)(x-3)}$. Note that $x = 3$ is a vertical asymptote, while $x = 2$ appears to be a candidate but isn't one. We have $\displaystyle\lim_{x\to3^+}f(x) = \lim_{x\to3^+}\frac{x-7}{x-3} = -\infty$ and $\displaystyle\lim_{x\to3^-}f(x) = \lim_{x\to3^-}\frac{x-7}{x-3} = \infty$, and thus $\displaystyle\lim_{x\to3}f(x)$ doesn't exist. Note that $\displaystyle\lim_{x\to2}f(x) = 5$.

2.4.33 $f(x) = \frac{x+1}{x^3-4x^2+4x} = \frac{x+1}{x(x-2)^2}$. There are vertical asymptotes at $x = 0$ and $x = 2$. We have $\displaystyle\lim_{x\to0^-}f(x) = \lim_{x\to0^-}\frac{x+1}{x(x-2)^2} = -\infty$, while $\displaystyle\lim_{x\to0^+}f(x) = \lim_{x\to0^+}\frac{x+1}{x(x-2)^2} = \infty$, and thus $\displaystyle\lim_{x\to0}f(x)$ doesn't exist.

Also we have $\displaystyle\lim_{x\to2^-}f(x) = \lim_{x\to2^-}\frac{x+1}{x(x-2)^2} = \infty$, while $\displaystyle\lim_{x\to2^+}f(x) = \lim_{x\to2^+}\frac{x+1}{x(x-2)^2} = \infty$, and thus $\displaystyle\lim_{x\to2}f(x) = \infty$ as well.

2.4.35 $\displaystyle\lim_{\theta\to0^+}\csc\theta = \lim_{\theta\to0^+}\frac{1}{\sin\theta} = \infty$.

2.4.37 $\displaystyle\lim_{x\to0^+}-10\cot x = \lim_{x\to0^+}\frac{-10\cos x}{\sin x} = -\infty$. (Note that as $x \to 0^+$, the numerator is near -10 and the denominator is near zero, but is positive. Thus the quotient is a negative number whose absolute value is large.)

2.4.39

a. $\displaystyle\lim_{x\to(\pi/2)^+}\tan x = -\infty$.

b. $\displaystyle\lim_{x\to(\pi/2)^-}\tan x = \infty$.

c. $\displaystyle\lim_{x\to(-\pi/2)^+}\tan x = -\infty$.

d. $\displaystyle\lim_{x\to(-\pi/2)^-}\tan x = \infty$.

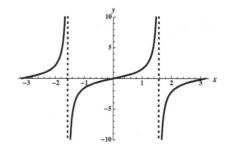

2.4.41

a. False. $\displaystyle\lim_{x\to1^-}f(x) = \lim_{x\to1^+}f(x) = \lim_{x\to1}f(x) = \lim_{x\to1}\frac{(x-1)(x-6)}{(x-1)(x+1)} = \frac{-5}{2}$.

b. True. For example, $\displaystyle\lim_{x\to-1^+}f(x) = \lim_{x\to-1^+}\frac{(x-1)(x-6)}{(x-1)(x+1)} = -\infty$.

c. False. For example $g(x) = \frac{1}{x-1}$ has $\displaystyle\lim_{x\to1^+}g(x) = \infty$, but $\displaystyle\lim_{x\to1^-}g(x) = -\infty$.

2.4.43 One example is $f(x) = \frac{1}{x-6}$.

2.4.45 $f(x) = \frac{x^2-3x+2}{x^{10}-x^9} = \frac{(x-2)(x-1)}{x^9(x-1)}$. f has a vertical asymptote at $x = 0$, because $\displaystyle\lim_{x\to0^+}f(x) = -\infty$ (and $\displaystyle\lim_{x\to0^-}f(x) = \infty$.) Note that $\displaystyle\lim_{x\to1}f(x) = -1$, so there isn't a vertical asymptote at $x = 1$.

2.4.47 $h(x) = \frac{e^x}{(x+1)^3}$ has a vertical asymptote at $x = -1$, because $\displaystyle\lim_{x\to-1^+}\frac{e^x}{(x+1)^3} = \infty$ (and $\displaystyle\lim_{x\to-1^-}h(x) = -\infty$.)

2.4.49 $g(\theta) = \tan(\pi\theta/10) = \frac{\sin(\pi\theta/10)}{\cos(\pi\theta/10)}$ has a vertical asymptote at each $\theta = 10n + 5$ where n is an integer. This is due to the fact that $\cos(\pi\theta/10) = 0$ when $\pi\theta/10 = \pi/2 + n\pi$ where n is an integer, which is the same as $\{\theta : \theta = 10n + 5, n$ an integer$\}$. Note that at all of these numbers which make the denominator zero, the numerator isn't zero.

2.4.51 $f(x) = \frac{1}{\sqrt{x}\sec x} = \frac{\cos x}{\sqrt{x}}$ has a vertical asymptote at $x = 0$.

2.4.53

a. Note that the numerator of the given expression factors as $(x - 3)(x - 4)$. So if $a = 3$ or if $a = 4$ the limit would be a finite number. In fact, $\displaystyle\lim_{x\to 3} \frac{(x - 3)(x - 4)}{x - 3} = -1$ and $\displaystyle\lim_{x\to 4} \frac{(x - 3)(x - 4)}{x - 4} = 1$.

b. For any number other than 3 or 4, the limit would be either $\pm\infty$. Because $x - a$ is always positive as $x \to a^+$, the limit would be $+\infty$ exactly when the numerator is positive, which is for a in the set $(-\infty, 3) \cup (4, \infty)$.

c. The limit would be $-\infty$ for a in the set $(3, 4)$.

2.4.55

a. The slope of the secant line is $\frac{f(h) - f(0)}{h} = \frac{h^{2/3}}{h} = h^{-1/3}$.

b. $\displaystyle\lim_{h\to 0^+} \frac{1}{h^{1/3}} = \infty$, and $\displaystyle\lim_{h\to 0^-} \frac{1}{h^{1/3}} = -\infty$. The tangent line is infinitely steep at the origin (i.e., it is a vertical line.)

2.5   Limits at Infinity

2.5.1

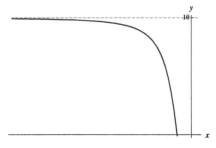

As $x < 0$ becomes large in absolute value, the corresponding values of f level off near 10.

2.5.3 If $f(x) \to 100,000$ as $x \to \infty$ and $g(x) \to \infty$ as $x \to \infty$, then the ratio $\frac{f(x)}{g(x)} \to 0$ as $x \to \infty$. (Because *eventually* the values of f are small compared to the values of g.)

2.5.5 $\displaystyle\lim_{x\to\infty} (-2x^3) = -\infty$, and $\displaystyle\lim_{x\to-\infty} (-2x^3) = \infty$.

2.5.7 $\displaystyle\lim_{x\to\infty} e^x = \infty$, $\displaystyle\lim_{x\to-\infty} e^x = 0$, and $\displaystyle\lim_{x\to\infty} e^{-x} = 0$.

2.5.9 $\displaystyle\lim_{x\to\infty} (3 + 10/x^2) = 3 + \lim_{x\to\infty} (10/x^2) = 3 + 0 = 3$.

2.5.11 $\displaystyle\lim_{\theta\to\infty} \frac{\cos\theta}{\theta^2} = 0$. Note that $-1 \le \cos\theta \le 1$, so $-\frac{1}{\theta^2} \le \frac{\cos\theta}{\theta^2} \le \frac{1}{\theta^2}$. The result now follows from the squeeze theorem.

2.5.13 $\lim\limits_{x \to \infty} \dfrac{\cos x^5}{\sqrt{x}} = 0$. Note that $-1 \le \cos x^5 \le 1$, so $\dfrac{-1}{\sqrt{x}} \le \dfrac{\cos x^5}{\sqrt{x}} \le \dfrac{1}{\sqrt{x}}$. Because $\lim\limits_{x \to \infty} \dfrac{1}{\sqrt{x}} = \lim\limits_{x \to \infty} \dfrac{-1}{\sqrt{x}} = 0$, we have $\lim\limits_{x \to \infty} \dfrac{\cos x^5}{\sqrt{x}} = 0$ by the squeeze theorem.

2.5.15 $\lim\limits_{x \to \infty} x^{12} = \infty$. Note that x^{12} is positive when $x > 0$.

2.5.17 $\lim\limits_{x \to \infty} x^{-6} = \lim\limits_{x \to \infty} \dfrac{1}{x^6} = 0$.

2.5.19 $\lim\limits_{x \to \infty} (3x^{12} - 9x^7) = \infty$.

2.5.21 $\lim\limits_{x \to -\infty} (-3x^{16} + 2) = -\infty$.

2.5.23 $\lim\limits_{x \to \infty} (-12x^{-5}) = \lim\limits_{x \to \infty} -\dfrac{12}{x^5} = 0$.

2.5.25 $\lim\limits_{x \to \infty} \dfrac{4x}{20x + 1} = \lim\limits_{x \to \infty} \dfrac{4x}{20x + 1} \cdot \dfrac{1/x}{1/x} = \lim\limits_{x \to \infty} \dfrac{4}{20 + 1/x} = \dfrac{4}{20} = \dfrac{1}{5}$. Thus, the line $y = \frac{1}{5}$ is a horizontal asymptote.

$\lim\limits_{x \to -\infty} \dfrac{4x}{20x + 1} = \lim\limits_{x \to -\infty} \dfrac{4x}{20x + 1} \cdot \dfrac{1/x}{1/x} = \lim\limits_{x \to -\infty} \dfrac{4}{20 + 1/x} = \dfrac{4}{20} = \dfrac{1}{5}$. This shows that the curve is also asymptotic to the asymptote in the negative direction.

2.5.27 $\lim\limits_{x \to \infty} \dfrac{(6x^2 - 9x + 8)}{(3x^2 + 2)} \cdot \dfrac{1/x^2}{1/x^2} = \lim\limits_{x \to \infty} \dfrac{6 - 9/x + 8/x^2}{3 + 2/x^2} = \dfrac{6 - 0 + 0}{3 + 0} = 2$. Similarly $\lim\limits_{x \to -\infty} f(x) = 2$. The line $y = 2$ is a horizontal asymptote.

2.5.29 $\lim\limits_{x \to \infty} \dfrac{3x^3 - 7}{x^4 + 5x^2} = \lim\limits_{x \to \infty} \dfrac{3x^3 - 7}{x^4 + 5x^2} \cdot \dfrac{3/x^4}{1/x^4} = \lim\limits_{x \to \infty} \dfrac{1/x - (7/x^4)}{1 + (5/x^2)} = \dfrac{0 - 0}{1 + 0} = 0$. Thus, the line $y = 0$ (the x-axis) is a horizontal asymptote.

$\lim\limits_{x \to -\infty} \dfrac{3x^3 - 7}{x^4 + 5x^2} = \lim\limits_{x \to -\infty} \dfrac{3x^3 - 7}{x^4 + 5x^2} \cdot \dfrac{3/x^4}{1/x^4} = \lim\limits_{x \to -\infty} \dfrac{1/x - (7/x^4)}{1 + (5/x^2)} = \dfrac{0 - 0}{1 + 0} = 0$. Thus, the curve is asymptotic to the x-axis in the negative direction as well.

2.5.31 $\lim\limits_{x \to \infty} \dfrac{(2x + 1)}{(3x^4 - 2)} \cdot \dfrac{1/x^4}{1/x^4} = \lim\limits_{x \to \infty} \dfrac{2/x^3 + 1/x^4}{3 - 2/x^4} = \dfrac{0 + 0}{3 - 0} = 0$. Similarly $\lim\limits_{x \to -\infty} f(x) = 0$. The line $y = 0$ is a horizontal asymptote.

2.5.33 $\lim\limits_{x \to \infty} \dfrac{(40x^5 + x^2)}{(16x^4 - 2x)} \cdot \dfrac{1/x^4}{1/x^4} = \lim\limits_{x \to \infty} \dfrac{40x + 1/x^2}{16 - 2/x^3} = \infty$. Similarly $\lim\limits_{x \to -\infty} f(x) = -\infty$. There are no horizontal asymptotes.

2.5.35

a. $f(x) = \dfrac{x^2 - 3}{x + 6} = x - 6 + \dfrac{33}{x + 6}$. The oblique asymptote of f is $y = x - 6$.

b. Because $\lim\limits_{x \to -6^+} f(x) = \infty$, there is a vertical asymptote at $x = -6$. Note also that $\lim\limits_{x \to -6^-} f(x) = -\infty$.

c.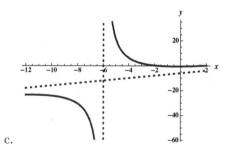

2.5.37

a. $f(x) = \frac{x^2 - 2x + 5}{3x - 2} = (1/3)x - 4/9 + \frac{37}{9(3x-2)}$. The oblique asymptote of f is $y = (1/3)x - 4/9$.

b. Because $\lim\limits_{x \to (2/3)^+} f(x) = \infty$, there is a vertical asymptote at $x = 2/3$. Note also that $\lim\limits_{x \to (2/3)^-} f(x) = -\infty$.

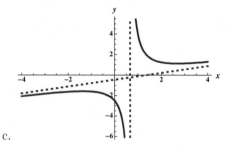

c.

2.5.39

a. $f(x) = \frac{4x^3 + 4x^2 + 7x + 4}{1 + x^2} = 4x + 4 + \frac{3x}{1+x^2}$. The oblique asymptote of f is $y = 4x + 4$.

b. There are no vertical asymptotes.

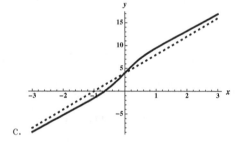

c.

2.5.41 First note that $\sqrt{x^6} = x^3$ if $x > 0$, but $\sqrt{x^6} = -x^3$ if $x < 0$. We have $\lim\limits_{x \to \infty} \frac{4x^3 + 1}{(2x^3 + \sqrt{16x^6 + 1})} \cdot \frac{1/x^3}{1/x^3} = $

$\lim\limits_{x \to \infty} \frac{4 + 1/x^3}{2 + \sqrt{16 + 1/x^6}} = \frac{4 + 0}{2 + \sqrt{16 + 0}} = \frac{2}{3}$.

However, $\lim\limits_{x \to -\infty} \frac{4x^3 + 1}{(2x^3 + \sqrt{16x^6 + 1})} \cdot \frac{1/x^3}{1/x^3} = \lim\limits_{x \to -\infty} \frac{4 + 1/x^3}{2 - \sqrt{16 + 1/x^6}} = \frac{4 + 0}{2 - \sqrt{16 + 0}} = \frac{4}{-2} = -2$.

So $y = \frac{2}{3}$ is a horizontal asymptote (as $x \to \infty$) and $y = -2$ is a horizontal asymptote (as $x \to -\infty$).

2.5.43 First note that $\sqrt[3]{x^6} = x^2$ and $\sqrt{x^4} = x^2$ for all x (even when $x < 0$.) We have $\lim\limits_{x \to \infty} \frac{\sqrt[3]{x^6 + 8}}{(4x^2 + \sqrt{3x^4 + 1})} \cdot$

$\frac{1/x^2}{1/x^2} = \lim\limits_{x \to \infty} \frac{\sqrt[3]{1 + 8/x^6}}{4 + \sqrt{3 + 1/x^4}} = \frac{1}{4 + \sqrt{3 + 0}} = \frac{1}{4\sqrt{3}}$.

The calculation as $x \to -\infty$ is similar. So $y = \frac{1}{4\sqrt{3}}$ is a horizontal asymptote.

2.5.45

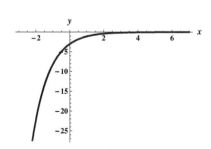

$\lim\limits_{x \to \infty} (-3e^{-x}) = -3 \cdot 0 = 0$. $\lim\limits_{x \to -\infty} (-3e^{-x}) = -\infty$.

2.5.47

$$\lim_{x \to \infty} (1 - \ln x) = -\infty. \quad \lim_{x \to 0^+} (1 - \ln x) = \infty.$$

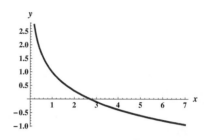

2.5.49

$y = \sin x$ has no asymptotes. $\lim_{x \to \infty} \sin x$ and $\lim_{x \to -\infty} \sin x$ do not exist.

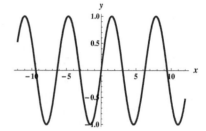

2.5.51

a. False. For example, the function $y = \frac{\sin x}{x}$ on the domain $[1, \infty)$ has a horizontal asymptote of $y = 0$, and it crosses the x-axis infinitely many times.

b. False. If f is a rational function, and if $\lim_{x \to \infty} f(x) = L \neq 0$, then the degree of the polynomial in the numerator must equal the degree of the polynomial in the denominator. In this case, both $\lim_{x \to \infty} f(x)$ and $\lim_{x \to -\infty} f(x) = \frac{a_n}{b_n}$ where a_n is the leading coefficient of the polynomial in the numerator and b_n is the leading coefficient of the polynomial in the denominator. In the case where $\lim_{x \to \infty} f(x) = 0$, then the degree of the numerator is strictly less than the degree of the denominator. This case holds for $\lim_{x \to -\infty} f(x) = 0$ as well.

c. True. There are only two directions which might lead to horizontal asymptotes: there could be one as $x \to \infty$ and there could be one as $x \to -\infty$, and those are the only possibilities.

2.5.53

a. $\lim_{x \to \infty} \frac{2x^3 + 10x^2 + 12x}{x^3 + 2x^2} \cdot \frac{(1/x^3)}{(1/x^3)} = \lim_{x \to \infty} \frac{2 + 10/x + 12/x^2}{1 + 2/x} = 2.$ Similarly, $\lim_{x \to -\infty} f(x) = 2.$ Thus, $y = 2$ is a horizontal asymptote.

b. Note that $f(x) = \frac{2x(x+2)(x+3)}{x^2(x+2)}$. So $\lim_{x \to 0^+} f(x) = \lim_{x \to 0^+} \frac{2(x+3)}{x} = \infty$, and similarly, $\lim_{x \to 0^-} f(x) = -\infty.$ There is a vertical asymptote at $x = 0$. Note that there is no asymptote at $x = -2$ because $\lim_{x \to -2} f(x) = -1$.

2.5.55

a. We have $\lim\limits_{x \to \infty} \dfrac{3x^4 + 3x^3 - 36x^2}{x^4 - 25x^2 + 144} \cdot \dfrac{(1/x^4)}{(1/x^4)} = \lim\limits_{x \to \infty} \dfrac{3 + 3/x - 36/x^2}{1 - 25/x^2 + 144/x^4} = 3$. Similarly, $\lim\limits_{x \to -\infty} f(x) = 3$. So $y = 3$ is a horizontal asymptote.

b. Note that $f(x) = \dfrac{3x^2(x+4)(x-3)}{(x+4)(x-4)(x+3)(x-3)}$. Thus, $\lim\limits_{x \to -3^+} f(x) = -\infty$ and $\lim\limits_{x \to -3^-} f(x) = \infty$. Also, $\lim\limits_{x \to 4^-} f(x) = -\infty$ and $\lim\limits_{x \to 4^+} f(x) = \infty$. Thus there are vertical asymptotes at $x = -3$ and $x = 4$.

2.5.57

a. $\lim\limits_{x \to \infty} \dfrac{x^2 - 9}{x^2 - 3x} \cdot \dfrac{(1/x^2)}{(1/x^2)} = \lim\limits_{x \to \infty} \dfrac{1 - 9/x^2}{1 - 3/x} = 1$. A similar result holds as $x \to -\infty$. So $y = 1$ is a horizontal asymptote.

b. Because $\lim\limits_{x \to 0^+} f(x) = \lim\limits_{x \to 0^+} \dfrac{x+3}{x} = \infty$ and $\lim\limits_{x \to 0^-} f(x) = -\infty$, there is a vertical asymptote at $x = 0$.

2.5.59

a. First note that $f(x) = \dfrac{\sqrt{x^2+2x+6}-3}{x-1} \cdot \dfrac{\sqrt{x^2+2x+6}+3}{\sqrt{x^2+2x+6}+3} = \dfrac{x^2+2x+6-9}{(x-1)(\sqrt{x^2+2x+6}+3)} = \dfrac{(x-1)(x+3)}{(x-1)(\sqrt{x^2+2x+6}+3)}$.

Thus

$$\lim\limits_{x \to \infty} f(x) = \lim\limits_{x \to \infty} \dfrac{x+3}{\sqrt{x^2+2x+6}+3} \cdot \dfrac{1/x}{1/x} = \lim\limits_{x \to \infty} \dfrac{1+3/x}{\sqrt{1+2/x+6/x^2}+3/x} = 1.$$

Using the fact that $\sqrt{x^2} = -x$ for $x < 0$, we have $\lim\limits_{x \to -\infty} f(x) = -1$. Thus the lines $y = 1$ and $y = -1$ are horizontal asymptotes.

b. f has no vertical asymptotes.

2.5.61

a. Note that when $x > 1$, we have $|x| = x$ and $|x - 1| = x - 1$. Thus

$$f(x) = (\sqrt{x} - \sqrt{x-1}) \cdot \dfrac{\sqrt{x} + \sqrt{x-1}}{\sqrt{x} + \sqrt{x-1}} = \dfrac{1}{\sqrt{x} + \sqrt{x-1}}.$$

Thus $\lim\limits_{x \to \infty} f(x) = 0$.

When $x < 0$, we have $|x| = -x$ and $|x - 1| = 1 - x$. Thus

$$f(x) = (\sqrt{-x} - \sqrt{1-x}) \cdot \dfrac{\sqrt{-x} + \sqrt{1-x}}{\sqrt{-x} + \sqrt{1-x}} = -\dfrac{1}{\sqrt{-x} + \sqrt{1-x}}.$$

Thus, $\lim\limits_{x \to -\infty} f(x) = 0$. There is a horizontal asymptote at $y = 0$.

b. f has no vertical asymptotes.

2.5.63

a. $\lim\limits_{x \to \infty} \sec^{-1} x = \pi/2$.

b. $\lim\limits_{x \to -\infty} \sec^{-1} x = \pi/2$.

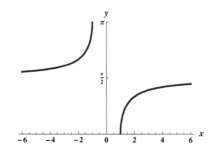

2.5.65

a. $\displaystyle\lim_{x\to\infty} \frac{e^x - e^{-x}}{2} = \infty$.

$\displaystyle\lim_{x\to-\infty} \frac{e^x - e^{-x}}{2} = -\infty$.

b. $\sinh(0) = \frac{e^0 - e^0}{2} = \frac{1-1}{2} = 0$.

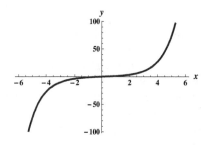

2.5.67

One possible such graph is:

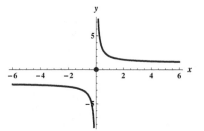

2.5.69 $\displaystyle\lim_{x\to 0^+} \frac{\cos x + 2\sqrt{x}}{\sqrt{x}} = \infty$. $\displaystyle\lim_{x\to\infty} \frac{\cos x + 2\sqrt{x}}{\sqrt{x}} = \lim_{x\to\infty}\left(2 + \frac{\cos x}{\sqrt{x}}\right) = 2$.
There is a vertical asymptote at $x = 0$ and a horizontal asymptote at $y = 2$.

2.5.71 $\displaystyle\lim_{t\to\infty} p(t) = \lim_{t\to\infty} \frac{3500t}{t+1} = 3500$. The steady state exists. The steady state value is 3500.

2.5.73 $\displaystyle\lim_{t\to\infty} v(t) = \lim_{t\to\infty} 1000 e^{0.065t} = \infty$. The steady state does not exist.

2.5.75 $\displaystyle\lim_{t\to\infty} a(t) = \lim_{t\to\infty} 2\left(\frac{t + \sin t}{t}\right) = \lim_{t\to\infty} 2\left(1 + \frac{\sin t}{t}\right) = 2$. The steady state exists. The steady state value is 2.

2.5.77 $\displaystyle\lim_{n\to\infty} f(n) = \lim_{n\to\infty} \frac{n-1}{n} = \lim_{n\to\infty} [1 - (1/n)] = 1$.

2.5.79 $\displaystyle\lim_{n\to\infty} f(n) = \lim_{n\to\infty} \frac{n+1}{n^2} = \lim_{n\to\infty} [1/n + 1/n^2] = 0$.

2.5.81 No. If $m = n$, there will be a horizontal asymptote, and if $m = n+1$, there will be an oblique asymptote.

2.5.83 $\displaystyle\lim_{x\to\infty} \frac{2e^x + 3e^{2x}}{e^{2x} + e^{3x}} = \lim_{x\to\infty} \frac{2e^x + 3e^{2x}}{e^{2x} + e^{3x}} \cdot \frac{1/e^{3x}}{1/e^{3x}} = \lim_{x\to\infty} \frac{2/e^x + 3/e^x}{1/e^x + 1} = \frac{0+0}{0+1} = 0$. Thus the line $y = 0$ is a horizontal asymptote.

$\displaystyle\lim_{x\to-\infty} \frac{2e^x + 3e^{2x}}{e^{2x} + e^{3x}} = \lim_{x\to-\infty} \frac{2e^x + 3e^{2x}}{e^{2x} + e^{3x}} \cdot \frac{1/e^{2x}}{1/e^{2x}} = \lim_{x\to-\infty} \frac{2e^{-x} + 3}{1 + e^x} = \infty$.

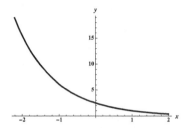

2.5.85 The numerator of f is defined for $-3 < x < 3$. The denominator is defined everywhere, but is zero when $2e^x = e^{-x}$. Simplifying gives $2e^{2x} = 1$, or $e^{2x} = 1/2$. This has the solution $x = (-\ln 2)/2 \approx -0.347$, which lies in the domain of the numerator. So the domain of f is $\{x : -3 < x < 3, x \neq (-\ln 2)/2\}$, and any questions about horizontal asymptotes are moot. As $x \to 3^-$ or as $x \to -3^+$, the numerator approaches $-\infty$, which follows because $\lim_{t \to 0^+} \ln t = -\infty$, and the denominator is approaching a positive constant as $x \to 3^-$ and a negative constant as $x \to -3^+$. Thus $\lim_{x \to 3^-} f(x) = -\infty$ and $\lim_{x \to -3^+} f(x) = \infty$, and there are vertical asymptotes at $x = 3$ and $x = -3$.

As $x \to -(\ln 2)/2$, the numerator is nonzero because $9 - x^2$ is not approaching 1. Thus, there is a vertical asymptote at $x = -(\ln 2)/2$. A graph of the function, with the vertical asymptotes shown in gray, verifies this analysis. Note that the vertical asymptotes at ± 3 require a different viewing window.

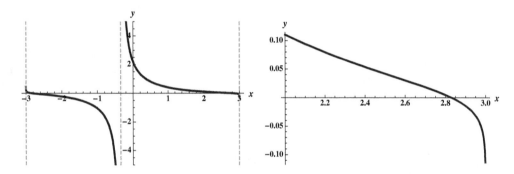

2.6   Continuity

2.6.1

a. $a(t)$ is a continuous function during the time period from when she jumps from the plane and when she touches down on the ground, because her position is changing continuously with time.

b. $n(t)$ is not a continuous function of time. The function "jumps" at the times when a quarter must be added.

c. $T(t)$ is a continuous function, because temperature varies continuously with time.

d. $p(t)$ is not continuous – it jumps by whole numbers when a player scores a point.

2.6.3 A function f is continuous on an interval I if it is continuous at all points in the interior of I, and it must be continuous from the right at the left endpoint (if the left endpoint is included in I) and it must be continuous from the left at the right endpoint (if the right endpoint is included in I.)

2.6.5

a. A function f is continuous from the left at $x = a$ if a is in the domain of f, and $\lim_{x \to a^-} f(x) = f(a)$.

b. A function f is continuous from the right at $x = a$ if a is in the domain of f, and $\lim_{x \to a^+} f(x) = f(a)$.

2.6.7 The domain of $f(x) = \frac{e^x}{x}$ is $(-\infty, 0) \cup (0, \infty)$, and f is continuous everywhere on this domain.

2.6.9 f is discontinuous at $x = 1$, at $x = 2$, and at $x = 3$. At $x = 1$, $f(1)$ does not exist (so the first condition is violated). At $x = 2$, $f(2)$ exists and $\lim\limits_{x \to 2} f(x)$ exists, but $\lim\limits_{x \to 2} f(x) \neq f(2)$ (so condition 3 is violated). At $x = 3$, $\lim\limits_{x \to 3} f(x)$ does not exist (so condition 2 is violated).

2.6.11 f is discontinuous at $x = 1$, at $x = 2$, and at $x = 3$. At $x = 1$, $\lim\limits_{x \to 1} f(x)$ does not exist, and $f(1)$ does not exist (so conditions 1 and 2 are violated). At $x = 2$, $\lim\limits_{x \to 2} f(x)$ does not exist (so condition 2 is violated). At $x = 3$, $f(3)$ does not exist (so condition 1 is violated).

2.6.13 The function is defined at 5, in fact $f(5) = \frac{50 + 15 + 1}{25 + 25} = \frac{66}{50} = \frac{33}{25}$. Also, $\lim\limits_{x \to 5} f(x) = \lim\limits_{x \to 5} \frac{2x^2 + 3x + 1}{x^2 + 5x} = \frac{33}{25} = f(5)$. The function is continuous at $a = 5$.

2.6.15 f is discontinuous at 1, because 1 is not in the domain of f.

2.6.17 f is discontinuous at 1, because $\lim\limits_{x \to 1} f(x) \neq f(1)$. In fact, $f(1) = 3$, but $\lim\limits_{x \to 1} f(x) = 2$.

2.6.19 f is discontinuous at 4, because 4 is not in the domain of f.

2.6.21 Because f is a polynomial, it is continuous on all of $\mathbb{R}$.

2.6.23 Because f is a rational function, it is continuous on its domain. Its domain is $(-\infty, -3) \cup (-3, 3) \cup (3, \infty)$.

2.6.25 Because f is a rational function, it is continuous on its domain. Its domain is $(-\infty, -2) \cup (-2, 2) \cup (2, \infty)$.

2.6.27 Because $f(x) = \left(x^8 - 3x^6 - 1\right)^{40}$ is a polynomial, it is continuous everywhere, including at 0. Thus $\lim\limits_{x \to 0} f(x) = f(0) = (-1)^{40} = 1$.

2.6.29 Because $f(x) = \left(\frac{x+5}{x+2}\right)^4$ is a rational function, it is continuous at all points in its domain, including at $x = 1$. Thus $\lim\limits_{x \to 1} f(x) = f(1) = 16$.

2.6.31 Because $x^3 - 2x^2 - 8x = x(x^2 - 2x - 8) = x(x - 4)(x + 2)$, we have (as long as $x \neq 4$)

$$\sqrt{\frac{x^3 - 2x^2 - 8x}{x - 4}} = \sqrt{x(x + 2)}.$$

Thus, $\lim\limits_{x \to 4} \sqrt{\dfrac{x^3 - 2x^2 - 8x}{x - 4}} = \lim\limits_{x \to 4} \sqrt{x(x + 2)} = \sqrt{24}$, using Theorem 2.12 and the fact that the square root is a continuous function.

2.6.33 Recall that $\lim\limits_{x \to 0} \dfrac{\sin x}{x} = 1$. Now noting that the function $f(x) = \ln 2x$ is continuous at 1, we have by Theorem 2.12 that $\lim\limits_{x \to 0} \ln\left(\dfrac{2 \sin x}{x}\right) = \ln\left(2 \left(\lim\limits_{x \to 0} \dfrac{\sin x}{x}\right)\right) = \ln(2 \cdot 1) = \ln 2$.

2.6.35 f is continuous on $[0, 1)$, on $(1, 2)$, on $(2, 3]$, and on $(3, 4)$.

2.6.37 f is continuous on $[0, 1)$, on $(1, 2)$, on $[2, 3)$, and on $(3, 5]$.

2.6.39

    a. f is defined at 1. We have $f(1) = 1^2 + (3)(1) = 4$. To see whether or not $\lim\limits_{x \to 1} f(x)$ exists, we investigate the two one-sided limits. $\lim\limits_{x \to 1^-} f(x) = \lim\limits_{x \to 1^-} 2x = 2$, and $\lim\limits_{x \to 1^+} f(x) = \lim\limits_{x \to 1^+} (x^2 + 3x) = 4$, so $\lim\limits_{x \to 1} f(x)$ does not exist. Thus f is discontinuous at $x = 1$.

b. f is continuous from the right, because $\lim\limits_{x \to 1^+} f(x) = 4 = f(1)$.

c. f is continuous on $(-\infty, 1)$ and on $[1, \infty)$.

2.6.41 f is continuous on $(-\infty, -\sqrt{8}]$ and on $[\sqrt{8}, \infty)$.

2.6.43 Because f is the composition of two functions which are continuous everywhere, it is continuous everywhere.

2.6.45 Because f is the composition of two functions which are continuous everywhere, it is continuous everywhere.

2.6.47 $\lim\limits_{x \to 2} \sqrt{\dfrac{4x+10}{2x-2}} = \sqrt{\dfrac{18}{2}} = 3$.

2.6.49 $\lim\limits_{x \to 3} \sqrt{x^2 + 7} = \sqrt{9 + 7} = 4$.

2.6.51 $f(x) = \csc x$ isn't defined at $x = k\pi$ where k is an integer, so it isn't continuous at those points. So it is continuous on intervals of the form $(k\pi, (k+1)\pi)$ where k is an integer. $\lim\limits_{x \to \pi/4} \csc x = \sqrt{2}$. $\lim\limits_{x \to 2\pi^-} \csc x = -\infty$.

2.6.53 f isn't defined for any number of the form $\pi/2 + k\pi$ where k is an integer, so it isn't continuous there. It is continuous on intervals of the form $(\pi/2 + k\pi, \pi/2 + (k+1)\pi)$, where k is an integer.

$\lim\limits_{x \to \pi/2^-} f(x) = \infty$. $\lim\limits_{x \to 4\pi/3} f(x) = \dfrac{1 - \sqrt{3}/2}{-1/2} = \sqrt{3} - 2$.

2.6.55 This function is continuous on its domain, which is $(-\infty, 0) \cup (0, \infty)$.

$\lim\limits_{x \to 0^-} f(x) = \lim\limits_{x \to 0^-} \dfrac{e^x}{1 - e^x} = \infty$, while $\lim\limits_{x \to 0^+} f(x) = \lim\limits_{x \to 0^+} \dfrac{e^x}{1 - e^x} = -\infty$.

2.6.57

a. Because A is a continuous function of r on $[0, .08]$, and because $A(0) = 5000$ and $A(.08) \approx 11098.2$, (and 7000 is an intermediate value between these two numbers) the Intermediate Value Theorem guarantees a value of r between 0 and .08 where $A(r) = 7000$.

b. Solving $5000(1 + (r/12))^{120} = 7000$ for r, we see that $(1 + (r/12))^{120} = 7/5$, so $1 + r/12 = \sqrt[120]{7/5}$, so $r = 12(\sqrt[120]{7/5} - 1) \approx 0.034$.

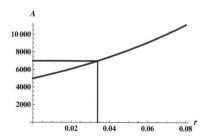

2.6.59

a. Note that $f(x) = 2x^3 + x - 2$ is continuous everywhere, so in particular it is continuous on $[-1, 1]$. Note that $f(-1) = -5 < 0$ and $f(1) = 1 > 0$. Because 0 is an intermediate value between $f(-1)$ and $f(1)$, the Intermediate Value Theorem guarantees a number c between -1 and 1 where $f(c) = 0$.

b. Using a graphing calculator and a computer algebra system, we see that the root of f is about 0.835.

c.

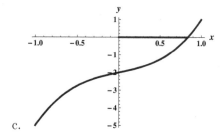

2.6.61

a. Note that $f(x) = x^3 - 5x^2 + 2x$ is continuous everywhere, so in particular it is continuous on $[-1, 5]$. Note that $f(-1) = -8 < -1$ and $f(5) = 10 > -1$. Because -1 is an intermediate value between $f(-1)$ and $f(5)$, the Intermediate Value Theorem guarantees a number c between -1 and 5 where $f(c) = -1$.

b. Using a graphing calculator and a computer algebra system, we see that there are actually three different values of c between -1 and 5 for which $f(c) = -1$. They are $c \approx -0.285$, $c \approx 0.778$, and $c \approx 4.507$.

c.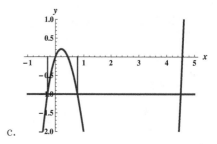

2.6.63

a. Note that $f(x) = e^x + x$ is continuous on its domain, so in particular it is continuous on $[-1, 0]$. Note that $f(-1) = \frac{1}{e} - 1 < 0$ and $f(0) = 1 > 0$. Because 0 is an intermediate value between $f(-1)$ and $f(0)$, the Intermediate Value Theorem guarantees a number c between -1 and 0 where $f(c) = 0$.

b. Using a graphing calculator and a computer algebra system, we see that the value of c guaranteed by the theorem is about -0.567.

c.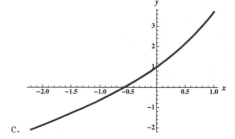

2.6.65

a. True. If f is right continuous at a, then $f(a)$ exists and the limit from the right at a exists and is equal to $f(a)$. Because it is left continuous, the limit from the left exists — so we now know that the limit as $x \to a$ of $f(x)$ exists, because the two one-sided limits are both equal to $f(a)$.

b. True. If $\lim_{x \to a} f(x) = f(a)$, then $\lim_{x \to a^+} f(x) = f(a)$ and $\lim_{x \to a^-} f(x) = f(a)$.

c. False. The statement would be true if f were continuous. However, if f isn't continuous, then the statement doesn't hold. For example, suppose that $f(x) = \begin{cases} 0 & \text{if } 0 \leq x < 1; \\ 1 & \text{if } 1 \leq x \leq 2, \end{cases}$ Note that $f(0) = 0$ and $f(2) = 1$, but there is no number c between 0 and 2 where $f(c) = 1/2$.

d. False. Consider $f(x) = x^2$ and $a = -1$ and $b = 1$. Then f is continuous on $[a, b]$, but $\frac{f(1) + f(-1)}{2} = 1$, and there is no c on (a, b) with $f(c) = 1$.

2.6.67 Because $f(x) = x^3 + 3x - 18$ is a polynomial, it is continuous on $(-\infty, \infty)$, and because the absolute value function is continuous everywhere, $|f(x)|$ is continuous everywhere.

2.6.69 Let $f(x) = \frac{1}{\sqrt{x} - 4}$. Then f is continuous on $[0, 16) \cup (16, \infty)$. So $h(x) = |f(x)|$ is continuous on this set as well.

2.6.71 $\lim_{x \to \pi} \dfrac{\cos^2 x + 3 \cos x + 2}{\cos x + 1} = \lim_{x \to \pi} \dfrac{(\cos x + 1)(\cos x + 2)}{\cos x + 1} = \lim_{x \to \pi} (\cos x + 2) = 1.$

2.6.73 $\lim\limits_{x\to\pi/2} \dfrac{\sin x - 1}{\sqrt{\sin x} - 1} = \lim\limits_{x\to\pi/2} (\sqrt{\sin x} + 1) = 2.$

2.6.75 $\lim\limits_{x\to0} \dfrac{\cos x - 1}{\sin^2 x} = \lim\limits_{x\to0} \dfrac{\cos x - 1}{1 - \cos^2 x} = \lim\limits_{x\to0} \dfrac{\cos x - 1}{(1 - \cos x)(1 + \cos x)} = \lim\limits_{x\to0} -\dfrac{1}{1 + \cos x} = -\dfrac{1}{2}.$

2.6.77 Recall that $-\pi/2 \le \tan^{-1} x \le \pi/2$. Thus for $x > 0$, $-\dfrac{\pi/2}{x} \le \dfrac{\tan^{-1} x}{x} \le \dfrac{\pi/2}{x}$. Thus $\lim\limits_{x\to\infty} \dfrac{\tan^{-1}(x)}{x} = 0$ by the Squeeze Theorem.

2.6.79 $\lim\limits_{x\to1^-} \dfrac{x}{\ln x} = -\infty.$

2.6.81

The graph shown isn't drawn correctly at the integers. At an integer a, the value of the function is 0, whereas the graph shown appears to take on all the values from 0 to 1.
Note that in the correct graph, $\lim\limits_{x\to a^-} f(x) = 1$ and $\lim\limits_{x\to a^+} f(x) = 0$ for every integer a.

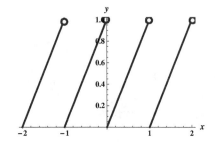

2.6.83 With slight modifications, we can use the examples from the previous two problems.

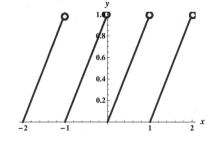

a. The function $y = x - \lfloor x \rfloor$ is defined at $x = 1$ but isn't continuous there.

b. The function $y = \frac{\sin(x-1)}{x-1}$ has a limit at $x = 1$, but isn't defined there, so isn't continuous there.

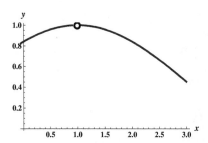

2.6.85

a. In order for g to be continuous from the left at $x = 1$, we must have $\lim\limits_{x\to1^-} g(x) = g(1) = a$. We have $\lim\limits_{x\to1^-} g(x) = \lim\limits_{x\to1^-} (x^2 + x) = 2$. So we must have $a = 2$.

b. In order for g to be continuous from the right at $x = 1$, we must have $\lim\limits_{x\to1^+} g(x) = g(1) = a$. We have $\lim\limits_{x\to1^+} g(x) = \lim\limits_{x\to1^+} (3x + 5) = 8$. So we must have $a = 8$.

c. Because the limit from the left and the limit from the right at $x = 1$ don't agree, there is no value of a which will make the function continuous at $x = 1$.

2.6.87 $\lim\limits_{x \to 0} \dfrac{2e^x + 10e^{-x}}{e^x + e^{-x}} = \dfrac{12}{2} = 6.$

$\lim\limits_{x \to -\infty} \dfrac{2e^x + 10e^{-x}}{e^x + e^{-x}} = \lim\limits_{x \to -\infty} \dfrac{2e^x + 10e^{-x}}{e^x + e^{-x}} \cdot \dfrac{e^x}{e^x} = \lim\limits_{x \to -\infty} \dfrac{2e^{2x} + 10}{e^{2x} + 1} = \dfrac{10}{1} = 10.$

$\lim\limits_{x \to \infty} \dfrac{2e^x + 10e^{-x}}{e^x + e^{-x}} = \lim\limits_{x \to \infty} \dfrac{2e^x + 10e^{-x}}{e^x + e^{-x}} \cdot \dfrac{e^{-x}}{e^{-x}} = \lim\limits_{x \to \infty} \dfrac{2 + 10e^{-2x}}{1 + e^{-2x}} = \dfrac{2}{1} = 2.$

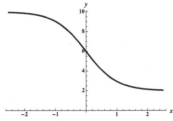

There are no vertical asymptotes. The lines $y = 2$ and $y = 10$ are horizontal asymptotes.

2.6.89 Let $f(x) = 70x^3 - 87x^2 + 32x - 3$. Note that $f(0) < 0$, $f(.2) > 0$, $f(.55) < 0$, and $f(1) > 0$. Because the given polynomial is continuous everywhere, the Intermediate Value Theorem guarantees us a root on $(0, .2)$, at least one on $(.2, .55)$, and at least one on $(.55, 1)$. Because there can be at most 3 roots and there are at least 3 roots, there must be exactly 3 roots. The roots are $x_1 = 1/7$, $x_2 = 1/2$ and $x_3 = 3/5$.

2.6.91

a. Note that $A(.01) \approx 2615.55$ and $A(.1) \approx 3984.36$. By the Intermediate Value Theorem, there must be a number r_0 between .01 and .1 so that $A(r_0) = 3500$.

b. The desired value is $r_0 \approx 0.0728$ or 7.28%.

2.6.93 We can argue essentially like the previous problem, or we can imagine an identical twin to the original monk, who takes an identical version of the original monk's journey up the winding path while the monk is taking the return journey down. Because they must pass somewhere on the path, that point is the one we are looking for.

2.6.95 The discontinuity is not removable, because $\lim\limits_{x \to a} f(x)$ does not exist. The discontinuity pictured is a jump discontinuity.

2.6.97 Note that $\lim\limits_{x \to 2} \dfrac{x^2 - 7x + 10}{x - 2} = \lim\limits_{x \to 2} \dfrac{(x - 2)(x - 5)}{x - 2} = \lim\limits_{x \to 2}(x - 5) = -3$. Because this limit exists, the discontinuity is removable.

2.6.99

a. Note that $-1 \le \sin(1/x) \le 1$ for all $x \ne 0$, so $-x \le x \sin(1/x) \le x$ (for $x > 0$. For $x < 0$ we would have $x \le x \sin(1/x) \le -x$.) Because both $x \to 0$ and $-x \to 0$ as $x \to 0$, the Squeeze Theorem tells us that $\lim\limits_{x \to 0} x \sin(1/x) = 0$ as well. Because this limit exists, the discontinuity is removable.

b. Note that as $x \to 0^+$, $1/x \to \infty$, and thus $\lim\limits_{x \to 0^+} \sin(1/x)$ does not exist. So the discontinuity is not removable.

2.6.101 Note that $h(x) = \dfrac{x^3 - 4x^2 + 4x}{x(x - 1)} = \dfrac{x(x - 2)^2}{x(x - 1)}$. Thus $\lim\limits_{x \to 0} h(x) = -4$, and the discontinuity at $x = 0$ is removable. However, $\lim\limits_{x \to 1} h(x)$ does not exist, and the discontinuity at $x = 1$ is not removable (it is infinite.)

2.6.103

a. Consider $g(x) = x + 1$ and $f(x) = \frac{|x-1|}{x-1}$. Note that both g and f are continuous at $x = 0$. However $f(g(x)) = f(x + 1) = \frac{|x|}{x}$ is not continuous at 0.

b. The previous theorem says that the composition of f and g is continuous at a if g is continuous at a and f is continuous at $g(a)$. It does not say that if g and f are both continuous at a that the composition is continuous at a.

2.6.105

a. Using the hint, we have

$$\sin x = \sin(a + (x - a)) = \sin a \cos(x - a) + \sin(x - a) \cos a.$$

Note that as $x \to a$, we have that $\cos(x - a) \to 1$ and $\sin(x - a) \to 0$.

So,

$$\lim_{x \to a} \sin x = \lim_{x \to a} \sin(a + (x - a)) = \lim_{x \to a} (\sin a \cos(x - a) + \sin(x - a) \cos a) = (\sin a) \cdot 1 + 0 \cdot \cos a = \sin a.$$

b. Using the hint, we have

$$\cos x = \cos(a + (x - a)) = \cos a \cos(x - a) - \sin a \sin(x - a).$$

So,

$$\lim_{x \to a} \cos x = \lim_{x \to a} \cos(a + (x - a)) = \lim_{x \to a} ((\cos a) \cos(x - a) - (\sin a) \sin(x - a)) = (\cos a) \cdot 1 - (\sin a) \cdot 0 = \cos a.$$

2.7　Precise Definitions of Limits

2.7.1 Note that all the numbers in the interval $(1, 3)$ are within 1 unit of the number 2. So $|x - 2| < 1$ is true for all numbers in that interval. In fact, $\{x : 0 < |x - 2| < 1\}$ is exactly the set $(1, 3)$ with $x \neq 2$.

2.7.3
$(3, 8)$ has center 5.5, so it is not symmetric about the number 5.
$(1, 9)$ and $(4, 6)$ and $(4.5, 5.5)$ are symmetric about the number 5.

2.7.5 $\lim_{x \to a} f(x) = L$ if for any arbitrarily small positive number ϵ, there exists a number δ, so that $f(x)$ is within ϵ units of L for any number x within δ units of a (but not including a itself).

2.7.7 We are given that $|f(x) - 5| < .1$ for values of x in the interval $(0, 5)$, so we need to ensure that the set of x values we are allowing fall in this interval.

Note that the number 0 is two units away from the number 2 and the number 5 is three units away from the number 2. In order to be sure that we are talking about numbers in the interval $(0, 5)$ when we write $|x - 2| < \delta$, we would need to have $\delta = 2$ (or a number less than 2). In fact, the set of numbers for which $|x - 2| < 2$ is the interval $(0, 4)$ which is a subset of $(0, 5)$.

If we were to allow δ to be any number greater than 2, then the set of all x so that $|x - 2| < \delta$ would include numbers less than 0, and those numbers aren't on the interval $(0, 5)$.

2.7.9

a. In order for f to be within 2 units of 5, it appears that we need x to be within 1 unit of 2. So $\delta = 1$.

b. In order for f to be within 1 unit of 5, it appears that we would need x to be within 1/2 unit of 2. So $\delta = .5$.

2.7.11

a. In order for f to be within 3 units of 6, it appears that we would need x to be within 2 units of 3. So $\delta = 2$.

b. In order for f to be within 1 unit of 6, it appears that we would need x to be within 1/2 unit of 3. So $\delta = 1/2$.

2.7.13

a. If $\epsilon = 1$, we need $|x^3 + 3 - 3| < 1$. So we need $|x| < \sqrt[3]{1} = 1$ in order for this to happen. Thus $\delta = 1$ will suffice.

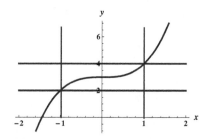

b. If $\epsilon = .5$, we need $|x^3 + 3 - 3| < .5$. So we need $|x| < \sqrt[3]{.5}$ in order for this to happen. Thus $\delta = \sqrt[3]{.5} \approx .79$ will suffice.

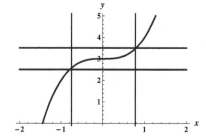

2.7.15

a. For $\epsilon = 1$, the required value of δ would also be 1. A larger value of δ would work to the right of 2, but this is the largest one that would work to the left of 2.

b. For $\epsilon = 1/2$, the required value of δ would also be 1/2.

c. It appears that for a given value of ϵ, it would be wise to take $\delta = \min(\epsilon, 2)$. This assures that the desired inequality is met on both sides of 2.

2.7.17

a. For $\epsilon = 2$, it appears that a value of $\delta = 1$ (or smaller) would work.

b. For $\epsilon = 1$, it appears that a value of $\delta = 1/2$ (or smaller) would work.

c. For an arbitrary ϵ, a value of $\delta = \epsilon/2$ or smaller appears to suffice.

2.7.19 For any $\epsilon > 0$, let $\delta = \epsilon/8$. Then if $0 < |x - 1| < \delta$, we would have $|x - 1| < \epsilon/8$. Then $|8x - 8| < \epsilon$, so $|(8x + 5) - 13| < \epsilon$. This last inequality has the form $|f(x) - L| < \epsilon$, which is what we were attempting to show. Thus, $\lim\limits_{x \to 1}(8x + 5) = 13$.

2.7.21 First note that if $x \neq 4$, $f(x) = \frac{x^2 - 16}{x - 4} = x + 4$.

Now if $\epsilon > 0$ is given, let $\delta = \epsilon$. Now suppose $0 < |x - 4| < \delta$. Then $x \neq 4$, so the function $f(x)$ can be described by $x + 4$. Also, because $|x - 4| < \delta$, we have $|x - 4| < \epsilon$. Thus $|(x + 4) - 8| < \epsilon$. This last inequality has the form $|f(x) - L| < \epsilon$, which is what we were attempting to show. Thus, $\lim\limits_{x \to 4} \frac{x^2 - 16}{x - 4} = 8$.

2.7.23 Let $\epsilon > 0$ be given. Let $\delta = \sqrt{\epsilon}$. Then if $0 < |x - 0| < \delta$, we would have $|x| < \sqrt{\epsilon}$. But then $|x^2| < \epsilon$, which has the form $|f(x) - L| < \epsilon$. Thus, $\lim_{x \to 0} f(x) = 0$.

2.7.25 Let $\epsilon > 0$ be given.

Because $\lim_{x \to a} f(x) = L$, we know that there exists a $\delta_1 > 0$ so that $|f(x) - L| < \epsilon/2$ when $0 < |x - a| < \delta_1$. Also, because $\lim_{x \to a} g(x) = M$, there exists a $\delta_2 > 0$ so that $|g(x) - M| < \epsilon/2$ when $0 < |x - a| < \delta_2$.

Now let $\delta = \min(\delta_1, \delta_2)$.

Then if $0 < |x - a| < \delta$, we would have $|f(x) - g(x) - (L - M)| = |(f(x) - L) + (M - g(x))| \leq |f(x) - L| + |M - g(x)| = |f(x) - L| + |g(x) - M| \leq \epsilon/2 + \epsilon/2 = \epsilon$. Note that the key inequality in this sentence follows from the triangle inequality.

2.7.27

a. Let $\epsilon > 0$ be given. It won't end up mattering what δ is, so let $\delta = 1$. Note that the statement $|f(x) - L| < \epsilon$ amounts to $|c - c| < \epsilon$, which is true for any positive number ϵ, without any restrictions on x. So $\lim_{x \to a} c = c$.

b. Let $\epsilon > 0$ be given. Let $\delta = \epsilon$. Note that the statement $|f(x) - L| < \epsilon$ has the form $|x - a| < \epsilon$, which follows whenever $0 < |x - a| < \delta$ (because $\delta = \epsilon$). Thus $\lim_{x \to a} x = a$.

2.7.29 Let $N > 0$ be given. Let $\delta = 1/\sqrt{N}$. Then if $0 < |x - 4| < \delta$, we have $|x - 4| < 1/\sqrt{N}$. Taking the reciprocal of both sides, we have $\frac{1}{|x-4|} > \sqrt{N}$, and squaring both sides of this inequality yields $\frac{1}{(x-4)^2} > N$. Thus $\lim_{x \to 4} f(x) = \infty$.

2.7.31 Let $N > 1$ be given. Let $\delta = 1/\sqrt{N-1}$. Suppose that $0 < |x - 0| < \delta$. Then $|x| < 1/\sqrt{N-1}$, and taking the reciprocal of both sides, we see that $1/|x| > \sqrt{N-1}$. Then squaring both sides yields $\frac{1}{x^2} > N-1$, so $\frac{1}{x^2} + 1 > N$. Thus $\lim_{x \to 0} f(x) = \infty$.

2.7.33

a. False. In fact, if the statement is true for a specific value of δ_1, then it would be true for any value of $\delta < \delta_1$. This is because if $0 < |x - a| < \delta$, it would automatically follow that $0 < |x - a| < \delta_1$.

b. False. This statement is not equivalent to the definition – note that it says "for an arbitrary δ there exists an ϵ" rather than "for an arbitrary ϵ there exists a δ."

c. True. This is the definition of $\lim_{x \to a} f(x) = L$.

d. True. Both inequalities describe the set of x's which are within δ units of a.

2.7.35 Assume $|x - 3| < 1$, as indicated in the hint. Then $2 < x < 4$, so $\frac{1}{4} < \frac{1}{x} < \frac{1}{2}$, and thus $\left|\frac{1}{x}\right| < \frac{1}{2}$.

Also note that the expression $\left|\frac{1}{x} - \frac{1}{3}\right|$ can be written as $\left|\frac{x-3}{3x}\right|$.

Now let $\epsilon > 0$ be given. Let $\delta = \min(6\epsilon, 1)$. Now assume that $0 < |x - 3| < \delta$. Then

$$|f(x) - L| = \left|\frac{x-3}{3x}\right| < \left|\frac{x-3}{6}\right| < \frac{6\epsilon}{6} = \epsilon.$$

Thus we have established that $\left|\frac{1}{x} - \frac{1}{3}\right| < \epsilon$ whenever $0 < |x - 3| < \delta$.

2.7.37 Assume $|x - (1/10)| < (1/20)$, as indicated in the hint. Then $1/20 < x < 3/20$, so $\frac{20}{3} < \frac{1}{x} < \frac{20}{1}$, and thus $\left|\frac{1}{x}\right| < 20$.

Also note that the expression $\left|\frac{1}{x} - 10\right|$ can be written as $\left|\frac{10x-1}{x}\right|$.

Let $\epsilon > 0$ be given. Let $\delta = \min(\epsilon/200, 1/20)$. Now assume that $0 < |x - (1/10)| < \delta$. Then

$$|f(x) - L| = \left|\frac{10x-1}{x}\right| < |(10x - 1) \cdot 20|$$

$$\leq |x - (1/10)| \cdot 200 < \frac{\epsilon}{200} \cdot 200 = \epsilon.$$

Thus we have established that $\left|\frac{1}{x} - 10\right| < \epsilon$ whenever $0 < |x - (1/10)| < \delta$.

2.7.39 Because we are approaching a from the right, we are only considering values of x which are close to, but a little larger than a. The numbers x to the right of a which are within δ units of a satisfy $0 < x - a < \delta$.

2.7.41

a. Let $\epsilon > 0$ be given. let $\delta = \epsilon/2$. Suppose that $0 < x < \delta$. Then $0 < x < \epsilon/2$ and

$$|f(x) - L| = |2x - 4 - (-4)| = |2x| = 2|x|$$
$$= 2x < \epsilon.$$

b. Let $\epsilon > 0$ be given. let $\delta = \epsilon/3$. Suppose that $0 < 0 - x < \delta$. Then $-\delta < x < 0$ and $-\epsilon/3 < x < 0$, so $\epsilon > -3x$. We have

$$|f(x) - L| = |3x - 4 - (-4)| = |3x| = 3|x|$$
$$= -3x < \epsilon.$$

c. Let $\epsilon > 0$ be given. Let $\delta = \epsilon/3$. Because $\epsilon/3 < \epsilon/2$, we can argue that $|f(x) - L| < \epsilon$ whenever $0 < |x| < \delta$ exactly as in the previous two parts of this problem.

2.7.43 Let $\epsilon > 0$ be given, and let $\delta = \epsilon^2$. Suppose that $0 < x < \delta$, which means that $x < \epsilon^2$, so that $\sqrt{x} < \epsilon$. Then we have

$$|f(x) - L| = |\sqrt{x} - 0| = \sqrt{x} < \epsilon.$$

as desired.

2.7.45

a. We say that $\lim\limits_{x \to a^+} f(x) = \infty$ if for each positive number N, there exists $\delta > 0$ such that

$$f(x) > N \quad \text{whenever} \quad a < x < a + \delta.$$

b. We say that $\lim\limits_{x \to a^-} f(x) = -\infty$ if for each negative number N, there exists $\delta > 0$ such that

$$f(x) < N \quad \text{whenever} \quad a - \delta < x < a.$$

c. We say that $\lim\limits_{x \to a^-} f(x) = \infty$ if for each positive number N, there exists $\delta > 0$ such that

$$f(x) > N \quad \text{whenever} \quad a - \delta < x < a.$$

2.7.47 Let $N > 0$ be given. Let $\delta = 1/N$, and suppose that $1 - \delta < x < 1$. Then $\frac{N-1}{N} < x < 1$, so $\frac{1-N}{N} > -x > -1$, and therefore $1 + \frac{1-N}{N} > 1 - x > 0$, which can be written as $\frac{1}{N} > 1 - x > 0$. Taking reciprocals yields the inequality $N < \frac{1}{1-x}$, as desired.

2.7.49 Let $M < 0$ be given. Let $\delta = \sqrt[4]{-10/M}$. Suppose that $0 < |x + 2| < \delta$. Then $(x+2)^4 < -10/M$, so $\frac{1}{(x+2)^4} > \frac{M}{-10}$, and $\frac{-10}{(x+2)^4} < M$, as desired.

2.7.51 Let $\epsilon > 0$ be given. Let $N = 1/\epsilon$. Suppose that $x > N$. Then $\frac{1}{x} < \epsilon$, and so $|f(x) - L| = |2 + \frac{1}{x} - 2| < \epsilon$.

2.7.53 Let $M > 0$ be given. Let $N = M - 1$. Suppose that $x > N$. Then $x > M - 1$, so $x + 1 > M$, and thus $\frac{x^2 + x}{x} > M$, as desired.

2.7.55 Let $\epsilon > 0$ be given. Let $N = \lfloor (1/\epsilon) \rfloor + 1$. By assumption, there exists an integer $M > 0$ so that $|f(x) - L| < 1/N$ whenever $|x - a| < 1/M$. Let $\delta = 1/M$.

Now assume $0 < |x - a| < \delta$. Then $|x - a| < 1/M$, and thus $|f(x) - L| < 1/N$. But then

$$|f(x) - L| < \frac{1}{\lfloor (1/\epsilon) \rfloor + 1} < \epsilon,$$

as desired.

2.7.57 Let $f(x) = \frac{|x|}{x}$ and suppose $\lim_{x \to 0} f(x)$ does exist and is equal to L. Let $\epsilon = 1/2$. There must be a value of δ so that when $0 < |x| < \delta$, $|f(x) - L| < 1/2$. Now consider the numbers $\delta/3$ and $-\delta/3$, both of which are within δ of 0. We have $f(\delta/3) = 1$ and $f(-\delta/3) = -1$. However, it is impossible for both $|1 - L| < 1/2$ and $|-1 - L| < 1/2$, because the former implies that $1/2 < L < 3/2$ and the latter implies that $-3/2 < L < -1/2$. Thus $\lim_{x \to 0} f(x)$ does not exist.

2.7.59 Because f is continuous at a, we know that $\lim_{x \to a} f(x)$ exists and is equal to $f(a) > 0$. Let $\epsilon = f(a)/3$. Then there is a number $\delta > 0$ so that $|f(x) - f(a)| < f(a)/3$ whenever $|x - a| < \delta$. Then whenever x lies in the interval $(a - \delta, a + \delta)$ we have $-f(a)/3 \le f(x) - f(a) \le f(a)/3$, so $2f(a)/3 \le f(x) \le 4f(a)/3$, so f is positive in this interval.

Chapter Two Review

1

    a. False. Because $\lim_{x \to 1} \dfrac{x - 1}{x^2 - 1} = \lim_{x \to 1} \dfrac{1}{x + 1} = \dfrac{1}{2}$, f doesn't have a vertical asymptote at $x = 1$.

    b. False. In general, these methods are too imprecise to produce accurate results.

    c. False. For example, the function $f(x) = \begin{cases} 2x & \text{if } x < 0; \\ 1 & \text{if } x = 0; \\ 4x & \text{if } x > 0 \end{cases}$ has a limit of 0 as $x \to 0$, but $f(0) = 1$.

    d. True. When we say that a limit exists, we are saying that there is a real number L that the function is approaching. If the limit of the function is ∞, it is still the case that there is no real number that the function is approaching. (There is no real number called "infinity.")

    e. False. It could be the case that $\lim_{x \to a^-} f(x) = 1$ and $\lim_{x \to a^+} f(x) = 2$.

    f. False.

    g. False. For example, the function $f(x) = \begin{cases} 2 & \text{if } 0 < x < 1; \\ 3 & \text{if } 1 \le x < 2, \end{cases}$ is continuous on $(0, 1)$, and on $[1, 2)$, but isn't continuous on $(0, 2)$.

    h. True. $\lim_{x \to a} f(x) = f(a)$ if and only if f is continuous at a.

3 This function is discontinuous at $x = -1$, at $x = 1$, and at $x = 3$. At $x = -1$ it is discontinuous because $\lim_{x \to -1} f(x)$ does not exist. At $x = 1$, it is discontinuous because $\lim_{x \to 1} f(x) \ne f(1)$. At $x = 3$, it is discontinuous because $f(3)$ does not exist, and because $\lim_{x \to 3} f(x)$ does not exist.

5

    a.

x	$.9\pi/4$	$.99\pi/4$	$.999\pi/4$	$.9999\pi/4$
$f(x)$	1.4098	1.4142	1.4142	1.4142

x	$1.1\pi/4$	$1.01\pi/4$	$1.001\pi/4$	$1.0001\pi/4$
$f(x)$	1.4098	1.4142	1.4142	1.4142

The limit appears to be approximately 1.4142.

b. $\lim\limits_{x\to\pi/4} \dfrac{\cos 2x}{\cos x - \sin x} = \lim\limits_{x\to\pi/4} \dfrac{\cos^2 x - \sin^2 x}{\cos x - \sin x} = \lim\limits_{x\to\pi/4} (\cos x + \sin x) = \sqrt{2}.$

7

There are infinitely many different correct functions which you could draw. One of them is:

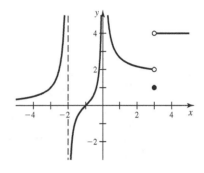

9 $\lim\limits_{x\to 1} \sqrt{5x + 6} = \sqrt{11}.$

11 $\lim\limits_{x\to 1} \dfrac{x^3 - 7x^2 + 12x}{4 - x} = \dfrac{1 - 7 + 12}{4 - 1} = \dfrac{6}{3} = 2.$

13 $\lim\limits_{x\to 1} \dfrac{1 - x^2}{x^2 - 8x + 7} = \lim\limits_{x\to 1} \dfrac{(1 - x)(1 + x)}{(x - 7)(x - 1)} = \lim\limits_{x\to 1} \dfrac{-(x + 1)}{x - 7} = \dfrac{1}{3}.$

15

$$
\begin{aligned}
\lim_{x\to 3} \frac{1}{x - 3}\left(\frac{1}{\sqrt{x + 1}} - \frac{1}{2}\right) &= \lim_{x\to 3} \frac{2 - \sqrt{x + 1}}{2(x - 3)\sqrt{x + 1}} \cdot \frac{(2 + \sqrt{x + 1})}{(2 + \sqrt{x + 1})} \\
&= \lim_{x\to 3} \frac{4 - (x + 1)}{2(x - 3)(\sqrt{x + 1})(2 + \sqrt{x + 1})} \\
&= \lim_{x\to 3} \frac{-(x - 3)}{2(x - 3)(\sqrt{x + 1})(2 + \sqrt{x + 1})} \\
&= \lim_{x\to 3} -\frac{1}{2\sqrt{x + 1}(2 + \sqrt{x + 1})} = -\frac{1}{16}.
\end{aligned}
$$

17 $\lim\limits_{x\to 3} \dfrac{x^4 - 81}{x - 3} = \lim\limits_{x\to 3} \dfrac{(x - 3)(x + 3)(x^2 + 9)}{x - 3} = \lim\limits_{x\to 3} (x + 3)(x^2 + 9) = 108.$

19 $\lim\limits_{x\to 81} \dfrac{\sqrt[4]{x} - 3}{x - 81} = \lim\limits_{x\to 81} \dfrac{\sqrt[4]{x} - 3}{(\sqrt{x} + 9)(\sqrt[4]{x} + 3)(\sqrt[4]{x} - 3)} = \lim\limits_{x\to 81} \dfrac{1}{(\sqrt{x} + 9)(\sqrt[4]{x} + 3)} = \dfrac{1}{108}.$

21 $\lim\limits_{x\to\pi/2} \dfrac{\frac{1}{\sqrt{\sin x}} - 1}{x + \pi/2} = \dfrac{0}{\pi} = 0.$

23

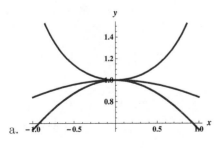

a.

b. Because $\lim\limits_{x\to 0} \cos x = \lim\limits_{x\to 0} \dfrac{1}{\cos x} = 1$, the squeeze theorem assures us that $\lim\limits_{x\to 0} \dfrac{\sin x}{x} = 1$ as well.

25 $\displaystyle\lim_{x\to 5} \frac{x-7}{x(x-5)^2} = -\infty.$

27 $\displaystyle\lim_{x\to 3^-} \frac{x-4}{x^2-3x} = \lim_{x\to 3^-} \frac{x-4}{x(x-3)} = \infty.$

29 $\displaystyle\lim_{x\to 0^-} \frac{2}{\tan x} = -\infty.$

31 $\displaystyle\lim_{x\to\infty} \frac{2x-3}{4x+10} = \lim_{x\to\infty} \frac{2-(3/x)}{4+(10/x)} = \frac{2}{4} = \frac{1}{2}.$

33 $\displaystyle\lim_{x\to -\infty} (-3x^3+5) = \infty.$

35 $\displaystyle\lim_{x\to\infty} (3\tan^{-1} x + 2) = \frac{3\pi}{2} + 2.$

37 $\displaystyle\lim_{x\to\infty} \frac{4x^3+1}{1-x^3} = \lim_{x\to\infty} \frac{4+(1/x^3)}{(1/x^3)-1} = \frac{4+0}{0-1} = -4.$ A similar result holds as $x\to -\infty$. Thus, $y=-4$ is a horizontal asymptote as $x\to\infty$ and as $x\to -\infty$.

39 $\displaystyle\lim_{x\to\infty} (1-e^{-2x}) = 1$, while $\displaystyle\lim_{x\to -\infty} (1-e^{-2x}) = -\infty$.
$y=1$ is a horizontal asymptote as $x\to\infty$.

41 Recall that $\tan^{-1} x = 0$ only for $x=0$. The only vertical asymptote is $x=0$.
$\displaystyle\lim_{x\to\infty} \frac{1}{\tan^{-1} x} = \frac{1}{\pi/2} = \frac{2}{\pi}.$
$\displaystyle\lim_{x\to -\infty} \frac{1}{\tan^{-1} x} = \frac{1}{-\pi/2} = -\frac{2}{\pi}.$ So $y=\frac{2}{\pi}$ is a horizontal asymptote as $x\to\infty$ and $y=-\frac{2}{\pi}$ is a horizontal asymptote as $x\to -\infty$.

43 $\displaystyle\lim_{x\to\infty} \frac{3x^2+2x-1}{4x+1} = \lim_{x\to\infty} \frac{3x^2+2x-1}{4x+1}\cdot\frac{1/x}{1/x} = \lim_{x\to\infty} \frac{3x+2-1/x}{4+1/x} = \infty.$
$\displaystyle\lim_{x\to -\infty} \frac{3x^2+2x-1}{4x+1} = \lim_{x\to -\infty} \frac{3x^2+2x-1}{4x+1}\cdot\frac{1/x}{1/x} = \lim_{x\to -\infty} \frac{3x+2-1/x}{4+1/x} = -\infty.$
By long division, we can write $f(x)$ as $f(x) = \frac{3x}{4} + \frac{5}{16} + \frac{-21/16}{4x+1}$, so the line $y = \frac{3x}{4} + \frac{5}{16}$ is the slant asymptote.

45 $\displaystyle\lim_{x\to\infty} \frac{1+x-2x^2-x^3}{x^2+1} = \lim_{x\to\infty} \frac{1+x-2x^2-x^3}{x^2+1}\cdot\frac{1/x^2}{1/x^2} = \lim_{x\to\infty} \frac{1/x^2+1/x-2-x}{1+1/x^2} = -\infty.$
$\displaystyle\lim_{x\to -\infty} \frac{1+x-2x^2-x^3}{x^2+1} = \lim_{x\to -\infty} \frac{1+x-2x^2-x^3}{x^2+1}\cdot\frac{1/x^2}{1/x^2} = \lim_{x\to -\infty} \frac{1/x^2+1/x-2-x}{1+1/x^2} = \infty.$
By long division, we can write $f(x)$ as $f(x) = -x-2 + \frac{2x+3}{x^2+1}$, so the line $y=-x-2$ is the slant asymptote.

47 f is discontinuous at 5, because $f(5)$ does not exist, and also because $\displaystyle\lim_{x\to 5} f(x)$ does not exist

49 h is not continuous at 3 because $\displaystyle\lim_{x\to 3^-} h(x)$ does not exist, so $\displaystyle\lim_{x\to 3} h(x)$ does not exist.

51 The domain of f is $(-\infty, -\sqrt{5}]$ and $[\sqrt{5}, \infty)$, and f is continuous on that domain.

53 The domain of h is $(-\infty, -5)$, $(-5, 0)$, $(0, 5)$, $(5, \infty)$, and like all rational functions, it is continuous on its domain.

55 In order for g to be left continuous at 1, it is necessary that $\displaystyle\lim_{x\to 1^-} g(x) = g(1)$, which means that $a=3$. In order for g to be right continuous at 1, it is necessary that $\displaystyle\lim_{x\to 1^+} g(x) = g(1)$, which means that $a+b = 3+b = 3$, so $b=0$.

57

One such possible graph is pictured to the right.

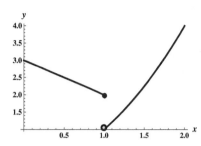

59

a. Note that $m(0) = 0$ and $m(5) \approx 38.34$ and $m(15) \approx 21.2$. Thus, 30 is an intermediate value between both $m(0)$ and $m(5)$, and $m(5)$ and $m(15)$. Note also that m is a continuous function. By the IVT, there must be a number c_1 between 0 and 5 with $m(c_1) = 30$, and a number c_2 between 5 and 15 with $m(c_2) = 30$.

b. A little trial and error leads $c_1 \approx 2.4$ and $c_2 \approx 10.8$.

c. No. The graph of the function on a graphing calculator suggests that it peaks at about 38.5

61 Let $\epsilon > 0$ be given. Let $\delta = \epsilon$. Now suppose that $0 < |x - 5| < \delta$.
Then

$$|f(x) - L| = \left| \frac{x^2 - 25}{x - 5} - 10 \right| = \left| \frac{(x - 5)(x + 5)}{x - 5} - 10 \right| = |x + 5 - 10|$$
$$= |x - 5| < \epsilon.$$

63 Let $N > 0$ be given. Let $\delta = 1/\sqrt[4]{N}$. Suppose that $0 < |x - 2| < \delta$. Then $|x - 2| < \frac{1}{\sqrt[4]{N}}$, so $\frac{1}{|x-2|} > \sqrt[4]{N}$, and $\frac{1}{(x-2)^4} > N$, as desired.

Chapter 3

Derivatives

3.1 Introducing the Derivative

3.1.1 The secant line through the points $(a, f(a))$ and $(x, f(x))$ for x near a, of the graph of f, is given by $m_{\text{sec}} = \frac{f(x)-f(a)}{x-a}$. As x approaches a, we obtain the limit $m_{\text{tan}} = \lim_{x \to a} \frac{f(x) - f(a)}{x - a} = \lim_{x \to a} m_{\text{sec}}$.

3.1.3 The average rate of change of f over $[a, x]$ is the slope of the secant line $m_{\text{sec}} = \frac{f(x)-f(a)}{x-a}$. As x approaches a, the length of the interval $x - a$ goes to zero, and in the limit we obtain the instantaneous rate of change of f at a given by $m_{\text{tan}} = \lim_{x \to a} \frac{f(x) - f(a)}{x - a}$.

3.1.5 $f'(a)$ is the value of the derivative of f at a. Also, $f'(a)$ is the slope of the tangent line to the graph of f at $(a, f(a))$. Furthermore, $f'(a)$ is the instantaneous rate of change of f at a.

3.1.7 $\frac{dy}{dx}$ is the limit of $\frac{\Delta y}{\Delta x}$ and is the rate of change of y with respect to x.

3.1.9

a. $m_{\text{tan}} = \lim_{x \to 3} \frac{x^2 - 5 - 4}{x - 3} = \lim_{x \to 3} \frac{x^2 - 9}{x - 3} =$
$\lim_{x \to 3} \frac{(x - 3)(x + 3)}{x - 3} = \lim_{x \to 3} (x + 3) = 6.$

b. Using the point-slope form of the equation of a line, we obtain $y - 4 = 6(x - 3)$, or $y = 6x - 14$.

c.

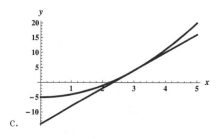

3.1.11

a. $m_{\text{tan}} = \lim_{x \to 1} \frac{-5x + 1 + 4}{x - 1} = \lim_{x \to 1} \frac{-5x + 5}{x - 1} =$
$\lim_{x \to 1} -5 \left(\frac{x - 1}{x - 1} \right) = -5.$

b. Using the point-slope form of the equation of a line, we get $y + 4 = -5(x - 1)$ which equals $y = -5x + 1$, the function itself.

c.

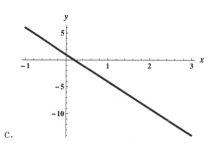

3.1.13

a. $m_{\tan} = \lim\limits_{x \to -1} \dfrac{\frac{1}{x} + 1}{x+1} = \lim\limits_{x \to -1} \dfrac{\frac{1+x}{x}}{x+1} = \lim\limits_{x \to -1} \dfrac{1}{x} = -1.$

b. $y - (-1) = -1(x+1)$, or $y = -x - 2.$

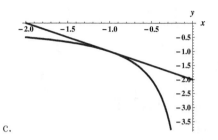

c.

3.1.15

a. $m_{\tan} = \lim\limits_{h \to 0} \dfrac{2(0+h) + 1 - 1}{h} = \lim\limits_{h \to 0} \dfrac{2h}{h} = 2.$

b. $y - 1 = 2x$, or $y = 2x + 1.$

3.1.17

a. $m_{\tan} = \lim\limits_{h \to 0} \dfrac{-7(-1+h) - 7}{h} = \lim\limits_{h \to 0} -\dfrac{7h}{h} = \lim\limits_{h \to 0} -7 = -7.$

b. $y - 7 = -7(x+1)$ or $y = -7x.$

3.1.19

a. $m_{\tan} = \lim\limits_{h \to 0} \dfrac{(2+h)^2 - 4 - 0}{h} = \lim\limits_{h \to 0} \dfrac{4 + 4h + h^2 - 4}{h} = \lim\limits_{h \to 0} (4 + h) = 4.$

b. $y - 0 = 4(x - 2)$, or $y = 4x - 8.$

3.1.21

a. $m_{\tan} = \lim\limits_{h \to 0} \dfrac{(1+h)^3 - 1}{h} = \lim\limits_{h \to 0} \dfrac{1 + 3h + 3h^2 + h^3 - 1}{h} = \lim\limits_{h \to 0} \dfrac{h(3 + 3h + h^2)}{h} = \lim\limits_{h \to 0} (3 + 3h + h^2) = 3.$

b. $y - 1 = 3(x - 1)$, or $y = 3x - 2.$

3.1.23

a. $m_{\tan} = \lim\limits_{h \to 0} \dfrac{\frac{1}{3 - 2(h-1)} - \frac{1}{5}}{h} = \lim\limits_{h \to 0} \dfrac{\frac{5 - (3 - 2h + 2)}{15 - 10(h-1)}}{h} = \lim\limits_{h \to 0} \dfrac{2}{15 - 10(h-1)} = \dfrac{2}{25}.$

b. $y - \frac{1}{5} = \frac{2}{25}(x+1)$, or $y = \frac{2}{25}x + \frac{7}{25}.$

3.1.25

a. $m_{\tan} = \lim\limits_{h \to 0} \dfrac{\sqrt{1+h+3} - 2}{h} = \lim\limits_{h \to 0} \dfrac{\sqrt{4+h} - 2}{h} \cdot \dfrac{\sqrt{4+h} + 2}{\sqrt{4+h} + 2} = \lim\limits_{h \to 0} \dfrac{4 + h - 4}{h(\sqrt{4+h} + 2)} =$

$\lim\limits_{h \to 0} \dfrac{1}{\sqrt{4+h} + 2} = \dfrac{1}{4}.$

b. $y - 2 = \frac{1}{4}(x - 1)$, or $y = \frac{1}{4}x + \frac{7}{4}.$

3.1.27

a. $f'(-3) = \lim\limits_{h \to 0} \dfrac{8(-3+h) + 24}{h} = \lim\limits_{h \to 0} \dfrac{8h}{h} = 8.$

b. $y - (-24) = 8(x+3)$, or $y = 8x.$

3.1.29

a. $f'(-2) = \lim\limits_{h \to 0} \dfrac{4(-2+h)^2 + 2(-2+h) - 12}{h} = \lim\limits_{h \to 0} \dfrac{16 - 16h + 4h^2 - 4 + 2h - 12}{h} =$
$\lim\limits_{h \to 0} \dfrac{-14h + 4h^2}{h} = -14.$

b. $y - 12 = -14(x+2)$, or $y = -14x - 16$.

3.1.31

a. $f'\left(\dfrac{1}{4}\right) = \lim\limits_{h \to 0} \dfrac{\frac{1}{\sqrt{\frac{1}{4}+h}} - 2}{h} = \lim\limits_{h \to 0} \dfrac{1 - 2\sqrt{\frac{1}{4}+h}}{h\sqrt{\frac{1}{4}+h}} = \lim\limits_{h \to 0} \dfrac{\left(1 - 2\sqrt{\frac{1}{4}+h}\right)\left(1 + 2\sqrt{\frac{1}{4}+h}\right)}{h\sqrt{\frac{1}{4}+h}\left(1 + 2\sqrt{\frac{1}{4}+h}\right)} =$
$\lim\limits_{h \to 0} \dfrac{1 - 4\left(\frac{1}{4}+h\right)}{h\sqrt{\frac{1}{4}+h}\left(1 + 2\sqrt{\frac{1}{4}+h}\right)} = \lim\limits_{h \to 0} -\dfrac{4}{\sqrt{\frac{1}{4}+h}\left(1 + 2\sqrt{\frac{1}{4}+h}\right)} = -4.$

b. $y - 2 = -4\left(x - \dfrac{1}{4}\right)$, or $y = -4x + 3$.

3.1.33

a. $f'(4) = \lim\limits_{h \to 0} \dfrac{\sqrt{2(4+h)+1} - 3}{h} = \lim\limits_{h \to 0} \dfrac{\sqrt{9+2h} - 3}{h} \cdot \dfrac{\sqrt{9+2h} + 3}{\sqrt{9+2h} + 3} = \lim\limits_{h \to 0} \dfrac{9 + 2h - 9}{h(\sqrt{9+2h} + 3)} =$
$\lim\limits_{h \to 0} \dfrac{2}{\sqrt{9+2h} + 3} = \dfrac{1}{3}.$

b. $y - 3 = \dfrac{1}{3}(x-4)$, or $y = \dfrac{1}{3}x + \dfrac{5}{3}$.

3.1.35

a. $f'(5) = \lim\limits_{h \to 0} \dfrac{\frac{1}{5+h+5} - \frac{1}{10}}{h} = \lim\limits_{h \to 0} \dfrac{10 - (10+h)}{10h(10+h)} = \lim\limits_{h \to 0} \dfrac{-1}{10(10+h)} = -\dfrac{1}{100}.$

b. $y - \dfrac{1}{10} = -\dfrac{1}{100}(x-5)$, or $y = -\dfrac{1}{100}x + \dfrac{3}{20}$.

3.1.37

a.

$$f'(x) = \lim\limits_{h \to 0} \dfrac{3(x+h)^2 + 2(x+h) - 10 - (3x^2 + 2x - 10)}{h}$$
$$= \lim\limits_{h \to 0} \dfrac{3x^2 + 6xh + 3h^2 + 2x + 2h - 10 - 3x^2 - 2x + 10}{h}$$
$$= \lim\limits_{h \to 0} \dfrac{6xh + 2h + 3h^2}{h} = \lim\limits_{h \to 0} (6x + 2 + 3h) = 6x + 2.$$

b. We have $f'(1) = 8$, and the tangent line is given by $y + 5 = 8(x-1)$, or $y = 8x - 13$.

c.

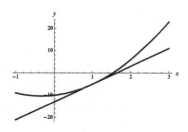

3.1.39

a. $f'(x) = \lim_{h \to 0} \dfrac{5(x+h)^2 - 6(x+h) + 1 - (5x^2 - 6x + 1)}{h} =$

$\lim_{h \to 0} \dfrac{5x^2 + 10xh + 5h^2 - 6x - 6h - 5x^2 + 6x}{h} = \lim_{h \to 0} \dfrac{10xh + 5h^2 - 6h}{h} = \lim_{h \to 0} (10x + 5h - 6) = 10x - 6.$

b. We have $f'(2) = 14$, so the tangent line is given by $y - 9 = 14(x - 2)$, or $y = 14x - 19$.

c.

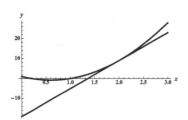

3.1.41

a. $\dfrac{d}{dx}\left(ax^2 + bx + c\right) =$

$\lim_{h \to 0} \dfrac{a(x+h)^2 + b(x+h) + c - \left(ax^2 + bx + c\right)}{h} = \lim_{h \to 0} \dfrac{ax^2 + 2axh + ah^2 + bx + bh + c - ax^2 - bx - c}{h}$

$= \lim_{h \to 0} \dfrac{2axh + ah^2 + bh}{h} = \lim_{h \to 0} (2ax + ah + b) = 2ax + b.$

b. With $a = 4, b = -3, c = 10$ we have $\dfrac{d}{dx}(4x^2 - 3x + 10) = 2 \cdot 4 \cdot x + (-3) = 8x - 3.$

c. From part (b), $f'(1) = 8 \cdot 1 - 3 = 5.$

3.1.43 $m_{\tan} = \lim_{h \to 0} \dfrac{\frac{1}{1+h+1} - \frac{1}{2}}{h} = \lim_{h \to 0} \dfrac{2 - (2+h)}{h(2+h)2} = \lim_{h \to 0} \dfrac{-1}{(2+h)2} = -\dfrac{1}{4}.$

3.1.45 $m_{\tan} = \lim_{h \to 0} \dfrac{2\sqrt{25+h} - 1 - (2\sqrt{25} - 1)}{h} = \lim_{h \to 0} \dfrac{2(\sqrt{25+h} - \sqrt{25})}{h} =$

$\lim_{h \to 0} \dfrac{2(\sqrt{25+h} - \sqrt{25})(\sqrt{25+h} + \sqrt{25})}{h(\sqrt{25+h} + \sqrt{25})} = \lim_{h \to 0} \dfrac{2(25+h-25)}{h(\sqrt{25+h} + \sqrt{25})} = \lim_{h \to 0} \dfrac{2}{\sqrt{25+h} + \sqrt{25}} = \dfrac{1}{5}.$

3.1.47

a. True. Because the graph is a line, any secant line has the same graph as the function and thus the same slope.

b. False. For example, take $f(x) = x^2$, $P = (0,0)$ and $Q = (1,1)$. Then the secant line has slope $m_{\sec} = \frac{1-0}{1-0} = 1$, but the the graph has a horizontal tangent at P so $m_{\tan} = 0$ and $m_{\sec} > m_{\tan}.$

c. True. $m_{\sec} = \dfrac{(x+h)^2 - x^2}{h} = \dfrac{2xh + h^2}{h} = 2x + h$, while $m_{\tan} = \lim_{h \to 0} (2x + h) = 2x.$ Because we assume that $h > 0$, we have $m_{\sec} = 2x + h > 2x = m_{\tan}.$

3.1.49

a.

$$f'(x) = \lim_{h \to 0} \dfrac{\sqrt{3(x+h) + 1} - \sqrt{3x+1}}{h}$$

$$= \lim_{h \to 0} \dfrac{\sqrt{3(x+h) + 1} - \sqrt{3x+1}}{h} \cdot \dfrac{\sqrt{3x + 3h + 1} + \sqrt{3x+1}}{\sqrt{3x + 3h + 1} + \sqrt{3x+1}}$$

$$= \lim_{h \to 0} \dfrac{3x + 3h + 1 - 3x - 1}{h(\sqrt{3x + 3h + 1} + \sqrt{3x+1})} = \lim_{h \to 0} \dfrac{3}{\sqrt{3x + 3h + 1} + \sqrt{3x+1}} = \dfrac{3}{2\sqrt{3x+1}}.$$

b. We have $f'(8) = \frac{3}{10}$. Using the point-slope form, we get that the tangent line has equation $y - 5 = \frac{3}{10}(x - 8)$, which can be written as $y = \frac{3}{10}x + \frac{13}{5}$.

3.1.51

a. $f'(x) = \lim\limits_{h \to 0} \dfrac{\frac{2}{3(x+h)+1} - \frac{2}{3x+1}}{h} = \lim\limits_{h \to 0} \dfrac{6x + 2 - (6x + 6h + 2)}{h(3x+1)(3x+3h+1)} = \lim\limits_{h \to 0} \dfrac{-6h}{h(3x+1)(3x+3h+1)} =$
$-\dfrac{6}{(3x+1)^2}$.

b. We have $f'(-1) = -\frac{3}{2}$. Using the point-slope form, we get that the tangent line has equation $y + 1 = -\frac{3}{2}(x+1)$, which can be written as $y = -\frac{3}{2}x - \frac{5}{2}$.

3.1.53

a. At C and D, the slope of the tangent line (and thus of the curve) is negative.

b. At A, B, and E, the slope of the curve is positive.

c. The graph is in its steepest ascent at A followed by B. At E it barely increases, at D it slightly decreases and at C it is decreasing the most, so the points in decreasing order of slope are A, B, E, D, C.

3.1.55

a. From the graph we approximate the derivative by the slope of a secant line: For example we see that $E(6) = 250$ kWh and $E(18) = 350$ kWh, so the power after 10 hours is approximately the slope of the secant line through these points, so $P(10) \approx m_{sec} = \frac{E(18) - E(6)}{18 - 6} = \frac{350\,\text{kWh} - 250\,\text{kWh}}{12\text{h}} \approx 8.3$ kW. Similarly, after 20 hours, using 18 hours and 25 hours, that $P(20) \approx m_{sec} = \frac{E(22) - E(18)}{22 - 18} = \frac{325\,\text{kWh} - 350\,\text{kWh}}{4\text{h}} \approx -6.25$kW.

b. The power is zero where the graph of $E(t)$ has a horizontal tangent line, which happens approximately at $t = 6$ hours and $t = 18$ hours.

c. The power has a maximum where the graph of $E(t)$ has the steepest increase, which is approximately at $t = 12$ hours.

3.1.57 Consider $a = 2$ and $f(x) = \frac{1}{x+1}$.

Then $f'(2) = \lim\limits_{x \to 2} \dfrac{\frac{1}{x+1} - \frac{1}{3}}{x - 2}$ as desired.

We have $f'(2) = \lim\limits_{x \to 2} \dfrac{\frac{1}{x+1} - \frac{1}{3}}{x - 2} = \lim\limits_{x \to 2} \dfrac{3 - (x+1)}{(x-2)3(x+1)} = \lim\limits_{x \to 2} \dfrac{-(x-2)}{(x-2)3(x+1)} = \lim\limits_{x \to 2} \dfrac{-1}{3(x+1)} = -\dfrac{1}{9}$.

3.1.59 Consider $a = 2$ and $f(x) = x^4$.

Then $f'(2) = \lim\limits_{h \to 0} \dfrac{(2+h)^4 - 16}{h}$ as desired.

We have

$$f'(2) = \lim_{h \to 0} \frac{(2+h)^4 - 16}{h} = \lim_{h \to 0} \frac{16 + 32h + 24h^2 + 8h^3 + h^4 - 16}{h}$$
$$= \lim_{h \to 0} \frac{h\left(32 + 24h + 8h^2 + h^3\right)}{h} = \lim_{h \to 0} \left(32 + 24h + 8h^2 + h^3\right) = 32.$$

3.1.61 It is not differentiable at $x = 2$. The denominator of f is zero when $x = 2$, so f is not defined at $x = 2$, and is therefore not differentiable there.

3.1.63 In order for f to be differentiable at $x = 1$, it would need to be continuous there. Thus, $\lim\limits_{x \to 1^-} f(x) =$
$\lim\limits_{x \to 1^-} 2x^2 = 2 = \lim\limits_{x \to 1^+} f(x) = \lim\limits_{x \to 1^+} ax - 2 = a - 2$, so the only possible value for a is 4. Now checking the differentiability at 1, we have (from the left)

$$\lim_{x \to 1^-} \frac{f(x) - f(1)}{x - 1} = \lim_{x \to 1^-} \frac{2x^2 - 2}{x - 1} = \lim_{x \to 1^-} 2(x + 1) = 4.$$

Also, from the right we have

$$\lim_{x \to 1^+} \frac{f(x) - f(1)}{x - 1} = \lim_{x \to 1^+} \frac{4x - 2 - 2}{x - 1} = \lim_{x \to 1^+} 4 = 4,$$

so f is differentiable at 1 for $a = 4$.

3.1.65

a. Note that the slope generated by the centered difference quotient is $\frac{f(4.5) - f(3.5)}{2(.5)} = \sqrt{4.5} - \sqrt{3.5} \approx$ 0.250492. The centered difference quotient line is very close to the tangent line, which closely approximates the function near the point of tangency.

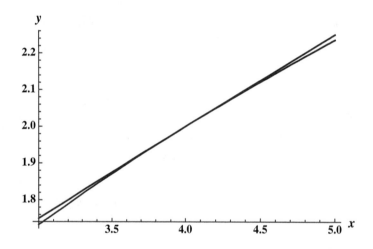

b.

h	Approximation	Error
0.1	0.25002	2.0×10^{-5}
0.01	$\approx .25000$	2.0×10^{-7}
0.001	$\approx .25000$	2.0×10^{-9}

c. The centered difference quotient is symmetric about zero, so using the corresponding negative values yields the same results.

d. The centered difference quotient appears to be more accurate than the approximation in the previous problem.

3.1.67

a. Forward:

$$\frac{\text{erf}(1.05) - \text{erf}(1)}{.05} = \frac{.862436 - .842701}{.05} = 0.3947.$$

Centered:

$$\frac{\text{erf}(1.05) - \text{erf}(.95)}{2(.05)} = \frac{.862436 - .820891}{0.1} = 0.41545.$$

b. Forward:
$$0.3947 - \frac{2}{e\sqrt{\pi}} \approx -0.0204075.$$

Centered:
$$0.41545 - \frac{2}{e\sqrt{\pi}} \approx 0.000342503.$$

3.2 Working with Derivatives

3.2.1 $f(x)$ refers to the value of the function at x, while $f'(x)$ refers to the slope of the graph. If the function is positive and increasing, such as $f(x) = x^2$ for $x = 2$, then $f(x) > 0$ and $f'(x) > 0$. But if the function is positive and decreasing, such as $f(x) = x^2$ for $x = -2$, then $f(x) > 0$ and $f'(x) < 0$.

3.2.3 Yes, differentiable functions are continuous by Theorem 3.1.

3.2.5

The function f is not differentiable at $x = -2, 0, 2$, so f' is not defined at those points. Elsewhere, the slope is constant.

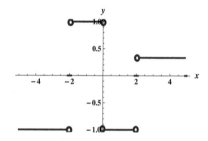

3.2.7 (c) is the only line with negative slope, so it corresponds to derivative (A). Since (d) contains the points $(2, 0)$ and $(0, 1)$, it has slope $\frac{1}{2}$, so it corresponds to derivative (B). Finally, lines (a) and (b) are parallel; since (b) contains the points $(0, 1)$ and $(-1, 0)$, it has slope 1, so that (a) has slope 1 as well. They both correspond to derivative (C).

3.2.9

a. The function has non-negative slope everywhere, and as there is a horizontal tangent at $x = 0$, so the derivative has to be zero at zero. The graph of the derivative has to be above the x-axis and touching it at $x = 0$, so (D) is the graph of the derivative.

b. The graph of this function has three horizontal tangent lines, at $x = -1, 0, 1$, and the matching graph of the derivative with three zeros is (C).

c. The function has negative slope on $(-1, 0)$, and positive slope on $(0, 1)$ and has a horizontal tangent at $x = 0$, so the derivative has to be negative on $(-1, 0)$, positive on $(0, 1)$ and zero at $x = 0$; the graph is (B).

d. The function has negative slope everywhere so the graph of the derivative has to be negative everywhere, which is graph (A).

3.2.11

The function always has non-negative slope, so the derivative is never below the x axis.
However, it does have slope zero at about $x = 2$.

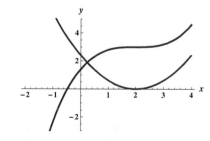

3.2.13 Note that f is undefined at $x = -2$ and $x = 1$, but is differentiable elsewhere. It is decreasing, and increasingly rapidly, as x increases towards $x = -2$. It decreases, but increasingly slowly, and towards a zero slope, as x increases from 1. Finally, between $x = -2$ and $x = 1$, the function increases, but increasingly slowly, until $x = 0$ and then decreases, but increasingly rapidly, as x approaches 1. A graph of the derivative is

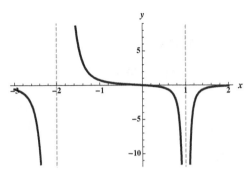

3.2.15

    a. The function f is not continuous at $x = 1$, because the graph has a jump there.

    b. The function f is not differentiable at $x = 1$ because it is not continuous at that point (Theorem 3.1 Alternate Version), and it is also not differentiable at $x = 2$ because the graph has a corner there.

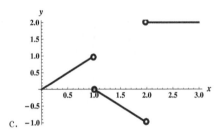

c.

3.2.17

    a. True. Differentiability implies continuity, by Theorem 3.1.

    b. True. Because the absolute value function is continuous, and $y = x + 1$ is continuous, and the composition of continuous functions is continuous, we know that this function is continuous. Note that it is not differentiable at $x = -1$ because the absolute value function is not differentiable at $x = 0$.

    c. False. In order for f to be differentiable on $[a, b]$, f would need to be defined at a and at b. Because the domain of f doesn't include these endpoints, this situation is not possible.

3.2.19

Because $f'(x) = x$ is negative for $x < 0$ and positive for $x > 0$, we have that the graph of f has to have negative slope on $(-\infty, 0)$ and positive slope on $(0, \infty)$ and has to have a horizontal tangent at $x = 0$. Because f' only gives us the slope of the tangent line and not the actual value of f, there are infinitely many graphs possible, they all have the same shape, but are shifted along the $y-$axis.

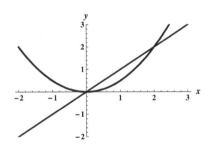

3.2.21 With $f(x) = 3x - 4$, we have

$$f'(x) = \lim_{h \to 0} \frac{f(x+h) - f(x)}{h} = \lim_{h \to 0} \frac{3(x+h) - 4 - (3x - 4)}{h} = \lim_{h \to 0} \frac{3h}{h} = \lim_{h \to 0} 3 = 3.$$

The slope of the tangent line at $(1, -1)$ is 3, so the slope of the normal line is $-\frac{1}{3}$. The equation of the normal line is thus $y - (-1) = -\frac{1}{3}(x - 1)$, or $y = -\frac{1}{3}x - \frac{2}{3}$.

3.2.23 With $f(x) = \frac{2}{x}$, we have $f'(x) = \lim\limits_{h\to 0} \dfrac{f(x+h) - f(x)}{h} = \lim\limits_{h\to 0} \dfrac{\frac{2}{x+h} - \frac{2}{x}}{h} = \lim\limits_{h\to 0} \dfrac{\frac{2x - (2(x+h))}{x(x+h)}}{h} =$
$\lim\limits_{h\to 0} \dfrac{-2h}{hx(x+h)} = \lim\limits_{h\to 0} \dfrac{-2}{x(x+h)} = -\dfrac{2}{x^2}$. At the point $(1,2)$ the slope of the tangent line is -2, so the slope of the normal line is $\frac{1}{2}$. The equation of the normal line is $y - 2 = \frac{1}{2}(x - 1)$ or $y = \frac{x}{2} + \frac{3}{2}$.

3.2.25 With $f(x) = x^2 + 1$, we have $f'(x) = \lim\limits_{h\to 0} \dfrac{f(x+h) - f(x)}{h} = \lim\limits_{h\to 0} \dfrac{(x+h)^2 + 1 - (x^2 + 1)}{h} =$
$\lim\limits_{h\to 0} \dfrac{x^2 + 2hx + h^2 + 1 - x^2 - 1}{h} = \lim\limits_{h\to 0} \dfrac{2hx + h^2}{h} = \lim\limits_{h\to 0} \dfrac{h(2x + h)}{h} = 2x$. We are looking for points $(x, x^2 + 1)$ where the slope of the line between this point and $Q(3, 6)$ is equal to $2x$. So we seek solutions to the equation

$$\frac{6 - (x^2 + 1)}{3 - x} = 2x,$$

which can be written as $5 - x^2 = 2x(3 - x)$, or $x^2 - 6x + 5 = 0$. Factoring, we obtain $(x - 5)(x - 1) = 0$, so the solutions are $x = 5$ and $x = 1$. Note that at the point $(5, 26)$ on the curve the tangent line is $y - 26 = 10(x - 5)$ which does contain the point $Q(3, 6)$ and at the point $(1, 2)$ the equation of the tangent line is $y - 2 = 2(x - 1)$, which also contains the point $Q(3, 6)$.

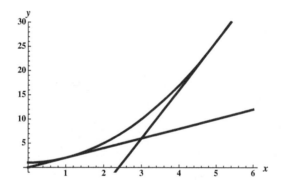

3.2.27 With $f(x) = \frac{1}{x}$, we have

$$f'(x) = \lim\limits_{h\to 0} \frac{f(x+h) - f(x)}{h} = \lim\limits_{h\to 0} \frac{\frac{1}{x+h} - \frac{1}{x}}{h} = \lim\limits_{h\to 0} \frac{\frac{x - (x+h)}{x(x+h)}}{h}$$

$$= \lim\limits_{h\to 0} \frac{-h}{hx(x+h)} = \lim\limits_{h\to 0} \frac{-1}{x(x+h)} = -\frac{1}{x^2}.$$

We are looking for points $(x, 1/x)$ where the slope of the line between this point and $Q(-2, 4)$ is equal to $\frac{-1}{x^2}$. So we seek solutions to the equation

$$\frac{1/x - 4}{x + 2} = -\frac{1}{x^2},$$

which can be written as $x - 4x^2 = -x - 2$, or $4x^2 - 2x - 2 = 0$, or $2x^2 - x - 1 = 0$. This factors as $(2x + 1)(x - 1) = 0$, so the solutions are $x = 1$ and $x = -1/2$. Note that at $x = 1$ the equation of the tangent line is $y - 1 = -1(x - 1)$ which does contain the point $Q(-2, 4)$, and at $x = -1/2$ the equation of the tangent line is $y + 2 = -4\left(x + \frac{1}{2}\right)$ or $y = -4x - 4$ which also contains the point $Q(-2, 4)$.

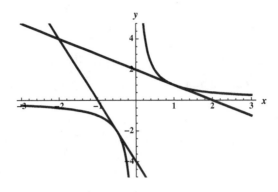

3.2.29

a. The tangent line for Q looks to be the steepest at $t = 0$.

b. All tangent lines for Q have positive slope, so Q' is positive for $t \geq 0$.

c. The tangent lines appear to be getting less steep as t increases, so Q' is decreasing.

d.

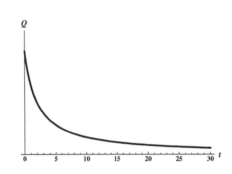

3.2.31

a.

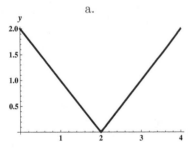

b. $f'_+(2) = \lim\limits_{h \to 0^+} \dfrac{|2 + h - 2| - 0}{h} = \lim\limits_{h \to 0^+} \dfrac{h}{h} = 1$, because for $h > 0$, we have $|h| = h$. Similarly, $f'_-(2) = \lim\limits_{h \to 0^-} \dfrac{|2 + h - 2| - 0}{h} = \lim\limits_{h \to 0^-} -\dfrac{h}{h} = -1$, because for $h < 0$, we have $|h| = -h$.

c. Because f is defined at $a = 2$ and the graph of f does not jump, f is continuous at $a = 2$. Because the left-hand and right-hand derivatives are not equal, f is not differentiable at $a = 2$.

3.2.33

a.   The graph has a vertical tangent at $x = 2$.

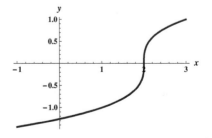

b. The graph has a vertical tangent at $x = 4$.

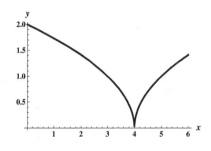

c. The graph has a vertical tangent at $x = -1$.

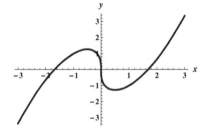

d. The graph has a vertical tangent at $x = 0$.

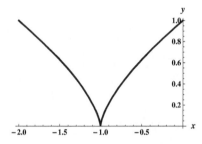

3.2.35 $f'(0) = \lim\limits_{h \to 0} \dfrac{h^{1/3}}{h} = \lim\limits_{h \to 0} \dfrac{1}{h^{2/3}} = +\infty$. Thus the graph of f has a vertical tangent at $x = 0$.

3.2.37

a.

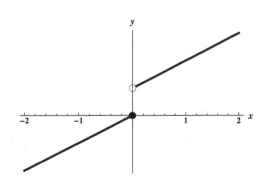

b. For $x < 0$, we have $f'(x) = \lim\limits_{h \to 0} \dfrac{x + h - x}{h} = \lim\limits_{h \to 0} \dfrac{h}{h} = \lim\limits_{h \to 0} 1 = 1$.

c. For $x > 0$, we have $f'(x) = \lim\limits_{h \to 0} \dfrac{x + h + 1 - (x + 1)}{h} = \lim\limits_{h \to 0} \dfrac{h}{h} = \lim\limits_{h \to 0} 1 = 1$.

d.

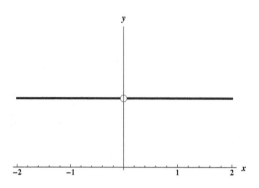

e. f is not differentiable at $x = 0$ as it is not continuous there. Also, if we were to compute the derivative of f from the right at 0 we would have

$$\lim_{h \to 0^+} \frac{f(0+h) - f(0)}{h} = \lim_{h \to 0^+} \frac{h + 1 - 0}{h} = \lim_{h \to 0^+} \frac{h + 1}{h},$$

which does not exist.

3.3   Rules of Differentiation

3.3.1 Often the limit definition of f' is difficult to compute, especially for functions which are reasonably complicated. The rules for differentiation allow us to easily compute the derivatives of complex functions.

3.3.3 The function $f(x) = e^x$ is an example of a function with this property.

3.3.5 By the constant multiple rule, the derivative of the function cf where c is a constant and f is a function is cf'. That is, the derivative of a constant times a function is that same constant times the derivative of the function.

3.3.7 By the power rule, $y' = 5x^{5-1} = 5x^4$.

3.3.9 By the constant rule, $f'(x) = 0$.

3.3.11 By the power rule $h'(t) = 1t^{1-1} = t^0 = 1$.

3.3.13 By the constant multiple rule and the power rule, $f'(x) = 5 \cdot \frac{d}{dx}x^3 = 5 \cdot 3x^2 = 15x^2$.

3.3.15 By the constant multiple and power rules, $p'(x) = 8 \cdot \frac{d}{dx}x = 8 \cdot 1 = 8$.

3.3.17 By the constant multiple and power rules, $g'(t) = 100\frac{d}{dt}t^2 = 100 \cdot 2t = 200t$.

3.3.19 $f'(x) = \frac{d}{dx}(3x^4 + 7x) = \frac{d}{dx}(3x^4) + \frac{d}{dx}(7x) = 12x^3 + 7$.

3.3.21 $f'(x) = \frac{d}{dx}(10x^4 - 32x + e^2) = \frac{d}{dx}(10x^4) - \frac{d}{dx}(32x) + \frac{d}{dx}(e^2) = 40x^3 - 32 - 0 = 40x^3 - 32$.

3.3.23 $g'(w) = \frac{d}{dw}(2w^3 + 3w^2 + 10w) = 2\frac{d}{dw}(w^3) + 3\frac{d}{dw}(w^2) + 10\frac{d}{dw}(w) = 2(3w^2) + 3(2w) + 10(1) = 6w^2 + 6w + 10$.

3.3.25 Expanding the product yields $f(x) = 6x^3 + 3x^2 + 4x + 2$. So

$$f'(x) = \frac{d}{dx}(6x^3 + 3x^2 + 4x + 2) = \frac{d}{dx}(6x^3) + \frac{d}{dx}(3x^2) + \frac{d}{dx}(4x) + \frac{d}{dx}(2)$$
$$= 18x^2 + 6x + 4.$$

3.3.27 Expanding the product yields $h(x) = x^4 + 2x^2 + 1$. So

$$h'(x) = \frac{d}{dx}(x^4 + 2x^2 + 1) = \frac{d}{dx}(x^4) + \frac{d}{dx}(2x^2) + \frac{d}{dx}(1)$$
$$= 4x^3 + 4x.$$

3.3.29 f simplifies as $f(w) = w^2 - 1$, so $f'(w) = 2w$ for $w \neq 0$.

3.3.31 g simplifies as $g(x) = \frac{(x-1)(x+1)}{x-1} = x + 1$. Thus $g'(x) = 1$ for $x \neq 1$.

3.3.33 y simplifies as $y = \frac{(\sqrt{x}-\sqrt{a})(\sqrt{x}+\sqrt{a})}{\sqrt{x}-\sqrt{a}} = \sqrt{x} + \sqrt{a}$. Thus $\frac{dy}{dx} = \frac{1}{2\sqrt{x}}$ for $x \neq a$.

3.3.35

   a. $y' = -6x$, so the slope of the tangent line at $a = 1$ is -6. Thus, the tangent line at the point $(1, -1)$ is $y + 1 = -6(x - 1)$, or $y = -6x + 5$.

   b.

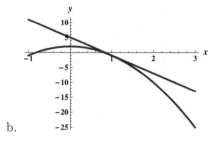

3.3.37

   a. $y' = e^x$, so the slope of the tangent line at $a = \ln 3$ is 3. Thus, the tangent line at the point $(\ln 3, 3)$ is $y - 3 = 3(x - \ln 3)$, or $y = 3x + 3 - 3\ln 3$.

   b.

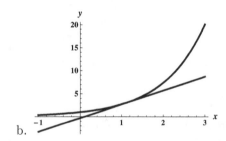

3.3.39

   a. $f'(x) = 2x - 6$, so the slope is zero when $2x - 6 = 0$, which is at $x = 3$.

   b. The slope is 2 when $2x - 6 = 2$ which is at $x = 4$.

3.3.41

   a. The slope of the tangent line is given by $f'(x) = 6x^2 - 6x - 12$, and this quantity is zero when $x^2 - x - 2 = 0$, or $(x - 2)(x + 1) = 0$. The two solutions are thus $x = -1$ and $x = 2$, so the points on the graph are $(-1, 11)$ and $(2, -16)$.

   b. The slope of the tangent line is 60 when $6x^2 - 6x - 12 = 60$, which is when $6x^2 - 6x - 72 = 0$. Simplifying this quadratic expression yields the equation $x^2 - x - 12 = 0$, which has solutions $x = -3$ and $x = 4$, so the points on the graph are $(-3, -41)$, and $(4, 36)$.

3.3.43

   a. The slope of the tangent line is given by $\frac{2}{\sqrt{x}} - 1$. This is equal to zero when $\sqrt{x} = 2$, or $x = 4$. The point on the graph is $(4, 4)$.

   b. The slope of the tangent line is $-\frac{1}{2}$ when $\frac{2}{\sqrt{x}} - 1 = -\frac{1}{2}$. Solving for x gives $x = 16$. The point on the graph is $(16, 0)$.

3.3.45 $f'(x) = 20x^3 + 30x^2 + 3$, $f''(x) = 60x^2 + 60x$, and $f^{(3)}(x) = 120x + 60$.

3.3.47 f simplifies as $f(x) = \frac{(x-8)(x+1)}{x+1} = x - 8$. So for $x \neq -1$, $f'(x) = 1$, $f''(x) = 0$, and $f^{(3)}(x) = 0$.

3.3.49

    a. False. 10^5 is a constant, so the constant rule assures us that $\frac{d}{dx}(10^5) = 0$.

    b. True. This follows because the slope is given by $f'(x) = e^x > 0$ for all x.

    c. False. $\frac{d}{dx}(e^3) = 0$.

    d. False. $\frac{d}{dx}(e^x) = e^x$, not xe^{x-1}.

    e. False. We have $\frac{d}{dx}(5x^3 + 2x + 5) = 15x^2 + 2$. Thus we have $\frac{d^2}{dx^2}(5x^3 + 2x + 5) = 30x$, and $\frac{d^3}{dx^3}(5x^3 + 2x + 5) = 30$. It is true that $\frac{d^n}{dx^n}(5x^3 + 2x + 5) = 0$ for $n \geq 4$.

3.3.51 First note that because the slope of $4x + 1$ is 4, it must be the case that $f'(2) = 4$. Also, at $x = 2$, we have $y = 4 \cdot 2 + 1 = 9$, so $f(2) = 9$. Because the line tangent to the graph of g at 2 has slope 3, we know that $g'(2) = 3$. The tangent line to g at $x = 2$ must be $y - (-2) = 3(x - 0)$, so the value of the tangent line at 2 (which must also be the value of $g(2)$) is 4. So $g(2) = 4$.

    a. $y'(2) = f'(2) + g'(2) = 4 + 3 = 7$. The line contains the point $(2, f(2) + g(2)) = (2, 13)$. Thus, the equation of the tangent line is $y - 13 = 7(x - 2)$, or $y = 7x - 1$.

    b. $y'(2) = f'(2) - 2g'(2) = 4 - 2 \cdot 3 = -2$. The line contains the point $(2, f(2) - 2g(2)) = (2, 1)$. Thus, the equation of the tangent line is $y - 1 = -2(x - 2)$, or $y = -2x + 5$.

    c. $y'(2) = 4f'(2) = 4 \cdot 4 = 16$. The line contains the point $(2, 4f(2)) = (2, 36)$. Thus, the equation of the tangent line is $y - 36 = 16(x - 2)$, or $y = 16x + 4$.

3.3.53 For $f(x) = x^2 + bx + c$ we have $f'(x) = 2x + b$, so $f'(1) = 2 + b$. Because the slope of $4x + 2$ is 4, we require $2 + b = 4$, so $b = 2$. Also, because the value of $4x + 2$ at $x = 1$ is 6, we must have $f(1) = 1 + 2 + c = 6$, so $c = 3$. Thus the curve $f(x) = x^2 + 2x + 3$ has $y = 4x + 2$ as its tangent line at $x = 1$.

3.3.55 $G'(2) = 3f'(2) - g'(2) = 3(-3) - 1 = -10$.

3.3.57 $G'(5) = 3f'(5) - g'(5) = 3 \cdot 1 - (-1) = 4$.

3.3.59 $\frac{d}{dx}[1.5f(x)]_{x=2} = 1.5f'(2) = 1.5 \cdot 5 = 7.5$.

3.3.61

    a. Let $f(x) = \sqrt{x}$ and $a = 9$. Then $\lim\limits_{h \to 0} \dfrac{f(a+h) - f(a)}{h} = \lim\limits_{h \to 0} \dfrac{\sqrt{9+h} - \sqrt{9}}{h} = f'(9)$.

    b. Because $f'(x) = \frac{1}{2\sqrt{x}}$, we have $f'(9) = \frac{1}{6}$, so this is the value of the original limit.

3.3.63

    a. Let $f(x) = x^{100}$ and $a = 1$. Then $\lim\limits_{x \to 1} \dfrac{f(x) - f(1)}{x - 1} = f'(1)$.

    b. Because $f'(x) = 100x^{99}$, we have $f'(1) = 100$, so this is the value of the original limit.

3.3.65 $\lim\limits_{x \to 0} \dfrac{e^{3x} - 1}{x} = 3$.

3.3.67 $\lim\limits_{x \to 0^+} x^x = 1$.

3.3.69 Let $f(x) = e^x$ and $a = 0$. Then we have $f'(a) = \lim\limits_{x \to a} \dfrac{f(x) - f(a)}{x - a} = \lim\limits_{x \to 0} \dfrac{e^x - 1}{x}$. Because $f'(0) = e^0 = 1$, this must be the value of $\lim\limits_{x \to 0} \dfrac{e^x - 1}{x}$.

3.3.71

a. $d'(t) = 32t$ is the velocity of the stone after t seconds, measured in feet per second.

b. The stone travels $d(6) = 16 \cdot 6^2 = 576$ feet and strikes the ground with a velocity of $32 \cdot 6 = 192$ feet per second. Converting to miles per hour, we have $192 \cdot \frac{3600}{5280} \approx 130.9$ miles per hour.

3.3.73

a. $A'(t) = -\frac{1}{25}t + 2$ square miles per year.

b. First we must find when $A(t) = 38$. This occurs when $-\frac{t^2}{50} + 2t + 28 = 38$, which can be written as $t^2 - 100t + 900 = 0$. This factors as $(t - 90)(t - 10) = 0$, so the only solution on the given domain is $t = 10$. At this time, we have $A'(10) = -0.4 + 2 = 1.6$ square miles per year.

c. Note that $A'(20) = -0.8 + 2 = 1.2$ square miles per year. In order to maintain a density of 1000 people per square mile, we must multiply the density of people per square mile times the number of square miles per year in order to obtain the rate of people per year required to maintain that density. Thus the population growth rate must be $1000 \cdot 1.2 = 1200$ people per year.

3.3.75

$$\frac{d}{dx}x^n = \lim_{h \to 0} \frac{(x + h)^n - x^n}{h} = \lim_{h \to 0} \left(\frac{x^n + nx^{n-1}h + \frac{n(n-1)}{2}x^{n-2}h^2 + \cdots + nxh^{n-1} + h^n - x^n}{h} \right)$$

$$= \lim_{h \to 0} \left(nx^{n-1} + \frac{n(n-1)}{2}x^{n-2}h + \cdots + nxh^{n-2} + h^{n-1} \right) = nx^{n-1} + 0 + 0 + \cdots + 0 = nx^{n-1}$$

3.3.77

a. $\frac{d}{dx}\left(\sqrt{x}\right) = \frac{d}{dx}x^{1/2} = \frac{1}{2} \cdot x^{-1/2} = \frac{1}{2\sqrt{x}}$.

b.

$$\frac{d}{dx}x^{3/2} = \lim_{h \to 0} \frac{(x + h)^{3/2} - x^{3/2}}{h} = \lim_{h \to 0} \frac{((x + h)^{3/2} - x^{3/2})((x + h)^{3/2} + x^{3/2})}{h((x + h)^{3/2} + x^{3/2})}$$

$$= \lim_{h \to 0} \frac{(x + h)^3 - x^3}{h((x + h)^{3/2} + x^{3/2})} = \lim_{h \to 0} \frac{x^3 + 3x^2h + 3xh^2 + h^3 - x^3}{h((x + h)^{3/2} + x^{3/2})}$$

$$= \lim_{h \to 0} \frac{3x^2 + 3xh + h^2}{((x + h)^{3/2} + x^{3/2})} = \frac{3x^2 + 0 + 0}{x^{3/2} + x^{3/2}} = \frac{3x^2}{2x^{3/2}} = \frac{3}{2}x^{1/2}.$$

c.

$$\frac{d}{dx}x^{5/2} = \lim_{h \to 0} \frac{(x + h)^{5/2} - x^{5/2}}{h} = \lim_{h \to 0} \frac{((x + h)^{5/2} - x^{5/2})((x + h)^{5/2} + x^{5/2})}{h((x + h)^{5/2} + x^{5/2})}$$

$$= \lim_{h \to 0} \frac{(x + h)^5 - x^5}{h((x + h)^{5/2} + x^{5/2})} = \lim_{h \to 0} \frac{x^5 + 5x^4h + 10x^3h^2 + 10x^2h^3 + 5xh^4 + h^5 - x^5}{h((x + h)^{5/2} + x^{5/2})}$$

$$= \lim_{h \to 0} \frac{5x^4 + 10x^3h + 10x^2h^2 + 5xh^3 + h^4}{((x + h)^{5/2} + x^{5/2})}$$

$$= \frac{5x^4 + 0 + 0 + 0 + 0}{x^{5/2} + x^{5/2}} = \frac{5x^4}{2x^{5/2}} = \frac{5}{2}x^{3/2}.$$

d. It appears that $\frac{d}{dx}x^{n/2} = \frac{n}{2} \cdot x^{(n/2)-1}$.

3.3.79

a. $\frac{d}{dx}(e^{2x}) = \lim\limits_{h \to 0} \frac{e^{2(x+h)} - e^{2x}}{h} = \lim\limits_{h \to 0} \frac{e^{2x}(e^{2h} - 1)}{h} = e^{2x} \lim\limits_{h \to 0} \frac{e^{2h} - 1}{h}.$

b. Let $z = 2h$. Then $\lim\limits_{h \to 0} \frac{e^{2h} - 1}{h} = \lim\limits_{z \to 0} \frac{e^z - 1}{z/2} = 2 \lim\limits_{z \to 0} \frac{e^z - 1}{z} = 2.$

c. $\frac{d}{dx}(e^{2x}) = e^{2x} \lim\limits_{h \to 0} \frac{e^{2h} - 1}{h} = 2e^{2x}.$

3.4   The Product and Quotient Rules

3.4.1 The derivative of the product fg with respect to x is given by $f'(x)g(x) + f(x)g'(x)$.

3.4.3 $\frac{d}{dx}(x^n) = nx^{n-1}$ for all integers n.

3.4.5 $\frac{d}{dx}e^{kx} = ke^{kx}$ for all real numbers k.

3.4.7 $f'(x) = 12x^3(2x^2 - 1) + 3x^4 \cdot 4x = 24x^5 - 12x^3 + 12x^5 = 36x^5 - 12x^3.$

3.4.9 $f'(t) = 5t^4 e^t + t^5 e^t = t^4 e^t (t + 5).$

3.4.11 $h'(x) = (1)(x^3 + x^2 + x + 1) + (x - 1)(3x^2 + 2x + 1) = x^3 + x^2 + x + 1 + 3x^3 + 2x^2 + x - 3x^2 - 2x - 1 = 4x^3.$

3.4.13 $g'(w) = e^w(w^3 - 1) + e^w \cdot 3w^2 = e^w(w^3 + 3w^2 - 1).$

3.4.15

a. $f'(x) = 1(3x + 4) + (x - 1) \cdot 3 = 6x + 1.$

b. $f'(x) = \frac{d}{dx}(3x^2 + x - 4) = 6x + 1.$

3.4.17

a. $g'(y) = (12y^3 - 2y)(y^2 - 4) + (3y^4 - y^2) \cdot 2y = 18y^5 - 52y^3 + 8y.$

b. $g'(y) = \frac{d}{dy}(3y^6 - 13y^4 + 4y^2) = 18y^5 - 52y^3 + 8y.$

3.4.19 $f'(x) = \frac{(x+1) \cdot 1 - x \cdot 1}{(x+1)^2} = \frac{1}{(x+1)^2}.$

3.4.21 $f'(x) = \frac{(e^x + 1)e^x - e^x(e^x)}{(e^x + 1)^2} = \frac{e^x}{(e^x + 1)^2}.$

3.4.23 $f'(x) = (1)e^{-x} + x(-e^{-x}) = e^{-x}(1 - x).$

3.4.25 $y' = \frac{d}{dt}\left(\frac{3t - 1}{2t - 2}\right) = \frac{(2t-2) \cdot 3 - (3t-1) \cdot 2}{(2t-2)^2} = -\frac{4}{(2t-2)^2} = -\frac{1}{(t-1)^2}.$

3.4.27 $g'(x) = \frac{(x^2 - 1) \cdot e^x - e^x \cdot 2x}{(x^2 - 1)^2} = \frac{e^x(x^2 - 2x - 1)}{(x^2 - 1)^2}.$

3.4.29

a. $f'(w) = \frac{w(3w^2 - 1) - (w^3 - w) \cdot 1}{w^2} = \frac{2w^3}{w^2} = 2w$ for $w \neq 0$.

b. For $w \neq 0$ this simplifies as $w^2 - 1$. $f'(w) = \frac{d}{dw}(w^2 - 1) = 2w.$

3.4.31

a. $y' = \frac{(x-a)(2x) - (x^2 - a^2)}{(x-a)^2} = \frac{2x^2 - 2ax - x^2 + a^2}{(x-a)^2} = \frac{x^2 - 2ax + a^2}{(x-a)^2} = \frac{(x-a)^2}{(x-a)^2} = 1$ for $x \neq a$.

b. For $x \neq a$, this simplifies as $y = \frac{(x+a)(x-a)}{x-a} = x + a$. $y' = \frac{d}{dx}(x+a) = 1$.

3.4.33

a. $y' = \frac{(x-1)-(x+5)}{(x-1)^2} = -\frac{6}{(x-1)^2}$.
At $a = 3$ we have $y' = -\frac{6}{4} = -\frac{3}{2}$ and $y = 4$, so the equation of the tangent line is $y - 4 = -\frac{3}{2} \cdot (x-3)$, or $y = -\frac{3}{2}x + \frac{17}{2}$.

b.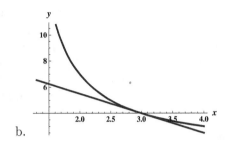

3.4.35

a. $y' = 2 + (1)e^x + xe^x$.
At $a = 0$ we have $y' = 2 + 1 + 0 = 3$ and $y = 1$. So the equation of the tangent line is $y - 1 = 3(x - 0)$, or $y = 3x + 1$.

b.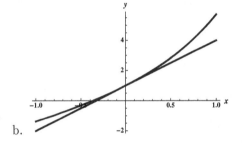

3.4.37 $f'(x) = (-9) \cdot 3 \cdot x^{-9-1} = -27x^{-10}$.

3.4.39 $g'(t) = \frac{d}{dt}(3t^2 + 6t^{-7}) = 6t - 42t^{-8}$.

3.4.41 $g'(t) = \frac{d}{dt}(1 + 3t^{-1} + t^{-2}) = -3t^{-2} - 2t^{-3}$.

3.4.43 $f'(x) = (1)e^{7x} + x(7e^{7x}) = e^{7x}(7x + 1)$.

3.4.45 $f'(x) = 3 \cdot 15 \cdot e^{3x} = 45e^{3x}$.

3.4.47 $g'(x) = \frac{d}{dx}(xe^{-3x}) = e^{-3x} - xe^{-3x}(3) = e^{-3x}(1 - 3x)$.

3.4.49 $y'(x) = \frac{d}{dx}\left(\frac{2}{3}e^x + e^{-x}\right) = \frac{2}{3}e^x - e^{-x}$.

3.4.51

a. $p'(t) = \frac{(t+2)200 - 200t}{(t+2)^2} = \frac{400}{(t+2)^2}$.

b. $p'(5) = \frac{400}{49} \approx 8.16$.

c. The value of p' is as large as possible when its denominator is as small as possible, which is when $t = 0$. The value of $p'(0)$ is 100.

d. $\lim_{t \to \infty} p'(t) = \lim_{t \to \infty} \frac{400}{(t+2)^2} = 0$. This means that the population eventually has a growth rate of 0, which means that the population approaches a steady state.

e.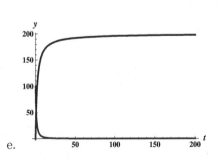

3.4.53

a. The instantaneous rate of change is $Q'(t) = -1.386e^{-0.0693t}$ mg/hr.

b. At $t = 0$ hours, we have $Q'(0) = -1.386$, so the amount of antibiotic is decreasing at a rate of 1.386 mg/hr. At $t = 2$ hours, we have $Q'(2) = -1.386e^{-0.1386} \approx -1.207$, so the amount of antibiotic is decreasing at a rate of about 1.207 mg/hr.

c. $\lim_{t \to \infty} Q(t) = 20 \lim_{t \to \infty} e^{-0.0693t} = 0$. In the long run, the antibiotic is all used up. $\lim_{t \to \infty} Q'(t) = -1.386 \lim_{t \to \infty} e^{-0.0693t} = 0$. The rate of change of the amount of antibiotic in the bloodstream also goes to zero as $t \to \infty$.

3.4.55

a. The slope is $f'(x) = e^{2x} + 2xe^{2x}$. This is zero when $e^{2x}(1 + 2x) = 0$, which occurs when $x = -\frac{1}{2}$.

b. The graph of f has a horizontal tangent line at $x = -1/2$.

3.4.57 $g'(x) = \frac{(x-2)((x+1)e^x + e^x) - (x+1)e^x}{(x-2)^2} = \frac{e^x}{(x-2)^2} \cdot \frac{(x-2)(x+2) - (x+1)}{1} = \frac{e^x}{(x-2)^2} \cdot (x^2 - x - 5)$.

3.4.59 $h'(x) = \frac{(x+1)e^4 - xe^4}{(x+1)^2} = \frac{e^4}{(x+1)^2}$.

3.4.61

a. False. In fact, because e^5 is a constant, its derivative is zero.

b. False. It is certainly a reasonable way to proceed, but one could also write the given quantity as $x + 3 + 2x^{-1}$, and then proceed using the sum rule and the power rule and the extended power rule.

c. False. $\frac{d}{dx}\left(\frac{1}{x^5}\right) = \frac{d}{dx}\left(x^{-5}\right) = -5x^{-6} = -\frac{5}{x^6}$.

d. True. The derivative of e^{3x} is $3e^{3x}$, and each succeeding derivative results in an extra factor of 3.

3.4.63
$f'(x) = x^2(3e^{3x}) + e^{3x}(2x) = e^{3x}(3x^2 + 2x)$.
$f''(x) = e^{3x}(6x + 2) + (3x^2 + 2x)3e^{3x} = e^{3x}(9x^2 + 12x + 2)$.
$f'''(x) = e^{3x}(18x + 12) + (9x^2 + 12x + 2)(3e^{3x}) = e^{3x}(27x^2 + 54x + 18) = 9e^{3x}(3x^2 + 6x + 2)$.

3.4.65
$$f'(x) = \frac{d}{dx}\left(\frac{x^2 - 7x}{x+1}\right) = \frac{(x+1)(2x-7) - (x^2-7x)\cdot 1}{(x+1)^2} = \frac{x^2 + 2x - 7}{x^2 + 2x + 1} = \frac{x^2 + 2x - 7}{(x+1)^2}.$$

$$f''(x) = \frac{d}{dx}\left(\frac{x^2 + 2x - 7}{x^2 + 2x + 1}\right) = \frac{(x^2 + 2x + 1)(2x+2) - (x^2 + 2x - 7)(2x+2)}{(x+1)^4}$$
$$= \frac{(2x^2 + 4x + 2) - (2x^2 + 4x - 14)}{(x+1)^3} = \frac{16}{(x+1)^3}.$$

3.4.67 $f'(x) = \frac{d}{dx}\left(4x^2 - \frac{2x}{5x+1}\right) = 8x - \frac{(5x+1)2 - (2x)(5)}{(5x+1)^2} = 8x - \frac{2}{(5x+1)^2}$.

3.4.69
$$h'(r) = \frac{(r+1)(-1 - \frac{1}{2\sqrt{r}}) - (2 - r - \sqrt{r})\cdot 1}{(r+1)^2} = \frac{-r - \frac{\sqrt{r}}{2} - 1 - \frac{1}{2\sqrt{r}} - 2 + r + \sqrt{r}}{(r+1)^2}$$
$$= \frac{\frac{\sqrt{r}}{2} - \frac{1}{2\sqrt{r}} - 3}{(r+1)^2} \cdot \frac{2\sqrt{r}}{2\sqrt{r}} = \frac{r - 1 - 6\sqrt{r}}{2\sqrt{r}(r+1)^2}.$$

3.4.71 $h'(x) = (35x^6 + 5)(6x^3 + 3x^2 + 3) + (5x^7 + 5x)(18x^2 + 6x) = 15((7x^6 + 1)(2x^3 + x^2 + 1) + (x^7 + x)(6x^2 + 2x)) = 300x^9 + 135x^8 + 105x^6 + 120x^3 + 45x^2 + 15.$

3.4.73

a.
$y' = -\frac{54x}{(x^2+9)^2}$. At $x = 2$, $y' = -\frac{108}{169}$ and $y = \frac{27}{13}$.
Thus the tangent line is given by

$$y - \frac{27}{13} = -\frac{108}{169}(x - 2),$$

or $y = -\frac{108}{169}x + \frac{567}{169}$.

b.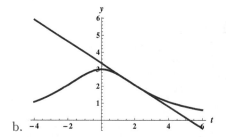

3.4.75 $\frac{d}{dx}\left[\frac{f(x)}{g(x)}\right]\Big|_{x=2} = \frac{g(2)f'(2)-f(2)g'(2)}{(g(2))^2} = \frac{2\cdot5-4\cdot4}{4} = -\frac{3}{2}.$

3.4.77 $\frac{d}{dx}\left[\frac{f(x)}{x+2}\right]\Big|_{x=4} = \frac{(4+2)f'(4)-f(4)}{36} = \frac{6-2}{36} = \frac{1}{9}.$

3.4.79 $\frac{d}{dx}\left[\frac{f(x)g(x)}{x}\right]\Big|_{x=4} = \frac{4(f'(4)g(4)+f(4)g'(4))-f(4)g(4)}{16} = \frac{4(1\cdot3+2\cdot1)-(2\cdot3)}{16} = \frac{14}{16} = \frac{7}{8}.$

3.4.81

a. The instantaneous rate of change is $\frac{d}{dx}F(x) = -\frac{2kQq}{x^3}$ N/m $= -\frac{1.8\times10^{10}Qq}{x^3}$ N/m.

b. $\left[\frac{d}{dx}F(x)\right]\Big|_{x=0.001} = -\frac{2(9\times10^9)}{(0.001)^3} = -\frac{18\times10^9}{10^{-9}} = -18 \times 10^{18} = -1.8 \times 10^{19}$ Newtons per meter.

c. Because the distance x appears in the denominator of $F'(x)$, the absolute value of the instantaneous rate of change decreases with the separation.

3.4.83 We attempt a solution with functions of the form $f(x) = e^{ax}$ and $g(x) = e^{bx}$, because these functions are multiples of their own derivatives. The derivative of fg is $(a + b)e^{(a+b)x}$, while the product of the derivatives is $abe^{(a+b)x}$. These would be equal if we could have $a + b = ab$, which occurs, for example, when $a = b = 2$. Thus the functions $f(x) = g(x) = e^{2x}$ have the desired property. In general we need $b = \frac{a}{a-1}$, $a \neq 1$.

3.4.85

a. The tangent line at $x = a$ is $y - a^2 = 2a(x - a)$ and at $x = b$ is $y - b^2 = 2b(x - b)$.
These intersect when $a^2 + 2ax - 2a^2 = b^2 + 2bx - 2b^2$, or $(2a - 2b)x = a^2 - b^2$, which is met when $x = \frac{a+b}{2}$. So $c = \frac{a+b}{2}$.

b. The tangent line at $x = a$ is $y - \sqrt{a} = \frac{1}{2\sqrt{a}}(x - a)$ and at $x = b$ is $y - \sqrt{b} = \frac{1}{2\sqrt{b}}(x - b)$.
These intersect when $\sqrt{a} + \frac{1}{2\sqrt{a}}(x - a) = \sqrt{b} + \frac{1}{2\sqrt{b}}(x - b)$, or $\left(\frac{1}{2\sqrt{a}} - \frac{1}{2\sqrt{b}}\right)x = \frac{\sqrt{b}-\sqrt{a}}{2}$, which is met when $x = \sqrt{ab}$. So $c = \sqrt{ab}$.

c. The tangent line at $x = a$ is $y - \frac{1}{a} = -\frac{1}{a^2}(x - a)$ and at $x = b$ is $y - \frac{1}{b} = -\frac{1}{b^2}(x - b)$.
These intersect when $\frac{1}{a} + -\frac{1}{a^2}(x - a) = \frac{1}{b} - \frac{1}{b^2}(x - b)$, or $\left(\frac{2}{a} - \frac{x}{a^2}\right) = \left(\frac{2}{b} - \frac{x}{b^2}\right)$, which is met when $x\left(\frac{1}{b^2} - \frac{1}{a^2}\right) = \frac{2}{b} - \frac{2}{a}$, or $x \cdot \left(\frac{a^2-b^2}{a^2b^2}\right) = \frac{2(a-b)}{ab}$. Thus we arrive at $x = \frac{2ab}{a+b}$. So $c = \frac{2ab}{a+b}$.

d. The tangent line at $x = a$ is $y - f(a) = f'(a)(x - a)$ and at $x = b$ is $y - f(b) = f'(b)(x - b)$.
These intersect when $f(a) + f'(a)(x - a) = f(b) + f'(b)(x - b)$, or $(f'(a) - f'(b))x = f(b) - f(a) - f'(b)b + f'(a)a$. Solving for x yields $x = \frac{f(b)-f(a)-f'(b)b+f'(a)a}{f'(a)-f'(b)}$ provided $f'(a) \neq f'(b)$ (which occurs when the tangent lines are parallel and don't intersect.)

3.4.87

$$\frac{d^2}{dx^2}(f(x)g(x)) = \frac{d}{dx}(f'(x)g(x) + f(x)g'(x)) = f''(x)g(x) + f'(x)g'(x) + f'(x)g'(x) + f(x)g''(x)$$
$$= f''(x)g(x) + 2f'(x)g'(x) + f(x)g''(x).$$

3.4.89 Let $k = -m$, where m is a positive integer. Then $\frac{d}{dx}(e^{kx}) = \frac{d}{dx}\left(\frac{1}{e^{mx}}\right) = \frac{0 - 1 \cdot me^{mx}}{(e^{mx})^2} = -me^{-mx} = ke^{kx}$.

3.4.91

   a.

$$\frac{d}{dx}[(f(x)g(x))h(x)] = \frac{d}{dx}[f(x)g(x)] \cdot h(x) + f(x)g(x) \cdot \frac{d}{dx}h(x)$$
$$= [f'(x)g(x) + f(x)g'(x)]h(x) + f(x)g(x)h'(x)$$
$$= f'(x)g(x)h(x) + f(x)g'(x)h(x) + f(x)g(x)h'(x).$$

   b. $\frac{d}{dx}[e^{2x}(x-1)(x+3)] = 2e^{2x}(x-1)(x+3) + e^{2x}(x+3) + e^{2x}(x-1) = e^{2x}(2x^2 + 4x - 6 + x + 3 + x - 1) = e^{2x}(2x^2 + 6x - 4) = 2e^{2x}(x^2 + 3x - 2)$.

3.5 Derivatives of Trigonometric Functions

3.5.1 A direct substitution would yield the quotient of zero with itself, which isn't defined

3.5.3 Because $\tan x = \frac{\sin x}{\cos x}$, and $\cot x = \frac{\cos x}{\sin x}$, we can use the quotient rule to compute these derivatives, because we know the derivatives of $\sin x$ and of $\cos x$.

3.5.5 $f'(x) = \cos x$ and $f'(\pi) = \cos \pi = -1$.

3.5.7 $\lim\limits_{x \to 0} \frac{\sin 3x}{x} = \lim\limits_{x \to 0} \frac{3\sin 3x}{3x} = 3\lim\limits_{x \to 0}\frac{\sin 3x}{3x} = 3 \cdot 1 = 3.$

3.5.9 $\lim\limits_{x \to 0} \frac{\sin 7x}{\sin 3x} = \lim\limits_{x \to 0} \frac{\frac{7\sin 7x}{7x}}{\frac{3\sin 3x}{3x}} = \frac{7}{3} \cdot \lim\limits_{x \to 0} \frac{\frac{\sin 7x}{7x}}{\frac{\sin 3x}{3x}} = \frac{7}{3} \cdot \frac{1}{1} = \frac{7}{3}.$

3.5.11 $\lim\limits_{x \to 0} \frac{\tan 5x}{x} = \lim\limits_{x \to 0} \frac{5\sin 5x}{5x\cos 5x} = 5\lim\limits_{x \to 0} \frac{\sin 5x}{5x} \cdot \lim\limits_{x \to 0} \frac{1}{\cos 5x} = 5 \cdot 1 \cdot 1 = 5.$

3.5.13 $\lim\limits_{x \to 0} \frac{\tan 7x}{\sin x} = \lim\limits_{x \to 0} \frac{\sin 7x}{\cos 7x \cdot \sin x} = \lim\limits_{x \to 0} \left(\frac{1}{\cos 7x} \cdot \frac{x}{\sin x} \cdot \frac{7\sin 7x}{7x}\right) =$
$7 \cdot \lim\limits_{x \to 0} \frac{1}{\cos 7x} \cdot \lim\limits_{x \to 0} \frac{x}{\sin x} \cdot \lim\limits_{x \to 0} \frac{\sin 7x}{7x} = 7 \cdot 1 \cdot 1 \cdot 1 = 7.$

3.5.15 $\lim\limits_{x \to 2} \frac{\sin(x-2)}{x^2 - 4} = \lim\limits_{x \to 2} \left(\frac{1}{x+2} \cdot \frac{\sin(x-2)}{x-2}\right) = \lim\limits_{x \to 2} \frac{1}{x+2} \cdot \lim\limits_{x \to 2} \frac{\sin(x-2)}{x-2} = \frac{1}{4} \cdot 1 = \frac{1}{4}.$

3.5.17 $y' = \cos x - \sin x.$

3.5.19 $y = -e^{-x}\sin x + e^{-x}\cos x = e^{-x}(\cos x - \sin x).$

3.5.21 $y' = \sin x + x\cos x.$

3.5.23 $y' = \dfrac{(\sin x + 1)(-\sin x) - (\cos x)(\cos x)}{(1 + \sin x)^2} = \dfrac{-1(\sin^2 x + \cos^2 x) - \sin x}{(1 + \sin x)^2} = \dfrac{-1(1 + \sin x)}{(1 + \sin x)^2} = -\dfrac{1}{1 + \sin x}.$

3.5.25 $y' = \cos x\cos x + \sin x \cdot (-\sin x) = \cos^2 x - \sin^2 x = \cos(2x).$

3.5.27 $y' = -\sin x \cos x + \cos x(-\sin x) = -2\sin x \cos x = -\sin(2x)$.

3.5.29 $\dfrac{d}{dx}(\cot x) = \dfrac{d}{dx}\left(\dfrac{\cos x}{\sin x}\right) = \dfrac{\sin x(-\sin x) - \cos x(\cos x)}{\sin^2 x} = \dfrac{-(\sin^2 x + \cos^2 x)}{\sin^2 x} = -\dfrac{1}{\sin^2 x} = -\csc^2 x$.

3.5.31 $\dfrac{d}{dx}(\csc x) = \dfrac{d}{dx}\left(\dfrac{1}{\sin x}\right) = \dfrac{0 - \cos x}{\sin^2 x} = -\dfrac{1}{\sin x} \cdot \dfrac{\cos x}{\sin x} = -\csc x \cot x$.

3.5.33 $y' = \sec x \tan x - \csc x \cot x$.

3.5.35 $y' = 5e^{5x}\csc x + e^{5x}(-\csc x \cot x) = e^{5x}\csc x(5 - \cot x)$.

3.5.37

$$y' = \frac{(1 + \csc x)(-\csc^2 x) - \cot x(-\csc x \cot x)}{(1 + \csc x)^2} = \frac{-\csc^2 x - \csc^3 x + \csc x(\csc^2 x - 1)}{(1 + \csc x)^2}$$
$$= \frac{-\csc x(1 + \csc x)}{(1 + \csc x)^2} = -\frac{\csc x}{1 + \csc x}$$

3.5.39

$$y' = \frac{0 - (\sec z \tan z \csc z - \sec z \csc z \cot z)}{\sec^2 z \csc^2 z} = \frac{\sec z \csc z(\cot z - \tan z)}{\sec^2 z \csc^2 z}$$
$$= \frac{\cot z - \tan z}{\sec z \csc z} = \cos^2 z - \sin^2 z = \cos(2z).$$

3.5.41 $y' = \sin x + x\cos x$, so $y'' = \cos x + \cos x + -x\sin x = 2\cos x - x\sin x$.

3.5.43 $y' = e^x \sin x + e^x \cos x$, so $y'' = e^x \sin x + e^x \cos x + e^x \cos x + e^x(-\sin x) = 2e^x \cos x$.

3.5.45 $y' = -\csc^2 x$ and $y'' = -((-\csc x \cot x)\csc x + \csc x(-\csc x \cot x)) = 2\cot x \csc^2 x$.

3.5.47

$$y' = \sec x \tan x \csc x - \sec x \csc x \cot x = \sec x \csc x(\tan x - \cot x) = \sec^2 x - \csc^2 x.$$

$$y'' = \sec x(\sec x \tan x) + (\sec x \tan x)\sec x - ((-\csc x \cot x)\csc x + \csc x(-\csc x \cot x))$$
$$= 2\sec^2 x \tan x + 2\csc^2 x \cot x.$$

3.5.49

   a. False. $\frac{d}{dx}\sin^2 x = \sin x \cos x + \cos x \sin x = 2\sin x \cos x \neq \cos^2 x$.

   b. False. $\frac{d^2}{dx^2}\sin x = \frac{d}{dx}\cos x = -\sin x \neq \sin x$.

   c. True. $\frac{d^4}{dx^4}\cos x = \frac{d^3}{dx^3}(-\sin x) = \frac{d^2}{dx^2}(-\cos x) = \frac{d}{dx}\sin x = \cos x$.

   d. True. In fact, $\pi/2$ isn't even in the domain of $\sec x$.

3.5.51 $\displaystyle\lim_{x\to 0}\frac{\sin ax}{\sin bx} = \lim_{x\to 0}\frac{a\sin ax}{ax} \cdot \frac{bx}{b\sin bx} = \frac{a}{b}\lim_{x\to 0}\frac{\sin ax}{ax} \cdot \lim_{x\to 0}\frac{bx}{\sin bx} = \frac{a}{b} \cdot 1 \cdot 1 = \frac{a}{b}$.

3.5.53 $\displaystyle\lim_{x\to 0}\frac{3\sec^5 x}{x^2 + 4} = \frac{3\sec^5(0)}{4} = \frac{3}{4}$.

3.5.55 $\displaystyle\lim_{x\to\pi/4} 3\csc(2x)\cot(2x) = \lim_{x\to\pi/4} 3\frac{1}{\sin 2x}\frac{\cos 2x}{\sin 2x} = 3\frac{\cos \pi/2}{(\sin \pi/2)^2} = 3 \cdot \frac{0}{1} = 0$.

3.5.57 $\frac{dy}{dx} = \cos x \sin x + x(-\sin x)\sin x + x\cos x\cos x = \sin x\cos x - x\sin^2 x + x\cos^2 x = \frac{1}{2}\sin 2x + x\cos 2x.$

3.5.59 $\frac{dy}{dx} = \frac{(\sin x - \cos x)\cos x - \sin x(\cos x + \sin x)}{(\sin x - \cos x)^2} = \frac{-(\sin^2 x + \cos^2 x)}{(\sin x - \cos x)^2} =$

$\frac{-1}{\sin^2 x - 2\sin x\cos x + \cos^2 x} = \frac{-1}{1 - \sin 2x} = \frac{1}{\sin(2x) - 1} = \frac{1}{2\sin x\cos x - 1}.$

3.5.61 $\frac{dy}{dx} = \frac{(1 + \cos x)\sin x - (1 - \cos x)(-\sin x)}{(1 + \cos x)^2} = \frac{2\sin x}{(1 + \cos x)^2}.$

3.5.63

a. $y' = 2\cos x$, so $y'(\pi/6) = \sqrt{3}$. $y(\pi/6) = 2$. The tangent line is thus given by $y - 2 = \sqrt{3}(x - \pi/6)$, or $y = \sqrt{3}x + 2 - \frac{\pi\sqrt{3}}{6}$.

b.

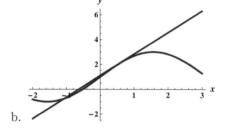

3.5.65

a. $y' = \frac{(1 - \cos x)(-\sin x) - \cos x\sin x}{(1 - \cos x)^2} = -\frac{\sin x}{(1 - \cos x)^2}$, so $y'(\pi/3) = -2\sqrt{3}$. $y(\pi/3) = 1$. The tangent line is thus given by $y - 1 = -2\sqrt{3}(x - \pi/3)$, or $y = -2\sqrt{3}x + \frac{2\sqrt{3}\pi}{3} + 1$.

b.

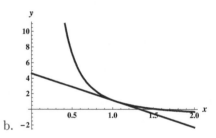

3.5.67 For a horizontal tangent line we need $f'(x) = 1 + 2\sin x = 0$, or $\sin x = -\frac{1}{2}$. This occurs for $x = \frac{7\pi}{6} + 2n\pi$ where n is any integer, or for $x = \frac{11\pi}{6} + 2n\pi$ where n is any integer.

3.5.69

a.

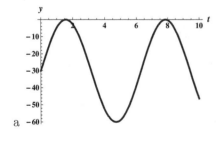

b. $v(t) = y'(t) = 30\cos t$ cm per second.

c.

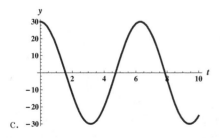

d. $v(t) = 30\cos t = 0$ when $t = \frac{2n+1}{2} \cdot \pi$ where n is a non-negative integer. At those times, the position is given by $\begin{cases} 0 & \text{if } n \text{ is even} \\ -60 & \text{if } n \text{ is odd.} \end{cases}$

e. The maximum velocity is 30 cm per second because $|\cos t| \leq 1$ for all t. We have $\cos t = 1$ for $t = 2n\pi$ for a positive integer n. At those times, $y(2n\pi) = -30$.

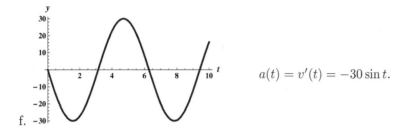

$a(t) = v'(t) = -30 \sin t.$

f.

3.5.71

a. $y'(t) = A \cos t$, $y''(t) = -A \sin t$, so $y''(t) + y(t) = -A \sin t + A \sin t = 0$ for all A and all t.

b. $y'(t) = -B \sin t$, $y''(t) = -B \cos t$, so $y''(t) + y(t) = -B \cos t + B \cos t = 0$ for all B and all t.

c. $y' = A \cos t - B \sin t$, $y'' = -A \sin t - B \cos t$, so $y''(t) + y(t) = -A \sin t - B \cos t + A \sin t + B \cos t = 0$ for all A, B, t.

3.5.73

$$\lim_{x \to 0} \frac{\cos x - 1}{x} = \lim_{x \to 0} \frac{(\cos x - 1)(\cos x + 1)}{x(\cos x + 1)} = \lim_{x \to 0} \frac{\cos^2 x - 1}{x(\cos x + 1)} = \lim_{x \to 0} -\frac{\sin^2 x}{x(\cos x + 1)}$$

$$= \lim_{x \to 0} \frac{\sin x}{x} \cdot \lim_{x \to 0} -\frac{\sin x}{(\cos x + 1)} = 1 \cdot \frac{0}{2} = 0.$$

3.5.75

$$\frac{d}{dx} \cos x = \lim_{h \to 0} \frac{\cos(x + h) - \cos x}{h} = \lim_{h \to 0} \frac{\cos x \cos h - \sin x \sin h - \cos x}{h}$$

$$= \cos x \left(\lim_{h \to 0} \frac{\cos h - 1}{h} \right) - \sin x \left(\lim_{h \to 0} \frac{\sin h}{h} \right) = \cos x \cdot 0 - \sin x \cdot 1 = -\sin x.$$

3.5.77 g is continuous at 0 if and only if $\lim_{x \to 0} g(x) = g(0)$. Because $\lim_{x \to 0} g(x) = \lim_{x \to 0} \frac{1 - \cos x}{2x} = \frac{1}{2} \cdot 0 = 0$, we require $a = 0$ in order for g to be continuous.

3.5.79

a. $\dfrac{d}{dx} \sin^2 x = \sin x \cos x + \cos x \sin x = 2 \sin x \cos x.$

b. $\dfrac{d}{dx} \sin^3 x = \dfrac{d}{dx}(\sin^2 x)(\sin x) = (2 \sin x \cos x) \sin x + \sin^2 x \cdot \cos x = 3 \sin^2 x \cos x.$

c. $\dfrac{d}{dx} \sin^4 x = \dfrac{d}{dx}(\sin^3 x)(\sin x) = (3 \sin^2 x \cos x)(\sin x) + (\sin^3 x)(\cos x) = 4 \sin^3 x \cos x.$

d. We guess that $\dfrac{d}{dx} \sin^n x = n \sin^{n-1} x \cos x.$

We have already seen that the claim is valid for $n = 2$. Suppose our guess is valid for a given positive integer n. Then

$$\frac{d}{dx} \sin^{n+1} x = \frac{d}{dx}(\sin^n x)(\sin x) = (n \sin^{n-1} x \cos x)(\sin x) + \sin^n x \cos x = (n + 1) \sin^n x \cos x.$$

Thus by induction, the result holds for all n.

3.5.81

a. $f(x) = \sin x$, $a = \pi/6$.

b. $\lim\limits_{h \to 0} \dfrac{\sin(\pi/6 + h) - (1/2)}{h} = f'(\pi/6) = \cos(\pi/6) = \sqrt{3}/2$.

3.5.83

a. $f(x) = \cot x$, $a = \pi/4$.

b. $\lim\limits_{x \to \pi/4} \dfrac{\cot(x) - 1}{x - \pi/4} = f'(\pi/4) = -\csc^2(\pi/4) = -2$.

3.5.85 Because D is a difference quotient, and because $h = 0.01$ is small, D is a good approximation to f'. Therefore, the graph of D is nearly indistinguishable from the graph of $f'(x) = \cos x$.

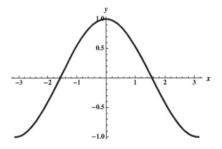

3.6   Derivatives as Rates of Change

3.6.1

The average rate of change over the interval $[a, a + \Delta x]$ is the slope of the line through $(a, f(a))$ and $(a + \Delta x, f(a + \Delta x))$, given by $m_{\text{avg}} = \dfrac{f(a+\Delta x)-f(a)}{\Delta x}$. The instantaneous rate of change is the limit of this expression as $\Delta x \to 0$, which is the slope of the tangent line at $(a, f(a))$.

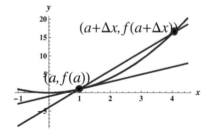

3.6.3 If $\frac{dy}{dx}$ is small, then small changes in x will result in relatively small changes in the value of y.

3.6.5 Acceleration is the instantaneous rate of change of the velocity; that is, if $s(t)$ is the position of an object at time t, then $s''(t) = \frac{d}{dt}(v(t)) = a(t)$ is the acceleration of the object at time t.

3.6.7 Each of the first 200 stoves cost on average \$70 to produce, while the 201st stove costs \$65 to produce.

3.6.9

a. $v_{\text{avg}} = \dfrac{f(0.75) - f(0)}{0.75} = \dfrac{30 - 0}{0.75} = 40$ mph.

b. $v_{\text{avg}} = \dfrac{f(0.75) - f(0.25)}{0.75 - 0.25} = \dfrac{30 - 10}{0.5} = 40$ mph.

This is a pretty good estimate, since the graph is nearly linear over that time interval.

c. $v_{avg} = \dfrac{f(2.25) - f(1.75)}{2.25 - 1.75} = \dfrac{-14 - 16}{0.5} = -60$ mph.

At 11 a.m. the velocity is $v(2) \approx -60$ mph. The car is moving south with a speed of approximately 60 mph.

d. From 9 a.m. until about 10:08 a.m., the car moves north, away from the station. Then it moves south, passing the station at approximately 11:02 a.m., and continues south until about 11:40 a.m. Then the car drives north until 12:00 noon stopping south of the station.

3.6.11

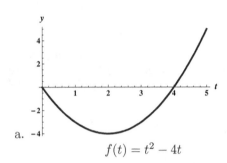

a. $f(t) = t^2 - 4t$

b. $f'(t) = 2t - 4$

b. $f'(t) = 0$ when $t = 2$ – that is when the object is stationary. For $0 \le t < 2$ we have $f'(t) < 0$ so the object is moving to the left. For $2 < t \le 5$ we have $f'(t) > 0$ so the object is moving to the right.

c. $f'(1) = -2$ ft/sec and $f''(t) = 2$ ft/sec^2, so in particular, $f''(1) = 2$ ft/sec^2.

d. $f'(t) = 0$ when $t = 2$ and $f''(2) = 2$ ft/sec^2.

e. On the interval $(2, 5]$ the velocity and acceleration are both positive, so the object's speed is increasing.

3.6.13

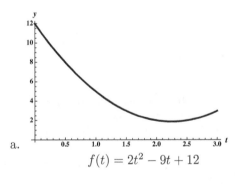

a. $f(t) = 2t^2 - 9t + 12$

b. $f'(t) = 4t - 9$

b. $f'(t) = 0$ when $t = 9/4$ – that is when the object is stationary. For $0 \le t < 9/4$ we have $f'(t) < 0$ so the object is moving to the left. For $9/4 < t \le 3$ we have $f'(t) > 0$ so the object is moving to the right.

c. $f'(1) = -5$ ft/sec and $f''(t) = 4$ ft/sec^2, so in particular, $f''(1) = 4$ ft/sec^2.

d. $f'(t) = 0$ when $t = 9/4$ and $f''(9/4) = 4$ ft/sec^2.

e. On the interval $(9/4, 3]$ both the velocity and acceleration are positive, so the object's speed is increasing.

3.6.15

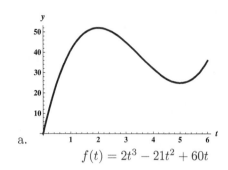

a. $f(t) = 2t^3 - 21t^2 + 60t$

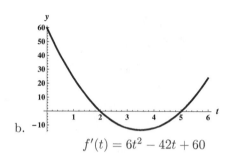

b. $f'(t) = 6t^2 - 42t + 60$

b. $f'(t) = 0$ when $6(t-2)(t-5) = 0$, which is at $t = 2$ and $t = 5$ – that is when the object is stationary. For $0 \le t < 2$ we have $f'(t) > 0$ so the object is moving to the right. For $2 < t < 5$ we have $f'(t) < 0$ so the object is moving to the left. For $5 < t \le 8$ we have $f'(t) > 0$, so the object is moving to the right again.

c. $f'(1) = 24$ ft/sec and $f''(t) = 12t - 42$, so $f''(1) = -30$ ft/sec^2.

d. $f'(t) = 0$ when $t = 2$ and $t = 5$. We have $f''(2) = -18$ ft/sec^2 and $f''(5) = 18$ ft/sec^2.

e. $f''(t) = 12t - 42$ is positive for $t > \frac{42}{12} = \frac{7}{2}$ and negative for $t < \frac{7}{2}$. So f' and f'' are both positive on $(5, 6]$ and are both negative on $(2, 3.5)$, so that is where the object is speeding up.

3.6.17

a. $v(t) = s'(t) = -32t + 64$ ft/sec.

b.   The highest point is reached at the instant when the stone changes from moving upward (where $v > 0$) to moving downward (where $v < 0$), so it must occur when $v = 0$, which is at $t = 2$.

c.   The height of the stone at its highest point is $s(2) = -16 \cdot 4 + 64 \cdot 2 + 32 = 96$ feet.

d.   The stone strikes the ground when $s(t) = 0$ for $t > 0$. Using the quadratic formula we see that this occurs when $t = 2 + \sqrt{6} \approx 4.45$ seconds.

e.   The velocity when the stone hits the ground is $v(2 + \sqrt{6}) = -32(2 + \sqrt{6}) + 64 = -32\sqrt{6} \approx -78.38$ feet per second.s

f.   The acceleration due to gravity is always negative, so the object is speeding up when its velocity is negative; that is, on its downward journey during the interval $(2, 2 + \sqrt{6})$.

3.6.19

a. The average growth rate from 1995 to 2005 is
$$\frac{p(10) - p(0)}{10 - 0} = \frac{8038 - 7055}{10} = 98.3 \text{ thousand}$$
people/year.

b The instantaneous growth rate is $p'(t) = -0.54t + 101$. In 1997 we have $p'(2) = 99.92$ thousand people per year and in 2005 we have $p'(10) = 95.6$ thousand people per year.

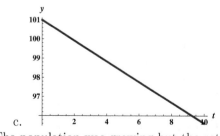

c.

The population was growing but the rate was slowing over this time interval.

3.6.21

a. The average cost function is given by $\overline{C}(x) = \frac{C(x)}{x} = \frac{1000}{x} + .1$. The marginal cost function is given by $M(x) = C'(x) = .1$.

b. At $a = 2000$ we have $\overline{C}(2000) = \frac{1000}{2000} + .1 = .6$, and $M(2000) = .1$.

c. The average cost per item when producing 2000 items is \$0.60. The cost of producing the next item is \$0.10.

3.6.23

a. The average cost function is given by $\overline{C}(x) = \frac{C(x)}{x} = \frac{100}{x} + 40 - 0.01x$. The marginal cost function is given by $M(x) = C'(x) = 40 - 0.02x$.

b. At $a = 1000$ we have $\overline{C}(1000) = \frac{100}{1000} + 40 - (.01)(1000) = 30.1$, and $M(1000) = 20$.

c. The average cost per item when producing 1000 items is \$30.10. The cost of producing the next item is \$20.00.

3.6.25

a. $D(10) = 40 - 20 = 20$ DVDs per day.

b. Demand is zero when $D(p) = 40 - 2p = 0$, which occurs for $p = 20$ dollars.

c. The elasticity is $E(p) = \frac{dD}{dp}\frac{p}{D} = -2\left(\frac{p}{40-2p}\right) = \frac{p}{p-20}$.

d. This quantity satisfies $-1 < E(p) < 0$ when $-1 < \frac{p}{p-20} < 0$ which occurs when $p < 20 - p$, or $p < 10$. So for prices in the interval $(0, 10)$ the demand is inelastic, while for prices in the interval $(10, 20)$ the demand is elastic.

e. If the price goes up from 10 to 10.25, that is a $\frac{.25}{10} = .025 = 2.5\%$ increase in price.

f. If the price goes up from 10 to 10.25, the demand goes from $D(10) = 40 - 20 = 20$ to $D(10.25) = 40 - 20.5 = 19.5$, which is a $\frac{.5}{20} = 2.5\%$ decrease.

3.6.27 $E(p) = \frac{dD}{dp}\frac{p}{D} = -abe^{-bp}\left(\frac{p}{ae^{-bp}}\right) = -bp$. Note that $-bp = -1$ for $p = \frac{1}{b}$. So the demand is elastic for $p > \frac{1}{b}$ and inelastic for $0 < p < \frac{1}{b}$.

3.6.29

a. False. For example, when a ball is thrown up in the air near the surface of the earth, its acceleration is constant (due to gravity) but its velocity changes during its trip.

b. True. If the rate of change of velocity is zero, then velocity must be constant.

c. False. If the velocity is constant over an interval, then the average velocity is equal to the instantaneous velocity over the interval.

d. True. For example, a ball dropped from a tower has negative acceleration and increasing speed as it falls toward the earth.

3.6.31 In each case, the stone reaches its maximum height when its velocity is zero.

On Mars, this occurs when $v(t) = s'(t) = 96 - 12t = 0$, or when $t = 8$ seconds. So the maximum height on Mars is $s(8) = 384$ feet.

On Earth, this occurs when $v(t) = s'(t) = 96 - 32t = 0$, or when $t = 3$ seconds. So the maximum height on Earth is $s(3) = 144$ feet.

The stone will travel $384 - 144 = 240$ feet higher on Mars.

3.6.33 The first stone reaches its maximum height when $f'(t) = -32t + 32 = 0$, so after 1 second, and its maximum height is therefore $f(1) = -16 + 32 + 48 = 64$ feet.

The second stone reaches its maximum height when $g'(t) = -32t + v_0 = 0$, so when $t = \frac{v_0}{32}$. Its height at that time is $g(v_0/32) = -16(v_0/32)^2 + (v_0^2/32) = \frac{v_0^2}{64}$. This is equal to 64 when $v_0 = 64$ feet per second.

3.6.35

a. The velocity is zero at $t = 1, 2,$ and 3.

b. The object is moving in the positive direction when the slope of s is positive, so from $t = 0$ to $t = 1$, and from $t = 2$ to $t = 3$. It is moving in the negative direction from $t = 1$ to $t = 2$, and for $t > 3$.

c.

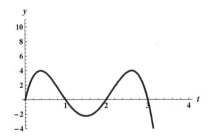

d. The speed is increasing on $(0, 1/2)$ as the velocity is positive and the acceleration is positive there. On $(1/2, 1)$ the speed is decreasing as the velocity is positive but the acceleration is negative. On $(1, 3/2)$ the speed is increasing as the velocity is negative and the acceleration is negative, but on $(3/2, 2)$ the speed is decreasing as the velocity is negative but the acceleration is positive. On approximately $(2, 2.6)$ the speed is increasing as the velocity is positive and the acceleration is positive, but on about $(2.6, 3)$ the velocity is positive but the acceleration is negative, so the speed is decreasing. On $(3, \infty)$ both the velocity and the acceleration are negative, so the object is speeding up.

3.6.37

a. $P(x) = xp(x) - C(x) = 100x + 0.02x^2 - 50x - 100 = 0.02x^2 + 50x - 100.$

b. The average profit is $\overline{P}(x) = \frac{P(x)}{x} = 0.02x + 50 - \frac{100}{x}$. The marginal profit is $P'(x) = .04x + 50.$

c. $\overline{P}(500) = 59.8.$ $P'(500) = 70.$

d. The average profit for the first 500 items sold is $59.80, while the profit on the 501st item is $70.00.

3.6.39

a. $P(x) = xp(x) - C(x) = 100x + 0.04x^2 - 800.$

b. The average profit is $\overline{P}(x) = \frac{P(x)}{x} = .04x + 100 - \frac{800}{x}$. The marginal profit is $P'(x) = .08x + 100.$

c. $\overline{P}(1000) = 139.2.$ $P'(1000) = 180.$

d. The average profit for the first 1000 items sold is $139.20, while the profit on the 1001st item is $180.00.

3.6.41

a. Because the graph represents the growth rate, the slowest rate (of about 1.1 million people per year) occurs at about $t = 30$, which corresponds to the year 1930.

b. The largest growth rate occurs at $t = 60$, so the year 1960 at the largest growth rate of about 2.9 million per year.

c. Because $p'(t) > 0$ for all t shown on the graph, $p(t)$ is never decreasing.

d. The population growth rate $p'(t)$ is increasing from about 1905 to 1915, from 1930 to 1960, and from 1980 to 1990.

3.6.43

a.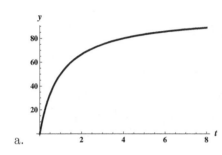

b. $v(t) = s'(t) = \frac{(t+1)100 - 100t \cdot 1}{(t+1)^2} = \frac{100}{(t+1)^2}$.

c.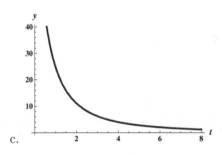

The velocity of the marble is decreasing.

d. $s(t) = 80$ when $\frac{100t}{t+1} = 80$, or $100t = 80t + 80$, which occurs when $t = 4$ seconds.

e. $v(t) = 50$ when $\frac{100}{(t+1)^2} = 50$, or $(t+1)^2 = 2$. This occurs for $t = \sqrt{2} - 1 \approx 0.414$ seconds.

3.6.45

a. The average cost function is $\overline{C}(x) = \frac{C(x)}{25000} = 50 + \frac{5000}{x} + 0.00006x$. The marginal cost function is $C'(x) = -\frac{125000000}{x^2} + 1.5$.
The average cost decreases to about 50 per unit as the batch size increases, while the marginal cost is negative but increases.

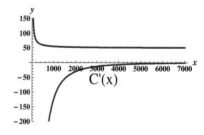

b. $\overline{C}(5000) = 51.3$, $C'(5000) = -3.5$.

c. If the batch size is 5000, then the average cost of producing 25000 items is $51.30 per item. If the batch size is increased from 5000 to 5001, then the cost of producing 25000 items would decrease by about $3.50.

3.6.47

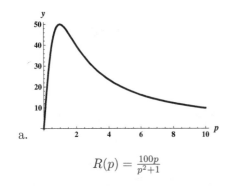

a. $R(p) = \frac{100p}{p^2+1}$

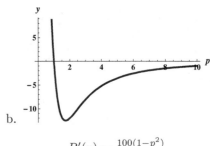

b. $R'(p) = \frac{100(1-p^2)}{(p^2+1)^2}$

c. $R'(p)$ is zero at $p = 1$, and the maximum of $R(p)$ occurs at this same value of p, so that is the price to charge in order to maximize revenue. The revenue at this price is $50.00.

3.6.49

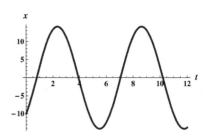

a. The mass oscillates about the equilibrium point.

b. $\frac{dx}{dt} = 10\cos t + 10\sin t$ is the velocity of the mass at time t.

c. $\frac{dx}{dt} = 0$ when $\sin t = -\cos t$, which occurs when $t = \frac{4n+3}{4} \cdot \pi$ where n is any positive integer.

d. The model is unrealistic as it ignores the effects of friction and gravity. In reality, the amplitude would decrease as the mass oscillates.

3.6.51

a. Juan starts out faster, but slows toward the end, while Jean starts slower but increases her speed toward the end.

b. Because both start and finish at the same time, they finish with the same average angular velocity.

c. It is a tie.

d. Jean's velocity is given by $\theta'(t) = \frac{\pi t}{4}$. At $t = 2$, $\theta'(2) = \frac{\pi}{2}$ radians per minute. Her velocity is greatest at $t = 4$.

e. Juan's velocity is given by $\phi'(t) = \pi - \frac{\pi t}{4}$. At $t = 2$, $\phi'(2) = \frac{\pi}{2}$ radians per minute as well. His velocity is greatest at $t = 0$.

3.6.53

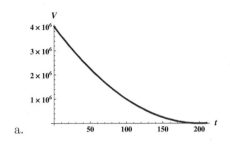

a.

At the beginning the volume is 4,000,000 cubic meters.

b. The tank is empty when $V(t) = 100(200 - t)^2 = 0$, which occurs when $t = 200$.

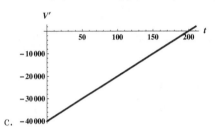

c.

Because $V(t)$ can be written as $V(t) = 4,000,000 - 40,000t + 100t^2$, the flow rate is $V'(t) = -40,000 + 200t$ cubic meters per minute.

d. The flow rate is largest (in absolute value) when $t = 0$ and smallest when $t = 200$.

3.6.55

a. $v(t) = y'(t) = -15e^{-t}\cos t - 15e^{-t}\sin t$, so $v(1) \approx -7.625$ meters per second, and $v(3) \approx .63$ meters per second.

b. She is moving down for approximately 2.4 seconds, and then up until about 5.5 seconds, and then down again until about 8.6 seconds, and then up again.

c. The maximum velocity going up appears to be about about 0.65 meters per second.

3.6.57

a. $T'(t) = 160 - 80x$, so $T'(1) = 80$, so the heat flux at 1 is -80. At $x = 3$ we have $T'(3) = -80$, so the heat flux at 3 is 80.

b. The heat flux $-T'(x)$ is negative for $0 \le x < 2$ and positive for $2 < x \le 4$.

c. At any point other than the midpoint of the rod, heat flows toward the closest end of the rod, and "out the end."

3.7 The Chain Rule

3.7.1 If $y = f(x)$ and $u = g(x)$ then $\dfrac{dy}{dx} = \dfrac{dy}{du} \cdot \dfrac{du}{dx}$. Alternatively, we have $\dfrac{d}{dx}(f(g(x))) = f'(g(x))g'(x)$.

3.7.3 The derivative of $f(g(x))$ equals f' evaluated at $g(x)$ multiplied by g' evaluated at x.

3.7.5 The inner function is $x^2 + 10$ and the outer function is u^{-5}, so with $y = f(u)$ and $u = g(x)$, we have $f(u) = u^{-5}$ and $g(x) = x^2 + 10$. Then $y = (x^2 + 10)^{-5}$.

3.7.7 With $u = 3x + 7$ and $y = u^{10}$ we have $\dfrac{dy}{dx} = \dfrac{dy}{dx} \cdot \dfrac{du}{dx} = 10u^9 \cdot 3 = 30(3x + 7)^9$.

3.7.9 With $u = \sin x$ and $y = u^5$ we have $\dfrac{dy}{dx} = \dfrac{dy}{du} \cdot \dfrac{du}{dx} = 5u^4 \cdot \cos x = 5\sin^4 x \cos x$.

3.7.11 With $u = 5x - 7$ and $y = e^u$, we have $\frac{dy}{dx} = \frac{dy}{du}\frac{du}{dx} = e^u(5) = 5e^{5x-7}$.

3.7.13 With $u = x^2 + 1$ and $y = \sqrt{u}$ we have $\frac{dy}{dx} = \frac{dy}{du} \cdot \frac{du}{dx} = \frac{1}{2\sqrt{u}} \cdot (2x) = \frac{x}{\sqrt{x^2+1}}$.

3.7.15 With $u = 5x^2$ and $y = \tan u$ we have $\frac{dy}{dx} = \frac{dy}{du} \cdot \frac{du}{dx} = \sec^2 u \cdot (10x) = 10x \sec^2 5x^2$.

3.7.17 With $u = e^x$ and $y = \sec u$ we have $\frac{dy}{dx} = \frac{dy}{du} \cdot \frac{du}{dx} = (\sec u \cdot \tan u) \cdot (e^x) = e^x \cdot \sec e^x \cdot \tan e^x$.

3.7.19 With $g(x) = 3x^2 + 7x$ and $f(u) = u^{10}$ we have $\frac{d}{dx}[f(g(x))] = f'(g(x))g'(x) = 10(3x^2 + 7x)^9(6x + 7)$.

3.7.21 With $g(x) = 10x + 1$ and $f(u) = \sqrt{u}$, we have $\frac{d}{dx}[f(g(x))] = f'(g(x))g'(x) = \frac{1}{2\sqrt{10x+1}} \cdot 10 = \frac{5}{\sqrt{10x+1}}$.

3.7.23 With $g(x) = 7x^3 + 1$ and $f(u) = 5u^{-3}$ we have $\frac{d}{dx}[f(g(x))] = f'(g(x))g'(x) = -15(7x^3+1)^{-4}(21x^2) = -315(7x^3 + 1)^{-4} \cdot x^2$.

3.7.25 With $g(x) = 3x + 1$ and $f(u) = \sec u$, we have $\frac{d}{dx}[f(g(x))] = f'(g(x))g'(x) = \sec(3x + 1)\tan(3x + 1) \cdot 3 = 3\sec(3x + 1)\tan(3x + 1)$.

3.7.27 With $g(x) = e^x$ and $f(u) = \tan u$ we have $\frac{d}{dx}[f(g(x))] = f'(g(x))g'(x) = \sec^2 u \cdot e^x = e^x \sec^2 e^x$.

3.7.29 With $g(x) = 4x^3 + 3x + 1$ and $f(u) = \sin u$ we have $\frac{d}{dx}[f(g(x))] = f'(g(x))g'(x) = \cos u \cdot (12x^2 + 3) = (12x^2 + 3) \cdot \cos(4x^3 + 3x + 1)$.

3.7.31 With $g(x) = 2\sqrt{x}$ and $f(u) = \sin u$, we have $\frac{d}{dx}[f(g(x))] = f'(g(x))g'(x) = \cos(2\sqrt{x}) \cdot \frac{1}{\sqrt{x}} = \frac{\cos(2\sqrt{x})}{\sqrt{x}}$.

3.7.33 With $g(x) = \sec x + \tan x$ and $f(u) = u^5$ we have $\frac{d}{dx}[f(g(x))] = f'(g(x))g'(x) = 5u^4 \cdot (\sec x \tan x + \sec^2 x) = 5(\sec x + \tan x)^4(\sec x \tan x + \sec^2 x) = 5\sec x(\sec x + \tan x)^5$.

3.7.35

a. $u = g(x) = \cos x$, $y = f(u) = u^3$. So $\frac{dy}{dx} = \frac{dy}{du} \cdot \frac{du}{dx} = 3\cos^2 x \cdot (-\sin x) = -3\cos^2 x \sin x$.

b. $u = g(x) = x^3$, $y = f(u) = \cos u$. So $\frac{dy}{dx} = \frac{dy}{du} \cdot \frac{du}{dx} = -\sin x^3 \cdot 3x^2 = -3x^2 \sin x^3$.

3.7.37

a. $h'(3) = f'(g(3))g'(3) = f'(1) \cdot 20 = 5 \cdot 20 = 100$.

b. $h'(2) = f'(g(2))g'(2) = f'(5) \cdot 10 = -10 \cdot 10 = -100$.

c. $p'(4) = g'(f(4))f'(4) = g'(1) \cdot (-8) = 2 \cdot (-8) = -16$.

d. $p'(2) = g'(f(2))f'(2) = g'(3) \cdot 2 = 20 \cdot 2 = 40$.

e. $h'(5) = f'(g(5))g'(5) = f'(2) \cdot 20 = 2 \cdot 20 = 40$.

3.7.39 Note that $a(70) = 13330$. $\frac{d}{dt}p(a(t))|_{t=70} = p'(a(70))a'(70) \approx \frac{738-765}{14330-13330} \cdot \frac{13440-13330}{80-70} = -.297$ hPa per minute.

3.7.41 Take $g(x) = 2x^6 - 3x^3 + 3$, and $n = 25$. Then $y' = n(g(x))^{n-1}g'(x) = 25(2x^6 - 3x^3 + 3)^{24}(12x^5 - 9x^2)$.

3.7.43 Take $g(x) = 1 + 2\tan x$, and $n = 15$. Then $y' = n(g(x))^{n-1}g'(x) = 15(1 + 2\tan x)^{14}(2\sec^2 x) = 30(1 + 2\tan x)^{14}\sec^2 x$.

3.7.45

$$\frac{d}{dx}\sqrt{1 + \cot^2 x} = \frac{1}{2\sqrt{1 + \cot^2 x}} \cdot \frac{d}{dx}(1 + \cot^2 x) = \frac{1}{2\sqrt{1 + \cot^2 x}} \cdot 2\cot x \cdot \frac{d}{dx}\cot x$$

$$= \frac{1}{2\sqrt{1 + \cot^2 x}} \cdot 2\cot x \cdot (-\csc^2 x) = -\frac{\cot x \csc^2 x}{\sqrt{1 + \cot^2 x}}.$$

3.7.47

$$\frac{d}{dx}\sin(\sin(e^x)) = \cos(\sin(e^x))\frac{d}{dx}\sin(e^x)$$
$$= \cos(\sin(e^x)) \cdot \cos(e^x) \cdot e^x$$

3.7.49

$$\frac{d}{dx}\sin^5(\cos 3x) = 5\sin^4(\cos 3x) \cdot \frac{d}{dx}(\sin(\cos 3x))$$
$$= 5\sin^4(\cos 3x) \cdot \cos(\cos 3x) \cdot \frac{d}{dx}\cos 3x$$
$$= 5\sin^4(\cos 3x) \cdot \cos(\cos 3x) \cdot (-\sin 3x) \cdot 3$$
$$= -15\sin^4(\cos 3x)\cos(\cos 3x)\sin 3x.$$

3.7.51

$$\frac{d}{dx}\tan(e^{\sqrt{3x}}) = \sec^2(e^{\sqrt{3x}}) \cdot \frac{d}{dx}e^{\sqrt{3x}} = \sec^2(e^{\sqrt{3x}}) \cdot e^{\sqrt{3x}} \cdot \frac{d}{dx}\sqrt{3x}$$
$$= \sec^2(e^{\sqrt{3x}}) \cdot e^{\sqrt{3x}} \cdot \frac{3}{2\sqrt{3x}}.$$

3.7.53 $\frac{d}{dx}\sqrt{x+\sqrt{x}} = \frac{1}{2\sqrt{x+\sqrt{x}}} \cdot \frac{d}{dx}(x+\sqrt{x}) = \frac{1}{2\sqrt{x+\sqrt{x}}} \cdot \left(1+\frac{1}{2\sqrt{x}}\right).$

3.7.55 $\frac{d}{dx}f(g(x^2)) = f'(g(x^2)) \cdot \frac{d}{dx}(g(x^2)) = f'(g(x^2)) \cdot g'(x^2) \cdot 2x.$

3.7.57 $y' = 5\left(\frac{x}{x+1}\right)^4 \cdot \frac{(x+1)(1) - x(1)}{(x+1)^2} = \frac{5x^4}{(x+1)^6}.$

3.7.59 $y' = e^{x^2+1}(2x)\sin x^3 + e^{x^2+1}(\cos x^3)3x^2 = xe^{x^2+1}(2\sin x^3 + 3x\cos x^3).$

3.7.61 $\frac{dy}{d\theta} = 2\theta\sec 5\theta + \theta^2(5\sec 5\theta \tan 5\theta) = \theta\sec 5\theta(2 + 5\theta \tan 5\theta).$

3.7.63 $y' = 4((x+2)(x^2+1))^3 \cdot ((1)(x^2+1) + (x+2)(2x)) = 4((x+2)(x^2+1))^3(3x^2+4x+1) = 4(x+2)^2(x^2+1)^3(3x+1)(x+1).$

3.7.65 $y' = \frac{1}{2}(x^4 + \cos 2x)^{-1/2}(4x^3 - 2\sin 2x) = \frac{2x^3 - \sin 2x}{\sqrt{x^4 + \cos 2x}}.$

3.7.67 $y' = 2(p+\pi)^1\sin p^2 + (p+\pi)^2(\cos p^2)(2p) = (p+\pi)(2\sin p^2 + 2p^2\cos p^2 + 2p\pi\cos p^2) = 2(p+\pi)(\sin p^2 + p^2\cos p^2 + p\pi\cos p^2).$

3.7.69

a. True. The product rule alone will suffice.

b. True. This function is the composition of e^x with $\sqrt{x+1}$.

c. True. The derivative of the composition $f(g(x))$ is the product of $f'(g(x))$ with $g'(x)$, so it is the product of two derivatives.

d. False. In fact, $\frac{d}{dx}P(Q(x)) = P'(Q(x))Q'(x).$

3.7.71

$$\frac{d^2}{dx^2}\sin x^2 = \frac{d}{dx}(2x\cos x^2) = 2(\cos x^2 - 2x^2\sin x^2)$$
$$= 2\cos x^2 - 4x^2\sin x^2.$$

Note that in the middle of this calculation we used a result from the middle of the previous problem – namely the derivative of $x\cos x^2$.

3.7.73 $\frac{d^2}{dx^2}e^{-2x^2} = \frac{d}{dx}\left(-4xe^{-2x^2}\right) = -4e^{-2x^2} + 16x^2e^{-2x^2} = 4e^{-2x^2}(4x^2 - 1).$

3.7.75 $\frac{d}{dx}\sqrt{f(x)} = \frac{1}{2\sqrt{f(x)}}\cdot f'(x).$

3.7.77

$y' = \frac{(x^3 - 6x - 1)(2)(x^2 - 1)(2x) - (x^2 - 1)^2(3x^2 - 6)}{(x^3 - 6x - 1)^2},$

so $y'(3) = \frac{(27 - 18 - 1)(2)(8)(6) - (64)(21)}{64} = \frac{768 - 1344}{64} = -\frac{576}{64} = -9.$ The equation of the tangent line is thus $y - 8 = -9(x - 3)$, or $y = -9x + 35.$

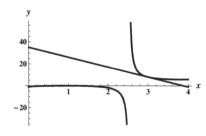

3.7.79

a. $g'(4) = 3$, $g(4) = 3\cdot 4 - 5 = 7.$ $f'(7) = -2$, $f(7) = -2\cdot 7 + 23 = 9.$ Thus, $h(4) = f(g(4)) = f(7) = 9,$ and $h'(4) = f'(g(4))g'(4) = f'(7)\cdot 3 = -2\cdot 3 = -6.$

b. The tangent line to h at $(4, 9)$ is given by $y - 9 = -6(x - 4)$, or $y = -6x + 33.$

3.7.81

$y'(x) = 2e^{2x}$, so $y'\left(\frac{\ln 3}{2}\right) = 2e^{\ln 3} = 6.$ Also, $y\left(\frac{\ln 3}{2}\right) = e^{\ln 3} = 3.$ The tangent line is therefore given by $y - 3 = 6\left(x - \frac{\ln 3}{2}\right)$, or $y = 6x + 3 - 3\ln 3.$

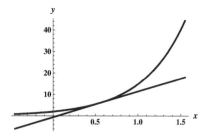

3.7.83 First, note that $g'(x) = \cos(\pi f(x))\cdot \pi f'(x).$

a. $g'(0) = \cos(\pi\cdot f(0))\cdot \pi f'(0) = \cos(-3\pi)\cdot 3\pi = -3\pi.$

b. $g'(1) = \cos(\pi\cdot f(1))\cdot \pi f'(1) = \cos(3\pi)\cdot 5\pi = -5\pi.$

3.7.85

a. $\frac{d^2y}{dt^2} = \frac{d}{dt}\left(-y_0\sqrt{\frac{k}{m}}\sin\left(t\sqrt{\frac{k}{m}}\right)\right) = -y_0\cdot \frac{k}{m}\cdot \cos\left(t\sqrt{\frac{k}{m}}\right).$

b. $-\frac{k}{m}y = -\frac{k}{m}\left(y_0\cos\left(t\sqrt{\frac{k}{m}}\right)\right) = \frac{d^2y}{dt^2}.$

3.7.87

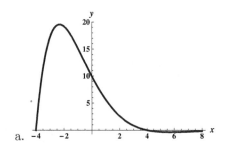

a.

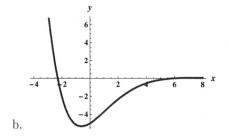

b.

$$\frac{dy}{dt} = -5e^{-t/2}\cos\left(\frac{\pi t}{8}\right) - \frac{5\pi}{4}e^{-t/2}\sin\left(\frac{\pi t}{8}\right).$$

c. The velocity is zero at about -2.3 and at about 5.7, and the displacement has a maximum and a minimum at these points.

3.7.89

a. Assuming a non leap year, March 1st corresponds to $t = 59$. We have $D(59) = 12 - 3\cos\left(\frac{2\pi(69)}{365}\right) \approx 10.88$ hours.

b. $\frac{d}{dt}D(t) = 3 \cdot \frac{2\pi}{365}\sin\left(\frac{2\pi(t+10)}{365}\right)$ hours per day.

c. $D'(59) \approx 0.048$ hours per day ≈ 2 minutes and 52 seconds per day. This means that on March 1st, the days are getting longer by just shy of 3 minutes per day.

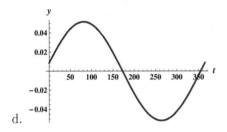

d.

e. The largest increase in the length of the days appears to be at about $t = 81$, and the largest decrease at about $t = 265$. These correspond to March 22nd and to September 22nd. The least rapid changes occur at about $t = 172$ and $t = 355$. These correspond to June 21st and December 21st.

3.7.91

a. $E'(t) = 400 + 200\cos\left(\frac{\pi t}{12}\right)$ MW.

b. Because the maximum value of $\cos\theta$ is 1, the maximum value of $E'(t)$ will be 600 MW, where $\cos\left(\frac{\pi t}{12}\right) = 1$, which is where $t = 0$, which corresponds to noon.

c. Because the minimum value of $\cos\theta$ is -1, the minimum value of $E'(t)$ will be 200 MW, where $\cos\left(\frac{\pi t}{12}\right) = -1$, which is where $\frac{\pi t}{12} = \pi$, or $t = 12$, which corresponds to midnight.

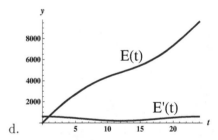

d.

3.7.93

a. $f'(x) = \frac{d}{dx}(\cos^2 x + \sin^2 x) = 2(\cos x)(-\sin x) + 2\sin x\cos x = 0$.

b. If $f(x)$ is a constant, then the output value must be the same at any input value, so we choose to evaluate f at a nice value like $x = 0$. We see that $f(0) = \cos^2 0 + \sin^2 0 = 1^2 + 0^2 = 1$, so we must have $\cos^2 x + \sin^2 x = 1$ for all x.

3.7.95 $\frac{d}{dx}\left(f(x)(g(x))^{-1}\right) = f'(x)(g(x))^{-1} + f(x)(-(g(x))^{-2}g'(x)) = \frac{f'(x)}{g(x)} - \frac{f(x)g'(x)}{(g(x))^2} = \frac{g(x)f'(x) - f(x)g'(x)}{(g(x))^2}$.

3.7.97

a. $h(x) = (x^2 - 3)^5$, $a = 2$.

b. $h'(x) = 5(x^2 - 3)^4(2x) = 10x(x^2 - 3)^4$, so the value of this limit is $h'(2) = 20$.

3.7.99

a. $h(x) = \sin x^2$, $a = \frac{\pi}{2}$.

b. $h'(x) = (\cos x^2)(2x)$, so the value of this limit is $h'\left(\frac{\pi}{2}\right) = \pi \cdot \cos\left(\frac{\pi^2}{4}\right) \approx -2.45$.

3.7.101 $\lim\limits_{x \to 5} \dfrac{f(x^2) - f(25)}{x - 5} = \dfrac{d}{dx}\left[f(x^2)\right]_{x=5} = 2 \cdot 5 \cdot f'(25) = 10f'(25)$.

3.7.103

a. $\lim\limits_{v \to u} H(v) = \lim\limits_{v \to u}\left(\dfrac{f(v) - f(u)}{v - u} - f'(u)\right) = \lim\limits_{v \to u}\left(\dfrac{f(v) - f(u)}{v - u}\right) - f'(u) = f'(u) - f'(u) = 0$.

b. Suppose $u = v$. Then clearly both sides of the given expression are 0, so they are equal. Suppose $u \neq v$. Then $H(v) = \dfrac{f(v) - f(u)}{v - u} - f'(u)$, so $H(v) + f'(u) = \dfrac{f(v) - f(u)}{v - u}$, so the result holds by multiplying both sides of this equation by $v - u$.

c.
$$h'(a) = \lim_{x \to a} \frac{f(g(x)) - f(g(a))}{x - a} = \lim_{x \to a} \frac{H(g(x)) + f'(g(a))}{x - a} \cdot (g(x) - g(a))$$
$$= \lim_{x \to a}\left[(H(g(x)) + f'(g(a))) \cdot \frac{g(x) - g(a)}{x - a}\right].$$

d. $h'(a) = \lim\limits_{x \to a}\left[(H(g(x)) + f'(g(a))) \cdot \dfrac{g(x) - g(a)}{x - a}\right] = (0 + f'(g(a))) \cdot g'(a) = f'(g(a))g'(a)$.

3.8 Implicit Differentiation

3.8.1 Implicit differentiation gives a single unified derivative, whereas solving for y explicitly yields two different functions.

3.8.3 The result of implicit differentiation is often an expression involving both the dependent and independent variables, so one would need to know both in order to calculate the value of the derivative.

3.8.5

a. $4x^3 + 4y^3 \dfrac{dy}{dx} = 0$. Thus $4y^3 \dfrac{dy}{dx} = -4x^3$, so $\dfrac{dy}{dx} = -\dfrac{x^3}{y^3}$.

b. When $x = 1$ and $y = -1$, we have $\dfrac{dy}{dx} = \dfrac{-1}{-1} = 1$.

3.8.7

a. $2y\dfrac{dy}{dx} = 4$, so $\dfrac{dy}{dx} = \dfrac{2}{y}$.

b. $\dfrac{dy}{dx}\Big|_{(1,2)} = \dfrac{2}{2} = 1$.

3.8.9

a. $\dfrac{dy}{dx}\cos y = 20x^3$, so $\dfrac{dy}{dx} = \dfrac{20x^3}{\cos y}$.

b. $\dfrac{dy}{dx}\Big|_{(1,\pi)} = \dfrac{20}{\cos \pi} = -20$.

3.8.11

a. $-\dfrac{dy}{dx}\sin y = 1$, so $\dfrac{dy}{dx} = -\dfrac{1}{\sin y} = -\csc y$.

b. $\dfrac{dy}{dx}\Big|_{(0,\pi/2)} = -\csc(\pi/2) = -1$.

3.8.13 $\left(y + x\dfrac{dy}{dx}\right)\cos(xy) = 1 + \dfrac{dy}{dx}$, so $y\cos(xy) + x\dfrac{dy}{dx}\cos(xy) = 1 + \dfrac{dy}{dx}$. If we rearrange terms in order to have the terms with a factor of $\dfrac{dy}{dx}$ all on the same side, we obtain $y\cos(xy) - 1 = \dfrac{dy}{dx} - x\dfrac{dy}{dx}\cos(xy)$. Factoring out the $\dfrac{dy}{dx}$ factor gives $y\cos(xy) - 1 = \dfrac{dy}{dx}(1 - x\cos(xy))$, so $\dfrac{dy}{dx} = \dfrac{y\cos(xy) - 1}{1 - x\cos(xy)}$.

3.8.15 $1 + \frac{dy}{dx} = -\sin y \cdot \frac{dy}{dx}$, so $\frac{dy}{dx} + (\sin y)\frac{dy}{dx} = -1$, and $\frac{dy}{dx} = -\frac{1}{1+\sin y}$.

3.8.17 $-2y\frac{dy}{dx}\sin y^2 + 1 = \frac{dy}{dx}e^y$, which we can write as $1 = \frac{dy}{dx}e^y + 2y\frac{dy}{dx}\sin y^2$, or $1 = \frac{dy}{dx}(e^y + 2y\sin y^2)$. Thus, $\frac{dy}{dx} = \frac{1}{e^y + 2y\sin y^2}$.

3.8.19

$$3x^2 = \frac{(x-y)(1 + \frac{dy}{dx}) - (x+y)(1 - \frac{dy}{dx})}{(x-y)^2}$$

$$3x^2(x-y)^2 = x + x\frac{dy}{dx} - y - y\frac{dy}{dx} - x + x\frac{dy}{dx} - y + y\frac{dy}{dx}$$

$$3x^2(x-y)^2 + 2y = 2x\frac{dy}{dx}$$

$$\frac{dy}{dx} = \frac{3x^2(x-y)^2 + 2y}{2x}$$

3.8.21

$$18x^2 + 21\frac{dy}{dx}y^2 = 13(y + x\frac{dy}{dx})$$

$$21\frac{dy}{dx}y^2 - 13x\frac{dy}{dx} = 13y - 18x^2$$

$$\frac{dy}{dx} = \frac{13y - 18x^2}{21y^2 - 13x}.$$

3.8.23

$$\frac{4x^3 + 2y\frac{dy}{dx}}{2\sqrt{x^4 + y^2}} = 5 + 6y^2\frac{dy}{dx}$$

$$y\frac{dy}{dx} - 6\frac{dy}{dx}y^2\sqrt{x^4 + y^2} = 5\sqrt{x^4 + y^2} - 2x^3$$

$$\frac{dy}{dx} = \frac{5\sqrt{x^4 + y^2} - 2x^3}{y - 6y^2\sqrt{x^4 + y^2}}.$$

3.8.25

a. $2^2 + 2 \cdot 1 + 1^2 = 7$, so the point $(2,1)$ does lie on the curve.

b. $2x + y + xy' + 2yy' = 0$, which can be written $(x+2y)y' = -2x - y$. Solving for y' yields $y' = \frac{-2x-y}{x+2y}$. Thus, at the point $(2,1)$ we have $y' = -\frac{5}{4}$. The equation of the tangent line is therefore $y - 1 = -\frac{5}{4}(x-2)$, or $y = -\frac{5}{4}x + \frac{7}{2}$.

3.8.27

a. $\sin \pi + 5\frac{\pi^2}{5} = \pi^2$, so the point $(\pi^2/5, \pi)$ does lie on the curve.

b. $y'\cos y + 5 = 2yy'$, so $5 = y'(2y - \cos y)$, so $y' = \frac{5}{2y - \cos y}$. At the given point we have $y' = \frac{5}{2\pi + 1}$. The equation of the tangent line is therefore $y - \pi = \frac{5}{1+2\pi}\left(x - \pi^2/5\right)$, or $y = \frac{5}{1+2\pi}x + \frac{\pi(1+\pi)}{1+2\pi}$.

3.8.29

a. $\cos(\pi/2 - \pi/4) + \sin(\pi/4) = (\sqrt{2}/2) + (\sqrt{2}/2) = \sqrt{2}$, so the point $(\pi/2, \pi/4)$ does lie on the curve.

b. $(1 - y')(-\sin(x-y)) + y'\cos y = 0$, which can be written as $y'(\cos y + \sin(x-y)) = \sin(x-y)$, so $y' = \frac{\sin(x-y)}{\cos y + \sin(x-y)}$. At the given point we have $y' = 1/2$. The equation of the tangent line is therefore $y - (\pi/4) = (1/2)(x - \pi/2)$, or $y = \frac{1}{2}x$.

3.8.31 $1 + 2yy' = 0$, so $y' = -\frac{1}{2y}$. Differentiating again, we obtain

$$y'' = -\frac{1}{2} \cdot \frac{-y'}{y^2} = \frac{y'}{2y^2} = \left(-\frac{1}{2y}\right) \cdot \frac{1}{2y^2} = -\frac{1}{4y^3}.$$

3.8.33 $1 + \frac{dy}{dx} = (\cos y)\frac{dy}{dx}$, so $1 = \frac{dy}{dx}(\cos y - 1)$, and thus $\frac{dy}{dx} = \frac{1}{\cos y - 1}$. Thus

$$\frac{d^2y}{dx^2} = -\frac{1}{(\cos y - 1)^2} \cdot \left(-\sin y \frac{dy}{dx}\right) = \frac{\sin y}{(\cos y - 1)^2} \cdot \frac{1}{(\cos y - 1)} = \frac{\sin y}{(\cos y - 1)^3}.$$

3.8.35 $2y'e^{2y} + 1 = y'$, so $y' = \frac{1}{1 - 2e^{2y}}$. Differentiating again, we obtain

$$y'' = -\left(1 - 2e^{2y}\right)^{-2}\left(-4e^{2y}y'\right) = \frac{4e^{2y}}{(1 - 2e^{2y})^3}.$$

3.8.37 $\frac{dy}{dx} = \frac{5}{4}x^{\frac{5}{4}-1} = \frac{5}{4}x^{\frac{1}{4}}.$

3.8.39 $\frac{dy}{dx} = 5 \cdot \frac{2}{3}(5x + 1)^{-\frac{1}{3}} = \frac{10}{3(5x+1)^{\frac{1}{3}}}.$

3.8.41 $\frac{dy}{dx} = \frac{1}{4}\left(\frac{2x}{4x-3}\right)^{-\frac{3}{4}} \cdot \frac{2(4x-3) - 2x \cdot 4}{(4x-3)^2} = -\frac{3}{2}\left(\frac{4x-3}{2x}\right)^{\frac{3}{4}} \cdot \frac{1}{(4x-3)^2} = -\frac{3}{2^{7/4}x^{3/4}(4x-3)^{5/4}}.$

3.8.43 Note that $y = (1 + x^{1/3})^{2/3}$, so $y' = (2/3)(1 + x^{1/3})^{-1/3} \cdot (1/3)x^{-2/3} = \frac{2}{9x^{2/3}(1+x^{1/3})^{1/3}}.$

3.8.45 $\frac{1}{3}x^{-\frac{2}{3}} + \frac{4}{3}y^{\frac{1}{3}}y' = 0$, so at the given point we have $\frac{1}{3} + \frac{4}{3}y' = 0$, so $y' = -\frac{1}{4}.$

3.8.47 $y^{\frac{1}{3}} + \frac{1}{3}xy^{-\frac{2}{3}}y' + y' = 0$, so at the given point we have $2 + \frac{1}{3} \cdot 1 \cdot \frac{1}{4}y' + y' = 0$, so $\frac{13}{12}y' = -2$, so $y' = -\frac{24}{13}.$

3.8.49 $y + xy' + \frac{3}{2}x^{\frac{1}{2}}y^{-\frac{1}{2}} - \frac{1}{2}x^{\frac{3}{2}}y^{-\frac{3}{2}}y' = 0$, so at the given point we have $1 + y' + \frac{3}{2} - \frac{1}{2}y' = 0$, so $\frac{1}{2}y' = -\frac{5}{2}$, so $y' = -5.$

3.8.51

    a. False. For example, the equation $y\cos(xy) = x$, cannot be solved explicitly for y in terms of x.

    b. True. We have $2x + 2yy' = 0$, and the result follows by solving for y'.

    c. False. The equation $x = 1$ doesn't represent any sort of function – it is either just a number, or perhaps a vertical line, but it doesn't represent a differentiable function.

    d. False. $y + xy' = 0$, so $y' = -\frac{y}{x}$, $x \neq 0$.

3.8.53

    a. There are two points on the curve associated with $x = 1$. When $x = 1$, we have $1 + y^2 - y = 1$, so $y(y - 1) = 0$. The two points are thus $(1, 0)$ and $(1, 1)$. Differentiating yields $1 + 2yy' - y' = 0$, so $y' = \frac{1}{1 - 2y}$.
    At $(1, 0)$, we have $y' = 1$, so the tangent line is given by $y = x - 1$.
    At $(1, 1)$, we have $y' = -1$, so the tangent line is given by $y - 1 = -1(x - 1)$, or $y = -x + 2$.

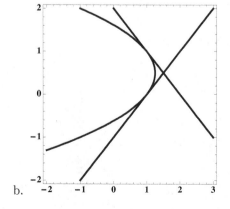

    b.

3.8.55

a. $y(2x) + (x^2 + 4)y' = 0$, so $y' = -\frac{2xy}{x^2+4}$.

b. At $y = 1$ we have $x^2 + 4 = 8$, so $x = \pm 2$. At the point $(2, 1)$ we have $y' = -\frac{4}{8} = -\frac{1}{2}$. At the point $(-2, 1)$ we have $y' = \frac{4}{8} = \frac{1}{2}$. Thus, the equations of the tangent lines are given by $y - 1 = -\frac{1}{2}(x - 2)$ and $y - 1 = \frac{1}{2}(x + 2)$, or $y = -\frac{1}{2}x + 2$ and $y = \frac{1}{2}x + 2$.

c. $y = \frac{8}{x^2+4}$, so $y' = \frac{0 - 8 \cdot 2x}{(x^2+4)^2} = -\frac{16x}{(x^2+4)^2}$.

d. $y' = -\frac{16x}{(x^2+4)^2} = -\frac{2x}{x^2+4} \cdot \frac{8}{x^2+4} = -\frac{2x}{x^2+4} \cdot y = -\frac{2xy}{x^2+4}$.

3.8.57

a. From number 53, we have that $y' = \frac{1}{1-2y}$. A vertical tangent would occur at a point whose y value would make $1 - 2y$ equal to zero. So we are looking for where $2y = 1$ or $y = \frac{1}{2}$.

If $y = \frac{1}{2}$, then $x + \frac{1}{4} - \frac{1}{2} = 1$, so $x = \frac{5}{4}$, and there is a vertical tangent at $\left(\frac{5}{4}, \frac{1}{2}\right)$.

b. Because y' is never zero, there are no horizontal tangent lines.

3.8.59 Differentiating with respect to x gives $18x + 2y\frac{dy}{dx} - 36 + 6\frac{dy}{dx} = 0$, so

$$2y\frac{dy}{dx} + 6\frac{dy}{dx} = -18x + 36$$
$$(2y + 6)\frac{dy}{dx} = -18x + 36$$
$$\frac{dy}{dx} = \frac{-9x + 18}{y + 3}.$$

This is zero when $x = 2$. Using the original equation, we have $36 + y^2 - 72 + 6y + 36 = 0$, or $y^2 + 6y = 0$, or $y = 0$ and $y = -6$. Thus there are horizontal tangent lines at $(2, 0)$ and $(2, -6)$. So $y = 0$ and $y = -6$ are horizontal tangent lines.

This curve has vertical tangent lines when $y = -3$. Using the original equation, we have $9x^2 + 9 - 36x - 18 + 36 = 0$ or $9x^2 - 36x + 27 = 0$, or $x^2 - 4x + 3 = 0$. This factors as $(x - 3)(x - 1) = 0$, so the corresponding values of x are 3 and 1. Thus the vertical tangent lines occur at $(3, -3)$ and $(1, -3)$.

3.8.61

a. If we write $y^3 - 1 = xy - x$, we have $(y - 1)(y^2 + y + 1) = x(y - 1)$, so $y^2 + y + 1 = x$. Differentiating gives $2y\frac{dy}{dx} + \frac{dy}{dx} = 1$, so $\frac{dy}{dx} = \frac{1}{1+2y}$. Note also that $y = 1$ satisfies the equation; $y' = 0$ on this branch.

b.

$$y^3 - 1 = x(y - 1)$$
$$(y - 1)(y^2 + y + 1) = x(y - 1)$$
$$y^2 + y + 1 = x$$
$$y^2 + y + (1 - x) = 0,$$

so by the quadratic formula we have $y = \frac{-1 \pm \sqrt{4x-3}}{2}$. Note that this means that $\pm\sqrt{4x - 3} = 2y + 1$.

c.

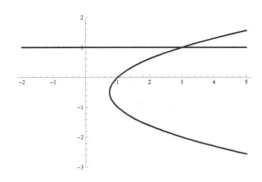

3.8.63

a. $4x^3 = 4x - 4yy'$, so $y' = \frac{x - x^3}{y}$.

b. $y = \pm\sqrt{x^2 - \frac{x^4}{2}}$.

c.

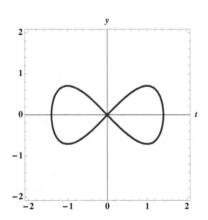

3.8.65

The slope of the normal line is the negative reciprocal of the slope of the tangent line. From 25: $y' = -\frac{5}{4}$, so the slope of the normal line is $\frac{4}{5}$. At the point $(2, 1)$ we have the line $y - 1 = \frac{4}{5}(x - 2)$, or $y = \frac{4}{5}x - \frac{3}{5}$.

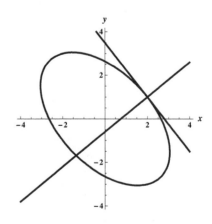

3.8.67

The slope of the normal line is the negative reciprocal of the slope of the tangent line. From 27: $y' = \frac{5}{2\pi+1}$, so the slope of the normal line is $\frac{-2\pi-1}{5}$. At the point $(\frac{\pi^2}{5}, \pi)$ we have the line $y - \pi = \frac{-2\pi-1}{5}(x - \frac{\pi^2}{5})$, or $y = \frac{-2\pi-1}{5}x + \frac{2\pi^3+\pi^2+25\pi}{25}$.

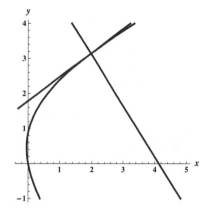

3.8.69

The slope of the normal line is the negative reciprocal of the slope of the tangent line. From 29: $y' = \frac{1}{2}$, so the slope of the normal line is -2. At the point $(\frac{\pi}{2}, \frac{\pi}{4})$ we have the line $y - \frac{\pi}{4} = -2(x - \frac{\pi}{2})$, or $y = -2x + \frac{5\pi}{4}$.

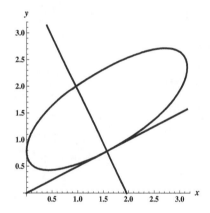

3.8.71

We have $9x^2 + 21y^2y' = 10y'$, so at the point $(1,1)$ we have $9 + 21y' = 10y'$, so $y' = -\frac{9}{11}$.
Thus, the tangent line is given by $y - 1 = -\frac{9}{11}(x - 1)$, or $y = \frac{-9}{11}x + \frac{20}{11}$. The normal line is given by $y - 1 = \frac{11}{9}(x - 1)$, or $y = \frac{11}{9}x - \frac{2}{9}$.

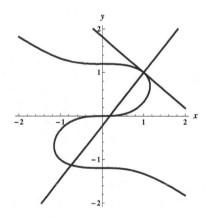

3.8.73

We have $2(x^2+y^2-2x)(2x+2yy'-2) = 4x+4yy'$, so at the point $(2,2)$ we have $2(4+4-4)(4+4y'-2) = 8+8y'$, so $16+32y' = 8+8y'$, so $y' = -\frac{1}{3}$. Thus, the tangent line is given by $y-2 = -\frac{1}{3}(x-2)$, or $y = \frac{-1}{3}x + \frac{8}{3}$. The normal line is given by $y-2 = 3(x-2)$, or $y = 3x-4$.

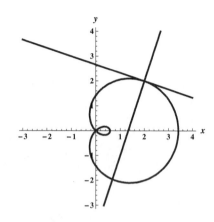

3.8.75

a. $1280 = 40L^{1/3}K^{2/3}$, so $0 = \frac{40}{3}L^{-2/3}K^{2/3} + \frac{80}{3}L^{1/3}K^{-1/3} \cdot \frac{dK}{dL}$. Multiplying both sides by $\frac{3}{40}L^{2/3}K^{1/3}$ yields

$$0 = K + 2L\frac{dK}{dL}, \text{ so } \frac{dK}{dL} = -\frac{1}{2}\frac{K}{L}.$$

b. With $L = 8$ and $K = 64$, $\frac{dK}{dL} = -\frac{64}{16} = -4$.

3.8.77 $V = \frac{\pi h^2(3r-h)}{3} = \frac{5\pi}{3}$. So

$$\frac{1}{3}[2\pi h(3r-h) + \pi h^2(3r'-1)] = 0,$$

$$6rh - 2h^2 + 3h^2r' - h^2 = 0,$$

so $r' = 1 - \frac{2r}{h}$.

At $r = 2$ and $h = 1$, we have $r' = 1 - 4 = -3$.

3.8.79 Note for $y = mx$, $\frac{dy}{dx} = m = \frac{y}{x}$, and for $x^2+y^2 = a^2$, $\frac{dy}{dx} = -\frac{x}{y}$. So for any point (x,y), we have $\frac{y}{x}$ and $-\frac{x}{y}$ are negative reciprocals.

3.8.81 For $xy = a$ we have $xy' + y = 0$, so $y' = -\frac{y}{x}$. For $x^2 - y^2 = b$, we have $2x - 2yy' = 0$, so $y' = \frac{x}{y}$. Let (c,d) be a point on both curves. Then the slope of the normal line to the first curve is $\frac{c}{d}$, but that is the slope of the tangent line to the second curve. Thus the two curves are orthogonal at any points of intersection.

3.8.83

$$(2x+2yy')(x^2+y^2+x) + (x^2+y^2)(2x+2yy'+1) = 8y^2 + 16xyy'$$

$$2yy'(x^2+y^2+x) + (x^2+y^2)2yy' - 16xyy' = 8y^2 - 2x(x^2+y^2+x) - (x^2+y^2)(2x+1)$$

$$y' = \frac{8y^2 - 2x(x^2+y^2+x) - (x^2+y^2)(2x+1)}{2y(x^2+y^2+x) + 2y(x^2+y^2) - 16xy}$$

$$= \frac{8y^2 - 2x^3 - 2xy^2 - 2x^2 - 2x^3 - x^2 - 2xy^2 - y^2}{2y(x^2+y^2+x+x^2+y^2-8x)}$$

$$= \frac{7y^2 - 3x^2 - 4xy^2 - 4x^3}{2y(2x^2+2y^2-7x)}.$$

3.8.85 $\dfrac{y'}{2\sqrt{y}} + y + xy' = 0$, so $y' + 2x\sqrt{y}y' = -2y\sqrt{y}$, so $y' = \dfrac{-2y\sqrt{y}}{2x\sqrt{y} + 1} = -\dfrac{2y^{3/2}}{2x\sqrt{y} + 1}$.

Differentiating again we obtain

$$y'' = -\frac{(2x\sqrt{y} + 1)(3\sqrt{y}y') - 2y^{3/2}\left(2\sqrt{y} + \frac{xy'}{\sqrt{y}}\right)}{(2x\sqrt{y} + 1)^2} = \frac{-(2x\sqrt{y} + 1)(3\sqrt{y}y') + 4y^2 + 2xyy'}{(2x\sqrt{y} + 1)^2}$$

$$= \left(\frac{-(2x\sqrt{y} + 1)(3\sqrt{y})\left(\frac{-2y\sqrt{y}}{2x\sqrt{y}+1}\right) + 4y^2 + 2xy\left(\frac{-2y\sqrt{y}}{1+2x\sqrt{y}}\right)}{(2x\sqrt{y} + 1)^2}\right) \cdot \frac{2x\sqrt{y} + 1}{2x\sqrt{y} + 1}$$

$$= \frac{(2x\sqrt{y} + 1)(6y^2) + 4y^2(1 + 2x\sqrt{y}) - 4xy^{5/2}}{(2x\sqrt{y} + 1)^3} = \frac{10y^2 + 16xy^2\sqrt{y}}{(2x\sqrt{y} + 1)^3}.$$

3.8.87 Differentiating with respect to x yields $2x(3y^2 - 2y^3) + x^2(6y - 6y^2)\dfrac{dy}{dx} = 0$. Solving for $\dfrac{dy}{dx}$ yields $\dfrac{dy}{dx} = \dfrac{-2x(3y^2 - 2y^3)}{6x^2(y - y^2)} = \dfrac{3y^2 - 2y^3}{3x(y^2 - y)} = \dfrac{3y - 2y^2}{3x(y - 1)}$. The numerator is zero when $y = 0$ or when $y = \dfrac{3}{2}$. Using the original equation, there are no points where $y = 0$, and there are also no points where $y = \dfrac{3}{2}$ because we obtain the equation $x^2(\dfrac{27}{4} - \dfrac{27}{4}) = 4$, which has no solutions. So there are no horizontal tangent lines.

There could be vertical tangent lines where $x = 0$ or $y = 1$; in fact, when $y = 1$ the original equation becomes $x^2(3 - 2) = 4$, so $x = \pm 2$. There are vertical tangents at $(2, 1)$ and $(-2, 1)$. Letting $x = 0$ doesn't yield any points in the original equation.

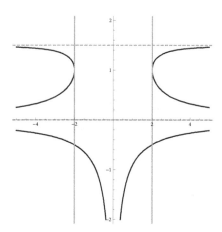

3.8.89 Differentiating with respect to x yields $(1 - y^2) + x(-2yy') + 3y^2y' = 0$. Solving for y' yields $y' = \dfrac{y^2 - 1}{3y^2 - 2xy} = \dfrac{y^2 - 1}{y(3y - 2x)}$. There could be a horizontal tangent line where $y = \pm 1$, but the original equation with $y = \pm 1$ yields $\pm 1 = 0$, so there are no horizontal tangent lines.

There could be a vertical tangent line for $y = 0$ or for $y = \dfrac{2}{3}x$. Using the original equation, letting $y = 0$ yields $x = 0$, and letting $y = \dfrac{2}{3}x$ yields $x\left(1 - \dfrac{4x^2}{9}\right) + \dfrac{8x^3}{27} = 0$. For $x \neq 0$, this yields $27 - 12x^2 + 8x^2 = 0$, or $x^2 = \dfrac{27}{4}$, so $x = \pm\dfrac{\sqrt{27}}{2} = \pm\dfrac{3\sqrt{3}}{2}$. The corresponding y values are $y = \pm\dfrac{2}{3}x = \pm\sqrt{3}$. So there are vertical tangent lines at $(0, 0)$ and at $(3\sqrt{3}/2, \sqrt{3})$ and $(-3\sqrt{3}/2, -\sqrt{3})$.

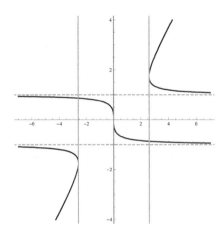

3.9   Derivatives of Logarithmic and Exponential Functions

3.9.1 $y = \ln x$ if and only if $x = e^y$. Differentiating implicitly yields $1 = e^y \cdot y'$, so $y' = \frac{1}{e^y} = \frac{1}{e^{\ln x}} = \frac{1}{x}$ for $x > 0$.

3.9.3 $\frac{d}{dx} \ln(kx) = \frac{1}{kx} \cdot k = \frac{1}{x}$. This is valid for $x > 0$ if $k > 0$ and $x < 0$ if $k < 0$. Also, we can write $\ln(kx) = \ln(k) + \ln(x)$, so its derivative is $0 + \frac{1}{x} = \frac{1}{x}$.

3.9.5 $\frac{d}{dx} \log_b x = \frac{1}{x \ln b}$ for $b > 0$, $b \neq 1$ and $x > 0$. If $b = e$, we have $\frac{d}{dx} \log_e x = \frac{1}{x \ln e} = \frac{1}{x}$.

3.9.7 $f(x) = e^{\ln(g(x)^{h(x)})} = e^{h(x) \cdot \ln(g(x))}$.

3.9.9 $\frac{d}{dx} \ln(7x) = \frac{1}{7x} \cdot 7 = \frac{1}{x}$.

3.9.11 $\frac{d}{dx} \ln(x^2) = \frac{1}{x^2} \cdot (2x) = \frac{2}{x}$.

3.9.13 $\frac{d}{dx}(\ln |\sin x|) = \frac{1}{\sin x} \cdot (\cos x) = \cot x$.

3.9.15 $\frac{d}{dx}\left[\ln\left(\frac{x+1}{x-1}\right)\right] = \frac{x-1}{x+1}\left(\frac{(x-1)-(x+1)}{(x-1)^2}\right) = -\frac{2}{(x+1)(x-1)} = \frac{2}{1-x^2}$.

3.9.17 $\frac{d}{dx}((x^2+1)\ln x) = 2x \ln x + \frac{x^2+1}{x}$.

3.9.19 $\frac{d}{dx}(\ln \ln x) = \frac{1}{\ln x} \cdot \frac{1}{x}$.

3.9.21 $\frac{d}{dx}\left(\frac{\ln x}{\ln x + 1}\right) = \frac{(\ln x + 1)(1/x) - (\ln x)(1/x)}{(\ln x + 1)^2} = \frac{1}{x(\ln x + 1)^2}$.

3.9.23 $\frac{dy}{dx} = 8^x \ln 8$.

3.9.25 $y' = 5 \cdot \frac{d}{dx} 4^x = 5 \cdot \ln 4 \cdot 4^x$.

3.9.27 $y' = 3x^2 3^x + x^3 3^x \ln 3 = 3^x x^2 (3 + x \ln 3)$.

3.9.29 $\frac{dA}{dt} = 250(1.045)^{4t} \cdot \ln(1.045) \cdot 4 = 1000 \cdot \ln 1.045 \cdot (1.045^{4t})$.

3.9.31

   a. $T = 10 \cdot 2^{-0.274 \cdot 16}$ minutes ≈ 28.7 seconds.

   b. $\frac{\Delta T}{\Delta a} = \frac{10 \cdot 2^{-0.274 \cdot 8} - 10 \cdot 2^{-0.274 \cdot 2}}{8 - 2} \approx -0.78$ minutes per 1000 feet, which is about -46.512 seconds per 1000 feet.

c. $\frac{dT}{da} = -2.74 \cdot 2^{-0.274 \cdot a} \cdot \ln 2$. At $a = 8$ we have $\frac{dT}{da} = -2.74 \cdot 2^{-0.274 \cdot 8} \cdot \ln 2 \approx -0.42$ minutes per 1000 feet. Every 1000 feet the airplane climbs, leaves about .42 minutes less time of consciousness, which corresponds to about 24.94 seconds.

3.9.33

a. At $Q = 10\mu\text{Ci}$ we have $10 = 350 \cdot \left(\frac{1}{2}\right)^{t/13.1}$, so $\ln(1/35) = \frac{t}{13.1} \ln(1/2)$, so $t = 13.1 \cdot \frac{\ln 35}{\ln 2} \approx 67.19$ hours.

b. $\frac{dQ}{dt} = \frac{350}{13.1} \cdot \ln\left(\frac{1}{2}\right) \cdot \left(\frac{1}{2}\right)^{t/13.1}$. We have $Q'(12) \approx -9.81453$, $Q'(24) \approx -5.20136$, and $Q'(48) \approx -1.46087$. The rate at which the iodine decreases is decreasing in absolute value as time increases.

3.9.35 $f'(x) = 2^x (\ln 2)$.

3.9.37 $g'(y) = e^y y^e + e^{y+1} y^{e-1}$.

3.9.39 $r'(\theta) = e^{2\theta} \cdot 2 = 2e^{2\theta}$.

3.9.41 $f'(x) = 2x^{3/2} + \frac{3}{2}(2x - 3)x^{1/2} = 5x^{3/2} - \frac{9}{2}x^{1/2}$.

3.9.43 $f'(x) = \frac{(2^x+1)2^x \ln 2 - 2^x(2^x \ln 2)}{(2^x+1)^2} = \frac{2^x \ln 2}{(2^x+1)^2}$.

3.9.45 Let $y = x^{\cos x}$. Then $\ln y = \cos x \ln x$. Differentiating both sides gives

$$\frac{1}{y}y' = (-\sin x)\ln x + \cos x \cdot \frac{1}{x}.$$

Therefore,

$$y' = x^{\cos x}\left(\frac{\cos x}{x} - \sin x \ln x\right).$$

At $\pi/2$ we have $y'(\pi/2) = (\pi/2)^0(0/(\pi/2) - \ln(\pi/2)) = -\ln(\pi/2)$.

3.9.47 Let $y = x^{\sqrt{x}}$. Then $\ln y = \sqrt{x} \cdot \ln x$. Differentiating both sides gives

$$\frac{1}{y}y' = \frac{1}{2\sqrt{x}}\ln x + \frac{\sqrt{x}}{x}.$$

Therefore,

$$y' = x^{\sqrt{x}}\left(\frac{\ln x + 2}{2\sqrt{x}}\right).$$

At 4 we have $y'(4) = 4^2\left(\frac{\ln 4 + 2}{4}\right) = 4\ln 4 + 8$.

3.9.49 Because $f(x) = (\sin x)^{\ln x}$, we have $\ln f(x) = \ln x \ln \sin x$. Differentiating both sides gives

$$\frac{1}{f(x)}f'(x) = \frac{1}{x} \cdot \ln \sin x + \ln x \cdot \frac{1}{\sin x}\cos x.$$

Therefore,

$$f'(x) = (\sin x)^{\ln x}\left(\frac{\ln \sin x + x \ln x \cot x}{x}\right).$$

We have $f'(\pi/2) = 0$ because $\cot \pi/2 = 0$ and $\ln \sin(\pi/2) = \ln 1 = 0$.

3.9.51 Let $y = x^{\sin x}$. Then $\ln y = \sin x \ln x$, so $\frac{1}{y}y' = \cos x \ln x + \frac{\sin x}{x}$. At the point $(1, 1)$ we have $y' = \sin 1$, so the tangent line is given by $y - 1 = (\sin 1)(x - 1)$, or $y = (\sin 1)x + 1 - \sin 1$.

3.9.53 Let $y = (x^2)^x = x^{2x}$. Then $\ln y = x \ln x^2$ and $\frac{1}{y}y' = \ln x^2 + 2$, so $y' = x^{2x}(\ln x^2 + 2)$. This quantity is zero when $\ln x^2 = -2$, or $x^2 = e^{-2}$. Thus there are horizontal tangents at $|x| = e^{-1}$, so for $x = \pm\frac{1}{e}$. The two tangent lines are given by $y = \frac{1}{e^{2/e}}$ (at $\left(\frac{1}{e}, \frac{1}{e^{2/e}}\right)$) and $y = e^{2/e}$ (at $\left(-\frac{1}{e}, e^{2/e}\right)$.)

3.9.55 $y' = 4 \cdot \frac{2x}{(x^2-1)\cdot \ln 3} = \frac{8x}{(x^2-1)\cdot \ln 3}$.

3.9.57 $y' = -\sin x (\ln(\cos^2 x)) + \cos x \cdot \left(\frac{2 \cos x(-\sin x)}{\cos^2 x} \right) = (-\sin x)(\ln(\cos^2 x) + 2)$.

3.9.59 $y' = \frac{d}{dx}(\log_4 x)^{-1} = -(\log_4 x)^{-2} \cdot \frac{1}{x \ln 4} = -\frac{1}{x(\ln 4)(\log_4 x)^2} = -\frac{\ln 4}{x \ln^2 x}$.

3.9.61 Let $y = \frac{(x+1)^{10}}{(2x-4)^8}$, so $\ln y = \ln \left(\frac{(x+1)^{10}}{(2x-4)^8} \right) = 10 \ln(x+1) - 8 \ln(2x-4)$. Then

$$\frac{1}{y} y' = \frac{10}{x+1} - \frac{8}{2x-4} \cdot 2,$$

$$y' = \frac{(x+1)^{10}}{(2x-4)^8} \cdot \left(\frac{10}{x+1} - \frac{8}{x-2} \right).$$

3.9.63 Let $y = x^{\ln x}$. Then $\ln y = (\ln x)^2$. Thus $\frac{1}{y} y' = 2 \ln x \cdot \frac{1}{x}$, so $y' = x^{\ln x} \left(\frac{2 \ln x}{x} \right)$.

3.9.65 Let $y = \frac{(x+1)^{3/2}(x-4)^{5/2}}{(5x+3)^{2/3}}$. Then $\ln y = \ln \left(\frac{(x+1)^{3/2}(x-4)^{5/2}}{(5x+3)^{2/3}} \right) = \frac{3}{2} \ln(x+1) + \frac{5}{2} \ln(x-4) - \frac{2}{3} \ln(5x+3)$. Then

$$\frac{1}{y} y' = \frac{3}{2(x+1)} + \frac{5}{2(x-4)} - \frac{10}{3(5x+3)},$$

$$y' = \frac{(x+1)^{3/2}(x-4)^{5/2}}{(5x+3)^{2/3}} \cdot \left(\frac{3}{2(x+1)} + \frac{5}{2(x-4)} - \frac{10}{3(5x+3)} \right).$$

3.9.67 Let $y = (\sin x)^{\tan x}$, and assume $0 < x < \pi$, $x \neq \frac{\pi}{2}$. Then $\ln y = (\tan x) \ln(\sin x)$. Then

$$\frac{1}{y} y' = (\sec^2 x) \ln(\sin x) + \frac{\tan x \cos x}{\sin x},$$

$$y' = (\sin x)^{\tan x} \left((\sec^2 x) \ln(\sin x) + 1 \right).$$

3.9.69

   a. False. $\log_2 9$ is a constant, so its derivative is 0.

   b. False. If $x < -1$, then the right-hand side is defined while the left-hand side isn't.

   c. False. The correct way to write that function would be $e^{(x+1)\ln 2}$.

   d. False. $\frac{d}{dx}(\sqrt{2})^x = (\sqrt{2})^x \ln(\sqrt{2})$.

   e. True. This follows from the generalized power rule.

3.9.71 $\frac{d^2}{dx^2}(\log x) = \frac{d}{dx} \left(\frac{1}{x \ln 10} \right) = -\frac{1}{x^2 \ln 10}$.

3.9.73 $\frac{d^3}{dx^3}(x^2 \ln x) = \frac{d^2}{dx^2}(2x \ln x + x) = \frac{d}{dx}(2 \ln x + 2 + 1) = \frac{2}{x}$.

3.9.75

   a. $y' = \frac{d}{dx} \left(e^{x \ln 3} \right) = (e^{x \ln 3}) \cdot \ln 3 = 3^x \ln 3$.

   b. Let $y = 3^x$. Then $\ln y = x \ln 3$. So $\frac{1}{y} y' = \ln 3$, and $y' = 3^x \ln 3$.

3.9.77 $f'(x) = \frac{d}{dx}(4 \ln(3x+1)) = \frac{4}{3x+1} \cdot 3 = \frac{12}{3x+1}$.

3.9.79 $f'(x) = \frac{d}{dx} \left(\frac{1}{2} \ln 10x \right) = \frac{d}{dx} \frac{1}{2}[\ln 10 + \ln x] = \frac{1}{2x}$.

3.9.81 $f'(x) = \frac{d}{dx}(\ln(2x-1) + 3 \ln(x+2) - 2 \ln(1-4x)) = \frac{2}{2x-1} + \frac{3}{x+2} + \frac{8}{1-4x}$.

3.9.83

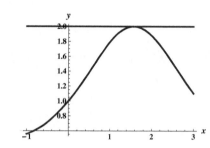

$y' = \frac{d}{dx}e^{\sin x \ln 2} = (\cos x)(\ln 2)2^{\sin x}$. At $x = \pi/2$ we have $y' = 0$, so the tangent line is given by $y = 2$.

3.9.85 Let $y = x^{10x}$. Then $\ln y = 10x \ln x$, so $\frac{1}{y}y' = 10 \ln x + 10$, and $y' = x^{10x}(10)(\ln x + 1)$.

3.9.87 Let $y = x^{\cos x}$. Then we have $\ln y = \cos x \ln x$, and $\frac{1}{y}y' = -\sin x \ln x + \frac{\cos x}{x}$. Thus, $y' = x^{\cos x}\left(\frac{\cos x}{x} - \sin x \ln x\right)$.

3.9.89 Let $y = \left(1 + \frac{1}{x}\right)^x$. Then $\ln y = x \ln\left(1 + \frac{1}{x}\right)$, so $\frac{1}{y}y' = \ln\left(1 + \frac{1}{x}\right) + x\left(\frac{-1/x^2}{1+1/x}\right) = \ln\left(1 + \frac{1}{x}\right) - \frac{1}{x+1}$. Therefore, $y' = \left(1 + \frac{1}{x}\right)^x\left(\ln\left(1 + \frac{1}{x}\right) - \frac{1}{x+1}\right)$.

3.9.91 Let $y = x^{x^{10}}$. Then $\ln y = x^{10} \ln x$, so $\frac{1}{y}y' = 10x^9 \ln x + \frac{x^{10}}{x} = x^9(10 \ln x + 1)$. Thus $y' = x^{x^{10}} \cdot x^9(10 \ln x + 1)$.

3.9.93

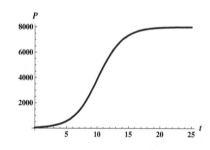

a. We used a graphing rectangle of $[0, 25] \times [0, 8000]$.

b. To find when $P(t)$ hits 5000, we solve $5000 = \frac{400000}{50+7950e^{-0.5t}}$, or $50 + 7950e^{-0.5t} = 80$. This leads to $7950e^{-0.5t} = 30$, or $-0.5t = \ln\left(\frac{30}{7950}\right)$. So we have $t = 2\ln(265) \approx 11.16$ years.

The carrying capacity is $\lim_{t\to\infty} P(t) = \frac{400,000}{50} = 8000$. Ninety percent of 8000 is 7200, so we seek the time when $P(t) = 7200$. We have $7200 = \frac{400000}{50+7950e^{-0.5t}}$, or $50 + 7950e^{-0.5t} = \frac{500}{9}$. This leads to $7950e^{-0.5t} = \frac{50}{9}$, or $-0.5t = \ln\left(\frac{50}{71550}\right)$. So we have $t = 2\ln\left(\frac{71550}{50}\right) \approx 14.53$ years.

c. $\frac{dP}{dt} = -\frac{400000}{(50+7950e^{-0.5t})^2} \cdot (7950)(-0.5)e^{-0.5t}$.

At $t = 0$ we have $P'(0) = \frac{400,000 \cdot 7950 \cdot .5}{8000^2} = \frac{1,590,000,000}{8000^2} \approx 25$ fish per year.

At $t = 5$ we have $P'(5) = \frac{1,590,000,000e^{-5/2}}{(50+7950e^{-5/2})^2} \approx 264$ fish per year.

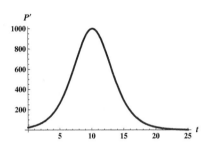

d. The maximum is at about $t = 10$ years.

3.9.95

a. $\ln(P(t)) = \ln(3 \cdot 10^{10}) - \ln(2 + 3e^{-0.025t})$. $\frac{d}{dt} \ln(P(t)) = \frac{P'(t)}{P(t)} = r(t) = \frac{0.075 \cdot e^{-0.025t}}{2 + 3e^{-0.025t}}$. $r(0) = \frac{0.075}{5} = 0.015$, so the population is growing at 1.5% per year in 1999.

b. $r(11) = \frac{0.075 e^{-0.275}}{2 + 3e^{-0.275}} \approx 0.0133$.

   $r(21) = \frac{0.075 e^{-0.525}}{2 + 3e^{-0.525}} \approx 0.0118$.

   The relative growth rate decreases over time.

c. $\lim\limits_{t \to \infty} r(t) = \lim\limits_{t \to \infty} \frac{0.075}{3 + 2e^{0.025t}} = 0$, because the denominator increases without bound. The relative growth rate becomes smaller and smaller as the population nears the carrying capacity.

3.9.97

a.

t	$A(t)$
5	\$17,442.50
15	\$72,704.68
25	\$173,248.49
35	\$356,177.57

Average growth on $[5, 15]$ is $\frac{A(15) - A(5)}{10} \approx \$5526$ per year. Average growth on $[15, 25]$ is $\frac{A(25) - A(15)}{10} \approx \$10,054$ per year. Average growth on $[25, 35]$ is $\frac{A(35) - A(25)}{10} \approx \$18,293$ per year.

b. $A(40) \approx \$497,872.68$.

c. $A'(t) = 50,000 \cdot 12 \cdot (1.005)^{12t} \cdot \ln(1.005) \approx 2993 \cdot (1.005)^{12t}$. The rate of growth of the investment increases over time, so the earlier you start saving, the higher the rate of increase will be when you retire.

3.9.99 We search for a solution to $x = p^x$. If the two curves will have only one point of intersection, then they should be tangent at the point of intersection. So we need $1 = p^x \ln p$, or $\frac{1}{\ln p} = p^x = x$. So $\ln p = \frac{1}{x}$ and $p = e^{1/x}$. Then we have $x = p^x = (e^{1/x})^x = e$. So the point of intersection is (e, e) and the value of p is $e^{1/e} \approx 1.44467$.

3.9.101 Let $f(x) = \ln x$ and $a = e$. Then $f'(e) = \lim\limits_{x \to e} \frac{\ln x - 1}{x - e} = \frac{1}{e}$.

3.9.103 Let $f(x) = x^x$ and $a = 3$. Then $f'(3) = \lim\limits_{h \to 0} \frac{(3+h)^{3+h} - 27}{h} = 3^3 \cdot (\ln 3 + 1) = 27(1 + \ln 3)$.

3.9.105 Let $y = u(x)^{v(x)}$. Then $\ln y = v(x) \ln u(x)$, so $\frac{1}{y} y' = v'(x) \ln u(x) + v(x) \cdot \frac{u'(x)}{u(x)}$. Thus we have $y' = u(x)^{v(x)} \cdot \left(v'(x) \ln u(x) + v(x) \cdot \frac{u'(x)}{u(x)} \right) = u(x)^{v(x)} \cdot \left(\frac{v(x)}{u(x)} \frac{du}{dx} + \ln u(x) \frac{dv}{dx} \right)$.

3.10 Derivatives of Inverse Trigonometric Functions

3.10.1 $\frac{d}{dx}\sin^{-1}x = \frac{1}{\sqrt{1-x^2}}$, $-1 < x < 1$.

$\frac{d}{dx}\tan^{-1}x = \frac{1}{1+x^2}$, $-\infty < x < \infty$.

$\frac{d}{dx}\sec^{-1}x = \frac{1}{|x|\sqrt{x^2-1}}$, $|x| > 1$.

3.10.3 $y' = \frac{1}{1+x^2}$. At $x = -2$ we have $y'(-2) = \frac{1}{1+4} = \frac{1}{5}$.

3.10.5 $(f^{-1})'(8) = \frac{1}{f'(2)} = \frac{1}{4}$.

3.10.7 $\frac{d}{dx}\sin^{-1}(2x) = \frac{2}{\sqrt{1-4x^2}}$.

3.10.9 $\frac{d}{dw}\cos(\sin^{-1}(2w)) = (-\sin(\sin^{-1}(2w))) \cdot \frac{d}{dw}\left(\sin^{-1}(2w)\right) = -2w \cdot \frac{2}{\sqrt{1-4w^2}} = -\frac{4w}{\sqrt{1-4w^2}}$.

3.10.11 $\frac{d}{dx}\sin^{-1}(e^{-2x}) = \frac{1}{\sqrt{1-e^{-4x}}} \cdot \frac{d}{dx}e^{-2x} = -\frac{2e^{-2x}}{\sqrt{1-e^{-4x}}}$.

3.10.13 $f'(x) = \frac{1}{1+100x^2} \cdot 10 = \frac{10}{100x^2+1}$.

3.10.15 $\frac{d}{dy}\tan^{-1}(2y^2 - 4) = \frac{1}{1+(2y^2-4)^2} \cdot \frac{d}{dy}(2y^2 - 4) = \frac{4y}{1+(2y^2-4)^2}$.

3.10.17 $\frac{d}{dz}\cot^{-1}\sqrt{z} = -\frac{1}{1+\sqrt{z}^2} \cdot \frac{d}{dz}\sqrt{z} = -\frac{1}{1+z} \cdot \frac{1}{2\sqrt{z}} = -\frac{1}{2\sqrt{z}(1+z)}$.

3.10.19 $\frac{d}{dx}\cos^{-1}\frac{1}{x} = -\frac{1}{\sqrt{1-\frac{1}{x^2}}} \cdot \left(-\frac{1}{x^2}\right) = \frac{1}{x^2\sqrt{\frac{x^2-1}{x^2}}} = \frac{|x|}{x^2\sqrt{x^2-1}} = \frac{1}{|x|\sqrt{x^2-1}}$, for $|x| > 1$.

3.10.21 $\frac{d}{du}\csc^{-1}(2u + 1) = -\frac{1}{|2u+1|\sqrt{(2u+1)^2-1}} \cdot 2 = -\frac{2}{|2u+1|\sqrt{(2u+1)^2-1}} = -\frac{1}{|2u+1|\sqrt{u^2+u}}$.

3.10.23 $\frac{d}{dy}\cot^{-1}\left(\frac{1}{1+y^2}\right) = \left(-\frac{1}{1+\left(\frac{1}{1+y^2}\right)^2}\right) \cdot \left(-\frac{2y}{(1+y^2)^2}\right) = \frac{2y}{(1+y^2)^2+1}$.

3.10.25 $\frac{d}{dx}\sec^{-1}(\ln x) = \frac{1}{|\ln x|\sqrt{(\ln x)^2-1}} \cdot \frac{1}{x} = \frac{1}{x|\ln x|\sqrt{(\ln x)^2-1}}$.

3.10.27 $\frac{d}{dx}\csc^{-1}(\tan e^x) = -\frac{1}{|\tan e^x|\sqrt{(\tan e^x)^2-1}} \cdot (\sec^2 e^x) \cdot e^x$.

3.10.29 $\frac{d}{ds}\cot^{-1}(e^s) = -\frac{1}{1+e^{2s}} \cdot e^s = -\frac{e^s}{1+e^{2s}}$.

3.10.31 $f'(x) = \frac{1}{1+4x^2} \cdot 2$, so $f'(1/2) = \frac{1}{1+1} \cdot 2 = 1$. Thus the equation of the tangent line is $y - \pi/4 = 1(x - 1/2)$, or $y = x + \frac{\pi}{4} - \frac{1}{2}$.

3.10.33 $f'(x) = -\frac{1}{\sqrt{1-x^4}} \cdot 2x = -\frac{2x}{\sqrt{1-x^4}}$, so $f'(1/\sqrt{2}) = -\frac{\sqrt{2}}{\sqrt{1-(1/4)}} = -\frac{2\sqrt{2}}{\sqrt{3}}$. Thus the equation of the tangent line is $y - \pi/3 = -\frac{2\sqrt{2}}{\sqrt{3}}\left(x - 1/\sqrt{2}\right)$, or $y = -\frac{2\sqrt{2}}{\sqrt{3}}x + \frac{\pi}{3} + \frac{2}{\sqrt{3}}$.

3.10.35

a. $\frac{x}{150} = \cot\theta$, so $\theta = \cot^{-1}\left(\frac{x}{150}\right)$. Then $\frac{d\theta}{dx} = -\frac{1}{1+\left(\frac{x}{150}\right)^2} \cdot \frac{1}{150} = -\frac{150}{(150)^2+x^2}$. When $x = 500$, we have

$\frac{d\theta}{dx} = -\frac{150}{150^2+500^2} \approx -0.00055$ radians per meter.

b. The most rapid change is at $x = 0$ where $\frac{d\theta}{dx} = -\frac{1}{150} \approx -0.0067$ radians per meter.

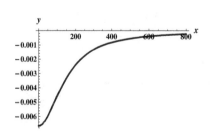

3.10.37 $f(4) = 16$ so $(f^{-1})'(16) = \frac{1}{f'(4)} = \frac{1}{3}$.

3.10.39 $f(1) = -1$ so $(f^{-1})'(-1) = \frac{1}{f'(1)} = \frac{1}{-5} = -\frac{1}{5}$.

3.10.41 $f\left(\frac{\pi}{4}\right) = 1$ so $(f^{-1})'(1) = \frac{1}{f'\left(\frac{\pi}{4}\right)} = \frac{1}{\sec^2\left(\frac{\pi}{4}\right)} = \frac{1}{2}$.

3.10.43 $f(4) = 2$ so $(f^{-1})'(2) = \frac{1}{f'(4)} = \frac{1}{(1/2\sqrt{4})} = 4$.

3.10.45 $f(4) = 36$ and $(f^{-1})'(36) = \frac{1}{f'(4)} = \frac{1}{2(4+2)} = \frac{1}{12}$.

3.10.47 Note that $f(1) = 3$. So $(f^{-1})'(3) = \frac{1}{f'(1)} = \frac{1}{4}$.

3.10.49 $(f^{-1})'(4) = \frac{1}{f'(7)} = \frac{4}{5}$, so $f'(7) = \frac{5}{4}$.

3.10.51

    a. Note that $f(0) = 4$, so $f^{-1}(4) = 0$. $(f^{-1})'(4) = \frac{1}{f'(0)} = \frac{1}{2}$.

    b. Note that $f(1) = 6$, so $f^{-1}(6) = 1$. $(f^{-1})'(6) = \frac{1}{f'(1)} = \frac{1}{3/2} = \frac{2}{3}$.

    c. Note that there is no given x so that $f(x) = 1$, so the desired derivative cannot be determined.

    d. From the table directly, $f'(1) = \frac{3}{2}$.

3.10.53

    a. True, because $\frac{d}{dx}\sin^{-1}x = -\frac{d}{dx}\cos^{-1}x$.

    b. False. $\frac{d}{dx}\tan^{-1}x = \frac{1}{1+x^2}$ for all x, and this doesn't equal $\sec^2 x$ anywhere except at the origin (one curve is always less than or equal to one, and the other is always greater than or equal to one).

    c. True. $\frac{d}{dx}\sin^{-1}x = \frac{1}{\sqrt{1-x^2}}$, and this is minimal when its denominator is as big as possible, which occurs when $x = 0$. So the smallest possible slope of a tangent line for this function on $(-1, 1)$ is $\frac{1}{\sqrt{1-0^2}} = 1$.

    d. True. $\frac{d}{dx}\sin x = \cos x$ and $\cos x = 1$ for $x = 0$ and $-1 \leq \cos x \leq 1$ for all x. Thus 1 is the largest possible slope for a tangent line to the sine function.

    e. True. This follows because the function $\frac{1}{x}$ is its own inverse. (Note that $f(f(x)) = \frac{1}{f(x)} = \frac{1}{1/x} = x$.) Thus, the derivative of the inverse of f is the derivative of f, which is $-\frac{1}{x^2}$.

3.10.55

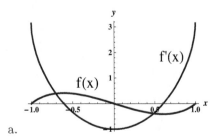

a.

b. $f'(x) = 2x\sin^{-1}(x) + \frac{x^2-1}{\sqrt{1-x^2}}$.

c. Note that f' is zero and f has a horizontal tangent line at about $x = -0.61$ and at about $x = 0.61$.

3.10.57

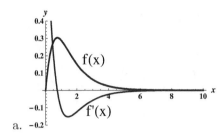

a.

b. $f'(x) = -e^{-x} \tan^{-1} x + e^{-x} \frac{1}{1+x^2}$.

c. Note that f' is zero and f has a horizontal tangent line at about $x = .75$.

3.10.59 Let $f(y) = 3y - 4$. Then $f'(y) = 3$ for all y in the domain of f. Let $y = f^{-1}(x)$. $(f^{-1})'(x) = \frac{1}{f'(y)} = \frac{1}{3}$.

3.10.61 Let $x = f(y) = y^2 - 4$ for $y > 0$. Note that this means that $y = \sqrt{x+4}$. Then $f'(y) = 2y$. So $(f^{-1})'(x) = \frac{1}{f'(y)} = \frac{1}{2y} = \frac{1}{2\sqrt{x+4}}$.

3.10.63 For $y \geq -2$, let $x = \sqrt{y+2}$. Note that it then follows that $x \geq 0$. Then $1 = \frac{y'}{2\sqrt{y+2}}$, and $x^2 = y+2$, so $y = x^2 - 2$. Thus we have $(f^{-1})'(x) = y' = 2\sqrt{x^2 - 2 + 2} = 2|x| = 2x$, because $x \geq 0$.

3.10.65 For $y > 0$, let $x = y^{-1/2}$. Then $1 = -\frac{1}{2}y^{-3/2}y'$, so $y' = -2y^{3/2} = -2(x^{-2})^{3/2} = -2x^{-3}$ where $x > 0$.

3.10.67

a. Because $\frac{l}{10} = \csc(\theta)$, $\theta = \csc^{-1}\left(\frac{l}{10}\right)$, and $\frac{d\theta}{dl} = -\frac{1}{(l/10)\sqrt{(l/10)^2 - 1}} \cdot \frac{1}{10} = -\frac{10}{l\sqrt{l^2 - 100}}$.

b. $\frac{d\theta}{dl}\Big|_{l=50} = -\frac{10}{50\sqrt{2500-100}} \approx -0.0041$ radians per foot.

$\frac{d\theta}{dl}\Big|_{l=20} = -\frac{10}{20\sqrt{400-100}} \approx -0.029$ radians per foot.

$\frac{d\theta}{dl}\Big|_{l=11} = -\frac{10}{11\sqrt{121-100}} \approx -0.198$ radians per foot.

c. $\lim_{l \to 10^+} -\frac{10}{l\sqrt{l^2 - 100}} = -\infty$. The angle changes very quickly as we approach the dock.

d. $\frac{d\theta}{dl}$ is negative because this measures the change in θ as l increases – but when the boat is approaching the dock, l is decreasing.

3.10.69

a. $\sin\theta = \frac{c}{D}$, so $\theta = \sin^{-1}\left(\frac{c}{D}\right)$. Thus $\frac{d\theta}{dc} = \frac{1/D}{\sqrt{1 - \left(\frac{c}{D}\right)^2}} = \frac{1}{\sqrt{D^2 - c^2}}$.

b. $\frac{d\theta}{dc}\Big|_{c=0} = \frac{1}{\sqrt{D^2}} = \frac{1}{D}$.

3.10.71 $(f^{-1})'(y_0) = \frac{1}{f'(x_0)}$ where $y_0 = f(x_0)$.

$\frac{d}{dx}\sin^{-1} x = \frac{1}{\cos(\sin^{-1} x)} = \frac{1}{\sqrt{1 - \sin^2(\sin^{-1} x)}} = \frac{1}{\sqrt{1-x^2}}$.

3.10.73 Using the identity $\cot^{-1} x + \tan^{-1} x = \frac{\pi}{2}$, we have the $\frac{d}{dx}\cot^{-1} x + \frac{d}{dx}\tan^{-1} x = 0$, so $\frac{d}{dx}\cot^{-1} x = -\frac{d}{dx}\tan^{-1} x$. Likewise, because $\csc^{-1} x + \sec^{-1} x = \frac{\pi}{2}$, we have $\frac{d}{dx}\csc^{-1} x + \frac{d}{dx}\sec^{-1} x = 0$, so $\frac{d}{dx}\csc^{-1} x = -\frac{d}{dx}\sec^{-1} x$.

3.10.75 $\cos(\sin^{-1}(x)) = \sqrt{1 - \sin^2(\sin^{-1}(x))} = \sqrt{1 - x^2}$ for $-1 \leq x \leq 1$.

3.10.77 $\tan(2\tan^{-1}(x)) = \frac{2\tan(\tan^{-1}(x))}{1-\tan^2(\tan^{-1}(x))} = \frac{2x}{1-x^2}$ for $-1 < x < 1$.

3.10.79

a.
$$\frac{d}{dx}\tan^{-1}(2/x^2) = \frac{1}{1+4/x^4}\cdot-\frac{4}{x^3} = \frac{1}{1+4/x^4}\cdot-\frac{4}{x^3}\cdot\frac{x}{x} = -\frac{4x}{x^4+4}.$$

$$\begin{aligned}
\frac{d}{dx}\left(\tan^{-1}(x+1) - \tan^{-1}(x-1)\right) &= \frac{1}{1+(x+1)^2} - \frac{1}{1+(x-1)^2} \\
&= \frac{x^2 - 2x + 2 - (x^2 + 2x + 2)}{1+(x+1)^2 + (x-1)^2 + (x^2-1)^2} \\
&= -\frac{4x}{1+x^2+2x+1+x^2-2x+1+x^4-2x^2+1} \\
&= -\frac{4x}{x^4+4}.
\end{aligned}$$

Because these two functions have the same derivative, they differ by a constant. So for any n, $\tan^{-1}(2/n^2) - \left(\tan^{-1}(n+1) - \tan^{-1}(n-1)\right)$ is a constant.

b. Because the two function in part (a) differ by a constant, we can compute the constant by evaluating for a specific number n. Choosing $n = 1$, we have $\tan^{-1}2 - \left(\tan^{-1}2 - \tan^{-1}0\right) = 0$, so the constant is 0, and we have
$$\tan^{-1}(2/n^2) = \left(\tan^{-1}(n+1) - \tan^{-1}(n-1)\right).$$

3.11   Related Rates

3.11.1 The area of a circle of radius r is $A(r) = \pi r^2$. If the radius $r = r(t)$ changes with time, then the area of the circle is a function of r and r is a function of t, so ultimately A is a function of t. If the radius changes at rate $\frac{dr}{dt}$, then the area changes at rate $2\pi r\frac{dr}{dt}$.

3.11.3 Because area is width times height, if one increases, the other must decrease in order for the area to remain constant.

3.11.5
$A(x) = x^2$, $\frac{dx}{dt} = 2$ meters per second.

a. $\frac{dA}{dt} = 2x\frac{dx}{dt}$, so at $x = 10$ meters we have $\frac{dA}{dt} = 2\cdot 10\text{m}\cdot 2\text{m/s} = 40\text{m}^2/\text{s}$.

b. At $x = 20$m we have $\frac{dA}{dt} = 2\cdot 20\text{m}\cdot 2\text{m/s} = 80\text{m}^2/\text{s}$.

c.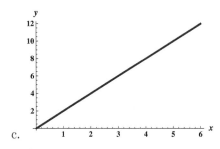

3.11.7

a. Let x be the length of a leg of an isosceles right triangle. Then $\frac{dx}{dt} = 2$ meters per second. The area is given by $A(x) = \frac{1}{2}x^2$. Thus, $\frac{dA}{dt} = \frac{dA}{dx}\frac{dx}{dt} = x\cdot 2 = 2x$ square meters per second. When $x = 2$, we have $\frac{dA}{dx} = 4$, so the area is increasing at 4 square meters per second.

b. When the hypotenuse is 1 meter long, the legs are $1/\sqrt{2}$ meters long. So $A'(1/\sqrt{2}) = 2\cdot\frac{1}{\sqrt{2}} = \sqrt{2}$, so the area is increasing at $\sqrt{2}$ square meters per second.

   c. If h is the length of the hypotenuse, then $x^2 + x^2 = h^2$, so $h = \sqrt{2}x$. So $\frac{dh}{dt} = \frac{dh}{dx}\frac{dx}{dt} = \sqrt{2}\frac{dx}{dt} = \sqrt{2} \cdot 2 = 2\sqrt{2}$ meters per second.

3.11.9

   a. Let r be the radius of the circle and A the area, and note that we are given $\frac{dA}{dt} = 1$ square cm per second. Because $A = \pi r^2$, we have $\frac{dA}{dt} = \frac{dA}{dr}\frac{dr}{dt}$, so

$$1 = 2\pi r \frac{dr}{dt},$$

and thus

$$\frac{dr}{dt} = \frac{1}{2\pi r}.$$

When $r = 2$, we have $\frac{dr}{dt} = \frac{1}{4\pi}$ cm per second.

   b. When $c = 2\pi r = 2$, we have $r = 1/\pi$. At this time, $\frac{dr}{dt} = \frac{1}{2\pi r} = \frac{1}{2\pi(1/\pi)} = \frac{1}{2}$ cm per second.

3.11.11 $A(x) = \pi x^2$, so $\frac{dA}{dt} = 2\pi x \frac{dx}{dt}$. At $x = 10\,\text{ft}$ and $\frac{dx}{dt} = -2\,\text{ft/min}$ we have $\frac{dA}{dt} = 2\pi \cdot 10 \cdot (-2) = -40\pi\,\text{ft}^2/\text{min}$.

3.11.13 $V(r) = \frac{4}{3}\pi r^3$, so $\frac{dV}{dt} = 4\pi r^2 \frac{dr}{dt} = 15\,\text{in}^3/\text{min}$. At $r = 10$ inches we have $4\pi(10\,\text{in})^2\frac{dr}{dt} = 15\,\text{in}^3/\text{min}$. Thus, $\frac{dr}{dt} = \frac{3}{80\pi}\,\text{in/min} \approx 0.012\,\text{in/min}$.

3.11.15 $V(r) = \frac{4}{3}\pi r^3$, and $S(r) = 4\pi r^2$. $\frac{dV}{dt} = 4\pi r^2 \frac{dr}{dt} = k \cdot 4\pi r^2$, so $\frac{dr}{dt} = k$, the constant of proportionality.

3.11.17 Using the results of the previous exercise, we are seeking the value of x where $\frac{dx}{dt} = \frac{dy}{dt} = 2x\frac{dx}{dt}$. This occurs for $x = 1/2$, so the desired points is $(1/2, 1/4)$.

3.11.19

By similar triangles, $\frac{2}{50} = \frac{h}{b}$, so $b = 25h$. Also, $A = \frac{1}{2}bh = 12.5h^2$, so the volume for $0 \leq h \leq 2$ is $V(h) = 12.5 \cdot h^2 \cdot 20 = 250h^2$. For $2 < h \leq 3$, $V(h) = 250 \cdot 2^2 + 50 \cdot 20 \cdot (h-2) = 1000h - 1000$. When $t = 250$ minutes, then $V = 250\,\text{min} \cdot 1\,\text{m}^3/\text{min} = 250\,\text{m}^3$. So $V(h) = 250h^2 = 250$, so $h = 1\,\text{m}$. At that time $\frac{dV}{dt} = 500h\frac{dh}{dt} = 500 \cdot 1 \cdot \frac{dh}{dt} = 1\,\text{m}^3/\text{min}$. So $\frac{dh}{dt} = \frac{1}{500}\,\text{m/min} = 0.002\,\text{m/min} = 2\,\text{mm/min}$.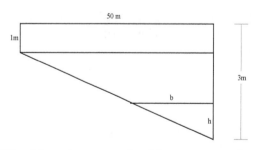

Fill time: The volume of the entire swimming pool is 2000 cubic meters, so at 1 cubic meter per minute, it will take 2000 minutes.

3.11.21

Let x be the distance the surface ship has traveled and D the depth of the submarine. We have $\frac{dx}{dt} = 10\,\text{km/hr}$. Note that $\frac{D}{x} = \tan 20°$, so $D = x \cdot \tan 20° \approx 0.364x$. We have $\frac{dD}{dt} = 0.364\frac{dx}{dt} = 3.64\,\text{km/hr}$. The depth of the submarine is increasing at a rate of 3.64 km/hr.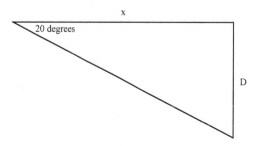

3.11.23

Let h be the vertical distance from the ground to the top of the ladder, and let x be the horizontal distance from the wall to the bottom of the ladder. By the Pythagorean Theorem, we have that $x^2 + h^2 = 169$. Thus, $2x\frac{dx}{dt} + 2h\frac{dh}{dt} = 0$, so $\frac{dh}{dt} = -\frac{x}{h}\frac{dx}{dt}$, and we are given that $\frac{dx}{dt} = 0.5$ feet per second. At $x = 5$ we have $h = \sqrt{169 - 25} = 12$ feet. Thus, $\frac{dh}{dt} = -\frac{5}{12} \cdot \frac{1}{2} = -\frac{5}{24}$ feet per second. So the top of the ladder slides down the wall at $\frac{5}{24}$ feet per second.

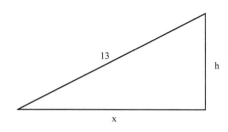

3.11.25

By similar triangles, $\frac{x+y}{20} = \frac{y}{5}$, so $x + y = 4y$, so $x = 3y$, and $\frac{dx}{dt} = 3\frac{dy}{dt}$. Because we are given that $\frac{dx}{dt} = -8$, we have $\frac{dy}{dt} = -\frac{8}{3}$ feet per second. The tip of her shadow is therefore moving at $-8 - \frac{8}{3} = -\frac{32}{3}$ feet per second.

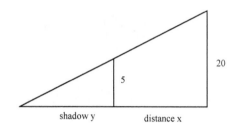

3.11.27 $V = \frac{1}{3}\pi r^2 h$ where $r = 3h$, so $V = 3\pi h^3$. We have that $\frac{dV}{dt} = 9\pi h^2 \frac{dh}{dt}$, and we given that $\frac{dh}{dt} = 2$ at the moment when $h = 12$, so at that time, $\frac{dV}{dt} = 9\pi \cdot 144\,\text{cm}^2 \cdot 2\,\text{cm/sec} = 2592\pi\,\text{cm}^3/\text{s}$. This is the rate at which the volume of the sandpile is increasing, so it must also be the rate at which the sand is leaving the bin, because there is no other sand involved.

3.11.29 Let h be the depth of the water in the tank at time t, and let r be the radius of the cone-shaped water at time t. By similar triangles, we have that $\frac{h}{r} = \frac{12}{6}$, so $h = 2r$. The volume of the water in the tank is given by $V = \frac{1}{3}\pi r^2 h = \frac{1}{3}\pi \frac{h^2}{4} \cdot h = \frac{\pi h^3}{12}$. Thus, $\frac{dV}{dt} = \frac{\pi h^2}{4}\frac{dh}{dt}$, and so when $h = 3$ we have $-2\,\text{ft}^3/\text{s} = \frac{9\pi\,\text{ft}^2}{4}\frac{dh}{dt}$, so $\frac{dh}{dt} = -\frac{8}{9\pi}\,\text{ft/s}$. So the depth of the water is decreasing at a rate of $8/(9\pi)$ feet per second.

3.11.31 Let h be the depth of the water in the tank at time t, and let r be the radius of the cone-shaped water at time t. By similar triangles, we have that $\frac{h}{r} = \frac{12}{6}$, so $h = 2r$. The volume of the water in the tank is given by $V = \frac{1}{3}\pi r^2 h = \frac{1}{3}\pi \frac{h^2}{4} \cdot h = \frac{\pi h^3}{12}$. Thus, $\frac{dV}{dt} = \frac{\pi h^2}{4}\frac{dh}{dt}$. When $\frac{dh}{dt} = -1$, we have $\frac{dV}{dt} = -\frac{\pi h^2}{4}$. when $h = 6$, we have $\frac{dV}{dt} = -9\pi$, so the water is draining from the tank at 9π cubic feet per minute.

3.11.33 Let r be the radius of the exposed surface of the water of height h at time t. Consider the right triangle with legs of length r and $10 - h$ (from the center of the sphere measured down to where the water level is). The hypotenuse is given by the radius of the sphere, which is 10. By the Pythagorean theorem, we have

$$r^2 + (10 - h)^2 = 10^2,$$

which can be written as $r^2 + 100 - 20h + h^2 = 100$, so $r^2 + h^2 = 20h$. So $20\frac{dh}{dt} = 2h\frac{dh}{dt} + 2r\frac{dr}{dt}$. When $h = 5$, we have $10 \cdot \frac{1}{25\pi} = 5 \cdot \frac{1}{25\pi} + 5\sqrt{3}\frac{dr}{dt}$, so $\frac{dr}{dt} = \frac{\sqrt{3}}{75\pi}$. The surface area is given by $S = \pi r^2$, so $\frac{dS}{dt} = 2\pi r\frac{dr}{dt}$, so at this moment it is given by $\frac{dS}{dt} = 2\pi \cdot 5\sqrt{3} \cdot \frac{\sqrt{3}}{75\pi} = \frac{2}{5}$ square meters per minute.

3.11.35 Let x be the distance the motorcycle has traveled since the instant it went under the balloon, and let y be the height of the balloon above the ground t seconds after the motorcycle went under it. We have $x^2 + y^2 = D^2$ where D is the distance between the motorcycle and the balloon. Thus, $2x\frac{dx}{dt} + 2y\frac{dy}{dt} = 2D\frac{dD}{dt}$, and we are given that $\frac{dy}{dt} = 10$ feet per second, and $\frac{dx}{dt} = 40\,\text{mph} = \frac{176}{3}\,\text{ft/s}$. After 10 seconds have passed, we have that $y = 150 + 100 = 250\,\text{ft}$, $x = \frac{1760}{3}\,\text{ft}$ and $D = \sqrt{250^2 + \left(\frac{1760}{3}\right)^2} \approx 638\,\text{ft}$. Thus, $\frac{dD}{dt} \approx \frac{1}{638}\left(\frac{1760}{3} \cdot \frac{176}{3} + 2500\right) \approx 57.86$ feet per second.

3.11.37

Let x be the distance between the fish and the fisherman's feet, and let D be the distance between the fish and the tip of the pole. Then $D^2 = x^2 + 144$, so $2D(dD/dt) = 2x(dx/dt)$. Note that $dD/dt = -1/3$ ft/sec, so when $x = 20$ ft, we have $dx/dt = \sqrt{400 + 144}/20 \cdot (-1/3) \approx -0.3887$ ft/sec ≈ -4.66 in/sec. The fish is moving toward the fisherman at about 4.66 in/sec.

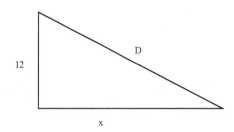

3.11.39

Let D be the length of the rope from the boat to the capstan, and let x be the horizontal distance from the boat to the dock. By the Pythagorean Theorem, $x^2 + 25 = D^2$, so $2x\frac{dx}{dt} = 2D\frac{dD}{dt}$, so $\frac{dx}{dt} = \frac{D}{x}\frac{dD}{dt}$. We are given that $\frac{dD}{dt} = -3$ feet per second, so when $x = 10$, we have $\frac{dx}{dt} = \frac{\sqrt{125}}{10} \cdot (-3) = -\frac{3\sqrt{5}}{2}$ feet per second. The boat is approaching the dock at $\frac{3\sqrt{5}}{2}$ feet per second.

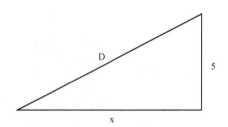

3.11.41 Let x be the distance the westbound airliner has traveled between noon and t hours after 1:00, and let y be the distance the northbound airliner has traveled t hours after 1:00, and let D be the distance between the planes. We have $D^2 = x^2 + y^2$, so $2D\frac{dD}{dt} = 2x\frac{dx}{dt} + 2y\frac{dy}{dt}$. We are given that $\frac{dx}{dt} = 500$ mph and $\frac{dy}{dt} = 550$ mph. At 2:30, we have that $x = 500 + 500 \cdot 1.5 = 1250$, and $y = 550 \cdot 1.5 = 825$ miles. $D = \sqrt{2243125} \approx 1497.7$ miles. Thus $\frac{dD}{dt} \approx \frac{1250 \cdot 500 + 825 \cdot 550}{1497.7} \approx 720.27$ miles per hour.

3.11.43 Let θ be the angle between the hands of the clock, and D the distance between the tips of the hands. By the law of cosines, $D^2 = 2.5^2 + 3^2 - 15\cos\theta$. So $2D\frac{dD}{dt} = 15\sin\theta\frac{d\theta}{dt}$. At 9:00 AM, we have $D^2 = 6.25 + 9$, so $D = \sqrt{15.25}$. Also, $\theta = \pi/2$ so $\sin\theta = 1$. Thus, $\frac{dD}{dt} = \frac{15}{2\sqrt{15.25}}\frac{d\theta}{dt}$. Now $\frac{d\theta}{dt} = \frac{d\theta_1}{dt} - \frac{d\theta_2}{dt}$ where $\frac{d\theta_1}{dt}$ is the angular change of the minute hand and $\frac{d\theta_2}{dt}$ is the angular change of the hour hand. We have $\frac{d\theta_1}{dt} = \frac{\pi}{30}$ radians per minute and $\frac{d\theta_2}{dt} = \frac{\pi}{360}$ radians per minute, so $\frac{d\theta}{dt} = \frac{11\pi}{360}$ radians per minute. Thus $\frac{dD}{dt} = \frac{15}{2\sqrt{15.25}} \cdot \frac{11\pi}{360} \approx .18436$ meters per minute, or about 11.06 meters per hour.

3.11.45

a. Let A be the point where the dragster started, let B be the point where camera 1 is located and let $C = y(t)$ be the position of the car at time t. Let θ be angle ABC. Note that $\tan\theta = \frac{y}{50}$, so $\sec^2\theta \cdot \frac{d\theta}{dt} = \frac{1}{50}\frac{dy}{dt}$. At time $t = 2$, we have that $\tan^2\theta = 4$, so $\sec^2\theta = \tan^2\theta + 1 = 5$. So $\frac{dy}{dt} = 5 \cdot 50 \cdot .75 = 187.5$ feet per second.

b. Let D be the point where camera 2 is located, and let ϕ be angle ADC. The $\phi = \tan^{-1}\left(\frac{y}{100}\right)$, so $\frac{d\phi}{dt} = \frac{1}{100\left(1 + \left(\frac{y}{100}\right)^2\right)} \cdot \frac{dy}{dt}$. After 2 seconds, we know that $y = 100$ and $\frac{dy}{dt} = 187.5$. Thus $\frac{d\phi}{dt} = \frac{100}{20,000} \cdot 187.5 = .9375$ radians per second.

3.11.47 By the Law of Sines, $\frac{\sin\theta}{s} = \frac{\sin\left(\frac{3\pi}{4} - \theta\right)}{2}$, so $2\sin\theta = s\sin\left(\frac{3\pi}{4} - \theta\right) = s\left(\sin\left(\frac{3\pi}{4}\right)\cos\theta - \cos\left(\frac{3\pi}{4}\right)\sin\theta\right)$.

We have

$$2\sin\theta = \frac{\sqrt{2}}{2}s(\sin\theta + \cos\theta)$$

$$2\tan\theta = \frac{\sqrt{2}}{2}s(\tan\theta + 1)$$

$$\tan\theta = \frac{(\sqrt{2}/2)\cdot s}{2 - (\sqrt{2}/2)s} = \frac{\sqrt{2}s}{4 - \sqrt{2}s}$$

$$\theta = \tan^{-1}\left(\frac{\sqrt{2}s}{4 - \sqrt{2}s}\right).$$

Thus, $\frac{d\theta}{dt} = \frac{\sqrt{2}\cdot\frac{ds}{dt}}{4 - 2\sqrt{2}s + s^2}$. When $\frac{ds}{dt} = 15$ and $s = 7.5$ we arrive at $\frac{d\theta}{dt} = 0.54$ radians per hour.

3.11.49

Let h be the vertical distance between the point on the elevator shaft positioned directly opposite the observer and the point on the elevator shaft that the observer is observing. So $h > 0$ corresponds to $\theta > 0$ and $h < 0$ corresponds to $\theta < 0$. We have $\frac{h}{20} = \tan\theta$, so $\frac{1}{20}\frac{dh}{dt} = \sec^2\theta\frac{d\theta}{dt}$. We are given that $\frac{dh}{dt} = 5\,\text{m/s}$. At $h = -10$, we have $\tan\theta = -.5$, so $\sec^2\theta = 1 + \tan^2\theta = 1 + (.5)^2 = 1.25$. So $\frac{d\theta}{dt} = \frac{1}{20\cdot 1.25}\cdot 5 = \frac{1}{5}$ radian per second. When $h = 20$, we have that $\tan\theta = 1$, so $\sec^2\theta = 1 + 1^2 = 2$, and thus $\frac{d\theta}{dt} = \frac{1}{20\cdot 2}\cdot 5 = \frac{1}{8}$ radian per second.

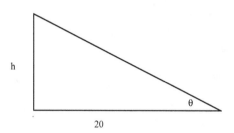

3.11.51 Let x be the distance the eastbound boat has traveled at time t and let s be the distance the northeastbound boat has traveled. Note the diagram shown. By the Law of Sines, $\frac{\sin\left(\frac{\pi}{2} - \theta\right)}{s} = \frac{\sin\left(\frac{\pi}{4} + \theta\right)}{x}$. Thus,

$$x\left(\sin\left(\frac{\pi}{2}\right)\cos\theta - \cos\left(\frac{\pi}{2}\right)\sin\theta\right) =$$
$$s\left(\sin\left(\frac{\pi}{4}\right)\cos\theta + \cos\left(\frac{\pi}{4}\right)\sin\theta\right)$$

So

$$x\cos\theta = \frac{\sqrt{2}}{2}\cdot s\cdot\cos\theta + \frac{\sqrt{2}}{2}\cdot s\cdot\sin\theta,$$

$$x = \frac{\sqrt{2}}{2}\cdot s + \frac{\sqrt{2}}{2}\cdot s\cdot\tan\theta,$$

and thus $\tan\theta = \frac{x - \frac{\sqrt{2}}{2}s}{\frac{\sqrt{2}}{2}s} = \frac{\sqrt{2}x - s}{s}$, and therefore $\theta = \tan^{-1}\left(\frac{\sqrt{2}x - s}{s}\right)$.

We have

$$\frac{d\theta}{dt} = \frac{1}{1 + \left(\frac{\sqrt{2}x - s}{s}\right)^2}\cdot\frac{\left(\sqrt{2}\left(\frac{dx}{dt}\right) - \left(\frac{ds}{dt}\right)\right)\cdot s - \left(\sqrt{2}x - s\right)\cdot\frac{ds}{dt}}{s^2} = \frac{\sqrt{2}\left(s\frac{dx}{dt} - x\frac{ds}{dt}\right)}{s^2 + (\sqrt{2}x - s)^2}.$$

At time t, we have $s(t) = 15t$ and $x(t) = 12t$. Note that

$$s\frac{dx}{dt} - x\frac{ds}{dt} = 15t\cdot 12 - 12t\cdot 15 = 0.$$

Thus $\theta' = 0$ for every value of t, so that the angle is constant.

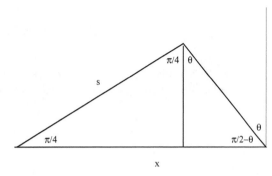

3.11.53 Let α be the angle between the line of sight to the bottom of the screen and the line of sight to the point 3 feet below where the floor and the wall meet. Note that $\cot\alpha = \frac{x}{3}$ and $\cot(\alpha + \theta) = \frac{x}{10}$, so $\alpha = \cot^{-1}(\frac{x}{3})$ and $\alpha + \theta = \cot^{-1}(\frac{x}{10})$. Thus, $\theta = \cot^{-1}(\frac{x}{10}) - \cot^{-1}(\frac{x}{3})$. So

$$\frac{d\theta}{dt} = -\frac{10x'}{100 + x^2} + \frac{3x'}{9 + x^2},$$

and at $x = 30$ feet, and with $\frac{dx}{dt} = 3$ feet per second, we have $\frac{d\theta}{dt} = -\frac{30}{1000} + \frac{9}{909} \approx -0.0201$ radians per second.

3.11.55

a. The volume of the water in the tank (as a function of h – the depth of the water in the tank) is given by 5 times the area of the segment of water in a cross-sectional circle. For a tank of radius 1, the formula for such a segment is $\cos^{-1}(1 - h) - (1 - h)\sqrt{2h - h^2}$. Thus the volume of the water in the tank is given by $V = 5(\cos^{-1}(1 - h) - (1 - h)\sqrt{2h - h^2})$. We have

$$\frac{dV}{dt} = 5 \cdot \left(-\frac{1}{\sqrt{1 - (1 - h)^2}} \cdot \left(-\frac{dh}{dt} \right) + \frac{dh}{dt}\sqrt{2h - h^2} - \frac{(1 - h)^2}{\sqrt{2h - h^2}}\frac{dh}{dt} \right)$$

$$= 5\left(\sqrt{2h - h^2} + \frac{1 - (1 - h)^2}{\sqrt{2h - h^2}} \right)\frac{dh}{dt}$$

$$= 5\left(\frac{2h - h^2 + 1 - 1 + 2h - h^2}{\sqrt{2h - h^2}} \right)\frac{dh}{dt}$$

$$= 5\left(\frac{2(2h - h^2)}{\sqrt{2h - h^2}} \right)\frac{dh}{dt}$$

$$= 10\sqrt{2h - h^2} \cdot \frac{dh}{dt}$$

When $h = .5$, we have $-\frac{3}{2} = \frac{dV}{dt} = 5\sqrt{3}\frac{dh}{dt}$, so $\frac{dh}{dt} = -\frac{\sqrt{3}}{10}$ meters per hr.

b. The surface area of the water is given by $S = 5 \cdot 2\sqrt{2h - h^2}$. So $\frac{dS}{dt} = 10 \cdot \frac{2 - 2h}{2\sqrt{2h - h^2}} \cdot \frac{dh}{dt}$, so at $h = .5$, we have $\frac{5}{\sqrt{3/4}} \cdot -\frac{\sqrt{3}}{10} = -1$ square meter per hr.

Chapter Three Review

1

a. False. This function is not differentiable at $x = -\frac{1}{2}$. It is possible for a function to be continuous at a point and not differentiable at that point.

b. False. For example, $f(x) = x^2 + 3$ and $g(x) = x^2 + 100$ have the same derivative, but aren't the same function.

c. False. For example, $\frac{d}{dx}|e^{-x}| = \frac{d}{dx}e^{-x} = -e^{-x} \neq |-e^{-x}|$.

d. False. For example, the function $f(x) = |x|$ has no derivative at 0, but there is no vertical tangent there.

e. True. For example, a ball dropping from a high tower has acceleration due to gravity which is negative, but it is speeding up as it falls because the velocity (which is negative also) is in the same direction as the acceleration.

3

a. $f'(1) = \lim\limits_{h \to 0} \dfrac{5(1+h)^3 + (1+h) - 6}{h}$. Expanding

yields $\lim\limits_{h \to 0} \dfrac{5(1 + 3h^2 + 3h + h^3) + 1 + h - 6}{h} =$

$\lim\limits_{h \to 0} \dfrac{5 - 15h^2 + 15h + 5h^3 + h - 5}{h}$. This can be

written as $\lim\limits_{h \to 0} \dfrac{5h^3 - 15h^2 + 16h}{h} = \lim\limits_{h \to 0} (5h^2 - 15h + 16) = 16$.

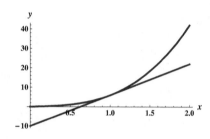

b. The tangent line at $(1, 6)$ is given by $y - 6 = 16(x - 1)$, or $y = 16x - 10$.

5

a. $f'(0) = \lim\limits_{h \to 0} \dfrac{\frac{1}{2\sqrt{3h+1}} - \frac{1}{2}}{h}$

$= \lim\limits_{h \to 0} \dfrac{1 - \sqrt{3h+1}}{2\sqrt{3h+1} \cdot h} =$

$\lim\limits_{h \to 0} \dfrac{(1 - \sqrt{3h+1})(1 + \sqrt{3h+1})}{2\sqrt{3h+1} \cdot h(1 + \sqrt{3h+1})} =$

$\lim\limits_{h \to 0} \dfrac{1 - (3h+1)}{2\sqrt{3h+1} \cdot h(1 + \sqrt{3h+1})}$. Simplifying

yields $\lim\limits_{h \to 0} -\dfrac{3}{2\sqrt{3h+1}(1 + \sqrt{3h+1})}$, and this

last limit can be seen to be $-\frac{3}{4}$.

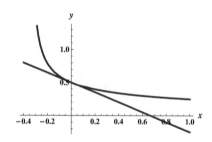

b. The tangent line at $\left(0, \frac{1}{2}\right)$ is given by $y - \frac{1}{2} = -\frac{3}{4}x$, or $y = -\frac{3}{4}x + \frac{1}{2}$.

7

a. Average growth is $\frac{p(60) - p(50)}{10} = 2.7$ million people per year.

b. The curve is pretty straight between $t = 50$ and $t = 60$, so the secant line between these two points is approximately as steep as the tangent line at a point in between.

c. A reasonable estimate to the instantaneous grow rate at 1985 would be the slope of the secant line between $t = 80$ and $t = 90$. This is $\frac{p(90) - p(80)}{10} = 2.217$ million people per year.

9

a. $v(15) \approx \frac{400 - 200}{5} = 40$ meters per second.

b. Because the graph is a straight line for $t \geq 30$, $v(70) = \frac{D(90) - D(60)}{30} = \frac{1600 - 1400}{30} = \frac{20}{3}$ meters per second. The points at 60 and 90 were chosen because it is easier to detect the function values at those points using the given grid.

c. The average velocity is $\frac{D(90)-D(20)}{70} \approx \frac{1600-550}{70} = 15$ meters per second.

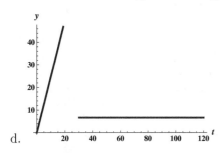

e. The parachute was deployed.

d.

11

$$g'(x) = \lim_{h \to 0} \frac{\sqrt{2(x+h)-3} - \sqrt{2x-3}}{h} = \lim_{h \to 0} \frac{\sqrt{2(x+h)-3} - \sqrt{2x-3}}{h} \cdot \frac{\sqrt{2(x+h)-3} + \sqrt{2x-3}}{\sqrt{2(x+h)-3} + \sqrt{2x-3}}$$

$$= \lim_{h \to 0} \frac{2(x+h)-3-(2x-3)}{h(\sqrt{2(x+h)-3} + \sqrt{2x-3})} = \lim_{h \to 0} \frac{2}{\sqrt{2(x+h)-3} + \sqrt{2x-3}} = \frac{2}{2\sqrt{2x-3}} = \frac{1}{\sqrt{2x-3}}.$$

13

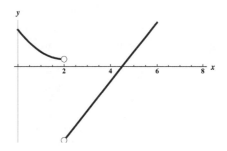

15 $f'(x) = 2x^2 + 2\pi x + 7.$

17 $f'(t) = 10t \sin t + 5t^2 \cos t.$

19 $f'(\theta) = (4\sec^2(\theta^2 + 3\theta + 2)) \cdot (2\theta + 3) = (8\theta + 12)\sec^2(\theta^2 + 3\theta + 2).$

21 $f'(u) = \frac{(8u+1)(8u+1)-(4u^2+u)(8)}{(8u+1)^2} = \frac{64u^2+16u+1-32u^2-8u}{(8u+1)^2} = \frac{32u^2+8u+1}{(8u+1)^2}.$

23 $f'(\theta) = \sec^2(\sin\theta) \cdot \cos\theta.$

25 $f'(x) = 2(\sin x)\sqrt{3x-1} + 2x(\cos x)\sqrt{3x-1} + \frac{3x \sin x}{\sqrt{3x-1}}.$

27 $f'(x) = \ln^2 x + x \cdot 2\ln x \cdot \left(\frac{1}{x}\right) = \ln x \cdot (\ln x + 2).$

29 $f'(x) = 2^{x^2-x} \cdot \ln 2 \cdot (2x - 1).$

31 $f'(x) = \frac{1}{\sqrt{1-\left(\frac{1}{x}\right)^2}} \cdot -\frac{1}{x^2} = -\frac{1}{|x|\sqrt{x^2-1}}.$

33 $\frac{d}{dx}x^{1/x} = \frac{d}{dx}e^{\frac{\ln x}{x}} = e^{\frac{\ln x}{x}} \cdot \left(\frac{1-\ln x}{x^2}\right) = x^{1/x}\left(\frac{1-\ln x}{x^2}\right)$. So $\frac{d}{dx}x^{1/x}\big|_{x=1} = 1 \cdot \frac{1-0}{1^2} = 1.$

35 $f'(x) = \sec^{-1} x + \frac{1}{\sqrt{x^2-1}}$. So $f'(2/\sqrt{3}) = \frac{\pi}{6} + \sqrt{3}.$

37 Because

$$y' = \frac{(1+\sin x)y'e^y - e^y \cos x}{(1+\sin x)^2},$$

collecting terms gives

$$y'\left(1 - \frac{e^y}{1+\sin x}\right) = -\frac{\cos x\, e^y}{(1+\sin x)^2},$$

so

$$y'(1-y) = -\frac{\cos x}{1+\sin x}\cdot y.$$

Thus $y' = -\frac{y\cos x}{(1-y)(1+\sin x)}$. This can also be written as $y' = \frac{y\cos x}{e^y - 1 - \sin x}$.

39 $y'\sqrt{x^2+y^2} + y\cdot\frac{x+yy'}{\sqrt{x^2+y^2}} = 0$, and thus $y'\left(\sqrt{x^2+y^2} + \frac{y^2}{\sqrt{x^2+y^2}}\right) = -\frac{xy}{\sqrt{x^2+y^2}}$. This can be written as

$y'\left(\frac{x^2+2y^2}{\sqrt{x^2+y^2}}\right) = -\frac{xy}{\sqrt{x^2+y^2}}$, so $y' = -\frac{xy}{x^2+2y^2}$.

41 $y' = 9x^2 + \cos x$. At $x = 0$, $y' = 1$. So the tangent line is given by $y - 0 = 1(x - 0)$, or $y = x$.

43 $y' + \frac{y+xy'}{2\sqrt{xy}} = 0$. At the point $(1,4)$, we have $y' + \frac{4+y'}{4} = 0$, so $y' = -\frac{4}{5}$. The tangent line is given by $y - 4 = -\frac{4}{5}(x - 1)$, or $y = -\frac{4}{5}x + \frac{24}{5}$.

45 We are looking for values of x so that $y'(x) = 0$. We have $y' = \sqrt{6-x} - \frac{x}{2\sqrt{6-x}}$, and this quantity is zero when $2(6-x) - x = 0$, or $12 - 3x = 0$, so when $x = 4$. So at the point $(4, 4\sqrt{2})$ there is a horizontal tangent line. There is a vertical tangent line at $x = 6$, because $\lim\limits_{x\to 6^-} y'(x) = -\infty$.

47

$y' = \frac{1}{2}x^{-1/2}\cos\sqrt{x}$.

$y'' = -\frac{1}{4}x^{-3/2}\cos\sqrt{x} + -\frac{1}{4}x^{-1}\sin\sqrt{x}$.

$y''' = \frac{3}{8}x^{-5/2}\cos\sqrt{x} + \frac{1}{8}x^{-2}\sin\sqrt{x} + \frac{1}{4}x^{-2}\sin\sqrt{x} - \frac{1}{8}x^{-3/2}\cos\sqrt{x} = \frac{3}{8}x^{-5/2}\cos\sqrt{x} + \frac{3}{8}x^{-2}\sin\sqrt{x} - \frac{1}{8}x^{-3/2}\cos\sqrt{x}$.

49 $\frac{d}{dx}[x^2 f(x)] = 2xf(x) + x^2 f'(x)$.

51 $\frac{d}{dx}\left(\frac{xf(x)}{g(x)}\right) = \frac{(f(x)+xf'(x))g(x) - xf(x)g'(x)}{g(x)^2}$.

53

a. $\frac{d}{dx}[f(x)+2g(x)]_{x=3} = f'(3) + 2g'(3) = 9 + 2\cdot 9 = 27$.

b. $\frac{d}{dx}\left[\frac{xf(x)}{g(x)}\right]_{x=1} = \frac{g(1)(1\cdot f'(1)+f(1))-1\cdot f(1)\cdot g'(1)}{(g(1))^2} = \frac{9\cdot[7+3]-15}{81} = \frac{25}{27}$.

c. $\frac{d}{dx}f(g(x^2))\big|_{x=3} = f'(g(9))\cdot g'(9)\cdot 2\cdot 3 = f'(1)\cdot 7\cdot 6 = 7\cdot 42 = 294$.

d. $\frac{d}{dx}(f(x))^3\big|_{x=5} = 3f(5)^2 f'(5) = 3(9)^2\cdot 5 = 1215$.

e. $(g^{-1})'(7) = \frac{1}{g'(3)} = \frac{1}{9}$.

55 Let $a = 5$ and $f(x) = \tan(\pi\sqrt{3x-11})$. Note that $f'(5) = \frac{3\pi\sec^2(2\pi)}{2} = \frac{3\pi}{2} = \frac{3\pi}{4}$.

So $\lim\limits_{x\to 5}\frac{f(x)-f(5)}{x-5} = \lim\limits_{x\to 5}\frac{\tan(\pi\sqrt{3x-11})-0}{x-5} = f'(5) = \frac{3\pi}{4}$.

57 Note that for $x = 2$, we have $y = \sqrt{8+2-1} = 3$. $\left(f^{-1}(x)\right)'\big|_{x=f(2)} = \frac{1}{f'(2)} = \frac{1}{\frac{3(2^2)+1}{2\sqrt{2^3+2-1}}} = \frac{6}{13}$.

59 If $f(x) = x^{-1/3}$, then $f^{-1}(x) = x^{-3}$. So $\left(f^{-1}\right)'(x) = -3x^{-4}$ for $x \neq 0$.

61

  a. $\left(f^{-1}\right)'\left(\frac{1}{\sqrt{2}}\right) = \frac{1}{f'\left(\frac{\pi}{4}\right)} = \frac{1}{\cos\left(\frac{\pi}{4}\right)} = \sqrt{2}$.

  b. $\frac{d}{dx}\sin^{-1}(x)\big|_{x=1/\sqrt{2}} = \frac{1}{\sqrt{1-(1/2)}} = \frac{1}{\sqrt{1/2}} = \sqrt{2}$.

63

  a. Because $f^{-1}(7) = 3$, we have $\left(f^{-1}\right)'(7) = \frac{1}{f'(3)} = \frac{1}{4}$.

  b. Because $f^{-1}(3) = 1$, we have $\left(f^{-1}\right)'(3) = \frac{1}{f'(1)} = 1$.

  c. $\left(f^{-1}\right)'(f(2)) = \frac{1}{f'(2)} = \frac{1}{3}$.

65

  a. The average cost is $\frac{C(3000)}{3000} = \frac{1025000}{3000} \approx \$341.67$. The marginal cost is $C'(3000) = -0.04(3000) + 400 = \$280$.

  b. The average cost of producing 3000 lawnmowers is \$341.67 per mower. The cost of producing the 3001st lawnmower is approximately \$280.

67

  a. The average growth rate is $\frac{p(50)-p(0)}{50} = \frac{407500-80000}{50} = 6550$ people per year.

  b. The growth rate in 1990 is $p'(40) = -5.1(40^2) + 144 \cdot 40 + 7200 = 4800$ people per year.

69

Let x be the distance the eastbound boat has traveled, and y the distance the southbound boat has traveled. By the Pythagorean Theorem, $D^2 = x^2 + y^2$, so $2D\frac{dD}{dt} = 2x\frac{dx}{dt} + 2y\frac{dy}{dt}$, so $\frac{dD}{dt} = \frac{x \cdot x' + y \cdot y'}{D}$. We are given that $x' = 40$, $y' = 30$, and at $t = .5$ hours, we have $x = 20$, $y = 15$, and $D = 25$. Thus, $\frac{dD}{dt} = \frac{20 \cdot 40 + 30 \cdot 15}{25} = 50$ mph.

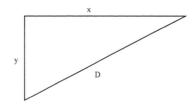

71 Let h be the elevation of the balloon, and s the length of the rope. We have $h = s\sin(65°)$, so $h' = s'\sin(65°) = -5 \cdot \sin(65°) \approx -4.53$ feet per second.

73

Let x be the distance the jet has flown since it went over the spectator. Let θ be the angle of elevation between the ground and the line from the spectator to the jet. Note that θ is also the angle pictured, and that $\cot\theta = \frac{x}{500}$. Thus, $\theta = \cot^{-1}\left(\frac{x}{500}\right)$. We are given that $x' = 450\,\text{mph} = 660\,\text{ft/sec}$.
$\theta' = -\frac{x'}{500 \cdot \left(1 + \left(\frac{x}{500}\right)^2\right)} = -\frac{500x'}{250{,}000 + x^2}$. After 2 seconds, $x = 1320$ feet, so at this time $\theta' = -\frac{500 \cdot 660}{250{,}000 + (1320)^2} \approx -0.166$ radians per second.

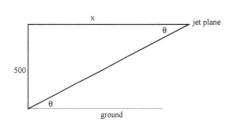

Chapter 4

Applications of the Derivative

4.1 Maxima and Minima

4.1.1 A number $M = f(c)$ where $c \in [a, b]$ with the property that $f(x) \leq M$ for all $x \in [a, b]$ is an absolute maximum for f on $[a, b]$, and a number $m = f(d)$ where $d \in [a, b]$ with the property that $f(x) \geq m$ for all $x \in [a, b]$ is an absolute minimum for f on $[a, b]$.

4.1.3 The function must be a continuous function defined on a closed interval.

4.1.5 The function shown has no absolute minimum on $[0, 3]$ because $\lim\limits_{x \to 0^+} f(x) = -\infty$. It has an absolute maximum near $x = 1$ and a local minimum near $x = 2.5$.

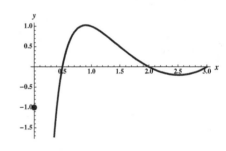

4.1.7 Note the existence of a horizontal tangent line at $x = 0$ where the maximum occurs.

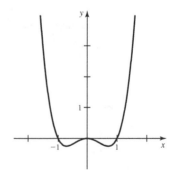

4.1.9 First find all the critical points by seeking all points x in the domain of f so that $f'(x) = 0$ or $f'(x)$ doesn't exist. Now compare the y-values of all of these points, together with the y-values of the endpoints. The largest y-value from among these is the maximum, and the smallest is the minimum.

4.1.11 $y = h(x)$ has an absolute maximum at $x = b$ and an absolute minimum at $x = c_2$.

4.1.13 $y = g(x)$ has no absolute maximum, but has an absolute minimum at $x = a$.

4.1.15 $y = f(x)$ has an absolute maximum at $x = b$ and an absolute minimum at $x = a$. It has local maxima at $x = p$ and $x = r$, and local minima at $x = q$ and $x = s$.

4.1.17 $y = g(x)$ has an absolute minimum at $x = b$ and an absolute maximum at $x = p$. It has local maxima at $x = p$ and $x = r$. It has a local minimum at $x = q$.

4.1.19   Note the horizontal tangent lines at 1 and 2, and the minimum at 0 and the maximum at 4.

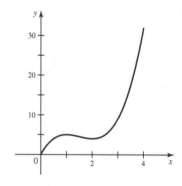

4.1.21   Note the horizontal tangent line at $x = 2$, and the "corners" at $x = 1$ and $x = 3$. Also note the absolute maximum at $x = 3$ and the absolute minimum at $x = 4$.

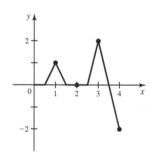

4.1.23

a. $f'(x) = 6x - 4$, which is zero when $x = 2/3$.

b. At $x = 2/3$ there is a local minimum.

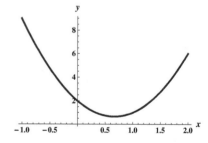

4.1.25

a. $f'(x) = x^2 - 9$, which is zero for $x = \pm 3$.

b. There is a local maximum at $x = -3$ and a local minimum at $x = 3$.

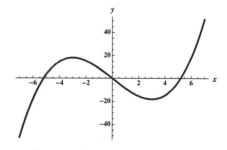

4.1.27

a. $f'(x) = 9x^2 + 3x - 2 = (3x + 2)(3x - 1)$, which is zero for $x = -2/3$ and $x = 1/3$.

b. There is a local maximum at $x = -2/3$ and a local minimum at $x = 1/3$.

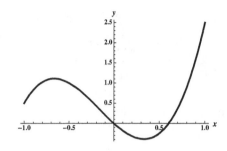

4.1.29

a. $f'(x) = \frac{(x^2+1)(1)-x(2x)}{(x^2+1)^2} = \frac{1-x^2}{(x^2+1)^2}$. This quantity is zero exactly when $1 - x^2 = 0$, so at $x = 1$ and $x = -1$.

b. At $x = 1$ there is a local maximum (which is also an absolute maximum) and at $x = -1$ there is a local minimum (which is also an absolute minimum.)

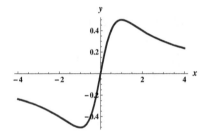

4.1.31

a. $f'(x) = \frac{e^x - e^{-x}}{2}$, which is zero when $e^x = e^{-x}$ or $x = -x$, so only for $x = 0$.

b. There is a local (and absolute) minimum at $x = 0$.

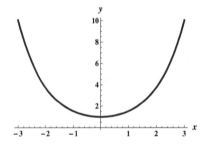

4.1.33

a. $f'(x) = -\frac{1}{x^2} + \frac{1}{x} = \frac{x-1}{x^2}$. There is a critical point at $x = 1$.

b. The critical point at $x = 1$ is a local minimum.

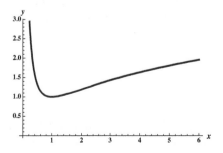

4.1.35

a. $f'(x) = 2x\sqrt{x+1} + x^2 \cdot \frac{1}{2\sqrt{x+1}} = \frac{4x(x+1)}{2\sqrt{x+1}} +$
$\frac{x^2}{2\sqrt{x+1}} = \frac{5x^2+4x}{2\sqrt{x+1}}$. This is zero when $5x^2 + 4x =$
$x(5x + 4)$ is zero, which occurs for $x = 0$ and
$x = -4/5$. The critical points are $(0,0)$ and
$(-4/5, 16/(25\sqrt{5}))$.

b. There is a local maximum at $x = -4/5$ and a local
minimum at $x = 0$.

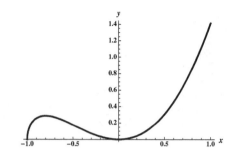

4.1.37

a. $f'(x) = 2x$, which is zero for $x = 0$.

b. We have that $f(-2) = -6$, $f(0) = -10$, and
$f(3) = -1$, so the maximum value of f on this
interval is -1 and the minimum is -10.

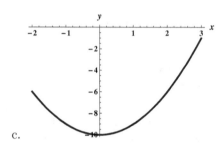

c.

4.1.39

a. $f'(x) = -2\cos x \sin x$, which is zero for $x = 0$,
$x = \pi/2$, and $x = \pi$. Because there are endpoints
at $x = 0$ and $x = \pi$, only $(\pi/2, 0)$ is a critical
point.

b. We have that $f(0) = 1$, $f(\pi/2) = 0$, and $f(\pi) = 1$,
so the maximum value of f on this interval is 1
and the minimum is 0.

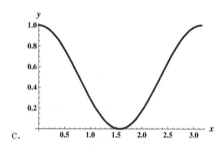

c.

4.1.41

a. $f'(x) = 3\cos 3x$, which is zero when

$$3x = \ldots, -\pi/2, \pi/2, 3\pi/2, \ldots,$$

so when $x = \ldots, -\pi/6, \pi/6, \pi/2, \ldots$. The only
such values on the given interval are $x = -\pi/6$
and $x = \pi/6$.

b. We have

$$f(-\pi/4) = -\sqrt{2}/2 \approx -0.707,$$

$f(-\pi/6) = -1$, $f(\pi/6) = 1$, and $f(\pi/3) = 0$, so
the absolute maximum of f is 1 and the absolute
minimum is -1.

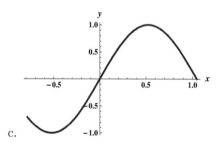

c.

4.1.43

a. Let $y = (2x)^x$, so that $\ln y = x \ln(2x)$. Then $\frac{1}{y} y' = \ln(2x) + \frac{x}{2x} \cdot 2 = 1 + \ln(2x)$. Thus $y' = (2x)^x (1 + \ln(2x))$. This quantity is zero when $1 + \ln(2x) = 0$, which occurs when $\ln(2x) = -1$, or $x = \frac{1}{2e} \approx .184$.

b. We have $f(.1) \approx .851$, $f\left(\frac{1}{2e}\right) = e^{-(1/2e)} \approx .832$, and $f(1) = 2$. So the absolute minimum is $e^{-(1/2e)}$ and the absolute maximum is 2.

c.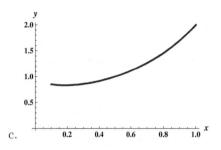

4.1.45

a. $f'(x) = 2x - \frac{1}{\sqrt{1-x^2}} = \frac{2x\sqrt{1-x^2}-1}{\sqrt{1-x^2}}$. This is zero on $(-1, 1)$ when the numerator is zero, which is when $2x\sqrt{1-x^2} = 1$, so when $(4x^2)(1-x^2) = 1$, or $4x^4 - 4x^2 + 1 = 0$. This factors as $(2x^2 - 1)(2x^2 - 1) = 0$, so we have solutions for $x = \pm\sqrt{1/2}$.

b. $f(-1) = 1 + \pi$, $f(-1/\sqrt{2}) = \frac{1}{2} + \frac{3\pi}{4}$, $f(1/\sqrt{2}) = \frac{1}{2} + \frac{\pi}{4}$, and $f(1) = 1$. So the maximum for f is $1 + \pi$ and the minimum is 1.

c.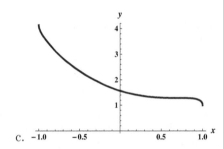

4.1.47

a. $f'(x) = 6x^2 - 30x + 24 = 6(x^2 - 5x + 4) = 6(x - 4)(x - 1)$. This is zero at $x = 4$ and $x = 1$.

b. $f(1) = 11$ and $f(4) = -16$. At the endpoints we have $f(0) = 0$ and $f(5) = -5$. The absolute maximum is 11 and the absolute minimum is -16.

c.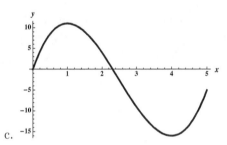

4.1.49

a. $f'(x) = 4x^2 + 10x - 6 = 2(2x^2 + 5x - 3) = 2(x + 3)(2x - 1)$. This is zero when $x = -3$ and when $x = 1/2$.

b. $f(-3) = 27$ and $f(1/2) = -19/12$. At the endpoints we have $f(-4) = 56/3 \approx 18.7$, and $f(1) = 1/3$. The absolute maximum is 27 and the absolute minimum is $-19/12$.

c.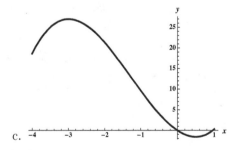

4.1.51 The stone will reach its maximum height when its velocity is zero, which occurs at the only critical point for this inverted parabola. We have that $v(t) = s'(t) = -32t + 64$, which is zero when $t = 2$. The height at this time is $s(2) = 256$, the maximum height.

4.1.53

a. Note that $P(n) = 50n - .5n^2 - 100$, so $P'(n) = 50 - n$, which is zero when $n = 50$. It is clear that this is a maximum, since the graph of P is an inverted parabola.

b. Given a domain of $[0, 45]$, since the only critical point is not in the domain, the maximum must occur at an endpoint. Because $P(0) = -100$, and $P(45) = \$1137.50$, he should take 45 people on the tour.

4.1.55

a. False. The derivative $f'(x) = \frac{1}{2\sqrt{x}}$ is never zero, and the function has no critical points.

b. False. For example, the function $f(x) = \begin{cases} \sin x & \text{if } -5 \le x \le 0, \\ -8 & \text{if } 0 < x \le 5 \end{cases}$ is not continuous on $[-5, 5]$, but has an absolute maximum of 1.

c. False. For example, the function $f(x) = (x - 2)^3$ satisfies $f'(2) = 0$, but it has neither a maximum nor a minimum at $x = 2$.

d. True. This follows from the theorems in this section.

4.1.57

a. $f'(x) = 2^x \cdot \ln 2 \cdot \sin x + 2^x \cos x = 2^x((\ln 2) \cdot \sin x + \cos x)$. Because 2^x is never zero, this expression is zero only when $(\ln 2) \cdot \sin x + \cos x = 0$, or $(\ln 2) \cdot \tan x = -1$, or $\tan x = \left(-\frac{1}{\ln 2}\right)$. So one solution is $x = \tan^{-1}\left(-\frac{1}{\ln 2}\right) \approx -.9647$. And since the tangent function is periodic with period π, we also have solutions at approximately $-.9647 + \pi \approx 2.1769$, and $-.9647 + 2\pi \approx 5.3185$. These are the only solutions on the given interval.

b. $f(-2) \approx -0.2273$, $f(-.9647) \approx -0.4211$, $f(2.1769) \approx 3.7164$, $f(5.3185) \approx -32.7968$, and $f(6) \approx -17.8826$. Thus the absolute maximum is about 3.7164 and the absolute minimum is about -32.7968.

c.

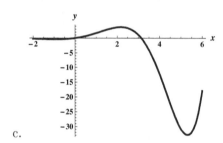

4.1.59

a. $f'(x) = \sec x \tan x$ which is zero when $\tan x = 0$ (since $\sec x$ is never zero.) So we are looking for where $\frac{\sin x}{\cos x} = 0$, which is when $\sin x = 0$, which is at $x = 0$.

b. $f(-\pi/4) = \sqrt{2} = f(\pi/4)$ and $f(0) = 1$. So the absolute maximum for f is $\sqrt{2}$ and the absolute minimum is 1.

c.

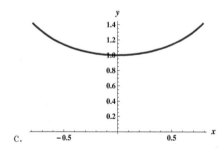

4.1.61

a. $f'(x) = 3x^2 e^{-x} + x^3 \cdot (-e^{-x}) = e^{-x} \cdot (3x^2 - x^3) = e^{-x} \cdot x^2 \cdot (3 - x)$. This expression is zero when $x = 0$ and when $x = 3$, so $(0, 0)$ and $(3, (27/e^3))$ are the critical points.

b. $f(-1) = -e$, $f(0) = 0$, $f(3) = \frac{27}{e^3} \approx 1.344$, and $f(5) \approx .8422$. So the absolute maximum of f on the given interval is about 1.344, and the absolute minimum is $-e \approx -2.718$.

c.

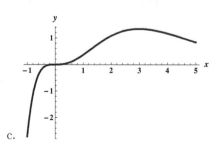

4.1.63

a. $f'(x) = \frac{\sqrt{x-4}\cdot 1 - x \cdot \frac{1}{2\sqrt{x-4}}\cdot 1}{x-4} = \frac{\sqrt{x-4}\cdot 1 - x\cdot \frac{1}{2\sqrt{x-4}}\cdot 1}{x-4} \cdot$
$\frac{2\sqrt{x-4}}{2\sqrt{x-4}} = \frac{2x-8-x}{2(x-4)^{3/2}} = \frac{x-8}{2(x-4)^{3/2}}$. This expression is 0 when $x = 8$. So $(8,4)$ is the only critical point.

b. $f(6) = 3\sqrt{2} = f(12)$, and $f(8) = 4$. Note that $3\sqrt{2} \approx 4.24 > 4$. So the absolute maximum of f on this interval is $3\sqrt{2}$, and the absolute minimum is 4.

c.

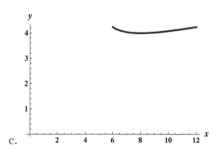

4.1.65 $f'(x) = \sqrt{x-a} + \frac{x}{2\sqrt{x-a}} = \frac{2x-2a+x}{2\sqrt{x-a}} = \frac{3x-2a}{2\sqrt{x-a}}$. This expression is zero when $x = \frac{2a}{3}$; however, that number is not in the domain of f if $a > 0$. However, if $a < 0$, then $\frac{2a}{3}$ is in the domain, and thus gives a critical point.

4.1.67 $f'(x) = x^4 - a^4$, which is zero when $x^4 = a^4$, or $|x| = a$. So there are critical points at $x = a$ and at $x = -a$.

4.1.69

a. $f'(\theta) = 2\cos\theta - \sin\theta$, which is zero when $\tan\theta = 2$. So one critical point occurs at $\theta = \tan^{-1}(2) \approx 1.107$. And since the tangent function is periodic with period π, there are will also be solutions at this number plus or minus integer multiples of π. On the given interval, these are located at approximately $1.107 - 2\pi \approx -5.176$, at $1.107 - \pi \approx -2.034$, and at $1.107 + \pi \approx 4.249$.

b. From the graph, it appears that there is a local minimum at about $\theta = -2.034$ and at $\theta = 4.249$, and there is a local maximum at about $\theta = -5.176$, and at about $\theta = 1.107$.

c. From the graph, it appears that the local minimum at about $\theta = -2.034$ is also an absolute minimum, as is the one at $\theta = 4.249$. The local maximum at about $\theta = -5.176$, and at about $\theta = 1.107$ are also absolute maxima. The value of the absolute maximum appears to be about 2.24 and the value of the absolute minimum appears to be about -2.24.

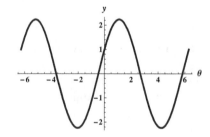

4.1.71

a. $f'(x) = (x-3)^{5/3} + (x+2)\cdot\frac{5}{3}(x-3)^{2/3} = \frac{(x-3)^{2/3}}{3}(3x-9+5x+10) = \frac{(x-3)^{2/3}}{3}(8x+1)$. This is zero when $x = 3$ and when $x = -\frac{1}{8}$. There are critical points at $x = -\frac{1}{8}$ and at $x = 3$.

b. From the graph, it appears that there is a local minimum of about -12.52 at $x = -\frac{1}{8}$.

c. The local minimum mentioned above is also an absolute minimum. The absolute maximum occurs at the left endpoint $x = -4$, where the value of f is about 51.23.

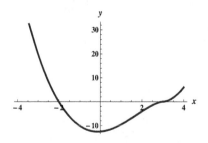

4.1.73

a. $h'(x) = \frac{(x^2+2x-3)(-1)-(5-x)(2x+2)}{(x^2+2x-3)^2} = \frac{x^2-10x-7}{(x^2+2x-3)^2}$.
By the quadratic formula, the numerator is
zero (making the quotient zero) when $x = \frac{10\pm\sqrt{100-4(-7)}}{2} = 5 \pm \frac{1}{2}\sqrt{128} = 5 \pm 4\sqrt{2}$. Note
that $5 + 4\sqrt{2}$ isn't in the domain, so the only crit-
ical point is at $x = 5 - 4\sqrt{2}$.

b. From the graph, it appears that the one critical
point mentioned above yields a local maximum.

c. The function has no absolute maximum and no
absolute minimum on the given interval.

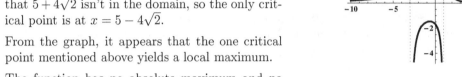

4.1.75

Note that

$$g(x) = \begin{cases} 3 - x + 2x + 2 = x + 5 & \text{if } -2 \le x \le -1, \\ 3 - x - 2x - 2 = 1 - 3x & \text{if } -1 \le x \le 3. \end{cases}$$

There is an absolute maximum of 4 and an absolute minimum of -8. The absolute maximum
occurs at $x = -1$, and the absolute minimum occurs at a $x = 3$.

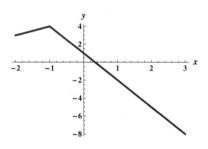

4.1.77

a. Because distance is rate times time, the time will
be distance over rate. The swim distance is given
by $\sqrt{2500 + x^2}$ meters, so the time for swimming
is $\frac{\sqrt{2500+x^2}}{2}$. For running, the distance is $50 - x$, so
the time is $\frac{50-x}{4}$. Thus we have $T(x) = \frac{\sqrt{2500+x^2}}{2} + \frac{50-x}{4}$.

b. $T'(x) = \frac{1}{2} \cdot \frac{1}{2} \left(x^2 + 2500\right)^{-1/2} \cdot 2x - \frac{1}{4} = \frac{x}{2\sqrt{x^2+2500}} - \frac{1}{4}$. This expression is zero when $\frac{x^2}{x^2+2500} = \frac{1}{4}$, so
when $4x^2 = x^2 + 2500$, which occurs when $x^2 = \frac{2500}{3}$. So $x = \sqrt{\frac{2500}{3}} \approx 28.868$.

c. $T(0) = 37.5$, $T(28.868) \approx 34.151$, and $T(50) = 25\sqrt{2} \approx 35.355$. The absolute minimum occurs at
the only critical point. The minimal crossing time
is approximately 34.151 seconds.

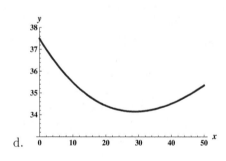

d.

4.1.79

a. Note that since there is a local extreme value at 2 for f and since f is differentiable everywhere, we
must have $f'(2) = 0$.

$g(2) = 2f(2) + 1 = 1$.

$h(2) = 2f(2) + 2 + 1 = 3$.

$g'(2) = 2 \cdot f'(2) + f(2) = 0$.

$h'(2) = 2f'(2) + f(2) + 1 = 1$.

b. h doesn't, since its derivative isn't zero at $x = 2$. However g might: for example, if $f(x) = (x - 2)^2$ then $g(x) = x(x - 2)^2 + 1$ has a local minimum at $x = 2$.

4.1.81

a. Because of the symmetry about the y-axis for an even function, a minimum at $x = c$ will correspond to a minimum at $x = -c$ as well.

b. Because of the symmetry about the origin, a minimum at $x = c$ will correspond to a maximum at $x = -c$. It is helpful to think about the symmetry about the origin as being the result of flipping about the y-axis and then flipping about the x-axis.

4.1.83

a. If $f(c)$ is a local maximum, then when x is near c but not equal to c, $f(c) \geq f(x)$, so $f(x) - f(c) \leq 0$.

b. When x is near to c but a little bigger than c, $x - c > 0$. So in this case, $\frac{f(x) - f(c)}{x - c} \leq 0$, since the numerator is negative (or 0) and the denominator is positive.

Thus, $\lim_{x \to c^+} \dfrac{f(x) - f(c)}{x - c} = f'(c) \leq 0$

c. When x is near to c but a little smaller than c, $x - c < 0$. So in this case, $\frac{f(x) - f(c)}{x - c} \geq 0$, since the numerator is negative (or 0) and the denominator is negative, making the quotient positive (or 0).

Thus, $\lim_{x \to c^-} \dfrac{f(x) - f(c)}{x - c} = f'(c) \geq 0$.

d. From the above, we have that $f'(c) \leq 0$ and $f'(c) \geq 0$, so $f'(c) = 0$.

4.2   What Derivatives Tell Us

4.2.1 If f' is positive on an interval, f is increasing on that interval. If f' is negative on an interval, f is decreasing on that interval.

4.2.3

One such example is $f(x) = x^3$ at $x = 0$.

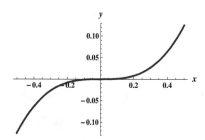

4.2.5 Under these circumstances the tangent lines lie below the graph of f.

4.2.7 An inflection point is a point on the graph of a function where the concavity changes. Thus, if $(c, f(c))$ is an inflection point, either $f''(x) < 0$ for x a little less than c and $f''(x) > 0$ for x a little bigger than c, or vice versa.

4.2.9

Yes, for example, consider $f(x) = 100 - x^2$ on the interval $(-8, 0)$. It is above the x axis, increasing, and concave down on that interval.

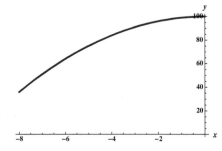

4.2.11

Such a function would be decreasing until $x = 2$, then increasing until $x = 5$, and then decreasing again after that.

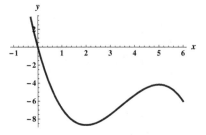

4.2.13

Such a function has extrema (minima) at 0 and 4, where the y value is zero. The function should never go below the x axis.

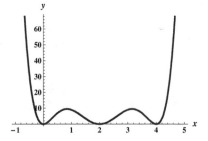

4.2.15

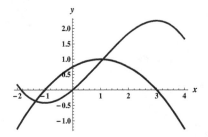

4.2.17

$f'(x) = -2x$, which is zero exactly when $x = 0$. On $(-\infty, 0)$ we note that $f' > 0$, so that f is increasing on this interval. On $(0, \infty)$, we note that $f' < 0$, so f is decreasing on this interval.

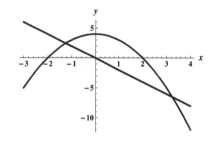

4.2.19

$f'(x) = 2(x-1)$, which is zero exactly when $x = 1$. On $(-\infty, 1)$ we note that $f' < 0$, so that f is decreasing on this interval. On $(1, \infty)$, we note that $f' > 0$, so f is increasing on this interval.

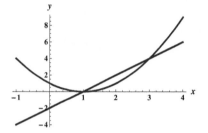

4.2.21

$f'(x) = 1 - 2x$, which is 0 when $x = 1/2$. On $(-\infty, 1/2)$ $f' > 0$ so f is increasing on this interval, while on $(1/2, \infty)$ $f' < 0$, so f is deceasing on this interval.

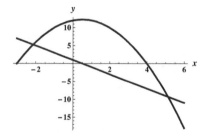

4.2.23

$f'(x) = -x^3 + 3x^2 - 2x = -x(x^2 - 3x + 2) = -x(x-1)(x-2)$. This is zero when $x = 0$, $x = 1$, and $x = 2$. Note that $f'(-1) > 0$, and $f'(1.5) > 0$, while $f'(.5) < 0$, and $f'(3) < 0$. So f is increasing on $(-\infty, 0)$ and on $(1, 2)$, while it is decreasing on $(0, 1)$ and on $(2, \infty)$.

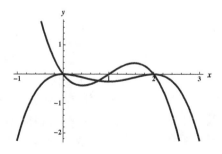

4.2.25

$f'(x) = 2x \ln x^2 + x^2 \cdot \frac{1}{x^2} \cdot 2x = 2x(\ln x^2 + 1)$. This is undefined for $x = 0$, and when $\ln x^2 + 1 = 0$. For $x > 0$, this occurs when $2\ln x + 1 = 0$, which occurs when $\ln x = -1/2$, or $x = \frac{1}{\sqrt{e}}$. By symmetry, we also have that $f'(x)$ is zero for $x = -\frac{1}{\sqrt{e}}$. Note that $\frac{1}{\sqrt{e}} \approx .6$, and that $f'(-1) < 0$, $f'(-1/2) > 0$, $f'(1/2) < 0$, and $f'(1) > 0$. Thus, f is decreasing on $(-\infty, -1/\sqrt{e})$ and on $(0, 1/\sqrt{e})$, and is increasing on $(-1/\sqrt{e}, 0)$ and on $(1/\sqrt{e}, \infty)$.

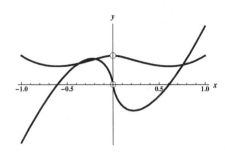

4.2.27 $f'(x) = -9\sin 3x$, which is 0 for $3x = -3\pi, -2\pi, -\pi, 0, \pi, 2\pi,$ and 3π, which corresponds to $x = -\pi, -2\pi/3, -\pi/3, 0, \pi/3, 2\pi/3$ and π. Note that $f'(-5\pi/6) = 9 > 0$, $f'(-\pi/2) = -9 < 0$, $f'(-\pi/6) = 9 > 0$, $f'(\pi/6) = -9 < 0$, $f'(\pi/2) = 9 > 0$, and $f'(5\pi/6) = -9 < 0$. Thus f is increasing on $(-\pi, -2\pi/3)$, on $(-\pi/3, 0)$, and on $(\pi/3, 2\pi/3)$, while f is decreasing on $(-2\pi/3, -\pi/3)$, on $(0, \pi/3)$, and on $(2\pi/3, \pi)$.

4.2.29 $f'(x) = (2/3)x^{-1/3}(x^2 - 4) + x^{2/3} \cdot 2x = \frac{2(x^2-4)}{3x^{1/3}} + \frac{2x^{5/3}}{1} \cdot \frac{3x^{1/3}}{3x^{1/3}} = \frac{8x^2-8}{3x^{1/3}} = \frac{8(x+1)(x-1)}{3x^{1/3}}$. This is zero for $x = \pm 1$ and is undefined for $x = 0$. Note that $f'(-8) = -84 < 0$, $f'(-1/8) = \frac{21}{4} > 0$, $f'(1/8) = \frac{-21}{4} < 0$, and $f''(8) = 84 > 0$. Thus f is decreasing on $(-\infty, -1)$ and on $(0, 1)$, while f is increasing on $(-1, 0)$ and on $(1, \infty)$.

4.2.31 $f'(x) = \frac{1}{x^2+1}$, which is always positive, so f is increasing on $(-\infty, \infty)$.

4.2.33 $f'(x) = -60x^4 + 300x^3 - 240x^2 = -60x^2(x^2 - 5x + 4) = -60x^2(x-4)(x-1)$. This is 0 for $x = 0$, $x = 1$, and $x = 4$. Note that $f'(-1) = -600 < 0$, $f'(1/2) = -26.25 < 0$, $f'(2) = 480 > 0$, and $f'(5) = -6000 < 0$. Thus f is increasing on $(1, 4)$ and is decreasing on $(-\infty, 1)$ and on $(4, \infty)$.

4.2.35 $f'(x) = -8x^3 + 2x = -2x(4x^2 - 1) = -2x(2x+1)(2x-1)$. This is zero for $x = 0$ and $x = \pm 1/2$. Note that $f'(-1) > 0$, $f'(-1/4) < 0$, $f'(1/4) > 0$, and $f'(1) < 0$, so f is increasing on $(-\infty, -1/2)$ and on $(0, 1/2)$, while it is decreasing on $(-1/2, 0)$ and on $(1/2, \infty)$.

4.2.37 We have $f'(x) = e^{-x^2/2} + xe^{-x^2/2} \cdot (-x) = (1-x^2)e^{-x^2/2}$. This is zero only when $x = \pm 1$. Note that $f'(-2) = -3e^{-2} < 0$, $f'(0) = 1 > 0$, and $f'(2) = -3e^{-2} < 0$. Thus f is decreasing on $(-\infty, -1)$ and on $(1, \infty)$, and is increasing on $(-1, 1)$.

4.2.39

   a. $f'(x) = 2x$, so $x = 0$ is the only critical point.

   b. Note that $f' < 0$ for $x < 0$ and $f' > 0$ for $x > 0$, so f has a local minimum of $f(0) = 3$ at $x = 0$.

   c. Note that $f(-3) = 12$, $f(0) = 3$ and $f(2) = 7$, so the absolute maximum is 12 and the absolute minimum is 3.

4.2.41

   a. $f'(x) = x \cdot \frac{1}{2}(4 - x^2)^{-1/2} \cdot (-2x) + \sqrt{4 - x^2} \cdot 1 = \frac{4 - 2x^2}{\sqrt{4-x^2}}$, which exists everywhere on $(-2, 2)$ and is zero only for $x = \pm\sqrt{2}$, so those are the only critical points.

   b. Note that $f'(-1.5) < 0$, $f'(0) > 0$ and $f'(1.5) < 0$, so f has a local minimum of $f(-\sqrt{2}) = -2$ and a local maximum of $f(\sqrt{2}) = 2$.

   c. Note that $f(-2) = 0 = f(2)$. So the absolute maximum is 2 at $x = \sqrt{2}$ and the absolute minimum is -2 at $x = -\sqrt{2}$.

4.2.43

a. $f'(x) = -3x^2 + 9$, which is zero when $9 = 3x^2$, or $x^2 = 3$. So the critical points are at $x = \pm\sqrt{3}$.

b. Note that $f'(-2) < 0$, $f'(0) > 0$, and $f'(2) < 0$, so there is a local minimum of $f(-\sqrt{3}) = -6\sqrt{3}$ and a local maximum of $f(\sqrt{3}) = 6\sqrt{3}$.

c. There is an absolute maximum of 28 at $x = -4$ and an absolute minimum of $-6\sqrt{3}$ at $x = -\sqrt{3}$.

4.2.45

a. $f'(x) = x^{2/3} + (x - 5) \cdot \frac{2}{3}x^{-1/3} = \frac{5x-10}{3x^{1/3}}$, which is undefined at $x = 0$ and is 0 at $x = 2$. So these are the two critical points.

b. Note that $f'(-1) > 0$ and $f'(1) < 0$, and $f'(3) > 0$ so f has a local maximum at $x = 0$ of $f(0) = 0$ and a local minimum at $x = 2$ of $-3\sqrt[3]{4} \approx -4.762$.

c. Note that $f(-5) = -10\sqrt[3]{25} \approx -29.24$, $f(0) = 0$, and $f(5) = 0$, so the absolute maximum of f on $[-5, 5]$ is 0 and the absolute minimum is $-10\sqrt[3]{25}$.

4.2.47

a. $f'(x) = \frac{\sqrt{x}}{x} + \frac{\ln x}{2\sqrt{x}} = \frac{2 + \ln x}{2\sqrt{x}}$. This is defined everywhere on $(0, \infty)$ and is 0 only at $x = e^{-2}$.

b. Note that $f' < 0$ on $(0, \frac{1}{e^2})$ and $f' > 0$ on $(\frac{1}{e^2}, \infty)$, so there is a local minimum at $x = \frac{1}{e^2}$.

c. Because there is only one critical point, the local minimum at $x = \frac{1}{e^2}$ yields an absolute minimum of $f(1/e^2) = -\frac{2}{e} \approx -.736$. There is no absolute maximum because f increases without bound as $x \to \infty$.

4.2.49 $f'(x) = -xe^{-x} + e^{-x} = e^{-x}(1 - x)$, which is 0 only for $x = 1$. Note that f is continuous on $(-\infty, \infty)$ and contains only one critical point.

Note that $f' > 0$ for $x < 1$ and $f' < 0$ for $x > 1$. So there is a local maximum of $f(1) = 1/e$ at $x = 1$. The local maximum of $1/e$ at $x = 1$ is an absolute maximum. There is no absolute minimum, because the function is unbounded in the negative direction as $x \to -\infty$.

4.2.51 Note that A is continuous on $(0, \infty)$.

$A'(r) = -\frac{24}{r^2} + 4\pi r = \frac{4\pi r^3 - 24}{r^2}$, which is 0 for $r = \sqrt[3]{6/\pi}$, so there is only one critical point on the stated interval.

Note that $A' < 0$ on $(0, \sqrt[3]{6/\pi})$ and $A' > 0$ on $(\sqrt[3]{6/\pi}, \infty)$, so there is a local minimum of $A(\sqrt[3]{6/\pi}) = 36\sqrt[3]{\pi/6}$.

The local minimum mentioned above is an absolute minimum. There is no absolute maximum, because A is unbounded as $r \to \infty$.

4.2.53

The function sketched should be increasing and concave up everywhere.

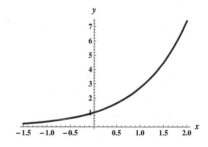

4.2.55

The function sketched should be decreasing everywhere, concave down for $x < 0$, and concave up
for $x > 0$.

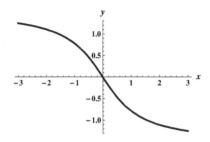

4.2.57 $f'(x) = 4x^3 - 6x^2$, so $f''(x) = 12x^2 - 12x = 12x(x-1)$. Note that f'' is zero when $x = 0$ and $x = 1$, so these are potential inflection points. Also note that $f''(-1) > 0$, $f''(.5) < 0$, and $f''(2) > 0$, so f is concave up on $(-\infty, 0)$ and on $(1, \infty)$, and is concave down on $(0, 1)$. There are inflection points at $(0, 1)$ and $(1, 0)$.

4.2.59 $f'(x) = 20x^3 - 60x^2$, and $f''(x) = 60x^2 - 120x = 60x(x-2)$. This is 0 for $x = 0$ and for $x = 2$. Note that $f''(-1) > 0$, $f''(1) < 0$, and $f''(3) > 0$. So f is concave up on $(-\infty, 0)$, concave down on $(0, 2)$, and concave up on $(2, \infty)$. There are inflection points at $x = 0$ and $x = 2$.

4.2.61 $f'(x) = e^x(x-3) + e^x = e^x(x-3+1) = e^x(x-2)$. $f''(x) = e^x(x-2) + e^x = e^x(x-2+1) = e^x(x-1)$. Note that f'' is zero only at $x = 1$. Also note that $f''(0) < 0$ and $f''(2) > 0$, so f is concave down on $(-\infty, 1)$ and is concave up on $(1, \infty)$. The point $(1, -2e)$ is an inflection point.

4.2.63 $g'(t) = \frac{6t}{3t^2+1}$, and $g''(t) = \frac{(3t^2+1)\cdot 6 - 6t(6t)}{(3t^2+1)^2} = \frac{6-18t^2}{(3t^2+1)^2}$. Note that g'' is 0 for $t = \pm\sqrt{1/3}$. Also, $g''(-1) < 0$, $g''(0) > 0$, and $g''(1) < 0$, so g is concave down on $(-\infty, -\sqrt{1/3})$ and on $(\sqrt{1/3}, \infty)$, and is concave up on $(-\sqrt{1/3}, \sqrt{1/3})$. There are inflection points at $t = \pm\sqrt{1/3}$.

4.2.65 $f'(x) = -xe^{-x^2/2}$, and $f''(x) = (-x)(-xe^{-x^2/2}) + e^{-x^2/2} \cdot -1 = e^{-x^2/2}(x^2-1)$. Note that $f''(x)$ is 0 for $x = \pm 1$. Also note that $f'' > 0$ on $(-\infty, -1)$ and on $(1, \infty)$, so f is concave up there, while on $(-1, 1)$ f is concave down because $f'' < 0$ on that interval. The inflection points are at $(\pm 1, e^{-1/2})$.

4.2.67 $f'(x) = \sqrt{x}/x + (\ln x)\left(\frac{1}{2\sqrt{x}}\right) = \frac{2+\ln x}{2\sqrt{x}}$. $f''(x) = \frac{2\sqrt{x}/x - (2+\ln x)/\sqrt{x}}{(2\sqrt{x})^2} = -\frac{\ln x}{4\sqrt{x^3}}$. Note that f'' is 0 only at $x = 1$. On $(0, 1)$ we note that $f'' > 0$ so f is concave up, and on $(1, \infty)$ we note that $f'' < 0$ so f is concave down. There is an inflection point at $(1, 0)$.

4.2.69 $g'(t) = 15t^4 - 120t^3 + 240t^2$, and $g''(t) = 60t^3 - 360t^2 + 480t = 60t(t-2)(t-4)$. Note that g'' is 0 for $t = 0, 2$, and 4. Note also that $g'' < 0$ on $(-\infty, 0)$ and on $(2, 4)$, so g is concave down on those intervals, while $g'' > 0$ on $(0, 2)$ and on $(4, \infty)$, so g is concave up there. There are inflection points at $t = 0, 2$, and 4.

4.2.71 $f'(x) = 3x^2 - 6x = 3x(x-2)$. This is zero when $x = 0$ and when $x = 2$, and these are the critical points. $f''(x) = 6x - 6$. Note that $f''(0) < 0$ and $f''(2) > 0$. Thus by the Second Derivative Test, there is a local maximum at $x = 0$ and a local minimum at $x = 2$.

4.2.73 $f'(x) = -2x$, so $x = 0$ is a critical point. $f''(x) = -2$, so $f''(0) = -2$ and the critical point yields a local maximum.

4.2.75 $f'(x) = e^x(x-7) + e^x = e^x(x-6)$. This is zero when $x = 6$, and this is a critical point. $f''(x) = e^x(x-6) + e^x = e^x(x-5)$. Note that $f''(6) > 0$, so there is a local minimum at $x = 6$.

4.2.77 $f'(x) = 6x^2 - 6x = 6x(x-1)$, so $x = 0$ and $x = 1$ are critical points. $f''(x) = 12x - 6$, so $f''(1) = 6 > 0$, so the critical point at $x = 1$ yields a local minimum. Also, $f''(0) = -6 < 0$, so the critical point at 0 yields a local maximum.

4.2.79 $f'(x) = x^2 \cdot (-e^{-x}) + e^{-x} \cdot 2x = e^{-x}(2x - x^2)$, which is zero for $x = 0$ and $x = 2$, so these are the critical points. $f''(x) = e^{-x}(2 - 2x) + (2x - x^2)(-e^{-x}) = e^{-x}(2 - 4x + x^2)$. Note that $f''(0) = 2 > 0$, so there is a local minimum at $x = 0$. Also, $f''(2) = -2e^{-2} < 0$, so there is a local maximum at $x = 2$.

4.2.81 $f'(x) = 4x \ln x + 2x^2 \cdot \frac{1}{x} - 22x = 4x \ln x - 20x = 4x(\ln x - 5)$. This is zero for $x = e^5$, so that is the critical point. $f''(x) = 4 \ln x + 4x \cdot \frac{1}{x} - 20 = 4 \ln x - 16$. Note that $f''(e^5) > 0$, so there is a local minimum at e^5.

4.2.83

a. True. $f'(x) > 0$ implies that f is increasing, and $f''(x) < 0$ implies that f' is decreasing. So f is increasing, but at a decreasing rate.

b. False. In fact, if $f'(c)$ exists and isn't zero, then there isn't any kind of local extrema at $x = c$.

c. True. In fact, if two functions differ by a constant, then all of their derivatives are the same.

d. False. For example, consider $f(x) = x$ and $g(x) = x - 10$. Both are increasing, but $f(x)g(x) = x^2 - 10x$ is decreasing on $(-\infty, 5)$.

e. False. A continuous function with two local maxima must have a local minimum in between.

4.2.85

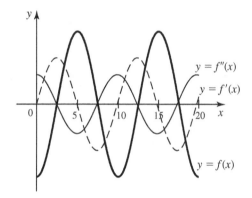

4.2.87 The graphs match as follows: (a) – (f) – (g); (b) – (e) –(i); (c) – (d) –(h). Note that (a) is always increasing, so its derivative must be always positive, and (f) switches from decreasing to increasing at 0, so its derivative must be negative for $x < 0$ and positive for $x > 0$.

Note that (b) has three extrema where there are horizontal tangent lines, so its derivative must cross the x-axis three times, and (e) has two extrema, so its derivative must cross the x-axis two times.

4.2.89

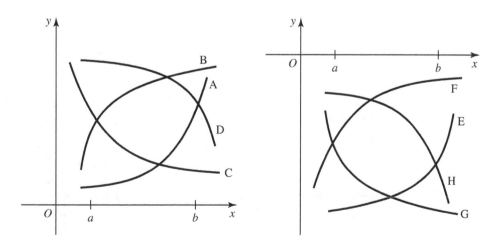

4.2.91

The graph sketched must have a flat tangent line at $x = -3/2$, $x = 0$, and $x = 1$, and must contain the points $(-2, 0)$, $(0, 0)$, and $(1, 0)$. The example to the right is only one possible such graph.

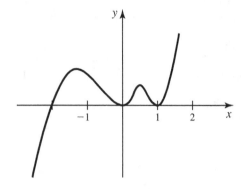

4.2.93

The graph sketched must be concave up on $(-\infty, -2)$ and on $(1, 3)$, and concave down on $(-2, 1)$ and on $(3, \infty)$. The example to the right is only one possible such graph.

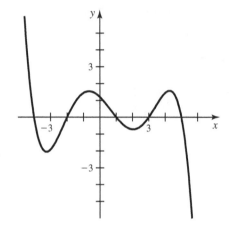

4.2.95

a. f is increasing on $(-2, 2)$. It is decreasing on $(-3, -2)$.

b. There are critical points of f at $x = -2$ and at $x = 0$. There is a local minimum at $x = -2$ and no extremum at $x = 0$.

c. There are inflection points of f at $x = -1$ and at $x = 0$.

d. f is concave up on $(-3, -1)$ and on $(0, 2)$, while it is concave down on $(-1, 0)$.

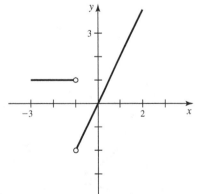

e.

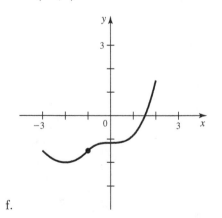

f.

4.2.97 $f'(x) = x^3 - 5x^2 - 8x + 48 = (x-4)^2(x+3)$. (This can be obtained by using trial-and-error to determine that $x = 4$ is a root, and then using long division of polynomials to see that $f'(x) = (x-4)(x^2 - x - 12)$.) Note that $f''(x) = 3x^2 - 10x - 8$, so $f''(-3) = 49 > 0$ and $f''(4) = 0$. So there is a local minimum at $x = -3$, but the test is inconclusive for $x = 4$. The first derivative test shows that there is neither a maximum nor a minimum at $x = 4$.

4.2.99 $f'(x) = 3x^2 + 4x + 4$, which is never 0. (Note that the discriminant $4^2 - 4 \cdot 3 \cdot 4 < 0$, so this quadratic has no real roots.) So there are no critical points.

4.2.101

a. $E = \frac{dD}{dp} \cdot \frac{p}{D} = -10 \frac{p}{500 - 10p} = \frac{p}{p - 50}$.

b. $E = \frac{12}{12 - 50} \cdot .045 = -1.42\%$.

c. If $D(p) = a - bp$, then $E(p) = -b \cdot \frac{p}{a - bp} = \frac{bp}{bp - a}$. So $E'(p) = \frac{(bp - a)b - bpb}{(bp - a)^2} = -\frac{ab}{(bp - a)^2}$, which is less than 0 for $a, b > 0$ and $p \neq a/b$.

d. If $D(p) = \frac{a}{p^b}$, then $E(p) = -\frac{ab}{p^{b+1}} \cdot \frac{p}{a/p^b} = -b$.

4.2.103

a. $\lim_{t \to \infty} \frac{300t^2}{t^2 + 30} \cdot \frac{1/t^2}{1/t^2} = \lim_{t \to \infty} \frac{300}{1 + (30/t^2)} = 300$.

b. Note that $P'(t) = \frac{(t^2 + 30)(600t) - 300t^2(2t)}{(t^2 + 30)^2} = \frac{18000t}{(t^2 + 30)^2}$. We want to maximize this, so we compute its derivative $P''(t) = \frac{(t^2 + 30)^2 \cdot 18000 - 18000t \cdot 2(t^2 + 30) \cdot 2t}{(t^2 + 30)^4} = \frac{54000(10 - t^2)}{(t^2 + 30)^3}$. This is 0 for $t = \sqrt{10}$, and an analysis of $P''(t)$ reveals that $P''(t) > 0$ for $t < \sqrt{10}$ and $P''(t) < 0$ for $t > \sqrt{10}$ so there is a local maximum for $P'(t)$ at $t = \sqrt{10}$.

c. Following the outline from the previous problem, we see that $P'(t) = \frac{2bKt}{(t^2 + b)^2}$, and $P''(t) = \frac{2bK(b - 3t^2)}{(t^2 + b)^3}$. $P''(t)$ is 0 for $t = \sqrt{b/3}$, and the first derivative test reveals that this is a local maximum.

4.2.105

a. $f'(x) = 3x^2 + 2ax + b$, and $f''(x) = 6x + 2a$, which is 0 only for $x = -\frac{a}{3}$. Note that the sign of $f''(x)$ is different for $x < -a/3$ and $x > -a/3$, so this does represent an inflection point.

b.

$$f(x^*) - f(x^* + x)$$
$$= f(-a/3) - f(-a/3 + x) = (-a/3)^3 + a(-a/3)^2 + b(-a/3) + c$$
$$- ((-a/3 + x)^3 + a(-a/3 + x)^2 + b(-a/3 + x) + c)$$
$$= (-a/3)^3 + a(-a/3)^2 + b(-a/3) + c$$
$$- (-a/3)^3 - 3(-a/3)^2 x - 3(-a/3)x^2 - x^3 - a(-a/3)^2 - 2a(-a/3)x - ax^2 - b(-a/3) - bx - c$$
$$= -x^3 + \left(\frac{a^2}{3} - b\right)x.$$

Also,

$$f(x^* - x) - f(x^*) = f(-a/3 - x) - f(-a/3)$$
$$= (-a/3)^3 + 3(-a/3)^2(-x) + 3(-a/3)(-x)^2 + (-x)^3$$
$$+ a(-a/3)^2 + 2a(-a/3)(-x) + a(-x)^2$$
$$+ b(-a/3) + b(-x) + c - (-a/3)^3 - a(-a/3)^2 - b(-a/3) - c$$
$$= -x^3 + \left(\frac{a^2}{3} - b\right)x.$$

Thus the two expressions are the same for all x.

4.2.107

a. $f(-x) = \frac{1}{((-x)^2)^n+1} = \frac{1}{x^{2n}+1} = f(x)$, so f is even.

b. Note that $f(\pm 1) = \frac{1}{((-1)^2)^n+1} = \frac{1}{2}$, for all n.

c. $f'(x) = -(x^{2n}+1)^{-2}(2nx^{2n-1}) = -2nx^{2n-1}(x^{2n}+1)^{-2}$. So $f''(x) = -2nx^{2n-1} \cdot (-2(x^{2n}+1)^{-3}) \cdot 2nx^{2n-1} + (x^{2n}+1)^{-2} \cdot (-2n(2n-1)x^{2n-2}) = \frac{-2nx^{2n-2}((-2n-1)x^{2n}+2n-1)}{(x^{2n}+1)^3}$. This is 0 when $x = 0$ for $n \geq 2$, and when $x = \pm \sqrt[2n]{\frac{2n-1}{2n+1}}$ for all positive n. An analysis of the sign of f'' shows that there is no sign change at $x = 0$, and f has inflection points at $x = \pm \sqrt[2n]{\frac{2n-1}{2n+1}}$.

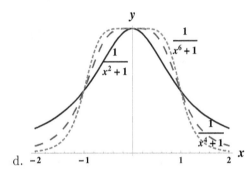

e. As n increases, the inflection points move further away from the y-axis, and closer to the point $(1, 1/2)$, although this movement is slight. The graphs become steeper and more "box-like."

d.

4.2.109 $f'(x) = 4x^3 + 3ax^2 + 2bx + c$, and $f''(x) = 12x^2 + 6ax + 2b = 2(6x^2 + 3ax + b)$. Note that $f''(x) = 0$ exactly when $x = \frac{-3a \pm \sqrt{9a^2 - 24b}}{12}$. This represents no real solutions when $9a^2 - 24b < 0$, which occurs when $b > 3a^2/8$. When $b = 3a^2/8$, there is one root, but in this case the sign of f'' doesn't change at the double root $x = -a/4$, so there are no inflection points for f. In the case $b < 3a^2/8$, there are two roots of f'', both of which yield inflection points of f, as can be seen by the change in sign of f'' at its two roots.

4.3   Graphing Functions

4.3.1 Because the intervals of increase and decrease and the intervals of concavity must be subsets of the domain, it is helpful to know what the domain is at the outset.

4.3.3 No. Polynomials are continuous everywhere, so they have no vertical asymptotes. Also, polynomials in x always tend to $\pm\infty$ as $x \to \pm\infty$.

4.3.5 The maximum and minimum must occur at either an endpoint or a critical point. So to find the absolute maximum and minimum, it suffices to find all the critical points, and then compare the values of the function at those points and at the endpoints. The largest such value is the maximum and the smallest is the minimum.

4.3.7

The function sketched should be decreasing and concave down for $x < 3$ and decreasing and concave up for $x > 3$.

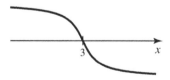

4.3.9 The domain of f is $(-\infty, \infty)$, and there is no symmetry. The y intercept is $f(0) = 0$, and the x-intercepts are 0 and 3 because $f(x) = x(x-3)^2$. $f'(x) = 3x^2 - 12x + 9 = 3(x^2 - 4x + 3) = 3(x-3)(x-1)$. This is zero when $x = 1$ and $x = 3$. Note that $f'(0) > 0$, $f'(2) < 0$ and $f'(4) > 0$, so f is increasing on

$(-\infty, 1)$ and on $(3, \infty)$. It is decreasing on $(1, 3)$. Note that $f''(x) = 6x - 12$ which is zero at $x = 2$. Because $f''(1) < 0$ and $f''(3) > 0$, we conclude that f is concave down on $(-\infty, 2)$ and concave up on $(2, \infty)$. There is an inflection point at $(2, 2)$, a local maximum at $(1, 4)$ and a local minimum at $(3, 0)$.

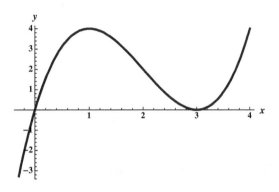

4.3.11

The domain of f is $(-\infty, \infty)$, and there is even symmetry, because $f(-x) = f(x)$. $f'(x) = 4x^3 - 12x = 4x(x^2 - 3)$. This is 0 when $x = \pm\sqrt{3}$ and when $x = 0$. $f''(x) = 12x^2 - 12 = 12(x^2 - 1)$, which is 0 when $x = \pm 1$. Note that $f'(-2) < 0$, $f'(-1) > 0$, $f'(1) < 0$, and $f'(2) > 0$. So f is decreasing on $(-\infty, -\sqrt{3})$ and on $(0, \sqrt{3})$. It is increasing on $(-\sqrt{3}, 0)$ and on $(\sqrt{3}, \infty)$. There is a local maximum of 0 at $x = 0$ and local minima of -9 at $x = \pm\sqrt{3}$. Note also that $f''(x) > 0$ for $x < -1$ and for $x > 1$ and $f''(x) < 0$ for $-1 < x < 1$, so there are inflection points at $x = \pm 1$. Also, f is concave down on $(-1, 1)$ and concave up on $(-\infty, -1)$ and on $(1, \infty)$. There is a y-intercept at $f(0) = 0$ and x-intercepts where $f(x) = x^4 - 6x^2 = x^2(x^2 - 6) = 0$, which is at $x = \pm\sqrt{6}$ and $x = 0$.

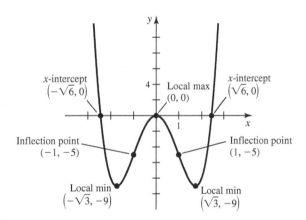

4.3.13 The domain of f is $(-\infty, \infty)$, and there is no symmetry. The y-intercept is $f(0) = -216$. The x-intercepts are 6 and -6.

$f'(x) = (x + 6)^2 + (x - 6)2(x + 6) = (x + 6)(x + 6 + 2x - 12) = (x + 6)(3x - 6) = 3(x + 6)(x - 2)$. The critical numbers are -6 and 2. Note that $f'(-7) > 0$, $f'(-2) < 0$, and $f'(3) > 0$, so f is increasing on $(-\infty, -6)$ and on $(2, \infty)$. It is decreasing on $(-6, 2)$. There is a local maximum of 0 at -6 and a local minimum of -256 at $x = 2$.

$f''(x) = 3(x - 2) + 3(x + 6) = 3(x - 2 + x + 6) = 3(2x + 4) = 6(x + 2)$, which is zero for $x = -2$. Note that $f''(x) < 0$ for $x < -2$ and $f''(x) > 0$ for $x > -2$, so f is concave down on $(-\infty, -2)$ and concave up on $(-2, \infty)$. The point $(-2, -128)$ is an inflection point.

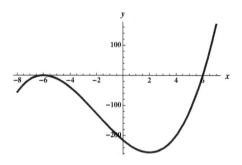

4.3.15

The domain of f is $(-\infty, 2) \cup (2, \infty)$, and there is no symmetry. Note that $\lim\limits_{x \to 2^+} f(x) = \infty$ and $\lim\limits_{x \to 2^-} f(x) = -\infty$, so there is a vertical asymptote at $x = 2$. There isn't a horizontal asymptote, because $\lim\limits_{x \to \pm\infty} f(x) = \pm\infty$.

$f'(x) = \frac{(x-2) \cdot 2x - x^2}{(x-2)^2} = \frac{x(x-4)}{(x-2)^2}$. This is 0 when $x = 4$ and when $x = 0$.

$f''(x) = \frac{(x-2)^2(2x-4) - (x^2-4x) \cdot 2 \cdot (x-2)}{(x-2)^4} = \frac{8}{(x-2)^3}$. This is never 0.

Note that $f'(-1) > 0$, $f'(1) < 0$, $f'(3) < 0$ and $f'(5) > 0$. So f is decreasing on $(0, 2)$ and on $(2, 4)$. It is increasing on $(-\infty, 0)$ and on $(4, \infty)$. There is a local maximum of 0 at $x = 0$ and a local minimum of 8 at $x = 4$.

Note that $f''(x) > 0$ for $x > 2$ and $f''(x) < 0$ for $x < 2$, So f is concave up on $(2, \infty)$ and concave down on $(-\infty, 4)$. There are no inflection points, because the only change in concavity occurs at a vertical asymptote. The only intercept is $(0, 0)$.

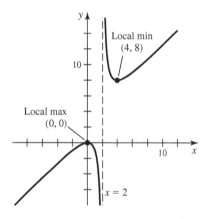

4.3.17

The domain of f is $(-\infty, -1) \cup (-1, 1) \cup (1, \infty)$, and there is odd symmetry, because $f(-x) = \frac{3(-x)}{(-x)^2 - 1} = -\frac{3x}{x^2 - 1} = -f(x)$. The only intercept is $(0, 0)$ which is both the y- and x-intercept.

Note that $\lim\limits_{x \to -1^+} f(x) = \infty$ and $\lim\limits_{x \to -1^-} f(x) = -\infty$, so there is a vertical asymptote at $x = -1$. Also, $\lim\limits_{x \to 1^+} f(x) = \infty$ and $\lim\limits_{x \to 1^-} f(x) = -\infty$, so there is a vertical asymptote at $x = 1$

Note that $\lim\limits_{x \to \pm\infty} \frac{3x}{x^2 - 1} \cdot \frac{1/x^2}{1/x^2} = \lim\limits_{x \to \pm\infty} \frac{3/x}{1 - (1/x^2)} = 0$, so $y = 0$ is a horizontal asymptote.

$f'(x) = \frac{(x^2-1) \cdot 3 - 3x \cdot 2x}{(x^2-1)^2} = \frac{-3x^2 - 3}{(x^2-1)^2} = -\frac{3(x^2+1)}{(x^2-1)^2}$. This is never 0, and is in fact negative wherever it is defined. Thus, f is decreasing on $(-\infty, -1)$, on $(-1, 1)$, and on $(1, \infty)$. There are no extrema.

$f''(x) = \frac{(x^2-1)^2(-6x) + 3(x^2+1) \cdot 2 \cdot (x^2-1) \cdot 2x}{(x^2-1)^4} = \frac{-6x^3 + 6x + 12x^3 + 12x}{(x^2-1)^3} = \frac{6x(x^2+3)}{(x^2-1)^3}$. This is 0 for $x = 0$. The point $(0, 0)$ is an point of inflection, because it is an interior point on the domain, and the second derivative changes from positive to negative there. The other concavity changes take place at the asymptotes. Note that f is concave down on $(-\infty, -1)$ and on $(0, 1)$, and concave up on $(-1, 0)$ and on $(1, \infty)$.

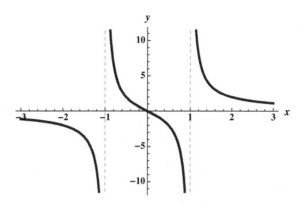

4.3.19

The domain of f is $(-\infty, -1/2) \cup (-1/2, \infty)$, and there is no symmetry.

Because $\lim\limits_{x \to \pm\infty} \dfrac{x^2 + 12}{2x + 1} \cdot \dfrac{1/x}{1/x} = \lim\limits_{x \to \pm\infty} \dfrac{x + (12/x)}{2 + (1/x)} = \pm\infty$, there is no horizontal asymptote. However, there is an oblique asymptote of $y = \frac{x}{2} - \frac{1}{4}$, because we can write f as $f(x) = \frac{x}{2} - \frac{1}{4} + \frac{49/4}{2x+1}$ by long division.

Also, because $\lim_{x \to (-1/2)^-} f(x) = -\infty$ and $\lim_{x \to (-1/2)^+} f(x) = \infty$, there is a vertical asymptote at $x = -1/2$.

$f'(x) = \dfrac{(2x+1)\cdot 2x - (x^2+12)\cdot 2}{(2x+1)^2} = \dfrac{2x^2 + 2x - 24}{(2x+1)^2} = \dfrac{2(x+4)(x-3)}{(2x+1)^2}$. This is 0 for $x = -4$ and $x = 3$. $f''(x) = \dfrac{(2x+1)^2(4x+2) - (2x^2+2x-24)\cdot 2(2x+1)\cdot 2}{(2x+1)^4} = \dfrac{98}{(2x+1)^3}$, which is never 0.

Note that $f'(x) > 0$ on $(-\infty, -4)$ and on $(3, \infty)$. So f is increasing on $(-\infty, -4)$ and on $(3, \infty)$. Also, $f'(x) < 0$ on $(-4, -1/2)$ and on $(-1/2, 3)$. So f is decreasing on those intervals. There is a local maximum of -4 at $x = -4$ and a local minimum of 3 at $x = 3$.

Note also that $f''(x) < 0$ for $x < -1/2$, and $f''(x) > 0$ for $x > -1/2$, so f is concave down on $(-\infty, -1/2)$ and is concave up on $(-1/2, \infty)$. There are no inflection points because the only change in concavity occurs at the vertical asymptote. There are no x-intercepts because $x^2 + 12 > 0$ for all x, and the y-intercept is $f(0) = 12$.

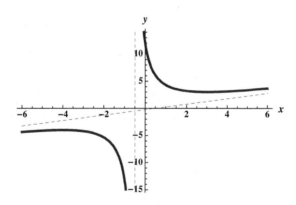

4.3.21

The domain of f is $(-\infty, \infty)$, and f is symmetric about the y-axis, because $f(-x) = \tan^{-1}((-x)^2) = \tan^{-1}(x^2) = f(x)$. The only intercept is $(0,0)$. Note that $\lim\limits_{x \to \pm\infty} \tan^{-1}(x^2) = \dfrac{\pi}{2}$, so $y = \pi/2$ is a horizontal asymptote in both directions.

$f'(x) = \frac{2x}{1+x^4}$, which is zero for $x = 0$. Note that f' is negative when x is negative and positive when x is positive, so f is decreasing on $(-\infty, 0)$ and increasing on $(0, \infty)$, and there is a local (in fact, absolute) minimum at $(0,0)$.

$f''(x) = \frac{(1+x^4)\cdot 2 - 2x \cdot 4x^3}{(1+x^4)^2} = \frac{2 - 6x^4}{(1+x^4)^2} = \frac{2(1-3x^4)}{(1+x^4)^2}$. This is zero for $x = \pm\sqrt[4]{1/3}$. Also note that $f''(-2) < 0$, $f''(0) > 0$, and $f''(2) < 0$, so f is concave down on $(-\infty, -\sqrt[4]{1/3})$ and on $(\sqrt[4]{1/3}, \infty)$, and is concave up on $(-\sqrt[4]{1/3}, \sqrt[4]{1/3})$. There are inflection points at $(-\sqrt[4]{1/3}, \pi/6)$ and $(\sqrt[4]{1/3}, \pi/6)$.

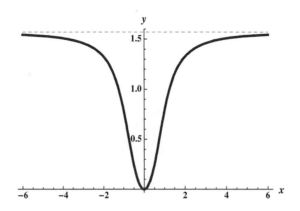

4.3.23

The domain of f is given to be $[-2\pi, 2\pi]$, and there is no symmetry, and no vertical asymptotes. There are no horizontal asymptotes to consider on this restricted domain.

$f'(x) = 1 - 2\sin x$. This is 0 when $\sin x = 1/2$, which occurs on the given interval for $x = -11\pi/6$, $-7\pi/6$, $\pi/6$, and $5\pi/6$. $f''(x) = -2\cos x$, which is 0 for $x = -3\pi/2, -\pi/2, \pi/2$, and $3\pi/2$.

Note that $f'(x) > 0$ on $(-2\pi, -11\pi/6)$, and on $(-7\pi/6, \pi/6)$, and on $(5\pi/6, 2\pi)$. So f is increasing on those intervals, while $f'(x) < 0$ on $(-11\pi/6, -7\pi/6))$ and on $(\pi/6, 5\pi/6)$, so f is decreasing there. f has local maxima at $x = -11\pi/6$ and at $x = \pi/6$ and local minima at $x = -7\pi/6$ and at $x = 5\pi/6$. Note also that $f''(x) < 0$ on $(-2\pi, -3\pi/2)$ and on $(-\pi/2, \pi/2)$ and on $(3\pi/2, 2\pi)$, so f is concave down on those intervals, while $f''(x) > 0$ on $(-3\pi/2, -\pi/2)$ and on $(\pi/2, 3\pi/2)$, so f is concave up there and there are inflection points at $x = \pm 3\pi/2$ and $x = \pm\pi/2$. The y-intercept is $f(0) = 2$ and the x-intercept is at approximately -1.030.

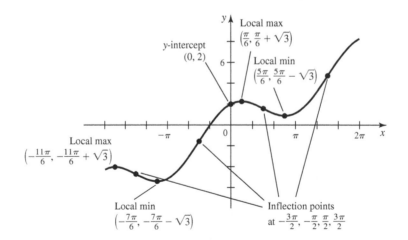

4.3.25

The domain of f is $(-\infty, \infty)$. There are no asymptotes. There are x-intercepts at $(0,0)$ and $(\pm 3\sqrt{3}, 0)$. f does have odd symmetry, because $f(-x) = -x - 3((-x)^{1/3}) = -(x - 3x^{1/3}) = -f(x)$.

$f'(x) = 1 - \frac{1}{\sqrt[3]{x^2}} = \frac{\sqrt[3]{x^2}-1}{\sqrt[3]{x^2}}$. This is undefined at $x = 0$, and is equal to zero at ± 1. Note that $f'(-2) > 0$, $f'(-1/2) < 0$, $f'(1/2) < 0$, $f'(2) > 0$. Thus, f is increasing on $(-\infty, -1)$ and on $(1, \infty)$. Because f is continuous at 0 (even though f' doesn't exist there), we can combine the intervals $(-1, 0)$ and $(0, 1)$ and state that f is decreasing on $(-1, 1)$. There is a local maximum at $(-1, 2)$ and a local minimum at $(1, -2)$.

$f''(x) = \frac{2}{3\sqrt[3]{x^5}}$, which is never zero, but is undefined at $x = 0$. Note that $f''(x) < 0$ for $x < 0$ and $f''(x) > 0$ for $x > 0$, so f is concave down on $(-\infty, 0)$ and is concave up on $(0, \infty)$. There is an inflection point at $(0, 0)$.

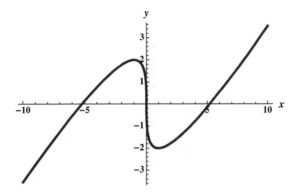

4.3.27

The domain of f is given to be $[0, 2\pi]$, so questions about symmetry and horizontal asymptotes aren't relevant. There are no vertical asymptotes.

$f'(x) = \cos x - 1$. This is never 0 on $(0, 2\pi)$. $f''(x) = -\sin x$, which is 0 on the given interval only for $x = \pi$. Note that $f'(x) < 0$ on $(0, 2\pi)$, so f is decreasing on the given interval and there are no relative extrema. Note also that $f''(x) < 0$ on $(0, \pi)$ and $f''(x) > 0$ on $(\pi, 2\pi)$, so f is concave down on $(0, \pi)$ and is concave up on $(\pi, 2\pi)$, and there is an inflection point at $x = \pi$. The only intercept is the origin $(0, 0)$.

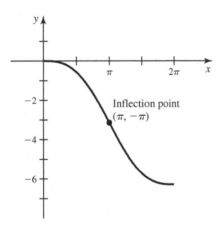

4.3.29

The domain of g is given to be $[-\pi, \pi]$, and there is no symmetry and no vertical asymptotes. Because the domain is finite, questions about horizontal asymptotes are not relevant.

$g'(t) = e^{-t} \cos t + \sin t \cdot (-e^{-t}) = e^{-t}(\cos t - \sin t)$. This is 0 on the given interval for $t = -3\pi/4$ and $t = \pi/4$. $g''(t) = e^{-t}(-\sin t - \cos t) + (\cos t - \sin t)(-e^{-t}) = -2e^{-t} \cos t$, which is 0 for $t = -\pi/2$ and $t = \pi/2$.

Note that $g'(t) < 0$ on $(-\pi, -3\pi/4)$ and on $(\pi/4, \pi)$, so g is decreasing on those intervals. On $(-3\pi/4, \pi/4)$ we have $g'(t) > 0$ and so g is increasing. There is a local minimum of about -7.460 at $t = -3\pi/4$ and a local maximum of about 0.322 at $t = \pi/4$.

Note also that $g''(t) > 0$ on $(-\pi, -\pi/2)$ and on $(\pi/2, \pi)$, while $g''(t) < 0$ on $(-\pi/2, \pi/2i)$, so g is concave down on $(-\pi/2, \pi/2)$ and is concave up on $(\pi/2, \pi)$ and on $(-\pi, -\pi/2)$. There are inflection points at $t = \pm\pi/2$. The origin is both the y−intercept and an x-intercept. The endpoints are x-intercepts as well.

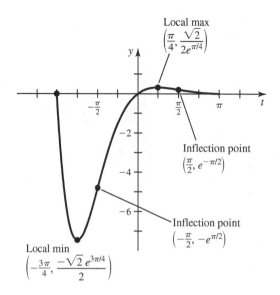

4.3.31

The domain of f is given to be $(-3\pi/2, 3\pi/2)$, but note that the function is not defined at $x = \pm\pi/2$, so the domain is actually $(-3\pi/2, -\pi/2) \cup (-\pi/2, \pi/2) \cup (\pi/2, 3\pi/2)$. Note that $f(-x) = -x + \tan(-x) = -x - \tan x = -(x + \tan x) = -f(x)$, so f has odd symmetry. f has vertical asymptotes at $x = \pm - 3\pi/2$ and at $x = \pm\pi/2$, because the tangent function increases or decreases without bound as x approaches these values.

$f'(x) = 1 + \sec^2 x$ which is always greater than 0. Thus f is increasing on each interval on which it is defined, and it has no extrema. $f''(x) = 2\sec x \cdot \sec x \tan x = 2\sec^2 x \tan x$. This is 0 at $x = \pm\pi$ and $x = 0$.

Note that $f''(x)$ is positive on $(-\pi, -\pi/2)$ and on $(0, \pi/2)$ and on $(\pi, 3\pi/2)$, so f is concave up on these intervals. Also, $f''(x)$ is negative on $(-3\pi/2, -\pi)$ and on $(-\pi/2, 0)$, and on $(\pi/2, \pi)$, so f is concave down on these intervals. There are points of inflection at $x = \pm\pi$ and at $x = 0$. The other changes in concavity occur at the vertical asymptotes.

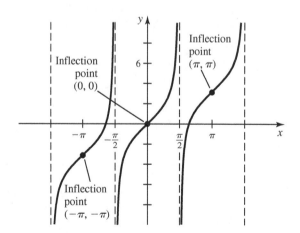

4.3.33

The domain of f is $(0, \infty)$, so questions about symmetry aren't relevant. There are no asymptotes.

$f'(x) = x \cdot 1/x + \ln x = 1 + \ln x$. This is 0 for $x = 1/e$. Note that $f'(x) < 0$ for $0 < x < 1/e$ and $f'(x) > 0$ for $x > 1/e$, so f is decreasing on $(0, 1/e)$ and increasing on $(1/e, \infty)$ and there is a local minimum (which is also an absolute minimum) at $x = 1/e$.

$f''(x) = 1/x$, which is always positive on the domain, so f is concave up on its domain and there are no inflection points.

There is an x-intercept at $x = 1$.

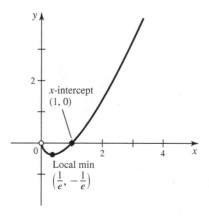

4.3.35

The domain of p is $(-\infty, \infty)$. There are no vertical asymptotes. Note that $p(-x) = -xe^{-(-x)^2} = -(xe^{-x^2}) = -p(x)$, so p has odd symmetry. Later in this chapter we will show that $\lim\limits_{x \to \pm\infty} p(x) = 0$, so $y = 0$ is a horizontal asymptote.

$p'(x) = x \cdot (-2xe^{-x^2} + e^{-x^2} \cdot 1 = e^{-x^2}(1 - 2x^2)$. This is 0 for $x = \pm\sqrt{2}/2$. Note that $p'(x) < 0$ on $(-\infty, -\sqrt{2}/2)$ and on $(\sqrt{2}/2, \infty)$, so p is decreasing on those intervals, and $p'(x) > 0$ on $(-\sqrt{2}/2, \sqrt{2}/2)$, so p is increasing on that interval. There is a local maximum at $x = \sqrt{2}/2$ and a local minimum at $x = -\sqrt{2}/2$.

$p''(x) = e^{-x^2}(-4x) + (1 - 2x^2) \cdot (-2x)e^{-x^2} = 2x(2x^2 - 3)e^{-x^2}$, which is 0 at $x = 0$ and at $x = \pm\sqrt{3/2}$. Note that $p''(x) > 0$ on $(-\sqrt{3/2}, 0)$ and on $(\sqrt{3/2}, \infty)$, so p is concave up on those intervals, while $p''(x) < 0$ on $(-\infty, -\sqrt{3/2})$ and on $(0, \sqrt{3/2})$, so p is concave down on those intervals. There are inflection points at each of $x = \pm\sqrt{3/2}$ and at $x = 0$.

There is an x-intercept at $(0, 0)$, which is also the y-intercept.

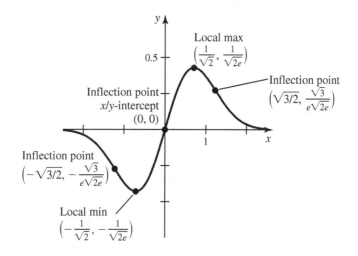

4.3.37

The domain of f is $(-\infty, \infty)$, and there is no symmetry. $f'(x) = x^2 - 4x - 5 = (x - 5)(x + 1)$. This is 0 when $x = -1, 5$. $f''(x) = 2x - 4$, which is 0 when $x = 2$. Note that $f'(-2) > 0$, $f'(0) < 0$, and $f'(6) > 0$. So f is increasing on $(-\infty, -1)$ and on $(5, \infty)$. It is decreasing on $(-1, 5)$. There is a local maximum of $14/3$ at $x = -1$ and a local minimum of $-94/3$ at $x = 5$. Note also that $f''(x) < 0$ for $x < 2$ and $f''(x) > 0$ for $x > 2$, so there is an inflection point at $(2, -40/3)$, and f is concave down on $(-\infty, 2)$ and concave up on $(2, \infty)$. The y intercept is $f(0) = 2$.

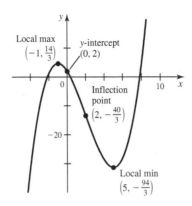

4.3.39

The domain of f is $(-\infty, \infty)$, and there is no symmetry. $f'(x) = 12x^3 + 12x^2 - 24x = 12x(x+2)(x-1)$. This is 0 when $x = -2$, when $x = 1$, and when $x = 0$. $f''(x) = 36x^2 + 24x - 24 = 12(3x^2 + 2x - 2)$, which is 0 when $x = \frac{-1 \pm \sqrt{7}}{3}$. These values are at approximately -1.215 and 0.549. Note that $f'(-3) < 0$, $f'(-1) > 0$, $f'(.5) < 0$, and $f'(2) > 0$. So f is decreasing on $(-\infty, -2)$ and on $(0, 1)$. It is increasing on $(-2, 0)$ and on $(1, \infty)$. There is a local maximum of 0 at $x = 0$ and a local minimum of -32 at $x = -2$ and a local minimum of -5 at $x = 1$. Let $r_1 < r_2$ be the two roots of $f''(x)$ mentioned above. Note that $f''(x) > 0$ for $x < r_1$ and for $x > r_2$ and $f''(x) < 0$ for $r_1 < x < r_2$, so there are inflection points at $x = r_1$ and at $x = r_2$. Also, f is concave down on (r_1, r_2) and concave up on $(-\infty, r_1)$ and on (r_2, ∞). There is a y-intercept at $f(0) = 0$ and x-intercepts where $f(x) = 3x^4 + 4x^3 - 12x^2 = x^2(3x^2 + 4x - 12) = 0$, which is at $x = \frac{-2 \pm 2\sqrt{10}}{3}$ and $x = 0$.

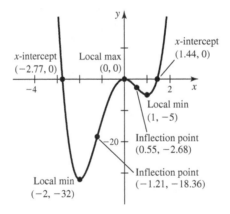

4.3.41

The domain of f is $(-\infty, -1) \cup (-1, 1) \cup (1, \infty)$, and there is no symmetry. Note that $\lim\limits_{x \to -1^+} f(x) = \infty$ and $\lim\limits_{x \to -1^-} f(x) = -\infty$, so there is a vertical asymptote at $x = -1$. Also, $\lim\limits_{x \to 1^+} f(x) = -\infty$ and $\lim\limits_{x \to 1^-} f(x) = \infty$, so there is a vertical asymptote at $x = 1$

Note that $\lim\limits_{x \to \pm\infty} \dfrac{3x - 5}{x^2 - 1} \cdot \dfrac{1/x^2}{1/x^2} = \lim\limits_{x \to \pm\infty} \dfrac{3/x}{1 - (1/x^2)} = 0$, so $y = 0$ is a horizontal asymptote.

$f'(x) = \dfrac{(x^2-1)\cdot 3 - (3x-5)\cdot 2x}{(x^2-1)^2} = \dfrac{-3x^2 + 10x - 3}{(x^2-1)^2} = \dfrac{(-3x+1)(x-3)}{(x^2-1)^2}$. This is 0 when $x = 3$ and when $x = 1/3$. $f''(x) = \dfrac{(x^2-1)^2(-6x+10) - (-3x^2+10x-3)(2)(x^2-1)\cdot 2x}{(x^2-1)^4} = \dfrac{2(3x^3 - 15x^2 + 9x - 5)}{(x^2-1)^3}$. This is 0 for $x \approx 4.405$. Let r be this root of $f''(x)$.

Note that $f'(-2) < 0$, $f'(-1/2) < 0$, $f'(1/2) > 0$, $f'(2) > 0$ and $f'(4) < 0$. So f is decreasing on $(-\infty, -1)$, on $(-1, 1/3)$ and on $(3, \infty)$. It is increasing on $(1/3, 1)$ and on $(1, 3)$. There is a local maximum of $1/2$ at $x = 3$ and a local minimum of $9/2$ at $x = 1/3$.

Note that $f''(x) < 0$ for $x < -1$ and $f''(x) < 0$ for $1 < x < r$, while $f''(x) > 0$ for $-1 < x < 1$, and for $x > r$. Thus f is concave up on $(-1, 1)$ and on (r, ∞) and concave down on $(-\infty, -1)$ and on $(1, r)$. There is an inflection point at r. There is a y-intercept at $f(0) = 5$ and an x-intercept at $(5/3, 0)$.

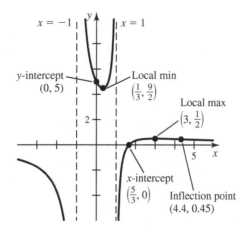

4.3.43

a. False. Maxima and minima can also occur at points where $f'(x)$ doesn't exist. Also, it is possible to have a zero of f' which doesn't correspond to an extreme point.

b. False. Inflection points can also occur at points where $f''(x)$ doesn't exist, and a zero of f'' might not correspond to an inflection point.

c. False. For example, $f(x) = \frac{(x^2-9)(x^2-16)}{(x+3)(x-4)}$ doesn't have a vertical asymptote at $x = -3$ or $x = 4$.

d. True. The limit of a rational function as $x \to \infty$ is a finite number when the degree of the denominator is greater than or equal to that of the numerator. If they both have the same degree, the limit is the ratio of the leading coefficients, and this is also true of the limit as $x \to -\infty$. In the case where the denominator has greater degree than the numerator, the limit is 0 as $x \to -\infty$ and as $x \to \infty$.

4.3.45

$f'(x)$ is 0 on the interior of the given interval at $x = \pm 3\pi/2$, $x = \pm\pi$, $x = \pm\pi/2$, and at $x = 0$.

$f'(x) > 0$ on $(-2\pi, -3\pi/2)$, $(-\pi, -\pi/2)$, $(0, \pi/2)$, and on $(\pi, 3\pi/2)$, so f is increasing on those intervals. $f'(x) < 0$ on $(-3\pi/2, -\pi)$, $(-\pi/2, 0)$, $(\pi/2, \pi)$, and on $(3\pi/2, 2\pi)$, so f is decreasing on those intervals. There are local maxima at $x = \pm 3\pi/2$ and $x = \pm\pi/2$, and local minima at $x = 0$ and at $x = \pm\pi$. An example of such a function is sketched.

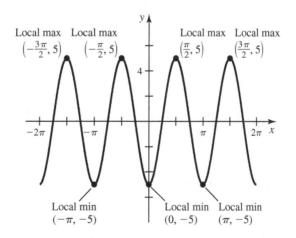

4.3.47

$f'(x)$ is 0 at $x = 0$, $x = -2$, and $x = 1$. $f'(x) > 0$ on $(-\infty, -2)$ and on $(1, \infty)$, so f is increasing on those intervals. $f'(x) < 0$ on $(-2, 0)$ and on $(0, 1)$, so f is decreasing on those intervals. There is a local maximum at $x = -2$ and a local minimum at $x = 1$. There isn't an extremum at $x = 0$.

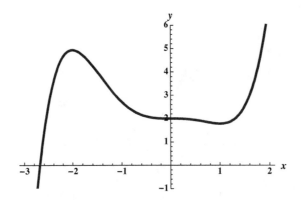

4.3.49

$f'(x)$ is 0 at $x = 1$ and $x = 3$.

$f'(x) > 0$ on $(0, 1)$ and on $(3, 4)$, so f is increasing on those intervals. $f'(x) < 0$ on $(1, 3)$, so f is decreasing on that interval. There is a local maximum at $x = 1$ and a local minimum at $x = 3$.

$f''(x)$ changes sign at $x = 2$ from negative to positive, so $x = 2$ is an inflection point where the concavity of f changes from down to up. An example of such a function is sketched.

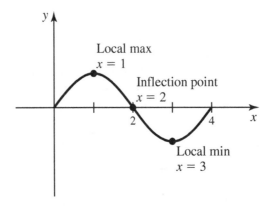

4.3.51

The domain of f is $(-\infty, \infty)$ and there is no symmetry. There are no asymptotes because f is a polynomial.

$f'(x) = 3x^2 - 12x - 135 = 3(x - 9)(x + 5)$, which is 0 for $x = 9$ and $x = -5$. $f'(x) > 0$ on $(-\infty, -5)$ and on $(9, \infty)$, so f is increasing on those intervals. $f'(x) < 0$ on $(-5, 9)$, so f is decreasing on that interval. There is a local maximum at $x = -5$ and a local minimum at $x = 9$.

$f''(x) = 6x - 12$, which is 0 for $x = 2$. $f''(x) > 0$ on $(2, \infty)$, so f is concave up on that interval. $f''(x) < 0$ on $(-\infty, 2)$, so f is concave down on that interval. There is a point of inflection at $x = 2$. The y-intercept is 0 and the x-intercepts are -9 and 15.

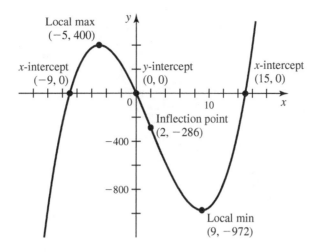

4.3.53

The domain of f is $(-\infty, \infty)$ and there is no symmetry. There are no asymptotes because f is a polynomial.

$f'(x) = 3x^2 - 6x - 144 = 3(x + 6)(x - 8)$, which is 0 for $x = -6$ and $x = 8$. $f'(x) > 0$ on $(-\infty, -6)$ and on $(8, \infty)$, so f is increasing on those intervals. $f'(x) < 0$ on $(-6, 8)$, so f is decreasing on that interval. There is a local maximum at $x = -6$ and a local minimum at $x = 8$.

$f''(x) = 6x - 6$, which is 0 for $x = 1$. $f''(x) > 0$ on $(1, \infty)$, so f is concave up on that interval. $f''(x) < 0$ on $(-\infty, 1)$, so f is concave down on that interval. There is a point of inflection at $x = 1$. The y-intercept is -140 and the x-intercepts are at -10, -1, and 14.

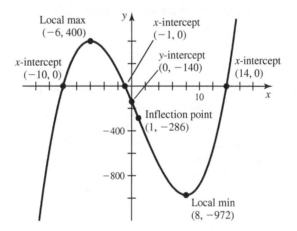

4.3.55

f can be written as $f(x) = e^{(\ln x)/x}$. $f'(x) = e^{(\ln x)/x} \left(\frac{1 - \ln x}{x^2} \right)$. This is 0 for $x = e$, and is positive on $(0, e)$ and negative on (e, ∞). There is a local maximum at $x = e$ of $e^{1/e}$.

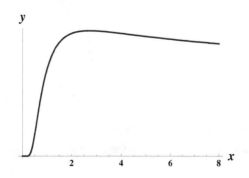

4.3.57

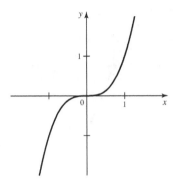

4.3.59

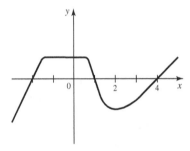

4.3.61

The domain of f is $(-\infty, -2) \cup (2, \infty)$ and there is no symmetry. There is a vertical asymptote at $x = 2$ because $\lim_{x \to 2^+} -\frac{x\sqrt{x^2-4}}{x-2} = -\infty$. There are no horizontal asymptotes.

$f'(x) = \frac{(x-2)(-x^2(x^2-4)^{-1/2}+(x^2-4)^{1/2}(-1))-((-x)(x^2-4)^{1/2})}{(x-2)^2}$. This can be written as $\frac{-x^2+2x+4}{(x-2)\sqrt{x^2-4}}$, and this quantity is 0 on the given domain only for $x = 1 + \sqrt{5} \approx 3.236$.

$f'(x) > 0$ on $(-\infty, -2)$ and on $(2, 1+\sqrt{5})$, so f is increasing on those intervals. $f'(x) < 0$ on $(1+\sqrt{5}, \infty)$, so f is decreasing on that interval. There is a local maximum at $x = 1 + \sqrt{5}$.

$f''(x)$ simplifies to be $-\frac{4(x+4)}{(x-2)^2(x+2)\sqrt{x^2-4}}$, which is 0 at $x = -4$

$f''(x) > 0$ on $(-4, -2)$, so f is concave up on that interval. $f''(x) < 0$ on $(-\infty, -4)$ and on $(1+\sqrt{5}, \infty)$, so f is concave down on those intervals. There is a point of inflection at $x = -4$.

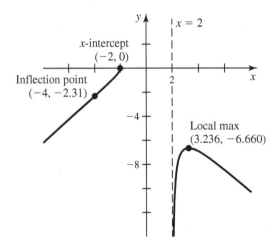

4.3.63

The domain of f is $(-\infty, \infty)$ and there is no symmetry. There are no asymptotes because f is a polynomial.

$f'(x) = 12x^3 - 132x^2 + 120x = 12x(x - 10)(x - 1)$, which is 0 for $x = 0$, $x = 1$, and $x = 10$.

$f'(x) > 0$ on $(0, 1)$ and on $(10, \infty)$, so f is increasing on those intervals. $f'(x) < 0$ on $(-\infty, 0)$ and on $(1, 10)$, so f is decreasing on those intervals. There is a local maximum at $x = 1$, and local minima at $x = 0$ and at $x = 10$.

$f''(x) = 36x^2 - 264x + 120 = 12(3x^2 - 22x + 10)$. This is 0 at approximately $x = .487$ and $x = 6.846$. Let these two roots be r_1 and r_2 with $r_1 < r_2$. $f''(x) > 0$ on $(-\infty, r_1)$ and on (r_2, ∞), so f is concave up on those intervals. $f''(x) < 0$ on (r_1, r_2), so f is concave down on that interval. There are points of inflection at $x = r_1$ and $x = r_2$.

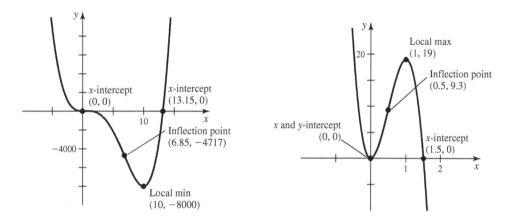

4.3.65

The domain of f is $(-\infty, \infty)$ and there is no symmetry. There are no asymptotes because f is a polynomial.

$f'(x) = 60x^5 - 180x^4 - 300x^3 + 900x^2 + 240x - 720 = 60(x + 2)(x + 1)(x - 1)(x - 2)(x - 3)$, which is 0 for $x = -2$, $x = -1$, $x = 1$, $x = 2$, and $x = 3$.

$f'(x) > 0$ on $(-2, -1)$, $(1, 2)$ and on $(3, \infty)$, so f is increasing on those intervals. $f'(x) < 0$ on $(-\infty, -2)$, $(-1, 2)$ and on $(2, 3)$, so f is decreasing on those intervals. There are local minima at $x = -2$, $x = 1$, and $x = 3$, and local maxima at $x = -1$ and $x = 2$.

$f''(x) = 300x^4 - 720x^3 - 900x^2 + 1800x + 240 = 60(5x^4 - 12x^3 - 15x^2 + 30x + 4)$. Using a computer algebra system, we find that this has 4 real roots, which we will call $r_1 < r_2 < r_3 < r_4$. They values of these roots are approximately -1.605, -0.125, 1.502, and 2.629.

$f''(x) > 0$ on $(-\infty, r_1)$, and on (r_2, r_3) and on (r_4, ∞), so f is concave up on those intervals. $f''(x) < 0$ on (r_1, r_2) and on (r_3, r_4), so f is concave down on those intervals. There are points of inflection at each r_i for i from 1 to 4.

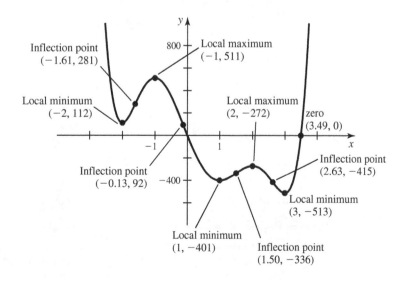

4.3.67

The domain of f is $(-\infty, \infty)$ and there is odd symmetry, because $f(-x) = -f(x)$. There are no vertical asymptotes, but $y = 0$ is a horizontal asymptote, because

$$\lim_{x \to \infty} \frac{x\sqrt{|x^2 - 1|}}{x^4 + 1} \cdot \frac{1/x^4}{1/x^4} = \lim_{x \to \infty} \frac{\sqrt{(1/x^4) - (1/x^6)}}{1 + (1/x^4)} = 0.$$

Note that $f(x) = \begin{cases} \frac{x\sqrt{x^2-1}}{x^4+1} & \text{if } |x| \geq 1; \\ \frac{x\sqrt{1-x^2}}{x^4+1} & \text{if } |x| < 1. \end{cases}$

Differentiating each part of the above and simplifying yields

$$f'(x) = \begin{cases} \dfrac{-2x^6 + 3x^4 + 2x^2 - 1}{(x^4 + 1)^2 \sqrt{x^2 - 1}} & \text{if } |x| > 1; \\ \dfrac{2x^6 - 3x^4 - 2x^2 + 1}{(x^4+1)^2 \sqrt{1-x^2}} & \text{if } |x| < 1. \end{cases}$$

The roots of this expression (on the respective domains) are approximately ± 1.374 and ± 0.596. Also, this derivative doesn't exist at $x = \pm 1$. Let the roots of f' be $\pm r_1$ and $\pm r_2$ where $0 < r_1 < r_2$. An analysis of the sign of f' shows that f is increasing on $(-r_2, -1)$ on $(-r_1, r_1)$ and on $(1, r_2)$, while f is decreasing on $(-\infty, -r_2)$, $(-1, -r_1)$, $(r_1, 1)$ and on (r_2, ∞), so there are local maxima at $x = -1$, $x = r_1$, and $x = r_2$, and local minima at $x = -r_1$, $x = -r_2$, and $x = 1$.

An analysis without computer of $f''(x)$ is not for the fainthearted. In the case $|x| > 1$ the second derivative is given by $\dfrac{x\left(6x^{10} - 19x^8 - 12x^6 + 42x^4 - 18x^2 - 3\right)}{(x^2 - 1)^{3/2}\left(x^4 + 1\right)^3}$, and for the case $|x| < 1$ we have $\dfrac{x\left(6x^{10} - 19x^8 - 12x^6 + 42x^4 - 18x^2 - 3\right)}{\left(1 - x^2\right)^{3/2}\left(x^4 + 1\right)^3}$. There is a root of approximately ± 1.790, and 0 is a root as well. Let the non-zero roots be $\pm r_3$ where $r_3 > 0$. An analysis of the sign of f'' reveals that f is concave down on $(-\infty, -r_3)$, $(0, 1)$ and on $(1, r_3)$, while it is concave up on $(-r_3, -1)$, $(-1, 0)$ and on (r_3, ∞). There are inflection points at $\pm r_3$ and at 0. The x-intercepts are ± 1 and 0.

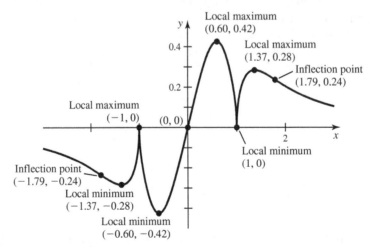

4.3.69

a. f has even symmetry, so we will analyze the function on $(0, 2\pi]$, and use the symmetry to graph the function over $[-2\pi, 0)$.

$f'(x) = \frac{x^2(-3\cos^2 x(-\sin x)) - (1 - \cos^3 x) \cdot 2x}{x^4} = \frac{3x \sin x \cos^2 x - 2(1 - \cos^3 x)}{x^3}$. This has no roots on $(0, 2\pi)$, and in fact is always negative, so f is decreasing on $(0, 2\pi)$.

$f''(x)$ when simplified is given by $\frac{3\left((x^2 - 2)\cos^3(x) - 2x^2 \sin^2(x)\cos(x) - 4x\sin(x)\cos^2(x) + 2\right)}{x^4}$. The roots of f'' on $(0, 2\pi)$ are $r_1 \approx .89$, $r_2 \approx 2.47$, $r_3 \approx 3.48$, $r_4 \approx 4.76$, and $r_5 \approx 5.5$. An analysis of the sign of f''

reveals that there is a change in concavity at each of these roots, starting with concavity downward on $(-r_1, r_1)$. So each of $\pm r_i$ is an inflection point.

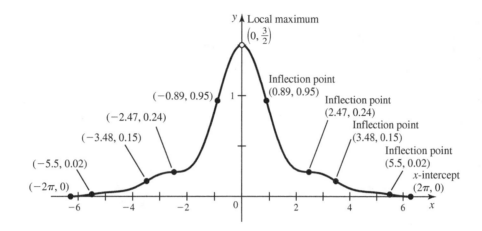

b. f has even symmetry, so we will analyze the function on $(0, 2\pi]$, and use the symmetry to graph the function over $[-2\pi, 0)$.

$$f'(x) = \frac{x^2(-5\cos^4 x(-\sin x) - (1 - \cos^5 x)(2x))}{x^4} = \frac{5x\cos^4 x \sin x - 2(1 - \cos^5 x)}{x^3}.$$

This has roots on $(0, 2\pi)$ of $r_1 \approx 2.41$ and $r_2 \approx 2.83$. An analysis of the sign of f' shows that f is decreasing on $(0, r_1)$, increasing on (r_1, r_2), decreasing on $(r_2, 2\pi)$, so there is a local minimum at r_1 and a local maximum at r_2.

$f''(x)$ when simplified is given by

$$\frac{(5x^2 - 6)\cos^5(x) - 20x^2\sin^2(x)\cos^3(x) - 20x\sin(x)\cos^4(x) + 6}{x^4}.$$

The roots of f'' on $(0, 2\pi)$ are $r_3 \approx .63$, $r_4 \approx 2.62$, $r_5 \approx 3.45$, $r_6 \approx 4.96$, and $r_7 \approx 5.74$. An analysis of the sign of f'' reveals that there is a change in concavity at each of these roots, starting with concavity downward on $(-r_3, r_3)$. So each of $\pm r_i$ is an inflection point for $i = 3, 4, 5, 6$ and 7.

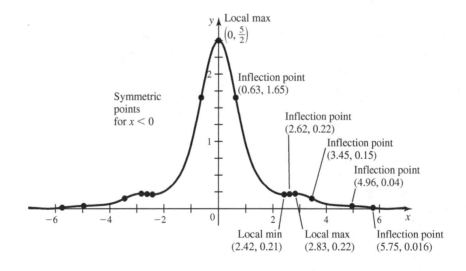

4.3.71

    (a)   (b)   (c)

a.

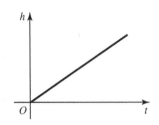 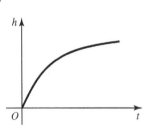 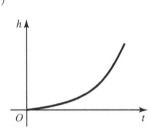

    (d)   (e)   (f)

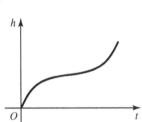 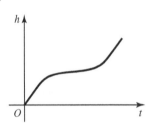 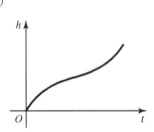

b. The water is being poured in at a constant rate, so the depth is always increasing, so $y = h(t)$ is an increasing function.

c.   (a) No concavity   (b) Always concave down.   (c) Always concave up.

(d) Concave down for for the first half and concave up for the second half.

(e) At the beginning, in the middle, and at the end, there is no concavity. In the lower middle it is concave down and in the upper middle it will be concave up.

(f) This is concave down for the first half, and concave up for the second half.

d.   (a) $h'(t)$ is constant, so there is no local max/min.

(b) $h'(t)$ is maximal at $t = 0$.

(c) $h'(t)$ is maximal at $t = 10$.

(d) $h'(t)$ is maximal at $t = 0$ and $t = 10$.

(e) $h'(t)$ is maximal on the first and last straight parts of $h(t)$.

(f) $h'(t)$ is maximal at $t = 0$ and $t = 10$.

4.3.73

If $f''(x) > 0$ on $(-\infty, 0)$ and on $(0, \infty)$, then $f'(x)$ is increasing on both of those intervals. But if there is a local max at 0, the function f must be switching from increasing to decreasing there. This means that f' must be switching from positive to negative. But if f' is switching from positive to negative, but increasing, there must be a cusp at $x = 0$, so $f'(0)$ does not exist.

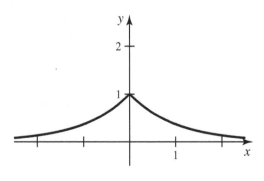

4.3.75

The equation is valid on only for $|x| \leq 1$ and $|y| \leq 1$. Using implicit differentiation, we have $(2/3)x^{-1/3} + (2/3)y^{-1/3}y' = 0$, so $y' = \frac{-y^{1/3}}{x^{1/3}}$. This is 0 for $y = 0$ (in which case $x = \pm 1$) and doesn't exist for $x = 0$ (in which case $x = \pm 1$.) In the first quadrant the curve is decreasing, in the 2nd it is increasing, in the 3rd it is decreasing, and in the 4th it is increasing. Differentiating y' yields $y'' = \frac{x^{1/3}(-1/3)y^{-2/3}y' + y^{1/3}(1/3)(x^{-2/3})}{x^{2/3}} = \frac{y^{2/3} + x^{2/3}}{3x^{4/3}y^{1/3}}$, which is positive when y is positive and negative when y is negative, so the curve is concave up in the first and 2nd quadrants, and concave down in the 3rd and 4th.

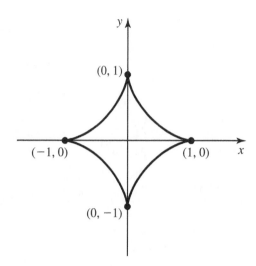

4.3.77

First note that the expression is symmetric when x and y are switched, so the curve should be symmetric about the line $y = x$. Also, if $y = x$, then $2x^3 = 3x^2$, so either $x = 0$ or $x = 3/2$, so this is where the curve intersects the line $y = x$.

Differentiating implicitly yields $3x^2 + 3y^2y' = 3xy' + 3y$, so $y' = \frac{y - x^2}{y^2 - x}$. This is 0 when $y = x^2$, but this occurs on the curve when $x^3 + x^6 = 3x^3$, which yields $x = 0$ (and $y = 0$), or $x^3 = 2$, so $x = \sqrt[3]{2} \approx 1.260$. Note also that the derivative doesn't exist when $x = y^2$, which again yields $(0,0)$ and $y^6 + y^3 = 3y^3$, or $y = \sqrt[3]{2}$. So there should be a flat tangent line at approximately $(1.260, 1.587)$ and a vertical tangent line at about $(1.587, 1.260)$.

Differentiating again and solving for y'' yields $y''(x) = \frac{2xy(x^3 - 3xy + y^3 + 1)}{(x - y^2)^3} = \frac{2xy}{(x - y^2)^3}$. In the first quadrant, when $x > y^2$, the curve is concave up, when $x < y^2$, the curve is concave down. In both the 2nd and 4th quadrants, the curve is concave up.

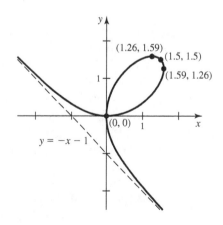

4.3.79

Note that the curve is symmetric about both the x-axis and the y-axis, so we can just consider the first quadrant, and obtain the rest by reflection.

Differentiating implicitly and solving for y' yields $y'(x) = \frac{2x^3 - 5x}{2y(y^2 - 2)}$. The numerator is negative on $(0, \sqrt{5/2})$ and positive on $(\sqrt{5/2}, \infty)$, while the denominator is negative for $0 < y < \sqrt{2}$ and positive for $y > \sqrt{2}$. Thus the relation is increasing in the rectangle $(0, \sqrt{5/2}) \times (0, \sqrt{2})$ and in the region $(\sqrt{5/2}, \infty) \times (\sqrt{2}, \infty)$, while it is decreasing in the other regions in the first quadrant. There are vertical tangent lines when $y = \sqrt{2}$. When $y = 2$ and $x = 0$ there is a horizontal tangent line.

Note that when $x = 0$, we have $y = 0$ or $y = \pm 2$, while if $y = 0$, we have $x = 0$ or $x = \pm\sqrt{5}$. Also, if $y = \sqrt{2}$ then $x = 1$ or $x = 2$. So some sample points to plot are $(0, 0)$, $(\pm\sqrt{5}, 0)$, $(0, \pm 2)$, $(\pm 1, \pm\sqrt{2})$, and $(\pm\sqrt{5}, \pm\sqrt{2})$. Also, when $1 < x < 2$, there are no corresponding y values on the curve.

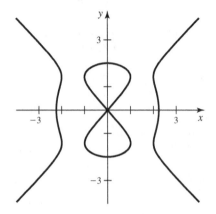

4.3.81

Note that the curve requires $-1 \le x < 1$.

Note also that the curve is symmetric about both the x-axis and the y-axis, so we can just consider the first quadrant, and obtain the rest by reflection.

Differentiating implicitly yields $4x^3 - 2x + 2yy' = 0$, so $y' = \frac{x - 2x^3}{y}$. This is 0 in the first quadrant for $x = \sqrt{2}/2$. Note also that there is a vertical tangent line at the point $(1, 0)$. The derivative is positive on $(0, \sqrt{2}/2)$ and negative on $(\sqrt{2}/2, 1)$, so in the first quadrant the curve is increasing on that first interval and decreasing on the second.

Differentiating again and solving for y'' (and rewriting) yields $y''(x) = \frac{x^4(2x^2 - 3)}{y}$, which is negative in the first quadrant for $0 < x < 1$, so this curve is concave down in the first quadrant.

The rest of the curve can be found by reflection.

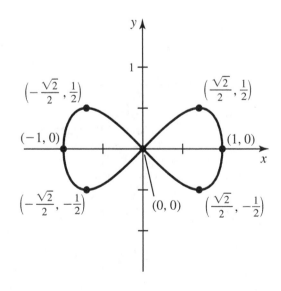

4.3.83

As n increases, the curves retain their symmetry, but move "outward." That is, the curves enclose a greater area. It appears that the figures approach the 2×2 square centered at the origin with sides parallel to the coordinate axes.

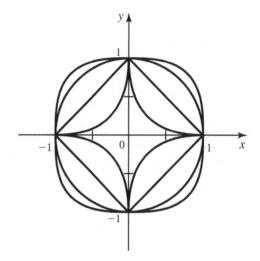

4.3.85

a. The domain is $(-\infty, a]$, because the base must be non-negative.

b. $\lim\limits_{x \to a^-} f(x) = 0$, $\lim\limits_{x \to -\infty} f(x) = 0$.

c. Write $f(x) = e^{x \ln(a-x)}$. Then $f'(x) = e^{x \ln(a-x)} \left(x \cdot -\frac{1}{a-x} + \ln(a-x) \right) = (a-x)^x \left(-\frac{x}{a-x} + \ln(a-x) \right)$.

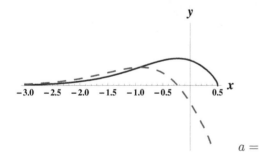

$a = .5$

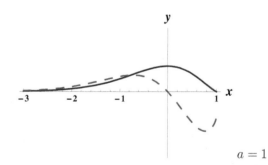

$a = 1$

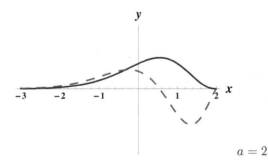

$a = 2$

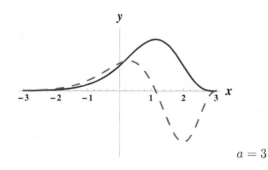

$a = 3$

d. $f'(x) = (a-x)^x \left(-\frac{x}{a-x} + \ln(a-x) \right) = \frac{-(x+(x-a)\ln(a-x))}{(a-x)^{1-x}}$. The numerator is 0 when $x = (a-x)(\ln(a-x))$. If z is a solution to the above, note that z gives a maximum, because f is continuous and positive, and the end behavior of the function is 0 at each end of its domain.

e. As a increases, the value of z increases, and the value of $f(z)$ increases as well, as demonstrated in the above graphs.

4.3.87

The domain of p is $(-\infty, \infty)$. There are no vertical asymptotes. Note that $f(-x) = \frac{\tan^{-1}(-x)}{(-x)^2+1} = -\frac{\tan^{-1}(x)}{x^2+1} = -f(x)$, so f has odd symmetry. Because $\lim_{x \to \pm\infty} \tan^{-1}(x) = \pm\pi/2$, $\lim_{x \to \pm\infty} f(x) = 0$, so $y = 0$ is a horizontal asymptote.

$f'(x) = \frac{(x^2+1)(1/(x^2+1)) - \tan^{-1}x \cdot 2x}{(x^2+1)^2} = \frac{1 - 2x \tan^{-1} x}{(x^2+1)^2}$. Using a computer algebra system shows that the numerator has two roots at approximately $\pm.765$. Let the roots be $\pm r_1$ where $r_1 > 0$. Note that $f'(x) < 0$ on $(-\infty, -r_1)$ and on (r_1, ∞), so f is decreasing there, while $f'(x) > 0$ on $(-r_1, r_1)$, so f is increasing on that interval. There is a local minimum at $-r_1$ and a local maximum at r_1.

$$f''(x) = \frac{(x^2+1)^2 \left[(-2x)(1/(x^2+1)) - \tan^{-1} x \cdot 2\right] - (1 - 2x \tan^{-1} x) \cdot 2(x^2+1)(2x)}{(x^2+1)^4}$$
$$= \frac{(6x^2 - 2)\tan^{-1} x - 6x}{(x^2+1)^3}.$$

Again, using a computer algebra system reveals roots at approximately ± 1.330 in addition to the root at 0. Let the non-zero roots of the numerator be $\pm r_2$ where $r_2 > 0$. We see that $f''(x) < 0$ on $(-\infty, -r_2)$, and on $(0, r_2)$, so f is concave down on those intervals, while $f''(x) > 0$ on $(-r_2, 0)$ and on (r_2, ∞), so f is concave up on those intervals, and there are points of inflection at $-r_2$, 0, and r_2.

There is an x-intercept at $(0,0)$, which is also the y-intercept.

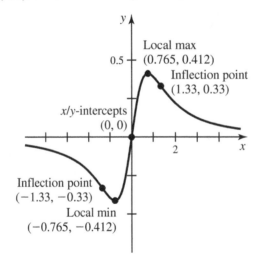

4.3.89

The domain of f is given to be $[-2\pi, 2\pi]$. There are no vertical asymptotes. Note that $f(-x) = \frac{(-x)(\sin(-x))}{((-x)^2+1)} = \frac{x \sin x}{x^2+1} = f(x)$, f has even symmetry. Questions about horizontal asymptotes aren't relevant because the given domain is an interval with finite length.

$f'(x) = \frac{(x^2+1)(x \cos x + \sin x) - x \sin x \cdot (2x)}{(x^2+1)^2}$, which can be simplified to $\frac{x(x^2+1)\cos x + (1-x^2)\sin x}{(x^2+1)^2}$, and with the aid of a computer algebra system, the roots of this expression can be found to be approximately ± 4.514 and ± 1.356, as well as $x = 0$. We will call the non-zero roots $\pm r_1$ and $\pm r_2$ where $0 < r_1 < r_2$. Note that $f'(x) < 0$ on $(-2\pi, -r_2)$ and on $(-r_1, 0)$ and (r_1, r_2), so f is decreasing there, while $f'(x) > 0$ on $(-r_2, -r_1)$, on $(0, r_1)$, and on $(r_2, 2\pi)$, so f is increasing on these intervals. There are local maxima at $x = \pm r_1$ and local minima at $x = 0$ and at $x = \pm r_2$.

$f''(x)$ has numerator $(x^2+1)^2((x^3+x)(-\sin x) + \cos x(3x^2+1) + (1-x^2)(\cos x) + \sin x(-2x)) - ((x^3 + x)\cos x + (1-x^2)\sin x)(4x)(x^2+1)$ and denominator $(x^2+1)^4$. This simplifies to

$$f''(x) = \frac{(-x^5 - 7x)\sin x + (-2x^4 + 2)\cos x}{(x^2+1)^3},$$

which is 0 at approximately ± 5.961 and ± 2.561 and ± 0.494. We will call these 6 roots $\pm r_3$, $\pm r_4$ and $\pm r_5$ where $0 < r_3 < r_4 < r_5$. Note that $f''(x) < 0$ on $(-2\pi, -r_5)$ and on $(-r_4, -r_3)$, and on (r_3, r_4), and on $(r_5, 2\pi)$, so f is concave down on these intervals, while $f''(x) > 0$ on $(-r_5, -r_4)$, and on $(-r_3, r_3)$, and on (r_4, r_5), so f is concave up on these intervals. There are points of inflection at each of $\pm r_3$, $\pm r_4$, and $\pm r_5$.

There is an x-intercept at $(0,0)$, which is also the y-intercept, as well as x-intercepts at $\pm 2\pi$.

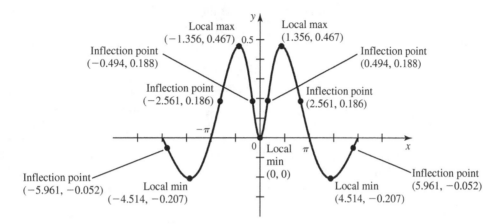

4.4   Optimization Problems

4.4.1 ...objective...constraints ....

4.4.3 The constraint is $x + y = 10$, so we can express $y = 10 - x$ or $x = 10 - y$. Therefore the objective function can be expressed $Q = x^2(10 - x)$ or $Q = (10 - y)^2 y$.

4.4.5 Let x and y be the dimensions of the rectangle. The perimeter is $2x + 2y$, so the constraint is $2x + 2y = 10$, which gives $y = 5 - x$. The objective function to be maximized is the area of the rectangle, $A = xy$. Thus we have $A = xy = x(5 - x) = 5x - x^2$. We have $x, y \geq 0$, which also implies $x \leq 5$ (otherwise $y < 0$). Therefore we need to maximize $A(x) = 5x - x^2$ for $0 \leq x \leq 5$. The critical points of the objective function satisfy $A'(x) = 5 - 2x = 0$, which has the solution $x = 5/2$. To find the absolute maximum of A, we check the endpoints of $[0, 5]$ and the critical point $x = 5/2$. Because $A(0) = A(5) = 0$ and $A(5/2) = 25/4$, the absolute maximum occurs when $x = y = 5/2$, so width = length = $5/2$ m.

4.4.7 Let x and y be be the dimensions of the rectangle. The area is $xy = 100$, so the constraint is $y = 100/x$. The objective function to be minimized is the perimeter of the rectangle, $P = 2x + 2y$. Using $y = 100/x$, we have $P = 2x + 2y = 2x + \frac{200}{x}$. Because $xy = 100 > 0$ we must have $x > 0$, so we need to minimize $P(x) = 2x + 200/x$ on the interval $(0, \infty)$. The critical points of the objective function satisfy $P'(x) = 2 - \frac{200}{x^2} = 0$, which has the solution $x = 10$. By the First (or Second) Derivative Test, this critical point corresponds to a local minimum, and by Theorem 4.5, this solitary local minimum is also the absolute minimum on the interval $(0, \infty)$. Therefore the dimensions of the rectangle with minimum perimeter are $x = 10$ and $y = \frac{100}{10} = 10$, so width = length = 10.

4.4.9 Let x and y be the two non-negative numbers. The constraint is $x + y = 23$, which gives $y = 23 - x$. The objective function to be maximized is the product of the numbers, $P = xy$. Using $y = 23 - x$, we have $P = xy = x(23 - x) = 23x - x^2$. Now x must be at least 0, and cannot exceed 23 (otherwise $y < 0$). Therefore we need to maximize $P(x) = 23x - x^2$ for $0 \leq x \leq 23$. The critical points of the objective function satisfy $P'(x) = 23 - 2x = 0$, which has the solution $x = 23/2$. To find the absolute maximum of P, we check the endpoints of $[0, 23]$ and the critical point $x = 23/2$. Because $P(0) = P(23) = 0$ and $P(23/2) = (23/2)^2$, the absolute maximum occurs when $x = y = 23/2$.

4.4.11 Let x and y be the two positive numbers. The constraint is $xy = 50$, which gives $y = 50/x$. The objective function to be minimized is the sum of the numbers, $S = x + y$. Using $y = 50/x$, we have $S = x + y = x + \frac{50}{x}$. Now x can be any positive number, so we need to maximize $S(x) = x + 50/x$ on the interval $(0, \infty)$. The critical points of the objective function satisfy $S'(x) = 1 - \frac{50}{x^2} = 0$, which has the solution $x = \sqrt{50} = 5\sqrt{2}$. By the First (or Second) Derivative Test, this critical point corresponds to a local minimum, and by Theorem 4.5, this solitary local minimum is also the absolute minimum on the interval $(0, \infty)$. Therefore the numbers with minimum sum are $x = 5\sqrt{2}$ and $y = \frac{50}{5\sqrt{2}} = \frac{10}{\sqrt{2}} = 5\sqrt{2}$, so $x = y = 5\sqrt{2}$.

4.4.13 We seek to minimize $S = 2x + y$ subject to the constraint $y = 12/x$. Substituting gives $S = 2x + 12/x$, so $S'(x) = 2 - 12/x^2$. This is zero when $x^2 = 6$, or $x = \sqrt{6}$. Note that for $0 < x < \sqrt{6}$ we have $S'(x) < 0$, and for $x > \sqrt{6}$ we have $S'(x) > 0$, so we have a minimum at $x = \sqrt{6}$. Note that when $x = \sqrt{6}$, we have $y = 12/x = 12/\sqrt{6} = 2\sqrt{6}$.

4.4.15 Let x be the length of the sides of the base of the box and y be the height of the box. The volume is $x \cdot x \cdot y = 100$, so the constraint is $x^2 y = 100$, which gives $y = 100/x^2$. The objective function to be minimized is the surface area S of the box, which consists of $2x^2$ (for the top and base) $+ 4xy$ (for the 4 sides); therefore $S = 2x^2 + 4xy$. Using $y = 100x^2$, we have $S = 2x^2 + 4xy = 2x^2 + 4x \cdot \frac{100}{x^2} = 2x^2 + \frac{400}{x}$. The base side length can be any $x > 0$, so we need to maximize $S(x) = 2x^2 + 400/x$ on the interval $(0, \infty)$. The critical points of the objective function satisfy $S'(x) = 4x - \frac{400}{x^2} = 0$; clearing denominators gives $4x^3 = 400$ so $x = \sqrt[3]{100}$. By the First (or Second) Derivative Test, this critical point corresponds to a local minimum, and by Theorem 4.5, this solitary local minimum is also the absolute minimum on the interval $(0, \infty)$. Therefore the dimensions of the box with minimum surface area are $x = \sqrt[3]{100}$ and $y = 100/\sqrt[3]{100}^2 = \sqrt[3]{100}$, so length $=$ width $=$ height $= \sqrt[3]{100}$ m.

4.4.17 Let x be the length of the sides of the base of the box and y be the height of the box. The volume of the box is $x \cdot x \cdot y = x^2 y$, so the constraint is $x^2 y = 16$, which gives $y = 16/x^2$. Let c be the cost per square foot of the material used to make the sides. Then the cost to make the base is $2cx^2$, the cost to make the 4 sides is $4cxy$, and the cost to make the top is $\frac{1}{2}cx^2$. The objective function to be minimized is the total cost, which is $C = 2cx^2 + 4cxy + \frac{1}{2}cx^2 = \frac{5}{2}cx^2 + 4cx \cdot \frac{16}{x^2} = c\left(\frac{5x^2}{2} + \frac{64}{x}\right)$. The base side length can be any $x > 0$, so we need to maximize $C(x) = c(5x^2/2 + 64/x)$ on the interval $(0, \infty)$. The critical points of the objective function satisfy $5x - \frac{64}{x^2} = 0$, which gives $x^3 = 64/5$ or $x = 4/\sqrt[3]{5}$. By the First (or Second) Derivative Test, this critical point corresponds to a local minimum, and by Theorem 4.5, this solitary local minimum is also the absolute minimum on the interval $(0, \infty)$. Therefore the box with minimum cost has base $4/\sqrt[3]{5}$ ft by $4/\sqrt[3]{5}$ ft and height $y = 16/(4/\sqrt[3]{5})^2 = 5^{2/3}$ ft.

4.4.19 The distance between $(x, 3x)$ and $(50, 0)$ is $d(x) = \sqrt{(3x - 0)^2 + (x - 50)^2}$. Instead of working with the distance, we can instead work with the square of the distance, because these two functions have minima which occur at the same place. So consider

$$(d(x))^2 = D(x) = (3x)^2 + (x - 50)^2 = 9x^2 + x^2 - 100x + 2500 = 10(x^2 - 10x + 250).$$

$\frac{dD}{dx} = 10(2x - 10)$, which is zero for $x = 5$. Because $\frac{d^2D}{dx^2} = 20 > 0$, we see that the critical point at $x = 5$ is a minimum. So the minimum of D (and d) occurs at $x = 5$. The value of d at the point $(5, 15)$, is $d(5) = \sqrt{15^2 + (-45)^2} = 15\sqrt{10} \approx 47.4$.

4.4.21

a. Let x be the distance from the point on the shoreline nearest to the boat to the point where the woman lands on shore; then the remaining distance she must travel on shore is $6 - x$. By the Pythagorean theorem, the distance the woman must row is $\sqrt{x^2 + 16}$. So the time for the rowing leg is $\frac{\text{distance}}{\text{rate}} = \frac{\sqrt{x^2+16}}{2}$ and the time for the walking leg is $\frac{\text{distance}}{\text{rate}} = \frac{6-x}{3}$. The total travel time for the trip is the objective function $T(x) = \frac{\sqrt{x^2+16}}{2} + \frac{6-x}{3}$. We wish to minimize this function for $0 \le x \le 6$. The critical points of the objective function satisfy $T'(x) = \frac{x}{2\sqrt{x^2+16}} - \frac{1}{3} = 0$, which when simplified gives $5x^2 = 64$, so $x = 8/\sqrt{5}$ is the only critical point in $(0, 6)$. From the First Derivative Test we see that T has a local minimum at this point, so $x = 8/\sqrt{5}$ must give the minimum value of T on $[0, 6]$.

b. Let $v > 0$ be the woman's rowing speed. Then the total travel time is now given by $T(x) = \frac{\sqrt{x^2+16}}{v} + \frac{6-x}{3}$. The derivative of the objective function is $T'(x) = \frac{x}{v\sqrt{x^2+16}} - \frac{1}{3}$. If we try to solve the equation $T'(x) = 0$ as in part (a) above, we see that there is at most one solution $x > 0$. Therefore there can be at most one critical point of T in the interval $(0,6)$. Observe also that $T'(0) = -1/3 < 0$ so the absolute minimum of T on $[0,6]$ cannot occur at $x = 0$. So one of two things must happen: there is a unique critical point for T in $(0,6)$ which is the absolute minimum for T on $[0,6]$, and then $T'(6) > 0$; or, T is decreasing on $[0,6]$, and then $T'(6) \leq 0$ (the quickest way to the restaurant is to row directly in this case). The condition $T'(6) \leq 0$ is equivalent to $\frac{6}{\sqrt{6^2+16}} \leq \frac{v}{3}$ which gives $v \geq 9/\sqrt{13}$ mi/hr.

4.4.23 Let L be the ladder length and x be the distance between the foot of the ladder and the fence. The Pythagorean theorem gives the relationship $L^2 = (x+5)^2 + b^2$, where b is the height of the top of the ladder. We see that $b/(x+5) = 8/x$ by similar triangles, which gives $b = 8(x+5)/x$. Substituting in the expression for L^2 above gives $L^2 = (x+5)^2 + 64\frac{(x+5)^2}{x^2} = (x+5)^2\left(1 + \frac{64}{x^2}\right)$. It suffices to minimize L^2 instead of L. However in this case x and b must satisfy $x, b \leq 20$. Solving $20 = 8(x+5)/x$ for x gives $x = 10/3$, so the condition $b \leq 20$ corresponds to $x \geq 10/3$, and we see that we must minimize L^2 for $10/3 \leq x \leq 20$. We have $\frac{d}{dx}L^2 = (x+5)^2\left(-\frac{128}{x^3}\right) + 2(x+5)\left(1 + \frac{64}{x^2}\right) = \frac{2(x+5)(x^3-320)}{x^3}$. Because $x > 0$, the only critical point is $x = \sqrt[3]{320} \approx 6.840$. By the First Derivative Test, this critical point corresponds to a local minimum, and by Theorem 4.5, this solitary local minimum is also the absolute minimum on the interval $[10/3, 20]$. Substituting $x \approx 6.840$ in the expression for L^2 we find the length of the shortest ladder $L \approx 18.220$ ft.

4.4.25 Let the coordinates of the base of the rectangle be $(x,0)$ and $(-x,0)$ where $0 \leq x \leq 5$. Then the width of the rectangle is $2x$ and the height is $\sqrt{25 - x^2}$, so the area A is given by $A(x) = 2x\sqrt{25 - x^2}$. The critical points of this function satisfy $A'(x) = 2\sqrt{25-x^2} + \frac{2x\cdot(-x)}{\sqrt{25-x^2}} = \frac{2(25-2x^2)}{\sqrt{25-x^2}} = 0$, which has unique solution $x = 5/\sqrt{2}$ in $(0,5)$. We have $A(0) = A(5) = 0$, so the rectangle of maximum area has width $2x = 10/\sqrt{2}$ cm, height $y = \sqrt{25 - (25/2)} = 5/\sqrt{2}$ cm.

4.4.27 If we remove a sector of angle θ from a circle of radius 20, the remaining circumference is $2\pi\cdot20 - \theta\cdot20 = 20(2\pi - \theta)$, so the base of the cone formed has radius $r = \frac{20(2\pi-\theta)}{2\pi} = \frac{10(2\pi-\theta)}{\pi}$. As θ varies from 0 to 2π, the radius ranges from 0 to 20, but all possible cones formed have side length 20. The height h of the cone is given by the Pythagorean theorem: $h^2 + r^2 = 20^2$, so $h = \sqrt{400 - r^2}$. The volume of the cone given by $V = \frac{\pi}{3}r^2h = \frac{\pi}{3}r^2\sqrt{400 - r^2}$.

Thus

$$V'(r) = \frac{2\pi}{3}r\sqrt{400 - r^2} + \frac{\pi}{3}r^2(400 - r^2)^{-1/2} \cdot \frac{1}{2} \cdot (-2r)$$
$$= \frac{\pi}{3} \cdot \frac{2r(400 - r^2) - r^3}{\sqrt{400 - r^2}}$$
$$= \frac{\pi}{3} \cdot \frac{800r - 3r^3}{\sqrt{400 - r^2}}.$$

The only positive critical point occurs where $r = \sqrt{\frac{800}{3}} = 20\sqrt{\frac{2}{3}}$. An application of the First Derivative Test shows that this is a maximum. So

$$h = \sqrt{400 - \left(20\sqrt{\frac{2}{3}}\right)^2} = \sqrt{400 - 400\cdot\frac{2}{3}} = 20\sqrt{\frac{1}{3}}.$$

4.4.29 Let x and y be the dimensions of the flower garden; the area of the flower garden is 30, so we have the constraint $xy = 30$ which gives $y = 30/x$. The dimensions of the garden and borders are $x + 4$ and $y + 2$, so the objective function to be minimized for $x > 0$ is $A = (x+4)(y+2) = (x+4)\left(\frac{30}{x} + 2\right) = 2x + \frac{120}{x} + 38$. The critical points of $A(x)$ satisfy $A'(x) = 2 - \frac{120}{x^2} = 0$, which has unique solution $x = \sqrt{60} = 2\sqrt{15}$. By the First (or Second) Derivative test, this critical point gives a local minimum, which by Theorem 4.5 must be the absolute minimum of A over $(0,\infty)$. The corresponding value of y is $30/2\sqrt{15} = \sqrt{15}$, so the dimensions are $\sqrt{15}$ by $2\sqrt{15}$ m.

4.4.31 The radius r and height h of the barrel satisfy the constraint $r^2 + h^2 = d^2$, which we can rewrite as $r^2 = d^2 - h^2$. The volume of the barrel is given by $V = \pi r^2 h = \pi (d^2 - h^2) h = \pi (d^2 h - h^3)$. The height h must satisfy $0 \le h \le d$, so we need to maximize $V(h)$ on the interval $[0, d]$. The critical points of V satisfy $V'(h) = \pi(d^2 - 3h^2) = 0$. The only critical point in $(0, d)$ is $h = d/\sqrt{3}$, which gives the maximum volume because at the endpoints $V(0) = V(d) = 0$. The corresponding r value satisfies $r^2 = d^2 - d^2/3 = 2d^2/3$, so $r = \sqrt{2}d/\sqrt{3}$ and we see that the ratio r/h that maximizes the volume is $\sqrt{2}$.

4.4.33 Let h be the height of the cylindrical tower and r the radius of the dome. The cylinder has volume $\pi r^2 h$, and the hemispherical dome has volume $2\pi r^3/3$ (half the volume of a sphere of radius r). The total volume is 750, so we have the constraint $\pi r^2 h + \frac{2\pi r^3}{3} = 750$ which gives $h = \frac{750}{\pi r^2} - \frac{2r}{3}$. We must have $h \ge 0$, which is equivalent to $r \le \sqrt[3]{1125/\pi}$. The objective function to be maximized is the cost of the metal to make the silo, which is proportional to the surface area of the cylinder ($= 2\pi rh$) plus 1.5 times the surface area of the hemisphere ($= 2\pi r^2$). So we can take as objective function $C = 2\pi rh + 1.5 \cdot 2\pi r^2 = 2\pi r \left(\frac{750}{\pi r^2} - \frac{2r}{3} \right) + 3\pi r^2 = \frac{1500}{r} + \frac{5}{3}\pi r^2$. The critical points of $C(r)$ satisfy $C'(r) = -\frac{1500}{r^2} + \frac{10}{3}\pi r = 0$, which gives $\pi r^3 = 450$ and hence $r = \sqrt[3]{450/\pi}$. The corresponding value of h is $h = \frac{750}{\pi r^2} - \frac{2r}{3} = \frac{750r}{\pi r^3} - \frac{2r}{3} = \left(\frac{750}{450} - \frac{2}{3} \right) r = r$. By the First (or Second) Derivative Test, this critical point corresponds to a local minimum, and by Theorem 4.5, this solitary local minimum is also the absolute minimum on the interval $[0, \sqrt[3]{1125/\pi}]$. Therefore the dimensions that minimize the cost are $r = h = \sqrt[3]{450/\pi}$ m.

4.4.35 Let x be the distance between the point and the weaker light source; then $12 - x$ is the distance to the stronger light source. The intensity is proportional to $I(x) = \frac{1}{x^2} + \frac{2}{(12-x)^2}$, so we can take this as our objective function to be minimized for $0 < x < 12$. The critical points of $I(x)$ satisfy $I'(x) = -\frac{2}{x^3} + \frac{4}{(12-x)^3} = 0$ which gives $\left(\frac{12-x}{x} \right)^3 = 2$, or $\frac{12-x}{x} = \sqrt[3]{2}$, or $x = \frac{12}{\sqrt[3]{2}+1} \approx 5.310$. By the First (or Second) Derivative Test, this critical point corresponds to a local minimum, and by Theorem 4.5, this solitary local minimum is also the absolute minimum on the interval $(0, 12)$. Therefore the intensity is weakest at the point $12/(\sqrt[3]{2}+1) \approx 5.310$ m from the weaker source.

4.4.37 Let x be the distance from the point on shore nearest the island to the point where the underwater cable meets the shore, and let y be the be the length of the underwater cable. By the Pythagorean theorem, $y = \sqrt{x^2 + 3.5^2}$. The objective function to be minimized is the cost given by $C(x) = 2400\sqrt{x^2 + 3.5^2} + 1200 \cdot (8-x) = 2400\sqrt{x^2 + 3.5^2} - 1200x + 9600$. We wish to minimize this function for $0 \le x \le 8$. The critical points of $C(x)$ satisfy $C'(x) = \frac{2400x}{\sqrt{x^2+3.5^2}} - 1200 = 1200 \left(\frac{2x}{\sqrt{x^2+3.5^2}} - 1 \right) = 0$, which we solve to obtain $x = 7\sqrt{3}/6$. By the First Derivative Test, this critical point corresponds to a local minimum, and by Theorem 4.5, this solitary local minimum is also the absolute minimum on the interval $[0, 8]$. Therefore the optimal point on shore has distance $x = 7\sqrt{3}/6$ mi from the point on shore nearest the island, in the direction of the power station.

4.4.39

a. Using the Pythagorean theorem, we find that the height of this triangle is 2. Let x be the distance from the point P to the base of the triangle; then the distance from P to the top vertex is $2 - x$ and the distance to each of the base vertices is $\sqrt{x^2 + 4}$, again by the Pythagorean theorem. Therefore the sum of the distances to the three vertices is given by $S(x) = 2\sqrt{x^2 + 4} + 2 - x$. We wish to minimize this function for $0 \le x \le 2$. The critical points of $S(x)$ satisfy $S'(x) = \frac{2x}{\sqrt{x^2+4}} - 1 = 0$, which has unique solution $x = 2/\sqrt{3}$ in $(0, 2)$. By the First Derivative Test, this critical point corresponds to a local minimum, and by Theorem 4.5, this solitary local minimum is also the absolute minimum on the interval $[0, 2]$. Therefore the optimal location for P is $2/\sqrt{3}$ units above the base.

b. In this case the objective function to be minimized is $S(x) = 2\sqrt{x^2 + 4} + h - x$ where $0 \le x \le h$. Exactly as above, we find that the only critical point $x > 0$ is $x = 2/\sqrt{3}$. This will give the absolute minimum on $[0, h]$ as long as $h \ge 2/\sqrt{3}$. When $h < 2/\sqrt{3}$, $S(x)$ is decreasing on $[0, h]$ and the minimum occurs at the endpoint $x = h$.

4.4.41 Let r and h be the radius and height of the cone; then we have the constraint $r^2 + h^2 = 3^2 = 9$, which gives $r^2 = 9 - h^2$. The objective function to be maximized is the volume of the cone, given by $V = \frac{\pi}{3}r^2 h = \frac{\pi}{3}(9 - h^2)h = \frac{\pi}{3}(9h - h^3)$. Because $r, h \geq 0$ we must have $0 \leq h \leq 3$. Therefore we need to maximize $V(h)$ over $[0, 3]$. The critical points of $V(h)$ satisfy $V'(h) = \frac{\pi}{3}(9 - 3h^2) = \pi(3 - h^2) = 0$, so $h = \sqrt{3}$ is the only critical point in $[0, 3]$. Because $V(0) = V(3) = 0$, the cone of maximum volume has height $h = \sqrt{3}$ and radius $r = \sqrt{6}$.

4.4.43 The critical points of the function $a(\theta)$ satisfy

$$a'(\theta) = \omega^2 r \left(-\sin\theta - \frac{2r\sin 2\theta}{L} \right) = -\omega^2 r \sin\theta \left(1 + \frac{4r\cos\theta}{L} \right) = 0,$$

using the identity $\sin 2\theta = 2\sin\theta\cos\theta$. There are two cases to consider separately: (a) $0 < L < 4r$ and (b) $L \geq 4r$. In case (a) the critical points in $[0, 2\pi]$ are $\theta = 0, \pi, 2\pi$ and also $\theta = \cos^{-1}(-L/(4r))$ and $2\pi - \cos^{-1}(-L/(4r))$. Comparing the values of $a(\theta)$ at these points shows that the maximum acceleration occurs at $\theta = 0$ and 2π and the minimum occurs at $\theta = \cos^{-1}(-L/(4r))$ and $2\pi - \cos^{-1}(-L/(4r))$. (There is a local maximum at $\theta = \pi$.) In case (b) the only critical points are $\theta = 0, \pi$ and 2π, and comparing the values of $a(\theta)$ at these points shows that the maximum acceleration occurs at $\theta = 0$ and 2π as in case (a), whereas the minimum occurs at $\theta = \pi$ in this case.

4.4.45

a. Let r and h be the radius and height of the can. The volume of the can is $V = \pi r^2 h$, which gives the constraint $\pi r^2 h = 354$ or $h = 354/(\pi r^2)$. The objective function to be minimized is the surface area, which consists of $2\pi r^2$ (for the top and bottom of the can) and $2\pi rh$ (for the side of the can). Therefore the objective function to be minimized is $A = 2\pi r^2 + 2\pi rh = 2\pi \left(r^2 + r\left(\frac{354}{\pi r^2}\right) \right) = 2\pi \left(r^2 + \frac{354}{\pi r} \right)$. We need to minimize $A(r)$ for $r > 0$. The critical points of $A(r)$ satisfy $A'(r) = 2\pi \left(2r - \frac{354}{\pi r^2} \right) = 0$, which gives $r = \sqrt[3]{(177/\pi)} \approx 3.834$ cm. The corresponding value of h is $h = \frac{354}{\pi r^2} = \frac{354r}{\pi r^3} = 2r \cdot \frac{177}{\pi r^3} = 2r$, so $h = 2\sqrt[3]{(177/\pi)} \approx 7.667$ cm. By the First (or Second) Derivative Test, this critical point corresponds to a local minimum, and by Theorem 4.5, this solitary local minimum is also the absolute minimum on the interval $(0, \infty)$.

b. We modify the objective function in part (a) above to account for the fact that the top and bottom of the can have double thickness: $A = 4\pi r^2 + 2\pi rh = 2\pi \left(2r^2 + r\left(\frac{354}{\pi r^2}\right) \right) = 4\pi \left(r^2 + \frac{177}{\pi r} \right)$. We need to minimize $A(r)$ for $r > 0$. The critical points of $A(r)$ satisfy $A'(r) = 4\pi \left(2r - \frac{177}{\pi r^2} \right) = 0$, which gives $r = \sqrt[3]{(177/2\pi)} \approx 3.043$ cm. The corresponding value of h is $h = \frac{354}{\pi r^2} = \frac{354r}{\pi r^3} = 4r \cdot \frac{177}{2\pi r^3} = 4r$, so $h = 4\sqrt[3]{(177/2\pi)} \approx 12.171$ cm. These dimensions are closer to those of a real soda can.

4.4.47 The viewing angle θ is given by $\theta = \cot^{-1}\left(\frac{x}{10}\right) - \cot^{-1}\left(\frac{x}{3}\right)$, and we wish to maximize this function for $x > 0$. The critical points satisfy $\theta'(x) = -\frac{1}{1+\left(\frac{x}{10}\right)^2} \cdot \frac{1}{10} - (-)\frac{1}{1+\left(\frac{x}{3}\right)^2} \cdot \frac{1}{3} = \frac{3}{x^2+3^2} - \frac{10}{x^2+10^2} = 0$ which simplifies to $3(x^2 + 100) = 10(x^2 + 9)$ or $x^2 = 30$. Therefore $x = \sqrt{30} \approx 5.477$ ft is the only critical point in $(0, \infty)$. By the First (or Second) Derivative Test, this critical point corresponds to a local maximum, and by Theorem 4.5, this solitary local maximum must be the absolute maximum on the interval $(0, \infty)$.

4.4.49 Let the radius of the ferris wheel have length r, and let α be the angle the specific seat on the ferris wheel makes with the center of the wheel (see the figure in the text). This point has coordinates $(r\cos\alpha, r + r\sin\alpha)$ so the distance from the seat to the base of the wheel is

$$d = \sqrt{r^2\cos^2\alpha + r^2(1 + \sin\alpha)^2} = \sqrt{2}r\sqrt{1 + \sin\alpha}.$$

Therefore the observer's angle satisfies $\tan\theta = \frac{r\sqrt{2}}{20}\sqrt{1 + \sin\alpha}$. Think of θ and α as functions of time t and differentiate: $\sec^2\theta\frac{d\theta}{dt} = \frac{r\sqrt{2}}{20} \cdot \frac{\cos\alpha}{2\sqrt{1+\sin\alpha}}\frac{d\alpha}{dt} = \frac{\pi r\sqrt{2}}{40} \cdot \frac{\cos\alpha}{\sqrt{1+\sin\alpha}}$. Therefore

$$\frac{d\theta}{dt} = \frac{\pi r\sqrt{2}}{40}\frac{\cos^2\theta\cos\alpha}{\sqrt{1 + \sin\alpha}}.$$

Observe that $\left|\frac{d\theta}{dt}\right| = \frac{\pi r\sqrt{2}}{40}\frac{\cos^2\theta|\cos\alpha|}{\sqrt{1+\sin\alpha}}\frac{\sqrt{1-\sin\alpha}}{\sqrt{1-\sin\alpha}}$, which can be written as $\frac{\pi r\sqrt{2}}{40}\cos^2\theta\sqrt{1-\sin\alpha}$. When the seat on the ferris wheel is at its lowest point we have $\theta = 0$ and $\alpha = -\pi/2$, which gives $\cos^2\theta = 1$ and $\sqrt{1-\sin\alpha} = \sqrt{2}$. At any other point on the wheel we have $\cos^2\theta \le 1$ and $\sqrt{1-\sin\alpha} < \sqrt{2}$, so θ is changing most rapidly when the seat is at its lowest point.

4.4.51 Let r and h be the radius and height of the cylinder. The distance d from the centroid of the cylinder (the midpoint of the cylinder's axis of rotation) to any point on the top or bottom edge satisfies $d^2 = r^2 + \left(\frac{h}{2}\right)^2$ so the constraint is $r^2 + (h/2)^2 = R^2$. The volume of the cylinder is given by $V = \pi r^2 h = \pi\left(R^2 - \left(\frac{h}{2}\right)^2\right)h = \pi\left(R^2 h - \frac{h^3}{4}\right)$. Because $r, h \ge 0$ we must have $0 \le h \le 2R$. We wish to maximize $V(h)$ on this interval. The critical points of $V(h)$ satisfy $V'(h) = \pi\left(R^2 - \frac{3h^2}{4}\right) = 0$ which gives $h = 2R/\sqrt{3}$, and from the constraint we obtain $r = \sqrt{2}R/\sqrt{3}$. The volume $V(h) = 0$ at the endpoints $h = 0$ and $h = 2R$, so the maximum volume must occur at this critical point.

4.4.53

a. Let r and h be the radius and height of the inscribed cylinder. The region that lies above the cylinder inside the cone is a cone with radius r and height $H - h$; by similar triangles we have $\frac{H-h}{r} = \frac{H}{R}$ so $h = \frac{H}{R}(R - r)$. The volume of the cylinder is $V = \pi r^2 h = \frac{\pi H}{R}\left(Rr^2 - r^3\right)$, which we must maximize over $0 \le r \le R$. The critical points of $V(r)$ satisfy $V'(r) = \frac{\pi H}{R}\left(2Rr - 3r^2\right) = 0$, which has unique solution $r = 2R/3$ in $(0, R)$. Because $V(r) = 0$ at the endpoints $r = 0$ and $r = R$, the cylinder with maximum volume has radius $r = 2R/3$, height $h = H/3$ and volume $V = \pi r^2 h = \frac{4\pi}{27}R^2 H = \frac{4}{9}\cdot\frac{\pi}{3}R^2 H$; i.e. $4/9$ the volume of the cone.

b. The lateral surface area of the cylinder is $A = 2\pi rh = 2\pi r\cdot\frac{H}{R}(R - r) = \frac{2\pi H}{R}r(R - r)$. This function takes its maximum over $0 \le r \le R$ at $r = R/2$, so the cylinder with maximum lateral surface area has dimensions $r = R/2$ and $h = H/2$.

4.4.55 Let R and H be the radius and height of the larger cone and let r and h be the radius and height of the smaller inscribed cone. The region that lies above the smaller cone inside the larger cone is a cone with radius r and height $H - h$; by similar triangles we have $\frac{H-h}{r} = \frac{H}{R}$ so $h = \frac{H}{R}(R - r)$. The volume of the smaller cone is $V = \frac{\pi}{3}r^2 h = \frac{\pi H}{3R}\left(Rr^2 - r^3\right)$, which we must maximize over $0 \le r \le R$. The critical points of $V(r)$ satisfy $V'(r) = \frac{\pi H}{3R}\left(2Rr - 3r^2\right) = 0$ which has unique solution $r = 2R/3$ in $(0, R)$. Because $V(r) = 0$ at the endpoints $r = 0$ and $r = R$, the smaller cone with maximum volume has radius $r = 2R/3$ and height $h = H/3$, so the optimal ratio of the heights is 3:1.

4.4.57

Following the hint, place two points P and Q above the midpoint of the base of the square, at distances x and y to the sides (see figure), where $0 \leq x, y \leq 1/2$. Then join the bottom vertices of the square to P, the upper vertices to Q and join P to Q. This road system has total length $L = 2\sqrt{x^2 + \frac{1}{4}} + 2\sqrt{y^2 + \frac{1}{4}} + (1 - x - y) = 1 + \left(\sqrt{4x^2 + 1} - x\right) + \left(\sqrt{4y^2 + 1} - y\right)$. We can minimize the contributions from x and y separately; the critical points of the function $f(x) = \sqrt{4x^2 + 1} - x$ satisfy $f'(x) = \frac{4x}{\sqrt{4x^2 + 1}} - 1 = 0$ which gives $\sqrt{4x^2 + 1} = 4x$, so $12x^2 = 1$ and $x = 1/(2\sqrt{3})$. By the First (or Second) Derivative Test, this critical point corresponds to a local minimum, and by Theorem 4.5, this solitary local minimum is also the absolute minimum on the interval $[0, 1/2]$. The minimum value of $f(x)$ on this interval is $f(1/(2\sqrt{3})) = \sqrt{3}/2$, so the shortest road system has length $L = 1 + 2 \cdot \frac{\sqrt{3}}{2} = 1 + \sqrt{3} \approx 2.732$.

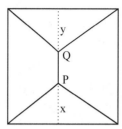

4.4.59 Let x be the distance between the point on the track nearest your initial position to the point where you catch the train. If you just catch the back of the train, then the train will have travelled $x + 1/3$ miles, which will require time $T = \frac{\text{distance}}{\text{rate}} = \frac{x + \frac{1}{3}}{20}$. The distance you must run is $\sqrt{x^2 + 1/(16)}$, so your running speed must be $v = \frac{\text{distance}}{\text{time}} = \frac{20\sqrt{x^2 + \frac{1}{16}}}{x + \frac{1}{3}}$. We wish to minimize this function for $x \geq 0$. The derivative of $v(x)$ can be written $v'(x) = \left(\frac{x}{x^2 + \frac{1}{16}} - \frac{1}{x + \frac{1}{3}}\right) v(x)$, so the critical points of $v(x)$ satisfy $\frac{x}{x^2 + \frac{1}{16}} = \frac{1}{x + \frac{1}{3}}$ so $x\left(x + \frac{1}{3}\right) = x^2 + \frac{1}{16}$ which gives $x = 3/16$ mi. By the First (or Second) Derivative Test, this critical point corresponds to a local minimum, and by Theorem 4.5, this solitary local minimum is also the absolute minimum on the interval $[0, \infty)$. The minimum running speed is $v\left(\frac{3}{16}\right) = \frac{20\sqrt{\left(\frac{3}{16}\right)^2 + \frac{1}{16}}}{\frac{3}{16} + \frac{1}{3}} = \frac{60\sqrt{9 + 16}}{9 + 16} = 12$ mph.

4.4.61

a. A point on the line $y = 3x + 4$ has the form $(x, 3x + 4)$, which has distance L to the origin given by $L^2 = x^2 + (3x + 4)^2 = 10x^2 + 24x + 16$. Because L is positive, it suffices to minimize L^2. The quadratic function $10x^2 + 24x + 16$ takes its minimum at $x = -24/20 = -6/5$, and the corresponding value of $y = 2/5$. Therefore the point closest to the origin on this line is $(-6/5, 2/5)$.

b. A point on the parabola $y = 1 - x^2$ has the form $(x, 1 - x^2)$, which has distance L to the point $(1,1)$ given by $L^2 = (x - 1)^2 + \left(1 - (1 - x^2)\right)^2 = x^4 + x^2 - 2x + 1$. Because L is positive, it suffices to minimize L^2. The critical points of L^2 satisfy $\frac{dL^2}{dx} = 4x^3 + 2x - 2 = 2(2x^3 + x - 1) = 0$ This cubic equation has a unique root $x \approx 0.590$, so the point closest to $(1, 1)$ on this parabola is approximately $(0.590, 0.652)$.

c. A point on the curve $y = \sqrt{x}$ has the form $(x, \sqrt{x})$, which has distance L to the point $(p,0)$ given by $L^2 = (x - p)^2 + \sqrt{x}^2 = x^2 + (1 - 2p)x + p^2$. Because L is positive, it suffices to minimize L^2 for $x \geq 0$. This quadratic function takes its minimum at $x = -(1 - 2p)/2 = p - 1/2$, so in case (i) the minimum occurs at the point $(p - 1/2, \sqrt{p - 1/2})$ and in case (ii) there are no critical points for $x > 0$, the function L^2 is increasing on $[0, \infty)$ so the minimum occurs at $(0, 0)$.

4.4.63

a. We find $g(0) = 0$, $g(40) = 30$ and $g(60) = 25$ miles per gallon. The value at $v = 0$ is reasonable because when a car first starts moving it needs a lot of power from its engine, so the gas mileage is very low. The decline from 30 to 25 mi/gal as v increases from 40 mi/hr to 60 mi/hr reflects the fact that gas mileage tends to decrease at speeds over 55 mi/hr.

b. The quadratic function $g(v) = (85v - v^2)/60$ takes its maximum value at $v = 85/2 = 42.5$ mi/hr.

c. At speed v the amount of gas needed to drive one mile is $1/g(v)$ and the time it takes is $1/v$. Hence the cost of gas for one mile is $p/g(v)$ and the cost for the driver is w/v, and so the cost for L miles is $C(v) = Lp/g(v) + Lw/v$.

d. We have $C(v) = 400\left(\frac{4}{g(v)} + \frac{20}{v}\right) = 1600\left(\frac{1}{g(v)} + \frac{5}{v}\right)$. The critical points of $C(v)$ satisfy $\frac{g'(v)}{g(v)^2} + \frac{5}{v^2} = 0$, which simplifies to $v^2 g'(v) + 5g(v)^2 = 0$. Substituting the formula for $g(v)$ above and using $g'(v) = (85 - 2v)/60$, we can factor out v^2 and reduce to the quadratic equation $v^2 - 194v + 8245 = 0$, which has roots $v \approx 62.883, 131.117$. The First (or Second) Derivative Test shows that $C(v)$ has a local minimum at $v \approx 62.9$, which is the unique critical point for $0 \le v \le 131$. Therefore the cost is minimized at this value of v.

e. Because L is a constant factor in the cost function $C(v)$, changing L will not change the critical points of $C(v)$.

f. The critical points of $C(v)$ now satisfy the equation $\frac{4.2g'(v)}{g(v)^2} + \frac{20}{v^2} = 0$, which simplifies to $4.2v^2 g'(v) + 20g(v)^2 = 0$. As above, substituting the formula for $g(v)$ above and using $g'(v) = (85 - 2v)/60$, we can factor out v^2 and reduce to the quadratic equation $v^2 - 195.2v + 8296 = 0$, which has roots $v \approx 62.532, 132.668$. As in part (d), the minimum cost occurs for $v \approx 62.532$, slightly less than the speed in part (d).

g. The critical points of $C(v)$ now satisfy the equation $\frac{4g'(v)}{g(v)^2} + \frac{15}{v^2} = 0$, which simplifies to $4v^2 g'(v) + 15g(v)^2 = 0$. As above, substituting the formula for $g(v)$ above and using $g'(v) = (85 - 2v)/60$, we can factor out v^2 and reduce to the quadratic equation $v^2 - 202v + 8585 = 0$, which has roots $v \approx 60.800, 141.200$. As in part (d), the minimum cost occurs for $v \approx 60.8$, less than the speed in part (d).

4.4.65

a. Let x, $d-x$ be the distances from the point where the rope meets the ground to the poles of height m, n respectively. Then the rope has length $L(x) = \sqrt{x^2 + m^2} + \sqrt{(d-x)^2 + n^2}$. We wish to minimize this function for $0 \le x \le d$. The critical points of $L(x)$ satisfy $L'(x) = \frac{x}{\sqrt{x^2+m^2}} - \frac{d-x}{\sqrt{(d-x)^2+n^2}} = 0$, which is equivalent to $\frac{x}{\sqrt{x^2+m^2}} = \frac{d-x}{\sqrt{(d-x)^2+n^2}}$, or in terms of the angles θ_1 and θ_2 in the figure, $\sec\theta_1 = \sec\theta_2$ and therefore $\theta_1 = \theta_2$. Observe that $L'(0) < 0$ and $L'(d) > 0$, so the minimum value of $L(x)$ must occur at some $x \in (0, d)$. There must be exactly one critical point, because as x ranges from 0 to d, θ_1 decreases and θ_2 increases, and so $\theta_1 = \theta_2$ can occur for at most one value of x.

b. Because the speed of light is constant, travel time is minimized when distance is minimized, which we saw in part (a) occurs when $\theta_1 = \theta_2$.

4.4.67 Let the angle of the cuts with the horizontal be ϕ_1 and ϕ_2, where $\phi_1 + \phi_2 = \theta$. The volume of the notch is proportional to $\tan\phi_1 + \tan\phi_2 = \tan\phi_1 + \tan(\theta - \phi_1)$, so it suffices to minimize the objective function $V(\phi_1) = \tan\phi_1 + \tan(\theta - \phi_1)$ for $0 \le \phi_1 \le \theta$. The critical points of $V(\phi_1)$ satisfy $\sec^2\phi_1 - \sec^2(\theta - \phi_1) = 0$, which is equivalent to the condition $\cos\phi_1 = \cos(\theta - \phi_1)$. This is satisfied if $\phi_1 = \theta - \phi_1$ which gives $\phi_1 = \theta/2$. There are no other solutions in $(0, \theta)$, because $\cos\phi_1$ is decreasing and $\cos(\theta - \phi_1)$ is increasing on $(0, \theta)$ and therefore can intersect at most once. So the only critical point occurs when $\phi_1 = \phi_2 = \theta/2$, and the First Derivative Test shows that this critical point is a local minimum; by Theorem 4.5, this must be the absolute minimum on $[0, \theta]$.

4.4.69 Let x and y be the lengths of the sides of the pen, with y the side parallel to the barn. The diagonal has length $\sqrt{x^2 + y^2}$, by the Pythagorean theorem. Therefore the constraint is $2x + y + \sqrt{x^2 + y^2} = 200$, which we rewrite as $2x + y = 200 - \sqrt{x^2 + y^2}$. Square both sides to obtain $4x^2 + 4xy + y^2 = 40{,}000 - 400\sqrt{x^2 + y^2} + x^2 + y^2$, which simplifies to $3x^2 + 4xy = 40{,}000 - 400\sqrt{x^2 + y^2}$. Now substitute $\sqrt{x^2 + y^2} = 200 - 2x - y$ in this equation and simplify to obtain $(3x - 200)(x - 200) = 4(100 - x)y$ so $y = \frac{(3x-200)(x-200)}{4(100-x)}$. The objective function to be maximized is the area of the pen, $A = xy$. Using the expression above for y in terms of x, we have $A = xy = \frac{x(3x-200)(x-200)}{4(100-x)} = -\frac{1}{4} \cdot \frac{x(3x-200)(x-200)}{(x-100)}$. The length x must be at least 0, and because the diagonal is at least as long as x, we must have $3x \le 200$; so x cannot exceed $200/3$. Therefore we need to maximize the function $A(x)$ defined above for $0 \le x \le 200/3$. We have $A'(x) = -\frac{1}{4} \cdot \left(\frac{(3x-200)(x-200)}{(x-100)} + \frac{x \cdot 3(x-200)}{(x-100)} + \frac{x(3x-200)}{(x-100)} - \frac{x(3x-200)(x-200)}{(x-100)^2} \right) = \left(\frac{1}{x} + \frac{3}{3x-200} + \frac{1}{x-200} - \frac{1}{x-100} \right) A(x)$. Because $A(x) > 0$ for $0 < x < 200/3$, the critical points of the objective function satisfy $\frac{1}{x} + \frac{3}{3x-200} + \frac{1}{x-200} = \frac{1}{x-100}$ which when simplified gives the equation $6x^3 - 1700x^2 + 160{,}000x - 4{,}000{,}000 = 0$. Using a numerical solver, we find that this equation has exactly one solution in the interval $(0, 200/3)$, which is $x \approx 38.81$. To find the absolute maximum of A, we check the endpoints of $[0, 200/3]$ and the critical point $x \approx 38.814$. We have $A(0) = A(200/3) = 0$, so the absolute maximum occurs when $x \approx 38.814$ m; using the formula for y in terms of x above gives $y \approx 55.030$ m.

4.5   Linear Approximation and Differentials

4.5.1

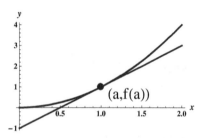

4.5.3 If f is differentiable at the point, then near that point, f is approximately linear, so the function nearly coincides with the tangent line at that point.

4.5.5 The relationship is given by $dy = f'(x)dx$, which is the linear approximation of the change Δy in $y = f(x)$ corresponding to a change dx in x.

4.5.7 The approximate average speed is $L(-1) = 60 - (-1) = 61$ miles per hour. The exact speed is $\frac{3600}{59}$ miles per hour which is about 61.02 miles per hour.

4.5.9 Let $T(x) = \frac{60D}{60+x}$. Then $T'(x) = -\frac{60D}{(60+x)^2}$, so $T'(0) = -\frac{D}{60}$. The linear approximation is given by $L(x) = T(0) - \frac{D}{60}(x - 0)$, or $L(x) = D\left(1 - \frac{x}{60}\right)$.

4.5.11 With $D = 80$, we have $T(-3) \approx L(-3) = 80(1 - \frac{-3}{60}) = 80 + 4 = 84$ minutes. The exact time required is $T(-3) = \frac{60 \cdot 80}{60 - 3} \approx 84.211$ minutes.

4.5.13

a. Note that $f(a) = f(2) = 8$ and $f'(a) = -2a = -4$, so the linear approximation has equation

$$y = L(x) = f(a) + f'(a)(x-a) = 8 + (-4)(x-2) = -4x + 16.$$

c. We have $f(2.1) \approx L(2.1) = 7.6$.

d. The percentage error is $100 \cdot \frac{|7.6-7.59|}{7.59} \approx 0.13\%$.

b.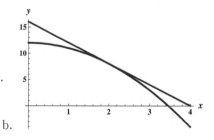

4.5.15

    a. Note that $f(a) = f(0) = \ln 1 = 0$ and $f'(a) = 1/(1 + a) = 1$, so the linear approximation has equation

$$y = L(x) = f(a) + f'(a)(x - a) = x.$$

    c. We have $f(0.9) \approx L(0.9) = 0.9$.

    d. The percentage error is $100 \cdot \frac{|0.9 - \ln 1.9|}{|\ln 1.9|} \approx 40\%$.

    b.

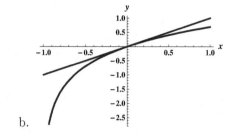

4.5.17

    a. Note that $f(a) = f(0) = \cos 0 = 1$ and $f'(a) = -\sin a = 0$, so the linear approximation has equation

$$y = L(x) = f(a) + f'(a)(x - a) = 1.$$

    c. We have $f(-0.01) \approx L(-0.01) = 1$.

    d. The percentage error is $100 \cdot \frac{|1 - \cos(-0.01)|}{\cos(-0.01)} \approx 0.005\%$.

    b.

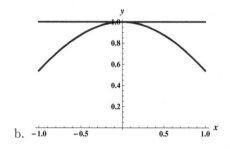

4.5.19

    a. Note that $f(a) = 8^{-1/3} = 1/2$ and $f'(a) = (-1/3)(8)^{-4/3} = -1/48$, so the linear approximation has equation

$$y = L(x) = f(a) + f'(a)(x - a) = \frac{1}{2} + \frac{-1}{48}x.$$

    c. We have $f(-0.1) \approx L(-0.1) \approx .50208333$

    d. The percentage error is $100 \cdot \frac{|7.9^{-1/3} - .50208333|}{(7.9)^{-1/3}} \approx 0.003\%$.

    b.

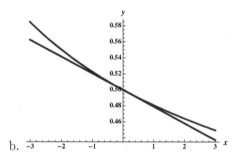

4.5.21 Let $f(x) = 1/x$, $a = 200$. Then $f(a) = 0.005$ and $f'(a) = -1/a^2 = -0.000025$, so the linear approximation to f near $a = 200$ is $L(x) = f(a) + f'(a)(x - a) = 0.005 - 0.000025(x - 200)$. Therefore $\frac{1}{203} = f(203) \approx L(203) = .004925$.

4.5.23 Let $f(x) = \sqrt{x}$, $a = 144$. Then $f(a) = 12$ and $f'(a) = 1/(2\sqrt{a}) = 1/24$, so the linear approximation to f near $a = 144$ is $L(x) = f(a) + f'(a)(x - a) = 12 + \frac{1}{24}(x - 144)$. Therefore $\sqrt{146} = f(146) \approx L(146) = \frac{145}{12}$.

4.5.25 Let $f(x) = \ln x$, $a = 1$. Then $f(a) = 0$ and $f'(a) = 1/a = 1$, so the linear approximation to f near $a = 1$ is $L(x) = f(a) + f'(a)(x - a) = x - 1$. Therefore $\ln(1.05) = f(1.05) \approx L(1.05) = .05$.

4.5.27 Let $f(x) = e^x$, $a = 0$. Then $f(a) = 1$ and $f'(a) = e^a = 1$, so the linear approximation to f near $a = 0$ is $L(x) = f(a) + f'(a)(x - a) = 1 + x$. Therefore $e^{0.06} = f(0.06) \approx L(0.06) \approx 1.060$.

4.5.29 Let $f(x) = 1/\sqrt[3]{x}$, $a = 512$. Then $f(a) = 1/8$ and $f'(a) = -1/(3a^{4/3}) = -1/12{,}288$, so the linear approximation to f near $a = 512$ is $L(x) = f(a) + f'(a)(x - a) = \frac{1}{8} - \frac{1}{12{,}288}(x - 512)$. Therefore $\frac{1}{\sqrt[3]{510}} = f(510) \approx L(510) = \frac{769}{6144} \approx 0.1252$.

4.5.31

a. With $f(x) = \frac{2}{x}$ and $a = 1$, we have $f(a) = 2$ and $f'(a) = -\frac{2}{a^2} = -2$. Thus the linear approximation to $f(x)$ at $x = 1$ is $L(x) = f(1) + f'(1)(x-1) = 2 + -2(x-1) = -2x + 4$.

b. A plot of f with L in gray:

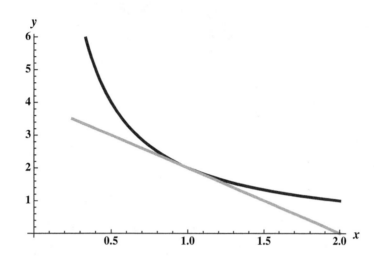

c. The linear approximation in part (b) appears to be an underestimate everywhere, because it lies below the graph of f.

d. Because $f'(x) = -\frac{2}{x^2}$, we have $f''(x) = \frac{4}{x^3}$, so that $f''(1) > 0$, and f is concave up at $x = 1$. This is consistent with L being an underestimate near $x = 1$.

4.5.33

a. With $f(x) = e^{-x}$ and $a = \ln 2$, we have $f(a) = \frac{1}{2}$ and $f'(a) = -e^{-a} = -\frac{1}{2}$. Thus the linear approximation to f at $x = \ln 2$ is $L(x) = f(\ln 2) + f'(\ln 2)(x-\ln 2) = \frac{1}{2} + -\frac{1}{2}(x-\ln 2) = -\frac{1}{2}x + \frac{1}{2}(1+\ln 2)$.

b. A plot of f with L in gray:

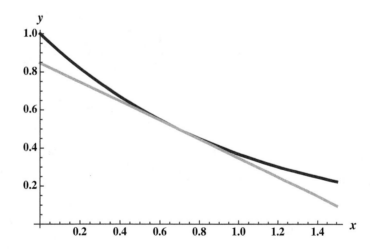

c. The linear approximation in part (b) appears to be an underestimate everywhere, because it lies below the graph of f

d. Because $f'(x) = -e^{-x}$, we have $f''(x) = e^{-x}$, so that $f''(x) > 0$ for all values of x and f is therefore concave up everywhere. This is consistent with L being an underestimate.

4.5.35 Note that $V'(r) = 4\pi r^2$, so $\Delta V \approx V'(a)\Delta r = 4\pi a^2 \Delta r$. Substituting $a = 5$ and $\Delta r = 0.1$ gives $\Delta V \approx 4\pi \cdot 25 \cdot 0.1 = 10\pi \approx 31.416$ ft^3.

4.5.37 Note that V is a linear function of h with $V'(h) = \pi r^2 = 400\pi$, so $\Delta V = V'(a)\Delta r = 400\pi\Delta r$. Substituting $\Delta r = -0.1$ gives $\Delta V = -40\pi \approx -125.664$ cm^3.

4.5.39 Note that $S'(r) = \pi\sqrt{r^2 + h^2} + \pi r \cdot \frac{r}{\sqrt{r^2+h^2}} = \pi\frac{2r^2+h^2}{\sqrt{r^2+h^2}}$, so $\Delta S \approx S'(a)\Delta r = \pi\frac{2a^2+h^2}{\sqrt{a^2+h^2}}\Delta r$. Substituting $h = 6$, $a = 10$ and $\Delta r = -0.1$ gives $\Delta S \approx \pi\frac{236}{\sqrt{136}}(-0.1) = \frac{-59\pi}{5\sqrt{34}} \approx -6.358$ m^2.

4.5.41 We have $f'(x) = 2$, so $dy = 2\,dx$.

4.5.43 We have $f'(x) = -3/x^4$, so $dy = -\frac{3}{x^4}dx$.

4.5.45 We have $f'(x) = a\sin x$, so $dy = a\sin x\,dx$.

4.5.47 We have $f'(x) = 9x^2 - 4$, so $dy = (9x^2 - 4)\,dx$.

4.5.49 We have $f'(x) = \sec^2 x$, so $dy = \sec^2 x\,dx$.

4.5.51

a. True. Note that $f(0) = 0$ and $f'(0) = 0$, so the linear approximation at 0 is in fact $L(x) = 0$.

b. False. The function $f(x) = |x|$ is not differentiable at $x = 0$, so there is no good linear approximation at 0.

c. True. For linear functions, the linear approximation at any point and the function are equal.

d. True. Note that $f'(x) = \frac{1}{x}$, so that $f''(x) = \frac{-1}{x^2}$, and $f''(e) < 0$, so f is concave down near $x = e$. Thus L is an overestimate of f.

4.5.53 We have $L(x) = f(4) + f'(4)(x - 4) = 3 + 2(x - 4)$. So $f(3.85) \approx L(3.85) = 3 + 2(3.85 - 4) = 3 - .3 = 2.7$.

4.5.55 Note that $f(a) = f(0) = 1$ and $f'(a) = -1/(1+a)^2 = -1$, so the linear approximation has equation $y = L(x) = f(a) + f'(a)(x - a) = 1 - x$.

b. The linear approximation to $1/1.1$ is $\frac{1}{1.1} \approx L(0.1) = 0.9$.

c. The percentage error is $100 \cdot \frac{|0.9 - \frac{1}{1.1}|}{\frac{1}{1.1}} = 1\%$.

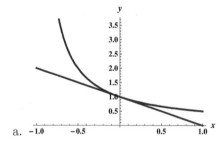

a.

4.5.57 Note that $f(a) = f(0) = 1$ and $f'(a) = -e^{-a} = -1$, so the linear approximation has equation $y = L(x) = f(a) + f'(a)(x - a) = 1 - x$.

b. The linear approximation to $e^{-0.03}$ is $e^{-0.03} \approx L(0.03) = 0.97$.

c. The percentage error is $100 \cdot \frac{|0.97 - e^{-0.03}|}{e^{-0.03}} \approx 0.046\%$.

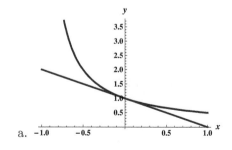

a.

4.5.59 $E(x) = |L(x) - s(x)| = \left| 60 - x - \frac{3600}{60-x} \right|$. A graph is shown below, for x from -7.26 to 8.26.

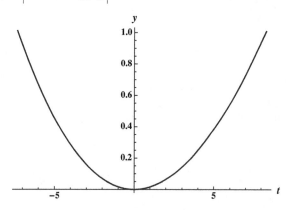

$E(x) \leq 1$ when $-7.26 \leq x \leq 8.26$, which corresponds to driving times for 1 mi from about 53 s to 68 s. Therefore, $L(x)$ gives approximations to $s(x)$ that are within 1 mi/hr of the true value when you drive 1 mile in t seconds, where $53 < t < 68$.

4.5.61 Note that $f(a) = f(8) = 2$ and $f'(a) = (1/3)a^{-2/3} = 1/12$, so the linear approximation has equation $y = L(x) = f(a) + f'(a)(x-a) = 2 + \frac{1}{12}(x-8) = \frac{x}{12} + \frac{4}{3}$.

x	Linear approx	Exact value	Percent error
8.1	$2.008\overline{3}$	2.00829885	1.717×10^{-3}
8.01	$2.0008\overline{3}$	2.000832986	1.734×10^{-5}
8.001	$2.00008\overline{3}$	2.00008333	1.736×10^{-7}
8.0001	$2.000008\overline{3}$	2.00000833	1.736×10^{-9}
7.9999	$1.999991\overline{6}$	1.999991667	1.736×10^{-9}
7.999	$1.99991\overline{6}$	1.999916663	1.736×10^{-7}
7.99	$1.9991\overline{6}$	1.999166319	1.738×10^{-5}
7.9	$1.991\overline{6}$	1.991631701	1.756×10^{-3}

The percentage errors become extremely small as x approaches 8 In fact, each time we decrease Δx by a factor of 10, the percentage error decreases by a factor of 100.

4.5.63

a. The linear approximation near $x = 1$ is more accurate for f because the rate at which f' is changing at 1 is smaller than the rate at which g' is changing at 1. The graph of f bends away from the linear function more slowly than the graph of g.

b. The larger the value of $|f''(a)|$, the greater the deviation of the curve $y = f(x)$ from the tangent line at points near $x = a$.

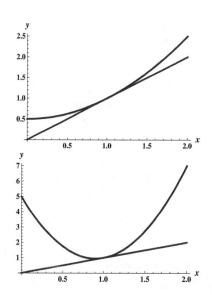

4.6   Mean Value Theorem

4.6.1 If f is a continuous function on the closed interval $[a, b]$ and is differentiable on (a, b) and the slope of the secant line that joins $(a, f(a))$ and $(b, f(b))$ is zero, then there is at least one value c in (a, b) at which the slope of the line tangent to f at $(c, f(c))$ is also zero.

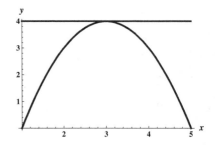

4.6.3 The function $f(x) = |x|$ is not differentiable at 0.

4.6.5 We seek a function over an interval for which it isn't true that there is a tangent line parallel to the secant line between the endpoints.

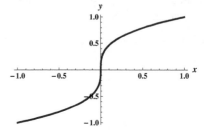

4.6.7 The function f is differentiable on $[0, 1]$ and $f(0) = f(1) = 0$, so Rolle's theorem applies. We wish to find a point x in $(0, 1)$ such that $f'(x) = 0$; we have $f'(x) = (x - 1)^2 + 2x(x - 1) = (x - 1)(3x - 1)$, so $x = 1/3$ satisfies the conclusion of Rolle's theorem.

4.6.9 The function f is differentiable on $[\pi/8, 3\pi/8]$ and $f(\pi/8) = f(3\pi/8) = 0$, so Rolle's theorem applies. We wish to find a point x in $(\pi/8, 3\pi/8)$ such that $f'(x) = 0$; we have $f'(x) = -4\sin 4x$, so $x = \pi/4$ satisfies the conclusion of Rolle's theorem.

4.6.11 The function f is not differentiable at $x = 0$, so Rolle's theorem does not apply.

4.6.13 g is continuous on $[-1, 3]$ and differentiable on $(-1, 3)$, and $g(-1) = 0 = g(3)$, so Rolle's theorem does apply. $g'(x) = 3x^2 - 2x - 5 = (x + 1)(3x - 5)$. This is zero for $x = -1$ (which is not on $(-1, 3)$) and for $x = 5/3$ (which is on $(-1, 3)$.) So $x = 5/3$ satisfies the conclusion of Rolle's theorem.

4.6.15 The average rate of change of the temperature from 3.2 km to 6.1 km is $\frac{-10.3 - 8.0}{6.1 - 3.2} \approx -6.3°/\text{km}$. Based on this, we cannot conclude that the lapse rate exceeds the critical value of $7°/\text{km}$.

4.6.17

   a. The function f is differentiable on $[-1, 2]$ so the Mean Value Theorem applies.

   b. The average rate of change of f on $[-1, 2]$ is $\frac{f(2) - f(-1)}{2 - (-1)} = \frac{3 - 6}{3} = -1$. We wish to find a point c in $(-1, 2)$ such that $f'(c) = -1$, or equivalently $-2c = -1$ which gives $c = 1/2$.

   c.

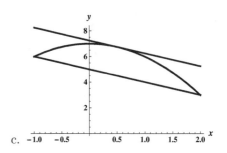

4.6.19

a. The function f is differentiable on $[0, \ln 4]$ so the Mean Value Theorem applies.

b. The average rate of change of f on $[0, \ln 4]$ is $\frac{f(\ln 4) - f(0)}{\ln 4 - 0} = \frac{4-1}{\ln 4} = \frac{3}{\ln 4}$. We wish to find a point c in $(0, \ln 4)$ such that $f'(c) = 3/\ln 4$, or equivalently $e^c = 3/\ln 4$ which gives $c = \ln\left(\frac{3}{\ln 4}\right)$.

c.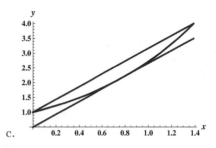

4.6.21

a. The function f is differentiable on $[0, 1/2]$ so the Mean Value Theorem applies.

b. The average rate of change of f on $[0, 1/2]$ is $\frac{f(1/2) - f(0)}{\frac{1}{2} - 0} = \frac{\frac{\pi}{6} - 0}{\frac{1}{2}} = \frac{\pi}{3}$.
We wish to find a point c in $(0, 1/2)$ such that $f'(c) = \pi/3$, or equivalently $\frac{1}{\sqrt{1-c^2}} = \frac{\pi}{3}$, so $c = \sqrt{1 - \frac{9}{\pi^2}}$.

c.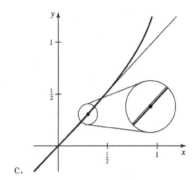

4.6.23

a. The Mean Value Theorem does not apply because the function f is not differentiable at $x = 0$.

b. Even though the Mean Value Theorem doesn't apply, it still happens to be the case that there are numbers c between -8 and 8 where the tangent line has slope $\frac{f(8) - f(-8)}{8 - (-8)} = \frac{1}{2}$. This occurs where $\frac{2}{3}c^{-2/3} = 1/2$, which gives $c = \pm\frac{8}{9} \cdot \sqrt{3}$.

c.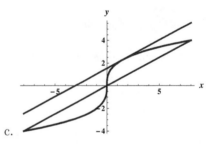

4.6.25

a. False. The function f is not differentiable at $x = 0$.

b. True. If $f(x) - g(x) = c$ is constant, then $f'(x) - g'(x) = 0$.

c. False. If $f'(x) = 0$ then we can conclude that $f(x) = c$ for some constant.

4.6.27 The functions $h(x)$ and $p(x)$ have the same derivative as $f(x)$ because they differ from $f(x)$ by a constant.

4.6.29 The secant line between the endpoints has slope $\frac{f(4) - f(-4)}{4 - (-4)} = \frac{4-1}{8} = \frac{3}{8}$.

The slope of the tangent line to the graph appears to have this value at approximately -2.5 and at about 2.6. These are eyeballed estimates, so your personal estimate may differ.

4.6.31 Because $f(1) \approx 2$ and $f(3) \approx 2$, the average rate of change of f on $[1, 3]$ is $\frac{f(3) - f(1)}{3 - 1} = 0$. However, the tangent to f between $x = 1$ and $x = 2$ is the graph of f itself, which has slope 2, and the tangent to f between $x = 2$ and $x = 3$ is also the graph of f, which has slope 1. So there is no point in $(1, 3)$ where the tangent line has slope 0. This does not contradict the Mean Value Theorem because f is not continuous everywhere on $[1, 3]$, nor differentiable everywhere on $(1, 3)$ both of these hypotheses fail at x = 2.

4.6.33 The average speed of the car over the 28 minute period ($= 28/60$ hr) is $\frac{30-0}{28/60} \approx 64.3$mi/hr, so the officer can conclude by the Mean Value Theorem that at some point the car exceeded the speed limit.

4.6.35 The runner's average speed is $6.2/(32/60) \approx 11.6$ mi /hr. By the Mean Value Theorem, the runner's speed was 11.6 mi/hr at least once. By the intermediate value theorem, all speeds between 0 and 11.6 mi/hr were reached. Because the initial and final speed was 0 mi/hr, the speed of 11 mi/hr was reached at least twice.

4.6.37 Observe that

$$\frac{f(b) - f(a)}{b - a} = \frac{A(b^2 - a^2) + B(b - a)}{b - a} = A(a + b) + B$$

and $f'(c) = 2Ac + B$, so the point c that satisfies the conclusion of the Mean Value Theorem is $c = (a+b)/2$.

4.6.39 Note that $f'(x) = 2\tan x \sec^2 x$ and $g'(x) = 2\sec x \sec x \tan x = 2\tan x \sec^2 x$, so $f'(x) = g'(x)$. This implies that $f - g$ is a constant, which also follows from the trigonometric identity $\sec^2 x = \tan^2 x + 1$.

4.6.41 Bolt's average speed during the race was $\frac{100}{9.58}$ m/s $= \frac{100}{9.58} \cdot \frac{3600}{1000}$ km/hr ≈ 37.58 km/hr, so by the Mean Value Theorem he must have exceeded 37 km/hr during the race.

4.6.43

a. If $g(x) = x$ then $g'(x) = 1$ and hence $\frac{f(b)-f(a)}{g(b)-g(a)} = \frac{f(b)-f(a)}{b-a} = \frac{f'(c)}{g'(c)} = f'(c)$.

b. We have $\frac{f(b)-f(a)}{g(b)-g(a)} = \frac{0-(-1)}{6-2} = \frac{1}{4}$; $\frac{f'(c)}{g'(c)} = \frac{2c}{4} = \frac{c}{2}$; so $c = 1/2$.

4.7   L'Hôpital's Rule

4.7.1 If $\lim\limits_{x\to a} f(x) = 0$ and $\lim\limits_{x\to a} g(x) = 0$, then we say $\lim\limits_{x\to a} f(x)/g(x)$ is of indeterminate form $0/0$.

4.7.3 Take the limit of the quotient of the derivatives of the numerator and denominator.

4.7.5 If $\lim\limits_{x\to a} f(x)g(x)$ has the form $0 \cdot \infty$, then $\lim\limits_{x\to a} \dfrac{f(x)}{1/g(x)}$ has the indeterminate form $0/0$ or ∞/∞.

4.7.7 If $\lim\limits_{x\to a} f(x) = 1$ and $\lim\limits_{x\to a} g(x) = \infty$, then $f(x)^{g(x)} \to 1^\infty$ as $x \to a$, which is meaningless; so direct substitution does not work.

4.7.9 This means $\lim\limits_{x\to\infty} \dfrac{g(x)}{f(x)} = 0$.

4.7.11 By Theorem 4.15, we have $\ln x, x^3, 2^x, x^x$ in order of increasing growth rates.

4.7.13 L'Hôpital's rule gives $\lim\limits_{x\to 2} \dfrac{x^2 - 2x}{8 - 6x + x^2} = \lim\limits_{x\to 2} \dfrac{2x - 2}{-6 + 2x} = \dfrac{2}{-2} = -1$.

4.7.15 L'Hôpital's rule gives $\lim\limits_{x\to 1} \dfrac{\ln x}{4x - x^2 - 3} = \lim\limits_{x\to 1} \dfrac{1/x}{4 - 2x} = \dfrac{1}{2}$.

4.7.17 L'Hôpital's rule gives $\lim\limits_{x\to e} \dfrac{\ln x - 1}{x - e} = \lim\limits_{x\to e} \dfrac{1/x}{1} = \dfrac{1}{e}$.

4.7.19 L'Hôpital's rule gives $\lim\limits_{x\to 0} \dfrac{3\sin 4x}{5x} = \lim\limits_{x\to 0} \dfrac{12\cos 4x}{5} = \dfrac{12}{5}$.

4.7.21 L'Hôpital's rule gives $\lim\limits_{u\to\pi/4} \dfrac{\tan u - \cot u}{u - \pi/4} = \lim\limits_{u\to\pi/4} \dfrac{\sec^2 u + \csc^2 u}{1} = 2 + 2 = 4$.

4.7.23 Apply l'Hôpital's rule twice: $\displaystyle\lim_{x\to 0}\frac{1-\cos 3x}{8x^2}=\lim_{x\to 0}\frac{3\sin 3x}{16x}=\lim_{x\to 0}\frac{9\cos 3x}{16}=\frac{9}{16}$.

4.7.25 Apply l'Hôpital's rule twice:

$$\lim_{x\to\pi}\frac{\cos x+1}{(x-\pi)^2}=\lim_{x\to\pi}\frac{-\sin x}{2(x-\pi)}=\lim_{x\to\pi}\frac{-\cos x}{2}=\frac{1}{2}.$$

4.7.27 Apply l'Hôpital's rule twice:

$$\lim_{x\to 0}\frac{e^x-\sin x-1}{x^4+8x^3+12x^2}=\lim_{x\to 0}\frac{e^x-\cos x}{4x^3+24x^2+24x}=\lim_{x\to 0}\frac{e^x+\sin x}{12x^2+48x+24}=\frac{1}{24}.$$

4.7.29 L'Hôpital's rule gives:

$$\lim_{x\to\infty}\frac{e^{1/x}-1}{1/x}=\lim_{x\to\infty}\frac{e^{1/x}(-1/x^2)}{(-1/x^2)}=\lim_{x\to\infty}e^{1/x}=1.$$

4.7.31 Apply l'Hôpital's rule twice:

$$\lim_{x\to -1}\frac{x^3-x^2-5x-3}{x^4+2x^3-x^2-4x-2}=\lim_{x\to -1}\frac{3x^2-2x-5}{4x^3+6x^2-2x-4}=\lim_{x\to -1}\frac{6x-2}{12x^2+12x-2}=4.$$

4.7.33 L'Hôpital's rule gives $\displaystyle\lim_{v\to 3}\frac{v-1-\sqrt{v^2-5}}{v-3}=\lim_{v\to 3}\frac{1-\dfrac{v}{\sqrt{v^2-5}}}{1}=-\frac{1}{2}$.

4.7.35 Apply l'Hôpital's rule twice:

$$\lim_{x\to 2}\frac{x^2-4x+4}{\sin^2\pi x}=\lim_{x\to 2}\frac{2x-4}{2\pi(\sin\pi x)(\cos\pi x)}=\lim_{x\to 2}\frac{2x-4}{\pi\sin 2\pi x}=\lim_{x\to 2}\frac{2}{2\pi^2\cos 2\pi x}=\frac{2}{2\pi^2}=\frac{1}{\pi^2}.$$

4.7.37 Apply l'Hôpital's rule three times:

$$\lim_{x\to\infty}\frac{3x^4-x^2}{6x^4+12}=\lim_{x\to\infty}\frac{12x^3-2x}{24x^3}=\lim_{x\to\infty}\frac{36x^2-2}{72x^2}=\lim_{x\to\infty}\frac{72x}{144x}=\frac{1}{2}.$$

4.7.39 Apply l'Hôpital's rule three times:

$$\lim_{x\to\pi/2^-}\frac{\tan x}{3/(2x-\pi)}=\lim_{x\to\pi/2^-}\frac{\sec^2 x}{-6/(2x-\pi)^2}=-(1/6)\lim_{x\to\pi/2^-}\frac{(2x-\pi)^2}{\cos^2 x}=(-1/6)\lim_{x\to\pi/2^-}\frac{4(2x-\pi)}{2\cos x(-\sin x)}=$$

$$(-1/6)\lim_{x\to\pi/2^-}\frac{8x-4\pi}{-\sin(2x)}=(-1/6)\lim_{x\to\pi/2^-}\frac{8}{-2\cos(2x)}=-\frac{2}{3}.$$

4.7.41 Applying l'Hôpital's rule twice gives:

$$\lim_{x\to\infty}\frac{\ln(3x+5)}{\ln(7x+3)+1}=\lim_{x\to\infty}\frac{3/(3x+5)}{7/(7x+3)}=\frac{3}{7}\lim_{x\to\infty}\frac{7x+3}{3x+5}=\frac{3}{7}\lim_{x\to\infty}\frac{7}{3}=1.$$

4.7.43 Applying l'Hôpital's rule twice gives:

$$\lim_{x\to\infty}\frac{x^2-\ln(2/x)}{3x^2+2x}=\lim_{x\to\infty}\frac{2x+(1/x)}{6x+2}=\lim_{x\to\infty}\frac{2-1/x^2}{6}=\frac{2}{6}=\frac{1}{3}.$$

4.7.45 L'Hôpital's rule gives $\displaystyle\lim_{x\to\infty}x\ln\left(1+\frac{1}{x}\right)=\lim_{x\to\infty}\frac{\ln\left(1+\frac{1}{x}\right)}{\frac{1}{x}}=\lim_{x\to\infty}\frac{1}{1+(1/x)}\cdot\frac{\frac{-1}{x^2}}{\frac{-1}{x^2}}=1$.

4.7.47 Observe that the given limit can be written $\displaystyle\lim_{x\to 0}\frac{\sin 7x}{\sin 6x}=\lim_{x\to 0}\frac{7\cos 7x}{6\cos 6x}=\frac{7}{6}$.

4.7.49 Observe that $\displaystyle\lim_{x\to(\pi/2)^-}\left(\frac{\pi}{2}-x\right)\sec x=\lim_{x\to(\pi/2)^-}\frac{\pi/2-x}{\cos x}=\lim_{x\to(\pi/2)^-}\frac{-1}{-\sin x}=1$ by l'Hôpital's rule.

4.7.51 Observe that $\displaystyle\lim_{x\to 0}\left(\cot x-\frac{1}{x}\right)=\lim_{x\to 0}\left(\frac{\cos x}{\sin x}-\frac{1}{x}\right)=\lim_{x\to 0}\frac{x\cos x-\sin x}{x\sin x}$. Apply l'Hôpital's rule twice:

$$\lim_{x\to 0}\frac{x\cos x-\sin x}{x\sin x}=\lim_{x\to 0}\frac{\cos x-x\sin x-\cos x}{\sin x+x\cos x}$$

$$=-\lim_{x\to 0}\frac{x\sin x}{\sin x+x\cos x}=-\lim_{x\to 0}\frac{\sin x+x\cos x}{\cos x+\cos x-x\sin x}=-\frac{0}{2}=0.$$

4.7.53 Observe that $\displaystyle\lim_{\theta\to(\pi/2)^-}(\tan\theta-\sec\theta)=\lim_{\theta\to(\pi/2)^-}\left(\frac{\sin\theta}{\cos\theta}-\frac{1}{\cos\theta}\right)=\lim_{\theta\to(\pi/2)^-}\frac{\sin\theta-1}{\cos\theta}$. By l'Hôpital's rule $\displaystyle\lim_{\theta\to(\pi/2)^-}\frac{\sin\theta-1}{\cos\theta}=\lim_{\theta\to(\pi/2)^-}\frac{\cos\theta}{-\sin\theta}=\frac{0}{-1}=0.$

4.7.55 Note that $\ln x^{2x}=2x\ln x$, so we evaluate $\displaystyle L=\lim_{x\to 0^+}2x\ln x=2\lim_{x\to 0^+}\frac{\ln x}{1/x}=2\lim_{x\to 0^+}\frac{1/x}{-1/x^2}=$ $2\displaystyle\lim_{x\to 0^+}(-x)=0$ by l'Hôpital's rule. Therefore $\displaystyle\lim_{x\to 0^+}x^{2x}=e^L=1.$

4.7.57 Note that $\ln(\tan\theta)^{\cos\theta}=\cos\theta\ln\tan\theta$, so we evaluate $\displaystyle L=\lim_{\theta\to\pi/2^-}\cos\theta\ln\tan\theta=\lim_{\theta\to\pi/2^-}\frac{\ln\tan\theta}{\sec\theta}$. L'Hôpital's rule gives $\displaystyle\lim_{\theta\to\pi/2^-}\frac{\ln\tan\theta}{\sec\theta}=\lim_{\theta\to\pi/2^-}\frac{\sec^2\theta/\tan\theta}{\sec\theta\tan\theta}=\lim_{\theta\to\pi/2^-}\frac{\sec\theta}{\tan^2\theta}=\lim_{\theta\to\pi/2^-}\frac{\cos\theta}{\sin^2\theta}=0$, so $\displaystyle\lim_{\theta\to\pi/2^-}(\tan\theta)^{\cos\theta}=e^L=1.$

4.7.59 Note that $\ln(1+x)^{\cot x}=\cot x\ln(1+x)$, so we evaluate $\displaystyle L=\lim_{x\to 0^+}\cot x\ln(1+x)=\lim_{x\to 0^+}\frac{\ln(1+x)}{\tan x}=$ $\displaystyle\lim_{x\to 0^+}\frac{1/(1+x)}{\sec^2 x}=\lim_{x\to 0^+}\frac{\cos^2 x}{1+x}=1$ by l'Hôpital's rule. Therefore $\displaystyle\lim_{x\to 0^+}(1+x)^{\cot x}=e^L=e.$

4.7.61 Note that $\ln(1+a/x)^x=x\ln(1+a/x)$, so we evaluate

$$L=\lim_{x\to\infty}x\ln(1+a/x)=\lim_{x\to\infty}\frac{\ln(1+a/x)}{1/x}=\lim_{x\to\infty}\frac{\frac{1}{1+a/x}\cdot\frac{-a}{x^2}}{\frac{-1}{x^2}}=\lim_{x\to\infty}\frac{a}{1+a/x}=a$$

by l'Hôpital's rule. Therefore $\displaystyle\lim_{x\to\infty}(1+a/x)^x=e^L=e^a.$

4.7.63 Note that $\ln(e^{ax}+x)^{1/x}=\frac{1}{x}\ln(e^{ax}+x)$, so we evaluate

$$L=\lim_{x\to 0}\frac{\ln(e^{ax}+x)}{x}=\lim_{x\to 0}\frac{(ae^{ax}+1)/(e^{ax}+x)}{1}=\frac{(a+1)/1}{1}=a+1.$$

Therefore, $\displaystyle\lim_{x\to 0}(e^{ax}+x)^{1/x}=e^{a+1}.$

4.7.65 Note that $\ln(\tan x)^x=x\ln\tan x$, so we evaluate

$$L=\lim_{x\to 0+}x\ln\tan x=\lim_{x\to 0+}\frac{\ln\tan x}{1/x}=\lim_{x\to 0+}\frac{\sec^2 x/\tan x}{-1/x^2}=-\lim_{x\to 0+}\frac{x^2}{\sin x\cos x}$$

by l'Hôpital's rule. Next, observe that $\displaystyle\lim_{x\to 0+}\frac{x^2}{\sin x\cos x}=\lim_{x\to 0+}\frac{x}{\sin x}\cdot\lim_{x\to 0+}\frac{x}{\cos x}=1\cdot 0=0$. Therefore $L=0$ and $\displaystyle\lim_{x\to 0+}(\tan x)^x=e^L=1.$

4.7.67 Note that $\ln(x + \cos x)^{1/x} = (\ln(x + \cos x))/x$, so we evaluate

$$L = \lim_{x \to 0} \frac{\ln(x + \cos x)}{x} = \lim_{x \to 0} \frac{(x + \cos x)^{-1}(1 - \sin x)}{1} = 1$$

by l'Hôpital's rule. Therefore $\lim_{x \to 0}(x + \cos x)^{1/x} = e^L = e$.

4.7.69 By Theorem 4.15, $e^{0.01x}$ grows faster than x^{10} as $x \to \infty$.

4.7.71 Note that $\ln x^{20} = 20 \ln x$, so $\ln x^{20}$ and $\ln x$ have comparable growth rates as $x \to \infty$.

4.7.73 By Theorem 4.15, x^x grows faster than 100^x as $x \to \infty$.

4.7.75 By Theorem 4.15, 1.00001^x grows faster than x^{20} as $x \to \infty$.

4.7.77 Observe that $\lim\limits_{x \to \infty} \dfrac{(x/2)^x}{x^x} = \lim\limits_{x \to \infty} 2^{-x} = 0$, so x^x grows faster than $(x/2)^x$ as $x \to \infty$.

4.7.79 Note that $\lim\limits_{x \to \infty} \dfrac{e^{x^2}}{e^{10x}} = \lim\limits_{x \to \infty} e^{x^2 - 10x} = \infty$, so e^{x^2} grows faster than e^{10x} as $x \to \infty$.

4.7.81

a. False; $\lim\limits_{x \to 2} x^2 - 1 = 3$, so l'Hôpital's rule does not apply. In fact, $\lim\limits_{x \to 2} \dfrac{x - 2}{x^2 - 1} = \dfrac{0}{3} = 0$.

b. False; l'Hôpital's rule does not say $\lim\limits_{x \to a} f(x)g(x) = \lim\limits_{x \to a} f'(x) \lim\limits_{x \to a} g'(x)$. In fact, $\lim\limits_{x \to 0} x \sin x = 0 \cdot 0 = 0$.

c. False; this limit has the form $0^\infty = 0$.

d. False; this limit has the indeterminate form 1^∞ which is not always 1.

e. True; $\ln x^{100} = 100 \ln x$.

f. True; note that $\lim\limits_{x \to \infty} \dfrac{e^x}{2^x} = \lim\limits_{x \to \infty} \left(\dfrac{e}{2}\right)^x = \infty$ because $e/2 > 1$.

4.7.83 Observe that $\lim\limits_{x \to \infty} \dfrac{2x^3 - x^2 + 1}{5x^3 + 2x} = \dfrac{2}{5}$ by Theorem 2.7. We can also use l'Hôpital's rule:

$$\lim_{x \to \infty} \frac{2x^3 - x^2 + 1}{5x^3 + 2x} = \lim_{x \to \infty} \frac{6x^2 - 2x}{15x^2 + 2} = \lim_{x \to \infty} \frac{12x - 2}{30x} = \lim_{x \to \infty} \frac{12}{30} = \frac{2}{5}.$$

4.7.85 By l'Hôpital's rule, $\lim\limits_{x \to 6} \dfrac{(5x + 2)^{1/5} - 2}{x^{-1} - 6^{-1}} = \lim\limits_{x \to 6} \dfrac{(5x + 2)^{-4/5}}{-x^{-2}} = -\dfrac{9}{4}$.

4.7.87 Observe that $(\sqrt{x - 2} - \sqrt{x - 4}) \cdot \frac{\sqrt{x-2}+\sqrt{x-4}}{\sqrt{x-2}+\sqrt{x-4}} = \frac{x-2-(x-4)}{\sqrt{x-2}+\sqrt{x-4}} = \frac{2}{\sqrt{x-2}+\sqrt{x-4}}$, so $\lim\limits_{x \to \infty} \sqrt{x - 2} -$ $\sqrt{x - 4} = \lim\limits_{x \to \infty} \dfrac{2}{\sqrt{x - 2} + \sqrt{x - 4}} = 0$.

4.7.89 Make the substitution $t = 1/x$; then $\lim\limits_{x \to \infty} x^3 \left(\dfrac{1}{x} - \sin \dfrac{1}{x}\right) = \lim\limits_{t \to 0+} \dfrac{t - \sin t}{t^3} = \lim\limits_{t \to 0+} \dfrac{1 - \cos t}{3t^2} =$ $\lim\limits_{t \to 0+} \dfrac{\sin t}{6t} = \lim\limits_{t \to 0+} \dfrac{\cos t}{6} = \dfrac{1}{6}$, using l'Hôpital's rule.

4.7.91 Observe that $\lim\limits_{x \to 1+} \left(\dfrac{1}{x - 1} - \dfrac{1}{\sqrt{x - 1}}\right) = \lim\limits_{x \to 1+} \dfrac{1 - \sqrt{x - 1}}{x - 1} = \infty$.

4.7.93 Note that $\log_2 x = \ln x / \ln 2$ and $\log_3 x = \ln x / \ln 3$; therefore $\lim\limits_{x \to \infty} \dfrac{\log_2 x}{\log_3 x} = \dfrac{\ln 3}{\ln 2}$.

4.7.95 Use the identity $1 + 2 + \cdots + n = \frac{n(n+1)}{2}$; then

$$\lim_{n\to\infty} \frac{1 + 2 + \cdots + n}{n^2} = \lim_{n\to\infty} \frac{n(n+1)}{2n^2} = \lim_{n\to\infty} \frac{n+1}{2n} = \frac{1}{2}.$$

4.7.97

$$\lim_{x\to1} \frac{x\ln x - x + 1}{x\ln^2 x} = \lim_{x\to1} \frac{\ln x + x \cdot \frac{1}{x} - 1}{\ln^2 x + 2x\ln x \cdot \frac{1}{x}} = \lim_{x\to1} \frac{\ln x}{\ln^2 x + 2\ln x} = \lim_{x\to1} \frac{1}{\ln x + 2} = \frac{1}{2},$$

where the first equality follows from l'Hôpital's rule and the penultimate follows by dividing the numerator and denominator by $\ln x$.

4.7.99 Let $z = \ln x^{\frac{1}{1+\ln x}}$. Then $z = \frac{\ln x}{1+\ln x}$, and $\displaystyle\lim_{x\to0^+} z = \lim_{x\to0^+} \frac{\ln x}{1 + \ln x} = \lim_{x\to0^+} \frac{1/x}{1/x} = \lim_{x\to0^+} 1 = 1$. Then $\displaystyle\lim_{x\to0^+} e^z = \lim_{x\to0^+} x^{\frac{1}{1+\ln x}} = e^1 = e$.

4.7.101 Let $z = \frac{1}{n}$. Then as $n \to \infty$ we have $z \to 0^+$. Then

$$\lim_{n\to\infty} n\cot(1/n) - n^2 = \lim_{z\to0^+} \frac{\cot z}{z} - \frac{1}{z^2}$$

$$= \lim_{z\to0^+} \frac{z\cos z - \sin z}{z^2 \sin z}$$

$$= \lim_{z\to0^+} \frac{\cos z - z\sin z - \cos z}{2z\sin z + z^2 \cos z}$$

$$= \lim_{z\to0^+} \frac{-\sin z}{2\sin z + z\cos z}$$

$$= \lim_{z\to0^+} \frac{-\cos z}{2\cos z + \cos z - z\sin z}$$

$$= -\frac{1}{2+1-0} = -\frac{1}{3},$$

where the third and fifth equalities follow from l'Hôpital's rule.

4.7.103

a. Approximately 3.43×10^{15}.

b. Approximately 3536.

c. We can explicitly solve for x in this case: $x^{x/100} = e^x \implies x^{1/100} = e \implies x = e^{100}$.

d. Approximately 163.

4.7.105 Note that $\ln(a^x - b^x)^x = x\ln(a^x - b^x)$, so we evaluate

$$L = \lim_{x\to0^+} x\ln(a^x - b^x) = \lim_{x\to0^+} \frac{\ln(a^x - b^x)}{1/x} = \lim_{x\to0^+} -x^2 \left(\frac{(\ln a)a^x - (\ln b)b^x}{a^x - b^x} \right)$$

by l'Hôpital's rule. We have $\displaystyle\lim_{x\to0^+} -x^2 \left(\frac{(\ln a)a^x - (\ln b)b^x}{a^x - b^x} \right) = -\lim_{x\to0^+} x\Big((\ln a)a^x - (\ln b)b^x\Big)\frac{x}{a^x - b^x}$ and one more application of l'Hôpital's rule gives $\displaystyle\lim_{x\to0^+} \frac{x}{a^x - b^x} = \lim_{x\to0^+} \frac{1}{(\ln a)a^x - (\ln b)b^x} = \frac{1}{\ln a - \ln b}$, so $L = 0$ and therefore $\displaystyle\lim_{x\to0^+} (a^x - b^x)^x = e^L = 1$.

4.7.107 Apply l'Hôpital's rule: $\displaystyle\lim_{x\to0} \frac{a^x - b^x}{x} = \lim_{x\to0} \frac{(\ln a)a^x - (\ln b)b^x}{1} = \ln a - \ln b$.

4.7.109

a. After each year the balance increases by the factor $1 + r$; therefore the balance after t years is $B(t) = P(1 + r)^t$.

b. Observe that

$$\lim_{m \to \infty} (1 + r/m)^m = \lim_{m \to \infty} \left(1 + \frac{1}{m/r}\right)^{(m/r)r} = e^r,$$

because $\lim_{n \to \infty} \left(1 + \frac{1}{n}\right)^n = e$. So with continuous compounding the balance after t years is $B(t) = Pe^{rt}$.

4.7.111 L'Hôpital's rule gives $\lim_{x \to \infty} \dfrac{\sqrt{ax + b}}{\sqrt{cx + d}} = \lim_{x \to \infty} \dfrac{a}{\sqrt{ax + b}} \cdot \dfrac{\sqrt{cx + d}}{c} = \dfrac{a}{c} \lim_{x \to \infty} \dfrac{\sqrt{cx + d}}{\sqrt{ax + b}}$, which is the same form as the original limit, so l'Hôpital's rule fails in this case. We can evaluate this limit as follows: first observe that $\lim_{x \to \infty} \dfrac{ax + b}{cx + d} = \dfrac{a}{c}$ by l'Hôpital's rule; therefore $\lim_{x \to \infty} \dfrac{\sqrt{ax + b}}{\sqrt{cx + d}} = \lim_{x \to \infty} \sqrt{\dfrac{ax + b}{cx + d}} = \sqrt{\dfrac{a}{c}}$.

4.7.113 Let $t = b^x$, as in Example 8; then $x = \ln t / \ln b$ and we have $\lim_{x \to \infty} \dfrac{x^p}{b^x} = \lim_{t \to \infty} \dfrac{\ln^p t}{t \ln^p b} = 0$, by Theorem 4.15.

4.7.115 Note that $\log_a x = \ln x / \ln a$, so $\dfrac{\log_a x}{\log_b x} = \dfrac{\ln b}{\ln a}$, and therefore $\log_a x$ and $\log_b x$ grow at a comparable rate as $x \to \infty$.

4.7.117 The triangle ABP has base $1 - \cos\theta$ and height $\sin\theta$, so its area is $f(\theta) = \frac{1}{2}\sin\theta(1 - \cos\theta)$. The sector OBP has area $\theta/2$, and the triangle OBP has base 1 and height $\sin\theta$; therefore $g(\theta) = \frac{1}{2}(\theta - \sin\theta)$. We have $\lim_{\theta \to 0} \dfrac{g(\theta)}{f(\theta)} = \lim_{\theta \to 0} \dfrac{\theta - \sin\theta}{\sin\theta(1 - \cos\theta)} = \lim_{\theta \to 0} \dfrac{\theta - \sin\theta}{\sin\theta - (1/2)\sin 2\theta}$. Three applications of l'Hôpital's rule gives $\lim_{\theta \to 0} \dfrac{g(\theta)}{f(\theta)} = \lim_{\theta \to 0} \dfrac{1 - \cos\theta}{\cos\theta - \cos 2\theta} = \lim_{\theta \to 0} \dfrac{\sin\theta}{2\sin 2\theta - \sin\theta} = \lim_{\theta \to 0} \dfrac{\cos\theta}{4\cos 2\theta - \cos\theta} = \dfrac{1}{3}$.

4.7.119 Note that $\ln\left(1 + \frac{a}{x}\right)^x = \dfrac{\ln(1 + a/x)}{1/x}$ so we evaluate $L = \lim_{x \to \infty} \dfrac{\ln(1 + a/x)}{1/x} = \lim_{x \to \infty} \dfrac{1}{1 + a/x} \cdot -\dfrac{a}{x^2} \cdot \dfrac{1}{-1/x^2} = \lim_{x \to \infty} \dfrac{a}{1 + a/x} = a$ by l'Hôpital's rule. Therefore $\lim_{x \to \infty} \left(1 + \dfrac{a}{x}\right)^x = e^L = e^a$.

4.7.121

a. Observe that $\lim_{x \to \infty} \dfrac{b^x}{e^x} = \lim_{x \to \infty} \left(\dfrac{b}{e}\right)^x$. This limit is ∞ exactly when $b > e$.

b. Observe that $\lim_{x \to \infty} \dfrac{e^{ax}}{e^x} = \lim_{x \to \infty} e^{(a-1)x}$. This limit is ∞ exactly when $a > 1$.

4.8 Newton's Method

4.8.1 Newton's method generates a sequence of x-intercepts of lines tangent to the graph of f to approximate the roots of f.

4.8.3 Generally, if two successive Newton approximations agree in their first p digits, then those approximations have p digits of accuracy. The method is terminated when the desired accuracy is reached.

4.8.5 Because $f'(x_n) = 2x_n$, we have

$$x_{n+1} = x_n - \frac{x_n^2 - 6}{2x_n} = \frac{2x_n^2 - x_n^2 + 6}{2x_n} = \frac{x_n^2 + 6}{2x_n}.$$

$x_1 = 2.5$ and $x_2 = 2.45$.

4.8.7 Because $f'(x_n) = -e^{-x_n} - 1$, we have

$$x_{n+1} = x_n - \frac{e^{-x_n} - x_n}{-e^{-x_n} - 1} = \frac{(-e^{-x_n} - 1)x_n - (e^{-x_n} - x_n)}{-e^{-x_n} - 1} = \frac{-e^{-x_n}x_n - e^{-x_n}}{-e^{-x_n} - 1} = \frac{x_n + 1}{e^{x_n} + 1}.$$

$x_1 = 0.564382$ and $x_2 = 0.567142$.

n	x_n
0	4.0
1	3.25
2	3.163462
3	3.162278
4	3.162278
5	3.162278
6	3.162278
7	3.162278
8	3.162278
9	3.162278
10	3.162278

4.8.9 Because $f'(x_n) = 2x_n$, we have
$x_{n+1} = x_n - \frac{x_n^2 - 10}{2x_n} = \frac{2x_n^2 - (x_n^2 - 10)}{2x_n} = \frac{x_n^2 + 10}{2x_n}.$

n	x_n
0	1.5
1	0.101436
2	0.501114
3	0.510961
4	0.510973
5	0.510973
6	0.510973
7	0.510973
8	0.510973
9	0.510973
10	0.510973

4.8.11 Because $f'(x_n) = \cos(x_n) + 1$, we have
$$x_{n+1} = x_n - \frac{\sin x_n + x_n - 1}{\cos x_n + 1}.$$

n	x_n
0	1.5
1	1.44389
2	1.36198
3	1.26818
4	1.19618
5	1.16857
6	1.16559
7	1.16556
8	1.16556
9	1.16556
10	1.16556

Because $f'(x_n) = \sec^2(x_n) - 2$, we have

4.8.13
$$x_{n+1} = x_n - \frac{\tan x_n - 2x_n}{\sec^2(x_n) - 2}.$$

4.8.15 A preliminary sketch of the two curves seems to indicate that they intersect once near $x = 2$.
Let $f(x) = \sin x - x/2$. Then $f'(x_n) = \cos x_n - 1/2$. The Newton's method formula becomes

$$x_{n+1} = x_n - \frac{\sin x_n - x_n/2}{\cos x_n - 1/2}.$$

If we use an initial estimate of $x_0 = 2$, we obtain $x_1 = 1.901$, $x_2 = 1.89551$, $x_3 = 1.89549$ and $x_4 = 1.89549$, so the point of intersection appears to be at approximately $x = 1.89549$.

4.8.17 A preliminary sketch of the two curves seems to indicate that they intersect three times, once between -2.5 and -2, once between 0 and $1/2$, and once between 1.5 and 2.
Let $f(x) = 4 - x^2 - 1/x$. Then $f'(x_n) = -2x_n + (1/x_n^2)$. The Newton's method formula becomes

$$x_{n+1} = x_n - \frac{4 - x_n^2 - (1/x_n)}{-2x_n + (1/x_n^2)}.$$

If we use an initial estimate of $x_0 = -2.25$, we obtain $x_1 = -2.11843$, $x_2 = -2.11491$, $x_3 = -2.11491$, so there appears to be a point of intersection near $x = -2.115$.
If we use an initial estimate of $x_0 = .25$, we obtain $x_1 = .254032$, $x_2 = .254102$, so there appears to be a point of intersection near $x = .254$.
If we use an initial estimate of $x_0 = 1.75$, we obtain $x_1 = 1.86535$, $x_2 = 1.86081$, so there appears to be another point of intersection near $x = 1.86$.

4.8.19 A preliminary sketch of the two curves seems to indicate that they intersect twice, once just to the right of 0, and once between 2 and 2.5.
Let $f(x) = 4\sqrt{x} - (x^2 + 1)$. Then $f'(x_n) = 2/\sqrt{x_n} - 2x_n$. The Newton's method formula becomes

$$x_{n+1} = x_n - \frac{4\sqrt{x_n} - (x_n^2 + 1)}{2/\sqrt{x_n} - 2x_n}.$$

If we use an initial estimate of $x_0 = .1$, we obtain $x_1 = .0583788$, $x_2 = .0629053$, $x_3 = .0629971$, so there appears to be a point of intersection near $x = .06299$.
If we use an initial estimate of $x_0 = 2.25$, we obtain $x_1 = 2.23026$, $x_2 = 2.23012$, $x_3 = 2.23012$, so there appears to be a point of intersection near $x = 2.23012$.

4.8.21 $f'(x) = \frac{-x \sin x - \cos x}{x^2}$, which is zero when $x \sin x + \cos x = 0$. Note that $f'(1) < 0$ and $f'(\pi) > 0$, so there must be a local minimum on the interval $(1, \pi)$. Let $g(x) = x \sin x + \cos x$. Then $g'(x_n) = \sin x_n + x_n \cos x_n - \sin x_n = x_n \cos x_n$, and the Newton's method formula becomes

$$x_{n+1} = x_n - \frac{x_n \sin x_n + \cos x_n}{x_n \cos x_n}.$$

If we use an initial estimate of $x_0 = 2.5$, we obtain $x_1 = 2.84702$, $x_2 = 2.79918$, $x_3 = 2.79839$, $x_4 = 2.79839$, so the smallest local minimum of f on $(0, \infty)$ occurs at approximately 2.79839.

4.8.23 $f'(x) = 9x^4 - 30x^3 + 7x^2 + 60x$ and $f''(x) = 36x^3 - 90x^2 + 14x + 60 = 2(18x^3 - 45x^2 + 7x + 30)$. We are seeking roots of $f''(x)$. If we apply Newton's method to f'' we obtain the recursion

$$x_{n+1} = x_n - \frac{36x_n^3 - 90x_n^2 + 14x_n + 60}{108x_n^2 - 180x_n + 14}.$$

Starting with an initial estimate of $x_0 = 1$, we obtain $x_1 = 1.34483$, $x_2 = 1.45527$, $x_3 = 1.49284$, $x_4 = 1.49974$, and $x_5 \approx 1.5$. We check directly that 1.5 is a root of f'', so $2x - 3$ is a factor of f'', and using long division, we see that $f''(x) = 2(2x - 3)(9x^2 - 9x - 10) = 2(2x - 3)(3x + 2)(3x - 5)$. So the potential inflection points of f are located at $x = -2/3$, $x = 3/2$, and $x = 5/3$. A check of the sign of f'' on the various intervals confirms that these are all the locations of inflection points.

4.8.25 The recursion for $f(x)$ is $x_{n+1} = x_n - \frac{(x_n - 1)^2}{2x_n - 2} = \frac{2x_n^2 - 2x_n - (x_n^2 - 2x_n + 1)}{2x_n - 2} = \frac{x_n^2 - 1}{2(x_n - 1)} = \frac{x_n + 1}{2}$.

The recursion for $g(x)$ is $y_{n+1} = y_n - \frac{y_n^2 - 1}{2y_n} = \frac{2y_n^2 - (y_n^2 - 1)}{2y_n} = \frac{y_n^2 + 1}{2y_n}$. The comparison below shows that Newton's method converges much faster for $g(x) = x^2 - 1$. This is because it is steeper near the root $x = 1$ – the value of $g'(1) = 2$, while $f'(1) = 0$. The flatness of f near 1 causes slow convergence.

n	x_n
0	2
1	1.5
2	1.25
3	1.125
4	1.0625
5	1.03125
6	1.01563
7	1.00781
8	1.00391
9	1.00195
10	1.00098

n	y_n
0	2
1	1.25
2	1.025
3	1.0003
4	≈ 1

4.8.27

a. True.

b. False. The quadratic formula gives exact values.

c. False. It sometime fails depending on factors such as the shape of the curve and the closeness of the initial estimate.

4.8.29 Let $g(x) = x^3/10 + 1 - x$. Fixed points of f are roots of g. The Newton's method recursion for g is given by

$$x_{n+1} = x_n - \frac{x_n^3/10 + 1 - x_n}{3x_n^2/10 - 1} = x_n - \frac{x_n^3 + 10 - 10x_n}{3x_n^2 - 10} = \frac{2(x_n^3 - 5)}{3x_n^2 - 10}.$$

A preliminary sketch of g indicates that there are three roots, near -3.5, 1, and 2.5.

n	x_n
0	-3.5
1	-3.57944
2	-3.57709
3	-3.57709

n	x_n
0	1
1	1.14286
2	1.1534
3	1.15347
4	1.15347

n	x_n
0	2.5
1	2.42857
2	2.42365
3	2.42362
4	2.42362

The fixed points of f are approximately -3.57709, 1.15347, and 2.42362.

4.8.31 Let $g(x) = 2x \cos x - x$. Fixed points of f are roots of g. Clearly $x = 0$ is a root of g. The Newton's method recursion for g is given by

$$x_{n+1} = x_n - \frac{2x_n \cos x_n - x_n}{2\cos x_n - 2x \sin x_n - 1}.$$

A preliminary sketch of g indicates that there is only one nonzero root on $[0, 2]$, near $x = 1$. We have:

n	x_n
0	1
1	1.0503
2	1.04721
3	1.0472
4	1.0472

The fixed points are 0 and approximately 1.0472.

4.8.33 A preliminary sketch of f indicates that there are two roots, near $x = -0.4$. and $x = 1.3$
The Newton's method recursion for f is given by

$$x_{n+1} = x_n - \frac{\cos(2x_n) - x_n^2 + 2x_n}{-2\sin(2x_n) - 2x_n + 2}.$$

We have:

n	x_n
0	-0.4
1	-0.337825
2	-0.335412
3	-0.335408
4	-0.335408

n	x_n
0	1.3
1	1.33256
2	1.33306
3	1.33306

The roots are approximately -0.335408 and 1.33306.

4.8.35 A preliminary sketch of f indicates that there is one root, near $x = 0.2$
The Newton's method recursion for f is given by

$$x_{n+1} = x_n - \frac{e^{-x_n} - (x_n + 4)/5}{-e^{-x_n} - 1/5}.$$

We have:

n	x_n
0	0.2
1	0.179122
2	0.179295
3	0.179295

The root is approximately 0.179295.

4.8.37 A preliminary sketch of f indicates that there are two roots, near $x = .5$ and near $x = 3$. The Newton's method recursion for f is given by

$$x_{n+1} = x_n - \frac{\ln x_n - x_n^2 + 3x_n - 1}{(1/x_n) - 2x_n + 3}.$$

We have:

n	x_n
0	.5
1	.610787
2	.620655
3	.620723
4	.620723

n	x_n
0	3
1	3.03698
2	3.03645
3	3.03645

The roots are approximately .620723 and 3.03645.

4.8.39 Because the residuals become small quickly, the convergence of x_n is quite slow. This is related to the extreme flatness of the graph of x^{10} between 0 and 1/2.

n	x_n	Error	Residual
0	.5	.5	.000976563
1	.45	.45	.000340506
2	.405	.405	.000118727
3	.3645	.3645	.0000413976
4	.32805	.32805	.0000144345
5	.295245	.295245	5.03298×10^{-6}
6	.265721	.265721	1.75489×10^{-6}
7	.239148	.239148	6.11893×10^{-7}
8	.215234	.215234	2.13354×10^{-7}
9	.19371	.19371	7.43919×10^{-8}
10	.174339	.174339	2.59389×10^{-8}

4.8.41 The graphs of $y = x$ together ith $y = e^{x/a}$ for $a = 1$, $a = 3$, and a such that there is precisely one point of intersection are shown below:

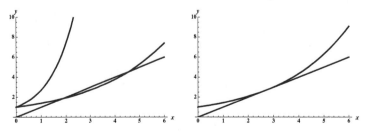

We want to find a point (b, b) on the graph of $y = e^{x/a}$. where the slope is 1. Hence we need $b = e^{b/a}$ and $1 = \frac{1}{a}e^{b/a}$. Dividing these equations gives $b = a$ and thus $a = e^{a/a} = e$.

4.8.43

a. The Newton's method formula would be:

$$x_{n+1} = x_n - \frac{1/x_n - a}{-1/x_n^2} = x_n + x_n - ax_n^2 = 2x_n - ax_n^2 = (2 - ax_n)x_n.$$

b. The approximation to $1/7$ is .14285714.

n	x_n
0	.1
1	.13
2	.1417
3	.14284777
4	.14285714
5	.14285714

4.8.45

a. We are seeking the time t when first $y(t) = 2.5e^{-t}\cos 2t$ is zero. This occurs first for $t = \pi/4$.

b. We are seeking the minimum value for y. We have $y'(t) = -2.5e^{-t}\cos 2t + 2.5e^{-t}(-2\sin 2t) = -2.5e^{-t}(\cos 2t + 2\sin 2t)$. This is zero when $\cos 2t = -2\sin 2t$, or $\tan 2t = \frac{-1}{2}$. Let $f(t) = \tan 2t + \frac{1}{2}$. If we apply Newton's method to $f(t)$ with a starting point of $t_0 = 1$, we obtain a root of 1.33897 after five iterations. An application of the First Derivative Test shows that there is a local minimum for y at this number. The displacement at this time is -0.586107. This local minimum is in fact an absolute minimum.

c. The second time that $y(t) = 2.5e^{-t}\cos 2t$ is zero is when $2t = \frac{3\pi}{2}$, or $t = 3\pi/4$.

d. Following our work in part b, we look for a root of $f(t) = \tan 2t + \frac{1}{2}$ that is bigger than 1.33897. From the graph, we are looking near $t = 3$. Applying Newton's method to $f(t)$ with an initial value of $x_0 = 3$ gives a root 2.90977 after three iterations. Applying the First Derivative Test, we see that there is a local maximum of 0.12181 at $x = 2.90977$.

4.8.47 Let $f(\lambda) = \tan(\pi\lambda) - \lambda$. We are looking for the first three positive roots of f. A preliminary sketch indicates that they are located near 1.4, 2.4, and 3.4. The Newton's method recursion is given by

$$x_{n+1} = x_n - \frac{\tan(\pi x_n) - x_n}{\pi\sec^2(\pi x_n) - 1}.$$

We obtain the following results:

n	x_n
0	1.4
1	1.34741
2	1.30555
3	1.29121
4	1.29012
5	1.29011
6	1.29011

n	x_n
0	2.4
1	2.37876
2	2.37331
3	2.37305
4	2.37305

n	x_n
0	3.4
1	3.4101
2	3.40919
3	3.40918
4	3.40918

The first three positive eigenvalues are approximately 1.29011, 2.37305, and 3.40918.

4.8.49 This problem can be solved (approximately) by setting up a computer or calculator program to run Newton's method, and then experimenting with different starting values. If this is done, it can be seen that any initial estimate between -4 and the local maximum at approximately -1.53 converges to the root at -2. Initial values between approximately -1.52 and -1.486 converge to the root at 3, while starting values between -1.485 and -1.475 converge to the root at -2. From -1.474 to approximately $.841$, starting values lead to convergence to the root at -1, while from $.842$ to $.846$ they lead to convergence to the root at -2. From about $.847$ to $.862$ they lead to convergence to the root at 3, while from $.863$ to the local minimum at 1.528 they lead to convergence to the root at -2. From about 1.528 to 4, the convergence is to the root at 3. Thus the approximate basis of convergence for -2 is $[-4, -1.53] \cup [-1.485, -1.475] \cup [.842, .846]$. For -1 the approximate basis of convergence is $[-1.474, .841]$, and for 3, it is $[-1.52, -1.486] \cup [.847, .862] \cup [1.53, 4]$.

4.9   Antiderivatives

4.9.1 Derivative, antiderivative.

4.9.3 $x + C$, where C is any constant.

4.9.5 $\dfrac{x^{p+1}}{p+1} + C$, where C is any real number and $p \neq -1$.

4.9.7 $\ln|x| + C$, where C is any constant.

4.9.9 Observe that $F(-1) = 4 + C = 4$, so $C = 0$.

4.9.11 The antiderivatives of $5x^4$ are $x^5 + C$. Check: $\frac{d}{dx}(x^5 + C) = 5x^4$.

4.9.13 The antiderivatives of $\sin 2x$ are $-(1/2)\cos 2x + C$. Check: $\frac{d}{dx}(-\frac{1}{2}\cos 2x + C) = \sin 2x$.

4.9.15 The antiderivatives of $3\sec^2 x$ are $3\tan x + C$. Check: $\frac{d}{dx}(3\tan x + C) = 3\sec^2 x$.

4.9.17 The antiderivatives of $-2/y^3 = -2y^{-3}$ are $y^{-2} + C$. Check: $\frac{d}{dy}(y^{-2} + C) = -2y^{-3}$.

4.9.19 The antiderivatives of e^x are $e^x + C$. Check: $\frac{d}{dx}(e^x + C) = e^x$.

4.9.21 The antiderivatives of $\frac{1}{s^2+1}$ are $\tan^{-1}s + C$. Check: $\frac{d}{ds}(\tan^{-1}(s) + C) = \frac{1}{s^2+1}$.

4.9.23 $\int (3x^5 - 5x^9)\, dx = 3 \cdot \frac{x^6}{6} - 5 \cdot \frac{x^{10}}{10} + C = \frac{1}{2}x^6 - \frac{1}{2}x^{10} + C$. Check: $\frac{d}{dx}(\frac{1}{2}x^6 - \frac{1}{2}x^{10} + C) = 3x^5 - 5x^9$.

4.9.25 $\int \left(4\sqrt{x} - \frac{4}{\sqrt{x}}\right) dx = \int (4x^{1/2} - 4x^{-1/2})\, dx = 4 \cdot \frac{x^{3/2}}{3/2} - 4 \cdot \frac{x^{1/2}}{1/2} + C = \frac{8}{3}x^{3/2} - 8x^{1/2} + C$. Check: $\frac{d}{dx}(\frac{8}{3}x^{3/2} - 8x^{1/2} + C) = 4\sqrt{x} - \frac{4}{\sqrt{x}}$.

4.9.27 Note that $\frac{d}{ds}(5s + 3)^3 = 15(5s + 3)^2$; therefore $\int (5s + 3)^2\, ds = \frac{(5s+3)^3}{15} + C$.

4.9.29 $\int (3x^{1/3} + 4x^{-1/3} + 6)\, dx = 3 \cdot \frac{3}{4}x^{4/3} + 4 \cdot \frac{3}{2}x^{2/3} + 6x + C = \frac{9}{4}x^{4/3} + 6x^{2/3} + 6x + C$. Check: $\frac{d}{dx}(\frac{9}{4}x^{4/3} + 6x^{2/3} + 6x + C) = 3x^{1/3} + 4x^{-1/3} + 6$.

4.9.31 $\int (3x + 1)(4 - x)\, dx = \int (12x - 3x^2 + 4 - x)\, dx = \int (-3x^2 + 11x + 4)\, dx = -x^3 + \frac{11}{2}x^2 + 4x + C$. Check: $\frac{d}{dx}\left(\frac{9}{2}x^{4/3} + C\right) = 6\sqrt[3]{x}$.

4.9.33 $\int (3x^{-4} + 2 - 3x^{-2})\, dx = -x^{-3} + 2x + 3x^{-1} + C$. Check: $\frac{d}{dx}\left(-x^{-3} + 2x + 3x^{-1} + C\right) = 3x^{-4} + 2 - 3x^{-2}$.

4.9.35 $\int \frac{4x^4 - 6x^2}{x}\, dx = \int \left(\frac{4x^4}{x} - \frac{6x^2}{x}\right) dx = \int (4x^3 - 6x)\, dx = x^4 - 3x^2 + C$. Check: $\frac{d}{dx}\left(x^4 - 3x^2 + C\right) = 4x^3 - 6x$.

4.9.37 Using Table 4.9 (formulas 1 and 2), $\int (\sin 2y + \cos 3y)\, dy = -\frac{1}{2} \cos 2y + \frac{1}{3} \sin 3y + C$.
Check: $\frac{d}{dy} \left(-\frac{1}{2} \cos 2y + \frac{1}{3} \sin 3y + C \right) = \sin 2y + \cos 3y$.

4.9.39 Using Table 4.9 (formula 3), $\int (\sec^2 x - 1)\, dx = \tan x - x + C$. Check: $\frac{d}{dx}(\tan x - x + C) = \sec^2 x - 1$.

4.9.41 Using Table 4.9 (formulas 3 and 5), $\int (\sec^2 \theta + \sec \theta \tan \theta)\, d\theta = \tan \theta + \sec \theta + C$. Check: $\frac{d}{d\theta}(\tan \theta + \sec \theta + C) = \sec^2 \theta + \sec \theta \tan \theta$.

4.9.43 $\int (3t^2 + \sec^2 2t)\, dt = t^3 + (1/2) \tan 2t + C$.

4.9.45 $\int \sec 4\theta \tan 4\theta\, d\theta = \frac{1}{4} \sec 4\theta + C$. Check: $\frac{d}{d\theta}(\frac{1}{4} \sec 4\theta + C) = \frac{1}{4}(4 \sec 4\theta \tan 4\theta) = \sec 4\theta \tan 4\theta$.

4.9.47 $\int \frac{1}{2y}\, dy = \frac{1}{2} \int y^{-1}\, dy = \frac{1}{2} \ln |y| + C$. Check: $\frac{d}{dy}(\frac{1}{2} \ln |y| + C) = \frac{1}{2y}$.

4.9.49 Using Table 4.10 (formula 10, $a = 5$), $\int \frac{6}{\sqrt{25 - x^2}}\, dx = 6 \sin^{-1} \left(\frac{x}{5} \right) + C$. Check: $\frac{d}{dx}(6 \sin^{-1} \left(\frac{x}{5} \right) + C) = \frac{6}{\sqrt{1 - (x^2/25)}} \cdot \frac{1}{5} = \frac{6}{\sqrt{25 - x^2}}$.

4.9.51 Using Table 4.10 (formula 12, $a = 10$), $\int \frac{1}{x\sqrt{x^2 - 100}}\, dx = \frac{1}{10} \sec^{-1} \left| \frac{x}{10} \right| + C$. Check: $\frac{d}{dx}(\frac{1}{10} \sec^{-1} \left| \frac{x}{10} \right| + C) = \frac{1}{10} \cdot \frac{1}{(x/10) \cdot \sqrt{(x^2/100) - 1}} \cdot \frac{1}{10} = \frac{1}{x\sqrt{x^2 - 100}}$.

4.9.53 Using Table 4.10 (formula 12, $a = 5$), $\int \frac{1}{x\sqrt{x^2 - 25}}\, dx = \frac{1}{5} \sec^{-1} \left| \frac{x}{5} \right| + C$. Check: $\frac{d}{dx} \left(\sec^{-1} \left| \frac{x}{5} \right| + C \right) = \frac{1}{5} \cdot \frac{5}{x\sqrt{x^2 - 25}} = \frac{1}{x\sqrt{x^2 - 25}}$.

4.9.55 $\int \frac{t+1}{t}\, dt = \int \left(\frac{t}{t} + \frac{1}{t} \right)\, dt = \int \left(1 + \frac{1}{t} \right)\, dt = t + \ln |t| + C$. Check: $\frac{d}{dt}(t + \ln |t| + C) = 1 + \frac{1}{t} = \frac{t+1}{t}$.

4.9.57 $\int e^{x+2}\, dx = \int e^2 e^x\, dx = e^2 \int e^x\, dx = e^2 e^x + C = e^{x+2} + C$. Check $\frac{d}{dx}(e^{x+2} + C) = e^{x+2}$.

4.9.59 We have $F(x) = \int (x^5 - 2x^{-2} + 1)\, dx = \frac{x^6}{6} + 2x^{-1} + x + C$; substituting $F(1) = 0$ gives $\frac{1}{6} + 2 + 1 + C = 0$, so $C = -\frac{19}{6}$, and thus $F(x) = \frac{x^6}{6} + \frac{2}{x} + x - \frac{19}{6}$.

4.9.61 We have $F(v) = \int \sec v \tan v\, dv = \sec v + C$; substituting $F(0) = 2$ gives $\sec 0 + C = 1 + C = 2$, so $C = 1$, and thus $F(v) = \sec v + 1$.

4.9.63 We have $F(x) = \int (8x^3 - 2x^{-2})\, dx = 2x^4 + 2x^{-1} + C$; substituting $F(1) = 5$ gives $2 + 2 + C = 5$, so $C = 1$, and thus $F(x) = 2x^4 + 2x^{-1} + 1$.

4.9.65 We have $F(y) = \int \frac{3y^3 + 5}{y}\, dy = \int \left(\frac{3y^3}{y} + \frac{5}{y} \right)\, dy = \int \left(3y^2 + \frac{5}{y} \right)\, dy = y^3 + 5 \ln |y| + C$; substituting $F(1) = 3$ gives $1 + 0 + C = 3$, so $C = 2$, and thus $F(y) = y^3 + 5 \ln |y| + 2$.

4.9.67 We have $f(x) = \int (2x - 3)\, dx = x^2 - 3x + C$; substituting $f(0) = 4$ gives $C = 4$, so $f(x) = x^2 - 3x + 4$.

4.9.69 We have $g(x) = \int 7x \left(x^6 - \frac{1}{7} \right)\, dx = \int (7x^7 - x)\, dx = \frac{7}{8}x^8 - \frac{x^2}{2} + C$; substituting $g(1) = 2$ gives $\frac{7}{8} - \frac{1}{2} + C = 2$, so $C = \frac{13}{8}$, and thus $g(x) = \frac{7}{8}x^8 - \frac{x^2}{2} + \frac{13}{8}$.

4.9.71 We have $f(u) = \int 4(\cos u - \sin 2u)\, du = 4(\sin u + \frac{1}{2} \cos 2u) + C = 4 \sin u + 2 \cos 2u + C$; substituting $f(\pi/6) = 0$ gives $4 \sin \frac{\pi}{6} + 2 \cos \frac{\pi}{3} + C = 2 + 1 + C = 0$, so $C = -3$, and thus $f(u) = 4 \sin u + 2 \cos 2u - 3$.

4.9.73 We have $y(t) = \int \left(\frac{3}{t} + 6 \right)\, dt = 3 \ln |t| + 6t + C$; substituting $y(1) = 8$ gives $0 + 6 + C = 8$, so $C = 2$, and thus $y(t) = 3 \ln |t| + 6t + 2$.

4.9.75 We have $y(\theta) = \int \frac{\sqrt{2} \cos^3 \theta + 1}{\cos^2 \theta}\, d\theta = \int \left(\frac{\sqrt{2} \cos^3 \theta}{\cos^2 \theta} + \frac{1}{\cos^2 \theta} \right)\, d\theta = \int \left(\sqrt{2} \cos \theta + \sec^2 \theta \right)\, d\theta = \sqrt{2} \sin \theta + \tan \theta + C$; substituting $y(\pi/4) = 3$ gives $1 + 1 + C = 3$, so $C = 1$, and thus $y(\theta) = \sqrt{2} \sin \theta + \tan \theta + 1$.

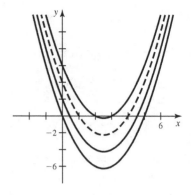

4.9.77   We have $f(x) = \int (2x - 5)\, dx = x^2 - 5x + C$; substituting $f(0) = 4$ gives $C = 4$, so $f(x) = x^2 - 5x + 4$.

4.9.79   We have $f(x) = \int (3x + \sin \pi x)\, dx = \frac{3x^2}{2} - \frac{\cos \pi x}{\pi} + C$; substituting $f(2) = 3$ gives $6 - \frac{\cos 2\pi}{\pi} + C = 6 - \frac{1}{\pi} + C = 3$, so $C = \frac{1}{\pi} - 3$, and thus $f(x) = \frac{3x^2}{2} - \frac{\cos \pi x}{\pi} + \frac{1 - 3\pi}{\pi}$.

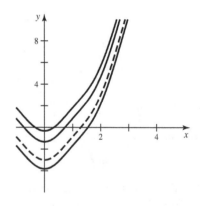

4.9.81   We have $f(t) = \int \frac{1}{t}\, dt = \ln t + C$; substituting $f(1) = 4$ gives $C = 4$, so $f(t) = \ln t + 4$.

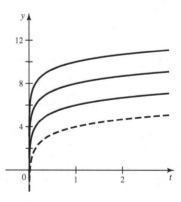

4.9.83 We have $s(t) = \int (2t + 4)\,dt = t^2 + 4t + C$; substituting $s(0) = 0$ gives $C = 0$, so $s(t) = t^2 + 4t$.

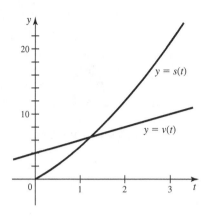

4.9.85 We have $s(t) = \int 2\sqrt{t}\,dt = 2 \cdot \frac{2}{3}t^{3/2} + C = \frac{4}{3}t^{3/2} + C$; substituting $s(0) = 1$ gives $C = 1$, so $s(t) = \frac{4}{3}t^{3/2} + 1$.

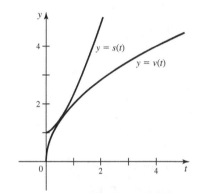

4.9.87 We have $s(t) = \int (6t^2 + 4t - 10)\,dt = 2t^3 + 2t^2 - 10t + C$; substituting $s(0) = 0$ gives $C = 0$, so $s(t) = 2t^3 + 2t^2 - 10t$.

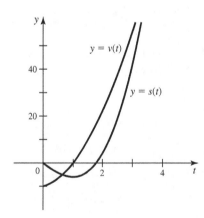

4.9.89 $v(t) = \int a(t)\,dt = \int -32\,dt = -32t + C_1$. Because $v(0) = 20$, we have $0 + C_1 = 20$, so $v(t) = -32t + 20$.
$s(t) = \int v(t)\,dt = \int (-32t + 20)\,dt = -16t^2 + 20t + C_2$. Because $s(0) = 0$, we have $C_2 = 0$, and thus $s(t) = -16t^2 + 20t$.

4.9.91 $v(t) = \int a(t)\,dt = \int .2t\,dt = .1t^2 + C_1$. Because $v(0) = 0$, we have $C_1 = 0$.
$s(t) = \int v(t)\,dt = \int .1t^2\,dt = \frac{1}{30}t^3 + C_2$. Because $s(0) = 1$, we have $C_2 = 1$, and thus $s(t) = \frac{1}{30}t^3 + 1$.

4.9.93 $v(t) = \int a(t)\,dt = \int 3\sin 2t\,dt = (-3/2)\cos 2t + C_1$. Because $v(0) = 1$, we have $-3/2 + C_1 = 1$, so $C_1 = 5/2$.
$s(t) = \int v(t)\,dt = \int [(-3/2)\cos 2t + 5/2]\,dt = (-3/4)\sin 2t + (5/2)t + C_2$. Because $s(0) = 10$, we have $C_2 = 10$, so $s(t) = (-3/4)\sin 2t + (5/2)t + 10$.

4.9.95 Runner A has position function $s(y) = \int \sin t\, dt = -\cos t + C$; the initial condition $s(0) = 0$ gives $C = 1$, so $s(t) = 1 - \cos t$. Runner B has position function $S(t) = \int \cos t\, dt = \sin t + C$; the initial condition $S(0) = 0$ gives $C = 0$, so $S(t) = \sin t$. The smallest $t > 0$ where $s(t) = S(t)$ is $t = \pi/2$ s.

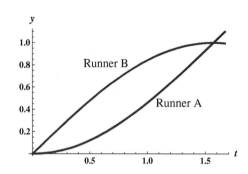

4.9.97

a. We have $v(t) = -9.8t + v_0$ and $v_0 = 30$, so $v(t) = -9.8t + 30$.

b. The height of the softball above ground is given by $s(t) = \int(-9.8t + 30)\, dt = -4.9t^2 + 30t + s_0 = -4.9t^2 + 30t$.

c. The ball reaches its maximum height when $v(t) = -9.8t + 30 = 0$, which gives $t = 30/9.8 \approx 3.06$ s; the maximum height is $s(30/9.8) \approx 45.92$ m.

d. The ball strikes the ground when $s(t) = 0$ (and $t > 0$), which gives $t(30 - 4.9t) = 0$, so $t = 30/4.9 \approx 6.12$ s.

4.9.99

a. We have $v(t) = -9.8t + v_0$ and $v_0 = 10$, so $v(t) = -9.8t + 10$.

b. The height of the payload above ground is given by $s(t) = \int(-9.8t + 10)\, dt = -4.9t^2 + 10t + s_0 = -4.9t^2 + 10t + 400$.

c. The payload reaches its maximum height when $v(t) = -9.8t + 10 = 0$, which gives $t = 10/9.8 \approx 1.02$ s; the maximum height is $s(10/9.8) \approx 405.10$ m.

d. The payload strikes the ground when $s(t) = 0$ (and $t > 0$), which gives $-4.9t^2 + 10t + 400 = 0$, so $t \approx 10.11$ s.

4.9.101

a. True, because $F'(x) = G'(x)$.

b. False; f is the derivative of F.

c. True; $\int f(x)\, dx$ is the most general antiderivative of $f(x)$, which is $F(x) + C$.

d. False; a function cannot have more than one derivative.

e. False; one can only conclude that $F(x)$ and $G(x)$ differ by a constant.

4.9.103 $\int \frac{e^{2x} - e^{-2x}}{2}\, dx = \frac{1}{2}\left(\frac{e^{2x}}{2} - \frac{e^{-2x}}{-2}\right) + C = \frac{e^{2x} + e^{-2x}}{4} + C$. Check: $\frac{d}{dx}\left(\frac{e^{2x} + e^{-2x}}{4} + C\right) = \frac{e^{2x} - e^{-2x}}{2}$.

4.9.105 $\int(\csc^2\theta + 2\theta^2 - 3\theta)\, d\theta = -\cot\theta + \frac{2}{3}\theta^3 - \frac{3}{2}\theta^2 + C$. Check: $\frac{d}{d\theta}\left(-\cot\theta + \frac{2}{3}\theta^3 - \frac{3}{2}\theta^2 + C\right) = \csc^2\theta + 2\theta^2 - 3\theta$.

4.9.107 $\int \frac{1 + \sqrt{x}}{x}\, dx = \int(x^{-1} + x^{-1/2})\, dx = \ln|x| + 2x^{1/2} + C = \ln|x| + 2\sqrt{x} + C$. Check: $\frac{d}{dx}(\ln|x| + 2\sqrt{x} + C) = \frac{1}{x} + \frac{1}{\sqrt{x}} = \frac{1 + \sqrt{x}}{x}$.

4.9.109 $\int \sqrt{x}(2x^6 - 4\sqrt[3]{x})\, dx = \int(2x^{13/2} - 4x^{5/6})\, dx = 2 \cdot \frac{2}{15}x^{15/2} - 4 \cdot \frac{6}{11}x^{11/6} + C = \frac{4}{15}x^{15/2} - \frac{24}{11}x^{11/6} + C$.
Check: $\frac{d}{dx}\left(\frac{4}{15}x^{15/2} - \frac{24}{11}x^{11/6} + C\right) = 2x^{13/2} - 4x^{5/6} = \sqrt{x}(2x^6 - 4\sqrt[3]{x})$.

4.9.111 We have $F'(x) = \int \cos x \, dx = \sin x + C$; $F'(0) = 3$ so $C = 3$. Then $F(x) = \int (\sin x + 3) \, dx = -\cos x + 3x + C$; $F(\pi) = 4$ gives $1 + 3\pi + C = 4$ so $C = 3 - 3\pi$ and $F(x) = -\cos x + 3x + 3 - 3\pi$.

4.9.113 We have $F''(x) = \int (672x^5 + 24x) \, dx = 672 \cdot \frac{x^6}{6} + 24 \cdot \frac{x^2}{2} + C$; $F''(0) = 0$ so $C = 0$. Next $F'(x) = \int (112x^6 + 12x^2) \, dx = 112 \cdot \frac{x^7}{7} + 12 \cdot \frac{x^3}{3} + C$; $F'(0) = 2$ so $C = 2$. Finally $F(x) = \int (16x^7 + 4x^3 + 2) \, dx = 16 \cdot \frac{x^8}{8} + 4 \cdot \frac{x^4}{4} + 2x + C$; $F(0) = 1$ so $C = 1$ and $F(x) = 2x^8 + x^4 + 2x + 1$.

4.9.115

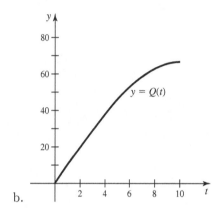

a. We have $Q(t) = \int 0.1(100 - t^2) \, dt = 0.1\left(100t - \frac{t^3}{3}\right) + C$; $Q(0) = 0$, so $C = 0$ and $Q(t) = 10t - t^3/30$ gal.

b.

c. $Q(10) = 200/3 \approx 67$ gal.

4.9.117 $\int \sin^2 x \, dx = \frac{1}{2}\int (1 - \cos 2x) \, dx = \frac{1}{2}\left(x - \frac{\sin 2x}{2}\right) + C = \frac{x}{2} - \frac{\sin 2x}{4} + C$; $\int \cos^2 x \, dx = \frac{1}{2}\int (1 + \cos 2x) \, dx = \frac{1}{2}\left(x + \frac{\sin 2x}{2}\right) + C = \frac{x}{2} + \frac{\sin 2x}{4} + C$.

4.9.119 Check that $\frac{d}{dx}(\sqrt{x^2 + 1}) = \frac{2x}{2\sqrt{x^2+1}} = \frac{x}{\sqrt{x^2+1}}$.

4.9.121 Check that $\frac{d}{dx}\left(-\frac{1}{2(x^2-1)}\right) = -\frac{1}{2}\frac{d}{dx}(x^2-1)^{-1} = -\frac{1}{2}(-1)(x^2-1)^{-2}(2x) = \frac{x}{(x^2-1)^2}$.

Chapter Four Review

1

a. False. The point $(c, f(c))$ is a critical point for f, but is not necessarily a local maximum or minimum. Example: $f(x) = x^3$ at $c = 0$.

b. False. The fact that $f''(c) = 0$ does not necessarily imply that f changes concavity at c. Example: $f(x) = x^4$ at $c = 0$.

c. True. Both are antiderivatives of $2x$.

d. True. The function has a maximum on the closed interval determined by the two local minima, and the only way the maximum can occur at the endpoints is if the function is constant, in which case every point is a local max and min.

e. True. The slope of the linearization is given by $f'(0) = \cos(0) = 1$, and the line has y-intercept $(0, f(0)) = (0, 0)$.

f. False. For example, $\lim_{x \to \infty} x^2 = \infty$ and $\lim_{x \to \infty} x = \infty$, but $\lim_{x \to \infty}(x^2 - x) = \infty$.

3

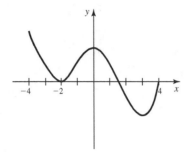

5

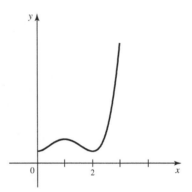

7 The critical points satisfy $f'(x) = 6x^2 - 6x - 36 = 6(x-3)(x+2) = 0$, so the critical points are $x = 3, -2$. Because $\lim\limits_{x \to \infty} f(x) = \infty$ and $\lim\limits_{x \to -\infty} f(x) = -\infty$, this function has no absolute max or min on $(-\infty, \infty)$.

9 The critical points satisfy $f'(x) = 2\ln x + 2x \cdot \frac{1}{x} = 2\ln x + 2 = 0$, which has solution $x = 1/e$. The Second Derivative Test shows that this critical point is a local minimum, so by Theorem 4.5 the absolute minimum value on the interval $(0, \infty)$ is $f(\frac{1}{e}) = -\frac{2}{e} + 10$. Because $\lim\limits_{x \to \infty} x\ln x = \infty$, this function does not have an absolute maximum on $(0, \infty)$.

11

All points in the interval $[-3, 2]$ are critical points. The absolute max occurs at $(4, 9)$; there are no local maxima. All points $(x, 5)$ for x in the interval $[-3, 2]$ are absolute and local minima.

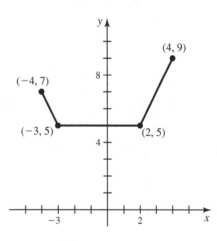

13 The derivatives of f are $f'(x) = 2x^3 - 6x + 4$, $f''(x) = 6x^2 - 6$. Observe that $f'(x) = 2(x-1)^2(x+2)$, so we have critical points $x = 1, -2$. Solving $f''(x) = 6(x^2 - 1) = 0$ gives possible inflection points at $x = \pm 1$. Testing the sign of $f'(x)$ shows that f is decreasing on the interval $(-\infty, -2)$ and is increasing on $(-2, \infty)$.

The First Derivative Test shows that a local minimum occurs at $x = -2$, and that the critical point $x = 1$ is neither a local max or min.

Testing the sign of $f''(x)$ shows that f is concave down on the interval $(-1, 1)$ and is concave up on the intervals $(-\infty, -1)$ and $(1, \infty)$. Therefore inflection points occur at $x = \pm 1$. Using a numerical solver, we see that the graph has x-intercepts at $x \approx -2.917, -0.215$. We also observe that $\lim\limits_{x \to \pm\infty} f(x) = \infty$, so f has no absolute maximum and an absolute minimum at $x = -2$.

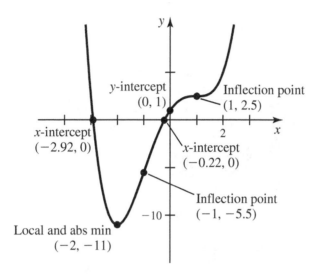

15 The derivatives of f are $f'(x) = -4\pi \sin[\pi(x - 1)]$, $f''(x) = -4\pi^2 \cos[\pi(x - 1)]$. Solving $f'(x) = 0$ gives critical point $x = 1$, and solving $f''(x) = 0$ gives possible inflection points at $x = 1/2, 3/2$. Testing the sign of $f'(x)$ shows that f is decreasing on the interval $(1, 2)$ and increasing on $(0, 1)$. The First Derivative Test shows that a local maximum occurs at $x = 1$. By Theorem 4.5, this solitary local maximum must be the absolute maximum for f on the interval $[0, 2]$.

Testing the sign of $f''(x)$ shows that f is concave down on the interval $(1/2, 3/2)$ and concave up on the intervals $(0, 1/2)$ and $(3/2, 2)$. Therefore inflection points occur at $x = 1/2, 3/2$. These points are also the x-intercepts of the graph. We also observe that $f(0) = f(2) = -4$, so f takes its absolute minimum at these points.

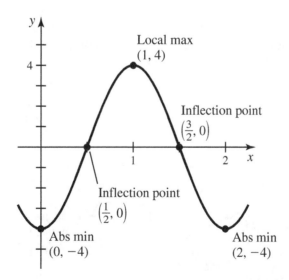

17 Note that the domain of f is the interval $(0, \infty)$. The derivatives of f are $f'(x) = \frac{1}{3}x^{-2/3} - \frac{1}{2}x^{-1/2}$, and $f''(x) = -\frac{2}{9}x^{-5/3} + \frac{1}{4}x^{-3/2}$. Solving $f'(x) = 0$ gives critical point $x = (2/3)^6$, and solving $f''(x) = 0$ gives a possible inflection point at $x = (8/9)^6$. Testing the sign of $f'(x)$ shows that f is increasing on the interval

$(0, (2/3)^6)$ and decreasing on the interval $((2/3)^6, \infty)$. The First Derivative Test shows that a local maximum occurs at $x = (2/3)^6$ and By Theorem 4.5 this solitary local maximum must be the absolute maximum of f on the interval $(0, \infty)$.

Testing the sign of $f''(x)$ shows that f is concave down on the interval $(0, (8/9)^6)$ and concave up on the interval $((8/9)^6, \infty)$. Therefore an inflection point occurs at $x = (8/9)^6$. Using a numerical solver, we find that the graph has x-intercept at $x \approx 23.767$. Because $\lim\limits_{x \to \infty} f(x) = -\infty$, f has no absolute minimum on the interval $(0, \infty)$.

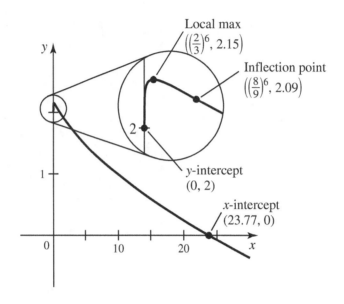

19 The derivatives of f are $f'(x) = \frac{2}{3}x^{-1/3} + \frac{1}{3}(x+2)^{-2/3}$, $f''(x) = -\frac{2}{9}\left(x^{-4/3} + (x+2)^{-5/3}\right)$. Solving $f'(x) = 0$ gives critical points $x \approx -2.57, -1.559$; we also have critical points at $x = -2, 0$ because $f'(x)$ is undefined at these points. Solving $f''(x) = 0$ numerically gives a possible inflection point at $x \approx -6.434$. We also have possible inflection points at $x = -2, 0$ because $f''(x)$ is undefined at these points. Testing the sign of $f'(x)$ shows that f is decreasing on the intervals $(-\infty, -2.566)$ and $(-1.559, 0)$ and increasing on $(-2.566, -1.559)$ and $(0, \infty)$. The First Derivative Test shows that local mins occur at $x \approx -2.566$ and $x = 0$ and a local max occurs at $x \approx -1.559$.

Testing the sign of $f''(x)$ shows that f is concave down on the intervals $(-\infty, -6.434)$, $(-2, 0)$ and $(0, \infty)$ and concave up on the interval $(-6.434, -2)$. Therefore inflection points occur at $x \approx -6.434$ and $x = -2$. Because $\lim\limits_{x \to \pm\infty} f(x) = \infty$, f has no absolute maximum. The absolute minimum occurs at $x \approx -2.566$.

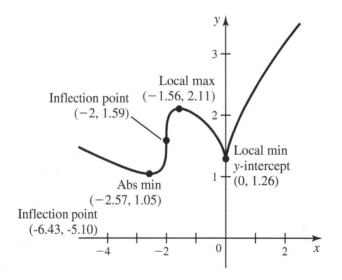

21 The objective function to be maximized is the volume of the cone, given by $V = \pi r^2 h/3$. By the Pythagorean theorem, r and h satisfy the constraint $h^2 + r^2 = 16$, which gives $r^2 = 16 - h^2$. Therefore $V(h) = \frac{\pi}{3}h(16 - h^2) = \frac{\pi}{3}(16h - h^3)$. We must maximize this function for $0 \leq h \leq 4$. The critical points of $V(h)$ satisfy $V'(h) = \frac{\pi}{3}(16 - 3h^2) = 0$, which has unique solution $h = 4/\sqrt{3} = 4\sqrt{3}/3$ in $(0, 4)$. Because $V(0) = V(4) = 0$, $h = 4\sqrt{3}/3$ gives the maximum value of $V(h)$ on $[0, 4]$. The corresponding value of r satisfies $r^2 = 16 - \frac{16}{3} = \frac{32}{3}$, so $r = \frac{4\sqrt{2}}{\sqrt{3}} = \frac{4\sqrt{6}}{3}$.

23 We have that $xy = 98$, and we want to maximize $p = (y-2)(x-1) = (y-2)(98/y-1) = 98 - y - 196/y + 2$. Note that $p'(y) = -1 + 196/y^2$, which is zero when $y^2 = 196$, so $y = \sqrt{196} = 14$. Also note that $p'(13) > 0$ and $p'(15) < 0$, so there is a local (in fact, absolute) maximum at $y = 14$. The value of x when $y = 14$ is $x = 98/14 = 7$.

25 The area of the triangle is $\frac{1}{2}pq$, and the constraint is $\sqrt{p^2 + q^2} = 10$, or $p^2 + q^2 = 100$. So we can write the area of the triangle as $A(p) = (1/2)p\sqrt{100 - p^2}$. We have $A'(p) = (1/2)\sqrt{100 - p^2} + \frac{1}{2}p \cdot \frac{-p}{\sqrt{100-p^2}} = \frac{100-p^2-p^2}{2\sqrt{100-p^2}} = \frac{100-2p^2}{2\sqrt{100-p^2}}$. This is zero for $p = \sqrt{50} = 5\sqrt{2}$. An application of the First Derivative Test shows that there is a local (in fact, absolute) maximum at this value of p. The value of q for this value of p is $\sqrt{100 - 50} = 5\sqrt{2}$ as well. So the area of the triangle is maximized when $p = q = 5\sqrt{2}$.

27

a. $f'(x) = \frac{2}{3}x^{-1/3}$, so $f'(27) = \frac{2}{3\sqrt[3]{27}} = \frac{2}{9}$. Thus $L(x) - 9 = \frac{2}{9}(x - 27)$, or $L(x) = 9 + \frac{2}{9}(x - 27) = \frac{2}{9}x + 3$.

b. $f(29) \approx L(29) = 9 + \frac{4}{9} \approx 9.44$. This is an overestimate, because $f''(27) < 0$. Note that the calculator value of $f(29)$ is about 9.43913.

29 Let $f(x) = 1/x^2$ and let $a = 4$. Then $f'(x) = \frac{-2}{x^3}$ so $f'(4) = \frac{-2}{64} = \frac{-1}{32}$. The linearization is $L(x) = \frac{1}{16} + (-1/32)(x - 4)$. Then $f(4.2) = 1/(4.2)^2 \approx L(4.2) = \frac{1}{16} - \frac{1}{32} \cdot \frac{2}{10} = .05625$.

31 $\Delta h \approx h'(a)\Delta t = -32 \cdot 5 \cdot 0.7 = -112$ feet.

33

a. The average rate of change of $P(t)$ on the interval $[0, 8]$ is $\frac{P(8)-P(0)}{8-0} = \frac{800/9-0}{8} = \frac{100}{9}$ cells/week.

b. We solve $P'(t) = \frac{100}{(t+1)^2} = \frac{100}{9}$ which gives $(t + 1)^2 = 9$, so $t = 2$ weeks.

35 It is possible to note that 1 is a root by inspection. Then by long division by $x - 1$, we have $f(x) = (x - 1)(3x^2 - x - 1)$. We apply Newton's method to the function $g(x) = 3x^2 - x - 1$.

The Newton's method recursion is given by $x_{n+1} = x_n - \frac{3x_n^2-x_n-1}{6x_n-1}$. Applying this recursion to the initial estimates of $-.5$ and $.8$ yields:

n	x_n		n	x_n
0	$-.5$		0	.8
1	$-.4375$		1	.768421
2	$-.434267$		2	.767592
3	$-.434259$		3	.767592
4	$-.434259$		4	.767592

The roots are thus 1, and approximately -.434259 and .767592.

37 First note that $f'(x) = 10x^4 - 18x^2 - 4$ and $f''(x) = 40x^3 - 36x = 4x(10x^2 - 9)$. This is clearly 0 when $x = 0$, and when $10x^2 - 9 = 0$. Applying Newton's method to the function $g(x) = 10x^2 - 9$ with initial estimates of -1 and 1 yields:

n	x_n
0	-1
1	$-.95$
2	$-.948684$
3	$-.948683$
4	$-.948683$
5	$-.948683$

n	x_n
0	1
1	$.95$
2	$.948684$
3	$.948683$
4	$.948683$
5	$.948683$

Checking the signs of $f''(x)$ on the appropriate intervals leads to the conclusion that these are all the locations of inflection points of f. So the inflection points of f are located at 0 and approximately $\pm.948683$.

39 L'Hôpital's rule gives $\displaystyle\lim_{t\to 0}\frac{1-\cos 6t}{2t}=\lim_{t\to 0}\frac{6\sin 6t}{2}=0.$

41 Observe that $\displaystyle\lim_{\theta\to 0}\frac{3\sin^2 2\theta}{\theta^2}=3\left(\lim_{\theta\to 0}\frac{\sin 2\theta}{\theta}\right)^2$; l'Hôpital's rule gives $\displaystyle\lim_{\theta\to 0}\frac{\sin 2\theta}{\theta}=\lim_{\theta\to 0}\frac{2\cos 2\theta}{1}=2$, so $\displaystyle\lim_{\theta\to 0}\frac{3\sin^2 2\theta}{\theta^2}=3\cdot 2^2=12.$

43 Observe that $2\theta\cot 3\theta=2\cos 3\theta\cdot\frac{\theta}{\sin 3\theta}$; $\displaystyle\lim_{\theta\to 0}\frac{\theta}{\sin 3\theta}=\lim_{\theta\to 0}\frac{1}{3\cos 3\theta}=\frac{1}{3}$ by l'Hôpital's rule, so

$$\lim_{\theta\to 0}2\theta\cot 3\theta=2\cdot 1\cdot\frac{1}{3}=\frac{2}{3}.$$

45 Make the change of variables $x=1/y$; then $\ln^{10}y=(\ln y)^{10}=(-\ln x)^{10}=\ln^{10}x$, and so $\displaystyle\lim_{y\to 0^+}\frac{\ln^{10}y}{\sqrt{y}}=\lim_{x\to\infty}\sqrt{x}\ln^{10}x=\infty.$

47 Apply l'Hôpital's rule twice:

$$\lim_{x\to 1}\frac{x^4-x^3-3x^2+5x-2}{x^3+x^2-5x+3}=\lim_{x\to 1}\frac{4x^3-3x^2-6x+5}{3x^2+2x-5}=\lim_{x\to 1}\frac{12x^2-6x-6}{6x+2}=0.$$

49 $\displaystyle\lim_{x\to 0}\csc x\sin^{-1}x=\lim_{x\to 0}\frac{\sin^{-1}x}{\sin x}=\lim_{x\to 0}\frac{1/\sqrt{1-x^2}}{\cos x}=1,$ by l'Hôpital's rule.

51 Observe that $\displaystyle\lim_{x\to\infty}\frac{x+1}{x-1}=1,$ either by l'Hôpital's rule or Theorem 2.7. Hence $\displaystyle\lim_{x\to\infty}\ln\left(\frac{x+1}{x-1}\right)=\ln 1=0.$

53 Note that $\ln(\sin x)^{\tan x}=\tan x\ln\sin x$, so we evaluate $L=\displaystyle\lim_{x\to\pi/2^-}\tan x\ln\sin x=\lim_{x\to\pi/2^-}\frac{\ln\sin x}{\cot x}=\lim_{x\to\pi/2^-}\frac{\cot x}{-\csc^2 x}=\lim_{x\to\pi/2^-}(-\cos x\sin x)=0$ by l'Hôpital's rule. Therefore $\displaystyle\lim_{x\to\pi/2^-}(\sin x)^{\tan x}=e^L=1.$

55 Note that for $0<x<1$, we have $\ln x<0$, so $|\ln x|=-\ln x$. Then $|\ln x|^x=(-\ln x)^x$. Consider the natural logarithm of this quantity, $x\ln(-\ln x)=\frac{\ln(-\ln x)}{\frac{1}{x}}$. Using lHôpital's rule we have

$$\lim_{x\to 0^+}\frac{\ln(-\ln x)}{\frac{1}{x}}=\lim_{x\to 0^+}\frac{\frac{1}{x\ln x}}{\frac{-1}{x^2}}=\lim_{x\to 0^+}\frac{-x}{\ln x}=0.$$

Thus $\lim_{x\to 0^+}|\ln x|^x=e^0=1.$

57 Note that $\ln\left(1 - \frac{3}{x}\right)^x = x\ln\left(1 - \frac{3}{x}\right) = \frac{\ln(1-3/x)}{1/x}$, so we evaluate

$$L = \lim_{x\to\infty}\frac{\ln(1-3/x)}{1/x} = \lim_{x\to\infty}\frac{(1-3/x)^{-1}(3/x^2)}{-1/x^2} = -3$$

by l'Hôpital's rule. Therefore $\lim_{x\to\infty}\left(1 - \frac{3}{x}\right)^x = e^L = e^{-3}$.

59 Let $y = (x-1)^{\sin\pi x}$. Then $\ln y = \sin\pi x\ln(x-1) = \frac{\ln(x-1)}{\csc\pi x}$. Then

$$\lim_{x\to 1}\ln y = \lim_{x\to 1}\frac{\ln(x-1)}{\csc\pi x} = \lim_{x\to 1}\frac{\frac{1}{x-1}}{-\pi\csc\pi x\cot\pi x} = \lim_{x\to 1}\frac{\sin^2\pi x}{-\pi(x-1)\cos\pi x}$$

$$= \lim_{x\to 1}\frac{1}{-\pi\cos\pi x}\cdot\lim_{x\to 1}\frac{\sin^2\pi x}{x-1} = \frac{1}{\pi}\lim_{x\to 1}\frac{2\pi\sin\pi x\cos\pi x}{1} = \frac{1}{\pi}\cdot 0 = 0.$$

Then $\lim_{x\to 1}y = \lim_{x\to 1}e^{\ln y} = e^0 = 1$.

61 Observe that $\lim_{x\to\infty}\frac{x^{1/2}}{x^{1/3}} = \lim_{x\to\infty}x^{1/6} = \infty$, so $x^{1/2}$ grows faster than $x^{1/3}$ as $x\to\infty$.

63 By Theorem 4.15, $\sqrt{x}$ grows faster than $\ln^{10}x$ as $x\to\infty$.

65 Observe that $\lim_{x\to\infty}\frac{e^x}{3^x} = \lim_{x\to\infty}\left(\frac{e}{3}\right)^x = 0$ because $e/3 < 1$. Therefore 3^x grows faster than e^x as $x\to\infty$.

67 Observe that $4^{x/2} = (4^{1/2})^x = 2^x$, so these functions are identical and hence have comparable growth rates as $x\to\infty$.

69 $\int(2x+1)^2\,dx = \int(4x^2+4x+1)\,dx = \frac{4}{3}x^3 + 2x^2 + x + C$.

71 $\int\left(\frac{1}{x^2} - \frac{2}{x^{5/2}}\right)dx = \int(x^{-2} - 2x^{-5/2})\,dx = -x^{-1} - 2\cdot\left(-\frac{2}{3}\right)x^{-3/2} = -\frac{1}{x} + \frac{4}{3}x^{-3/2} + C$.

73 Using Table 4.5 (formula 1), $\int(1 + \cos 3\theta)\,d\theta = \theta + \frac{\sin 3\theta}{3} + C$.

75 Using Table 4.5 (formula 5), $\int\sec 2x\tan 2x\,dx = \frac{1}{2}\sec 2x + C$.

77 Using Table 4.6 (formula 8), $\int\frac{12}{x}\,dx = 12\ln|x| + C$.

79 Using Table 4.6 (formula 10), $\int\frac{dx}{x^2+1} = \tan^{-1}x + C$.

81 $\int\left(\sqrt[4]{x^3} + \sqrt{x^5}\right)dx = \int(x^{3/4} + x^{5/2})\,dx = \frac{4}{7}x^{7/4} + \frac{2}{7}x^{7/2} + C$.

83 We have $f(t) = \int(\sin t + 2t)\,dt = -\cos t + t^2 + C$; $f(0) = -1 + C = 5$, so $C = 6$ and $f(t) = -\cos t + t^2 + 6$.

85 Using the identity $\sin^2 x = (1 - \cos 2x)/2$ and Table 4.5 (formula 1), we see that $h(x) = \frac{1}{2}\int(1 - \cos 2x)\,dx = \frac{1}{2}\left(x - \frac{\sin 2x}{2}\right) + C = \frac{x}{2} - \frac{\sin 2x}{4} + C$. We have $h(1) = \frac{1}{2} - \frac{\sin 2}{4} + C = 1$, so $C = \frac{1}{2} + \frac{\sin 2}{4}$ and so $h(x) = \frac{x}{2} - \frac{\sin 2x}{4} + \frac{1}{2} + \frac{\sin 2}{4}$.

87 The velocity of the rocket is given by $v(t) = -9.8t + v_0 = -9.8t + 120$, and the position function of the rocket is $s(t) = \int(-9.8t + 120)\,dt = -4.9t^2 + 120t + s_0 = -4.9t^2 + 120t + 125$. The rocket reaches its maximum height when $v(t) = 0$, which occurs at $t = 120/9.8 \approx 12.24$ s; the maximum height is $s(120/9.8) \approx 859.69$ m. The rocket hits the ground when $s(t) = 0$; solving this quadratic equation gives $t \approx 25.49$ s.

89

For the second limit, let $y = x^2$:
$$\lim_{x \to 0} \frac{x^2}{1 - e^{-x^2}} = \lim_{y \to 0} \frac{y}{1 - e^{-y}} = \lim_{y \to 0} \frac{1}{e^{-y}} = 1$$
by l'Hôpital's rule.   For the first, observe
that for $x > 0$ $\frac{x}{\sqrt{1-e^{-x^2}}} = \left(\frac{x^2}{1-e^{-x^2}}\right)^{1/2}$, so

$$\lim_{x \to 0^+} \frac{x}{\sqrt{1 - e^{-x^2}}} = 1 \text{ as well.}$$

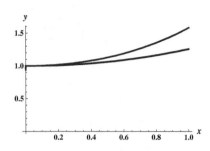

91 Observe that $\lim\limits_{x \to \infty} \dfrac{2x^5 - x + 1}{5x^6 + x} = 0$ by Theorem 2.7. We can also use l'Hôpital's rule:

$$\lim_{x \to \infty} \frac{2x^5 - x + 1}{5x^6 + x} = \lim_{x \to \infty} \frac{10x^4 - 1}{30x^5 + 1} = \lim_{x \to \infty} \frac{40x^3}{150x^4} = \lim_{x \to \infty} \frac{4}{15x} = 0.$$

93 Note that $\lim\limits_{x \to 0^+} x^x = 1$, as shown in Example 6 a. Therefore $\lim\limits_{x \to 0^+} f(x) = \lim\limits_{x \to 0^+} (x^x)^x = 1^0 = 1$, and $\lim\limits_{x \to 0} g(x) = \lim\limits_{x \to 0} x^{(x^x)} = 0^1 = 0.$

95 First, observe that $\lim\limits_{x \to \infty} \left(1 + \dfrac{1}{x}\right)^{x+a} = \lim\limits_{x \to \infty} \left(1 + \dfrac{1}{x}\right)^x \left(1 + \dfrac{1}{x}\right)^a = e \cdot 1 = e.$ Therefore $\lim\limits_{x \to \infty} \ln g(x) = 1.$ It suffices to determine whether $\ln g(x) - 1$ is positive or negative as $x \to \infty$. To do this, consider $\lim\limits_{x \to \infty} x(\ln g(x) - 1) = \lim\limits_{t \to 0} \dfrac{(1 + at)\ln(1 + t) - t}{t^2}$, where we make the change of variables $t = 1/x$. This limit can be evaluated by using l'Hôpital's rule twice: $\lim\limits_{t \to 0} \dfrac{(1 + at)\ln(1 + t) - t}{t^2} = a - \dfrac{1}{2}.$ Therefore when $a > 1/2$ we have $g(x) > e$ as $x \to \infty$, and when $0 < a < 1/2$, $g(x) < e$ as $x \to \infty$. In the case $a = 1/2$ we consider the limit $\lim\limits_{x \to \infty} x^2(\ln g(x) - 1) = \lim\limits_{t \to 0} \dfrac{(1 + at)\ln(1 + t) - t}{t^3}$, which can be evaluated by using l'Hôpital's three times: $\lim\limits_{t \to 0} \dfrac{(1 + t/2)\ln(1 + t) - t}{t^3} = \dfrac{1}{12}.$ Therefore $g(x) > e$ as $x \to \infty$ in this case as well.

Chapter 9

Power Series

9.1 Approximating Functions With Polynomials

9.1.1 Let the polynomial be $p(x)$. Then $p(0) = f(0)$, $p'(0) = f'(0)$, and $p''(0) = f''(0)$.

9.1.3 The approximations are $p_0(0.1) = 1$, $p_1(0.1) = 1 + \frac{0.1}{2} = 1.05$, and $p_2(0.1) = 1 + \frac{0.1}{2} - \frac{.01}{8} = 1.04875$.

9.1.5 The remainder is the difference between the value of the Taylor polynomial at a point and the true value of the function at that point, $R_n(x) = f(x) - p_n(x)$.

9.1.7

    a. Note that $f(1) = 8$, and $f'(x) = 12\sqrt{x}$, so $f'(1) = 12$. Thus, $p_1(x) = 8 + 12(x - 1)$.

    b. $f''(x) = 6/\sqrt{x}$, so $f''(1) = 6$. Thus $p_2(x) = 8 + 12(x - 2) + 3(x - 1)^2$.

    c. $p_1(1.1) = 12 \cdot 0.1 + 8 = 9.2$. $p_2(1.1) = 3(.1)^2 + 12 \cdot 0.1 + 8 = 9.23$.

9.1.9

    a. $f'(x) = -e^{-x}$, so $p_1(x) = f(0) + f'(0)x = 1 - x$.

    b. $f''(x) = e^{-x}$, so $p_2(x) = f(0) + f'(0)x + \frac{1}{2}f''(0)x^2 = 1 - x + \frac{1}{2}x^2$.

    c. $p_1(0.2) = 0.8$, and $p_2(0.2) = 1 - 0.2 + \frac{1}{2}(0.04) = 0.82$.

9.1.11

    a. $f'(x) = -\frac{1}{(x+1)^2}$, so $p_1(x) = f(0) + f'(0)x = 1 - x$.

    b. $f''(x) = \frac{2}{(x+1)^3}$, so $p_2(x) = f(0) + f'(0)x + \frac{1}{2}f''(0)x^2 = 1 - x + x^2$.

    c. $p_1(0.05) = 0.95$, and $p_2(0.05) = 1 - 0.05 + 0.0025 = 0.953$.

9.1.13

    a. $f'(x) = (1/3)x^{-2/3}$, so $p_1(x) = f(8) + f'(8)(x - 8) = 2 + \frac{1}{12}(x - 8)$.

    b. $f''(x) = (-2/9)x^{-5/3}$, so $p_2(x) = f(8) + f'(8)(x - 8) + \frac{1}{2}f''(8)(x - 8)^2 = 2 + \frac{1}{12}(x - 8) - \frac{1}{288}(x - 8)^2$.

    c. $p_1(7.5) \approx 1.958$, $p_2(7.5) \approx 1.957$.

9.1.15 $f(0) = 1, f'(0) = -\sin 0 = 0, f''(0) = -\cos 0 = -1$, so that $p_0(x) = 1$, $p_1(x) = 1$, $p_2(x) = 1 - \frac{1}{2}x^2$.

399

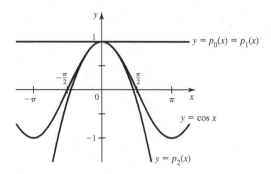

9.1.17 $f(0) = 0$, $f'(0) = -\frac{1}{1-0} = -1$, $f''(0) = -\frac{1}{(1-0)^2} = -1$, so that $p_0(x) = 0$, $p_1(x) = -x$,
$p_2(x) = -x - \frac{1}{2}x^2$.

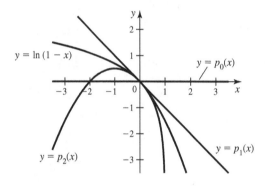

9.1.19 $f(0) = 0$. $f'(x) = \sec^2 x$, $f''(x) = 2\tan x \sec^2 x$, so that $f'(0) = 1$, $f''(0) = 0$. Thus $p_0(x) = 0$,
$p_1(x) = x$, $p_2(x) = x$.

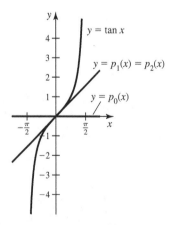

9.1.21 $f(0) = 1$, $f'(0) = -3(1+0)^{-4} = -3$, $f''(0) = 12(1+0)^{-5} = 12$, so that $p_0(x) = 1$, $p_1(x) = 1 - 3x$,
$p_2(x) = 1 - 3x + 6x^2$.

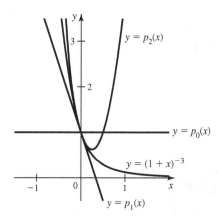

9.1.23

a. $p_2(0.05) \approx 1.025$.

b. The absolute error is $\sqrt{1.05} - p_2(0.05) \approx 7.68 \times 10^{-6}$.

9.1.25

a. $p_2(0.08) \approx 0.962$.

b. The absolute error is $p_2(0.08) - \frac{1}{\sqrt{1.08}} \approx 1.5 \times 10^{-4}$.

9.1.27

a. $p_2(0.15) \approx 0.861$.

b. The absolute error is $p_2(0.15) - e^{-0.15} \approx 5.4 \times 10^{-4}$.

9.1.29

a. Note that $f(1) = 1$, $f'(1) = 3$, and $f''(1) = 6$. Thus, $p_0(x) = 1$, $p_1(x) = 1 + 3(x - 1)$, and $p_2(x) = 1 + 3(x - 1) + 3(x - 1)^2$.

b.

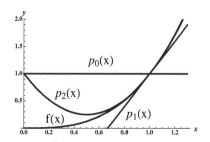

9.1.31

a. $p_0(x) = \frac{\sqrt{2}}{2}$, $p_1(x) = \frac{\sqrt{2}}{2} + \frac{\sqrt{2}}{2}(x - \frac{\pi}{4})$, $p_2(x) = \frac{\sqrt{2}}{2} + \frac{\sqrt{2}}{2}(x - \frac{\pi}{4}) - \frac{\sqrt{2}}{4}(x - \frac{\pi}{4})^2$.

b.

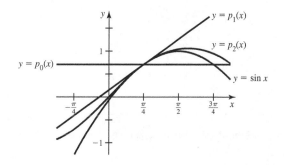

9.1.33

a. $p_0(x) = 3$, $p_1(x) = 3 + \frac{1}{6}(x - 9)$, $p_2(x) = 3 + \frac{1}{6}(x - 9) - \frac{1}{216}(x - 9)^2$.

b.

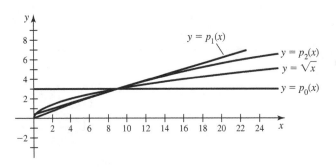

9.1.35

a. $p_0(x) = 1$, $p_1(x) = 1 + \frac{1}{e}(x - e)$, $p_2(x) = 1 + \frac{1}{e}(x - e) - \frac{1}{2e^2}(x - e)^2$.

b.

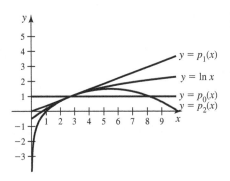

9.1.37

a. $f(1) = \frac{\pi}{4} + 2$, $f'(1) = \frac{1}{2} + 2 = \frac{5}{2}$. $f''(1) = -\frac{1}{2} + 2 = \frac{3}{2}$. $p_0(x) = 2 + \frac{\pi}{4}$, $p_1(x) = 2 + \frac{\pi}{4} + \frac{5}{2}(x - 1)$, $p_2(x) = 2 + \frac{\pi}{4} + \frac{5}{2}(x - 1) + \frac{3}{4}(x - 1)^2$.

b.

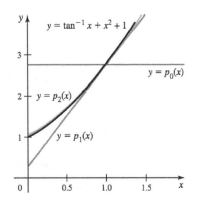

9.1.39

a. Ue the Taylor polynomial centered at 0 with $f(x) = e^x$. We have $p_3(x) = 1 + x + \frac{1}{2}x^2 + \frac{1}{6}x^3$. $p_3(0.12) \approx 1.127$.

b. $|f(0.12) - p_3(0.12)| \approx 8.9 \times 10^{-6}$.

9.1.41

a. Use the Taylor polynomial centered at 0 with $f(x) = \tan(x)$. We have $p_3(x) = x + \frac{1}{3}x^3$. $p_3(-0.1) \approx -0.100$.

b. $|p_3(-0.1) - f(-0.1)| \approx 1.3 \times 10^{-6}$.

9.1.43

a. Use the Taylor polynomial centered at 0 with $f(x) = \sqrt{1+x}$. We have $p_3(x) = 1 + \frac{1}{2}x - \frac{1}{8}x^2 + \frac{1}{16}x^3$. $p_3(0.06) \approx 1.030$.

b. $|f(0.06) - p_3(0.06)| \approx 4.9 \times 10^{-7}$.

9.1.45

a. Use the Taylor polynomial centered at 100 with $f(x) = \sqrt{x}$. We have $p_3(x) = 10 + \frac{1}{20}(x - 100) - \frac{1}{8000}(x - 100)^2 + \frac{1}{1600000}(x - 100)^3$. $p_3(101) \approx 10.050$.

b. $|p_3(101) - f(101)| \approx 3.9 \times 10^{-9}$.

9.1.47

a. Use the Taylor polynomial centered at 0 with $f(x) = \sinh(x)$. Note that $f(0) = 0$, $f'(0) = 1$, $f''(0) = 0$ and $f'''(0) = 1$. Then we have $p_3(x) = x + x^3/6$, so $\sinh(.5) \approx (.5)^3/6 + .5 \approx 0.521$.

b. $|p_3(.5) - \sinh(.5)| \approx 2.6 \times 10^{-4}$.

9.1.49 With $f(x) = \sin x$ we have $R_n(x) = \dfrac{f^{(n+1)}(c)}{(n+1)!} x^{n+1}$ for c between 0 and x.

9.1.51 With $f(x) = e^{-x}$ we have $f^{(n+1)}(x) = (-1)^{n+1}e^{-x}$, so that $R_n(x) = \dfrac{(-1)^{n+1}e^{-c}}{(n+1)!} x^{n+1}$ for c between 0 and x.

9.1.53 With $f(x) = \sin x$ we have $R_n(x) = \dfrac{f^{(n+1)}(c)}{(n+1)!} \left(x - \dfrac{\pi}{2}\right)^{n+1}$ for c between $\frac{\pi}{2}$ and x.

9.1.55 $f(x) = \sin x$, so $f^{(5)}(x) = \cos x$. Because $\cos x$ is bounded in magnitude by 1, the remainder is bounded by $|R_4(x)| \leq \frac{0.3^5}{5!} \approx 2.0 \times 10^{-5}$.

9.1.57 $f(x) = e^x$, so $f^{(5)}(x) = e^x$. Because $e^{0.25}$ is bounded by 2, $|R_4(x)| \leq 2 \cdot \frac{0.25^5}{5!} \approx 1.63 \times 10^{-5}$.

9.1.59 $f(x) = e^{-x}$, so $f^{(5)}(x) = -e^{-x}$. Because $f^{(5)}$ achieves its maximum magnitude in the range at $x = 0$, which has absolute value 1, $|R_4(x)| \leq 1 \cdot \frac{0.5^5}{5!} \approx 2.6 \times 10^{-4}$.

9.1.61 Here $n = 3$ or 4, so use $n = 4$, and $M = 1$ because $f^{(5)}(x) = \cos x$, so that $R_4(x) \leq \frac{(\pi/4)^5}{5!} \approx 2.49 \times 10^{-3}$.

9.1.63 $n = 2$ and $M = e^{1/2} < 2$, so $|R_2(x)| \leq 2 \cdot \frac{(1/2)^3}{3!} \approx 4.2 \times 10^{-2}$.

9.1.65 $n = 2$; $f^{(3)}(x) = \frac{2}{(1+x)^3}$, which achieves its maximum at $x = -0.2$: $|f^{(3)}(x)| = \frac{2}{0.8^3} < 4$. Then $|R_2(x)| \leq 4 \cdot \frac{0.2^3}{3!} \approx 5.4 \times 10^{-3}$.

9.1.67 Use the Taylor series for e^x at $x = 0$. The derivatives of e^x are e^x. On $[-0.5, 0]$, the maximum magnitude of any derivative is thus 1 at $x = 0$, so $|R_n(-0.5)| \leq \frac{0.5^{n+1}}{(n+1)!}$, so for $R_n(-0.5) < 10^{-3}$ we need $n = 4$.

9.1.69 Use the Taylor series for $\cos x$ at $x = 0$. The magnitude of any derivative of $\cos x$ is bounded by 1, so $|R_n(-0.25)| \leq \frac{0.25^{n+1}}{(n+1)!}$, so for $|R_n(-0.25)| < 10^{-3}$ we need $n = 3$.

9.1.71 Use the Taylor series for $f(x) = \sqrt{x}$ at $x = 1$. Then $|f^{(n+1)}(x)| = \frac{1 \cdot 3 \cdots (2n-1)}{2^{n+1}} x^{-(2n+1)/2}$, which achieves its maximum on $[1, 1.06]$ at $x = 1$. Then

$$|R_n(1.06)| \leq \frac{1 \cdot 3 \cdots (2n-1)}{2^{n+1}} \cdot \frac{(1.06 - 1)^{n+1}}{(n+1)!},$$

and for $|R_n(0.06)| < 10^{-3}$ we need $n = 1$.

9.1.73

a. False. If $f(x) = e^{-2x}$, then $f^{(n)}(x) = (-1)^n 2^n e^{-2x}$, so that $f^{(n)}(0) \neq 0$ and all powers of x are present in the Taylor series.

b. True. The constant term of the Taylor series is $f(0) = 1$. Higher-order terms all involve derivatives of $f(x) = x^5 - 1$ evaluated at $x = 0$; clearly for $n < 5$, $f^{(n)}(0) = 0$, and for $n > 5$, the derivative itself vanishes. Only for $n = 5$, where $f^{(5)}(x) = 5!$, is the derivative nonzero, so the coefficient of x^5 in the Taylor series is $f^{(5)}(0)/5! = 1$ and the Taylor polynomial of order 10 is in fact $x^5 - 1$. Note that this statement is true of any polynomial of degree at most 10.

c. True. The odd derivatives of $\sqrt{1 + x^2}$ vanish at $x = 0$, while the even ones do not.

d. True. Clearly the second-order Taylor polynomial for f at a has degree at most 2. However, the coefficient of $(x - a)^2$ is $\frac{1}{2} f''(a)$, which is zero because f has an inflection point at a.

9.1.75

a. This matches (C) because for $f(x) = (1 + 2x)^{1/2}$, $f''(x) = -(1 + 2x)^{-3/2}$ so $\frac{f''(0)}{2!} = -\frac{1}{2}$.

b. This matches (E) because for $f(x) = (1 + 2x)^{-1/2}$, $f''(x) = 3(1 + 2x)^{-5/2}$, so $\frac{f''(0)}{2!} = \frac{3}{2}$.

c. This matches (A) because $f^{(n)}(x) = 2^n e^{2x}$, so that $f^{(n)}(0) = 2^n$, which is (A)'s pattern.

d. This matches (D) because $f''(x) = 8(1 + 2x)^{-3}$ and $f''(0) = 8$, so that $f''(0)/2! = 4$

e. This matches (B) because $f'(x) = -6(1 + 2x)^{-4}$ so that $f'(0) = -6$.

f. This matches (F) because $f^{(n)}(x) = (-2)^n e^{-2x}$, so $f^{(n)}(0) = (-2)^n$, which is (F)'s pattern.

9.1.77

a. $p_2(0.1) = 0.1$. The maximum error in the approximation is $1 \cdot \frac{0.1^3}{3!} \approx 1.67 \times 10^{-4}$.

b. $p_2(0.2) = 0.2$. The maximum error in the approximation is $1 \cdot \frac{0.2^3}{3!} \approx 1.33 \times 10^{-3}$.

9.1.79

a. $p_3(0.1) = 1 - .01/2 = 0.995$. The maximum error is $1 \cdot \frac{0.1^4}{4!} \approx 4.2 \times 10^{-6}$.

b. $p_3(0.2) = 1 - .04/2 = 0.98$. The maximum error is $1 \cdot \frac{0.2^4}{4!} \approx 6.7 \times 10^{-5}$.

9.1.81

a. $p_1(0.1) = 1.05$. Because $|f''(x)| = \frac{1}{4}(1 + x)^{-3/2}$ has a maximum value of $1/4$ at $x = 0$, the maximum error is $\frac{1}{4} \cdot \frac{0.1^2}{2} \approx 1.3 \times 10^{-3}$.

b. $p_1(0.2) = 1.1$. The maximum error is $\frac{1}{4} \cdot \frac{0.2^2}{2} = 5 \times 10^{-3}$.

9.1.83

a. $p_1(0.1) = 1.1$. Because $f''(x) = e^x$ is less than 2 on $[0, 0.1]$, the maximum error is less than $2 \cdot \frac{0.1^2}{2!} = 10^{-2}$.

b. $p_1(0.2) = 1.2$. The maximum error is less than $2 \cdot \frac{0.2^2}{2!} = .04 = 4 \times 10^{-2}$.

9.1.85

a.

	$|\sec x - p_2(x)|$	$|\sec x - p_4(x)|$
-0.2	3.4×10^{-4}	5.5×10^{-6}
-0.1	2.1×10^{-5}	8.5×10^{-8}
0.0	0	0
0.1	2.1×10^{-5}	8.5×10^{-8}
0.2	3.4×10^{-4}	5.5×10^{-6}

b. The errors are equal for positive and negative x. This makes sense, because $\sec(-x) = \sec x$ and $p_n(-x) = p_n(x)$ for $n = 2, 4$. The errors appear to get larger as x gets farther from zero.

9.1.87

a.

	$|e^{-x} - p_1(x)|$	$|e^{-x} - p_2(x)|$
-0.2	2.14×10^{-2}	1.40×10^{-3}
-0.1	5.17×10^{-3}	1.71×10^{-4}
0.0	0	0
0.1	4.84×10^{-3}	1.63×10^{-4}
0.2	1.87×10^{-2}	1.27×10^{-3}

b. The errors are different for positive and negative displacements from zero, and appear to get larger as x gets farther from zero.

9.1.89

a.

	$|\tan x - p_1(x)|$	$|\tan x - p_3(x)|$
-0.2	2.71×10^{-3}	4.34×10^{-5}
-0.1	3.35×10^{-4}	1.34×10^{-6}
0.0	0	0
0.1	3.35×10^{-4}	1.34×10^{-6}
0.2	2.71×10^{-3}	4.34×10^{-5}

b. The errors are equal for positive and negative x. This makes sense, because $\tan(-x) = -\tan x$ and $p_n(-x) = -p_n(x)$ for $n = 1, 3$. The errors appear to get larger as x gets farther from zero.

9.1.91 The true value of $e^{0.35} \approx 1.419067549$. The 6th-order Taylor polynomial for e^x centered at $x = 0$ is

$$p_6(x) = 1 + x + \frac{x^2}{2} + \frac{x^3}{6} + \frac{x^4}{24} + \frac{x^5}{120} + \frac{x^6}{720}.$$

Evaluating the polynomials at $x = 0.35$ produces the following table:

n	$p_n(0.35)$	$|p_n(0.35) - e^{0.35}|$
1	1.350000000	6.91×10^{-2}
2	1.411250000	7.82×10^{-3}
3	1.418395833	6.72×10^{-4}
4	1.419021094	4.65×10^{-5}
5	1.419064862	2.69×10^{-6}
6	1.419067415	1.33×10^{-7}

The 6th-order Taylor polynomial for e^x centered at $x = \ln 2$ is

$$p_6(x) = 2 + 2(x - \ln 2) + (x - \ln 2)^2 + \frac{1}{3}(x - \ln 2)^3 + \frac{1}{12}(x - \ln 2)^4$$
$$+ \frac{1}{60}(x - \ln 2)^5 + \frac{1}{360}(x - \ln 2)^6.$$

Evaluating the polynomials at $x = 0.35$ produces the following table:

n	$p_n(0.35)$	$\lvert p_n(0.35) - e^{0.35} \rvert$
1	1.313705639	1.05×10^{-1}
2	1.431455626	1.24×10^{-2}
3	1.417987101	1.08×10^{-3}
4	1.419142523	7.50×10^{-5}
5	1.419063227	4.32×10^{-6}
6	1.419067762	2.13×10^{-7}

Comparing the tables shows that using the polynomial centered at $x = 0$ is more accurate for all n. To see why, consider the remainder. Let $f(x) = e^x$. By Theorem 9.2, the magnitude of the remainder when approximating $f(0.35)$ by the polynomial p_n centered at 0 is:

$$|R_n(0.35)| = \frac{|f^{(n+1)}(c)|}{(n+1)!}(0.35)^{n+1} = \frac{e^c}{(n+1)!}(0.35)^{n+1}$$

for some c with $0 < c < 0.35$ while the magnitude of the remainder when approximating $f(0.35)$ by the polynomial p_n centered at $\ln 2$ is:

$$|R_n(0.35)| = \frac{|f^{(n+1)}(c)|}{(n+1)!}|0.35 - \ln 2|^{n+1} = \frac{e^c}{(n+1)!}(\ln 2 - 0.35)^{n+1}$$

for some c with $0.35 < c < \ln 2$. Because $\ln 2 - 0.35 \approx 0.35$, the relative size of the magnitudes of the remainders is determined by e^c in each remainder. Because e^x is an increasing function, the remainder in using the polynomial centered at 0 will be less than the remainder in using the polynomial centered at $\ln 2$, and the former polynomial will be more accurate.

9.1.93

a. The slope of the tangent line to $f(x)$ at $x = a$ is by definition $f'(a)$; by the point-slope form for the equation of a line, we have $y - f(a) = f'(a)(x - a)$, or $y = f(a) + f'(a)(x - a)$.

b. The Taylor polynomial centered at a is $p_1(x) = f(a) + f'(a)(x - a)$, which is the tangent line at a.

9.1.95

a. We have

$$f(0) = f^{(4)}(0) = \sin 0 = 0 \qquad f(\pi) = f^{(4)}(\pi) = \sin \pi = 0$$
$$f'(0) = f^{(5)}(0) = \cos 0 = 1 \qquad f'(\pi) = f^{(5)}(0) = \cos \pi = -1$$
$$f''(0) = -\sin 0 = 0 \qquad f''(\pi) = -\sin \pi = 0$$
$$f'''(0) = -\cos 0 = -1 \qquad f'''(\pi) = -\cos \pi = 1.$$

Thus

$$p_5(x) = x - \frac{x^3}{3!} + \frac{x^5}{5!}$$
$$q_5(x) = -(x - \pi) + \frac{1}{3!}(x - \pi)^3 - \frac{1}{5!}(x - \pi)^5.$$

b. A plot of the three functions, with $\sin x$ the black solid line, $p_5(x)$ the dashed line, and $q_5(x)$ the dotted line is below.

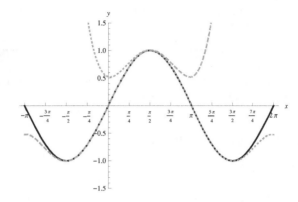

$p_5(x)$ and $\sin x$ are almost indistinguishable on $[-\pi/2, \pi/2]$, after which $p_5(x)$ diverges pretty quickly from $\sin x$. $q_5(x)$ is reasonably close to $\sin x$ over the entire range, but the two are almost indistinguishable on $[\pi/2, 3\pi/2]$. $p_5(x)$ is a better approximation than $q_5(x)$ on about $[-\pi, \pi/2)$, while $q_5(x)$ is better on about $(\pi/2, 2\pi]$.

c. Evaluating the errors gives

x	$|\sin x - p_5(x)|$	$|\sin x - q_5(x)|$
$\frac{\pi}{4}$	3.6×10^{-5}	7.4×10^{-2}
$\frac{\pi}{2}$	4.5×10^{-3}	4.5×10^{-3}
$\frac{3\pi}{4}$	7.4×10^{-2}	3.6×10^{-5}
$\frac{5\pi}{4}$	2.3	3.6×10^{-5}
$\frac{7\pi}{4}$	20.4	7.4×10^{-2}

d. $p_5(x)$ is a better approximation than $q_5(x)$ only at $x = \frac{\pi}{4}$, in accordance with part (b). The two are equal at $x = \frac{\pi}{2}$, after which $q_5(x)$ is a substantially better approximation than $p_5(x)$.

9.1.97

a. We have

$$f(36) = \sqrt{36} = 6 \qquad\qquad f(49) = \sqrt{49} = 7$$
$$f'(36) = \frac{1}{2} \cdot \frac{1}{\sqrt{36}} = \frac{1}{12} \qquad\qquad f'(49) = \frac{1}{2} \cdot \frac{1}{\sqrt{49}} = \frac{1}{14}.$$

Thus

$$p_1(x) = 6 + \frac{1}{12}(x - 36) \qquad\qquad q_1(x) = 7 + \frac{1}{14}(x - 49).$$

b. Evaluating the errors gives

x	$|\sqrt{x} - p_1(x)|$	$|\sqrt{x} - q_1(x)|$
37	5.7×10^{-4}	6.0×10^{-2}
39	5.0×10^{-3}	4.1×10^{-2}
41	1.4×10^{-2}	2.5×10^{-2}
43	2.6×10^{-2}	1.4×10^{-2}
45	4.2×10^{-2}	6.1×10^{-3}
47	6.1×10^{-2}	1.5×10^{-3}

c. $p_1(x)$ is a better approximation than $q_1(x)$ for $x \leq 41$, and $q_1(x)$ is a better approximation for $x \geq 43$. To see why this is true, note that $f''(x) = -\frac{1}{4}x^{-3/2}$, so that on $[36, 49]$ it is bounded in magnitude by $\frac{1}{4} \cdot 36^{-3/2} = \frac{1}{864}$. . Thus (using P_1 for the error term for p_1 and Q_1 for the error term for q_1)

$$P_1(x) \leq \frac{1}{864} \cdot \frac{|x-36|^2}{2!} = \frac{1}{1728}(x-36)^2, \qquad Q_1(x) \leq \frac{1}{864} \cdot \frac{|x-49|^2}{2!} = \frac{1}{1728}(x-49)^2.$$

It follows that the relative sizes of $P_1(x)$ and $Q_1(x)$ are governed by the distance of x from 36 and 49. Looking at the different possibilities for x reveals why the results in part (b) hold.

9.2   Properties of Power Series

9.2.1 $c_0 + c_1 x + c_2 x^2 + c_3 x^3$.

9.2.3 Generally the Ratio Test or Root Test is used.

9.2.5 The radius of convergence does not change, but the interval of convergence may change at the endpoints.

9.2.7 $|x| < \frac{1}{4}$.

9.2.9 Using the Root Test: $\lim_{k \to \infty} \sqrt[k]{|a_k|} = \lim_{k \to \infty} |2x| = |2x|$. So the radius of convergence is $\frac{1}{2}$. At $x = 1/2$ the series is $\sum 1$ which diverges, and at $x = -1/2$ the series is $\sum (-1)^k$ which also diverges. So the interval of convergence is $(-1/2, 1/2)$.

9.2.11 Using the Root Test, $\lim_{k \to \infty} \sqrt[k]{|a_k|} = \lim_{k \to \infty} \frac{|x-1|}{k^{1/k}} = |x - 1|$. So the radius of convergence is 1. At $x = 2$, we have the harmonic series (which diverges) and at $x = 0$ we have the alternating harmonic series (which converges). Thus the interval of convergence is $[0, 2)$.

9.2.13 Using the Ratio Test: $\lim_{k \to \infty} \left| \frac{a_{k+1}}{a_k} \right| = \lim_{k \to \infty} \left| \frac{(k+1)^{k+1} x^{k+1}}{k^k x^k} \right| = \lim_{k \to \infty} (k+1) \left(\frac{k+1}{k} \right)^k |x| = \infty$ (for $x \neq 0$) because $\lim_{k \to \infty} \left(\frac{k+1}{k} \right)^k = e$. Thus, the radius of convergence is 0, the series only converges at $x = 0$.

9.2.15 Using the Root Test: $\lim_{k \to \infty} \sqrt[k]{|a_k|} = \lim_{k \to \infty} \sin(1/k)|x| = \sin(0)|x| = 0$. Thus, the radius of convergence is ∞ and the interval of convergence is $(-\infty, \infty)$.

9.2.17 Using the Root Test: $\lim_{k \to \infty} \sqrt[k]{|a_k|} = \lim_{k \to \infty} \frac{|x|}{3} = \frac{|x|}{3}$, so the radius of convergence is 3. At -3, the series is $\sum (-1)^k$, which diverges. At 3, the series is $\sum 1$, which diverges. So the interval of convergence is $(-3, 3)$.

9.2.19 Using the Root Test: $\lim_{k \to \infty} \sqrt[k]{|a_k|} = \lim_{k \to \infty} \frac{|x|}{k} = 0$, so the radius of convergence is infinite and the interval of convergence is $(-\infty, \infty)$.

9.2.21 Using the Ratio Test: $\lim_{k \to \infty} \left| \frac{(k+1)^2 x^{2k+2}}{(k+1)!} \cdot \frac{k!}{k^2 x^{2k}} \right| = \lim_{k \to \infty} \frac{k+1}{k^2} x^2 = 0$, so the radius of convergence is infinite, and the interval of convergence is $(-\infty, \infty)$.

9.2.23 Using the Ratio Test: $\lim_{k \to \infty} \left| \frac{a_{k+1}}{a_k} \right| = \left| \frac{x^{2k+3}}{3^k} \cdot \frac{3^{k-1}}{x^{2k+1}} \right| = \frac{x^2}{3}$ so that the radius of convergence is $\sqrt{3}$. At $x = \sqrt{3}$, the series is $\sum 3\sqrt{3}$, which diverges. At $x = -\sqrt{3}$, the series is $\sum (-3\sqrt{3})$, which also diverges, so the interval of convergence is $(-\sqrt{3}, \sqrt{3})$.

9.2.25 Using the Root Test: $\lim_{k \to \infty} \sqrt[k]{|a_k|} = \lim_{k \to \infty} \frac{(|x-1|)k}{k+1} = |x - 1|$, so the series converges when $|x - 1| < 1$, so for $0 < x < 2$. The radius of convergence is 1. At $x = 2$, the series diverges by the Divergence Test. At $x = 0$, the series diverges as well by the Divergence Test. Thus the interval of convergence is $(0, 2)$.

9.2.27 Using the Ratio Test: $\lim\limits_{k\to\infty}\left|\frac{a_{k+1}}{a_k}\right| = \left|\frac{(k+1)^{20}x^{k+1}}{(2k+3)!}\cdot\frac{(2k+1)!}{x^k k^{20}}\right| = \lim\limits_{k\to\infty}\left(\frac{k+1}{k}\right)^{20}\frac{|x|}{(2k+2)(2k+3)} = 0$, so the radius of convergence is infinite, and the interval of convergence is $(-\infty,\infty)$.

9.2.29 $f(3x) = \frac{1}{1-3x} = \sum_{k=0}^{\infty}3^k x^k$, which converges for $|x| < 1/3$, and diverges at the endpoints.

9.2.31 $h(x) = \frac{2x^3}{1-x} = \sum_{k=0}^{\infty}2x^{k+3}$, which converges for $|x| < 1$ and is divergent at the endpoints.

9.2.33 $p(x) = \frac{4x^{12}}{1-x} = \sum_{k=0}^{\infty}4x^{k+12} = 4\sum_{k=0}^{\infty}x^{k+12}$, which converges for $|x| < 1$. It is divergent at the endpoints.

9.2.35 $f(3x) = \ln(1-3x) = -\sum_{k=1}^{\infty}\frac{(3x)^k}{k} = -\sum_{k=1}^{\infty}\frac{3^k}{k}x^k$. Using the Ratio Test:

$$\lim_{k\to\infty}\left|\frac{a_{k+1}}{a_k}\right| = \lim_{k\to\infty}\frac{3k}{k+1}|x| = 3|x|,$$

so the radius of convergence is $1/3$. The series diverges at $1/3$ (harmonic series), and converges at $-1/3$ (alternating harmonic series).

9.2.37 $h(x) = x\ln(1-x) = -\sum_{k=1}^{\infty}\frac{x^{k+1}}{k}$. Using the Ratio Test: $\lim\limits_{k\to\infty}\left|\frac{a_{k+1}}{a_k}\right| = \lim\limits_{k\to\infty}\frac{k}{k+1}|x| = |x|$, so the radius of convergence is 1, and the series diverges at 1 (harmonic series) but converges at -1 (alternating harmonic series).

9.2.39 $p(x) = 2x^6\ln(1-x) = -2\sum_{k=1}^{\infty}\frac{x^{k+6}}{k}$. Using the Ratio Test: $\lim\limits_{k\to\infty}\left|\frac{a_{k+1}}{a_k}\right| = \lim\limits_{k\to\infty}\frac{k}{k+1}|x| = |x|$, so the radius of convergence is 1. The series diverges at 1 (harmonic series) but converges at -1 (alternating harmonic series).

9.2.41 The power series for $f(x)$ is $\sum_{k=0}^{\infty}(2x)k$, convergent for $-1 < 2x < 1$, so for $-1/2 < x < 1/2$. The power series for $g(x) = f'(x)$ is $\sum_{k=1}^{\infty}k(2x)^{k-1}\cdot 2 = 2\sum_{k=1}^{\infty}k(2x)^{k-1}$, also convergent on $|x| < 1/2$.

9.2.43 The power series for $f(x)$ is $\sum_{k=0}^{\infty}x^k$, convergent for $-1 < x < 1$, so the power series for $g(x) = \frac{1}{6}f'''(x)$ is $\frac{1}{6}\sum_{k=3}^{\infty}k(k-1)(k-2)x^{k-3} = \frac{1}{6}\sum_{k=0}^{\infty}(k+1)(k+2)(k+3)x^k$, also convergent on $|x| < 1$.

9.2.45 The power series for $\frac{1}{1-3x}$ is $\sum_{k=0}^{\infty}(3x)^k$, convergent on $|x| < 1/3$. Because $g(x) = \ln(1-3x) = -3\int\frac{1}{1-3x}\,dx$ and because $g(0) = 0$, the power series for $g(x)$ is $-3\sum_{k=0}^{\infty}3^k\frac{1}{k+1}x^{k+1} = -\sum_{k=1}^{\infty}\frac{3^k}{k}x^k$, also convergent on $[-1/3, 1/3)$.

9.2.47 Start with $g(x) = \frac{1}{1+x}$. The power series for $g(x)$ is $\sum_{k=0}^{\infty}(-1)^k x^k$. Because $f(x) = g(x^2)$, its power series is $\sum_{k=0}^{\infty}(-1)^k x^{2k}$. The radius of convergence is still 1, and the series is divergent at both endpoints. The interval of convergence is $(-1, 1)$.

9.2.49 Note that $f(x) = \frac{3}{3+x} = \frac{1}{1+(1/3)x}$. Let $g(x) = \frac{1}{1+x}$. The power series for $g(x)$ is $\sum_{k=0}^{\infty}(-1)^k x^k$, so the power series for $f(x) = g((1/3)x)$ is $\sum_{k=0}^{\infty}(-1)^k 3^{-k}x^k = \sum_{k=0}^{\infty}\left(\frac{-x}{3}\right)^k$. Using the Ratio Test: $\lim\limits_{k\to\infty}\left|\frac{a_{k+1}}{a_k}\right| = \lim\limits_{k\to\infty}\left|\frac{3^{-(k+1)}x^{k+1}}{3^{-k}x^k}\right| = \frac{|x|}{3}$, so the radius of convergence is 3. The series diverges at both endpoints. The interval of convergence is $(-3, 3)$.

9.2.51 Note that $f(x) = \ln\sqrt{4-x^2} = \frac{1}{2}\ln(4-x^2) = \frac{1}{2}\left(\ln 4 + \ln\left(1-\frac{x^2}{4}\right)\right) = \ln 2 + \frac{1}{2}\ln\left(1-\frac{x^2}{4}\right)$. Now, the power series for $g(x) = \ln(1-x)$ is $-\sum_{k=1}^{\infty}\frac{1}{k}x^k$, so the power series for $f(x)$ is $\ln 2 - \frac{1}{2}\sum_{k=1}^{\infty}\frac{1}{k}\frac{x^{2k}}{4^k} = \ln 2 - \sum_{k=1}^{\infty}\frac{x^{2k}}{k2^{2k+1}}$. Now, $\lim\limits_{k\to\infty}\left|\frac{a_{k+1}}{a_k}\right| = \lim\limits_{k\to\infty}\left|\frac{x^{2k+2}}{(k+1)2^{2k+3}}\cdot\frac{k2^{2k+1}}{x^{2k}}\right| = \lim\limits_{k\to\infty}\frac{k}{4(k+1)}x^2 = \frac{x^2}{4}$, so that the radius of convergence is 2. The series diverges at both endpoints, so its interval of convergence is $(-2, 2)$.

9.2.53

  a. True. This power series is centered at $x = 3$, so its interval of convergence will be symmetric about 3.

  b. True. Use the Root Test.

  c. True. Substitute x^2 for x in the series.

  d. True. Because the power series is zero on the interval, all its derivatives are as well, which implies (differentiating the power series) that all the c_k are zero.

9.2.55 Using the Ratio Test: $\lim\limits_{k \to \infty} \left| \frac{a_{k+1}}{a_k} \right| = \lim\limits_{k \to \infty} \left| \frac{(k+1)!\, x^{k+1}}{(k+1)^{k+1}} \cdot \frac{k^k}{k!\, x^k} \right| = \lim\limits_{k \to \infty} \left(\frac{k}{k+1} \right)^k |x| = \frac{1}{e}|x|$. The radius of convergence is therefore e.

9.2.57 $\sum_{k=0}^{\infty} (-1)^k \frac{1}{k+1} x^k$

9.2.59 $\sum_{k=1}^{\infty} (-1)^k \frac{x^{2k}}{k!}$

9.2.61 The power series for $f(x-a)$ is $\sum c_k (x-a)^k$. Then $\sum c_k (x-a)^k$ converges if and only if $|x - a| < R$, which happens if and only if $a - R < x < a + R$, so the radius of convergence is the same.

9.2.63 This is a geometric series with ratio $\sqrt{x} - 2$, so its sum is $\frac{1}{1 - (\sqrt{x} - 2)} = \frac{1}{3 - \sqrt{x}}$. Again using the Root Test, $\lim\limits_{k \to \infty} \sqrt[k]{|a_k|} = |\sqrt{x} - 2|$, so the interval of convergence is given by $|\sqrt{x} - 2| < 1$, so $1 < \sqrt{x} < 3$ and $1 < x < 9$. The series diverges at both endpoints.

9.2.65 This is a geometric series with ratio e^{-x}, so its sum is $\frac{1}{1 - e^{-x}}$. By the Root Test, $\lim\limits_{k \to \infty} \sqrt[k]{|a_k|} = e^{-x}$, so the power series converges for $x > 0$.

9.2.67 This is a geometric series with ratio $(x^2 - 1)/3$, so its sum is $\frac{1}{1 - \frac{x^2 - 1}{3}} = \frac{3}{3 - (x^2 - 1)} = \frac{3}{4 - x^2}$. Using the Root Test, the series converges for $|x^2 - 1| < 3$, so that $-2 < x^2 < 4$ or $-2 < x < 2$. It diverges at both endpoints.

9.2.69 The power series for e^x is $\sum_{k=0}^{\infty} \frac{x^k}{k!}$. Substitute $-x$ for x to get $e^{-x} = \sum_{k=0}^{\infty} (-1)^k \frac{x^k}{k!}$. The series converges for all x.

9.2.71 Substitute $-3x$ for x in the power series for e^x to get $e^{-3x} = \sum_{k=0}^{\infty} \frac{(-3x)^k}{k!} = \sum_{k=0}^{\infty} (-1)^k \frac{3^k}{k!} x^k$. The series converges for all x.

9.2.73 The power series for $x^m f(x)$ is $\sum c_k x^{k+m}$. The radius of convergence of this power series is determined by the limit

$$\lim_{k \to \infty} \left| \frac{c_{k+1} x^{k+1+m}}{c_k x^{k+m}} \right| = \lim_{k \to \infty} \left| \frac{c_{k+1} x^{k+1}}{c_k x^k} \right|,$$

and the right-hand side is the limit used to determine the radius of convergence for the power series for $f(x)$. Thus the two have the same radius of convergence.

9.2.75

  a. $f(x)g(x) = c_0 d_0 + (c_0 d_1 + c_1 d_0)x + (c_0 d_2 + c_1 d_1 + c_2 d_0)x^2 + \ldots$

  b. The coefficient of x^n in $f(x)g(x)$ is $\sum_{i=0}^{n} c_i d_{n-i}$.

9.2.77

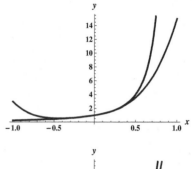

a. For both graphs, the difference between the true value and the estimate is greatest at the two ends of the range; the difference at 0.9 is greater than that at -0.9.

b. The difference between $f(x)$ and $S_n(x)$ is greatest for $x = 0.9$; at that point, $f(x) = \frac{1}{(1-0.9)^2} = 100$, so we want to find n such that $S_n(x)$ is within 0.01 of 100. We find that $S_{111} \approx 99.98991435$ and $S_{112} \approx 99.99084790$, so $n = 112$.

9.3 Taylor Series

9.3.1 The nth Taylor Polynomial is the nth sum of the corresponding Taylor Series.

9.3.3 The nth coefficient is $\frac{f^{(n)}(a)}{n!}$.

9.3.5 Substitute x^2 for x in the Taylor series. By theorems proved in the previous section about power series, the interval of convergence does not change except perhaps at the endpoints of the interval.

9.3.7 It means that the limit of the remainder term is zero.

9.3.9

a. Note that $f(0) = 1$, $f'(0) = -1$, $f''(0) = 1$, and $f'''(0) = -1$. So the Maclaurin series is $1 - x + x^2/2 - x^3/6 + \cdots$.

b. $\sum_{k=0}^{\infty} (-1)^k \frac{x^k}{k!}$.

c. The series converges on $(-\infty, \infty)$, as can be seen from the Ratio Test.

9.3.11

a. Because the series for $\frac{1}{1+x}$ is $1 - x + x^2 - x^3 + \cdots$, the series for $\frac{1}{1+x^2}$ is $1 - x^2 + x^4 - x^6 + \cdots$.

b. $\sum_{k=0}^{\infty} (-1)^k x^{2k}$.

c. The absolute value of the ratio of consecutive terms is x^2, so by the Ratio Test, the radius of convergence is 1. The series diverges at the endpoints by the Divergence Test, so the interval of convergence is $(-1, 1)$.

9.3.13

   a. Note that $f(0) = 1$, and that $f^{(n)}(0) = 2^n$. Thus, the series is given by $1 + 2x + \frac{4x^2}{2} + \frac{8x^3}{6} + \cdots$.

   b. $\sum_{k=0}^{\infty} \frac{(2x)^k}{k!}$.

   c. The absolute value of the ratio of consecutive terms is $\frac{2|x|}{n}$, which has limit 0 as $n \to \infty$. So by the Ratio Test, the interval of convergence is $(-\infty, \infty)$.

9.3.15

   a. By integrating the Taylor series for $\frac{1}{1+x^2}$ (which is the derivative of $\tan^{-1}(x)$), we obtain the series $x - \frac{x^3}{3} + \frac{x^5}{5} - \frac{x^7}{7} + \cdots$. Then by replacing x by $x/2$ we have $\frac{x}{2} - \frac{x^3}{3 \cdot 2^3} + \frac{x^5}{5 \cdot 2^5} - \frac{x^7}{7 \cdot 2^7} + \cdots$.

   b. $\sum_{k=0}^{\infty} (-1)^k \frac{1}{(2k+1) \cdot 2^{2k+1}} x^{2k+1}$.

   c. By the Ratio Test (the ratio of consecutive terms has limit $\frac{x^2}{4}$), the radius of convergence is $|x| < 2$. Also, at the endpoints we have convergence by the Alternating Series Test, so the interval of convergence is $[-2, 2]$.

9.3.17

   a. Note that $f(0) = 1$, $f'(0) = \ln 3$, $f''(0) = \ln^2 3$, $f''(0) = \ln^3 3$. So the first four terms of the desired series are $1 + (\ln 3)x + \frac{\ln^2 3}{2}x^2 + \frac{\ln^3 3}{6}x^3 + \cdots$.

   b. $\sum_{k=0}^{\infty} \frac{(\ln^k 3)x^k}{k!}$.

   c. The ratio of successive terms is $\frac{(\ln^{k+1} 3)x^{k+1}}{(k+1)!} \cdot \frac{k!}{(\ln^k 3)x^k} = \frac{\ln 3}{k+1}x$, and the limit as $k \to \infty$ of this quantity is 0, so the interval of convergence is $(-\infty, \infty)$.

9.3.19

   a. Note that $f(0) = 1$, $f'(0) = 0$, $f''(0) = 9$, $f'''(0) = 0$, etc. The first terms of the series are $1 + 9x^2/2 + 81x^4/4! + 3^6x^6/6! + \cdots$.

   b. $\sum_{k=0}^{\infty} \frac{(3x)^{2k}}{(2k)!}$.

   c. The absolute value of the ratio of successive terms is $\left| \frac{(3x)^{2k+2}}{(2k+2)!} \cdot \frac{(2k)!}{(3x)^{2k}} \right| = \frac{1}{(2k+2)(2k+1)} \cdot 9x^2$, which has limit 0 as $x \to \infty$. The interval of convergence is therefore $(-\infty, \infty)$.

9.3.21

   a. Note that $f(\pi/2) = 1$, $f'(\pi/2) = \cos(\pi/2) = 0$, $f''(\pi/2) = -\sin(\pi/2) = -1$, $f'''(\pi/2) = -\cos(\pi/2) = 0$, and so on. Thus the series is given by $1 - \frac{1}{2}\left(x - \frac{\pi}{2}\right)^2 + \frac{1}{24}\left(x - \frac{\pi}{2}\right)^4 - \frac{1}{720}\left(x - \frac{\pi}{2}\right)^6 + \cdots$.

   b. $\sum_{k=0}^{\infty} (-1)^k \frac{1}{(2k)!} \left(x - \frac{\pi}{2}\right)^{2k}$.

9.3.23

   a. Note that $f^{(k)}(1) = (-1)^k \frac{k!}{1^{k+1}} = (-1)^k \cdot k!$. Thus the series is given by $1 - (x-1) + (x-1)^2 - (x-1)^3 + \cdots$.

   b. $\sum_{k=0}^{\infty} (-1)^k (x - 1)^k$.

9.3.25

   a. Note that $f^{(k)}(3) = (-1)^{k-1} \frac{(k-1)!}{3^k}$. Thus the series is given by $\ln(3) + \frac{x-3}{3} - \frac{1}{18}(x-3)^2 + \frac{1}{81}(x-3)^3 + \cdots$.

   b. $\ln 3 + \sum_{k=1}^{\infty} (-1)^{k+1} \frac{1}{k \cdot 3^k} (x - 3)^k$.

9.3.27

a. Note that $f(1) = 2$, $f'(1) = 2 \ln 2$, $f''(1) = 2 \ln^2 2$, $f'''(1) = 2 \ln^3 2$. The first terms of the series are $2 + (2 \ln 2)(x - 1) + (\ln^2 2)(x - 1)^2 + \frac{(\ln^3 2)(x-1)^3}{3} + \cdots$.

b. $\sum_{k=0}^{\infty} \frac{2(x-1)^k \ln^k 2}{k!}$.

9.3.29 Because the Taylor series for $\ln(1 + x)$ is $x - \frac{x^2}{2} + \frac{x^3}{3} - \frac{x^4}{4} + \cdots$, the first four terms of the Taylor series for $\ln(1 + x^2)$ are $x^2 - \frac{x^4}{2} + \frac{x^6}{3} - \frac{x^8}{4} + \cdots$, obtained by substituting x^2 for x.

9.3.31 Because the Taylor series for $\frac{1}{1-x} = 1 + x + x^2 + x^3 + \cdots$, the first four terms of the Taylor series for $\frac{1}{1-2x}$ are $1 + 2x + 4x^2 + 8x^3 + \cdots$ obtained by substituting $2x$ for x.

9.3.33 The Taylor series for $e^x - 1$ is the Taylor series for e^x, less the constant term of 1, so it is $x + \frac{x^2}{2} + \frac{x^3}{3!} + \frac{x^4}{4!} + \cdots$. Thus, the first four terms of the Taylor series for $\frac{e^x - 1}{x}$ are $1 + \frac{x}{2!} + \frac{x^2}{3!} + \frac{x^3}{4!} + \cdots$, obtained by dividing the terms of the first series by x.

9.3.35 Because the Taylor series for $(1 + x)^{-1}$ is $1 - x + x^2 - x^3 + \cdots$, if we substitute x^4 for x, we obtain $1 - x^4 + x^8 - x^{12} + \cdots$.

9.3.37 The Taylor series for $\sinh x$ is $x + \frac{x^3}{6} + \frac{x^5}{120} + \frac{x^7}{5040} + \cdots$. Thus, the Taylor series for $\sinh x^2$ is $x^2 + \frac{x^6}{6} + \frac{x^{10}}{120} + \frac{x^{14}}{5040} + \cdots$ obtained by substituting x^2 for x.

9.3.39

a. The binomial coefficients are $\binom{-2}{0} = 1$, $\binom{-2}{1} = \frac{-2}{1!} = -2$, $\binom{-2}{2} = \frac{(-2)(-3)}{2!} = 3$, $\binom{-2}{3} = \frac{(-2)(-3)(-4)}{3!} = -4$.

Thus the first four terms of the series are $1 - 2x + 3x^2 - 4x^3 + \cdots$.

b. $1 - 2 \cdot 0.1 + 3 \cdot 0.01 - 4 \cdot 0.001 = 0.826$

9.3.41

a. The binomial coefficients are $\binom{1/4}{0} = 1$, $\binom{1/4}{1} = \frac{1/4}{1} = \frac{1}{4}$, $\binom{1/4}{2} = \frac{(1/4)(-3/4)}{2!} = -\frac{3}{32}$, $\binom{1/4}{3} = \frac{(1/4)(-3/4)(-7/4)}{3!} = \frac{7}{128}$, so the first four terms of the series are $1 + \frac{1}{4}x - \frac{3}{32}x^2 + \frac{7}{128}x^3 + \cdots$.

b. Substitute $x = 0.12$ to get approximately 1.029.

9.3.43

a. The binomial coefficients are $\binom{-2/3}{0} = 1$, $\binom{-2/3}{1} = -\frac{2}{3}$, $\binom{-2/3}{2} = \frac{(-2/3)(-5/3)}{2!} = \frac{5}{9}$, $\binom{-2/3}{3} = \frac{(-2/3)(-5/3)(-8/3)}{3!} = -\frac{40}{81}$, so the first four terms of the series are $1 - \frac{2}{3}x + \frac{5}{9}x^2 - \frac{40}{81}x^3 + \cdots$.

b. Substitute $x = 0.18$ to get 0.89512.

9.3.45 $\sqrt{1 + x^2} = 1 + \frac{x^2}{2} - \frac{x^4}{8} + \frac{x^6}{16} - \cdots$. By the Ratio Test, the radius of convergence is 1. At the endpoints, the series obtained are convergent by the Alternating Series Test. Thus, the interval of convergence is $[-1, 1]$.

9.3.47 $\sqrt{9 - 9x} = 3\sqrt{1 - x} = 3 - \frac{3}{2}x - \frac{3}{8}x^2 - \frac{3}{16}x^3 - \cdots$. The interval of convergence is $[-1, 1]$.

9.3.49 $\sqrt{a^2 + x^2} = a\sqrt{1 + \frac{x^2}{a^2}} = a + \frac{x^2}{2a} - \frac{x^4}{8a^3} + \frac{x^6}{16a^5} - \cdots$. The series converges when $\frac{x^2}{a^2}$ is less than 1 in magnitude, so the radius of convergence is a. The series given by the endpoints is convergent by the Alternating Series Test, so the interval of convergence is $[-a, a]$.

9.3.51 $(1 + 4x)^{-2} = 1 - 2(4x) + 3(4x)^2 - 4(4x)^3 + \cdots = 1 - 8x + 48x^2 - 256x^3 + \cdots$.

9.3.53 $\frac{1}{(4+x^2)^2} = (4+x^2)^{-2} = \frac{1}{16}(1+(x^2/4))^{-2} = \frac{1}{16}\left(1 - 2\cdot\frac{x^2}{4} + 3\cdot\frac{x^4}{16} - 4\cdot\frac{x^6}{64} + \cdots\right) = \frac{1}{16} - \frac{1}{32}x^2 + \frac{3}{256}x^4 - \frac{1}{256}x^6 + \cdots$

9.3.55 $(3+4x)^{-2} = \frac{1}{9}\left(1 + \frac{4x}{3}\right)^{-2} = \frac{1}{9} - \frac{2}{9}\left(\frac{4x}{3}\right) + \frac{3}{9}\left(\frac{4x}{3}\right)^2 - \frac{4}{9}\left(\frac{4x}{3}\right)^3 + \cdots.$

9.3.57 The interval of convergence for the Taylor series for $f(x) = \sin x$ is $(-\infty, \infty)$. The remainder is $R_n(x) = \frac{f^{(n+1)}(c)}{(n+1)!}x^{n+1}$ for some c. Because $f^{(n+1)}(x)$ is $\pm\sin x$ or $\pm\cos x$, we have

$$\lim_{n\to\infty} |R_n(x)| \le \lim_{n\to\infty} \frac{1}{(n+1)!}\left|x^{n+1}\right| = 0$$

for any x.

9.3.59 The interval of convergence for the Taylor series for e^{-x} is $(-\infty, \infty)$. The remainder is $R_n(x) = \frac{(-1)^{n+1}e^{-c}}{(n+1)!}x^{n+1}$ for some c. Thus $\lim_{n\to\infty} |R_n(x)| = 0$ for any x.

9.3.61

  a. False. Not all of its derivatives are defined at zero - in fact, none of them are.

  b. True. The derivatives of $\csc x$ involve positive powers of $\csc x$ and $\cot x$, both of which are defined at $\pi/2$, so that $\csc x$ has continuous derivatives at $\pi/2$.

  c. False. For example, the Taylor series for $f(x^2)$ doesn't converge at $x = 1.9$, because the Taylor series for $f(x)$ doesn't converge at $1.9^2 = 3.61$.

  d. False. The Taylor series centered at 1 involves derivatives of f evaluated at 1, not at 0.

  e. True. The follows because the Taylor series must itself be an even function.

9.3.63

  a. The relevant Taylor series are: $e^x = 1 + x + \frac{x^2}{2!} + \frac{x^3}{3!} + \frac{x^4}{4!} + \frac{x^5}{5!} + \frac{x^6}{6!} + \cdots$ and $e^{-x} = 1 - x + \frac{x^2}{2!} - \frac{x^3}{3!} + \frac{x^4}{4!} - \frac{x^5}{5!} + \frac{x^6}{6!} + \cdots$. Thus the first four terms of the resulting series are $\frac{1}{2}(e^x + e^{-x}) = 1 + \frac{x^2}{2!} + \frac{x^4}{4!} + \frac{x^6}{6!} + \cdots$.

  b. Because each series converges (absolutely) on $(-\infty, \infty)$, so does their sum. The radius of convergence is ∞.

9.3.65

  a. Use the binomial theorem. The binomial coefficients are $\binom{-2/3}{0} = 1$, $\binom{-2/3}{1} = -\frac{2}{3}$, $\binom{-2/3}{2} = \frac{(-2/3)(-5/3)}{2!} = \frac{5}{9}$, $\binom{-2/3}{3} = \frac{(-2/3)(-5/3)(-8/3)}{3!} = -\frac{40}{81}$ and then, substituting x^2 for x, we obtain $1 - \frac{2}{3}x^2 + \frac{5}{9}x^4 - \frac{40}{81}x^6 + \cdots$.

  b. From Theorem 9.6 the radius of convergence is determined from $\left|x^2\right| < 1$, so it is 1.

9.3.67

  a. From the binomial formula, the Taylor series for $(1-x)^p$ is $\sum \binom{p}{k}(-1)^k x^k$, so the Taylor series for $(1-x^2)^p$ is $\sum \binom{p}{k}(-1)^k x^{2k}$. Here $p = 1/2$, and the binomial coefficients are $\binom{1/2}{0} = 1$, $\binom{1/2}{1} = \frac{1/2}{1!} = \frac{1}{2}$, $\binom{1/2}{2} = \frac{(1/2)(-1/2)}{2!} = -\frac{1}{8}$, $\binom{1/2}{3} = \frac{(1/2)(-1/2)(-3/2)}{3!} = \frac{1}{16}$ so that $(1-x^2)^{1/2} = 1 - \frac{1}{2}x^2 - \frac{1}{8}x^4 - \frac{1}{16}x^6 + \cdots$.

  b. From Theorem 9.6 the radius of convergence is determined from $\left|x^2\right| < 1$, so it is 1.

9.3.69

  a. $f(x) = (1+x^2)^{-2}$; using the binomial series and substituting x^2 for x we obtain $1 - 2x^2 + 3x^4 - 4x^6 + \cdots$.

  b. From Theorem 9.6 the radius of convergence is determined from $\left|x^2\right| < 1$, so it is 1.

9.3.71 Because $f(64) = 4$, and $f'(x) = \frac{1}{3}x^{-2/3}$, $f'(64) = \frac{1}{48}$, $f''(x) = -\frac{2}{9}x^{-5/3}$, $f''(64) = -\frac{1}{4608}$, $f'''(x) = \frac{10}{27}x^{-8/3}$, and $f'''(64) = \frac{10}{1769472} = \frac{5}{884736}$, the first four terms of the Taylor series are $4 + \frac{1}{48}(x-64) - \frac{1}{4608 \cdot 2!}(x-64)^2 + \frac{5}{884736 \cdot 3!}(x-64)^3$. Evaluating at $x = 60$, we get 3.914870274.

9.3.73 Because $f(16) = 2$, and $f'(x) = \frac{1}{4}x^{-3/4}$, $f'(16) = \frac{1}{32}$, $f''(x) = -\frac{3}{16}x^{-7/4}$, $f''(16) = -\frac{3}{2048}$, $f'''(x) = \frac{21}{64}x^{-11/4}$, and $f'''(16) = \frac{21}{131072}$, the first four terms of the Taylor series are $2 + \frac{1}{32}(x-16) - \frac{3}{2048 \cdot 2!}(x-16)^2 + \frac{21}{131072 \cdot 3!}(x-16)^3$. Evaluating at $x = 13$, we get 1.898937225.

9.3.75 Evaluate the binomial coefficient $\binom{1/2}{k} = \frac{(1/2)(-1/2)(-3/2)\cdots(1/2-k+1)}{k!} = \frac{(1/2)(-1/2)\cdots((3-2k)/2)}{k!} = (-1)^{k-1}2^{-k}\frac{1\cdot3\cdots(2k-3)}{k!} = (-1)^{k-1}2^{-k}\frac{(2k-2)!}{2^{k-1}\cdot(k-1)!\cdot k!} = (-1)^{k-1}2^{1-2k} \cdot \frac{1}{k}\binom{2k-2}{k-1}$. This is the coefficient of x^k in the Taylor series for $\sqrt{1+x}$. Substituting $4x$ for x, the Taylor series becomes $\sum_{k=0}^{\infty}(-1)^{k-1}2^{1-2k} \cdot \frac{1}{k}\binom{2k-2}{k-1}(4x)^k = \sum_{k=0}^{\infty}(-1)^{k-1}\frac{2}{k}\binom{2k-2}{k-1}x^k$. If we can show that k divides $\binom{2k-2}{k-1}$, we will be done, for then the coefficient of x^k will be an integer. But $\binom{2k-2}{k-1}-\binom{2k-2}{k-2} = \frac{(2k-2)!}{(k-1)!(k-1)!} - \frac{(2k-2)!}{(k-2)!k!} = \frac{(2k-2)!}{(k-1)!(k-1)!} - \frac{(2k-2)!(k-1)}{(k-1)!(k-1)!k} = \frac{k(2k-2)!-(k-1)(2k-2)!}{k(k-1)!(k-1)!} = \frac{1}{k}\frac{(2k-2)!}{(k-1)!(k-1)!} = \frac{1}{k}\binom{2k-2}{k-1}$ and thus we have shown that k divides $\binom{2k-2}{k-1}$.

9.3.77

a. The Maclaurin series for $\sin x$ is $x - \frac{1}{3!}x^3 + \frac{1}{5!}x^5 - \frac{1}{7!}x^7 + \cdots$. Squaring the first four terms yields

$$\left(x - \frac{1}{3!}x^3 + \frac{1}{5!}x^5 - \frac{1}{7!}x^7\right)^2$$
$$= x^2 - \frac{2}{3!}x^4 + \left(\frac{2}{5!} + \frac{1}{3!3!}\right)x^6 + \left(-2\cdot\frac{1}{7!} - 2\cdot\frac{1}{3!5!}\right)x^8$$
$$= x^2 - \frac{1}{3}x^4 + \frac{2}{45}x^6 - \frac{1}{315}x^8.$$

b. The Maclaurin series for $\cos x$ is $1 - \frac{1}{2}x^2 + \frac{1}{4!}x^4 - \frac{1}{6!}x^6 + \frac{1}{8!}x^8 - \cdots$. Substituting $2x$ for x in the Maclaurin series for $\cos x$ and then computing $(1 - \cos 2x)/2$, we obtain

$$(1 - (1-\frac{1}{2}(2x)^2 + \frac{1}{4!}(2x)^4 - \frac{1}{6!}(2x)^6 + \frac{1}{8!}(2x)^8)/2$$
$$= (2x^2 - \frac{2}{3}x^4 + \frac{4}{45}x^6 - \frac{2}{315}x^8)/2$$
$$= x^2 - \frac{1}{3}x^4 + \frac{2}{45}x^6 - \frac{1}{315}x^8,$$

and the two are the same.

c. If $f(x) = \sin^2 x$, then $f(0) = 0$, $f'(x) = \sin 2x$, so $f'(0) = 0$. $f''(x) = 2\cos 2x$, so $f''(x) = 2$, $f'''(x) = -4\sin 2x$, so $f'''(0) = 0$. Note that from this point $f^{(n)}(0) = 0$ if n is odd and $f^{(n)}(0) = \pm 2^{n-1}$ if n is even, with the signs alternating for every other even n. Thus, the series for $\sin^2 x$ is

$$2x^2/2 - 8x^4/4! + 32x^6/6! - 128x^8/8! + \cdots = x^2 - \frac{1}{3}x^4 + \frac{2}{45}x^6 - \frac{1}{315}x^8 + \cdots.$$

9.3.79 There are many solutions. For example, first find a series that has $(-1, 1)$ as an interval of convergence, say $\frac{1}{1-x} = \sum_{k=0}^{\infty} x^k$. Then the series $\frac{1}{1-x/2} = \sum_{k=0}^{\infty} \left(\frac{x}{2}\right)^k$ has $(-2, 2)$ as its interval of convergence. Now shift the series up so that it is centered at 4. We have $\sum_{k=0}^{\infty} \left(\frac{x-4}{2}\right)^k$, which has interval of convergence $(2, 6)$.

9.3.81 $\frac{1\cdot3\cdot5\cdot7}{2\cdot4\cdot6\cdot8}x^4 - \frac{1\cdot3\cdot5\cdot7\cdot9}{2\cdot4\cdot6\cdot8\cdot10}x^5$.

9.3.83 Use the Taylor series for $\cos x$ centered at $\pi/4$: $\frac{\sqrt{2}}{2}(1 - (x - \pi/4) - \frac{1}{2}(x - \pi/4)^2 + \frac{1}{6}(x - \pi/4)^3 + \cdots)$. The remainder after n terms (because the derivatives of $\cos x$ are bounded by 1 in magnitude) is $|R_n(x)| \leq \frac{1}{(n+1)!} \cdot \left(\frac{\pi}{4} - \frac{2\pi}{9}\right)^{n+1}$.

Solving for $|R_n(x)| < 10^{-4}$, we obtain $n = 3$. Evaluating the first four terms (through $n = 3$) of the series we get 0.7660427050. The true value is ≈ 0.7660444431.

9.3.85 Use the Taylor series for $f(x) = x^{1/3}$ centered at 64: $4 + \frac{1}{48}(x - 64) - \frac{1}{9216}(x - 64)^2 + \cdots$. Because we wish to evaluate this series at $x = 83$, $|R_n(x)| = \frac{|f^{(n+1)}(c)|}{(n+1)!}(83 - 64)^{n+1}$. We compute that $|f^{(n+1)}(c)| = \frac{2 \cdot 5 \cdots (3n-1)}{3^{n+1}c^{(3n+2)/3}}$, which is maximized at $c = 64$. Thus

$$|R_n(x)| \leq \frac{2 \cdot 5 \cdots (3n-1)}{3^{n+1}64^{(3n+2)/3}(n+1)!}19^{n+1}$$

Solving for $|R_n(x)| < 10^{-4}$, we obtain $n = 5$. Evaluating the terms of the series through $n = 5$ gives 4.362122553. The true value is ≈ 4.362070671.

9.3.87

    a. Use the Taylor series for $(125 + x)^{1/3}$ centered at $x = 0$. Using the first four terms and evaluating at $x = 3$ gives a result (5.03968) accurate to within 10^{-4}.

    b. Use the Taylor series for $x^{1/3}$ centered at $x = 125$. Note that this gives the identical Taylor series except that the exponential terms are $(x - 125)^n$ rather than x^n. Thus we need terms up through $(x - 125)^3$, just as before, evaluated at $x = 128$, and we obtain the identical result.

    c. Because the two Taylor series are the same except for the shifting, the results are equivalent.

9.3.89 Consider the remainder after the first term of the Taylor series. Taylor's Theorem indicates that $R_1(x) = \frac{f''(c)}{2}(x - a)^2$ for some c between x and a, so that $f(x) = f(a) + f'(a)(x - a) + \frac{f''(c)}{2}(x - a)^2$. But $f'(a) = 0$, so that for every x in an interval containing a, there is a c between x and a such that $f(x) = f(a) + \frac{f''(c)}{2}(x - a)^2$.

    a. If $f''(x) > 0$ on the interval containing a, then for every x in that interval, we have $f(x) = f(a) + \frac{f''(c)}{2}(x - a)^2$ for some c between x and a. But $f''(c) > 0$ and $(x - a)^2 > 0$, so that $f(x) > f(a)$ and a is a local minimum.

    b. If $f''(x) < 0$ on the interval containing a, then for every x in that interval, we have $f(x) = f(a) + \frac{f''(c)}{2}(x - a)^2$ for some c between x and a. But $f''(c) < 0$ and $(x - a)^2 > 0$, so that $f(x) < f(a)$ and a is a local maximum.

9.4   Working with Taylor Series

9.4.1 Replace f and g by their Taylor series centered at a, and evaluate the limit.

9.4.3 Substitute -0.6 for x in the Taylor series for e^x centered at 0. Note that this series is an alternating series, so the error can easily be estimated by looking at the magnitude of the first neglected term.

9.4.5 The series is $f'(x) = \sum_{k=1}^{\infty} kc_k x^{k-1}$, which converges for $|x| < b$.

9.4.7 Because $e^x = 1 + x + x^2/2! + x^3/3! + \cdots$, we have $\frac{e^x - 1}{x} = 1 + x/2! + \cdots$, so $\lim_{x \to 0} \frac{e^x - 1}{x} = 1$.

9.4.9 Because $-\ln(1 - x) = x + \frac{x^2}{2} + \frac{x^3}{3} + \frac{x^4}{4} + \frac{x^5}{5} + \cdots$, we have $\frac{-x - \ln(1-x)}{x^2} = \frac{1}{2} + \frac{x}{3} + \frac{x^2}{4} + \cdots$, so $\lim_{x \to 0} \frac{-x - \ln(1-x)}{x^2} = \frac{1}{2}$.

9.4.11 We compute that

$$\frac{e^x - e^{-x}}{x} = \frac{1}{x}\left(\left(1 + x + \frac{x^2}{2} + \frac{x^3}{6} + \cdots\right) - \left(1 - x + \frac{x^2}{2} - \frac{x^3}{6} + \cdots\right)\right)$$

$$= \frac{1}{x}\left(2x + \frac{x^3}{3} + \cdots\right) = 2 + \frac{x^2}{3} + \cdots$$

so the limit of $\dfrac{e^x - e^{-x}}{x}$ as $x \to 0$ is 2.

9.4.13 We compute that

$$\frac{2\cos 2x - 2 + 4x^2}{2x^4} = \frac{1}{2x^4}\left(2(1 - \frac{(2x)^2}{2} + \frac{(2x)^4}{24} - \frac{(2x)^6}{720} + \cdots) - 2 + 4x^2\right)$$

$$= \frac{1}{2x^4}\left(\frac{(2x)^4}{12} - \frac{(2x)^6}{360} + \cdots\right) = \frac{2}{3} - \frac{4x^2}{45} + \cdots$$

so the limit of $\dfrac{2\cos 2x - 2 + 4x^2}{2x^4}$ as $x \to 0$ is $\dfrac{2}{3}$.

9.4.15 We have $\ln(1+x) = x - \frac{1}{2}x^2 + \frac{1}{3}x^3 - \frac{1}{4}x^4 + \cdots$, so that

$$\frac{\ln(1+x) - x + x^2/2}{x^3} = \frac{x^3/3 - x^4/4 + \cdots}{x^3} = \frac{1}{3} - \frac{x}{4} + \cdots$$

so that $\displaystyle\lim_{x\to 0} \frac{\ln(1+x) - x + x^2/2}{x^3} = \frac{1}{3}$.

9.4.17 We compute that

$$\frac{3\tan^{-1}x - 3x + x^3}{x^5} = \frac{1}{x^5}\left(3\left(x - \frac{x^3}{3} + \frac{x^5}{5} - \frac{x^7}{7} + \cdots\right) - 3x + x^3\right)$$

$$= \frac{1}{x^5}\left(\frac{3x^5}{5} - \frac{3x^7}{7} + \cdots\right) = \frac{3}{5} - \frac{3x^2}{7} + \cdots$$

so the limit of $\dfrac{3\tan^{-1}x - 3x + x^3}{x^5}$ as $x \to 0$ is $\dfrac{3}{5}$.

9.4.19 The Taylor series for $\sin 2x$ centered at 0 is

$$\sin 2x = 2x - \frac{1}{3!}(2x)^3 + \frac{1}{5!}(2x)^5 - \frac{1}{7!}(2x)^7 + \cdots = 2x - \frac{4}{3}x^3 + \frac{4}{15}x^5 - \frac{8}{315}x^7 + \cdots.$$

Thus

$$\frac{12x - 8x^3 - 6\sin 2x}{x^5} = \frac{12 - 8x^3 - (12x - 8x^3 + \frac{8}{5}x^5 - \frac{16}{105}x^7 + \cdots)}{x^5}$$

$$= -\frac{8}{5} + \frac{16}{105}x^2 - \cdots,$$

so $\displaystyle\lim_{x\to 0} \frac{12x - 8x^3 - 6\sin 2x}{x^5} = -\frac{8}{5}$.

9.4.21 The Taylor series for $\ln(x-1)$ centered at 2 is

$$\ln(x-1) = (x-2) - \frac{1}{2}(x-2)^2 + \cdots.$$

We compute that

$$\frac{x-2}{\ln(x-1)} = \frac{x-2}{(x-2) - \frac{1}{2}(x-2)^2 + \cdots} = \frac{1}{1 - \frac{1}{2}(x-2) + \cdots}$$

so the limit of $\dfrac{x-2}{\ln(x-1)}$ as $x \to 2$ is 1.

9.4.23 Computing Taylor series centers at 0 gives

$$e^{-2x} = 1 - 2x + \frac{1}{2!}(-2x)^2 + \frac{1}{3!}(-2x)^3 + \cdots = 1 - 2x + 2x^2 - \frac{4}{3}x^3 + \cdots$$

$$e^{-x/2} = 1 - \frac{x}{2} + \frac{1}{2!}\left(-\frac{x}{2}\right)^2 + \frac{1}{3!}\left(-\frac{x}{2}\right)^3 + \cdots = 1 - \frac{x}{2} + \frac{1}{8}x^2 - \frac{1}{48}x^3 + \cdots.$$

Thus

$$\frac{e^{-2x} - 4e^{-x/2} + 3}{2x^2} = \frac{1 - 2x + 2x^2 - \frac{4}{3}x^3 + \cdots - (4 - 2x + \frac{1}{2}x^2 - \frac{1}{12}x^3 + \cdots) + 3}{2x^2}$$

$$= \frac{\frac{3}{2}x^2 - \frac{5}{4}x^3 + \cdots}{2x^2}$$

$$= \frac{3}{4} - \frac{5}{8}x + \cdots$$

so $\lim\limits_{x \to 0} \dfrac{e^{-2x} - 4e^{-x/2} + 3}{2x^2} = \dfrac{3}{4}$.

9.4.25

a. $f'(x) = \frac{d}{dx}\left(\sum_{k=0}^{\infty} \frac{x^k}{k!}\right) = \sum_{k=1}^{\infty} k\frac{x^{k-1}}{k!} = \sum_{k=0}^{\infty} \frac{x^k}{k!} = f(x)$.

b. $f'(x) = e^x$ as well.

c. The series converges on $(-\infty, \infty)$.

9.4.27

a. $f'(x) = \frac{d}{dx}(\ln(1+x)) = \frac{d}{dx}\left(\sum_{k=1}^{\infty}(-1)^{k+1}\frac{1}{k}x^k\right) = \sum_{k=1}^{\infty}(-1)^{k+1}x^{k-1} = \sum_{k=0}^{\infty}(-1)^k x^k$.

b. This is the power series for $\frac{1}{1+x}$.

c. The Taylor series for $\ln(1+x)$ converges on $(-1, 1)$, as does the Taylor series for $\frac{1}{1+x}$.

9.4.29

a.

$$f'(x) = \frac{d}{dx}(e^{-2x}) = \frac{d}{dx}\left(\sum_{k=0}^{\infty} \frac{(-2x)^k}{k!}\right) = \frac{d}{dx}\left(\sum_{k=0}^{\infty}(-2)^k\frac{x^k}{k!}\right) = -2\sum_{k=1}^{\infty}(-2)^{k-1}\frac{x^{k-1}}{(k-1)!} = -2\sum_{k=0}^{\infty}\frac{(-2x)^k}{k!}.$$

b. This is the Taylor series for $-2e^{-2x}$.

c. Because the Taylor series for e^{-2x} converges on $(-\infty, \infty)$, so does this one.

9.4.31

a. $\tan^{-1} x = x - \frac{x^3}{3} + \frac{x^5}{5} - \cdots$, so $\frac{d}{dx}\tan^{-1}x^2 = 1 - x^2 + x^4 - x^6 + \cdots$.

b. This is the series for $\frac{1}{1+x^2}$.

c. Because the series for $\tan^{-1} x$ has a radius of convergence of 1, this series does too. Checking the endpoints shows that the interval of convergence is $(-1, 1)$.

9.4.33

a. Because $y(0) = 2$, we have $0 = y'(0) - y(0) = y'(0) - 2$ so that $y'(0) = 2$. Differentiating the equation gives $y''(0) = y'(0)$, so that $y''(0) = 2$. Successive derivatives also have the value 2 at 0, so the Taylor series is $2\sum_{k=0}^{\infty}\frac{t^k}{k!}$.

b. $2\sum_{k=0}^{\infty}\frac{t^k}{k!} = 2e^t$.

9.4.35

a. $y(0) = 2$, so that $y'(0) = 16$. Differentiating, $y''(t) - 3y'(t) = 0$, so that $y''(0) = 48$, and in general $y^{(k)}(0) = 3y^{(k-1)}(0) = 3^{k-1} \cdot 16$. Thus the power series is $2 + \frac{16}{3}\sum_{k=1}^{\infty}\frac{(3t)^k}{k!} = 2 + \sum_{k=1}^{\infty}\frac{3^{k-1}16}{k!}t^k$.

b. $2 + \frac{16}{3}\sum_{k=1}^{\infty}\frac{(3t)^k}{k!} = 2 + \frac{16}{3}(e^{3t} - 1) = \frac{16}{3}e^{3t} - \frac{10}{3}$.

9.4.37 The Taylor series for e^{-x^2} is $\sum_{k=0}^{\infty}(-1)^k\frac{x^{2k}}{k!}$. Thus, the desired integral is $\int_0^{0.25}\sum_{k=0}^{\infty}(-1)^k\frac{x^{2k}}{k!}\,dx = $
$\sum_{k=0}^{\infty}(-1)^k\frac{x^{2k+1}}{(2k+1)k!}\Big|_0^{0.25} = \sum_{k=0}^{\infty}(-1)^k\frac{1}{(2k+1)k!4^{2k+1}}$. Because this is an alternating series, to approximate it to within 10^{-4}, we must find n such that $a_{n+1} < 10^{-4}$, or $\frac{1}{(2n+3)(n+1)!\cdot4^{2n+3}} < 10^{-4}$. This occurs for $n = 1$, so $\sum_{k=0}^{1}(-1)^k\frac{1}{(2k+1)\cdot k!\cdot4^{2k+1}} = \frac{1}{4} - \frac{1}{192} \approx 0.245$.

9.4.39 The Taylor series for $\cos 2x^2$ is $\sum_{k=0}^{\infty}(-1)^k\frac{(2x^2)^{2k}}{(2k)!} = \sum_{k=0}^{\infty}(-1)^k\frac{4^k x^{4k}}{(2k)!}$. Note that $\cos x$ is an even function, so we compute the integral from 0 to 0.35 and double it:

$$2\int_0^{0.35}\sum_{k=0}^{\infty}(-1)^k\frac{4^k x^{4k}}{(2k)!}\,dx = 2\left(\sum_{k=0}^{\infty}(-1)^k\frac{4^k x^{4k+1}}{(4k+1)(2k)!}\right)\Big|_0^{0.35} = 2\left(\sum_{k=0}^{\infty}(-1)^k\frac{4^k(0.35)^{4k+1}}{(4k+1)(2k)!}\right).$$

Because this is an alternating series, to approximate it to within $\frac{1}{2}\cdot10^{-4}$, we must find n such that $a_{n+1} < \frac{1}{2}\cdot10^{-4}$, or $\frac{4^{n+1}(0.35)^{4n+5}}{(4n+3)(2n+2)!} < \frac{1}{2}\cdot10^{-4}$. This occurs first for $n = 1$, and we have $2\left(.35 - \frac{4\cdot(0.35)^5}{5\cdot2!}\right) \approx 0.696$.

9.4.41 $\tan^{-1}x = x - x^3/3 + x^5/5 - x^7/7 + x^9/9 - \cdots$, so $\int\tan^{-1}x\,dx = \int(x - x^3/3 + x^5/5 - x^7/7 + x^9/9 - \cdots)\,dx = C + \frac{x^2}{2} - \frac{x^4}{12} + \frac{x^6}{30} - \frac{x^8}{56} + \cdots$. Thus, $\int_0^{0.35}\tan^{-1}x\,dx = \frac{(0.35)^2}{2} - \frac{(0.35)^4}{12} + \frac{(0.35)^6}{30} - \frac{(0.35)^8}{56} + \cdots$. Note that this series is alternating, and $\frac{(0.35)^6}{30} < 10^{-4}$, so we add the first two terms to approximate the integral to the desired accuracy. Calculating gives approximately 0.060.

9.4.43 The Taylor series for $(1+x^6)^{-1/2}$ is $\sum_{k=0}^{\infty}\binom{-1/2}{k}x^{6k}$, so the desired integral is $\int_0^{0.5}\sum_{k=0}^{\infty}\binom{-1/2}{k}x^{6k}\,dx$ $= \sum_{k=0}^{\infty}\frac{1}{6k+1}\binom{-1/2}{k}x^{6k+1}\Big|_0^{0.5} = \sum_{k=0}^{\infty}\frac{1}{6k+1}\binom{-1/2}{k}(0.5)^{6k+1}$. This is an alternating series because the binomial coefficients alternate in sign, so to approximate it to within 10^{-4}, we must find n such that $a_{n+1} < 10^{-4}$, or $\left|\frac{1}{6n+7}\binom{-1/2}{n+1}(0.5)^{6n+7}\right| < 10^{-4}$. This occurs first for $n = 1$, so we have $\binom{-1/2}{0}0.5 + \frac{1}{7}\binom{-1/2}{1}(0.5)^7 \approx 0.499$.

9.4.45 Use the Taylor series for e^x at 0: $1 + \frac{2}{1!} + \frac{2^2}{2!} + \frac{2^3}{3!}$.

9.4.47 Use the Taylor series for $\cos x$ at 0: $1 - \frac{2^2}{2!} + \frac{2^4}{4!} - \frac{2^6}{6!}$

9.4.49 Use the Taylor series for $\ln(1+x)$ evaluated at $x = 1/2$: $\frac{1}{2} - \frac{1}{2}\cdot\frac{1}{4} + \frac{1}{3}\cdot\frac{1}{8} - \frac{1}{4}\cdot\frac{1}{16}$.

9.4.51 The Taylor series for f centered at 0 is $\frac{-1+\sum_{k=0}^{\infty}\frac{x^k}{k!}}{x} = \frac{\sum_{k=1}^{\infty}\frac{x^k}{k!}}{x} = \sum_{k=1}^{\infty}\frac{x^{k-1}}{k!} = \sum_{k=0}^{\infty}\frac{x^k}{(k+1)!}$. Evaluating both sides at $x = 1$, we have $e - 1 = \sum_{k=0}^{\infty}\frac{1}{(k+1)!}$.

9.4.53 The Maclaurin series for $\ln(1+x)$ is $x - \frac{1}{2}x^2 + \frac{1}{3}x^3 - \frac{1}{4}x^4 + \cdots = \sum_{k=1}^{\infty}(-1)^{k+1}\frac{x^k}{k}$. By the Ratio Test, $\lim_{k\to\infty}\left|\frac{a_{k+1}}{a_k}\right| = \lim_{k\to\infty}\left|\frac{x^{k+1}k}{x^k(k+1)}\right| = |x|$, so the radius of convergence is 1. The series diverges at -1 and converges at 1, so the interval of convergence is $(-1, 1]$. Evaluating at 1 gives $\ln 2 = \sum_{k=1}^{\infty}(-1)^{k+1}\frac{1}{k} = 1 - \frac{1}{2} + \frac{1}{3} - \frac{1}{4} + \cdots$.

9.4.55 $\sum_{k=0}^{\infty}\frac{x^k}{2^k} = \sum_{k=0}^{\infty}\left(\frac{x}{2}\right)^k = \frac{1}{1-\frac{x}{2}} = \frac{2}{2-x}$.

9.4.57 $\sum_{k=0}^{\infty}(-1)^k\frac{x^{2k}}{4^k} = \sum_{k=0}^{\infty}\left(\frac{-x^2}{4}\right)^k = \frac{1}{1+\frac{x^2}{4}} = \frac{4}{4+x^2}.$

9.4.59 $\ln(1+x) = -\sum_{k=1}^{\infty}(-1)^k\frac{x^k}{k}$, so $\ln(1-x) = -\sum_{k=1}^{\infty}\frac{x^k}{k}$, and finally $-\ln(1-x) = \sum_{k=1}^{\infty}\frac{x^k}{k}$.

9.4.61

$$
\begin{aligned}
\sum_{k=1}^{\infty}(-1)^k\frac{kx^{k+1}}{3^k} &= \sum_{k=1}^{\infty}(-1)^k\frac{k}{3^k}x^{k+1} = \sum_{k=1}^{\infty}k\left(-\frac{1}{3}\right)^k x^{k+1} \\
&= x^2\sum_{k=1}^{\infty}\left(-\frac{1}{3}\right)^k kx^{k-1} = x^2\sum_{k=1}^{\infty}\left(-\frac{1}{3}\right)^k \frac{d}{dx}(x^k) \\
&= x^2\frac{d}{dx}\left(\sum_{k=1}^{\infty}\left(-\frac{x}{3}\right)^k\right) = x^2\frac{d}{dx}\left(\frac{1}{1+\frac{x}{3}}\right) = -\frac{3x^2}{(x+3)^2}.
\end{aligned}
$$

9.4.63 $\sum_{k=2}^{\infty}\frac{k(k-1)x^k}{3^k} = x^2\sum_{k=2}^{\infty}\frac{k(k-1)x^{k-2}}{3^k} = x^2\frac{d^2}{dx^2}\left(\sum_{k=2}^{\infty}\frac{x^k}{3^k}\right)$
$= x^2\frac{d^2}{dx^2}\left(\sum_{k=2}^{\infty}\left(\frac{x}{3}\right)^k\right) = x^2\frac{d^2}{dx^2}\left(\frac{x^2}{9}\cdot\frac{1}{1-\frac{x}{3}}\right) = x^2\frac{d^2}{dx^2}\left(\frac{x^2}{9-3x}\right) = x^2\frac{-6}{(x-3)^3} = \frac{-6x^2}{(x-3)^3}.$

9.4.65

a. False. This is because $\frac{1}{1-x}$ is not continuous at 1, which is in the interval of integration.

b. False. The Ratio Test shows that the radius of convergence for the Taylor series for $\tan^{-1}x$ centered at 0 is 1.

c. True. $\sum_{k=0}^{\infty}\frac{x^k}{k!} = e^x$. Substitute $x = \ln 2$.

9.4.67 The Taylor series for $\sin x$ centered at 0 is

$$\sin x = x - \frac{x^3}{6} + \frac{x^5}{120} - \cdots.$$

We compute that

$$
\begin{aligned}
\frac{\sin ax}{\sin bx} &= \frac{ax - \frac{(ax)^3}{6} + \frac{(ax)^5}{120} - \cdots}{bx - \frac{(bx)^3}{6} + \frac{(bx)^5}{120} - \cdots} \\
&= \frac{a - \frac{a^3x^2}{6} + \frac{a^5x^4}{120} - \cdots}{b - \frac{b^3x^2}{6} + \frac{b^5x^4}{120} - \cdots}
\end{aligned}
$$

so the limit of $\dfrac{\sin ax}{\sin bx}$ as $x \to 0$ is $\dfrac{a}{b}$.

9.4.69 Compute instead the limit of the log of this expression, $\lim_{x\to 0}\frac{\ln(\sin x/x)}{x^2}$. If the Taylor expansion of $\ln(\sin x/x)$ is $\sum_{k=0}^{\infty}c_kx^k$, then $\lim_{x\to 0}\frac{\ln(\sin x/x)}{x^2} = \lim_{x\to 0}\sum_{k=0}^{\infty}c_kx^{k-2} = \lim_{x\to 0}c_0x^{-2} + c_1x^{-1} + c_2$, because the higher-order terms have positive powers of x and thus approach zero as x does. So compute the terms of the Taylor series of $\ln\left(\frac{\sin x}{x}\right)$ up through the quadratic term. The relevant Taylor series are: $\frac{\sin x}{x} = 1 - \frac{1}{6}x^2 + \frac{1}{120}x^4 - \cdots$, $\ln(1+x) = x - \frac{1}{2}x^2 + \frac{1}{3}x^3 - \cdots$ and we substitute the Taylor series for $\frac{\sin x}{x} - 1$ for x in the Taylor series for $\ln(1+x)$. Because the lowest power of x in the first Taylor series is 2, it follows that only the linear term in the series for $\ln(1+x)$ will give any powers of x that are at most quadratic. The only term that results is $-\frac{1}{6}x^2$. Thus $c_0 = c_1 = 0$ in the above, and $c_2 = -\frac{1}{6}$, so that $\lim_{x\to 0}\frac{\ln(\sin x/x)}{x^2} = -\frac{1}{6}$ and thus $\lim_{x\to 0}\left(\frac{\sin x}{x}\right)^{1/x^2} = e^{-1/6}$.

9.4.71 The Taylor series we need are $\cos x = 1 - \frac{1}{2}x^2 + \frac{1}{24}x^4 + \ldots$, $e^t = 1 + t + \frac{1}{2!}t^2 + \frac{1}{3!}t^3 + \frac{1}{4!}t^4 + \ldots$. We are looking for powers of x^3 and x^4 that occur when the first series is substituted for t in the second series. Clearly there will be no odd powers of x, because $\cos x$ has only even powers. Thus the coefficient of x^3 is zero, so that $f^{(3)}(0) = 0$. The coefficient of x^4 comes from the expansion of $1 - \frac{1}{2}x^2 + \frac{1}{24}x^4$ in each term of e^t. Higher powers of x clearly cannot contribute to the coefficient of x^4. Thus consider $\left(1 - \frac{1}{2}x^2 + \frac{1}{24}x^4\right)^k$. The term $-\frac{1}{2}x^2$ generates $\binom{k}{2}$ terms of value $\frac{1}{4}x^4$ for $k \geq 2$, while the other term generates k terms of value $\frac{1}{24}x^4$ for $k \geq 1$. These terms all have to be divided by the $k!$ appearing in the series for e^t. So the total coefficient of x^4 is $\frac{1}{24}\sum_{k=1}^{\infty}\frac{k}{k!} + \frac{1}{4}\sum_{k=2}^{\infty}\binom{k}{2}\frac{1}{k!}$, $= \frac{1}{24}\sum_{k=1}^{\infty}\frac{1}{(k-1)!} + \frac{1}{4}\sum_{k=2}^{\infty}\frac{1}{2\cdot(k-2)!}$, $= \frac{1}{24}\sum_{k=0}^{\infty}\frac{1}{k!} + \frac{1}{8}\sum_{k=0}^{\infty}\frac{1}{k!}$, $= \frac{1}{24}e + \frac{1}{8}e = \frac{e}{6}$ Thus $f^{(4)}(0) = \frac{e}{6} \cdot 4! = 4e$.

9.4.73 The Taylor series for $\sin t^2$ is $\sin t^2 = t^2 - \frac{1}{3!}t^6 + \frac{1}{5!}t^{10} - \ldots$, so that $\int_0^x \sin t^2\, dt = \frac{1}{3}t^3 - \frac{1}{7\cdot 3!}t^7 + \ldots \Big|_0^x = \frac{1}{3}x^3 - \frac{1}{7\cdot 3!}x^7 + \ldots$. Thus $f^{(3)}(0) = \frac{3!}{3} = 2$ and $f^{(4)}(0) = 0$.

9.4.75 Consider the series $\sum_{k=1}^{\infty} x^k = \frac{x}{1-x}$. Differentiating both sides gives $\frac{1}{(1-x)^2} = \sum_{k=0}^{\infty} kx^{k-1} = \frac{1}{x}\sum_{k=0}^{\infty} kx^k$ so that $\frac{x}{(1-x)^2} = \sum_{k=0}^{\infty} kx^k$. Evaluate both sides at $x = 1/2$ to see that the sum of the series is $\frac{1/2}{(1-1/2)^2} = 2$. Thus the expected number of tosses is 2.

9.4.77

a. We look first for a Taylor series for $(1 - k^2\sin^2\theta)^{-1/2}$. Because $(1 - k^2x^2)^{-1/2} = (1 - (kx)^2)^{-1/2} = \sum_{i=0}^{\infty}\binom{-1/2}{i}(kx)^{2i}$, and $\sin\theta = \theta - \frac{1}{3!}\theta^3 + \frac{1}{5!}\theta^5 - \ldots$, substituting the second series into the first gives $\frac{1}{\sqrt{1 - k^2\sin^2\theta}} = 1 + \frac{1}{2}k^2\theta^2 + \left(-\frac{1}{6}k^2 + \frac{3}{8}k^4\right)\theta^4 + \left(\frac{1}{45}k^2 - \frac{1}{4}k^4 + \frac{5}{16}k^6\right)\theta^6 + \left(\frac{-1}{630}k^2 + \frac{3}{40}k^4 - \frac{5}{16}k^6 + \frac{35}{128}k^8\right)\theta^8 + \ldots$.

Integrating with respect to θ and evaluating at $\pi/2$ (the value of the antiderivative is 0 at 0) gives $\frac{1}{2}\pi + \frac{1}{48}k^2\pi^3 + \frac{1}{160}\left(-\frac{1}{6}k^2 + \frac{3}{8}k^4\right)\pi^5 + \frac{1}{896}\left(\frac{1}{45}k^2 - \frac{1}{4}k^4 + \frac{5}{16}k^6\right)\pi^7 + \frac{1}{4608}\left(-\frac{1}{630}k^2 + \frac{3}{40}k^4 - \frac{5}{16}k^6 + \frac{35}{128}k^8\right)\pi^9$. Evaluating these terms for $k = 0.1$ gives $F(0.1) \approx 1.574749680$. (The true value is approximately 1.574745562.)

b. The terms above, with coefficients of k^n converted to decimal approximations, is $1.5707 + .3918 \cdot k^2 + .3597 \cdot k^4 - .9682 \cdot k^6 + 1.7689 \cdot k^8$. The coefficients are all less than 2 and do not appear to be increasing very much if at all, so if we want the result to be accurate to within 10^{-3} we should probably take n such that $k^n < \frac{1}{2} \times 10^{-3} = .0005$, so $n = 4$ for this value of k.

c. By the above analysis, we would need a larger n because $0.2^n > 0.1^n$ for a given value of n.

9.4.79

a. By the Fundamental Theorem, $S'(x) = \sin x^2$, $C'(x) = \cos x^2$.

b. The relevant Taylor series are $\sin t^2 = t^2 - \frac{1}{3!}t^6 + \frac{1}{5!}t^{10} - \frac{1}{7!}t^{14} + \ldots$, and $\cos t^2 = 1 - \frac{1}{2!}t^4 + \frac{1}{4!}t^8 - \frac{1}{6!}t^{12} + \ldots$. Integrating, we have $S(x) = \frac{1}{3}x^3 - \frac{1}{7\cdot 3!}x^7 + \frac{1}{11\cdot 5!}x^{11} - \frac{1}{15\cdot 7!}x^{15} + \ldots$, and $C(x) = x - \frac{1}{5\cdot 2!}x^5 + \frac{1}{9\cdot 4!}x^9 - \frac{1}{13\cdot 6!}x^{13} + \ldots$.

c. $S(0.05) \approx \frac{1}{3}(0.05)^3 - \frac{1}{42}(0.05)^7 + \frac{1}{1320}(0.05)^{11} - \frac{1}{75600}(0.05)^{15} \approx 4.166664807 \times 10^{-5}$. $C(-0.25) \approx (-0.25) - \frac{1}{10}(-0.25)^5 + \frac{1}{216}(-0.25)^9 - \frac{1}{9360}(-0.25)^{13} \approx -.2499023616$.

d. The series is alternating. Because $a_{n+1} = \frac{1}{(4n+7)(2n+3)!}(0.05)^{4n+7}$, and this is less than 10^{-4} for $n = 0$, only one term is required.

e. The series is alternating. Because $a_{n+1} = \frac{1}{(4n+5)(2n+2)!}(0.25)^{4n+5}$, and this is less than 10^{-6} for $n = 1$, two terms are required.

9.4.81

a. $J_0(x) = 1 - \frac{1}{4}x^2 + \frac{1}{16\cdot 2!^2}x^4 - \frac{1}{2^6\cdot 3!^2}x^6 + \ldots$.

b. Using the Ratio Test: $\left|\frac{a_{k+1}}{a_k}\right| = \frac{x^{2k+2}}{2^{2k+2}((k+1)!)^2} \cdot \frac{2^{2k}(k!)^2}{x^{2k}} = \frac{x^2}{4(k+1)^2}$, which has limit 0 as $k \to \infty$ for any x. Thus the radius of convergence is infinite and the interval of convergence is $(-\infty, \infty)$.

c. Starting only with terms up through x^8, we have $J_0(x) = 1 - \frac{1}{4}x^2 + \frac{1}{64}x^4 - \frac{1}{2304}x^6 + \frac{1}{147456}x^8 + \cdots$, $J_0'(x) = -\frac{1}{2}x + \frac{1}{16}x^3 - \frac{1}{384}x^5 + \frac{1}{18432}x^7 + \cdots$, $J_0''(x) = -\frac{1}{2} + \frac{3}{16}x^2 - \frac{5}{384}x^4 + \frac{7}{18432}x^6 + \cdots$ so that $x^2 J_0(x) = x^2 - \frac{1}{4}x^4 + \frac{1}{64}x^6 - \frac{1}{2304}x^8 + \frac{1}{147456}x^{10} + \cdots$, $x J_0'(x) = -\frac{1}{2}x^2 + \frac{1}{16}x^4 - \frac{1}{384}x^6 + \frac{1}{18432}x^8 + \cdots$, $x^2 J_0''(x) = -\frac{1}{2}x^2 + \frac{3}{16}x^4 - \frac{5}{384}x^6 + \frac{7}{18432}x^8 + \cdots$, and $x^2 J_0''(x) + x J_0'(x) + x^2 J_0(x) = 0$.

9.4.83

a. The power series for $\cos x$ has only even powers of x, so that the power series has the same value evaluated at $-x$ as it does at x.

b. The power series for $\sin x$ has only odd powers of x, so that evaluating it at $-x$ gives the opposite of its value at x.

9.4.85

a. Because $f(a) = g(a) = 0$, we use the Taylor series for $f(x)$ and $g(x)$ centered at a to compute that

$$\lim_{x \to a} \frac{f(x)}{g(x)} = \lim_{x \to a} \frac{f(a) + f'(a)(x-a) + \frac{1}{2}f''(a)(x-a)^2 + \cdots}{g(a) + g'(a)(x-a) + \frac{1}{2}g''(a)(x-a)^2 + \cdots}$$

$$= \lim_{x \to a} \frac{f'(a)(x-a) + \frac{1}{2}f''(a)(x-a)^2 + \cdots}{g'(a)(x-a) + \frac{1}{2}g''(a)(x-a)^2 + \cdots}$$

$$= \lim_{x \to a} \frac{f'(a) + \frac{1}{2}f''(a)(x-a) + \cdots}{g'(a) + \frac{1}{2}g''(a)(x-a) + \cdots} = \frac{f'(a)}{g'(a)}.$$

Because $f'(x)$ and $g'(x)$ are assumed to be continuous at a and $g'(a) \neq 0$,

$$\frac{f'(a)}{g'(a)} = \lim_{x \to a} \frac{f'(x)}{g'(x)}$$

and we have that

$$\lim_{x \to a} \frac{f(x)}{g(x)} = \lim_{x \to a} \frac{f'(x)}{g'(x)}$$

which is one form of L'Hôpital's Rule.

b. Because $f(a) = g(a) = f'(a) = g'(a) = 0$, we use the Taylor series for $f(x)$ and $g(x)$ centered at a to compute that

$$\lim_{x \to a} \frac{f(x)}{g(x)} = \lim_{x \to a} \frac{f(a) + f'(a)(x-a) + \frac{1}{2}f''(a)(x-a)^2 + \frac{1}{6}f'''(a)(x-a)^3 + \cdots}{g(a) + g'(a)(x-a) + \frac{1}{2}g''(a)(x-a)^2 + \frac{1}{6}g'''(a)(x-a)^3 + \cdots}$$

$$= \lim_{x \to a} \frac{\frac{1}{2}f''(a)(x-a)^2 + \frac{1}{6}f'''(a)(x-a)^3 + \cdots}{\frac{1}{2}g''(a)(x-a)^2 + \frac{1}{6}g'''(a)(x-a)^3 + \cdots}$$

$$= \lim_{x \to a} \frac{\frac{1}{2}f''(a) + \frac{1}{6}f'''(a)(x-a) + \cdots}{\frac{1}{2}g''(a) + \frac{1}{6}g'''(a)(x-a) + \cdots} = \frac{f''(a)}{g''(a)}.$$

Because $f''(x)$ and $g''(x)$ are assumed to be continuous at a and $g''(a) \neq 0$,

$$\frac{f''(a)}{g''(a)} = \lim_{x \to a} \frac{f''(x)}{g''(x)}$$

and we have that

$$\lim_{x \to a} \frac{f(x)}{g(x)} = \lim_{x \to a} \frac{f''(x)}{g''(x)}$$

which is consistent with two applications of L'Hôpital's Rule.

Chapter Nine Review

1

    a. True. The approximations tend to get better as n increases in size, and also when the value being approximated is closer to the center of the series. Because 2.1 is closer to 2 than 2.2 is, and because $3 > 2$, we should have $|p_3(2.1) - f(2.1)| < |p_2(2.2) - f(2.2)|$.

    b. False. The interval of convergence may or may not include the endpoints.

    c. True. The interval of convergence is an interval centered at 0, and the endpoints may or may not be included.

    d. True. Because $f(x)$ is a polynomial, all its derivatives vanish after a certain point (in this case, $f^{(12)}(x)$ is the last nonzero derivative).

3 $p_2(x) = 1$.

5 $p_3(x) = x - \frac{x^2}{2} + \frac{x^3}{3}$.

7 $p_2(x) = x - 1 - \frac{1}{2}(x-1)^2$.

9 $p_3(x) = \frac{5}{4} + \frac{3(x - \ln 2)}{4} + \frac{5(x - \ln 2)^2}{8} + \frac{(x - \ln 2)^3}{8}$.

11

    a. $p_0(x) = 1$, $p_1(x) = 1 + x$, and $p_2(x) = 1 + x + \frac{x^2}{2}$.

    b.

n	$p_n(-0.08)$	$\left|p_n(-0.08) - e^{-0.08}\right|$
0	1	7.7×10^{-2}
1	0.92	3.1×10^{-3}
2	0.923	8.4×10^{-5}

13

    a. $p_0(x) = \frac{\sqrt{2}}{2}$, $p_1(x) = \frac{\sqrt{2}}{2}(1 + (x - \pi/4))$, and $p_2(x) = \frac{\sqrt{2}}{2}\left(1 + (x - \pi/4) - \frac{1}{2}(x - \pi/4)^2\right)$.

    b.

n	$p_n(\pi/5)$	$\left|p_n(\pi/5) - \sin(\pi/5)\right|$
0	0.707	1.2×10^{-1}
1	0.596	8.2×10^{-3}
2	0.587	4.7×10^{-4}

15 The derivatives of $\sin x$ are bounded in magnitude by 1, so $|R_n(x)| \le M \frac{|x|^{n+1}}{(n+1)!} \le \frac{|x|^{n+1}}{(n+1)!}$. But $|x| < \pi$, so $|R_3(x)| \le \frac{\pi^4}{24}$.

17 Using the Ratio Test, $\lim\limits_{k \to \infty} \left|\frac{a_{k+1}}{a_k}\right| = \lim\limits_{k \to \infty} \left|\frac{(k+1)^2 x^{k+1}}{(k+1)!} \cdot \frac{k!}{k^2 x^k}\right| = \lim\limits_{k \to \infty} \left(\frac{k+1}{k}\right)^2 \frac{|x|}{k+1} = 0$, so the interval of convergence is $(-\infty, \infty)$.

19 Using the Ratio Test, $\lim\limits_{k \to \infty} \frac{a_{k+1}}{a_k} = \lim\limits_{k \to \infty} \left|\frac{(x+1)^{2k+2}}{(k+1)!} \cdot \frac{k!}{(x+1)^{2k}}\right| = \lim\limits_{k \to \infty} \frac{1}{k+1}(x+1)^2 = 0$, so the interval of convergence is $(-\infty, \infty)$.

21 By the Root Test, $\lim\limits_{k\to\infty} \sqrt[k]{|a_k|} = \lim\limits_{k\to\infty} \left(\frac{|x|}{9}\right)^3 = \frac{|x^3|}{729}$, so the series converges for $|x| < 9$. The series given by letting $x = \pm 9$ are both divergent by the Divergence Test. Thus, $(-9, 9)$ is the interval of convergence.

23 By the Ratio Test, $\lim\limits_{k\to\infty} \left| \frac{(x+2)^{k+1}}{2^{k+1}\ln(k+1)} \cdot \frac{2^k \ln k}{(x+2)^k} \right| = \lim\limits_{k\to\infty} \frac{\ln k}{2\ln(k+1)} |x+2| = \frac{|x+2|}{2}$. The radius of convergence is thus 2, and a check of the endpoints gives the divergent series $\sum \frac{1}{\ln k}$ at $x = 0$ and the convergent alternating series $\sum \frac{(-1)^k}{\ln k}$ at $x = -4$. The interval of convergence is therefore $[-4, 0)$.

25 The Maclaurin series for $f(x)$ is $\sum_{k=0}^{\infty} x^{2k}$. By the Root Test, this converges for $|x^2| < 1$, so $-1 < x < 1$. It diverges at both endpoints, so the interval of convergence is $(-1, 1)$.

27 The Maclaurin series for $f(x)$ is $\sum_{k=0}^{\infty}(-5x)^k = \sum_{k=0}^{\infty}(-5)^k x^k$. By the Root Test, this has radius of convergence $1/5$. Checking the endpoints, we obtain an interval of convergence of $(-1/5, 1/5)$.

29 Note that $\frac{1}{1-10x} = \sum_{k=0}^{\infty}(10x)^k$, so $\frac{1}{10} \cdot \frac{1}{1-10x} = \frac{1}{10}\sum_{k=0}^{\infty}(10x)^k$. Taking the derivative of $\frac{1}{10} \cdot \frac{1}{1-10x}$ gives $f(x)$. Thus, the Maclaurin series for $f(x)$ is $\frac{1}{10}\sum_{k=1}^{\infty} 10k(10x)^{k-1} = \sum_{k=1}^{\infty} k(10x)^{k-1}$. Using the Ratio Test, we see that the radius of convergence is $1/10$, and checking endpoints we obtain an interval of convergence of $(-1/10, 1/10)$.

31 The first three terms are $1 + 3x + \frac{9x^2}{2}$. The series is $\sum_{k=0}^{\infty} \frac{(3x)^k}{k!}$.

33 The first three terms are $-(x - \pi/2) + \frac{1}{6}(x - \pi/2)^3 - \frac{1}{120}(x - \pi/2)^5$. The series is

$$\sum_{k=0}^{\infty}(-1)^{k+1}\frac{1}{(2k+1)!}\left(x - \frac{\pi}{2}\right)^{2k+1}.$$

35 The first three terms are $4x - \frac{1}{3}(4x)^3 + \frac{1}{5}(4x)^5$. The series is $\sum_{k=0}^{\infty}(-1)^k \frac{(4x)^{2k+1}}{2k+1}$.

37 The nth derivative of $\cosh 3x$ at $x = 0$ is 0 if n is odd and is 3^n if n is even. The first 3 terms of the series are thus $1 + \frac{9x^2}{2!} + \frac{81x^4}{4!}$. The whole series can be written as $\sum_{k=0}^{\infty} \frac{(3x)^{2k}}{(2k)!}$.

39 $f(x) = \binom{1/3}{0} + \binom{1/3}{1}x + \binom{1/3}{2}x^2 + \cdots = 1 + \frac{1}{3}x - \frac{1}{9}x^2 + \cdots$.

41 $f(x) = \binom{-3}{0} + \binom{-3}{1}\frac{x}{2} + \binom{-3}{2}\frac{x^2}{4} + \cdots = 1 - \frac{3}{2}x + \frac{3}{2}x^2 + \cdots$.

43 $R_n(x) = \frac{(-1)^{n+1}e^{-c}}{(n+1)!}x^{n+1}$ for some c between 0 and x, and $\lim\limits_{n\to\infty}|R_n(x)| \le e^{-|x|}\lim\limits_{n\to\infty}\frac{|x|^{n+1}}{(n+1)!} = 0$, because $n!$ grows faster than $|x|^n$ as $n \to \infty$ for all x.

45 $R_n(x) = \frac{f^{(n+1)}(c)}{(n+1)!}x^{n+1}$ for some c in $(-1/2, 1/2)$. Now, $\left|f^{(n+1)}(c)\right| = \frac{n!}{(1+c)^{n+1}}$, so $\lim\limits_{n\to\infty}|R_n(x)| \le \lim\limits_{n\to\infty}(2|x|)^{n+1} \cdot \frac{1}{n+1} \le \lim\limits_{n\to\infty} 1^{n+1}\frac{1}{n+1} = 0$.

47 The Taylor series for $\cos x$ centered at 0 is

$$\cos x = 1 - \frac{x^2}{2} + \frac{x^4}{24} - \frac{x^6}{720} + \cdots.$$

We compute that

$$\begin{aligned} \frac{x^2/2 - 1 + \cos x}{x^4} &= \frac{1}{x^4}\left(x^2/2 - 1 + \left(1 - \frac{x^2}{2} + \frac{x^4}{24} - \frac{x^6}{720} + \cdots\right)\right) \\ &= \frac{1}{x^4}\left(\frac{x^4}{24} - \frac{x^6}{720} + \cdots\right) = \frac{1}{24} - \frac{x^2}{720} + \cdots \end{aligned}$$

so the limit of $\dfrac{x^2/2 - 1 + \cos x}{x^4}$ as $x \to 0$ is $\dfrac{1}{24}$.

49 The Taylor series for $\ln(x-3)$ centered at 4 is

$$\ln(x-3) = (x-4) - \frac{1}{2}(x-4)^2 + \frac{1}{3}(x-4)^3 - \cdots .$$

We compute that

$$
\begin{aligned}
\frac{\ln(x-3)}{x^2-16} &= \frac{1}{(x-4)(x+4)}\left((x-4) - \frac{1}{2}(x-4)^2 + \frac{1}{3}(x-4)^3 - \cdots\right) \\
&= \frac{1}{(x-4)(x+4)}\left((x-4)\left(1 - \frac{1}{2}(x-4) + \frac{1}{3}(x-4)^2 - \cdots\right)\right) \\
&= \frac{1}{x+4}\left(1 - \frac{1}{2}(x-4) + \frac{1}{3}(x-4)^2 - \cdots\right)
\end{aligned}
$$

so the limit of $\dfrac{\ln(x-3)}{x^2-16}$ as $x \to 4$ is $\dfrac{1}{8}$.

51 The Taylor series for $\sec x$ centered at 0 is

$$\sec x = 1 + \frac{x^2}{2} + \frac{5x^4}{24} + \frac{61x^6}{720} + \cdots$$

and the Taylor series for $\cos x$ centered at 0 is

$$\cos x = 1 - \frac{x^2}{2} + \frac{x^4}{24} - \frac{x^6}{720} + \cdots .$$

We compute that

$$
\begin{aligned}
&\frac{\sec x - \cos x - x^2}{x^4} \\
&= \frac{1}{x^4}\left(\left(1 + \frac{x^2}{2} + \frac{5x^4}{24} + \frac{61x^6}{720} + \cdots\right) - \left(1 - \frac{x^2}{2} + \frac{x^4}{24} - \frac{x^6}{720} + \cdots\right) - x^2\right) \\
&= \frac{1}{x^4}\left(\frac{x^4}{6} + \frac{31x^6}{360} + \cdots\right) = \frac{1}{6} + \frac{31x^2}{360} + \cdots
\end{aligned}
$$

so the limit of $\dfrac{\sec x - \cos x - x^2}{x^4}$ as $x \to 0$ is $\dfrac{1}{6}$.

53 We have $e^{-x^2} = 1 - x^2 + \frac{x^4}{2} - \frac{x^6}{6} + \frac{x^8}{24} - \cdots$, so $\int e^{-x^2}\,dx = \int(1 - x^2 + \frac{x^4}{2} - \frac{x^6}{6} + \frac{x^8}{24} - \cdots)\,dx = C + x - \frac{x^3}{3} + \frac{x^5}{10} - \frac{x^7}{42} + \cdots$. Thus, $\int_0^{1/2} e^{-x^2}\,dx = (0.5) - \frac{(0.5)^3}{3} + \frac{(0.5)^5}{10} - \frac{(0.5)^7}{42} + \cdots$. Because $(0.5)^7/42 < .001$, we can calculate the approximation using the first three numbers shown, arriving at approximately 0.461.

55 $x\cos x = x - \frac{x^3}{2} + \frac{x^5}{24} - \frac{x^7}{720} + \cdots$, so $\int x\cos x\,dx = \int(x - \frac{x^3}{2} + \frac{x^5}{24} - \frac{x^7}{720} + \cdots)\,dx = C + \frac{x^2}{2} - \frac{x^4}{8} + \frac{x^6}{144} - \frac{x^8}{5760} + \frac{x^{10}}{403200} - \cdots$. Thus $\int_0^1 x\cos x\,dx = \frac{1}{2} - \frac{1}{8} + \frac{1}{144} - \frac{1}{5760} + \cdots$. Because $\frac{1}{5760} < .001$, we add the first three terms to approximate to the desired accuracy. Calculating gives $\int_0^1 x\cos x\,dx \approx 0.382$.

57 The series for $f(x) = \sqrt{x}$ centered at $a = 121$ is $11 + \frac{x-121}{22} - \frac{(x-121)^2}{10648} + \frac{(x-121)^3}{2576816} + \cdots$. Letting $x = 119$ gives $\sqrt{119} \approx 11 - \frac{1}{11} - \frac{1}{2\cdot11^3} - \frac{1}{2\cdot11^5}$.

59 $\tan^{-1} x = x - x^3/3 + x^5/5 - x^7/7 + x^9/9 + \cdots$, so $\tan^{-1}(-1/3) \approx \frac{-1}{3} + \frac{1}{3\cdot3^3} - \frac{1}{5\cdot3^5} + \frac{1}{7\cdot3^7}$.

61 Because $y(0) = 4$, we have $y'(0) - 16 + 12 = 0$, so $y'(0) = 4$. Differentiating the equation $n-1$ times and evaluating at 0 we obtain $y^{(n)}(0) = 4y^{(n-1)}(0)$, so that $y^{(n)}(0) = 4^n$. The Taylor series for $y(x)$ is thus $y(x) = 4 + 4x + \frac{4^2x^2}{2!} + \frac{4^3x^3}{3!} + \cdots$, or $y(x) = 3 + e^{4x}$.

63

a. The Taylor series for $\ln(1+x)$ is $\sum_{k=1}^{\infty}(-1)^{k+1}\frac{x^k}{k}$. Evaluating at $x=1$ gives $\ln 2 = \sum_{k=1}^{\infty}(-1)^{k+1}\frac{1}{k}$.

b. The Taylor series for $\ln(1-x)$ is $-\sum_{k=1}^{\infty}\frac{x^k}{k}$. Evaluating at $x=1/2$ gives $\ln(1/2) = -\sum_{k=1}^{\infty}\frac{1}{k2^k}$, so that $\ln 2 = \sum_{k=1}^{\infty}\frac{1}{k2^k}$.

c. $f(x) = \ln\left(\frac{1+x}{1-x}\right) = \ln(1+x) - \ln(1-x)$. Using the two Taylor series above we have $f(x) = \sum_{k=1}^{\infty}(-1)^{k+1}\frac{x^k}{k} - \left(-\sum_{k=1}^{\infty}\frac{x^k}{k}\right) = \sum_{k=1}^{\infty}(1+(-1)^{k+1})\frac{x^k}{k} = 2\sum_{k=0}^{\infty}\frac{x^{2k+1}}{2k+1}$.

d. Because $\frac{1+x}{1-x} = 2$ when $x = \frac{1}{3}$, the resulting infinite series for $\ln 2$ is $2\sum_{k=0}^{\infty}\frac{1}{3^{2k+1}(2k+1)}$.

e. The first four terms of each series are: $1 - \frac{1}{2} + \frac{1}{3} - \frac{1}{4} \approx 0.5833333333$, $\frac{1}{2} + \frac{1}{8} + \frac{1}{24} + \frac{1}{64} \approx 0.6822916667$, $\frac{2}{3} + \frac{2}{81} + \frac{2}{1215} + \frac{2}{15309} \approx 0.6931347573$ The true value is $\ln 2 \approx 0.6931471806$. The third series converges the fastest, because it has 3^{k+1} in the denominator as opposed to 2^k, so its terms get small faster.

GRAPHS OF ELEMENTARY FUNCTIONS

Linear functions

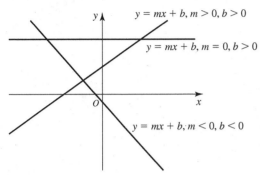

$y = mx + b, m > 0, b > 0$

$y = mx + b, m = 0, b > 0$

$y = mx + b, m < 0, b < 0$

Quadratic functions

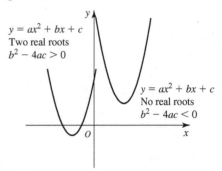

$y = ax^2 + bx + c$
Two real roots
$b^2 - 4ac > 0$

$y = ax^2 + bx + c$
No real roots
$b^2 - 4ac < 0$

Positive even powers

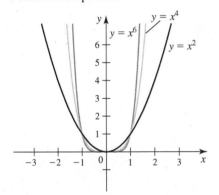

$y = x^6$ $y = x^4$ $y = x^2$

Positive odd powers

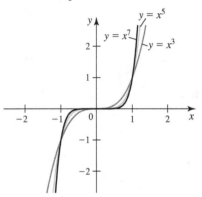

$y = x^5$ $y = x^7$ $y = x^3$

Negative even powers

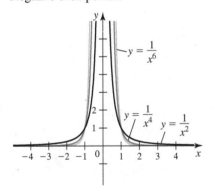

$y = \dfrac{1}{x^6}$ $y = \dfrac{1}{x^4}$ $y = \dfrac{1}{x^2}$

Negative odd powers

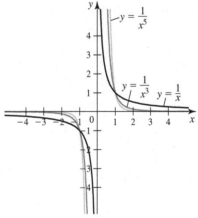

$y = \dfrac{1}{x^5}$ $y = \dfrac{1}{x^3}$ $y = \dfrac{1}{x}$

Exponential functions

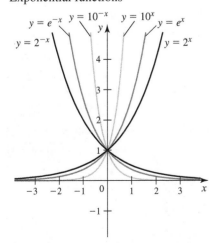

$y = e^{-x}$ $y = 10^{-x}$ $y = 10^x$ $y = e^x$

$y = 2^{-x}$ $y = 2^x$

Natural logarithmic and exponential functions

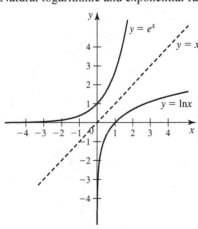

$y = e^x$ $y = x$

$y = \ln x$

DERIVATIVES

General Formulas

$$\frac{d}{dx}(c) = 0 \qquad\qquad \frac{d}{dx}(cf(x)) = cf'(x)$$

$$\frac{d}{dx}(f(x) + g(x)) = f'(x) + g'(x) \qquad\qquad \frac{d}{dx}(f(x) - g(x)) = f'(x) - g'(x)$$

$$\frac{d}{dx}(f(x)g(x)) = f'(x)g(x) + f(x)g'(x) \qquad\qquad \frac{d}{dx}\left(\frac{f(x)}{g(x)}\right) = \frac{g(x)f'(x) - f(x)g'(x)}{(g(x))^2}$$

$$\frac{d}{dx}(x^n) = nx^{n-1}, \text{ for real numbers } n \qquad\qquad \frac{d}{dx}[f(g(x))] = f'(g(x)) \cdot g'(x)$$

Trigonometric Functions

$$\frac{d}{dx}(\sin x) = \cos x \qquad\qquad \frac{d}{dx}(\cos x) = -\sin x$$

$$\frac{d}{dx}(\tan x) = \sec^2 x \qquad\qquad \frac{d}{dx}(\cot x) = -\csc^2 x$$

$$\frac{d}{dx}(\sec x) = \sec x \tan x \qquad\qquad \frac{d}{dx}(\csc x) = -\csc x \cot x$$

Inverse Trigonometric Functions

$$\frac{d}{dx}(\sin^{-1} x) = \frac{1}{\sqrt{1 - x^2}} \qquad\qquad \frac{d}{dx}(\cos^{-1} x) = -\frac{1}{\sqrt{1 - x^2}}$$

$$\frac{d}{dx}(\tan^{-1} x) = \frac{1}{1 + x^2} \qquad\qquad \frac{d}{dx}(\cot^{-1} x) = -\frac{1}{1 + x^2}$$

$$\frac{d}{dx}(\sec^{-1} x) = \frac{1}{|x|\sqrt{x^2 - 1}} \qquad\qquad \frac{d}{dx}(\csc^{-1} x) = -\frac{1}{|x|\sqrt{x^2 - 1}}$$

Exponential and Logarithmic Functions

$$\frac{d}{dx}(e^x) = e^x \qquad\qquad \frac{d}{dx}(b^x) = b^x \ln b$$

$$\frac{d}{dx}(\ln |x|) = \frac{1}{x} \qquad\qquad \frac{d}{dx}(\log_b x) = \frac{1}{x \ln b}$$

Hyperbolic Functions

$$\frac{d}{dx}(\sinh x) = \cosh x \qquad\qquad \frac{d}{dx}(\cosh x) = \sinh x$$

$$\frac{d}{dx}(\tanh x) = \operatorname{sech}^2 x \qquad\qquad \frac{d}{dx}(\coth x) = -\operatorname{csch}^2 x$$

$$\frac{d}{dx}(\operatorname{sech} x) = -\operatorname{sech} x \tanh x \qquad\qquad \frac{d}{dx}(\operatorname{csch} x) = -\operatorname{csch} x \coth x$$

Inverse Hyperbolic Functions

$$\frac{d}{dx}(\sinh^{-1} x) = \frac{1}{\sqrt{x^2 + 1}} \qquad\qquad \frac{d}{dx}(\cosh^{-1} x) = \frac{1}{\sqrt{x^2 - 1}} \quad (x > 1)$$

$$\frac{d}{dx}(\tanh^{-1} x) = \frac{1}{1 - x^2} \quad (|x| < 1) \qquad\qquad \frac{d}{dx}(\coth^{-1} x) = \frac{1}{1 - x^2} \quad (|x| > 1)$$

$$\frac{d}{dx}(\operatorname{sech}^{-1} x) = -\frac{1}{x\sqrt{1 - x^2}} \quad (0 < x < 1) \qquad\qquad \frac{d}{dx}(\operatorname{csch}^{-1} x) = -\frac{1}{|x|\sqrt{1 + x^2}} \quad (x \neq 0)$$